The Oxford Handbook of Women and Competition

OXFORD LIBRARY OF PSYCHOLOGY

Editor-in-Chief PETER E. NATHAN

The Oxford Handbook of Women and Competition

Edited by

Maryanne L. Fisher

OXFORD
UNIVERSITY PRESS

OXFORD
UNIVERSITY PRESS

Oxford University Press is a department of the University of Oxford. It furthers
the University's objective of excellence in research, scholarship, and education
by publishing worldwide. Oxford is a registered trade mark of Oxford University
Press in the UK and certain other countries.

Published in the United States of America by Oxford University Press
198 Madison Avenue, New York, NY 10016, United States of America.

Library of Congress Cataloging-in-Publication Data
Names: Fisher, Maryanne, editor.
Title: The Oxford handbook of women and competition /
edited by Maryanne L. Fisher.
Description: New York : Oxford University Press, [2017] |
Series: Oxford library of psychology
Identifiers: LCCN 2017001588 | ISBN 9780199376377 (jacketed hardcover : alk. paper)
Subjects: LCSH: Women—Psychology. | Competition (Psychology)
Classification: LCC HQ1206 .O94 2017 | DDC 155.3/339—dc23
LC record available at https://lccn.loc.gov/2017001588

9 8 7 6 5 4 3 2 1

Printed by Sheridan Books, Inc., United States of America

SHORT CONTENTS

The *Oxford Library of Psychology*, a landmark series of handbooks, is published by Oxford University Press, one of the world's oldest and most highly respected publishers, with a tradition of publishing significant books in psychology. The ambitious goal of the *Oxford Library of Psychology* is nothing less than to span a vibrant, wide-ranging field and, in so doing, to fill a clear market need.

Encompassing a comprehensive set of handbooks, organized hierarchically, the *Library* incorporates volumes at different levels, each designed to meet a distinct need. At one level are a set of handbooks designed broadly to survey the major subfields of psychology; at another are numerous handbooks that cover important current focal research and scholarly areas of psychology in depth and detail. Planned as a reflection of the dynamism of psychology, the *Library* will grow and expand as psychology itself develops, thereby highlighting significant new research that will impact on the field. Adding to its accessibility and ease of use, the *Library* will be published in print and, later on, electronically.

The *Library* surveys psychology's principal subfields with a set of handbooks that capture the current status and future prospects of those major subdisciplines. This initial set includes handbooks on social and personality psychology, clinical psychology, counseling psychology, school psychology, educational psychology, industrial and organizational psychology, cognitive psychology, cognitive neuroscience, methods and measurements, history, neuropsychology, personality assessment, developmental psychology, and more. Each handbook undertakes to review one of psychology's major subdisciplines with breadth, comprehensiveness, and exemplary scholarship. In addition to these broadly conceived volumes, the *Library* also includes a large number of handbooks designed to explore in depth more specialized areas of scholarship and research, such as stress, health and coping, anxiety and related disorders, cognitive development, and child and adolescent assessment. In contrast to the broad coverage of the subfield handbooks, each of these latter volumes focuses on an especially productive, more highly focused line of scholarship and research. Whether at the broadest or most specific level, however, all of the *Library* handbooks offer synthetic coverage that reviews and evaluates the relevant past and present research and anticipates research in the future. Each handbook in the *Library* includes introductory and concluding chapters written by its editor to provide a roadmap to the handbook's table of contents and to offer informed anticipation of significant future developments in that field.

An undertaking of this scope calls for handbook editors and chapter authors who are established scholars in the areas about which they write. Many of the nation's and world's most productive and best-respected psychologists have agreed to edit *Library* handbooks or write authoritative chapters in their areas of expertise.

For whom has the *Oxford Library of Psychology* been written? Because of its breadth, depth, and accessibility, the *Library* serves a diverse audience, including graduate students in psychology and their faculty mentors, scholars, researchers, and practitioners in psychology and related fields. Each will find in the *Library* the information they seek on the subfield or focal area of psychology in which they work or are interested.

Befitting its commitment to accessibility, each handbook includes a comprehensive index, as well as extensive references to help guide research. And because the *Library* was designed from its inception as an online as well as a print resource, its structure and contents will be readily and rationally searchable online. Further, once the *Library* is released online, the handbooks will be regularly and thoroughly updated.

In summary, the *Oxford Library of Psychology* will grow organically to provide a thoroughly informed perspective on the field of psychology, one that reflects both psychology's dynamism and its increasing interdisciplinarity. Once published electronically, the *Library* is also destined to become a uniquely valuable interactive tool, with extended search and browsing capabilities. As you begin to consult this handbook, we sincerely hope you will share our enthusiasm for the more-than-500-year tradition of Oxford University Press for excellence, innovation, and quality, as exemplified by the *Oxford Library of Psychology*.

Peter E. Nathan
Editor-in-Chief
Oxford Library of Psychology

ABOUT THE EDITOR

Maryanne L. Fisher

Maryanne L. Fisher is Full Professor in the Department of Psychology at Saint Mary's University in Halifax, Canada, and an Affiliate Faculty member at the Kinsey Institute in Indiana, USA. She is an award-winning educator and has published over 90 journal articles spanning a variety of topics, with most related to women's intrasexual competition. She has recently coedited *Evolution's Empress: Darwinian Perspectives on the Nature of Women* (Oxford University Press, 2013).

CONTRIBUTORS

Lora E. Adair
Department of Psychology
University of Central Arkansas
Conway, AR

Grace L. Anderson
Office of Institutional Research
Great Falls College–Montana State
    University
Great Falls, MT

Steven Arnocky
Department of Psychology
Nipissing University
North Bay, Ontario, Canada

Ashley Rae Arsena
College of Business
The University of Texas at San Antonio
San Antonio, TX

Fiona Kate Barlow
School of Psychology
The University of Queensland
St. Lucia, Queensland, Australia

Melanie L. Beaussart
Department of Psychology
California State University–
    San Bernardino
San Bernardino, CA

Robert Biegler
Department of Psychology
Norwegian University of Science and
    Technology
Trondheim, Norway

Gary L. Brase
Department of Psychological Sciences
Kansas State University
Manhattan, KS

Gayle Brewer
School of Psychology
University of Central Lancashire
Preston, England, UK

Rebecca L. Burch
Department of Human Development
State University of New York–Oswego
Oswego, NY

Lorne Campbell
Department of Psychology
University of Western Ontario
London, Ontario, Canada

Rachael A. Carmen
Department of Psychology
State University of New York–New Paltz
New Paltz, NY

Gregory L. Carter
Department of Psychology
York St. John University
York, England, UK

Kelly Cobey
Department of Psychology
University of Stirling
Stirling, Scotland, UK
Centre for Journalology,
    Ottawa Methods Centre,
    Clinical Epidemiology Program,
    Ottawa, Ontario, Canada
School of Epidemiology, Public Health,
    and Preventative Medicine, University
    of Ottawa, Ontario, Canada

Raquel Costa
Department of Psychobiology
University of Valencia
Valencia, Spain

Delphine S. Courvoisier
Faculty of Medicine
University Hospitals of Geneva
Geneva, Switzerland

Alita J. Cousins
Department of Psychology
Eastern Connecticut State University
Willimantic, CT

Charlotte J. S. De Backer
Department of Communication Studies
University of Antwerp
Antwerp, Belgium

Danielle J. DelPriore
Department of Psychology
University of Utah
Salt Lake City, UT

Haley M. Dillon
Department of Psychology
State University of New York, Plattsburgh
Plattsburgh, NY

Lori Dithurbide
School of Health and Human
    Performance
Dalhousie University
Halifax, Nova Scotia, Canada

Shelli L. Dubbs
School of Psychology
The University of Queensland
St. Lucia, Queensland, Australia

Kristina M. Durante
Rutgers Business School
Newark and New Brunswick
Newark, NJ

Julia Dutove
Department of Human Performance
Minnesota State University, Mankato
Mankato, MN

Ana María Fernández
School of Psychology
Universidad de Santiago de Chile
Santiago, Chile

Maryanne L. Fisher
Department of Psychology
Saint Mary's University
Halifax, Nova Scotia, Canada

Andrew C. Gallup
Department of Psychology
State University of New York–Oneonta
Oneonta, NY

Glenn Geher
Department of Psychology
State University of New York–New Paltz
New Paltz, NY

Amanda E. Guitar
Department of Anthropology
Binghamton University
Binghamton, NY

Amanda Hahn
Department of Psychology
Humboldt State University
Arcata, CA

Nicole H. Hess
Department of Anthropology
Washington State University
    at Vancouver
Vancouver, WA

Sarah E. Hill
Department of Psychology
Texas Christian University
Fort Worth, TX

P. Lynne Honey
Department of Psychology
MacEwan University
Edmonton, Alberta, Canada

Liselot Hudders
Department of Communication
    Studies
Ghent University
Ghent, Belgium

Laura L. Johnsen
Department of Anthropology
Binghamton University
Binghamton, NY

Ashleigh J. Kelly
School of Psychology
The University of Queensland
St. Lucia, Queensland, Australia

Leif Edward Ottesen Kennair
Department of Psychology
Norwegian University of Science and
    Technology
Trondheim, Norway

Lucie Kocum
Department of Psychology
Saint Mary's University
Halifax, Nova Scotia, Canada

Linda S. Krajewski
Division of Social Sciences
Human Development
    and Physical Education
San Bernardino Valley College
San Bernardino, CA

Norman P. Li
School of Social Sciences
Singapore Management University
Singapore

Laurette T. Liesen
Department of Political Science
Lewis University
Romeoville, IL

Bobbi Low
School of Natural Resources and
Environment
University of Michigan
Ann Arbor, MI

Melanie MacEacheron
Department of Psychology
University of Western Ontario
London, Ontario, Canada

Francis T. McAndrew
Department of Psychology
Knox College
Galesburg, IL

Tami M. Meredith
Department of Mathematics and
Computing Science
Saint Mary's University
Halifax, Nova Scotia, Canada

Alissa A. Miller
Department of Anthropology
Washington State University
Pullman, WA

Craig Morris
Department of Anthropology
Binghamton University
Binghamton, NY

Chenthila Nagamuthu
Department of Psychology
University of Toronto
Scarborough
Toronto, Ontario, Canada

Lambrianos Nikiforidis
College of Business
The University of Texas at
San Antonio
San Antonio, TX

Megan Oaten
School of Applied Psychology
Griffith University
Southport, Queensland, Australia

Elizabeth Page-Gould
Department of Psychology
University of Toronto
Toronto, Ontario, Canada

Theresa Porter
Connecticut Valley Hospital
Middletown, CT

Marjorie L. Prokosch
Department of Psychology
Texas Christian University
Fort Worth, TX

Chris Reiber
Thousand Oaks, CA

Stacey L. Rucas
Department of Social Sciences
California Polytechnic
State University
San Luis Obispo, CA

Hayley C. Russell
Department of Health and Exercise
Science
Gustavus Adolphus College
Saint Peter, MN

Catherine Salmon
Department of Psychology
University of Redlands
Redlands, CA

Alicia Salvador
Department of Psychobiology-IDOCAL
University of Valencia
Valencia, Spain

Nicole M. Scott
Ape Cognition and Conservation
Initiative
Des Moines, IA

Miguel A. Serrano
Department of Psychobiology
University of Valencia
Valencia, Spain

Rebecca L. Shaiber
Department of Psychology
Loyola University
Chicago, IL

April R. Smith
Department of Psychology
Miami University
Oxford, OH

Rosemarie I. Sokol-Chang
Department of Psychology
State University of New
York–New Paltz
New Paltz, NY

Emily A. Stone
Center for Community and Business
Research
University of Texas at San Antonio
San Antonio, TX

Katelin A. Sutton
Division of Student Learning
Charles Sturt University
Sydney, New South Wales, Australia

Tracy Vaillancourt
School of Psychology
University of Ottawa
Ottawa, Ontario, Canada

Katherine A. Valentine
Crean College of Health and Behavioral
Sciences
Chapman University
Orange, CA

Jaroslava Varella Valentova
Institute of Psychology
University of São Paulo
São Paulo, Brazil

Marco Antonio Corrêa Varella
Institute of Psychology
University of Brasília
Brasília, Brazil

Saundra Vernon
Department of Psychology
Saint Mary's University
Halifax, Nova Scotia, Canada

Jose C. Yong
School of Social Sciences
Singapore Management University
Singapore

TABLE OF CONTENTS

ACKNOWLEDGMENTS

The Oxford Handbook of Women and Competition represents a fulfilled goal. Twenty years ago, research by Sarah Hrdy, Anne Campbell, Helen Fisher, and David Buss (among others) provided me, the Editor, with inspiration to study women and intrasexual competition. I hoped that one day the field would progress to the extent that full volumes on the topic would be possible, and here is tangible evidence of this advancement. Collaborating with the contributors for the *Oxford Handbook of Women and Competition* has been a pleasure, and I am grateful for their hard work, patience, and shared vision in what the book was to become. I am also thankful for the support and assistance from the people at Oxford University Press (OUP), namely Abby Gross. Due to these individuals, OUP firmly remains one of the premier publishers for scholars to share their ideas. In addition, I thank Saint Mary's University for their openness to research topics that are at the edges of mainstream psychology and oftentimes controversial, and to my fantastic collaborators who have worked with me on various topics pertaining to women over the years. I also have a deep appreciation for the undergraduate students who have worked with me, especially their enthusiasm for research, as well as for my son (Maxwell) who greets the world with a highly curious mind. Thanks also to my nonacademic (and academic) friends and family who have had countless discussions with me on related topics, and to my husband, Mark, for his support from the very start of this project. I am grateful to all of you, and am delighted to have had this opportunity.

The Oxford Handbook of Women and Competition

Introduction

Introduction

Maryanne L. Fisher

Abstract

The topic of women's competition has gained recent momentum, as evidenced by the proliferation of articles in the scientific literature. There has been a considerable body of new research highlighting competition in several domains, including access to and retention of mates, access to resources related to mothering, interaction with virtual media, issues faced in the workplace, and engagement with sport and physical activity. The chapters in this volume provide a definitive view on the contemporary state of knowledge regarding women's competition. The majority of chapters rely on an evolutionary framework; other chapters argue that sociocultural sources shape women's competition. While the book is primarily about women, some contributors focus on issues faced by adolescent girls, or mention developmental trajectories for young girls through adulthood. It is hoped that the information within this volume will serve as a source of inspiration to help guide future directions for research.

Key Words: women, competition, indirect aggression, behavior, intrasexual competition, same-sex, review

Introduction

For those of us with an interest in women and competition, it is truly an exciting era. Never before has there been such a dedicated focus on the topic, with numerous articles and books detailing the wide assortment of venues in which women engage in competition and associated behavioral, cognitive, and hormonal considerations. Indeed, the issue has gained significant momentum in the scholarly literature over the last two decades. These developments span a noteworthy range of topics, as exemplified in the chapters listed in the table of contents for this volume.

The goal of this volume is to provide a definitive overview of the field of women and competition. Some chapters expand this view to incorporate girls and adolescents, aiming to provide a fuller understanding of issues pertaining to women. A second, equally important goal is to shed light on topics that require further exploration, and thereby serve as a springboard to help direct future research. Indeed, every chapter contains concrete ideas for new research directions.

To set the stage, I begin this introduction with a discussion on why this book is about women. Some readers may argue that such a section is entirely unnecessary, and that books that focus on men would not typically include such a review. However, I feel strongly compelled to document shifts in the scholarship over time, and to suggest plausible reasons that led to the dedicated study of women and competition. Such change has been slow and often difficult, and it has taken decades to arrive. Thus, I feel it must be documented for posterity, so that new generations of scholars may comprehend some of the hurdles researchers in this area have likely faced.

I then turn to a brief overview of the current theoretical state of the field, including a short discussion of areas that have remained seemingly overlooked by the research community. This section is followed by a presentation of the layout of the book, and a short conclusion.

Turning the Focus toward Women

The overwhelming majority of modern research on competition pertains to that which occurs within-sex (intrasexual) rather than between-sex (intersexual). It is important to start with a clear statement that scholarly developments in the study of women and intrasexual competition have not been at the expense of understanding men and their forms of intrasexual competition, which was (e.g., Daly & Wilson, 1990; Fischer & Mosquera, 2001; Geary et al., 2003; Marlowe, 2000; Mazur & Booth, 1998; Polk, 1994; Symons, 1979; Van de Vliert & Janssen, 2002; Wilson & Daly, 1985)—and remains (see, e.g., Buunk & Massar, 2012; Ponzi et al., 2015)—a topic of much interest for researchers. Some of this past research, as well as current scholarship, reflects an interest in exploring the sexes together, showing how they converge and diverge in their forms of intrasexual competition. Indeed, some of the chapters in this volume similarly rely on comparisons of women with men, while others focus solely on women. Regardless, the constantly growing body of scientific literature shows that there is a need to understand the sexes both together and individually, in terms of their competitive behaviors, motivations, and cognitions.

It is indisputable that there has been an academic shift from the focus on men and competition to studying women and competition. There are several potential explanations for why this has happened, five of which are now discussed.

As mentioned, the majority of chapters in the current volume incorporate an evolutionary perspective. It has been reviewed elsewhere (Fisher, Sokol-Chang, & Garcia, 2013) that women are typically perceived as being relatively passive in the evolutionary process, particularly within the traditional evolutionary psychology paradigm (see Liesen, 2007, 2013). Viewing women as competitive therefore reflects a shift toward perceiving women as active agents. Moreover, much of the prior work pertaining to women and evolution has been oriented toward what happens *to* women rather than women's active influence on human evolution (Fisher, Sokol-Chang, & Garcia, 2013). Hence, this paradigm shift toward viewing women as active agents within the evolution of humans has directly led to an outpouring of new work.

Another reason underpinning the change may be temporal societal shifts. Societal views of women (and men) are revised over time, and for most Western cultures, this shift has meant a movement toward gender equality (see, e.g., Crompton & Lyonette, 2008). For instance, in 1977, 65% of interview respondents in the United States believed in "traditional" gender roles, where men should be the primary earners, with women taking care of the home and family, while in 2012, that number dipped to 31% of respondents (Roper Center, 2015). Inglehart and Norris (2003) state that while there is a general global movement toward gender equality, such that some countries have achieved major gains in legal, educational, economic, and political gender equality, "in many places, the lives of women remain wretched" (p. 3). This remaining cultural difference in gender equality may be due to numerous factors. Manago and colleagues (2014) document how environmental change in terms of increased urbanization, and technological and commercial growth, leads to a shift away from ascribed gender roles and toward chosen and equality-based roles.

Moreover, gender roles may directly impinge upon competitive attitudes and behaviors. Cultures that become less patriarchal show a decrease in sex differences in attitudes toward engaging in direct, overt competition. Andersen et al. (2013) investigated ball-throwing activity where there was an economic reward for performance when individuals outperformed others; they found that adolescent girls had a lower propensity than boys to compete in such a task in a patriarchal society, with no sex difference in a matriarchal society. They argue that traditional gender roles exhibited by patriarchal societies cause girls to typically show a decline in competitiveness during adolescence, and that this decline presumably decreases as society shifts from patriarchal to matriarchal (Andersen et al., 2013). Hence, by extension, if there is a cultural shift over time toward egalitarian gender roles, there should be less stigma associated with girls and women competing in a direct manner for the resources, mates, and status that they seek.

Perhaps this shift is also a result of the growing number of women involved in research. Reiter (1975), when discussing the study of women in anthropology, comments: "A great deal of information on women exists, but it frequently comes from questions asked of men about their wives, daughters, and sisters, rather than from the women themselves. Men's information is too often presented as a group's reality, rather than as only a part of a cultural whole. Too often women and their roles are glossed over, under-analyzed, or absent from all but the edges of their description" (p. 12). With the growing number of women entering academia (e.g., CAUT, 2008), there is presumably an associated shift in the focus of research, coupled with new, critical questions about potential biases in past theories and findings.

Maybe, too, it is due to increasingly sophisticated methodologies. Hrdy (1981/1999, pp. 129–130) states that:

> Women are no less competitive than other primates, and the evidence will be forthcoming when we begin to devise methodologies sufficiently ingenious to measure it. Efforts to date have sought to find "lines of authority" and hierarchies comparable to those males form in corporations. No scientist has yet trained a systematic eye on women competing with one another in the spheres that really matter to them.

Thus, she proposed that one of the obstacles to studying women's intrasexual competition is subtlety, and consequently researchers need to invent or discover research methods that are able to detect covert behaviors. Further, researchers need to determine the spheres in which women compete, rather than simply examine hierarchies and dominance, as women compete in many arenas and these traditional schemas may not be relevant. Turning one's research focus to these previously unexplored areas was critical, given that women's intrasexual competition rarely involves escalating contests (Clutton-Brock & Huchard, 2013), and that women suppress it when men are present in order to avoid seeming undesirable (Cashdan, 1999; Fisher et al., 2010). The chapters in this book indicate there have been sufficient advances in methodologies and research design that have enabled empirical examination of women's notoriously subtle and covert intrasexual competition.

The State of the Field

The topic of female competition has gained considerable recent momentum, as evidenced by the proliferation of articles in the scientific literature. This expansion of inquiry and theoretical development has been noticeable within the area of women's competition, as well as in the competition of other mammals and birds. Indeed, the general topic has developed to the extent that there was a recent issue of a top-tier scientific journal dedicated to this topic (i.e., Campbell & Stockley, 2013; a theme issue on "Female Competition and Aggression" for *Philosophical Transactions of the Royal Society, Series B, Biological Sciences*). While there has been an absence of academic books singularly devoted to women's intrasexual competition, several authors have meaningfully raised the issue in the larger context of the evolved psychology of women (e.g., Campbell, 2002; Hrdy, 1981/1999) or while studying the similarities and differences between the sexes (e.g., Benenson, 2014). It should be noted that there have been a handful of books that have solely explored women and competition, but often these are more popularist accounts, with the majority using interview data and providing a look into individual experiences, or relying on general statements without academic support (e.g., Chesler, 2009; Holiday & Rosenberg, 2009; Shapiro Barash, 2007; Tanenbaum, 2002). These books remain informative works, certainly, but do not typically include the same level of scientific rigor as more academically marketed volumes. Looking more broadly, there are mass market books aimed at helping women remove themselves from competition altogether (e.g., DiMarco, 2008). Recently, there have been publications oriented toward addressing how women are treating themselves overly harshly, and thus acting as a "mean girl" to themselves and competing with imaginary rivals (e.g., Ahlers & Arylo, 2015). Regardless of the intended audience or approach, one fact is clear: collectively, these works provide direct evidence that there is an interest in the lives of girls and women, as pertaining to their aggressive and competitive interactions with same-sex others.

In my opinion (outlined in Fisher, 2013), one of the most influential catalysts that propelled scientific developments in the area of women and intrasexual competition was a call by Sarah Blaffer Hrdy (1981), quoted earlier in this chapter. Hrdy writes that when she originally published *The Woman That Never Evolved*, the field had only been examining female intrasexual competition within the context of nonhuman primates, not among humans. After the initial release of her book, articles started to appear that pertained to sex differences in competition (e.g., Cashdan, 1998), and some researchers focussed on these differences within competition for mates (e.g., Buss, 1988; Buss & Dedden, 1990). These developments were followed by early research on women's competitive tactics and behavior within an evolutionary context (e.g., Campbell, 1995, 1999; Cashdan, 1999; but see also an early mention in Fisher, 1983). More recently, there has been a growth in the literature dedicated toward women intrasexually competing with friends (Bleske & Shackelford, 2001) or in the workplace (e.g., Buunk & Dijkstra, 2012).

I propose that once the door was opened by Hrdy (1981), researchers started to earnestly explore evolutionary accounts of women's intrasexual competition, and then this focus shifted outward, moving into domains outside of evolutionary-based (sub) disciplines. Although many scholars prior to Hrdy studied competition, they often concluded with the statement that girls and women are simply less competitive relative to boys and men (e.g., Skarin & Moely, 1976; for a review, see Cashdan, 1998). Such conclusions were based on overt, direct measures of competition, such as winning a game, or social comparison with friends and concerns with appearing to be inferior to them (e.g., Berndt, 1982). In many instances, sex differences typically manifest when competition is expressed using physical aggression, with men using this form far more than women (e.g., table 3, Cashdan, 1998). Thus, the critical catalyst that drove the academic movement toward studying women's intrasexual competition, and led to incredible progress over the past decades, was when Hrdy rallied scholars to start to examine women's competition in ways that truly mattered to them. Hence, there was a shift away from examining direct methods for establishing hierarchies, for example, and toward covert, indirect means to gain access to mates, status, dominance, or resources (e.g., Björkqvist, 1994; Björkqvist, Lagerspetz, & Kaukiainen, 1992; Campbell, 1999).

Researchers have proposed a link between aggression and competition, such that aggression is necessary for competition to occur (e.g., Schuster, 1983). Indeed, as may be deduced from this review thus far, there was a breakthrough when findings from studies on aggression began to be included in frameworks for examining women's intrasexual competition. Those studying aggression showed women's experiences in interpersonal relationships often led to gains with respect to resources, mates, status, or reputation (e.g., Burbank, 1987; Olson, 1994; Schuster, 1983, 1985). Those who linked the findings from indirect aggression with theories of competition were able to, at long last, comprehend the subtle nature of women's intrasexual competition.

Rather than provide an overview of developments since the integration of these areas, I leave it to readers to peruse the chapters of this book. The contributors provide evidence of the ways in which women compete, and the underlying causes and motivations of their behavior. What is abundantly clear is that women do compete (typically with each other), and that the form of their competition is often indirect, covert, and circuitous. Many of the authors review how girls and women rely on indirect aggression to perform their intrasexually competitive acts. Based on the chapters in this volume, it is safe to conclude that women rarely compete via direct, physically aggressive means.

Future Research Directions

There are still many areas within women's intrasexual competition that are neglected by researchers; as mentioned, each chapter outlines directions for future work. However, for the sake of transparency, it is important to note that there are several omissions from this volume, which is primarily due to an overall lack of research on specific topics. I have identified six such areas, although I presume there remain others not listed here.

To begin, there is a mainly theoretical limitation regarding work that is situated using evolutionary theory. Darwin, in *The Descent of Man* (1871/ 1998), argued that the weapons and ornaments observed in males but rarely in females of many species were secondary sexual characteristics. These features were not primarily the result of increased survival, but instead the consequence of intrasexual competition for access to mates or to attract members of the opposite sex. Sexual selection, as Darwin named the process, was dependent on the advantages that some members of the species had over other members, exclusively framed in terms of reproduction. According to Clutton-Brock (2007, p. 1885), since the days of Darwin, sexual selection is now perceived to be

> a process operating through intrasexual competition for mates or mating opportunities, with the result that selection pressures arising from intrasexual competition between females to conceive or rear young are generally excluded and sexual selection is, by definition, a process that is largely confined to males. An unfortunate consequence of this is that characteristics that increase the competitive ability of individuals are likely to be attributed to sexual selection if they occur in males—but not if they occur in females.... [There remain] many important questions about the operation of sexual selection in females and the evolution of sex differences have yet to be answered. Where females compete directly with each other, it is often unclear precisely

what they are competing for. Where females have developed obvious secondary sexual characteristics, it is often uncertain whether these are used principally to attract males or in intrasexual competition for resources, and how their development is limited is unknown.

Thus, while we have made large strides in our understanding of women's intrasexual competition for limited resources (including quality mates), the ultimate motivation and consequences of competition is at times obscured.

The remaining five areas that are not addressed in this volume are less theoretical, but highly important. First, there is minimal research on mating psychology related to nonheterosexual women, as applied to competition for access to, and retention of, mates (see for exceptions, Li et al., 2010, who studied eating disorders; and Lindenbaum, 1985, who reports as a psychotherapist on competition within lesbian relationships). Indeed, while there exists work, for example, on women's sexual fluidity as a mechanism for shared parenting (i.e., allomothering; Kuhle & Radtke, 2013, but also Apostolou, 2016) as a form of cooperation, there remains a heteronormative bias in the literature for women's mating competition. Moreover, there is seemingly no literature addressing how nonheterosexual women compete for access to resources that are necessary for successfully raising children (who may be present from a prior heterosexual relationship, or a result of planned insemination), or access to resources that may assist their families' survival (for further reading, see Kirkpatrick, 1987).

Second, this volume only touches on co-wives and the forms of their competition among various cultures (see, e.g., the chapter by Sokol-Chang, Burch, & Fisher). There has been research on co-wives and competition within individual cultures (e.g., Burbank, 1987) and, albeit rarely, at a multicultural level (see Jankowiak et al., 2005; and for coding issues in the Standard Cross-Cultural Sample, see White, 1988). However, it remains vastly understudied and is rarely a central topic of inquiry. Related to this point, there is a lack of specific, focused investigation into issues faced by co-wives who are mothers, specifically dealing with the resources that they need to support their children, although presumably such data exist as part of other projects.

Third, there is also an apparent lack of investigation into the acute and chronic health consequences for women who engage in intrasexual competition on a long-term basis in the workplace, within their families (e.g., in the case of co-wives, between sisters, or between mothers and daughters, or among in-laws), or for access to mates. In one study, young adult women reported higher levels of distress resulting from competition within their friendships and in academic domains (McGuire & Leaper, 2016), but the long-term outcome of this distress remains unknown. In this volume, the chapter by Miller and Rucas does partly address this topic, as they examine how the loss of sleep due to rumination over social situations with other women influences well-being and health outcomes. This topic is highly important, given the direct consequences for women's overall health and well-being, which affects not only themselves but also those who may depend on them for care, such as children, elderly parents, or mates.

Fourth, much of the work that conceptually relies on an evolutionary framework pertains to women's intrasexual competition for access to mates. In her chapter in this volume, Low discusses the theoretical underpinnings of women's intrasexual competition, and asserts, "Intrasexual selection always concerns resources important for survival and reproduction, or resources that have in the past filled that role" (p. 17). She states that the majority of work in this area deals with mating, yet it also plays a very important part in other areas of girls' and women's lives, starting in the womb. One explanation for the focus on mating is that Darwin considered intrasexual competition in his theory of sexual selection, such that it occurs when members of the same sex compete for access to mates. Perhaps scholars using an evolutionary perspective have been slow to move away from this limited scope and expand competition to being a phenomenon that happens in many life-stages and in a variety of contexts.

This focus on mating access has led to several areas of neglect; for example, competition for retention of mates, or competition among women who are already in a romantic relationship. Indeed, the overwhelming majority of the research findings are based on single young women participating in studies for course credit while at university, and hence, are members of a WEIRD sample (i.e., Western, Educated, Industrialized, Rich, and Democratic societies; Henrich, Heine, & Norenzayan, 2010). For example, it remains unknown how women who have been married for over a decade, with children or grandchildren, compete to retain their mates, or even if they engage in such activity. Moreover, we have no research on how these women would compare if they lived in, for example, a Western and non-Western culture. This focus on younger women competing for access to mates has resulted in a lack of research on competition among women in their later reproductive years or among postmenopausal women; for a first exploration of these issues, see MacEacheron and Campbell in this volume. This lack of attention to older women is a noteworthy exception, given the research on the importance of grandmothers (see Sokol-Chang et al., this volume, for a review).

Fifth, there has been a dearth of research into the influence of individual differences on women's intrasexual competition (although see, for an exception, Buunk & Fisher, 2009). However, there needs to be much deeper exploration into factors related to, for example, personality traits, time perspective orientation, life history strategy, developmental history, self-monitoring, dominance seeking, and social conformity. Likewise, cultural influences remain overlooked, including how one's cultural orientation (e.g., collectivistic/individualist) plays a role. There is some promising recent work, though, which deals with individual differences in father presence versus absence within the Caribbean island of Curaçao (van Brummen-Girigori & Buunk, 2016).

Structure and Contents of the Book

This book consists of 39 chapters organized into 10 sections, with an additional concluding chapter. At times, there is some overlapping content in a portion of the chapters that helps to reinforce key points from multiple perspectives, while still enabling the chapters to stand alone.

Section two is devoted to theory and overview of women's intrasexual competition. Low opens the book with a broad overview of the types of female intrasexual competition, and outlines how it occurs over the span of a woman's lifetime, starting in the womb and then later in life for social status or mates. Given that the bulk of the existing literature pertains to mating competition, it was decided that the next chapter would deal specifically with theory surrounding this form of competition. Thus, Arnocky and Vaillancourt examine mating competition, as caused by biparental care and individual variation in men's mate value. To close this section and provide the reader with ideas about general sociality, and how competition may work in tandem with needs for affiliation and cooperation, Scott examines the sociality of female nonhuman primates. She extrapolates about the potential lives of women if they lived in various social environments.

Section three deals with social status and aggression. Liesen begins this section with an examination of women's aggression and status seeking within their social networks, arguing that they may be both supportive and competitive, and largely impact on women's lives, as well as the lives of their children. Gallup's chapter serves as an example of some of the arguments posed by Liesen, and he investigates adolescent girls' intrasexual peer aggression from an evolutionary perspective, positing that it serves to influence the dating relationships of rivals, as well as enabling one to gain access to desired partners. Rucas presents the idea of social capital as driving women's intrasexual competition, and investigates how relationships with particular individuals lead to benefits that offset costs in maintaining social networks, for example. Nagamuthu and Page-Gould explore women's same-sex friendships, and address whether intrasexual competition is highest among friends, or if friendship nullifies the existence of competition in favor of cooperation. Honey adds a different perspective, focusing instead on how the Dark Triad of personality traits (subclinical psychopathy, Machiavellianism, and narcissism) is used by women to exploit and manipulate others, often for purposes of gaining status, resources, or mates.

Section four pertains to communication and gossip. Anderson presents a model of women's communication of aggression, where women functionally match the form and frequency of their aggression to environmental triggers and individual differences between competitors. McAndrew turns the focus of the rest of this section to gossip. He explores women's use of gossip, and shows that it may be used in an aggressive, competitive way to effectively exclude potential competitors from the social group, as well as harming competitors' ability to establish or maintain a social network. Sutton and Oaten then use the perspective of gossip as informational aggression, and conclude that it is an effective, low-risk strategy to use in intrasexual competition for mates, particularly within the framework of altering reputations and poaching potential mates. Hess addresses coalitional relationships, and suggests that they serve aggressive functions in competitions involving one's reputation. She argues that intrasexually competing via gossip is typically more effective than using physical aggression for within-group competitive contexts.

Section five is centered on mate availability and mating relationships. Stone opens this section with a review of the research on how imbalances in the number of men and women (i.e., the sex ratio) influence mating competition. Her investigation reveals that while men's mating competition is increased when there is a surplus of available mates, women's behavior is more mixed, possibly due to socioeconomic factors, patriarchy, or variance in mate quality. Dillion, Adair, and Brase take a closer look at sex ratios, focusing instead on the operational sex ratio (i.e., the ratio of men to women who are viable and available mates in a given mating market). They posit that women who are in environments where there is a surplus of women demonstrate systematic changes in their behaviors, including increased intrasexual competition. Continuing the theme of mating markets, Fisher and Fernández discuss strategies for intrasexual competition in relation to women's mate value, and suggest that mate value may be manipulated by rivals. Brewer adds novelty with her examination of the specific mating-related threats that women face, depending on whether they are single or romantically partnered, and how these threats influence their use of competitive tactics. Adair, Dillon, and Brase turn to how women may use the mating preferences of other women to provide information concerning their own mate choice (e.g., for the purposes of mate copying, mate poaching, or mate retention). They investigate how women's interest in other women's mate choice may lead to increased competition for mates, as well as the contexts in which this competition is most likely to be observed. In the last chapter of this section, Morris, Beaussart, Reiber, and Krajewski look at how women cope with the long-term effects of romantic relationship dissolution, and propose that associated negative emotions may provide motivation to avoid similar situations in the future. Specifically, they argue that dissolution due to women's intrasexual competition via losing a mate to a rival may lead to several advantages.

Section six details endocrinological and psychobiological considerations. Costa, Serrano, and Salvador suggest that women engaged in competition show a psychobiological response pattern that is effectively captured by their coping competition model. In this model, they propose a multistep process that emphasizes one's cognitive appraisal of the situation, which begins before the competition, as well as one's appraisal about the outcome, which influences future competitions. Using a narrower perspective, Cobey and Hahn exclusively focus on the hormonal regulation of competitive behavior in women, using a comparative and lifespan approach that ranges from birth through to after menopause. Nikiforidis, Arsena, and Durante narrow the

hormonal focus one step further and examine the influence of the ovulatory cycle on women's intrasexual competition. Their review highlights ovulatory influences on women's motivation to enhance their appearance for purposes of outperforming rivals, but also on patterns of consumption and financial decision-making as a way to compete in terms of status and resources.

Section seven pertains to topics spanning health and aging. Miller and Rucas examine how women's intrasexual competition and aggression within their social networks gives rise to problems for sleep, for example via ruminations or in sleep tradeoffs against waking activities, when more time and mental energy are needed for social actions. Sleep issues in turn impact on women's health and well-being. Turning to diet, Salmon reviews women's intrasexual competition for status and dominance, as well as for mates, and posits that it may lead to reproductive suppression. She proposes such suppression may be self-induced or caused by others, via extreme dieting behavior. In the last chapter of this section, MacEacheron and Campbell review potential factors that influence women's intrasexual mating competition as they age, arguing that the majority of research is exclusively performed on young women. To demonstrate potential areas of future development, they review reproductive advantages that women may experience when they are considered a successful mother.

Section eight focuses on motherhood and family. Valentine, Li, and Yong provide a thorough cross-species review of how mammalian mothers engage in various types of competition that ultimately influence the success of their offspring surviving and reproducing. In a related vein, Sokol-Chang, Burch, and Fisher focus on human mothers and separately investigate the advantages of cooperative versus competitive mothering, arriving at the conclusion that integrating both cooperation and competition is the most beneficial strategy. Kennair and Biegler extend the focus of this section to other family members and study mother-daughter conflict over choice of the daughter's mate, if the daughter's mate value is perceived as a valuable commodity in terms of a tradable resource for the family. In some cases, parents may provide benefits to some daughters, but not others, causing intrasexual competition between sisters. The section ends with Cousins' and Porter's examination of infanticide. They explore the specific circumstances that may lead to infanticide, such that it allows the mother to be able to intrasexually compete for access to better-quality mates.

Section nine presents chapters on physical appearance. DelPriore, Prokosch, and Hill begin this section with a focus on the advantages and disadvantages faced by beautiful women. They discuss how and why women strategically enhance their physical attractiveness to facilitate intrasexual competition. Dubbs, Kelly, and Barlow contend that women's fixation on improving their physical appearance for mating competition can lead them to take risks, such as unnecessary medical procedures. Shaiber, Johnsen, and Geher depart from examining individual attractiveness per se and instead present a review of adult and children's beauty pageants, arguing that they elicit competitive behaviors and strategies typically seen in mating contexts. Further, they suggest that the emphasis on status and resources that are bestowed on a winner enhance motivation to intrasexually compete. Johnsen and Geher examine fashion, viewing it as a tool women may use to enhance their attractiveness and hence effectively compete with rivals. They also review how women alter their clothing choices in relation to their ovulatory cycle status, in order to best compete for mating access.

Section ten deals with competition in virtual contexts. Yong, Li, Valentine, and Smith examine women's intrasexual competition for mates via virtual means. They propose that women engage in social comparison and competition with same-sex others who they see in print and electronic media, and explore the ways that women are influenced by this pervasive exposure. Keeping with the theme of virtual media, Guitar and Carmen examine a social network site, Facebook, and how it provides a novel platform for women to engage in intrasexual competition via behaviors such as stalking, bullying, and self-promotion, as well as other competitive strategies. Meredith turns to the issue of women's computer gaming, and contends that women engage in intrasexually competitive behaviors while gaming, if provided with the opportunities to do so. She argues that the style of women's play mirrors competitive strategies that have been documented in real life, including mating competitions, contests for status, and the formation and maintenance of alliances.

Section eleven pertains to competition in applied settings, and the included chapters span a wide assortment of areas. Kocum, Courvoisier, and Vernon investigate intrasexual competition among women in the workplace, and argue that zero-sum situations lead to the creation of intrasexual prejudice and discrimination. De Backer, Hudders, and Fisher examine the ways one may study competition in relation to food preparation and consumption, and propose many lines of potential inquiry to bridge evolutionary theory with food studies. Varella, Varella Valentová, and Fernández discuss how women's interest in various artistic pursuits, such as bodily ornamentation, creating objects, and beautifying places, represent important venues for examining intrasexual competition. The final chapter of the book is by Russell, Dutove, and Dithurbide, and they review women's competition in sport and physical activity. They provide a developmental perspective on girls and sport, and then turn to how women learn about competition, issues surrounding dispositional competitiveness, outcomes of competitiveness, and general consequences for women's competition in sport.

Concluding Remarks

This volume represents a comprehensive examination of women's competition. The topic is highly important, given that competition has the potential to influence many aspects of women's lives, including their overall biological development, coupled with attitudes toward their physical health and appearance, their interactions with family members and same-sex friends, how they form romantic and sexual relationships, the ways they interact with virtual media, and their participation in sport and physical activity. The contributors address how competition starts early in life, even while still in the womb, and carries on throughout girlhood and adolescence into adulthood. The fact that competition is so pervasive throughout women's lives clearly indicates its importance as an area of academic study.

Collectively, we have made significant advances in the study of this topic. However, there remain areas that have yet to be examined. In addition, there are topics being explored that are not included in the volume (mostly due to their infancy). Two such examples are hormonal fluctuations in contest sports (Casto & Edwards, 2016), and interest in running for political positions (Preece & Stoddard, 2015). Clearly, there are no signs that the momentum of research on women's competition will slow in the near future.

This volume is timely and needed. There has been an exciting increase in the number of studies over the last decades pertaining to women's intrasexual competition in particular. Still, there has not been a parallel increase in the number of academic books on the topic. As mentioned, the majority of relevant books are oriented toward a popular-readership audience, with little examination of the overall academic literature. What is truly novel about this volume is the definitive voice that the chapters provide on the academic study of women's competition. The chapters not only represent the current state of the field from multiple perspectives, but also provide solid guidelines for future directions for research. Hopefully, this volume will be an inspiring one for the next generation of scholars, and serve as a solid foundation to their work.

References

Ahlers, A., & Arylo, C. (2015). *Reform your inner mean girl: 7 steps to stop bullying yourself and start loving yourself.* Old Saybrook, CT: Tantor Audio.

Andersen, S., Ertac, S., Gneezy, U., List, J. A., & Maximiano, S. (2013). Gender, competitiveness, and socialization at a young age: Evidence from a matrilineal and patrilineal society. *Review of Economics and Statistics, 95*(4), 1438–1443.

Apostolou, M. (2016). The evolution of female same-sex attractions: The weak selection pressures hypothesis. *Evolutionary Behavioral Sciences, 10*(4), 270–283.

Benenson, J. (2014). *The survival of the sexes: Warriors and worriers.* New York: Oxford University Press.

Berndt, T. J. (1982). The features and effects of friendship in early adolescence. *Child Development, 53*(6), 1447–1460.

Björkqvist, K. (1994). Sex differences in physical, verbal, and indirect aggression: A review of recent research. *Sex Roles, 30,* 177–188.

Björkqvist, K., Lagerspetz, K. M., & Kaukiainen, A. (1992). Do girls manipulate and boys fight? Developmental trends in regard to direct and indirect aggression. *Aggressive Behavior, 18,* 117–127.

Bleske, A. L., & Shackelford, T. K. (2001). Poaching, promiscuity, and deceit: Combatting mating rivalry in same-sex friendships. *Personal Relationships, 8*(4), 407–424.

Burbank, V. K. (1987). Female aggression in cross-cultural perspective. *Behavior Science Research, 21,* 70–100.

Buunk, A. P., & Dijkstra, P. (2012). The social animal within organizations. In S. C. Roberts (Ed.), *Applied evolutionary psychology* (pp. 36–54). New York: Oxford University Press.

Buunk, A., & Fisher, M. (2009). Individual differences in intrasexual competition. *Journal of Evolutionary Psychology, 7,* 37–48.

Buunk, A. P., & Massar, K. (2012). Intrasexual competition among males: Competitive towards men, prosocial towards women. *Personality and Individual Differences, 52*(7), 818–821.

Buss, D. M. (1988). The evolution of human intrasexual competition: Tactics of mate attraction. *Journal of Personality and Social Psychology, 54,* 616–628.

Buss, D. M., & Dedden, L. A. (1990). Derogation of competitors. *Journal of Social and Personal Relationships, 7,* 395–422.

Campbell, A. (1995). A few good men: Evolutionary psychology and female adolescent aggression. *Ethology and Sociobiology, 16,* 99–123.

Campbell, A. (1999). Staying alive: Evolution, culture and women's intra-sexual aggression. *Behavioural and Brain Sciences, 22,* 203–252.

Campbell, A. (2002). *A mind of her own: The evolutionary psychology of women.* New York: Oxford University Press.

Campbell, A., & Stockley, P. (Eds.). (2013). Female competition and aggression special issue. *Philosophical Transactions of the Royal Society B, 368* (1631).

Cashdan, E. (1998). Are men more competitive than women? *British Journal of Social Psychology, 37,* 213–229.

Cashdan, E. (1999). How women compete. *Behavioral and Brain Sciences, 22,* 221.

Casto, K. V., & Edwards, D. A. (2016). Before, during, and after: How phases of competition differentially affect testosterone, cortisol, and estradiol levels in women athletes. *Adaptive Human Behavior and Physiology, 2*(1), 11–25.

CAUT (2008). Narrowing the gender gap. *CAUT Equity Review, 2.* Retrieved from https://www.caut.ca/docs/equity-review/narrowing-the-gender-gap-mdash-women-academics-in-canadian-universities-(mar-2008).pdf?sfvrsn=12.

Chesler, P. (2009). *Women's inhumanity to women.* Chicago: Chicago Review Press.

Clutton-Brock, T. (2007). Sexual selection in males and females. *Science, 318,* 1882–1885.

Clutton-Brock, T. H., & Huchard, E. (2013). Social competition and selection in males and females. *Philosophical Transactions of the Royal Society B, 368*(1631), 1–15.

Crompton, R., & Lyonette, C. (2008). Who does the housework? The division of labour within the home. In A. Park, J. Curtice, K. Thomson, M. Phillips, M. Johnson, & E. Clery (Eds.), *British social attitudes* (24th report, pp. 53–80). London: Sage.

Daly, M., & Wilson, M. (1990). Killing the competition: Female/female and male/male homicide. *Human Nature, 1*(1), 81–107.

Darwin, C. (1871/1998). *The expression of emotion in man and animals.* London: Harper Collins.

DiMarco, H. (2008). *Mean girls: Facing your beauty turned beast.* Grand Rapids, MI: Revell.

Fischer, A. H., & Mosquera, P. M. (2001). What concerns men? Women or other men?: A critical appraisal of the evolutionary theory of gender differences. *Psychology, Evolution and Gender, 3,* 5–26.

Fisher, H. E. (1983). *The sex contract.* New York: William Morrow.

Fisher, M. (2013). Women's intrasexual competition. In M. Fisher, J. Garcia, & R. Chang (Eds.), *Evolution's empress: Darwinian perspectives on the nature of women* (pp. 19–42). New York: Oxford University Press.

Fisher, M., Shaw, S., Worth, K., Smith, L., & Reeve, C. (2010). How we view those who derogate: Perceptions of female competitor derogators. *Journal of Social, Evolutionary, and Cultural Psychology, 4*(4), 265–276.

Fisher, M., Sokol Chang, R., & Garcia, J. (2013). Introduction to *Evolution's Empress.* In M. Fisher, J. Garcia, & R. Chang (Eds.), *Evolution's empress: Darwinian perspectives on the nature of women* (pp. 1–16). New York: Oxford University Press.

Geary, D. C., Byrd-Craven, J., Hoard, M. K., Vigil, J., & Numtee, C. (2003). Evolution and development of boys' social behavior. *Developmental Review, 23*(4), 444–470.

Henrich, J., Heine, S. J., & Norenzayan, A. (2010). The weirdest people in the world? *Behavioural Brain Science, 33*(2/3), 61–83.

Holiday, E., & Rosenberg, J. I. (2009). *Mean girls, meaner women: Understanding why women backstab, betray and trash-talk each other and how to heal.* Bangkok, Thailand: Orchid Press.

Hrdy, S. (1981/1999). *The women that never evolved.* Cambridge, MA: Harvard University Press.

Inglehart, R., & Norris, P. (2003). *Rising tide: Gender equality and cultural change around the world.* Cambridge, UK: Cambridge University Press.

Jankowiak, W., Sudakov, M., & Wilreker, B. C. (2005). Co-wife conflict and co-operation. *Ethnology, 44*(1), 81–92.

Kirkpatrick, M. (1987). Clinical implications of lesbian mother studies. *Journal of Homosexuality, 14*(1/2), 201–211.

Kuhle, B. X., & Radtke, S. (2013). Born both ways: The alloparenting hypothesis for sexual fluidity in women. *Evolutionary Psychology, 11*, 304–323.

Li, N. P., Smith, A. R., Griskevicius, V., Cason, M. J., & Bryan, A. (2010). Intrasexual competition and eating restriction in heterosexual and homosexual individuals. *Evolution and Human Behavior, 31*(5), 365–372.

Liesen, L. T. (2007). Women, behavior, and evolution: Understanding the debate between feminist evolutionists and evolutionary psychologists. *Politics and the Life Sciences, 26*(1), 51–70.

Liesen, L. T. (2013). Feminists need to look beyond evolutionary psychology for insights into human reproductive strategies: A commentary. *Sex Roles, 69*, 484.

Lindenbaum, J. P. (1985). The shattering of an illusion: The problem of competition in lesbian relationships. *Feminist Studies, 11*(1), 85–103.

Manago, A. M., Greenfield, P. M., Kim, J. L, & Ward, L. M. (2014). Changing cultural pathways through gender role and sexual development: A theoretical framework. *Journal of the Society for Physical Anthropology, 42*(2), 198–221.

Marlowe, F. (2000). Paternal investment and the human mating system. *Behavioural Processes, 51*, 45–61.

Mazur, A., & Booth, A. (1998). Testosterone and dominance in men. *Behavioral and Brain Sciences, 21*, 353–397.

McGuire, J. E., & Leaper, C. (2016). Competition, coping, and closeness in young heterosexual adults' same-gender friendships. *Sex Roles, 74*, 422–435.

Olson, E. (1994). Female voices of aggression in Tonga. *Sex Roles, 30*, 237–248.

Polk, K. (1994). *When men kill.* Cambridge: Cambridge University Press.

Ponzi, D., Henry, A., Kubicki, K, Nickels, N., Wilson, M. C., & Maestripieri, D. (2015). Morningness-eveningness and intrasexual competition in men. *Personality and Individual Differences, 76*, 228–231.

Preece, J., & Stoddard, O. (2015). Why women don't run: Experimental evidence on gender differences in political competition aversion. *Journal of Economic Behavior and Organization, 117*, 296–308.

Reiter, R., ed. (1975). *Toward an anthropology of women.* 6th ed. New York: Monthly Review Press.

Roper Center. (2015) Retrieved from http://ropercenter.cornell.edu/general-social-survey/.

Schuster, I. (1983). Women's aggression: An African case study. *Aggressive Behaviour, 9*, 319–331.

Schuster, I. (1985). Female aggression and resource scarcity: A cross-cultural perspective. In M. Haug, D. Benton, P. F. Brain, B. Olivier, & J. Moss (Eds.), *The aggressive female* (pp. 185–208). Den Haag, Netherlands: CIP-Gegevens Koninklijke Bibloteheek.

Shapiro Barash, S. (2007). *Tripping the prom queen: The truth about women and rivalry.* New York: St. Martin's Griffin.

Skarin, K., & Moely, B. E. (1976). Altruistic behavior: An analysis of age and sex differences. *Child Development, 47*(4), 1159–1165.

Symons, D. (1979). *The evolution of human sexuality.* New York: Oxford University Press.

Tanenbaum, L. (2002). *Catfight: Women and competition.* New York: Seven Stories Press.

van Brummen-Girigori, O., & Buunk, A. P. (2016). Intrasexual competitiveness and non-verbal seduction strategies to attract males: A study among teenage girls from Curaçao. *Evolution and Human Behavior, 37*(2), 134–141.

Van de Vliert, E., & Janssen, O. (2002). Competitive societies are happy if the women are less competitive than the men. *Cross-Cultural Research: The Journal of Comparative Social Science, 36*, 321–337.

White, D. R. (1988). Rethinking polygyny: Co-wives, codes, and cultural systems. *Current Anthropology, 29*(4), 529–572.

Wilson, M. I., & Daly, M. (1985). Competitiveness, risk taking, and violence: The young male syndrome. *Ethology and Sociobiology, 6*, 59–73.

Theory and Overview

Competition Throughout Women's Lives

Bobbi Low

Abstract

From conception to the grave, girls and women face competition with others. In this chapter, I focus only on competition with other females: in the womb, the fetus's needs compete with her mother's and any sister's; after birth, she competes throughout her life: with her sisters, other female relatives, and unrelated female competitors for social status or mates. Although seldom as overt as male–male competition, female–female competition is equally serious in terms of lifetime impacts and may occasionally become violent. Here I follow a female lifetime, exploring the kinds, intensity, and impact of female–female competition.

Key Words: female–female competition, behavioral ecology, life history theory, lifespan, sex differences

The *Oxford English Dictionary* defines "competition" as "the activity or condition of striving to gain or win something by defeating or establishing superiority over others." Today, we may find ourselves competing for prizes that are rather trivial in the sense of competition for real resources and their relationship to a struggle for existence: beauty pageants and high school athletic prizes, for example. Darwin, in making his argument for the existence of natural selection, was quite cogent about the importance of competition for limited resources in the "struggle for existence" throughout organisms' lifetimes. His argument (somewhat rephrased) was simple. In any species (he gives a great example of elephants), (1) numbers increase geometrically: more individuals are produced than can be supported indefinitely by existing resources; (2) this geometric rate of increase is never seen; (3) this means that some struggle for existence (read "competition for resources") must occur; and (4) heritable variation exists. We can infer, then, from his reasoning that in any environment, not all individuals survive and reproduce equally well. Of course, we have learned a considerable amount about genetics

and subtle environmental influences in the ensuing decades since Darwin. Nonetheless, in his basic points, Darwin (1859, p. 62) was quite prescient:

> I should premise that I use the term Struggle for Existence in a large and metaphorical sense, including dependence of one being on another, and including (which is more important) not only the life of the individual, but success in leaving progeny. Two canine animals in a time of dearth may be truly said to struggle with each other over which shall get food and live. But a plant on the edge of the desert is said to struggle for life against the drought, though more properly it should be said to be dependent on the moisture.

Darwin then went on to discuss competition issues for parasitic plants like mistletoe, which competes against other mistletoes and other fruiting plants to attract the birds that disseminate their seeds. Competition for resources, across many species and throughout lifetimes, was central to his work.

Darwin found it easy to see how surviving and reproducing would be favored by natural selection. At first, though, he had trouble seeing how "ordinary" natural selection could favor risky and potentially lethal behaviors, so he separated sexual selection—the competition for mates—from ordinary natural selection. It was difficult for him to see the utility of behaviors, such as fights among elephant seals or red deer, that were dangerous and likely to get individuals killed. Today, because we understand the utility of risk-taking for high reproductive rewards, we consider sexual selection as a subset of natural selection (e.g., Mayr, 1972, p. 88). Much (typically male) intrasexual selection is simply a very high-risk, high-gain form of competition. For example, 30% of adult male red deer deaths arise from injuries received in fights; however, a male that does not fight has no reproductive success at all (Clutton-Brock, Guinness, & Albon, 1982).

For males, then, often being highly successful in reproducing involves taking serious, potentially lethal risks. Most mammals tend to have polygynous mating systems, because females are specialized for feeding newborns; males, thus freed from the utility of parental assistance, may then specialize in competing for mates (e.g., Clutton-Brock et al., 1982; Davies, Krebs, & West, 2012). In such systems—especially in terrestrial mammals—males are more expensive than females for a mother to produce successfully: males are carried longer in utero, they weigh more at birth, they nurse more often and consume more milk at each nursing bout, and they wean at a few days older so they can grow larger. Such trends result from the fact that, in physical combat, larger males are likely to be more successful than smaller males (Clutton-Brock et al., 1982; Le Boeuf & Reiter, 1988), especially in terrestrial (rather than aquatic or aerial) species. However, because of intense male intrasexual competition and resultant injuries, males die earlier than females.

Female mammals, in contrast, have the highest success when they can raise healthy, successful offspring. They are specialized to feed infants, and, being physically close, attend to much other parental care; as a result, there tends to be a sexual dichotomy: males spend effort on finding mates, whereas females spend more parental effort than males on their offspring.

In northern elephant seals (*Mirounga angustirostris*), although 82% of males die before reproductive age, and most males sire no offspring, the most successful male sires ten times as many offspring as the most successful female (Le Boeuf & Reiter, 1988). Thus, becoming a successfully reproducing male is a high-risk, high-gain endeavor. On the other hand, a male mammal that has been castrated lives

longer than its fertile competitors (e.g., Hoffman et al., 2013) but is unsuccessful at leaving offspring. Thus, male striving and risk-taking are important in terms of siring offspring: that is, not only *surviving*, but also *reproducing* successfully, are important. Today, then, we treat sexual selection as a part of natural selection, because reproduction is as important as survivorship in terms of lineage success. That is, natural selection and its subsets of sexual selection (e.g., attracting an excellent mate), social selection (e.g., having a successful lineage), and reciprocity (e.g., helping individuals who will return that help) all contribute to the differential success of individuals.

Importantly, although often so subtle as to go unnoticed, females, like males, undergo considerable intrasexual selection—competition with others of the same sex—principally for matings. This is in contrast to intersexual selection—mate choice by the opposite sex, in which the usual case is female choice of particular males.

In all cases, we are asking what traits, in any particular environment, help an individual to survive and reproduce and its lineage to persist and grow compared to another. We have come to understand that measuring and understanding these differences can be a complex and subtle business; maximizing reproductive success in terms of number of offspring may not lead to optimization of lineage persistence and growth relative to other family lines—it depends on the environment. For example, in highly competitive environments, every offspring may need great investment to be competitive. And there is a tradeoff: one cannot make more *and* larger offspring. So, when competition is low, high fertility—and low investment in each offspring—is common; when competition is high, the winning strategy is to make fewer but intensely invested offspring (Low, 2001, 2013; MacArthur & Wilson, 1967). In all these cases, competition, in the Darwinian sense, is focused on survival and reproduction, or, more properly, lineage persistence and relative lineage increase.

With this "large and metaphorical" understanding of competition, it is easy to see that each of us faces competition of various sorts at every stage in our lives. There are many ways to compete, as discussed at length in subsequent chapters: the actors can vary, the specific resources at stake (in terms of contributing to reproductive and lineage success) vary, and the strategies vary (e.g., having many babies with little care vs. few babies with intensive care). But, in all cases, competition is for rewards (e.g., status, wealth, high-quality mates) that contribute to successful reproduction and to continuing family lineages. A moment's thought will probably reflect what we find in the literature. Although the specifics may differ between the sexes—in seeking a mate, men value youth or reproductive value more than do women; women value resources more than men—no one wants a sickly, socially inept, poor individual as a lifetime mate.

Particulars can also vary across societies. Thus, among the Ache of Paraguay, the best hunters, a form of status, have more wives over their lifetimes than do poorer hunters (Hill & Hurtado, 1996). Among the Yanomamö, if a man kills someone on a revenge raid, he is accorded the status of *unokai*; *unokai* marry earlier and more often than other men and have more children (Chagnon, 1988). Even in late-marrying, no-divorce nineteenth-century Sweden, wealthy men married younger wives than did poorer men and had, on average, 1.5 more children than other men (Low, 1994; Low & Clarke, 1991). In essentially every traditional or historical society for which these questions were asked, wealth and/or high status allowed men to increase their reproductive success.

At each stage in a woman's life history, the importance of any particular resource may vary. For example, nutritional resources in infancy help growth (and thus competitive ability), status in school or sports influences other students and perhaps even teachers to respect one, and being able to obtain the best available mate as an adult helps in a variety of ways: enhanced resources or an ability to have either more or better-invested children than others. In contrast, some types of competitiveness may be stable through several life history stages. Even though we think of nutrition as of highest priority in infancy, it remains an important resource through the lifespan. On the other hand, physical strength, hormonal balance, and other resources that require effort to develop may not be important until puberty. Similarly, both intelligence and knowledge become increasingly important as a child grows into an adult.

Intrasexual selection always concerns resources important for survival and reproduction or resources that have in the past filled that role. Probably the most-studied female–female competition is that centered on finding good (e.g., wealthy, high-status, companionable) mates—strategies such as derogation of competitors and self-promotion. These are covered in excellent detail in later chapters, so here I only leave signposts to them. Let us begin, then, with conception and follow how competition plays out in each stage of a woman's life history.

Competition in the Womb

Even before the moment of fertilization, what may become a human female faces intense competition. Within the mother, whose sex chromosomes are XX, each protogamete, through the process of meiosis, produces four cells. There is competition to become a part of the new fetus because, of the four cells the mother produces, only one will become a viable egg; the others, which are called "polar bodies," have almost no protoplasm and are not viable. There is considerable chromosomal influence and competition, at least in studies of mice (Wang, Racowsky, & Deng, 2011). It is even possible that the monthly process of egg and polar body production, the generation of one egg and three useless cells that will die, may contribute to menopause (Reiber, 2010). Thus, *whether and which* X chromosome from the mother, and its associated half-genome, make it into the functioning egg is an important example of intrasexual competition.

Men, who are XY, produce four sperm through meiosis. Some of these will bear an X chromosome, from the father's mother, and some will have a Y chromosome, from the man's father. Therefore, there is competition to determine whether an X-bearing or a Y-bearing sperm is the successful penetrator of the egg. Furthermore, if a man has what is called a "driving Y" chromosome, he will produce mostly or all Y-bearing sperm, and our protodaughter has little or no chance of entering the world (Hamilton, 1967).

Assume that fertilization has indeed produced a female fetus. The fetus's genes and her mother's genes are not identical, so neither are their reproductive interests. The fetus is always in competition with her mother for resources. The mother's interests often are best served by providing less investment than would be ideal for the fetus (e.g., if food is in short supply). Both the mother's own total reproduction and the interests of other offspring matter to the mother, but the interests of the fetus are simply to maximize what she alone can get from her mother (Hrdy, 1999). This means that mother and fetus compete both for simple nutrition and for essential nutrients like calcium. When conditions are harsh, it is not unlikely that the mother will reabsorb or spontaneously abort the fetus—a severe and deadly competitive loss indeed for the daughter fetus. Even when resources are relatively rich and further maternal nutritional investment in this daughter would yield no increased survival or improved condition, the daughter's interests are still dedicated toward getting more resources for less effort, thus putting pressure on the mother's resources. This intense conflict over the distribution of the mother's resources is why Trivers (1974) noted the intense maternal–offspring conflict at the termination of parental care (e.g., weaning).

This maternal–fetal conflict is exacerbated by the fact that half of the fetus's genes come from the father, and the father's interests are allied with the fetus even if the mother's investment causes her harm (Haig, 1993). Neither the fetus nor the father bears the costs; the mother's body has the task of allocating effort in the optimal way for herself and *all* her offspring, which is of no import for the fetus or father—again, the fetus has an "interest" simply in getting the most investment possible. I return to this problem later because women face this problem again, from the other side, when they become mothers.

If our fetal girl shares the womb with siblings, competition is yet more severe. As an aside, this is especially true if she shares the womb with a male twin (intersexual selection). In virtually all mammals, males grow faster and are carried longer in utero. After birth, males nurse longer and more often than female offspring (e.g., Davies et al., 2012). All these conflicting interests regarding resource allocation—father's and fetus's interests against mother's—mean greater resource drains on the mother. Furthermore, if a male and female share the womb, there will be fiercer competition for female fetuses and infants against larger, stronger brother(s). But a female twin also imposes a cost on our focal female fetus, although not so severe as a male twin.

Preadolescence: Sugar and Spice— Are Little Girls Nice?

Cross-culturally, in the 93 odd-numbered societies of the Standard Cross-Cultural Sample (one of the standard ways to make cross-cultural comparisons), from about age 7 on, boys, but not girls, are taught to be aggressive and to show fortitude, whereas girls are taught to be industrious, responsible, and obedient. Curiously, there was no significant difference in the degree to which either sex was taught to be competitive (although it is not clear how this was defined; Barry, Josephson, Lauer, & Marshall, 1976; Low, 1989). So, although today we see many sex differences in type and apparent

intensity of competitiveness, in traditional societies, girls, as well as boys, were taught to be competitive.

Anyone who has spent time around small children will have noticed that even preschool children choose with whom to play; at this stage, inclusion/exclusion choices appear to be largely stereotypic and based on children's perceptions of social convention (Killen, Pisacane, Lee-Kim, & Ardilla-Rey, 2001). In many circumstances, little boys play in mixed-age groups more than do girls; boys engage in more rough-and-tumble play (Berenbaum, Martin, Hanish, & Fabes, 2008; DiPietro, 1981) and are often fiercely and overtly competitive, fighting for what they want. No matter how often an adult separates the fighters, boys tend toward head-on aggression more than girls do.

So, are little girls really sweet and less competitive than little boys? Perhaps not. Girls do seem to be more subtle in the ways they compete (Benenson, Antonellis, Cotton, Noddin, & Campbell, 2008; Benenson, Hodgson, Heath, & Welch, 2008): they appear to avoid potentially risky direct aggression. Instead, they turn away at critical moments, shift their voice tone, and spread rumors. It would be hard to assess their behavior as less competitive than that of boys; the competition is just conducted differently (e.g., Kokko & Pulkkinen, 2005). These differences (e.g., girls competing by manipulating status and by exclusion) may underlie the fact that girls do not generally play in such mixed-age groups as do boys.

There is evidence that girls' patterns of competition and exclusion are somewhat malleable; usually this is noted in studies of sex differences in competition. Cotton et al. (2013) found, in repeated mathematics competitions in elementary school, that boys outperformed girls in the first competition but that, in later competition, girls were at no disadvantage and sometimes outperformed the boys. This raises the question of how girls are socialized to compete with each other. In a sample of girls slightly younger than age 15, Booth and Nolen (2012) found that girls from single-sex schools competed more like boys than did girls from mixed-sex schools: that is, with rougher play and more direct aggression. Similarly, we must be careful in trying to generalize about girls' competitive strategies from samples taken mainly from one or two countries. When Cárdenas et al. (2012) compared girls' competitiveness in Sweden (a high gender-equity country; Low, 2011) and Colombia, which ranks far lower in macro measures of gender equity, they found that boys and girls (aged 9–12) in Colombia were equally competitive in all tasks and in all measures used. In Sweden, boys tended to be more competitive in general, but girls tended to be competitive about improving performance on tasks (e.g., school assignments, recitals).

For girls as well as boys, though, there are more- and less-aggressive individuals; by age 8, one can predict some important aspects about aggression in later life. Individuals with low impulse control and high aggressiveness can show these traits early and continue showing them throughout life. Furthermore, a variety of interventions (e.g., tutoring, peer-pairing) appears to have no impact on this pattern. That is, the level and type of aggressiveness (direct, verbal, or physical attacks) are relatively stable throughout life (e.g., Ogilvie, 1968; Salmivalli & Kaukiainen, 2004).

Adolescence and Young Adulthood

Not surprisingly, sex differences in competitiveness increase in adolescence as hormonal changes set the stage for direct mate competition. Overt female–female competition becomes heightened in adolescence and young adulthood, and its intensity continues through mating and marriage; at its extreme, it can become violent (e.g., Sikes, 1998). Competition can be a double-edged sword, as many other chapters in this volume illustrate (also, e.g., Hibbard & Buhrmester, 2010). At this life stage, too, the ways in which boys and girls compete tend to differ: although both sexes frequently express their motivation as competing to "excel" (e.g., to surpass a personal best), boys are more likely than girls to compete to "win." In formal educational settings, girls are often as competitive as boys, but their competition takes different (less direct, more subtle) forms. In fact, for girls, formal competition to win may be associated with relatively high levels of depression and loneliness and fewer close friendships (Hibbard & Buhrmester, 2010).

Even from late primary school, popularity is a major aim of competition and a likely proxy for later success in mate competition, The "popular" girls get the higher-status dates and, perhaps later, higher-status mates. To be sought after is clearly advantageous, although this striving for popularity may be variously modeled (Read, 2011; Read, Francis, & Skelton, 2011). Duncan (2004) found that girls felt their relationships tended to shift once they entered secondary school from intimate dyadic pairings to more fluid—and strategic—groups often focused on sexual competition and popularity. Popularity is often associated with cliques and with exclusionary "meanness" as individuals begin to sort themselves into groups of similar status (Merton, 2005).

Girls and young women tend to participate in organized sports less than do boys and young men. Cross-culturally, using the Human Relations Area Files (which contain more society data than the Standard Cross-Cultural Sample but may contain observations by others than experienced ethnographers), Deaner and Smith (2013) found that in 50 societies, there were more male sports than female sports and that some (e.g., hunting, combat sports) were exclusively male, thus reflecting a robust sex difference. In the contemporary United States, women represented 51% of noncompetitive exercisers, 24% of total sports participants, and 20% of team sports participants (Deaner et al., 2012). There was little evidence that these trends were reversing. As Deaner has noted, through evolutionary time, men likely gained status in a variety of male–male competitions, both as individuals and in teams; such competitors gained better access to mates. Perhaps it is not surprising that women's intrasexual competition is far more common in other (e.g., individual, personal, and directly reproductive) contexts rather than, for example, in organized sports.

To infer the importance of socialization in female intrasexual competition, Andersen et al. (2012) found that, in the patriarchal society they studied, girls' competitiveness declined as puberty began. Cross-culturally today, Finnish, Israeli, Italian, and Polish girls ages 8, 11, and 15 all used indirect aggression most commonly (e.g., subtle snubs, snide comments), followed by verbal aggression directed at the victim, with physical aggression least common (Österman et al., 1998). Which strategy is most common changes with age: from adolescence onward, *physical* aggression, typically in the context of attracting the approval of boys in the group, can increase in some circumstances. For example, female associates of gang members may try to prove they also are "tough" and therefore worthy and desirable (Levy, 2012), sometimes to the extent of considerable violence and even murder (Lin, 2011; Sikes, 1998).

Competition for Mates and Competition Among Co-Wives

As girls mature and become actively interested in mating and marriage, life becomes more complicated, in part because our lives today differ so greatly from our lives in the past. Across most mammals, including primates, as noted earlier, males compete and display "good genes" as reflected by hierarchical status, fighting ability, and so forth. This has been studied more in nonhuman species and in traditional societies: in general, a male that can dominate is preferable as a mate than a male that loses to others, and, as with all behaviors, there are genetic as well as environmental and ontogenetic contributions. Frequently, we can see the gene–behavior connections most clearly in abnormal or pathological cases, although they are usually simplified examples. Consider the Dutch family in which a point mutation resulted in males showing borderline mental retardation and abnormally impulsive aggressive behavior (Brunner, Nelen, Breakefield, Ropers, & van Oost, 1993).

Humans are among the most intensely male-parental of mammals because human fathers tend give more parental care than do males of other primates. Thus, finding an excellent husband usually becomes a matter of competition among families because free female choice—which is common in other mammals—was largely superseded by parents and often fathers and uncles who chose (and sometimes still choose) children's spouses (Whyte, 1979). This appears to be true not only for traditional societies such as hunter-gatherers and agriculturalists, but also even in more recent recorded history. Shakespeare captured this in *Romeo and Juliet*: when 12-year-old Juliet complained as her father betrothed her to a middle-aged man (who would be a good ally for her father) although she loved young handsome Romeo. Her father responded (Act 3, Scene 5):

An you will not wed, I'll pardon you!
Graze where you will, you shall not house
  with me:. . .
An you be mine, I'll give you to my friend;
An you be not, hang, beg, starve, die in the streets,
For by my soul, I'll ne'er acknowledge thee
Nor what is mine shall never do thee good.

Even though female choice was not widespread in our evolutionary and historical past, women did and do have some ability to exert influence in some societies. Today, in large nation-states (in which most competition studies are done), most women have the ability to choose their spouse. At this point, female–female competition is critical. All else equal, those who excel at intrasexual competition will be favored by selection (e.g., Buss & Dedden, 1990).

Both men and women derogate their competitors. Women, far more than men, were likely to call other women promiscuous (a great threat to

male investment) and to degrade other women's appearance. They also were more likely than males ($p = 0.047$) to question another woman's fidelity. Other tactics women employed to "dis" other women were to spread rumors and to call other women unintelligent, insensitive, exploitative, and boring. Not all of these tactics were equally effective, especially when men's tactics versus women's tactics were analyzed (e.g., Buss & Dedden, 1990). But how are women who derogate their competitors viewed by men and by other women? Fisher et al. (2010) found that others' perceptions do change. Men saw female derogators as less friendly, kind, and trustworthy and overall less desirable as a mate—so there may be costs to derogation. Women saw women derogators in similar ways but also saw derogators as less fit to be a parent and less attractive.

Derogation is certainly not the only competitive strategy women use; another is self-promotion: advertising one's positive attributes such as, "I am intelligent, responsible, beautiful." Fisher, Cox, and Gordon (2009) found that women tend to use self-promotion more than do men, whereas men derogated competitors more strongly than did women. Self-promotion was particularly apparent for individuals who were romantically unattached or dating compared to those in a committed relationship. Both derogation and self-promotion are more indirect and subtle forms of competition than, for example, overt aggression; it is clear that one can compete subtly or overtly and aggressively. The social environment may have strong influence here: depending on circumstances (gang members vs. professional women CEOs, for example), each can be highly effective.

From an evolutionary point of view, the fact that most peoples in traditional societies are polygynous suggests that competition and cooperation among co-wives have done much to shape modern female–female competition. It is true that co-wives can become allies (Yanca & Low, 2004), although this may not be the predominant pattern. In a cross-cultural study of 160 societies for which data exist in the Standard Cross-Cultural Sample (a standardized sample controlling for geographic region and, within region, language group, and for which trained ethnographers' reports exist), Betzig (1989) found that conflict among co-wives was the eighth most commonly stated cause of divorce after such obvious causes as infertility. She also argued that because co-wives were in competition in polygynous societies, such conflict might reasonably be lumped with adultery. If this were done, such conflict would be part of the second most common cause of conjugal dissolution. In a detailed study of 69 societies for which the ethnographers specifically commented about co-wife relationships, Jankowiak, Sudakov, and Wilreker (2005) found considerable pragmatic cooperation (e.g., in gathering) and a few life-long friendships among co-wives; nonetheless, they found conflict in the majority of co-wife relationships. They found that first wives (typically older than subsequent wives) frequently reacted with suspicion, fear, and anger to the addition of a new wife.

Pregnancy: Neither Rosy nor Romantic

Pregnancy has never been the rosy, romanticized picture some might imagine (Hrdy, 1999). In pregnancy, in addition to the fact that a woman must compete with her fetus for resources, a father's reproductive interests are also at stake—and not in the mother's favor. "Genomic imprinting" (Haig, 1993) reflects the fact that fetal genes from the father can act in the fetus's favor (i.e., forcing more parental investment by the mother even when that is counter to the mother's interests). So, for example, there are paternally imprinted genes (well-studied in rodents and humans) such as *Ig/2* and *Pg1/Mest* that cause the fetus to grow faster and thus take more resources from the mother (Burt & Trivers, 2006). (These often help the offspring with early growth: bigger babies typically do better than smaller, thinner infants.) Other paternal genes have similar effects a little later: *Pg3* not only enhances embryonic growth, but also increases nursing behavior; *Rasgrf1* increases infant growth (again, at the mother's expense), with peak influence around weaning. In all these cases, the father's imprinted genes aid the fetus or newborn at little or no cost to the father but often at considerable cost to the mother. Because genomic imprinting occurs whether the fetus is a girl or boy, it obviously involves more than intrasexual competition; nonetheless, a woman's ability to rebuff paternally imprinted genes may give her a competitive advantage against other women. Again, this is an arena for future work.

Mothers: Competing Through One's Children and Having It All

In life's next stage, women become mothers. Do mothers (or both parents) use their children to brag, to gain status? There are two main ways in which this is feasible. First, parents may use children as "billboards" of parental wealth in their social competitions, much as wealthy men may adorn their wives in sexual competition (e.g., Low, 1979). Second, parents may both pressure children to excel (in academics or athletics, for example) and brag about their children's accomplishments to other parents, again in the context of social selection. There is little in the primary literature about these possibilities, but web sites and popular articles, from *Time* magazine's coverage of children's styles (e.g., dresses for 3-year-olds costing hundreds of dollars) to *Battle Hymn of the Tiger Mother* (Chua, 2011) and *Joy Luck Club* (Tan, 1989), suggest that this is a fairly common phenomenon and one ripe for study.

In the matter of women competing to "have it all" (i.e., to have both well-provided and well-taught children and high-level professional careers), early feminists in the 1970s seem to have had no idea of the difficulties inherent in becoming superwoman. Nonetheless, from a reading of *Lean In* (Sandberg, 2013), it is clear that with enough advantages, some women—supercompetitors—can become superwoman... if they can afford a nursery next to their CEO office.

Postreproductive Life: Do Grandmothers Compete?

Unless they die prematurely, all organisms experience senescence: the decay in system functions that comes with age. In humans, many systems (e.g., lung function, muscle amount and tone) show significant decay by the time a person reaches around 70 years of age. Of course, this can vary depending on such things as smoking or intense exercise. But human female reproductive systems senesce as early as 40–45 years of age, with an average in the 50s. Human females are unusual in living almost a third of their lifetime in the years after ceasing reproduction; in most other mammals, females might spend perhaps 10% of their lifetimes postreproductive. Why?

To take a comparative perspective, some other species do show early female reproductive senescence: odontocyte whales (Marsh & Kasuya, 1984, 1986), baboons (Packer, Tatar, & Collins, 1998), bonobos (de Waal, 1997), rhesus monkeys (Walker, 1995), lions (Packer et al., 1998), and elephants (Poole, 1997). Many of these species share with humans an intense level of maternal care and a long time to independence for offspring. These phenomena have given rise to the Grandmother Hypothesis (e.g., Hawkes, O'Connell, Blurton Jones, Alvarez, & Charnov, 1998, 1999), which argues that because children take so very long to become independent, very late-born children of late-reproducing mothers might die, and grandmothers may work to help the success of their grandchildren. If this is so, then it would be competitively advantageous for mothers to switch relatively early from reproduction to simply caring for existing children.

Despite the attractiveness of this hypothesis, there are few data and results conflict. The first analysis of human lifetime fertility among women who stopped earlier versus later is that of Hill and Hurtado (1991, 1996), who worked with the Ache of Paraguay. They found some positive effects of grandmothers' help: men and women with a living mother experienced slightly higher fertility than did others, and children with a living grandmother survived slightly better than others. But these effects were small, and women who remained fertile longer had higher lifetime reproductive success than other women. Selection is weak at older ages because (1) it affects relatively few women (many have died), and (2) it affects little or none of their reproductive lives (Hamilton, 1966; Williams, 1957). Thus, grandmothering benefits (in terms of, e.g., enhanced survivorship of grandchildren or daughter's fertility) are not likely to be large enough to be highly beneficial (Kachel, Premo, & Hublin, 2011).

Because the value of a grandmother's efforts may vary with age-specific fertility and mortality patterns, a grandmother's value to a mother's fertility may vary across societies. Studies in the Gambia have found that maternal grandmothers improve the survivorship of their grandchildren (Sear, Mace, & McGregor, 2000) and that the presence of a woman's in-laws increases her fertility (Sear, Mace, & McGregor, 2002). In contrast, no such effects existed in Malawi (Sear, 2008). Similarly, conflicting results arise from cross-cultural reviews (Hill & Hurtado, 1991, 2009; Sear & Mace, 2008; Shanley, Sear, Mace, & Kirkwood, 2007). In different societies, various relatives may or may not affect women's fertility and children's survival. Strassmann and Garrard (2011), in a meta-analysis of 17 studies, found that the survival of the maternal (but not paternal) grandparents enhanced grandchildren's survivorship. Their results suggested another hypothesis: that of local resource competition, with individuals competing against relatives (often same-sex relatives) for resources, which is usually detrimental. Here, as Darwin might say, is a problem for future analysis.

Given the similarities to human female senescence in other species (e.g., with elephants, odontocyte whales, baboons, lions, and rhesus monkeys), it is worth asking if there is evidence of a grandmother effect in these species. Packer et al. (1998) tested the grandmother hypothesis with field data from baboons and lions—in these species, two results countered the grandmother hypothesis: first, old-reproducing females had no higher mortality costs of reproduction than younger females; and second, grandmother help did not improve the fitness of either grandchildren or reproductive-age offspring.

Are There Universals?

It is safe to say that some intrasexual competition exists in every stage of a human female's life; it can be severe, even lethal (ending up in a polar body or being shot by a rival girl-gang member), and there are often striking tradeoffs. Sometimes the competition is directly over survival and reproduction; often, competition is for proxies for these two central biological phenomena, such as gaining nutrition competitively as a child, joining the popular clique at school, or attracting an outstanding mate. Maternal–fetal conflict and genomic imprinting are likely to be similar in all populations, for example. On the other hand, the effect of kin on children's survival appears quite mixed across populations. Finally, at different life history stages and across populations, the particular proxies for survival and lineage success can differ greatly, depending on health, growth, competence as a result of intense schooling, and more (see Low, 2013). Nonetheless, the end point in most cases is to gain the best available possible mate, whether that is a corporate CEO or a successful drug dealer, and to have healthy, well-invested children. Today, in most developed nations, (some) women have the option of gaining CEO positions themselves; typically, this incurs a fertility cost as a result of long and expensive schooling, which usually delays the age at which a woman has her first child (the most important predictor of lineage growth) and reduces her total fertility (Low, Simon, & Anderson, 2002). For example, in 2005, the 87 male US senators had, on average, three children; the 13 female senators averaged 0.8 children (author's data). Thus, competition, conflicts of interest, and tradeoffs rule women's lives from before becoming an egg to grandmotherhood.

References

Andersen, S., Ertac, S., Gneezy, U., List, J., & Maximiano, S. (2012). Gender, competitiveness and socialization at a young age: Evidence from a matrilineal and a patriarchal society. *Review of Economics and Statistics*. doi: 10.1162/REST_a_00312

Barry, H. III, Josephson, L., Lauer, E., & Marshall, C. (1976). Traits inculcated in childhood. 5. Cross-cultural codes. *Ethnology*, 15, 83–114.

Benenson, J., Antonellis, T., Cotton, B., Noddin, K., & Campbell, K. (2008). Sex differences in children's formation of exclusionary alliances under scarce resource conditions. *Animal Behaviours*, 76, 497–505.

Benenson, J., Hodgson, L., Heath, S., & Welch, P. (2008). Human sexual differences in the use of social ostracism as a competitive tactic. *International Journal of Primatology*, 29, 1019–1035.

Berenbaum, S., Martin, C., Hanish, L., & Fabes, R. (2008). Sex differences in children's play. In J. Becker, K. Berkeley, N. Geary, & E. Hampton (Eds.), *Sex differences in the brain: From genes to behavior* (pp. 275–290). Oxford: Oxford University Press.

Betzig, L. (1989). Causes of conjugal dissolution: A cross-cultural study. *Current Anthropology*, 30(5), 654–676.

Booth, A., & Nolen, P. (2012). Choosing to compete: How different are boys and girls? *Journal of Economic Behavior and Organization*, 81, 542–555.

Brunner, H. G., Nelen, M., Breakefield, X. O., Ropers, H. H., & van Oost, B. A. (1993). Abnormal behavior associated with a point mutation in the structural gene for monoamine oxidase A. *Science*, 262, 578–580.

Burt, A., & Trivers, R. L. (2006). *Genes in conflict*. Cambridge, MA: Belknap.

Buss, D. M., & Dedden, L. A. (1990). Derogation of competitors. *Social and Personal Relationships*, 7, 395–422.

Cárdenas, J.–C., Dreber, A., von Essen, E,. & Ranchill, E. (2012). Gender differences in competitiveness and risk taking: Comparing children in Colombia and Sweden. *Journal of Economic Behavior and Organization*, 83, 11–23.

Chagnon, N. A. (1988). Life histories, blood revenge, and warfare in a tribal population. *Science*, 239(26), 985–992.

Chua, A. (2011). *Battle hymn of the tiger mother*. New York: Penguin Press.

Clutton-Brock, T. H., Guinness, F. E., & Albon, S. D. (1982). *Red deer: Behavior and ecology of two sexes*. Chicago: University of Chicago Press.

Cotton, C., McIntyre, F., & Price, J. (2013). Gender differences in repeated competition: Evidence from school math contests. *Journal of Economic Behavior and Organization*, 86, 52–66.

Darwin, C. (1859). *On the origin of species by means of natural selection*. Facsimile of the first edition, with an introduction by Ernst Mayr, published 1987. Cambridge, MA: Harvard University Press.

Davies, N. B., Krebs, J. R., & West, S. A. (2012). *An introduction to behavioral ecology* (4th ed.). London: Wiley-Blackwell.

Deaner, R., Geary, D., Puts, D., Ham, S., Kruger, J., Fles, E.,. . . Grandis, T. (2012). A sex difference in the predisposition for physical competition: Males play sports much more than females even in the contemporary US. *PLOS One*, 7(11), 1–15.

Deaner, R., & Smith, B. (2013). Sex differences in sports across 50 societies. *Cross-Cultural Research*, 47, 268–309.

de Waal, F. (1997). *The forgotten ape*. Berkeley: University of California Press.

DiPietro, J. (1981). Rough and tumble play: A function of gender. *Developmental Psychology*, 17(1), 50–58.

Duncan, N. (2004). It's important to be nice, but it's nicer to be important: Girls, popularity, and sexual competition. *Sex Education: Sexuality, Society, and Learning*, 4(2), 137–152.

Fisher, M. L., Cox, A., & Gordon, F. (2009). Self-promotion versus competitor derogation: The influence of sex and romantic relationship status on intrasexual competition strategy selection. *Journal of Evolutionary Psychology*, 7(4), 287–808.

Fisher, M. L., Shaw, S., Worth, K., Smith, L., & Reeve, C. (2010). How we view those who derogate: Perceptions of female competitor derogators. *Journal of Social, Evolutionary, and Cultural Psychology*, 4(4), 265–276.

Haig, D. (1993). Genetic conflicts in human pregnancy. *The Quarterly Review of Biology*, 68(4), 495–532.

Hamilton, W. D. (1967). Extraordinary sex ratios. *Science*, 156, 477–488.

Hamilton, W. D. (1966). The moulding of senescence by natural selection. *Theoretical Biology*, 12, 12–45.

Hawkes, K., O'Connell, J. F., Blurton Jones, N. G., Alvarez, H., & Charnov, E. L. (1998). Grandmothering, menopause, and the evolution of human life histories. *Proceedings of the National Academy of Science of the United States of America*, 95, 1336–1339.

Hawkes, K., O'Connell, J. F., Blurton Jones, N. G., Alvarez, H., & Charnov, E. L. (1999). The grandmother hypothesis and human evolution. In L. Cronk, N. A. Chagnon, & W. G. Irons (Eds.), *Adaptation and human behavior: An anthropological perspective* (pp. 237–258). Hawthorne, NY: Aldine de Gruyter.

Hibbard, D. R., & Buhrmester, D. (2010). Competitiveness, gender, and adjustment among adolescents. *Sex Roles*, 63, 412–424.

Hill, K., & Hurtado, A. M. (1991). The evolution of premature reproductive senescence and menopause in human females: An evaluation of the "Grandmother Hypothesis." *Human Nature*, 2, 313–350.

Hill, K., & Hurtado, A. M. (1996). *Ache life history: The ecology and demography of a foraging people*. New York: Aldine de Gruyter.

Hill, K., & Hurtado, A. M. (2009). Cooperative breeding in South American hunter-gatherers. *Proceeding of the Royal Society B*, 276, 3863–3870.

Hoffman, J. M., Creevey, K. E., & Promislow, D. E. L. (2013). Reproductive capability is associated with lifespan and cause of death in companion dogs. *PLoS ONE*, 8(4), e61082. doi: 10.1371/journal.pone.0061082

Hrdy, S. B. (1999). *Mother nature*. New York: Pantheon Books.

Jankowiak, W., Sudakov, M., & Wilreker, B. (2005). Co-wife conflict and cooperation. *Ethnology*, 44(1), 81–98.

Kachel, A., Premo, L., & Hublin, J. (2011). Grandmothering and natural selection. *Proceeding of the Royal Society B*, 278, 384–391.

Killen, M., Pisacane, K., Lee-Kim, J., & Ardilla-Rey, A. (2001). Fairness or stereotypes? Young children's priorities when evaluating group exclusion and inclusion. *Developmental Psychology*, 37(5), 587–596.

Kokko, K., & Pulkkinen, L. (2005). Stability of aggressive behavior from childhood to middle age in women and men. *Aggressive Behavior*, 31, 485–497.

Le Boeuf, B. J., & Reiter, J. (1988). Lifetime reproductive success in Northern elephant seals. In T. H. Clutton-Brock (Ed.), *Reproductive success: Studies of individual variation in contrasting breeding systems* (pp. 344–383). Chicago: University of Chicago Press.

Levy, M. (2012). Boys fight, girls fight. *Girlhood Studies*, 5(2), 45–64.

Lin, Y. -H. (2011). Constructing alternative femininity: The gender identity of "Bad Girls" in Taiwan. In L. E. Bass & D. A. Kinney (Eds.), *The well-being, peer cultures and rights of children*

(Sociological studies of children and youth, volume 14) (pp. 159–179). Bingley, West Yorkshire: Emerald Groups Publishing.

Low, B. (1979). Sexual selection and human ornamentation. In N. A. Chagnon & W. G. Irons (Eds.), *Evolutionary theory and human social organization* (pp. 462–486). North Scituate, MA: Duxbury.

Low, B. (2001). *Why sex matters*. Princeton, NJ: Princeton University Press.

Low, B. (2011). Gender equity in evolutionary perspective. In C. Roberts (Ed.), *Applied evolutionary psychology* (pp. 131–148). Oxford: Oxford University Press.

Low, B. (2013). Fertility: Life history and ecological aspects. In M. L. Fisher, J. Garcia, & R. S. Chang (Eds.), *Evolution's empress: Darwinian perspectives on the nature of women* (pp. 222–242). New York: Oxford University Press.

Low, B., Simon, C., & Anderson, K. (2002). An evolutionary perspective on demographic transitions: Modeling multiple currencies. *American Journal of Human Biology, 14*, 149–167.

Low, B. S. (1989). Cross-cultural patterns in the training of children: An evolutionary perspective. *Journal of Comparative Psychology, 103*(4), 311–319.

Low, B. S. (1994). Men in the demographic transition. *Human Nature, 5*, 223–253.

Low, B. S., & Clarke, A. L. (1991). Family patterns in 19th-century Sweden—Impact of occupational-status and landownership. *Journal of Family History, 16*(2), 117–138.

MacArthur, R., & Wilson, E. (1967). *The theory of island biogeography*. Princeton, NJ: Princeton University Press.

Marsh, H., & Kasuya, T. (1984). Changes in the ovaries of the short-finned pilot whale, *Globocephala macrorhynchus*, with age and reproductive activity. *Reports of the International Whaling Commission, Special Issue 6*, 259–310.

Marsh, H., & Kasuya, T. (1986). *Evidence for reproductive senescence in female cetaceans* (pp. 83–95). International Whaling Commission (Special Issue 8).

Mayr, E. (1972). Sexual selection and natural selection. In B. Campbell (Ed.), *Sexual selection and the descent of man: The Darwinian pivot*. Rutgers: Transaction Publishers.

Merton, D. (2005). The meaning of meanness: Popularity, competition, and conflict among junior high school girls. In R. Matson (Ed.), *The spirit of sociology: A reader* (pp. 358–368). Boston: Pearson/Allyn & Bacon.

Ogilvie, B. (1968). Psychological consistencies within the personality of high-level competitors. *Journal of the American Medical Association, 205*(11), 780–786.

Österman, K., Björkqvist, K., Lagerspetz, K., Kaukianen, A., Landau, S., Fraczek, A., & Caparana, G. (1998). Cross-cultural evidence of female indirect aggression. *Aggressive Behavior, 24*, 1–8.

Packer, C., Tatar, M., & Collins, A. (1998). Reproductive cessation in female mammals. *Nature, 392*, 807–810.

Poole, J. (1997). *Elephants*. Stillwater, MN: Voyageur Press.

Read, B. (2011). Britney, Beyonce, and me—primary school girls' role models and constructions of the "popular" girl. *Gender and Education, 23*(1), 1–13.

Read, B., Francis, B., & Skelton, C. (2011). Gender, popularity and notions of in/authenticity amongst 12-year-old to 13-year-old school girls. *British Journal of Sociology and Education, 32*(2), 169–183.

Reiber, C. (2010). Female gamete competition: A new evolutionary perspective on menopause. *Journal of Social, Evolutionary, and Cultural Psychology, 4*(4), 215–240.

Salmivalli, C., & Kaukiainen, A. (2004). "Female aggression" revisited: Variable- and person-centered approaches to studying gender differences in different types of aggression. *Aggressive Behavior, 30*, 158–163.

Sandberg, S. (2013). *Lean in: Women, work, and the will to lead*. New York: Knopf.

Sear, R. (2008). Kin and child survival in rural Malawi. *Human Nature, 19*, 277–293.

Sear, R., & Mace, R. (2008). Who keeps children alive? A review of the effects of kin on child survival. *Evolution and Human Behavior, 29*, 1–18.

Sear, R., Mace, R., & McGregor, I. (2000). Maternal grandmothers improve nutritional status and survival of children in rural Gambia. *Proceeding of the Royal Society B, 267*, 1641–1647.

Sear, R., Mace, R., & McGregor, I. (2002). The effects of kin on female fertility in rural Gambia. *Evolution and Human Behavior, 24*, 25–42.

Shanley, D., Sear, R., Mace, R., & Kirkwood, T. (2007). Testing evolutionary theories of menopause. *Proceeding of the Royal Society B, 274*, 2943–2949.

Sikes, G. (1998). *8 Ball chicks*. New York: Anchor Books Doubleday.

Strassmann, B., & Garrard, W. (2011). Alternatives to the grandmother hypothesis. *Human Nature, 22*, 201–222.

Tan, A. (1989). *The joy luck club*. New York: Putnam.

Trivers, R. L. (1974). Parent-offspring conflict. *American Zoologist, 14*, 249–264.

Walker, M. (1995). Menopause in female rhesus monkeys. *American Journal of Primatology, 35*, 59–71.

Wang, Q., Racowsky, C., & Deng, M. (2011). Mechanism of the chromosome-induced polar body extrusion in mouse eggs. *Cell Division, 6*(17). doi: 10.1186/1747-1028-6-17

Whyte, M. K. (1979). *The status of women in pre-industrial societies*. Princeton, NJ: Princeton University Press.

Williams, G. C. (1957). Pleiotropy, natural selection, and the evolution of senescence. *Evolution, 11*, 398–411.

Yanca, C., & Low, B. (2004). Female allies and female power: A cross-cultural analysis. *Evolution and Human Behavior, 25*(1), 9–23.

Sexual Competition among Women: A Review of the Theory and Supporting Evidence

Steven Arnocky *and* Tracy Vaillancourt

Abstract

Darwin (1871) observed in his theory of evolution by means of sexual selection that "it is the males who fight together and sedulously display their charms before the female" (p. 272). Researchers examining intrasexual competition have since focused disproportionately on male competition for mates, with female competition receiving far less attention. In this chapter, we review evidence that women do indeed compete with one another to secure and maintain reproductive benefits. We begin with an overview of the evolutionary theory of competition among women, with a focus on biparental care and individual differences in men's mate value. We discuss why competition among women is characteristically different from that of men and highlight evidence supporting women's use of epigamic display of physical attractiveness characteristics and indirect aggression toward same-sex peers and opposite-sex romantic partners as sexually competitive tactics. Finally, individual differences in competition among women are discussed.

Key Words: female competition, parental investment theory, sexual selection, indirect aggression, epigamic display

The sexual struggle is of two kinds; in the one it is between individuals of the same sex, generally the males, in order to drive away or kill their rivals, the females remaining passive; whilst in the other, the struggle is likewise between the individuals of the same sex, in order to excite or charm those of the opposite sex, generally the females, which no longer remain passive, but select the more agreeable partners.

(Darwin, 1871, p. 398)

Competition pervades many important aspects of human existence. Over the course of recorded history, individuals and groups have rivaled one another for status, wealth, territory, food, resources, and mating opportunities, with the victors typically gaining an advantage in terms of survival and reproduction (Darwin, 1859, 1871). From an evolutionary perspective, such competition has been regarded to occur most frequently among males (Darwin, 1871) and only trivially among females who sometimes assume "characters which properly belong to the males" (Darwin, 1871, p. 614). Yet recent advances in evolutionary theory and supporting empirical evidence have begun to challenge this view, suggesting instead that female competition exists as an adaptive behavioral strategy in its own right: competition among females may aid in the acquisition of reproductively relevant resources (e.g., Clutton-Brock, 2009; Rosvall, 2011), as well as mating access (e.g., Campbell, 1995; Vaillancourt, 2005, 2013), and mate retention (Arnocky, Sunderani, Miller, & Vaillancourt, 2012).

In this chapter we provide an overview of the evolutionary view of competition as it applies to women. Toward this end, competition is first defined within the context of natural and sexual selection. The adaptive role of female competition is then reviewed and applied to human behavior, suggesting that female–female competition should be expected to occur among humans (Arnocky et al., 2012; Campbell, 1995, 1999; Rosvall, 2011; Vaillancourt, 2005, 2013). Two common forms of female competition are placed within this evolutionary framework: the use of physical attractiveness characteristics as a mechanism for attracting members of the opposite sex (i.e., epigamic display) and indirect aggression toward same-sex peers and opposite-sex romantic partners. Finally, individual differences in competition among women are discussed.

Why Do Humans Compete?

In the mid-nineteenth century, Charles Darwin (1859) put forth the theory of evolution by natural selection, which suggests that survival and reproduction become enhanced among organisms that are best suited to the prevailing environmental condition. The offspring of well-suited individuals will become more abundant, and the population will evolve according to their more appropriate characteristics (see also Darwin & Wallace, 1858). Darwin, however, noted many physical and behavioral characteristics that seemed to undermine his theory. One prototypical example is the brilliant plumage of the peacock, which is physically costly to produce and may detract from survival by increasing visibility to predators. This was a source of great frustration for Darwin, who wrote, "The sight of a feather in a peacock's tail, whenever I gaze at it, makes me sick!" (Darwin, April 3, 1860, in a letter to botanist Asa Gray).

Darwin eventually came to recognize that such traits likely evolved in the context of reproductive success, even if at the expense of an individual's survival. In his seminal work on the subject, *The Descent of Man, and Selection in Relation to Sex* (1871), Darwin proposed that sexual selection, as a special case of natural selection, is a driving force behind evolutionary change. Sexual selection refers to the success of certain individuals over others of the same sex, in relation to the propagation of offspring (Darwin, 1871). Specifically, it is the heritable traits possessed by successful reproducers that will be passed on to, and exhibited more frequently in, subsequent generations. In the case of the

peacock's plumage, for instance, research has shown that train coloration predicts males' mating success. Males with more brilliant plumage are more sexually desirable to peahens and may therefore have greater opportunity than males with duller coloration to pass on their genes to offspring who, in turn, will be more likely to possess similarly bright train feathers (Petrie & Halliday, 1994; Petrie, Halliday, & Sanders, 1991).

Intersexual and Intrasexual Selection

Sexual selection is the result of two important interrelated phenomena. First, *intersexual selection* refers to the degree of selectivity or choosiness of mating partners between the sexes. This choosiness is often based on epigamic display of secondary sexual characteristics, which are irrelevant to reproduction yet are attractive to members of the opposite sex because they indicate genotypic and phenotypic quality (Starratt & Shackelford, 2015). For example, peahens prefer to mate with brightly colored peacocks, perhaps because bright trains are a costly signal of a male's genetic quality—only sufficiently healthy males will produce the brightest colorations (Zahavi, 1975). Second, *intrasexual selection* refers to competition between members of the same sex over contested mating resources and opportunities. Members of one sex rival one another by displaying their value to potential mates or through direct dominance and threat displays or other aggressive behavior (e.g., Thornhill & Alcock, 1983). For instance, among elephant seals, males engage in direct physical combat in order to acquire and control harems of females, with successful male competitors typically achieving the greatest reproductive success (Hoelzel, Le Boeuf, Reiter, & Campagna, 1999; Le Boeuf, 1974). It is important to note that intrasexual competition need not be limited to mate acquisition: after copulation, sperm competition, as a form of indirect competition, (Hoelzel et al., 1999) as well as mate-guarding behavior (Galimberti, Boitani, & Marzetti, 2000), also serve to maintain the likelihood of paternity.

Darwin observed a striking sex difference among the two aspects of sexual selection. He noted that, in the vast majority of species, adult males more often engage in intrasexual selection. Males are usually more "modified" and "fight together and sedulously display their charms before the female" (Darwin, 1871, p. 272). Conversely, females more often act as sexual gatekeepers, selecting their mates from the more competitive male population (see Andersson, 1994).

Yet Darwin was unable to determine the cause of this commonly reported sex difference (Cronin, 1991), and it took nearly a century for researchers to begin to understand why males are often considered to be more competitive than females and, importantly, under what circumstances exceptions to this phenomenon arise.

Differential Parental Investment Influences Sexual Selection

Sexual selection is driven by the reproductive constraints imposed on one sex by the other. Lindenfors and Tullberg (2011) noted that "most often it is females who are the limiting resource for the reproductive success of males due to a fundamental asymmetry between males and females in their defining characteristic, their gametes" (p. 10). Many researchers have suggested that by the time of fertilization, females have invested considerably more reproductive effort because of anisogamy; females produce a limited number of energy-rich eggs and males produce many energetically cheaper sperm (Dawkins, 1976; Trivers, 1972). Females, being limited by the number of eggs they can produce, will exhibit a corresponding limitation in reproductive outcomes. A female will produce roughly the same number of offspring in a given breeding season, regardless how many males she mates with. Conversely, male reproductive success increases significantly alongside the number of females they can access and inseminate (Bateman, 1948).

Sex differences in the energy expended toward offspring production and survival are by no means limited to anisogamous gametes. Parental investment theory (Trivers, 1972) contends that the expenditure of *any* parental effort, including time, energy, risk, feeding, and other resources toward the production and survival of offspring, carries with it a cost that could otherwise be spent on procuring mating opportunities or rearing additional offspring (Barash, 1979; Trivers, 1972). Females, when bearing the heavier parental investment, have the most to lose from making poor mating decisions and must therefore express greater choosiness in determining with whom they will mate (Trivers, 1972).

In turn, these differential reproductive constraints lead to greater variability in reproductive fitness among males. Some particularly successful males will access multiple females and produce many offspring, whereas many less successful males will be shut out from reproducing altogether

(Bateman, 1948; cf. Birkhead, 2001). Accordingly, males more than females exhibit behavioral biases toward preferring and competing for multiple mating opportunities; "there is nearly always a combination of an undiscriminating eagerness in the males and a discriminating passivity in the females" (Bateman, 1948, p. 365).

Due to increased competitive pressure among males, natural and sexual selection will, over deep evolutionary time, begin to favor the competitively adaptive morphological and behavioral male features of successful maters, leading to increased sexual dimorphism of those traits (Alcock, 2001; Lande, 1980; Moore, 1990; Selander, 1972). For instance, sexually dimorphic body size among species of snake in which males are larger than females confers a distinct competitive advantage in physical combat (Shine, 1978). As another example, the horns of male ungulates have evolved not for antipredatory defense but rather for fighting male competitors during rutting season (Lindenfors & Tullberg, 2011). Sexually dimorphic features become most pronounced among species with strong sexual selectivity (Alexander, Hoogland, Howard, Noonan, & Sherman, 1979). At the extreme end of this spectrum, male members of a highly polygynous gorilla species compete to control and mate with a harem of females. These males are typically twice as large as their female counterparts (Larsen, 2003; Plavcan, 2001; Robbins & Czekala, 1997). Conversely, biparental care in most monogamously mating species counters male reproductive variance and reduces sexual dimorphism (Archer & Coyne, 2005).

This trend has also been observed in sex-role-reversed species wherein males invest significant parental care and have a reproductive rate below that of their female counterparts. In sex-role-reversed pipefish, males are choosier in their mate selection, whereas females tend to exhibit mating effort by way of ornamentation/courtship displays toward males as well as dominance displays toward intrasexual competitors (Berglund & Rosenqvist, 2001, 2009).

A Framework for Female Competition

In more than 95% of mammalian species, females are the sole providers of parental care (Clutton-Brock, 1989, 1991; Kleiman & Malcolm, 1981; Woodroffe & Vincent, 1994). It may, therefore, be tempting to conclude that females are primarily passive mate selectors who engage in low levels of competition. However, recent evidence is beginning to challenge this assumption, suggesting instead that evolutionary theory does not disqualify females from competing in order to benefit their survival and reproductive fitness (Rosvall, 2011; see also Hrdy, 1981). Across a wide variety of species, females have indeed been shown to compete over mating-relevant resources such as food (Baird & Sloan, 2003) and nesting sites (Rosvall, 2008), as well as for the protection of offspring (Christenson & LeBoeuf, 1978). Females have also been shown to engage in more direct forms of mating competition. Some intrasexually aggressive female birds are more likely to be monogamously (vs. polygamously) mated and may consequently receive increased benefits from males (e.g., Sandell, 1998; Searcy & Yasukawa, 1996). Among primates, dominant females have been observed to harass subordinate females. This harassment can cause enough stress that the female subordinates may fail to come into estrus or might spontaneously abort pregnancies (Campbell, 1995).

Rosvall (2011) argued that researchers' relative ignorance of female–female competition may be rooted in how researchers define sexual selection. If the definition is restricted merely to competition for the *number* of mates or copulations, as has traditionally been the case, then its applicability is biased toward males because female reproductive fitness benefits less from mating with multiple partners (Bateman, 1948). Conversely, if the definition of sexual selection is broadened to encompass all manifestations of competition for mates, including competition for mate quality and mating-relevant resources, then females' intrasexual competition should be viewed as compatible with that of males (Rosvall, 2011). For instance, in species with extensive female care and little male parental investment, female competition primarily surrounds accessing males who can provide good genetic benefits (i.e., copulating with visibly high-quality males; Fisher, 1930), as well as protecting offspring and accessing resources to bolster the capacity for maternal care (Rosvall, 2008). Among polygynous primates, females who achieve dominant status reach sexual maturity and conceive earlier, and they produce more offspring who live longer (e.g., Pusey, Williams, & Goodall, 1997). Conversely, when males engage in parental care, females often compete for exclusive mating access to the males who are most likely or able to provide parental care, resources, or territories (e.g., Andersson, 1994; Rosvall, 2011; Whiteman & Cote, 2003), as well as to prevent extra-pair mating (Roberts & Searcy, 1988). As the research literature grows in this area of inquiry, it is becoming increasingly clear that female competition pervades a wide variety of species. These findings have led some researchers to suggest that female–female competition confers many benefits to survival and reproductive fitness and is therefore "unlikely to exist merely as non-adaptive byproducts of selection on males" (Rosvall, 2011, p. 1135). Researchers have recently begun to explore whether competition among human females might also have been sexually selected for, and, if so, how such competition might manifest within our modern social structure.

Applying Sexual Selection to Human Competition

Consistent with most mammalian species, human females have greater requisite parental investment than human males (Trivers, 1972). The internal fertilization process of human reproduction involves women bearing the greater cost of gamete production relative to men. For women, fertilization is then followed by a requisite nine months of gestation and up to four years of lactation, along with the caloric costs of carrying, protecting, and providing nutrition for the infant (Campbell, 1999). Anisogamy and differential parental care in humans suggests that women should be choosier than men when selecting their sexual partners. Research findings have largely supported this hypothesis, showing that women are less willing than men to go on a date with (and to have sex with) an attractive member of the opposite sex (Clark & Hatfield, 1989; Kurzban & Weeden, 2005; Townsend & Wasserman, 1998). Women's greater selectivity, in turn, leads men to compete with one another in order to gain and maintain mating access to choosy females (Campbell, 1995; Daly & Wilson, 1988).

Sexual selection explains many of the broad sex differences that exist in human behavior (e.g., Archer, 2009; Daly & Wilson, 1990). Men compete for dominance, resources, and social status among other intangibles that may contribute to reproductive opportunity or that serve to quell rivals (Daly & Wilson, 1988, 1994). For instance, men are more likely than women to signal their desirability by displaying high status and wealth (buying women nice dinners, getting a high-paying job, and flashing money; Buss, 1988). Men are also more likely to compete with one another using physical prowess and combat. Among men, one's proportion of fat-free muscle mass predicts his total number of past-year sex partners (Lassek & Gaulin, 2009). Some men use physical aggression in order to attain or guard sexual partners, even at the risk of incurring injury or death (e.g., Wilson & Daly, 1985). The decision to utilize aggression hinges on a fundamental cost–benefit analysis. Men are more likely to aggressively compete if they perceive a high likelihood of coming out victorious (Archer & Thanzami, 2007; Parker, 1974). Across cultural and contextual boundaries, males engage in more risk taking as well as more physically and sexually aggressive behavior surrounding their status and mating relationships compared to females (Archer & Coyne, 2005; Daly & Wilson, 1983; Vaillancourt, 2005).

Biparental Care

At first glance, humans seem to fit well within the prototypical mammalian model of greater female choosiness and male competition for varied mating opportunities. Men can certainly benefit their reproductive fitness by increasing the number of women with whom they copulate. For instance, serially monogamous men (but not women) produce more children than those who remain in one purely monogamous pair-bond (Forsberg & Tullberg, 1995; Jokela, Rotkirch, Rickard, Pettay, & Lummaa, 2010). Although women might also improve their reproductive fitness by copulating with multiple partners via sperm competition (i.e., engaging in short-term mating with men who exhibit "good gene" characteristics such as physical attractiveness; Sunderani, Arnocky, & Vaillancourt, 2013; Weatherhead & Robertson, 1979), their mating strategies nevertheless also include a greater preference for establishing long-term pair-bonds with men who will contribute a significant degree of parental care toward offspring (Buunk & Fisher, 2009).

Why do women exhibit a preference for monogamy and biparental care? Researchers have suggested that, over our evolutionary history, an increase in men's parenting efforts likely would have led to greater reproductive success (Miller, 1994). Evidence suggests that biparental care can enhance the survival and well-being of offspring. For instance, in preindustrial Europe and the United States, paternal investment has been linked to infant and child survival rates (Geary, 2000). Among the Ache, a Paraguayan hunter-gatherer society, father-present children are three times more likely to survive compared to father-absent children (Hill & Hurtado, 1996). Paternal investment is also indicative of offspring "quality." Children whose fathers provide paternal investment tend to have better social and academic skills, as well as higher income during adulthood (Geary, 2000; Pleck,

1997). From a fitness perspective, it is therefore in a woman's best interest to secure a man who can not only provide good genes but is also able and willing to invest in their offspring (Campbell, 2004). This is reflected in the priority of women's mate preferences. Women are attracted to both good-gene indicators, such as facial symmetry and skin quality (Jones et al., 2004), as well as to behavioral and personality cues to a potential mate's willingness to invest in her and her offspring (Buss, 2012).

Evidence of men's increased monogamy and parental investment can be observed in the degree of sexual dimorphism of modern humans. Males and females of biparental species tend to be morphologically similar. Although men are on average larger (approximately 15%) and stronger than women, this appears to constitute a significant reduction in sexual dimorphism compared to that of our ancestors (Geary, 2000). Hominids preceding Homo sapiens, such as *Australopithecus afarensis*, are believed to have displayed greater sexual dimorphism, with estimates of males being significantly larger than females, and of mating polygynously while contributing little in the way of parental investment (Geary, 2000; Gibbons, 2007; Larsen, 2003; cf. Reno, Meindl, McCollum, & Lovejoy, 2003). Conversely, the mating system of modern human society is typically described as one of serial monogamy, mild polygyny, and biparental care (see Schmitt & Rohde, 2013).

By engaging in long-term mating relationships, men might increase the quality of mate they can attract, as well as their degree of paternity certainty (Buss & Schmitt, 1993; Starratt & Shackelford, 2015). Yet biparental care also constrains male reproductive variance. Fewer men will have a large number of offspring from numerous women, and many more men will find opportunity to mate (Geary, 2000). Thus, due to the "heavy commitment that he will make in their joint progeny, it pays a male to be choosy ... [and] women must compete with one another to secure the best men, just as men vie for the best women" (Campbell, 2004, p. 17). Indeed, when men invest in a long-term mating strategy, they tend to be more discriminating in their mate choice than if they were adopting a short-term, low-investment strategy. For instance, Buss and Schmitt (1993) found that men tend to relax their standards for a potential mate when considering short-term but not long-term mating contexts. Not all men will be equal providers of good genes, of reproductively relevant resources (e.g., food, shelter, protection, social influence), or of parental effort (e.g., teaching, emotional support). Thus, women must also exhibit competitive attitudes (Buunk & Fisher, 2009) and behavior (Griskevicius et al., 2009; Vaillancourt, 2005, 2013) toward same-sex conspecifics for access to the highest-quality mates, who may themselves be highly selective in their mate choice (Campbell, 2004). Females who could secure the most reproductively viable mates (e.g., men who will invest in offspring, provide resources, care, etc.) would have had the greatest opportunity of producing surviving offspring. For example, it has been noted that, in some preindustrial societies, the ability of a woman to secure a high-status man was linked to more surviving offspring compared to women with lower-status partners (e.g., Voland, 1990; Voland & Engel, 1990). Because these desirable men represent only a portion of the population, it is conceivable that competition for their favor will occur (Vaillancourt, 2005).

Mate Poaching

Women, like men, do not compete merely for mating access to unattached individuals. In all human societies, some individuals will attempt to attract mates who are themselves already in an existing romantic relationship, a behavioral tactic termed "mate poaching" (Buss, 2006; Schmitt & Buss, 2001). In a large cross-cultural study, Schmitt et al. (2004) found that 35% of women admitted to attempting to poach a man from an existing romantic relationship for the purpose of a short-term liaison, and 44% reported doing so for the purpose of establishing a long-term romantic relationship. Women can benefit their reproductive fitness through short-term mating with high-quality men via sperm competition—copulating with multiple men in a short period of time creates a scenario whereby the sperm of the best genetic quality may be more likely to fertilize the women's egg (Baker & Bellis, 1995; Goetz et al., 2005; Weatherhead & Robertson, 1979). Women might also use short-term sexual encounters to "upgrade" to a better-quality romantic partner (Greiling & Buss, 2000). By poaching a man who has demonstrated his desirability and willingness to commit to other women, a female might benefit her long-term mating success (Schmitt & Buss, 2001). Arnocky, Sunderani, and Vaillancourt (2013) found that successful mate poaching by women predicted having had a greater number of lifetime sex partners, more lifetime casual sex partners, as well as more lifetime dating relationship

partners, indicating greater mating success among those women willing to compete for mates who are already "taken." Consistent with findings from studies of intrasexual competition among women, physically attractive women are more frequently the targets of a male mate poacher's desire and are more successful in their own poaching attempts compared to less physically attractive women (Sunderani et al., 2013).

Divergent Sexual Strategies and Strategic Interference

The competitive strategies of women are by no means limited to intrasexual (female–female) conflict. Women can also benefit their reproductive fitness by competing with mating partners in order to express their preferred sexual strategy. For example, it is well established that men, more than women, prefer sexual variety (Symons, 1979). For women, however, a long-term partner's infidelity is undesirable given that it can result in the division of important financial, social, and emotional resources with other women (Buss & Shackelford, 1997b), or in relationship dissolution, leading to significant loss of investment, resources, and parenting assistance (see Buss, 2003; Fisher, 1992). It may therefore benefit women to employ various mate-guarding tactics (Buss, 2002). Such behavior is common, with approximately 75% of married women (and men) reporting that they engage in some form of mate-retention behavior (Buss & Shackelford, 1997a). For women, the most common mate-retention strategies were providing love and care, physical appearance enhancement, and physical possession signals. In attempting to retain a mate, women are more likely than men to engage in appearance enhancement, verbal possession signals (e.g., discussing being off the market), and threatening punishment for a mate's infidelity (e.g., notifying her partner that she will dissolve the relationship if he cheats on her); such tactics are most likely to be employed by women who are paired with a desirable mate who is high in income and/or status striving (Buss & Shackelford, 1997a).

Why Competition among Women Differs from That among Men

The competitive strategies employed by women seem to differ fundamentally from those of men. Women, in comparison to men, less often exhibit extreme forms of overt physical and sexual aggression (Archer, 2004; Daly & Wilson, 1988; Vaillancourt, 2005). Women have more to lose in terms of reproductive fitness from potential physically damaging confrontations (Daly & Wilson, 1989). Campbell (1999, 2004) has argued that females' greater parental investment requires greater risk aversion. Even though humans are effectively a biparental species, women still provide the bulk of *obligatory* parental care (Hrdy, 1999). Thus, a mother's death is more debilitating to a child's survival compared to the death of a father (Sear, Mace, & McGregor, 2000). Whereas a man's inclusive fitness may rely on copulatory opportunity, a women's inclusive fitness relies more heavily on her successfully rearing her children through early life (Campbell, 2004). Accordingly, the costs associated with direct aggression and other risky forms of competition become amplified—for a woman (and for other female nonhuman primates), it is more important to remain alive in order to rear their offspring (see also Björkqvist, 1994; Campbell, 2004; Liesen, 2013; Smuts, 1987). It has been suggested that women instead compete using a variety of epigamic-display tactics and (relatively) less risky aggressive strategies in order to achieve dominance, attract mates, and quell rivals (Archer & Coyne, 2005; Vaillancourt, 2005, 2013). In the following section we review the evolutionary underpinnings of two commonly researched forms of competition among women: epigamic display (appearance enhancement) and indirect aggression.

Epigamic Display: Competition over Physical Attractiveness Characteristics

Across diverse human cultural groups, men are remarkably consistent in their expressed preference for physically attractive women (Buss, Shackelford, Kirkpatrick, & Larsen, 2001; Cunningham, Roberts, Wu, Barbee, & Druen, 1995). Men find attractive women who best display various cues to health and fertility. These include youth, lustrous hair, clear skin, feminine and symmetrical facial features, and a low waist-to-hip ratio (WHR; ranging between .67 and .80), typically constituting an hourglass-like figure (Buss, 1989; Fisher & Voracek, 2006; Gangestad & Scheyd, 2005; Hinsz, Matz, & Patience, 2001; Singh & Randall, 2007; Symons, 1979). Given men's selectivity in choosing long-term mating partners, women should be expected to compete with one another in the display of these desirable characteristics (Symons, 1979). Indeed, when asked how they compete with rivals and attract mates, women often report attempting to enhance their appearance (Cashdan, 1998) through the use of makeup, suntanning, nail polish,

and flattering clothing (Tooke & Camire, 1991). In their book titled *Why Women Have Sex*, Meston and Buss (2009) review evidence that women, more than men, attempt to enhance their physical appearance as a competitive mating strategy. Women are twice as likely as men to spend more than one hour working on their physical appearance each day. Western women are also 50% more likely than men to bronze their skin and are willing to spend almost ten times the amount of money that men spend on appearance-enhancement products (Meston & Buss, 2009). Seock and Bailey (2008) found women to enjoy shopping more, and to be more brand-conscious (aware and desiring of high-end brands) compared to men. For women, shopping seems to be more closely linked to enhancement of their self-image (Dittmar & Drury, 2000).

A woman's effort toward enhancing her appearance may therefore be an adaptive competition tactic. Hill and Durante (2011) found that women who were primed with intrasexual competition motives (by viewing photos of attractive women and rating their attractiveness, friendliness, and extraversion) were more willing to take health risks in order to enhance their physical appearance (via skin tanning and taking diet pills) compared to women in a control condition. Single women were also more likely to engage in risk behavior when exposed to a mating prime (viewing photos of men and rating their attractiveness, friendliness, and extraversion). Hill, Rodeheffer, Griskevicius, Durante, and White (2012) have further shown that in an economic recession (when spending on most products decreases), women nevertheless exhibit a propensity toward increasing spending on appearance-enhancing products (termed "the lipstick effect"). The researchers found that such spending is driven largely by an increased desire to attract mates with resources. Indeed, physical attractiveness is positively related to women's mating success. Rhodes, Simmons, and Peters (2005) found that women with highly attractive faces became sexually active earlier in life (i.e., had a longer period of reproductive potential) and had more long-term dating partners, compared to their less attractive peers. Physically attractive women are also more adept at stealing desirable men from already-existing romantic relationships (Sunderani et al., 2013). Rhodes et al. noted that "Attractive traits can certainly be altered by grooming practices and need not be entirely honest signals of mate quality" (p. 198). In other words, if a female can mimic or enhance facial attractiveness through the use of products and/or grooming, she may, to a degree, be able to improve her long-term mating success. Women are also more likely than men to report attempting to enhance their physical appearance as a mate-guarding tactic (Buss, 2002).

Rhodes et al. (2005) also note that the association between features of attractiveness and health and fertility is clearer for bodies (Singh, 1993) than for faces (Rhodes, Chan, Zebrowitz, & Simmons, 2003). Disordered body image and eating disordered behavior have been conceptualized as being born out of competition for mate acquisition and retention (Abed, 1998). This is because a low WHR in women is viewed as an honest signal of her health, indicating a greater estrogen-to-androgen ratio and greater fecundity. For instance, in a sample of women presenting for artificial sperm donor insemination, Zaadstra et al. (1993) showed that an increase in WHR predicted a statistically significant decrease in the probability of conception. WHR was a stronger predictor of fecundity than either age or obesity. Perhaps, then, it is not surprising that males find women with a low WHR to be more physically attractive, healthier, and reproductively viable than women with a higher WHR (Singh, 1993).

This raises the question of whether women compete within the domain of body shape. The uniquely human cognitive ability to link food and exercise to body weight and shape affords individuals the capacity to purposefully alter their WHR (Abed, 1998). In extreme form, women who are unhappy with their body's appearance might engage in excessive compensatory behavior in attempting to lose weight and are at an increased risk for developing an eating disorder (Parry-Jones & Parry-Jones, 1995). Abed et al. (2012) have argued that competition over displaying youth and thinness has become intensified in recent decades due in part to declining fertility (leading to extended periods of "pseudonubility" among older women who remain thinner), increased sexual autonomy, and high concentrations of attractive same-sex competitors in our local mating environments. This may help to explain the concurrent rise in eating disorders over the same time period (Abed et al., 2012). For example, eating disorders are significantly more common among heterosexual women who are in their prime reproductive years, compared to men, older women who are outside of reproductive age, and homosexual women (e.g., Abed et al., 2012; Li, Smith, Griskevicius, Cason, & Bryan, 2010). Moreover, intrasexual competition for mates has been shown to correlate positively with body dissatisfaction,

drive for thinness, and disordered eating behavior in both cross-sectional and experimental studies (Faer, Hendriks, Abed, & Figueredo, 2005; Li et al., 2010). For example, Li et al. (2010) exposed participants to one of two photo conditions depicting either (a) high-status competitive or (b) low-status noncompetitive intrasexual rivals. Results showed that heterosexual women (but not men or homosexual women) were more likely to report body dissatisfaction and more restrictive eating attitudes following exposure to the high-status but not low-status competitor photos. Eating disorder behavior has also recently been shown to be predicted by a fast life history (i.e., greater reproductive and mating effort) among college-age women (Abed et al., 2012). Taken together, these findings suggest that competition via the epigamic display of a desirable body morphology may, in some women, lead to the use of extreme and disordered attempts at weight loss. Recent research suggests that enhancing one's own physical appearance is merely "half the battle" in the struggle for mating success. Women sometimes also seek to disparage, exclude, humiliate, and derogate their competitors along dimensions of status, fidelity, and physical attractiveness, through the use of indirect aggression.

Indirect Aggression

Evidence suggests that the degree to which women compete extends beyond mere epigamic display (i.e., attempting to attract desirable men by demonstrating the characteristics most valued by men). Women have also been shown to compete via attack on rivals' social status, attractiveness, and sexual reputation (Campbell, 1995, 1999; Vaillancourt, 2005, 2013). These attacks are often covert and surreptitious, reducing the likelihood of retaliation and of physical, social, or legal consequence (Björkqvist, 1994; Campbell, 1999; Vaillancourt, 2005, 2013). Indirect aggression involves purposefully and often covertly manipulating interpersonal relationships through acts of social exclusion, gossip, and rumor spreading in order to harm others (Crick & Grotpeter, 1995; Lagerspetz, Björkqvist, & Peltonen, 1988). The vast majority of peer aggression occurs within rather than between the sexes (Gallup, O'Brien, White, & Wilson, 2009), and a greater proportional amount of aggression among girls and women is indirect in nature (Vaillancourt et al., 2010). This is not surprising given that women's use of indirect aggression has been shown to increase the perpetrators' status within the social hierarchy (Vaillancourt

& Hymel, 2006; Zimmer-Gembeck, Geiger, & Crick, 2005) and to promote depression, lower self-esteem, school dropout, and suicide among victims (e.g., Marr & Field, 2001; Owens, Slee, & Shute, 2000).

Interestingly, the content of women's indirect aggression corresponds to men's mate preferences. For example, given the degree of paternity uncertainty associated with human reproduction, men value sexual fidelity in a romantic partner. Predictably, girls and women often verbally attack female competitors' sexual reputation (e.g., by calling other women promiscuous or by calling them a tease; Buss & Dedden, 1990) and will limit their social interactions with those deemed to be promiscuous (see Campbell, 2004, for review). Similar indirect attacks surrounding women's physical appearance are common. Vaillancourt and Sharma (2011) showed that almost all women who were randomly exposed to an attractive female confederate engaged in derogatory behavior toward her when she was dressed in sexually provocative versus conservative clothing. Indirect attack of a woman's physical appearance may have adaptive value. Derogatory statements made about a woman's physical appearance can in fact reduce men's perceptions of that target woman's attractiveness and are more likely to be perpetrated by women who are, at the time, high in estrogen and thus maximally fertile (Fisher, 2004). Women have also been found to use indirect aggression during intersexual conflict. For instance, women are more likely than men to flirt with someone in front of their romantic partner as a mate-retention strategy (Buss, 2002).

Arnocky and Vaillancourt (2012) explored whether peer aggression does in fact confer mating benefits to perpetrators. The researchers followed adolescents over the course of one year. At time 1, participants completed both self-report and peer-report measures of physical and indirect aggression, as well as self-reports of peer victimization. At time 2, participants reported on their current dating status. Controlling for age, initial dating status, popularity, and physical attractiveness, results demonstrated that for both males and females, indirect aggression at time 1 predicted having a romantic partner one year later. In addition, being victimized by one's peer group negatively predicted having a dating partner at one-year follow-up.

Individual Differences in Competition

It is important to note that the basic principles of sexually selected female competition outlined in this chapter are contingent on various environmental factors that can either increase or decrease the propensity for competition among individuals. One condition driving the frequency and ferocity of competition among humans and other vertebrate species is the operational sex ratio, or the proportion of fertilizable females to sexually active males in a given population (Emlen & Oring, 1977). When the sex ratio is skewed, members of the scarcer sex have better mating prospects (Fisher, 1930) and can therefore express greater choosiness regarding with whom they mate (Berglund, 1994). Conversely, mating opportunities are scarcer for the abundant sex, resulting in greater intrasexual competition (Emlen & Oring, 1977). In India, for example, there are more males than females in large part because of sex-selective abortions (Jha et al., 2006). This leaves many men (typically those of low socioeconomic status) lacking mating opportunity. Research has found a strong correlation between the operational sex ratio in various states in India and homicide rates, even after controlling for urbanization and socioeconomic status (Drèze & Reetika, 2000).

Women have been found to engage in more casual sex under conditions of relative mate scarcity (perhaps conforming to a male-biased mating strategy; Schmitt, 2005; South & Trent, 1988; Stone, Shackelford, & Buss, 2007). If indirect aggression has evolved among women for the purpose of mate competition, then its use can be expected to increase under conditions of women's abundance relative to men. To test this hypothesis, Arnocky, Ribout, Mirza, and Knack (2014) exposed participants to one of two bogus magazine articles, one reporting fictitious research findings suggesting that quality mates are a scarce resource and the other suggesting that quality mates are easy to come by. The researchers found that women were more intrasexually competitive, more jealous, and more willing to use indirect aggression against a same-sex rival after being primed to believe that mates were scarce (vs. abundant). Future research would benefit from exploring whether epigamic display variables (e.g., cosmetic use, perceived skin-tanning risk, desire to diet) similarly increase in mate-scarcity versus mate-abundance conditions. Indeed, research has found that under conditions of mate scarcity, women tended to wear more revealing clothing (Barber, 1999). Cross-culturally, competition among women seems to be contextually sensitive in that it becomes intensified when suitable men are a scarce commodity (Campbell, 1995). See chapters 14 and 15 of this book for additional review of how the operational sex ratio influences competition among women.

Mate Value

Competition may be more frequent and extreme among those who are otherwise limited in their mating opportunities. Mate value is defined as "the total value of the characteristics that an individual possesses in terms of the potential contribution to his or her mate's reproductive success" (Waynforth, 2001, p. 207). Men and women share many similarities in terms of what they consider to be a high-mate-value partner. Buss and Barnes (1986) found that both men and women desire kind, healthy, intelligent partners with exciting and easygoing personalities. However, Buss also observed sex differences in that men more than women preferred physically attractive partners, whereas women more than men preferred mates with good earning capacity.

Research has previously shown that men who do not conform well to women's mate preferences may compete more intensely for mating opportunities or for mating-relevant resources. For example, Wilson and Daly (1985) showed that poor or unmarried men were more likely to commit murder than were their wealthier or married counterparts. Men are also more likely to engage in mate-retention tactics when they are of particularly low mate value (Miner, Starratt, & Shackelford, 2009) or when they are mated with a woman of particularly high mate value (Buss & Shackelford, 1997a). Men are also more likely to engage in mate retention when they perceive an increased likelihood of a partner's infidelity (Starratt, Shackelford, Goetz, & McKibbin, 2007). This phenomenon is likely grounded in our ancestral past, whereby unnecessary or misdirected attempts at retaining partners would have detracted from other important mating and survival functions (Graham-Kevan & Archer, 2009). Thus, individuals who could best approximate the need for such efforts would probably have been more likely to survive and reproduce. Being of relatively low mate value is one particularly salient cue to an increased likelihood of cuckoldry or partner defection from the relationship, qualifying the expenditure of mate-retention effort (Arnocky et al., 2012).

If women have simultaneously evolved a propensity for the use of competitive strategies to attain and maintain desired mating opportunities, then women should also be expected to exhibit more competition and mate-retention behavior in the face of increased reproductive threat. In support of this argument, Graham-Kevan and Archer (2009) found both men and women of low mate value to exhibit increased controlling behavior compared to their high-mate-value counterparts. Arnocky et al. (2012) found that women who perceived themselves to be of low physical attractiveness compared to their friends were more likely to perpetrate indirect aggression toward both peers (as a form of intrasexual competition) and partners (as a form of mate retention). Moreover, highly attractive women reported being indirectly victimized by their peers to a greater extent compared to less physically attractive females (Arnocky et al., 2012; Leenaars, Dane, & Marini, 2008). Arnocky et al. have suggested that low-mate-value women may be at particular risk of partner defection, given the greater proportion of more desirable competitors within the local mating market. Less attractive women (and men) have been found to worry more about a partner's potential involvement with others compared to their more attractive counterparts (e.g., White, 1980). Women who perceive themselves as being less physically attractive are also more romantically jealous (Arnocky et al., 2012). This may, in turn, warrant the perpetration of indirectly aggressive measures as a strategy for both intrasexual competition and mate retention. Future research would benefit from examining these links experimentally. Cross-sectional data are limited in that directional conclusions about the effects of low perceived mate value and jealousy on female competition cannot be made. By temporarily priming low versus high self-perceived mate value, researchers could effectively examine group differences in inducing competition, be it indirect aggression, enhanced orientation toward epigamic display, or other competition-related variables.

Conclusion

Studies of human sexual selection have disproportionately focused on the relevance of competition for men, neglecting the potential evolutionary origins of competition among women. Yet it has become increasingly clear that competition among women may be an adaptive behavioral strategy meant to augment mating and reproductive success. The amount of parental investment provided by men is unparalleled by any of our closest primate relatives (Geary,

2000). Parental investment constrains reproductive variance and increases men's choosiness in selecting long-term mates (Campbell, 1999). Because men also vary considerably in their own mate value, both in terms of their willingness and ability to invest in partner(s) and offspring as well as in their genotypic and phenotypic quality, women can bolster their reproductive fitness by competing for the most desirable mates (Arnocky et al., 2012; Vaillancourt, 2005, 2013). Buss and Dedden (1990) have argued that successful intrasexual competition relies on enhancing one's desirability to members of the opposite sex by (a) causing rivals to be less appealing and/or (b) enhancing one's own appeal. Each of these goals may be satisfied through successful competition along dimensions of men's mate preferences for physically attractive, youthful, and sexually faithful mates (Buss, 2012). Evidence supporting this hypothesis has been robustly observed in terms of both women's epigamic display (i.e., self-promotion via physical appearance; Abed, 1998), as well as in their use of indirect aggression perpetrated against their peers (Arnocky et al., 2012). Physically attractive (Buss, 1989; Walster, Aronson, Abrahams, & Rottman, 1966) and indirectly aggressive girls and women have been shown to be more likely to attract mates (e.g., Arnocky & Vaillancourt, 2012; Gallup et al., 2011). Conversely, women who are victimized by their peers may be viewed as lustful or unfaithful, as less physically attractive, and as less desirable to men (Arnocky & Vaillancourt, 2012; Fisher, 2004; Vaillancourt, 2005, 2013). Though there remains much to be discovered, it is seems to be the case that competition among women is intimately tied to the competition for mating success. The strategies employed by women do not merely mimic those employed by men but rather appear to reflect behavioral adaptations that are unique to the struggle for female mating success, suggesting that female competition exists not merely as a spandrel derived from sexual selection among males but rather as an adaptive behavioral strategy in its own right.

References

Abed, R. T. (1998). The sexual competition hypothesis for eating disorders. *British Journal of Medical Psychology, 71*(4), 525–547. doi: 10.1111/j.2044-8341.1998.tb01007.x

Abed, R. T., Mehta, S., Figueredo, A. J., Aldridge, S., Balson, H., Meyer, C., & Palmer, R. (2012). Eating disorders and intrasexual competition: Testing an evolutionary hypothesis among young women. *The Scientific World Journal, 1*, 1–8. doi: 10.1100/2012/290813

Alexander, R. D., Hoogland, J. L., Howard, R. D., Noonan, K. M., & Sherman, P. W. (1979) Sexual dimorphisms and breeding systems in pinnipeds, ungulates, primates, and humans In N. Chagnon & W. Irons (Eds.), *Evolutionary biology and human social behavior: An anthropological perspective* (pp. 402–435). North Sciate, MA: Duxbury.

Alcock, J. (2001). *Animal behavior.* 7th ed. Sunderland, MA: Sinauer Associates, Inc.

Andersson, M. (1994). *Sexual selection.* Princeton, NJ: Princeton University Press.

Archer, J. (2004). Sex differences in aggression in real-world setting: A meta-analytic review. *Review of General Psychology, 8*, 291–322. doi: 10.1037/1089-2680.8.4.291

Archer, J. (2009). Does sexual selection explain human sex differences in aggression? *Behavioral and Brain Sciences, 32*(3–4), 249–266. doi: 10.1017/S0140525X09990951

Archer, J., & Coyne, S. M. (2005). An integrated review of indirect, relational and social aggression. *Personality and Social Psychology Review, 9*(3), 212–230. doi: 10.1207/s15327957pspr0903_2

Archer, J., & Thanzami, V. L. (2007). The relation between physical aggression, size and strength, among a sample of young Indian men. *Personality and Individual Differences, 43*(3), 627–633. doi: 10.1016/j.paid.2007.01.005

Arnocky, S., Ribout, A., Mirza, R., & Knack, J. M. (2014). Perceived mate availability influences intrasexual competition, jealousy, and mate guarding behavior. *Journal of Evolutionary Psychology, 12*(1), 45–64. doi: 10.1556/JEP.12.2014.1.3

Arnocky, S., Sunderani, S., Miller, J., & Vaillancourt, T. (2012). Jealousy mediates the relationship between attractiveness comparison and females' indirect aggression. *Personal Relationships, 19*(2), 290–303. doi: 10.1111/j.1475-6811.2011.01362.x

Arnocky, S., Sunderani, S., & Vaillancourt, T. (2013). Mate poaching and mating success in humans. *Journal of Evolutionary Psychology, 11*(2), 65–83. doi: 10.1556/JEP.11.2013.2.2

Arnocky, S., & Vaillancourt, T. (2012). A multi-informant longitudinal study on the relationship between aggression, peer victimization, and adolescent dating status. *Evolutionary Psychology, 10*(2), 253–270.

Baker, R. R. & Bellis, M. A. (1995). *Human sperm competition: Copulation, masturbation and infidelity.* London: Chapman & Hall.

Baird, T. A., & Sloan, C. L. (2003). Interpopulation variation in the social organization of female collared lizards, *Grotaphytus collaris. Ethology, 109*(11), 879–894. doi: 10.1046/j.0179-1613.2003.00925.x

Barash, D. P. (1979). *The whisperings within.* New York: Harper & Row.

Barber, N. (1999). Women's dress fashions as a function of reproductive strategy. *Sex Roles, 40*(5–6), 459–471. doi: 10.1023/A:1018823727012

Bateman, A. J. (1948). Intra-sexual selection in Drosophila. *Heredity, 2*, 349–368.

Berglund, A. (1994). The operational sex ratio influences choosiness in a pipefish. *Behavioral Ecology, 5*(3), 254–258. doi: 10.1093/beheco/5.3.254

Berglund. A., & Rosenqvist, G. (2001). Male pipefish prefer dominant over attractive females. *Behavioral Ecology, 12*(4), 402–406. doi: 10.1093/beheco/12.4.402

Berglund, A., & Rosenqvist, G. (2009). An intimidating ornament in a female pipefish. *Behavioral Ecology, 20*(1), 54–59. doi: 10.1093/beheco/arn114

Birkhead, T. (2001). *Promiscuity: An evolutionary history of sperm competition.* Cambridge, MA: Harvard University Press.

Björkqvist, K. (1994). Sex differences in physical, verbal, and indirect aggression: A review of recent research. *Sex Roles, 30*(3–4), 177–188. doi: 10.1007/BF01420988

Buss, D. M. (1988). The evolution of human intrasexual competition: Tactics of mate attraction. *Journal of Personality and Social Psychology, 54*(4), 616–628. doi: 10.1037/0022-3514.54.4.616

Buss, D. M. (1989). Sex differences in human mate preferences: Evolutionary hypotheses tested in 37 cultures. *Behavioral and Brain Sciences, 12*(1), 1–49. doi: 10.1017/S0140525X00023992

Buss, D. M. (2002). Human mate guarding. *Neuroendocrinology Letters, 23*(Suppl. 4), 23–29.

Buss, D. M. (2003). *The evolution of desire: Strategies of human mating.* New York: Basic Books.

Buss, D. M. (2006). Strategies of human mating. *Psychological Topics, 15*(2), 239–260.

Buss, D. M. (2012). *Evolutionary psychology: The new science of the mind* (4th ed.). Boston: Allyn & Bacon.

Buss, D. M., & Barnes, M. (1986). Preferences in human mate selection. *Journal of Personality and Social Psychology, 50*(3), 559–570. doi: 10.1037/0022-3514.50.3.559

Buss, D. M., & Dedden, L. A. (1990). Derogation of competitors. *Journal of Personal and Social Relationships, 7*(3), 395–422. doi: 10.1177/0265407590073006

Buss, D. M., & Schmitt, D. P. (1993). Sexual strategies theory: An evolutionary perspective on human mating. *Psychological Review, 100*(2), 204–232. doi: 10.1037/0033-295X.100.2.204

Buss, D. M., & Shackelford, T. K. (1997a). From vigilance to violence: Mate retention tactics in married couples. *Journal of Personality and Social Psychology, 72*(2), 346–361. doi: 10.1037/0022-3514.72.2.346

Buss, D. M., & Shackelford, T. K. (1997b). Susceptibility to infidelity in the first year of marriage. *Journal of Research in Personality, 31*(2), 193–221. doi: 10.1006/jrpe.1997.2175

Buss, D. M., Shackelford, T. K., Kirkpatrick, L. A., & Larsen, R. J. (2001). A half century of American mate preferences. *Journal of Marriage and the Family, 63*(2), 491–503. doi: 10.1111/j.1741-3737.2001.00491.x

Buunk, A. P., & Fisher, M. (2009). Individual differences in intrasexual competition. *Journal of Evolutionary Psychology, 7*(1), 37–48. doi: 10.1556/JEP.7.2009.1.5

Campbell, A. (1995). A few good men: Evolutionary psychology and female adolescent aggression. *Ethology and Sociobiology, 16,* 99–123. doi: 10.1016/0162-3095(94)00072-F

Campbell, A. (1999). Staying alive: Evolution, culture, and women's intrasexual aggression. *Behavioral and Brain Sciences, 22*(2), 203–252.

Campbell, A. (2004). Female competition: Causes, constraints, content, and contexts. *Journal of Sex Research, 41*(1), 16–26. doi: 10.1080/00224490409552210

Cashdan, E. (1998). Smiles, speech, and body posture: How women and men display sociometric status and power.

Journal of Nonverbal Behavior, 22(4), 209–228. doi: 10.1023/A:1022967721884

Christenson, T. E., & LeBoeuf, B. J. (1978). Aggression in female northern elephant seal, *Mirounga angustirostris. Behavior, 64,* 158–172.

Clark, R. D., & Hatfield, E. (1989). Gender differences in receptivity to sexual offers. *Journal of Psychology and Human Sexuality, 2*(1), 39–55. doi: 10.1300/J056v02n01_04

Clutton-Brock, T. H. (1989). Mammalian mating systems. *Proceedings of the Royal Society B: Biological Sciences, 236*(1285), 339–372. doi: 10.1098/rspb.1989.0027

Clutton-Brock, T. H. (1991). *The evolution of parental care.* Princeton, NJ: Princeton University Press.

Clutton-Brock, T. H. (2009). Sexual selection in females. *Animal Behavior, 77,* 3–11. doi: 10.1016/j.anbehav.2008.08.026

Crick, N. R., & Grotpeter, J. K. (1995). Relational aggression, gender and social-psychological adjustment. *Child Development, 66*(3), 710–722. doi: 10.1111/j.1467-8624.1995.tb00900.x

Cronin, H. (1991). *The ant and the peacock.* Cambridge: Cambridge University Press.

Cunningham, M. R., Roberts, A. R., Wu, C. H., Barbee, A. P., & Druen, P. B. (1995). "Their ideas of beauty are, on the whole, the same as ours": Consistency and variability in the cross-cultural perception of female attractiveness. *Journal of Personality and Social Psychology, 68,* 261–279. doi: 10.1037/0022-3514.68.2.261

Daly, M., & Wilson, M. (1983). *Sex, evolution and behavior.* Boston, MA: Wadsworth.

Daly, M., & Wilson, M. (1988). *Homicide.* New York: Aldine.

Daly, M., & Wilson, M. (1989). Homicide and cultural evolution. *Ethology and Sociobiology 10*(1–3), 99–110. doi: 0.1016/0162-3095(89)90014-9

Daly, M., & Wilson, M. (1990). Killing the competition. *Human Nature, 1*(1), 81–107. doi: 10.1007/BF02692147

Daly, M., & Wilson, M. (1994). Evolutionary psychology of male violence. In J. Archer (Ed.), *Male violence* (pp. 253–288). London: Routledge, Chapman & Hall.

Darwin, C. (1859). *On the origin of species.* Cambridge, MA: Harvard University Press.

Darwin, C. (1860). Letter 2743—Darwin, C. R. to Gray, Asa, 3 April (1860). Cambridge, UK: University of Cambridge, Darwin Correspondence Project.

Darwin, C. (1871). *The descent of man and selection in relation to sex.* London: John Murray.

Darwin, C., & Wallace, A. (1858). On the tendency of species to form varieties, and on the perpetuation of varieties and species by natural means of selection. *Journal of the Linnean Society of London, Zoology, 3,* 45–62.

Dawkins, R. (1976). *The selfish gene.* New York: Oxford University Press.

Dittmar, H., & Drury, J. (2000). Self-image—Is it in the bag? A qualitative comparison between "ordinary" and "excessive" consumers. *Journal of Economic Psychology, 21*(2), 109–142. doi: 10.1016/S0167-4870(99)00039-2

Drèze, J., & Reetika, K. (2000). Crime, gender, and society in India: Insights from homicide data. *Population and Development Review, 26*(2), 335–352. doi: 10.1111/j.1728-4457.2000.00335.x

Emlen, S., & Oring, L. W. (1977). Ecology, sexual selection, and the evolution of mating systems. *Science, 197*(4300), 215–223. doi: 10.1126/science.327542

Faer, L. M., Hendriks, A., Abed, R. T., & Figueredo, A. J. (2005). The evolutionary psychology of eating disorders: Female competition for mates or for status? *Psychology and Psychotherapy, 78*(3), 397–417. doi: 10.1348/147608305X42929

Forsberg, A. J. L., & Tullberg, B. S. (1995). The relationship between cumulative number of cohabiting partners and number of children for men and women in modern Sweden. *Ethology and Sociobiology, 16*(3), 221–232. doi: 10.1016/0162-3095(95)00003-4

Fisher, H. E. (1992). *Anatomy of love: The natural history of monogamy, adultery, and divorce.* New York: W. W. Norton.

Fisher, M. L. (2004). Female intrasexual competition decreases female facial attractiveness. *Proceedings of the Royal Society of London B: Biological Sciences, 271*(Suppl. 5), S283–S285. doi: 10.1098/rsbl.2004.0160

Fisher, M. L., & Voracek M. (2006). The shape of beauty: Determinants of female physical attractiveness. *Journal of Cosmetic Dermatology, 5*(2), 190–194. doi: 10.1111/j.1473-2165.2006.00249.x

Fisher, R. A. (1930). *The genetical theory of natural selection.* Oxford: Clarendon Press.

Galimberti, F., Boitani, L., & Marzetti, I. (2000). Harassment during arrival on land and departure to sea in southern elephant seals. *Ethology Ecology & Evolution, 12*(4), 389–404. doi: 10.1080/08927014.2000.9522794

Gallup, A. C., O'Brien, D. T., White, D. D., & Wilson, D. S. (2009). Peer victimization in adolescence has different effects on the sexual behavior of male and female college students. *Personality and Individual Differences, 46*(5-6), 611–615. doi: 10.1016/j.paid.2008.12.018

Gallup, A. C., O'Brien, D. T., and Wilson, D. S. (2011). Intrasexual peer aggression and dating behavior during adolescence: An evolutionary perspective. *Aggressive Behavior, 37*(3), 258–267. doi: 10.1002/ab.20384

Gangestad, S. W., & Scheyd, G. J. (2005). The evolution of physical attractiveness. *Annual Review of Anthropology, 34*, 523–548. doi: 10.1146/annurev.anthro.33.070203.143733

Geary, D. C. (2000). Evolution and proximate expression of human paternal investment. *Psychological Bulletin, 126*(1), 55–77. doi: 10.1037/0033-2909.126.1.55

Gibbons, A. (2007). Hominid harems: Big males competed for small Australopithecine females. *Science, 318*(5855), 1363. doi: 10.1126/science.318.5855.1363a

Goetz, A. T., Shackelford, T. K., Weekes-Shackelford, V. A., Euler, H. A., Hoier, S., Schmitt, D. P., & LaMunyon, C. W. (2005). Mate retention, semen displacement, and human sperm competition: A preliminary investigation of tactics to prevent and correct female infidelity. *Personality and Individual Differences, 38*(4), 749–763. doi: 10.1016/j.paid.2004.05.028

Graham-Kevan, N., & Archer, J. (2009). Control tactics and partner violence in heterosexual relationships. *Evolution & Human Behavior, 30*(6), 445–452. doi: 10.1016/j.evolhumbehav.2009.06.007

Greiling, H., & Buss, D. M. (2000). Women's sexual strategies: The hidden dimension of extra pair mating. *Personality and Individual Differences, 28*(5), 929–963. doi: 10.1016/S0191-8869(99)00151-8

Griskevicius, V., Tybur, J. M., Gangestad, S. W., Perea, E. F., Shapiro, J. R., & Kenrick, D. T. (2009). Aggress to impress: Hostility as an evolved context-dependent strategy. *Journal of Personality and Social Psychology, 96*(5), 980–994. doi: 10.1037/a0013907

Hill, K., & Hurtado, A. M. (1996). *Ache life history: The ecology and demography of a foraging people.* New York: Aldine.

Hill, S. E., & Durante, K. M. (2011). Courtship, competition, and the pursuit of attractiveness: Mating goals facilitate health-related risk taking and strategic risk suppression in women. *Personality and Social Psychology Bulletin, 37*(3), 383–394. doi: 10.1177/0146167210395603

Hill, S. E., Rodeheffer, C. D., Griskevicius, V., Durante, K., & White, A. E. (2012). Boosting beauty in an economic decline: Mating, spending, and the lipstick effect. *Journal of Personality and Social Psychology, 103*(2), 275–291. doi: 10.1037/a0028657

Hinsz, V. B., Matz, D. C., & Patience, R. A. (2001). Does women's hair signal reproductive potential? *Journal of Experimental Social Psychology, 37*(2), 166–172. doi: 10.1006/jesp.2000.1450

Hoelzel, A. R., Le Boeuf, B. J., Reiter, J., & Campagna, C. (1999). Alpha-male paternity in elephant seals. *Behavioral Ecology and Sociobiology, 46*(5), 298–306. doi: 10.1007/s002650050623

Hrdy, S. B. (1981). *The woman that never evolved.* Cambridge, MA: Harvard University Press.

Hrdy, S. B. (1999). *Mother nature: A history of mothers, infants and natural selection.* New York: Pantheon.

Jha, P., Kumar, R., Vasa, P., Dhingra, N., Thiruchelvam, D., & Moineddin, R. (2006). Low male-to-female sex ratio of children born in India: National survey of 1.1 million households. *The Lancet, 367*(9506), 211–218. doi: 10.1016/S0140-6736(06)67930-0

Jokela, M., Rotkirch, A., Rickard, I. J., Pettay, J., & Lummaa, V. (2010). Serial monogamy increases reproductive success in men but not in women. *Behavioral Ecology, 21*(5), 906–912. doi: 10.1093/beheco/arq078

Jones, B. C., Little, A. C., Feinberg, D. R., Penton-Voak, I. S., Tiddeman, B. P., & Perrett, D. I. (2004). The relationship between shape symmetry and perceived skin condition in male facial attractiveness. *Evolution and Human Behavior, 25*(1), 24–30. doi: 10.1016/S1090-5138(03)00080-1

Kleiman, D. G., & Malcolm, J. R. (1981). The evolution of male parental investment in mammals. In D. G. Gubernick & P. H. Klopfer (Eds.), *Parental care in mammals* (pp. 347–387). New York: Plenum Press.

Kurzban, R., & Weeden, J. (2005). Hurrydate: Mate preferences in action. *Evolution and Human Behavior, 26*(3), 227–244. doi: 1 0.1016/j.evolhumbehav.2004.08.012

Lagerspetz, K. M. J., Björkqvist, K., & Peltonen, T. (1988). Is indirect aggression typical of females? Gender differences in aggressiveness in 11- to 12-year-old children. *Aggressive Behavior, 14*(6), 403–416. doi: 10.1002/1098-2337(1988)14:6<403::AID-AB2480140602>3.0.CO;2-D

Lande, R. (1980). Sexual dimorphism, sexual selection, and adaptation in polygenetic characters. *Evolution, 34*(2), 292–305.

Larsen, C. S. (2003). Equality for the sexes in human evolution? Early hominid sexual dimorphism and implications for mating systems and social behavior. *Proceedings of the National Academy of Science of the United States of America, 100*(16), 9103–9104. doi: 10.1073/pnas.1633678100

Lassek, W. D., & Gaulin, S. J. C. (2009). Costs and benefits of fat-free muscle mass in men: Relationship to mating success, dietary requirements, and native immunity. *Evolution and Human Behavior*, *30*(5), 322–328. doi: 10.1016/j.evolhumbehav.2009.04.002

LeBoeuf, B. J. (1974). Male–male competition and reproductive success in elephant seals. *American Zoologist*, *14*(1), 163–176. doi: 10.1093/icb/14.1.163

Leenaars, L. S., Dane A. V., & Marini Z. A. (2008). Evolutionary perspective on indirect victimization in adolescence: The role of attractiveness, dating and sexual behavior. *Aggressive Behavior*, *34*(4), 404–415. doi: 10.1002/ab.20252

Li, N. P., Smith, A. R., Griskevicius, V., Cason, M. J., & Bryan, A. (2010). Intrasexual competition and eating restriction in heterosexual and homosexual individuals. *Evolution and Human Behavior*, *31*(5), 365–372. doi: 10.1016/j.evolhumbehav.2010.05.004

Liesen, L. (2013). The tangled web she weaves: The evolution of female–female aggression and status-seeking. In M. L. Fisher, J. R. Garcia, & R. S. Chang (Eds.), *Evolution's empress: Darwinian perspectives on the nature of women* (pp. 43–62). New York: Oxford University Press.

Lindenfors, P., & Tullberg, B. S. (2011). Evolutionary aspects of aggression: The importance of sexual selection. *Advances in Genetics*, *75*, 7–22. doi: 10.1016/B978-0-12-380858-5.00009-5

Marr, N., & Field, T. (2001). *Bullycide: Death at playtime*. Oxfordshire, UK: Success Unlimited.

Meston, C. M., & Buss, D. M. (2009). *Why women have sex: The psychology of sex in women's own voices*. New York: Times Books.

Miller, E. M. (1994). Paternal provisioning versus mate seeking in human populations. *Personality and Individual Differences*, *17*(2), 227–255. doi: 10.1016/0191-8869(94)90029-9

Miner, E. J., Starratt, V. G., & Shackelford, T. K. (2009). It's not all about her: Men's mate value and mate retention. *Personality and Individual Differences*, *47*(3), 214–218. doi: 10.1016/j.paid.2009.03.002

Moore, A. J. (1990). The evolution of sexual dimorphism by sexual selection: The separate effects of intrasexual selection and intersexual selection. *Evolution*, *44*(2), 315–331.

Owens, L., Slee, P., & Shute, R. (2000). It hurts a hell of a lot: The effects of indirect aggression on teenage girls. *School Psychology International*, *21*(4), 359–376. doi: 10.1177/0143034300214002

Parker, G. A. (1974). Assessment strategy and the evolution of fighting behavior. *Journal of Theoretical Biology*, *47*(1), 223–243. doi: 10.1016/0022-5193(74)90111-8

Parry-Jones, W. L. L., & Parry-Jones, B. (1995). Eating disorders: Social section. In G. E. Berrios & R. Porter (Eds.), *History of clinical psychiatry: The origin and history of psychiatric disorders* (pp. 602–611). London: Athlone.

Petrie, M., & Halliday, T. (1994). Experimental and natural changes in the peacock's (*Pavo cristatus*) train can affect mating success. *Behavioral Ecology and Sociobiology*, *35*(3), 213–217. doi: 10.1007/BF00167962

Petrie, M., Halliday, T., & Sanders, C. (1991). Peahens prefer peacocks with more elaborate trains. *Animal Behaviour*, *41*, 323–331. doi: 10.1016/S0003-3472(05)80484-1

Plavcan, J. M. (2001). Sexual dimorphism in primate evolution. *American Journal of Physical Anthropology*, *116*(S33), 25–53. doi: 10.1002/ajpa.10011

Pleck, J. H. (1997). Paternal investment: Levels, sources, and consequences. In M. E. Lamb (Ed.), *The role of the father in child development* (3rd ed., pp. 66–103). New York: Wiley.

Pusey, A., Williams, J., & Goodall, J. (1997). The influence of dominance rank on the reproductive success of female chimpanzees. *Science*, *277*(5327), 823–831. doi: 10.1126/science.277.5327.828

Reno, P. L., Meindl, R. S., McCollum, M. A., & Lovejoy, C. O. (2003). Sexual dimorphism in *Australopithecus afarensis* was similar to that of modern humans. *Proceedings of the National Academy of Sciences of the United States of America*, *100*(16), 9404–9409. doi: 10.1073/pnas.1133180100

Rhodes, G., Chan, J., Zebrowitz, L. A., & Simmons, L. W. (2003). Does sexual dimorphism in human faces signal health? *Proceedings of the Royal Society of London. Series B*, *270*(Suppl. 1), S93–S95.

Rhodes, G., Simmons, L. W., & Peters, M. (2005). Attractiveness and sexual behavior: Does attractiveness enhance mating success? *Evolution and Human Behavior*, *26*(2), 186–201. doi: 10.1016/j.evolhumbehav.2004.08.014

Robbins, M. M., & Czekala, N. M. (1997). A preliminary investigation of urinary testosterone and cortisol levels in wild male mountain gorillas. *American Journal of Primatology*, *43*, 51–64. doi: 10.1002/(SICI)1098-2345(1997)43:1<51::AID-AJP4>3.0.CO;2-X

Roberts, L. B., & Searcy, W. A. (1988). Dominance relationships in harems of female red-winged blackbirds. *Auk*, *105*, 89–96.

Rosvall, K. A. (2008). Sexual selection on aggressiveness in females: Evidence from an experimental test with tree swallows. *Animal Behavior*, *75*(5), 1603–1610. doi: 10.1016/j.anbehav.2007.09.038

Rosvall, K. A. (2011). Intrasexual competition in females: Evidence for sexual selection? *Behavioral Ecology*, *22*(6), 1131–1140. doi: 10.1093/beheco/arr106

Sandell, M. I. (1998). Female aggression and the maintenance of monogamy: Female behavior predicts male mating status in European starlings. *Proceedings of the Royal Society of London B: Biological Sciences*, *265*(1403), 1307–1311. doi: 10.1098/rspb.1998.0434

Schmitt, D. P. (2005). Sociosexuality from Argentina to Zimbabwe: A 48-nation study of sex, culture, and strategies of human mating. *Behavioral and Brain Sciences*, *28*(2), 247–311. doi: 10.1017/S0140525X05000051

Schmitt, D. P., Alcalay, L., Allik, J., Angleitner, A., Ault, L., Austers, I., ... Zupanèiè, A. (2004). Patterns and universals of mate poaching across 53 nations: The effects of sex, culture, and personality on romantically attracting another person's partner. *Journal of Personality and Social Psychology*, *86*(4), 560–584. doi: 10.1037/0022-3514.86.4.560

Schmitt, D. P., & Buss, D. M. (2001). Human mate poaching: Tactics and temptations for infiltrating existing relationships. *Journal of Personality and Social Psychology*, *80*(6), 894–917. doi: 10.1037/0022-3514.80.6.894

Schmitt, D. P., & Rohde, P. A. (2013). The human polygyny index and its ecological correlates: Testing sexual selection and life history theory at the cross-national level. *Social Science Quarterly*, *94*(4), 1159–1184. doi: 10.1111/ssqu.12030

Sear, R., Mace, R., & McGregor, I. A. (2000). Maternal grandmothers improve nutritional status and survival of children in rural Gambia. *Proceedings of the Royal Society of London B: Biological Sciences*, *267*(1453), 1641–1647. doi: 10.1098/rspb.2000.1190

Searcy, W. A., & Yasukawa, K. (1996). The reproductive success of secondary females relative to that of monogamous and primary females in red-winged blackbirds. *Journal of Avian Biology, 27*(3), 225–230.

Selander, R. K. (1972). Sexual selection and dimorphism in birds. In B. Campbell (Ed.), *Sexual selection and the descent of man* (pp. 180–230). Chicago: Aldine.

Seock, Y. K., & Bailey, L. R. (2008). The influence of college students' shopping orientations and gender differences on online information searches and purchase behaviours. *International Journal of Consumer Studies, 32*(2), 113–121. doi: 10.1111/j.1470-6431.2007.00647.x

Shine, R. (1978). Sexual size dimorphism and male combat in snakes. *Oecologia, 33,* 269–277.

Singh, D. (1993). Adaptive significance of female physical attractiveness: Role of waist-to-hip ratio. *Journal of Personality and Social Psychology, 65*(2), 293–307. doi: 10.1037/0022-3514.65.2.293

Singh, D., & Randall, P. K. (2007). Beauty is in the eye of the plastic surgeon: Waist–hip ratio (WHR) and women's attractiveness. *Personality and Individual Differences, 43*(2), 329–340. doi: 10.1016/j.paid.2006.12.003

Smuts, B. (1987). Gender, aggression, and influence. In B. Smuts, D. Cheney, R. Seyfarth, R. Wrangham, & T. Strusaker (Eds.), *Primate societies* (pp. 400–412). Chicago: University of Chicago Press.

South, S. J., & Trent, K. (1988). Sex ratios and women's roles: A cross-national analysis. *American Journal of Sociology, 93*(5), 1096–1115. doi: 10.1086/228865

Starratt, V. G., & Shackelford, T. K. (2015). Intersexual competition. In P. Whelan & A. Bolin (Eds.), *Encyclopedia of human sexuality.* Hoboken, NJ: Wiley-Blackwell.

Starratt, V. G., Shackelford, T. K., Goetz, A. T., & McKibbin, W. F. (2007). Male mate retention behaviors vary with risk of female infidelity and sperm competition. *Acta Psychologica Sinica, 39*(3), 523–527.

Stone, E. A, Shackelford, T. K., & Buss, D. M. (2007). Sex ratio and mate preferences: A cross-cultural investigation. *European Journal of Social Psychology, 37*(2), 288–296. doi: 10.1002/ejsp.357

Sunderani, S., Arnocky, S., & Vaillancourt, T. (2013). Individual differences in mate poaching: An examination of hormonal, dispositional, and behavioral mate-value traits. *Archives of Sexual Behavior, 42*(4), 533–542. doi: 10.1007/s10508-012-9974-y

Symons D. (1979). *The evolution of human sexuality.* New York: Oxford University Press.

Thornhill, R., & Alcock, J. (1983). *The evolution of insect mating systems.* Cambridge, MA: Harvard University Press.

Tooke, J., & Camire, L. (1991). Patterns of deception in intersexual and intrasexual mating strategies. *Ethology and Sociobiology, 12*(5), 345–364. doi: 10.1016/0162-3095 (91)90030-T

Townsend, J. M., & Wasserman, T. (1998). Sexual attractiveness: Sex differences in assessment and criteria. *Evolution and Human Behavior, 19*(3), 171–191. doi: 10.1016/S1090-5138(98)00008-7

Trivers, R. L. (1972). Parental investment and sexual selection. In B. Campbell (Ed.), *Sexual selection and the descent of man* (pp. 136–179). Chicago: Aldine.

Vaillancourt, T. (2005). Indirect aggression among humans: Social construct or evolutionary adaptation? In R. E. Tremblay, W.W. Hartup, & J. Archer (Eds.), *Developmental origins of aggression* (pp. 158–177). New York: Guilford.

Vaillancourt, T. (2013). Do human females use indirect aggression as an intrasexual competition strategy? *Philosophical Transactions of the Royal Society B, 368,* 1–7. doi: 10.1098/rstb.2013.0080

Vaillancourt, T., & Hymel, S. (2006). Aggression and social status: The moderating roles of sex and peer-valued characteristics. *Aggressive Behavior, 32*(4), 396–408. doi: 10.1002/ab.20138

Vaillancourt, T., Miller, J. L., & Sharma, A. (2010). "Tripping the prom queen": Female intrasexual competition and indirect aggression. In K. Österman (Ed.), *Indirect and direct aggression* (pp. 17–32). Frankfurt: Peter Lang.

Vaillancourt, T., & Sharma, A. (2011). Intolerance of sexy peers: Intrasexual competition among women. *Aggressive Behavior, 37*(6), 569–577. doi: 10.1002/ab.20413

Voland, E. (1990). Differential reproductive success within the Krummhörn population (Germany, 18th and 19th centuries). *Behavioral Ecology and Sociobiology, 26*(1), 65–72. doi: 10.1007/BF00174026

Voland, E., & Engel, C. (1990). Female choice in humans: A conditional mate selection strategy of the Krummhörn Women (Germany, 1720–1874). *Ethology, 84*(2), 144–154. doi: 10.1111/j.1439-0310.1990.tb00791.x

Walster, E., Aronson, J., Abrahams, D., & Rottman, L. (1966). Importance of physical attractiveness in dating behaviour. *Journal of Personality and Social Psychology, 4*(5), 508–516. doi: 10.1037/h0021188

Waynforth, D. (2001). Mate choice trade-offs and women's preference for physically attractive men. *Human Nature, 12*(3), 207–219. doi: 10.1007/s12110-001-1007-9

Weatherhead, P. J., & Robertson, R. J. (1979). Offspring quality and the polygyny threshold: The "sexy son" hypothesis. *American Naturalist, 113*(2), 201–208.

White, G. L. (1980). Physical attractiveness and courtship progress. *Journal of Personality and Social Psychology, 39*(4), 660–668. doi: 10.1037/0022-3514.39.4.660

Whiteman, E. A., & Cote, I. M. (2003). Social monogamy in the cleaning goby *Elacatinus evelynae*: Ecological constraints or net benefit? *Animal Behaviour, 66*(2), 281–291. doi: 10.1006/anbe.2003.2200

Wilson, M., & Daly, M. (1985). Competitiveness, risk-taking and violence: The young male syndrome. *Ethology and Sociobiology, 6*(1), 59–73. doi: 0.1016/0162-3095(85)90041-X

Woodroffe, R., & Vincent, A. (1994). Mother's little helpers: Patterns of male care in mammals. *Trends in Ecology & Evolution, 9*(8), 294–297. doi: 10.1016/0169-5347(94)90033-7

Zaadstra, B. M., Seidell, J. C., Vannoord, P. A., Tevelde, E. R., Habbema, J. D., Vrieswijk, B., & Karbaat. J. (1993). Fat and female fecundity: Prospective study of effect of body fat distribution on conception rates. *British Medical Journal, 306*(6876), 484–487.

Zahavi, A. (1975). Mate selection—A selection for a handicap. *Journal of Theoretical Biology, 53*(1), 205–214. doi: 10.1016/0022-5193(75)90111-3

Zimmer-Gembeck, M. J., Geiger, T. C., & Crick, N. R. (2005). Relational and physical aggression, prosocial behavior, and peer relations: Gender moderation and bidirectional associations. *Journal of Early Adolescence, 25*(4), 421–452. doi: 10.1177/0272431605279841

Female Intrasexual Competition in Primates: Why Humans Aren't as Progressive as We Think

Nicole M. Scott

Abstract

Males and females compete with each other and amongst their own sex, but often for different reasons. This chapter enriches current understanding of female-female competition in humans by examining competition in other primates; it explores why females compete and discusses when affiliation and cooperation may lead to better outcomes. Socioecological constraints on a species—such as social organization, food competition, and dispersal preference—play a major role in the structure of female-female relationships; notable attention is given to factors that affect social relationships: food competition, reproduction, dispersal, and dominance. Bond maintenance behaviors and communication strategies are also discussed relative to female-female relationships. Three nonhuman primate societies are examined, and potential lessons from these structures are gleaned where possible. The chapter reviews human progress in overcoming phylogenetic and ecological constraints in favor of women's societal liberties.

Key Words: socioecology, primate sociality, resource competition, phylogeny, chimpanzee, dominance

Introduction

In recent decades, researchers have increasingly recognized that females can be competitive and aggressive (for possible historical reasons on the delay of interest, see Hrdy, 2013b). Although the immediate, or proximate, function of competition and use of aggression by females differs from that of males, the ultimate (in the sense of Tinbergen, 1963) reasons are similar: to increase their *fitness* or reproductive success. It is now evident that female competition and aggression occur throughout the animal kingdom (e.g., chimpanzees: Goodall, 1986; Pusey et al., 2008; Scott, 2013; cichlids: Tubert, Lo Nostro, Villafane, & Pandolfi, 2012; Walter & Trillmich, 1994; blackbirds: Yasukawa & Searcy, 1982; to name a few). Sources, or proximate causes, of female aggression stem from many levels of explanation: from population-level social structure to molecular-level circulating hormone concentrations

(Nelson, 2006). Humans are subject to many of the same physiological, ecological, and social constraints that other animals experience. This chapter is focused on female-female competition in human's closest relatives, the other primates. I specifically focus on three primate species—chimpanzees, hamadryas baboons, and ring-tailed lemurs—giving special consideration to the different ecological and social pressures of these and other species.

I have three goals for this chapter beyond providing an introduction to primates. The first goal is to place female-female competition and aggression in an evolutionary context to better understand the evolutionary advantage of the different strategies for dealing with each. Specifically, a number of theories regarding primate social relationships will be described. The second goal is to discuss competition in a variety of primate species while highlighting some of the general factors underlying competition. The third goal is to describe the lives of female primates from three diverse social structures: chimpanzee multimale-multifemale societies, hamadryas baboon harems, and ring-tailed lemur female-dominated hierarchies. These three species provide insights into the lives of females living under different societal pressures, sharing different relationships with group males, and balancing different levels of aggressive and affiliative interactions with a special emphasis on cooperation. The main goal of this chapter is to thus provide an evolutionary story of women's social relationships by presenting information on female nonhuman primates; I refrain from making direct comparisons between the two and, instead, invite readers to keep the nonhuman primate story in mind as they continue to read the other chapters in this volume (see also Hrdy, 2013a).

In this chapter, I present an ethological approach to understanding the evolutionary values of aggression and competition. I discuss the current evidence suggesting that female primates compete for social status, for access to the best resources, and for the opportunity to raise healthy offspring. However, I also illustrate that aggression is not the only means for attaining those goals. Affiliation (via mutualism, kin selection, or coalitionary support) is the other side of the competition coin, and I spend some time discussing how it at times can be more useful than aggression. One common mechanism of competition shared between the contexts of affiliation and aggression is cooperation because cooperation often involves affiliation between individuals who then direct aggression against a third party. I highlight some of the evolutionary and environmental adaptations shared by women and other female primates in the context of primate social evolution. There exists a misconception that humans are the pinnacle of evolution. This chapter will highlight areas of primate life where humans could, in observing particular patterns of behavior in other primates, use that knowledge to understand its underlying causes and take note of when aggression is typically useful in competing or perhaps when more affiliative cooperation is better in navigating social life.

Introduction to Primates

It is likely that the first primates were nocturnal, insectivorous, and limited in their gregariousness (Charles-Dominique, 1977). From the last common ancestor, primates evolved and diversified into many ecological niches, dietary preferences, and social categories. There are two major divisions

of primates—made according to when they split from a shared common ancestor—that are useful in comparing primate species: Strepsirrhines (previously referred to as prosimians) and Haplorhines—which are further divided into Tarsiiformes (which will not be discussed further) and Anthropoids (Fleagle, 2013; see Appendix). Anthropoids are further divided into Platyrrhines (also known as New World monkeys) and Catarrhines (which include Old World monkeys and apes; see Fleagle, 2013). Each of these divisions and their respective species has experienced different evolutionary pressures and adapted accordingly; therefore, a myriad of traits have been added, subtracted, and modified in a nonlinear, temporally sporadic fashion that has added to diversity both within and between divisions. Recently, the evolutionary relationships or *phylogeny* among primates has been questioned and re-evaluated according to a number of different traits (e.g., Arnold, Matthews, & Nunn, 2010). As additional traits continue to be included in analyses of phylogeny, these relationships will continue to change. This chapter refers only to broad phylogenetic relationships because the order of divergence is widely accepted even if the approximate dates are not.

The Strepsirrhines or *prosimians* retain many ancestral traits in addition to their more recently derived traits and are estimated to have diverged from the other primates around 76 million years ago (mya; Horvath et al., 2008; Matsui, Rakotondraparany, Munechika, Hasegawa, & Horai, 2009; although see Steiper & Seiffert (2012) for a more recent divergence). The earliest lemur colonization of the island of Madagascar is estimated to be around 65 mya (Horvath et al., 2008; Matsui et al., 2009), where they diversified and continue to live today. New World monkeys split from Old World monkeys and apes around 35–45 mya (Goodman et al., 1998; Schrago & Russo, 2003), whereas Old World monkeys and apes separated around 20–30 mya (Goodman et al., 1998; Kumar & Hedges, 1998). Humans split from chimpanzees and bonobos around 5–7 mya (Goodman et al., 1998; Kumar & Hedges, 1998; Robson & Wood, 2008). The appendix at the end of this chapter maps out the relationship of each species mentioned in this chapter and indicates to which division a species belongs.

One of the hallmarks of primates is their ability to fill ecological and social niches (Fleagle, 2013); thus, the ecology of species within taxonomic divisions is almost as diverse as it is between divisions.

For instance, lemurs, one taxonomic family of pro-simians that has been recently popularized in movies and television, are found only in Madagascar. The "land of lemurs" has few predators (Goodman, O'Connor, & Langrand, 1993), and their uniquely low predation risk likely played a role in their adaptation (Macedonia, 1993). New World monkeys—such as tamarins, spider monkeys, and squirrel monkeys—are only found in the Americas (hence the name), from northern Argentina through central Mexico. The ancestral monkeys who first colonized the Americas adapted according to the demands of a forest environment (despite having access to other biomes) and without competition from other, established primate orders. Old World monkeys—such as baboons, macaques, and patas monkeys—and nonhuman apes are found throughout Africa and parts of Asia and Europe, and their habitats include forests, savanna and open grassland, mountains, and even deserts. Complementing these diverse ecologies and adaptive pressures, primate social relationships exist in many varieties and complexities: some societies are more prone to aggressive interactions while others tend toward more affiliative behaviors wherein levels of competition drive the emphasis of each. This observation illustrates how it is key to view primate sociality in light of the environment or local ecological pressures in addition to considering phylogenetically inherited traits. After all, adaptation can only work with the materials that phylogeny has given to a species.

Although they are intimately intertwined, both ecology and sociality are potential common denominators when contrasting different primate groups. However, primate sociality can be assessed in three different ways: based on social organization (e.g., spatial proximity and ranging behavior), social structure (dyadic relationships and group hierarchies), or mating system (Schülke & Ostner, 2012). At this point, it should not be surprising that primate social groupings range the full spectrum from predominantly solitary living within a loose social group, pair-bonding, one-male-multifemale group (e.g., harem), and multimale-multifemale group (Fleagle, 2013; Schülke & Ostner, 2012). In some species, groups splinter and form smaller foraging parties only to come together at the end of the day to sleep as a large group (e.g., hamadryas baboons; Kummer, 1968) or come together days or weeks later (e.g., chimpanzees; Goodall, 1986)—a practice commonly referred to as *fission-fusion*. Societies can be male-bonded (in which males form strong social bonds), female-bonded

(in which females form strong social bonds), or both and may have linear and stable or nonlinear dominance hierarchies. Mating may occur between only the dominant female and males living in her social group (e.g., tamarins: Terborgh & Goldizen, 1985), between an otherwise solitary male and female (e.g., orangutans: Galdikas, 1981), between a bonded pair (e.g., gibbons: Carpenter, 1940), within a one-male-multifemale group (e.g., gorillas: Harcourt, Stewart, & Fossey, 1981; hamadryas baboons: Kummer, 1968), or within a multimale-multifemale group (e.g., chimpanzees: Goodall, 1986; Tutin & McGinnis, 1981; ring-tailed lemurs: Jolly, 1966; Sauther, 1991).

In general, female primates are free to choose their mating partner; however, their choice is generally limited with respect to the social structure, mating strategy, and various instantiations of coercion (Kappeler, 2012). One type of coercion, rape, is relatively rare within the different primate species with the notable exceptions of orangutans and humans (Muller & Wrangham, 2009; Muller & Thompson, 2012). Different societal structures can exist between species of a taxonomic grouping, as just illustrated in apes (orangutans, gibbons, gorillas, and chimpanzees; see also Jolly (1998) for a similar contrast in lemurs) as well as within a single genus (e.g., squirrel monkeys: Strier, 1999). Along a similar vein, social structures and, subsequently, social relationships are largely habitat-specific, and differences are evident between wild and captive populations (see Gartlan (1968) for discussion), although there is also evidence of species-specific (or phylogenetic) constraints (Thierry, 2007). Overall, and generally speaking, primates—humans included—are social, adaptive, and diverse. The overlapping diversity of social and environmental characteristics shared by human and nonhuman primates—along with their close genetic relatedness—lends a fruitful comparison in the endeavor to elucidate humans' propensity to certain behaviors.

Why Compare Nonhuman Primates to Humans

Understanding the societal pressures and adaptive behavior of other primates helps to explain why people behave the way they do. Nonhuman primate behavior not only helps explain the current pressures experienced by women, but also elucidates how past pressures shaped the evolution of ancestral women. Uncovering the social structure and behavior of ancestral humans is more difficult than uncovering their fossils. Reconstructing the behavioral repertoire of extinct species requires comparisons to extant species under a range of assumptions. These assumptions include the idea that limited evolution has occurred for certain traits (e.g., life histories: Jones, 2011; Robson & Wood, 2008; Roff, 1992), that suboptimal traits have been retained via strong phylogenetic inertia (see Blomberg & Garland (2002) for a review), or that the same trait has evolved in different species by means of convergent evolution (Fleagle, 2013). Thus, the process of reconstructing the behaviors of our ancestors culminates as a number of approximations toward the truth as additional evidence is collected. For instance, studying percussive stone tool use in monkeys and apes aids in hypothesis testing of how this technology emerged in early humans (e.g., Whiten, 2013; see also Hall, 1968).

One specific reason to compare nonhuman primate behavior to humans, rather than the behavior of other animals, is close genetic relatedness. For instance, chimpanzees and bonobos (sometimes referred to as pygmy chimpanzees) are humans' closest living relatives, sharing 90–99% of the same genetic information, depending on the level of genetic analysis (e.g., Anzai et al., 2003). The great apes, in particular, are the group most often studied for identifying how our proto-human ancestors behaved. Much has been learned about our own behavior from observing these animals. However, these apes do not always make for the best comparisons to humans because evolution does not necessarily lead to constancy in behavioral repertoires across closely related species. For instance, orangutans spend much of their time in solitude, so their social interactions, when they occur, likely do not reflect common human experience. On the other hand, chimpanzees and gorillas lack the pair-bonding common in many human societies, and their social relationships are shaped accordingly. Therefore, it is important to note where there are similarities and where there are differences and then select and construct comparisons appropriately.

In summary, taking phylogeny into account when comparing socioecological traits is important for understanding adaptive strategies of species and how these transform over evolutionary time. As mentioned, adaptation can only work with the materials at hand, which are constrained by phylogeny, and prepare the individual for the environment in which it lives. When phylogenetic constraints are appropriately applied, then more meaningful comparisons can be made (e.g., Arnold et al., 2010). However, convergent evolution—where the same trait evolves in different lines—can muddle the picture and may lead researchers to misattribute phylogenic origins or their subsequent constraints. Therefore, the remainder of this chapter will largely ignore phylogeny and will mostly be concerned with the ecological and social pressures that shape female-female social relationships.

Evolutionary Context of Competition and Aggression

Viewing female-female competition and aggression in an evolutionary context illuminates the adaptive benefits of each despite their associated costs. There are many factors that play into competition and aggression, but it is extraordinarily difficult to account for all of them within a single theory or model. Therefore, this section discusses a number of general theories of how primate social relationships evolved, including their merits and shortfalls. I also give consideration to general factors affecting female-female relationships, including food competition, reproduction, dispersal, and dominance.

Theories of Primate Sociality

Many attempts have been made to explain social relationships in primates (Silk, Cheney, & Seyfarth, 2013), and many theories have been devised to explain the evolution of primate social relationships (e.g., Clutton-Brock & Harvey, 1977; Isbell, 1991; Isbell & Young, 2002; Kappeler & van Schaik, 2002; Sterck, Watts, & van Schaik, 1997; van Schaik, 1989), but it was Wrangham (1980) who first used female behavior as a central explaining factor. Many of these theories have attempted to categorize female social behavior by its various traits (see Table 4.1; see also Isbell & Young, 2002). In some cases, all social categories can be found within a single taxonomic family, although family trends can be also apparent (e.g., hamadryas baboons are an exception to the otherwise "typical" baboon trend of matrilineal group organization and strong female bonds; see Cords, 2012). The different traits that make up a social category cannot be attributed to a single cause, and the diversity of social categories makes it difficult to develop a single, compatible theory of how primates evolved these systems. Figure 4.1 illustrates some of the factors that affect female social relationships—and female sociality more broadly—and demonstrates how these factors interact. These factors will be discussed throughout this section and the next section.

Theories for explaining primate social relationships range from attributing change in social

Table 4.1. Categories of Female-Female Relationships in Nonhuman Primates.

Social Category[1]	Competitive Regime[2]				Social Response		Example[1]
	Contest Competition		Scramble Competition		Female Philopatry	Female Dominance	Species
	Within-Group	Between-Group	Within-Group	Between-Group			
Dispersing-Egalitarian	Low	Low	Low[3]	Low	No	Egalitarian	Chimpanzee, Ring-tailed lemur, Hamadryas baboon
Resident-Egalitarian	Low	High	Low[3]	High	Yes	Egalitarian	Patas monkey
Resident-Nepotistic	High	High?[4,5]	High[5]	High	Yes	Nepotistic, Despotic	Japanese macaque
Resident-Nepotistic-Tolerant	High?[5]	High	High[5]	High	Yes	Nepotistic, Tolerant	Sulawesi macaque

[1] Sterck, Watts, & van Schaik (1997)
[2] Modified from Isbell & Young (2002)
[3] Classified as *high* in van Schaik (1989)
[4] Classified as *low* in Sterck, Watts, & van Schaik (1997)
[5] Classified as *low* in van Schaik (1989)

Categories are described by the type and amount of feeding competition and the social response to female gregariousness. Table is modified from Sterck, Watts, and van Schaik (1997), but similar categories proposed by other authors are also included. Differences between authors' categories are noted.

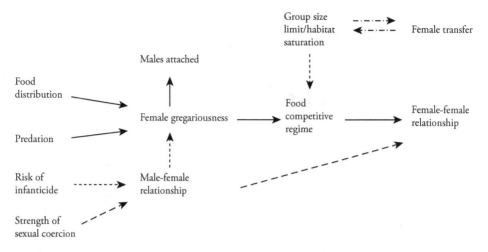

Figure 4.1 Schematic of factors affecting female-female relationships in nonhuman primates. Solid lines represent factors explained in van Schaik (1989). Dotted lines represent factors explained in Sterck, Watts, and van Schaik (1997). Dashed line roughly represents factors explained in Brereton (1995). Compound dash-dot lines represent likely other factors.

structure to primarily male-driven causes to primarily female-driven. Specific theories stretch from the idea of a reproductive arms race—in which males and females evolve to counteract each other's adaptation to secure fitness and mate choice (Brereton, 1995; see also Treves, 1998)—to protection from predators (see Sterck et al., 1997; see Figure 4.1). For instance, Brereton (1995; see also Hrdy, 1977; van Schaik & Kappeler, 1993; Watts, 1989) suggested in the *coercion-defense hypothesis* that males who live in societies where females choose their mating partner and who remain unselected by a female will develop coercive strategies to gain access to sex—such as by developing a larger body size or another method of overpowering females to force the matter (however, see Plavcan (1999) for a discussion of other possible factors affecting the evolution of sexual dimorphism). On the other hand, females adapt to this threat by evolving new traits, such as forming coalitions with other females against these "undesirables" (see the section "Dispersal, Dominance, and Female Sociality" for a discussion of female coalitions), by recruiting a higher-ranking male for support, or by concealing estrus (i.e., the point in the female's reproductive cycle when she is receptive). The "undesirables" would have to respond to regain a reproductive advantage, so they (i.e., the next generation or so) further evolve new traits, such as committing infanticide or some other abuse, and so the war rages on (i.e., because natural selection works only on those who succeed in reproducing). Building on previous work on female choice (Trivers, 1972; see also Smuts & Smuts (1993)

for review), Treves (1998) modified this dynamic approach of males and females directing adaptation in the *conspecific threat hypothesis*, which explains shifts in sociality as primarily caused by fluctuations in the probability of males who are not part of the group or other unrelated males interacting with females. This theory places a greater emphasis on the selective pressure exerted from the general aggressiveness of an unrelated male toward a female (and her offspring), whereas the previous theory focuses primarily on sexual coercion alone without regard to group membership.

Both the coercion-defense and conspecific threat theories explain current primate behavior but do so under different assumptions of female response and adaptations to male aggression (see also Smuts & Smuts, 1993) and are narrowly focused on reproductive strategies. An ecologically based model, on the other hand, assumes that primate sociality is an adaptation to a particular ecology rather than to social pressures (e.g., male aggression), although some of these models place a greater emphasis on the energetic costs to the individual (e.g., Isbell, 1991; Isbell & Young, 2002) rather than on group-level competition (van Schaik, 1989; Wrangham, 1980). This perspective places a greater emphasis on the selective pressures supporting social organization than on social interactions.

An *ecological model* (according to van Schaik, 1989) assumes that female gregariousness is determined by a combination of food distribution and predation risk (see Figure 4.1). Female gregariousness, in turn, determines male distribution within their social group as well as female competitive regime, within and between groups, in terms of food availability. The interaction of these factors results in the varied social relationships seen in female primates. There is support for this version of the model in the observation that females use aggression to manipulate the number of males associated with their social group (e.g., squirrel monkeys: Baldwin, 1968; talapoins: Rowell & Dixon, 1975; ring-tailed lemurs: Sussman, 1977; olive baboons: Packer & Pusey, 1979). For instance, female Japanese macaques limit the number of males in their troop by acting aggressively toward an unwanted male, thus driving him to withdraw from their troop (Packer & Pusey, 1979). This may reflect a female strategy of limiting competition for food or other resources, especially in species where size dimorphism (in this case, when males are larger than females) is not great or where males are less likely to provide protection or parental care (Clutton-Brock & Harvey, 1977; Packer & Pusey, 1979). For instance, hanuman langur females form coalitions against aggressive males, and the size of these coalitions increases as the number of aggressive males increases (Hrdy, 1974, 1977; Sommer, 1987; Treves & Chapman, 1996).

Despite the power in explaining certain tendencies, the ecological model is not always directly supported. The female-female relationship classes are derived from an ecological standpoint in consideration of both individual- and group-level competition, however, there are shortfalls which can be addressed by adding an additional layer of explanation. A *socioecological model* (Sterck et al., 1997) is based on the ecological model but adds demographic components to help account for the behaviors of species that the latter cannot explain. This model has the added power of accounting for social phenomena such as group size limits (i.e., habitat saturation) and infanticide (see Figure 4.1). For instance, an ecological model (see van Schaik, 1989) considers female relationships with males as a byproduct of female sociality rather than as a contributing factor (i.e., feedback loop).

Although the socioecological theory does well in explaining female-female social relationships, Sterck, Watts, and van Schaik (1997) discussed other alternative theories concerning demographics and social issues. Concerning demographic influences, they presented female philopatry (i.e., remaining in the natal group rather than dispersing) with kin selection as the ultimate source of female-female social relationships. They also suggested that interbirth interval (i.e., the time between births) could

be a supporting factor, but then argued against both interbirth interval and philopatry as prominent producers of female sociality. In terms of social issues, they discussed male policing, male harassing (i.e., the coercion-defense hypothesis), and costly reproduction, but only supported costly reproduction as a viable source of influence, citing the other two as failing to account for the full variation of female relationships. They also suggested that it could all just be an ecological effect of between-group competition. This could be especially true when the individual female and her dependent offspring are considered to be the main social unit.

As yet, there is no single theory that completely explains primate sociality, but it is clear that aggression and competition are not the only contributing factors to female social relationships. Cooperation and affiliation are important factors in female sociality, and the influence of these factors should not be underestimated (Sussman, Garber, & Cheverud, 2005). These are discussed in detail in the section "Female Competition and Cooperation in Primates;" however, to establish a background, the general principles that affect female sociality will be discussed first.

General Principles Affecting Female-Female Sociality

Sterck, Watts, and van Schaik (1997) described in detail the different types of female social relationships of primate groups (see Table 4.1), as well as how social relationships evolved (see Figure 4.1). Throughout the remainder of this chapter, a number of contributing factors to primate sociality will be discussed, especially with respect to how these factors affect female social relationships. Specifically, the effects of food competition, dispersal, and dominance (see Table 4.1) will serve as recurring themes in the following sections.

With respect to existing models of primate social evolution, the effects from predation, female transfer, group size limits, group cohesiveness, and within-group competitive regime have been recognized as major contributing factors determining female social relationships (see Figure 4.1); however, the importance of the interaction of these factors with phylogeny, demography, sexual and social selection pressures, and life histories is still being debated (see Strier (1999) for discussion and references). In this section, different aspects of female primate social life will be considered with respect to their effect on female-female social relationships and sociality.

FOOD COMPETITION AND FEMALE SOCIALITY

Competition for high-quality foods affects both a female primate's interpersonal relationships and her group's social structure (see Table 4.1). Particularly, the distribution of food in her environment influences the level and type of feeding competition (Isbell & Young, 2002; van Schaik, 1989; Wrangham, 1980). Feeding competition comes in two intersecting sets: *scramble* or *contest* and within or between groups (Figure 4.2). Scramble competition is indirect, whereby the first to arrive at a food patch has sole access to it (by virtue of being the only one there) and otherwise cannot monopolize the bounty (unless they deplete the food before company arrives). Contest competition is direct, and the winner is based on dominance or agonistic exchange, although it can also promote the formation of alliances. These types of competition and the resulting social structures vary with diet (see Isbell (1991) for discussion). Preferred foods found in clumped, defensible patches, such as fruit, promote within-group contest competition, and females benefit from remaining in their natal group and forming affiliative and agonistic dominance relationships (Wrangham, 1980). In this case, nepotism—favoritism granted to kin—would benefit all kin, and dispersal would be costly to the individual. This type of distribution also promotes between-group competition, which itself promotes cooperation within the group in protecting food patches. Food that is abundant and evenly distributed requires less competition both between and within groups and incurs a lower cost to a dispersing female because it would not be likely that she would wander into a desolate area where she would starve. In this case,

agonistic or dominance relationships provide little added benefit to the female.

As just illustrated, scramble and contest competition occur between and within groups and factor into group structure and social relationships. Within-group scramble competition is nearly unavoidable (Isbell, 1991), whereas within-group contest competition depends on the available resources (e.g., abundance, distribution, and quality; Sterck et al., 1997; but see Pruetz & Isbell (2000) for emphasis on food depletion time). More generally, between-group competition appears more dependent on food abundance according to diet (i.e., fruit vs. leaves vs. insects), whereas within-group competition is tied to food distribution (Isbell, 1991). When foods are spatially clumped and of high quality, females are more likely to be philopatric (stay within their group) and exhibit strong aggression toward other groups because such food patches are defensible (Isbell & Young, 2002; Wrangham, 1980). However, if there is typically variable food quality within patches, then females will form dominance relationships within their group, and nepotism will likely be prevalent (Isbell & Young, 2002; Wrangham, 1980; see next section for a more detailed discussion). According to specific diets, insectivore primates have a greater preponderance of solitary life because their food is highly dispersed and not defensible, whereas folivores (i.e., leaf-eaters) have an abundance of greens to chew on, and, for them, the costs of grouping are much lower (however, for a discussion of food competition in folivores, see Snaith & Chapman, 2007). On the other hand, frugivores (i.e., fruit-eaters) rely on seasonal, highly dispersed, patchy fruit distribution; for these species, both within- and between-group competition are high, and the benefits of social grouping outweigh the costs. Due to the variability in social grouping in the face of diet and subsequent competitive regime, each factor should be considered as one of many that affect social relationships rather than as defining factors. This goes for predation (van Schaik, 1989) and the other myriad of factors that affect social grouping and female-female relationships, in particular.

DISPERSAL, DOMINANCE, AND FEMALE SOCIALITY

As just described, the different types of feeding competition help to shape the social structure of the group, especially female-female relationships. There are four types of female-female relationships that can describe a group (see Table 4.1; Sterck et al., 1997; see also Isbell & Young, 2002).

Competing how?

	Within-group scramble	Within-group contest
Competing with who?	Between-group scramble	Between-group contest

Figure 4.2 Matrix of the two intersecting sets of competition types. As illustrated, scramble and contest competition strategies can occur within or between established groups. A group will experience one type of within-group competition and one type of between-group competition.

These relationships are partly delineated and identified according to the social category continua described by Vehrencamp (1983) as egalitarian-despotic, individualistic-nepotistic, and tolerant-intolerant. The first is called *dispersing-egalitarian*. In this type of society, females disperse from their natal group and enter into their new group without the aggression associated with dominance relationships because these societies have no or poorly defined hierarchies; therefore, females share relatively equal access to resources. The second type of female-female relationship is *resident-nepotistic*, and it is described as females inheriting their mothers' ranks (or rank closely to her and any sisters) in a highly hierarchical, female-philopatric society. In this type of society, aggression would be used early in life to assert the female's inherited position and her privileged access to resources. She would do this by instigating fights with her playmates only to be supported by her mother in any counterattack from the assailed playmates' mothers. The third type, *resident-nepotistic-tolerant*, is similar to the second, but, in this society, aggression directed up the hierarchy (i.e., toward higher-ranking individuals) is more common. Reconciliatory behavior following aggression is also common in this social structure. Relationships benefit from mending after aggressive interactions, and such mending helps to secure coalitionary support from the aggressed in the future. Such support is imperative for rank maintenance. The fourth type of female-female relationship is *resident-egalitarian*. In this society, females remain in their natal group within a poorly defined dominance hierarchy.

It is important to note that these female-female relationship classes can exist within phylogenetic taxa (e.g., genera, species) and so cannot be used to define a particular phylogenetic group (taxon). This observation highlights the importance of ecology over a purely phylogenetic explanation of social relationships, although the observation that these systems tend to be maintained even in captive groups suggests that species-typical patterns may persist in a wide range of ecological settings. Take for consideration the observation that, compared to eastern chimpanzees, female western chimpanzees have higher grooming frequencies and form alliances and strong bonds with each other (Boesch, 1996; Boesch & Boesch-Achermann, 2000) even though chimpanzees as a species were classified as dispersing-egalitarian (Sterck et al., 1997) at a time when such population differences were not considered. Additionally, it should be noted that these

social relationship categories have limited descriptive fidelity in terms of capturing the specifics of female-female relationships, despite their usefulness in partitioning species into comparative groups. For instance, chimpanzees, ring-tailed lemurs, and hamadryas baboons are all considered dispersing-egalitarian despite the three species having very different social organizations (see the section "Lessons from Three Primate Species" for further discussion).

As noted earlier, coalitionary support is key to maintaining dominance. Coalitions can form between close relatives (e.g., mothers or sisters) or between unrelated group members (see Langergraber (2012) and Gilby (2012) for discussions). Coalitions can be formed against lower-ranking individuals, higher-ranking individuals, or against an individual ranking between the coalition members, and females decide who to compete with versus assist depending on the immediate (e.g., resource access) or long-term (e.g., reinforce rank) benefit (Chapais, 2006). For instance, a lower-ranking sister may join an unrelated individual in a dispute with her higher-ranking sister in order to acquire a higher rank, even though the higher-ranking sister likely helped the lower-ranking sister acquire her current (albeit lower) rank (Japanese macaques: Chapais, Prud'homme, & Teijeiro, 1994). Generally, coalitionary support decreases with decreasing maternal relatedness, and this pattern likely supports the maintenance of matrilineal dominance hierarchies within groups (Chapais, Girard, & Primi, 1991; Chapais, Girard, Prud'homme, & Vasey, 1997; Silk, Alberts, & Altmann, 2004).

Infanticide is a less mutualistic mechanism of dominance ascension or maintenance that is also used as a general competitive tactic. Simply put, infanticide is often attributed to being an evolved trait in males because they benefit from stopping the mother's lactation—which suppresses estrus—thus returning her to estrus sooner (Hrdy, 1974; Palombit, 2012). However, competing females also use infanticide to their advantage. Females have been observed killing the infant of another female (e.g., chimpanzees: Goodall, 1986; Pusey et al., 2008; marmosets: Saltzman, 2003) or indirectly causing the death of another's infant (e.g., lemurs: Jolly, 1998). Female-led infanticide can be the result of a lack of available food or a lack of help in rearing the infant and is sometimes inflicted by the mother rather than by a dominant female (Culot et al., 2011). Early on, it was thought that infanticide was rare in nonhuman primates (Goodall, 1986; Palombit, 2012), but more cases have been observed as field studies continue. Some researchers have suggested *disequilibrium* (Sterck et al., 1997), a situation of nonadaptive change, such as change resulting from habitat fragmentation or human pressure, as an explanation for this otherwise difficult-to-explain phenomenon, but others maintain that infanticide is an evolutionary adaptation (e.g., Hausfater & Hrdy, 1984; Lyon, Pandit, van Schaik, & Pradhan, 2011; Wilson et al., 2014) and is the result of competition for survival within a stressed group (e.g., Townsend, Slocombe, Thompson, & Zuberbühler, 2007).

Summary on Social Evolution

Essentially, predation risk favors group formation in females whereas food availability limits grouping (see Figure 4.1). Competition for food and other resources within a group strains female-female relationships and leads to aggression; thus, mitigating behaviors, such as affiliation and reconciliation, and cooperative behaviors, such as coalition formation, developed to promote group cohesion. Males go where the females are located and respond according to female social and grouping strategies (Wrangham, 1980). The proposed ecological and socioecological models do reasonably well in predicting the social relationships of female primates and other mammals, and these predictions are generally supported by what is observed in the wild, although exceptions have been found (e.g., Pruetz & Isbell, 2000).

So why, then, is it surprising to hear new evidence showing the aggressiveness of and competition between females? Perhaps it is historical and is owed to the male-dominated academy's failure to consider competition in females as a viable topic of study in parallel to the study of male traits (e.g., Hrdy, 2013a, 2013b). Or, perhaps it is because these are "animals," and there is a tendency to view humans as separate from the other animals, in which case there would be no useful parallel to consider. There, historically, has been a sense of human superiority over animals such that the selective pressures and the principles that govern animal behavior are not viewed as equally constraining human behavior (e.g., Hume, 1777/1975). In line with that view, some researchers believe that human behavior differs from other animals in kind rather than in degree; however, in these last two sections, I make an effort to illustrate parallels in human and nonhuman primate lives. I draw specific examples of the social and ecological pressures experienced by females from a number of different species,

including how these affect aggression and cooperation. This theme will continue in the final section of the chapter with a discussion of female life in three distinct species of nonhuman primates—chimpanzees, hamadryas baboons, and ring-tailed lemurs—with special consideration directed as parallels in modern women.

Female Competition and Cooperation in Primates

In discussing the value of a social life, primatologist Hans Kummer (1979) described an individual A's need to view any group member, B, as a potential resource of some future benefit. In this sense, B is a resource for present or future ecological, social, emotional, or psychological benefit, and each interaction with B is an investment in their social bond. However, every time A meets B, their social bond is tested and evaluated as ally or competitor. These tests come in the forms of agonistic encounters, displays of ability, greetings, affiliative behaviors (such as grooming), and even play. Only through the creation and maintenance of social bonds can the benefits of social living—improved access to food, protection from predators, access to mates, and help caring for young (see discussions in Fleagle (1988) and Silk (2012))—be reaped by primates; however, social living also results in competition and, inevitably, conflict.

The varied types of competition are mediated differentially by aggression, but there are situations in which aggression is useful and others in which more affiliative behaviors may lead to a better outcome. Examples of such situations—which have been discussed throughout this chapter—include dispersal, dominance, and reproduction. Communication is a key mechanism for addressing aggression and cooperation, and so it will be discussed where applicable. For instance, a number of species use gestural (apes and monkeys: Call & Tomasello, 2007; Pika & Liebal, 2012) or vocal communication (chimpanzees: van Hooff, 1973; baboons: Cheney, Seyfarth, & Silk, 1995) to signal friendly intent or express submission (i.e., in order to avoid attack from another), to signal a threat of attack, or to recruit an ally for coalitionary support. Mechanisms of bond maintenance, such as grooming, can also aid in dampening the effects of competition and even foster cooperation in some future event. Grooming, in particular, has the added advantages of decreasing stress for both the groomer and the groomed (e.g., Boccia, Reite, & Laudenslager, 1989; Shutt, MacLarnon, Heistermann, & Semple, 2007) and inhibiting aggression (Carpenter, 1964, in Coelho,

Turner, & Bramblett, 1983). Bonding mechanisms will be discussed also in this section; however, it should be noted that the full function of grooming is still contested (see Barrett, Henzi, Weingrill, Lycett, & Hill, 1999; Colmenares, Zaragoza, & Hernandez-Lloreda, 2002; Seyfarth, 1977, for discussions).

Female Dispersal

Dispersal is an important means of avoiding inbreeding and, consequently, of maintaining genetic diversity within a group. In some primate species, females typically disperse from their natal group (chimpanzees: Goodall, 1986; hamadryas baboons: Abegglen, 1984; but see Swedell, Saunders, Schreier, Davis, Tesfaye, & Pines, 2011), whereas in other species it is males who typically disperse (ring-tailed lemurs: Sussman, 1991; olive baboons: Packer, 1979; Smuts, 1985) or sometimes both sexes disperse to varying degrees (gorillas: Watts, 2003). Sometimes females (or males) disperse from their natal group with a kin or age cohort member (also referred to as *co-transfer*: ring-tailed lemurs: Sussman, 1991). However, dispersal does not always occur by choice. Sometimes females leave their natal group in response to male coercion (e.g., hamadryas baboons: Swedell & Plummer, 2012). Sometimes females are pushed out of their group by other females through targeted aggression only to be met with similar aggression by the females in their new group (Kappeler, 2012). In these situations, resident group members will likely be unwilling to share resources with the new immigrant member. Aggression serves the residents in establishing priority access to the group's resources, whereas aggression would not benefit the immigrant who needs to be accepted into the group; in her case, it would be better to show affiliation. For example, when a male (of almost any primate species) immigrates into a new social group, he will benefit from resorting to aggression against resident males to secure his new residency (and place in the hierarchy) and aggression against resident females in the form of infanticide (to increase his own fitness; see Smuts & Smuts, 1993, for discussion), whereas aggression will work against a female immigrant because males will likely come to the aid of a resident female who is under attack (as will other resident females). Instead, an immigrant female benefits most from finding a "sponsor" in either a resident male (e.g., chimpanzees: Pusey, 1979; mantled howler monkeys: Glander, 1992) or female (e.g., bonobos: Idani, 1991) and befriending the sponsor while slowly gaining acceptance by the remaining residents.

Individuals who disperse from their natal group experience different ecological and social pressures than do conspecifics who remain in their natal group (Isbell & van Vuren, 1996). Within an established social group, members of the philopatric sex are likely to be more closely genetically related to each other than are members of the sex that disperses (see Di Fiore (2012) for discussion). Therefore, individuals who remain in their natal group have the potential to form longer-lasting, more positive social bonds than if they had left their natal group under the assumptions that (1) time spent together and familiarity can increase social bonding (e.g., Hinde, 1977; Langergraber, Mitani, & Vigilant, 2009), and (2) kin selection (i.e., the phenomenon of showing preference to more closely related individuals as a means of increasing one's own fitness; Hamilton, 1964a, 1964b) promotes bonding. In turn, these individuals have more to gain from maintaining social bonds with their philopatric peers because those are the individuals whom they will need for future coalitional competition, kinship aside. In other words, a large repertoire of affiliative behaviors may be more beneficial than an arsenal of aggressive behaviors. Such affiliative interactions should be expected to occur more often, at least for those who remain in their natal groups, because these individuals will need to establish and service a large and complex network of long-term relationships (see Scott (2013) for evidence in communication strategies). Because aggression certainly has its place in maintaining one's position in the social hierarchy, it would be expected that aggressive interactions would still be necessary.

From this point, it may be expected that differential bonding and communication strategies of the philopatric versus the dispersing sex would be evident. In agreement with this argument, an immigrant female might use affiliative behaviors, such as grooming, to create a new social bond (Dunbar & Schultz, 2010), whereas a resident female will (and does) groom selective peers in order to maintain valuable social relationships (Aureli, Fraser, Schaffner, & Schino, 2012). Current evidence suggests that the philopatric sex spends significantly more time involved in grooming than does the dispersing sex (e.g., Assamese macaques: Cooper & Bernstein, 2000; bonnet macaques: Sugiyama, 1971; patas monkeys: Kaplan & Zucker, 1980; spider monkeys: Slater, Schaffner, & Aureli, 2009), including a higher proportion of time in same-sex rather than mixed-sex grooming. Similarly, evidence from a number of primate species (e.g., vocal communication: red-capped mangabey: Bouchet, Pellier, Blois-Heulin, & Lemasson, 2010; rhesus macaque: Greeno & Semple, 2009; vervet monkey: Locke & Hauser 1999; gestural communication: spider monkey: Slater et al., 2009) indicates that the philopatric sex has a much greater reliance on communication in terms of frequency. However, similar studies of chimpanzees found no clear differences between the sexes in the general rate of production of vocalizations (Clark, 1993; Marler, 1976) or gestural communication (Scott, 2013), although differences did emerge when contexts of dominance and competition were examined more closely (sex: Mitani & Gros-Louis, 1995; Wilson, Hauser, & Wrangham, 2007; submission: Clark, 1993; Scott, 2013).

Female Competition for Food and Social Resources

Given that many species exhibit a positive relationship between social status and reproductive success (females: Pusey, 2012; Silk, 2012; males: Alberts, 2012; but also see Gartlan (1968) for exceptions), competition surrounding dominance relationships can be intense. An individual can establish dominance through his or her physical attributes, direct and indirect aggression, inheritance, or sometimes cooperation. For instance, in nepotistic societies such as Japanese macaques, close maternal kin (i.e., grandmother, mother, sister) will provide coalitionary support to a young female until she can dominate all other females that her mother outranks, including her older sisters (Kawamura, 1958; see Cords (2012) and Langergraber (2012) for discussions). However, as discussed earlier (see the section "General Principles Affecting Female-Female Sociality"), maternal kin also compete with each other to gain a higher rank and will sometimes gain the coalitionary support of an unrelated individual in order to rise in rank (e.g., Japanese macaques: Chapais et al., 1994). The influence of paternal relatedness is currently being investigated for similar effects (e.g., Schülke & Ostner, 2008).

Female dominance hierarchies are common when there is within-group contest competition (Chapais et al., 1991; see also Schülke & Ostner (2012) for discussion) because food distribution for these groups is patchy and varies in quality (Isbell, 1991). In this environment, it would be energetically beneficial to defer the better patches to the more dominant group members rather than fighting

for them; thus, the most dominant individual gets the largest, highest-quality patch and so on down the hierarchy (Schülke & Ostner, 2012). However, these conditions also promote coalition formation (Chapais et al., 1991), especially among relatives (Sterck et al., 1997; van Schaik, 1989; Wrangham, 1980). For example, by providing friends with access to highly desired foods, as is the case in meat sharing by chimpanzees, the "fruits" of contingent reciprocity may be reaped or future coalition partnering may be "bought" (see Mitani (2006) and Gilby (2012) for discussions). Even if playing favorites or buying favors is not the impetus for food sharing, in the very least, individuals benefit from their own generosity by giving in to those who harass them for a share: the more quickly they give in to such coercion, the more quickly they can continue eating (Stevens & Gilby, 2004; see Gilby (2012) for discussion). On the other hand, when food competition between groups is high, then cooperation in protecting food sources within their home range or territory becomes necessary, and dominance relationships may become more lax (van Schaik, 1989).

Friendships are an important means of staying competitive beyond just preferred access to food. There are adaptive benefits in terms of psychological and physiological health as well as reproductive success (Langergraber et al., 2009; Silk et al., 2009). In fact, it may be common for female primates to "tend and befriend" rather than "fight or flee" each other (Taylor et al., 2000). If females completely lacked affiliative bonds such as friendship, then not only would they suffer, but so too would their offspring. For instance, the infants of females who share strong social bonds with other females live longer than do infants of females who share weak bonds with others, surviving longer even in adulthood (baboons: Silk, Alberts, & Altmann, 2003a; Silk et al., 2009). The active maintenance of friendships through affiliative behaviors such as grooming also provides benefits by lowering anxiety and stress, as measured by glucocorticoid levels (baboons: Crockford, Wittig, Whitten, Seyfarth, & Cheney, 2008). On the flip side, following the death of a friend, the survivor may show higher levels of glucocorticoids (chacma baboons: Engh et al., 2006), indicating that she feels anxiety (or some other form of stress) in face of her social loss.

That is not to say that friendship or coalitionary support is free, as alluded to earlier in this section with the example of meat sharing. The cost of kin support is presumably usually outweighed by the ultimate (indirect) gain in fitness (Langergraber,

2012). Like any (human) friendship, supporters need something in return. This can come in the form of contingent reciprocity, mutual benefit, or market value (Gilby, 2012; see also de Waal & Brosnan (2006) for altruistic reciprocity). For example, longtailed macaques trade grooming for sex, and the rates for the grooming–mating exchange were influenced by social rank and the supply of available partners (Gumert, 2007). Grooming is a common commodity across primate species and can be used to drive up an individual's market value (by providing extended grooming services) or can be used in a more "I'll scratch your back if you scratch mine" kind of deal (e.g., contingent reciprocity: Gilby, 2012; or reciprocal altruism: Mitani, 2006). Other currencies of friendship include returned coalitionary support, sex, and food sharing (see Gilby (2012) for discussion and additional references). In fact, having male friends provides the female with the added benefit of infant protection (Setchell, 2008; see also Smuts & Smuts, 1993). In baboons, this friendship is initiated and maintained by the female after she has copulated with the male (possibly as a source of paternal confusion) and ends if the infant dies (Palombit, Seyfarth, & Cheney, 1997). One negative to having a male friend is that other males may indirectly attack him through a direct attack on his close female friend (chimpanzees: de Waal, 1982; baboons: Smuts, 1985).

Overall, friendships often exist outside of dominance and kinship boundaries (e.g., Gilby, 2012; chimpanzees: Langergraber et al., 2009; baboons: Silk et al., 2009) and are not limited to the same sex. Friendships are useful in competitive societies because they can provide coalitionary support against aggressive interactions or in cases of dominance disputes. They also have the added benefits of providing preferred access to food (e.g., food sharing). However, by simply being more dominant than others, an individual can eschew "payment" and directly gain preferential access to food and coalitionary support.

Competition for Mating Opportunities

Reproduction is the major source of competition in primates, although it can be considered to be the ultimate source of all competition. As discussed in the section "Theories of Primate Sociality," some theories center on reproductive competition as the source of the evolution of social traits in primates. Females evolved social or morphological traits to aid them in competing for mating opportunities. These adaptations include behavioral responses that have direct (e.g., infanticide) or indirect (e.g., reproductive suppression) influences on the reproductive success of other females, as well as on the physical development of secondary sexual characteristics (e.g., sexual swellings).

Infanticide is one example of a social strategy for reproductive competition. Typically, when the male is the aggressor, he is an outsider to the group and the alpha male has already been killed (by the intruder or other causes; Palombit, 2012). When the attacker is a female, though, she is usually a resident of the group, and the attack occurs outside the view of the alpha male (if the societal structure includes a male-dominance hierarchy). For instance, one account reports the continued harassment and attack on a lower-ranking female and her infant twins by a small group of resident females over the span of days during which the victim sought passive protection from resident males and in which infanticide was prevented (chimpanzees: Pusey et al., 2008). One way a female can avoid infanticide is by maintaining a male friend, as discussed in the previous section, who will protect her from attacks by males and females alike. Another strategy is to use the space in their group's territory that is best protected by resident males and offers the best source of food: females who spend the majority of their time in these spaces have higher reproductive success than do females who range elsewhere or who switch groups (chimpanzees: Williams, Pusey, Carlis, Farm, & Goodall, 2002).

Another example of female-female reproductive competition is reproductive suppression, in which one female, usually the most dominant female, suppresses the reproduction of other female group members (see Kappeler, 2012; Pusey, 2012). She can do this directly by preventing or interrupting mating (Setchell & Kappeler, 2003) or indirectly by hormonal suppression (Abbott, 1989; cottontop tamarins: Snowdon, Ziegler, & Widowski, 1993). Daughters are not immune to this treatment or from getting kicked out of the group once they reach a "critical" size (lemurs: Vick & Pereira, 1989). Hormonal suppression is reversible and may actually benefit a subordinate. By waiting until she obtains the dominant position in the group, she gains mothering experience, and, upon achieving breeding status, she gains alloparenting resources from her subordinates, thereby increasing her reproductive success (for species and discussions see Setchell (2008) and van Noordwijk (2012)). However, it is also possible that the costs associated with waiting to reproduce do not create enough pressure for evolving a counter-strategy, rather than there being any actual benefit.

Alternatively, females can prevent the pregnancy of a rival by physically intervening in the mating process. The competing female can use aggression or other harassment to disrupt or prevent mating (Kappeler, 2012; Setchell, 2008). For example, the presence of a dominant female may be enough to halt any interactions between a subordinate female and a nearby male before mating ever begins (e.g., brown capuchins: Janson, 1984, in Setchell, 2008). Like males, female primates in some species have evolved morphological traits, such as increased canine size (Plavcan, van Schaik, & Kappeler, 1995), to help them compete with others of their own sex.

In summary, female primates have evolved a number of behavioral and physiological traits that help them to compete for reproductive success through dispersal patterns, competition for food and social resources, and competition for mating opportunities. Cooperation is also prevalent and can occur between kin and unrelated individuals, as well as between the sexes. However, when it comes to pregnancy and birth, competition is fierce between family and friends alike.

Up to this point, a basic introduction to primate sociality has been laid out. In the next section, the information will be applied in a discussion of three distinct primate species. In discussing each species, the general principles affecting female-female sociality will be discussed in greater detail. Examples of female competition and cooperation as these pertain to the general principles will be considered with respect to the social structure and social organization of each species.

Lessons from Three Primate Species

Up to this point, a number of aspects of primate competition have been discussed, including a number of theories that have been devised to explain the evolution of and variations in female-female relationships. The third and final goal of this chapter is to illustrate where lessons may be gleaned from other primates with respect to similarities found in human cultures. Specifically, the aspects of dispersal, reproduction, dominance, and friendship will be described in further detail for three distinct species. The species to be evaluated are from three distinct clades (see Appendix): ape (chimpanzees), Old World monkey (hamadryas baboons), and prosimian (ring-tailed lemurs). Chimpanzees, hamadryas baboons, and ring-tailed lemurs provide examples

of female-female competition from distinct societies and evolutionarily distinct paths (see Appendix).

Reviewing these three species provides the opportunity to view the life of females through a different lens: a lens through which women would view the world if humans had a social structure more like these species. Because every aspect of social life is interconnected and also connected with the greater environment, when certain aspects of life get shifted, then the entire social system shifts as well. In the case of chimpanzees, their social structure is in many ways like modern (Western) humans in terms of (historically) female dispersal and male dominance. Hamadryas baboons live in harem societies that characterize some modern societies and some ancestral traditions, as well as reflect what life is like when groups depend on a centralized male protector. Lemurs, on the other hand, live in a female-dominated society, and their experiences may shed some light on what we could expect if women ruled the world. This section will conclude with some remarks on what can be learned about female life in each of these species and how women can apply knowledge gleaned from these observations to navigate their own social structures.

Chimpanzees
SOCIAL STRUCTURE

Chimpanzees live in a multimale-multifemale fission–fusion society of up to 150 individuals, although they spend the majority of their time in groups of 1–20 individuals (Goodall, 1986; Lwanga, Struhasker, Struhasker, Butynski, & Mitani, 2011; Nishida, 1968). Some of the traits that chimpanzees exhibit appear human-like; including tool use, communication strategies, and lethal intergroup aggression (or what may be referred to as "war" in human culture). Although differences have been found between chimpanzee communities (e.g., Whiten et al., 1999; Wilson & Wrangham, 2003), these differences are attributed to habitat and cultural traditions rather than genetics (Boesch & Boesch-Achermann, 2000; but see Langergraber & Vigilant, 2011). For instance, chimpanzees exhibit intelligent strategies for visits to border regions of their territory (border patrols), including traveling in larger groups and adjusting the volume of their vocalizations, assumingly to remain undetected or to advertise their territory ownership and coalitionary strength (Wilson et al., 2007; see also Clark (1993) and Fedurek, Donnellan, & Slocombe (2014) for other social and ecological contexts affecting call rates). Overall, males in chimpanzee society tend to be more gregarious than females (Boesch & Boesch-Achermann, 2000; Kawanaka, 1984; Nishida, 1968), although a female's participation in cooperative group activities, such as border patrols and hunting, is largely dependent on her stage in estrus (Goodall, 1986).

The fission–fusion society of chimpanzees means that individuals travel in parties of varying size to forage, sleep, or copulate. The advantages of this societal structure include decreased competition on a day-to-day basis, but there are disadvantages, too. One disadvantage is the excitement caused by group fusion when members of the group reunite. Reunions entail affiliative gestures, a chorus of vocalizations, and sometimes violent displays (Goodall, 1986). Displays advertise male might and often end with the displayer beating (hands and feet) on another chimpanzee. Infants are not immune to these indiscretions, sometimes getting picked up and flung if caught in the path of the displayer. One solution that chimpanzees have developed is signaling with *greeting* gestures that mitigate fusion excitement and redirect the energy of potential aggression. In fact, chimpanzees have a large repertoire of vocalizations, gestures, postures, and facial expressions that function to promote affiliation, cooperation, aggression, and dominance (Goodall, 1986; Pollick & de Waal, 2007; Scott, 2013; van Hooff, 1973). Overall, communication is a key aspect of chimpanzee life, acting to create, maintain, and mend friendships, as well as to avoid or threaten aggressive action.

DISPERSAL AND REPRODUCTION

In chimpanzee society, a female and her offspring form the basic social unit. When a female reaches sexual maturity around the age of 10–11 years (Goodall, 1986), she may transfer to a new group where she can start a family. Female dispersal helps to avoid incest, but the transfer may only be temporary, and she may return to her natal group after some time. Transfer usually involves aggression once she has joined her new group, and she will typically stay close to a resident male (a new friend) for protection (Pusey, 1979) because all males are more dominant than all females in most situations (for contexts of situational dominance see Noë, de Waal, & van Hooff, 1980). This arrangement benefits the male because he is most likely to copulate with her in the near future (an example of mutualism or reciprocity).

Females generally have the choice to mate, but sometimes the matter is forced on the spot or in the form of a consortship (de Waal, 1982; Goodall,

1986; Muller, Emery Thompson, Kahlenberg, & Wrangham, 2011; Yerkes & Elder, 1936). A consortship is the chimpanzee equivalent of a weekend vacation to a bed-and-breakfast whether she likes it or not: an unwilling female can incur aggression until she either gets help from others nearby in resisting his advances or is finally coerced into following the male (Goodall, 1986). When the female is mature, experienced, and familiar with the courting male, she has complete control over when the copulation occurs and for how long, but an inexperienced female easily can be coerced by an assertive male even when she is not in estrus (Muller, Emery Thompson, & Wrangham, 2006; Yerkes & Elder, 1936; but see Muller et al. (2011) for other factors affecting female choice). In some communities, males may show remarkable tolerance when ignored by females and may not force the situation nor attack (western chimpanzees: Goodall, 1986); however, when a female is at her most fertile point in estrus and thus most likely to conceive, then males may maintain high aggression rates against her in order to secure paternity (eastern chimpanzees: Muller et al., 2011).

Male tolerance is one example of the conditions under which females have influence in a male's social life despite the dominance discrepancy. Males may involve females in rank disputes through election by female choice (e.g., western chimpanzees: Goodall, 1986; captive chimpanzees: de Waal, 1982), and males will sometimes defer access to intriguing objects to females (captive chimpanzees: Noë et al., 1980). However, the full reality of female choice is still debated (Muller et al., 2011; Muller & Wrangham, 2009), although the extent to which choice varies by population has yet to be determined. Furthermore, although adolescent males batter and harrass females while climbing the status ladder, adult males will not try to dominate their own mothers and continue to show respect to them (Goodall, 1982), although males have been reported to sire offspring with their mothers (Wroblewski, Murray, Keele, Schumacher-Stankey, Hahn, & Pusey, 2009). Females appear to take full advantage of males' dependence on their future support—for instance, in future coalitions—by sometimes taking a passive role when recruiting a male ally (e.g., she stays behind and watches as her male friend exacts the punishment; Goodall, 1968). However, there may be population differences between eastern and western chimpanzees (e.g., Whiten et al., 1999), as well as between captive and wild chimpanzees (e.g., Arnold & Whiten, 2001), so generalization is fairly limited until further studies are conducted directly comparing these populations. Overall, females seem to enjoy some situations of special social status but only in the case of their relationships with males; female–female relationships can be more contentious.

DOMINANCE AND FRIENDSHIPS

Females are less gregarious than males, but this is confounded by dependent offspring. Females with dependent offspring tend to spend time either away from others as a family unit or with a nursing party of other family units (Goodall, 1986; Nishida, 1968). Current evidence suggests that females at some sites share same-sex relationships that are more similar to male-male relationships than previously believed (western chimpanzees: Lehmann & Boesch, 2008, 2009). Although evident, the dominance hierarchy of females is typically difficult to assess and describe, so it is best described as nonlinear (e.g., Goodall, 1986; Nishida, 1970; but see de Waal (1982, p. 186) for an exception in a captive group) or categorical (e.g., high rank, middle rank, or low rank; Scott, 2007).

Some of the factors that affect rank for females differ from those for males, such as how many offspring she has in the community, especially in terms of her number of sons, but similarities exist, too, such as her ability to recruit allies and form coalitions (Goodall, 1968). Some researchers have described female dominance as primarily attributed by respect from below or what has been called a *subordinance hierarchy* (de Waal, 1982; Rowell, 1974) because aggression does not appear to be a factor in determining rank (i.e., dominance cannot be assessed from the *winner* of fights, but rather is determined from direction of greeting and reassurance; Scott, 2007). This may be true in maintaining rank in an established group, but, in captivity, females seem to go through the same processes as males when establishing rank in a new colony (Yerkes, 1943).

Without clear-cut dominance relationships, female-female aggression appears to result from competition rather than from power struggles for status. Subsequently, female chimpanzees lack the motivation to mitigate their agonistic acts toward other females, although they do share these signals with males. Reconciliation is important for maintaining rank, yet, unlike males, females do not use signals of reassurance following acts of aggression. The same pattern of same-sex interactions

and different-sex interactions exists for contexts of submission (another important context for securing social status; Scott, 2013). That is not to say, though, that female chimpanzees completely lack social bonds with other females.

Females may lack the buffering mechanisms that mitigate the effects of aggression (de Waal, 1986; see Benenson et al. (2014) for a similar argument in humans) but may still manage to share strong, long-lasting social bonds with another female. These bonds resemble male-male social bonds and can exist outside familial bounds (Gilby & Wrangham, 2008; Langergraber et al., 2009; Lehmann & Boesch, 2009)—these are often referred to as *close friends*. As mentioned previously, the gregariousness of females is not to the same extent as it is in males (e.g., Goodall, 1986, p. 156): rates of male-male association are higher than female-female rates (Langergraber et al., 2009) and so are intrasexual grooming rates (Stumpf, 2007). Despite the lack of large-scale bonding, females may sometimes form a coalition against a male when he tries to force a consortship or copulation and otherwise act aggressively toward another female (captive chimpanzees: de Waal, 1982; see discussion in Smuts & Smuts (1993) for examples in other species). Females can also solicit the help of a more dominant female when an altercation with another female is imminent or occurring, as illustrated in this example from de Waal (1982, p. 47):

> Jimmie and Tepel are sitting. . . while their two children play. . . . Between the two mothers the oldest female, Mama, lies asleep. Suddenly the children start screaming, hitting and pulling each other's hair. Jimmie admonishes them. . . Tepel anxiously shifts her position. . . and eventually Tepel wakes Mama by poking her in the ribs several times. As Mama gets up Tepel points to the two quarrelling children. . . . Mama takes one threatening step forward, waves her arm in the air and barks loudly [and] the children stop quarrelling.

In light of this example, female chimpanzees use gestures more sparingly and more acutely than do males, seemingly catering their communicative exchange to the identity of their partners (Scott, 2013). This not only highlights the social intelligence of this species, but also may suggest that females value a stable network of social bonds. Males, by contrast, appear to treat all other adults the same regardless of their sex—at least in terms of their gesture use (Scott, 2013)—and constantly strive to assert themselves in their ranks and their needs. This sounds similar to behavior in humans (e.g., Luxen, 2005), so what can we learn?

In summary, female chimpanzees are able to come together when there is physical threat or other altercation; if only they could assert themselves and act as a cohesive unit more often, they just might enjoy more dominance privileges than they currently do, although males do defer to females in certain situations. Furthermore, when emigrating, females are most at risk of severe attack when they are alone near the border regions of neighboring communities, especially when anestrus (i.e., not cycling). Immigrants often face aggression, particularly from resident females, although it does seem to bring together otherwise competing females to redirect their aggression away from each other and toward the new female. This may be a rather small benefit, but it serves to illustrate that cooperation is possible despite the lack of reconciliatory behaviors. In chimpanzee society, females are generally dependent on males for protection, as in the case with immigration, although it should now be clear that in the rare case when females team together they can overcome their subordinate position under males and maintain the social order themselves (at least in captivity, e.g., de Waal, 1982). The advantage of this type of society is that politics is everything. That certainly seems to be the case in humans, too.

Hamadryas Baboons

SOCIAL STRUCTURE

Like chimpanzees, hamadryas baboons (*Papio hamadryas*) live in a sexually dimorphic (males are bigger than females) fission–fusion society. These baboons gather in troops numbering in the hundreds, but form separate one-male units in which they do their feeding, mating, and most of their socializing. These one-male units, also referred to as *harems*, consist of a single dominant adult male, one or more females, and sometimes one or more *follower* males (Abegglen, 1984; Kummer, 1968). These units were initially characterized by male-female relationships because it appeared that females shared comparatively weak bonds; however, more recent evidence suggests that females can share social bonds within their unit and sometimes with a female from a different unit (Swedell, 2002). The troop is characterized by male-male relationships because the majority of communication between units in the troop occurs between dominant males, and the majority of social mixing is performed by

infants, juveniles, and subadult males (Kummer, 1968).

This one-male unit social structure is maintained by male aggressiveness to other males and to females of his own unit. A male maintains the cohesiveness of his unit by *herding* his females, usually by staring at an individual and sometimes by biting her neck after she moves too far away from him (Kummer, 1968). This kind of aggression is similar to that experienced by a female during chimpanzee consort formation. The cohesiveness of the entire troop is maintained by male-male relationships through aggressive interactions and cooperative support surrounding the control of and access to females. This can be likened to an honor system in which males do not cheat with another male's female.

DISPERSAL AND REPRODUCTION

A female hamadryas typically becomes part of a one-male unit before she is sexually mature, some time between the ages of 1 and 3 years, and as the result of an adult male forcing her into consortship through repeated aggression until she willingly follows him (Kummer, 1968). If she lags behind as the group moves, he will swiftly bite her on the nape of the neck. If she struggles in her movements, though, he may carry her on his back (Kummer, 1968). In fact, male hamadryas baboons display care-taking behaviors, and these could be an important root for the formation of the one-male unit (e.g., Kummer, 1967); this situation has clear benefits for females and would explain females' tendency to organize around a central individual. Following their care-taking tendencies, males act as the main protector of their units. During aggressive interactions, a female will rush to be close to her leader male and either turn to threaten her aggressor from his side or solicit him, such as by presenting her rump (a common *asking* gesture in other primate species: e.g., chimpanzees) to threaten the aggressor instead. Sometimes the alleged victim deceptively instigates the interaction on an unsuspecting victim, as in this example from Kummer (1967, p. 66):

> Adult IV quietly sat cradling her infant. Subadult female 3a lingered around without being noticed. Suddenly 3a started screaming, rushed past IV pulling her tail violently, and ran on to their group leader. Female IV jumped to her feet, screamed, and ran toward the male, where 3a was already in the protected threat position. The male aimed a slight brow-lifting threat at IV.

DOMINANCE AND FRIENDSHIPS

Like chimpanzees, adult hamadryas females are known to form positive, stable social bonds with other females. Unlike chimpanzees, some female baboons show evidence of bonding outside their primary social unit, although this phenomenon appears to be closely tied to the number of other females in her unit (Swedell, 2002) and may be tied to kinship (see Schreier & Swedell, 2009; but additional evidence is needed). This could be an effect of the leader male's decreased ability to watch all of his females because it does not appear to be an effect of the leader male's unavailability as a social partner. One reason that females seem to be drawn to other females, even those from outside their social group, is access to infants (e.g., Kummer, 1968; Swedell, 2002). Many baboon species use grunts to signal benign intent when approaching a mother to request to hold her infant (Crockford et al., 2008; Silk, Rendall, Cheney, & Seyfarth, 2003b), but no work has been done to my knowledge on female hamadryas. Without this positive signal, mothers would likely move away to avoid potential harm coming to their infants. Another reason that females momentarily seek the attention of others is personality: some females appear more intrinsically motivated than others to seek out and maintain positive interactions with other females (Swedell, 2002). However, the identity of *others* as kin could be an important factor (e.g., Chalyan, Lapin, & Meishvili, 1994, in Swedell, 2002). Age seems to be an important factor as well because juvenile females are much more likely to socialize with other females, especially females of other groups (Kummer, 1968).

Within the one-male unit, females are rather undifferentiated in rank in wild populations (Abegglen 1984; Swedell, 2002) but can show linear dominance hierarchies in captivity (Kummer, 1968; Leinfelder, de Vries, Deleu, & Nelissen, 2001); however, the degree of female bonding is highly variable in the species as a whole and seems to be dependent on the size of one-male units (Colmenares et al., 2002; Swedell, 2002). In circumstances under which the dominant male is removed from the group, a female will take his place as most dominant, and the typical interactions with respect to this rank will resume (e.g., Coelho et al., 1983; Stammbach, 1978). This tendency of females to organize around a central dominant individual appears to be instigated by the females rather than imposed on them by a male (Coelho et al., 1983; Stammbach, 1978). Females do not compete with each other for rank or food, but rather appear to compete for the right to groom their leader (Kummer, 1968; Swedell, 2002).

What can we learn from hamadryas baboons? Generally, female competition is limited: mate choice is constrained by her recruitment into a one-male unit, and access to food is abundant. The greatest competition is for attention from the central individual. Female baboons are drawn to a central, dominant individual and choose to be subordinate under that individual, even if the dominant other is another female. Personality clearly is an important factor in females' decisions on what constrains their social world and whether they choose to lead or follow. This could be the result of evolutionary adaptation (e.g., as response to paternal care of infants or group protection by males), but individual choice (in the face of local pressures) seems to provide the simplest explanation. The male social code makes it difficult for females to choose a male or to change social units without changing troops (hence leaving her family behind). Nevertheless, some females seem to be more outgoing than others, much like humans, and seek friends outside of their units. Effective communication plays a key role in this social mixing. The advantage to this society is the unconditional protection provided by the leader male, and his security in knowing the integrity of his fellow troop males allows the female to pursue her social interests.

Ring-tailed Lemurs

SOCIAL STRUCTURE

Ring-tailed lemur groups consist of a few adult males, a few adult females, and their young offspring making up a group of 15 individuals, on average (Jolly, 1966; Sauther & Sussman, 1993). These lemurs share many attributes with (savanna) baboons in their societal structures but not with the peculiar hamadryas baboons. Ring-tailed lemur societies consist of polygamous kin groups with dominant males and dominant females (Jolly, 1966). One important difference from savanna baboon society is that, for lemurs, society is unconditionally female-dominated. However, there are many other differences. For instance, typical (savanna) baboon dominance structures radiate from large kin groups (Smuts, 1985), whereas lemur dominance relationships are mainly dyadic and clear-cut—either the pair is wholly affiliate or wholly agonistic (see Jolly, 1998, for discussion). Unlike chimpanzees and baboons, however, this is not a sexually dimorphic species, meaning that males and females are the same size. In terms of female-female bonds, as in some chimpanzee groups, mothers and daughters may share strong bonds, and affiliative interactions are generally between kin (e.g., Jolly, 1998; Taylor & Sussman, 1985). Also like chimpanzees, social groups can sometimes fission, and severe aggression between former groupmates may follow (Hood & Jolly, 1995).

DISPERSAL AND REPRODUCTION

Like other species of lemurs, female ring-tailed lemurs have seasonal receptivity in which all females of a social group (and surrounding groups) are in estrus for only a few hours out of the year (Jolly, 1967). Females will mate first with the group's dominant male and then with other group and immigrant males (Sauther, 1991). Male mate competition with female choice is the rule, although both sexes show increased aggression during the mating and birthing seasons (Jolly, 1967; Vick & Pereira, 1989); however, dominance hierarchies appear to remain intact (Pereira & Weiss, 1991; Sauther, 1991). Male-female aggression is especially high during the breeding season, as is male-male aggression (Jolly, 1967). Aggression between males and females is often instigated by males, but females usually win (Jolly, 1966). This is true even in pair-bonded lemur species (indri: Pollock, 1979). Rates of female-female aggression usually peak during the birth season when the risks of infanticide (e.g., Hood, 1994; Pereira & Weiss, 1991; although see Sauther & Sussman (1993) for possible arguments) and feeding competition are highest (Jolly et al., 1993).

Males typically disperse to new groups during the birthing season, and females must be wary of male infanticide (Pereira & Weiss, 1991), although other females may become responsible for the death of a groupmate's infant. For instance, a mother may be chased and subsequently drop her infant. When she attempts to retrieve her infant, the other group members may chase her away repeatedly (Gould, 1990): without access to its mother, the infant eventually dies. Taylor (1986, cited in Gould, 1990) noted that some infants were injured or killed when a higher-ranking female attacked the infant's lower-ranking mother as the infant was clinging to her body.

During the birth season, males may transfer to new groups in pairs, which they do every 3–4 years (Sussman, 1992). Males transfer to new groups regularly, and this serves as an indication of their low paternal investment—lack of rearing or other infant care. With so little investment in offspring, and without dominance over females, males provide little agonistic support to females in disputes, and, in return, they receive little agonistic support from females when they are similarly imperiled (Pereira & Kappeler, 1997). This is different from both chimpanzee and baboon intersexual relationships.

As with chimpanzees and baboons, troop fission can occur, and the new and "parent" troops may fight despite their recent positive associations— moving out of the "us" group entails moving into the "them" group. Lemurs appear to have an exceptionally high degree of physical conflict with their formerly same-group female kin (Hood & Jolly, 1995; Ichino, 2006). This emphasizes an *every female for herself* attitude, especially considering the almost complete lack of male agonistic support.

DOMINANCE AND FRIENDSHIPS

Unlike baboons, lemurs are not nepotistic: daughters do not inherit their mother's rank, and mothers do not intervene in conflicts against their daughter, although mothers and daughters may cooperate in aggression against another (as do sisters; see Jolly (1998) for a discussion; Kappeler, 1993a, 1993b; Pereira, 1995). Rank-reversals can occur yearly, especially around the breeding season when all females in the group enter estrus at the same time (Jolly, 1967), and dominance can be circular (i.e., A is dominant to B who is dominant to C who is dominant to A; Pereira, 1995). Females associate preferentially with each other, although generally they have few close friends and show little affiliative behavior outside of grooming (Kappeler, 1993a, 1993b; see also Jolly (1998) for discussion).

Female lemurs are more aggressive than males: females exchange more aggression within and between troops (Jolly et al., 1993; Kappeler, 1999; Sauther & Sussman, 1993; although see Jolly, 1966). Lemurs lack the social repair mechanisms seen in baboons and chimpanzees, such as reconciliation. Reconciliation after conflict is rare (Kappeler, 1993b), as is coalitionary support in terms of recruitment of allies during an attack against another or in terms of retaliation against an attacker, although polyadic attack can occur (see Jolly, 1998, for discussion). Lemurs may target specific individuals, including members of their troop, and repeatedly attack them, sometimes leading to expulsion from the group or death (Jolly et al., 1993; Vick & Pereira, 1989). This occurs in other primate groups as well (see discussion in Sterck et al., 1997).

In summary, female ring-tailed lemurs have the advantage of dominance over males, leading to a decreased threat of male aggression. It has been suggested that females have this advantage over males because they are in higher need of limited available resources (e.g., food), and their similar size to males makes them good contenders in a fight and because male paternal investment is low (Dunham, 2008). So, the cost of being dominant and non-pair-bonded is raising young without the help of the father. Lemurs are, however, female-bonded, wherein mothers and daughters or sisters share the strongest bonds. Despite this, there are still high rates of female-female aggression within the troop, including targeted aggression that can result in group expulsion for some unlucky females. One issue to consider in making comparisons to humans is that lemurs may be constrained in their social development by their limited ability to identify each other at a distance (as a result of their relatively poor eyesight compared to other primates: Pereira, 1995; see also Kappeler (1999) for discussion). So, they may not be able to monitor the activities of others from a distance, thereby severely limiting their ability to intervene in unsanctioned interactions. Some researchers consider this to potentially limit their social intelligence, but, in considering their many shared societal attributes with savanna baboons and other cercopithecines, their behavior is likely more reflective of their socioecology than of any physiological constraint. The most important lesson to be learned from lemurs is that even when females are the most dominant individuals, female-female aggression and competition are still high, even between kin. An *every female for herself* attitude has its personal benefits, but it also has its societal limits.

Conclusion

Overall, the aim for this chapter was to provide a detailed account of female competition in other primates in order to put into perspective the types of female-female competition that occur in human societies. Within this chapter, I provided a number of examples in which other primates appear to mirror human behavior in a similar situation. The main focus has been concentrated on describing nonhuman primate behavior without making direct comparisons to humans: readers can make those assessments as they continue reading this volume. Rather, this chapter has provided an assessment of the value of aggression, cooperation, and competition from the viewpoint of nonhuman primates with respect to the social and ecological factors they may face. The different social structures and

relationship types that exist throughout the primate order emerge from the intertwining of many factors (e.g., phylogenic, biological, ecological, psychological), and these factors should be similarly considered in studies of human behavior.

The socioecological constraints on a species have been given notable attention, and much discussion proceeded from this approach. The behavioral repertoires used for aggression and affiliation were explained largely from a socioecological standpoint, and many examples of species that fit the model (or are exceptions) were provided in an attempt to provide a holistic view of the many factors that played into human evolution and the behavioral consequences seen today.

It appears that there is no single solution for female primates to the problem of competition. The discussion in the final section involved the effects of social structure on female choices and, subsequently, what kind of life females could expect in that situation. Excluded from the discussion was an example of monogamy, although there are some clear advantages to it in terms of female-female competition: competition would move from day-to-day battles for resources to solely battling to keep her mate's eye from straying. That is not say, however, that aggression would mostly disappear; instead, it would be used more often in territorial battles and within family unit disputes—given that dominance would be shared between the male and female (e.g., gibbons: Carpenter, 1940).

The question remains: why are humans not as progressive as expected compared to the other primates? There remain many parallels between women and other female primates, many of which I have presented in this chapter. Like women, female primates compete for social status, for access to the best resources, and for the opportunity to raise healthy offspring. More times than not, females are alone in their battles, especially when they fight against their own kin. In few primate species do males provide a supportive role to females outside the realm of physical aggression toward an aggressor—including in the rearing of offspring. So, the answer is simple: it is because humans are subject to the same phylogenetic and environmental constraints as the other primates, and these constraints impose limits on all aspects of social life that are difficult to rise above despite humans' "superior" cognition or morality. However, as humans, women (and men) are supposed to have the advantage of using contemplative decision making to make the more difficult yet more beneficial choice that leads to the more positive outcome in their social relationships, especially while knowing that the outcomes of certain social situations typically and consistently emerge in specified ways. However, humans have yet to fully illustrate this ability (or "superior" morality), as evidenced by the observation that women in many countries (e.g., Saudi Arabia, Yemen, Syria) do not enjoy the same liberties as women in other societies, and they currently lack many of the rights men enjoy (e.g., right to an education, right to bear witness) or the same protections under law (as in cases of rape or other abuse). In fact, it was only relatively recently that women in some of the most liberal countries (e.g., United States) were granted similar rights to men, such as the right to vote (19th Amendment to the US Constitution in 1920) or equal pay (Equal Pay Act of 1963; Civil Rights Act of 1964; although this is yet to be fully realized in practice). As is the case in many primate species, there is a continued absence of both intra- and intercultural harmony.

Acknowledgments

I would like to thank Maryanne Fisher for the invitation to write this chapter and for her outstanding editorial support throughout the writing process. I would also like to thank Jill Pruetz, Michael Wilson, Carson Murray, and two anonymous reviewers for their helpful suggestions and comments.

References

Abbott, D. H. (1989). Social suppression of reproduction in primates. In V. Standen & R. A. Foley (Eds.), *Comparative socioecology: The behavioural ecology of humans and other animals* (pp. 285–304). Oxford: Blackwell Scientific.

Abegglen, J. J. (1984). *On socialization in hamadryas baboons: A field study.* Cranbury, NJ: Associated University Presses.

Alberts, S. C. (2012). Magnitude and sources of variation in male reproductive performance. In J. C. Mitani, J. Call, P. M. Kappeler, R. A. Palombit, & J. B. Silk (Eds.), *The evolution of primate societies* (pp. 412–433). Chicago: University of Chicago Press.

Anzai, T., Shiina, T., Kimura, N., Yanagiya, K., Kohara, S., Shigenari, A., ... Inoko, H. (2003). Comparative sequencing of human and chimpanzee MHC class I regions unveils insertions/deletions as the major path to genomic divergence. *Proceedings of the National Academy of Sciences of the United States of America, 100*(13), 7708–7713. doi:10.1073/pnas.1230533100

Arnold, C., Matthews, L. J., & Nunn, C. L. (2010). The 10kTrees website: A new online resource for primate phylogeny. *Evolutionary Anthropology: Issues, News, and Reviews, 19*(3), 114–118. doi:10.1002/evan.20251

Arnold, K., & Whiten, A. (2001). Post-conflict behaviour of wild chimpanzees (*Pan troglodytes schweinfurthii*) in the Budongo Forest, Uganda. *Behaviour, 138*(5), 649–690.

Aureli, F., Fraser, O. N., Schaffner, C. M., & Schino, G. (2012). The regulation of social relationships. In J. C. Mitani, J. Call, P. M. Kappeler, R. A. Palombit, & J. B. Silk (Eds.), *The evolution of primate societies* (pp. 531–551). Chicago: University of Chicago Press.

Baldwin, J. D. (1968). The social behavior of adult male squirrel monkeys (*Samimiri sciureus*) in a seminatural environment. *Folia Primatologica, 9*, 281–314.

Barrett, L., Henzi, S. P., Weingrill, T., Lycett, J. E., & Hill, R. A. (1999). Market forces predict grooming reciprocity in female baboons. *Proceedings of the Royal Society of London, B, 266*, 665–670.

Benenson, J. F., Kuhn, M. N., Ryan, P. J., Ferranti, A. J., Blondin, R., Shea, M.,. . . . Wrangham, R. W. (2014). Human males appear more prepared than females to resolve conflicts with same-sex peers. *Human Nature, 25*, 251–268.

Blomberg, S. P., & Garland, T. (2002). Tempo and mode in evolution: Phylogenetic inertia, adaptation and comparative methods. *Journal of Evolutionary Biology, 15*(6), 899–910.

Boccia, M. L., Reite, M., & Laudenslager, M. (1989). On the physiology of grooming in a pigtail macaque. *Physiology & Behavior, 45*(3), 667–670. Retrieved from http://www.ncbi.nlm.nih.gov/pubmed/2756061

Boesch, C. (1996). Social grouping in Tai chimpanzees. In W. McGrew, L. Merchant, & T. Nishida (Eds.), *Great ape societies* (pp. 101–113). Cambridge, UK: Cambridge University Press.

Boesch, C., & Boesch-Achermann, H. (2000). *The chimpanzees of the Tai forest: Behavioural ecology and evolution.* Oxford: Oxford University Press.

Bouchet, H., Pellier, A., Blois-Heulin, C., & Lemasson, A. (2010). Sex differences in the vocal repertoire of adult red-capped mangabeys (*Cercocebus torquatus*): A multi-level acoustic analysis. *American Journal of Primatology, 72*, 360–375. doi:10.1002/ajp.20791

Brereton, A. R. (1995). Coercion-defense hypothesis: The evolution of primate sociality. *Folia Primatologica, 64*, 207–214.

Call, J., & Tomasello, M. (Eds.). (2007). *The gestural communication of apes and monkeys.* Mahwah, NJ: Lawrence Erlbaum Associates.

Carpenter, C. R. (1940). A field study in Siam of the behavior and social relations of the gibbon (*Hylobates lar*). *Comparative Psychology Monographs, 16*(5), 1–212.

Carpenter, C. R. (1964). *Naturalistic behavior of nonhuman primates.* University Park, PA: The Pennsylvania State University Press.

Chalyan, V. G., Lapin, B. A., & Meishvili, N. V. (1994). Kinship and troop structure formation in baboon in Gumista Reserve. *Congress of the International Primatological Society, 15*, 238.

Chapais, B. (2006). Kinship, competence and cooperation in primates. In P. M. Kappeler & C. van Schaik (Eds.), *Cooperation in primates and humans* (pp. 47–64). Heidelberg: Springer.

Chapais, B., Girard, C., & Primi, G. (1991). Non-kin alliances, and the stability of matrilineal dominance relations in Japanese macaques. *Animal Behaviour, 41*, 481–491.

Chapais, B., Girard, C., Prud'homme, J., & Vasey, P. (1997). Relatedness threshold for nepotism in Japanese macaques. *Animal Behaviour, 53*, 1089–1101.

Chapais, B., Prud'homme, J., & Teijeiro, S. (1994). Dominance competition among siblings in Japanese macaques: Constraints on nepotism. *Animal Behaviour, 48*, 1335–1347.

Charles-Dominique, P. (1977). *Ecology and behaviour of nocturnal primates: Prosimians of equatorial West Africa.* New York: Columbia University Press.

Cheney, D. L., Seyfarth, R. M., & Silk, J. B. (1995). The role of grunts in reconciling opponents and facilitating interactions among adult female baboons. *Animal Behaviour, 50*, 249–257.

Clark, A. P. (1993). Rank differences in the production of vocalizations by wild chimpanzees as a function of social context. *American Journal of Primatology, 31*(3), 159–179. doi:10.1002/ajp.1350310302

Clutton-Brock, T. H., & Harvey, P. H. (1977). Primate ecology and social organization. *Journal of Zoology, 183*, 1–39.

Coelho, A. M. J. M., Turner, S. A., & Bramblett, C. A. (1983). Allogrooming and social status: An assessment of the contributions of female behavior to the social organization of hamadryas baboons (*Papio hamadryas*). *Primates, 24*(April), 184–197.

Colmenares, F., Zaragoza, F., & Hernandez-Lloreda, M. V. (2002). Grooming and coercion in one-male units of hamadryas baboons: Market forces or relationship constraints? *Behaviour, 139*, 1525–1553.

Cooper, M., & Bernstein, I. S. (2000). Social grooming in Assamese macaques (*Macaca assamensis*). *American Journal of Primatology, 50*, 77–85.

Cords, M. (2012). The behavior, ecology, and social evolution of cercopithecine monkeys. In J. C. Mitani, J. Call, P. M. Kappeler, R. A. Palombit, & J. B. Silk (Eds.), *The evolution of primate societies* (pp. 91–112). Chicago: University of Chicago Press.

Crockford, C., Wittig, R. M., Whitten, P. L., Seyfarth, R. M., & Cheney, D. L. (2008). Social stressors and coping mechanisms in wild female baboons (*Papio hamadryas ursinus*). *Hormones and Behavior, 53*(1), 254–265. doi:10.1016/j.yhbeh.2007.10.007

Culot, L., Lledo-Ferrer, Y., Hoelscher, O., Muñoz Lazo, F. J. J., Huynen, M.-C., & Heymann, E. W. (2011). Reproductive failure, possible maternal infanticide, and cannibalism in wild moustached tamarins, *Saguinus mystax*. *Primates; Journal of Primatology, 52*(2), 179–186. doi:10.1007/s10329-011-0238-6

de Waal, F. B. M. (1982). *Chimpanzee politics: Power and sex among apes.* New York: Harper & Row.

de Waal, F. B. M. (1986). The integration of dominance and social bonding in primates. *The Quarterly Review of Biology, 61*(4), 459–478.

de Waal, F. B. M., & Brosnan, S. F. (2006). Simple and complex reciprocity in primates. In P. M. Kappeler & C. van Schaik (Eds.), *Cooperation in primates and humans* (pp. 85–106). Heidelberg: Springer.

Di Fiore, A. (2012). Genetic consequences of primate social organization. In J. C. Mitani, J. Call, P. M. Kappeler, R. A. Palombit, & J. B. Silk (Eds.), *The evolution of primate societies* (pp. 269–292). Chicago: University of Chicago Press.

Dunbar, R. I. M., & Shultz, S. (2010). Bondedness and sociality. *Behaviour, 147*, 775–803.

Dunham, A. E. (2008). Battle of the sexes: cost asymmetry explains female dominance in lemurs. *Animal Behaviour, 76*, 1435–1439.

Engh, A. L., Beehner, J. C., Bergman, T. J., Whitten, P. L., Hoffmeier, R. R., Seyfarth, R. M., & Cheney, D. L. (2006).

Behavioural and hormonal responses to predation in female chacma baboons (*Papio hamadryas ursinus*). *Proceedings of the Biological Sciences/The Royal Society, 273*(1587), 707–712. doi:10.1098/rspb.2005.3378

Fedurek, P., Donnellan, E., & Slocombe, K. (2014). Social and ecological correlates of long-distance pant-hoot calls in male chimpanzees. *Behavioral Ecology and Sociobiology, 68*(8), 1345–1355.

Fleagle, J. G. (2013). *Primate adaptation and evolution* (3rd ed.). San Diego, CA: Academic Press.

Galdikas, B. M. F. (1981). Orangutan reproduction in the wild. In C. E. Graham (Ed.), *Reproductive biology of the great apes* (pp. 281–300). New York: Academic Press.

Gartlan, J. S. (1968). Structure and function in primate society. *Folia Primatologica, 8*, 89–120.

Gilby, I. C. (2012). Cooperation among non-kin: Reciprocity, markets, and mutualism. In J. C. Mitani, J. Call, P. M. Kappeler, R. A. Palombit, & J. B. Silk (Eds.), *The evolution of primate societies* (pp. 514–530). Chicago: University of Chicago Press.

Gilby, I. C., & Wrangham, R. W. (2008). Association patterns among wild chimpanzees (*Pan troglodytes schweinfurthii*) reflect sex differences in cooperation. *Behavioral Ecology and Sociobiology, 62*(11), 1831–1842. doi:10.1007/s00265-008-0612-6

Glander, K. E. (1992). Disperal patterns in Costa Rican mantled howling monkeys. *International Journal of Primatology, 13*(4), 415–435.

(van Lawick-) Goodall, J. (1968). A preliminary report on expressive movements and communication in the Gombe Stream chimpanzees. In P. Jay (Ed.), *Primates: Studies in adaptation and variability* (pp. 313–374). New York: Holt, Rinehart and Winston.

Goodall, J. (1982). Order without law. *Journal of Social and Biological Structures, 5*(4), 353–360.

Goodall, J. (1986). *The chimpanzees of Gombe: Patterns of behavior.* London: Belknap Press of Harvard University Press.

Goodman, S. M., O'Connor, S., & Langrand, O. (1993). A review of predation on lemur: Implications for the evolution of social behavior in small, nocturnal primates. In P. M. Kappeler & J. U. Ganzhorn (Eds.), *Lemur social systems and their ecological basis* (pp. 51–66). New York: Plenum Press.

Goodman, M., Porter, C., Czelusniak, J., Page, S. L., Schneider, H., Shoshani, J.,. . . Groves, C. P. (1998). Toward a phylogenetic classification of primates based on DNA evidence complemented by fossil evidence. *Molecular Phylogenetics and Evolution, 9*(3), 585–598. doi:10.1006/mpev.1998.0495

Gould, L. (1990). The social development of free-ranging infant *lemur catta* at Berenty Reserve, Madagascar. *International Journal of Primatology, 11*(4), 297–318.

Greeno, N., & Semple, S. (2009). Sex differences in vocal communication among adult rhesus macaques. *Evolution and Human Behavior, 30*, 141–145.

Gumert, M. D. (2007). Payment for sex in a macaque mating market. *Animal Behaviour, 74*, 1655–1667.

Hall, K. R. L. (1968). Tool-using performances as indicators of behavioral adaptability. In P. Jay (Ed.), *Primates: Studies in adaptation and variability* (pp. 131–148). New York: Holt, Rinehart & Winston.

Hamilton, W. D. (1964a). The genetical evolution of social behavior. I. *Journal of Theoretical Biology, 7*, 1–16.

Hamilton, W. D. (1964b). The genetical evolution of social behavior. II. *Journal of Theoretical Biology, 7*, 17–52.

Harcourt, A. H., Stewart, K. J., & Fossey, D. (1981). Gorilla reproduction in the wild. In C. E. Graham (Ed.), *Reproductive biology of the great apes* (pp. 265–279). New York: Academic Press.

Hausfater, G., & Hrdy, S. B. (1984). *Infanticide: Comparative and evolutionary perspectives.* Hawthorne, NY: Aldine.

Hinde, R. A. (1977). On assessing the bases of partner preferences. *Behaviour, 62,* 1–9.

Hood, L. C. (1994). Infanticide among ringtailed lemurs (*Lemur catta*) at Berenty Reserve, Madagascar. *American Journal of Primatology, 33,* 65–69.

Hood, L. C., & Jolly, A. (1995). Troop fission in female *Lemur catta* at Berenty Reserve, Madagascar. *International Journal of Primatology, 16,* 997–1015.

Horvath, J. E., Weisrock, D. W., Embry, S. L., Fiorentino, I., Balhoff, J. P., Kappeler, P.,... Yoder, A. D. (2008). Development and application of a phylogenomic toolkit: Resolving the evolutionary history of Madagascar's lemurs. *Genome Research, 18*(3), 489–499. doi:10.1101/gr.7265208

Hrdy, S. B. (1974). Male-male competition and infanticide among the langurs (*Presbytis entellus*) of Abu, Rajasthan. *Folia Primatologica, 22,* 19–58. doi:10.1159/000155616

Hrdy, S. B. (1977). *The langurs of Abu.* Cambridge, MA: Harvard University Press.

Hrdy, S. B. (2013a). *The woman that never evolved.* Cambridge, MA: Harvard University Press.

Hrdy, S. B. (2013b). The "one animal in all creation about which man knows the least." *Philosophical Transactions of the Royal Society B, 368*(1631), 20130072. doi:10.1098/rstb.2013.0072

Hume, D. (1777/1975). *Enquiries concerning human understanding* (3rd ed.). L. A. Selby-Bigge & P. H. Nidditch (Eds.). New York: Oxford University Press.

Ichino, S. (2006). Troop fission in wild ring-tailed lemurs (*Lemur catta*) at Berenty, Madagascar. *American Journal of Primatology, 68,* 97–102. doi:10.1002/ajp

Idani, G. (1991). Social relationships between immigrant and resident bonobo (*Pan paniscus*) females at Wamba. *Folia Primatologica, 57,* 83–95.

Isbell, L. A. (1991). Contest and scramble competition: Patterns of female aggression and ranging behavior among primates. *Animal Behaviour, 2,* 143–155.

Isbell, L. A., & van Vuren, D. (1996). Differential costs of locational and social dispersal and their consequences for female group-living primates. *Behaviour, 133*(1), 1–36.

Isbell, L. A., & Young, T. P. (2002). Ecological models of female social relationships in primates: Similarities, disparities, and some directions for future clarity, *Behaviour, 139,* 177–202.

Janson, C. (1984). Female choice and the mating system of the brown capuchin monkey (*Cebus apella*). *Zeitschrift für Tierpsychologie, 65,* 177–200.

Jolly, A. (1998). Pair-bonding, female aggression and the evolution of lemur societies. *Folia Primatologica, 69,* 1–13.

Jolly, A. (1966). *Lemur behavior.* Chicago: University of Chicago Press.

Jolly, A. (1967). Breeding synchrony in *Lemur catta.* In S. A. Altmann (Ed.), *Social communication among primates* (pp. 1–14). Chicago: University of Chicago Press.

Jolly, A., Rasamimanana, H. R., Kinnaird, M. F., O'Brien, T. G., Crowley, H. M., Harcourt, C. S., et al. (1993). Territoriality in *Lemur catta* groups during the birth season at Berenty, Madagascar. In P. M. Kappeler & J. U. Ganzhorn (Eds.), *Lemur social systems and their ecological basis* (pp. 85–109). New York: Plenum Press.

Jones, J. H. (2011). Primates and the evolution of long, slow life histories. *Current Biology, 21*(18), R708–R717. doi:10.1016/j.cub.2011.08.025

Kaplan, J. R., & Zucker, E. (1980). Social organization in a group of free ranging patas monkeys. *Folia Primatologica, 34,* 196–213.

Kappeler, P. M. (1993a). Variation in social structure: The effects of sex and kinship on social interactions in three lemur species. *Ethology, 93,* 125–145.

Kappeler, P. M. (1993b). Reconciliation and post-conflict behaviour in ringtailed lemurs, *Lemur catta* and redfronted lemurs, *Eulemur fulvus rufus. Animal Behaviour, 45,* 901–915.

Kappeler, P. M. (1999). Lemur social structure and convergence in primate socioecology. In P. C. Lee (Ed.), *Comparative primate socioecology* (pp. 273–299). Cambridge, UK: Cambridge University Press.

Kawamura, S. (1958). Matriarchal social ranks and the Minoo-B troop: A study of the rank system of Japanese monkeys. *Primates, 1–2,* 149–156.

Kawanaka, K. (1984). Association, ranging, and the social unit in chimpanzees of the Mahale mountains. *Tanzania. International Journal of Primatology, 5,* 411–434.

Kumar, S., & Hedges, S. B. (1998). A molecular timescale for vertebrate evolution. *Nature, 392,* 917–920.

Kappeler, P. M. (2012). Mate choice. In J. C. Mitani, J. Call, P. M. Kappeler, R. A. Palombit, & J. B. Silk (Eds.), *The evolution of primate societies* (pp. 367–386). Chicago: University of Chicago Press.

Kappeler, P. M., & van Schaik, C. P. (2002). Evolution of primate social systems. *International Journal of Primatology, 23*(4), 707–740.

Kummer, H. (1967). Tripartite relations in hamadryas baboons. In S. A. Altmann (Ed.), *Social communication among primates* (pp. 63–72). Chicago: University of Chicago Press.

Kummer, H. (1968). Two variations in the social organization of baboons. In P. Jay (Ed.), *Primates: Studies in adaptation and variability* (pp. 293–312). New York: Holt, Rinehart & Winston.

Kummer, H. (1979). Intra- and intergoup relationships in primates. In M. von Cranach, K. Foppa, W. Lepenies, & D. Ploog (Eds.), *Human ethology: Claims and limits of a new discipline* (pp. 381–434). Cambridge, UK: Cambridge University Press.

Langergraber, K. (2012). Cooperation among kin. In J. C. Mitani, J. Call, P. M. Kappeler, R. A. Palombit, & J. B. Silk (Eds.), *The evolution of primate societies* (pp. 491–513). Chicago: University of Chicago Press.

Langergraber, K., Mitani, J., & Vigilant, L. (2009). Kinship and social bonds in female chimpanzees (*Pan troglodytes*), *American Journal of Primatology, 71,* 840–851.

Langergraber, K. E., & Vigilant, L. (2011). Genetic differences cannot be excluded from generating behavioural differences among chimpanzee groups. *Proceedings of the Royal Society B-Biological Sciences, 278*(1715), 2094–2095.

Lehmann, J., & Boesch, C. (2008). Sexual differences in chimpanzee sociality. *International Journal of Primatology, 29*(1), 65–81. doi:10.1007/s10764-007-9230-9

Lehmann, J., & Boesch, C. (2009). Sociality of the dispersing sex : The nature of social bonds in West African female chimpanzees, *Pan troglodytes. Animal Behaviour, 77*(2), 377–387. doi:10.1016/j.anbehav.2008.09.038

Leinfelder, I., de Vries, H., Deleu, R., & Nelissen, M. (2001). Rank and grooming reciprocity among females in a mixed-sex group of captive hamadryas baboons. *American Journal of Primatology, 55*(1), 25–42. doi:10.1002/ajp.1036

Locke, J., & Hauser, M. D. (1999). Sex and status effects on primate volubility: Clues to the origin of vocal languages? *Evolution and Human Behavior, 20*, 151–158.

Luxen, M. F. (2005). Gender differences in dominance and affiliation during a demanding interaction *Journal of Psychology: Interdisciplinary and Applied, 139*, 331–347.

Lwanga, J. S., Struhsaker, T. T., Struhsaker, P. J., Butynski, T. M., & Mitani, J. C. (2011). Primate population dynamics over 32.9 years at Ngogo, Kibale National Park, Uganda. *American Journal of Primatology, 73*(10), 997–1011.

Lyon, J. E., Pandit, S. A., van Schaik, C. P., & Pradhan, G. R. (2011). Mating strategies in primates: A game theoretical approach to infanticide. *Journal of Theoretical Biology, 274*(1), 103–108. doi:10.1016/j.jtbi.2011.01.005

Macedonia, J. M. (1993). Adaptation and phylogenetic constraints in the antipredator behavior of ringtailed and ruffed lemurs. In P. M. Kappeler & J. U. Ganzhorn (Eds.), *Lemur social systems and their ecological basis* (pp. 67–84). New York: Plenum Press.

Marler, P. (1976). Social organization, communication, and graded signals: The chimpanzee and the gorilla. In R. Hinde & P. Bateson (Eds.), *Growing points in ethology* (pp. 239–280). Cambridge, UK: Cambridge University Press.

Matsui, A., Rakotondraparany, F., Munechika, I., Hasegawa, M., & Horai, S. (2009). Molecular phylogeny and evolution of prosimians based on complete sequences of mitochondrial DNAs. *Gene, 441*(1–2), 53–66. doi:10.1016/j.gene.2008.08.024

Mitani, J. C. (2006). Reciprocal exchange in chimpanzees and other primates. In P. M. Kappeler & C. van Schaik (Eds.), *Cooperation in primates and humans* (pp. 107–120). Heidelberg: Springer.

Mitani, J. C., & Gros-Louis, J. (1995). Species and sex differences in the screams of chimpanzees and bonobos. *International Journal of Primatology, 16*, 393–411.

Muller, M. N., Emery Thompson, M., Kahlenberg, S. M., & Wrangham, R. W. (2011). Sexual coercion by male chimpanzees shows that female choice may be more apparent than real. *Behavioral Ecology and Sociobiology, 65*(5), 921–933.

Muller, M. N., Emery Thompson, M., & Wrangham, R. W. (2006). Male chimpanzees prefer mating with old females. *Current Biology, 16*, 2234–2238.

Muller, M. N., & Thompson, M. E. (2012). Mating, parenting, and male reproductive performance. In J. C. Mitani, J. Call, P. M. Kappeler, R. A. Palombit, & J. B. Silk (Eds.), *The evolution of primate societies* (pp. 387–411). Chicago: University of Chicago Press.

Muller, M. N., & Wrangham, R. W. (2009). *Sexual coercion in primates and humans.* Cambridge, MA: Harvard University Press.

Nelson, R. (2006). *Biology of aggression.* Oxford: Oxford University Press.

Nishida, T. (1968). The social group of wild chimpanzees in the Mahale Mountains. *Primates, 9*, 167–224.

Nishida, T. (1970). Social behaviour and relationship among wild chimpanzees of the Mahali Mountains. *Primates, 11*, 47–87.

Noë, R., de Waal, F. B. M., & van Hooff, J. A. R. A. M. (1980). Types of dominance in a chimpanzee colony. *Folia Primatologica, 34*, 90–110.

Packer, C. (1979). Inter-troop transfer and inbreeding avoidance in *Papio anubis. Animal Behaviour, 27*(1), 1–36.

Packer, C., & Pusey, A. E. (1979). Female aggression and male membership in troops of Japanese macaques and olive baboons. *Folia Primatologica, 31*, 212–218.

Palombit, R. (2012). Infanticide: Male strategies and female counterstrategies. In J. C. Mitani, J. Call, P. M. Kappeler, R. A. Palombit, & J. B. Silk (Eds.), *The evolution of primate societies* (pp. 432–468). Chicago: University of Chicago Press.

Palombit, R., Seyfarth, R., & Cheney, D. (1997). The adaptive value of "friendships" to female baboons: Experimental and observational evidence. *Animal Behaviour, 54*(3), 599–614. Retrieved from http://www.ncbi.nlm.nih.gov/pubmed/9299045

Pereira, M. E. (1995). Development and social dominance among group-living primates. *American Journal of Primatology, 37*(2), 143–175. doi:10.1002/ajp.1350370207

Pereira, M. E., & Kappeler, P. M. (1997). Divergent systems of agonistic relationship in lemurid primates. *Behaviour, 134*, 225–274.

Pereira, M. E., & Weiss, M. L. (1991). Female mate choice, male migration, and the threat of infanticide in ringtailed lemurs. *Behavioral Ecology and Sociobiology, 28*(2), 141–152.

Pika, S., & Liebal, K. (Eds.). (2012). *Developments in primate gesture research.* Amsterdam: John Benjamins.

Plavcan, J. M. (1999). Mating systems, intrasexual competition and sexual dimorphism in primates. In P. C. Lee (Ed.), *Comparative primate socioecology* (pp. 241–269). Cambridge, UK: Cambridge University Press.

Plavcan, J. M., van Schaik, C. P., & Kappeler, P. M. (1995). Competition, coalitions and canine size in primates. *Journal of Human Evolution, 28*, 245–276.

Pollick, A. S., & de Waal, F. B. M. (2007). Ape gestures and language evolution. *Proceedings of the National Academy of Sciences, 104*, 8184–8189.

Pollock, J. I. (1979). Female dominance in *Indri indri. Folia Primatologica, 31*, 143–164.

Pruetz, J. D., & Isbell, L. A. (2000). Correlations of food distribution and patch size with agonistic interactions in female vervets (*Chlorocebus aethiops*) and patas monkeys (*Erythrocebus patas*) living in simple habitats. *Behavioral Ecology and Sociobiology, 49*(1), 38–47.

Pusey, A. (2012). Magnitude and sources of variation in female reproductive performance. In J. C. Mitani, J. Call, P. M. Kappeler, R. A. Palombit, & J. B. Silk (Eds.), *The evolution of primate societies* (pp. 343–366). Chicago: University of Chicago Press.

Pusey, A., Murray, C., Wallauer, W., Wilson, M., Wroblewski, E., & Goodall, J. (2008). Severe aggression among female *Pan troglodytes schweinfurthii* at Gombe National Park, Tanzania. *International Journal of Primatology, 29*(4), 949–973. doi:10.1007/s10764-008-9281-6

Pusey, A. E. (1979). Intercommunity transfer of chimpanzees in Gombe National Park. In D. A. Hamburg & E. R. McCown (Eds.), *The great apes* (pp. 465–480). Menlo Park, CA: Benjamin/Cummings.

Robson, S. L., & Wood, B. (2008). Hominin life history: Reconstruction and evolution. *Journal of Anatomy, 212*(4), 394–425. doi:10.1111/j.1469-7580.2008.00867.x

Roff, D. A. (1992). *The evolution of life histories: Theory and analysis*. New York: Chapman and Hall.

Rowell, T. E. (1974). The concept of social dominance. *Behavioural Biology, 11*, 131–154.

Rowell, T. E., & Dixon, A. F. (1975). Changes in social organization during the breeding season of wild talapoin monkeys. *Journal of Reproduction and Fertility, 43*, 419–434.

Saltzman, W. (2003). Reproductive competition among female common marmosets (*Callithrix jacchus*): Proximate and ultimate causes. In C. B. Jones (Ed.), *Sexual selection and reproductive competition in primates: New perspectives and directions* (pp. 197–229). Norman, OK: American Society of Primatologists.

Sauther, M. L. (1991). Reproductive behavior of free-ranging *Lemur catta* at Beza Mahafaly Special Reserve, Madagascar. *American Journal of Physical Anthropology, 84*(4), 463–477.

Sauther, M. L., & Sussman, R. W. (1993). A new interpretation of the social organization and mating system of the ringtailed lemur (*Lemur catta*). In P. M. Kappeler & J. U. Ganzhorn (Eds.), *Lemur social systems and their ecological basis* (pp. 111–121). New York: Plenum Press.

Schreier, A., & Swedell, L. (2009). The fourth level of social structure in a multi-level society: ecological and social functions of clans in hamadryas baboons. *American Journal of Primatology, 71*, 1–8.

Schrago, C. G., & Russo, C. M. (2003). Timing the origin of New World monkeys. *Molecular Biology and Evolution, 20*(10), 1620–1625. doi:10.1093/molbev/msg172

Schülke, O., & Ostner, J. (2008). Male reproductive skew, paternal relatedness and female social relationships. *American Journal of Primatology, 70*, 1–4.

Schülke, O., & Ostner, J. (2012). Ecological and social influences on sociality. In J. C. Mitani, J. Call, P. M. Kappeler, R. A. Palombit, & J. B. Silk (Eds.), *The evolution of primate societies* (pp. 195–219). Chicago: University of Chicago Press.

Scott, N. M. (2007). *Communicating dominance: Chimpanzee use of gestures* (Unpublished doctoral dissertation). Roehampton University, London.

Scott, N. M. (2013). Gesture use by chimpanzees (*Pan troglodytes*): Differences between sexes in inter- and intra-sexual interactions. *American Journal of Primatology, 75*(6), 555–567. doi:10.1002/ajp.22133

Setchell, J. M. (2008). Alternative reproductive tactics in primates. In R. F. Olivieri, M. Taborsky, & H. J. Brockmann (Eds.), *Alternative reproductive tactics: An integrative approach* (pp. 373–398). Cambridge, UK: Cambridge University Press.

Setchell, J. M., & Kappeler, P. M. (2003). Selection in relation to sex in primates. *Advances in the Study of Behavior, 33*, 87–137.

Seyfarth, R. M. (1977). A model of social grooming among adult female monkeys. *Journal of Theoretical Biology, 65*, 671–698.

Shutt, K., MacLarnon, A., Heistermann, M., & Semple, S. (2007). Grooming in Barbary macaques: Better to give than to receive? *Biology Letters, 3*(3), 231–233. doi:10.1098/rsbl.2007.0052

Silk, J. B. (2012). The adaptive value of sociality. In J. C. Mitani, J. Call, P. M. Kappeler, R. A. Palombit, & J. B. Silk (Eds.), *The evolution of primate societies* (pp. 552–564). Chicago: University of Chicago Press.

Silk, J. B., Alberts, S. C., & Altmann, J. (2003a). Social bonds of female baboons. *Science, 302*(November), 1231–1234.

Silk, J. B., Alberts, S. C., & Altmann, J. (2004). Patterns of coalition formation by adult female baboons in Amboseli, Kenya. *Animal Behaviour, 67*, 573–582.

Silk, J. B., Beehner, J. C., Bergman, T. J., Crockford, C., Engh, A. L., Moscovice, L. R.,... Cheney, D. L. (2009). The benefits of social capital: Close social bonds among female baboons enhance offspring survival. *Proceedings. Biological Sciences/ The Royal Society, 276*(1670), 3099–3104. doi:10.1098/rspb.2009.0681

Silk, J., Cheney, D., & Seyfarth, R. (2013). A practical guide to the study of social relationships. *Evolutionary Anthropology, 22*, 213–225.

Silk, J. B., Rendall, D., Cheney, D. L., & Seyfarth, R. M. (2003b). Natal attraction in adult female baboons (*Papio cynocephalus ursinus*) in the Moremi Reserve. *Ethology, 109*, 627–644.

Slater, K. Y., Schaffner, C. M., & Aureli, F. (2009). Sex differences in the social behavior of wild spider monkeys (*Ateles geoffroyi yucatanensis*). *American Journal of Primatology, 71*, 21–29.

Smuts, B. B. (1985). *Sex and friendship in baboons*. Hawthorne, NY: Aldine.

Smuts, B. B., & Smuts, R. W. (1993). Male aggression and sexual coercion of females in nonhuman primates and other mammals: Evidence and theoretical implications. *Advances in the Study of Beahvior, 22*, 1–63.

Snaith, T., & Chapman, C. (2007). Primate group size and interpreting socioecological models: Do folivores really play by different rules? *Evolutionary Anthropology, 16*, 94–106.

Snowdon, C. T., Ziegler, T. E., & Widowski, T. M. (1993). Further hormonal suppression of eldest daughter cottontop tamarins following birth of infants. *American Journal of Primatology, 31*(1), 11–21. doi:10.1002/ajp.1350310103

Sommer, V. (1987). Infanticide among free-ranging langurs (*Presbytis entellus*) at Jodhpur (Rajasthan/India): Recent observations and a reconsideration of hypotheses. *Primates, 28*, 163–197.

Stammbach, E. (1978). On social differentiation in groups of captive female hamadryas baboons. *Behaviour, 67*, 322–338.

Steiper, M. E., & Seiffert, E. R. (2012). Evidence for a convergent slowdown in primate molecular rates and its implications for the timing of early primate evolution. *Proceedings of the National Academy of Sciences, 109*(16), 6006–6011.

Sterck, E. H. M., Watts, D. P., & van Schaik, C. P. (1997). The evolution of female social relationships in nonhuman primates. *Behavioral Ecology and Sociobiology, 41*(5), 291–309. doi:10.1007/s002650050390

Stevens, J. R., & Gilby, I. C. (2004). A conceptual framework for nonkin food sharing: Timing and currency of benefits. *Animal Behaviour, 67*, 603–614.

Strier, K. B. (1999). Why is female kin bonding so rare? Comparative sociality of neotropical primates. In P. C. Lee (Ed.), *Comparative primate socioecology* (pp. 300–319). Cambridge, UK: Cambridge University Press.

Stumpf, R. (2007). Chimpanzees and bonobos: Diversity within and between species. In C. J. Campbell, A. Fuentes, K. C. Mackinnon, M. Panger, D. K. Beader (Eds.), *Primates in perspective* (pp. 321–344). Oxford: Oxford University Press.

Sugiyama, Y. (1971). Characteristics of the social life of bonnet macaques (*Macaca radiata*). *Primates, 12*, 247–266.

Sussman, R. W. (1977). Feeding behavior of *Lemur catta* and *Lemur fulvis*. In T. H. Clutton-Brock (Ed.), *Primate ecology: Studies of feeding and ranging behavior in lemurs, monkeys, and apes* (pp. 1–36). London: Academic Press.

Sussman, R. W. (1991). Demography and social organization of free-ranging *Lemur catta* in the Beza Mahafaly Reserve, Madagascar. *American Journal of Physical Anthropology, 84*, 43–58.

Sussman, R. W. (1992). Male life history and intergroup mobility among ringtailed lemurs (*Lemur catta*). *International Journal of Primatology, 13*, 395–414.

Sussman, R. W., Garber, P. A., & Cheverud, J. I. M. M. (2005). Importance of cooperation and affiliation. *American Journal of Physical Anthropology, 128*(1), 84–97. doi:10.1002/ajpa.20196

Swedell, L. (2002). Affiliation among females in wild hamadryas baboons (*Papio hamadryas hamadryas*). *International Journal of Primatology, 23*(6), 1205–1226.

Swedell, L., & Plummer, T. (2012). A papionin multilevel society as a model for hominin social evolution. *International Journal of Primatology, 33*(5), 1165–1193.

Swedell, L., Saunders, J., Schreier, A., Davis, B., Tesfaye, T., & Pines, M. (2011). Female "dispersal" in hamadryas baboons: Transfer among social units in a multilevel society. *American Journal of Physical Anthropology, 145*(3), 360–370.

Taylor, L., & Sussman, R. W. (1985). A preliminary study of kinship and social organization in a semi-free-ranging group of *Lemur catta*. *International Journal of Primatology, 6*(6), 601–614.

Taylor, L. L. (1986). *Kinship, dominance, and social organization in a semi-free-ranging group of ringtailed lemurs (Lemur catta)*. Ph.D. thesis, Washington University, St. Louis.

Taylor, S. E., Klein, L. C., Lewis, B. P., Gruenewald, T. L., Gurung, R. A. R., & Updegraff, J. A. (2000). Biobehavioral responses to stress in females: Tend-and-befriend, not fight-or-flight. *Psychological Review, 107*(3), 411–429.

Terborgh, J., & Goldizen, A. W. (1985). On the mating system of the cooperatively breeding saddle-backed tamarin (*Saquinis fuscicollis*). *Behavioral Ecology & Sociobiology, 16*, 293–299.

Thierry, B. (2007). Unity in diversity: Lessons from macaque societies. *Evolutionary Anthropology: Issues, News, and Reviews, 16*(6), 224–238. doi:10.1002/evan.20147

Tinbergen, N. (1963). On aims and methods of ethology. *Zeitschrift für Tierpsychologie, 20*, 410–433.

Townsend, S. W., Slocombe, K. E., Thompson, M. E., & Zuberbühler, K. (2007). Female-led infanticide in wild chimpanzees. *Current Biology, 17*, R355–R356.

Treves, A. (1998). Primate social systems: Conspecific threat and coercion-defense hypotheses. *Folia Primatologica, 69*, 81–88.

Treves, A., & Chapman, C. A. (1996). Conspecific threat, predation avoidance and resource defense: Implications of grouping in langurs. *Behavioral Ecology and Sociobiology, 39*, 43–53.

Trivers, R. (1972). Parental investment and sexual selection. In B. Campbell (Ed.), *Sexual selection and the descent of man* (pp. 136–179). Chicago: Aldine.

Tubert, C., Lo Nostro, F., Villafane, V., & Pandolfi, M. (2012). Aggressive behavior and reproductive physiology in females of the social cichlid fish *Cichlasoma dimerus*. *Physiology & Behavior, 106*, 193–200.

Tutin, C. E. G., & McGinnis, P. R. (1981). Chimpanzee reproduction in the wild. In C. E. Graham (Ed.), *Reproductive biology of the great apes* (pp. 239–264). New York: Academic Press.

van Hooff, J. A. R. A. M. (1973). Structural analysis of behaviour in chimpanzees. In M. von Cranach & I. Vine (Eds.), *Social communication and movements: Studies in interaction and expression in man and chimpanzee* (pp. 75–162). London: Academic Press.

van Noordwijk, M. A. (2012). From maternal investment to lifetime maternal care. In J. C. Mitani, J. Call, P. M. Kappeler, R. A. Palombit, & J. B. Silk (Eds.), *The evolution of primate societies* (pp. 321–342). Chicago: University of Chicago Press.

van Schaik, C. P. (1989). The ecology of social relationships amongst female primates. In V. Standen & R. A. Foley (Eds.), *Comparative socioecology: The behavioural ecology of humans and other animals* (pp. 195–218). Oxford: Blackwell Scientific.

van Schaik, C. P., & Kappeler, P. M. (1993). Life history, activity period and lemur social systems. In P. M. Kappeler & J. U. Ganzhorn (Eds.), *Lemur social systems and their ecological basis* (pp. 241–260). New York, Plenum Press.

Vehrencamp, S. L. (1983). A model for the evolution of despotic versus egalitarian societies. *Animal Behavior, 31*, 667–682.

Vick, L. G., & Pereira, M. E. (1989). Episodic targeting aggression and the histories of lemur social groups. *Behavioral Ecology and Sociobiology, 25*(1), 3–12.

Walter, B., & Trillmich, F. (1994). Female aggression and male peace-keeping in a cichlid fish harem: Conflict between and within the sexes in *Lamprologus ocellatus*. *Behavioral Ecology and Sociobiology, 34*(2), 105–112. doi:10.1007/BF00164181

Watts, D. P (1989). Infanticide in mountain gorillas: New cases and a reconsideration of the evidence. *Ethology, 81*, 1–18.

Watts, D. P. (2003). Gorilla social relationships: A comparative overview. In A. B. Taylor & M. L. Goldsmith (Eds.), *Gorilla biology: A multidisciplinary perspective* (pp. 302–327). Cambridge, UK: Cambridge University Press.

Whiten, A. (2013). Archaeology meets primate technology. *Nature, 498*(7454), 303–304.

Whiten, A., Goodall, J., McGrew, W. C., Nishida, T., Reynolds, V., Sugiyama, Y.,... Boesch, C. (1999). Chimpanzee cultures. *Nature, 399*, 682–685.

Williams, J. M., Pusey, A. E., Carlis, J. V., Farm, B. P., & Goodall, J. (2002). Female competition and male territorial behaviour influence female chimpanzees' ranging patterns. *Animal Behaviour, 63*(2), 347–360. doi:10.1006/anbe.2001.1916

Wilson, M. L., Boesch, C., Fruth, B., Furuichi, T., Gilby, I. C., Hashimoto, C.,... Wrangham, R. W. (2014). Lethal aggression in Pan is better explained by adaptive strategies than human impacts. *Nature, 513*, 414–417.

Wilson, M. L., Hauser, M. D., & Wrangham, R. W. (2007). Chimpanzees (*Pan troglodytes*) modify grouping and vocal behaviour in response to location-specific risk. *Behaviour, 144*, 1621–1653.

Wilson, M. L., & Wrangham, R. W. (2003). Intergroup relations in chimpanzees. *Annual Review of Anthropology, 32*, 363–392. doi:10.1146/annurev.anthro.32.061002.120046

Wrangham, R. W. (1980). An ecological model of female-bonded primate groups. *Behaviour, 75*, 262–300.

Wroblewski, E. E., Murray, C. M., Keele, B. F., Schumacher-Stankey, J., Hahn, B. H., & Pusey, A. E. (2009). Male dominance rank and reproductive success in chimpanzees, *Pan troglodytes schweinfurthii*. *Animal Behaviour, 77*(4), 873–885.

Yasukawa, K., & Searcy, W. A. (1982). Aggression in female red-winged blackbirds: A strategy to ensure male parental investment. *Behavioral Ecology and Sociobiology*, *11*(1), 13–17.

Yerkes, R. (1943). *Chimpanzees: A laboratory colony*. New Haven, CT: Yale University Press.

Yerkes, R., & Elder, J. H. (1936). Oestrus, receptivity, and mating in the chimpanzee. *Comparative Psychology Monographs*, *13*, 1–39.

Appendix

Phylogenetic tree representing the order in which groups split. Examples of species are given for each major division and are color-coded: only species mentioned in the chapter are included. Apes are further divided into major species (other taxonomic information, such as genera, is ignored). Tree is not drawn to evolutionary time scale.

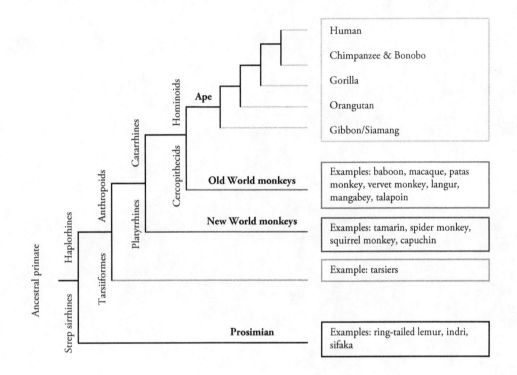

Social Status and Aggression

Feminist and Evolutionary Perspectives of Female-Female Competition, Status Seeking, and Social Network Formation

Laurette T. Liesen

Abstract

During the 1980s and 1990s, feminist evolutionists were instrumental in demonstrating that primate females, including girls and women, can be aggressive and seek status within their groups. Building on their insights, researchers from across disciplines have found that females use a variety of direct and indirect tactics as they pursue their reproductive success. To better understand women's aggression and status seeking, one also must examine their social networks. Women must not only deal with the dynamics within their groups, they also must deal with pressures from other groups. Success in maintaining connections in one's social network is vital for access to the various resources women need for their own reproductive success and to keep competitors in check. Overall, women's social networks, while serving both supportive and competitive functions, profoundly impact on the reproductive future of women and especially the survival and future reproductive strategies of their children.

Key Words: female aggression, status seeking, social networks, reproductive strategies, female competition

Navigating social groups can be both a rewarding and daunting experience. The friendships girls and women create provide companionship, advice, and support that is vital to their social and reproductive futures. Although these networks of friendships have great benefits, their intimacy and intensity can also make girls and women vulnerable, especially if these networks weaken or fall apart. In addition, if girls or women find themselves on the outside and a target of a particular strong female social network, the costs can be heavy in terms of their status and future reproductive success. Many popular books have been written about the competitiveness and aggression that can emerge between and among girls and women. For example, Rachel Simmons's *Odd Girl Out: The Hidden Culture of Aggression in Girls* (2002) and Rosalind Wiseman's *Queen Bees and Wannabees: Helping your Daughter Survive Cliques, Gossip, Boyfriends, and the New Realities of Girl World* (2009) are just a couple of the books that have provided detailed and descriptive accounts of how girls have dealt with the ostracism and bullying that can occur. However, none of these authors has included an evolutionary perspective that attempts to explain why women are aggressive and competitively strive for status.

Prior to the 1980s, female aggression and dominance were invisible to scholars within the evolutionary sciences. Many assumed that because females had few physical conflicts and their relationships were not obviously hierarchical, they did not pursue dominance, rank, or status. By the early 1980s, feminist evolutionists and primatologists were conducting groundbreaking research, informed by feminism, that looked beyond sexual stereotypes in examining female aggression, dominance, and status seeking and their long-term reproductive benefits (Fedigan, 1982; Hrdy, 1981/1999; Smuts,

1987). By the late 1990s and 2000s, and building on the insights of feminist evolutionists, researchers began to examine human female aggression (e.g., Björkqvist, Österman, & Kaukiainen, 1992; Campbell, 1999, 2002) and dominance structures among female adolescents (e.g., Benenson, 1999, 2009; Hawley, 1999, 2003, 2007). Currently, there is ongoing research on indirect aggression tactics among women, such as gossip, derogation, manipulation, and social exclusion (Benenson et al., 2013; Fisher, 2013; Fisher & Cox, 2011; Hess & Hagen, 2006).

Because women's social networks are not hierarchical and do not usually involve overt aggression, they can be complex and difficult to understand, not only for researchers but also for the women who are attempting to navigate the social dynamics of their own networks. While women compete for status within their groups, the groups themselves can acquire status, too, and compete with other groups of women. Therefore, women not only have to deal with the social and competitive dynamics within their social networks, they have to deal with pressures from other groups.

Success in maintaining connections in one's social network, cooperating with others, and keeping competitors in check is vital for access to the various resources women need for their own reproductive success. Another layer of complexity is that women's own childhood experiences influence their ability to navigate their social networks, and their success or failure will also affect the lives and reproductive choices of their children. Therefore, the stakes are incredibly high. Overall, women's social networks, while serving both supportive and competitive functions, profoundly influence the reproductive future of women and especially the survival and reproductive strategies of their children.

Legacy of Feminist Evolutionists in Primatology

Research in the evolutionary sciences prior to the 1980s was dominated by men who considered the sexual stereotypes of male dominance and aggression and female passivity and lack of concern about status to be true (Hrdy, 1981/1999). By the late 1970s and early 1980s, primatologists, informed by feminist perspectives, began examining nonhuman primate female reproductive behavior, including female aggression and dominance structures. These scientists incorporated the theories and methodologies of sociobiology, evolutionary biology, and behavioral ecology while paying particularly

close attention to female reproductive behavior. Primatologists such as Sarah Blaffer Hrdy (1977, 1981/1999), Linda Fedigan (1982), Jane Lancaster (1985, 1991), and Barbara Smuts (1987, 1992) challenged prevailing assumptions that females passively pursued their own reproductive interests and that males were innately aggressive and the only sex that competed for dominance and status (Barash, 1982; Wilson, 1978). Feminist evolutionists' observations of nonhuman primate females provided the foundations for current research on girls and women's aggressive, competitive, and status-seeking behaviors.

Primatologists include various types of behavior in their definition of aggression. It is intentional behavior that may cause physical injury to another individual, and it is also nonphysical or self-assertive behaviors, such as displays, supplantations, harassment, and territorial vocalizations (Fedigan, 1982). These types of behavior may not cause physical harm, but they may cause an individual to withdraw from a territory and from the resources necessary for survival, rank, or reproductive success. Smuts (1987) found no consistent sex differences between primate males and females in the frequency of supplantations, threats, chases, and fights. In a more recent study, Strier (2011) cites several instances among different primate groups in which high-ranking females have forced lower-ranked females out of their territories when there was scarcity of food. These lower-ranked females were then forced to find lesser-quality food sources on the periphery of their territory, making them vulnerable to attack by outsiders. Also, in their analysis of female chimpanzee behavior, Pusey and Schroepfer-Walker (2013) found that resident females aggressively would force immigrant females out of their territories to maintain their access to high-quality food sources. Overall, just because primate females do not always exhibit physical aggression often does not mean that they are passive and noncompetitive.

There are a variety of contexts in which nonhuman primate females use various aggressive behaviors, all of which relate to individual survival and reproductive success. Linda Fedigan (1982) observed female aggressive behavior among macaques during their daily interactions between dominant and subordinate individuals over higher rank. This behavior was observed also by Smuts (1987) among wild female baboons who used ritualized threats, face lacerations, and mounting of potential allies, all of which had been considered male dominance behavior. To protect their infants, female macaques, lemurs, and baboons have attacked males and higher-ranking females (Fedigan, 1982; Hrdy, 1981/1999; Smuts, 1987). In addition, female macaques, lemurs, baboons, and chimpanzees have used aggression to secure scarce resources, such as food, water, territory, or mates (Fedigan, 1982; Hrdy, 1981/1999; Pusey & Schroepfer-Walker, 2013; Smuts, 1987). Both Fedigan (1982) and Smuts (1987) observed female aggression during encounters with unfamiliar animals or predators. Finally, various researchers have observed high-ranking chimpanzee females committing infanticide against the infants of low-ranking females (Hrdy, 1981/1999; Pusey et al., 2008; Pusey & Schoepfer-Walker, 2013; Pusey, Williams, & Goodall, 1997). Not only do these various nonhuman female primates use both physical and indirect aggression to enhance their long-term reproductive success, they also use these tactics to obtain and maintain their dominance within their social networks.

Dominance and status are necessary for reproductive success, which is definitely evident among nonhuman female primates. Prior to the work done by feminist evolutionists and primatologists, researchers interested in dominance and rank only observed male behavior because it was more physical and overt (Fedigan, 1982). As a result, evolutionists of the 1960s and 1970s defined dominance only as a relationship among individuals (males) in which one demonstrates the ability to achieve goals against the striving of others through conflict, self-assertions, or physical aggression (Fedigan, 1982). In addition, female dominance structures were not researched because researchers assumed that competitiveness, status seeking, and ambition were not compatible with being a good mother (Hrdy, 1999).

Dominance can be defined as the preferential access to valuable resources, such as food, water, territory, or mates (Barkow, 1975), and it can also refer to the ability of an individual to take resources away from another individual (Lee & Johnson, 1992). It is important to note that dominant individuals do not always exhibit physical aggression; they can use indirect methods, such as self-assertions or threats. Individual dominance or subordinance is determined by rank, which is defined in terms of basic rank and dependent rank. *Basic rank* is a dominance relationship that occurs when an identified individual is alone with no allies present, whereas *dependent rank* is a dominance relationship that occurs when an individual has a dominant relative or ally present (de Waal & Harcourt, 1992). Among primates, including humans, an individual's rank is

contextual, as well as changeable. In one situation, an individual may achieve her goals rather easily, but among another group or in another context, it may be more difficult because of the presence of higher-ranked individuals. Nonhuman female primates who face increased competition over resources use physical and nonphysical aggression to gain and maintain their dominance rank. This leads to a better quality of life in terms of greater access to resources, more offspring, and less harassment and injury from others. According to Hrdy, competition among nonhuman primate females is:

> The central organizing principle of primate social life. . . .. Whereas males compete for transitory status and transient access to females, it is females who tend to play for more enduring stakes. For many species, female rank is long-lived and can be translated into longstanding benefits for descendants of both sexes. Females should be, if anything, *more* competitive than males, not less, although the manner in which females compete may be less direct, less boisterous, and hence more difficult to measure. (1981/1999, pp. 128–129)

This research by feminist evolutionists is foundational to our understanding of human female aggression and status seeking in the context of their social networks and has influenced many researchers' work on human female behavior for past two decades. These behaviors are shared with our closest relatives and have been maintained despite changes in species over time. Not only do these behaviors have adaptive significance for nonhuman female primates, it is clear that they also have adaptive significance for girls and women, too.

The Influence of Social Networks

The feminist evolutionists' research on nonhuman female primates shows that social bonds and coalitions are key to their longevity and reproductive success (Hrdy, 1981/1999), and their work prompted other researchers to look at human female social structures more closely. According to de Waal and Harcourt (1992), a coalition involves three or more individuals who cooperate and assist each other within an aggressive or competitive context. There are several contexts in which female coalitions are formed:

- Repulsing males that have entered the group (Smuts, 1992)
- Protecting another adult female from an attack by a male (Smuts, 1987)

- Protecting infants (Hrdy, 1981/1999; Smuts, 1985, 1987)
- Harassing and attacking lower-ranked females and their offspring (Hrdy, 1981/1999; Pusey et al., 2008)
- Excluding other females from their groups to reduce competition for food (Benenson, Hodgson, Heath, & Welch, 2008).

Within these social groupings, individuals can gain greater fitness by facilitating greater rank, and alliances can be key to achieving dominance status (Moscovice, 2013). In their recent study, Silk et al. (2010) report that female savanna baboons form strong equitable bonds and long-lasting relationships with female kin and with those close in age. The quality of these bonds influences their ability to cope with the stress from their environment, and, in many cases, nonhuman primate females depend on their allies to maintain their rank above lower-ranked females (Chapais, 1992). If female baboons form long-lasting and stable social bonds, it also enhances their longevity and lowers cortisol levels (Moscovice, 2013), leading to greater reproductive success. If nonhuman female primates do not have the support of their coalitions, they are at risk of ongoing harassment that can cause such stress that, over time, will reduce their fertility or cause spontaneous abortions (Hrdy, 1981/1999). In addition, Engh et al. (2006) found that when a female's social bonds were disrupted by the death of a close ally, the affected female's cortisol levels increased in the month following her ally's death. Not only do strong bonds improve survival and reproductive success of the mothers, Silk et al. (2010) found that the offspring of female baboons lived significantly longer than those who formed weak bonds.

In examining women and girls' social networks or friendships, it is clear that they involve behavioral, psychological, and physiological components. They are not only defined by particular behaviors, but they involve underlying feelings, motivations, and, in turn, physiological responses. According to Hruschka (2010), a girl's behavior influences her friends' feelings, thoughts, and physiological responses, and vice versa. Friends are motivated to be kind and benevolent to each other. They want to improve a friend's welfare and avoid doing things that may be hurtful. In addition, friends want to spend time together; they feel secure, relaxed, and happy when they are in each other's company. Friends expect reciprocity in gift giving and in how they are treated. Among girls and women, friends

do not want to compete for another's attention, and they do not want to be excluded.

There are many benefits that women perceive from their friendships. They enjoy the companionship and emotional support they receive. When they are looking for men, they can receive advice about dating and have friends accompany them on mate-seeking excursions (Bleske-Rechek & Lighthall, 2010). In addition, female friends can also provide low-cost assistance with child care (Benenson, 2013). Finally, groups of female friends provide protection of each other's reputations and can deter harmful gossip or actions by competitors (Hess, 2006). Overall, there are many supportive behaviors that friends exhibit, and those who have fewer social connections receive fewer opportunities and resources throughout their lives (Christakes & Fowler, 2009; Putnam, 2000).

At the same time, there are several psychological and social traits that people find attractive in good friends. They have a reputation for being helpful and share an individual's personal attitudes and values. Friends usually are from similar social classes and ethnicities, and people want friends whom they perceive to have high status (Hruschka, 2010). In their study about women's friendships, attractiveness, and rivalry, Bleske-Rechek and Lighthall (2010) found that friends are similar in their levels of attractiveness. Finally, people like to form friendships with those who like them as well (Hruschka, 2010).

Just as social bonds have adaptive benefits to nonhuman primate females, they also provide physiological benefits to girls and women. According to Moscovice (2013), several longitudinal, cross-cultural studies indicate that people who maintain strong social bonds have greater longevity and a reduced risk of physical and mental health problems (see also Putnam, 2000). These social relationships may improve an individual's health by providing the physical resources, emotional support, and information that help her cope better with stressful situations. Those who lack these relationships have increased neuroendocrine responses to acute and chronic stressors, such as illness, life events, and life transitions (Holt-Lunstad, Smith, & Layton, 2010). Women who maintain a larger and more diverse range of social networks are more active in giving and receiving support and have better overall health outcomes (Moscovice, 2013). According to Holt-Lunstad et al.'s (2010) meta-analysis on social relationships and mortality risk, "individuals with adequate social relationships have a 50% greater likelihood of survival compared to those with poor or insufficient social relationships" (p. 14). In other words, social relationships impact individual health outcomes among adults.

Although there are many benefits to girls and women's friendships and social networks, there also can be some costs. Not only can friends be supporters, they can also be competitors for time, energy, and men. To communicate one's friendship, there are demanding behaviors of exclusivity, such as hanging out or spending time together, sharing meals, gift giving, and, in the 21st century, talking on the cell phone, writing texts, and sending emails (Hruschka, 2010). Indeed, girls and women can become very protective of their friends and try to guard them from being "poached" by a rival (Hess, 2006). In addition to demands of time, there are expectations of trust and allowing oneself to be vulnerable by sharing information that can affect one's reputation, identity, and social status (Hess, 2006). Finally, another possible cost to friendship is readiness to help and share, which can take time and material resources (Hruschka, 2010). When the costs of these friendships increase, and as various resources become scarcer, it can lead to increased competition and aggression between and among friends within a specific social network.

Not only do female social networks provide support, they can also be used to control or eliminate rivals. Like our nonhuman female primate relatives, girls and women can leverage their friendships and social networks to promote themselves or to exclude a competitor for resources, status, or men (Arnocky & Vaillancourt, 2012). As Fisher (2013) points out, there is definitely a dichotomy that exists in women's relationships with each other—they are coalition builders and cooperators, but can also be fierce competitors in terms of pursuing their reproductive interests. As the next section discusses, girls and women do not hesitate to use a variety of aggressive tactics to compete for those resources that promote their reproductive success.

Intrasexual Competition: Aggression and Status Seeking in Girls and Women

Much of the competition and aggression that occurs between and among girls and women is related to boys and men. Consequently, girls and women seek status and resources that will enhance their reproductive success. This intrasexual competition can become intense when there are fewer males available, especially men who are willing to provide resources such as food, space, and parental care (Fisher, 2013; Rosvall, 2011). The strategies girls and women use range from subtle (e.g., the use of cosmetics) to aggressive physical fighting. When women decide to use aggressive tactics, it is usually when they have their friends or allies with them (Fisher, 2013). In the competition for men, resources, and status, like our nonhuman female primate relatives, girls and women rely on their social networks to achieve their goals and enhance their reproductive success (Benenson, 2013).

Feminist evolutionists' research of nonhuman female primate behavior (Hrdy, 1981/1999; Smuts, 1987) has helped other researchers learn to observe the more subtle examples of human female aggression, as well as to ask why some girls and women intentionally use aggression and why they can be so competitive. Human female aggression is reported in all regions of the world, with women displaying a wide range of aggressive behaviors ranging from insulting, excluding, or silently snubbing a person, to physically fighting, destroying property, and killing (Björkqvist et al., 1992; Burbank, 1987; Campbell, 2002; Hess & Hagen, 2006; Österman et al., 1998).

In response to their anger and frustration, women and girls use both direct and indirect tactics. Direct aggression includes physical assaults, threats, and verbal insults, whereas indirect aggression includes exclusion, gossip, and social manipulation. Indirect aggression enables the aggressor to avoid direct physical contact with her competitor while causing great damage to her victim, ranging from anxiety and depression to illness. In a study by White, Gallup, and Gallup (2010), the top tactics used by adolescent girls against other girls were teasing and exclusion. In addition, Campbell (2004) found that female physical aggression occurs more often among lower socioeconomic classes, presumably because the competition for resources is more intense. While scholars have been researching aggression in females, the popular literature has many accounts of American adolescent girls and the damage they can do by using relational aggression (Simmons, 2002; Tanenbaum, 2002; Valen, 2010; Wiseman, 2009). For example, Simmons (2002) describes relational aggression among girls as "ignoring someone to punish them or get one's own way,... using negative body language or facial expressions, sabotaging someone else's relationships, or threatening to end a relationship unless a friend agrees to a request" (p. 21). Overall, girls and women are aggressive and tend to use direct verbal and indirect aggression more often than direct physical aggression.

As nonhuman female primates use various aggressive techniques and seek dominance within their social groups, women also use aggression to get the resources and status they need for their own reproductive success and that of their children. Among human groups, status refers to the standing an individual has within face-to-face group, not just high levels of socioeconomic success (Anderson, John, Keltner, & Krieg, 2001) (although when social networks compete with each other, this measure is relevant). Thus, higher status results in prominence (i.e., being visible and known), respect (i.e., peers holding an individual in high regard), and influence over the group (i.e., controlling decisions within the group; Anderson et al., 2001). Another term for dominance in the research on children and adolescence is the term "popular," which refers to higher-ranked children who are more visible and well known (Adler & Adler, 1998).

Based on feminist evolutionists' work on female primates, there has been a great deal of research on status and dominance structures among girls, which contributes to our understanding of how and why women seek status. For example, Hawley (1999) examined the adaptiveness of social dominance, which she defines as the "differential ability to control resources" (p. 97). The resources humans want to control are resources related to growth, survival, and cognitive and behavioral development. Hawley's (2007) resource control theory focuses on the function of behavior as individuals attempt to control scarce material, social, and informational resources. Although children are not directly competing for food, water, and territory, they are competing with other children for cognitive stimulation from toys, interaction with others, and new exciting situations (Hawley, 1999). Individuals also compete for social resources, including alliances, mates, and models for social learning (friends whom they like, admire, and respect). Finally, the information humans compete for include material and social resources that contribute to reproductive success. Whereas children and adolescents want to know what is going on with their peers and what is considered "cool" in terms of material goods and behaviors, women need informational resources to secure jobs and to help find mates.

There are different strategies for securing the various resources that children and adults use over the course of their life-times. Some individuals use prosocial strategies, such as cooperation, assistance, and persuasion. These tend to be individuals with good social skills who are agreeable and conscientious and

who are well-liked by their peers. In contrast, there are others who rely primarily on coercive strategies, such as aggression, threats, and insults. These individuals are not well liked and are not considered popular by their peers, who usually try to avoid them (Hawley, 2003). Finally, there are individuals who use both prosocial and coercive strategies, and Hawley (1999, 2003, 2007) calls them "bi-strategic controllers." They use aggression to maintain popularity in the eyes of their peers and manage competitors within their groups. There have been several studies analyzing Western school-aged girls who are bi-strategic controllers and who use both overt and relational aggression strategically to achieve or maintain their popularity (Benenson, Sinclair, & Dolenszky, 2006; Cillessen & Mayeux, 2004; Cillessen & Rose, 2005). According to Sitsema et al. (2010) in their longitudinal social network analysis on friendship selection, adolescent individuals who used relational aggression had a perceived sense of humor, leadership, and popularity in terms of reputational status. This behavior helped these individuals select similar friends and maintain those relationships. In another study, Sijtsema, Veenstra, Lindenberg, and Salmivalli (2009) used dyadic network analysis and found that adolescent female bullies sought prestige and popularity when they targeted their victims. As Hawley, Little, and Card (2008) found, these girls had many friends, attracted social attention, and had peers who wanted to be like them because they were socially prominent and had access to the resources important to them—status, information, and boys.

During the past decade, there have been many studies conducted on aggressive tactics, competition, and status seeking among women. According to Fisher (2013), several types of intrasexual competition occur among women and these are dependent on the type of relationship they are seeking. If women are pursuing short-term relationships with men, they tend to advertise their physicality, sexuality, and lack of commitment. If they are pursuing long-term relationships, women will demonstrate their parenting abilities, as well as their fidelity, and they may emphasize their competitors' promiscuity. Finally, women will compete to keep their men, claiming that their competitors are cruel or have a poor reputation.

Women use various strategies in their competition for men, some of which begin during childhood and adolescence. Self-promotion is a very common strategy that women use to enhance their positive qualities. They will use tactics that enhance their appearance, their body, or their athleticism. These are very effective strategies because they can be used against any number of rivals and no one in particular (Fisher & Cox, 2011). Another common tactic women use is competitor derogation, which decreases a rival's attractiveness to men. This tactic targets a specific competitor and tends to be used more by women who are already in a romantic relationship than by those who are not. However, women who derogate may find this to be a risky tactic because they may be regarded as less friendly, unkind, and untrustworthy by men (Fisher, 2013; Fisher & Cox, 2011; Fisher, Shaw, Worth, Smith, & Reeve, 2010) and because they may be harshly judged by other women (Fisher et al., 2010). Less common and definitely more subtle tactics include either mate manipulation by sequestering or displacing attention from a potential rival or manipulation of the competitor by attempting to convince the rival that the potential mate is not worth the competition (Fisher, 2013; Fisher & Cox, 2011). Finally, Benenson et al. (2013) argue that social exclusion is a common and very effective strategy used against vulnerable females that can enhance the dominant female's access to resources, such as food, territory, assistance, and sexual partners.

The tactics women use in their competition for men can become more effective and damaging with the help of their friends. Female social networks definitely can wield power and cause damage within and outside their groups. These coalitions can eliminate potential competitors for physical resources, mates, and status within their social networks (Benenson, 2013). Girls and women may use indirect or relational aggression against friends with whom they have shared personal information (Benenson et al., 2006) in order to maintain status quo within the group or to maintain or strengthen their social bonds (Fisher, 2013; Hess, 2006; Hruschka, 2010).

One way in which girls and women use their social networks to control rivals is through gossip. They can suppress the sexuality of other girls by using derogatory gossip, thus punishing them for seeming to make sex too readily available to the males (Sutton & Oaten, 2014; Vaillancourt, 2013). One's reputation may provide or prevent access to various social and material resources. For example, a damaged reputation could lead to the loss of one's social group, which can impact access to males. The loss of a well-connected social group could impact job and career prospects as well. Hess (2006) argues that women can use "informational warfare" against

rivals' reputation with the help of their own social networks much more effectively than as individuals (see also McAndrew, 2014). These social networks are better at collecting accurate information about competitors, as well as for providing a more thorough analysis. Multiple individuals can provide additional details, as well as offer various interpretations of the gossip. Discussions among these social networks can provide a better cost-benefit analysis about the best way to disseminate the information. Finally, these coalitions of friends can do a much more effective job of spreading gossip than a single individual. Information that is repeated by multiple individuals will appear to be more believable (Hess & Hagen, 2006). Overall, women's social networks play a key role in their competition for status and reproductive success.

At the same time, gossip serves several functions for female social networks. It can maintain group unity as well as the morals and values of the group. Although it can provide a means for social bonding, gossip can also be a source of cultural and norm learning and enforcement (Hess & Hagen, 2006). When one fails to conform to the group's norms or begins to compete directly for resources, girls and women may socially exclude and isolate that individual (Benenson, 2009). As a group, they can spread gossip and rumors in order to secure the group's social position, thus enhancing its power, credibility, and status (Hess, 2006; Hess & Hagen, 2006).

The costs for those girls and women on the receiving end of aggression and competition can be social, psychological, and even physical damage. Children and adolescents who are victimized find themselves marginalized from their peer groups (Martin, 2009), and this isolation can have negative effects on their health, social learning, and academic performance. The popular literature provides numerous accounts of how girls suffer at the hands of their peers as they are shunned, struggle at school, and, in some cases, deal with depression and eating disorders (Simmons, 2002; Wiseman, 2009).

Not only can female-female aggression and competition affect individuals, but powerful female social networks can also impact on and harm girls and women in other social networks. In research conducted by Linda Mealey (1999, 2000, 2003), she argues that the increased levels of anorexia in modern Western countries are a direct consequence of intrasexual competition among women. According to Vaillancourt (2013), there is cross-cultural evidence that a thin body shape is perceived as attractive, particularly among women in high socioeconomic regions of the world. Mealey (2000) suggests that the self-imposed starvation is subordinate behavior in response to the manipulation by more socially dominant women and their access to media and social trends. In the 1990s, women's fashion magazines started the trend of portraying extremely thin models, and, in terms of assessing what is physically attractive, women are influenced by other women's opinions more than by men's opinions (Mealey, 2000). According to Mealey (2003), anorexia develops almost exclusively in girls and young women in the richest, most developed countries' middle and upper classes. The symptoms include a psychological focus on the body image, an increase in exercise, avoidance of food, weight loss, menstrual irregularity, and hormonal imbalances. From an evolutionary perspective, anorexia has a significant impact on a girl's or young woman's reproductive capacity. The changes in hormonal and physical profile in anorexic women lead to the reduction in sex drive, sexual attractiveness, and sexual activity. At the same time, the reduction in body fat affects anorexic women's overall fertility in terms of ovulation and the ability to become pregnant, maintain a pregnancy, and lactate (Mealey, 2003).

In some cases, anorexia may be considered adaptive. If a woman is under social and psychological stress, she may not be suited for pregnancy and childrearing at that time. However, with greater access to birth control and health care in Western societies, the increase in anorexia is puzzling. As a type of intrasexual competition, Mealey (2000) maintains that dominant women's goal is to reduce competitors' attractiveness while maintaining their own social and economic success and status. Not only is there evidence of reproductive suppression in other nonhuman female primates (Hrdy, 1981/1999), but anorexia is "adaptive for those who are actually triggering the suppression. In [her] model, dominant women co-opt the existing capacity to adaptively self-suppress by triggering the mechanism in their reproductive competitors" (Mealey, 2003, p. 8).

It is clear that girls and women use a variety of aggressive tactics to gain status, and these tactics can be considered aspects of their reproductive strategies that lead to the resources and status necessary for reproductive success (Benenson, 2013). For many women, their reproductive success depends on their reputation and status as good long-term mates and on their ability to attract males who will invest in resources over a long period of time to help raise

their children. Like nonhuman primate females, girls and women form their own social networks as part of the competition for men, resources, and status (Liesen, 2013). Not only do these social networks provide support and resources for girls and women, but they also can enable them to be more aggressive if they choose. Strong social networks not only empower women, they also can influence the futures of their children.

The Influence of Women's Social Networks on Reproductive Strategies

The strength or weakness of women's social networks is rooted in their childhood experiences, family structures, and environments, and these can have a profound effect on their abilities to compete with other women as well as impact on their reproductive strategies. Life history theory is very helpful in understanding the development of individual reproductive strategies. It is a branch of modern evolutionary biology that analyzes patterns of growth, development, and reproduction. Specifically, it examines how individuals allocate their limited resources, such as time and energy, during their lifetimes to maximize their reproductive success (Del Giudice, Angelieri, & Manera, 2009; Kaplan & Gangestad, 2005). Although the reproductive choices individuals make are not conscious, natural selection has shaped human psychology and physiology to be responsive to environmental cues so that an individual can maximize his or her fitness (Kaplan & Gangestad, 2005). According to Gowaty (2013), sex-differentiated behavior is individually flexible, influenced by and responsive to both nature and nurture. These developmentally plastic sex roles consist of adaptively flexible behavior and physiology, serving the fitness interests of individuals in their current environments. Researchers using life history theory use the terms "life history strategies" and "reproductive strategies" interchangeably. Both refer to adaptive solutions to simultaneous fitness tradeoffs, such as somatic effort versus reproductive effort, mating versus parenting, current reproduction versus future reproduction, and quality of offspring versus quantity of offspring (Del Giudice et al., 2009). Over evolutionary time, natural selection has favored those strategies that result in greater fitness or reproductive success. The best strategy for a particular individual depends on the ecology, availability of resources, mortality risk, and environmental uncertainty.

Reproductive strategies refer to sexual/mating behavior, pair-bonding, and parenting styles.

Humans have a variety of long-term reproductive strategies that include monogamy (exclusive pair-bonds that can last a lifetime), serial monogamy (series of exclusive pair-bonds over a lifetime), polygyny (a single male who has multiple wives), and polyandry (a single female who has multiple husbands, which is extremely rare) (Schmitt, 2005). Humans can also opt for short-term mating opportunities. They can have brief, nonexclusive encounters with multiple partners, such as premarital and extramarital relationships and mate poaching. These types of relationships are also found across cultures (Schmitt, 2005).

At the same time, reproductive strategies can also be fast or slow depending on the environment. Faster reproductive strategies are adaptive in those environments that are dangerous or have limited resources, or where there is also greater predation, risk of injury, disease, or starvation. Thus, it is more beneficial for an individual to pursue immediate or early reproduction since her lifespan may be limited. In contrast, slower reproductive strategies involve long-term planning, less risk taking, less aggression, and delayed gratification. Individuals choosing this strategy delay sexual activity, and, when they do reproduce, they invest more parental resources in fewer children (Simpson, Griskevicius, I-Chun Kua, Sung, & Collins, 2012). Overall, an evolutionary perspective contends that both supportive and stressful environments have long been a part of human history and that human developmental systems have been shaped by natural selection to respond adaptively to both environmental contexts (Ellis et al., 2012).

Women's lives—their relationships, environments, access to resources, and social networks—have a significant impact on their children's development, health, and future reproductive strategies. They need to be both cooperative as well as competitive because their reproductive success and that of their children depend on utilizing both strategies. The influences on individuals' reproductive strategies begin in utero with the physical and environmental impacts or stressors experienced by mothers. The research done by feminist evolutionists found that, among nonhuman primates, if a mother experiences extreme stress and harassment, it can lead to spontaneous abortion of her offspring (Hrdy, 1981/1999). Even among humans, maternal stress can influence the fetus, altering the cognitive, endocrine, and neurochemical responses later in life (Cameron & Garcia, 2013). Among mammals in general, maternal nutrition during pregnancy and lactation has a direct impact on the physiology of the offspring. In humans, undernourished mothers have babies with low birth weights, which in turn influences the baby's short-term health, as well as increasing its risk of cardiovascular disease and diabetes when he or she is an adult (Cameron & Garcia, 2013).

Once a child is born, the quality of maternal care, levels of stress in the household, and access to resources all can affect the development of a child's reproductive strategy. Jay Belsky (2012) and other developmental psychologists (Del Giudice, 2009; Del Giudice et al., 2009; Ellis, Figuerdo, Blumbach, & Schlomer, 2009) using evolutionary theory have proposed the *psychosocial acceleration theory*, which links childhood experiences, interpersonal orientation, and reproductive strategies. They have found that stressful or supportive extrafamilial environments influence family dynamics, particularly parent–child and marital relationships. These relationships in turn shape and regulate children's early emotional and behavioral development, including their attachment security and later the endocrine processes that affect their own sexual/mating behavior, pair-bonding, and future parenting styles (Belsky, 2012).

The quality of maternal care can have an impact on girls' timing of sexual maturity. In a study by Belsky, Steinberg, Houts, and Halpern-Felsher (2010), they examined maternal harshness and its impact on girls' age of menarche. They examined maternal harshness when a group of children were 4.5 years old. Mothers were considered harsh when they spanked their children, expected them to be quiet and respectful in the presence of adults, expected children to obey and not ask questions, regarded respect for authority as the most important lesson for a child to learn, believed praise spoils a child, and did not give their child lots of hugs and kisses. Daughters of harsh mothers had earlier ages of menarche, which resulted in early sexual experiences and more sexual risk taking. This developmental system evolved as a means of preparing individuals for their anticipated social and physical environments in order to enhance their reproductive fitness (Belsky, 2012). In other words, these children developed a faster reproductive strategy that enabled them to have the best chance of successfully reproducing in stressful and harsh environment that may shorten their future opportunities to reproduce.

At the same time, the availability of material and social resources for the family affects children's future reproductive strategies. A stressful childhood environment can be either harsh and/or unpredictable (Ellis et al., 2009). In this context, harshness refers to age-specific rates of morbidity and mortality in a local environment. In Western societies, harshness could be measured in terms of socioeconomic status, whereas unpredictability refers to fluctuations in the harshness in the environment. It can include job changes, moving, and divorce/remarriage of parents (Simpson et al., 2012). Ellis et al. (2009) found that the number of parental transitions is definitely an important predictor of whether a child develops a fast reproductive strategy. In addition, the availability of basic material resources (food, shelter, etc.) is also an environmental factor that influences the development of reproductive strategies (Griskevicius, Delton, Roberton, & Tybur, 2010). According to Dishion, Ha, and Veronneau (2012), the low socioeconomic status of a child's family can be a predictor of peer rejection, isolation, and exclusion, negatively influencing the child's social, emotional, and reproductive development.

If harshness and unpredictability are consistently present in a child's life, they also affect the security of her attachments, which then influence future relationships and reproductive behavior. Attachment relationships have an adaptive function in terms of both survival and reproduction. They act as a "summary" of the safeness of a child's local ecology (Belsky, Schlomer, & Ellis, 2012; Del Giudice et al., 2009). Parent–child relationships can be either conflictual or supportive, and the nature of this relationship impacts on whether a child has a secure attachment with his or her parents. This relationship then influences a child's general outlook on the world (trustful vs. mistrustful), his or her orientation toward others (exploitative/opportunistic vs. cooperative), and his or her behavior in general (Belsky, 2012). According to Hrdy (2009), "a baby confident of a rapid response by a mother committed to his well-being is likely to become a child who will be quicker to soothe and adapt to new situations, and likely to grow up to feel confident about human relations in general" (p. 83).

In an attempt to link attachment theory to evolutionary theory, Del Giudice and Belsky (2010) argue that a safe and predictable physical and social environment will lead to later reproduction and increased parenting effort in raising fewer, high-quality children. They call this a "secure strategy." If a child were raised in a risky and unpredictable environment, the optimal reproductive strategy would

be increased mating effort at the expense of parenting effort for a greater number of children. They call this an "insecure strategy." These environments and resulting attachments influence the development of these children by the time they are 7 years old and have an impact on their reproductive choices as adults.

In terms of relationships with others outside of the family, insecure attachments lead to either anxiety or avoidance behaviors. Those who are anxious tend to be clingy and dependent, whereas those who exhibit avoidance tend to be self-reliant, detached, and dismissive. Children who develop anxiety within their insecure attachments exhibit passivity and victimization and tend to internalize their disorders. By the time they are adults, they have impulsive sexual attitudes. These women tend to engage in sexual activity at an early age and have an intense desire for intimate relationships. This "insecure strategy" for women can be a way to extract help and secure resources from family and men. On the other hand, boys with avoidance tend to be aggressive and have inflated self-esteem. As adult men, they exhibit low commitment in their romantic relationships and tend to be promiscuous. This "insecure strategy" for men leads to risk taking, early reproduction, and low parental investment (Del Giudice, 2009; Del Giudice & Belsky, 2010).

So, for example, if a child matures in an environment containing various stressors, such as resource insecurity, violence, marital discord, and insensitive/inconsistent parenting, he or she will develop insecure attachments, exploit relationships, and be mistrustful of the world. These experiences lead to endocrine and hormonal changes, so that child would experience earlier puberty and earlier sexual experiences. In a long-term study of more than 4,500 British women, Nettle et al. (2011) found that short duration of breastfeeding, separation from mothers, lack of paternal involvement, and frequent family moves lowered the age of these women's first pregnancies. Thus, these girls then pursued reproductive strategies that were short-term, focusing on mating and having many children rather than on intensive and attentive parenting styles. According to Cameron and Garcia (2013), "under high risk environmental conditions, when the probability of extended period of growth and survival are low, the optimal strategy is to shift efforts to maximize the number of offspring through accelerated mating, increasing the chances that at least some of the offspring will survive to reproductive maturity" (p. 141).

In contrast, those children whose families have stable financial resources, see spousal harmony, and experience a supportive childrearing environment will have secure attachments, a trustful orientation toward the world, and reciprocally beneficial interpersonal relationships. When a child's physical and social environment is safe and predictable, his or her puberty and sexual activity will be delayed, he or she will tend to pursue longer-lasting pair-bonds and will tend to provide greater parental investment in fewer children in the future (Belsky, 2012; Del Giudice & Belsky, 2010).

In addition to the influence of early attachment, researchers have also found that different periods of children's lives have impacts on their future reproductive strategies and related behaviors. Simpson et al. (2012) found that the first 5 years of a child's life may be a sensitive period for the development of reproductive strategies. Their findings showed that the strongest predictor of sexual and risky behavior by age 23 was the exposure to an unpredictable environment. The children they studied developed a faster reproductive strategy consisting of more sex partners, had sex at an earlier age (among males), engaged in more delinquent and aggressive behavior, and were more likely to be associated with criminal behavior.

At the same time, Del Giudice et al. (2009) found that the transition from early to middle childhood, also called juvenility, has a broad impact on children's later development and affects attachment, sexuality, and aggression. This period is one that involves physical changes that occur in response to the environment. The transition from childhood to juvenility requires a phenotypic switch provided by adrenarche, the prepubertal secretion of adrenal androgens that can start between 6 and 8 years of age. During this transition, children once again adjust their reproductive strategies to their local environments and genetic predispositions.

The period of juvenility is one of intense social learning and interaction with peers. It is a time when parental influence is reduced, and it becomes more adaptive in the transition to adulthood to spend more time with friends. A child's relationship with his or her peers is influenced by the attachments made with his or her parents. Girls with anxious or ambivalent attachments tend to be fearful, withdrawn, and passive around their peers, and this has lasting effects on their adult lives, as well as placing them at risk of being victimized by bullies (Del Giudice, 2009). Those with avoidant attachments tend to be more aggressive with their peers and can

engage in bullying behavior (Del Giudice, 2009). Overall, "during juvenility, vital social abilities (such as parenting, competition, coalition building, and sometimes sexuality) are first practiced, and can significantly affect the individual's social standing and future opportunities" (Del Giudice et al., 2009, p. 2).

The variations in attachment and environment result not only in differences in sexual maturity or fecundity, but also in a range of behaviors related to reproductive strategies. According to Del Giudice et al. (2009), these variations "will often involve a suite of reproduction-related *behavioral* traits such as risk taking, dominance-seeking, aggression, altruism/cooperation, and long-term attachments to mates" (p. 6). Sex differences in aggression begin to appear between 3 and 6 years of age. Whereas boys tend to be more physically aggressive by this age, girls exhibit more verbal and relational aggression (Del Giudice et al., 2009). Del Giudice and Belsky (2010) found that girls with anxious attachments exhibited more relational and indirect aggression. Those girls who demeaned, teased, and excluded others during their middle school years started dating earlier and had sex earlier than their victims (Gallup, O'Brien, & Wilson, 2011; White et al., 2010).

According to life history theory, the period of adolescence is another very sensitive period for change that influences a young person's sense of status, resource control, and mating success (Ellis et al., 2012). For both males and females, this is a time when there are higher levels of aggression, competition, and social dominance, reflecting the much higher stakes for sexual partners, status, and social alliances. If teens are in a harsh and unpredictable environment, death and disability increase dramatically along with depression, eating disorders, alcohol and substance abuse, suicide, and risky sexual behavior (Ellis et al., 2012). In response to this type of environment, teenage girls have shorter periods of adolescent subfertility; they have sex, pregnancies, and children earlier; they engage in more delinquent and aggressive behavior; and they attain lower educational levels and occupational status (Ellis et al., 2012). At the same time, if they are also victims of indirect and relational aggression, they may exhibit markers of low fitness, such as depression, anxiety, low self-esteem, peer rejection, somatic and cognitive problems, social dissatisfaction, and suicide (Arnocky & Vaillancourt, 2012).

In addition, studies have shown that children and adolescents tend to form social networks of peer groups that share similar attitudes, behavior, and circumstances, as well as reproductive strategies. In a study conducted by Dishion et al. (2012), the authors found support for their hypothesis that deviant peer clustering is the strongest predictor of early and sexually promiscuous activity among adolescence. As teenagers become more engaged with their deviant peer groups, they receive increased social status among their peers, engage in increased sexual activity, and produce more children. Overall, these peer groups reinforce and support a faster reproductive strategy that leads to early sexual activity and lower parental investment.

In sum, there are multiple points at which family environment, resources, and social networks—or lack thereof—impact on the development of an individual's reproductive strategy and future fitness. This creates an incredibly competitive and complex environment for girls and women as they choose various strategies to pursue the resources, status, and mates that they need for their own reproductive success. The journey begins with each individual's own mother's experiences, her environment, and how she is able to cope with possible harshness and unpredictability. If she can compete with other females and successfully establish a strong social network—family members, husband, and friends—who can provide material resources, emotional support, and assist in the care of her child, she will be able to raise a well-attached, secure, collaborative child. If a woman fails to compete successfully, she may negatively affect her own reproductive success, as well as the physical and psychological health of her children.

It is imperative to remember that behavior, especially in humans, is responsive to current environmental cues. Humans, as well as other species, have a behavioral flexibility that enables them to respond to current environmental variables and pressures in order to make the most adaptive reproductive decisions (West-Eberhard, 2003). Feminist evolutionist Patricia Adair Gowaty (2013) reminds us that sex-differentiated behavior is individually flexible and influenced by both biology and the environment. Individuals determine the fitness costs and benefits based on the available alternatives in current ecological time. As is evident from the various disciplines that study female behavior, aggression, and social networks, reproductive strategies are chosen in "real time," based on the ecological and social circumstances in which an individual finds herself.

Consequently, a mother's competition and cooperation with others cannot stop during her lifetime. The maintenance of social networks must be ongoing because a child is constantly assessing her environment from infancy through adolescence to determine the best type of reproductive strategy, one that will be based on her circumstances at any given time. The quality of the child's physical and social environment triggers developmental changes that can lead to either fast or slow reproductive strategies that enable her to compete with her peers in that specific environment. At the same time, the quality of the attachments children establish influence their ability to create strong social networks and avoid being victims of aggressive behavior and social exclusion. Therefore, women must strive, and at times aggressively and competitively, to create and maintain strong and supportive social networks not just for themselves, but also for the survival and reproductive success of their children.

Feminist evolutionists have provided evidence of the importance of social networks not only for non-human female primates, but also among hunter-gatherer societies. According to Hrdy (2005), shared care or cooperative breeding has been a part of our primate and hominid history, in which members of the group, in addition to the parents, have cared and provided resources for children. These cooperative efforts not only increased the lifespan of mothers, they kept children safe from predators and prevented their starvation. At the same time, women can be incredibly aggressive and competitive when it comes to attaining the status and resources that they deem necessary for their reproductive success. Not only will they turn to their social networks for support and various resources, they also can use direct and indirect aggression as well as their social networks to suppress competitors and rivals who could interfere with their individual reproductive strategies. Consequently, women find themselves trying to strike a balance between cooperating with other women while staving off competitors who may take the resources, support, and mates that they need for their own reproductive success and that of their children.

Conclusion and Future Research Questions

In the examination of female-female aggression and status seeking, women's social networks serve both supportive and competitive functions in women's pursuit of reproductive success (see also Fisher & Moule, 2013). Foundational to this understanding is the various works by feminist evolutionists in primatology (Fedigan, 1983; Hrdy, 1981/1999; Smuts, 1987) who uncovered the male bias that pervaded evolutionary thinking at the time and who took the pains to observe female nonhuman primate aggressive and dominance behaviors. Their work had great implications for and applications in the lives of girls and women (Gowaty, 1997; Hrdy, 1981/1999, 1999; Smuts, 1995) even though their research did not always directly measure girls' and women's aggressive and reproductive behaviors. Nonetheless, their research questions led to more quantitative analyses of human female aggression and status seeking from various disciplines, thus supporting their arguments regarding the competitive and cooperative reproductive lives of girls and women.

Additional research has used social network analysis of peer groups, both male and female (Sijtsema et al., 2009, 2010), to provide insights into the dynamics of how dominant individuals use aggression to pursue their goals. However, social network analyses studies specifically focusing on the social networks of girls and women would be especially helpful in understanding how girls and women seek and use their status as they competitively pursue their reproductive interests. As Liesen (2013) argues, women tend to organize themselves in webs or matrices of peer groups in which the higher-status female is the center of attention, and lower-status females are on the periphery. Like nonhuman primate females, dominant girls/women have central and very visible roles within their groups and are well known by those outside of their groups. In addition to survey analyses, observational analysis of these human female aggressive and status-seeking behaviors would provide additional insights into the competitive dynamics of human female social networks.

At the same time, groups of girls or women compete with each other as they pursue competing reproductive strategies. For example, girls or women who pursue fast, short-term pair-bonds with men will certainly clash with those who are pursuing slow, long-term relationships with men in order to have them invest their time, energy, and resources into raising children. These conflicts of interest can play out on junior high playgrounds (Hawley, 2003, 2007; Simmons, 2002; Wiseman, 2009) and in high schools and colleges (Anderson et al., 2001; Hess, 2006). Future research can certainly be done on differing reproductive strategies and competing reproductive interests among groups of women. When politics is defined as the management of conflicts of interests (i.e., interests such as resources, men, or status), women's struggles within their social networks, as well as against other women and their social networks, are very political. Whereas women who live in middle-class and upper-middle-class communities in developed countries have the resources, support, and social networks to assist them in rearing their children, women in impoverished communities struggle to rear their children. In 2011, 22% of all children in the United States lived in poverty, and 48% of these poor children lived in single-parent, female-headed households (FIFCFS, 2013). Several factors contribute to this phenomenon—lack of job opportunities for poor men and women, violent and abusive environments, lack of health care, and premature death. Not only do many of these women have these experiences, but, in too many cases, they may also lack the social networks and support that would enable them to avoid the same problems for their children. As discussed earlier, children who grow up in poverty, who also experience harsh and unpredictable environments, have been found to be more aggressive and prone to violence and abuse. At the same time, they tend to pursue faster reproductive strategies that consist of short-term mating opportunities, reduced parenting effort, and an increased number of children. In an environment of the continued cycle of weak social networks, these children may live lives similar to their parents.

Strong social networks are key to women and their children in overcoming some of these obstacles. As Hrdy (2009) maintains, we have definitely underestimated the importance of shared care and support of children by group members other than their parents and how this community effort shapes future prosocial behavior. Although scholars and policy makers tend to think that only mothers provide the best care for their children, Hrdy (2009) argues that there is no one universal pattern of infant care among primates in general and that it is part of our evolutionary history to rely on shared care. Therefore, mothers with strong social networks will be able to provide additional care and resources for their children and have a better chance of creating a stable and predictable environment for their children. Human mothers learn to care for their children from their own experiences with their parents and caregivers, but they also learn from others in their communities. Not only do these networks assist with immediate needs and care, they also may play a role in future reproductive strategies chosen by individuals, as well as in their ability to function productively and cooperatively in the community.

So, how do we strengthen weak social networks while manage competing interests within communities? Many of those who have lived in harsh and unpredictable environments have relied on faster reproductive strategies in order to have children before they possibly experience premature death. Yet, those who rely on slower reproductive strategies tend not to be sympathetic or understanding about their reproductive choices. Rarely is it discussed among policy makers that women and their children who face these problems are trying to make the best of very bad situations by being aggressive and having many children early in their lives. Their bodies already knew at very young ages that their future reproductive success depended on maturing and reproducing quickly because of the harshness and unpredictability of their environments.

In an effort to address the problems faced by the poor and disadvantaged, policy makers have tried to address the symptoms of teen pregnancy and violence by providing sexual education, birth control, and self-esteem-building programs (Ellis et al., 2012). However, they are not addressing the environmental conditions that may trigger aggression, violence, short-term relationships, and low investment in parenting. What these communities need is a strengthening of social networks. This can be accomplished in a variety of ways, such as by improving economic opportunities by challenging the private sector to take the risk of creating jobs in impoverished areas, by having state and local governments facilitate the building of networks through a variety of supportive community programs for children and parents, and, most importantly, by teaching people in general the vital importance of social networks and community building. As Robert Putnam demonstrates (2000) in his book *Bowling Alone: The Collapse and Recovery of American Community*, declines in social capital and weak social networks affect children's education, health, safety, and future economic success. Our social networks are intertwined; if one sector of society is struggling, suffering, and dying from violence or disease, it impacts all of us in terms of economic growth, safety, and civic unity. We need to decide as communities whether there we have the political will and if it is in all our reproductive interests to support more effectively those whose choices are limited by their harsh and unpredictable environments.

In conclusion, women's social networks serve both supportive and competitive functions, and this also profoundly influences their reproductive futures and the survival and reproductive strategies of their children. Based on feminist evolutionists' foundational research on primate female aggression and status seeking, we see that girls and women can aggressively pursue their own reproductive success both competitively and cooperatively. As discussed earlier, various researchers have expanded the understanding of girls' and women's various aggressive behavior, whereas others have examined how their social networks are used to eliminate competitors. Not only are the stakes high for women and mothers as they pursue the status, resources, and mates that they need for their own reproductive success, but their behavior and choices also continually affect the behavior and choices of their children's physical, social, and reproductive development.

References

Adler, P. A., & Adler, P. (1998). *Peer power: Preadolescent culture and identity.* New Brunswick, NJ: Rutgers University Press.

Anderson, C., John, O., Keltner, D., & Krieg, A. (2001). Who attains social status? Effects of personality and physical attractiveness in social groups. *Journal of Personality and Social Psychology, 81*(1), 116–132.

Arnocky, S., & Vaillancourt, T. (2012). A multi-informant longitudinal study on the relationship between aggression, peer victimization, and dating status in adolescence. *Evolutionary Psychology, 10*(2), 253–270.

Barash, D. (1982). *Sociobiology and behavior* (2nd ed.). New York, NY: Elsevier Science.

Barkow, J. (1975). Prestige and culture: A biosocial interpretation. *Current Anthropology, 16*, 553–752.

Belsky, J. (2012). The development of human reproductive strategies: Progress and prospects. *Current Directions in Psychological Science, 21*(5), 310–316.

Belsky, J., Schlomer, G. L., & Ellis, B. (2012). Beyond cumulative risk: Distinguishing harshness and unpredictability as determinants of parenting and early life history strategy. *Developmental Psychology, 48*(3), 662–673.

Belsky, J., Steinberg, L., Houts, R. M., & Halpern-Felsher, B. L. (2010). The development of reproductive strategy in females: Early maternal harshness → earlier menarche → increased sexual risk taking. *Developmental Psychology, 46*(1), 120–128.

Benenson, J. (1999). Females' desire for status cannot be measured using male definitions. *Behavioral and Brain Sciences, 22*, 216–217.

Benenson, J. (2009). Dominating versus eliminating the competition: Sex differences in human intrasexual aggression. *Behavioral and Brain Sciences, 32*(3), 268–269.

Benenson, J. (2013). The development of human female competition: Allies and adversaries. *Philosophical Transactions of the Royal Society B, 368*, 20130079.

Benenson, J., Hodgson, L., Heath, S., & Welch, P. (2008). Human sexual differences in the use of social ostracism as a competitive tactic. *International Journal of Primatology, 29*, 1019–1035.

Benenson, J. F., Markovits, H., Hultgren, B., Nguyen, T., Bullock, G., & Wrangham, R. (2013). Social exclusion: More important to human females than males. *PLOS One*, *8*(2), e55851.

Benenson, J., Sinclair, N., & Dolenszky, E. (2006). Children and adolescents' expectation of aggressive responses to provocation: Females predict more hostile reactions in compatible dyadic relationships. *Social Development*, *15*(11), 65–81.

Björkqvist, K., Österman, K., & Kaukiainen, A. (1992). The development of direct and indirect aggression in males and females. In K. Björkqvist & P. Niemela (Eds.), *Of mice and women: Aspects of female aggression* (pp. 51–66). San Diego CA: Academic Press.

Bleske-Rechek, A., & Lighthall, M. (2010). Attractiveness and rivalry in women's friendships with women. *Human Nature*, *21*, 82–97.

Burbank, V. (1987). Female aggression in cross-cultural perspective. *Behavioral Science Research*, *21*, 71–100.

Cameron, N. M., & Garcia, J. K. (2013). Maternal effect and offspring development. In M. L. Fisher, J. R. Garcia, & R. Sokol Chang (Eds.), *Evolution's empress: Darwinian perspectives on the nature of women* (pp. 133–150). New York: Oxford University Press.

Campbell, A. (1999). Staying alive: Evolution, culture, and women's intrasexual aggression. *Behavioral and Brain Sciences*, *22*, 203–252.

Campbell, A. (2002). *A mind of her own: The evolutionary psychology of women*. Oxford: Oxford University Press.

Campbell, A. (2004). Female competition: Causes, constraints, content, and contexts. *Journal of Sex Research*, *41*(1), 16–26.

Chapais, B. (1992). The role of alliances in social inheritance of rank among female primates. In A. H. Harcourt & F. B. de Waal (Eds.), *Coalitions and alliances in humans and other animals* (pp. 29–60). Oxford: Oxford University Press.

Christakes, N. A., & Fowler, J. H. (2009). *Connected: How your friends' friends' friends affect everything you feel, think, and do*. New York: Back Bay Books.

Cillessen, A. H. N., & Mayeux, L. (2004). From censure to reinforcement: Developmental change in the association between aggression and social status. *Child Development*, *75*(1), 147–163.

Cillessen, A. H. N., & Rose, A. J. (2005). Understanding popularity in the peer system. *Current Directions in Psychological Science*, *14*(2), 102–105.

Del Giudice, M. (2009). Sex, attachment, and the development of reproductive strategies. *Behavioral and Brain Sciences*, *32*, 1–67.

Del Giudice, M., Angelieri, R., & Manera, V. (2009). The juvenile transition: A developmental switch point in human life history. *Developmental Review*, *29*, 1–31.

Del Giudice, M., & Belsky, J. (2010). Sex differences in attachment emerge in middle childhood: An evolutionary hypothesis. *Child Development Perspectives*, *4*(2), 97–105.

de Waal, F. B., & Harcourt, A. H. (1992). Coalitions and alliances: A history of ethological research. In A. H. Harcourt & F. B. de Waal (Eds.), *Coalitions and alliances in humans and other animals* (pp. 1–22). Oxford: Oxford University Press.

Dishion, T. J., Ha, T., & Veronneau, M. H. (2012). An ecological analysis of the effects of deviant peer clustering on sexual promiscuity, problem behavior, and childbearing from early adolescence and adulthood: An enhancement of the life history framework. *Developmental Psychology*, *48*(3), 703–717.

Ellis, B., Del Giudice, M., Dishion, T., Figuerdo, A. J., Gray, P., Griskevicius, V., . . . Wilson, D. S. (2012). The evolutionary basis of risky adolescent behavior: Implications for science, policy, and practice. *Developmental Psychology*, *48*(3), 598–623.

Ellis, B., Figuerdo, A. J., Blumbach, B. H., & Schlomer, G. L. (2009). Fundamental dimensions of environmental risk: The impact of harsh versus unpredictable environments on the evolution and development of life history strategies. *Human Nature*, *20*, 204–268.

Engh, A. L., Beehner, J. C., Bergman, T. J., Whitten, P. L., Hoffmeier, R. R., Seyfarth, R. M., Cheney, D. L. (2006). Behavior and hormonal responses to predation in female chacma baboons (*Papio hamadryas ursinus*). *Proceedings of the Royal Society of London, Series B*, *273*(1587), 707–712.

Federal Interagency Forum on Child and Family Statistics (FIFCFS). (2013). *America's children: Key national indicators of well being, 2013*. Washington: US Government Printing Office.

Fedigan, L. (1982). *Primate paradigms: Sex roles and social bonds*. Montreal, Canada: Eden Press.

Fedigan, L. (1983). Dominance and reproductive success in primates. *Yearbook of Physical Anthropology*, *26*, 91–129.

Fisher, M. L. (2013). Women's intrasexual competition for mates. In M. L. Fisher, J. R. Garcia, & R. Sokol Chang (Eds.), *Evolution's empress: Darwinian perspectives on the nature of women* (pp. 19–42). New York: Oxford University Press.

Fisher, M. L., & Cox, A. (2011). Four strategies used during intrasexual competition for mates. *Personal Relationships*, *18*, 20–38.

Fisher, M. L., & Moule, K. R. (2013). A new direction for intrasexual competition research: Cooperative versus competitive motherhood. *Journal of Social, Evolutionary, and Cultural Psychology*, *7*(4), 318–325.

Fisher, M. L., Shaw, S., Worth, K., Smith, L., & Reeve, C. (2010). How we view those who derogate: Perceptions of female competitor derogators. *Journal of Social, Evolutionary, and Cultural Psychology*, *4*(4), 265–276.

Gallup, A. C., O'Brien, D. T., & Wilson, D. S. (2011). Intrasexual peer aggression and dating behavior during adolescence: An evolutionary perspective. *Aggressive Behavior*, *37*, 258–267.

Gowaty, P. A. (1997). Darwinian feminists and feminist evolutionists. In P. A. Gowaty (Ed.), *Feminism and evolutionary biology* (pp. 1–18). New York: Chapman Hall.

Gowaty, P. A. (2013). A sex-neutral theoretical framework for making strong inferences about the origins of sex roles. In M. L. Fisher, J. R. Garcia, & R. Sokol Chang (Eds.), *Evolution's empress: Darwinian perspectives on the nature of women* (pp. 85–112). New York: Oxford University Press.

Griskevicius, V., Delton, A. W., Robertson, T. E., & Tybur, J. M. (2010). Environmental contingency in life history strategies: The influence of mortality and socioeconomic status on reproductive timing. *Journal of Personality and Social Psychology*, *100*(2), 241–254.

Hawley, P. (1999). The ontogenesis of social dominance: A strategy-based evolutionary perspective. *Developmental Review*, *19*, 97–132.

Hawley, P. (2003). Prosocial and coercive configuration of resource control in early adolescence: A case for the well adapted Machiavellian. *Merrill-Palmer Quarterly*, *49*(3), 279–309.

Hawley, P. (2007). Social dominance in childhood and adolescence: Why social competence and aggression may go hand in hand. In P. H. Hawley, T. D. Little, & P. C. Rodkin (Eds.), *Aggression and adaptation: The bright side to bad behavior* (pp. 1–30). Mahwah, NJ: Erlbaum.

Hawley, P., Little, T. D., & Card, N. (2008). The myth of the alpha male: A new look at dominance-related beliefs and behaviors among adolescent males and females. *International Journal of Behavioral Development*, *32*(1), 76–88.

Hess, N. H. (2006). *Informational warfare: Female friendship and coalitional manipulation of reputation* (Unpublished doctoral dissertation). University of California, Santa Barbara.

Hess, N. H., & Hagen, E. H. (2006). Psychological adaptations for assessing gossip veracity. *Human Nature*, *17*(3), 337–354.

Holt-Lunstad, J., Smith, T. B., & Layton, J. B. (2010). Social relationships and mortality risk: A meta-analytic review. *PLoS Medicine*, *7*(7), 1–20.

Hrdy, S. B. (1977). *Langurs of Abu: Female and male strategies of reproduction*. Cambridge, MA: Harvard University Press.

Hrdy, S. B. (1981/1999). *The woman that never evolved*. Cambridge, MA: Harvard University Press.

Hrdy, S. B. (1999). *Mother nature: A history of mothers, infants, and natural selection*. New York: Pantheon Books.

Hrdy, S. B. (2009). *Mothers and others: The evolutionary origins of mutual understanding*. Cambridge, MA: Belknap Press.

Hruschka, D. J. (2010). *Friendship: Development, ecology, and evolution of a relationship*. Berkeley, CA: University of California Press.

Kaplan, H. S., & Gangestad, S. W. (2005). Life history theory and evolutionary psychology. In D. M. Buss (Ed.), *The handbook of evolutionary psychology* (pp. 68–95). Hoboken, NJ: Wiley.

Lancaster, J. (1985). Evolutionary perspectives on sex differences in higher primates. In A. S. Rossi (Ed.), *Gender and the life course* (pp. 3–28). New York: Aldine Press.

Lancaster, J. (1991). A feminist and evolutionary biology looks at women. *Yearbook of Physical Anthropology*, *34*, 1–11.

Lee, P. C., & Johnson, J. A. (1992). Sex difference in alliances and the acquisition and maintenance of dominance status among immature primates. In A. H. Harcourt & F. B. de Waal (Eds.), *Coalitions and alliances in humans and other animals* (pp. 391–414). Oxford: Oxford University Press.

Liesen, L. (2013). The tangled web she weaves: The evolution of female-female aggression and status seeking. In M. L. Fisher, J. R. Garcia, & R. Sokol Chang (Eds.), *Evolution's empress: Darwinian perspectives on the nature of women* (pp. 43–62). New York: Oxford University Press.

Martin, J. L. (2009). Formation and stabilization of vertical hierarchies among adolescents: Towards a quantitative ethology of dominance among humans. *Social Psychology Quarterly*, *72*(3), 241–264.

McAndrew, F. T. (2014). How "the gossip" became a woman and how "gossip" became her weapon of choice. In M. Fisher (Ed.), *Handbook of women and competition*. New York: Oxford University Press.

Mealey, L. (1999). Evolutionary models of female intrasexual competition. *Behavioral and Brain Sciences*, *22*, 234.

Mealey, L. (2000). Anorexia: A "losing" strategy? *Human Nature*, *11*(1), 105–116.

Mealey, L. (2003). Anorexia: A "dis-ease" of low, low fertility. In J. L. Rodgers & H. P. Kohler (Eds.), *The biodemography of human reproduction and fertility* (pp. 1–21). Boston: Kluwer Academic.

Moscovice, L. R. (2013). Getting by with a little help from friends. In M. L. Fisher, J. R. Garcia, & R. Sokol Chang (Eds.), *Evolution's empress: Darwinian perspectives on the nature of women* (pp. 63–84). New York: Oxford University Press.

Nettle, D., Coall, D. A., & Dickens, T. E. (2011). Early life conditions and age at first pregnancy in British women. *Proceedings of the Royal Society B: Biological Sciences*, *278*, 1721–1727.

Österman, K., Björkqvist, K., Lagerspetz, K. M. J., Kaukianien, A., Landau, S. F., Fraczek, A., & Caprara, G. V. (1998). Cross-cultural evidence of female indirect aggression. *Aggressive Behavior*, *24*, 1–8.

Pusey, A., Murray, C., Wallauer, W., Wilson, M., Wrobelewski, E., & Goodall, J. (2008, July 29). Severe aggression among female *pan troglodytes schweinfurthii* at Gombe National Park, Tanzania. *International Journal of Primatology*, *29*. Published online.

Pusey, A., & Schroepfer-Walker, K. (2013). Female competition in chimpanzees. *Philosophical Transactions of the Royal Society B*, *368*, 20130077.

Pusey, A., Williams, J., & Goodall, J. (1997). The influence of dominance rank on the reproductive success of female chimpanzees. *Science*, *277*, 828–831.

Putnam, R. D. (2000). *Bowling alone: The collapse and revival of American community*. New York: Simon and Schuster.

Rosvall, K. A. (2011). Intrasexual competition in females: Evidence for sexual selection? *Behavioral Ecology*, *22*, 1131–1140.

Schmitt, D. P. (2005). Fundamentals of human mating strategies. In D. M. Buss (Ed.), *The handbook of evolutionary psychology* (pp. 258–291). Hoboken, NJ: Wiley.

Sijtsema, J. J., Ojanen, T., Veenstra, R., Lindenberg, S., Hawley, P. H., & Little, T. D. (2010). Forms and functions of aggression in adolescent friendship selection and influence: A longitudinal social network analysis. *Social Development*, *19*(3), 515–534.

Sijtsema, J. J., Veenstra, R., Lindenberg, S., & Salmivalli, C. (2009). Empirical test of bullies' status goals: Assessing direct goals, aggression, and prestige. *Aggressive Behavior*, *35*, 57–67.

Silk, J. B., Beeher, J. C., Bergman, T. J. Crockford, C., Engh, A. L., Moscovice, L. R., . . . Cheney, D. L. (2010). Strong and consistent social bonds enhance the longevity of female baboons. *Current Biology*, *20*, 1359–1361.

Simmons, R. (2002). *Odd girl out: The hidden culture of aggression in girls*. New York: Harcourt.

Simpson, J. A., Griskevicius, V., I-Chun Kuo, S., Sung, S., & Collins, W. A. (2012). Evolution, stress, and sensitive periods: The influence of unpredictability in early versus late childhood on sex and risky behavior. *Developmental Psychology*, *48*(3), 674–686.

Smuts, B. (1985). *Sex and friendship in baboons*. New York: Aldine.

Smuts, B. (1987). Gender, aggression, and influence. In B. Smuts, D. Cheney, R. Seyfarth, R. Wrangham, & T.

Strusaker (Eds.), *Primate societies* (pp. 400–412). Chicago: University of Chicago Press.

Smuts, B. (1992). Male aggression against women: An evolutionary perspective. *Human Nature, 3,* 1–44.

Smuts, B. (1995). The evolutionary origins of patriarchy. *Human Nature, 6*(1), 1–32.

Strier, K. (2011). *Primate behavioral ecology* (4th ed.). Boston: Prentice Hall.

Sutton, K. A., & Oaten, M. J. (2014). Women's talk? Exploring the relationship between gossip, gender, mate competition and mate poaching. In M. Fisher (Ed.), *Handbook of women and competition.* New York: Oxford University Press.

Tanenbaum, L. (2002). *Catfight: Women and competition.* New York: Seven Stories Press.

Vaillancourt, T. (2013). Do human females use indirect aggression as an intrasexual competition strategy? *Philosophical Transactions of the Royal Society B, 368:* 20130080.

Valen, K. (2010). *The twisted sisterhood: Unraveling the dark legacy of female friendships.* New York: Ballantine Books.

West-Eberhard, M. J. (2003). *Developmental plasticity and evolution.* New York: Oxford University Press.

White, D. D., Gallup, A., & Gallup, G. (2010). Indirect peer aggression in adolescence and reproductive behavior. *Evolutionary Psychology, 8*(1), 49–65.

Wilson, E. O. (1978). *On human nature.* New York: Bantam Books.

Wiseman, R. (2009). *Queen bees and wannabees: Helping your daughter survive cliques, gossip, boyfriends, and the new realities of girl world* (2nd ed.). New York: Crown.

Adolescent Peer Aggression and Female Reproductive Competition

Andrew C. Gallup

Abstract

Research suggests that intrasexual aggression during adolescence functions in competition over dating and reproductive opportunities and that aggressive strategies are more adaptive for females at this developmental stage. This sex difference appears to be related to the differential use of aggressive behavior and slightly uneven developmental trajectory between adolescent males and females. Competition over males is a common motive for female aggression during middle and high school, and, similar to adults, adolescent aggressors often use tactics of competitor derogation to lower the mate value of rivals. Taking an evolutionary perspective, findings demonstrate that adolescent females who engage in intrasexual peer aggression tend to have adaptive dating and sexual patterns, whereas those who are frequently victimized suffer maladaptive fitness outcomes. Recent research also shows that directed female intrasexual aggression during early stages of adolescence can be effective in both disrupting dating relationships of rivals and gaining access to desired dating partners.

Key Words: peer aggression, intrasexual competition, dating behavior, adolescence, victimization

Adolescent Aggression as an Adaptation

Humans show a dramatic peak in aggression during the period of adolescence, and this can come in many different forms, ranging from physical violence to social exclusion. The prevalence of bullying, defined as a specific type of aggression including an imbalance of power and repeated physical and/or nonphysical aggressive acts toward a weaker party (Olweus, 1993), has been thoroughly investigated and occurs at high levels around the world. Cross-cultural research has shown that involvement in bullying is quite common in adolescent students between the ages of 11 and 16 years (Craig et al., 2009; Nansel et al., 2004). For example, Nansel et al. (2004) provided an analysis of bullying in 25 countries showing that involvement varied from 9% to as high as 54%. In an analysis of 40 countries, Craig et al. (2009) found that prevalence rates in bullying ranged from 4.8% to 45.2% and were highest in Baltic countries and lowest in European countries. In the United States, recent research

indicates that as many as 48% of males and 39% of females are involved in various forms of peer aggression, peer victimization, or both during middle and high school (White, Gallup, & Gallup, 2010).

The high level of participation in aggressive adolescent interactions has become a serious public concern in many cultures (e.g., Kim, Koh, & Leventhal, 2005). Although there is large variation in involvement at the international scale, participation in bullying as the aggressor and/or the victim is associated with poorer psychosocial functioning, health problems, and social adjustment across cultures (Nansel et al., 2004). Being a frequent target of various forms of peer aggression (not necessarily bullying) has also been linked to a range of negative consequences associated with psychosocial maladjustment, including depression, loneliness, low global self-esteem, poor social self-concept, and social and general anxiety (for a meta-analytic review, see Hawker & Boulton, 2000). Involvement in aggression during middle and high school also appears to reduce cooperative interactions in early adulthood as measured by choices in behavioral economics games (Gallup, O'Brien, & Wilson, 2010). Similarly, experiencing routine peer victimization in childhood and adolescence has been associated with a variety of negative outcomes later in life, such as long-term unemployment (Varhama & Björkqvist, 2005), lower lifetime income levels (Brown & Taylor, 2008), and a higher likelihood of being single in adulthood (Fosse & Holen, 2004). In addition, some research shows that children who perpetrate frequent aggression toward peers tend to be considered less positively (Cillessen & Mayeux, 2004; Zimmer-Gembeck, Hunter, & Pronk, 2007) and have difficulty adjusting socially later in life (Campbell, Spieker, Vandergrift, Belsky, Burchinal, & the NICHD Early Child Care Research Network, 2010). Therefore, developing a better understanding of the motives and mechanisms behind adolescent aggression is of utmost importance when evaluating the effectiveness of various prevention programs (Volk, Camerilli, Dane, & Marini, 2012).

Although it has traditionally been believed that overtly aggressive adolescents have experienced developmental problems or present with social and cognitive deficits (e.g., Crick & Dodge, 1994; Dodge, 1986), the ubiquity of aggression in the animal kingdom supports the view that it is an evolved adaptation (Archer, 1988). A number of domain-specific forms of aggression in nonhuman animals have been categorized (Moyer, 1968), and, similar to other animals, aggression in humans is sensitive to social context, providing unique functionality that has been shaped by natural and sexual selection (Griskevicius et al., 2009). In other words, aggressive behavior evolved because it can serve to enhance the survival and reproduction of the individual (Buss & Shackelford, 1997). For example, human aggression can provide many adaptive benefits in competition for resources or status (Archer, 2009; Buss & Shackelford, 1997) or in resolving other evolutionarily important conflicts directly related to reproductive competition (Daly & Wilson, 1988; Wilson & Daly, 1985). Simply put, the use of aggression can impose costs upon rivals while benefiting the perpetrator with adaptive fitness outcomes (Hawley, Little, & Rodkin, 2007). Consistent with the view that aggression is an evolved adaptation, the psychological mechanisms underlying human aggression are hypothesized to be solutions to particular adaptive problems associated with specific social interactions. Buss and Shackelford (1997) identify several such problems, including but not limited to

co-opting the resources of others, defending against attack, inflicting costs on same-sex rivals, and negotiating status and power hierarchies. Whereas aggression among humans is just one of many social strategies involved in gaining status and resources (Hawley, 1999, 2003; Wilson, Near, & Miller, 1996), the widespread nature of aggressive behavior provides support for the effectiveness of such interactions.

Following this evolutionary interpretation, some developmental psychologists have recently tried to explain aggression from a behavioral ecological perspective in terms of social dominance, in which a combination of aggressive and affiliative strategies relate to individuals' resource control, social competence, reduced group-level aggression, and increased social cohesion (see Pellegrini, 2008). Similarly, others have argued that specific forms of bullying behavior function to promote individual somatic and sexual benefits, as well as group-based benefits of dominance; these researchers point out how bullies are often better off than average adolescents in terms of mental and physical health, popularity, and social skills (reviewed by Volk et al., 2012). Extensive research has also shown positive associations between the utilization of various forms of peer aggression and high status and popularity during adolescence (Prinstein & Cillessen, 2003; Rodkin, Farmer, Pearl, & Van Acker, 2000; Salmivalli, Kaukiainen, & Lagerspetz, 2000; Vaillancourt & Hymel, 2006; Zimmer-Gembeck et al., 2005). The heightened involvement in peer aggression during this period may therefore be understood as one of several social strategies employed within a competitive and hierarchical environment such as that of formal educational systems (Gallup et al., 2010; Gallup, O'Brien, & Wilson, 2011; Hawley, 2003).

Furthermore, the mismatch between contemporary educational settings and ancestral community learning environments may act to exacerbate the level of aggression during adolescence. Industrialized school systems provide a novel social setting from an evolutionary perspective, placing large groups of unrelated children with varying ability and backgrounds together in constructed age cohorts for formal educational training. Ancestral human populations were clearly void of such institutions, and children would have moved around and interacted more freely, spending time learning around more related, closely affiliated individuals across the spectrum of age and development. Because of this, it has been suggested that modern school systems remove natural expressions of play behavior in children, which are common to hunter-gatherer societies and provide benefits to the social group by counteracting tendencies toward aggressive dominance (Gray, 2009). In industrialized school systems, for example, disparities between similar-aged peers are likely to become pronounced during adolescence due to the timing of physical maturity (i.e., onset of puberty and development of secondary sexual characteristics), social and cognitive development, and transitions first from primary to middle school and then from middle to high school that further alter the peer landscape. When children and adolescents change schools as they progress through the grade system, they are reshuffled from being the oldest members of their previous institution to the youngest ones in the new. This restructuring seems to amplify aggressive behavior. For instance, there is an initial increase in aggressive competition among adolescents as they move from primary to secondary school (11–14 years of age), and this form of aggressive behavior appears to mediate dominance status during this transition (Pellegrini & Long, 2002). Thus, the contemporary educational system provides a more rigid, yet fluctuating hierarchical environment that may facilitate continuous aggressive and coercive strategies through temporal changes in competition for rank.

From an evolutionary perspective, studying this time period of development may provide important insight into the psychological mechanisms of aggressive social competition, resource acquisition, and mating. Adolescent populations represent a critical developmental stage in the human lifespan in which sophisticated social-cognitive skills (e.g., Björkqvist, 1994; Underwood, 2003) and reproductive capacity both emerge. Perhaps one of the more evolutionarily significant features accompanying the rise in peer aggression during adolescence (Campbell, 1995) is the onset of dating activity that follows puberty at this time The available fossil evidence suggests that the lifespan of early hominids was drastically reduced in comparison to contemporary populations, with a striking increase in longevity for modern humans only occurring in the Early Upper Paleolithic (Caspari & Lee, 2004). This may explain why, even in contemporary populations in the United States, initial romantic relationships begin quite early on in adolescence (Connolly, Pepler, Craig, & Taradash, 2000; Natsuaki, Biehl, & Ge, 2009; Zimmer-Gembeck, 1999; Zimmer-Gembeck, Siebenbruner, & Collins, 2001) when compared to the median age of marriage (28.7 for males; 26.5 for females; US Bureau of the Census,

2011). For example, a recent study showed that more than 70% of adolescent males and females reported involvement in romantic dating between the ages of 12 and 16 years (Natsuaki et al., 2009). Still other samples show that the majority of adolescents are involved in dating relations by 11–14 years of age (Connolly et al., 2000). Although it is true that dating and sexual behavior can be disconnected from reproductive consequences or lifetime fitness in contemporary societies, the same could not be said for ancestral conditions, whereby the formation of lasting romantic relationships by postpubescent adolescents would likely result in pregnancy. Therefore, there seems to be a strong ancestral selective pressure for the emergence of strategic, reproductively relevant behaviors and psychology during the adolescent years.

The vast majority of adolescent aggressive behaviors occur between members of the same sex (Gallup, O'Brien, White, & Wilson, 2009; Gallup et al., 2010, 2011; Gallup & Wilson, 2009; White et al., 2010), which suggests that they may play a role in intrasexual competition for status and mates (Pellegrini, 2007; Pellegrini & Archer, 2005). Because individuals begin to date and initiate their first romantic relationships—and thus become active participants in mating competition—at the same time of heightened intrasexual conflict and peer aggression, it is reasonable that the two may be directly related. The evidence suggests that this may be particularly the case for females, rather than males, during this stage of development. Qualitative research shows that preferred mating partners serve as valuable resources motivating adolescent aggression in females (Campbell, 1986, 1995; Gallup & Wilson, 2012; Marsh & Paton, 1984), and quantitative studies show stronger correlations between the level of adolescent peer aggression and adaptive dating/sexual behavior for females than males (e.g., Gallup et al., 2009; 2011; Pellegrini & Long, 2003; White et al., 2010). It has recently been proposed that the majority of aggressive interactions reported by female adolescents on a day-to-day basis, including much of what would not be categorized as bullying per se, may be central to competition for dating and mating opportunities (Gallup et al., 2011).

The remainder of this chapter focuses on the growing literature on female aggression and adaptive reproductive outcomes during the adolescent years (i.e., middle and high school). First, sex differences in forms and trends of aggressive interaction during adolescence are discussed in terms of parental investment theory and sexual selection.

Next, evidence is presented on methods of female intrasexual competition for mates and how aggressive social strategies during adolescence compare to research in adult populations. Literature is then presented demonstrating a clear and consistent association between peer aggression and adaptive dating and sexual behavior during adolescence and into adulthood for females. Concluding remarks summarize this work in terms of improving the fundamental understanding of peer aggression during adolescence. Suggestions are provided for further basic research directly investigating the contexts and outcomes of intrasexual aggression in middle and high school populations, rather than in adult samples, because the developmental stage of the teenage years may provide greater insight into evolved psychological mechanisms of female social competition, resource acquisition, and mating.

Sex Differences in Aggression
Forms and Trends of Adolescent Aggression

Human aggression can take many forms, ranging from direct physical violence to gossip and the spreading of rumors. During adolescence, aggression can be broken down into physical, social, relational, and indirect categories. Physical aggression is the most explicit and has been traditionally studied in school populations, whereas the latter three have only recently gained attention, particularly in female interactions (Underwood, 2003). Researchers commonly disagree on the distinctiveness of the various forms. Some differentiate between physical, social, indirect, and relational aggression (Heilbron & Prinstein, 2008). Social aggression can be direct (i.e., verbal) or indirect actions aimed at damaging another's self-esteem or social status (Galen & Underwood, 1997), whereas relational aggression involves the direct manipulation of peer relationships (Crick, 1995, 1997). For example, involvement in relational aggression positively predicts future measures of social standing and perceived popularity (Rose, Swenson, & Waller, 2004; Zimmer-Gembeck, Geiger, & Crick, 2005). Still others point to the similarities between the three nonphysical types of aggression, simply distinguishing between direct and indirect forms (Archer & Coyne, 2005). However, indirect aggression has also been argued to be a unique form of hostility in which a perpetrator attempts to harm the target while concurrently trying to obscure their intent (Björkqvist, Österman, & Kaukianen, 1992). Thus, for the

purposes of this chapter, it is useful to identify all forms of aggression as they have been studied in adolescent encounters.

Extensive research has shown that some general trends and patterns of aggression exist during the course of adolescence. First, as previously discussed, the vast majority of aggressive acts between adolescent peers are reported to be intrasexual (Gallup et al., 2009, 2010, 2011; Gallup & Wilson, 2009; White et al., 2012). In other words, for example, females are more likely to aggress and be victimized by other females. Second, direct forms of aggression appear to decrease for both males and females during adolescence (Björkqvist, 1994; Côté, Vaillancourt, Le Blanc, Nagin, & Tremblay, 2006), whereas indirect forms peak during this period for both sexes (Card, Stucky, Sawalani, & Little, 2008; Miller, Vaillancourt, & Boyle, 2009). Relating to the potential functionality of the heightened use of nonphysical forms of hostility during adolescence, research shows that this type of aggression is positively associated with peer acceptance and future perceived popularity for the aggressor because its use tends to be accompanied by high status (Salmivalli et al., 2000; Vaillancourt & Hymel, 2006; Zimmer-Gembeck et al., 2005). On the contrary, being the routine victim of such acts can directly diminish one's reputation and social support (Cross & Campbell, 2011), as well as produce anxiety, loss of self-esteem, and depression (Owens, Shute, & Slee, 2000a).

Although it is becoming increasingly apparent that the overall quantity of aggressive acts may be similar between the sexes (see Björkqvist, 1994), males and females do show noticeable differences in terms of the trajectory and quality of aggressive behavior during adolescence. For example, research consistently shows that females tend to engage in more social, relational, and indirect forms of aggression than do males, with this gap growing during later childhood (8–11 years) and ultimately peaking during adolescence (reviewed by Archer & Coyne, 2005). Behaviors that are commonly observed among adolescent girls engaging in social and indirect forms of aggression include anger, conflict/disagreement, name-calling, teasing, embarrassment, breaking of confidences, criticizing of appearance and/or clothing, gossip, and spreading of rumors targeted at one's reputation (e.g., Owens, Shute, & Slee, 2000b; Underwood, 2003). Conversely, physical forms of aggression tend to be more frequent in males at all ages, with this sex difference beginning in early childhood and becoming most divergent in early adulthood between the ages of 18 and 30 years (reviewed by Archer, 2004).

In addition to the varying strategies used between the sexes, involvements in violent actions tend to peak a few years earlier for adolescent girls than for boys (reviewed by Campbell, 1995). For example, both official statistics and self-reports show the initiation of violent crimes to be between the ages of 12 and 15 for females and between 15 and 18 for males (Elliot, Huizinga, & Morse, 1983; Piper, 1983). Assault arrest records also show a similar disparity, with peak engagement occurring between the ages of 15 and 19 for females and 20 and 24 for males (Kruttschnitt, 1994). Campbell (1995) suggests that the earlier rise in these types of aggressive acts for females could reflect the advanced sexual development and earlier competition for high-quality mates. In males, physical maturity is delayed in relation to females, and time is required to obtain the status and resources necessary for successfully attracting mates (Buss, 1989); consequently the onset of peak intrasexual aggression may lag behind. In females, however, the fact that males show mate preferences for youth and physical attractiveness (Buss, 1989) allows for an earlier engagement in effective mating competition via aggressive strategies.

Parental Investment and Costs of Physical Aggression

From an evolutionary perspective, differential parental investment theory provides a powerful framework for understanding the divergent strategies and trends of aggressive behavior during adolescence and into young adulthood. Parental investment refers to the costs associated with the production of viable offspring, and, among mammals, females are obligated to invest significantly more than males (Trivers, 1972). This disparity in lengthy periods of gestation and lactation, which makes maternal investment more critical to offspring survival, means that direct physical forms of aggression are more costly to females (see Campbell, 1999). Therefore, instead of using violent forms of intrasexual competition, females have evolved to be choosier when selecting a potential mate. Accordingly, cross-cultural research shows that females preferentially seek high status and cues of resource acquisition when choosing mates (e.g., Buss, 1989; Shackelford, Schmitt, & Buss, 2005). Female choice, however, leads to greater fitness variance among males, and because status and resource acquisition are positively associated with the reproductive success of men (e.g., Cronk, 1991; Hopcroft, 2006; Turke & Betzig, 1985), it can be costly from a reproductive fitness perspective for males not to engage in direct aggressive competition (Daly & Wilson, 1988).

Accordingly, the cost-benefit ratio of physical aggression varies considerably between the sexes. It has been suggested that females have evolved to generally avoid physically risky forms of aggression during their prime reproductive years in order to safely compete with rivals and ensure investment in rearing offspring, perhaps using fear as an adaptive mechanism to reduce exposure to direct physical conflict (Cross & Campbell, 2011). For example, females show a lower threshold to fear and heightened neurological reactivity to threatening stimuli (reviewed by Campbell, 2013). Importantly, indirect aggression offers an effective and low-cost strategy for females to utilize during intrasexual competition by decreasing the risk of physical injury while retaining many benefits in inflicting harm (Björkqvist, 1994; Owens et al., 2000a; Owens, Slee, & Shute, 2000c; Underwood, 2003). Conversely, due to a greater variance in mating opportunities, physical forms of aggression may provide a selective advantage in males depending on the context (Wilson & Daly, 1985). Consistent with this framework, experimental research shows that status and mating motives increase direct forms of aggression in males and indirect forms of aggression in females (Griskevicius et al., 2009).

Aggressive Strategies of Intrasexual Competition
Expression of Aggressive Competition in Adult Populations

The use of aggression against rival peers is one of multiple strategies that could be employed when competing for resources, including preferred dating/mating partners. Research on adult populations has shown that both males and females will act to diminish the status or reputation of rivals in an attempt to make them less desirable to members of the opposite sex (Buss & Dedden, 1990). Similarly, indirect aggression has been utilized in mate competition behavior in adult females seemingly to increase reproductive opportunity at the expense of rivals (Arnocky, Sunderani, Miller, & Vaillancourt, 2012; Campbell, 1999; Fisher, 2004; Griskevicius et al., 2009). Indeed, growing research suggests that females use indirect aggression as an intrasexual competition strategy (Vaillancourt, 2013).

Female competition for mates is only recently being understood (Campbell, 2013; Fisher, 2012; see this edited volume), and researchers have identified four primary categories of tactics: self-promotion, competitor derogation, competitor manipulation, and mate manipulation (Fisher & Cox, 2011). One strategy in which adolescents may gain fitness advantages over their peers via social, relational, or indirect peer aggression is through the use of competitor derogation. This can be an effective strategy for competing with members of the same sex (Schmitt & Buss, 1996) but only if it causes suitable mates to decrease their assessment of targeted rivals while not hindering the reputation or assessment of the aggressor. Consistent with these predictions, Fisher and Cox (2009) found that female's derogations of rivals cause adult males, as well as females, to decrease their initial attractiveness ratings of rival female faces. Furthermore, research has shown that derogation of competitors does not significantly influence males' perceptions of a female aggressor's physical attractiveness, promiscuity, parenting ability, or how willing they would be to consider her for either a long-term relationship or short-term sexual relationship (Fisher, Shaw, Worth, Smith, & Reeve, 2010). Taken together, these findings suggest that the use of social, relational, and indirect forms of aggression can produce negative perceptions of rival peers and do not hold negative reputational consequences, thus providing a relative fitness advantage to the aggressor. That said, research shows that the effectiveness of this strategy also depends on the individual traits of the aggressor. For instance, it has been shown that derogations made by a physically attractive female have significantly more sway compared to those made by someone who is unattractive (Fisher & Cox, 2009).

Jealousy over mating is a strong motivator for aggression in adult females. In a cross-cultural review of adult female aggression, Burbank (1987) found that 52% of all aggression between women is precipitated by a husband's adultery. Research shows that females often compete by derogating the qualities most valued by males, such as fidelity and physical attractiveness (Campbell, 2004; Cross & Campbell, 2011; Vaillancourt, Miller, & Sharma, 2010). Women are threatened by other females' promiscuous activity (Baumeister & Twenge, 2002), and methods of derogating rivals by questioning sexual exclusivity and highlighting promiscuous behavior are documented features of indirect aggression in adult populations (Buss & Dedden, 1990; Vaillancourt & Sharma, 2011). Although

males may show initial attraction toward promiscuous females in regards to a short-term mating strategy, research suggests that they are less likely to pursue these females for long-term and committed relationships due to the prospect of paternal uncertainty (Buss & Schmitt, 1993). For instance, when assessing characteristics preferred in a short-term versus long-term mating partner on a 7-point scale (3 extremely desirable; −3 extremely undesirable), males rate traits such as faithful and sexually loyal as significantly more important for long-term partners. Similarly, males rate traits such as unfaithful and promiscuous as undesirable (ranging from −0.40 to −2.93) for both short- and long-term partners, although these are seen as significantly less desirable for long-term mates (Buss & Schmitt, 1993).

Similar to issues of fidelity, adult females often compete with one another in regards to physical attractiveness (reviewed by Fisher, 2012). Cross-culturally, women are distressed and become jealous when they believe potential rivals are more physically attractive than they are (Arnocky et al., 2012; Buss, Shackelford, Choe, Buunk, & Dijkstra, 2000), and social comparisons are positively correlated with intrasexual competition (Buunk & Fisher, 2009). Consistent with research on the use of competitor derogation to vie with rivals (Fisher & Cox, 2009), females in romantic relationships have been shown to make more appearance comparisons and are more likely to engage in aggressive behaviors toward female peers (Arnocky et al., 2012). Because appearance comparisons are highly correlated with the degree of body dissatisfaction (Huon, Piira, Hayne, & Strong, 2002), females who make appearance comparisons might perceive themselves as being low on relative mate value and thus be more inclined to engage in aggressive tactics of intrasexual competition.

Expression of Aggressive Competition in Adolescent Populations

In line with the literature on intrasexual female competition in adults, female peer aggression during adolescence is also used as a means to target same-sex rivals that may be found most desirable by males. For example, focus groups and interviews of 15- to 16-year-old girls show that competition over boys is a common explanation for intrasexual aggression (Owens et al., 2000a, 2000b). Jealousy over romantic partners is also a frequent motive for engaging in female-female fights or other forms of intrasexual aggression among adolescents (Campbell, 1986; Gallup et al., 2011; Marsh &

Paton, 1984). These reports therefore suggest that aggressive tactics of female adolescents are used intentionally for the purposes of acquiring and/or maintaining mates. Using questionnaires to assess reasons for fighting among 16-year-old schoolgirls, Campbell (1986) discovered that 46% of the female fights revolved around issues of personal integrity and sexual reputation, with accusations of promiscuity being the most frequent. Indirect aggression is also used among adolescent girls (aged 13–16 years) to highlight the sexual promiscuity or perceived flaws in physical appearance of rival peers (Eder & Enke, 1991; Owens et al., 2000a, 2000b). Because males put a premium on fidelity and physical attractiveness in potential committed partners, adolescent females perceived as deviating from these qualities may be regarded as less desirable, and, as a consequence, these individuals may be less willing or able to compete for male romantic interest due to heightened social anxiety and depression from peer victimization (Vaillancourt, 2005).

Because indirect forms of aggression are on the rise during adolescence, particularly for females, this tactic, in combination with others, may provide similar relative fitness benefits to perpetrators by inflicting fitness costs to victims during this time as well. In particular, it has been hypothesized that indirect aggression during adolescence functions by diminishing the relative mate value or desire of rivals by reducing social standing or reputation (Vaillancourt, 2005) and diminishing physical attractiveness and/or sexual fidelity (Leenaars, Dane, & Marini, 2008). Also consistent with the adult literature, qualitative research has shown that envy over physical appearance is an important cause for indirect aggression by adolescent females (Owens et al., 2000a). Naturalistic studies also show that sneering comments about other girls' physical appearance are frequently the topic of gossip (Brown, 1998; Duncan, 1999; Simmons, 2002).

Pellegrini (2007) has proposed that the use of indirect or relational aggression by adolescent females to access heterosexual relationships may be mediated by physical attractiveness, with less attractive females targeting their more attractive counterparts for victimization. One reason for this is because the most attractive females pose the greatest threat in dating competition. In accord with this, peer ratings of physical attractiveness predict future dating relationships during adolescence (Arnocky & Vaillancourt, 2012), which is also consistent with the view that adolescent males, much like their adult counterparts, place an emphasis on physical

appearance in romantic partners. Supporting these findings, a recent study on a large middle and high school population (aged 13–18 years) revealed that female self-perceived physical attractiveness was positively correlated with reported indirect peer victimization (Leenaars et al., 2008). Although these studies do not identify the specific features that make an adolescent female physically attractive (e.g., symmetry, nice clothes, developed breasts, etc.), in a study of students aged 14–16 years, Gallup and Wilson (2009) found that female intrasexual aggression in the form of demeaning, diminishing, and embarrassing was positively correlated with body mass index (BMI). Because BMI is negatively associated with ratings of attractiveness in females, accounting for more than 70% of variance in this measure (Tovée, Reinhardt, Emery, & Cornelissen, 1998), it has been interpreted that some overweight females aggress against rival peers in an attempt to diminish their social standing, reputation, and appeal to high-quality mates. In other words, similar to research on adult populations, the most physically attractive females pose the greatest threat in dating and mating competition during adolescence and may be selectively targeted by rivals of equal or lesser attractiveness as a consequence.

Adolescent Aggression and Female Reproductive Competition
Connections Between Peer Aggression and Dating

It was the pioneering work of Campbell (1995) that first attributed the increase in female aggression during adolescence to the evolved psychology of mate competition. The trajectory of heightened peer aggression during the teenage years corresponds tightly with the development of sexual maturity and the onset of dating behavior. Most adolescents begin to date and have their first romantic relationships around the age of 15 years (Zimmer-Gembeck, 1999; Zimmer-Gembeck et al., 2001), with other studies showing that 56–71% of adolescents are involved in dating relations by 11–14 years of age (Connolly et al., 2000). The development of romantic interests has been identified as a hallmark of adolescence (Hartup, 1993; Havighurst, 1972), and the formation of dyadic relationships with romantic partners is an important part of life at this time (Douvan & Adelson, 1966; Furman, 1993; Sharabany, Gershoni, & Hofman, 1981). For example, dating can provide personal support and intimacy, companionship, and positive self-perceptions for young adolescents (Furman & Buhrmester, 1992; Neemann, Hubbard, & Masten, 1995; Richards, Crowe, Larson, & Swarr, 1998; Sharabany et al., 1981). This period is therefore critical for the development of interpersonal relations, and much of the aggressive interactions that adolescent students experience on a day-to-day basis may be central to competition in the realm of dating and mating (Gallup et al., 2011).

A number of studies have identified a link between adolescent aggression and mate competition. In an investigation of fifth- to eighth-grade students, individuals who self-reported bullying their peers were more involved in dating than were those who did not bully others (Connolly et al., 2000). For example, self-reported bullies began dating at earlier ages and had more dating activities and a higher frequency of heterosexual contact. In addition, a significantly greater proportion of bullies had a current boyfriend or girlfriend at the time of the study compared to nonbullying adolescents. Similarly, a significantly smaller proportion of bullies had never had a boyfriend or girlfriend compared to nonbullying peers. In a separate study in which direct observations of 12- to 14-year-old middle school students were made at monthly dances across a school year, peer aggression was found to predict opposite-sex interaction (Pellegrini & Long, 2007).

Longitudinal designs have documented similar associations between aggression and dating during adolescence. In a longitudinal study of young adolescents transitioning from elementary to middle school (fifth–sixth grade), it was shown that as students grew older, peer nominations of aggression (e.g., how fellow students rated their tendency to be mean and pick on other kids) were positively correlated with opposite-sex friendship (Bukowski, Sippola, & Newcomb, 2000). In a more recent study, Arnocky and Vaillancourt (2012) performed a longitudinal analysis of adolescents in grades 6–9 (aged 11–14). They tested whether perpetrators of aggression at time 1 were more likely to have a dating partner at time 2 (1 year later) and whether victims of aggression were less likely to have a dating partner in the future. Both predictions were confirmed: the use of indirect aggression was positively associated with having a dating partner the following year for both males and females, whereas self-reported victimization from bullying negatively predicted time 2 dating for both sexes.

Whereas this literature shows a correlation between aggression and dating behavior both for males and females, retrospective studies demonstrate a stronger relationship for females (Gallup et al., 2009, 2011; White et al., 2010). Consistent with these findings, a separate longitudinal study of students in grades 6–8 (12–14 years of age) showed that dominance-related strategies (i.e., activities pertaining to resource competition), and not aggressive behaviors per se, were best predictive of dating popularity in males, whereas the same analysis found that dating popularity increases in early adolescent females who use frequent relational peer aggression (Pellegrini & Long, 2003). These findings are consistent with both female preferences for status in males and research on the effectiveness of female derogation of rivals in mate competition.

Peer Aggression and Adaptive Dating Outcomes

The research in the previous section supports the view that peer aggression may provide fitness benefits to the perpetrator while inflicting costs on rival victims. If adolescent peer aggression functions in intrasexual competition, its use should be correlated with both adaptive dating patterns for perpetrators and maladaptive dating outcomes for victims. Due to fundamental sex differences in human reproductive biology (i.e., reproductive potential, parental investment, and parental certainty), the behaviors and outcomes of this hypothesis remain sex-specific. Biologically, a male has a relatively greater reproductive potential than a female simply due to sizeable differences in gamete production and reproductive lifespan. In addition, as previously discussed, females have a greater obligatory investment in the development and care of offspring (Trivers, 1972), which further limits the pace of reproduction. Evidence suggests that men achieve increases in reproductive fitness mainly through increases in the number of reproductive partners (Betzig, 1986), but such promiscuity fails to provide similar fitness benefits to females who are limited by extended gestation and lactation periods. For example, research shows that having more spouses is associated with greater offspring production for males, but not females (Jokela, Rotkirch, Rickard, Pettay, & Lummaa, 2010). Likewise, as mentioned earlier, due to the prospect of infidelity and paternal uncertainty, males put a premium on fidelity in potential permanent partners, and for this reason females known to be promiscuous may suffer reputational damage that could affect the quality of their future long-term mates (Buss & Schmitt, 1993). Therefore, females are more likely to improve reproductive success by beginning lasting, committed relationships at earlier ages (Wood, 1994).

In the first study of its kind, Gallup et al. (2011) used a retrospective analysis in college students (aged 18–21 years) to explicitly investigate the relationship between adaptive dating responses and the frequency of intrasexual aggression/victimization during adolescence (middle and high school), including features such as the onset of dating behavior, total dating partners, length of longest dating relationship, opposite-sex flirtation, and self-perceived attractiveness. Based on sex differences in reproductive biology, the first main hypothesis was that female peer aggression would positively associate with the length of longest romantic relationship and with opposite-sex flirtation, as well as predict an earlier onset of dating behavior, whereas male peer aggression would predict more total dating partners, more opposite-sex flirtation, and an earlier onset of dating behavior. For the second main hypothesis, the following predictions were made: female peer victimization would predict a later onset of dating behavior, more total dating partners, shorter romantic relationships, and less opposite-sex flirtation, whereas male peer victimization would predict fewer total dating partners, less opposite-sex flirtation, and a later onset of dating behavior. Overall, these can be considered sex-specific adaptive or maladaptive outcomes based on their relation to reproductive fitness. Whereas opposite-sex interest is advantageous to both sexes, males benefit more from having multiple partners, and females benefit more from initiating earlier relationships and having long-lasting committed partners.

In regards to the first hypothesis, results showed that females who perpetrated high levels of social, relational, and indirect aggression (teasing, demeaning, isolating, and excluding) reported an earlier onset of dating compared to their peers, and there were also trends for aggressive females having longer dating relationships and experiencing more male flirtation. Importantly, although the onset of dating behavior is positively associated with the total number of dating partners, female intrasexual aggression was not connected with having more dating partners after controlling for the length of longest relationship and years spent dating. This provides support that females may use these aggressive tactics in the pursuit of adaptive dating outcomes and not simply for an increase in dating activity in general. There was also an adaptive outcome for aggressive males because greater perpetration of social and indirect aggression predicted more total dating partners, higher female flirtation, and greater self-perceived physical attractiveness in adolescence. Unlike with females, however, male-male aggression did not predict the onset of dating activity or the length of the longest romantic relationship.

Gallup et al. (2011) also asked participants to report on whether they had ever become involved in a direct fight during middle or high school that was specifically over access to a preferred member of the opposite sex. Results demonstrated that more than 20% of males and females identified doing so, but this action was associated with adaptive dating outcomes for females only. For instance, females who fought with other girls in this context during adolescence began dating at earlier ages, had more romantic relationships, had longer dating relationships, and reported higher levels of male flirtation than those who did not. For males, however, fighting over access to a girlfriend during middle and high school did not correspond with significant differences in dating behavior.

In regards to the second hypothesis, results for females showed that intrasexual peer victimization was indeed correlated with a later onset of dating behavior, more total dating partners, less male flirtation, and lower self-perceived physical attractiveness while growing up during adolescence. Therefore, victimized females show reduced reproductive potential by delaying the onset of romantic relationships while also displaying an overinvolvement in dating thereafter that could have damaging reputational effects down the line when pursuing high-quality long-term mates. Patterns of overinvolvement in dating have been linked to behavioral problems and lower psychosocial functions (Zimmer-Gembeck et al., 2001). These outcomes of dating behavior and self-image (lower perceived physical attractiveness) are likely to coincide with reduced fitness in the future because this is likely to reduce self-esteem, which may inhibit competition for mates. In addition, having shorter and more frequent dating relationships has been linked to other behavioral problems and lower psychosocial functions (Zimmer-Gembeck et al., 2001). Adolescent peer victimization therefore appears to be linked to negative fitness consequences in females by promoting an increase in dating activity that may be accompanied by damaging personal effects. For males, however, frequent peer victimization was unrelated to dating patterns, opposite-sex interest, or self-perceived attractiveness during adolescence.

Overall, the results of this study support many of the evolutionary predictions regarding the dating outcomes associated with peer aggression/victimization in adolescent females. Conversely, the findings for males only partially support the predictions of the hypothesized relationship between aggression and adaptive dating outcomes and do little to support the predicted association between victimization and maladaptive dating outcomes. It is proposed that both the slightly earlier onset of peak aggression and reproductive maturity, as well as the different forms of aggression utilized by males and females during adolescence, may be contributing to the effectiveness of these strategies in mating competition.

Peer Aggression and Adaptive Sexual Behaviors

The formation of dating relationships by adolescents would have resulted in fitness consequences (i.e., pregnancy) during the vast majority of human evolutionary history, and there are a number of reasons why adolescent dating behavior provides a valid reflection of reproductive fitness. Adolescent dating relationships represent the initial stages of human courtship, and because adolescent females perceive norms that sexual behavior should not occur outside of dating relationships (Collins, Welsh, & Furman, 2009), it has been argued that most of adolescent sexual behavior occurs within the context of dating (Arnocky & Vaillancourt, 2012). Being in a quality dating relationship during adolescence also predicts future involvement in committed relationships during adolescence (Seiffge-Krenke & Lang, 2002) and greater odds of being married or living with a committed partner by 25 years of age (Raley, Crissey, & Muller, 2007). Therefore, studying how social interactions influence adolescent dating relationships may well provide important insight into evolved psychological mechanisms for fitness maximization.

Consistent with the growing literature on female aggression and adolescent dating, recent research shows a similar connection between intrasexual peer aggression/victimization and sexual behavior during adolescence (de Bruyn, Cillessen, & Weisfeld, 2012; Gallup et al., 2009; Leenaars et al., 2008; White et al., 2010). For example, males and females (aged 14–15) judged as having dominant and aggressive profiles by their peers report the highest levels of sexual activity as measured by heavy petting and/or intercourse (de Bruyn et al., 2012). In two separate retrospective studies, it was also shown that females using frequent indirect aggression during middle school (sixth–eighth grade) reported having an earlier onset of heterosexual intercourse, whereas females targeted for frequent social, relational, or indirect victimization during this time reported a later onset of sexual activity, more total sexual partners, and a higher rate of promiscuous behavior (Gallup et al., 2009; White et al., 2010). In a natural fertility population, age at first sexual intercourse is a proximate determinant of total fertility and provides an important evolutionary advantage to females who compete successfully for mating opportunities (Wood, 1994). Therefore, in the absence of contraceptive techniques, there appears to be adaptive value for indirect aggression in females during adolescence. Consistent with the aforementioned reports of dating behavior, these studies (Gallup et al., 2009; White et al., 2010) found a greater association between sexual behavior and female adolescent aggression.

Peer Aggression and Mate Acquisition

Although a number of reports have drawn correlations among female adolescent aggression, intrasexual mating competition, and enhanced dating/sexual activity, few studies have investigated the direct effectiveness of this strategy in acquiring preferred mating partners. By providing an extended questionnaire to a selected sample of early adolescent females (grades 6–8) enrolled in an aggression prevention program, Gallup and Wilson (2012) partially tested whether intrasexual aggression functioned in dating competition. Specifically, it was hypothesized that (1) dating/mating competition was a motive behind intrasexual peer aggression, and (2) perpetrating these acts was actually utilized in the acquisition of preferred dating partners and the disruption of existing dating relationships. Results supported both predictions. When asked to identify the top three reasons for female-female aggression in their middle school, the top two responses (31.3% each) were specifically related to boys/dating relationships and status/popularity, replicating previous work (Campbell, 1995; Marsh & Paton, 1984; Owens et al., 2000a; Prinstein & Cillessen, 2003). The next top responses, each listed by 18.8% of the sample, were physical appearance and jealousy, which is also consistent with previous research (Brown, 1998; Duncan, 1999; Owens et al., 2000b; Simmons, 2002).

In regards to the use of directed aggression in mate acquisition, 19.0% admitted that they had acted aggressively toward another girl in the past specifically because she was in a relationship with a preferred dating partner. Of these aggressors, 50% stated that their repeated hostility ultimately resulted in breaking up the rival's relationship and that they began dating the desired boy shortly thereafter. Conversely, 38.1% reported that they had been a victim of female aggression simply because they were in a relationship with a boy the aggressive girl liked. Of this sample, 50% stated that this aggression caused these dating relationships to end as consequence of this victimization. In total, 14% reported experiencing the role of both aggressor and victim in the context of peer aggression as a form of mate disruption.

This research adds substantially to evolutionary predictions of females utilizing peer aggression in intrasexual mating competition by demonstrating that at least a small proportion of female adolescents actually employ aggressive behavioral strategies with the specific function of disrupting the existing relationships of rivals and acquiring dating opportunities with desired males (Gallup & Wilson, 2012). Although the majority of female students in this study did not report involvement in aggression revolving around dating competition, responses indicate that it was a relatively successful strategy when employed. Half of the female victims reporting this type of aggression indicated that it caused their dating relationships to end as a result. Only one girl responded to the question of who decided to end the relationship following the peer victimization, revealing that her boyfriend broke up with her as a consequence. Perhaps more importantly, of the females who admitted perpetrating this type of aggression, half stated that this behavior resulted in them dating that boy instead. One of the open-ended responses illustrates how intrasexual aggression is used specifically as a social strategy to gain access to preferred dating partners. For example, when responding to whether she had ever acted aggressively toward another girl in this context, one participant stated the following:

> Yes I did. And no I did not end up dating him. Not yet anyways. I just broke them up and any other girls he dates.

These results are consistent with previous research showing that intrasexual aggression can function in competitor derogation by diminishing rivals in an attempt to make them less desirable to their current partner or other members of the opposite sex (e.g., Buss & Dedden, 1990; Fisher, 2004; Vaillancourt, 2013).

Conclusion and Future Directions

The heightened levels of aggression during the adolescent years correspond well with the onset of puberty, the development of advanced social-cognitive abilities, and the initiation of romantic relationships. The majority of adolescents are involved in dating at young ages, and growing research suggests a large proportion of the aggressive peer interactions during this period revolve around intrasexual competition over preferred dating partners. Longitudinal and cross-sectional studies show both male and female peer aggression is predictive of opposite-sex friendship and interaction, an earlier onset of dating and sexual experiences, and involvement in future dating relationships, whereas more specific retrospective investigations show seemingly greater functionality to female aggression in producing evolutionary adaptive dating outcomes for aggressors and negative fitness outcomes for victims. Frequently used aggressive behaviors among adolescent girls, such as social exclusion or spreading of false accusations, can operate by inflicting costs upon rivals that in turn could provide relative fitness benefits to the perpetrator. For example, aggressive teenage girls report dating and having sexual intercourse at earlier ages and have longer committed dating relationships, whereas those who are frequently victimized suffer negative fitness outcomes such as a delayed onset of dating, shorter dating relationships, and greater sexual promiscuity. Similar to research on adult populations, competition over males is a frequent motive for female aggression during middle and high school, and aggressors preferentially target the mate value of rivals (i.e., fidelity and physical appearance) and often use tactics of competitor derogation to deter peer fitness. These tactics could work to produce negative reputational effects while also making the victims less willing or able to compete for high-quality committed relationships due to heightened social anxiety and depression from peer victimization. Moreover, recent research shows that direct female intrasexual hostility during early stages of adolescence can be motivated by and is effective in both disrupting dating relationships of rival victims and gaining access to desired dating partners. Together, these findings provide strong support for the view that female aggression is used in intrasexual competition during adolescence.

As evidenced by the studies referenced throughout this chapter, some female aggressive strategies during adolescence are associated with, motivated by, and functional in achieving adaptive dating behavior and mating outcomes during this time. Potential reasons for the sex difference in terms of the relationship between aggressive tendencies and adaptive mating/dating outcomes include the uneven developmental trajectories between adolescent males and females and differential tactics of aggressive behavior and/or cognitive ability, all of which are founded in evolutionary biology. Consistent with this view, the onset of dating and sexual behavior is negatively correlated with the use of social, relational, and indirect peer aggression among teenage girls (Gallup et al., 2011; White et al., 2010). In addition, because adolescent females make more use of these nonphysical forms of aggression than do males, it could be that these tactics are simply more effective in regards to interpersonal attraction and reproductive opportunities via competitor derogation. Another possibility is that the type of physical aggression employed by adolescent populations could be less socially acceptable than other forms of aggressive behavior (i.e., gossip), and therefore it loses potential adaptive significance in regards to reproductive competition in this context. This may suggest a difference in the functionality of the diverging aggressive strategies used by males and females during adolescence and early adulthood (i.e., males showing highest relative physical aggression between 18 and 30 years of age, females showing highest relative indirect aggression in adolescence; Archer, 2004; Archer & Coyne, 2005). Physically violent forms of aggression are highest among males in early adulthood and can be evolutionarily adaptive at this time depending on the local circumstances (e.g., Wilson & Daly, 1985), whereas indirect and social forms of aggression are highest among females in childhood and adolescence and can be very effective in terms of the distress caused to victims (Owens et al., 2000c; Underwood, 2003).

Limitations to the existing body of literature include a lack of precision when it comes to identifying and measuring actual aggressive behaviors pertaining to reproductive competition during adolescence. Although some studies have investigated the various aggressive behaviors used by adolescents (e.g., false accusations, spreading rumors and gossiping, direct and indirect harassment), other studies have relied more heavily on surveys to characterize general forms and features of aggressive behavior (e.g., indirect, relational, etc.) This is in part due to the challenges in observing and identifying common

nonphysical forms of adolescent aggression behaviors in real time. In addition, detailed self-reports on such interaction can also present bias. Furthermore, it remains likely that multiple social strategies are effective in attaining adaptive reproductively oriented behaviors during adolescence (see Pellegrini, 2008). For example, some manipulative and antisocial strategies involve a combination of cooperative tactics to obtain status and resources (e.g., Wilson et al., 1996). Hawley (1999) has proposed that the control of resources (preferred dating partners in this case) can be multidimensional, employing both coercive and prosocial behaviors. Evidence has shown that, in fact, individuals who use aggressive and prosocial behavior ("bi-strategics") are found to be socially attractive to peers (Hawley, 2003). Most of the current research has focused exclusively on aggressive peer interactions, and therefore future research should investigate whether the most reproductively relevant strategies during adolescence are strictly coercive, bi-strategic, or both.

Moving forward, using a comprehensive analysis of multiple sources of data is likely to be most effective (Pellegrini & Long, 2002). Future cross-sectional and longitudinal research should work to develop reliable strategies for measuring actual aggressive and dating behavior through a combination of survey use and ethnographic methodology of behavior (e.g., Eder, 1985; Eder & Enke, 1991; Pellegrini & Long, 2007) and continue to explore motives behind peer aggression through the use of interviews and open-ended survey responses (Gallup & Wilson, 2012; Paquette & Underwood, 1999; Owens et al., 2000a, 2000b, 2000c) and diary methods at the individual level (e.g., Pellegrini & Long, 2002). Methods could also be expanded to track larger patterns of aggression and dating interactions, the sex ratio of available partners, and the frequency and forms of aggressive behaviors at the population level, particularly near important social events such as organized school dances (e.g., Pellegrini & Long, 2007). Furthermore, experimental methods could be used at various levels of adolescent development to pinpoint the onset, context, and interpersonal variables predicting aggressive mate competition in middle and high school populations. Although complexity arises when following these recommendations for implementing multiple methods for studying students in schools, extensive research collaborations with community school systems have been executed with great success and can serve as a model for future developments at various scales (Wilson, 2011; Wilson, O'Brien, & Sesma, 2009).

Despite the challenges of studying adolescent populations, future research investigating the contexts and outcomes of intrasexual aggression in middle and high school students has the potential to vastly improve the fundamental understanding of the evolved psychology of interpersonal attraction and female mating competition. Mate poaching, for example, which is defined by the psychology of romantically attracting someone who is already in a relationship, is quite a common and successful mating strategy for various samples of adults populations (Schmitt & Buss, 2001) and seems to emerge very early in female adolescent development, at least in part through intrasexual forms of peer aggression (Gallup & Wilson, 2012). The personality characteristics that are negatively associated with mate poaching attempts in adult populations (i.e., agreeableness and conscientiousness; Schmitt & Buss, 2001) are also negatively correlated with forms of relational aggression in adolescent females (Burton, Hafetz, & Henninger, 2007). Given this consistency, researchers could explore these and other types of reproductive strategies in middle and high school populations. Similarly, due to the relatively high frequency of aggression in the context of mate competition, it is expected that even during early adolescence females should begin to develop defenses for countering various intrasexual aggressive tactics. Human mate guarding, for example, is a well-documented phenomenon in evolutionary psychology (see Buss, 2002) but has yet to be formally studied in adolescents. This could be just one of many fruitful areas of future research in evolutionary developmental psychology because these sophisticated mating strategies may be initiated at this period in life. Furthermore, a more thorough investigation into the perceptions and predictors of mate quality among adolescent victims and aggressors would also be valuable for testing specific hypotheses.

Evolutionary theory provides considerable heuristic value in regards to investigating and explaining phenomena such as adolescent peer aggression and victimization. Effective long-term applications for reducing aggressive behaviors can only be made through a better understanding of the fundamental biological correlates contributing to these actions. For example, Volk and colleagues (2012) highlight some evolutionarily important points to promote effective bullying interventions that would likely also be useful for other forms of aggression during adolescence. For one, they indicate an importance in altering the cost-benefit ratio associated with aggressive behavior. This may be done through disciplinary actions of teachers and parents, but, more importantly, through more effective teaching of students by authorities and peers that aggressive social strategies are unacceptable whereas more prosocial alternatives are preferred. In other words, if a culture is created in which aggressive individuals are seen as socially unattractive in peer groups, this could promote the use of more prosocial efforts as adolescents compete to gain access to preferred dating partners. Future research in this area will be vital to improving the highly aggressive climate of adolescent student populations.

Acknowledgment

I am grateful to Craig Bielert for providing comments on an earlier draft of the chapter.

References

Arnocky, S., Sunderani, S., Miller, J., & Vaillancourt, T. (2012). Jealousy mediates the relationship between attractiveness comparison and females' indirect aggression. *Personal Relationships, 19*, 290–303.

Arnocky, S., & Vaillancourt, T. (2012). A multi-informant longitudinal study on the relationship between aggression, peer victimization, and dating status in adolescence. *Evolutionary Psychology, 10*, 253–270.

Archer, J. (1988). *The behavioural biology of aggression*. Cambridge, MA: Cambridge University Press.

Archer, J. (2004). Sex differences in aggression in real-world settings: A meta-analytic review. *Review of General Psychology, 8*, 291–322.

Archer, J. (2009). The nature of human aggression. *International Journal of Law and Psychiatry, 32*, 202–208

Archer, J., & Coyne, S. M. (2005). An integrated review of indirect, relational, and social aggression. *Personality and Social Psychology Review, 9*, 212–230.

Baumeister, R. F., & Twenge, J. M. (2002). Cultural suppression of female sexuality. *Review of General Psychology, 6*, 166–203.

Betzig, L. L. (1986). *Despotism and differential reproduction: A Darwinian view of history*. Hawthorne, NY: Aldine.

Björkqvist, K. (1994). Sex differences in physical, verbal, and indirect aggression: A review of recent research. *Sex Roles, 30*, 177–188.

Björkqvist, K., Österman, K., & Kaukiainen, A. (1992). The development of direct and indirect aggressive strategies in males and females. In K. Björkqvist & P. Niemela (Eds.), *Of mice and women: Aspects of female aggression*. San Diego: Academic Press.

Brown, L. M. (1998). *Raising their voices: The politics of girls' anger*. Cambridge, MA: Harvard University Press.

Brown, S., & Taylor, K. (2008). Bullying, education and earnings: Evidence from the National Child Development Study. *Economics of Education Review, 27*, 387–401.

Bukowski, W. M., Sippola, L. K., & Newcomb, A. F. (2000). Variations in patterns of attraction of same- and other-sex peers during early adolescence. *Developmental Psychology, 36*, 147–154.

Burbank, V. (1987). Female aggression in cross-cultural perspective. *Cross-Cultural Research, 21*, 70–100.

Burton, L. A., Hafetz, J., & Henninger, D. (2007). Gender differences in relational and physical aggression. *Social Behavior and Personality, 35*, 41–50.

Buss, D. M. (1989). Sex differences in human mate preferences: Evolutionary hypotheses tested in 37 cultures. *Behavioral and Brain Sciences, 12*, 1–14.

Buss, D. M. (2002). Human mate guarding. *Neuroendocrinology Letters Special Issue, Suppl. 4, 23*, 23–29.

Buss, D. M., & Dedden, L. A. (1990). Derogation of competitors. *Journal of Social and Personal Relationships, 7*, 395–422.

Buss, D. M., & Schmitt, D. P. (1993). Sexual strategies theory: An evolutionary perspective on human mating. *Psychological Review, 100*, 204–232.

Buss, D. M., & Shackelford, T. K. (1997). Human aggression in evolutionary psychology perspective. *Clinical Psychology Review, 17*, 605–619.

Buss, D. M., Shackelford, T. K., Choe, J., Buunk, B. P., & Dijkstra, P. (2000). Distress about mating rivals. *Personal Relationships, 7*, 235–243.

Buunk, A., & Fisher, M. (2009). Individual differences in intrasexual competition. *Journal of Evolutionary Psychology, 7*, 37–48.

Campbell, A. (1986). Self-report of fighting by females. *British Journal of Criminology, 26*, 28–46.

Campbell, A. (1995). A few good men: Evolutionary psychology and female adolescent aggression. *Ethology and Sociobiology, 16*, 99–123.

Campbell, A. (1999). Staying alive: Evolution, culture and women's intrasexual aggression. *Behavioral and Brain Sciences, 22*, 203–252.

Campbell, A. (2004). Female competition: Causes, constraints, content, and contexts. *Journal of Sex Research, 41*, 16–26.

Campbell, A. (2013). The evolutionary psychology of women's aggression. *Philosophical Transactions of the Royal Society, 368*, 20130078.

Campbell, S. B., Spieker, S., Vandergrift, N., Belsky, J., Burchinal, M., & NICHD Early Child Care Research Network. (2010). Predictors and sequelae of trajectories of physical aggression in school-age boys and girls. *Development and Psychopathology, 22*, 133–150.

Card, N. A., Stucky, B. D., Sawalani, G. M., & Little, T. D. (2008). Direct and indirect aggression during childhood and adolescence: A meta-analytic review of gender differences, intercorrelations, and relations to maladjustment. *Child Development, 79*, 1185–1229.

Caspari, R., & Lee, S. H. (2004). Older age becomes common late in human evolution. *Proceedings of the National Academy of Sciences of the United States of America, 101*(30), 10895–10900.

Cillessen, A. H. N., & Mayeux, L. (2004). From censure to reinforcement: Developmental changes in the association between aggression and social status. *Child Development, 75*, 147–163.

Collins, W. A., Welsh, D. P., & Furman, W. (2009). Adolescent romantic relationships. *Annual Review of Psychology, 60*, 631–652.

Connolly, J., Pepler, D., Craig, W., & Taradash, A. (2000). Dating experiences of bullies in early adolescence. *Child Maltreatment, 5*, 299–310.

Côté, S. M., Vaillancourt, T., Le Blanc, J. C., Nagin, D. S., & Tremblay, R. E. (2006). The development of physical aggression from toddlerhood to pre-adolescence: A nationwide longitudinal study of Canadian children. *Journal of Abnormal Child Psychology, 34*, 71–85.

Craig, W., Harel-Fisch, Y., Fogel-Grinvald, H., Dostaler, S., Hetland, J., Simons-Morton, B., Molcho, M., de Mato, M. G., Overpeck, M., Due, P., Pickett, W., HBSC Violence & Injuries Prevention Focus Group, & HSBC Bullying Writing Group (2009). A cross-national profile of bullying and victimization among adolescents in 40 countries. *International Journal of Public Health, 54*, 216–224.

Crick, N. R. (1995). Relational aggression: The role of intent attributions, feelings of distress, and provocation type. *Development and Psychopathology, 7*, 313–322.

Crick, N. R. (1997). Engagement in gender normative versus nonnormative forms of aggression: Links to social-psychological adjustment. *Developmental Psychology, 33*, 610–617.

Crick, N. R., & Dodge, K. A. (1994). A review and reformulation of social information-processing mechanisms in children's social adjustment. *Psychological Bulletin, 115*, 74–101.

Cronk, L. (1991). Wealth, status, and reproductive success among the Mukogodo of Kenya. *American Anthropologist, 93*, 345–360.

Cross, C. P., & Campbell, A. (2011). Women's aggression. *Aggression and Violent Behavior, 16*, 390–398.

Daly, M., & Wilson, M. (1988). *Homicide.* New York: Aldine de Gruyter.

de Bruyn, E. H., Cillessen, A. H. N., & Weisfeld, G. E. (2012). Dominance-popularity status, behavior, and the emergence of sexual activity in young adolescents. *Evolutionary Psychology, 10*, 296–319.

Dodge, K. A. (1986). A social information processing model of social competence in children. In M. Perlmutter (Ed.), *Minnesota symposium on child psychology* (pp. 77–125). Hillsdale, NJ: Erlbaum.

Douvan, E., & Adelson, J. (1966). *The adolescent experience.* New York: Wiley & Sons.

Duncan, N. (1999). *Sexual bullying: Gender conflict and pupil culture in secondary schools.* London: Routledge.

Eder, D. (1985). The cycle of popularity: Interpersonal relations among female adolescents. *Sociology of Education, 58*, 154–165.

Eder, D., & Enke, J. L. (1991). The structure of gossip: Opportunities and constraints on collective expression among adolescents. *American Sociological Review, 56*, 494–508.

Elliott, D., Huizinga, D., & Morse, B. (1983). Self-reported violent offending: A descriptive analysis of juvenile violent offenders and their offending careers. *Journal of Interpersonal Violence, 1*, 472–514.

Fisher, M. (2004). Female intrasexual competition decreases female facial attractiveness. *Proceedings of the Royal Society of London, Series B (Supplemental), 271*, S283–S285.

Fisher, M. (2012). Women's intrasexual competition for mates. In M. L. Fisher, J. R. Garcia, & R. Sokol Chang (Eds.), *Evolution's empress: Darwinian perspectives on the nature of women* (pp. 19–42). Oxford: Oxford University Press.

Fisher, M., & Cox, A. (2009). The influence of female attractiveness on the effectiveness of competitor derogation. *Journal of Evolutionary Psychology, 7,* 141–155.

Fisher, M., & Cox, A. (2011). Four strategies used during intrasexual competition for mates. *Personal Relationships, 18,* 20–38.

Fisher, M., Shaw, S., Worth, K., Smith, L., & Reeve, C. (2010). How we view those who derogate: Perceptions of female competitor derogators. *Journal of Social, Evolutionary, and Cultural Psychology, 4,* 265–276.

Fosse, G. K., & Holen, A. (2004). Cohabitation, education, and occupation of psychiatric outpatients bullied as children. *Journal of Nervous and Mental Disease, 192,* 385–388.

Furman, W. (1993). Theory is not a four-letter word: Needed directions in the study of adolescent friendships. *New Directions for Child and Adolescent Development, 1993,* 89–103.

Furman, W., & Buhrmester, D. (1992). Age and sex differences in perceptions of networks of personal relationships. *Child Development, 63,* 103–115.

Galen, B. R., & Underwood, M. K. (1997). A developmental investigation of social aggression among children. *Developmental Psychology, 33,* 589–600.

Gallup, A. C., O'Brien, D. T., White, D. D., & Wilson, D. S. (2009). Peer victimization in adolescence has different effects on the sexual behavior of male and female college students. *Personality and Individual Differences, 46,* 611–615.

Gallup, A. C., O'Brien, D. T., & Wilson, D. S. (2010). The relationship between adolescent peer aggression and responses to a sequential prisoner's dilemma game during college: An explorative study. *Journal of Social, Evolutionary and Cultural Psychology, 4,* 277–289.

Gallup, A. C., O'Brien, D. T., & Wilson, D. S. (2011). Intrasexual peer aggression and dating behavior during adolescence: An evolutionary perspective. *Aggressive Behavior, 37,* 258–267.

Gallup, A. C., & Wilson, D. S. (2009). Body mass index (BMI) and peer aggression in adolescent females: An evolutionary perspective. *Journal of Social, Evolutionary and Cultural Psychology, 3,* 356–371.

Gallup, A. C., & Wilson, D. S. (2012). Peer aggression and intrasexual competition over dating opportunities among adolescent females. In B. C. Guevara & N. A. Becerra (Eds.), *Psychology of aggression: New research* (pp. 165–173). Hauppauge, NY: Nova Science.

Gray, P. (2009). Play as a foundation for hunter-gatherer social existence. *American Journal of Play, 1*(4), 476–522.

Griskevicius, V., Tybur, J. M., Gangestad, S. W., Perea, E. F., Shapiro, J. R., & Kenrick, D. T. (2009). Aggress to impress: Hostility as an evolved context-dependent strategy. *Journal of Personality and Social Psychology, 86,* 980–994.

Hartup, W. W. (1993). Adolescents and their friends. *New Directions for Child and Adolescent Development, 1993,* 3–22.

Havighurst, R. J. (1972). *Developmental tasks and education.* New York: Davis McKay.

Hawker, D. S. J., & Boulton, M. J. (2000). Twenty years' research on peer victimization and psychosocial maladjustment: A meta-analytic review of cross-sectional studies. *Journal of Child Psychology and Psychiatry, 41,* 441–455.

Hawley, P. H. (1999). The ontogenesis of social dominance: A strategy-based evolutionary perspective. *Developmental Review, 19,* 97–132.

Hawley, P. H. (2003). Prosocial and coercive configurations of resource control in early adolescence: A case for the well-adapted Machiavellian. *Merrill-Palmer Quarterly, 49,* 279–309.

Hawley, P. H., Little, T. D., & Rodkin, P. C. (2007). *Aggression and adaptation: The bright side to bad behavior.* Mahwah, NJ: Lawrence Erlbaum.

Heilbron, N., & Prinstein, M. J. (2008). A review and reconceptualization of social aggression: Adaptive and maladaptive correlates. *Clinical Child and Family Review, 11,* 176–217.

Hopcroft, R. L. (2006). Sex, status, and reproductive success in the contemporary United States. *Evolution and Human Behavior, 27,* 104–120.

Huon, G. F., Piira, T., Hayne, A., & Strong, K. G. (2002). Assessing body and eating peer-focused comparisons: The Dieting Peer Competitiveness (DPC) scale. *European Eating Disorders Review, 10,* 428–446.

Jokela, M., Rotkirch, A., Rickard, I. J., Pettay, J., & Lummaa, V. (2010). Serial monogamy increases reproductive success in men but not in women. *Behavioral Ecology, 21,* 906–912.

Kim, Y. S., Koh, Y. J., & Leventhal, B. (2005). School bullying and suicidal risk in Korean middle school students. *Pediatrics, 115*(2), 357–363.

Kruttschnitt, C. (1994). Gender and interpersonal violence. In A. Reiss & J. Roth (Eds.), *Understanding and preventing violence* (pp. 293–377). Washington, DC: National Academy Press.

Leenaars, L. S., Dane, A. V., & Marini, Z. A. (2008). Evolutionary perspective on indirect victimization in adolescence: The role of attractiveness, dating and sexual behavior. *Aggressive Behavior, 34,* 1–12.

Marsh, P., & Paton, R. (1984). Unpublished interview transcripts, Volumes 1–5. Research supported by Social Science Research Council (HR 8379) and the Economic and Social Research Council (GOO230113). Oxford: Oxford Brookes University.

Miller, J. L., Vaillancourt, T., & Boyle, M. H. (2009). Examining the heterotypic continuity of aggression using teacher reports: Results from a national Canadian study. *Social Development, 18,* 164–180.

Moyer, K. E. (1968). Kinds of aggression and their physiological basis. *Communications in Behavioral Biology, 2*(2), 65–87.

Nansel, T. R., Craig, W., Overpeck, M. D., Saluja, G., Ruan, W. J., & the Health Behaviour in School-Aged Children Bullying Analyses Working Group. (2004). Crossnational consistency in the relationship between bullying behaviors and psychosocial adjustment. *Archives of Pediatrics and Adolescent Medicine, 158,* 730–736.

Natsuaki, M. N., Biehl, M. C., & Ge, X. (2009). Trajectories of depressed mood from early adolescence to young adulthood: The effects of pubertal timing and adolescent dating. *Journal of Research on Adolescence, 19*(1), 47–74.

Neemann, J., Hubbard, J., & Masten, A. S. (1995). The changing importance of romantic relationship involvement to competence from late childhood to late adolescence. *Development and Psychopathology, 7,* 727–750.

Olweus, D. (1993). *Bullying at school: What we know and what we can do.* Oxford: Blackwell.

Owens, L., Shute, R., & Slee, P. (2000a). "I'm in and you're out ... " Explanations for teenage girls' indirect aggression. *Psychology, Evolution and Gender, 2,* 19–46.

Owens, L., Shute, R., & Slee, P. (2000b). Guess what I just heard!: Indirect aggression among teenage girls in Australia. *Aggressive Behavior*, 26, 67–83.

Owens, L., Slee, P., & Shute, R. (2000c). "It hurts a hell of a lot . . . ": The effects of indirect aggression on teenage girls. *School Psychology International*, 21, 359–376.

Paquette, J. A., & Underwood, M. K. (1999). Young adolescents' experiences of peer victimization: Gender differences in accounts of social and physical aggression. *Merrill-Palmer Quarterly*, 45(2), 233–258.

Pellegrini, A. D. (2007). Is aggression adaptive? Yes: Some kinds are and in some ways. In P. H. Hawley, T. D. Little, & P. C. Rodkin (Eds.), *Aggression and adaptation: The bright side to bad behavior* (pp. 85–105). Mahwah, NJ: Lawrence Erlbaum.

Pellegrini, A. D. (2008). The roles of aggressive and affiliative behaviors in adolescence: A behavioral ecological perspective. *Developmental Review*, 28, 461–487.

Pellegrini, A. D., & Archer, J. (2005). Sex differences in competitive and aggressive behavior: A view from sexual selection theory. In B. J. Ellis & D. J. Bjorklund (Eds.), *Origins of the social mind: Evolutionary psychology and child development* (pp. 219–244). New York: Guilford.

Pellegrini, A. D., & Long, J. D. (2002). A longitudinal study of bullying, dominance, and victimization during the transition from primary school through secondary school. *British Journal of Developmental Psychology*, 20, 259–280.

Pellegrini, A. D., & Long, J. D. (2003). A sexual selection theory longitudinal analysis of sexual segregation and integration in early adolescence. *Journal of Experimental Child Psychology*, 85, 257–278.

Pellegrini, A. D., & Long, J. D. (2007). An observational study of early heterosexual interaction at middle school dances. *Journal of Research on Adolescence*, 17, 613–618.

Piper, E. (1983). *Patterns of violent juvenile recidivism* (Unpublished doctoral dissertation). University of Pennsylvania, Philadelphia.

Prinstein, M. J., & Cillessen, A. H. N. (2003). Forms and functions of adolescent peer aggression associated with high levels of peer status. *Merrill-Palmer Quarterly*, 49, 310–342.

Raley, R. K., Crissey, S., & Muller, C. (2007). Of sex and romance: Later adolescent relationships and young adult union formation. *Journal of Marriage and Family*, 69, 1210–1226.

Richards, M. H., Crowe, P. A., Larson, R., & Swarr, A. (1998). Developmental patterns and gender differences in the experience of peer companionship during adolescence. *Child Development*, 69, 154–163.

Rodkin, P. C., Farmer, P. W., Pearl, R., & Van Acker, R. (2000). Heterogeneity of boys popularity: Antisocial and prosocial configurations. *Developmental Psychology*, 36, 14–24.

Rose, A. J., Swenson, L. P., & Waller, E. M. (2004). Overt and relational aggression and perceived popularity: Developmental differences in concurrent and prospective relations. *Developmental Psychology*, 40, 378–387.

Salmivalli, C., Kaukiainen, A., & Lagerspetz, K. (2000). Aggression and sociometric status among peers: Do gender and type of aggression matter? *Scandinavian Journal of Psychology*, 41, 17–24.

Schmitt, D., & Buss, D. (1996). Strategic self-promotion and competitor derogation: Sex and content effects on the perceived effectiveness of mate attraction tactics. *Journal of Personality and Social Psychology*, 70, 1185–1204.

Schmitt, D. P., & Buss, D. M. (2001). Human mate poaching: Tactics and temptations for infiltrating existing mateships. *Journal of Personality and Social Psychology*, 80, 894–917.

Seiffge-Krenke, I., & Lang, J. (2002). Forming and maintaining romantic relations from early adolescence to young adulthood: Evidence of a developmental sequence. Presented at Biennial Meeting of the Society for Research on Adolescence, New Orleans, LA.

Simmons, R. (2002). *Odd girl out: The hidden culture of aggression in girls*. London: Harcourt.

Shackelford, T. K., Schmitt, D. P., & Buss, D. M. (2005). Universal dimensions of human mate preferences. *Personality and Individual Differences*, 39, 447–458.

Sharabany, R., Gershoni, R., & Hofman J. E. (1981). Girlfriend, boyfriend: Age and sex differences in intimate friendship. *Developmental Psychology*, 17, 800–808.

Tovée, M. J., Reinhardt, S., Emery, J. L., & Cornelissen, P. L. (1998). Optimal BMI = maximum sexual attractiveness. *Lancet*, 352, 548.

Trivers, R. (1972). Parental investment and sexual selection. In B. Campbell (Ed.), *Sexual selection and the descent of man* (pp. 136–179). Chicago: Aldine-Atherton.

Turke, P. W., & Betzig, L. L. (1985). Those who can do: Wealth, status, and reproductive success on Ifaluk. *Ethology and Sociobiology*, 6, 79–87.

Underwood, M. K. (2003). *Social aggression among girls*. New York: Guilford.

US Bureau of the Census Table MS-2. (2011). Estimated median age at first marriage, by sex: 1890 to the present. Families and Living Arrangements. Retrieved June 2, 2011, http://www.census.gov/population/socdemo/hh-fam/ms2.xls.

Vaillancourt, T. (2005). Indirect aggression among humans: Social construct or evolutionary adaptation? In R. E. Tremblay, W. W. Hartup, & J. Archer (Eds.), *Developmental origins of aggression* (pp. 158–177). New York: Guilford.

Vaillancourt, T. (2013). Do human females use indirect aggression as an intrasexual competition strategy? *Philosophical Transactions of the Royal Society*, 368, 20130080.

Vaillancourt, T., & Hymel, S. (2006). Aggression and social status: The moderating roles of sex and peer-valued characteristics. *Aggressive Behavior*, 32, 396–406.

Vaillancourt, T., Miller, J. L., & Sharma, A. (2010). "Tripping the Prom Queen": Female intrasexual competition and indirect aggression. In K. Österman (Ed.), *Indirect and direct aggression* (pp. 17–32). Frankfurt, Germany: Peter Lang.

Vaillancourt, T., & Sharma, A. (2011). Intolerance of sexy peers: Intrasexual competition among women. *Aggressive Behavior*, 37, 569–577.

Varhama, L. M., & Björkqvist, K. (2005). Relation between school bullying during adolescence and subsequent long-term unemployment in adulthood in a Finnish sample. *Psychological Reports*, 96, 269–272.

Volk, A. A., Camilleri, J. A., Dane, A. V., & Marini, Z. A. (2012). Is adolescent bullying an evolutionary adaptation? *Aggressive Behavior*, 38, 222–238.

White, D. D., Gallup, A. C., & Gallup, G. G., Jr. (2010). Indirect peer aggression in adolescence and reproductive behavior. *Evolutionary Psychology*, 8, 49–65.

Wilson, D. S. (2011). *The neighborhood project: Using evolution to improve my city, one block at a time*. New York: Little, Brown and Company.

Wilson, D. S., Near, D., & Miller, R. R. (1996). Machiavellianism: A synthesis of the evolutionary and psychological literatures. *Psychological Bulletin, 119*, 285–299.

Wilson, D. S., O'Brien, D. T., & Sesma, A. (2009). Human prosociality from an evolutionary perspective: Variation and correlations at a city-wide scale. *Evolution and Human Behavior, 30*(3), 190–200.

Wilson, M., & Daly, M. (1985). Competitiveness, risk taking, and violence: The young male syndrome. *Ethology and Sociobiology, 6*, 59–73.

Wood, J. W. (1994). *Dynamics of human reproduction: Biology, biometry, demography*. Hawthorne, NY: Aldine de Gruyter.

Zimmer-Gembeck, M. J. (1999). Stability, change and individual differences in the involvement with friends and romantic partners among adolescent females. *Journal of Youth and Adolescence, 28*, 419–438.

Zimmer-Gembeck, M. J., Geiger, T. C., & Crick, N. R. (2005). Relational and physical aggression, prosocial behavior, and peer relations: Gender moderation and bidirectional associations. *Journal of Early Adolescence, 25*, 421–452.

Zimmer-Gembeck, M. J., Hunter, T. A., & Pronk, R. (2007). A model of behaviors, peer relations, and depression: Perceived social acceptance as a mediator and the divergence of perceptions. *Journal of Social and Clinical Psychology, 26*, 273–302.

Zimmer-Gembeck, M. J., Siebenbruner, J., & Collins, W. A. (2001). Diverse aspects of dating: Associations with psychosocial functioning from early to middle adolescence. *Journal of Adolescence, 24*, 313–336.

Cooperation Drives Competition among Tsimane Women in the Bolivian Amazon

Stacey L. Rucas

Abstract

This chapter connects work conducted among the Tsimane of Bolivia with others and highlights the value and scope of social capital as a driver of competition among women. It further examines proximate and ultimate levels of causation to understand what forces instigate women to seek relationships with certain individuals and what benefits might be reaped through costly investments in maintenance of social status and networks. In particular, women invest in social resources such as friendships, kin-groups, and social status because they may increase inclusive fitness through higher quantity or quality of offspring. Finally, the chapter connects the ultimate effects with their underlying proximate levels of causation, showing that women view cooperators, helpers, and advisors as more interpersonally attractive. The conclusion offers a robust connection between proximate and ultimate causation effects and helps explain in richer theoretical detail the extent, progression, and complexity of women's same-sex relationships over evolutionary time.

Key Words: competition, cooperation, friendship, Tsimane, social capital

Introduction

With a few notable exceptions, very little evolutionary ecological research has been conducted on women's social dynamics within small-scale societies. However, the few studies that have been conducted have illuminated one very important fact: social manipulation via competition and cooperation by women for access to resources is cross-cultural and observed in different societies and environments throughout the world, such as among Australian Aborigines (Burbank, 1987, 1994), Polynesian Bellonese (Kuschel, 1992), Bolivian Tsimane (Rucas, Gurven, Kaplan, & Winking, 2010; Rucas et al., 2006), Mexican Zapotecs (Fry, 1998), Venezuelan Margariteños (Cook, 1992), and Central African Republic Aka (Helfrecht, 2009; Hess, Helfrecht, Hagen, Sell, & Hewlett, 2010).

Evolutionary biology posits that male reproductive success is limited mostly by men's access to mates, driving their greater interest in short-term mating and multiple partners (Schmitt, Shackelford,

& Buss, 2001). In contrast, reproductive success is limited for women by their access to resources, which for species other than humans typically refers mostly to the caloric content (food), needed to drive developmental energy until offspring can produce sufficiently for themselves. But human offspring are among the costliest in nature to raise to adulthood, as defined by the time and caloric parental demands needed across 18 to 22 years of cumulative child development, throughout which children wage little production yet accumulate significant consumption (Kaplan, 1994, 1996, 1997). Women in particular supply much of this investment and in natural-fertility populations are the primary caregivers for the first several years of a child's life (Hawkes, O'Connell, & Blurton Jones, 1997; Wood & Eagly, 2002). These sex differences in the limitations on reproductive success are directly derived from the sex differences in reproductive rate, lifetime reproductive potential, and the differential cost of reproduction. For example, men who can attract multiple mates can reproduce very quickly, whereas the same is less true for women due to the reproductive physiological constraints they face in gestation and lactation that is required for each successive offspring, resulting in years of comparatively greater parental investment by women than men (Parker, Baker, & Smith, 1972; Trivers, 1972). Similarly, since the cost of reproduction is higher for women due to these constraints, access to resources disproportionately improves the reproductive success of one woman over another. However, rivalry over resources by women has evolved far beyond the basic physical contest competition observed in other primates that ensues over choice pieces of fruit. The vast production requirements needed to raise expensive human offspring has resulted in a multitude of new strategies for acquiring and increasing the variety of resources used to drive women's reproduction. Probably the best adaptation women have acquired that has paid off exponentially in this respect has been that of expanded social intelligence, which is positively related to sophisticated forms of indirect aggression (Björkqvist, Österman, & Kaukiainen, 2000). It has also given rise to women's abilities to compete for social capital such as cooperative, resource-sharing partners, higher social status, and more social supporters who can supply years or even a lifetime of diverse resources.

In other species, evolutionary biology has proven that female mate choice is driven largely by the good genes obtained from potential mates, an effect strongest in species that supply little paternal investment. While evidence with humans supports similar competition for physically attractive men, there is also evidence that shows that women are more likely than men to trade off physical attraction in one mate for strong resource production and commitment potential in another (Buss, 1989). This trend in mating priorities among women began to appear as early as a million years ago and involves a growing preference for extensive paternal provisioning of offspring and women via the biological and culturally reinforced mechanism of pair-bonding. In effect, women actively seek to mate with men who can produce resources such as food, housing, security, and social status and who show important traits of commitment, loyalty, and dedication, offering the continued promise of replenishing reserves far into the future. Since men may adopt different strategies of mate acquisition based upon their inherent phenotypic makeup and character, good paternal investors drive women to compete with one another in order to secure a cooperative mate

who will willingly offer provisioning in the way of time, energy, and emotional support.

The mental adaptations of social cognition and intelligence, which facilitate better pair-bonds, also lend heavily to development and maintenance of social relationships outside the immediate partnership, such as friendships and kinships. These relationships are conduits to resource acquisition and for preventing shares of social resources such as friendships and social status to competitors. Such cooperative friendships, similar to cooperative life-mates, became reproductively limiting resources whereby larger and more loyal social networks improved the health and happiness of self and offspring. As with all traits in nature, variation exists, and thus some social relationships are more cooperative and therefore beneficial to inclusive fitness, while others are more antagonistic and costly. Further, some potential female friends are more connected to others due to a variety of attractive qualities they may possess. For example, Tsimane women of Bolivia, a group of forager-horticulturalists, who were portrayed as better mothers, harder workers, and better advisors and described as better communicators tended to have higher interpersonal attractiveness ratings by others and subsequently larger social networks. On the contrary, women's identified social rivals who were gossiping about them, frequent liars, and mean-spirited exhibited significantly lower attractiveness ratings (Rucas, 2004; Rucas et al., 2006). In this way, good cooperative and connected social partners with robust social skills may instigate competition among women to secure additional friends and maintain constructive relationships with them. They may do this by spending more time socializing with cooperators, thereby strengthening friendship bonds. Women may also invest in gaining social status in their human hierarchies through advances in skill development, education, income, and material resource acquisition and by enhancing physical appearance in order to attract friends. Finally, they may also invest in monitoring and directing improvements to their social reputations by practicing and emphasizing the skills and character traits indicative of higher social intelligence, such as empathy, loyalty, information exchange, social cognition, and authenticity. These points are examined further, with a focus on social research that was conducted among the Tsimane women, followed by a brief introduction and narrative illustrating the typical life-course and social existence of Tsimane people.

Tsimane Women
Daily Lives

The Tsimane are a natural-fertility group of South American Indians numbering approximately 10,000 individuals who live in the lowland jungles of the Beni region of Bolivia on native community land where they form extended-kin households. They engage in a combination of fishing, hunting, and gathering subsistence strategies, in addition to varying degrees of shift-and-burn horticulture. In their garden plots they grow foods such as plantains, manioc, corn, and rice. Women's most common daily activities typically involve food production, cooking, child care, and socializing.

The women who participated in the social research live in relatively stable communities ranging in size from 30 to 550 individuals. Tsimane marriages are fairly steady, monogamous unions. Polygyny is accepted in the society, but frequency is low at <10% of unions. Postmarital residence can be highly opportunistic with couples sometimes deciding where to live postmarriage based upon their best chances of being welcomed and engaging in resource sharing. Women typically have their first child by age 19, exhibit a total fertility rate of approximately nine children throughout their lifetimes, and are grandmothers by about 38 years of age. In fact, the typical life-course of reproduction is one in which women's own reproduction overlaps considerably with that of their daughters, and the standard investment of grandmothers as envisioned in Western societies is not observed among the Tsimane at least for the first few grandchildren. This difference is because young Tsimane grandmothers are still reproducing and thus face own-child versus grandchild investment tradeoffs. Still, grandmothers funnel significant time, energy, food, and social capital to children and grandchildren, since typically by their age they are reaping cumulative production rewards due to many years of skill development and practice.

Tsimane women exhibit shared social network sizes with other women in their community due to years of social interaction and extended family networks and depending on whether they were able to remain in their natal villages. Typically via implicit social contracts, women share food, friendships, garden plots, households, work duties, and the occasional polygynous husband. They form coalitions to cooperate and engage in varying amounts of social aggression and gossip, reputational manipulation, and relational aggression similar to that observed in societies elsewhere. Coalitions of women are made up mostly by those with varying degrees of relatedness, and many coalitions also contain members with little or no relatedness to others. Sources of intrasexual conflict vary across the life-course and include arguments over mate acquisition and food thefts, more often when young. As they age, however, conflicts switch and more often revolve around mate retention and social contract defections, whereby sharing has been initiated but reciprocation has failed to follow. These social contracts are often about meat sharing, but they can also be about factors such as social visitation invitations that have not been reciprocated. These forms of social ostracization by Tsimane women prevent access by rivals to social events where they might gain friendships and social status or even find potential mates. The basic economy of social exchange means that relationships with others and social standing are very important predictors of happiness and success in life. In fact, the Tsimane hold a belief that social aggression, mostly by way of negative gossip and witchcraft from adversaries, is the root cause of many physical and mental ailments.

Tsimane women cooperate with each other for food sharing, collective action tasks (i.e., building ovens and making roofing panels), foraging, gardening, socializing, mate acquisition, and allocaretaking of children. They also sometimes compete within their social networks over the very same targeted resources that spur the cooperative activities in part due to the greater number of interactions that coalition members share and also because cooperation does not always pay off even among friends. For example, many Tsimane women reported having different current best friends now than when they were younger and enemies who had at least occasionally previously been friends, highlighting similar dynamic processes in shifting social network positions and identities as has been observed in other, even modern, societies.

The Tsimane offer an excellent opportunity to study evolved human behavior, because unlike university students or modern community populations in Western societies, which are often used for such studies, the Tsimane inhabit an ecology and environment with life-ways and natural fertility that more closely approximate our human ancestors and therefore offer a peek into the environments of the past that have helped shape our current social adaptations.

Social Lives: As Illustrated through a Socioeconomic Game

Economic games data have elucidated many important evolutionary ecological facets of the *Homo social economicus* brain (Fehr & Fischbacher, 2004; Hagen & Hammerstein, 2006; Haley & Fessler, 2005; Hoffman, McCabe, & Smith, 1998). While there are now a growing number of exceptions, the bulk of this work is still largely constrained to modern societies that typically deal with anonymous participant interactions (Chuah, Hoffmann, Jones, & Williams, 2007; Gintis, 2000; Gurven, 2004; Henrich et al., 2004). On the contrary, much less is understood about how the specific nature of social relationships, reputations, kinship, social status, and social intelligence affect broadly defined cultural material resource exchanges, particularly among women, and what this may tell us about the quality and attributes of social dyads; recent exceptions can be made for some vital emerging work among Fijians (Gervais, 2013). Previously published research with Tsimane women sought also to address this knowledge gap by designing a new experimental game, termed the Social Strategy Game, that could capture the effects of the characteristics of women's social relationships with specific targets and how they impact on inclinations to behave prosocially or competitively with them in the context of a game (Rucas et al., 2010). In this work, jewelry beads were used as the currency of cultural material resource competition between pairs of women. During ethnographic interviews, women were prompted to point to photographs of other women who were friends, cooperators, kin, desired friends, enemies, social antagonists, neighbors, and those they were quarreling with about mates, thefts of food, and failed social exchange contracts. Effectively, the game was designed to test, for example, whether women would be more cooperative with kin versus rivals as determined by their disinclination to take valued cultural material resources, in this case jewelry beads as established in the game, away from them.

It was found that women behaved more prosocially, taking fewer beads from cooperative kin than noncooperative kin. Women also behaved more altruistically, taking fewer beads from those women with whom they desired new friendship and those who lived closer in proximity. In effect, women are less competitive, taking fewer resources from those perceived as social supporters. Further consistent with predictions, Tsimane women behaved more competitively with social antagonists. In particular, they tended to take more jewelry beads away from those they described as gossiping about them behind their backs and those with whom all social communication had broken down from previous fallouts, including those who were past but not current friends. They also took more beads from women designated as friends who were currently defecting on some form of a social contract such as food sharing or friendship, which illustrates the dynamic nature of women's relationships and that they can abruptly shift from positive to negative based on immediate circumstances. The findings, however, failed to show that women take more beads from their enemies. Most likely the reason for this finding is that one punishes social contract defectors, whose normal status is as friends or kin, in order to encourage future cooperation. However, on average, Tsimane women do not see a positive future with their enemies, because these dyads, though rare, tend to be longstanding, tempestuous, antisocial relationships. Women suspect and fear enemies for their retributional, sorcery abilities and thus are unwilling to further antagonize such relationships with heightened competition or punishment.

Since women played the game only within their village, it cannot be said that they behave cooperatively or prosocially within their own groups as a general rule. In fact, the Social Strategy Game data imply the opposite—that women's groups exhibit significant levels of competition, even sometimes between friends when social contracts have gone awry or cooperative relationships have soured to selfishness. For cross-cultural comparison, a previous study uncovered similar results whereby women were found to gossip more about in-group members compared to men, showing that women encounter most competition from *within* their social networks (Levin & Arluke, 1985), and they also physically and verbally retaliate more against female rather than male competitors (Fitzgerald & Ketterer, 2011). The Tsimane data also highlighted that kin preference in social decision-making is insufficient to explain all women's behaviors in small-scale societies, since the noncooperativeness of a kin member may shift prosociality toward cooperative non-kin individuals when the benefits of reciprocity pay off more than behaving altruistically to kin. Indeed, on many anecdotal occasions we found instances where women behaved more prosocially with a friend than with a cousin, sister, or aunt. Even among kin, women preferred those with a reputation for being helpful, as evidenced by their strong disinclination to take as many jewelry beads away from them during economic games.

Therein lays the crux, which is that the affiliative, cooperative, or helpful nature of the social relationship between two women, often irrespective of the coefficient of relatedness, is perhaps the greatest predictor of the inclination to be prosocial rather than competitive. Moreover, those women most desired as friends received the most cultural resources (in this case jewelry beads but that theoretically could be any other resource) by those women who wanted their friendship. For these reasons, women can be said to behave in ways that benefit their friends and those they desire to have in their social network because the nature of resource acquisition through channeling within these relationships is more often positive. This work also highlights that women actively strive to restrict flows of broadly defined resources to those who are not cooperative and who socially antagonize them. Cultural investigations and descriptions indicate that they do this, just as women do in other societies, through a variety of socially aggressive behaviors such as gossip, social exclusion, relationship manipulation, and social status or reputational damage (Burbank, 1987; Rucas et al., 2006, 2010; Rucas, Gurven, Winking, & Kaplan, 2012).

The Relevance of Social Capital

The socioeconomics games research has clearly highlighted some of the patterns, complexity, and investments that Tsimane women make in time and energy devoted to social pursuits. Following these results, even more lines of research with Tsimane women uncovered that social resources such as friendships, social status, reputations, and social-exchange contracts are perhaps more important competitive resources to women than food and mates (Rucas et al., 2012). This discovery led to meaningful reevaluation about how much influence social capital might exert on women's reproductive success, health, and happiness. Unfortunately, the characteristics and specific influences on women's social capital have been little studied among small-scale societies. Following cultural investigations and several years of analysis, a model has been developed (see Figure 7.1), which attempts to define some of the attributes that directly or reciprocally impact on one's social capital and how social capital might in turn affect women's reproductive success. In this model, social capital is the sum of all of the material, labor, time, or aid that others are willing to provide for a woman at any given point in time. The model

highlights certain proximate, close variables such as social status and attractiveness that increase social capital. For example, physical and interpersonal attractiveness are expected to boost social capital by drawing or "attracting" others into the social sphere of women, the best of whom will end up as helpful allies and friends. In fact, it is predicted that interpersonal attraction in particular may function as a way to increase frequency of interaction between positive social partners. On the ultimate end of the causation model, social capital is expected to increase lifetime reproductive success through quantity and quality of offspring. Some specific relationships or predictions of the model are further discussed and tests conducted to evaluate potential proximate and ultimate causation outcomes.

A Closer Look at Some Relationships of the Social Capital Model
Mates as Cooperative Partners Who Share-Bond

Research on mate attraction has undoubtedly proven that cues of physical attractiveness, as indicated by higher immunocompromising hormones resulting in testosteronized features, are important in female mate selection and operate as costly signals of better health (Little & Perrett, 2002; Rikowski & Grammer, 1999; Thornhill & Gangestad, 1993; Thornhill et al., 2003). However, research also shows that these features are sometimes traded off in favor of other traits that are more important for facilitating long-term mate bonds with cooperative partners such as warmth, kindness, family orientation, and commitment (Bereczkei, Voros, Gal, & Bernath, 1997).

Pair-bond longevity is key to female reproductive success since cooperative paternal investors can significantly improve offspring quantity and quality and decrease interbirth intervals of their wives (Marlowe, 2001). In fact, the strength of the marital bond and the mutual cooperative investments may be greatly influenced by the relatedness of marital partners seen cross-culturally, a trend that Hamamy (2012) describes as "deeply rooted . . . among one-fifth of the world's population" (p. 185). For example, the prevalence of kin-preference marriage rules across societies indicates that situations may make marrying kin better than marrying strangers, even in the presence of greater genetic risks. Several studies comparing consanguineous (i.e., marriages between cousins) with nonconsanguineous marriages show that blood-related unions have higher overall fertility (Bittles,

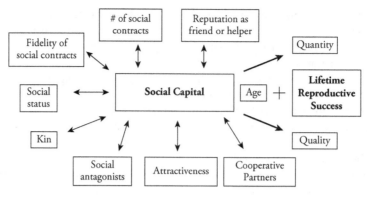

Figure 7.1 Social capital effects on lifetime reproductive success.

Grant, Sullivan, & Hussain, 2002; Bittles, Mason, Greene, & Rao, 1991; Tunçbilek & Koc, 1994). Cultural investigations into the matter indicate this may result from the greater social resources that these marriages reportedly enjoy through more durable mutual bonds, longer marriages, and widespread beliefs that they have stronger, more solid families. People further report that kin marriages are more compatible and offer a more comfortable and cooperative situation for the bride, whose in-laws will effectively be her own kin, thus improving their welcome of her (Hussain, 1999). In these ways, the benefits of greater resource acquisition through more socially cooperative, closely related networks among consanguineous marriages may help outweigh the costs of greater genetic disorder risks.

Evolutionary ecological theory points out that the sex that invests the most is the choosier about mate selection; therefore, women should be relatively more discerning about mate choice than men, since they have more to lose from poor choices due to their greater parental demands of gestation and lactation. Owing to the scarcity of quality mates (i.e., men of high genetic quality who possess resources they are willing to commit to offspring), women are expected to compete intensely with each other for these men, and such expectations should be worldwide, not limited to modern societies. In fact, according to a study of the ethnographic atlas, women were found to be the targets of other women's aggression in more than 90% of societies, and it was further discovered that female–female competition is widespread, with women fighting about men in cultures all over the world (Burbank, 1987). Burbank's extended work with Australian Aborigines and

their physical stick fights shows not only that female competition is again cross-cultural but also that mate competition is especially true elsewhere and can instigate even costlier and, more rare at least for women, physically aggressive behaviors (Burbank, 1994).

Total resource production in cooperative marriages, whereby both spouses are actively involved in sex-labor-divided but complementary productive activities, is positively correlated to total reproductive success among forager-horticulturalists (Gurven, Winking, Kaplan, von Rueden, & McAllister, 2009). Indeed, choosing the right mate is not just about securing cooperative help, whereby an alternative mate may provide little or nothing. It is also about protecting against significant detriment to inclusive fitness when, for example, choosing an aggressive uncooperative mate could result in paternal disinvestment and perhaps even spousal abuse, thus harming not only current offspring health but also future reproductive success (Stieglitz, Gurven, & Kaplan, 2012; Stieglitz, Kaplan, Gurven, Winking, & Vie Tayo, 2011). A side benefit of a species evolving away from strong male polygyny dominance of the mating structure to one that is more pair-bonded is that over time it reduces male aggression rates and lowers testosterone (Surbeck, Deschner, Schubert, Weltring, & Hohmann, 2012). The reason for this change is that sexual dimorphism, whereby males are larger than females, is largely a result of male–male physical competition for access to quantity mates, a feature most pronounced in promiscuous, polygynously mating species whereby larger aggressive males can prevent access by other males to females (Gaulin & Sailer, 1984). Pair-bonding, by comparison, significantly reduces male–male competition, since most adult males are mated already with a female, and over evolutionary time males may become smaller relative to females than is true among polygynous species, in part due to lowered testosterone that functions to divert somatic energy through development away from mating effort and physical fighting apparatus and toward other processes such as immune function and paternal investment (Alvergne, Faurie, & Raymond, 2009; Muller, Marlowe, Bugumba, & Ellison, 2009). A perhaps unintended consequence of this transition in mating systems and women's attraction for cooperative, helpful traits in a mate for long-term pair-bonding would be reduced male-directed aggression toward women and children and a concurrent increase in women's overall fitness (Hohmann & Fruth, 2003).

Humans, and at least one other primate species, *Pan paniscus* (bonobos), may have evolved traits protecting them against opposite-sex dominance and aggression, thereby limiting the risks associated with poor mate choices. Indeed, few species, prosimians aside, have evolved psychological adaptations among their females to facilitate their potential for social dominance over males. Common chimpanzees (*Pan troglodytes*) appear to more rarely, and only under specific ecological conditions, exhibit the trait of female coalition formation to retaliate against aggressive males (Newton-Fisher, 2006). Conversely, both humans and bonobos more readily exhibit this feature, which is even more puzzling since, unlike among hyena species for example, where females are strongly dominant over males, human and bonobo females are often smaller than their male rivals. Regardless, at some point in time both bonobos and humans evolved abilities and tendencies for females to create long-term affiliative bonds with nonrelatives. In fact, across primates, only the bonobo comes close to replicating, albeit in distant form and not magnitude, the female–female bonds observed in humans today that extend so far beyond kinship (Demuru & Palagi, 2012; Parish, 1996). Given that bonobos are among our closest genetic relatives, it either indicates that our common ancestor passed the adaptation to us or that there is something uniquely shared about the ecologies of bonobos and ourselves, different from our other close genetic relative, the common chimpanzee (*Pan troglodytes*), that has resulted in the evolution of strong extra-kin female relationships and female social dominance (Parish, Waal, & Haig, 2000). One aspect of this adaptation that makes it remarkably unique is

the willingness of females of both species to occasionally form coalitions in defense against aggressive and overtly dominant or demanding males (Parish, 1996). Further, the steady presence and readily recruited nature of durable female coalitions among humans and bonobos likely functions to persistently deter male aggression. In humans, cross-cultural research shows that the intensity and amount of male-initiated family violence are reduced by stronger female alliances (Gelles, 1993; Stieglitz et al., 2011). In fact, some aggressive men, in order to further subjugate and control wives, may act in ways that attempt to curtail contacts with female friends, presumably because such relationships may interfere with spousal attempts to dominate wives (Wilson & Daily, 1996). In this way, female cooperative friendships may dramatically improve offspring survivorship by indirectly protecting mothers and their offspring from male-directed aggression. Comparatively, aggression against immigrant, non-kin females is frequent and sometimes severe among common chimpanzees where there is a fear of loss of food and mating opportunities (Baker & Smuts, 1994; Pusey, 1980; Pusey & Schroepfer-Walker, 2013). In fact, especially violent acts of infanticide and vicious attacks against nonresident mothers by ingroup female coalitions have been observed among common chimps experiencing resources shortage and female-skewed sex ratios (Townsend, Slocombe, Thompson, & Zuberbühler, 2007). Such circumstances are largely absent among bonobos, who also exhibit female outgrouping at adulthood. Instead, young new incoming bonobo females sit closer to established resident females who sometimes defend them against potential harassment by others (Idani, 1991), and they tend to engage in homosexual activities with resident females as both a bonding mechanism and to improve social status (Clay & Zuberbühler, 2012; Hohmann & Fruth, 2000). By making strong extra-kin female cooperative coalitions marked by considerably less physical aggression, human females may be similarly able to protect each other from poor mate choices and outgroup women or ingroup social antagonists.

Cooperative Friendships and Ultimate Causation

The relationships between physical aggression, coalition making, dominance (Wilson & Daly, 1985), wealth and social status (Cronk, 1991;

Gurven & Rueden, 2006; Turke & Betzig, 1985), and grouping on the acquisition of reproductive fitness have been largely studied among men (Low, 1999; Sanderson, 2001). More recently, evidence among largely modern populations has been emerging that women are just as likely as men to form coalitions that engage in aggressive behaviors, albeit social over physical (Campbell, 1995; Fisher & Candea, 2012; Fisher, Tran, & Voracek, 2008), and that they spend significant time and energy in the creation and maintenance of formal social networks of cooperators and allies in order to better compete over resources (Campbell, 1999, 2002; Campbell, Muncer, & Bibel, 1998; Campbell, Muncer, Guy, & Banim, 1996; Cashdan, 1995, 2003; Hess & Hagen, 2006). Still, the benefits of women's social networks, coalitions, and friendships on fitness outcomes are perhaps among the least studied aspects of evolutionary ecology among natural-fertility populations; exceptions can be found with work conducted on nonhuman primates (Cheney, Seyfarth, & Silk, 1995; Silk, 1980; Silk, Alberts, & Altmann, 2003, 2004; Silk, Altmann, & Alberts, 2006; Silk et al., 2009, 2010). To the contrary, a large body of work exists that supports the positive effects of food intake and low work output on the reproductive function of women (Ellison, 2003). Data also support that higher-quality mates are sought by women, sometimes even when they are already mated, through a process called mate-switching, in order to further increase offspring quality (Greiling & Buss, 2000; Thornhill & Gangestad, 2008). Still, women spend extensive time and effort on social affairs beyond the topics of mates and food, leading to the hypothesis that the creation and investment in social capital is offset by strong fitness payoffs. Previous Tsimane data support this prediction whereby it was uncovered that social resources may instigate more or at least as much conflict among women as either food or men (Rucas et al., 2012).

Both in traditional and nontraditional societies, individuals devote a large part of every day to the acquisition of food through direct and indirect methods. The importance of food as an energy source is clear in that it fuels all physiological functions. However, humans are a highly social species that pay enormous time and energy costs to developing and maintaining special relationships with others and securing positions within their communities (Barton & Dunbar, 1997). Social grouping provides many benefits to help outweigh its costs, such as protection from conspecifics and predators, increased food sharing, and benefits from division of labor and specialization of productive activities. Throughout the life-course, women make complex, never-ending tradeoffs to optimally produce and rear quality children, and social networks may provide some of the best avenues to access other resources that limit reproductive success (Lancaster, 1991). For example, evidence indicates that lactating women are in a net deficit of food production, potentially negatively influencing not only themselves but also their children (Hurtado, Hill, Kaplan, & Hurtado, 1992; Kaplan, Hill, Lancaster, & Hurtado, 2000). During breastfeeding, they reduce their work output while at the same time increasing food consumption to fuel feeding bouts. Because of this net deficit, they must rely on their social ties and influential skills in order to obtain sufficient food from others such as husbands, friends, and relatives. In these ways, sociality assists women in their reproductive struggle by decreasing mortality through protection from predators and other conspecifics and also increasing access to food and other necessities via extended social networks.

Several lines of evidence provide support for the idea that social networks positively impact on the reproductive rate of mammals. Coalition building and maintenance of alliances with female kin increases reproductive success in red howler monkeys (Pope, 2000), and a higher frequency of group helpers is associated with lower interbirth intervals and earlier age of reproduction among meerkats (Russell, Brotherton, McIlrath, Sharpe, & Clutton-Brock, 2003). Achieved social dominance resulting from intrasexual competition among female meerkats improves overall breeding success (Clutton-Brock et al., 2006). Social familiarity plays a part in fitness too, whereby groups of rats raised together produce more offspring than groups where individuals were unfamiliar and reared apart (Schultz & Lore, 1993). Even lions employ social intelligence to increase fitness by engaging in cooperative territorial defense, and it is the females who utilize memory of past behaviors of their companions to assess the riskiness of intruder encounters (Grinnell, 2002). Female bonding and cooperation among bonobos increases fitness due to greater control over food resources by females (Parish, 1996), and social status and group size increase fertility among savanna baboons (Altmann & Alberts, 2003). Susan Perry's (2003) rather extensive fieldwork among white-faced capuchins led her to speculate that alliance formation and associated social skills might enhance the fitness of individuals through quality, rather than quantity, of offspring. This was confirmed by research among baboons that demonstrated a relationship between sociality and infant survivorship (Perry, 2003; Silk et al., 2003). Allocaretakers among a variety of primate species can significantly increase infant growth, leading to the hypothesis that variation in social intelligence facilitating cooperative friendships may differentially aid some females in eliciting help from others for child-care assistance (Hrdy, 1999; Meehan, 2009; Meehan & Hawks, 2013; Mitani & Watts, 1997). This line of reasoning is further confirmed with research on pigtail macaques showing that sociability and social investment increase future adult and infant survivorship (Fairbanks, 1976). Socially learned maternal competence skills among chimpanzees exhibit a strong positive effect on the quality of offspring and ultimately the fitness of the mother and her future generations (Bloomsmith et al., 2003). Ultimately, all of this work with other mammals provides clear, widespread support that costly investments in social capital (e.g., through social skills, social status, and social intelligence) pay off with measurable increases in fertility and offspring survivorship. Over time, selection has favored female mammals who spend more energy and time socializing.

While no corollary work among humans living in small-scale groups directly correlates friendship with reproductive success, an astonishing array of scientific data exists that points to both proximate and ultimate causation-level benefits for women who have more friends. For example, a wide variety of medical studies implicate an even broader array of health, and thus fitness, benefits to be gained by one's friendships. For example, women with increased social networks and task helpers, in contemporary societies, enjoy reduced mortality at varying ages as exemplified in several studies (Avlund, Damsgaard, & Holstein, 1998; Bygren, Konlaan, & Johansson, 1996; Iwasaki et al., 2002; Skolnik, 1998; Tucker, Schwartz, Clark, & Friedman, 1999; Yasuda et al., 1997). Dissatisfaction with social support is associated with higher morbidity (Rennemark & Hagberg, 1999), and larger social networks and greater perceived social support enhance participation in life-extending, pro-health behaviors, such as cancer screening, breast examination, and exercise (Oka, King, & Young, 1994; Suarez, Lloyd, Weiss, Rainbolt, & Pulley, 1994; Wagle, Komorita, & Lu, 1997). On the other hand, it was found that female patients with fewer social supporters are at greater risk of death and life-threatening addictions (Reynolds et al., 1994; Thundal, Granbom, & Allebeck, 1999). Social networks have been shown

to improve psychological and mental health functioning and significantly decrease the risk of dementia, an effect more pronounced among women than men, indicating the possibility of sex-differentiated social capital benefits (Achat et al., 1998; Fratiglioni, Wang, Ericsson, Maytan, & Winblad, 2000; Olstad, Sexton, & Sogaard, 2001; Sapp et al., 2003; Walen & Lachman, 2000). Investment in physical activity and better physical functioning are strongly correlated with social network variables such as presence of kin, friends, and confidants (Kelsey et al., 2000; Michael, Colditz, Coakley, & Kawachi, 1999; Unger, McAvay, Bruce, Berkman, & Seeman, 1999).

For women, but not for men, a small social network is correlated positively with early retirement and negatively with preplanning for that retirement, pointing to a relationship between poor social support and reduced productivity (Elovainio et al., 2003). Effectively, women with fewer friends stop working earlier in their life-cycle, thus underscoring diminished overall lifetime productivity and implying that social networks are especially important for encouraging productive activities that ultimately help women meet the demands of reproduction, such as childrearing, wage earning, and successful parental and grandparental investment strategies.

Social networks have also been shown to directly increase child survivorship (Adams, Madhaven, & Simon, 2002). For example, having close friends is correlated with a decreased risk of brain and spinal cord birth defects in offspring (Carmichael, Shaw, Neri, Schaffer, & Selfin, 2003), an outcome that results from the positive effects that social resources have on cardiovascular, endocrine, and immune functions (Uchino, Cacioppo, & Kiecolt-Glaser, 1996). Conversely, a lack of social support increases the probability of delivering a small-for-gestational-age infant (Dejin-Karlsson et al., 2000), and it further decreases the likelihood of breastfeeding newborns (Humphreys, Thompson, & Miner, 1998). Among first-time mothers, those who perceived receiving little social support from friends and family were at greater risk of becoming mentally depressed following childbirth (Brugha et al., 1998), which could ultimately result in maternal disinvestment as those mothers turn psychological attention from their children to themselves. Indeed, being willing to engage in active social exchange with others signals social competence and motivation, which affects one's success at gaining benefits from others. In point of fact, extroverts have been shown to exhibit greater overall reproductive success

(Eaves, Martin, & Hewitt, 1990), and individuals with higher levels of cooperation, as evidenced from research in small communities, have lower mortality rates (Hewner, 1997).

Similar scientific research continues to emerge, adding credence to the argument that females of many species have adapted social skills and traits to better facilitate the demands of reproduction. Countless pieces of evidence now exist proving that social capital resources, whether measured as friendships, social status, attractiveness, or social skills, improve inclusive fitness through a variety of mechanisms (Jokela, 2009; Rhodes, Simmons, & Peters, 2005; Uchino et al., 1996). Sociality costs time, money, and energy, and so the question remains: With ever-elaborate, evolving social adaptations, do the reproductive benefits outweigh the mounting costs? Because, just as friendships can supply resources, they can also take them away when friendships are ill chosen or have soured to selfishness and social aggression ensues. For humans, domains of social intelligence facilitated by linguistic features may include the evolution and use of social emotions, knowledge of detailed history of third-party interactions, recognizing mental states behind verbal expressions, and complex coalitional formation for the purpose of resource competition and cooperation. For example, more socially intelligent women will have stronger friendships due to their greater mutual empathy and communication skills, which will in turn facilitate longer-term cooperative iterations. Hence their friendly alliances and higher social intelligence will be better able to protect them from competitive singletons or coalitions of other women who might seek through social aggression to take resources such as mates or social status away from them. Coalitional formation, otherwise termed social networking, and its successful implementation is achieved only through combining together many of the mental domains of social, emotional, and Machiavellian intelligence (i.e., the ability to manipulate social situations in one's favor). In addition, while women may sometimes compete directly for items such as a piece of food, if social networks can help them gain access to many different yet equally important resources, the payoff might be greater for competition over social capital rather than for items obtained independently. Effectively, social capital operates as the conduit, securing one admittance to everything from food to help with productive activities, better mates, clothing, allocaretaking, support in social wars, and protection from predators and conspecifics, just to name a few.

To answer questions about the significance of social capital resources in comparison to other important fitness factors such as food and mates, data were previously gathered among Tsimane women that sought to ascertain the source of women's intrasexual conflicts (Rucas et al., 2012). Tsimane women were asked in semistructured interviews whether they were quarreling with others and about the nature of the conflict. They were further prompted to expound upon the root cause of competition between the parties. Based on the mating focus of the majority of chapters within this volume, one might deduce that mate competition is the single greatest driver of social aggression; however, we found this was not true for the Tsimane and therefore may also not be true for women living in similar ecological conditions where the basic economy is one of widespread social exchange. The presumption of the method of this particular work was that women should compete most frequently over those resources with the greatest potential to influence reproductive success. As the majority of chapter authors in this book would predict, it was found that Tsimane women did compete over men, both for mate acquisition and mate retention. They also occasionally fought as an extension of the quarreling of mutual children, the context of which was nearly always about teenage daughters who wished to marry the same unattached man. While rare overall, these conflicts illustrated a form of competitive motherhood (Fisher & Moule, 2013), whereby mothers attempted to secure mating resources for adult offspring at the expense of others. Women also fought over food items stolen from household stores and garden plots. Taken as a whole, it was found that social resources were at the root of more conflicts than other categories. In fact, social contract defections about failed reciprocity concerns such as defections in food sharing and socializing (e.g., women who would not return invitations to social chicha-drinking events) accounted for nearly 20% of all types of quarrels reported among women. The general category of all social resource quarrels, made up by a combination of failed social contracts and loyalty fights (defined by women who joined a friend's quarrel to support them in a social war with a third party), was the greatest of the three most common quarrel types. If assumptions are correct, it would indicate that social resources are especially significant predictors of women's reproductive success.

All of this research with humans, with other species, and across disciplines combines to form a basis for the reality that women invest in social capital resources such as friends, social networks, social status, and social contracts in order to improve their inclusive fitness. In this way the social world becomes a valuable resource in and of itself, rivaling the influence of food and mates. Therefore, the acquisition of affiliative cooperative friendships should not only be under competition but also provide one of the best mechanisms by which to compete with adversaries and extract more assets from the environment at the expense of rival women. While the social world is costly, following an evolutionary ecological line of thinking, investment in friendships among woman should be offset by higher reproductive gains. This particular hypothesis, never yet tested among women in small-scale societies, is explored next using Tsimane data.

The model depicted in Figure 7.1 indicates the various pathways by which different variables influence, often reciprocally, the nature of women's social capital. The main ultimate-level causation hypothesis (H_1) derived from the model is that the more social capital a woman has, as measured by social status, social power, and social network size, the greater her predicted lifetime reproductive success, whether through offspring quantity, quality, or both. This effect would be due to the greater resource gains delivered to women in the form of time, energy, and material goods provided by their friends and better social standing.

In order to test this idea, women were interviewed about their social capital, friendships, and social status. Each woman's social network size was defined and measured as the total number of times that she named others as cooperative helpers and the number of times she was named as a helper, and then divided by 2 to obtain an average social network size for each woman. The social status of each woman was estimated by adding up the total number of times each woman was mentioned during all social interviews in her community, regardless of whether the content was negative or positive. This variable attempts to ascertain social status by measuring an individual's notoriety or prominence in the larger community consciousness.

Figure 7.2 illustrates a general linear model regression test of H_1 and depicts the positive effect of social status on reproductive success controlling for log age, percentile attractiveness, and community size. Women with higher social status, as measured by the total number of times their names were mentioned during all-female interviews, exhibited marginally more total births ($\beta = .015$, $p = .14$) and significantly more children who survived ($\beta = .026$, $p = .008$). The adjusted variance accounted for by all predictors in the social status model explains approximately 69% of the variance in total births.

Social status is another form of social capital, and this study demonstrates that measured social position is influenced by the size of women's cooperative networks. Further, social status boosts the number of surviving offspring while only marginally affecting fertility rates. Controlling for the influencing effects of attractiveness and age, it was found that women had on average one extra surviving child for every extra 38 times they were mentioned during all social interviews. A Tsimane woman, for example, named only 50 times across all interviews fell into the lower social status linear distribution and, controlling for age, had only four surviving children, while women named 125 times across all interviews, and thus at the higher end of the social status distribution, mothered an average of six children. These results indicate that social status, as measured by notoriety or prominence within the cultural consciousness, helped improve women's abilities to produce higher-quality offspring.

Figure 7.3 illustrates an additional test for H_1 that predicts inclusive fitness effects from social capital investments. Controlling for log age, women reported by others as being the most socially powerful, identified by the influence and respect they elicited within their communities, had higher total fertility ($\beta = .766$, $p < .05$), and more surviving offspring ($\beta = .949$, $p < .01$).

At most, women had only two others who named them directly as being the most powerful who elicited respect and demonstrated influence among their groups. This variance spread indicates that social dominance among women is dispersed and likely localized in this case to one's extended household clusters. Still, women singled out by at least two others as being the most socially powerful mothered on average nearly two extra surviving children as compared to those not named as socially influential. Thus, Tsimane women reported as having higher social status due to perceptions that they are socially powerful are somehow able to turn that social capital into higher fertility and child survivorship. These independent social status measures of notoriety and social power provide strong support for the notion that, in small-scale societies, inclination to invest in social status is the product of an evolutionary adaptation.

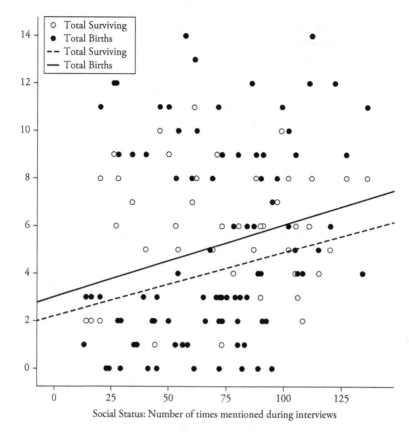

Figure 7.2 Social status effects on fitness outcomes.

Note: Women with higher social status have more surviving children.

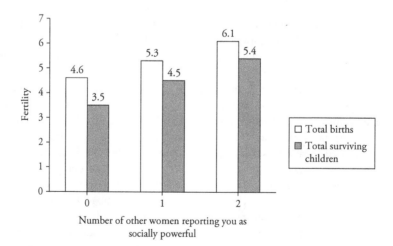

Figure 7.3 Social status effects on fertility.

Note: Controlling for log age, socially powerful women have more children and more who survive.

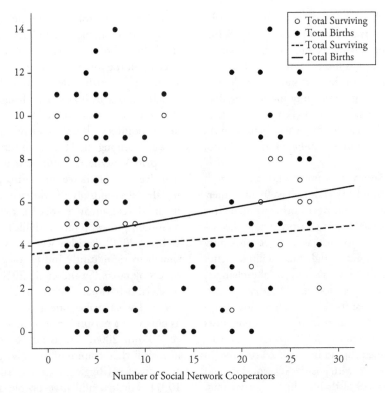

Figure 7.4 Social capital effects on fitness outcomes.

Note: Women with more helping friends have higher fertility and marginally higher child survivorship.

Figure 7.4 illustrates the general linear model regression test of H_1 and depicts the positive effect of social network size, measured as the total number of cooperative helpers, on fertility ($\beta = .19$, $p = .01$) and quality of offspring as measured by total surviving births ($\beta = .12$, $p = .11$), controlling for log age, percentile attractiveness, and community size. The adjusted variance accounted for by all predictors in the social network size model explains approximately 76% of the variance in total births.

For all the reasons documented in previous studies with other species and modern populations, social networks confer fitness benefits among native populations. Friends are especially important because they fill a variety of roles such as relationship allies, reciprocal partners, cooperators, and social supporters. Friends may help their female companions in mutual social conflicts with other coalitions of women, and they may also help in more direct instances of resource acquisition such as food sharing and social contract making. The benefits of friends and social networks can positively impact on the health, well-being, and status of women and by extension their children

and future generations. These data indicate that controlling for the effects of age and attractiveness, each additional 5.26 cooperative same-sex helpers results in a one-unit increase in fertility. However, the effects of helpers on children surviving to five years of age is less influential, indicating that cooperative friendships may improve fertility rates more than offspring quality.

Cooperativeness and Social Status Make You More Attractive: Testing the Proximate Perspective

If social capital has an effect on fitness, then what proximate mechanisms might exist to help women grow their social resources and interact in repeated iterations with the right people? Achieving a better position in the social hierarchy, for example, might facilitate women's abilities to garner and preserve larger social networks by increasing the deference bestowed by a greater quantity of others. Social standing operates in part by attracting individuals to those possessing greater resource-acquisition abilities and who are willing to fulfill social contracts. Effectively there are two mechanisms at play: (a) the willingness of another to repay a debt rather than defect and (b) their ability to repay. These can be thought of as loyalty and wealth, respectively. While the latter may be equally relevant for both women and men, the former is more influential for women whose same-sex relationships are more often defined by reciprocal exchange and equity monitoring than has been observed among men (Felmlee, Sweet, & Sinclair, 2012; Geary, 2002; Geary, Byrd-Craven, Hoard, Vigil, & Numtee, 2003; Geary & Flinn, 2002; Hall, 2011).

Therefore, wealthier women and those with greater reciprocal fidelity should have higher interpersonal attractiveness ratings by other women. This interpersonal attractiveness is a proximate mechanism that operates to instigate closer proximity between pairs of women and thus facilitate better and more frequent economic and social exchanges. If this is so, it is hypothesized (H$_2$) that women should rank their best friends and cooperative helpers as more attractive than their social antagonists who defect or refuse to initiate reciprocal contracts. In this way, women should be expected to strive to fill out their networks with positive relationships and filter out, to the best of their ability, negative ones. The social system is rather dynamic though, and while cooperative friendships may drive resources in one's direction, antagonistic relationships diminish fitness by directing resources away. In some cases, these result in extraordinary costs to reproductive success across the life-course. An example of such an occurrence happens when one or more women attempt to prevent another from high-quality mateships via social aggression, derogation, and damage to her reputation, thus blighting her attractiveness and desirability to others (Buss & Dedden, 1990; Campbell, 1995; Fisher, 2004; Rucas et al., 2006). For the reasons that social relationships can greatly improve inclusive fitness if they go well—or destroy fitness if they go poorly—social intelligence has been under strong selection among women, whereby those who were better able to navigate the byzantine terrain of female intrasexual social dynamics would have fared better over time.

The theory previously outlaid essentially predicts the evolution of proximate mechanisms that influence the motivations of women to locate and socially bond with other women who make better cooperative friends. Previous work (Rucas et al., 2006) with the Tsimane hypothesized that one such motivator, attractiveness to specific others, may be a socially salient feature operating between and within the sexes and that it may have not only physical but also nonphysical components, such as the behavior and personality of others that may make them more desirable social partners. It is likely that the behavior of prosociality holds a greater influence upon the interpersonal attractiveness of same-sex others in small-scale societies like the Tsimane, which rely heavily on social exchange as the basis for their economy, than would be true of modern market economies with independently achieved wealth. Research among the Hiwi, a hunting and gathering group in Venezuela, confirms that individuals are selective in their choices of sharing partners, meaning that decisions about whom one is attracted to in the development of social networks is far from a random process (Gurven, Hill, Kaplan, Hurtado, & Lyles, 2000). Positive personality traits have been shown to significantly impact on attractiveness of others by raters (Swami et al., 2010), and a variety of social behavioral characteristics that are components of what makes one a good cooperator, such as how well a person is respected and liked (Kniffin & Wilson, 2004; Townsend & Levy, 1990) and how well they communicate, also greatly enhance attractiveness (Riggio, Widaman, Tucker, & Salinas, 1991). Further, affiliative people are consistently rated more attractive (LaCrosse, 1975), and in smaller-scale societies other behaviors such as warriorship, hunting ability, and social status are positively correlated with attractiveness (Escasa, Gray, & Patton, 2010).

There is, however, some contradictory evidence suggesting that personality and behavior are unimportant next to physical attractiveness when it comes to considering the likelihood of choosing a partner (Kurzban & Weeden, 2005; Walster, Aronson, Abrahams, & Rottman, 1966); however, these studies are unique from the evolutionary ecological perspective for at least two reasons. First, they are conducted on modern populations who exhibit greater economic autonomy, and therefore couples may not rely on each other as much as is true in sex-labor–divided societies such as the Tsimane. Second, they introduce an ecological component that would have been incredibly rare in the evolutionary past: one of total anonymity between partners. Without previous reputational information, which is more consistently and amply available in smaller-scale societies, people in dense modern cultures may have to rely more heavily on physical cues simply because they have greater reliability when there is limited time or opportunity to get to know the reputations, behaviors, and personalities of others who would inform one about their ability to reciprocate on diverse social contracts.

Because behavior is made known often through linguistic channels, one's reputation can be manipulated via social aggression that operates through language such as gossip. Moreover, if the cooperative reputation of others is a component of interpersonal attraction, this introduces the possibility that attractiveness may be altered by social aggression such as true, false, positive, or negative gossip. Indeed, one study illustrated this effect by testing whether eavesdroppers lowered their attractiveness ratings of targets after overhearing false negative gossip about them (Aronson & Linder, 1965). The results confirm strong support for the idea that not only does behavior affect the attractiveness of others but someone's attractiveness can be manipulated by interested parties. In this way, women may be able to competitively damage the friendship opportunities of their social antagonists through social aggression, gossip, exclusion, and equity enforcement designed to steer potential cooperators away from them (Benenson, 2013; McAndrew, 2014). Arguably, this valuable strategy could assist some individuals in attaining greater access to social status and cooperative friendships at the expense of their competitors. However, when derogation of competitors is overt and easily recognized by others, it introduces the cost that negative gossipers may be perceived of as less attractive by both male and female observers (Fisher, Shaw, Worth, Smith, & Reeve, 2010). The result may be an evolutionary arms race for women to recognize and punish social aggressors and for social manipulators to better avoid detection.

Tsimane data are again useful for testing the proximate causation prediction that women view their positive social coalition partners as more interpersonally attractive then social antagonists. To do this, 120 women (92 of reproductive age) participated in confidential questionnaires and interviews regarding the state of current and recent quarrels or conflicts they were having with other women and girls in their community. Demographic details such as family size, total fertility, and child survivorship were also collected.

Polaroids were taken of all adult women in the study communities, and subjects were presented with photographs and asked to indicate whether or not the woman in the photograph was a helper in her social network. A helper was defined as someone who reciprocates with activities such as allocaretaking, fieldwork, or food sharing. They further identified all other women from the photographs who were desired friends, kin, best friends, good advisors, socially powerful in their communities,

gossiping about them behind their backs, enemies, and defecting on some form of social contract. Polaroid photographs were also used to determine attractiveness. In viewing a pair of random photographs, women were asked to identify the more attractive of the two. Following this, another random Polaroid was chosen from the pile of all women's pictures and compared with the other two to determine its relative position. This same method was repeated for all photographs, until each woman had ranked all other women in attractiveness from ascending to descending order. While this strategy is especially time consuming, a particular value of this unique method of rating attractiveness is that it forces greater variation and wider distribution of possible ranking options. Conversely, the more common method of rapid assignment of 1 to 10 values tends to result in remarkable overlap of ratings among women who might not actually be viewed as having the same interpersonal attractiveness. Further, this methodology makes more natural sense to people in small-scale societies not used to assigning quantitative numbers to people.

Multiple regression in SPSS 20 was used to evaluate the hypothesis (H_2) that if interpersonal attractiveness is one proximate mechanism driving women to socially bond with one another, then women should rank their friends, kin, and helpers with higher attractiveness than their social competitors in order to facilitate cooperation and helping behavior between the right individuals. In this way, good cooperators become more attractive and gain social capital, and, likewise, their social capital makes them attractive to others. This mechanism allows trustworthy cooperators to find each other in order to maximize the effects of social capital on inclusive fitness.

Figure 7.5 illustrates the multiple regression test of H_2 and depicts the absolute differences in mean percentile attractiveness rankings for different social identities after controlling for age and kinship (in all cases other than the kin condition). For each bar, the zero baseline represents the attractiveness of those women not named in that social category. For example, women who were desired as friends were ranked on average 6.42% higher in attractiveness by the women who named them than women who were not desired friends.

Figure 7.6 shows the results of a general linear model, controlling for age and community, that tests whether women with higher social status are more attractive as a friend as measured by the total number of times that other Tsimane women

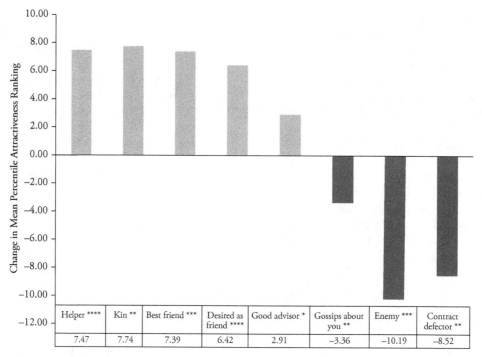

Figure 7.5 Attractiveness of social cooperators versus competitors.
Note: *sig. < .1; **sig. < .05; ***sig. < .01, ****sig. < .001.

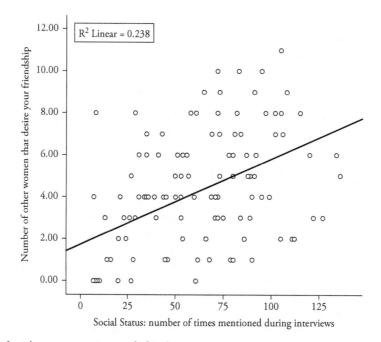

Figure 7.6 Effects of social status on attractiveness of a friend.
Note: Women with higher social status (notoriety) are more attractive as friends.

identified them as desired cooperative friends ($\beta = .04$, $p < .001$). Further, a multiple linear regression test of cooperative network size effects on social status was conducted to assess whether social position is at least partly determined by the size of a woman's social network ($\beta = .03$, $p < .01$). Previous primatologists proposed that higher-ranking females would be more attractive as social partners and draw more interest because they are more capable of assisting others with coalitional conflicts (Cheney & Seyfarth, 2008).

Figure 7.6 supports this assertion among Tsimane women by showing that women with higher social status are more desired as friends. This fact indicates that rank correlates with social network size and helps explain why social status, measured independently by social power and notoriety, correlates with inclusive fitness.

Various forms of proximate mechanisms facilitate women's abilities to bond with others who will make better cooperators. This work explored one of these—interpersonal attractiveness—and it was observed that women tend to rate their positive social network participants as higher in attractiveness than either noncooperators or other neutral parties. Women are also significantly less attracted, as would be predicted, to their rivals. They were especially less attracted to women who were defecting on social contracts, enemies, and other women who were gossiping about them when they are not around. Where helpers, kin, and best friends received the largest boosts in attractiveness, enemies and social contract defectors by comparison suffered especially sizeable losses to attractiveness. This was true particularly in the case of enemies and social contract defectors, who received reduced interpersonal attractiveness ratings by over 10 and 8 percentage points, respectively. This result provides strong support for the notion that attractiveness to others who are perceived as prosocial may function to increase the likelihood that women orient themselves around others who are more likely to provide assistance and less likely to orient themselves around others who are cheating or defecting on social sharing agreements.

Previous research with Tsimane women and other researchers in diverse disciplines and among varied populations was reviewed to form a basis for the understanding that women's social dynamics are best understood using an evolutionary ecological framework. Of important note is the development of a new understanding about what resources drive the reproductive success of women in our species

and the knowledge that social capital is as important as mates or food for improving inclusive fitness, since it acts as an important conduit driving energy, time, and material goods in one's favor. The need to secure cooperative social sharing partners and social status drives competition between women in part because not all women are equally good cooperators. Women further compete for social status and social power, or respect, because they attract larger social networks.

A limitation of this study is that while theory and statistical analysis predict and test for cause and effect, it is possible that the variable relationships are in the opposite direction. For example, perhaps an increase in the number of offspring drives investment in social networks for similar purposes of providing greater access to resources. In the future, longitudinal data on changes in network size and associated fertility across the life-course would be most helpful in confirming the direction of the effect. A further limitation of the study rests with the small-scale nature of the society and the fact that the Tsimane, like most societies in our evolutionary past, depend heavily on social exchange for their basic form of economy, and therefore the effects may not be so easily reinterpreted to explain women's relationships within modern society. For example, in cultures where women can more easily, independently gain access to resources, they may not rely as heavily on cooperative social relationships, and therefore the effects of social capital on reproductive success might be greatly reduced or at least altered according to other unique variables. A corollary effect might be greater competition for other reproductively limiting resources such as food, material goods, and physically attractive mates who can provide children with good genes. The real question in ascertaining predictive power would be intense examination of the possible theoretical affects that same-sex friendships and social status may confer on women in modern societies, whether similar or different from small-scale ones.

In conclusion, scientific work on women's social dynamics among the Tsimane has illuminated many significant findings, the most important being that women have evolved adaptations to secure social capital. Economic games research illustrated that Tsimane women are more resource competitive with social antagonists as a form of punishment that attempts to secure more faithful future cooperation from women who have recently defected on social contracts. Likewise, they are less resource competitive with helpful friends and kin because cooperation is a better strategy than competition. Quarreling data demonstrated that loyalty to friendships and good cooperative partnerships among Tsimane women are important enough resources to warrant social aggression, even though in doing so they draw valuable time and energy away from other important activities such as direct investment in food production and reproduction.

All of this previous work, combined with new analyses testing aspects of the pathway model, proves that social capital increases lifetime reproductive success, which makes it a resource worth fighting for. The need to locate and maintain good cooperative networks and attract good friends through social status gains are prime drivers of competition between and among women.

Discussion
Theory and Further Connections

Evolutionary biological theory predicts that access to females is the variable that best controls men's reproductive success. To the contrary, for women, access to resources best controls their inclusive fitness. Across the nonhuman primate order, no other species of males invests nearly so much in their offspring as do humans, and cooperative investments by men contribute to pair-bond stability (Quinlan & Quinlan, 2007). This fact puts a tremendous foraging and provisioning burden on nonhuman primate females and is why access to food is the resource that best predicts their inclusive fitness. Comparatively, extensive writings in this volume and previous work by its authors strongly emphasize the value of men as a reproductive resource that extends beyond their ability to simply contribute high-quality sperm. Due to the provisioning motivations and productive potential of some men over others, women have spent boundless time engaged in intense intrasexual competition, battling over their attention and their retention. Tsimane, Hadza, and other cross-cultural sample data support this notion by highlighting the robust effect that cooperative husbands can have on fertility, and the majority of this result is due to the reciprocal social exchange they engage in with mates and the provisioning provided to families (Gurven et al., 2009; Marlowe, 2001; Quinlan & Quinlan, 2008). In other words, the social exchange nature of the pair-bond is more important to many women than the good genes offered by some men in exchange for little postcopulatory investment. This helps explain why pair-bonding is the most common human adult social condition throughout the world—that and the fact that mates typically share

in the mutual inheritance of offspring. Overall, marriage increases fertility and exhibits astonishing effects on reducing morbidity and mortality for both men and women due to the antirisk behavioral shifts it produces, the emotional and social support provided by spouses, and the proximate endocrine and immune function benefits it delivers (Lillard & Waite, 1995; Waite & Gallagher, 2002). All of these benefits hail from the social nature and social value of the share-bonded relationship.

The Tsimane have illuminated other puzzling aspects of women's social dynamics, however. For example, women have many conflicts and arguments that are not about men, indicating quite clearly that there are other reproductively limiting resources that call for greater attention from social science researchers. In fact, much of women's conflicts are about soured social exchanges and other forms of social capital. Moreover, evidence persists proving that females of several species are acutely aware of social relationships among third-party others and this knowledge influences and instigates flexible changes in individual decision-making and associated behaviors (Liesen, 2013; Seyfarth & Cheney, 2012). This information is then utilized by females for Machiavellian purposes, such as resolving relationships, postconflict. For example, when chimpanzee females receive affiliative entreaties from the friend of their enemy, it helps them reconcile with their former opponent following bouts of competition (Wittig & Boesch, 2010). Women, however, possess far greater social intelligence than all nonhuman primates, and their social skills and abilities commonly extend to multiple orders of intentionality and theory of mind and include extensive empathizing (Baron-Cohen & Wheelwright, 2004; Christov-Moore et al., 2014). In other words, with some degree of accuracy women have the ability to read the mind of someone who is reading the mind of someone else (and perhaps even further, depending on their degree of social cognition and the extent of their social intelligence). Women's complexity and skill regarding the social world is a phenomenal outlier in the animal kingdom, and this is precisely because social capital exhibited powerful influences on their inclusive fitness (Herrmann, Call, Hernández-Lloreda, Hare, & Tomasello, 2007). A fact that has greatly contributed to this effect involves the sex differences in style of aggression, whereby women and girls far prefer social over physical aggression as a means of competing with others due to the lower cost ratio (Björkqvist, Lagerspetz, & Kaukiainen, 1992;

Crick & Grotpeter, 1995). Ultimately, intrasexual and sexual selection both act to produce males with predispositions in upper-body strength and muscle mass to better facilitate physical aggression (Buss & Shackelford, 1997; Wells, 2007) and women with complex social cognition (Hall, 1990; Saxena & Jain, 2013) in order to facilitate better social aggression (Campbell, 1995, 2002).

Work in related disciplines such as sociology and, more recently, public health has concluded that social capital investments and maintenance are a major motivator of human behavior (Astone, Nathanson, Schoen, & Kim, 1999). For example, modern datasets have linked reduced social capital with higher rates of conflict through homicides, suggesting a lack of social resources is correlated to greater and more intense within-group competition, whereas in localities that exhibit greater social capital, cooperation is more prevalent and reflected in lower rates of homicides (Rosenfeld, Baumer, & Messner, 2001). While competition among women may result from a lack of resources, cooperation among social others can help buffer women from resource shortages, as well as provide emotional support and companionship (Roberts, Arrow, Lehmann, & Dunbar, 2014). Thus, social capital becomes something worthy of contestation and may have selected for tendencies to befriend rather than engage in fight-or-flight behavior when exposed to competitive stress responses, a trait that is present among women and appears as early as infancy (David & Lyons-Ruth, 2005; Taylor, 2006; Taylor et al., 2000).

The ultimate connection between social capital and reproduction has mostly been explored only within primatology (Archie, Tung, Clark, Altmann, & Alberts, 2014). Comparatively less work has been done among humans aside from the bulk of research that tests for sociality impacts on health pathways. Still, there are a handful of studies on preexisting datasets recorded in modern populations, such as Bulgaria and Poland, showing that reciprocity and social networks influence women's decisions to have additional children (Bühler & Fratczak, 2007; Philipov, Spéder, & Billari, 2006), and researchers in the United States have modeled that teenage birth-rates among girls positively correlate with income inequality. They concluded that this effect operates mostly through pathways of reduced social capital present alongside poverty disparity (Gold, Kennedy, Connell, & Kawachi, 2002). Each of these studies highlights the prominence of social-capital variables

in predicting individual fertility; however, much more work needs to be done in this area.

If primate models are any evidence of human behavior, though, there is much to compare. For example, the strength of social bonds are especially important and independent predictors of offspring survival, and companionship among female baboons raises inclusive fitness via pathways of increasing longevity (Silk et al., 2009, 2010). Reciprocity in grooming exists between nongenetically related female companions, proving that cooperation is a component of their friendships (Cheney, Moscovice, Heesen, Mundry, & Seyfarth, 2010). Among capuchins, extensively grooming females who preferentially interact also tend to have closer, more tightly connected social groups that should ultimately confer social benefits (Crofoot, Rubenstein, Maiya, & Berger Wolf, 2011). Social capital lowers physiological stress among macaques as measured by glucocorticoid levels, suggesting proximate health benefits from social contacts (Brent, Semple, Dubuc, Heistermann, & MacLarnon, 2011). Finally, in Bornean orangutans, a female philopatric species where males outgroup upon adulthood, females restrict offspring play around unrelated mothers. It therefore follows that should a primate species evolve the capacity to make strong affiliative relationships with nonrelated females, such as humans and bonobos have done, they would have higher-quality offspring that exhibit improved social and physical skills due to more time spent playing with others during growth and development (van Noordwijk et al., 2012).

Research among Tsimane women has significantly advanced our understanding of the theoretical underpinnings of intrasexual competition among women by specifying the exact nature of the resources that cause conflict. In particular, social capital is among the most important resources that women strive to optimize in order to maximize their inclusive fitness, an outcome confirmed through several social-variable effects on offspring quantity and quality. Because social capital proved so useful in this respect, selection favored a variety of proximate pathways through which women might have achieved social ends. A prime example was the co-opting of attraction mechanisms, which likely evolved more to facilitate parent–offspring and pair-bond associations and extended them to interpersonal relationships with other women. This resulted in women viewing their friendships and prosocial others as having significantly greater interpersonal attractiveness than null parties, especially rivals. Ultimately this facilitated more interactions among groups of women who cooperated, reciprocated, and supported one another, and it limited their interactions with social antagonists and rivals who would seek to damage or even destroy fitness.

Future Avenues of Investigation

Future work on women's social relationships could do more to identify which aspects or qualities within dyadic social relationships are most responsible for providing fitness benefits. In this vein, a recent guide was developed based on years of research with baboons to provide better comparable and useful metrics to assess the quality of relationships within groups (Silk, Cheney, & Seyfarth, 2013). The guide goes a long way toward integrating and bringing together a diversity of methods used in social capital research, and while it is particular to nonhuman primates and other animals, many if not all of the variables could be used to evaluate women's dyadic relationships. Another value of using these metrics lies in the nature of the behavioral observation data required, which eliminates some of the problems of linguistic biasing and manipulation that may happen during social interviews with smart women. Still, human language offers a rich area of work relevant to understanding women's social dynamics, so researchers working with humans might try to develop a similar best practices, definition, and methodological guide for studies targeting women's competitive and cooperative behaviors.

Results on the social lives of Tsimane women may not equally parallel those of women living in modern developed societies, since social exchange is no longer the basis of our economies. However, there is much anecdotal evidence to indicate that significant competition among modern women ensues for reasons that go far beyond gaining or retaining a mate, indicating strong potential for the existence of other resources with reproductive relevance. Future work with modern populations needs to better consider the possibility of social resources as instigators of interpersonal conflict driven by the nature of their ability to enhance reproductive success.

Further lines of inquiry might also pay greater attention to factors that affect interpersonal attractiveness as a complement to work conducted on physical attractiveness. With respect to evolutionary studies, the bulk of work on attractiveness has mostly related to physical features driving mate attraction. But Tsimane women's data clearly indicates that a host of social factors, relationship status, and prosocial behaviors affect perceptions of other's

interpersonal attractiveness. Importantly, this variable of interpersonal attractiveness may help drive individuals toward others who are more helpful and kind and steer them away from those who have hurt and damaged their reputations and social prospects. Such a line of inquiry will better assist in explaining how and through what mechanisms women associate with particular others. Other proximate mechanisms also need further investigation and integration into models of social capital and how these work to determine fitness. For example, recent research connects oxytocin to food-sharing bouts among common chimpanzees (Wittig et al., 2014). In small-scale societies, food sharing is an essential and common form of the social exchange economy, and similar proximate mechanisms may have evolved in humans to facilitate improved social bonds with bread-breaking partners regardless of kinship affiliation. Studies might search for similar connections among pairs of women that regularly share meals. Certainly such an inquiry need not be limited to small-scale foragers and might also be applied to women's friendships in modern societies.

Still other proximate avenues of research could be explored. For example, it was discovered that primate friends who play together and those with more friends at age one ended up with higher social-bonding hormones such as oxytocin and vasopressin, both of which exhibit positive health effects on the body and well-being (Weinstein, Bales, Maninger, Hostetler, & Capitanio, 2014). No such corollary longitudinal work with women exists that suggests exposure to friendship in early growth and development patterns hormonal shifts, ultimately resulting in a host of adult consequences such as better health, more cooperative partners, and improved attachments between mothers and infants and among pair-bonds.

While research among female competition and cooperation is demonstrably and rapidly increasing, it has also highlighted how little we really do know about the nature of women's social dynamics and how much more there is to do in this area. At some point, however, supplementing the academic research with applied perspectives, efforts, and goals for improving the lives and happiness of women everywhere should be a paramount aspiration.

Conclusion and Future Directions

Intrasexual selection theory predicts the evolution of traits that improve women's chances at competition for reproductively limiting resources. Social intelligence and social aggression, broadly defined, helped women in their wars with other women throughout millennia, and most certainly social capital became an ever-increasing resource worth fighting over. Prosociality and social cooperation would have delivered strong advantages to groups of women in the evolutionary past where economies were based on social exchange and women were more likely to outgroup, or disperse, thus leaving valuable kinship networks behind. As a corollary, a host of proximate connections between physiology and prosociality would have evolved, conferring fitness and health advantages and also driving further avenues through which women might have engaged the social world around them in order to increase their overall social capital. Unfortunately, though, cheating strategies would have appeared, such as taking advantage of helpers and cooperators in these social exchange societies, necessitating development of similar social manipulation mechanisms to defend one against rivals in order to buffer negative fitness consequences from socially aggressive competitors. As a result, interpersonal attractiveness to specific others, especially those with positive prosocial characteristics who ultimately inhabit positive "friendly" positions in one's social network, evolved to better facilitate affiliation with the right women. Tsimane data support all of the tested connections within the social capital model but also highlight how much more work there is to do, not only with testing the other connections but also with identifying added variables of causative influence that might improve model development. In many ways, the job to be done is as complex as the world of women's social dynamics.

References

Achat, H., Kawachi, I., Levine, S., Berkey, C., Coakley, E., & Colditz, G. (1998). Social networks, stress and health-related quality of life. *Quality of Life Research, 7*(8), 735–750.

Adams, A. M., Madhaven, S., & Simon, D. (2002). Women's social networks and child survival in Mali. *Social Science & Medicine, 54*(2), 165–178.

Altmann, J., & Alberts, S. C. (2003). Variability in reproductive success viewed from a life-history perspective in baboons. *American Journal of Human Biology, 15*(3), 401–409.

Alvergne, A., Faurie, C., & Raymond, M. (2009). Variation in testosterone levels and male reproductive effort: Insight from a polygynous human population. *Hormones and Behavior, 56*(5), 491–497.

Archie, E. A., Tung, J., Clark, M., Altmann, J., & Alberts, S. C. (2014). Social affiliation matters: Both same-sex and opposite-sex relationships predict survival in wild female baboons. *Proceedings of the Royal Society B: Biological Sciences, 281*(1793), 20141261.

Aronson, E., & Linder, D. (1965). Gain and loss of esteem as determinants of interpersonal attractiveness. *Journal of Experimental Social Psychology, 1*(2), 156–171.

Astone, N. M., Nathanson, C. A., Schoen, R., & Kim, Y. J. (1999). Family demography, social theory, and investment in social capital. *Population and Development Review, 25*(1), 1–31.

Avlund, K., Damsgaard, M. T., & Holstein, B. E. (1998). Social relations and mortality. An eleven-year follow-up study of 70-year old men and women in Denmark. *Social Science and Medicine, 47*(5), 635–643.

Baker, K. C., & Smuts, B. B. (1994). Social relationships of female chimpanzees. In R. W. Wrangham (Ed.), *Chimpanzee cultures* (pp. 227–242). Cambridge, MA: Harvard University Press.

Baron-Cohen, S., & Wheelwright, S. (2004). The empathy quotient: An investigation of adults with Asperger syndrome or high-functioning autism, and normal sex differences. *Journal of Autism and Developmental Disorders, 34*(2), 163–175.

Barton, R., & Dunbar, R. I. M. (1997). Evolution of the social brain. In A. Whiten & R. W. Bryne (Eds.), *Machiavellian intelligence II* (pp. 240–263). Cambridge, UK: Cambridge University Press.

Benenson, J. F. (2013). The development of human female competition: Allies and adversaries. *Philosophical Transactions of the Royal Society B, 368*(1631), 20130079.

Bereczkei, T., Voros, S., Gal, A., & Bernath, L. (1997). Resources, attractiveness, family commitment: Reproductive decisions in human mate choice. *Ethology, 103*(8), 681–699.

Bittles, A. H., Grant, J. C., Sullivan, S. G., & Hussain, R. (2002). Does inbreeding lead to decreased human fertility? *Annals of Human Biology, 29*(2), 111–130.

Bittles, A. H., Mason, W. M., Greene, J., & Rao, N. A. (1991). Reproductive behavior and health in consanguineous marriages. *Science, 252*(5007), 789–794.

Björkqvist, K., Lagerspetz, K. M., & Kaukiainen, A. (1992). Do girls manipulate and boys fight? Developmental trends in regard to direct and indirect aggression. *Aggressive Behavior, 18*(2), 117–127.

Björkqvist, K., Österman, K., & Kaukiainen, A. (2000). Social intelligence – empathy = aggression? *Aggression and Violent Behavior, 5*(2), 191–200.

Bloomsmith, M. A., Kuhar, C., Baker, K., Lambeth, S., Brent, L., Ross, S. R., & Fritz, J. (2003). Primiparous chimpanzee mothers: Behavior and success in a short-term assessment of infant rearing. *Applied Animal Behaviour Science, 84*(3), 235–250.

Brent, L., Semple, S., Dubuc, C., Heistermann, M., & MacLarnon, A. (2011). Social capital and physiological stress levels in free-ranging adult female rhesus macaques. *Physiology & Behavior, 102*(1), 76–83.

Brugha, T. S., Sharp, H. M., Cooper, S. A., Weisender, C., Britto, D., Shinkwin, R., ... Kirwan, P. H. (1998). The Leicester 500 Project: Social support and the development of postnatal depressive symptoms, a prospective cohort survey. *Psychological Medicine, 28*(1), 63–79.

Bühler, C., & Fratczak, E. (2007). Learning from others and receiving support: The impact of personal networks on fertility intentions in Poland. *European Societies, 9*(3), 359–382.

Burbank, V. (1987). Female aggression in cross-cultural perspective. *Behavioral Science Research, 21*, 70–100.

Burbank, V. (1994). *Fighting women*. Berkeley: University of California Press.

Buss, D. M. (1989). Sex differences in human mate preferences: Evolutionary hypotheses tested in 37 cultures. *Behavioral and Brain Sciences, 12*, 1–49.

Buss, D. M., & Dedden, L. A. (1990). Derogation of competitors. *Journal of Social and Personal Relationships, 7*(3), 395–422.

Buss, D. M., & Shackelford, T. K. (1997). Human aggression in evolutionary psychological perspective. *Clinical Psychology Review, 17*(6), 605–619.

Bygren, L. O., Konlaan, B. B., & Johansson, S. E. (1996). Attendance at cultural events, reading books or periodicals, and making music or singing in a choir as determinants for survival: Swedish interview survey of living conditions. *British Medical Journal, 313*(7072), 1577–1580.

Campbell, A. (1995). A few good men: Evolutionary psychology and female adolescent aggression. *Ethology and Sociobiology, 16*(2), 99–123.

Campbell, A. (1999). Staying alive: Evolution, culture, and women's intrasexual aggression. *Behavioral and Brain Sciences, 22*, 203–252.

Campbell, A. (2002). *A mind of her own: The evolutionary psychology of women.* New York: Oxford University Press.

Campbell, A., Muncer, S., & Bibel, D. (1998). Female-female criminal assault: An evolutionary perspective. *Journal of Research in Crime and Delinquency, 35*(4), 413–428.

Campbell, A., Muncer, S., Guy, A., & Banim, M. (1996). Social representation of aggression: Crossing the sex barrier. *European Journal of Social Psychology, 26*, 135–147.

Carmichael, S. L., Shaw, G. M., Neri, E., Schaffer, D. M., & Selfin, S. (2003). Social networks and risk of neural tube defects. *European Journal of Epidemiology, 18*(2), 129–133.

Cashdan, E. (1995). Hormones, sex, and status in women. *Hormones and Behavior, 29*(3), 354–366.

Cashdan, E. (2003). Hormones and competitive aggression in women. *Aggressive Behavior, 29*(2), 107–115.

Cheney, D. L., Moscovice, L. R., Heesen, M., Mundry, R., & Seyfarth, R. M. (2010). Contingent cooperation between wild female baboons. *Proceedings of the National Academy of Sciences, 107*(21), 9562–9566.

Cheney, D. L., & Seyfarth, R. M. (2008). *Baboon metaphysics: The evolution of a social mind.* Chicago: University of Chicago Press.

Cheney, D. L., Seyfarth, R. M., & Silk, J. B. (1995). The role of grunts in reconciling opponents and facilitating interactions among adult female baboons. *Animal Behaviour, 50*(1), 249–257.

Christov-Moore, L., Simpson, E. A., Coudé, G., Grigaityte, K., Iacoboni, M., & Ferrari, P. F. (2014). Empathy: Gender effects in brain and behavior. *Neuroscience & Biobehavioral Reviews, 39*, 34–50.

Chuah, S.-H., Hoffmann, R., Jones, M., & Williams, G. (2007). Do cultures clash? Evidence from cross-national ultimatum game experiments. *Journal of Economic Behavior and Organization, 64*(1), 35–48.

Clay, Z., & Zuberbühler, K. (2012). Communication during sex among female bonobos: effects of dominance, solicitation and audience. *Scientific Reports, 2*, article 291.

Clutton-Brock, T., Hodge, S., Spong, G., Russell, A., Jordan, N., Bennett, N., ... Manser, M. (2006). Intrasexual competition and sexual selection in cooperative mammals. *Nature, 444*(7122), 1065–1068.

Cook, H. B. K. (1992). Matrifocality and female aggression in Margariteno society. In K. Björkqvist & P. Niemela (Eds.), *Of mice and women: Aspects of female aggression* (pp. 149–162). San Diego: Academic Press.

Crick, N. R., & Grotpeter, J. K. (1995). Relational aggression, gender and social-psychological adjustment. *Child Development, 66*(3), 710–722.

Crofoot, M. C., Rubenstein, D. I., Maiya, A. S., & Berger Wolf, T. Y. (2011). Aggression, grooming and group-level cooperation in white-faced capuchins (*Cebus capucinus*): Insights from social networks. *American Journal of Primatology, 73*(8), 821–833.

Cronk, L. (1991). Wealth, status, and reproductive success among the Mukogodo of Kenya. *American Anthropologist, 93*, 345–360.

David, D. H., & Lyons-Ruth, K. (2005). Differential attachment responses of male and female infants to frightening maternal behavior: Tend or befriend versus fight or flight? *Infant Mental Health Journal, 26*(1), 1–18.

Dejin-Karlsson, E., Hanson, B. S., Ostergren, P. O., Lindgren, A., Sjoberg, N. O., & Marsal, K. (2000). Association of a lack of psychosocial resources and the risk of giving birth to small for gestational age infants: A stress hypothesis. *British Journal of Obstetrics and Gynaecology, 107*(1), 89–100.

Demuru, E., & Palagi, E. (2012). In bonobos yawn contagion is higher among kin and friends. *PloS ONE, 7*(11), 1–7.

Eaves, L. J., Martin, N. G., & Hewitt, J. K. (1990). Personality and reproductive fitness. *Behavior Genetics, 20*(5), 563–568.

Ellison, P. T. (2003). Energetics and reproductive effort. *American Journal of Human Biology, 15*, 342–351.

Elovainio, M., Kivimaki, M., Vahtera, J., Ojanlatva, A., Korkeila, K., Suominen, S., ... Koskenvuo, M. (2003). Social support, early retirement, and a retirement preference: A study of 10,489 Finnish adults. *Journal of Occupational and Environmental Medicine, 45*(4), 433–439.

Escasa, M., Gray, P. B., & Patton, J. Q. (2010). Male traits associated with attractiveness in Conambo, Ecuador. *Evolution and Human Behavior, 31*(3), 193–200.

Fairbanks, L. A. (1976). Behavioral correlates of reproductive success in a pigtail macaque breeding colony. *Bulletin of the Psychonomic Society, 8*(5), 389–391.

Fehr, E., & Fischbacher, U. (2004). Third-party punishment and social norms. *Evolution and Human Behavior, 25*(2), 63–87.

Felmlee, D., Sweet, E., & Sinclair, H. C. (2012). Gender rules: Same- and cross-gender friendships norms. *Sex Roles, 66*(7–8), 518–529.

Fisher, M. L. (2004). Female intrasexual competition decreases female facial attractiveness. *Proceedings of the Royal Society of London, Series B: Biological Sciences, 271*(Suppl 5), S283–S285.

Fisher, M. L., & Candea, C. (2012). You ain't woman enough to take my man: Female intrasexual competition as portrayed in songs. *Journal of Social, Evolutionary, and Cultural Psychology, 6*(4), 480–493.

Fisher, M. L., & Moule, K. R. (2013). A new direction for intrasexual competition research: Cooperative versus competitive motherhood. *Journal of Social, Evolutionary, and Cultural Psychology, 7*(4), 318.

Fisher, M. L., Shaw, S., Worth, K., Smith, L., & Reeve, C. (2010). How we view those who derogate: Perceptions of female competitor derogators. *Journal of Social, Evolutionary, and Cultural Psychology, 4*(4), 265–276.

Fisher, M. L., Tran, U. S., & Voracek, M. (2008). The influence of relationship status, mate seeking, and sex on intrasexual competition. *Journal of Social Psychology, 148*(4), 493–512.

Fitzgerald, C. J., & Ketterer, H. L. (2011). Examining verbal and physical retaliation against kinship insults. *Violence and Victims*, 26(5), 580–592.

Fratiglioni, L., Wang, H. X., Ericsson, K., Maytan, M., & Winblad, B. (2000). Influence of social network on occurrence of dementia: A community-based longitudinal study. *Lancet*, 355(9212), 1315–1319.

Fry, D. P. (1998). Anthropological perspectives on aggression: Sex differences and cultural variation. *Aggressive Behavior*, 24(2), 81–95.

Gaulin, S. J., & Sailer, L. D. (1984). Sexual dimorphism in weight among the primates: The relative impact of allometry and sexual selection. *International Journal of Primatology*, 5(6), 515–535.

Geary, D. C. (2002). Sexual selection and sex differences in social cognition. In A. V. McGillicuddy-De Lisi & R. D. Lisi (Eds.), *Biology, society, and behavior: The development of sex differences in cognition* (Vol. 21, pp. 23–53). Greenwich, CT: Ablex/Greenwood.

Geary, D. C., Byrd-Craven, J., Hoard, M. K., Vigil, J., & Numtee, C. (2003). Evolution and development of boys' social behavior. *Developmental Review*, 23(4), 444–470.

Geary, D. C., & Flinn, M. V. (2002). Sex differences in behavioral and hormonal response to social threat: Commentary on Taylor et al. (2000). *Psychological Review*, 109(4), 745–750.

Gelles, R. J. (1993). Family violence. In R. L. Hampton (Ed.), *Family violence: Prevention and treatment* (pp. 1–24). Issues in Children's and Families' Lives 1. Thousand Oaks, CA: SAGE.

Gervais, M. M. (2013). *Structures of sentiment: Mapping the affective bases of social relationships in Yasawa, Fiji* (Unpublished doctoral dissertation). University of California, Los Angeles.

Gintis, H. (2000). Beyond *Homo economicus*: Evidence from experimental economics. *Ecological Economics*, 35(3), 311–322.

Gold, R., Kennedy, B., Connell, F., & Kawachi, I. (2002). Teen births, income inequality, and social capital: Developing an understanding of the causal pathway. *Health & Place*, 8(2), 77–83.

Greiling, H., & Buss, D. M. (2000). Women's sexual strategies: The hidden dimension of extra-pair mating. *Personality and Individual Differences*, 28(5), 929–963.

Grinnell, J. (2002). Modes of cooperation during territorial defense by African lions. *Human Nature*, 13(1), 85–104.

Gurven, M. (2004). Economic games among the Amazonian Tsimane: Exploring the roles of market access, costs of giving, and cooperation on pro-social game behavior. *Experimental Economics*, 7(1), 5–24.

Gurven, M., Hill, K., Kaplan, H., Hurtado, A. M., & Lyles, R. (2000). Food transfers among Hiwi foragers of Venezuela: Tests of reciprocity. *Human Ecology*, 28(2), 171–218.

Gurven, M., & Rueden, C. V. (2006). Hunting, social status and biological fitness. *Social Biology*, 53(1–2), 81–99.

Gurven, M., Winking, J., Kaplan, H., von Rueden, C., & McAllister, L. (2009). A bioeconomic approach to marriage and the sexual division of labor. *Human Nature*, 20(2), 151–183.

Hagen, E. H., & Hammerstein, P. (2006). Game theory and human evolution: A critique of some recent interpretations of experimental games. *Theoretical Population Biology*, 69(3), 339–348.

Haley, K. J., & Fessler, D. M. (2005). Nobody's watching? Subtle cues affect generosity in an anonymous economic game. *Evolution and Human Behavior*, 26(3), 245–256.

Hall, J. A. (1990). *Nonverbal sex differences: Accuracy of communication and expressive style*. Baltimore, MD: Johns Hopkins University Press.

Hall, J. A. (2011). Sex differences in friendship expectations: A meta-analysis. *Journal of Social and Personal Relationships*, 28(6), 723–747.

Hamamy, H. (2012). Consanguineous marriages. *Journal of Community Genetics*, 3(3), 185–192.

Hawkes, K., O'Connell, J. F., & Blurton Jones, N. G. (1997). Hadza women's time allocation, offspring provisioning, and the evolution of long postmenopausal life spans. *Current Anthropology*, 38(4), 551–577.

Helfrecht, C. E. (2009). *Age and sex differences in aggression among the Aka foragers of the Central African Republic* (Unpublished master's thesis). Washington State University, Pullman, WA.

Henrich, J., Boyd, R., Bowles, S., Camerer, C., Fehr, E., & Gintis, H. (2004). *Foundations of human sociality: Economic experiments and ethnographic evidence from fifteen small-scale societies*. Oxford: Oxford University Press.

Herrmann, E., Call, J., Hernández-Lloreda, M. V., Hare, B., & Tomasello, M. (2007). Humans have evolved specialized skills of social cognition: The cultural intelligence hypothesis. *Science*, 317(5843), 1360–1366.

Hess, N. H., & Hagen, E. H. (2006). Sex differences in indirect aggression: Psychological evidence from young adults. *Evolution and Human Behavior*, 27(3), 231–245.

Hess, N. H., Helfrecht, C., Hagen, E., Sell, A., & Hewlett, B. (2010). Interpersonal aggression among Aka hunter-gatherers of the Central African Republic. *Human Nature*, 21(3), 330–354.

Hewner, S. J. (1997). Biocultural approaches to health and mortality in an older order Amish community. *Collegium Antropologicum*, 21(1), 67–82.

Hoffman, E., McCabe, K. A., & Smith, V. L. (1998). Behavioral foundations of reciprocity: Experimental economics and evolutionary psychology. *Economic Inquiry*, 36(3), 335–352.

Hohmann, G., & Fruth, B. (2000). Use and function of genital contacts among female bonobos. *Animal Behaviour*, 60(1), 107–120.

Hohmann, G., & Fruth, B. (2003). Intra- and inter-sexual aggression by bonobos in the context of mating. *Behaviour*, 140(11), 1389–1414.

Hrdy, S. B. (1999). *Mother nature: Maternal instincts and how they shape the human species*. Toronto: Ballantine Books.

Humphreys, A. S., Thompson, N. J., & Miner, K. R. (1998). Intention to breastfeed in low-income pregnant women: The role of social support and previous experience. *Birth*, 25(3), 169–174.

Hurtado, A. M., Hill, K., Kaplan, H., & Hurtado, I. (1992). Trade-offs between female food acquisition and child care among Hiwi and Ache foragers. *Human Nature*, 3(3), 185–216.

Hussain, R. (1999). Community perceptions of reasons for preference for consanguineous marriages in Pakistan. *Journal of Biosocial Science*, 31(4), 449–461.

Idani, G. (1991). Social relationships between immigrant and resident Bonobo (*Pan paniscus*) females at Wamba. *Folia Primatologica*, 57(2), 83–95.

Iwasaki, M., Otani, T., Sunaga, R., Miyazaki, H., Xiao, L., Wang, N., ... Suzuki, S. (2002). Social networks and mortality based on the Komo-Ise Cohort Study in Japan. *International Journal of Epidemiology, 31*(6), 1208–1218.

Jokela, M. (2009). Physical attractiveness and reproductive success in humans: Evidence from the late 20th century United States. *Evolution and Human Behavior, 30*(5), 342–350.

Kaplan, H. (1994). Evolutionary and wealth flows theories of fertility: Empirical tests and new models. *Population and Development Review, 20*(4), 753–791.

Kaplan, H. (1996). A theory of fertility and parental investment in traditional and modern human societies. *American Journal of Physical Anthropology, 101*(S23), 91–135.

Kaplan, H. (1997). The evolution of the human life course. In K. Wachter & C. Finch (Eds.), *Between Zeus and the salmon: The biodemography of longevity* (pp. 175–211). Washington, DC: National Academies Press.

Kaplan, H., Hill, K., Lancaster, J., & Hurtado, A. M. (2000). A theory of human life history evolution: Diet, intelligence, and longevity. *Evolutionary Anthropology, 9*(4), 156–185.

Kelsey, K. S., Campbell, M. K., Tessaro, I., Benedict, S., Belton, L., Fernandez, L. M., . . . DeVellis, B. (2000). Social support and health behaviors among blue-collar women workers. *American Journal of Health Behavior, 24*(6), 434–443.

Kniffin, K. M., & Wilson, D. S. (2004). The effect of nonphysical traits on the perception of physical attractiveness: Three naturalistic studies. *Evolution and Human Behavior, 25*(2), 88–101.

Kurzban, R., & Weeden, J. (2005). HurryDate: Mate preferences in action. *Evolution and Human Behavior, 26*(3), 227–244.

Kuschel, R. (1992). "Women are women and men are men": How Bellonese women get even. In K. Björkqvist & P. Niemela (Eds.), *Of mice and women: Aspects of female aggression* (pp. 173–185). San Diego, Academic Press.

LaCrosse, M. B. (1975). Nonverbal behavior and perceived counselor attractiveness and persuasiveness. *Journal of Counseling Psychology, 22*(6), 563.

Lancaster, J. B. (1991). A feminist and evolutionary biologist looks at women. *Yearbook of Physical Anthropology, 34*, 1–11.

Levin, J., & Arluke, A. (1985). An exploratory analysis of sex differences in gossip. *Sex Roles, 12*(3–4), 281–286.

Liesen, L. (2013). The tangled web she weaves. In M. Fisher, J. Garcia, & R. S. Chang (Eds.), *Evolution's empress: Darwinian perspectives on the nature of women* (pp. 43–62). New York: Oxford University Press.

Lillard, L. A., & Waite, L. J. (1995). 'Til death do us part: Marital disruption and mortality. *American Journal of Sociology, 100*(5), 1131–1156.

Little, A. C., & Perrett, D. I. (2002). Putting beauty back in the eye of the beholder. *Psychologist, 15*(1), 28–32.

Low, B. S. (1999). *Why sex matters: A Darwinian look at human behavior.* Princeton, NJ: Princeton University Press.

Marlowe, F. (2001). Male contribution to diet and female reproductive success among foragers. *Current Anthropology, 42*(5), 755–759.

McAndrew, F. T. (2014). The "sword of a woman": Gossip and female aggression. *Aggression and Violent Behavior, 19*(3), 196–199.

Meehan, C. L. (2009). Maternal time allocation in two cooperative childrearing societies. *Human Nature, 20*(4), 375–393.

Meehan, C. L., & Hawks, S. (2013). Cooperative breeding and attachment among the Aka foragers. In N. Quinn & J. M. Mageo (Eds.), *Attachment reconsidered: Cultural perspectives on a Western theory* (pp. 85–113). New York: Palgrave.

Michael, Y. L., Colditz, G. A., Coakley, E., & Kawachi, I. (1999). Health behaviors, social networks, and healthy aging: Cross-sectional evidence from the Nurses' Health Study. *Quality of Life Research, 8*(8), 711–722.

Mitani, J. C., & Watts, D. (1997). The evolution of non-maternal caretaking among anthropoid primates: Do helpers help? *Behavioral Ecology and Sociobiology, 40*(4), 213–220.

Muller, M. N., Marlowe, F. W., Bugumba, R., & Ellison, P. T. (2009). Testosterone and paternal care in East African foragers and pastoralists. *Proceedings of the Royal Society B: Biological Sciences, 276*(1655), 347–354.

Newton-Fisher, N. E. (2006). Female coalitions against male aggression in wild chimpanzees of the Budongo Forest. *International Journal of Primatology, 27*(6), 1589–1599.

Oka, R., King, A., & Young, D. R. (1994). Sources of social support as predictors of exercise adherence in women and men ages 50 to 65 years. *Women's Health, 1*(2), 161–175.

Olstad, R., Sexton, H., & Sogaard, A. J. (2001). The Finnmark study: A prospective population study of the social support buffer hypothesis, specific stressors and mental distress. *Social Psychiatry and Psychiatric Epidemiology, 36*(12), 582–589.

Parish, A. R. (1996). Female relationships in bonobos (*Pan paniscus*): Evidence for bonding, cooperation, and female dominance in a male-philopatric species. *Human Nature, 7*(1), 61–96.

Parish, A. R., de Waal, F. & Haig, D. (2000). The other "closest living relative": How bonobos (*Pan paniscus*) challenge traditional assumptions about females, dominance, intra-and intersexual interactions, and hominid evolution. *Annals of the New York Academy of Sciences, 907*(1), 97–113.

Parker, G. A., Baker, R. R., & Smith, F. C. F. (1972). The origin and evolution of gamete dimorphism and the male-female phenomenon. *Journal of Theoretical Biology, 36*, 529–553.

Perry, S. (2003). Case study 4A: Coalitionary aggression in white-faced capuchins. In F. B. M. de Waal & P. L. Tyack (Eds.), *Animal social complexity: Intelligence, culture and individualized societies* (pp. 111–114). Cambridge, MA: Harvard University Press.

Philipov, D., Spéder, Z., & Billari, F. C. (2006). Soon, later, or ever? The impact of anomie and social capital on fertility intentions in Bulgaria (2002) and Hungary (2001). *Population Studies, 60*(3), 289–308.

Pope, T. R. (2000). Reproductive success increases with degree of kinship in cooperative coalitions of female red howler monkeys (*Aloutta seniculus*). *Behavioral Ecology and Sociobiology, 48*(4), 253–267.

Pusey, A. E. (1980). Inbreeding avoidance in chimpanzees. *Animal Behaviour, 28*(2), 543–552.

Pusey, A. E., & Schroepfer-Walker, K. (2013). Female competition in chimpanzees. *Philosophical Transactions of the Royal Society B, 368*(1631), 20130077.

Quinlan, R. J., & Quinlan, M. B. (2007). Evolutionary ecology of human pair-bonds: Cross-cultural tests of alternative hypotheses. *Cross-Cultural Research, 41*(2), 149–169.

Quinlan, R. J., & Quinlan, M. B. (2008). Human lactation, pair-bonds, and alloparents. *Human Nature, 19*(1), 87–102.

Rennemark, M., & Hagberg, B. (1999). Gender specific associations between social network and health behavior in old age. *Aging & Mental Health, 3*(4), 320–327.

Reynolds, P., Boyd, P. T., Blacklow, R. S., Jackson, J. S., Greenberg, R. S., Austin, D. F., . . . Edwards, B. K. (1994). The relationship between social ties and survival among black and white breast-cancer patients. *Cancer Epidemiology Biomarkers & Prevention, 3*(3), 253–259.

Rhodes, G., Simmons, L. W., & Peters, M. (2005). Attractiveness and sexual behavior: Does attractiveness enhance mating success? *Evolution and Human Behavior, 26*(2), 186–201.

Riggio, R. E., Widaman, K. F., Tucker, J. S., & Salinas, C. (1991). Beauty is more than skin deep: Components of attractiveness. *Basic and Applied Social Psychology, 12*(4), 423–439.

Rikowski, A., & Grammer, K. (1999). Human body odour, symmetry and attractiveness. *Proceedings of the Royal Society of London, Series B: Biological Sciences, 266*(1422), 869–874.

Roberts, S., Arrow, H., Lehmann, J., & Dunbar, R. (2014). *Close social relationships: An evolutionary perspective.* New York: Oxford University Press.

Rosenfeld, R., Baumer, E. P., & Messner, S. F. (2001). Social capital and homicide. *Social Forces, 80*(1), 283–310.

Rucas, S. L. (2004). *Female intrasexual social behaviors among the Tsimane of Bolivia* (Unpublished doctoral dissertation). University of New Mexico, Albuquerque.

Rucas, S. L., Gurven, M., Kaplan, H., & Winking, J. (2010). The Social Strategy Game: Resource competition within female social networks among small-scale forager-horticulturalists. *Human Nature, 21*, 1–18.

Rucas, S. L., Gurven, M., Kaplan, H., Winking, J., Gangestad, S. W., & Crespo, M. (2006). Female intrasexual competition and reputational effects on attractiveness among the Tsimane of Bolivia. *Evolution and Human Behavior, 27*, 40–52.

Rucas, S. L., Gurven, M., Winking, J., & Kaplan, H. (2012). Social aggression and resource conflict across the female lifecourse in the Bolivian Amazon. *Aggressive Behavior, 38*(3), 194–207.

Russell, A. F., Brotherton, P. N. M., McIlrath, G. M., Sharpe, L. L., & Clutton-Brock, T. H. (2003). Breeding success in cooperative meerkats: Effects of helper number and maternal state. *Behavioral Ecology, 14*(4), 486–492.

Sanderson, S. (2001). *The evolution of human sociality: A Darwinian conflict perspective.* Lanham, MD: Rowman and Littlefield.

Sapp, A. L., Trentham-Dietz, A., Newcomb, P. A., Hampton, J. M., Moinpour, C. M., & Remington, P. L. (2003). Social networks and quality of life among female long-term colorectal cancer survivors. *Cancer, 98*(8), 1749–1758.

Saxena, S., & Jain, R. K. (2013). Social intelligence of undergraduate students in relation to their gender and subject stream. *IOSR Journal of Research and Method in Education, 1,* 1–4.

Schmitt, D. P., Shackelford, T. K., & Buss, D. M. (2001). Are men really more "oriented" toward short-term mating than women? A critical review of theory and research. *Psychology, Evolution and Gender, 3*(3), 211–239.

Schultz, L. A., & Lore, R. K. (1993). Communal reproductive success in rats (*Rattus-Norvegicus*): Effects of group composition and prior social experience. *Journal of Comparative Psychology, 107*(2), 216–222.

Seyfarth, R. M., & Cheney, D. L. (2012). The evolutionary origins of friendship. *Annual Review of Psychology, 63,* 153–177.

Silk, J. B. (1980). Kidnapping and female competition among captive bonnet macaques. *Primates, 21*(1), 100–110.

Silk, J. B., Alberts, S. C., & Altmann, J. (2003). Social bonds of female baboons enhance infant survival. *Science, 302*(5648), 1231–1234.

Silk, J. B., Alberts, S. C., & Altmann, J. (2004). Patterns of coalition formation by adult female baboons in Amboseli, Kenya. *Animal Behaviour, 67*(3), 573–582.

Silk, J. B., Altmann, J., & Alberts, S. C. (2006). Social relationships among adult female baboons (*Papio cynocephalus*) I: Variation in the strength of social bonds. *Behavioral Ecology and Sociobiology, 61*(2), 183–195.

Silk, J. B., Beehner, J. C., Bergman, T. J., Crockford, C., Engh, A. L., Moscovice, L. R., ... Cheney, D. L. (2009). The benefits of social capital: Close social bonds among female baboons enhance offspring survival. *Proceedings of the Royal Society, Series B: Biological Sciences, 276*(1670), 3099–3104.

Silk, J. B., Beehner, J. C., Bergman, T. J., Crockford, C., Engh, A. L., Moscovice, L. R., ... Cheney, D. L. (2010). Strong and consistent social bonds enhance the longevity of female baboons. *Current Biology, 20*(15), 1359–1361.

Silk, J. B., Cheney, D., & Seyfarth, R. (2013). A practical guide to the study of social relationships. *Evolutionary Anthropology: Issues, News, and Reviews, 22*(5), 213–225.

Skolnik, H. S. (1998). *A social ecological investigation of the associations among social network participation, psychological well-being, and survival* (Unpublished doctoral dissertation). University of California, Irvine.

Stieglitz, J., Gurven, M., & Kaplan, H. (2012). Infidelity, jealousy, and wife abuse among Tsimane forager-farmers: Testing evolutionary hypotheses of marital conflict. *Evolution and Human Behavior, 33*(5), 438–448.

Stieglitz, J., Kaplan, H., Gurven, M., Winking, J., & Vie Tayo, B. (2011). Spousal violence and paternal disinvestment among Tsimane forager-horticulturalists. *American Journal of Human Biology, 23,* 445–457.

Suarez, L., Lloyd, L., Weiss, N., Rainbolt, T., & Pulley, L. (1994). Effects of social networks on cancer-screening behavior of older Mexican-American women. *Journal of the National Cancer Institute, 86*(10), 775–779.

Surbeck, M., Deschner, T., Schubert, G., Weltring, A., & Hohmann, G. (2012). Mate competition, testosterone and intersexual relationships in bonobos, *Pan paniscus. Animal Behaviour, 83*(3), 659–669.

Swami, V., Furnham, A., Chamorro-Premuzic, T., Akbar, K., Gordon, N., Harris, T., ... Tovée, M. J. (2010). More than just skin deep? Personality information influences men's ratings of the attractiveness of women's body sizes. *Journal of Social Psychology, 150*(6), 628–647.

Taylor, S. E. (2006). Tend and befriend biobehavioral bases of affiliation under stress. *Current Directions in Psychological Science, 15*(6), 273–277.

Taylor, S. E., Klein, L. C., Lewis, B. P., Gruenewald, T. L., Gurung, R. A., & Updegraff, J. A. (2000). Biobehavioral responses to stress in females: Tend-and-befriend, not fight-or-flight. *Psychological Review, 107*(3), 411–429.

Thornhill, R., & Gangestad, S. (1993). Human facial beauty: Averageness, symmetry, and parasite resistance. *Human Nature, 4*(3), 237–269.

Thornhill, R., & Gangestad, S. W. (2008). *The evolutionary biology of human female sexuality.* New York: Oxford University Press.

Thornhill, R., Gangestad, S., Miller, R., Scheyd, G., McCullough, J. K., & Franklin, M. (2003). Major histocompatibility complex genes, symmetry, and body scent attractiveness in men and women. *Behavioral Ecology, 14*(5), 668–678.

Thundal, K. L., Granbom, S., & Allebeck, P. (1999). Women's alcohol dependence and abuse: The relation to social network and leisure time. *Scandinavian Journal of Public Health, 27*(1), 30–37.

Townsend, J. M., & Levy, G. (1990). Effects of potential partners' physical attractiveness and socioeconomic status on sexuality and partner selection. *Evolution and Human Behavior, 19*(2), 149–164.

Townsend, S. W., Slocombe, K. E., Thompson, M. E., & Zuberbühler, K. (2007). Female-led infanticide in wild chimpanzees. *Current Biology, 17*(10), R355–R356.

Trivers, R. (1972). Parental investment and sexual selection. In B. Campbell (Ed.), *Sexual selection and the descent of man* (pp. 136–179). Chicago: Aldine.

Tucker, J. S., Schwartz, J. E., Clark, K. M., & Friedman, H. S. (1999). Age-related changes in the associations of social network ties with mortality risk. *Psychology and Aging, 14*(4), 564–571.

Tunçbilek, E., & Koc, I. (1994). Consanguineous marriage in Turkey and its impact on fertility and mortality. *Annals of Human Genetics, 58*(4), 321–329.

Turke, P., & Betzig, L. (1985). Those who can do: Wealth, status, and reproductive success on Ifaluk. *Ethology and Sociobiology, 6*(2), 79–87.

Uchino, B. N., Cacioppo, J. T., & Kiecolt-Glaser, J. K. (1996). The relationship between social support and physiological processes: A review with emphasis on underlying mechanisms and implications for health. *Psychological Bulletin, 119*(3), 488.

Unger, J. B., McAvay, G., Bruce, M. L., Berkman, L., & Seeman, T. (1999). Variation in the impact of social network characteristics on physical functioning in elderly persons: MacArthur studies of successful aging. *Journals of Gerontology, Series B: Psychological Sciences and Social Sciences, 54*(5), S245–S251.

van Noordwijk, M. A., Arora, N., Willems, E. P., Dunkel, L. P., Amda, R. N., Mardianah, N., . . . van Schaik, C. P. (2012). Female philopatry and its social benefits among Bornean orangutans. *Behavioral Ecology and Sociobiology, 66*(6), 823–834.

Wagle, A., Komorita, N. I., & Lu, Z. Y. J. (1997). Social support and breast self-examination. *Cancer Nursing, 20*(1), 42–48.

Waite, L., & Gallagher, M. (2002). *The case for marriage: Why married people are happier, healthier and better off financially.* New York: Random House.

Walen, H. R., & Lachman, M. E. (2000). Social support and strain from partner, family, and friends: Costs and benefits for men and women in adulthood. *Journal of Social and Personal Relationships, 17*(1), 5–30.

Walster, E., Aronson, V., Abrahams, D., & Rottman, L. (1966). Importance of physical attractiveness in dating behavior. *Journal of Personality and Social Psychology, 4*(5), 508.

Weinstein, T. A., Bales, K. L., Maninger, N., Hostetler, C. M., & Capitanio, J. P. (2014). Early involvement in friendships predicts later plasma concentrations of oxytocin and vasopressin in juvenile rhesus macaques (*Macaca mulatta*). *Frontiers in Behavioral Neuroscience, 8*(295), 1–13.

Wells, J. C. (2007). Sexual dimorphism of body composition. *Best Practice and Research: Clinical Endocrinology and Metabolism, 21*(3), 415–430.

Wilson, M., & Daly, M. (1985). Competitiveness, risk-taking, and violence: The young male syndrome. *Ethology and Sociobiology, 6*(1), 59–73.

Wilson, M., & Daily, M. (1996). Male sexual proprietariness and violence against wives. *Current Directions in Psychological Science, 5*(1), 2–7.

Wittig, R. M., & Boesch, C. (2010). Receiving post-conflict affiliation from the enemy's friend reconciles former opponents. *PLoS ONE, 5*(11), e13995.

Wittig, R. M., Crockford, C., Deschner, T., Langergraber, K. E., Ziegler, T. E., & Zuberbühler, K. (2014). Food sharing is linked to urinary oxytocin levels and bonding in related and unrelated wild chimpanzees. *Proceedings of the Royal Society, Series B: Biological Sciences, 281*(1778), 20133096.

Wood, W., & Eagly, A. H. (2002). A cross-cultural analysis of the behavior of women and men: Implications for the origins of sex differences. *Psychological Bulletin, 128*(5), 699.

Yasuda, N., Zimmerman, S. I., Hawkes, W., Fredman, L., Hebel, J. R., & Magaziner, J. (1997). Relation of social network characteristics to 5-year mortality among young-old versus old-old white women in an urban community. *American Journal of Epidemiology, 145*(6), 516–523.

Competition between Female Friends

Chenthila Nagamuthu *and* Elizabeth Page-Gould

Abstract

Many theories of cross-group friendship are based on the assumption that friends are inherently equal in status. This chapter discusses the idea that, even among same-sex friends, this assumption may be premature. It compares evidence for two contrasting arguments concerning competition between female friends: (a) intrasexual competition is highest among friends, and (b) friendship nullifies competition between friends. The chapter argues that equality may not be as normative in close friendships as the field has intuitively assumed. It also discusses how acknowledging and embracing these differences can lead to better predictions for the role of close relationships in interpersonal dominance and cooperation.

Key Words: female friends, friendship, equality, competition, intrasexual competition, interpersonal dominance, cooperation

Competition between Female Friends

We compare ourselves to friends more than we do to acquaintances and strangers, and we overwhelmingly compare ourselves to members of the same sex (Wheeler & Miyake, 1992). However, friendship is typically conceptualized as being marked by equality and reciprocity among friends (Austin, 1980; Laursen & Hartup, 2002), and friendships are predominantly formed with members of the same sex (Rose, 1985). We explore this apparent paradox in this chapter by examining whether friends truly share equal status within their relationships or whether intrasexual competition is natural among female friends. According to the former position, friendship serves as a protective factor against competition, while the latter position holds that social hierarchy may serve the same functions within friendships as it serves in other social bonds. Note that, unless otherwise specified in this chapter, we are referring to competition between friends over anything from winning a contest, to attaining higher grades, to competing for a mate.

We focus on friendship rather than acquaintanceship (i.e., a social relationship that does not involve strong feelings of closeness) because friends have strong social norms pertaining to egalitarianism and support of each other's goals whereas acquaintances are not bound by the same social contract. Egalitarianism is considered a key feature of friendship. We view and treat our friends as our equals and exchange costly favors in the form of material and emotional support without expectations of repayment (Silk, 2003). While close friendship involves fair exchange of emotional and material support (Silk, 2003), individuals are uncomfortable with imbalances in their friendships and tend to engage in reciprocal sharing by engaging in social exchanges (Olk & Gibbons, 2010). Best friendship, in particular, is viewed as a status-leveling relationship, marked by equality and camaraderie. Thus, much of the literature on friendship focuses primarily on the egalitarian nature of these relationships. This focus has resulted in a gap in knowledge about the existence of power or status differentials between friends and the implications such a differential would have on the quality and effects of friendship (Veniegas & Peplau, 1997).

Equality, such as that between friends, can exist in different degrees across the dimensions of social power and social status. Social power refers to how much control a person holds over resources, and social status refers to how esteemed a person is considered within a social group (Anderson, Beer, Srivastava, Spataro, & Chatman, 2006; Magee & Galinsky, 2008). Status differentials can exist between friends through preexisting social status (e.g., friendships between members of majority and minority religious groups) or can develop informally within a social network of friends. Similarly, power differentials can exist between friends through a preexisting inequality in resources (e.g., a friendship that develops between a sports coach and a team member) or can develop over the course of the friendship (e.g., if one friend gets a much higher-paying job than the other). Although resource reciprocity and equality of status are considered major components of friendship relationships, we argue that equality is not a necessary characteristic of friendship.

We posit that status and power differences should be expected among friends and that these differentials will elicit competitive behavior. Social power and hierarchy pervade human society (Magee & Galinsky, 2008), so it seems unlikely that friendship is immune to these social processes. Friends frequently differ on a number of dimensions that are relevant to social status and power (e.g., attractiveness, socioeconomic status, age), and it is probable that friends are aware of how they differ from each other. This chapter outlines friendship as defined in the literature and provides an overview of studies examining status differences among female friends, competition among female friends (both among animals and humans), and friendship as a competition-nullifying force. Ultimately, the main objective of this chapter is to compare evidence for two arguments concerning female friendship and competition: (a) intrasexual competition occurs in female friendship, and (b) friendship nullifies competition between females. We begin, however, by reviewing what is known about friendship and equality.

Friendship

Friendship is defined in Western cultures as a voluntary and mutual relationship based on equality and psychological intimacy (Blieszner & Roberto, 2004; Matthews, 1983). This relationship differs from casual acquaintanceships through the way in which help is exchanged. Friendships are communal relationships in which friends exchange favors and benefits based on need, but acquaintanceships tend to operate under tit-for-tat reciprocity, whereby obligation exists to return previous favors (Clark & Mills, 1979). It is considered inappropriate for friends to keep track of benefits that have been exchanged or to expect the repayment of favors (Silk, 2003). In other words, cultural norms dictate that friends are to interact with one another as equals, existing in a state of neither superiority nor inferiority to one another. Furthermore, friendships are expected to have causal influence as an equalizer (Hays, 1988), whereby friends who differ on a significant dimension such as age, sex, or socioeconomic status are assumed to respond to each other symmetrically, as though the status differential were nonexistent.

However, it is unclear why equality continues to be presented as a fundamental component of friendship. Both humans and nonhuman primates exhibit friendships that differ in social status (Palombit, Cheny, & Seyfarth, 2001; Palombit, Seyfarth, & Cheney, 1997). Research on same-sex friendships has shown that individuals of equal power rate their friendships to be of higher quality than friendships of those with unequal power (Veniegas & Peplau, 1997), but these findings simultaneously demonstrate that friendships can exist in the absence of power equality. According to equity theory, equal distribution of a reward is a key feature of friendship (Hatfield, Utne, & Traupmann, 1979). Indeed, competition between friends is viewed as an attack on the equity that holds a friendship together (Charlesworth, 1996; Schneider, Woodburn, del Toro, & Udvari, 2005).

Researchers often generalize findings to all types of friendships, rather than making clear the distinction between different types of friendship relationships (Way & Chen, 2000). However, ignoring various features of friendship relationships may have contributed to muddled understanding regarding friendship and competition. Close friends differ from casual friends in a number of ways; most notably, the former more frequently interact with each other and across a wider range of locations (Hays, 1989). For instance, close friends were found to interact with one another in their own homes at a higher frequency than casual friends, who tended to interact more frequently on campus (Hays, 1989). Close friends describe their interactions as more exclusive than casual friends do, and close friends are more of a source of emotional and informational support (Hays, 1989). Compared to casual friends, close friends plan more to interact with each other (Hays, 1989). This chapter uses the term "friend" to specify close friendships that are beyond acquaintanceships.

Psychological Closeness and Equality

The nature of interpersonal closeness is one of the most widely studied topics in social psychology, and many theories have been put forth to explain the social cognitive processes of closeness. The self-expansion theory of closeness holds that we incorporate the characteristics of close others into our own sense of self (i.e., a close friend; Aron, Aron, Tudor, & Nelson, 1991; Weidler & Clark, 2011). It also seems that close others—such as siblings, teachers, and best friends—are chronically accessible in working memory and shape our interpretations of new people (Anderson, Glassman, Chen, & Cole, 1995). That is, we store mental representations of significant others, which contain information about the important people in our life (Anderson et al., 1995). A representation of a significant other can be activated when we meet a new person, causing us to remember and think about this new person as possessing the same qualities as the significant other (Anderson et al., 1995). Thus, we come to view our friends as a part of ourselves, and our closest friends are chronically accessible in our minds.

We propose that the defining feature of friendship is feeling psychologically close to another person in a platonic way, irrespective of whether the two friends are equals. Psychological closeness is a characteristic of any close relationship, but equality has only been applied as a condition of friendship relationships (e.g., romantic relationships are rarely equal in power; Felmlee, 1994). Theories of psychological closeness (e.g., self-expansion theory) do not impose equality as a necessary constraint on psychological closeness. Therefore, since we can feel close to someone who is not of equal status, it is unclear why equality has been largely emphasized in the literature for friendship relationships. Moreover, since our cognitive representations of our close friends become chronically accessible in working memory, friends should be the most likely competitors out of a social network (Anderson et al., 1995). Thus, we propose that a simpler, more inclusive definition is that friendship is simply the existence of platonic, psychological closeness, rather than also requiring equality across social status and power.

Removing the equality constraint from friendship is more reflective of people's everyday experiences of friendship. US undergraduates were interviewed about the meaning of friendship generally, as well as details of their friendships with their closest same- and cross-sex friends at school (Singelton & Vacca, 2007). Questions measured companionship (e.g., participating in activities for mutual enjoyment), intimacy (e.g., revealing information about oneself to one another), social conflict, friendship satisfaction, and interpersonal competition (e.g., social comparison motivated by a need to outdo one another). An example of an interpersonal competition item is disliking when one's friend gets better grades. The analyses in this study revealed that although all friendships included competition and conflict, male same-sex friendship pairs were most competitive, cross-sex friends were the second-most competitive, and female same-sex friendships were the least competitive (Singelton & Vacca, 2007).

Cross-group friendship refers to friendship between different groups of people (e.g., different sex, different ages, different ethnicities). Thus, cross-sex friendship is an example of cross-group friendship. Taking the aforementioned sex difference at face value, the finding is consistent with norms associating competitiveness with masculinity. However, alternative explanations have been suggested. It is possible that women display more covert forms of competition for power compared to male friendship pairs (Davidson & Duberman, 1982), such that competition is underestimated among female friends. An additional possibility is that women have more trouble identifying feelings of competitiveness against their female friends because they view competition within relationships as a negative trait (Rubin, 1985), so they were just less likely to discuss it. Whatever the explanation for the sex differences in relative competitiveness among friends, these findings demonstrate that competition exists within both same-sex and cross-sex friendships.

So far we have focused on whether equality of status and power should be defining characteristics of friendship. We argue that the internal dyadic structure of friendship involves power and status hierarchies (Adams & Blieszner, 1994), even among friends who are similar across social characteristics such as sex, race, age, and occupational status. Friends who occupy similar social positions do not necessarily share equal power or status within their relationship (Adams & Blieszner, 1994). Thus, despite the fact that friendships could be considered egalitarian relationships based on the propensity for friendships to be demographically homogeneous, it can be assumed that any two best friends will not share identical personality traits (Izard, 1963).

Preexisting Status Differentials

Friendship develops between people who have different social standings, which has the potential to color an ongoing relationship. Research on cross-group friendship (i.e., friendship between people who belong to different social groups, like cross-race friendships) has been driven by an assumption that cross-group friendship has status-leveling properties. For example, the original formulation of the contact hypothesis identified cross-group friendships as inherently containing the optimal conditions needed for prejudice reduction, namely the presence of an equal-status relationship where there is no intergroup competition (Allport, 1954). Given this assumption, many researchers have proposed that friendship is a fundamental condition under which contact with outgroup members will lead to reduced prejudice (Pettigrew, 1998; Wright, Brody, & Aron, 2005).

Somewhat in support of this view, adolescents reported less conflict with cross-ethnic friends than same-ethnic friends (Schneider, Dixon, & Udvari, 2007), although they also reported less closeness to cross-ethnic friends, relatively. Assuming that social status can be derived from one's ethnicity, then these findings suggest that preexisting status differentials do not necessarily elicit more competition among dissimilar friends. However, given that more conflict *and more closeness* was observed among same-ethnicity friends, these findings also support the idea that friendship does not necessarily reduce interpersonal competition. In addition, regardless of the sex composition, friendships that were characterized by conflict were more likely to dissolve at some point in the academic year (Schneider et al., 2007). Importantly, researchers found that male friends who enjoyed competition against one another in a nonhostile manner maintained their friendships (Schneider et al., 2007), which demonstrates that competition between friends can be functional and facilitate bonding, at least among men.

Sex Differences in Same-Sex Friendships

Before focusing on competition and friendship between females, we must first examine the sex differences between the same-sex friendships of men and women. Sex differences in friendship may occur on (a) a quantitative dimension (e.g., the number of friends people have, or the frequency of interactions between two same-sex friends), (b) the degree of intimacy in the friendship, and (c) the types of interactions friends engage in or prefer (Caldwell & Peplau, 1982). It appears that there are no sex differences in the number of friends men and women have, the amount of time they spend with their friends, or preferences for the degree of intimacy in the friendship (Caldwell & Peplau, 1982). However, research illustrates that sex differences exist in the types of interactions people prefer: women indicate greater preference for spending time conversing with friends relative to men, whereas men prefer engaging in activities with their friends (Caldwell & Peplau, 1982). Women emphasize talking about and sharing their emotional problems with their same-sex friends, while men emphasize engaging in activities together (Aukett, Ritchie, & Mill, 1988). This emphasis on conversation and emotional support in female friendships highlights how women bond with their same-sex friends and suggests that women are more emotionally available for one another. Moreover, if men are more likely to engage in shared activities that may have a competitive element, the processes involved in status may manifest differently in men's and women's same-sex friendships: men have more opportunity for dominance competitions while women have more fodder for relational aggression through greater personal disclosure.

Even in the workplace, where status and power hierarchies are typically formalized within organizational structure, sex differences in coworker friendships persist. Female professionals' same-sex friendships were rated higher in overall quality, intimacy, enjoyment, and nurturance than males' same-sex friendships (Sapadin, 1988). Male professionals, on the other hand, rated their cross-sex friendships higher in the aforementioned areas, except for intimacy (Sapadin, 1988). Overall, the findings from this study suggest that the social support features of women's same-sex friendships are reflected in their cross-sex friendships as well.

Taken together, the research we have reviewed in this section aligns to highlight that the content of interactions between friends may facilitate more or less competition among friends. Men are more likely than women to engage in shared activities like sports that allow for explicit competition between friends. Women are more likely than men to engage in conversations and exchange social support with their friends. When men and women become friends with each other, cross-sex friendships have more social support than men's same-sex friendships and more competition than women's same-sex friendships. Perhaps greater self-disclosure for men in cross-sex friendships mitigates the opportunity to engage in activities that incorporate competition, but opportunities still likely exist for competition between men and women. For instance, cross-sex friends at the workplace may have to compete for a promotion or for recognition from their boss. Interpersonally, male and female friends may also compete for social status within the informal hierarchies that make up their friendship networks.

To study the nature of friendships between same-sex adults other than university students, one study examined the same-sex friendships of the parents of university students (Aries & Johnson, 1983). Participants selected one person of the same sex they considered their close friend, and, if no such person existed, they selected a person of the same sex to whom they felt closest. The questionnaire that was administered focused on the frequency and nature of communication between close friends and on the frequency and depth of numerous conversation topics. Similar to findings with self-reports, women discussed intimate topics more frequently—as well as more mundane topics of daily and shared activities—compared to men. Furthermore, women demonstrated more depth than men in discussions of personal and family matter topics (Aries & Johnson, 1983). Once again, we see that women engage in more in-depth conversations, sharing their personal stories and their emotions. This can be considered a major benefit of female friendships, as women may confer therapeutic benefits of sharing personal matters and their emotions with one another. However, as we have already suggested, disclosing personal information equips an adversary for relational aggression (e.g., gossiping), which is a form of aggression that is more common in females than males (cf. McAndrew, this volume; Sutton & Oaten, this volume).

Functions of Hierarchy and Friendship
Benefits of Hierarchy

Hierarchies establish social order and facilitate social coordination (Magee & Galinsky, 2008). In other words, hierarchies function to coordinate activities and behavior in social groups (Magee & Galinsky, 2008). By establishing clear roles within a social group, hierarchy facilitates task coordination (Magee & Galinsky, 2008). Furthermore, groups that are more hierarchical perform better than those with a lesser degree of hierarchical differentiation

(Halevy, Chou, & Galinsky, 2011). More specifically, hierarchies establish defined roles of leadership and deference, which allow for maximized task coordination (Magee & Galinsky, 2008). In regard to organizational hierarchies, hierarchies confer incentives to obtain higher ranks, thereby providing individuals a sense of motivation (Magee & Galinsky, 2008). This motivation can come from a personal interest to satisfy material needs and a need for stability and comfort (Halevy, Chou, & Galinsky, 2011; Magee & Galinsky, 2008). Thus, hierarchy is generally thought to facilitate successful social relationships, which may be why informal hierarchical differentiation occurs spontaneously and quickly within social groups.

Benefits of Friendship

There are many benefits of friendship that likely serve to propagate these relationships, even when they are costly. Friendship research on baboons indicates that prosociality provides several benefits for females (Silk et al., 2009): bonds between females increased reproductive success. Furthermore, female baboons who formed stronger bonds with their own mothers and daughters bore offspring with higher survival rates than those females who formed weaker bonds (Silk et al., 2009). The authors conclude that these findings align with those of human studies, as they indicate that greater social integration goes hand in hand with decreased mortality and enhanced physical and mental health, at least for females (Silk et al., 2009).

Among humans, the need to belong to a social group is arguably a fundamental psychological need. Social exclusion is linked to the perception of pain (whether it be social or physical; cf. MacDonald & Leary, 2005), theoretically because humans do not want to be excluded from others, as exclusion limits survival. Moreover, friendship allows for reciprocal altruism, with resources, time, and efforts being freely shared within the friendship for the benefit of the other friend (Shackelford & Buss, 1996). Friendships also serve as a key contributor to one's general sense of well-being, as friends provide us emotional support, help us out when times are tough, and enjoy spending time with us (Veniegas & Peplau, 1997). Altogether, friendship confers many survival and psychological benefits, which is likely why platonic, nonkin relationships have developed.

However, the quality of a friendship is a key moderator in the value of the relationship and differentials in power and status are negatively related to friendship quality. The balance of power within friendship has even been cited as one of two important determinants of friendship quality, along with sex (i.e., individuals are most often closest to same-sex friends; Veniegas & Peplau, 1997). In friendships with an unequal balance of power, one individual exerts greater influence over the dyad's decision-making activities. Interestingly, only 40% of respondents reported that all of their same-sex friendships were equal-powered (Veniegas & Peplau, 1997). In another sample, while 75% of participants reported equal-power friendships, another quarter of the sample reported a covert struggle for dominance within their friendships (Davidson & Duberman, 1982). Friendships in which both friends had equal power were significantly higher on all measures of relationship quality than unequal-power friendships (Veniegas & Peplau, 1997). The fact that variance in social power between friendships relates meaningfully to friendship quality refutes the widely held assumption that friendships enforce equality and power sharing between friends (Veniegas & Peplau, 1997).

Competition between Female Friends

Although research among humans has downplayed the role of competition within friendships, extensive research has been conducted on the social behavior of nonhuman primates. A prime example is a study on chacma baboons (*Papio cynocephalus ursinus*) that assessed competition between females for a male partner to protect their offspring from infanticide by newly immigrated alpha males (Palombit et al., 2001). It was hypothesized that when two females shared a male friend, the higher-ranking female would interact with the male at a higher rate than her lower-ranking counterpart. Various social behaviors were recorded during direct competitive interactions between females, including rate of supplanting (i.e., any instance where a female withdrew within five seconds of another female approaching her within a 2-meter distance) and number of physical attacks such as biting, chasing, and hitting. A female's competitiveness, measured by assessing behavior and close proximity to males, was positively related to her social access to a shared male friend. For example, dominant females were able to maintain higher levels of close proximity and groom a shared male friend compared to their subordinate friends. These findings suggest that dominant behavior within a friendship dyad may pose a social advantage for females, since they are

more successful in accessing a mutual male friend (Palombit et al., 2001).

Earlier work involved testing the "anti-infanticide hypothesis," which posits that male friends provide female friends a benefit by protecting them against attacks by infanticidal males (Palombit et al., 1997). Other proposed benefits of female–male friendships include male protection of the female against abuse from dominant females and the attachment of the male to an infant that results in him caring for future offspring. Investigators played recordings of female screams for male baboons, and they observed that male friends responded more strongly than male control subjects (Palombit et al., 1997). A response to a female's screams constituted either ignoring it or orienting oneself toward the female. One such orienting response involved a male friend running toward the scream, leaping up and scanning the area with his eyes. Assuming that an orienting response is indicative of the male's willingness to intervene, his investment in his friendship with a female can be observed. Male friends also responded more strongly to the screams of female friends than those of female controls. Directly addressing the infanticide hypothesis, male friends also responded more strongly than control males to female screams that were paired with threat vocalizations from a potentially infanticidal alpha male but less strongly than control males to these screams following infant death. These patterns did not hold when female screams were paired with threat vocalizations from a non-infanticidal male or from an alpha female. These findings indicate that male–female friendships among chacma baboons offer the female a benefit of protection of her infants against infanticide (Palombit et al., 1997). Therefore, there is an advantage for female chacma baboons in competing against each other for male friends. Relating this back to humans, perhaps females may have to compete with one another either subconsciously or consciously for a male friend's attention, so as to receive the protection males can provide women and their children from potential danger or threats.

Our review of the literature on female competition and friendship among nonhuman primates reveals that competition between females can be an important quality to possess in order to secure protection from danger (e.g., via attainment of a male friend). Female friends can also collectively compete against outgroup females to defend their territory and reward each other for their efforts, thereby emphasizing the importance of their relationship to each other (Cords, 2002). This latter point is discussed later in the chapter.

However, among humans, competition among same-sex friends is inherently more complex. Humans do not need to win a physical fight to establish dominance; thus, humans engage in subtler forms of intrasexual competition with their female friends. Intrasexual competition refers to members of the same sex competing against one another to display traits that are attractive to the opposite sex (Bleske & Shackelford, 2001). We tend to select same-sex friends based on traits such as age, education level, intelligence, and social class, among other characteristics (Buss, 1984; Vandenberg (1972); we also select our potential mates based on similarity of these traits (Buss, 1984; Vandenberg, 1972). Therefore, our same-sex friends can very likely have many traits in common with our current or potential mates, which can lead to competition between friends for the attention of their friend's mate (Buss, 1984; Vandenberg, 1972). Such competition can arise because we are similar in age and have similar preferences for activities to our same-sex friends and their mates (Buss, 1984; Vandenberg, 1972). Similarity is highly related to interpersonal attraction (Byrne, 1971; Tan & Singh, 1995). Competition between same-sex friends can also arise because a same-sex friend has more knowledge about our mate (e.g., such as the status of the relationship, whether they are going through any difficulties) and may be a more successful rival than a same-sex stranger (Buss, 1984; Vadenberg, 1972). Finally, competition between same-sex friends may arise simply because same-sex friends have more opportunities to compete for our mates, compared to same-sex strangers, whom we only meet once in our life (Buss, 1984; Vandenberg, 1972).

To test humans' responses to intrasexual rivalry between same-sex friends for mates, university students were asked to list up to five of their closest same-sex friends and whether each was single or in a relationship (Bleske & Shackelford, 2001). The participants rated the desirability of 59 characteristics that might be found in same-sex friends and were asked how upset they would be if a same-sex friend engaged in each of 102 acts that people may use to attract their long-term mates (e.g., wearing makeup; Bleske & Shackelford, 2001; Buss, 1989). The investigators then assessed participants' level of upset by asking them to consider a stranger engaging in each of the 102 acts on which they had imagined their responses to a friend (Bleske & Shackelford, 2001). The results suggest that (a) both men and women are more upset in response to imagined rivalry from a same-sex friend than from a same-sex stranger; (b) women are more upset than men in response to a friend engaging in acts of sexual availability toward their mates, and in enhancing their appearance, compared to same-sex strangers; and (c) women regard sexual availability and promiscuity of same-sex friends as more undesirable than men do (Bleske & Shackelford, 2001). One explanation for this latter finding is that women are very selective with their friends because they tend to confide their secrets to them and reveal their insecurities, whereas male friendships tend to be activity- and task-specific (Bell, 1981; Davidson & Duberman, 1982; Sharabany, Gershon, & Hofman, 1981; Weiss & Lowenthal, 1975). As such, women tend to select friends whom they perceive as nonrivals for mates (Bleske & Shackelford, 2001). These findings support the investigators' hypothesis that humans evolved mechanisms that make us feel upset as a response to mate competition against our same-sex friends and influence our selection of friends to prevent competition for mates (Bleske & Shackelford, 2001). Women may feel more upset in response to their same-sex friend engaging in acts that attract their mates because they are concerned their friend will be able to succeed in attracting someone they are interested in (Bleske & Shackelford, 2001).

Friendship as a Competition-Nullifying Force

Research suggests that friends compete against each other more than nonfriends, among both adults and children (Fonzi, Schneider, Tani, & Tomada, 1997; Tesser & Smith, 1980). Hypercompetitiveness (defined as competition in which one has a need to prove one's own superiority) between friends is associated with a lack of closeness and the dissolution of friendships, and there is variance in competitiveness across friendship pairs (Schneider et al., 2005). Subjective portrayals of competition between friends vary. In a qualitative study, early adolescents were asked to recall instances where they played games with friends, compared grades or other performance scores, or participated in contests with their friends in which there was a winner and a loser (Schneider et al., 2005). The majority of interviewees indicated that they do not compete with friends because they do not want to discover that one is better than the other (Schneider et al., 2005). Several participants also indicated that they do not want to hurt their friends' feelings by outperforming them and that they would feel humiliated if their friends defeated them (Schneider et al., 2005). Thus, despite the fact the literature suggests that friends do compete with each other more than they do with nonfriends, it seems that friends nonetheless avoid at least overtly engaging in competition in order to maintain equality.

Cultural context moderates the effects of competition within friendship as well. North Americans are more competitive with their friends than people in most other societies, such as those from Latin American cultures (Schneider et al., 2005). People from more individualistic societies value personal autonomy and competition to achieve individual-focused goals, whereas many Latin American cultures are much more collectivist and value interdependence with friends and family and cooperation with fellow community members (Biesanz, Biesanz, & Biesanz, 1982; Griffiths & Griffiths, 1979; Moses, 2000). As such, hypercompetitiveness within friendship should be less normative for Latin American participants (Schneider et al., 2005). Thus, competition tends to exist at both a higher and lower extent between friends, depending on the cultural context. People from individualistic societies generally engage in more competition with friends compared to people from collectivist societies.

Although the influence on and responses to competition among friends differ by culture, the outcomes of this competition seem to be pervasive across cultures. Hypercompetitiveness is associated with conflict between friends, friendship dissolution, and less closeness, which may be why friends often avoid competing against each other in the first place (Schneider et al., 2005). These findings illustrate that competition between friends is perceived as a risk for potentially having negative emotions, such as feelings of hurt and humiliation (Schneider et al., 2005).

Again, women and men appear to differ in their responses to competition among friends. Hypercompetitiveness among boys typically yields nonhostile social comparison (e.g., comparing achievements without any hostility, jealousy, or anger) and enjoyment of engagement in competition. These dimensions of competition were positively associated with greater companionship among male friends (Schneider et al., 2005). However, these same dimensions of competition were negatively associated with the quality of female friendships, likely due to women's friendship norms (Maccoby, 1990; Patrick, Ryan & Pintrich, 1999; Schneider et al., 2005). Female friends are known to

value reciprocity from one another and punish any superiority behavior, thereby prohibiting competition between each other (Benenson, 2013; Maltz, Borker, & Gumperz, 1982; Winstead & Griffin, 2001). In addition, women tend to end friendships when conflicts arise in order to avoid future conflict (Benenson et al., 2009; MacEvoy, & Asher, 2012; Whitesell & Harter, 1996).

There may be developmental aspects to these friendship norms. For example, schoolchildren were paired with either a close friend or a classmate whom they neither liked nor disliked (Berndt, 1985). Among younger students in fourth and sixth grades, helpfulness and resource sharing was approximately equal between friends versus classmates toward whom they felt ambivalent. However, older students in eighth grade were more generous and helpful toward their own friends than their classmates (Berndt, 1985). Eighth-grade students also reported perceiving that their friends competed with them less and strived for equality in rewards than other classmates (Berndt, 1985). This study suggests that as children get older, their sense of camaraderie increases for their close friends, whereby they treat these friends differently than someone who is not a close friend.

Thus, it is clear that female friends are not in perpetual competition with one another, particularly as one becomes older. This conclusion is easily evidenced by the nonhuman primate literature, particularly blue monkeys. Among adult blue monkeys (*Cerocopithecus mitis*), friends become allies during intergroup competition, whereby females act aggressively toward outgroup members in order to defend their territory when outgroup members infringe upon territory boundaries (Butynski, 1990; Cords, 2002; Lawes & Henzi, 1995; Rudran, 1978). Following intergroup conflicts, females groom each other and their adult male peers, which facilitates ingroup bonding (Cords, 2002). Thus, postaggression grooming suggests that cooperation during intergroup conflict is an important component of the friendships that female blue monkeys have with ingroup members (Cords, 2002). This behavior is quite interesting, as blue monkeys do not typically interact with each other socially. We can deduce that female blue monkeys do not compete with female friends. Adult and subadult females spend an average of only 5% of their day on overt social activities such as grooming and sitting in contact with other monkeys (Cords, 2002). Importantly, postconflict grooming behavior does not occur among females following attacks by predators or males (Cords, 2002). Postconflict grooming is thought to be a means to reward or encourage an ingroup member who was more active than the groomer during the intergroup conflict (Cords, 2002). Blue monkeys are an interesting species that illustrate how female friends can cooperate together to compete against outgroup females. The evidence reveals that female blue monkey friends reinforce cooperation against outgroup females, despite being an otherwise socially distant species.

Status Differences between Friends: Preliminary Empirical Evidence

The previous section supports the argument that competition is not a hallmark of female same-sex friendships. In other words, social norms guide female friends to avoid conflicts such as competition. However, we have support from earlier in the chapter that power differentials between friends do not elicit competitive behavior. So do friendships with a power differential confer any benefits to the relationship? Is there a functional role to power differentials in friendships? If power differentials between friends do not elicit competition, perhaps they do the opposite: enhance cooperation. We conducted a preliminary study to examine the relationship between preexisting and externally imposed power differentials between same-sex friends and their effect on successful task cooperation. Our research addressed the question of the functional role of power differentials within friendships, examining the difference between power differentials created naturally through within-friendship differences in trait dominance and externally imposed power differentials. Following from the assumption that any two best friends will not share identical personality traits, it may be the case that one friend has a more dominant personality than the other. The relative paucity of research on power differentials between friends triggered our curiosity about its functionality within friendship. More specifically, our study tested whether power differentials serve any purpose in successful task cooperation between best friends, examining the relative influence of personality-based versus contextually imposed power differentials. In the following paragraphs we discuss our findings in terms of female friendships.

Our study included 88 same-sex best friends (70% female), of which at least one friend was an undergraduate student enrolled in a first-year introductory psychology course in Toronto, Canada. Participants and their friends completed International Personality Item Pool–Interpersonal Circumplex, which is a 32-item assessment that measures eight interpersonal dispositions, of which we were specifically interested in trait dominance (Markey & Markey, 2009). A sample item that measured trait dominance was "Demand to be the center of interest," whereas a sample item measuring trait submissiveness was "Let others finish what they are saying." Participants rated each item on a 1 (*very inaccurate*) to 5 (*very accurate*) scale in relation to other people they know of the same age and sex. To prepare for data analysis, responses to particular items from the International Personality Item Pool–Interpersonal Circumplex were used to score trait dominance. Higher averaged values of the four dominance items represented a greater level of trait dominance.

Participants then completed the "Lost on the Moon task," which measures group decision-making and leadership in a group setting and requires dyads to work cooperatively to come up with a consensual solution to solve the problem in the task. The task requires participants to imagine themselves as members of a space crew that were set to land on a specific surface of the moon but instead crash-landed 200 miles away from their intended destination. Participants were informed that most of their equipment on board has been damaged and only 15 intact pieces of equipment remain. Participants work together to rank each of the 15 pieces of equipment from 1 (*most important*) to 15 (*least important*) in helping them make the 200-mile trip to their intended location. Each friendship pair's Lost on the Moon score was computed by individually subtracting their ranking of each item from the rankings listed by NASA scientists. NASA scientists' rankings are used as the standard to which we compared successful performance (Hall, 1971). The absolute values of the differences were summed and provided us with the dyad's overall team score. Lower team scores indicated greater task success, as they deviated less from the "correct" responses.

Within each dyad, we randomly assigned one friend to be the "leader" and the other friend to be the "follower" during the Lost on the Moon task. Both participants were told that although they were supposed to work cooperatively together on the task, past research had shown that people completed the task better when one person was assigned to be the leader. Other than this piece of information, the leader and follower were given no specific instructions as to what these roles entailed. We hypothesized that both trait and state power differentials between friends would predict how successfully the friends could cooperate with each other.

Our analyses suggest that similarity of trait dominance within friendships predicts better cooperative performance than complementarity of trait dominance. In other words, power differentials predict worse performance among friends than observed among friends who were matched in their levels of dominance (Figure 8.1). When the participant was assigned to be the follower, then participant dominance predicted worse cooperative performance, but friend dominance predicted better performance. When the participant was assigned to be the leader, then participant dominance was unrelated cooperative performance, but partner dominance predicted significantly worse performance. Altogether, it seemed that experimentally imposed power differentials facilitated cooperative performance only when they were congruent with preexisting levels of trait dominance within the friendship dyad.

We found that equal-power friendships performed the best on the Lost on the Moon task, and friendships that were unequal in trait power performed the worst. As is represented by the non-overlapping error bars in Figure 8.1, equal-power friendships where both friends were low in dominance performed better on the cooperative task than friendships where both friends were high in dominance. Perhaps best friends who are both low in trait dominance find it easier to work in partnership to come to an agreement on solving the Lost on the Moon problem than friends who both possess a dominant disposition. Based on past findings that groups consisting mostly of highly dominant superstars tend to perform poorly (Magee & Galinsky, 2008), we expected that friendships with a natural power differential would find it easiest to cooperate together on the task, as they would be better able to coordinate with one another. It is important to note that Magee and Galinsky (2008) were summarizing research conducted in business organizations, where there are rarely norms of equality (i.e., business organizations typically represent formal hierarchies, with clear roles and power over resources). Our preliminary results suggest the opposite may be true in friendships, where norms of equality exist. Moreover, it seems that our experimental manipulation of power differential within friendships affected behavior only by moderating the relationship between preexisting trait dominance and cooperative behavior.

Future Directions

There are a few clear next steps for research on equality and friendship before we will know the true functionality of power and equality within friendships. The Lost on the Moon task that we used was designed to be performed best when participants cooperate with one another in a prosocial, collaborative way. Other types of tasks, such as competitive zero-sum games (e.g., Dictator Game) may elicit different levels of performance as a function

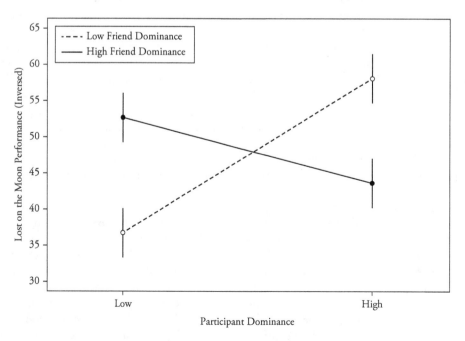

Figure 8.1 Success on Lost on the Moon task as a function of self's and best friend's level of trait dominance.

of differentials between friends' dominance. Our study aimed to examine whether power differences between best friends serve a functional role in successful task cooperation, but the function of power and equality within friendships may extend beyond performance domains to interpersonal relationships and group cohesion.

Our finding concerning unequal-power friendships fails to support Hay's (1988) hypothesis that friendships serve as equalizers, even when friends differ on status. This suggests that unequal-power friends did not respond to each other symmetrically, but rather one friend exerted greater influence than the other during the group task, which made consensual agreement tougher to achieve. Moreover, since unequal-power friends performed among the worst of dyads, our results suggest that power differentials do not serve any functionality toward friendship cooperation.

As our current findings suggest that power differentials do not serve a functional role in cooperation, our research provides the groundwork for examining why unequal-power friends remain friends. Past research has indicated that equal-power friends rate their friendship as significantly higher in quality than unequal-power friends (Veniegas & Peplau, 1997). If this holds true among the best friends in our sample, why do unequal-power friends remain in such voluntary relationships? We expect that the answer to this question may lead us to question other core assumptions that we hold about friendship, such as its voluntary nature. Cross-cultural research on friendship suggests that friendship is not a purely voluntary relationship, as feelings of obligation are usually high among friends (Adams & Plaut, 2003). In other words, sometimes people stay in bad friendships out of a sense of obligation just as they may maintain social contact with an antisocial family member out of obligation. As an additional factor, we assume that some people maintain nonegalitarian friendships out of optimism that the status differential will change.

At the very least, our findings demonstrate that it is important that friendship researchers not make the assumption that all friendships are egalitarian. We must explore whether nonegalitarian friendships provide us with the same benefits as egalitarian friendships, and, if not, we should investigate why certain adults remain in such voluntary relationships. Since friendships contribute to our general sense of well-being (Veniegas & Peplau, 1997), it seems perplexing that some individuals choose to remain in friendships where they hold more or less power than their friends. Thus, studying balance of power within friendship will allow us to better understand the dynamics of these unique relationships as a whole. If equality in status and power is not a necessary component of friendship, then people must be able to derive benefits from friendship nonetheless. By moving beyond the assumption that friendships are egalitarian, we may better understand why some friendships become equal and other friendships perpetuate pre-existing inequalities.

Conclusion

Considering female same-sex friendships and competition, status and power differentials within friendship seem natural, despite our preconceived notions. The idea of equality being a requisite quality of friendship should possibly be abandoned. The competition that we see among female friends likely stems from the fact that our friends are the most proximal and cognitively accessible people to us. Our friends make up part of our self-concept, and we are motivated to be as successful as they are when we compare ourselves to them. This comparison leads us to engage in friendly competition to meet our friends on the same playing field, so as to balance out any status or power differentials. Thus, we argue that equality in status or power is not a necessity for friendship, as we can achieve equality through reciprocal altruism and competition.

The evidence presented in this chapter suggests that both human and nonhuman-primate females compete with their female friends and that success in competition confers important benefits. Female chacma baboons, for instance, compete for male friends to receive protection from infanticidal males (Palombit et al., 1997). Female blue monkeys compete with outgroup females when they infringe on their territorial boundaries and then engage in grooming behavior with ingroup female friends to reward each other for their efforts against the outgroup members (Cords, 2002). Among humans, competition among female same-sex friends for each other's current or potential mates is likely, as we tend to have more similar traits to our friends and their current or potential mates than would a same-sex stranger (Buss, 1984; Vandenberg, 1972). Women are more sensitive than men in response to their same-sex friend making sexual advances toward their current or potential mates or enhancing their appearance (Bell, 1981; Davidson & Duberman, 1982; Sharabany et al., 1981; Weiss & Lowenthal, 1975). Therefore, competition among female friends can lead to a reassessment of the relationship—and perhaps its dissolution—when competition is motivated by selecting a mate (Bleske & Shackelford, 2001). This is contrary to competition among female friends that is motivated by a desire to do just as well as one's friend in other achievement domains to level the playing field.

This chapter's main goal was to examine support for or against two arguments concerning female friendships and competition: (a) intrasexual competition occurs among female friends, and (b) friendship nullifies competition among females. The evidence we examined reveals that while friendship may not necessitate equality between friends, normal degrees of competition among female friends help to reduce preexisting differentials between them. In addition, dominance behaviors among female friends yield success in accessing male friends. Competition between female friends for male friends can be necessary if a woman is interested in acquiring a male's protection of herself and her children (Palombit et al., 1997). The evidence also suggests that intrasexual competition between female friends can occur, and, if it does, humans have developed adaptive mechanisms that lead us to feel upset in response to our female friends competing with us for mates. These mechanisms likely exist so that we can reevaluate our friendships and dissolve them if we feel we cannot trust our female-friend competitor.

Cultural norms around friendship will always play an important role in the nature of this type of relationship. Female friends from individualistic societies are more likely than female friends from collectivist societies to engage in competition with each other. For the most part, female friends prefer to avoid competition between each other, so as to thwart off feelings of negativity, humiliation, and hurt in their relationship. Female friends are less competitive with each other than male friends and view competition as a threat to their relationship. Competition between female friends is likely at its lowest when females are school-aged, as girls view conflict in their friendships as harmful to the relationship and often will terminate these relationships. Girls prefer to avoid competition with their female friends. Moreover, culture (i.e., individualistic versus collectivist society) plays a role in whether friendship nullifies or confers competition between female friends.

Based on the evidence, we conclude that intrasexual competition does indeed exist between female friends but that friendship also confers equality between friends, thereby often nullifying competition between women. Thus, both arguments are partially true. We speculate that intrasexual competition is most probable between female friends when they are most actively seeking a mate or partner to care for them and their future offspring. This chapter has highlighted that the constructs of competition and friendship may be naturally intertwined, even if women prefer not to compete with their friends. As such, we must expand our theories of friendship to allow for competition and imbalances in status and power.

References

Adams, R. G., & Blieszner, R. (1994). An integrative conceptual framework for friendship research. *Journal of Social and Personal Relationships, 11*, 163–184.

Adams, G., & Plaut, V. C. (2003). The cultural grounding of personal relationship: Friendship in North American and West African worlds. *Personal Relationships, 10*, 333–347.

Allport, G. W. (1954). *The nature of prejudice* (25th ed.). Reading, MA: Addison-Wesley.

Anderson, C., Beer, J. S., Srivastava, S., Spataro, S. E., & Chatman, J. A. (2006). Knowing your place: Self-perceptions of status in face-to-face groups. *Journal of Personality and Social Psychology, 91*(6), 1094–1110.

Anderson, S. M., Glassman, N. S., Chen, S., & Cole, S. W. (1995). Transference in social perception: The role of chronic accessibility in significant-other representations. *Journal of Personality and Social Psychology, 69*(1), 41–57.

Aries, E. J., & Johnson, F. L. (1983). Close friendship in adulthood: Conversational content between same-sex friends. *Sex Roles, 9*(12), 1183–1196.

Aron, A., Aron, E. N., Tudor, M., & Nelson, G. (1991). Close relationships as including other in the self. *Journal of Personality and Social Psychology, 60*(2), 241–253.

Aukett, R., Ritchie, J., & Mill, K. (1988). Gender differences in friendship patterns. *Sex Roles, 19*(1/2), 57–66.

Austin, W. (1980). Friendship and fairness effects of type of relationship and task performance on choice of distribution rules. *Personality and Social Psychology Bulletin, 6*(3), 402–408.

Bell, R. R. (1981). Friendships of women and men. *Psychology of Women Quarterly, 5*, 402–417.

Benenson, J. F. (2013). The development of human female competition: Allies and adversaries. *Philosophical Transactions of the Royal Society, 386*.

Benenson, J. F., Markovits, H., Fitzgerald, C., Geoffroy, D., Flemming, J., Kahlenberg, S. M., & Wrangham, R. W. (2009). Males' greater tolerance of same-sex peers. *Psychological Science, 20*, 184–190.

Berndt, T. J. (1985). Prosocial behaviour between friends in middle childhood and early adolescence. *Journal of Early Adolescence, 5*(3), 307–317.

Biesanz, R., Biesanz, K. Z., & Biesanz, M. V. (1982). *The Costa Ricans.* Prospect Heights, IL: Waveland Press.

Bleske, A., & Shackelford, T. (2001). Poaching, promiscuity, and deceit: Combatting mating rivalry in same-sex friendships. *Personal Relationships, 8*, 407–424.

Blieszner, R., & Roberto, K. A. (2004). Friendships across the life span: Reciprocity in individual and relationship development. In F. R. Lang & K. L. Fingerman (Eds.), *Personal relationships across the life span* (pp. 159–182). New York: Cambridge University Press.

Buss, D. M. (1984). Marital assortment for personality dispositions: Assessment with three different data sources. *Behavior Genetics, 14*, 111–123.

Buss, D. M. (1989). Sex differences in human mate preferences: Evolutionary hypotheses tested in 37 cultures. *Behavioral and Brain Sciences, 12*, 1–14.

Butynski, T. M. (1990). Comparative ecology of blue monkeys (*Cerocopithecus mitis*) in high- and low-density subpopulations. *Ecological Monographs, 60*, 1–26.

Byrne, D. (1971). *The attraction paradigm.* New York: Academic Press.

Caldwell, M. A., & Peplau, L. A. (1982). Sex differences in same-sex friendship. *Sex Roles, 8*(7), 721–732.

Charlesworth, W. R. (1996). Co-operation and competition: Contributions to an evolutionary and developmental model. *International Journal of Behavioural Development, 19*, 25–39.

Clark, M. S., & Mills, J. (1979). Interpersonal attraction in exchange and communal relationships. *Journal of Personality and Social Psychology, 37*(1), 12–24.

Cords, M. (2002). Friendship among adult female blue monkeys (*Cercopithecus mitis*). *Behaviour, 139*, 291–314.

Davidson, L. R., & Duberman, L. (1982). Friendship: Communication and interactional patterns in same-sex dyads. *Sex Roles, 8*(8), 809–822.

Felmlee, D. H. (1994). Who's on top? Power in romantic relationships. *Sex Roles, 31*(516), 275–295.

Fonzi, A., Schneider, B. H., Tani, F., & Tomada, G. (1997). Predicting children's friendship status from their interaction in structured situations of potential conflict. *Child Development, 68*, 496–506.

Griffiths, J., & Griffiths, P. (1979). *Cuba: The second decade.* London: Writers and Readers Publishing.

Halevy, N., Chou, E., & Galinsky, A. D. (2011). A functional model of hierarchy: Why, how, and when vertical differentiation enhances group performance. *Organizational Psychology Review, 1*, 32–52.

Hall, J. (1971). Decisions, decisions, decisions. *Psychology Today*, 51–54, 86–88.

Hatfield, E., Utne, M. K., & Traupmann, J. (1979). Equity theory and intimate relationships. In R. L. Burgess. & T. L. Huston (Eds.), *Social exchange in developing relationships* (pp. 99–133). New York: Academic Press.

Hays, R. B. (1988). Friendship. In S. W. Duck (Ed.), *Handbook of personal relationships: Theory, research, and interventions* (pp. 391–408). New York: Wiley.

Hays, R. B. (1989). The day-to-day functioning of close versus casual friendships. *Journal of Social and Personal Relationships, 6*(21), 21–37.

Izard, C. E. (1963). Personality similarity and friendship: A follow-up study. *Journal of Abnormal and Social Psychology, 66*(6), 598–600.

Laursen, B., & Hartup, W. W. (2002). The origins of reciprocity and social exchange in friendships. *New Directions for Child and Adolescent Development, 95*, 27–40.

Lawes, M. J., & Henzi, S. P. (1995). Inter-group encounters in blue monkeys: How territorial must a territorial species be? *Animal Behaviour, 49*, 240–243.

Maccoby, E. (1990). Gender and relationships. *American Psychologist, 45*, 513–520.

MacDonald, G., & Leary, M. R. (2005). Why does social exclusion hurt? The relationship between social and physical pain. *Psychological Bulletin, 131*(2), 202–223.

MacEvoy, J. P., & Asher, S. R. (2012). When friends disappoint: Boys' and girls' responses to transgressions of friendship expectations. *Child Development, 83*, 104–119.

Magee, J. C., & Galinsky, A. D. (2008). Social hierarchy: The self-reinforcing nature of power and status. *The Academy of Management Annals, 2*(1), 351–398.

Maltz, D. N., Borker, R. A., & Gumperz, J. A. (1982). A cultural approach to male–female miscommunication. In L. Monaghan, J. E. Goodman, & J. M. Robinson (Eds.), *Language and social identity* (pp. 195–216). Marblehead, MA: Wiley.

Markey, P. M., & Markey, C. N. (2009). A brief assessment of the Interpersonal Circumplex: The IPIP–IPC. *Assessment, 16*(4), 52–361.

Matthews, S. H. (1983). Definitions of friendship and their consequences in old age. *Ageing and Society, 3*, 141–155.

Moses, C. (2000). *Everyday life in Castro's Cuba.* Wilmington, DE: Scholarly Resources.

Olk, P. M., & Gibbons, D. E. (2010). Dynamics of friendship reciprocity among professional adults. *Journal of Applied Social Psychology, 40*, 1146–1171.

Palombit, R. A., Cheney, D. L., & Seyfarth, R. M. (2001). Female–female competition for male "friends" in wild chacma baboons, *Papio cynocephalus ursinus. Animal Behaviour, 61*, 1159–1171.

Palombit, R. A., Seyfarth, R. M., & Cheney, D. L. (1997). The adaptive value of "friendships" to female baboons: Experimental and observational evidence. *Animal Behaviour, 54*, 599–614.

Patrick, H., Ryan, A. M., & Pintrich, P. R. (1999). The differential impact of extrinsic and mastery goal orientations on males' and females' self-regulated learning. *Learning and Individual Differences, 11*, 153–171.

Pettigrew, T. F. (1998). Intergroup contact theory. *Annual Review of Psychology, 49*, 65–85.

Rose, S. M. (1985). Same- and cross-sex friendships and the psychology of homosociality. *Sex Roles, 12*(1–2), 63–74.

Rubin, L. B. (1985). *Just friends: The role of friendship in our lives.* New York: Harper & Row.

Rudran, R. (1978). Socioecology of the blue monkeys (*Cercopithecus mitis stuhlmanni*) of the Kibale Forest, Uganda. *Smithsonian Contributions to Zoology, 249*, 1–88.

Sapadin, L. A. (1988). Friendship and gender: Perspectives of professional men and women. *Journal of Social and Personal Relationships, 5*(387), 389–403.

Schneider, B. H., Dixon, K., & Udvari, S. (2007). Closeness and competition in the inter-ethnic and co-ethnic friendships of early adolescents in Toronto and Montreal. *Journal of Early Adolescence, 27*(1), 115–138.

Schneider, B. H., Woodburn, S., del Toro, M. D. P. S., & Udvari, S. J. (2005). Cultural and gender differences in the implications of competition for early adolescent friendship. *Merrill-Palmer Quarterly, 51*(2), 163–191.

Shackelford, T. K., & Buss, D. M. (1996). Betrayal in mateships, friendships, and coalitions. *Personality and Social Psychology Bulletin, 22*, 1151–1164.

Sharabany, R., Gershon, R., & Hofman, J. E. (1981). Girlfriend, boyfriend: Age and sex differences in intimate friendship. *Developmental Psychology, 17*, 800–808.

Silk, J. B. (2003). Cooperation without counting. In P. Hammerstein (Ed.), *Genetic and cultural evolution of cooperation* (pp. 37–54). Cambridge, MA: MIT Press.

Silk, J. B., Beehner, J. C., Bergman, T. J., Crockford, C., Engh, A. L., Moscovice, L. R., ... Cheney, D. L. (2009). The benefits of social capital: Close social bonds among female baboons enhance offspring survival. *Proceedings of the Royal Society Biological Sciences, 276*, 3099–3104.

Singelton, R. A., & Vacca, J. (2007). Interpersonal competition in friendships. *Sex Roles, 57*, 617–627.

Tan, D. T. Y., & Singh, R. (1995). Attitudes and attraction: A developmental study of the similarity-attraction and dissimilarity-repulsion hypotheses. *Personality and Social Psychology Bulletin, 21*, 975–986.

Tesser, A., & Smith, J. (1980). Some effects of task relevance and friendship. *Journal of Experimental Social Psychology, 16*, 582–590.

Vandenberg, S. (1972). Assortative mating, or who married whom? *Behavior Genetics, 2*, 127–158.

Veniegas, R. C., & Peplau, L. A. (1997). Power and the quality of same-sex friendships. *Psychology of Women Quarterly, 21*, 279–297.

Way, N., & Chen, L. (2000). Close and general friendships among African American, Latino, and Asian American adolescents from low-income families. *Journal of Adolescent Research, 15*(2), 274–301.

Weidler, D. J., & Clark, E. M. (2011). A distinct association: Inclusion of other in the self and self-disclosure. *The New School of Psychology Bulletin, 9*(1), 34–44.

Weiss, L., & Lowenthal, M. F. (1975). Life-course perspectives on friendship. In M. F. Lowenthal, M. Turner, D. Chiriboga, & Associates (Eds.), *Four stages of life* (pp. 48–61). San Francisco: Jossey-Bass.

Wheeler, L., & Miyake, K. (1992). Social comparison in everyday life. *Journal of Personality and Social Psychology, 62*, 760–773.

Whitesell, N. R., & Harter, S. (1996). The interpersonal context of emotion: Anger with close friends and classmates. *Child Development, 67*, 1345–1359.

Winstead, B., & Griffin, J. (2001). Friendship styles. In J. Worrell (Ed.), *Encyclopedia of women and gender* (pp. 481–492). Boston: Academic Press.

Wright, S. C., Brody, S. A., & Aron, A. (2005). Intergroup contact: Still our best hope for reducing prejudice. In C. S. Crandall & M. Schaller (Eds.), *The social psychology of prejudice: Historical perspectives* (pp. 115–142). Seattle: Lewinian Press.

The Element of Surprise: Women of the Dark Triad

P. Lynne Honey

Abstract

The Dark Triad of personality (subclinical psychopathy, narcissism, and Machiavellianism) is associated with exploitative behavior. Although people with these traits may be perceived negatively, they often compete successfully for mates, resources, and power. Research on the Dark Triad highlights its utility for men and downplays the smaller, but still meaningful, samples of women with dark personalities. This chapter summarizes evidence about women's antisocial behaviors and traits, and hypothesizes that we underestimate women's ability to deceive and harm others. Women exploit others, and yet our expectations about women tend to be positive and women are generally viewed as nonthreatening. When women cause harm, it is often minimized, and women are held typically less responsible for their actions. Female criminals may have an advantage because their behavior is unexpected. This chapter outlines benefits for underestimated women and proposes additional research to clarify whether the Dark Triad is differentially adaptive for women.

Key Words: Dark Triad, Machiavellianism, narcissism, psychopathy, stereotypes, sex differences

Sugar and spice, and all things nice, that's what little girls are made of.

This nursery rhyme echoes a societal expectation about femininity that is rooted in pleasantness. On the other hand, another little poem described a different sort of girl:

There was a little girl, who had a little curl, right in the middle of her forehead. When she was good, she was very, very good, and when she was bad she was horrid!

Although most of us recognize that the second little girl is somewhat more realistic, with both pleasant and unpleasant characteristics, it is interesting to find that our stereotypes about women often reflect the first rhyme, such that our expectations of women are quite positive in many ways. We expect women to be nurturing, kind, and nonthreatening,

consistent with the "women are wonderful" effect (Eagly, Mladinic, & Otto, 1991), in which it is found that stereotypes about women tend to have a positive valence, even if women are perceived as having less agency or competence than men (Eagly & Mladinic, 1994). The "women are wonderful" effect is consistent with notions of benevolent sexism (Glick & Fiske, 2001) in which women are viewed in a positive light, generally as soft and generous nurturers, but are also seen as weak and in need of protection. In cross-cultural studies, endorsement of benevolent sexism (e.g., "Women should be cherished and protected by men"; "Women tend to have a superior moral sensibility") is negatively correlated with nation-level measures of gender equality (Glick & Fiske, 2001). Thus, countries with high levels of sex/gender discrimination exhibit greater endorsement of these positive views of women compared to men. Although positive and wholesome female stereotypes are often associated with patriarchal attitudes that are not particularly egalitarian, they are nonetheless espoused and embraced by many men and women who view women as the gentler sex.

Our schemas of women as wonderful are so pervasive that they seem to bias even our research questions about female misbehavior. Heidensohn (2010) points out that deviance is a cornerstone topic in social science and that feminist approaches to social science research are common, yet there is a surprising deficit in the study of female deviance, aggression, and crime when compared to the study of male deviance, aggression, and crime. It is reasonable to question whether our understanding of women as agents of aggression or deviance is biased by the research questions we ask and by the researchers who ask the questions. For example, when researchers who study intimate partner violence focus on the consequences of violence (i.e., injuries), they reliably find the expected pattern of male perpetrators causing more injuries and female victims being more injured. When researchers focus instead on the number of aggressive acts perpetrated by intimate partners, they find that women commit more acts of aggression, and men are the more frequent recipients of those aggressive acts (Archer, 2000). Although it is clear that the typically larger and stronger sex can cause more damage, it is not the case that the larger and stronger sex commits a greater number of aggressive acts in the context of intimate relationships. These sorts of results are regularly downplayed in research articles and in media reports about intimate partner violence (Archer, 2000, 2009). Scientists are not immune to socialized bias even when pursuing objective truth. Just as the risks, treatments, and prognoses for heart disease in women were ignored in research that included only men because men were seen as the primary victims of heart attack (Wenger, 2012), risks for men are minimized in research that focuses on women as victims of aggression.

Research in cognitive and social psychology has demonstrated repeatedly that our biases often blind us to objective reality. Our expectancies constrain our view of the world in powerful ways, leading us to overestimate our risk of minor dangers and underestimate our risk of more likely dangers (Ajzen, 1977). We also have varying levels of sensitivity when it comes to detecting the misbehavior of others. In 2010, ABC News staged and video-recorded a series of bicycle thefts in a park as part of a hidden-camera special called "What Would You Do?" The point of these staged scenarios was to determine whether average Americans would stop a bicycle theft as it was happening. The results were quite dramatic. When the "thief" was a young black man, he was repeatedly questioned, chased away, and physically threatened. When the "thief" was a young white man, he was watched carefully but was questioned or stopped only rarely. This demonstration of the sort of expectations and biases that people hold about race and crime was powerful and was the focus of the news piece. There was another set of thefts presented that also spoke volumes about our biases. When the "thief" was a young woman, no one seemed to assume that she was doing anything wrong. In fact, several people stopped to offer assistance as she cut the chains on bicycles that she freely admitted were not her own. If one were to imagine a situation in which the "ideal" thief must be chosen to steal an item in full view of the public, it would be reasonable to choose the person least likely to be suspected. That ideal thief would likely be a young woman. Note in this set of examples that one factor—race—leads one individual to be subject to a much higher level of social scrutiny. At the same time another factor—sex—leads to a much *lower* level of social scrutiny, for the woman compared to the men. The interesting question, then, is whether women are conferred direct advantages as a result of reduced scrutiny for their antisocial behaviors.

Underestimation of Antisocial Behavior by Women

Women are arrested for fewer crimes and are less likely to be incarcerated compared to men. Of all people arrested in the United States in 2009, only 25% were women (Traylor & Richie, 2012). Women were arrested for approximately 10% of the murders, 12% of the robberies, and 22% of the aggravated assaults. Women are more likely to be arrested for larceny or theft (44%), fraud (43%), forgery or counterfeiting (38%), and embezzlement (51%). In Canada, the pattern is similar (Boyce, 2013). Women represent 19% of cases that go to criminal court, and the most common offenses for women are theft (35%) and fraud (30%). Patterns are similar in Australia (Holmes, 2010) and in Europe (Heiskanen, 2010). Thus, women are charged with and convicted for far fewer violent crimes than are men, but there is a much smaller sex difference when it comes to nonviolent property or monetary crimes.

When women do commit crimes, they often receive different treatment than do men in various aspects of the justice system. Men are more likely to be convicted in court and, once convicted, are more likely to be imprisoned rather than experience some other consequence, such as a fine or community service (Boyce, 2013; Holmes, 2010; Traylor & Richie, 2012). There are a variety of reasons why men and women might have different patterns of conviction and incarceration, including the severity of the crimes, the behavior of the defendants during trial and sentencing, and the extenuating circumstances associated with the case. One example of a dramatic difference is associated with sexual crimes. Women are far more likely than men to be arrested for prostitution, and prostitution is a nonviolent crime for which incarceration is rarely a consequence. On the other hand, men are far more likely than women to be arrested for sexual assault, which is a violent crime, and incarceration is more likely for all violent crimes (Traylor & Richie, 2012). As mentioned, there are a variety of confounding variables that make it difficult to compare the consequences faced by men and women within the legal and penal systems. It is possible that men and women would experience different consequences even if the crimes and circumstances were identical, but to test such a hypothesis requires controlled laboratory conditions that realistically do not naturally occur.

Some experimental research has explored sex differences in attribution of guilt, and those studies have revealed that the behavior of participants in laboratory scenarios does produce patterns that are similar to those seen in actual legal settings. For example, in studies where participants read a variety of controlled scenarios about both violent crimes and property crimes, and the only factor that differed between scenarios was the sex of the perpetrator, female perpetrators were perceived as less culpable than male perpetrators who had committed the same crimes. Related to this finding of reduced culpability, participants also tend to suggest shorter jail times for female perpetrators (Ahola, Christianson, & Hellstrom, 2009). Kleinke and Baldwin (1993) examined attitudes toward hypothetical perpetrators who explained their behaviors with "insane" statements, such as "I control the forces of good and evil." When those behaviors were harmful, participants were likely to recommend that a man be sent to prison but a woman be sent to a mental institution. This result is consistent with other research that suggests that women's harmful behaviors are attributed to emotional problems or mental instability rather than character flaws or intentional actions.

These sorts of results, in which women are routinely described or perceived as less agentic than men, are hardly unique. Women are perceived as somewhat less responsible for their alcohol and drug use, especially by male raters (Hatgis, Friedmann, & Weiner, 2008). When women are described as initiating an aversive action (e.g., Mary bribes a politician or Susan threatens a rival), the action is more likely to be perceived as being caused by external forces (the politician expected it, or the rival deserved it). Men are more likely to be seen as causal in such situations (Lafrance, Brownell, & Hahn, 1997). When probation officers document behaviors by juvenile offenders, they are more likely to focus on emotional and social instability of female offenders, but male offenders are described as more intentional and autonomous (Mallicoat, 2007). Accounts in Israeli newspapers focus on the emotional outbursts (and beauty) of female suicide bombers, whereas their male counterparts are described in terms of their dedication and fearlessness (Sela-Shayovitz, 2007). In a psychiatric setting, clinicians must evaluate the risk that a patient will commit violence. Clinicians appear to underestimate the risk posed by female patients and are more accurate in estimating the risk posed by male patients (Skeem et al., 2005). This list of research findings illustrates a consistent theme. We attribute greater agency to the behavior of men and thus perceive women as less culpable, less autonomous, and less dangerous.

When looking at violent crimes like domestic abuse or sexual assault, women are again perceived as less dangerous, and their crimes are not viewed as particularly serious compared to those perpetrated by men. As mentioned previously, women are more likely to be injured as a result of intimate partner violence (Archer, 2000), and that pattern is even more severe in many places outside of North America (Archer, 2006). On the other hand, women also commit more individual acts of aggression within the context of intimate relationships (Archer, 2000), even if those acts are less likely to result in physical injury that requires medical treatment. Perhaps this difference in the consequences of aggression results in female-perpetrated assault being seen as less serious and that men who are victims of assault by their female partners are perceived as less masculine. Consistent with this, abused men often experience more blame (Lehmann & Santilli, 1996), and bystanders are more willing to intervene in a situation where a man is hitting a woman than in a situation where a woman is hitting a man (Chabot, Tracy, Manning, & Poisson, 2009). Henning, Jones, and Holdford (2005) interviewed people convicted of domestic assault in Tennessee and found that although there was a dramatic difference in the number of women convicted (n = 159) compared to men (n = 1,267), there were no significant demographic differences between the sexes, and details of their respective criminal cases were similar. Differences included the tendency for female assailants to blame their victims and to insist that they acted entirely in self-defense. Thus, women's attributions about their own behaviors are consistent with the tendency for others to perceive that women are less agentic than men. In a large-scale study of teen relationships, Gross (2009) found that in relationships where violence was reported, approximately 65% of them included mutual violence, in which both partners had physically harmed each other. In those relationships that reported one-sided violence, in which only one partner was the aggressor, the aggressor was approximately five times more likely to be the female partner. The same study reported that very few of the young men who had experienced physical assaults by their female partners felt that they were being abused, and most of them minimized the seriousness of their girlfriends' behaviors. Once again, female violence is minimized despite its relatively high rate of occurrence.

This same pattern is found when we examine sexual assault data. In sexual assault scenarios, female aggressors are seen as less guilty than male aggressors, and male victims receive more blame (Russell, Oswald, & Kraus, 2011; Rye, Greatrix, & Enright, 2006; Rylands & Nesca, 2012). Furthermore, there are systematic and institutionalized differences in how sexual assault is identified and recorded, and these differences affect the data that are available to help understand patterns of sexual assault. For example, in the United States, sexual assault is recorded and tracked using the Uniform Crime Reporting Program (UCR). Until 2012, the system of categorization used by the UCR defined forcible rape as "the carnal knowledge of a female forcibly and against her will" (Stemple & Meyer, 2014). Thus, there were *no* male victims of forcible rape in the UCR. In 2012, various UCR definitions of sexual assault were revised, but the definition of rape still includes reference to having been penetrated, which excludes victims who were "made to penetrate." The broader definition of sexual assault includes being made to penetrate, which includes a large number of cases of sexual assault with male

victims. If one were to only look at cases of "rape," as just defined, then women are disproportionately the victims of sexual assault. If, however, all cases of nonconsensual sex were considered, then the pattern changes. In 2010, there were 1,270,000 women raped; 1,267,000 men were made to penetrate; and comparable percentages of women (5.6%) and men (5.3%) experienced other forms of sexual violence (National Center for Injury Prevention and Control [NCIPC], 2011). Stemple and Meyer's (2014) analysis of the National Intimate Partner and Sexual Violence Survey, the National Inmate Survey, and the National Survey of Youth in Custody reveals that women perpetrate a large number of sexual assaults against men and against other women. Because those assaults do not typically include penetration and thus are categorized differently than rape, the way that the data are used does not reflect the risks posed by female sexual offenders. This is not to suggest that women are as likely as men to commit sexual assaults because that is simply not the case. More than 93% of cases of rape (of men and women) were perpetrated by men. For all other forms of sexual violence, men committed 93% of acts against women. The pattern with male victims of other forms of sexual violence is different, however. Women committed 79% of "made to penetrate" offenses, 84% of sexual coercion offenses, and 53.1% of unwanted sexual contact offenses against men (NCIPC, 2011). Despite the fact that women commit the majority of non-rape sexual offenses against men, women are not perceived as a risk to men. This failure to perceive women as potential perpetrators has the very damaging consequence that men who are victims of sexual assault are marginalized and are not supported by society or the legal system (Stemple & Meyer, 2014). The other consequence is that female perpetrators are not held as accountable for their actions, and the damage that they cause is underestimated.

What benefit is gained by committing sexual assault? Evolutionary theories of rape typically emphasize the reproductive benefit acquired by male rapists at the expense of the female victim (e.g., Thornhill & Palmer, 2000). Although it is outside the scope of this chapter to discuss the controversy associated with this line of reasoning, it is worth noting that a focus on penetrative rape of fertile women again ignores the broader scope of sexual violence against people of all ages and genders. Sexual assault may be motivated by sexual arousal, but it may also provide benefits that are nonsexual. Control of an intimate partner, threat and humiliation of rivals or subordinates (as is common in the context of incarceration), and immediate sexual gratification are all benefits that perpetrators of sexual assaults gain. Whether the perpetrator is male or female does not change those benefits. Any individual with a callous disregard for the well-being and integrity of another person can gain those benefits.

Although our cognitive templates about sexual assault and other criminal behaviors are clearly biased toward a pattern of male perpetrator and female victim, what about other unpleasant or antisocial behaviors that are not crimes? Lying is an example of a behavior that could result in a benefit for the liar at the expense of someone else. Men and women appear to tell equivalent numbers of lies, although the content and motivation of those lies does tend to differ between the sexes (Feldman, Forrest, & Happ, 2002; Tyler & Feldman, 2004). Additionally, among children (Gervais, Tremblay, Demarais-Gervais, & Vitaro, 2000) and adolescents (Haselton, Buss, Oubaid, & Angleitner, 2005), there are no clear sex differences in the number of lies told. Males and females do tend to differ when it comes to the content of lies, however. For example, adolescent girls are more likely than boys to conceal or deceive their parents about their sexual behaviors (Knox, Zusman, McGinty, & Gesheidler, 2001). Among adults, women tell more lies about other people, whereas men tell more lies about themselves (DePaulo, Kashy, Kirkendol, Wyer, & Epstein, 1996). Still, men and women tend to be equally likely to attempt to deceive others. Regarding attitudes toward various other unethical behaviors, a study of business and psychology students found no sex differences in attitudes toward deception, theft, or abuse of resources; women and men were equally likely to endorse unethical behaviors in certain circumstances, whether or not they had taken an ethics course (Tang & Chen, 2008). Given that men and women are equally likely to deceive or engage in other unethical behaviors including theft, we should be equally vigilant and suspicious of men and of women; and yet, when meeting strangers, women are consistently rated as seeming more conscientious and responsible compared to men (Marcus & Lehmann, 2002). Lying is so common that it might not be perceived as a relevant antisocial behavior, but it is still a behavior that allows one individual to gain a benefit or avoid a cost, potentially at another's expense. If we underestimate women's likelihood of such a common antisocial behavior, then we provide an opportunity for female liars to remain undetected.

The risk of antisocial behavior tends to be underestimated among women, even within populations where antisocial behavior is *expected*. Among psychiatric patients with risk factors, including recent violent behaviors, that suggest they could be violent after their release from the hospital, false-negative predictions are more likely for female patients than for male patients with identical indicators of violence, even when evaluated by highly trained clinicians (Skeem et al., 2005). Among adolescents diagnosed with conduct disorder, which is characterized by prolonged and repeated violation of norms, rules, and laws (American Psychiatric Association [APA], 2013), girls and boys have equivalent risk of aggression and crime, but girls are perceived as less symptomatic because their overall rates of physical violence are lower (Berkout, Young, & Gross, 2011). The distinction between danger associated with physical violence and other forms of aggression often minimizes the damaging impact of female-typical aggression. Girls and women typically employ indirect or relational aggression, which is characterized by social manipulation and a variety of behaviors that make targets feel self-conscious, inferior, or excluded; such forms of aggression are very effective tactics in intrasexual competition (Vaillancourt, 2013). It has been suggested that women's aggression is underestimated and understudied because it is less public and more personal (Logan, 2011). Victims of women's aggression tend to be family members or romantic partners (Archer, 2004; Skeem et al., 2005), but classmates and other peers are common targets as well (Björkqvist, Lagerspetz, & Kaukiainen, 2013).

The relationship between rates of physical aggression and expectations of aggression likely influences the way that we perceive the behavior of actual people in a manner that leads us to different attributions about men and women. When male and female professional dancers were instructed to perform identical body movements, observers perceived more aggression in postures executed by men and more grief in postures executed by women (De Meijer, 1991). Expectations about masculine and feminine preferences and strategies also lead us to see unknown individuals as either male or female based on very limited information about their level of competitiveness or aggression. Eden, Maloney, and Bowman (2010) presented participants with video clips of online games being played by unseen players, and participants were asked to rate the masculinity or femininity of the players. Skilled players in first-person shooter games were perceived as masculine, whereas skilled players in nonviolent puzzle games were perceived as feminine, as were unskilled players in other games. This is consistent with reported preferences by male and female gamers, such that female gamers often report that they prefer characters or games that are nonviolent and male gamers prefer combat games and characters that employ violence (Companion & Sambrook, 2008). In other "games," including the Prisoner's Dilemma, participants tend to assume that a competitive player (one who initially defects rather than cooperates) is male and that a cooperative player is female (King, Miles, & Kniska, 1991). Such biases raise the question of whether our expectations are based on real risks associated with interacting with men rather than women. That is, are we making occasional errors because our heuristics generally lead to accurate decisions?

In novel situations, we often behave as if we are minimizing risk by making attributions or choices that result in the lowest likelihood of loss or danger. According to error management theory (Haselton & Buss, 2000), we are predisposed to make decisions in a manner that reflects the risk associated with false-positive and false-negative judgments. For example, men should be sensitive to any cue of interest from women because the risk of missing a mating opportunity is large, whereas women should be less sensitive to cues of sexual interest because there is greater risk for women in pursuing every available mating opportunity. Likewise, there may be biases in our perception of risk associated with male and female behavior. If women are less likely to be violent than men, then people should be more sensitive to cues of aggression by men and less sensitive to cues of aggression by women. Moreover, because one is more likely to be physically harmed if a cue of male aggression is missed than if a cue of female aggression is missed, there should be a perceptual bias in favor of detecting male aggression. The risk of a false negative exists, but that risk is small and the costs of the false negative are perceived to be minimal. Consistent with this approach, it has been found that women are more suspicious of men than men are of women in terms of expectations of deception (Keenan, Gallup, Goulet, & Kulkarni, 1997). This expectation of deception may relate to a heightened ability to detect deception; within the context of dating relationships, women are better able to detect deceptive statements by their partners than are men (McCornack & Parks, 1990). It seems as if large differences between men and women for violence and direct aggression have led

to generalized differential thresholds for detection of risk.

Exploitation as Competition

We typically think of deceptive and destructive behaviors as "bad," and they generally are negative events for the targets or victims of those behaviors. For the perpetrators, however, there are benefits; people who lie, cheat, steal, intimidate, and even kill can acquire resources, avoid punishment, and gain status. Although there are individual and cooperative methods to acquire evolutionarily relevant resources, exploitative methods will simultaneously provide resources for the exploiter and deprive someone else of access to those resources (Buss & Duntley, 2008). In other words, although one might work hard to plant and maintain a garden in order to have food (an individual strategy), she could also share the work with neighbors in order to have a bigger garden and somewhat less work for each person (a cooperative strategy). A thief who raids the garden gets the benefit of the food without having expended the effort and time to grow it and has reduced the amount of food that is left for everyone else (an exploitative strategy).

Any trait that allows a person to exploit others would confer an advantage over targets and competitors alike. As will be described later, if exploitation can occur without detection, then the advantage is even greater because there is a reduction in the cost associated with social penalties or retaliation. Dugatkin (1992) provides a game theory model to support hypotheses about the evolution of the con artist within the context of a mobile, social group. In game theory terms, con artists are defectors or cheaters, and their victims are cooperators. The Prisoner's Dilemma is a game that is often used to test hypotheses about game theory. It involves a scenario in which two prisoners are being interrogated in separate rooms. If neither prisoner provides any information to the interrogators (each prisoner *cooperates* with the other), then both prisoners will go free. If each prisoner provides information about the other (each prisoner *defects* on the other), then both prisoners will be punished for the crime. If one prisoner stays silent (cooperates) but the other provides evidence (defects), then the defector goes free while the cooperator is punished. If each party trusts the other, then both will benefit from cooperation. Trusting an untrustworthy person, however, is a big risk. In a one-shot situation, in which the players would never encounter one another again, the most stable strategy is to defect. In an iterative situation, where players will encounter each other repeatedly, both players will benefit from mutual cooperation, and the most stable strategy is "tit-for-tat" in which initial cooperation is followed by a series of decisions that reward cooperation and punish defection. In a situation like the Prisoner's Dilemma, humans have fairly predictable approaches to making decisions under uncertainty, and, on average, we tend to cooperate with one another (Axelrod & Hamilton, 1981). It has been argued that our tendency to cooperate has been selected for because social species like humans benefit more from cooperation than from callous self-interest. Still, the need to detect cues of defection is important, and defectors benefit from deception (Cosmides, 1989).

In order for a con artist to succeed within a group, the overall number of con artists must remain relatively low. A con artist succeeds by exploiting the cooperative nature of others, but the likelihood of cooperation would be reduced if members of the group are either uncooperative because they are themselves cheaters or because they have had repeated experiences with cheaters, thus leading them to become vigilant and untrusting. Con artists are more likely to succeed when they are able to move between groups that do not communicate or avoid detection within their existing group. If being female reduces the likelihood of suspicion, then a female con artist could avoid detection for longer and have a greater opportunity to exploit a group before having to move on to the next. Although Dugatkin's (1992) model is focused on con artists, it could just as easily apply to a variety of antisocial behaviors including lying, theft, coercion, fraud, or identity theft. Regardless of the behavior, theory suggests that women who commit crimes, or merely manipulate others for small personal gains, may be readily camouflaged by their sex.

There are a variety of antisocial behaviors that allow some people to gain benefits at the expense of others. Both men and women benefit from exploitation and control of others in order to acquire resources, status, dominance, or direct reproductive benefits. Each individual faces the problems of both intersexual conflict and intrasexual competition (Buss & Schmitt, 1993). Intersexual conflict occurs when men and women have different reproductive goals or would benefit differently from sex or relationships. For example, men accrue greater benefits to reproductive potential by having a large number of sex partners in a short amount of time

because each coupling has the potential to produce an offspring. Although women may benefit from promiscuity in other ways, women do not require multiple partners to maximize the number of children they produce. Evidence of conflict is revealed in men's deception about willingness to commit and women's deception about willingness to engage in uncommitted sex. Intrasexual competition occurs within a sex, over mating opportunities. For example, women might compete with other women by attempting to be more attractive than a rival or by sabotaging a rival to remove her from competition. In both intersexual and intrasexual competition, deception is a useful strategy. Deception between the sexes allows the deceiver to benefit from access to sexual or relationship resources that the deceived partner might not have been otherwise willing to provide. For example, a man who lies about being in love with his partner might convince her to have sex with him, when she would otherwise refuse. In competition with same-sex rivals, the "winners" have greater access to more partners and higher-quality partners. The man who routinely lies about being in love might have more sex partners than a man who does not use this deceptive strategy. Thus, this strategy of deception could benefit the liar in both intersexual conflict and intrasexual competition.

There are a number of ways that women can be reproductively successful. Ideally, the goal is to have a large number of high-quality offspring and enough resources to ensure their survival to adulthood. Furthermore, having offspring with variable genes means that there is an increased likelihood that at least some of them will survive to adulthood in environments that are harsh or unpredictable (Ridley, 1993). Success in intersexual conflict and intrasexual competition can provide women with access to resources and care provided by partners, access to varied and high-quality genes for her offspring, and care and protection for those offspring (Trivers, 1972). Furthermore, some aspects of intersexual conflict and intrasexual competition are zero-sum games. If a man invests resources in a woman and her offspring, he will have fewer resources to invest in any other women or offspring. Thus, a woman who can outcompete another woman for access to a man who is willing to invest resources has not only acquired resources for herself, but she has also reduced the resources available to her competitors and reduced her partner's ability to distribute his resources in order to acquire additional reproductive advantages. We turn now to a discussion of a personality variant that may allow some women to have a competitive edge in both intersexual conflict and intrasexual competition, as well as in more general interpersonal competition.

The Dark Triad and Competition

The Dark Triad is a cluster of personality traits that includes subclinical psychopathy, narcissism, and Machiavellianism (Paulhus & Williams, 2002). As a personality variant, it represents a self-serving and often instrumental style of social interaction that allows those employing this strategy to manipulate and exploit social groups, or individuals, for resources (Jonason & Webster, 2012). Each of the three traits has antisocial aspects. Psychopathy is characterized by aggression and lack of empathy (Mealey, 1995). Narcissistic individuals are grandiose and entitled, with a sense of superiority (Raskin & Terry, 1988). Machiavellian individuals are cold and manipulative (Christie & Geis, 1970). Given its unique clustering of self-serving personality traits (Jonason, Li, & Teicher, 2010), the Dark Triad could be considered a marked disadvantage for individuals in a species as social as humans, but the growing literature in this area would indicate the opposite (McDonald, Donnellan, & Navarrete, 2012).

It should be noted that an individual may be considered to have traits consistent with the Dark Triad without having all the traits associated with the Dark Triad. Although some researchers have argued that there is sufficient overlap in the features of the three traits to warrant treating the Dark Triad as a singular construct (Webster & Jonason, 2013), others have argued that the three traits, although strongly correlated, are distinct constructs that differentially predict important behavior patterns (Furnham, Richards, & Paulhus, 2013). For example, in a workplace setting, the three Dark Triad traits predict different tactics used to manipulate or control the behavior of others: narcissists use soft tactics, like giving compliments or joking around, psychopaths use hard tactics including the use of threats and intimidation, whereas Machiavellians are flexible and use both types of tactics (Jonason, Slomski, & Partyka, 2012). An individual may express all three Dark Triad traits equally or may express one and not the others (Paulhus & Williams, 2002). That is, a psychopath, a narcissist, and a Machiavellian each have Dark Triad personalities, but each would have somewhat different behaviors.

There are certainly costs associated with antisocial behavior, and people with Dark Triad traits are not exempt from those costs (Jonason, Li, & Czarna, 2013). Social exclusion, physical retaliation, damaged reputation, and loss of resources may all result from treating others poorly. As with the tit-for-tat strategy that is most stable in the Prisoner's Dilemma (Axelrod & Hamilton, 1981), retaliation of all sorts typically follows cheating behavior. Whether that retaliation is simply that others refuse to share their resources or that the cheater loses her life or livelihood, there are typically penalties associated with breaking the social contract. Although it has been demonstrated that people with Dark Triad traits may downplay the likelihood of negative consequences (Jonason & Tost, 2010), if they are detected in their antisocial behaviors, then they typically cannot avoid all punishment. Rather, the benefits may outweigh the potential costs. In terms of reproductive benefits, the Dark Triad traits are linked to increased sexual success when measured as the number of partners and the variability associated with a disinhibited sexual style (Jonason, Li, Webster, & Schmitt, 2009). In addition, people with Dark Triad traits tend to engage in mate poaching (enticing a partner out of an existing relationship) and tend to use aggressive and manipulative behaviors in an attempt to keep their existing partners (Jonason, Li, & Buss, 2010). It should be noted that although Dark Triad traits are associated with investment in short-term mating, those same traits are essentially orthogonal to interest in long-term mating (Jonason et al., 2009) which suggests that many people with Dark Triad traits are in long-term relationships or are seeking them. Furthermore, each of the Dark Triad traits is associated with high levels of intrasexual competition (Hanusiak, Fisher, & Carter, 2013), which suggests that Dark Triad individuals are willing to engage in a variety of behaviors that increase mating opportunities by outcompeting rivals.

Dark Triad traits are also associated with status and social influence. In the workplace, Dark Triad traits are associated with a wide range of manipulative tactics, from ingratiation to threats, intended to control others (Jonason, Slomski et al., 2012). With friends, strangers, family, and coworkers, Dark Triad traits predict the use of social tactics including intimidation, charm, and the silent treatment as methods of controlling people or situations (Jonason & Webster, 2012). The style of social interaction for Dark Triad individuals tends to be focused on ruthless self-advancement, with a lack of coalition-building (Zuroff, Fournier, Patall, & Leybman, 2010), and each of the Dark Triad traits is associated with striving for social dominance (Semenyna & Honey, 2015). Each of these studies provides evidence that Dark Triad traits, far from being aversive or maladaptive, provide benefits that include control of others, access to resources, and reproductive advantages. From an evolutionary perspective, both social and sexual opportunities lead to greater ultimate fitness (Buss & Schmitt, 1993) in addition to any proximate reward experienced by the individual in the moment. It should also be noted that people with Dark Triad traits are not necessarily unpleasant people, despite the often-unpleasant consequences of their actions. Some can be quite charming, entertaining, fun, and personable (Jonason & Webster, 2012; McDonald et al., 2012). When combined with other traits like intelligence or physical attractiveness, Dark Triad traits are associated with a great deal of social success (Furnham, 2010).

Sex Differences in Dark Triad Traits

It has been repeatedly demonstrated that there are small but consistent sex differences in the expression of Dark Triad traits, such that men tend to have higher scores on the various measures. There are small but consistent sex differences in scores of narcissism (Paulhus & Williams, 2002), although some researchers have described those differences as marginal (Ames, Rose, & Anderson, 2006). Men also tend to have slightly higher scores for Machiavellianism (Christie & Geis, 1970). The largest sex difference is found on measures of psychopathy, where there is a persistent and robust sex difference with substantially more men represented among the highest scorers (Forth, Brown, Hart, & Hare, 1996). It is not clear why there is a large sex difference in measures of psychopathy. Many of the explanations of this sex difference are descriptive or reflect proximate mechanisms like hormone levels and socialization, rather than ultimate explanations that would address the evolutionary significance of this apparent behavioral dimorphism (see Cale & Lilienfeld, 2002).

Researchers repeatedly report that although men have higher average scores than women on all of the Dark Triad traits, the behavioral patterns associated with those traits are the same for men and women (Furnham et al., 2013). Dark Triad men and women tend to be impulsive (Jones & Paulhus, 2011), have lower levels of empathy (Jonason & Krause, 2013), and endorse more unethical behavior (Tang & Chen, 2008). They are also more likely to report cheating on a test or paper in high school and submitting plagiarized papers in college (Williams, Nathanson, & Paulhus, 2010), cheat

on multiple-choice examinations (Nathanson, Paulhus, & Williams, 2006), and engage in risky lifestyle behaviors including drug, alcohol, and cigarette use (Jonason, Koenig, & Tost, 2010). That is not to say that there is an absence of interesting interactions between Dark Triad traits and biological sex. For example, Machiavellian women tend to use self-disclosure as a manipulative tactic, but Machiavellian men do not (O'Connor & Simms, 1990). Men and women who cheat on their partners tend to have higher scores on Dark Triad measures, but unfaithful men and women tend to have different patterns of Dark Triad traits; psychopathy is associated with infidelity in both sexes, but Machiavellianism is more strongly associated with female infidelity. Furthermore, although psychopathy is associated with the end of the relationship, Machiavellianism is not (Jones & Weiser, 2014). Thus, Dark Triad traits may be associated with different methods of exploitation in men and women, but the important point is that Dark Triad traits are associated with exploitation by both sexes.

Research on the Dark Triad typically examines responses and behaviors by both men and women, and yet broad statements about the Dark Triad often emphasize the masculine nature of the traits, as well as the benefits for men with those traits. In an article that summarizes and describes popular culture examples of Dark Triad-type characters, Jonason, Webster, Schmitt, Li, and Crysel (2012) provide a series of excellent examples—from James Bond to Dr. Gregory House—of media portrayals of men who exhibit Dark Triad traits. Notably absent are examples of Dark Triad women. The authors stated

> Although women can score high on the Dark Triad traits, they often suffer more serious consequences than men do for pursuing a fast life strategy. For instance, pursuing a violent approach to life is more problematic for women than for men in that women are smaller in stature. . . . Female characters may more commonly conform to the stereotypic female gender roles of nurturance, caring, and compassion. It seems possible that if female characters violate these roles, the associated movies will not make it to mainstream audiences. It is possible there are female examples of antiheroes, and we cannot claim to be aware of every character in popular media.
> *(Jonason, Webster et al., 2012, p. 195)*

This statement falsely equates a fast life strategy with violence and is not followed by any supportive empirical evidence about the alleged "more serious consequences" for women. Aside from a statement that such women risk raising offspring alone (hardly a risk confined to women with Dark Triad traits), no clear examples support the maladaptedness of Dark Triad traits for women. The statement is also dismissive of the existence of a variety of women who exhibit similar traits to the men exemplified in their paper. For one example, although Tony Stark (Iron Man) is held up as an example of a Dark Triad antihero, a woman who attempted to assassinate Tony Stark could also have been profiled. Natasha Romanova (Black Widow) was an elite spy known for her seductive infiltration of a variety of agencies, as well as for her combat skill. Although she has received less attention than has Iron Man, she was included in the 2012 Hollywood blockbuster *The Avengers*. Although it is perfectly reasonable to state that the authors cannot be aware of every character in popular media, it is not unreasonable to be aware of characters within the same movie. Likewise, the titular *House* could be contrasted with the titular *Nurse Jackie*, who repeatedly violates ethical standards of practice, shares Dr. House's predilection for Vicodin, and trades sex for access to various drugs. James Bond is a classic antihero, but his existence does not negate the existence of other Fleming characters like Pussy Galore, who ran a crime syndicate, or real-life agents of espionage like Mata Hari. There are various sources of information and examples about women with dark personalities and antisocial behavior (e.g., Logan, 2011), so it is unclear why examples of such *femmes fatales* were so elusive to Jonason, Webster, and their colleagues (2012).

These authors are not alone, though. Buss and Duntley (2008) provided a compelling review of various means by which adaptations for exploitation may have been selected for throughout human evolution and how those adaptations manifest in modern humans. Although many of the adaptations are described as benefiting exploitative individuals in general, the preponderance of examples demonstrate how such adaptations benefit human men and, in particular, how male-typical violence and aggression are used to exploit women or gain access to them. Women are suggested to have evolved crucial anti-exploitation adaptations such as rape avoidance, but the only concrete mention of an exploitative female tactic is that of a woman concealing her intelligence in order to "exploit the exploiters." Although the examples provided are useful, there is a distinct bias toward men being described as exploiters and women being described as exploited. Although nonviolent methods of

exploitation are mentioned, including free riding, cheating, and cuckoldry, those methods are not explored in any detail. As there is evidence of similar rates of unethical behavior (Tang & Chen, 2008), cheating (Nathanson et al, 2006), and infidelity (Jones & Weiser, 2014) among high Dark Triad men and women, it cannot be argued that adaptations for exploitation benefit men only, nor are they expressed by men only. As discussed previously, it is clear that violence and intimidation are stereotypically male behaviors and that those methods of exploitation are disproportionately expressed by males. Buss and Duntley (2008) do provide a clear and compelling argument that the risks of engaging in physically violent behaviors are greater for women, who are on average smaller than men and often responsible for the care and indeed gestation of young and vulnerable children. Still, there are situations where women benefit from aggressive actions, and men and women tend to aggress for different reasons and in ways that are functional for each sex (Griskevicius, Tybur, Gangestad, Perea, Shapiro, & Kenrick, 2009). Even when women aggress against men, as in the case of intimate partner violence, it is not clear that fear of retaliation plays a large role in suppressing the behavior. Among college women who were violent toward their male partners, a common reason that they reported for their behavior was that they felt that there would be no retaliation (Fiebert & Gonzalez, 1997).

Furthermore, the benefits of antisocial behaviors and traits may be greater for men than for women because women require the social support of other women and often the larger community in order to support and protect offspring (Stockley & Campbell, 2013). Rejection from the social group can be more costly for human females (Benenson, 2013), as is the case in a variety of social species (Clutton-Brock & Huchard, 2013), so behaviors that lead to social exclusion are more risky for women. There are, however, many forms of exploitation that are covert and do not require violence. In fact, methods like free riding, cheating, and cuckoldry are successful only when the exploited party does not detect the behavior of the exploiter. Although a variety of hypotheses about the adaptive nature of Dark Triad traits emphasize that women would be at greater risk when expressing those traits, there is no cost associated with retaliation when the manipulative or exploitative acts are not detected.

It is clear that the upper end of the distribution of Dark Triad trait scores is disproportionately male, and this is especially true for psychopathy.

The populations of prisons are also disproportionately male, and men are more likely than women to use physical violence against others. It is also clear that media and literary examples of antiheros and con artists are also disproportionately male. As a corollary and perhaps a consequence of this set of statistical facts, evidence reviewed earlier in this chapter demonstrates that men are less trusted, more maligned for exploitative behavior, and offered less assistance than are women. Such stereotypes and bias exist despite consistent evidence that women—despite being less physically violent—are capable of exploitative and antisocial behavior. For those women who do score in the upper end of the Dark Triad distribution, it is possible that societal views of women as the weaker and more victimized sex may provide malevolent women a greater opportunity for exploiting others.

The Element of Surprise

The idea that women may be particularly well-suited to a variety of nefarious pursuits is not entirely novel. In 1886, Thomas Byrnes, then Inspector of Police and Chief of Detectives for New York City, stated that women "make the most patient and dangerous pickpockets" (p. 34) owing mainly to their ability to slip in and out of most locations undetected and unsuspected. Although there have been numerous depictions of female crime and deviance in both the academic and popular literature, from criminology texts (e.g., Mallicoat, 2012) to legends about historical icons like Calamity Jane (Sollid, 1995), the hypothesis that women with Dark Triad personality traits benefit from societal expectations of women as innocent and nonthreatening requires very specific examples. The following illustrations were selected because they point out not just that women are capable of competitive, devious, or harmful behavior, but also that their crimes and deceptions were minimized, undetected, or unpunished because of their sex. These examples are certainly not exhaustive, but they represent a range of people and behaviors from the sympathetic and justifiable to the horrific.

Serena Nicotine: Repeat Offender

On May 22, 2013, Serena Nicotine took another woman hostage while they were being held in a cell at the courthouse in Edmonton, Alberta, Canada. Nicotine was awaiting a hearing regarding her previous armed hostage-taking, and this most recent set of charges added to a long list of violent offenses.

Nicotine has proven that she is a risk to the safety of others. At the age of 12, she was charged in the death of a 3-year-old who drowned after Nicotine and another girl repeatedly held her head under water (Parker, 1996). At 15, she and a conspirator murdered the operator of the group home she lived in (Pruden, 2013). As an adult, she has been notorious for a series of hostage incidents and prison standoffs where guards and inmates alike have been captured and tortured ("Alleged courthouse," 2013). Why, then, is she repeatedly put into situations where she can harm others? In part, it is because the law does not see women as capable of the type of violence that she has inflicted on others.

In the Canadian federal prison system, the sorts of safeguards that would routinely be used on dangerous male offenders are not allowed to be used on women. These safeguards include the use of restraints or isolation from other prisoners. In an interview in 2005, after Nicotine had taken another inmate hostage, the president of the Union of Canadian Correctional Officers stated, "If she were a man, she'd be in a special handling unit and she'd never be given the opportunity to . . . continually do what she does. . . . You're dealing with a philosophy that women aren't as dangerous as men and we treat them differently in the correctional system. But their victims are still as victimized" (Monchuk, 2005, para. 1). When Nicotine was transferred in 2004 to the Edmonton Institution for Women, there was a special protocol created specifically to deal with her, and yet this protocol was still not enough to protect the other prisoners or even the guards from attack. She continued to take hostages and use a variety of ersatz weapons to terrorize others (Pruden, 2013).

Although the institutionalized protocols and biases inherent in any complex system could lead to an underestimation of the overall risk associated with female inmates, there is no question that this particular inmate is known to be dangerous and requires special handling. The creation of a special protocol by union and management officials points to that recognition. Ironically, Nicotine has been "described as sweet and naïve," and one guard suggested that "if you didn't know her history that you might let her babysit your children" ("Alleged courthouse," 2013, para. 2). Nicotine herself has made statements that suggest that she can control her behavior.

I'm very nice most of the time, I mean, people may look at me as very evil or heartless, whatever. But no,

I'm not. It only depends. I'm only like that once in a while—not all the time. . ... I controlled a lot of it though. Could have hurt a lot of people but I chose not to.

("Alleged courthouse," 2013, para. 2)

In terms of Dark Triad traits, Serena Nicotine has certainly demonstrated behaviors consistent with psychopathy, including callous disregard for the safety of others, impulsivity, criminal behavior, and failure to accept responsibility for her actions (Hare & Neumann, 2008). From the accounts of correctional officers, it is clear that she is afforded ample opportunity to harm others simply because she is not a man. Although it is difficult to argue that an incarcerated woman is at an advantage compared to women in the general population, it is clear that she has not experienced some of the harsher treatment that her behavior would elicit if she were male.

Lindsay Moran: International Spy

In 1997, Lindsay Moran became a case officer for the Central Intelligence Agency (CIA). Her job was to meet and recruit people in foreign countries, enticing them to provide her with information in exchange for payment (Moran, 2005). Prior to joining the CIA, she had always wanted to be a spy, and she had thought that being a woman might be a detriment to her career choice. As she progressed through training and became a valued agent, she came to realize that being a woman was not, in fact, a drawback:

> My first developmental luncheon with Barry was to take place at the T.G.I. Friday's in nearby Newport News. At this meeting, I should garner enough information from Barry that I could begin to determine his potential access to state secrets. I also should present myself as someone engaging enough that Barry might agree to another meeting with me. In reality, I would later learn, a foreign man/potential source rarely, if ever, turns down the opportunity to have lunch, dinner, or drinks with a young female American "diplomat." But this wouldn't become clear to me until long after my first date with Barry.
>
> *(Moran, 2005, ch. 5, p. 7)*

Moran found that foreign targets were comfortable sharing information with women and were often eager to show off their status by providing important confirmatory evidence about high-profile political or underworld figures. In this situation, men, who are prone to displays of status

and value as methods of impressing women (Buss, 1989), are vulnerable to a woman who conceals her true motives (Buss & Duntley, 2008). Tamir Pardo, Director of the Mossad, the national intelligence agency for Israel, has stated that female spies have a distinct advantage over men (Ziegler, 2012), and that advantage is based on being able to read and manipulate people and situations. On a darker note, a military source quoted in the Hebrew newspaper *Ma'Ariv* stated that women are important assets as suicide bombers because no one suspects them; they blend in better with the crowd and are not treated with the level of suspicion afforded to men (Kotes-Bar, 2004).

Although it is not possible to determine whether Lindsay Moran would score particularly high on all Dark Triad scales (and it is likely that her psych evaluation is classified!), the behaviors associated with recruiting foreign operatives are consistent with Machiavellianism at least (Christie & Geis, 1970). One must be quite manipulative and somewhat callous to successfully convince others to willingly provide potentially harmful information about their country, their government, and even their acquaintances, family, and friends. Although Moran was uncomfortable with the moral implications of her actions (2005), the behaviors themselves fit the Dark Triad profile. The title of Moran's book is *Blowing My Cover*, and that title reflects her decision to leave the CIA and publicly describe portions of her training and experiences. While she was an active case officer, her cover was intact and she was a successful spy, due in part to being female.

"Madeleine Blair": Gentlewoman Madame

Running a house of prostitution is a task that requires intellect, organization, and often subterfuge. In the early years of the 20th century, a woman who wrote under the pseudonym of Madeleine Blair was born into a poor family in the rural Midwest of the United States and, upon reaching adolescence, was required to go to work as a domestic servant in the city of St. Louis. An impetuous encounter with a young man left her socially "ruined," and she soon began a career as a prostitute who eventually became a successful brothel owner in what was then called the Northwest Territories of Canada (present-day Alberta, Canada). She published an account of her life in which she detailed her own memoirs as well as accounts of the lives of various women who made illegal profits in the sex trade. The entire book is a very flattering account of her shrewdness and resourcefulness, in which Madeleine Blair appears quite willing to take all credit for overcoming a series of personal and professional obstacles. She credited much of her success to her ability to blend in with "respectable" people, and she used her charm to convince others to give her money or other gifts. For Blair, there was no need to take someone's money if they were simply willing to hand it over. She also used her charm to convince legal authorities to turn a blind eye to her enterprises and even to deflect or hide from puritanical opposition. Upon learning that a preacher was intent on confronting her as the town madame, she graciously welcomed him into her home and place of business and, without giving her name, proceeded to discuss the finer points of morality:

> For an hour we discussed this subject on equal terms, he with no idea that I was the notorious woman that he had come to excoriate and I, oblivious of the fact that I was a harlot and a drunkard, who, in the very nature of things, was not supposed to know nor to think of those things which pertain to the Spirit.
>
> When we ended the discussion the man arose and told me that he had come into the neighborhood for the purpose of denouncing to her face a terrible woman named Madeleine Blair. Inadvertently he had come to my house, thinking it was the place he sought, but as soon as he had seen me he knew his mistake. He was holding services at the First Presbyterian Church, and hoped to see me there on the following Sunday. I gave an equivocal answer, and he went away after a gracious acknowledgement of a pleasant hour spent in my society.
>
> *(Anonymous, 1919, ch. 8, para. 17, 18)*

Thus, because it is so difficult to reconcile the schema of "harlot and drunkard" with the persona of a woman who politely discusses morality in the parlor, the good reverend was not to know that he had missed his opportunity to denounce Madeleine Blair in person. Blair had good impulse control and was able to manipulate others' impression of her very well. These traits are consistent with Machiavellianism (Christie & Geis, 1970). Furthermore, she displays no modesty regarding her skills or her superiority to others. Other women are less ambitious and clever, men are fools, and officials are corruptible tools for her use. She describes no one as being her equal. This attitude toward others is consistent

with narcissism (Raskin & Terry, 1988). Thus, Madeleine Blair displayed two Dark Triad traits that benefitted her career.

Moll Flanders: Dafoe's Antiheroine

The fictional account of Moll Flanders (Dafoe, 1722/2008) is filled with the sort of tawdry and sordid details that make a novel an instant classic. Fictional though it may be, it provides a depiction of a believable female character who overcomes hardship after hardship through her fierce sense of self-preservation and very flexible moral code. Flanders expresses Dark Triad traits on nearly every page of the book. She is vain and expects to be treated as a lady, despite her rough heritage and upbringing. She manipulates a variety of men into providing resources, including a series of marriages resulting in a number of children by different fathers. One marriage is to her brother, and she also bears him children. She disposes of her children, of varied paternity, by leaving them with nursemaids and others in various towns. She steals, connives, and cheats her way into better circumstances with the ongoing conviction of her own righteousness. Her occasional bouts of contrition are brief and resolved pragmatically.

> Then it occurred to me, "What an abominable creature am I! and how is this innocent gentleman going to be abused by me! How little does he think, that having divorced a whore, he is throwing himself into the arms of another! that he is going to marry one that has lain with two brothers, and has had three children by her own brother! one that was born in Newgate, whose mother was a whore, and is now a transported thief! one that has lain with thirteen men, and has had a child since he saw me! Poor gentleman!" said I, "what is he going to do?" After this reproaching myself was over, it following thus: "Well, if I must be his wife, if it please God to give me grace, I'll be a true wife to him, and love him suitably to the strange excess of his passion for me; I will make him amends if possible, by what he shall see, for the cheats and abuses I put upon him, which he does not see."
>
> *(Dafoe, 1722/2008, p. 195)*

Dafoe's Moll Flanders does suffer various punishments for her misdeeds, including imprisonment and transportation to the colonies, yet her story ends in her 70th year as she plans to live sedately with her husband as they repent their wicked—and ultimately successful—lives.

Flanders epitomizes the behavioral flexibility associated with Machiavellianism and the high self-regard of narcissism (Furnham et al., 2013). She utilizes multiple mating strategies, poaches the mates of others, has many children by different men, and invests very little in her offspring. Thus, her reproductive success is high as a result of the exploitation of her partners and of society as a whole.

Melissa Ann Shepard: Sweet Old Black Widow

Female serial killers are the topic of another chapter in this Handbook (see the work by Helen Gavin), and this group readily fits an analysis of Dark Triad traits. For example, a classic type of female serial killer is the Black Widow, named for the spider that kills her mates. The human version tends to seduce and often marry a series of men and then kill them in order to have their money and other resources (Holmes & Holmes, 2010). This sort of crime requires the victim to place a great deal of trust in the perpetrator.

One example is Melissa Shepard. In the fall of 2012, at the age of 78, she was arrested in Nova Scotia after her new husband, Fred Weeks, fell ill on their honeymoon. It was determined that he had been poisoned with an overdose of benzodiazepines and that his new wife chose to not seek treatment for his illness. While Weeks was in the hospital, his wife misinformed hospital staff about his physical and mental health status and interfered in various ways with his treatment ("Be careful," 2013).

If this were an isolated incident, it might be tempting to think that this elderly couple made some mistakes with medication, and, because the newlyweds apparently barely knew each other, Shepard was unfamiliar with Weeks's health history. Unfortunately, this was not an isolated incident (O'Connor, 2012). In fact, Melissa Shepard had previously poisoned her second husband Gordon Stewart and ran him over with her car twice, killing him, in 1991. She was convicted of manslaughter but spent only 2 years in jail before being paroled. Her third husband died in 2002 under suspicious circumstances consistent with poisoning, not long after changing his will to make Shepard the sole benefactor. Although she was charged with prescription fraud for obtaining multiple prescriptions for lorazepam from different doctors, prosecutors dropped the case. Then, in 2004, Shepard went out for dinner with Alex Strategos and moved in with him that night. Within months, he signed over power of attorney

to her while he was ill from benzodiazepine poisoning, and she robbed him of $18,000. Shepard was convicted of grand theft and forgery and spent 4 years in prison for those crimes.

Melissa Shepard, also known as Melissa Russell, Melissa Stewart, Melissa Friedrich, and Melissa Weeks, has successfully conned a variety of men out of their money, has been convicted of killing at least one husband, likely killed another husband, and nearly killed two more. Just before he died, Gordon Stewart wrote that even though he knew she had lied and cheated him, he took her back because he loved her and hoped she would change (O'Connor, 2012). Strategos was recently divorced when he met Shepard, and their relationship became serious quickly, judging by their immediate cohabitation and his willingness to give her control over all of his finances. What led him to be willing to trust her with so much of his life? According to Strategos, "I was lonely, and she was a woman" (O'Connor, 2012, para. 1).

Melissa Shepard demonstrates a callous disregard for the health of her male partners, to the point where she is willing to take their lives as well as their money. She was deceptive and manipulated each man into providing her with financial control. She traded romantic attention for financial payoff and then disposed of each partner. These behaviors are consistent with psychopathy as well as Machiavellianism, and she profited quite well until she was jailed.

The women profiled in these examples are not all the same. Each has exploited her environment, and the people in it, in a somewhat different way. Serena Nicotine's overt violence resulted in different outcomes than did Melissa Shepard's covert manipulations. Both women ended up in jail, but their lives have been very different otherwise. The life of a spy, as in the case of Lindsay Moran, is more secretive and yet somewhat more respected than the life of a madame like Madeleine Blair. Still, Blair had the longer and possibly more rewarding career! The fictional Moll Flanders experienced a variety of consequences for her amoral acts but also reaped a variety of resource and reproductive benefits. Machiavellianism, narcissism, and psychopathy are traits that are each adaptive and maladaptive in different ways for different people. The costs include loss of friends, freedom, and respect. The benefits include money, information, reproductive success, and social influence. What is common across each of these examples, and each of the Dark Triad personality traits, is the exploitation of others. The women in each of these examples are competing for a variety of benefits. Nicotine competes for power and dominance, alternating her use of intimidation and charm. Moran competed for information and professional respect. She risked the safety of her targets in order to be a top agent, and she then profited from a book that violated the secrecy associated with being a CIA agent. Blair competed with other women for the attentions of favored clients and with other madames for market share in the frontier. She, like the fictional Flanders, manipulated men for money and for protection. Shepard has thus far lived a relatively long and prosperous life by cheating men out of their life savings and then killing them. Their gains, at the expense of others, reflect the value of their Dark Triad tendencies. Although these are powerful examples of how women with dark personalities can exploit their environments, it is important to recognize that they are still just examples. The danger of anecdotal evidence is that it represents a select view of a topic and may not represent reality. In order to demonstrate whether Dark Triad traits are adaptive for women, it is necessary to have more than anecdotes.

Future Directions

There has already been more than a decade of research examining Dark Triad traits (Furnham et al., 2013), and there has been no evidence to suggest that women are disproportionately disadvantaged (in comparison to men) by expression of Dark Triad traits. A variety of studies have demonstrated that men tend to have much higher scores than women on measures of psychopathy (Forth et al., 1996) and that there are often small but consistent sex differences in both narcissism and Machiavellianism (Paulhus & Williams, 2002). Theorists have repeatedly focused on male competition as the selective pressure for male Dark Triad traits. The fact remains that women are well-represented in Dark Triad studies, and a small but consistent proportion of each study's female sample has high Dark Triad scores. Women with Dark Triad traits may be less numerous than men with Dark Triad traits, but they are not anomalies or outliers.

As analogy, it would be worth considering women with Dark Triad traits in the way that we think about women with strong spatial skills. Decades of research have provided evidence of a robust and consistent sex difference in mental rotation tasks and various other tests of spatial ability (Masters & Sanders, 1993), with much larger effect sizes than those found for sex differences in Dark Triad

studies. Differences in spatial ability exist at the population level, and expectancies and stereotypes about spatial abilities are skewed in the direction of male superiority at such tasks. Although men on average perform better than women do on average, it is not the case that most women are incapable of mental rotation, nor are women with better-than-average mental rotation abilities unusual or abnormal. Women benefit from having mental rotation abilities, just as men do. Likewise, women may have Dark Triad personalities, and there is nothing particularly unusual about a woman who has a tendency toward Machiavellianism, narcissism, and even psychopathy. A woman with Dark Triad traits may benefit from those traits, just as would a man with the same traits.

To determine how women might benefit from expressing Dark Triad traits, more research is necessary to determine whether women express those traits differently than do men. A good example of this type of research comes from O'Connor and Simms (1990), who demonstrated that women use self-disclosure as a manipulative tactic in interpersonal relationships, but men do not. Further research could determine whether women with Dark Triad traits have specific tactics for controlling social groups and friends or whether the types of indirect aggression frequently used by women (Vaillancourt, 2013) are predicted by the various Dark Triad personality measures. If Dark Triad women utilize specific tactics for social control, it would provide evidence that Dark Triad traits facilitate dominance in a manner that is sex-specific.

It has often been stated that Dark Triad men preferentially pursue a "fast" life strategy, in which multiple mates are acquired, and parental and partner investment is minimal (Jonason, Valentine, Li, & Harbeson, 2011). Women who employ a "love them and leave them" approach may be pregnant when they leave and thus are less able to avoid parental investment entirely. Do women with Dark Triad traits put their children up for adoption, abort, or abandon them at higher rates than do women with lower Dark Triad traits? Are such women more likely or somehow more able to exploit the efforts of grandparents or other secondary caregivers for their offspring? If Dark Triad women are able to reduce the costs of reproduction, and especially of short-term mating, it would provide evidence that the mating behaviors associated with the Dark Triad are not disproportionately risky for women.

In addition to the competitive benefits, including resources, mates, and power, that might be associated with the Dark Triad, there should be evidence that women are not unduly punished for Dark Triad behaviors. It would be useful to determine whether Dark Triad traits are detected equally in men and women and whether the social consequences are different. Do friends, coworkers, and strangers identify dangerous characteristics in women, or are women somewhat better at concealing their darker natures? How do other women react to Dark Triad behaviors? Are Dark Triad women excluded from social groups, or are they the subjects of more gossip? If Dark Triad women are able to conceal their behaviors or are able to maintain and even control their friendships, it would provide support for the hypothesis that Dark Triad traits are no more risky for women than for men. Furthermore, it would lend support for the hypothesis that women with Dark Triad traits may benefit from the covert and unexpected nature of their behaviors.

Finally, the hypothesis that Dark Triad women benefit from societal views of women as trustworthy and harmless must be directly tested. For example, it could be determined whether Dark Triad women are more likely to emphasize their stereotypically feminine traits in order to manipulate others or avoid punishment. Do they emphasize female solidarity in order to exploit other women? Do they pretend to be victimized in order to avoid punishment or gain protection and resources? Do they pretend to be more chaste or faithful than they actually are in order to convince men to commit to long-term relationships? Each of these methods or strategies could lead to successful competition for mates, social influence, or resources. If Dark Triad women are more likely than other women to use this sort of strategy, then it would provide support for the idea that being female provides an advantage for those with callous, selfish, and manipulative tendencies.

In summary, women may be conferred a competitive advantage in the expression of some antisocial behaviors because society does not expect women to behave in an antisocial manner. Women commit crimes at rates that are substantially lower than those of men, and women are far less likely to commit violent crimes. Even though women are equally likely to lie or otherwise deceive, and a significant proportion of women express Dark Triad traits, women are often given the benefit of the doubt and thus have the opportunity to capitalize on the trust and inattention toward their antisocial behaviors. We trust women more than we trust men; we expect women to be kind, cheerful, and nurturing; and we see women as less than fully responsible for their own behaviors. Society's benevolent view of women as nurturing creatures who are less dangerous than men is both entrenched and somewhat inaccurate. This sexist attitude toward the behavior and attributes of women may be benevolent, but it is an impediment to equality on a societal level. On an individual level, however, it can facilitate the acquisition of resources. Con artists, criminals, and spies alike may benefit from society's sexism. Although there are anecdotal examples of how Dark Triad traits may facilitate exploitation by women in a manner that is different from men, research is needed to explore whether Dark Triad traits are expressed, detected, and punished differently in men and women. The examples provided in this chapter reflect situations in which women have been given the opportunity to exploit their environments because of their gender, and, although we may not like these women or approve of their actions, we can still recognize their "successes."

References

ABC News. (2010, May 7). *What would you do?* New York: American Broadcasting Corporation.

Ahola, A. S., Christianson, S. A., & Hellstrom, A. (2009). Justice needs a blindfold: Effects of gender and attractiveness on prison sentences and attributions of personal characteristics in a judicial process. *Psychiatry, Psychology and Law, 16,* S90–S100.

Ajzen, I. (1977). Intuitive theories of events and effects of base-rate information on prediction. *Journal of Personality and Social Psychology, 35,* 305–314.

Alleged courthouse hostage-taker has violent history (2013, May 31). *CBC News.* Retrieved from http://www.cbcnews.ca

American Psychiatric Association (APA). (2013). *Diagnostic and statistical manual of mental disorders (5th ed.).* Arlington, VA: American Psychiatric Publishing.

Ames, D. R., Rose, P., & Anderson, C. P. (2006). The NPI-16 as a short measure of narcissism. *Journal of Research in Personality, 40,* 440–450.

Anonymous. (1919). *Madeleine: An autobiography.* New York: Harper & Brothers.

Archer, J. (2000). Sex differences in aggression between heterosexual partners: A meta-analytic review. *Psychological Bulletin, 126,* 651–680.

Archer, J. (2004). Sex differences in aggression in real-world settings: A meta-analytic review. *Review of General Psychology, 8,* 291–322.

Archer, J. (2006). Cross-cultural differences in physical aggression between partners: A social-role analysis. *Personality and Social Psychology Review, 10,* 133–153.

Archer, J. (2009). Does sexual selection explain human sex differences in aggression? *Behavioral and Brain Sciences, 32,* 249–311.

Axelrod, R., & Hamilton, W. D. (1981). The evolution of cooperation. *Science, 211*, 1390–1396.

Be careful of "Black Widow," judge warns at sentencing (2013, June 11). *Canadian Press.* Retrieved from http://atlantic.ctvnews.ca/be-careful-of-black-widow-judge-warns-at-sentencing-1.1320645

Benenson, J. F. (2013). The development of human female competition: Allies and adversaries. *Philosophical Transactions of the Royal Society B, 368*, 20130079. http://dx.doi.org/10.1098/rstb.2013.0079

Berkout, O. V., Young, J. N., & Gross, A. M. (2011). Mean girls and bad boys: Recent research on gender differences in conduct disorder. *Aggression and Violent Behavior, 16*, 503–511.

Björkqvist, K., Lagerspetz, K. M. J., & Kaukiainen, A. (2013). Do girls manipulate and boys fight? Developmental trends in regard to direct and indirect aggression. *Aggressive Behavior, 18*, 117–127.

Boyce, J. (2013). *Adult criminal court statistics in Canada, 2011/2012.* Ottawa: Statistics Canada. http://www.statcan.gc.ca/pub/85-002-x/2013001/article/11804-eng.htm

Buss, D. M. (1989). Sex differences in human mate preferences: Evolutionary hypotheses tested in 37 cultures. *Behavioral and Brain Sciences, 12*, 1–49.

Buss, D. M., & Duntley, J. D. (2008). Adaptations for exploitation. *Group Dynamics: Theory, Research, and Practice, 12*, 53–62.

Buss, D. M., & Schmitt, D. P. (1993). Sexual strategies theory: An evolutionary perspective on human mating. *Psychological Review, 100*, 204–232.

Byrnes, T. (1886). *Professional criminals of America.* New York: Cassell.

Cale, E. M., & Lilienfeld, S. O. (2002). Sex differences in psychopathology and antisocial personality disorder: A review and integration. *Clinical Psychology Review, 22*, 1179–1207.

Chabot, H. F., Tracy, T. L., Manning, C. A., & Poisson, C. A. (2009). Sex, attribution, and severity influence intervention decisions of informal helpers in domestic violence. *Journal of Interpersonal Violence, 24*, 1696–1713.

Christie, R., & Geis, F. (1970). *Studies in Machiavellianism.* New York: Academic.

Clutton-Brock, T. H., & Huchard, E. (2013). Social competition and selection in males and females. *Philosophical Transactions of the Royal Society B, 368*, 20130074. http://dx.doi.org/10.1098/rstb.2013.0074

Companion, M., & Sambrook, R. (2008). The influence of sex on character attribute preferences. *CyberPsychology and Behavior, 11*, 673–674.

Cosmides, L. (1989). The logic of social exchange: has natural selection shaped how humans reason? Studies with the Wason selection task. *Cognition 31*, 187–276.

Dafoe, D. (1722/2008). *The fortunes and misfortunes of the famous moll flanders.* Retrieved from http://www.gutenberg.org/files/370/370-h/370-h.htm (Original work published 1722.)

De Meijer, M. (1991). The attribution of aggression and grief to body movements: The effect of sex-stereotypes. *European Journal of Social Psychology, 21*, 249–259.

DePaulo, B., Kashy, D. A., Kirkendol, S. E., Wyer, M. M., & Epstein, J. A. (1996). Lying in everyday life. *Journal of Personality and Social Psychology, 70*, 979–995.

Dugatkin, L. A. (1992). The evolution of the "con artist." *Ethology and Sociobiology, 13*, 3–18.

Eagly, A. H., & Mladinic, A. (1994). Are people prejudiced against women? Some answers from research on attitudes, gender stereotypes, and judgments of competence. *European Review of Social Psychology 5*, 1–35.

Eagly, A. H., Mladinic, A., & Otto, S. (1991). Are women evaluated more favorably than men? An analysis of attitudes, beliefs and emotions. *Psychology of Women Quarterly, 15*, 203–216.

Eden, A., Maloney, E., & Bowman, N. D. (2010). Gender attribution in online video games. *Journal of Media Psychology, 22*, 114–124.

Feldman, R. S., Forrest, J. A., & Happ, B. R. (2002). Self-presentation and verbal deception: Do self-presenters lie more? *Basic and Applied Social Psychology, 24*, 163–170.

Fiebert, M. S., & Gonzalez, D. M. (1997). College women who initiate assaults on their male partners and the reasons offered for such behavior. *Psychological Reports, 80*, 583–590.

Forth, A. E., Brown, S. L., Hart, S. D., & Hare, R. D. (1996). The assessment of psychopathy in male and female non-criminals: Reliability and validity. *Personality and Individual Differences, 20*, 531–543.

Furnham, A. (2010). *The elephant in the boardroom: The causes of leadership derailment.* Basingstoke, UK: Palgrave MacMillan.

Furnham, A., Richards, S. C., & Paulhus, D. L. (2013). The Dark Triad of personality: A 10-year review. *Social and Personality Psychology Compass, 7*, 199–216.

Gervais, J., Tremblay, R. E., Demarais-Gervais, L., & Vitaro, F. (2000). *International Journal of Behavioral Development, 24*, 213–221.

Glick, P., & Fiske, S. T. (2001). An ambivalent alliance: Hostile and benevolent sexism as complementary justifications of gender inequality. *American Psychologist, 56*, 109–118.

Griskevicius, V., Tybur, J. M., Gangestad, S. W., Perea, E. F., Shapiro, J. R., & Kenrick, D. T. (2009). Aggress to impress: Hostility as an evolved context-dependent strategy. *Journal of Personality and Social Psychology, 96*, 980–994.

Gross, B. (2009). Battle of the sexes. *The Forensic Examiner, Summer*, 83–87.

Hanusiak, L., Fisher, M., & Carter, G. (2013, June). *The Dark Triad and intrasexual competition among women.* Poster presented at the annual meeting of the Canadian Psychological Association, Quebec City, Quebec.

Hare, R. D., & Neumann, C. S. (2008). Psychopathy as a clinical and empirical construct. *Annual Review of Clinical Psychology, 4*, 217–246.

Haselton, M. G., & Buss, D. M. (2000). Error management theory: A new perspective on biases in cross-sex mind reading. *Journal of Personality and Social Psychology, 78*, 81–91.

Haselton, M. G., Buss, D. M., Oubaid, V., & Angleitner, A. (2005). Sex, lies, and strategic interference: The psychology of deception between the sexes. *Personality and Social Psychology Bulletin, 31*, 3–23.

Hatgis, C., Friedmann, P. D., & Wiener, M. (2008). Attributions of responsibility for addiction: The effect of gender and type of substance. *Substance Use and Misuse, 43*, 700–708.

Heidensohn, F. (2010). The deviance of women: A critique and an inquiry. *British Journal of Sociology*, doi: 10.1111/j.1468-4446.2009.01242.x

Henning, K, Jones, A. R., & Holdford, R. (2005). "I didn't do it, but if I did I had a good reason": Minimization, denial, and attributions of blame among male and female domestic violence offenders. *Journal of Family Violence, 20*, 131–139.

Holmes, J. (2010). *Female offending: Has there been an increase?* Crime and Justice Statistics Bureau Brief, Issue paper 46. Sydney: New South Wales Bureau of Crime Statistics and Research.

Holmes, R. M., & Holmes, S. T. (2010). *Serial murder*, 3rd ed. Thousand Oaks, CA: Sage.

Heiskanen, M. (2010). Trends in police-recorded crime. In S. Harrendorf, M. Heiskanen, & S. Malby (Eds.), *International statistics on crime and justice* (pp. 21–48). Helsinki: European Institute for Crime Prevention and Control.

Jonason, P. K., Koenig, B., & Tost, J. (2010). Living a fast life: The Dark Triad and Life History Theory. *Human Nature, 21*, 428–442.

Jonason, P. K., & Krause, L. (2013). The emotional deficits associated with the Dark Triad traits: Cognitive empathy, affective empathy, and alexithymia. *Personality and Individual Differences, 55*, 532–537.

Jonason, P. K., Li, N. P., & Buss, D. M. (2010). The costs and benefits of the Dark Triad: Implications for mate poaching and mate retention tactics. *Personality and Individual Differences, 48*, 373–378.

Jonason, P. K., Li, N. P., & Czarna, A. Z. (2013). Quick and dirty: Some psychosocial costs associated with the Dark Triad in three countries. *Evolutionary Psychology, 11*, 172–185.

Jonason, P. K., Li, N. P., & Teicher, E. A. (2010). Who is James Bond?: The Dark Triad as an agentic social style. *Individual Differences Research, 8*, 111–120.

Jonason, P. K., Li, N. P., Webster, G. W., & Schmitt, D. P. (2009). The Dark Triad: Facilitating short-term mating in men. *European Journal of Personality, 23*, 5–18.

Jonason, P. K., Slomski, S., & Partyka, J. (2012). The Dark Triad at work: How toxic employees get their way. *Personality and Individual Differences, 52*, 449–453.

Jonason, P. K., & Tost, J. (2010). I just cannot control myself: The Dark Triad and self-control. *Personality and Individual Differences, 49*, 611–615.

Jonason, P. K., Valentine, K. A., Li, N. P., & Harbeson, C. L. (2011). Mate-selection and the Dark Triad: Facilitating a short-term mating strategy and creating a volatile environment. *Personality and Individual Differences, 51*, 759–763.

Jonason, P. K., & Webster, G. D. (2012). A protean approach to social influence: Dark Triad personalities and social influence tactics. *Personality and Individual Differences, 52*, 521–526.

Jonason, P. K., Webster, G. D., Schmitt, D. P., Li, N. P., & Crysel, L. (2012). The antihero in popular culture: A life history theory of the Dark Triad. *Review of General Psychology, 16*, 192–199.

Jones, D. N., & Paulhus, D. L. (2011). Differentiating the Dark Triad within the interpersonal circumplex. In L. M. Horowitz & S. Strack (Eds.), *Handbook of interpersonal psychology: Theory, research, assessment, and therapeutic interventions* (pp. 249–269). New York: Wiley & Sons.

Jones, D. N., & Weiser, D. A. (2014). Differential infidelity patterns among the Dark Triad. *Personality and Individual Differences, 57*, 20–24.

Keenan, J. P., Gallup, G. G., Jr., Goulet, N., & Kulkarni, M. (1997). Attributions of deception in human mating strategies. *Journal of Social Behavior and Personality, 12*, 45–52.

King, W. C. Jr., Miles, E. W., & Kniska, J. (1991). Boys will be boys (and girls will be girls): The attribution of gender role stereotypes in a gaming situation. *Sex Roles, 25*, 607–623.

Kleinke, C. L., & Baldwin, M. R. (1993). Responsibility attributions for men and women giving sane versus crazy explanations for good and bad behaviour. *Journal of Psychology, 127*, 37–50.

Knox, D., Zusman, M. E., McGinty, K., & Gescheidler, J. (2001). Deception of parents during adolescence. *Adolescence, 36*, 611–614.

Kotes-Bar, C. (2004, June 21). I dreamt of killing more than a hundred. *Ma'Ariv*, p. 14.

Lafrance, M., Brownell, H., & Hahn, E. (1997). Interpersonal verbs, gender, and implicit causality. *Social Psychology Quarterly, 60*, 138–152.

Logan, C. (2011). La femme fatale: The female psychopath in fiction and clinical practice. *Mental Health Review Journal, 16*, 118–127.

Lehmann, M., & Santilli, N. R. (1996). Sex differences in perceptions of spousal abuse. In R. Crandall (Ed.), Handbook of gender research (Special Issue). *Journal of Social Behavior and Personality, 11*, 229–238.

Mallicoat, S. L. (2007). Gendered justice: Attributional differences between males and females in the juvenile courts. *Feminist Criminology, 2*, 4–30.

Mallicoat, S. L. (2012). *Women and crime*. Thousand Oaks, CA: Sage.

Marcus, D. K., & Lehmann, S. J. (2002). Are there sex differences in interpersonal perception at zero acquaintance? A social relations analysis. *Journal of Research in Personality, 36*, 190–207.

Marvel Studios & Whedon, J. (2012). *The Avengers*. United States: Paramount.

Masters, M. S., & Sanders, B. (1993). Is the gender difference in mental rotation disappearing? *Behavior Genetics, 23*, 337–341.

McCornack, S. A., & Parks, M. R. (1990). What women know that men don't: Sex differences in determining the truth behind deceptive messages. *Journal of Social and Personal Relationships, 7*, 107–118.

McDonald, M. M., Donnellan, M. B., & Navarrete, C. D. (2012). A life history approach to understanding the Dark Triad. *Personality and Individual Differences, 52*, 601–605.

Mealey, L. (1995). The sociobiology of sociopathy: An integrated evolutionary model. *Behavioral and Brain Sciences, 18*, 523–599.

Monchuk, J. (2005, April 10). Prison plan for dangerous women not working on killer who prompted policy. The Canadian Press. Retrieved from http://www.prisontalk/forums/archive/index.php/t-117861.html

Moran, L. (2005). *Blowing my cover*. New York: G. P. Putnam.

Nathanson, C., Paulhus, D. L., & Williams, K. M. (2006). Predictors of a behavioral measure of scholastic cheating: Personality and competence but not demographics. *Contemporary Educational Psychology, 31*, 97–122.

National Center for Injury Prevention and Control (NCIPC). (2011). The National Intimate Partner and Sexual Violence Survey. Retrieved from http://www.cdc.gov/violenceprevention/pdf/nisvs_report2010-a.pdf. Accessed April 5, 2015.

O'Connor, E. M., & Simms, C. M. (1990). Self-revelation as manipulation: The effects of sex and Machiavellianism on self-disclosure. *Social Behavior and Personality, 18*, 95–100.

O'Connor, J. (2012, October 2). Romancing the "Internet Black Widow": Man recounts alleged poisoning as fresh accusations emerge in N. B. *National Post*. Retrieved from http://news.nationalpost.com/2012/10/02/romancing-the-internet-black-widow-man-recounts-alleged-poisoning-as-fresh-accusations-emerge-in-n-b/

Parker, S. (1996). All we did was drown her. *Alberta Report, 23*, 21.

Paulhus, D. L., & Williams, K. M. (2002). The dark triad of personality: Narcissism, Machiavellianism and psychopathy. *Journal of Research in Personality, 36*, 556–563.

Pruden, J. G. (2013, May 31). Notorious female inmate facing new charges in Edmonton hostage taking. *Edmonton Journal.* Retrieved from http://www.edmontonjournal.com

Raskin, R., & Terry, H. (1988). A principle-components analysis of the Narcissistic Personality Inventory and further evidence of its construct validity. *Journal of Personality and Social Psychology, 54*, 890–902.

Ridley, M. (1993). *The red queen: Sex and the evolution of human nature.* New York: Harper Collins.

Russell, B. L., Oswald, D. L., & Kraus, S. W. (2011). Evaluations of sexual assault: Perceptions of guilt and legal elements for male and female aggressors using various coercive strategies. *Violence and Victims, 26*, 799–815.

Rye, B. J., Greatrix, S. A., & Enright, C. S. (2006). The case of the guilty victim: The effects of gender of the victim and gender of the perpetrator on attributions of blame and responsibility. *Sex Roles, 54*, 639–649.

Rylands, K., & Nesca, M. (2012). More than just gender: The attribution of guilt in sexual assault cases. *American Journal of Forensic Psychology, 30*, 29–42.

Sela-Shayovitz, R. (2007). Female suicide bombers: Israeli newspaper reporting and the public construction of social reality. *Criminal Justice Studies, 20*, 197–215.

Semenyna, S. W., & Honey, P. L. (2015). Dominance styles mediate sex differences in Dark Triad traits., *83*, 37–43.

Skeem, J., Schubert, C., Stowman, S., Beeson, S., Mulvey, E., Gardner, W., & Lidz, C. (2005). Gender and risk assessment accuracy: Underestimating women's violence potential. *Law and Human Behavior, 29*, 173–186.

Sollid, R. B. (1995). *Calamity Jane.* Helena: Montana Historical Society Press.

Stemple, L., & Meyer, I. H. (2014). The sexual victimization of men in America: New data challenge old assumptions. *American Journal of Public Health, 104*, e19-e26. doi: 10.2105/AJPH.2014.301946

Stockley, P., & Campbell, A. (2013). Female competition and aggression: Interdisciplinary perspectives. *Philosophical Transactions of the Royal Society B, 368*, 20130073. http://dx.doi.org/10.1098/rstb.2013.0073

Tang, T. L. P., & Chen, Y. J. (2008). Intelligence vs. wisdom: The love of money, Machiavellianism, and unethical behavior across college major and gender. *Journal of Business Ethics, 82*, 1–26.

Thornhill, R., & Palmer, C. (2000). *A natural history of rape: Biological bases of sexual coercion.* Cambridge, MA: MIT Press.

Traylor, L., & Richie, B. (2012). Female offenders and women in prison. In J. Petersilia & K. R. Reitz (Eds.), *Oxford handbook of sentencing and corrections.* New York: Oxford University Press.

Trivers, R. L. (1972). Parental investment and sexual selection. In B. Campbell (Ed.), *Sexual selection and the descent of man, 1871–1971* (pp. 136–179). Chicago: Aldine-Atherton.

Tyler, J. M., & Feldman, R. S. (2004). Truth, lies, and self-presentation: How gender and anticipated future interaction relate to deceptive behaviour. *Journal of Applied Social Psychology, 34*, 2602–2615.

Vaillancourt, T. (2013). Do human females use indirect aggression as an intrasexual competition strategy? *Philosophical Transactions of the Royal Society B, 368*, 20130080. http://dx.doi.org/10.1098/rstb.2013.0080

Webster, G. D., & Jonason, P. K. (2013). Putting the "IRT" in "Dirty": Item Response Theory analyses of the Dark Triad Dirty Dozen—An efficient measure of narcissism, psychopathy, and Machiavellianism. *Personality and Individual Differences, 54*, 302–306.

Wenger, N. K. (2012). Women and coronary heart disease: A century after Herrick. *Circulation, 126*, 604–611.

Williams, K. M., Nathanson, C., & Paulhus, D. L. (2010). Identifying and profiling scholastic cheaters: Their personality, cognitive ability, and motivation. *Journal of Experimental Psychology: Applied, 16*, 293–307.

Ziegler, M. (2012, September 30). Why the best spies in Mossad and the CIA are women. *Forbes.* Retrieved from http://www.forbes.com/sites/crossingborders/2012/09/30/why-the-best-spies-in-mossad-and-the-cia-are-women/

Zuroff, D. C., Fournier, M. A., Patall, E. A., & Leybman, M. J. (2010). Steps toward an evolutionary personality psychology: Individual differences in the social rank domain. *Canadian Psychology, 51*, 58–66.

Communication and Gossip

Competitive Communication Among Women: The Pretty Prevail by Means of Indirect Aggression

Grace L. Anderson

Abstract

According to many communication scholars, aggression is a consequence of sociocultural experiences and less often considered an evolved response to environmental triggers. While there are many factors of aggression, an evolutionary rationale helps to isolate which of these factors are more crucial in explaining aggression among women, one of which is physical attractiveness. Far from superficial, attractive women enjoy better bargaining positions during intrasexual competition than those less attractive, and aggress to negotiate better treatment from rivals. However, evidence of this is mixed because women exaggerate their physical attractiveness during times of heightened ovulatory fertility. Consequently, women's competitive bargaining positions are based on the interplay between everyday attractiveness and their exaggerations of physical attractiveness. In comparison to traditional social psychology and communication models of aggression, human evolution more parsimoniously explains the ways women functionally match their communication of aggression to many environmental triggers and individual differences between competitors.

Key Words: aggression, communication, human evolution, intrasexual competition, ovulatory fertility, physical attractiveness

In the field of communication, competitive communication among women is often expressed as indirect aggression, which includes the investigation of social gossip, spreading rumors, and ostracism. Communication scholars create and refine questionnaires measuring its communication (e.g., Beatty & McCroskey, 1997; Infante & Rancer, 1982; Levine, Kotowski, Beatty, & Van Kelegom, 2012), examine the threat posed by indirect aggression to the recipient (e.g., Dailey, Lee, & Spitzber, 2007; Willer & Cupach, 2008; Willer & Soliz, 2010), and study the impact of witnessing aggressive behavior through media such as television and video games (e.g., Martins & Wilson, 2012; Sherry, 2001; Smith & Donnerstein, 1998). Some communication scholars investigate the biological underpinnings of aggressive communication (e.g., Beatty & McCroskey, 1997;

Shaw, Kotowski, Boster, & Levine, 2012; Valencic, Beatty, Rudd, Dobos, & Heisel, 1998). However, the form and frequency of aggression is often thought to be a derivative of previous social and cultural experiences of frustration, hostility, and witnessing the aggressive behavior of others. Many sociocultural explanations of aggression do not share much common ground with theories that offer biological explanations of aggression (Geen, 1998). According to biological explanations, aggression is a behavior that evolved to help individuals cope with primeval problems that continue to persist across many generations, like resource scarcity, territory defense, or mate poaching (Buss & Shackelford, 1997b; Campbell, 1999; Tooby, Cosmides, Sell, Lieberman, & Sznycer, 2008). As such, an evolutionary explanation of indirect aggression can seem conceptually distant from sociocultural explanations of indirect aggression. Yet this chapter illustrates ways in which evolutionary explanations of indirect aggression are reconcilable (but at times irreconcilable) with sociocultural explanations.

A complex behavior such as indirect aggression among women can be best explained by a multitheory approach. First sociocultural explanations are compared to evolutionary explanations of indirect aggression. Subsequent sections more specifically examine how indirect aggression among women corresponds with their biological traits of physical attractiveness (i.e., beauty). Far from superficial, physical attractiveness broadcasts much information about a woman's internal state (e.g., health, fertility, and fecundity; Symons, 1979, 1995), which is important information when women compete for mates (Tooke & Camire, 1991). It appears as though women who are physically attractive communicate greater indirect aggression toward those who are less attractive because they value their own welfare more than those who are less attractive, feel entitled to prevail during competition, and therefore aggress to negotiate better treatment from rivals (Sell, Tooby, & Cosmides, 2009). Women not only differ in their everyday attractiveness but also exaggerate their physical attractiveness at times. As a result, evidence linking physical attractiveness to aggression among women is somewhat mixed. Rather it seems that women's bargaining position during competition is based on the interplay between their everyday physical attractiveness and exaggerations of their physical attractiveness. This explanation comes to light by examining indirect aggression among women using two theories closely aligned with an evolutionary rationale: the recalibration theory of anger and costly signaling theory. In comparison to traditional social psychology and communication models of aggression, these theories offer a more complete explanation of why women communicate indirect aggression.

Being that indirect aggression is complex, one must clearly define it. While the differences between physical and verbal aggression are clear, the differences between direct and indirect verbal aggression are less clear (Anderson & Huesmann, 2003). Verbal aggression differs depending on whether it was communicated directly toward the target or indirectly toward mutual friends or acquaintances (Archer & Coyne, 2005). Indirect aggression has also been referred as social aggression or relational aggression because it can be considered a form of social manipulation whereby aggressors exploit their mutual social network to harm the targeted person indirectly (vs. face to face; Björkqvist & Niemelä, 1992).

Aggression as Explained by Communication and Social Psychology Scholars Versus Evolutionary Scholars

Extant communication models borrow heavily from social psychology models, which consider aggression an outcome of personality factors working in tandem with situational factors (Anderson & Huesmann, 2003). Some situational factors that have been linked with aggression are uncomfortably hot temperatures (Anderson, 1989; Anderson, Bushman, & Groom, 1997; Vrij, van der Steen, & Koppelaar, 1994), the presence of weapons (Anderson, Benjamin, & Bartholow, 1998; Bartholow, Anderson, Carnagey, & Benjamin, 2005; Berkowitz & LePage, 1967), viewing violent television (Anderson & Dill, 2000; Bushman, 1998; Hogben, 1998; Paik & Comstock, 1994), and video games (Bushman & Anderson, 2002; Hasan, Bègue, & Bushman, 2013; Lin, 2013; Sherry, 2001; Williams & Skoric, 2005), to name a few. Persistent association of these situational cues to negative affect, over time, leads to a stable perception that the external environment is stressful, threatening, or hostile (Berkowitz, 1989). Further, some people are more prone to aggress than others because they are highly aroused by situational stressors and have weak cognitive control of emotional outbursts (Berkowitz, 2008; Davidson, Putnam, & Larson, 2000). What causes an emotionally aggressive response to situational triggers is not necessarily the trigger itself but the significance of the trigger as appraised by the person who encounters it (Lazarus, 1993). Overall, this explanation of aggression emphasizes one's life experiences as formidable influencers of aggressive behavior.

Many communication scholars also think that the initial development of aggression among children can be explained by a process referred to as social learning (e.g., Geen, 1998; Smith & Donnerstein, 1998). At first, children acquire the ability to aggress by observing others acting aggressively, particularly adults (i.e., social modeling; Bandura, 1973). Whether or not the child actually behaves aggressively in the future depends on the consequences the child perceives associated with aggression. For example, if there are incentives to aggress without penalty or punishment, the child will likely aggress (Benenson & Christakos, 2003). Younger children are still forming their normative beliefs about aggression by acting aggressively and judging the consequences. However, by the time children are 8 or 9 years old, they have solidified their beliefs about aggression and their behavior is more resistant to change (Huesmann & Guerra, 1997). Consequently, scholars investigating aggression using social learning theory (and later refined as social cognitive theory) believe that it is relatively rare for severe and habitual aggression to appear in late adolescence (Anderson & Huesmann, 2003). Aggressive tendencies developed during childhood foreshadow the aggressive tendencies of adulthood.

Overall these models emphasize a sociocultural explanation of aggression by alleging that the form and frequency of aggression is largely determined by previous social and cultural experience. Although some acknowledge that aggression derives, in part, from inherited predispositions (e.g., Anderson & Bushman, 2002; Anderson & Huesmann, 2003), the theories behind biological explanations of aggression and sociocultural explanations of aggression do not share much common ground (Geen, 1998).

In comparison to biological and evolutionary explanations of aggression, sociocultural explanations of aggression consist of short-range explanations of aggression as an outcome of a milieu of individual differences and situational variables. Another way to describe these models is that they provide proximate explanations of aggression because they emphasize the immediate triggers of aggression. Some of these explanations of aggression have narrowly defined triggers, such as violent television (Anderson & Dill, 2000; Bushman, 1998; Hogben, 1998; Paik & Comstock, 1994) and video games (Bushman & Anderson, 2002; Sherry, 2001; Williams & Skoric, 2005). However, others can be broad and domain-general, like the frustration-aggression hypothesis (Dollard, Miller, Doob, Mowrer, & Sears, 1939) and the general aggression model. This model portrays aggression as a uniform reaction to many personality and environmental triggers, including self-esteem, sex, provocation, frustration, weapons, pain, and discomfort, to name a few (Anderson & Bushman, 2002).

Yet the consideration of all proximate triggers of aggression can become dizzyingly complex as many variables interact to influence the communication of aggression. For instance, women communicate aggression when uncomfortably hot (and presumably frustrated), but they primarily communicate aggression toward targets who do not share in their discomfort from the heat (i.e., targets who

feel comfortable; Berkowitz, Schrager, & Dunand, 2006). Misery loves company, because the shared plight of discomfort seems to mitigate aggression in response to frustration. This finding implies that situational conditions (e.g., heat) interact with social comparisons between people's emotional states to affect the extent to which frustration promotes aggression. This complex finding must also be considered in relation to other findings evidencing aggression in response to an accumulation other factors such as self-esteem and violent media.

Moreover, the relationships between these proximate factors of aggression can sometimes seem incongruous. Communication researchers, for example, have found that adolescent girls experience difficulty saving face when they are the target of aggression from those who are more popular and attractive (Willer & Cupach, 2008). However, it is puzzling why attractive girls would aggress because it contradicts the prevailing belief that aggression is a reaction to frustration (Dollard et al., 1939). People positively judge attractive women (Langlois et al., 2000) as more socially competent (Eagly, Ashmore, Makhijani, & Longo, 1991), more likely to enjoy happy social and professional lives (Dion, Berscheid, & Walster, 1972), and more likely to experience greater occupational success (Budesheim & DePaola, 1994; DeShields, Kara, & Kaynak, 1996; Mack & Rainey, 1990; Reingen & Kernan, 1993). In these ways, attractive women may experience less cumulative frustrations than those who are relatively unattractive. According to the frustration-aggression hypothesis, women who experience less frustration would presumably aggress less. Yet evidence suggests that attractive women are more aggressive (Fisher, Cox, & Gordon, 2009; Price, Dunn, Hopkins, & Kang, 2012; Price, Kang, Dunn, & Hopkins, 2011; Muñoz-Reyes, Gil-Burmann, Fink, & Turiegano, 2012; Sell, Tooby, et al., 2009) and less cooperative (Mulford, Orbell, Shatto, & Stockard, 1998) than women who are less attractive. Indeed, attractive women may have grown up under conditions in which their aggression was not as severely punished as compared to less attractive children (Dion et al., 1972). It would seem that the link between frustration, negative affect, and aggression depicts only part of the overall picture of women's aggression. A more complete picture can be painted by considering the biological underpinnings of physical attractiveness to more ultimately explain the origins of aggression.

Indeed it is this dilemma on which this chapter focuses. Proximate factors of aggression can sometimes seem incongruous, and there is mixed support for whether women aggress toward less attractive targets (Fisher et al., 2009; Muñoz-Reyes et al., 2012; Price et al., 2012; Price et al., 2011; Sell, Tooby, et al., 2009; Terrell, Patock-Peckham, & Nagoshi, 2009) or more attractive targets (Arnocky, Sunderani, Miller, & Vaillancourt, 2012; Gallup & Wilson, 2009; Leenaars, Dane, & Marini, 2008; Vaillancourt & Sharma, 2011). Such incongruity has not been adequately explained because interdisciplinary cross-referencing is not abundant.

Tinbergen (2005) explained this dilemma best when he said, "In [their] haste to step into the twentieth century and to become a respectable science, Psychology [and Communication Studies] skipped the preliminary descriptive stage that other natural sciences had gone through, and so was soon losing touch with the natural phenomena" (p. 299). When considering the milieu of factors of aggression, like physical attractiveness, those that are more compelling are those that can be argued in terms of both the proximate and ultimate mechanisms of human adaptation (Buss, 1986; Buss & Shackelford, 1997b; Sugiyama, 2005). Phrased another way, it is important to consider how proximate, contextual differences in physical attractiveness between competitors derive from ultimate, biological differences that explain *why* physical attractiveness is an important factor of aggression among women. While communication and social psychological research has evidenced *which* social cues trigger aggression and *how* they trigger aggression, adding an evolutionary rationale can explain *why* some social cues trigger aggression among specific populations of people.

An ultimate explanation generally makes clear that aggression has developed and been refined across many generations of humans and other animals. People who were aggressive in the appropriate circumstances were more likely to survive and reproduce (Buss & Shackelford, 1997b). The people alive today have inherited the (presumably successful) aggression tendencies of their ancestors. All of this is not to suggest that the investigation of biological mechanisms precludes or supersedes the investigation of proximate or more immediate triggers of aggression. Rather, evolutionary reasoning sheds light on the inherited neurocognitive mechanisms underlying the ways people react to proximate triggers of aggression. At its core, aggression is the behavioral outcome of a complex cascade of responses of the endocrine and nervous system, which evolved to help an individual cope with problems that have been historically pervasive, like resource scarcity, territory defense, or mate poaching (Tooby et al., 2008).

The remainder of this chapter pursues a number of goals. First, the functional origins of aggression among women are investigated in terms of how aggression helps women cope with the unique reproductive dilemmas they experience that men do not. Second, the ways in which communication and social psychological models can be enhanced by considering the adaptive problems aggression evolved to solve are illustrated. The evolutionary origins of aggression can be a scaffold in which to clarify the many proximal causes of aggression outlined by communication and social psychology theories. Third, the focus turns to how women calculate their relative bargaining position during aggression based, in part, on their physical attractiveness and reproductive value. By using two closely aligned theories, the recalibration theory of anger and costly signaling theory, it is possible to explain aggression among women in terms of their bargaining position and their motivation to compete. In so doing, this multitheory approach helps explain mixed findings about indirect aggression among women in terms of their physical attractiveness.

An Ultimate Explanation of Aggression

The starting point of any evolutionary investigation is first defining the function or the adaptive problem that human behavior has evolved to solve. Aggression functions to maintain status hierarchies among humans (Buss & Shackelford, 1997b; Cohen, Nisbett, Bowdle, & Schwarz, 1996; La Freniere & Charlesworth, 1983). A keen ability to aggressively negotiate and acquire high social status is valuable in the present as well as past environments (Buss, 2009). Those who successfully increase their social status, at times aggressively, typically have access to desirable resources that help ensure health and survival (Adler et al., 1994; Sapolsky, 2004), as well as attractive mating opportunities (Buss, 1988). Women, more than men, place great importance on attracting mates who possess social status and valuable resources that can be shared and passed to any potential offspring (Buss, 1988, 1989; Li, Bailey, Kenrick, & Linsenmeier, 2002; Townsend, 1989). Therefore, women may communicate aggression not necessarily to acquire high social status for themselves directly but to attract mates with high social status and deflect same-sex rivals from mate poaching. Those who successfully increase their social status or attract mates with high social status using aggression may pass on those traits to their children socially *and* biologically (if they reproduce). All humans have descended from a long and unbroken line of ancestors who successfully resolved many complex problems of survival and reproduction to which they needed to adapt (Buss, 1996; Williams, 1966).

Women encounter adaptive problems not faced by men, particularly with regard to parental investment, and therefore women have evolved different psychological mechanisms (i.e., modes of thought) than men (Trivers, 1972). Compared to other animals, human babies are vulnerable, costly, and require prolonged care, and historically women bear a greater parental burden than men. This adaptive problem has altered women's motivation to compete in addition to their methods of competition (Campbell, 1999). Because the costs of gestation and childrearing are high for mothers at the very beginning of their child's life and male investment is important to the survival and success of vulnerable offspring, the costs of abandonment from their mates are also relatively high compared to other species (Trivers, 1972). Therefore, women seem to have evolved a stronger preference for monogamous, long-term mating than men in order to force biparental care from their mates (Buss & Schmitt, 1993). Although women may also have evolved to prefer short-term mating (e.g., casual sex without relational commitment) to receive benefits like short-term resources from men (e.g., jewelry, free dinners, and career advancement), women seem to prefer short-term mating as a possible precursor to long-term mating with someone more desirable (Greiling & Buss, 2000). In line with this, women tend to prefer mates who have qualities of good parenting (Buss & Schmitt, 1993; Trivers, 1972), earning capacity, and social status (Buss, 1989; Feingold, 1992; Kenrick, Sadalla, Groth & Trost, 1990; Townsend, 1989). Unlike men, this circumstance has led women to evolve a motivation to compete over the quality of mates (e.g., handsome and resource-rich) rather than a larger quantity of mates (Kenrick, Sadalla, Groth, & Trost, 1990).

However, due to the presence of mate poaching, women risk losing their partner's long-term investment to other women (Buss & Shackelford, 1997a; Durante, Li, & Haselton, 2008; Kaighobadi, Shackelford, & Buss, 2010). Women must therefore continue to compete vigilantly with same-sex rivals and engage in mate-retention behaviors, even after securing a desirable mate (Buss, Larsen, Westen, & Semmelroth, 1992). As such, intrasexual competition is not simply a competition for single, unmated women. Research has indicated that women, both newlyweds and those established in marriage, engage in mate-retention tactics by means of social aggression toward same-sex rivals when their mates' income and status are high (Buss & Shackelford, 1997a; Kaighobadi, Shackelford, & Buss, 2010).

The greater parental investment burden encountered by women than men has also altered the methods women use to aggress. For example, Campbell (2004) postulates that women refrain from physical aggression because it is too costly in that they are more likely than men to experience reproductive costs from injury. In line with this, from an early age females have been found to show greater nonverbal discomfort (i.e., tightly crossed arms, stiff, unmoving, frowning, minimal eye contact) than males during competition with same-sex peers despite the outcome (i.e., win or lose; Benenson et al., 2002). It seems that women appraise aggressive encounters as more dangerous than men (Bettencourt & Miller, 1996; Eagly & Steffen, 1986). Women consequently rely upon social aggression and indirect communication (e.g., gossip, spreading rumors, and ostracism) rather than physical aggression to compete effectively with same-sex rivals (Hess & Hagen, 2006). Yet when resources are scarce (e.g., during unemployment, welfare support, and among single mothers), women can be motivated to commit violent crimes of assault as often as property crimes (e.g., credit card fraud and shoplifting; Campbell, 2004; Campbell, Muncer, & Bibel, 1998; 2001). In this way, the particular method of aggression women choose differs depending on how they functionally match their method of aggression to environmental circumstances (Griskevicius et al., 2009). Furthermore, resource scarcity is an environmental stressor that women have faced across evolutionary time. Consequently, women respond to contemporary environmental stressors, like resource scarcity and mate poaching, in ways that ancestrally predicted payoffs.

In sum, women functionally match their method of aggression (physical, direct verbal, and indirect aggression) to environmental circumstances in ways that have been rewarding during ancestral history (Tooby & Cosmides, 1990b). Adaptations from previous generations of humans have imbued women in the present day with particular modes of thought that increase their chances and their children's chances of survival and reproduction. An ultimate explanation of aggression makes clear that aggression is a consequence of tradeoffs between reproductive costs and benefits that gave rise to customary ways of aggression among women across evolutionary time (Griskevicius et al., 2009).

A Proximate Explanation of Aggression

Proximate explanations of aggression illuminate the socioecological or environmental factors that help women decide whether to communicate aggression (direct vs. indirect, verbal aggression vs. physical aggression) to functionally match a strategy of action to environmental circumstances. In essence, individuals have evolved to follow conditional rules (if condition x, then pursue strategy y) in part based on how rewarding that strategy was ancestrally (ultimate explanation) and further calibrated by the specific circumstances experienced by the individual (proximate explanation; Buss, 1995; Tooby & Cosmides, 1990a, 1992). For example, women can more easily deny hostile intent when gossiping with friends (i.e., indirect aggression) than when directly expressing threats to their targets (i.e., direct aggression). If women are averse to risk and retaliation, then they may be inclined to communicate indirect aggression (if at all) to strategically deny hostile intent and deflect retaliation by obscuring that they are the culprit. Aggression is employed when context-specific costs of behaving aggressively are relatively low compared to the potential benefits of behaving aggressively versus alternative plans of action (Griskevicius et al., 2009).

Furthermore, patterns of aggression are adjusted throughout life as the individual learns when and what kinds of aggression are likely successful from past experience and/or by witnessing others' aggression, which fine-tunes the individual's response to similar circumstances in the future (i.e., social learning; Bandura, 1973). For instance, observing another lose a good reputation because she aggressed too intensely by communicating direct verbal aggression may alter a woman's tendency to aggress more indirectly in the future to avoid costly retaliation.

Rather than evolving as a continuous biological response (like heart rate), aggression has instead evolved as a contingency plan in response to stress and environmental triggers (Wilson, 2000). Environmental stressors, such as scarce resources, sexual access, and encounters with strangers, have been historically pervasive, and the individual must be prepared to respond to these stressors as they occur in present environments (Wilson, 2000). Aggression, including indirect and direct verbal aggression as well as physical aggression, functions as a possible solution for these problems alongside of other alternative actions like acquiescence or avoidance (Griskevicius et al., 2009). This does not imply that strategies are always conscious, planned, or articulated, but rather women follow templates for behavior during competition shaped by evolution and proximate social constraints.

As discussed later, in some ways an evolutionary model of aggression is irreconcilable with a traditional social psychological approach. Yet in other ways they are not so different. Cognitive association models illustrate aggression as a reaction to aversive stimuli that produce negative affect associated with other hostile, aggressive thoughts conditioned over time (Anderson & Huesmann, 2003). For instance, the presence of weapons activates hostile thoughts and provokes aggression among men (Berkowitz & LePage, 1967) but not among those who hunt recreationally and therefore have positive affect surrounding weapons (Bartholow et al., 2005). Social learning models, on the other hand, better explain how aggressive knowledge structures are first acquired by observing and then modeling others' behavior, depending on whether the modeled behavior is seen as rewarding or punished (Bandura, 1973). The form, frequency, and situations that trigger aggression are largely learned by previous social experience developed during childhood and foreshadow aggressive tendencies into adulthood (Anderson & Huesmann, 2003). Specifically, girls feel that they will be more severely punished by their social peers for communicating aggression than boys (Perry, Perry, & Rasmussen, 1986). Women and men are differentially punished for aggression based on social gender roles during development, which alters their communication of aggression in adulthood.

Despite this, cognitive association and social learning modes of aggression assume that human children are born with minds somewhat untouched by cognitions they have inherited from their ancestors. Rather, it is primarily the experiences of childhood that shape a person's cognition. For this reason, social role and cognitive association models of aggression do not specify a priori why there would be gender roles associated with aggression (Griskevicius et al., 2009). Sex differences in aggression are treated as one class of individual differences, and these models do not define the adaptive problems that aggression was designed by selection to solve. However, an evolutionary approach recognizes that a person's cognition is constrained by traits they have inherited from their ancestors. As a part of human nature, sex-typed behaviors, such as aggression, cannot be fully explained by social variables, such as societal wealth distribution or contemporary sex roles (Wood & Eagly, 2002).

Consequently, some consider an evolutionary approach to human communication reductionistic (e.g., Infante, 1995; Nelson, 2004), and, indeed, current human behavior is constrained by adaptive influences during previous generations. Yet human behavior remains complex under an evolutionary approach. This is because many environmental cues act as "inputs" that inform women about the adaptive problem they are facing and the strategic solutions that are likely to be successful. As such, aggression among women is situation-dependent and, presumably, a consequence of the complicated endocrine response spurred by changes in one's environment, not terribly unlike cognitive association and social learning models of aggression.

In other ways, an evolutionary rational is irreconcilable with these models. Many social psychologists and communication scholars are quick to conclude that aggression is subjectively undesirable and viewed as being detrimental to one's healthy development (e.g., Frankenhuis & Del Giudice, 2012). Consequently, aggression is defined as pathological or maladaptive. Investigations, therefore, tend to focus on factors of poor development or ill health with the aim to subdue aggression (Infante, 1995). While there are cases of pathological aggression (e.g., Nelson & Trainor, 2007), there are many more cases of functional aggression communicated by those who are not pathological. Many behaviors, such as aggression, intimidation, and xenophobia (see Reid et al., 2012), that are subjectively unsavory are nevertheless functional in terms of survival or reproduction.

In comparison, an evolutionary approach defines pathological or maladaptive behavior more narrowly by referring to cases in which psychological mechanisms fail to fulfill their evolved function (due to genetic mutation, parasites, or exposure to toxins during gestation, for example; Buss & Greiling, 1999). For instance, a child may have an aggressive disposition and experience low subjective well-being. However, according to an evolutionary perspective, if this child grew up in a dangerous environment or even experienced prenatal stress (while in the womb of the mother; see Shaw et al., 2012), aggression may be associated with vigilance, which promotes survival in that specific environment (Frankenhuis & Del Giudice, 2012; Glover,

2011). This is because an aggressive response may have promoted vigilance in similar ancestral environments. Too liberally classifying aggression as maladaptive mistakes aggression as a pathological behavior rather than a functional response to environmental cues that human ancestors would have faced. For this reason, many social psychological and communication investigations too narrowly focus on a small subset of (pathological) aggressive encounters that humans experience (Frankenhuis & Del Giudice, 2012).

In sum, traditional social psychology and communication models do not often explain aggression in terms of an ultimate explanation of ancestral adaptation. Yet customary forms of indirect aggression evolved as a reaction to adaptive problems that women encountered ancestrally, like heavy parental investment burdens and mate poaching. For this reason, traditional social psychology and communication models differ from an evolutionary approach in that they allege human minds are born immaculate and somewhat untouched by inherited predispositions, and they are indeed not. These models are somewhat more reconcilable with proximate evolutionary models, with the exception that subjectively undesirable behavior, such as aggression, is not necessarily maladaptive.

Having compared an evolutionary explanation of aggression to traditional social psychology and communication models, we now turn to the utility of applying theories closely aligned with evolutionary psychology (recalibration theory of anger and costly signaling theory) to further explain aggression among women in greater detail. While previous sections discussed the evolutionary circumstances surrounding aggression among women from a bird's-eye view, the following sections illustrate the specific parameters of aggressive exchanges among women from a more microscopic view. As superficial as it may sound, these theories identify physical attractiveness as an important factor of bargaining position among women during competition and, in turn, their communication of aggression. While sociocultural theories of aggression have identified many factors of aggression, an evolutionary rationale helps to identify which of these factors, namely physical attractiveness, are more crucial in explaining aggression among women.

Recalibration Theory of Anger

During a specific instance of competition over resources or mates, the actions of one person influence the welfare of another. Thus, people may have evolved to levy the maximum amount of a resource from an opponent that the person can defend, cost-effectively, based on a person's bargaining position (Sell, Tooby, et al., 2009; Tooby & Cosmides, 2010; Tooby et al., 2008). Humans (Ermer, Cosmides, & Tooby, 2008) and animals (Maynard Smith & Harper, 2003; Maynard Smith & Price, 1973) have evolved to regulate risk-taking behavior during competition such that those who are less formidable than their opponents will concede to avoid injury during competition. Consequently, Tooby et al. (2008) proposed a recalibration theory of anger. Specifically, humans will strategically express and calibrate their anger and aggression depending on the relative formidability or bargaining position between competitors. For example, it is not wise to provoke a physical fight with Mike Tyson, as it never paid (historically) for the average person to compete with society's prize fighter (for the average person will surely lose). Similarly, it is not wise to verbally aggress toward a high-status competitor, such as one's employer, who has the ability to socially punish the aggressor (e.g., job loss). Competitors weigh the costs and rewards of aggression versus alternative courses of action (i.e., acquiescence or withdrawal) in an attempt to resolve the competition in favor of the angry individual. For example, competitors may engage in more than one strategy, such as engaging in both coercive and prosocial strategies interchangeably. From an early age, children learn the value of balancing both coercive (e.g., threats) and prosocial strategies (e.g., compassion) during competition to mitigate social punishment (Hawley, 2003; Hawley, Johnson, Mize, & McNamara, 2007; Hawley, Little, & Card, 2007).

According to the recalibration theory of anger, individuals become angry and aggressive when they feel entitled to win competitions because they value their own personal welfare as more important than their competitors'. Emotions such as anger are adaptive in that they keep competitors alert and defensive against rivals who interfere with their achieving a desirable outcome. Phrased another way, emotions are affective reactions to contextual problems or ambitions that need to be managed, increasing one's motivation to manage them (Maner et al., 2005). For instance, anger is a typical reaction when an acquaintance is spreading negative rumors, preventing one from achieving a positive reputation (i.e., indirect aggression). The characteristic feelings associated with an emotion, such as anger, motivate individuals to enact a number of possible behaviors that help the individual deal with the

environmental stressor that evoked that emotion (Tooby, 1985). An angry individual may behave in a number of ways, including through retaliatory aggression, avoidance, and acquiescence. Those who behave aggressively, versus taking other, alternative courses of action, are likely those who feel entitled to win because they perceive themselves as formidable competitors (i.e., they perceive a low likelihood of loss or the costs of loss as low). In other words, it is less risky to aggress toward a person who is inferior to oneself in terms of physical strength (during physical aggression) or ability to withhold benefits (during verbal aggression).

Two inputs that humans use to calculate formidability or bargaining position are their ability to inflict costs (e.g., because of physical prowess) and confer benefits (e.g., because of physical attractiveness; Sell, Tooby, et al., 2009). For men, physical strength (particularly upper-body strength) increases their ability to inflict the costs of injury on competitors during physical aggression (Sell, Cosmides, et al., 2009; Sell, Tooby, et al., 2009). For women, physical attractiveness increases their likelihood of being conferred benefits because they are perceived as more socially competent (Eagly et al., 1991) and occupationally successful (Budesheim & DePaola, 1994; DeShields et al., 1996; Dion et al., 1972; Mack & Rainey, 1990; Reingen & Kernan, 1993), providing them benefits that they could withhold and utilize during competition. Consequently, physically strong men and attractive women feel entitled to deference and value their own welfare more than others' and communicate this by directing anger at competitors with the aim of prevailing during conflict (Price et al., 2011; Sell, Tooby, et al., 2009; Tooby et al., 2008). For example, women who are not receiving rewards they feel owed to them from less attractive rivals become angry, whereas women who are less attractive should acquiesce (Sell, Tooby, et al., 2009). Indeed, those who are the target of peer aggression tend to experience less successful relational outcomes, including less flirtation from men and a later onset of dating (Gallup, O'Brien, White, & Wilson, 2009).

Anger and aggression can be thought of as part of a communicative process that negotiates a welfare tradeoff ratio between competitors that reflects their relative status. For women, relative status is calculated in part by their physical attractiveness because attractive women are conferred benefits and social status (Sell, Tooby, et al., 2009). Further, and more important, physical attractiveness conveys much information about a woman's internal state (e.g., health, fertility, and fecundity), which makes physical attractiveness an important cue of reproductive status to potential mates and same-sex rivals competing over the same mates (Sugiyama, 2005). The following sections illustrate the importance of women's physical attractiveness and reproductive status during intrasexual competition over mates and how the predictions of the recalibration theory of anger stand up to empirical evidence.

Physical attractiveness as a cue of reproductive value. This relates to the number of future offspring a woman will likely produce based on her age, health, and fertility (Sugiyama, 2005). Being that many reproductive and health processes are internal to a woman's body and therefore not directly observable (such as ovulation and hormonal status), reproductive value is noticeable to the naked eye only because some observable traits covary with reproductive value (Symons, 1979). These observable traits are referred to as phenotypes, or traits that are morphological, physiological, or behavioral, that affect an individual's ability to efficiently survive and reproduce (Symons, 1979). Many observable traits, or phenotypes, that are considered attractive by men also publicize women's underlying reproductive fitness, including genetic quality (of heritable traits), as well as current health condition (Symons, 1979, 1995). In fact, men have evolved to find feminine traits, like an hourglass figure and symmetrical facial features (discussed later), attractive *because* they inform men of a woman's underlying reproductive value (Symons, 1979, 1995).

Therefore, women who are physically attractive have a high mate value (the degree to which women promote the reproductive success of men who mate with them; Symons, 1995) and are in a position to actualize their own mate preferences, securing more male-provided resources and benefits (Buss, 1993; Rhodes, Simmons, & Peters, 2005; Thornhill & Gangestad, 2008). Furthermore, heterosexual women compete for mates among same-sex rivals by advertising phenotypic qualities valued by those of the opposite sex (Tooke & Camire, 1991). For instance, intelligence and kindness are two important traits in a good parent and are valued in a mate by both sexes. However, men tend to value attractive mates, whereas women find high-status, resource-rich mates attractive because these resources can be shared and help ensure the survival of any offspring (Buss, 1989; Li et al., 2002). Therefore, women alter their appearance to attract

resource-rich mates and intimidate same-sex rivals (Tooke & Camire, 1991), and physical attractiveness serves as an important "input" to calculate relative formidability when women compete for mates (Sell, Tooby, et al., 2009).

Ancestral men across many generations all faced the same adaptive problem of identifying which women were higher-quality mates (Symons, 1995). Ancestral women faced the adaptive problem of caring for vulnerable offspring in a changing environment, and not all women are equally equipped to conceive and rear offspring (Hrdy, 1999). For this reason men fastidiously seek certain qualities that indicate a woman's mate value, or the degree to which a potential mate would promote his reproductive success if he mated with her. Two categories of traits that men notice and find attractive in a mate are those that track endogenous estrogen levels and the symmetry of bilateral traits, which in turn inform the beholder of a woman's reproductive value. These two phenotypic categories are discussed as important cues of mate value and physical attractiveness, which in turn influence women's bargaining position during intrasexual competition.

Estrogen concentrations predict conception success in terms of ovulation, follicle size, egg quality, and the implantation and gestation of a zygote (Lipson & Ellison, 1996; Thornhill & Gangestad, 2008). As such, men find physical features that track estrogen levels attractive in a potential mate. For example, women who have higher estrogen levels have more feminine facial features (e.g., higher cheekbones and narrower chins; Law Smith et al., 2006; Perrett et al., 1998; Rhodes, Hickford, & Jeffery, 2000) and smaller waist to hip ratios (WHR), meaning that they carry their fat in the buttocks and thighs rather than in their waistline (i.e., an hourglass figure; Ziomkiewicz, Ellison, Lipson, Thune, & Jasiénska, 2008). Women with low WHR also become pregnant more easily than women with high WHR (Symons, 1995). Additionally, fat deposits in the thighs typically consist of gynoid fat, which is considered to be especially important for the development of fetal brains (Thornhill & Gangestad, 2008). As such, mothers with low WHR and the children of these women score significantly higher on cognitive tests than the offspring of women with high WHR (Lassek & Gaulin, 2008). As a result of these factors, men may have evolved to find women with low WHR and other traits that index endogenous estrogen attractive (Singh, 1995; Singh & Young, 1995).

A second category of phenotypic traits men use to calculate a woman's attractiveness is fluctuating asymmetry, which is any deviation from perfect symmetry on a bilateral trait that is typically symmetrical in the population (e.g., arms, legs, eyes, ears; Thornhill & Gangestad, 1994). Symmetrical features indicate heterozygosity, which is associated with developmental stability (i.e., one's capacity to resist genetic and environmental stress from disrupting their healthy development; Miller, 2000), health (i.e., pathogen resistance; Møller, 2006; Rhodes et al., 2001; Symons, 1995), and reproductive success (Perrett et al., 1999). Consequently, men may also have evolved to find women with symmetrical bilateral body features attractive.

Some believe that multiple traits of attractiveness each cue redundant information about a person's underlying reproductive value but imperfectly (Thornhill & Grammer, 1999). In other words, according to this perspective, WHR, breast size, and fluctuating asymmetry may all indicate the same source of developmental instability that is signaled across many channels, albeit imperfectly. However, others have suggested that multiple cues of attractiveness communicate overlapping yet distinct information about health and fertility. For example, the body fat of WHR varies as a consequence of estrogen fluctuations throughout life (Ziomkiewicz et al., 2008), whereas the body fat of breasts is less subject to change as a consequence of changing estrogen levels (Singh & Young, 1995) but does change as consequence of age (Sugiyama, 2005). In any case, a woman's reproductive value can be determined by any number of traits that are observable on her body.

Taken together, physical and behavioral traits that are associated with health, age, fertility, fecundity, intelligence, status, parenting skill, kindness, and a willingness to invest in offspring all contribute to calculating one's mate value (Sugiyama, 2005). All other things being equal, women who are physically attractive are more likely to fulfill their particular mate preferences than unattractive women (Buss, 1993; Rhodes et al., 2005; Thornhill & Gangestad, 2008). Consequently, attractive women may feel entitled to win mating competition against other women who are relatively less attractive and may become angry and aggressive when their opponents fail to acquiesce to them (Benderlioglu, Sciulli, & Nelson, 2004; Sell, Tooby, et al., 2009). Far from superficial, physical attractiveness thus confers to the beholder much information about a woman's internal state (e.g., health, fertility, and fecundity;

Symons, 1979, 1995). As a result, it may be a key player in the marketplace of mating for women and therefore a key factor of their aggression during intrasexual competition (Tooke & Camire, 1991).

However, not all women can simply rely on their good looks to prevail during competition. Environmental conditions and individual differences between women on dimensions other than physical attractiveness can alter women's ability to prevail during competition. For instance, there are some environments in which the ratio of men to women is low, as is unfortunately the case for many urban African Americans due to high mortality and incarceration rates of African American men. In this case, long-term relationships occur less often and women compete intensely over a small number of desirable long-term mates or switch their focus to men with short-term resources ("high rollers"; Campbell, 2004). On the other hand, when women differ in terms of their earning potential, those with high earning potential will seek mates with earning potential that surpasses their own (Townsend, 1989; Weiderman & Allgeier, 1992); the exact reasoning remains ambiguous. However, it seems that the "mating pool" of desirable men becomes increasingly small among some women due to environmental conditions (e.g., sex ratio) or individual differences (e.g., in terms of socioeconomic status). For these women, intrasexual competition will become fierce over a small number of elite men, even for those who are physically attractive with high mate value.

Conversely, there are times in women's lives during which intrasexual competition for mates is not intense. Specifically, physical attractiveness is not expected to predict aggression among women who are prepubescent and postmenopausal. This is because reproductive concerns are much lower for women within these age groups (Symons, 1979, 1995). As evidence for this, among females who are prepubescent, rates of physical aggression fall during early childhood at the same time that indirect aggression tactics become more common (Ingram, 2013). When utilizing samples ranging from children to young adults, these changes become particularly apparent. For instance, from ages 6 to 10 years old, children become increasingly egalitarian in the way they share toys but exhibit more self-interested forms of play (less sharing) when they can elude detection (Benenson & Christakos, 2003). By the age of 9 years, girls start to use competition tactics that deprive their competitors of the contested resource rather than purely seeking personal gain when resources are scarce (Roy & Benensen, 2002). Cross-culturally, peer aggression is prevalent among those who are 11 to 16 years old (Nansel, Craig, Overpeck, Saluja, & Ruan, 2004) and is associated with dating popularity (Pellegrini & Long, 2003). Later, when competition for mates intensifies by the ages 17 to 19 years, physical attractiveness appears as a predictor of aggression in that young women who are more attractive express hostility toward same-sex rivals (Muñoz-Reyes et al., 2012).

Later, as women age, they tend to gossip and indirectly aggress less (Forrest, Eatough, & Shevlin, 2005; Massar, Buunk & Rempt, 2012). Research has found that younger women are more likely to gossip than older women; however, this relationship is mediated by women's self-perceived mate value (Massar et al., 2012). Older women who are approaching 50 years of age experience swift declines in mate value (Miller, 2000; Symons, 1979, 1995); indeed, they receive fewer compliments about their appearance and fewer invitations for sex, which is associated with a decrease in gossip and intrasexual competition (Massar et al., 2012).

Taken as a whole, the link between physical attractiveness, mate value, and indirect aggression seems to apply to women experiencing heightened mating competition during adolescence and into adulthood but not as they approach menopause. Women who are physically attractive are more likely to fulfill their particular mate preferences (Buss, 1993; Rhodes et al., 2005; Thornhill & Gangestad, 2008), feel entitled to win mating competitions against other women who are relatively less attractive, and may become angry and aggressive when their opponents fail to acquiesce to them (Sell, Tooby, et al., 2009). However, the link between physical attractiveness and aggression primarily seems to occur when conception is likely during a woman's adult life, regardless of her relational status, and subsides when conception becomes less likely with age.

Empirical evidence linking physical attractiveness to aggression. Despite these connections, investigations of aggression among women in terms of physical attractiveness have produced mixed findings. Sell, Tooby, et al. (2009) found that attractive women feel entitled to deference from those less attractive and communicate this by directing anger and aggression at competitors with the aim of prevailing during conflict (see also Price et al., 2011; Tooby et al., 2008). Some researchers, however, have found evidence in opposition

to that of Sell, Tooby, et al. Women will aggress toward another woman who is relatively more attractive (Arnocky et al., 2012; Gallup & Wilson, 2009) and sexy (Vaillancourt & Sharma, 2011) and therefore a more formidable mating competitor. Conversely, attractive women report greater victimization from indirect aggression by as much as 35%, compared to unattractive women (Leenaars et al., 2008). Although it may seem that women should compete with those who are similarly attractive and comparable in mate value (i.e., to "pick on someone your own size"), preliminary evidence does not seem to suggest this (Anderson, Reid, & Gaulin, 2012). Some women seem to compete with those who are relatively more attractive despite this leading to a competitive disadvantage and making them less likely to prevail during mating competition. Two explanations have been used to explain why some women would compete with those who are relatively more attractive: (a) aggression against more attractive women is communicated out of frustration (Gallup & Wilson, 2009) and (b) behaving aggressively toward attractive women strategically mitigates the greatest threat to a female's mating success (Arnocky et al., 2012).

Although the rewards of effectively combating an attractive rival are great (i.e., avoiding the costly loss of a desirable mate), choosing to provoke or aggress against one's most formidable competitor is risky. A less attractive woman is less likely to prevail during a competition over mates at the outset because men strongly desire physical attractiveness in potential mates above other qualities (Li et al., 2002). Further, verbal derogations are more effective if the derogator is physically attractive herself (Fisher & Cox, 2009; Grabe, Bas, Pagano, & Samson, 2012). While derogators can be judged negatively, this tends to affect men's perceptions of a woman's personality only, with evaluations of her attractiveness as a mate unaffected (Fisher, Shaw, Worth, Smith, & Reeve, 2010). This then suggests that derogations made by those who are less attractive are relatively less effective. As a result, someone who provokes a more attractive competitor is subject to retaliation that is more effective and damaging. All told, it seems unreasonably costly to communicate aggression toward women who are relatively more attractive than oneself in competition over mates. Presumably, women, either consciously or unconsciously, weigh the likelihood and cost of losing a competition with a particular competitor before engaging them in competition.

It may be the case that women who are relatively less attractive mitigate their competition costs and levy rewards in other ways. Indeed, there is a larger set of potential inputs humans use to calculate a welfare tradeoff between competitors besides simply attractiveness (Sell, Tooby, et al., 2009; Tooby et al., 2008; see also Barkow, 2009). For instance, the presence of coalitional support seems to be a relevant environmental input that alters the calculation of costs and rewards during mating competition. Vaillancourt and Sharma (2011) found some evidence that women act "bitchier" (eye-rolling, staring emotionlessly, ridiculing outside of earshot) toward a sexy rival when in the presence of friends than in the presence of strangers. Among women in polygynous marriages, whereby women's access to male-provided resources is highly variable, those who have greater control of resources are those who are geographically close to their relatives and kin (e.g., biological sister wives; Yanca & Low, 2004). The presence of coalitional partners (friends or kin) who could come to one's defense thus seems to mitigate some of the costs of provoking a rival who is more attractive.

Another explanation for mixed evidence linking physical attractiveness to aggression could be that women may not be the most attractive in their social groups but instead target those who are *relatively* less attractive (Gallup, O'Brien, & Wilson, 2011). In other words, women may typically aggress against those who are less attractive and are themselves victimized by those who are relatively more attractive (i.e., like a chain reaction). Most evidence does not measure women's aggressiveness or victimization in relation to the relative attractiveness of her opponent. Instead, research tends to focus on whether the aggressor was more or less attractive globally (see Fisher et al., 2009; Leenaars et al., 2008; Price et al., 2011, 2012) or if the target of aggression was more or less attractive globally (Terrell et al., 2009; Vaillancourt & Sharma, 2011). However, rarely are these factors measured in relation to each other directly. Women presumably calculate their own attractiveness in relation to other women in their social networks. It may be that they do not have enough experience to know whether they are globally attractive beyond their particular social network. Women of similar physiological measurements may feel more or less attractive (self-perceived attractiveness) depending on how they relate to others in their immediate social groups.

Sell, Tooby, et al. (2009) did theorize that women need not be exceptionally attractive, just noticeably more attractive than their current rival, in order to feel entitled to aggress. In their study, however, they found evidence supporting predictions about self-reported, global attractiveness correlated with increased anger and aggression among women without relation to a particular rival. In sum, self-reported or physiological measurements of global attractiveness may not give adequate information in terms of relative differences of attractiveness in social groups. This may, in turn, produce inconsistent findings about how individual differences in physical attractiveness are linked to aggression that is presumably communicated within social groups.

Furthermore, the predictions of recalibration theory have primarily been supported when measuring women's self-perceived attractiveness rather than their physiological measures of attractiveness (Price et al., 2012; see also Price et al., 2011). Indeed, women's self-perceived facial attractiveness does not correspond with others' ratings of their attractiveness (Brewer, Archer, & Manning, 2007). Male ratings of female facial attractiveness corresponded with other body traits of attractiveness (i.e., WHR and body mass index) while women's self-perceived facial attractiveness did not. It appears that women do not accurately assess their own attractiveness as they place too much emphasis on their facial attractiveness, ignoring ways in which other body traits influence the way they are evaluated as attractive by men. This may perhaps be indicative of adaptive self-deception (Trivers, 2000), but evidence is mixed as to whether women overestimate (Brewer et al., 2007) or underestimate (Price et al., 2012) their self-perceived physical attractiveness. Recalibration theory does suggest that the association between physiological attractiveness and aggression is mediated by self-perceived attractiveness, but it is unclear exactly how self-deception about one's attractiveness is adaptive. Yet both male and female raters of women's facial beauty do agree, suggesting that other women are able to identify their same-sex rivals whom men find attractive but are unable to realistically judge their own beauty (Brewer et al., 2007).

In comparison to physiological attractiveness, self-perceived attractiveness is more malleable, and perhaps its influence on aggression is moderated by other factors of self-enhancement, such as jewelry, makeup, and revealing clothing. Self-perceived attractiveness may communicate a different message than physiological attractiveness. For instance, women of varying degrees of physiological attractiveness may feel more or less self-perceived attractiveness by enhancing their image by wearing revealing and figure-hugging clothing during times when they are actively seeking desirable mates (e.g., at a disco; see Grammer, Renninger, & Fischer, 2004). By contrast, physiological attractiveness indexes relative differences in mate value between women whether or not they are actively competing to mate. Women may signal their intent to compete for mates by enhancing their self-perceived attractiveness on some occasions but not others. Why this occurs may perhaps be better explained by costly signaling theory, a closely aligned theory to recalibration theory of anger that is discussed further in subsequent sections of this chapter.

In sum, the recalibration theory of anger predicts that women strategically express anger and aggression depending on relative differences in the physical attractiveness of competitors. Traits of attractiveness in women are valued by men and heeded by rival women because these traits cue women's underlying reproductive value. Women who are relatively more attractive than their same-sex rivals are more likely to actualize their own mate preferences for resource-rich men and will feel entitled to better treatment from less attractive same-sex rivals (Buss, 1993; Rhodes et al., 2005; Thornhill & Gangestad, 2008). However, physical attractiveness is not expected to influence aggression communicated by women who do not face the same reproductive concerns because of their age (before puberty or approaching menopause). The recalibration theory of anger stands up relatively well to empirical investigation, but evidence is somewhat mixed. Attractiveness may not be the only variable that explains women's aggressiveness in intrasexual competition. Additional environmental factors, such as coalitional support, also help women calculate their formidability as competitors and therefore influence their likelihood to aggress (Vaillancourt & Sharma, 2011; Yanca & Low, 2004). Mixed findings may also be due to the way physical attractiveness is typically measured globally rather than relative to the aggressor and victim. Finally, self-perceived attractiveness is typically measured but does not always correspond with physiological measures of attractiveness. Indirect aggression tends to be communicated within social groups where relative differences in self-perceived attractiveness are more likely to be the expounding factor of aggression among women. Yet the reasoning why many physiological traits of attractiveness

are not strongly associated with women's self-perceived attractiveness remains unclear. Some of this confusion can perhaps be resolved by considering the predictions of costly signaling theory.

Costly Signaling Theory

Since women's physical attractiveness is an important criterion of mate attraction, there should be selection pressures favoring women who display and even exaggerate their physical attractiveness, as a signal to men of their motivation to mate. Previously, we reviewed evidence suggesting that physical attractiveness is an important cue during mate competition because it carries reliable information about a woman's reproductive value. Moreover, at times of higher conception likelihood (i.e., during ovulation), women also signal a motivation or intent to mate by enhancing their baseline attractiveness, although this is not necessarily done consciously. This merits further scrutiny because *cues* and *signals* have distinct meanings according to costly signaling theory (Grammer et al., 2004; Haselton, Mortezaie, Pillsworth, Bleske-Rechek, & Frederick, 2007). Cues of physical attractiveness are relatively stable indexes of mate value (i.e., traits; discussed previously), whereas signals are fluctuating indications of a motivation to mate (i.e., states). Making this distinction represents a shift in focus from cues of physical attractiveness to the interplay between relatively stable physical cues and fluctuating signals of intent through self-enhancement. Thus, this distinction may serve to qualify the mixed conclusions of previous research on aggression among women in terms of their physical attractiveness.

Signals of physical attractiveness during ovulatory fertility. Just as physically attractive cues of reproductive value have been argued as a bargaining chip in both mate attraction and intrasexual competition, the same can be argued for ovulatory fertility. During periods of heightened ovulatory fertility, women have a heightened motivation to attract mates with desirable traits that could be inherited by potential offspring (Gangestad & Thornhill, 1998; Thornhill & Gangestad, 1999, 2008). These traits include masculine appearance (Johnston, Hagel, Franklin, Fink, & Grammer, 2001; Penton-Voak & Perrett, 2000; see also Roney & Simmons, 2008), scent (Grammer, 1993), lower vocal pitch (Feinberg et al., 2006; Puts, 2005, 2006), and dominant personality (Gangestad, Simpson, Cousins, Garver-Apgar, & Christensen, 2004; Havlicek, Roberts, & Flegr, 2005). In line with this, women in the fertile phase of their ovulatory cycle have been found to choose more attractive (Hill & Durante, 2009), sexy, and seductive clothing (Durante, Griskevicius, Hill, Perilloux & Li 2011; Durante et al., 2008; Grammer et al., 2004; Schwarz & Hassebrauck, 2008) in order to attract desirable men and perhaps signal their intent to mate.

In order for signals to be effective, responses to signals must also have evolved (Maynard Smith & Harper, 2003). Not only should sexual selection favor men who successfully choose quality mates based on attractiveness cues of reproductive value (i.e., women's baseline attractiveness), but they should also favor men who notice women's signals of an intention to mate (i.e., women's exaggerations of attractiveness). In so doing, men isolate women who are quality mates *as well as* those showing interest in mating at the time. Having directly tested the interplay between cues and signals of women's attractiveness, Zhang and Reid (2013) found that men's sexual cognition was spurred primarily when cues of women's attractiveness were coupled with a strong signal of women's intent to mate by using a flirtatious voice (i.e., high-pitched vocal variation). Conversely, men's motivation to mate is reduced when they perceive that a woman has no interest in them, regardless of her level of physical attractiveness. There is little point to exerting mating effort toward an uninterested recipient. Consequently, it appears as though women have evolved to signal to desirable men their intention to mate when conception is most likely. Conversely, it also appears that men have evolved to process the added information of such signals in order to augment the information they had already garnered from women's cues of reproductive value.

Having established that fertile women signal their motivation to mate by enhancing their attractiveness and that men have evolved to respond to these signals, it should also be noted that women's signals are constrained by reproductive and social costs that prevent them from dishonestly signaling an intent to mate. Research suggests that signals are worth attending to only when they are generally honest and when there is not a high density of "cheaters" who signal a quality they do not actually possess (Maynard Smith & Harper, 2003; Searcy & Nowicki, 2005). There are three possible explanations for why women would communicate honest rather than dishonest signals of mating intent (e.g., wearing revealing clothing when they are not interested in mating). First, physiologically speaking, signaling one's motivation to mate by exaggerating

one's attractiveness is difficult to do to an extreme. For example, women may enhance their physical attractiveness by wearing revealing clothing so long as they have attractive traits to reveal in the first place. Second, women would face a heavier cost of parental investment if they were to falsely signal a strong intent to mate and risk conceiving an unintended pregnancy (e.g., physiological costs of gestation, heavy parental burden, and lost mating opportunities). Third, strongly signaling one's intent to mate with a particularly desirable target may incur social costs in the form of aggression from other women also interested in mating with the same man. Not only may a woman enhance her physical attractiveness during times of heightened ovulation to signal her intent to mate with desirable men, but by doing so, a woman's signal may be observed by same-sex rivals who are motivated to thwart her mating attempts (thus discouraging her from signaling dishonestly).

It is this third explanation of signal honesty that helps to explain aggression among women. Signals that communicate intentions toward a potential mate may also elicit a retaliatory response from same-sex rivals. Negative social consequences of signaling an intent to mate, such as social gossip or a negative reputation, represent a cost that keeps the amount of dishonest signals communicated by women low. Furthermore, research indicates that the costs incurred when communicating intense signals are typically greater for women of lower quality (e.g., those who are less healthy or attractive) in comparison to women with more desirable traits (Grafen, 1990; Zahavi, 1975). Women who calculate that they are likely to win a mating competition at the outset (e.g., because they are more physically attractive than their same-sex rival) will likely continue to signal a motivation to compete for mates more intensely, even if experiencing retaliation. This is because the costs of social retaliation are not as great for an attractive woman as they would be for her less attractive rival. This contention is backed by evidence that indicates that verbal derogations are more effective if the derogator is physically attractive herself (Fisher & Cox, 2009). Further, while derogators can be judged negatively, this tends to affect men's perceptions of the female derogator on dimensions related to her personality only, with evaluations of her attractiveness as a mate remaining unchanged (Fisher et al., 2010). As such, physical attractiveness should perhaps not be considered as a stable cue of reproductive value. Rather, considering fluctuating displays or exaggerations of physical attractiveness as signals of mating motivation may prove more useful and cast mixed evidence of the relationship between attractiveness and aggression in a new light.

Empirical evidence linking attractive signaling to aggression. Evidence that seems contrary to the predictions of recalibration theory of anger can be explained by costly signaling theory. For instance, Vaillancourt and Sharma (2011) found that women are intolerant and communicate indirect aggression toward peers who dress in a sexy, provocative way. If one were to interpret provocative clothing as a signal rather than a cue (in terms of costly signaling theory), then a sexy peer may be communicating a motivation to compete for mates by exaggerating cues of her reproductive value, and also experiencing the costs of retaliation (indirect aggression) from rival women, thereby discouraging her from signaling dishonestly. Vaillancourt and Sharma manipulated the degree of sexiness of the target (i.e., a confederate), yet they did not measure the relative difference in attractiveness between both women (i.e., confederate and participant). Therefore, it cannot be determined whether attractive women or less attractive women aggress toward a sexy rival who is strongly signaling a motivation to compete for mates.

Indeed, attractive women report greater victimization from indirect aggression than unattractive women by as much as 35% (Leenaars et al., 2008). It may be that attractive women are recalling times during which they were signaling a motivation to mate during heightened ovulatory fertility. Conversely, Arnocky et al. (2012) found that women who negatively compare their own appearance to other women (e.g., "I do not like wearing a swimming costume because I don't think that I look as good as other girls"), self-report communicating more indirect aggression than women who positively compare their appearances to others. It may be that less attractive women recalled retaliating toward a signaling woman in the past (i.e., a woman exaggerating her physical attractiveness). Yet this cannot be concluded based on the findings of Arnocky et al. While they measured women's attractiveness in comparison to those in their social network, they did not do the same for indirect aggression; to whom unattractive women were communicating their aggression (those more or less attractive) was not measured.

Interpreting this evidence in terms of costly signaling theory leads one to think of interesting lines of future inquiry. According to costly signaling theory, one should find that the exaggeration of appearances during times of fertility corresponds with an increase in being the target of indirect aggression from same-sex peers. If true, it would seem that attractive women are not immune to retaliation when they exaggerate their physical attractiveness during ovulation; it is just less costly for them (Fisher & Cox, 2009; Fisher et al., 2010). Thus, attractive women may recall being the target of aggression (Leenaars et al., 2008) but perhaps may not have experienced great loss over it. Aggression is less damaging to a woman's image when communicated by others who are less physically attractive (Willer & Cupach, 2008).

Furthermore, perhaps the predictions of the recalibration theory still apply, as in women who are more attractive generally aggress more than those less attractive (Sell, Tooby, et al. 2009). However, this pattern of baseline attractiveness (i.e., cues) may interact with exaggerations of attractiveness (i.e., signals) to predict indirect aggression. In other words, do all signaling women, attractive and unattractive alike, experience retaliatory aggression for signaling? Conversely, do all women, attractive and unattractive alike, communicate aggression to signaling women? This remains to be investigated. One would need to test how women's baseline (everyday) attractiveness interacts with their exaggerated physical attractiveness (e.g., provocative dress) to predict their communication of indirect aggression.

The interplay of cues and signals casts the mixed evidence of aggression among women and physical attractiveness in a new light. It is important to recognize the differences between women's attractiveness cues of reproductive value and their signals of mating motivation. Relatedly, we should refrain from methodologically conflating women's baseline attractiveness with their exaggerations of attractiveness. Women's signals of mating motivation may have evolved to attract desirable mates, but they may also elicit social aggression from same-sex rivals who can either be more attractive or less attractive than the signaler (Leenaars et al., 2008; Vaillancourt & Sharma, 2011). Since social costs are greater for signalers of lower quality (Grafen, 1990; Zahavi, 1975), women who are more physically attractive than their rivals will continue to signal their intent to mate and compete despite being the target of social aggression.

Some evidence suggests that women's signals of mating motivation during ovulatory fertility are intended to communicate toward same-sex rivals and not just mates (Durante et al., 2008; Fisher, 2004). For example, women in the fertile phase of their ovulatory cycle derogate the appearances of other women (Fisher, 2004). Even women with long-term mates report a heightened desire to wear revealing clothing during the time they are more likely to conceive (Durante et al., 2008). It is argued that this occurs in order for these women to appear more attractive than their same-sex rivals and, in so doing, avoid the costly loss of a desirable long-term mate through mate-poaching attempts (Durante et al., 2008). One strong interpretation of these findings is that women evolved to signal their physical attractiveness to other women as well as men. Indeed, Hudders, De Backer, Fisher, and Vyncke (2014) recently found that women prefer luxury items that enhance attractiveness (e.g., a designer dress) when primed with an intrasexual competition scenario. These authors suggest that women who consume luxury items are doing so to signal their superiority toward other women, not necessarily toward potential mates, because men do not typically perceive luxury items as more attractive.

Yet since the effectiveness of signals is based on the mutual rewards garnered by both signalers and receivers (according to costly signaling theory; Maynard Smith & Harper, 2003), it is unclear what benefit signalers receive by signaling to same-sex rivals who target them with aggression. Rather, according to costly signaling theory, aggression from same-sex rivals is a cost that maintains the honesty of the signal that occurs between a woman and her potential mate. In other words, women may not have evolved to signal their physical attractiveness to other women but to primarily signal their mating intentions toward men. The indirect aggression that comes from rival women may be a costly byproduct ensuring that women will more honesty signal their intent to mate, which in turn makes the signal more worth attending to by men. It is the role of future research to directly test whether indirect aggression among women is primarily a costly byproduct of signaling an intent to mate with men or whether women express their indirect aggression as signals to other women of their superiority and formidability.

In sum, during times of heightened fertility women signal their mating motivation to men by wearing provocative clothing and, by the same token, broadcasting their motivation to compete to other same-sex rivals. Women are more likely to successfully endure the social retaliation costs associated with signaling when they have the physiological traits of attractiveness and high reproductive value. Consequently, signal effectiveness is a balance of reproductive payoffs from attracting desirable mates, as well as social costs inflicted by same-sex rivals. By considering physical attractiveness in terms of the interplay between evolved cues and signals, mixed evidence of aggression among women becomes clearer and new avenues are uncovered for future research.

Conclusion

In conclusion, this chapter raises a number of important issues. The current analysis focused exclusively on a psychological mechanism (i.e., a mode of thought) in which environmental cues trigger an evolved pattern of aggression as a consequence of anger. In other words, the association between relative physical attractiveness and aggression among women is mediated by an emotional response of anger. However, aggression has also been known to come from feelings of jealousy. All emotions are thought to be affective reactions to contextual problems or ambitions that are pressing and need to be managed, increasing one's motivation to manage them (Maner et al., 2005). For example, jealousy and anger are adaptive in that they keep women alert and defensive against sexual rivals who may interfere with their ability to achieve a desirable mating outcome (Buss et al., 1992; Buunk & Dijkstra, 2004; Dijkstra & Buunk, 2002; DeSteno & Salovey, 1996; Price et al., 2012; Tooby et al., 2008).

Anger tends to be spurred when the aggressor is well positioned to make the price of retaliation high (Price et al., 2012; Tooby et al., 2008). However, jealousy seems to be the emotional response of women who are less formidable and less attractive than their same-sex rival and, as a result, are less able to negotiate an outcome in their favor (Arnocky et al., 2012). Women become especially threatened by a rival who is physically attractive when imagining the emotional infidelity of her mate because it indicates that her mate's resources will be siphoned away to another woman (Buss et al., 1992; Buunk & Dijkstra, 2004). Further, women who self-report low mate value experience more overall jealousy than women with a high self-reported mate value (Massar, Buunk, & Dechesne, 2009). Evidence suggests that jealousy is felt among women confronted by an attractive rival (Dijkstra & Buunk, 2002), and they are, therefore, not in a good position to force their competitor to respect their welfare (Sell, Tooby, et al., 2009). This then leads one to question the utility of communicating aggression when feeling jealous if aggression is unlikely to result in success. As such, it is unclear whether jealousy is the "loser" emotional counterpart to the "winner" anger when competitors calculate their relative welfare tradeoff during competition. In future research, it would be interesting to inquire if both anger and jealousy are evoked among competitors who are assessing their relative welfares and whether these emotions primarily occur when competitors perceive a competitive advantage versus disadvantage, respectively.

Another issue worth addressing is that, while an adaptionist approach was taken in this chapter, it was not argued that aggression is a direct consequence of specific genetic polymorphisms. While this may be a potential argument for the evolution of aggression, this chapter considered an alternative way aggression may have evolved. It was argued that aggression and other personality traits are facultatively calibrated to (i.e., tied to) phenotypic traits, such as physical attractiveness, that are themselves a consequence of specific gene combinations. Evidence suggests that gene polymorphisms may explain relatively little variation in personality traits. This is because variations in personality traits are tied to the variation of other heritable traits, such as physical attractiveness, which then, in turn, are a consequence of specific gene combinations (Holtzman, Augustine, & Senne, 2011; Lukaszewski & Roney, 2011).

In close, it was the expressed goal of this chapter to first investigate the functional origins of aggression among women. A second goal was to illustrate the ways in which traditional communication and social psychological models can be reconcilable (and at times irreconcilable) with the adaptive problems aggression evolved to solve. Owing to the unique adaptive problems women face, particularly with regard to a high minimum parental investment, they may have evolved to compete with same-sex rivals for monogamous, long-term mates. One of the ways women remain vigilant against same-sex rivals may be by communicating indirect aggression (rather than physical aggression) throughout their reproductive lives (from puberty to menopause). By using two closely aligned theories, the recalibration theory of anger and costly signaling theory, aggression among women was explained in terms of women's differential reproductive value and their motivation to compete. The recalibration theory of anger posits that women strategically express anger and aggression depending on relatively stable

differences of reproductive value and physical attractiveness between competitors. Women who are relatively more attractive than their same-sex rivals are more likely to actualize their own mate preferences for resource-rich men (Buss, 1993; Rhodes et al., 2005; Thornhill & Gangestad, 2008) and will feel entitled to better treatment from less attractive rivals (Sell, Tooby, et al., 2009). According to costly signaling theory, women also change and exaggerate their physical attractiveness when they are experiencing heightened ovulatory fertility (Durante, Griskevicius, Hill, Perilloux & Li 2011; Durante et al., 2008; Grammer et al., 2004; Hill & Durante, 2009; Schwarz & Hassebrauck, 2008), signaling a changing motivation to mate with desirable men. However, intense signaling exposes women to retaliatory aggression from same-sex rivals. Those who can endure the social retaliation costs are women who have physiological traits of attractiveness and high reproductive value (Fisher & Cox, 2009; Fisher et al., 2010). Consequently, women's formidability during mating competition is based on the interplay between cues and signals of physical attractiveness. It is this model of aggression that more parsimoniously explains the motivations, methods, and strategic communication of aggression to functionally match the many environmental triggers and individual differences between competitors.

References

Adler, N. E., Boyce, T., Chesney, M. A., Cohen, S., Folkman, S., Kahn, R. L., & Syme, S. L. (1994). Socioeconomic status and health: The challenge of the gradient. *American Psychologist, 49*(1), 15–24.

Anderson, C. A. (1989). Temperature and aggression: Ubiquitous effects of heat on occurrence of human violence. *Psychological Bulletin, 106*(1), 74–96.

Anderson, C. A., Benjamin, A. J., & Bartholow, B. D. (1998). Does the gun pull the trigger? Automatic priming effects of weapon pictures and weapon names. *Psychological Science, 9*(4), 308–314.

Anderson, C. A., & Bushman, B. J. (2002). Human aggression. *Annual Review of Psychology, 53*, 27–51.

Anderson, C. A., Bushman, B. J., & Groom, R. W. (1997). Hot years and serious and deadly assault: Empirical tests of the heat hypothesis. *Journal of Personality and Social Psychology, 73*(6), 1213.

Anderson, C. A., & Dill, K. E. (2000). Video games and aggressive thoughts, feelings, and behavior in the laboratory and in life. *Journal of Personality and Social Psychology, 78*(4), 772.

Anderson, C. A., & Huesmann, L. R. (2003). Human aggression: A social-cognitive view. In M. A. Hogg & J. Cooper (Eds.), *Handbook of social psychology* (pp. 296–323). Thousand Oaks, CA: SAGE.

Anderson, G. L., Reid, S., & Gaulin, S. (2012, May). *How aggression among women is calibrated by physical attractiveness: An experimental test of the recalibration theory of anger.* Paper presented at the International Communication Association Convention, Phoenix, AZ.

Archer, J., & Coyne, S. M., (2005). An integrated review of indirect, relational, and social aggression. *Personality and Social Psychology Review, 9*(3), 212–230.

Arnocky, S., Sunderani, S., Miller, J. L., & Vaillancourt, T. (2012). Jealousy mediates the relationship between attractiveness comparison and females' indirect aggression. *Personal Relationships, 19*(2), 290–303.

Bandura, A. (1973). *Aggression: A social learning analysis.* Englewood Cliffs, NJ: Prentice Hall.

Barkow, J. H. (2009). Steps toward convergence: Evolutionary psychology's saga continues. *Proceedings of the National Academy of Sciences of the United States of America, 106*(35), 14743–14744.

Bartholow, B. D., Anderson, C. A., Carnagey, N. L., & Benjamin, A. J., Jr. (2005). Interactive effects of life experience and situational cues on aggression: The weapons priming effect in hunters and nonhunters. *Journal of Experimental Social Psychology, 41*(1), 48–60.

Beatty, M. J., & McCroskey, J. C. (1997). It's in our nature: Verbal aggressiveness as temperamental expression. *Communication Quarterly, 45*(4), 446–460.

Benderlioglu, Z., Sciulli, P. W., & Nelson R. (2004). Fluctuating asymmetry predicts human reactive aggression. *American Journal of Human Biology, 16*(4), 458–469.

Benenson, J. F., & Christakos, A. (2003). The greater fragility of females' versus males' closest same-sex friendships. *Child Development, 74*(4), 1123–1129.

Benenson, J. F., Roy, R., Waite, A., Goldbaum, S., Linders, L., & Simpson, A. (2002). Greater discomfort as a proximate cause of sex differences in competition. *Merrill-Palmer Quarterly, 48*(3), 225–247.

Berkowitz, L. (1989). Frustration-aggression hypothesis: Examination and reformulation. *Psychological Bulletin, 106*(1), 59–73.

Berkowitz, L. (2008). On the consideration of automatic as well as controlled psychological processes in aggression. *Aggressive Behavior, 34*(2), 117–129.

Berkowitz, L., & LePage, A. (1967). Weapons as aggression-eliciting stimuli. *Journal of Personality and Social Psychology, 7*(2 Part 1), 202–207.

Berkowitz, L., Schrager, S. M., & Dunand, M. A. (2006). Shared suffering can mitigate aversively-generated aggression. *Aggressive Behavior, 32*(1), 80–87.

Bettencourt, B., & Miller, N. (1996). Gender differences in aggression as a function of provocation: A meta-analysis. *Psychological Bulletin, 119*(3), 422–447.

Björkqvist, K., & Niemelä, P. (1992). *Of mice and women: Aspects of female aggression.* San Diego, CA: Academic Press.

Brewer, G., Archer, J., & Manning, J. (2007). Physical attractiveness: The objective ornament and subjective self-ratings. *Journal of Evolutionary Psychology, 5*(1), 29–38.

Budesheim, T. L., & DePaola, S. J. (1994). Beauty or the beast? The effects of appearance, personality, and issue information on evaluations of political candidates. *Personality and Social Psychology Bulletin, 20*(4), 339–348.

Bushman, B. J. (1998). Priming effects of media violence on the accessibility of aggressive constructs in memory. *Personality and Social Psychology Bulletin, 24*(5), 537–545.

Bushman, B. J., & Anderson, C. A. (2002). Violent video games and hostile expectations: A test of the general aggression model. *Personality and Social Psychology Bulletin, 28*(12), 1679–1686.

Buss, D. M. (1986). Can social science be anchored in evolutionary biology? Four problems and a strategic solution. *Revue Européenne des Sciences Sociales, 24*(73), 41–50.

Buss, D. M. (1988). The evolution of human intrasexual competition: tactics of mate attraction. *Journal of Personality and Social Psychology, 54*(4), 616.

Buss, D. M. (1989). Sex differences in human mate preferences: Evolutionary hypotheses tested in 37 cultures. *Behavioral and Brain Sciences, 12*(1), 1–14.

Buss, D. M. (1993). Strategic individual differences: The evolutionary psychology of selection, evocation, and manipulation. *Life Science Research Reports, 53*, 121-121.

Buss, D. M. (1995). Evolutionary psychology: A new paradigm for psychological science. *Psychological Inquiry, 6*, 1–49.

Buss, D. M. (1996). Social adaptation and five major factors of personality. In J. S. Wiggins (Ed.), *The five-factor model of personality: Theoretical perspectives* (pp. 180–207). New York: Guilford.

Buss, D. M. (2009). How can evolutionary psychology successfully explain personality and individual differences? *Perspectives on Psychological Science, 4*(4), 359–366.

Buss, D. M., & Greiling, H. (1999). Adaptive individual differences. *Journal of Personality, 67*(2), 209–243.

Buss, D. M., Larsen, R. J., Westen, D., & Semmelroth, J. (1992). Sex differences in jealousy: Evolution, physiology, and psychology. *Psychological Science, 3*(4), 252–255.

Buss, D. M., & Schmitt, D. P. (1993) Sexual strategies theory: An evolutionary perspective on human mating. *Psychological Review, 100*(2), 204–232.

Buss, D. M., & Shackelford, T. K. (1997a). From vigilance to violence: Mate retention tactics in married couples. *Journal of Personality and Social Psychology, 72*(2), 346–361.

Buss, D. M., & Shackelford, T. K. (1997b). Human aggression in evolutionary psychological perspective. *Clinical Psychology Review, 17*(6), 605–619.

Buunk, B. P., & Dijkstra, P. (2004). Gender differences in rival characteristics that evoke jealousy in response to emotional versus sexual infidelity. *Personal Relationships, 11*(4), 395–408.

Campbell, A. (1999). Staying alive: Evolution, culture, and women's intrasexual aggression. *Behavioral and Brain Sciences, 22*(2), 203–214.

Campbell, A. (2004). Female competition: Causes, constraints, content, and contexts. *Journal of Sex Research, 41*(1), 16–26.

Campbell, A., Muncer, S., & Bibel, D. (1998). Female-female criminal assault: An evolutionary perspective. *Journal of Research in Crime and Delinquency, 35*(4), 413–428.

Campbell, A., Muncer, S., & Bibel, D. (2001). Women and crime: An evolutionary approach. *Aggression and Violent Behavior, 6*(5), 481–497.

Cohen, D., Nisbett, R. E., Bowdle, B. F., & Schwarz, N. (1996). Insult, aggression, and the Southern culture of honor: An "experimental ethnography." *Journal of Personality and Social Psychology, 70*(5), 945–960.

Dailey, R. M., Lee, C. M., & Spitzber, B. H. (2007). Communicative aggression: Toward a more interactional view of psychological abuse. In B. H. Spitzberg & W. R. Cupach (Eds.), *The dark side of interpersonal communication* (pp. 297–396). Mahwah, NJ: Lawrence Erlbaum Associates.

Davidson, R. J., Putnam, K. M., & Larson, C. L. (2000). Dysfunction in the neural circuitry of emotion regulation—a possible prelude to violence. *Science, 289*(5479), 591–594.

DeShields, O. W. Jr., Kara, A., & Kaynak, E. (1996). Source effects in purchase decisions: The impact of physical attractiveness and accent of salesperson. *International Journal of Research in Marketing, 13*(1), 89–101.

DeSteno, D. A., & Salovey, P. (1996). Evolutionary origins of sex differences in jealousy? Questioning the "fitness" of the model. *Psychological Science, 7*(6), 367–372.

Dijkstra, P., & Buunk, B. P. (2002). Sex differences in the jealousy-evoking effect of rival characteristics. *European Journal of Social Psychology, 32*(6), 829–852.

Dion, K., Berscheid, E., & Walster, E. (1972). What is beautiful is good. *Journal of Personality and Social Psychology, 24*(3), 285–290.

Dollard, J., Miller, N. E., Doob, L. W., Mowrer, O. H., & Sears, R. R. (1939). *Frustration and aggression.* New Haven, CT: Yale University Press.

Durante, K. M., Griskevicius, V., Hill, S. E., Perilloux, C., & Li, N. P. (2011). Ovulation, female competition, and product choice: Hormonal influences on consumer behavior. *Journal of Consumer Research, 37*(6), 921–934.

Durante, K. M., Li, N. P., & Haselton, M. G. (2008). Changes in women's choice of dress across the ovulatory cycle: Naturalistic and laboratory task-based evidence. *Personality and Social Psychology Bulletin, 34*, 1451–1460.

Eagly, A. H., Ashmore, R. D., Makhijani, M. G., & Longo, L. C. (1991). What is beautiful is good, but. . . . : A meta-analytic review of research on the physical attractiveness stereotype. *Psychological Bulletin, 110*(1), 109–128.

Eagly, A. H., & Steffen, V. J. (1986). Gender and aggressive behavior: A meta-analytic review of the social psychological literature. *Psychological Bulletin, 100*(3), 309–330.

Ermer, E., Cosmides, L., & Tooby, J. (2008). Relative status regulates risky decision-making about resources in men: Evidence for the co-evolution of motivation and cognition. *Evolution and Human Behavior, 29*(2), 106–118.

Feinberg, D. R., Jones, B. C., Law Smith, M. J., Moore, F. R., DeBruine, L. M., Cornwell, R. E., . . . Perrett, D. I. (2006). Menstrual cycle, trait estrogen level, and masculinity preferences in the human voice. *Hormones and Behavior, 49*, 215–222.

Feingold, A. (1992). Gender differences in mate selection preferences: A test of the parental investment model. *Psychological Bulletin, 112*(1), 125–139.

Fisher, M. L. (2004). Female intrasexual competition decreases female facial attractiveness. *Proceedings of the Royal Society of London: Biology Letter, 271*, S283–S285.

Fisher, M., & Cox, A. (2009). The influence of female attractiveness on competitor derogation. *Journal of Evolutionary Psychology, 7*(2), 141–155.

Fisher, M., Cox, A., & Gordon, F. (2009). Self-promotion versus competitor derogation: The influence of sex and romantic relationship status on intrasexual competition strategy selection. *Journal of Evolutionary Psychology, 7*(4), 287–308.

Fisher, M., Shaw, S., Worth, K., Smith, L., & Reeve, C. (2010). How we view those who derogate: Perceptions of female competitor derogators. *Journal of Social, Evolutionary, and Cultural Psychology, 4*(4), 265–276.

Forrest, S., Eatough, V., & Shevlin, M. (2005). Measuring adult indirect aggression: The development and psychometric assessment of the indirect aggression scales. *Aggressive Behavior, 31*(1), 84–97.

Frankenhuis, W. E., & Del Giudice, M. (2012). When do adaptive developmental mechanisms yield maladaptive outcomes? *Developmental Psychology, 48*(3), 628.

Gallup, A. C., O'Brien, D. T., White, D. D., & Wilson, D. S. (2009). Peer victimization in adolescence has different effects on the sexual behavior of male and female college students. *Personality and Individual Differences, 46*(5), 611–615.

Gallup, A. C., O'Brien, D. T., & Wilson, D. S. (2011). Intrasexual peer aggression and dating behavior during adolescence: An evolutionary perspective. *Aggressive Behavior, 37*(3), 258–267.

Gallup, A. C., & Wilson, D. S. (2009). Body mass index (BMI) and peer aggression in adolescent females: An evolutionary perspective. *Journal of Social, Evolutionary, and Cultural Psychology, 3*(4), 356–371.

Gangestad, S. W., Simpson, J. A., Cousins, A. J., Garver-Apgar, C. E., & Christensen, P. N. (2004). Women's preference of male behavioral displays change across the menstrual cycle. *Psychological Science, 15*(2), 203–207.

Gangestad, S. W., & Thornhill, R. (1998). Menstrual cycle variation in women's preferences for the scent of symmetrical men. *Proceedings of the Royal Society: Biological Sciences, 265*(1399), 927–933.

Geen, R. G. (1998). Aggression and antisocial behavior. In D. T. Gilbert, S. T. Fiske, & G. Lindzey (Eds.), *The handbook of social psychology* (4th ed., Vol. 2, pp. 317–356). New York: McGraw-Hill.

Glover, V. (2011). Annual research review: Prenatal stress and the origins of psychopathology: an evolutionary perspective. *Journal of Child Psychology and Psychiatry, 52*(4), 356–367.

Grabe, M. E., Bas, O., Pagano, L. A., & Samson, L. (2012). The architecture of female competition: Derogation of a sexualized female news anchor. *Journal of Evolutionary Psychology, 10*(3), 107–133.

Grafen, A. (1990). Biological signals as handicaps. *Journal of Theoretical Biology, 144*, 517–546.

Grammer, K. (1993). 5-α-androst-16en-3α-on: A male pheromone? A brief report. *Ethology and Sociobiology, 14*, 201–208.

Grammer, K., Renninger, L. A., & Fischer, B. (2004). Disco clothing, female sexual motivation, and relationship status: Is she dressed to impress? *Journal of Sex Research, 41*, 66–74.

Greiling, H., & Buss, D. M. (2000). Women's sexual strategies: The hidden dimension of extra-pair mating. *Personality and Individual Differences, 28*(5), 929–963.

Griskevicius, V., Tybur, J. M., Gangestad, S. W., Perea, E. F., Shapiro, J. R., & Kenrick, D. T. (2009). Aggress to impress: Hostility as an evolved context-dependent strategy. *Journal of Personality and Social Psychology, 96*(5), 980–994.

Hasan, Y., Bègue, L., & Bushman, B. J. (2013). Violent video games stress people out and make them more aggressive. *Aggressive Behavior, 39*(1), 64–70.

Haselton, M. G., Mortezaie, M., Pillsworth, E. G., Bleske-Rechek, A., & Frederick, D. A. (2007). Ovulatory shifts in human female ornamentation: Near ovulation, women dress to impress. *Hormones and Behavior, 51*, 40–45.

Havlicek, J., Roberts, S. C., & Flegr, J. (2005). Women's preference for dominant male odour: Effects of menstrual cycle and relationship status. *Biology Letters, 1*, 256–259.

Hawley, P. H. (2003). Strategies of control, aggression, and morality in preschoolers: An evolutionary perspective. *Journal of Experimental Child Psychology, 85*(3), 213–235.

Hawley, P. H., Johnson, S. E., Mize, J. A., & McNamara, K. A. (2007). Physical attractiveness in preschoolers: Relationships with power, status aggression, and social sckills. *Journal of School Psychology, 45,* 499–521.

Hawley, P. H., Little, T. D., & Card, N. A. (2007). The allure of a mean friend: Relationship quality and processes of aggressive adolescents with prosocial skills. *International Journal of Behavioral Development, 31*(2), 170–180.

Hess, N. H., & Hagen, E. H. (2006). Sex differences in indirect aggression: Psychological evidence from young adults. *Evolution and Human Behavior, 27*(3), 231–245.

Hill, S. E., & Durante, K. M. (2009). Do women feel worse to look their best? Testing the relationship between self-esteem and fertility status across the menstrual cycle. *Personality and Social Psychology Bulletin, 35*(12), 1592–1601.

Hogben, M. (1998) Factors moderating the effect of televised aggression on viewer behavior. *Communication Research, 25*(2), 220–247.

Holtzman, N. S., Augustine, A. A., & Senne, A. L. (2011). Are pro-social or socially aversive people more physically symmetrical? Symmetry in relation to over 200 personality variables. *Journal of Research in Personality, 45,* 687–691.

Hrdy, S. B. (1999). *Mother nature.* New York: Pantheon Books.

Hudders, L., De Backer, C., Fisher, M., & Vyncke, P. (2014). The rival wears Prada: Luxury consumption as a female competition strategy. *Evolutionary Psychology, 12*(3), 570–587.

Huesmann, L. R., & Guerra, N. G. (1997). Children's normative beliefs about aggression and aggressive behavior. *Journal of Personality and Social Psychology, 72*(2), 408.

Infante, D. A. (1995). Teaching students to understand and control verbal aggression. *Communication Education, 44*(1), 51–63.

Infante, D. A., & Rancer, A. S. (1982). A conceptualization and measure of argumentativeness. *Journal of Personality Assessment, 46*(1), 72–80.

Ingram, G. P. (2013). From hitting to tattling to gossip: An evolutionary rationale for the development of indirect aggression. *Evolutionary Psychology, 12*(2), 343–363.

Johnston, V. S., Hagel, R., Franklin, M., Fink, B., & Grammer, K. (2001). Male facial attractiveness, Evidence for hormones-mediated adaptive design. *Evolution and Human Behavior, 22,* 251–267.

Kaighobadi, F., Shackelford, T. K., & Buss, D. M. (2010). Spousal mate retention in the newlywed year and three years later. *Personality and Individual Differences, 48*(4), 414–418.

Kenrick, D. T., Sadalla, E. K., Groth, G., & Trost, M. R. (1990). Evolution, traits, and the stages of human courtship: Qualifying the parental investment model. *Journal of Personality, 58*(1), 97–116.

La Freniere, P. L., & Charlesworth, W. R. (1983). Dominance, attention, and affiliation in a preschool group: A nine-month longitudinal study. *Ethology and Sociobiology, 4*(2), 55–67.

Langlois, J. H., Kalakanis, L., Rubenstein, A. J., Larson, A., Hallam, M., & Smoot, M. (2000). Maxims or myths of beauty? A meta-analytic and theoretical review. *Psychological Bulletin, 126*(3), 390–423.

Lassek, W. D., & Gaulin, S. J. (2008). Waist-hip ratio and cognitive ability: Is gluteofemoral fat a privileged store of neurodevelopmental resources? *Evolution and Human Behavior, 29*(1), 26–34.

Law Smith, M. J., Perrett, D. I., Jones, B. C., Cornwell, R. E., Moore, F. R., Feinberg, D. R., . . . Hillier, S. G. (2006). Facial appearance is a cue to oestrogen levels in women. *Proceedings of the Royal Society of London, Series B, 273,* 135–140.

Lazarus, R. S. (1993). From psychological stress to the emotions: A history of changing outlooks. *Annual Review of Psychology, 44*(1), 1–22.

Leenaars, L. S., Dane, A. V., & Marini, Z. A. (2008). Evolutionary perspective on indirect victimization in adolescence: The role of attractiveness, dating and sexual behavior. *Aggressive Behavior, 34*(4), 404–415.

Levine, T. R., Kotowski, M. R., Beatty, M. J., & Van Kelegom, M. J. (2012). A meta-analysis of trait-behavior correlations. *Journal of Language and Social Psychology, 31*(1), 95–111.

Li, N. P., Bailey, J. M., Kenrick, D. T., & Linsenmeier, J. A. (2002). Necessities and luxuries of mate preferences: Testing the tradeoffs. *Journal of Personality and Social Psychology, 82,* 947–955.

Lin, J. (2013). Do video games exert stronger effects on aggression than film? The role of media interactivity and identification on the association of violent content and aggressive outcomes. *Computers in Human Behavior, 29*(3), 535–543.

Lipson, S. F., & Ellison, P. T. (1996). Comparison of salivary steroid profiles in naturally occurring conception and non-conception cycles. *Human Reproduction, 11,* 2090–2096.

Lukaszewski, A. W., & Roney, J. R. (2011). The origins of extraversion: Joint effects of facultative calibration and genetic polymorphism. *Personality and Social Psychology Bulletin, 37,* 409–421.

Mack, D., & Rainey, D. (1990). Female applicants' grooming and personnel selection. *Journal of Social Behavior & Personality, 5*(5), 399–407.

Maner, J. K., Kenrick, D. T., Becker, D. V., Robertson, T. E., Hofer, B., Neuberg, S. L., & Schaller, M. (2005). Functional projection: How fundamental social motives can bias interpersonal perception. *Journal of Personality and Social Psychology, 88*(1), 63–78.

Martins, N., & Wilson, B. J. (2012). Mean on the screen: Social aggression in programs popular with children. *Journal of Communication, 62*(6), 991–1009.

Massar, K., Buunk, A. P., & Dechesne, M. (2009). Jealousy in the blink of an eye: Jealous reactions following subliminal exposure to rival characteristics. *European Journal of Social Psychology, 39,* 768–799.

Massar, K., Buunk, A. P., & Rempt, S. (2012). Age differences in women's tendency to gossip are mediated by their mate value. *Personality and Individual Differences, 52,* 106–109.

Maynard Smith, J., & Harper, D. (2003) *Animal signals.* Oxford: Oxford University Press.

Maynard Smith, J., & Price, G. R. (1973). The logic of animal conflict. *Nature, 246,* 15–18.

Miller, G. F. (2000). *The mating mind: How sexual selection shaped the evolution of human nature.* New York: Doubleday.

Møller, A. P. (2006). A review of developmental instability, parasitism and disease. *Infection, Genetics and Evolution, 6,* 133–140.

Mulford, M., Orbell, J., Shatto, C., & Stockard, J. (1998). Physical attractiveness, opportunity, and success in everyday exchange 1. *American Journal of Sociology, 103*(6), 1565–1592.

Muñoz-Reyes, J. A., Gil-Burmann, C., Fink, B., & Turiegano, E. (2012, October). *Facial asymmetry and aggressiveness in Spanish adolescents.* Paper presented at the Biennial International Conference on Human Ethology, Vienna.

Nansel, T. R., Craig, W., Overpeck, M. D., Saluja, G., & Ruan, W. (2004). Cross-national consistency in the relationship between bullying behaviors and psychosocial adjustment. *Archives of Pediatrics & Adolescent Medicine, 158*(8), 730–736.

Nelson, C. K. (2004). Classifying communibiology's texts: Implications for genre theory. *Communication Theory, 14*(2), 142–166.

Nelson, R. J., & Trainor, B. C. (2007). Neural mechanisms of aggression. *Nature Reviews Neuroscience, 8*(7), 536–546.

Paik, H., & Comstock, G. (1994). The effect of television violence on antisocial behavior: A meta-analysis 1. *Communication Research, 21*(4), 516–546.

Pellegrini, A. D., & Long, J. D. (2003). A sexual selection theory longitudinal analysis of sexual segregation and integration in early adolescence. *Journal of Experimental Child Psychology, 85*(3), 257–278.

Penton-Voak, I. S., & Perrett, D. I., (2000). Female preference for male faces changes cyclically: Further evidence. *Evolution and Human Behavior, 21*, 39–48.

Perrett, D. I., Burt, D. M., Penton-Voak, I. S., Lee, K. J., Rowland, D. A., & Edwards, R. (1999). Symmetry and human facial attractiveness. *Evolution and Human Behavior, 20*(5), 295–307.

Perrett, D. I., Lee, K. J., Penton-Voak, I., Rowland, D., Yoshikawa, S., Burt, D. M., ... Akamatsu, S. (1998). Effects of sexual dimorphism on facial attractiveness. *Nature, 394*, 884–887.

Perry, D. G., Perry, L. C., & Rasmussen, P. (1986). Cognitive social learning mediators of aggression. *Child Development, 57*(3), 700–711.

Price, M. E., Dunn, J., Hopkins, S., & Kang, J. (2012). Anthropometric correlates of human anger. *Evolution and Human Behavior, 33*(3), 174–181.

Price, M. E., Kang, J., Dunn, J., & Hopkins, S. (2011). Muscularity and attractiveness as predictors of human egalitarianism. *Personality and Individual Differences, 50*(5), 636–640.

Puts, D. A. (2005). Mating context and menstrual phase affect women's preferences for male voice pitch. *Evolution and Human Behavior, 26*, 388–397.

Puts, D. A. (2006). Cyclic variation in women's preferences for masculine traits, potential hormonal causes. *Human Nature, 17*(1), 114–127.

Reid, S. A., Zhang, J., Anderson, G. L., Gasiorek, J. Bonilla, D., & Peinado, S. (2012). Parasite primes make foreign accented English sound more distant to people who are disgusted by pathogens (but not by sex or morality). *Evolution and Human Behavior, 33*(5), 471–478.

Reingen, P. H., & Kernan, J. B. (1993). Social perception and interpersonal influence: Some consequences of the physical attractiveness stereotype in a personal selling setting. *Journal of Consumer Psychology, 2*(1), 25–38.

Rhodes, G., Hickford, C., & Jeffery, L. (2000). Sex-typicality and attractiveness: Are supermale and superfemale faces super-attractive? *British Journal of Psychology, 91*, 125–140.

Rhodes, G., Simmons, L. W., & Peters, M. (2005). Attractiveness and sexual behavior: does attractiveness enhance mating success? *Evolution and Human Behavior, 26*(2), 186–201.

Rhodes, G., Zebrowitz, L. A., Clark, A., Kalick, S. M., Hightower, A. & McKay, R. (2001). Do facial average and symmetry signal health? *Evolution and Human Behavior, 22*, 31–46.

Roney, J. R., & Simmons, Z. L. (2008). Women's estradiol predicts preference for facial cues of men's testosterone. *Hormones and Behavior, 53*, 14–19.

Roy, R., & Benenson, J. F. (2002). Sex and contextual effects on children's use of interference competition. *Developmental Psychology, 38*(2), 306.

Sapolsky, R. M. (2004). Social status and health in humans and other animals. *Annual Review of Anthropology, 33*, 393–418.

Schwarz, S., & Hassebrauck, M. (2008). Self-perceived and observed variations in women's attractiveness throughout the menstrual cycle: A diary study. *Evolution and Human Behavior, 29*(4), 282–288.

Searcy, W. A., & Nowicki, S. (2005). *The evolution of animal communication: Reliability and deception in signaling systems.* Princeton, NJ: Princeton University Press.

Sell, A., Cosmides, L., Tooby, J., Sznycer, D., von Rueden, C., & Gurven, M. (2009). Human adaptations for the visual assessment of strength and fighting ability from the body and face. *Proceedings of the Royal Society B: Biological Sciences, 276*(1656), 575–584.

Sell, A., Tooby, J., & Cosmides L. (2009). Formidability and the logic of human anger. *Proceedings of the National Academy of Sciences of the United States of America, 106*(35), 15073–15078.

Shaw, A. Z. Kotowski, M. R., Boster, F. J., Levine, T. R. (2012). The effect of prenatal sex hormones on the development of verbal aggression. *Journal of Communication, 62*, 778–793.

Sherry, J. (2001). The effects of violent video games on aggression. *Human Communication Research, 27*(3), 409–431.

Singh, D. (1995). Female health, attractiveness, and desirability for relationships: Role of breast asymmetry and waist-to-hip ratio. *Ethology and Sociobiology, 16*, 465–481.

Singh, D., & Young, R. K. (1995). Body weight, waist-to-hip ratio, breasts, and hips: Role in judgments of female attractiveness and desirability for relationships. *Ethology and Sociobiology, 16*, 483–507.

Smith, S. L., & Donnerstein, E. (1998). Harmful effects of exposure to media violence: Learning of aggression, emotional desensitization, and fear. In R. G. Geen & E. Donnerstein (Eds.), *Human aggression* (pp. 169–195). New York: Academic Press.

Sugiyama, L. S. (2005). Physical attractiveness in adaptationist perspective. In D. M. Buss (Ed.), *The handbook of evolutionary psychology* (pp. 292–343). Hoboken, NJ: John Wiley.

Symons, D. (1979). *The evolution of human sexuality.* New York: Oxford University Press.

Symons, D. (1995). Beauty is in the adaptations of the beholder: The evolutionary psychology of human female sexual attractiveness. In P. R. Abramson & S. D. Pinker (Eds.), *Sexual nature, sexual culture* (pp. 80–120). Chicago: University of Chicago Press.

Terrell, H. K., Patock-Peckham, J. A., & Nagoshi, C. T. (2009). Effects of sex, status, and mating cues on expected aggressive responses. *Aggressive Behavior, 35*(3), 259–273.

Thornhill, R., & Gangestad, S. W. (1994). Human fluctuating asymmetry and sexual behavior. *Psychological Science, 5*(5), 297–302.

Thornhill, R., & Gangestad, S. W. (1999). The scent of symmetry: A human sex pheromone that signals fitness? *Evolution and Human Behavior, 20*, 175–201.

Thornhill, R., & Gangestad, S. W. (2008). *The evolution biology of human female sexuality.* New York: Oxford University Press.

Thornhill, R., & Grammer, K. (1999). The body and face of a woman: One ornament that signals quality. *Evolution and Human Behavior, 20,* 105–120.

Tinbergen, N. (2005). On aims and methods of ethology. *Animal Biology, 55*(4), 297–321.

Tooby, J. (1985). The emergence of evolutionary psychology. Emerging syntheses in science. In *Proceedings of the founding workshops of the Santa Fe Institute.* Santa Fe, NM: Santa Fe Institute.

Tooby, J., & Cosmides, L. (1990a). On the universality of human nature and the uniqueness of the individual: The role of genetics and adaptation. *Journal of Personality, 58*(1), 17–67.

Tooby, J., & Cosmides, L. (1990b). The past explains the present: Emotional adaptations and the structure of ancestral environments. *Ethology and Sociobiology, 11*(4), 375–424.

Tooby, J., & Cosmides, L. (1992). Psychological foundations of culture. In J. Barkow, L. Cosmides, & J. Tooby (Eds.). *The adapted mind* (pp. 19–136). New York: Oxford University Press.

Tooby, J., & Cosmides, L. (2010). Groups in mind: The coalitional roots of war and morality. In H. Høgh-Olesen (Ed.), *Human morality and sociality: Evolutionary and comparative perspectives* (pp. 191–234). New York: Palgrave Macmillan.

Tooby, J., Cosmides, L., Sell, A., Lieberman, D., & Sznycer, D. (2008). Internal regulatory variables and the design of human motivation: A computational and evolutionary approach. In A. J. Elliot (Ed.), *Handbook of approach and avoidance motivation* (pp. 251–272). New York: Psychology Press.

Tooke, W., & Camire, L. (1991). Patterns of deception in intersexual and intrasexual mating strategies. *Ethology and Sociobiology, 12,* 345–364.

Townsend, J. M. (1989). Mate selection criteria: A pilot study. *Ethology and Sociobiology, 10*(4), 241–253.

Trivers, R. L. (1972). Parental investment and sexual selection. In E. B. Campbell (Ed.), *Sexual selection and the descent of man 1871–1971* (pp. 136–179). Chicago: Aldine.

Trivers, R. (2000). The elements of a scientific theory of self-deception. *Annals of the New York Academy of Sciences, 907*(1), 114–131.

Vaillancourt, T., & Sharma, A. (2011). Intolerance of sexy peers: Intrasexual competition among women. *Aggressive Behavior, 37*(6), 569–577.

Valencic, K. M., Beatty, M. J., Rudd, J. E., Dobos, J. A., & Heisel, A. D. (1998). An empirical test of a communibiological model of trait verbal aggressiveness, *Communication Quarterly, 46,* 327–341.

Vrij, A., Van der Steen, J., & Koppelaar, L. (1994). Aggression of police officers as a function of temperature: An experiment with the firearms training system. *Journal of Community & Applied Social Psychology, 4*(5), 365–370.

Weiderman M. W., & Allgeier, E. R. (1992). Gender differences in mate selection criteria: Sociobiological or socioeconomic explanation? *Ethology and Sociobiology, 13,* 115–124.

Willer, E. K., & Cupach, W. R. (2008). When "sugar and spice" turn to "fire and ice": Factors affecting the adverse consequences of relational aggression among adolescent girls. *Communication Studies, 59*(4), 415–429.

Willer, E. K., & Soliz, J. (2010). Face need, intragroup status, and women's reactions to socially aggressive face threats. *Personal Relationships, 17,* 557–571.

Williams, D., & Skoric, M. (2005). Internet fantasy violence: A test of aggression in an online game. *Communication Monographs, 72*(2), 217–233.

Williams, G. C. (1966). *Adaptation and natural selection: A critique of some current evolutionary thought.* Princeton, NJ: Princeton University Press.

Wilson, E. O. (2000). Sex and society. In E. O. Wilson, *Sociobiology: The new synthesis* (pp. 314–335). Cambridge, MA: Belknap Press.

Wood, W., & Eagly, A. H. (2002). A cross-cultural analysis of the behavior of women and men: Implications for the origins of sex differences. *Psychological Bulletin, 128*(3), 699–727.

Yanca, C., & Low, B. S. (2004). Female allies and female power: A cross-cultural analysis. *Evolution and Human Behavior, 25*(1), 9–23.

Zahavi, A. (1975). Mate selection: A selection for a handicap. *Journal of Theoretical Biology, 53,* 205–214.

Zhang, J., & Reid, S. A. (2013, June). *Women's voices as a cue of physical attractiveness and a courtship signal: The interaction effect of perceived vocal attractiveness and pitch shifts on men's mating psychology.* Paper presented as the annual International Communication Association Convention, London.

Ziomkiewicz, A., Ellison, P. T., Lipson, S. F., Thune, I., & Jasiénska, G. (2008). Body fat, energy balance and estradiol levels: A study based on hormonal profiles from complete menstrual cycles. *Human Reproduction, 23*(11), 2555–2563.

How "The Gossip" Became a Woman and How "Gossip" Became Her Weapon of Choice

Francis T. McAndrew

Abstract

Gossip is the weapon of choice in the indirect relationship aggression that occurs among women. However, gossip can also be a positive force in the life of groups. In this chapter, I maintain that gossip is an evolutionary adaptation that enabled our prehistoric ancestors to be socially successful and explore the complicated roles gossip plays in human social life. I argue that an interest in the affairs of same-sex others is especially strong among females and that this is not always benign. I review the evidence that women are more likely than men to use gossip in an aggressive, competitive manner and maintain that understanding the dynamics of competitive gossip may also give us insight into related social phenomena such as how people use social media such as Facebook and why men and women often have such different tastes in movies and television.

Key Words: gossip, sex differences, aggression, female competition, evolutionary psychology, Facebook

Gossip is an enigma. It can be a tool for building or destroying reputations, or it can be the cohesive glue that holds a group together. It can be a self-affirming source of social-comparison information or a devastating conduit of betrayal. It may even be the instrument used to banish an individual from the group entirely. In this chapter, I explore these seemingly contradictory functions of gossip and trace the path by which gossip has become historically and stereotypically more strongly associated with women than with men. I also examine the ways in which gossip serves as the primary vehicle for indirect aggression in social competition between women.

Although everyone seems to detest a person who is known as a "gossip," and few people would use that label to describe themselves, it is an exceedingly unusual individual who can walk away from a juicy story about one of his or her acquaintances. Each of us has had firsthand experience with the difficulty of keeping spectacular news about someone else

a secret, but why does private information about other people represent such an irresistible temptation for us? It is only in the past fifteen years or so that psychologists have turned their attention toward the study of gossip, partially because it is difficult to define exactly what it is. Most researchers agree that the practice involves talk about people who are not present and that this talk is relaxed, informal, and entertaining (Dunbar, Duncan, & Marriott, 1997; Levin & Arluke, 1987; Morreal, 1994; Rosnow & Fine, 1976; Spacks, 1985). Typically, the topic of conversation also concerns information that we can make moral judgments about (McAndrew, 2008). Beersma and Van Kleef (2012) distinguished four distinct motives for gossiping: to influence others negatively, to gather and validate information, for social enjoyment and entertainment, and to protect the group from some internal threat. Of these motives, the gathering and validating of information appears to be the most common one. In his book *Grooming, Gossip, and the*

Evolution of Language, British psychologist Robin Dunbar (1996) suggested that gossip is a mechanism for bonding social groups together, analogous to the grooming that is found in primate groups, and other researchers have proposed that gossip is one of the best tools that we have for comparing ourselves socially with others (Suls, 1977; Wert & Salovey, 2004). The ultimate question, however, is how did gossip come to serve these functions in the first place? Let us begin with the story of how gossip has become so strongly associated with women (Rosnow & Fine, 1976; Spacks, 1985).

How Did "The Gossip" Become a Woman?

The title of this chapter was inspired by an article published by Alexander Rysman (1977) in which he asks a very interesting question: How, in the convoluted linguistic history of the word "gossip," did this brand of social behavior become so intimately identified with women? The answer lies in the very root of the word itself.

The term is derived from the Old English phrase *God Sib,* which literally translates as "god parent." The term originally referred to companions who were not relatives but who were intimate enough to be named as godparents to one's child. These companions were almost always females, and they were usually present during labor and the birth of a child. Apparently, medieval European births were very social affairs restricted entirely to women. The hours were passed in conversation and moral support, and it undoubtedly was a strong bonding experience among those who were present (Rysman, 1977). Thus, the original word was a noun specifically referring to the female companions of a woman during childbirth, and it was entirely benign in its usage. However, by the 1500s, the word had taken on a decidedly negative connotation. The first known literary use of the word in this negative context occurred in Shakespeare's *Midsummer Night's Dream,* and the Oxford English Dictionary defines the sixteenth-century use of the word as describing a woman "of light and trifling character" who "delights in "idle talk" and was a "newsmonger" or a "tattler" (www.OED.com). Rysman suggested (perhaps facetiously) that the word acquired negative connotations over time because one of the side effects of women coming together in solidarity was an increase in hassles for men! It was not until the 1800s that the word was applied to a type of conversation rather than to the person engaging in the conversation.

The useful social role played by gossip in human groups is often overshadowed by the way it is employed by individuals to further their own reputations and selfish interests at the expense of others (Dunbar, 1996; Emler, 1994; Spacks, 1985). The recognition of gossip's potential for social disruption is everywhere reflected in a wide variety of laws, punishments, and moral codes designed to control it (Emler, 1994; Goodman & Ben-Ze'ev, 1994). One need look no further than the Bible for examples of societal efforts to stifle destructive gossip:

> A perverse man stirs up dissension, and a gossip separates close friends.
> *(Proverbs 16:28)*

> The words of a gossip are like choice morsels; they go down to a man's inmost parts.
> *(Proverbs 18:7–8)*

> For every kind of beast and bird, of reptile and sea creature, can be tamed and has been tamed by mankind, but no human being can tame the tongue. It is a restless evil, full of deadly poison.
> *(James 3:7–8)*

> They were filled with all manner of unrighteousness, evil, covetousness, malice. They are full of envy, murder, strife, deceit, maliciousness. They are gossips.
> *(James 3:7–8)*

A notable exception to the Bible's pervasive use of the male pronoun and references to men in general in its dictums can be found in an unkind description of widows:

> Besides that, they learn to be idlers, going about from house to house, and not only idlers, but also gossips and busybodies, saying what they should not.
> *(1 Timothy 5:13)*

And let us not forget that one of the Ten Commandments is "Thou shalt not bear false witness against thy neighbor."

Thus, there have always been legal and religious sanctions that could be brought to bear upon gossipers who crossed a line and gossiped about the wrong people at the wrong time. Most nations still have laws against slander on the books, and until relatively recently dueling to the death was considered an honorable way of dealing with those who had transgressed against one's reputation and good name. However, an examination of historical European tactics for handling gossipers reveals a persistent concern with clamping down on the gossip of women. The two most common punishments

Figure 11.1 The Scold's Bridle.

for gossipers in Europe and colonial America from the early 1500s to the early 1800s were almost exclusively reserved for women: the "Scold's Bridle" and the "Ducking Stool."

The Scold's Bridle (sometimes referred to as the "Brank's Bridle," or more simply, "The Branks") was a device used to publicly punish and humiliate women who were perceived as quarrelsome or as gossips, shrews, or scolds. It first appeared in Britain during the 1500s (Science Museum of London, 2013) and it gradually spread to several other European countries, becoming especially popular in Germany. The Scold's Bridle was a heavy iron mask,

somewhat like a cage, that fit tightly over a woman's head (see Figure 11.1). The mask included a flat piece of iron. This flat piece of iron was sometimes spiked, and it was thrust into the woman's mouth over her tongue. While wearing a Scold's Bridle, a woman would be completely unable to speak (Cox, 2003). Variations of the Scold's Bridle sometimes included a bell on top of it to attract attention and/ or a ring attached to a chain so that a husband could drag his wife around the village and subject her to the ridicule of others. The Scold's Bridle was employed with the approval of the church and local authorities, and in some villages the Bridle was actually kept in a cabinet in the church when not in use (Canadian Broadcasting Company, 2012).

The origins of the Ducking Stool are shrouded in the mist of time, but it was in wide use by the late medieval period, and it remained in use well into the 1800s in western Europe and colonial America. The Ducking Stool was reserved almost exclusively for women, although occasionally quarrelsome married couples were tied back-to-back and subjected to it together (Cox, 2003). Ducking Stools consisted of a chair fixed to the end of two long beams, usually between 12 and 15 feet in length (see Figure 11.2). The woman was strapped into the chair, hoisted out over a pond or river, and then plunged underwater by several men who operated the apparatus from land. The number of times she was dunked and the length of each submersion depended on the degree to which her gossip had been deemed harmful to the community, and it undoubtedly also depended on the political connections of the people she had offended. For especially serious offenses, a woman could be kept in the chair for hours and subjected to repeated dunkings. Beleaguered husbands could present their scolding wives for dunking with the blessing of the church. Given the condition of the

Figure 11.2 The Ducking Stool.

bodies of water located in or near towns during this period of history, what the woman was being immersed in was usually not much better than raw sewage, providing a strong incentive for her to keep her mouth tightly closed. Later in this chapter, we examine the evidence pertinent to the question of whether or not the perceived association between women and negative gossip is based on anything more than simple stereotypes.

How Might Gossip Have Become an Evolutionary Adaptation?

Gossip is central to the social life of humans. Most of our conversations are concerned with matters of social importance, and the available historical information and cross-cultural data suggest that this has always been the case. The prominent role played by gossip in the conversation of everyday people has been documented in populations as geographically diverse as medieval Europeans (Schein, 1994), the !Kung Bushmen of West Africa (Lee, 1990), the Hopi of North America (Cox, 1970), and the Kabana people of Papua New Guinea (McPherson, 1991). When evolutionary psychologists stumble upon something that is shared by people of all ages, times, and cultures, they usually suspect that they have identified a vital aspect of human nature—something that became a part of who we are in our long-forgotten prehistoric past. Examples of such evolutionary adaptations include our appreciation of landscapes containing fresh water and vegetation, our never-ending battle with our sweet tooth, and our infatuation with people who look a certain way. These adaptations enabled us to not only survive but to thrive in our prehistoric ancestral environments. In this chapter, I am exploring the possibility that our preoccupation with gossip is just another of these evolutionary adaptations.

It will be obvious to most readers that being drawn to environments that provide resources, food that provides energy, and romantic partners who appear able to help one bear and raise healthy children might very well be psychological adaptations that evolved because of their indisputable advantages. However, it may not be so clear at first glance how an interest in gossip could possibly be in the same league as these other human characteristics. If one thinks in terms of what it would have taken to be successful in our ancestral social environment, however, the idea may no longer seem quite so far-fetched.

Our ancestors lived their lives as members of small cooperative groups that were in competition with other relatively small groups (Dunbar, 1996; Lewin, 1993; Tooby & DeVore, 1987). To make matters more complicated, it was necessary to cooperate with in-group members so that the group as a whole could be successful, but competition between members of the same group was also unavoidable insofar as there was only a limited amount of food, mates, and other resources to go around (Krebs & Denton, 1997). Living in such groups, our ancestors faced a number of consistent adaptive problems that were social in nature, for example obtaining a reproductively valuable mate and successfully managing friendships, alliances, and family relationships (Shackelford, 1997). The social intelligence needed for success in this environment required an ability to predict and influence the behavior of others, and an intense interest in the private dealings of other people would have been handy indeed, and it would have been strongly favored by natural selection. In short, people who were fascinated with the lives of others were simply more successful than those who were not, and it is the genes of those individuals that have come down to us through the ages (Alexander, 1979; Barkow, 1989, 1992; Davis & McLeod, 2003; Humphrey, 1983; McAndrew, 2008). Like it or not, we are descended from busybodies, and our inability to ignore gossip and information about other individuals is as much a part of who we are as is our inability to resist doughnuts or sex—and for the same reasons.

A related social skill that would have had a big payoff is the ability to remember details about the temperament, predictability, and past behavior of individuals who were personally known. We need to be on guard against individuals who have taken advantage of us in the past so that it does not happen again (hence, our often regrettable tendency to hold grudges) and also to have clear recollections of those who have been helpful and can be counted on in future times of need. In our prehistoric past, there would have been little use for a mind that was designed to engage in abstract statistical thinking about large numbers of unknown outsiders. In today's world, it is advantageous to be able to think in terms of probabilities and percentages when it comes to people, because predicting the behavior of the strangers whom we deal with in everyday life requires that we do so. This task is difficult for many of us because the early wiring of the brain was guided by different needs. Thus, natural selection shaped a thirst for, and a memory to store, information about specific people. It is well established that we have a brain area specifically dedicated to the identification of human faces (de Haan, Pascalis, & Johnson, 2002; Nelson, 2001) and that we perceive and remember faces best when they have been paired with negative information about individuals who are described as cheaters or as socially undesirable in other ways (Anderson, Siegel, Bliss-Moreau, & Barrett, 2011; Mealey, Daood, & Krage, 1996). For better or worse, this is the mental equipment that we must rely on to navigate our way through a modern world filled with technology and strangers. I should not be surprised when the very same undergraduate students who get glassy-eyed at any mention of statistical data about human beings in general become riveted by case studies of individuals experiencing psychological or relationship problems. Successful politicians take advantage of this pervasive "power of the particular" (as cognitive psychologists call it) when they use anecdotes and personal narratives to make political points. Even the dictator Josef Stalin noted that "one death is a tragedy; a million deaths is a statistic." The prevalence of reality TV shows and nightly news programs focusing on stories about a missing child or the sexual scandals of politicians is a beast of our own creation.

Gossip may be one of the relatively few social behaviors that have been shaped by natural selection operating on individuals competing within groups as well as by natural selection acting on groups in competition with other groups (McAndrew, Bell, & Garcia, 2007). According to multilevel selection theorists such as David Sloan Wilson (1997), it is crucial to distinguish between the competition going on between individuals within the same group and the competition that occurs between individuals in different groups. Within-group selection follows the more accepted idea that individual organisms (or collections of genes) are in direct selfish competition with each other. Group-level adaptations, on the other hand, require thinking in terms of between-group selection in which groups can be thought of as adaptive units in their own right and not just as byproducts of individual self-interest (Wilson, Wilczynski, Wells, & Weiser, 2000). According to Multiple Level Selection Theory (MST), groups do not evolve into adaptive units for *all* traits but only for those that are adaptive in a group but not in an individual context. In other words, "group selection favors traits that increase the fitness of groups relative to other groups"(Wilson, 1997, p. S122).

Although MST is not inherently incompatible with more traditional evolutionary viewpoints, it is often presented as if this was the case. The most common attacks leveled against MST stem from a basic misunderstanding of what the theory is saying. Many mistakenly equate MST with long-discredited naïve theories of group selection based on organisms acting for "the good of the species" and think that MST discounts the importance of natural selection that occurs in units smaller than groups. MST does not deny that selection at lower levels of organization is vitally important; on the contrary, MST maintains that selection at the individual level occurs at a faster pace than selection at the group level (Boehm, 1997). In fact, MST maintains that traits such as altruism are selected at the group level precisely because they are ultimately adaptive to the individuals in successful groups. The confusion apparently arises over the fact that it is the individual's membership in a group faced with particular selection pressures that cause the group to become the vehicle for behaviors that benefit each individual.

If it is true that gossip evolved in response to both within-group and between-group selection pressures, the evolution of gossip as we now see it (or hear it?) would have been a delicate balancing act. Competition among members of a social group would remain adaptive to the individuals involved only so long as these competitive forces did not completely undermine the ability of the group to function as a cooperative unit. Similarly, a highly cooperative group that thwarted the reproductive fitness of too many of its members would not survive for long. Theoretically then, the gossip we see in modern humans is really a finely balanced double-bladed weapon, with one blade (a broadsword?) wielded on behalf of the group to deter free-riders and other disruptive individuals, while the other blade (a dagger?) is used more selectively and quietly by one group member against another in a quest to climb the social ladder. So, even though gossip has a bad reputation, it also serves essential positive social functions, and human society could not exist without it (Emler, 2001). I now compare what is known about self-serving, negative, within-group, "bad gossip" to the less selfish "good gossip" that serves the interests of the larger group.

"Bad Gossip": The Selfish Gossip Used Within One's Own Group

The average person's reaction to the word "gossip" is reflexively negative, probably because we most easily think of the negative, selfish use of gossip. It is true that when gossip is examined in the light of competition between people in the same social group, it is very much about enhancing one's own social success (Barkow, 1989). Gossip offers a means of manipulating others' reputations by passing on negative information about competitors or enemies as well as a means of detecting betrayal by others in our important relationships (Shackelford, 1997; Spacks, 1985). According to one of the pioneers of gossip research, anthropologist Jerry Barkow (1992), we should be especially interested in information about people who matter most in our lives: rivals, mates, relatives, partners in social exchange, and high-ranking figures whose behavior can affect us. Given the proposition that our interest in gossip evolved as a way of acquiring fitness-enhancing information, Barkow also suggests that the type of knowledge that we seek should be information that can affect our social standing relative to others. Hence, we would expect to find higher interest in negative news (such as misfortunes and scandals) about high-status people and potential rivals because we could exploit it. Negative information about those lower than us in status would not be as useful. There should also be less interest in passing along negative information about our friends and relatives than about people who are not allies. Conversely, positive information (good fortune and sudden elevation of status, for example) about allies should be likely to be spread around, whereas positive information about rivals or non-allies should be less enticing because it is not useful in advancing one's own interests.

For a variety of reasons, our interest in the doings of same-sex others ought to be especially strong. Wilson and Daly (1996), among others, have identified same-sex members of one's own species as our principal evolutionary competitors, and Shackelford (1997) has verified the cross-culturally universal importance of same-sex friendships and coalitional relationships. According to Shackelford, managing alliances and friendships posed important adaptive problems throughout human history because it was important to evaluate the quality and intentions of one's allies and rivals if one was to be successful. Given how critical such relationships are in all areas of life, and also given that such relationships would be most likely to exist between members of same-aged cohorts, we should be most interested in gossip about other people of the same sex who are close to us in age. Hence, the eighteen-year-old male caveman would have done much better by attending to the business of other eighteen-year-old males rather than to the business of fifty-year-old males or females of any age. Interest about members of the other sex should be strong only when their age and situational circumstances would make them appropriate as mates.

The gossip studies on which my students and I have worked at Knox College over the past fifteen years (e.g., Goranson & McAndrew, 2013; McAndrew & Milenkovic, 2002; McAndrew et al., 2007) have focused on uncovering what we are most interested in finding out about other people and what we are most likely to spread around. We have had people of all ages rank their interest in tabloid stories about celebrities, and we have asked college students to read gossip scenarios about unidentified individuals and tell us which types of people they would most like to hear such information about, whom they would gossip about, and with whom they would share gossip. In keeping with the evolutionary hypotheses suggested earlier, we have consistently found that people are most interested in gossip about individuals of the same sex as themselves who also happen to be around their own age. We have also found that information that is socially useful is always of greatest interest to us: we like to know about the scandals and misfortunes of our rivals and of high-status people because this information might be valuable in social competition. Positive information about such people tends to be uninteresting to us. Finding out that someone who is already higher in status than ourselves has just acquired something that puts him even further ahead of us does not supply us with ammunition that we can use to gain ground on him. Conversely, positive information about our friends and relatives is highly prized and likely to be used to our advantage whenever possible. For example, we consistently found that college students were not much interested in hearing about academic awards or a large inheritance if it involved one of their professors and that they were also not very interested in passing that news along to others. Yet the same information about their friends or romantic partners was rated as being quite interesting and likely to be spread around.

"Good Gossip": Gossip Can Serve the Interests of the Group as a Whole

In spite of its generally negative reputation, studies indicate that most gossip cannot be accurately described as malicious in its intent (Ben-Ze'ev, 1994; Dunbar et al., 1997; Fine & Rosnow, 1978; Goodman & Ben-Ze'ev, 1994; Spacks, 1985), and this is just as true for women as it is for men. Levin and Arluke (1987), among others, have proposed that gossip is universal because it is psychologically and socially useful. Anthropologists have frequently identified gossip as a cultural device that can be used not only by individuals to advance their own interests but also as a means by which groups can enforce conformity to group norms (Abrahams, 1970; Cox, 1970; Lee, 1990). It is this dual nature of gossip that creates so much ambivalence toward it. The recognition of its importance in maintaining group life makes acceptance of it a necessity, but its potential for advancing the interests of one individual at the expense of another poses a threat that must be contained if the group is to function effectively. Thus, paradoxically, gossip can serve both as a form of antisocial behavior *and* as a means of controlling antisocial behavior (Wilson et al., 2000).

Gossip probably evolved as a social control mechanism that served the interests of the group as well as the interests of individuals. Boehm (1999) proposes that gossip can serve as a "leveling mechanism" for neutralizing the dominance tendencies of others, making it a "stealthy activity by which other people's moral dossiers are constantly reviewed" (p. 73). Boehm believes that small-scale foraging societies such as those typical during human prehistory emphasized an egalitarianism that suppressed internal competition and promoted consensus seeking in a way that made the success of one's group extremely important to one's own fitness. These social pressures discouraged free-riders and cheaters and encouraged altruists (Boehm, 1997). He also believes that such egalitarian societies were necessary because of the relatively equal and unstable balance of power among individuals with access to weapons and shifting coalitions. In these societies, the manipulation of public opinion through gossip, ridicule, and ostracism became a key way of keeping potentially dominant group members in check (Boehm, 1993). Please note I am *not* proposing old-fashioned group selection here. Behaviors that favor the good of the group over the selfish interests of individuals can evolve only if the resulting success of the group trickles down and ultimately proves to be adaptive for the majority of the individuals in the group as well.

Ample evidence exists that gossip can indeed be a positive force in the life of a group. Gossip can be a way of learning the unwritten rules of social groups and cultures by resolving ambiguity about group norms and an avenue for socializing newcomers into the ways of the group (Ayim, 1994; Baumeister, Zhang, & Vohs, 2004; Laing, 1993; Noon & Delbridge, 1993; Suls, 1977). Gossip is also an efficient way of reminding group members about the importance of the group's norms and values, and it can be an effective deterrent to deviance and a low-cost form of punishment useful for enforcing cooperation in groups (Barkow, 1992; Feinberg, Cheng, & Willer, 2012; Levin & Arluke, 1987; Merry, 1984). Evolutionary biologist Robert Trivers (1971, 1985) has discussed the evolutionary importance of detecting "gross cheaters" (those who fail to reciprocate altruistic acts) and "subtle cheaters" (those who reciprocate but give much less than they get). Gossip can be an effective means of uncovering such information about others and an especially useful way of controlling these free-riders who may be tempted to violate group norms of reciprocity by taking more from the group than they give in return (Dunbar, 1996; Feinberg et al., 2012).

Studies in real-life groups such as California cattle ranchers (Ellickson, 1991), Maine lobster fishermen (Acheson, 1988), and college rowing teams (Kniffin & Wilson, 1998; Wilson & Kniffin, 1999) confirm that gossip is used in these quite different settings to maintain boundaries between the in-group and out-group and to enforce group norms when individuals fail to live up to the group's expectations. In all these groups, individuals who violated expectations about sharing resources and meeting responsibilities became frequent targets of gossip and ostracism, which put pressure on them to become better citizens. Anthropological studies of hunter-gatherer groups have typically revealed a similar social control function for gossip in these societies (Lee, 1990; McPherson, 1991). Experimental evidence also shows that prosocial gossip keeps people in line. Beersma and Van Kleef (2011) used a laboratory "dictator game" to study this problem. In their experimental game, people could contribute lottery tickets for a large monetary prize to a group pool (which would be spilt evenly among the group if there was a winning ticket), or they could keep the tickets for themselves. People who believed that other people in the group might gossip about them reduced their free-riding and increased the level of their contributions compared to people who did not believe that gossip about them would be possible or likely. Similarly, another study demonstrated that people will use gossip prosocially to rat out selfish, exploitative individuals in experimental game situations even when they have to spend money to do so (Feinberg, Willer, Stellar, & Keltner, 2012). In other words, prosocial gossip is so rewarding that people will even incur a cost for the opportunity to engage in it! In keeping with all of the findings described above, it has been documented that gossip that occurs in response to the violation of a social norm is met with approval and is often perceived as the "moral" thing to do (Beersma & Van Kleef, 2012; Wilson et al., 2000).

Individual Differences in Gossip

The jury is still out on how gossipers are perceived by others. Jaeger, Skleder, Rind, and Rosnow (1994) looked at gossip in a college sorority. They found that "low gossipers" scored higher in the need for social approval than "high gossipers." They also found that the high gossipers tended to have more close friends than low gossipers but paradoxically were perceived as less likeable than the low gossipers. Similarly, Farley (2011) discovered that high-frequency gossipers were liked significantly less than low-frequency gossipers and "negative" gossipers were liked less than "positive" gossipers. At least among fourth- through sixth-grade girls, however, gossipers are liked *more* than the targets of their gossip (Maloney, 1999). Given that being in possession of gossip gives an individual a position of power relative to others in the group, it might be expected that gossipers would be better liked and more influential. Part of the problem is that the few studies that have been conducted so far have simply looked at *how often* an individual does or does not participate in gossip, but no attempt has been made to study gossipers based on the quality of the gossip they provide or the skill with which they conduct themselves in gossip situations. I believe that using the mere frequency of gossiping as a research variable is something of a red herring, and it is quality, not quantity, that counts. It is probably the case that skillful gossipers are indeed well liked and wield a great deal of social power in groups (Farley, 2011).

I have suggested in the past that gossip is social skill rather than a character flaw, insofar as we only get in trouble when we do not do it well (McAndrew, 2008). After all, sharing gossip with another person is a sign of deep trust because the gossiper is clearly signaling that he or she believes that the person receiving the gossip will not use this sensitive information in a way that will have negative consequences for the gossiper; shared secrets also have a way of bonding people together. An individual who is not included in the office-gossip network is obviously an outsider who is not trusted or accepted by the group. Adopting the role of the self-righteous soul who refuses to participate in gossip at work or in other areas of social life ultimately will be self-defeating, and it will turn out to be nothing more

than a ticket to social isolation. On the other hand, indiscriminately blabbing everything one hears to anyone who will listen will quickly get one a reputation as an untrustworthy busybody. Successful gossiping is about being a good team player and sharing key information with others in a way that will not be perceived as self-serving and about understanding when to keep one's mouth shut. Future studies need to work on developing a valid and reliable way of assessing skill as a gossiper.

As with most psychological traits, the tendency to gossip and the need to compare one's self to others appear to be stable and measurable individual differences. Nevo, Nevo, and Derech-Zehavi (1993) have constructed a measure called the Tendency to Gossip Questionnaire, which appears to have acceptable validity and reliability. A subsequent study using the questionnaire found that individuals employed in people-oriented professions such as counselors and psychotherapists score especially high on this scale (Nevo et al., 1993). A high need to exert social power seems to be one factor that distinguishes heavy gossipers from others (Farley, Timme, & Hart, 2010).

Is Gossip Indeed the "Weapon of Choice" in Aggressive Competition Between Women?

I now return to the question of whether negative gossip is more prevalent in relationships among women. It is clear that throughout Western history, gossip was formally frowned upon and that the gossip of women in particular was identified as a serious social problem. The universality of the perceived link between women and malicious gossip is reflected in an ancient Chinese proverb stating that "the tongue is the sword of a woman—and she never lets it go rusty." However, is there any evidence to suggest that women are more prone to gossip than are men or that women are more likely to use gossip in an aggressive or socially destructive manner? The evidence suggests that the answer to these questions is "Yes."

An interest in the affairs of same-sex others is especially strong among females, and women have somewhat different patterns of sharing gossip than men do (McAndrew & Milenkovic, 2002; McAndrew et al., 2007). The studies by McAndrew and colleagues reveal that men report being far more likely to share gossip with their romantic partners than with anyone else, but women report that they would be just as likely to share gossip with their same-sex friends as with their romantic partners. And although men are usually more interested in news about other men, women are virtually obsessed with news about other women. This fact can be demonstrated by looking at the actual frequency with which men and women selected a same-sex person as the most interesting subject of the gossip scenarios presented to them in a study by McAndrew and Milenkovic (2002). On hearing about someone having a date with a famous person, forty-three out of forty-four women selected a woman as the most interesting person to know this about, as compared with twenty-four out of thirty-six men who selected a male as most interesting. Similarly, forty out of forty-two women (vs. twenty-two out of thirty-seven males) were most interested in same-sex academic cheaters, and thirty-nine out of forty-three were most interested in a same-sex leukemia sufferer (as opposed to only eighteen out of thirty-seven men). In fact, the only two scenarios among the thirteen studied in which men expressed more same-sex interest than women did involved hearing about an individual heavily in debt because of gambling or an individual who was having difficulty performing sexually.

A female preoccupation with the lives of other women has been noted by other researchers as well. For example, De Backer, Nelissen, and Fisher (2007) presented college students with gossip-like stories containing male or female characters in which the nature of the gossip presented in the stories was an important variable. After reading the stories, the participants were given a surprise recall test for the information they had been exposed to. Women remembered more about other women than men did about other men. Also, the attractiveness of female characters and the wealth of male characters were most easily recalled.

The fascination that women have with the doings of other women is not benign. It has been well established that men are more physically aggressive than women (McAndrew, 2009). However, women are much more likely to engage in indirect "relational" aggression (Vaillancourt, 2013), and gossip (with the goal of socially ostracizing rivals) is the weapon of choice in the female arsenal (Campbell, 2012; Hess & Hagen, 2006; Hines & Fry, 1994; Owens, Shute, & Slee, 2000a). Women are more likely than men to socially exclude others, a sex difference that appears as early as the age of six (Benenson, 2013). The motivation for this relational aggression can be as trivial as simple boredom, but it more often transpires in retaliation for perceived slights or envy over physical appearance or males (Owens, Shute,

& Slee, 2000b). The fact that highly attractive adolescent girls (who may be threatening because of their high mate value) are at greater risk for victimization by indirect aggression is consistent with the notion that mate competition is a motive for such aggression (Vaillancourt, 2013). Whatever the reason for it, the goal is usually to exclude competitors from one's social group and to damage their ability to maintain a reliable social network of their own (Geary & Flinn, 2002). As it turns out, this is a highly effective way of hurting other women. When a workplace bully is a woman, indirect relational aggression is the usual *modus operandi,* and her victim is almost always another woman. The levels of stress reported by the victims in these situations are extreme (Crothers, Lipinski, & Minutolo, 2009), and other studies have confirmed that females are more sensitive than males to indirect aggression and report being more devastated by it (Galen & Underwood, 1997). These findings may be connected to other research results that show that a majority of women who suffer from persecutory delusions identified familiar people such as friends and relatives as their persecutors and what they specifically feared was that they were being "talked about" or excluded from the in-group. Men suffering from persecutory delusions were much more likely to fear physical attacks by other men who were strangers (Walston, David, & Charlton, 1998).

Women spend more time gossiping overall than do men, and they are more likely to gossip about close friends and relatives (Levin & Arluke, 1985). Men, on the other hand, are more likely to talk about themselves, their work, and their own relationships and generally engage in more self-promotion than do women (Dunbar et al., 1997). The amount of gossiping that occurs between two people is a good predictor of friendship quality in men, especially if the gossip concerns achievement-related information, but the amount of gossip between two women does not predict the quality of their friendship in such a straightforward fashion (Watson, 2012). When pairs of friends gossip, it is rare for listeners to respond negatively to gossipy information, and such information usually evokes agreement and supportive responses rather than disapproval (Eder & Enke, 1991). Women in particular tend to demonstrate highly encouraging responses to gossip that they hear from their friends (Leaper & Holliday, 1995).

Evidence shows that it is specifically the gossip that occurs between women that is most likely to be aggressive and competitive. The nature of the topics that are discussed between women is qualitatively different from those that are featured in gossip between men or between a man and a woman, and the frequency of negative gossip is highest of all in gossip between female friends (Leaper & Holliday, 1995). The way that female-to-female gossip plays out is also consistent with what would be expected if gossip developed as a response to evolutionary pressures. Younger women are more likely to gossip about rivals than are older women, possibly because the competition for mates is more intense during the earlier, reproductive part of a woman's life (Massar, Buunk, & Rempt, 2012). Furthermore, the characteristics of rivals that are most likely to be attacked through malicious gossip are precisely those characteristics that have traditionally been most vital to a woman's reputation in the mating market: her physical appearance and sexual reputation (Buss & Dedden, 1990; Vaillancourt, 2013; Watson, 2012). A recent study fuels the perception that physical appearance is a primary arena of competition among women in that a woman with a "hypercompetitive personality" is significantly more likely to undergo cosmetic surgery than is a less competitive woman (Thornton, Ryckman, & Gold, 2013).

Applications: The Role of Gossip in Competition and Other Social Phenomenon

When gossip is discussed seriously, the goal usually is to suppress the frequency with which it occurs in an attempt to avoid the undeniably harmful effects it often has in work groups and other social networks. This tendency, however, overlooks that gossip is part of who we are and that it is an essential part of what makes groups function as well as they do. Understanding the nature of intrasexual competition and the role played by gossip in such competition can lead to an understanding of other seemingly unrelated phenomena. Thus, the gossip behaviors that developed to manage the social lives of our prehistoric ancestors provide the skeleton for the global social world of the Internet that we now inhabit. Theoretically, the same selection pressures that produced "good gossip" and "bad gossip" are alive and well and will continue to guide our interactions in this brave new world.

For example, understanding the dynamics of competitive gossip can generate hypotheses about how people will pursue social information and present themselves on the Internet through social media

channels such as Facebook. The Internet provides unprecedented opportunities to spread and track gossip, and it is self-evident that the face-to-face social competition that social scientists have traditionally studied now plays out in cyberspace. Given that gossip and ostracism are primarily female tactics of aggression, one would expect female aggression to be amplified by the Internet more than male aggression would be. Troubling media stories about cyberbullying on Facebook, sometimes even resulting in the suicide of the victim, usually involve female aggressors and almost always involve female victims. Studying Internet behavior in light of what we know about gossip shows great promise for helping us deal with this important problem.

Gossip studies by McAndrew et al. (2007), McAndrew and Milenkovic (2002), and De Backer, Nelisson, and Fisher (2007) discovered that most people have a greater interest in gossip about same-sex and same-age individuals, with women being especially interested in gossip about other women. The researchers concluded that this was rooted in the evolutionary necessity of keeping tabs on our competitors for status and mates, and traditionally our chief competitors are those in our own age and sex cohorts. Similarly, it is well replicated that men and women have very different mating strategies and preferences, with men seeking attractiveness, youth, and fertility in mates while advertising their own status, achievement, and access to resources and women showing the opposite pattern (Buss, 1989a, 1989b; Buss & Schmitt, 1993; Geary, 2010). These findings suggest the following predictions about how people might use Facebook.

First, everyone should spend more time looking at the Facebook pages of people about the same age as themselves. However, to the extent that this interest is driven by the social competition needs described earlier, older people should be under less pressure to do so and will exhibit less interest in same-sex peers and more interest in family. Second, there will be more interest in looking at the pages of same-sex others versus opposite-sex others, and this tendency will be even stronger in females than in males. Because of the greater emphasis placed on the physical appearance of women, females, compared to males, will spend more time on activities related to impression management with their profile pictures, and females will also spend more time looking at the photos of other people. Finally, males, compared to females, will spend more time looking at items on the pages of others that reflect an individual's status or prestige, such as educational background, work/career information, and number of Facebook friends.

Preliminary research regarding these predictions has been promising. In an Internet survey utilizing an international sample of 1,026 Facebook users (284 males, 735 females; mean age = 30.24) I conducted with one of my students, Hye Sun Jeong (McAndrew & Jeong, 2012), we discovered that, overall, women engaged in far more Facebook activity than did men. They spent more time on Facebook and they had more Facebook friends. Consistent with previous research on gossip-seeking behavior, women were more interested than men in the relationship status of others, and they were more interested in keeping tabs on the activity of other women than men were in keeping tabs on the activity of other men. They also expended more energy than men in using profile photographs as a tool for impression management and in studying the photographs of other people. On the other hand, men, aside from the fact that they were more interested in how many friends their Facebook friends had, were not more likely than women to attend to the educational and career accomplishments of others.

Evidence shows that time on Facebook is positively correlated with more frequent episodes of jealousy-related feelings and behaviors, especially among women (Elphinston & Noller, 2011; Morris, et al, 2009; Muise, Christofides, & Desmarais, 2009; Utz & Beukeboom, 2011). In one recent episode, a woman actually stabbed her boyfriend simply because he received a Facebook friend request from another woman (Timesleader.com, 2012). Overall, research indicates that men and women do not differ in the frequency or magnitude of episodes of experienced jealousy, but different factors serve as the triggers for jealousy for men than for women (Buss, 2012). Given its emphasis on relationships and physical appearance, Facebook seems to be more likely to pull the triggers relevant to female jealousy. The inherent ambiguity of many Facebook comments, photos, and other activities offers ample opportunity for flirting (or at least perceptions of flirting), creating new avenues for eliciting jealousy, intentional and otherwise. Sahil Shah (another one of my students) and I explored this issue in a study of sex differences in jealousy over Facebook activities. We confirmed that females are in fact more prone to Facebook-evoked jealousy than males, and, perhaps surprisingly, we also found that males are more sensitive to this sex difference than are females. This suggests that misunderstandings between romantic partners over Facebook use will more likely be due to females' misunderstanding their partners' reactions to Facebook activity than the other way around (McAndrew & Shah, 2013).

If the predisposition to gossip has evolved to facilitate an interest in those who are socially important to us and an interest in information that would be essential for success in social competition, learning about how it all works could even help us to understand the sex differences in what entertains us as well as our obsession with the lives of celebrities. Soap operas and similar entertainment venues press the buttons that pique women's interests in relationships, appearance, and competition for mates. These programs always feature deception, backstabbing, and, yes, gossip. The intrigue surrounding questions such as, "When will he catch her cheating on him?" or "When will everyone find out whose baby that *really* is?" plays directly into the competitive interests and tactics utilized by women. In contrast, male entertainment interests in movies and TV shows featuring physical violence, warfare, and athletic competition is more reflective of male competitive interests, and hence they become intrinsically entertaining to men. The otherwise inexplicable popularity of some American reality television programs such as *Survivor, Fear Factor,* and *The Amazing Race* may be due at least in part to the skill with which they tap into the competitive interests of men and women alike.

What about the fascination that people have with the lives of celebrities who are total strangers to them? One possible explanation may be found in the fact that celebrities are a recent occurrence, evolutionarily speaking. In the ancestral environment, any person about whom we knew intimate details of his or her private life was by definition a socially important member of the in-group. "There was never any selection pressure in favor of our distinguishing between genuine members of our community whose actions had real effects on our lives and those of our kin and acquaintances and the images and voices with which the entertainment industry bombards us" (Barkow, 1992, p. 630). Thus, the intense familiarity with celebrities provided by the modern media trips the same gossip mechanisms that have evolved to keep up with the affairs of in-group members. After all, anyone who we see *that* often and know *that* much about *must* be socially important to us. This is especially true for television actors in soap operas that are seen on a daily basis. In fact, it has been documented that tabloids prefer stories about TV actors who are seen regularly over movie stars who are seen less often; these famous people become familiar friends whose characters take on a life of their own (Levin & Arluke, 1987). Consequently, TV doctors receive letters asking for medical advice, and people send cards and gifts to celebrate the birth of soap-opera babies. The public's interest in these high-status members of our social world seems insatiable; circulation of supermarket tabloids and magazines such as *People* and *Us* run into the tens of millions per week. People seem to be interested in almost all aspects of celebrity lives, but unflattering stories about violations of norms or bad habits are most in demand. Stories about ordinary people typically make it into the tabloids only if they concern extraordinary events (Levin & Arluke, 1987).

In our modern world, celebrities may also serve another important social function. In a highly mobile, industrial society, celebrities may be the only "friends" people have in common with neighbors and coworkers. They provide a common interest and topic of conversation between people who otherwise might not have much to say to one another, and they facilitate the types of informal interaction that help people become comfortable in new surroundings. Hence, keeping up on the lives of actors, politicians, and athletes can make a person more socially adept during interactions with strangers and even provide segues into social relationships with new friends in the virtual world of the Internet. Research by De Backer, Nelissen, Vyncke, Braeckman, and McAndrew (2007) finds that young people even look to celebrities and popular culture for learning life strategies that would have been learned from role models within one's tribe in the old days. Teenagers in particular seem to be prone to learning how to dress, how to manage relationships, and how to be socially successful in general by tuning in to popular culture.

Conclusion

Regarding the overarching theme of this handbook, women and competition, studies of gender stereotypes have traditionally revealed "softer and gentler" impressions of women as creatures who are more likeable and just plain *nicer* than men. Such studies find that we expect women to be more cooperative, sensitive, and agreeable than men, who are perceived as more dominant, aggressive, and, yes, *competitive* (Eagly, Mladinic, & Otto, 1991; Haddock & Zanna, 1994). The eminent social psychologist Alice Eagly tagged this with the moniker "the *women-are-wonderful effect*" in an invited address at the American Psychological Association

convention in 1994 (Myers, 2013). While this may appear to represent a positive state of affairs for women, Glick and Fiske (1996) believe that it ultimately leads to a form of *benevolent sexism* by which women are excluded from competitive professional opportunities because such situations are not deemed to be compatible with their "nature."

The impressive collection of scholarship in this handbook puts to rest any idea that women are not competitive, and this chapter in particular puts a damper on the notion that they are particularly agreeable and nice when they *do* compete with each other. The seemingly universal historical preoccupation with controlling the gossip of women reflects a long-standing awareness of a competitive aspect of female social life that has only recently been recognized and confirmed by empirical research. We now have documentation that women are fascinated with the affairs of other women (e.g., DeBacker, Nelissen, and Fisher, 2007; McAndrew et al., 2007; McAndrew & Milenkovic, 2002) and that the gossip that erupts from this fascination is explicitly driven by competitive motives (e.g., Geary & Flinn, 2002; Vaillancourt, 2013; Watson, 2012). Given that ancient people as far removed from each other as Old Testament Hebrews and pre-Confucian Chinese seemed to be aware of the link between female competition and gossip, I have been puzzled by how long it has taken psychologists and other social scientists to discover it. After all, it is not as if we were unaware that gossip existed. I believe that its omnipresence and mundane everydayness is precisely the reason it was ignored for so long. There has been a peculiar history to the progression of the sciences in that the more intimately related to daily human experience a phenomenon is, the longer it has taken to become an object of scientific study. Humans probably had a working grasp of astronomy, complete with theories about the structure and mechanisms of the universe, long before we had a scientific understanding of anything else. And yet, what could possibly be farther removed from us than objects that are literally light years away? Eventually, an understanding of physics developed in ancient Greece. Chemistry began to take shape with the alchemists of the late medieval period, and it was only about 300 years ago that any progress of note began to occur in biology. Experimental psychology did not appear until the very end of the nineteenth century, and social psychology only blossomed after World War II. Whether the late development of the science of human social behavior is due to the difficulties of doing good science when so many variables are involved, a misplaced smugness that we already "know" how it all works, or a philosophical position that such things are simply beyond the reach of science is impossible to say. But for whatever reason, the study of gossip and the role that it plays in competition between women has come late to the party. The extensive list of references at the end of this chapter reveals that virtually nothing was written about it until the 1970s, and the first experimental work in the field did not appear until the dawn of the twenty-first century. Thus, the field is still in its infancy, and it will be exciting to see what develops over the next couple of decades. I hope that this chapter opens the door just a bit to allow us to take a peek at how understanding this backbone of social life will shed light on topics as diverse as aggression between women, why we become addicted to the Internet, and what makes us laugh and cry in the movies. If nothing else, accepting gossip as an innate part of human nature may help you feel just a bit less guilty the next time you find yourself hooked on some story about a B-List celebrity about your own age.

References

Abrahams, R. D. (1970). A performance-centered approach to gossip. *Man, 5,* 290–301.

Acheson, J. M. (1988). *The lobster gangs of Maine.* Hanover, NH University Press of New England.

Alexander, R. (1979). *Darwinism and human affairs.* Seattle: University of Washington Press.

Anderson, E., Siegel, E. H., Bliss-Moreau, E., & Barrett, L. F. (2011). The visual impact of gossip. *Science, 332,* 1446–1448.

Ayim, M. (1994). Knowledge through the grapevine: Gossip as inquiry. In R. F. Goodman & A. Ben-Ze'ev (Eds.), *Good gossip* (pp. 85–99). Lawrence: University of Kansas Press.

Barkow, J. H. (1989). *Darwin and status: Biological perspectives on mind and culture.* Toronto: University of Toronto Press.

Barkow, J. H. (1992). Beneath new culture is old psychology: Gossip and social stratification. In J. H. Barkow, L. Cosmides, & J. Tooby (Eds.), *The adapted mind: Evolutionary psychology and the generation of culture* (pp. 627–637). New York: Oxford University Press.

Baumeister, R. F., Zhang, L., & Vohs, K. D. (2004). Gossip as cultural learning. *Review of General Psychology, 8,* 111–121.

Beersma, B., & Van Kleef, G. A. (2011). How the grapevine keeps you in line: Gossip increases contributions to the group. *Social Psychological and Personality Science, 2,* 642–649.

Beersma, B., & Van Kleef, G. A. (2012). Why people gossip: An empirical analysis of social motives, antecedents, and consequences. *Journal of Applied Social Psychology, 42,* 2640–2670.

Benensen, J. F. (2013). The development of human female competition: Allies and adversaries. *Philosophical Transactions of the Royal Society B, 368,* 20130079.

Ben-Ze'ev, A. (1994). The vindication of gossip. In R. F. Goodman & A. Ben-Ze'ev (Eds.), *Good gossip* (pp. 11–24). Lawrence: University of Kansas Press.

Boehm, C. (1993). Egalitarian behavior and reverse dominance hierarchy. *Current Anthropology, 34,* 227–254.

Boehm, C. (1997). Impact of the human egalitarian syndrome on Darwinian selection mechanics. *American Naturalist, 150,* S100–S121.

Boehm, C. (1999). *Hierarchy in the forest: The evolution of egalitarian behavior.* Cambridge, MA: Harvard University Press.

Buss, D. M. (1989a). Conflict between the sexes: Strategic interference and the evocation of anger and upset. *Journal of Personality and Social Psychology, 56,* 735–747.

Buss, D. M. (1989b). Sex differences in human mate preferences: Evolutionary hypotheses tested in 37 cultures. *Behavioral and Brain Sciences, 12,* 1–49.

Buss, D. M. (2012). *Evolutionary psychology: The new science of the mind* (4th ed.). Boston: Allyn & Bacon.

Buss, D. M., & Dedden, L. (1990). Derogation of competitors. *Journal of Social and Personal Relationships, 7,* 395–422.

Buss, D. M., & Schmitt, D. P. (1993). Sexual strategies theory: An evolutionary perspective on human mating. *Psychological Review, 100,* 204–232.

Campbell, A. (2012). Women and aggression. In T. K. Shackelford & V. A. Weekes-Shackelford (Eds.), *The Oxford handbook of evolutionary perspectives on violence, homicide, and war* (pp. 197–217). New York: Oxford University Press.

Canadian Broadcasting Company. (2012, November). *The Real Dirt—On Gossip.* Banks Productions: Documentary film aired on November 8 and 12, 2012.

Cox, B. A. (1970). What is Hopi gossip about? Information management and Hopi factions. *Man, 5,* 88–98.

Cox, J. A. (2003, Spring). Bilboes, brands, and branks: Colonial crimes and punishments. *Colonial Williamsburg Journal.* Retrieved from http://history.org/Foundation/journal/spring03/branks.cfm#.

Crothers, L. M., Lipinski, J., & Minutolo, M. C. (2009). Cliques, rumors, and gossip by the watercooler: Female bullying in the workplace. *Psychologist-Manager Journal, 12,* 97–110.

Davis, H., & McLeod, S. L. (2003). Why humans value sensational news: An evolutionary perspective. *Evolution and Human Behavior, 24,* 208–216.

De Backer, C., Nelissen, M., Vyncke, P., Braeckman, J., & McAndrew, F. T. (2007). Celebrities: From teachers to friends. A test of two hypotheses on the adaptiveness of celebrity gossip. *Human Nature, 18,* 334–354.

De Backer, C. J. S., Nelissen, M., & Fisher, M. L. (2007). Let's talk about sex: A study on the recall of gossip about potential mates and sexual rivals. *Sex Roles, 56,* 781–791.

de Haan, M., Pascalis, O., & Johnson, M. H. (2002). Specialization of neural mechanisms underlying face recognition in human infants. *Journal of Cognitive Neuroscience, 14,* 199–209.

Dunbar, R. I. M. (1996). *Grooming, gossip, and the evolution of language.* Cambridge, MA: Harvard University Press.

Dunbar, R. I. M., Duncan, N. D. C., & Marriott, A. (1997). Human conversational behavior. *Human Nature, 8,* 231–246.

Eagly, A., Mladinic, A., & Otto, S. (1991). Are women evaluated more favorably than men? *Psychology of Women Quarterly, 15,* 203–216.

Eder, D., & Enke, J. L. (1991). The structure of gossip: Opportunities and constraints on collective expression among adolescents. *American Sociological Review, 56,* 494–508.

Ellickson, R. C. (1991). *Order without law: How neighbors settle disputes.* Cambridge, MA: Harvard University Press.

Elphinston, R. A., & Noller, P. (2011). Time to face it! Facebook intrusion and the implications for romantic jealousy and relationship satisfaction. *Cyberpsychology, Behavior, and Social Networking, 14,* 631–635.

Emler, N. (1994). Gossip, reputation, and social adaptation. In R. F. Goodman & A. Ben-Ze'ev (Eds.), *Good gossip* (pp. 117–138). Lawrence: University of Kansas Press.

Emler, N. (2001). Gossiping. In W. P. Robinson & H. Giles (Eds.), *The new handbook of language and social psychology* (pp. 317–338). New York: John Wiley & Sons.

Farley, S. D. (2011). Is gossip power? The inverse relationships between gossip, power, and likability. *European Journal of Social Psychology, 41,* 574–579.

Farley, S. D., Timme, D. R., & Hart, J. W. (2010). On coffee talk and break-room chatter: Perceptions of women who gossip in the workplace. *Journal of Social Psychology, 150,* 361–368.

Feinberg, M., Cheng, J. T., & Willer, R. (2012). Gossip as an effective and low-cost form of punishment. *Behavioral and Brain Sciences, 35,* 25.

Feinberg, M., Willer, R., Stellar, J., & Keltner, D. (2012). The virtues of gossip: Reputational information sharing as prosocial behavior. *Journal of Personality and Social Psychology, 102,* 1015–1030.

Fine, G., & Rosnow, R. L. (1978). Gossip, gossipers, gossiping. *Personality and Social Psychology Bulletin, 4,* 161–168.

Galen, B. R., & Underwood, M. K. (1997). A developmental investigation of social aggression among children. *Developmental Psychology, 33,* 589–600.

Geary, D. C. (2010). *Male, female: The evolution of human sex differences* (2nd ed.). Washington, DC: American Psychological Association.

Geary, D. C., & Flinn, M. V. (2002). Sex differences in behavioral and hormonal response to social threat: Commentary on Taylor et al. (2000). *Psychological Review, 109,* 745–750.

Glick, P., & Fiske, S. T. (1996). The ambivalent sexism inventory: Differentiating hostile and benevolent sexism. *Journal of Personality and Social Psychology, 70,* 491–512.

Goodman, R. F., & Ben-Ze'ev, A. (1994). *Good gossip.* Lawrence: University of Kansas Press.

Goranson, A., & McAndrew, F. T. (2013, July). *Does self-monitoring predict interest in gossip?* Poster presented at the annual meeting of the Human Behavior and Evolution Society, Miami, FL.

Haddock, G., & Zanna, M. P. (1994). Preferring "housewives" to "feminists." *Psychology of Women Quarterly, 18,* 25–52.

Hess, N. H., & Hagen, E. H. (2006). Sex differences in indirect aggression: Psychological evidence from young adults. *Evolution and Human Behavior, 27,* 231–245.

Hines, N. J., & Fry, D. P. (1994). Indirect modes of aggression among women of Buenos Aires, Argentina. *Special Issue: On aggression in women and girls: Cross-cultural perspectives. Sex Roles, 30,* 213–236.

Humphrey, N. K. (1983). *Consciousness regained: Chapters in the development of mind.* Oxford: Oxford University Press.

Jaeger, M. E., Skleder, A. A., Rind, B., & Rosnow, R. L. (1994). Gossip, gossipers, gossipees. In R. F. Goodman & A. Ben-Ze'ev (Eds.), *Good gossip* (pp. 154–168). Lawrence: University of Kansas Press.

Kniffin, K. M., & Wilson, D. S. (1998, July). *Gossiping for the good of the group.* Paper presented at the annual meeting of the Human Behavior and Evolution Society, Davis, CA.

Krebs, D. L., & Denton, K. (1997). Social illusions and self-deception. In J. A. Simpson & D. T. Kenrick (Eds.), *Evolutionary social psychology* (pp. 21–48). Mahwah, NJ: Lawrence Erlbaum Associates.

Laing, M. (1993). Gossip: Does it play a role in the socialization of nurses? *Journal of Nursing Scholarship, 25,* 37–43.

Leaper, C., & Holliday, H. (1995). Gossip in same-gender and cross-gender friends' conversations. *Personal Relationships, 2,* 237–246.

Lee, R. B. (1990). Eating Christmas in the Kalahari. In J. B. Spradley & D. W. McCurdy (Eds.), *Conformity and conflict: Readings in cultural anthropology* (7th ed.; pp. 30–37). Glenview, IL: Scott, Foresman & Company.

Levin, J., & Arluke, A. (1987). *Gossip: The inside scoop.* New York: Plenum Press.

Lewin, R. (1993). *Human evolution: An illustrated introduction.* Cambridge, MA: Blackwell.

Maloney, T. M. (1999). Social status, peer liking, and functions of gossip among girls in middle childhood. *Dissertation Abstracts International: Section B: The Sciences and Engineering, 59,* 6094.

Massar, K., Buunk, A. P., & Rempt, S. (2012). Age differences in women's tendency to gossip are mediated by their mate value. *Personality and Individual Differences, 52,* 106–109.

McAndrew, F. T. (2008). Can gossip be good? *Scientific American Mind Magazine, 19,* 26–33.

McAndrew, F. T. (2009). The interacting roles of testosterone and challenges to status in human male aggression. *Aggression and Violent Behavior, 14,* 330–335.

McAndrew, F. T., Bell, E. K., & Garcia, C. M. (2007). Who do we tell, and whom do we tell on? Gossip as a strategy for status enhancement. *Journal of Applied Social Psychology, 37,* 1562–1577.

McAndrew, F. T., & Jeong, H. S. (2012). Who does what on Facebook? Age, sex, and relationship status as predictors of Facebook use. *Computers in Human Behavior, 28,* 2359–2365.

McAndrew, F. T., & Milenkovic, M. A. (2002). Of tabloids and family secrets: The evolutionary psychology of gossip. *Journal of Applied Social Psychology, 32,* 1064–1082.

McAndrew, F. T., & Shah, S. S. (2013). Sex differences in jealousy over Facebook activity. *Computers in Human Behavior, 29,* 2603–2606.

McPherson, N. M. (1991). A question of morality: Sorcery and concepts of deviance among the Kabana, West New Britain. *Anthropologica, 33,* 127–143.

Mealey, L., Daood, C., & Krage, M. (1996). Enhanced memory for faces of cheaters. *Ethology and Sociobiology, 17,* 119–128.

Merry, S. E. (1984). Rethinking gossip and scandal. In D. Black (Ed.), *Toward a general theory of social control: Vol. 1. Fundamentals* (pp. 271–302). Orlando: Academic Press.

Morreal, J. (1994). Gossip and humor. In R. F. Goodman & A. Ben-Ze'ez (Eds.), *Good gossip* (pp. 56–64). Lawrence: University of Kansas Press.

Morris, J., Reese, J., Beck, R., & Mattis, C. (2009). Facebook usage as a measure of retention at a private 4-year institution. *Journal of College Student Retention: Research, Theory, and Practice, 11,* 311–322.

Muise, A., Christofides, E., & Desmarais, S. (2009). More information than you ever wanted: Does Facebook bring out the green-eyed monster of jealousy? *Cyber Psychology and Behavior, 12,* 441–444.

Myers, D. G. (2013). *Social psychology* (11th ed.). New York: McGraw-Hill.

Nelson, C. A. (2001). The development and neural bases of face recognition. *Infant and Child Development, 10,* 3–18.

Nevo, O., Nevo, B., & Derech-Zehavi, A. (1993). The development of the Tendency to Gossip Questionnaire: Construct and concurrent validation for a sample of Israeli college students. *Educational and Psychological Measurement, 53,* 973–981.

Nevo, O., Nevo, B., & Derech-Zehavi, A. (1993). Gossip and counseling: The tendency to gossip and its relation to vocational interests. *Counseling Psychology Quarterly, 6,* 229–238.

Noon, M., & Delbridge, R. (1993). News from behind my hand: Gossip in organizations. *Organization Studies, 14,* 23–36.

Owens, L., Shute, R., & Slee, P. (2000a). "Guess what I just heard!" Indirect aggression among teenage girls in Australia. *Aggressive Behavior, 26,* 67–83.

Owens, L., Shute, R., & Slee, P. (2000b). "I'm in and you're out . . .": Explanations for teenage girls' indirect aggression. *Psychology, Evolution, and Gender, 2,* 19–46.

Rosnow, R., & Fine, G. A. (1976). *Rumor and gossip: The social psychology of hearsay.* New York: Elsevier.

Rysman, A. (1977). How the "gossip" became a woman. *Journal of Communication, 27,* 176–180.

Schein, S. (1994). Used and abused: Gossip in medieval society. In R. F. Goodman & A. Ben-Ze'ev (Eds.), *Good gossip* (pp. 139–153). Lawrence: University of Kansas Press.

Science Museum of London. (2013). The Scold's Bridle. Retrieved from http://www.sciencemuseum.org.uk/brought-tolife/objects/displays.aspx?id=5343 on June 20, 2013.

Shackelford, T. K. (1997). Perceptions of betrayal and the design of the mind. In J. A. Simpson & D. T. Kenrick (Eds.), *Evolutionary social psychology* (pp. 73–107). Mahwah, NJ: Lawrence Erlbaum Associates.

Spacks, P. M. (1985). *Gossip.* New York: Alfred A. Knopf.

Suls, J. M. (1977). Gossip as social comparison. *Journal of Communication, 27,* 164–168.

Thornton, B., Ryckman, R. M., & Gold, J. A. (2013). Competitive orientations and women's acceptance of cosmetic surgery. *Psychology, 4,* 67–72.

Timesleader.com (2012, July 23). Man stabbed after receiving Facebook friend request. Timesleader.com (Wilkes-Barre, Pennsylvania). Retrieved from http://www.timesleader.com/stories/Police-Man-stabbed-after-receiving-Facebook-friend-request-,180035.

Tooby, J., & DeVore, I. (1987). The reconstruction of hominid behavioral evolution using strategic modeling. In W. G. Kinzey (Ed.), *Primate models for the origin of human behavior* (pp. 183–237). New York: SUNY Press.

Trivers, R. L. (1971). The evolution of reciprocal altruism. *Quarterly Review of Biology, 46,* 35–57.

Trivers, R. L. (1985). *Social evolution.* Menlo Park, CA: Benjamin Cummings.

Utz, S., & Beukeboom, C. J. (2011). The role of social network sites in romantic relationships: Effects on jealousy and relationship happiness. *Journal of Computer-Mediated Communication, 16,* 511–527.

Vaillancourt, T. (2013). Do human females use indirect aggression as an intrasexual competition strategy? *Philosophical Transactions of the Royal Society B, 368,* 20130080.

Walston, F., David, A. S., & Charlton, B. G. (1998). Sex differences in the content of persecutory delusions: A reflection of hostile threats in the ancestral environment? *Evolution and Human Behavior, 19,* 257–260.

Watson, D. C. (2012). Gender differences in gossip and friendship. *Sex Roles, 67,* 494–502.

Wert, S. R., & Salovey, P. (2004). A social comparison account of gossip. *Review of General Psychology, 8,* 122–137.

Wilson, D. S. (1997). Altruism and organism: Disentangling the themes of Multilevel Selection Theory. *American Naturalist, 150,* S122–S134.

Wilson, D. S., & Kniffin, K. M. (1999). Multilevel selection and the social transmission of behavior. *Human Nature, 10,* 291–310.

Wilson, D. S., Wilczynski, C., Wells, A., & Weiser, L. (2000). Gossip and other aspects of language as group-level adaptations. In C. Heyes and L. Huber (Eds.), *Evolution and cognition* (pp. 347–365). Cambridge, MA: MIT Press.

Wilson, M. I., & Daly, M. (1996). Male sexual proprietariness and violence against wives. *Current Directions in Psychological Science, 5,* 2–7.

Women's Talk? Exploring the Relationships Between Gossip, Sex, Mate Competition, and Mate Poaching

Katelin A. Sutton *and* Megan Oaten

Abstract

According to some feminist critiques, gossip is merely a form of women's talk and thus an activity that men do not participate in. Yet gossip may be an ideal strategy for both men and women to engage in when involved in mate competition, allowing the individual to covertly damage a competitor's reputation while simultaneously preserving his or her own. This chapter investigates the role of gossip in mate competition, considering the influence of variables including sex and attraction context on both the usage and success of a gossip-based competition strategy. Evidence shows that, although sex differences do exist in reputation-based gossip, both men and women are willing to use gossip strategically in order to gain a mating advantage. Overall, it appears that gossip is an effective, low-risk, and non-sex-specific intrasexual competition strategy for individuals to employ in both traditional and poaching attraction contexts.

Key Words: gossip, relationships, mate poaching, sex differences, evolutionary psychology

Gossip has developed from a positive term applied to both sexes into a derogatory term applied to women.
—*Rysman, 1977, p. 178*

According to some feminist critiques, gossip is simply a form of women's talk and thus may be considered an activity that men do not participate in (Coates, 1998; Spacks, 1982). The historical and social bases to this contention are discussed in detail by McAndrew in this volume. Yet evolutionary researchers investigating the functions of gossip have suggested that both men and women may gain benefit from utilizing a gossip-based strategy when involved in mate competition (De Backer, Nelissen, & Fisher, 2007; Power, 1998). The aim of this chapter is to investigate the relationships among gossip, sex, and mate competition. Rysman (1977) might suggest that "the gossip is a woman" (p. 178), and it is true that sex differences in reputation-based gossip do exist. However, this chapter will also present evidence that, first, both men and women are willing to use gossip strategically when involved in mate competition, and, second, that gossip functions as an effective intrasexual competition strategy in both conventional and poaching attraction settings.

Gossip as a Form of Intrasexual Competition

The scientific study of gossip initially became popular in the 1960s. However, in the ensuing 50 years it has not received the same level of scientific attention as other, related social behaviors, such as humor, ostracism, and bullying (De Backer,

2005). According to some prominent social psychological researchers, this is somewhat surprising because gossip is universal, uniquely human, shows up early in child development, and plays a crucial social role (Baumeister, Zhang, & Vohs, 2004; Bloom, 2004). It has been proposed that a potential explanation for why gossip has received less attention than other social behaviors is because it is a multifaceted concept that can be difficult to define (Foster, 2004).

Broadly, gossip has been defined in the literature as an exchange of personal information about absent third parties that can either be positive or negative upon evaluation (Foster, 2004). However, this broader classification of gossip (that includes both positive and negative information) is somewhat controversial because most adult conversation could be considered gossip under this definition (Levin & Arluke, 1985). Other definitions of gossip that have been offered in the literature include a form of societal control (Gluckman, 1963, 1968), a means of manipulating both one's own and others' reputations (Emler, 1994), an information management technique (Suls, 1977), and a social activity allowing for discreet indiscretion (Bergmann, 1993). For both the sake of simplicity and also to ensure that all facets of the behavior are studied, many current gossip researchers (e.g., De Backer & Fisher, 2012; Massar, Buunk, & Rempt, 2011) have utilized general and broad definitions of gossip. However, such inclusive definitions have not historically been utilized by all cross-disciplinary gossip researchers (Foster, 2004). Thus, as a whole, the scientific study of gossip has been somewhat disjointed and incoherent.

A second area of debate has focused on the function of gossip. Bloom (2004), for example, claims that gossip should not be a subject area open to psychological study and that, if anything, it's likely to be an arbitrary and unnatural category. In comparison, evolutionary psychologists have suggested that gossip may have a number of functional purposes and have considered the activity as both a strategy learning tool and as a means of reputation manipulation (De Backer, 2005). The two forms of gossip can be differentiated via the importance (or lack of) placed on the gossip target. For example, *strategy learning gossip* (here, gossip is considered a social learning tool) is gossip without importance placed on a specific individual. (For further information about strategy learning gossip, refer to McAndrew, this volume.) In comparison, *reputation-based gossip* (here, gossip is considered a method for intrasexual competition) is gossip with importance placed on a specific individual (De Backer, 2005). This chapter will focus on reputation-based gossip, and, throughout, we will consider the theoretical and empirical evidence in support of gossip functioning as an intrasexual competition strategy.

Competition often occurs when the individual seeks access to a fitness-enhancing resource that has limited availability. If one individual has access to the desired resource, this typically indicates that others will have to make do with either less of, or even without, the resource (Darwin, 1859; Walters & Crawford, 1994). Although individuals compete over access to numerous resources including food, water, and shelter, perhaps the resource that causes the most competition is access to high-quality mates (Graziano, Jensen-Campbell, Todd, & Finch, 1997). Some individuals possess more highly desired characteristics (e.g., physical attractiveness, positive personality characteristics, and high status) than others, and this makes them preferable mating partners (Buss et al., 1990). It has been proposed that men and women should compete among each other for access to such desirable mating targets (Cox & Fisher, 2008). Known as *intrasexual competition*, a number of evolutionary psychologists (including De Backer et al., 2007) have proposed that gossip might be a useful strategy in competition of this kind.

In its simplest form, mate competition can be thought of as conceptualizing three main protagonists: the individual, the romantic target, and the romantic competitor (or rival) (Buss, 1988). This mate competition triad is often used to describe the function and usage of intrasexual competition strategies. It has been contended that one of the primary reasons why gossip might be relied on during intrasexual competition is because it allows one to influence and alter the reputations of all three of these protagonists (De Backer, 2005). Solove (2007) noted that "our reputation is one of our most cherished assets" (p. 30). Furthermore, it is not just one's own reputation that is important, but also knowledge about others' reputations (Solove, 2007). It is proposed that gossip functions as a form of informational aggression, with men and women competing for resources by using information to attack a competitor's reputation (Hess & Hagen, 2002). Gossip may therefore provide the individual with a means of damaging a competitor's reputation while simultaneously maintaining or even improving his or her own (De Backer, 2005).

There are three main ways in which the individual might use gossip as a form of informational aggression in a mating scenario. First, by spreading negative gossip about a competitor (known as *competitor derogation*), the individual is able to alter a competitor's reputation and social standing (DiFonzo & Bordia, 2007). This ensures that, relative to oneself, the competitor's value is diminished (Buss & Dedden, 1990). Second, this type of gossip also allows the individual to alter his or her own reputation and enhance his or her own positive qualities relative to other individuals of the same sex (known as *self-promotion*; Buss, 1988; De Backer, 2005), insofar as the individual cannot plausibly accuse someone of behaviors that he or she also engages in. For example, in sharing derogatory gossip about a competitor's hygiene, the individual is implying that he or she is hygienic relative to the competitor.

These initial two functions of reputation-based gossip may be extremely useful in mate competition. This is because, in combination, competitor derogation and self-promotion enable the individual to appear maximally desirable to a potential mate relative to others of the same sex who are attempting to achieve the same goal (Buss & Dedden, 1990). However, gossip allows one to go beyond these initial two strategies. In listening to gossip, the individual is able to find out important information (e.g., current relationship status, relationship intentions, and personality traits) about targets and competitors. Furthermore, the individual is then able to potentially manipulate this information to his or her own advantage (De Backer, 2005).

This third function may be effective because the individual may also be able to recruit the help of family members and friends to achieve these goals. For example, Power (1998) has contended that men may use gossip to inform other men about women's sexual behavior and reproductive value. Women, in comparison, may use gossip to discuss the status of men and to warn female friends about potential cheaters (Power, 1998). Researchers have also claimed that reputation-based gossip need not only occur between individuals of the same sex (De Backer, 2005). Men and women might gossip with members of the opposite sex about the relationship status and suitability of potential mates (De Backer, 2005). Such information may thus indicate whether it is wise for the individual to spend time and energy engaging in mate competition.

Mate Poaching and Reputation-Based Gossip

In analyzing hypotheses put forth by evolutionary psychologists, it is clear that gossip might function as an ideal strategy for intrasexual competition. Through reputation-based gossip, the individual is able to derogate competitors, self-promote, and learn about the reputations of targets and competitors. Thus, the individual may be able to achieve a desirable mating outcome: becoming involved with a high-quality mate. The majority of studies investigating reputation-based gossip, and indeed intrasexual competition strategies in general, have tended to focus their methodologies on traditional attraction contexts involving romantically unattached individuals (Schmitt & Buss, 2001). Although we will consider such research throughout this chapter, it is important to note that reputation-based gossip need not only occur in these traditional contexts. In some ways, gossip may actually be ideally suited to usage in nontraditional attraction contexts such as mate poaching (Schmitt & Buss, 2001).

Mate poaching is defined as attempting to attract a mate who is already involved in a relationship (Schmitt & Buss, 2001). Researchers have suggested that it is a universal phenomenon, occurring across societies (Schmitt et al., 2004). Schmitt and colleagues (2004) have found that, cross-culturally, up to 60% of men and 40% of women admit that they have attempted to attract a partner already involved in a relationship.

Intrasexual competition strategies, and in particular, competitor derogation tactics, can involve challenges if used in mate poaching contexts. This is because the competitor is the target's current partner. Consequently, the individual is unlikely to win any favors by derogating the competitor directly to the target (Schmitt & Buss, 2001). However, gossip, as an indirect form of aggression, may allow the individual to overcome this challenge. Gossip involves the individual covertly derogating a competitor's reputation and thus may enable the individual to escape potential repercussions from both the target and the competitor.

A related advantage of using gossip in a mate poaching context may actually relate back to the competitor being the target's partner. In traditional attraction contexts, there can be numerous competitors, both known and unknown (Cox & Fisher, 2008). In comparison, in a poaching context there is a single, known competitor: the target's partner. Consequently, the individual can focus on tailoring gossip so that it is relevant to the competitor and effective in diminishing the competitor's reputation (Cox & Fisher, 2008; Fisher, Shaw, Worth, Smith, & Reeve, 2010).

However, having a known competitor can also be disadvantageous for the individual. This is because the gossip content that has been found to be effective in traditional attraction scenarios (e.g., derogating a competitor's physical attractiveness; Fisher & Cox, 2009) is often not as effective in mate poaching contexts. Because the competitor is the target's partner, derogations based on easily proved elements of reputation (e.g., physical attractiveness and status) are able to be readily verified as untruthful by the target (Hess & Hagen, 2002). In comparison, derogations based on harder-to-prove elements of reputation (e.g., sexual promiscuity) may be especially damaging in mate poaching contexts (Kaighobadi & Shackelford, 2012). Such gossip is not only more difficult to verify but may also cause negative relational outcomes for the competitor's relationship with the target (Bringle & Buunk, 1991).

Despite this, men and women may still remain unwilling to use gossip to derogate competitors in mate poaching contexts. This is primarily due to the potential negative ramifications that the individual may face by engaging in the tactic. Gossip is an indirect method of aggression and, as such, a low-risk strategy for competitor derogation (De Backer, 2005). However, there remains the possibility that the individual will be revealed as the gossiper (Schmitt & Buss, 1996; Schmitt & Shackelford, 2003). If the individual is found to be spreading derogatory gossip about a competitor with the aim of poaching the competitor's partner, it is likely that the individual will face negative repercussions from both the competitor and the target. Throughout this chapter, we will evaluate if the benefits that the individual might receive by utilizing a gossip-based poaching strategy (becoming involved with a desirable mate) outweigh these potential consequences.

Sex Differences in Reputation-Based Gossip

In investigating the role of reputation-based gossip in both traditional and nontraditional attraction contexts, the variable that has perhaps received the most attention from researchers is sex. Initial competition and aggression researchers from the 1970s and 1980s suggested that displays of intrafemale competitiveness were less salient as a sexual selection strategy than displays of intramale competitiveness (Gilligan, 1982; Goodwin, 1980). However,

evolutionary psychologists have more recently argued that, although there are universal sex differences in aggression and competition, both men and women should compete fiercely for a high-quality mate (Campbell, 2004). It is contended that both men and women should use intrasexual competition tactics to achieve mating goals (Campbell, 2004). Indeed, evidence from both human and nonhuman primates has proposed that females compete strenuously with rival females for access to high-quality mates and for the resources needed to support themselves and their progenies (Hrdy, 1981). It might be that it is the form of aggression adopted by men and women that differs. Basow, Cahill, Phelan, and Longshore (2007) found no sex differences in experiences of indirect aggression, either as a target or instigator. However, it was found that females tend to use indirect aggression more than physical aggression (Basow et al., 2007).

Interestingly, research has indicated that indirect aggression (including gossip) is no less damaging than physical aggression insofar as its potential to inflict stress and diminish a competitor's reputation and social support (Campbell, 2004). Gossip may therefore be a useful intrasexual competition tactic for both men and women. However, it has been hypothesized that indirect aggression is an especially useful competitor derogation tactic for women to employ in mate competition (Campbell, 2004; Hess & Hagen, 2002). This is because it allows a female to cause harm to a competitor while simultaneously attempting to appear harmless. By circuitously attacking a competitor's reputation, an individual can prevent retaliation from the victim of the aggression (Campbell, 2004).

From an evolutionary perspective, Campbell (1999) has contended that a female's willingness to use methods of indirect aggression in mate competition may be an evolved adaptation that has served to increase reproductive success. According to Campbell (1999), females should choose indirect aggression methods such as gossip to derogate competitors because being careless in respect to their safety and survival (e.g., by engaging in physical aggression with a competitor) may have greater consequences for a female's reproductive success than if a male had the same attitude (Campbell, 1999). Data from anthropological researchers provide some support for this argument, indicating that maternal death has a greater impact on infant mortality than paternal absence (Kaplan & Lancaster, 2003). According to Campbell (1999), women have thus evolved to be risk-avoidant.

An alternative evolutionary argument based on costly signaling theory suggests that men, conversely, may have evolved risk-acceptance mechanisms (Daly & Wilson, 2001; Wilson & Daly, 1985). Numerous studies have found that men are more risk-accepting than women (Daly & Wilson, 2001), and parental investment theory may provide an overarching explanation for this risk acceptance (Hoppe, Moldovanu, & Sela, 2009; Trivers, 1972). *Parental investment* has been defined as the time, energy, and effort a mother or father makes in a single child that improves that child's probability of survival relative to the parent's ability to invest in other children (Trivers, 1972). Women are often viewed as experiencing a higher level of parental investment than men. This is due to a variety of factors, including it being women who conceive and bear offspring, in addition to it historically being women who did the bulk of child-rearing (Bjorklund & Shackelford, 1999; Trivers, 1972). As a result of this sex difference in parental investment, men who compete successfully in mate competition are able to gain more reproduction opportunities than are women (Daly & Wilson, 2001). Thus, evolutionary psychologists suggest that men will achieve greater mating benefits than women if they engage in riskier behaviors. Consequently, from this perspective, men may have evolved to become more risk-accepting than women in order to increase their chances of achieving reproductive success (Daly & Wilson, 2001; Trivers, 1972).

In combination, these two arguments provide an evolutionary rationale for why men and women have evolved different risk-acceptance mechanisms. On the basis of these contentions, it might be hypothesized that women (being risk-avoidant) will be more likely than men (being risk-accepting) to engage in low-risk derogation strategies such as gossip when involved in mate competition.

However, women's predisposition to engage in reputation-based gossip may be a result of factors beyond sex differences in risk acceptance. For example, engaging in indirect aggression allows the individual to derogate a competitor while maintaining her reputation as a nice and reliable person. Studies have indicated that people generally prefer mates who are kind and trustworthy (Lukaszewski & Roney, 2010). Cross-cultural researchers have found this to be the case for both men and women (Buss, Shackelford, & LeBlanc, 2000). However, other researchers have contended that it may be women who are most concerned about being perceived as unkind or mean by targets (Fisher et al., 2010). In line with this, researchers have shown that females find being the victim of indirect aggression significantly more distressful than do males (Paquette & Underwood, 1999). As a consequence, a female competitor may be unwilling to continue to engage in mate competition after hearing derogatory gossip being shared about her reputation.

Finally, there is some evidence suggesting that indirect aggression may actually be a more successful strategy for women than for men. This is because women are more likely to have significant and close relationships than are men and typically spend more time and put more emphasis on building and maintaining relationships than do men (Golombok & Hines, 2002; Underwood, 2003). Whereas men's friendships are based around participating in common activities and giving and receiving practical assistance, women's friendships are characterized by emotional sharing and self-disclosure (de Vries, 1996). Researchers investigating sex differences in friendship and gossip have found that females are more likely to form and maintain social networks than are males (Dunbar, 2010). Additionally, females are more likely to view in-group gossiping as threatening to the friendship than are males (Watson, 2012).

In support of arguments about the usefulness of reputation-based gossip for women, Hess and Hagen (2002) have suggested that, due to differences in the evolutionary past, women may have evolved specialized adaptations for gossip. According to the researchers, historically, women may have been more vulnerable to inaccurate gossip and may have experienced more within-group competition than men for two main reasons (Hess & Hagen, 2002). First, some elements of female reputation (e.g., sexual promiscuity) may be more vulnerable to inaccurate gossip than elements of male reputation (due to concealed ovulation and the potential threat of paternity uncertainty; Hess & Hagen, 2002). Second, historically, following marriage, females typically moved tribes to be with their partners. Because there should be less competition between kin than nonkin (Rodseth, Wrangham, Harrigan, & Smuts, 1991), women would consequently have been exposed to more within-group competition than men. By using gossip as a form of informational aggression, women may have been able to disrupt existing reciprocal relationships between female tribe members (Hess & Hagen, 2002). Gossiping would thus have enabled a woman to effectively and covertly compete with other, unrelated females in her new tribe for access to limited resources such as food and protection. As a result, Hess and Hagen (2002) contend that women may have evolved specializations for gossiping both in dyads and in groups. It is therefore proposed that gossip may be a more important and useful mate competition strategy for women than for men.

However, other social-evolutionary researchers have disagreed with the notion that gossip is of specific benefit to females in mate competition. Miller (2000) has suggested that it is actually men who derive mating benefits as a result of sharing gossip. This is because, in doing so, men are able to show off their social intelligence and exclusive social knowledge (Miller, 2000). According to Miller's (2000) show-off hypothesis, by engaging in gossip, men may be able to signal to women that they have high ranking and intelligence. Because these are traits that women find desirable in potential mates (Miller, 2000; Pinker, 1995), gossip usage may thus allow men to compete effectively in mate competition.

Additionally, there is some evidence that women generally prefer to engage in methods of self-promotion over competitor derogation when involved in competition (Fisher, Cox, & Gordon, 2009). A potential explanation offered for this finding is that a woman may believe that engaging in derogation strategies will lead to others' perceiving her as mean and unkind, thus reducing her chances of securing a potential mate (Fisher et al., 2009; Schmitt & Buss, 1996). However, as has been previously discussed, gossip functions differently to many other methods of competitor derogation (e.g., controlling or dominating a competitor) insofar as it is an indirect method of aggression (Buss & Dedden, 1990). Gossip involves the individual covertly attacking a competitor's reputation and thus allows for the preservation of the individual's own reputation (De Backer, 2005). As a result, women may be more willing to engage in gossip than in other, more direct methods of competitor derogation.

Finally, in terms of sex differences, other researchers still have contended that reputation-based gossip is of equal importance and usefulness for both men and women. The central reason for this is that, throughout evolutionary history, both men and women faced the problem of acquiring and keeping a high-quality mate (De Backer, 2005). Because gossip potentially enables the individual to both attain a mate and retain a partnership (De Backer, 2005), the behavior should then be of no more importance for one sex than the other.

Empirical Research on Sex Differences in Gossip

A number of empirical studies investigating gossip have tested whether sex differences exist in time spent gossiping or gossip content. Leaper and Holliday (1995) examined gossip conversations among friendship dyads and found a number of interesting results. First, female pairs were more likely than male pairs or cross-sex pairs to engage in negative gossip. Second, female pairs were more likely to engage in negative gossip than positive gossip. Third, female pairs tended to encourage evaluative gossip. However, Levin and Arluke (1985) found no differences in the type of information (either positive or negative) that men and women shared when engaging in gossip. Leaper and Holliday (1995) have stated that one of the reasons that Levin and Arluke (1985) did not find any sex differences in either a positive or negative direction is that they failed to take into account whether the gossip was taking place between same-sex or cross-sex friends. More recent evidence has indicated that women often gossip in groups (rather than on a one-to-one basis), with the primary objective of this gossip being to diminish the reputations of other women (Hess & Hagen, 2002). Additional research has also indicated that one of the ways female friends achieve closeness is by derogating non-group members (Owens, Shute, & Slee, 2000). Furthermore, despite Levin and Arluke (1985) finding no sex differences in willingness to engage in either positive or negative gossip, the researchers did find an overall sex difference in time engaged in gossip. Seventy-one percent of women's conversation time was spent gossiping about others, as compared to 64% of men's conversation time (Levin & Arluke, 1985). Such research would appear to indicate that women (especially when with other women) devote more time to gossip than do men. However, gossip does appear to be an activity that comprises the majority of both men and women's conversations.

In addition to studying sex differences in time engaged in gossip, researchers have also investigated whether there are differences in the content of men and women's gossip (De Backer et al., 2007; Nevo, Nevo, & Derech Zehavi, 1993). From an evolutionary perspective, if gossip does function as an effective intrasexual competition strategy, the content of the gossip men and women engage in should be salient to mating decisions (De Backer et al., 2007). For example, if the individual chooses to actively engage in gossip in order to derogate a competitor's reputa-tion, the content of this gossip should be focused on manipulating the traits of the competitor that mating targets view as most important when mak-ing mating decisions (Hess & Hagen, 2002).

Several studies have investigated whether sex differences in competitor derogation strategies (including gossip) are in line with predictions from evolutionary psychology. First, it has been found that, cross-culturally, women desire partners with high status and availability of resources, described as *good provider indicators*. In comparison, men desire attractive mates, with attractiveness cueing genetic fitness (Buss, Shackelford, Choe, Buunk, & Dijkstra, 2000). Second, researchers have found that men and women do preferentially derogate competitors on traits salient to these sex differences (Buss & Dedden, 1990). For example, whereas women are more likely to derogate a competi-tor's appearance, fidelity, and sexual history, men have been found to derogate other men's financial resources, achievements, and ability to have sex (Buss & Dedden, 1990). Third, in conducting a meta-analytic review, Schmitt (2002) found that, regardless of the relationship context, women were perceived as being significantly more effective than men when using appearance-based derogations in mate competition. Conversely, men were perceived as significantly more effective than women when using resource-related derogation tactics (Schmitt, 2002). Based on such research, it might then be hypothesized that gossip should be a useful strategy for both men and women to employ in mate com-petition. However, for gossip to function effectively as a derogation tactic, there should be sex differ-ences in the information that individuals choose to spread about competitors.

Nevo and colleagues (1993) investigated men and women's tendency to gossip and found empiri-cal support for these hypotheses. The researchers found that women had a higher tendency to engage in physical appearance gossip than did men. In comparison, men tended to engage in achievement gossip more often than did women (Nevo et al., 1993). Additionally, in line with previous research (Leaper & Holliday, 1995; Levin & Arluke, 1985), women were also found to have a higher overall ten-dency to gossip than were men.

These findings are supported by research focused on the passive component of reputation-based gossip (De Backer et al., 2007; McAndrew & Milenkovic, 2002). For example, McAndrew and Milenkovic (2002) investigated sex differences in interest in gossip information. It was found that females were most interested in gossip about other females when it was concerned with promiscuity and sexual infidelity. In comparison, males were found to have equal interest in gossip about these topics, regardless of whether the subject was male or female (McAndrew & Milenkovic, 2002). In extending this research, De Backer and colleagues (2007) investigated men and women's ability to recall gossip content about both targets and compet-itors. In analyzing gossip specifically for attraction, the researchers found that men and women showed equal interest in information about potential mates' reputations (De Backer et al., 2007). However, the results also indicated that there were sex differences in the recall of gossip relevant to competitors. Cues of attractiveness were recalled more for female com-petitors (by females), whereas cues of wealth and status were recalled more for male competitors (by males). Overall, men and women were more likely to recall gossip about a competitor that research indicates should be salient in mate competition (De Backer et al., 2007). Based on these findings, the researchers concluded that reputation-based gossip is an efficient learning mechanism for both men and women (De Backer et al., 2007).

It appears, then, that men and women may tailor their gossip content in order to provide the most use to them in mate competition. However, other researchers have contended that when gossip is used actively as a method of competitor derogation it may be more effective for women than men (Hess & Hagen, 2002). The reason for this is that not all reputational elements are created equal. Some ele-ments of reputation (e.g., physical attractiveness or status) are able to be easily judged and quickly proved (Hess & Hagen, 2002). As a result, these reputational elements are difficult to impugn with derogatory gossip. However, other areas of reputa-tion are much more difficult to prove. These repu-tational elements are therefore more vulnerable to negative and untrue gossip (Hess & Hagen, 2002). Sexual reputation gossip, and particularly female sexual experience, for example, is hard to objectively verify as true or false due to concealed ovulation in females (Geary, 2000; Hess & Hagen, 2002). Three additional hard-to-prove elements of reputation that may be particularly relevant to females include fertility, fidelity, and child-care ability (Hess & Hagen, 2002). Accordingly, gossip may be effective as a competitor derogation strategy when it is used by women to manipulate and derogate these repu-tational elements of competitors.

The majority of researchers investigating sex differences in reputation-based gossip have only examined the strategy within traditional attraction contexts. However, from an evolutionary perspective, gossip may also be an effective strategy for women to employ in poaching contexts. The reason for this relates back to Campbell's (1999) contentions that women have evolved to be more risk-avoidant than men and are thus more likely to engage in low-risk derogation strategies when involved in mate competition than are men. As we have previously discussed, there are additional risks associated with mate poaching over and above those associated with conventional mate attraction (Schmitt & Buss, 2001). Consequently, as a result of the increased risks associated with mate poaching, it might be hypothesized that women will be more likely to engage in covert and low-risk derogation strategies, such as gossip, when attempting to poach a mate.

On the basis of these hypotheses, Sutton and Oaten (2014) conducted a study investigating men and women's willingness to share gossip in poaching contexts. Utilizing a cost-benefit methodology, the researchers asked male and female participants if they were willing to share derogatory gossip statements about a competitor in order to poach the competitor's partner. This gossip was based on derogating the competitor's sexual reputation (their fidelity toward their partner), and statement veracity, cost, and severity were also manipulated (Sutton & Oaten, 2014). The results from the study indicate that both men and women were willing to share derogatory gossip in a poaching context in order to achieve a desirable mating outcome. In looking specifically at sex differences, at low levels of potential risk (e.g., when there were no costs associated with sharing the gossip), men and women indicated a similar willingness to gossip. However, as the potential consequences for gossiping increased (e.g., when the gossip involved additional costs, was more severe, or was untrue), men indicated that they were significantly more willing to gossip than were women (Sutton & Oaten, 2014).

Researchers investigating reputation-based gossip in traditional attraction contexts have suggested that it is a competition strategy that should be particularly beneficial for women (Hess & Hagen, 2002; Massar et al., 2011). In addition, it was hypothesized that, as a result of the high-consequence nature mate poaching, women would be more likely to engage in the low-risk derogation strategy of gossip when attempting to poach a

mate than men (Campbell, 1999; Schmitt & Buss, 2001). Yet the results from Sutton and Oaten's (2014) study suggest that men are more willing to share derogatory gossip in poaching contexts than are women. Reconsidering Campbell's (1999) arguments on risk avoidance may actually provide an explanation for this finding. Specifically, arguments from evolutionary psychologists about the low-risk nature of reputation-based gossip are based on the usage of derogatory gossip in traditional attraction contexts. In such contexts, women may view covert tactics of aggression (such as gossip) as low-risk methods of derogation. This would explain why researchers investigating reputation-based gossip have traditionally found either no sex differences in willingness to gossip (De Backer et al., 2007) or that women are more likely to engage in the strategy than are men (Nevo et al., 1993). However, changing the attraction context to mate poaching may also change women's perceptions of the risks associated with gossip and, in particular, sharing derogatory gossip about a competitor. Campbell's (1999) research suggests that, as the potential consequences for engaging in intrasexual competition strategies increase, women become risk-avoidant (Campbell, 1999). In comparison, in line with research based on costly signaling theory, it appears that in high-risk scenarios, men are more risk-accepting than women (Daly & Wilson, 2001; Wilson & Daly, 1985). Thus, whereas reputation-based gossip may be a low-risk competition strategy when utilized in traditional attraction contexts, the additional consequences associated with mate poaching may shift gossip to a high-risk derogation strategy in this nontraditional attraction setting. This reasoning offers an explanation for why Sutton and Oaten (2014) found that women were less willing to share derogatory gossip about a competitor in order to poach their partner than were men, but only for increased risk factors.

Rather than simply being women's talk, gossip therefore appears to be a useful intrasexual competition strategy for both men and women to employ when involved in mate competition. Regardless of their sex, individuals appear willing to use gossip in order to achieve a desirable mating outcome in both traditional and poaching attraction contexts. Empirical research suggests, however, that how and when individuals choose to engage in the strategy depends on a number of factors. For example, in terms of gossip content, both men and women appear to focus their derogations on the content that is the most salient in mate competition (Nevo et al., 1993). In addition, whereas women appear to be willing to share derogatory gossip about competitors under traditional conditions of attraction (De Backer et al., 2007; Massar et al., 2011), this willingness appears to decrease in poaching settings, in particular as the risk factors associated with gossiping increase (e.g., the gossip is untrue; Sutton & Oaten, 2014). Men, too, appear to consider the potential risks associated with gossiping in deciding whether to engage in the strategy (Sutton & Oaten, 2014). However, due to an evolved risk acceptance, men appear to be more willing than women to share derogatory gossip in high-risk contexts in order to achieve a desirable mating outcome (Daly & Wilson, 2001; Sutton & Oaten, 2014). From an evolutionary perspective, it then appears that both men and women utilize gossip strategically when involved in mate competition.

The Effectiveness of Reputation-Based Gossip

However, simply showing that men and women are willing to use reputation-based gossip strategically does not necessarily provide an indication of the success of the strategy. This is because an effective intrasexual competition strategy, in particular one focused on competitor derogation, is a two-part process. Individuals must first be willing to engage in the strategy (Buss & Dedden, 1990). As we have discussed throughout this chapter, both men and women appear willing to use gossip in order to gain a mating advantage. In addition, however, the intrasexual competition strategy must make the target perceive the competitor as an undesirable mate choice, in particular, in comparison to the individual (Buss & Dedden, 1990). Therefore, when investigating intrasexual competition strategies, it is important to consider the target's perceptions, both of the competitor and of the individual.

In a meta-analytic review of intrasexual competition strategies, Schmitt (2002) found that numerous factors influence the effectiveness of both self-promotion and competitor derogation. Sex, attraction context, and type of strategy were all found to influence the perceived effectiveness of an intrasexual strategy (Schmitt, 2002). Regardless of attraction context (traditional, mate retention, or mate poaching), women were viewed as more effective when engaging in appearance-related tactics, whereas men were perceived as more effective when engaging in resource-related tactics. These sex differences were found in both self-promotion and competitor derogation contexts. However, sex

differences in resource-related tactics were larger in derogation contexts, with sex differences in appearance-based tactics larger in promotion contexts (Schmitt, 2002).

Fisher and Cox (2009) also considered variables that influence the effectiveness of intrasexual competition tactics, focusing on appearance-related derogations. Both men and women were found to be effective in diminishing a target's perceptions of a competitor's appearance. Additionally, attractive women were more effective at manipulating a target's perceptions of a competitor's appearance than were unattractive women (Fisher & Cox, 2009).

In investigating reputation-based gossip from the perspective of the target, it may also be useful to consider the target's perceptions of the individual (the gossiper). Throughout this chapter, gossip has been referred to as a covert, low-risk strategy for intrasexual competition. However, whereas engaging in gossip minimizes potential risks, as has been discussed, there remains the possibility that the individual will be revealed as the gossiper (Schmitt & Buss, 1996). If learning that the individual is using gossip to derogate others diminishes the target's perceptions of the individual, this may decrease the effectiveness of the strategy.

Fisher and colleagues (2010) conducted an empirical study investigating both male and female perceptions of female derogators. It was found that learning that a female is a derogator decreases men and women's perceptions of the individual. Both men and women viewed the derogator as less friendly, kind, trustworthy, and desirable in comparison to women who did not derogate competitors (Fisher et al., 2010). However, male perceptions of the derogator's physical attractiveness and promiscuity remained unchanged, as did male willingness to become involved in a relationship with the derogator.

Sutton and Oaten (2014) extended this research by considering gossip from the perspective of the target in a mate poaching context. Utilizing a qualitative methodology, the researchers asked men and women how hearing gossip about their partner's alleged sexual infidelity would influence their self-perceptions and their perceptions of their partner and their relationship. The results indicated that, for some targets, hearing this gossip would lead to either no changes or to positive relational consequences. However, the majority of men and women specified that hearing this gossip would lead to negative relational outcomes, including negatively valenced responses, relational conflict, and even relationship dissolution (Sutton & Oaten, 2014). When specifically asked about the potential long-term relational consequences of hearing this gossip about their partners, more than one-fourth of male participants and more than one-fifth of female participants stated that a consequence would be dissolution of their relationship. Despite this, targets were generally unwilling to retaliate toward the gossiper, preferring to focus their emotions on themselves and their partners. Indeed, when participants did indicate that they would like to retaliate toward the gossiper, nonaggressive retaliations (including talking to the gossiper) were endorsed over aggressive retaliations (such as punching the gossiper; Sutton & Oaten, 2014).

On the basis of this research, it appears that reputation-based gossip satisfies Buss and Dedden's (1990) two-step process for a successful intrasexual competition strategy. Not only are men and women willing to engage in the strategy, but it also appears to be effective in manipulating and diminishing target perceptions of competitors in both traditional and poaching attraction contexts. As with gossip willingness, sex does appear to impact the effectiveness of a gossip-based competition strategy. Research indicates that gossip will have the most effectiveness as a competitor derogation strategy when it is used by men and women to manipulate the traits of competitors that targets view as most salient in mate competition (Fisher & Cox, 2009; Schmitt, 2002). Such findings provide further evidence that gossip is an effective method of intrasexual competition when used strategically by men and women to compete for mates.

Gossip from the Perspective of the Derogated Individual

Finally, in investigating the role of gossip in mate competition, it is also important to consider the competitor, the third member of the mate competition triad. If the competitor learns that the gossiper is spreading gossip with the aim of derogating his or her (the competitor's) reputation, he or she may choose to retaliate against the gossiper. Although the chances that the individual will be revealed as the derogator are reduced when a gossip-based strategy is utilized, no derogation strategy is without risk (Fisher et al., 2010). If the individual is revealed as the derogator, the potential for retaliation from the competitor may lead to this strategy becoming high-risk and no longer cost-effective for the individual (the gossiper). As a result, despite the potential benefits that the individual might receive as a

result of choosing a gossip-based competition strategy, men and women might preferentially focus on methods of competition that have fewer risks associated with them (e.g., methods of self-promotion; Schmitt & Buss, 1996).

A number of studies have been conducted to investigate how men and women perceive derogators. Fisher and colleagues (2010), for example, found that both men and women decrease their perceptions of other women after learning that they are a derogator, although men still view the derogator as a potential romantic target. In addition, when investigating perceptions of derogators in poaching contexts, Sutton and Oaten (2014) found that, although both men and women perceive gossipers negatively, they are generally unwilling to respond to the gossiper aggressively. However, this research investigated perceptions of derogators who gossip about either an unknown other person (Fisher et al., 2010) or about one's partner (Sutton & Oaten, 2014). Learning that the derogator is sharing negative gossip about one's own reputation may lead the competitor to engage in additional acts of retaliation toward the gossiper.

For example, as has been discussed, signaling that a competitor is sexually promiscuous or unfaithful can be an ideal strategy when competing for a mate (Hess & Hagen, 2002). However, the individual may face a number of costs if he or she chooses to do so, insofar as the competitor will likely retaliate (De Backer, 2005). The retaliation may take the form of indirect aggression (i.e., by spreading gossip in return) or physical aggression (i.e., by punching the derogator; Bromley, 1993; Campbell, 2004). Studies have indicated that when females are in conflict with each other, the cause is generally over access to a relationship partner (Campbell, 1999, 2001). For females, sharing information about a competitor's sexual reputation may be a pertinent competition strategy (Hess & Hagen, 2002). However, spreading this gossip is considered such an extreme measure that it may lead a female to escalate retaliation to physical aggression. Campbell (1986) has found that the most common category for physical aggression among females (accounting for 46% of physical fights) is due to damaging another female's sexual reputation. Aggression between females is more likely to intensify if one makes accusations and gossips about another female's alleged promiscuity (Campbell, 2004). If the competitor does retaliate aggressively toward the individual as a result of hearing this information about her reputation, gossip may become high-risk, and individuals may become disinclined to participate in the strategy.

It might be expected that men and women who derogate competitors in order to mate poach will face a number of repercussions over and above those traditionally faced by derogators (Schmitt & Buss, 2001). This not only occurs as a result of the derogated individual attempting to protect his or her own reputation, but also is also due to the derogated individual's mate retention efforts. As we have previously noted, one of the underlying principles of mate competition is that men and women compete with other individuals of the same sex in order to become involved with high-quality mating partners. After gaining access to these desirable partners, it is unlikely that individuals will give them up without a fight. Indeed, researchers suggest that mate retention strategies may have co-evolved with mate poaching strategies as an adaptive means of guarding and maintaining a partnership with a high-quality mate (Schmitt, 2002). However, learning that the individual is sharing derogatory gossip about one's reputation may also lead the competitor to engage in further acts of retaliation toward the individual.

Sutton and Oaten (2014) conducted a study to investigate reputation-based gossip in poaching contexts from the perspective of the competitor (the derogated individual). Male and female participants were informed that they had overheard people sharing derogatory gossip about their sexual reputation (their fidelity toward their partner) and asked how they would respond to hearing such information. The results from the two-part study first indicated that both men and women were generally unwilling to respond to the gossiper with either physical or indirect aggression. Even when attempting to retain a mate from a would-be poacher, both men and women suggested that engaging in aggressive retaliations toward the gossiper was inappropriate (Sutton & Oaten, 2014). Rather, the derogated individual reported preferentially focusing on intersexual retention strategies (aimed at their partner) over intrasexual retention strategies (aimed at the gossiper). Men and women were most likely to engage in positive inducement behaviors (including being extra loving and kind) toward their partners as a result of hearing this gossip about themselves. Overall, men and women did report that they would engage in similar retention behaviors. However, when sex differences were specifically examined, men were significantly more likely to engage in intersexual manipulations after hearing this gossip than were women (Sutton & Oaten, 2014).

In terms of the mate competition triad, there is less research investigating reputation-based gossip from the perspective of the competitor than from the perspective of either the individual or the target. However, the current research findings provide additional evidence that gossip is a low-risk intrasexual competition strategy for usage in both traditional and nontraditional attraction contexts (Fisher et al., 2010; Sutton & Oaten, 2014). In the (relatively unlikely) event that the individual is exposed as a gossiper, both men and women do decrease their perceptions of the individual (Fisher et al., 2010; Sutton & Oaten, 2014). However, there is some conflicting evidence over whether the derogated individual will also choose to retaliate aggressively toward the gossiper. Although some research suggests that the primary cause for physical aggression among women is derogatory gossip (Campbell, 1986), more recent evidence suggests that men and women are generally unwilling to respond to gossipers aggressively (Sutton & Oaten, 2014). Additional research needs to be conducted investigating gossip from the perspective of the derogated individual in order to clarify these findings. Nevertheless, there appears to be significantly fewer risks associated with a gossip-based derogation strategy than with many other methods of competitor derogation.

Limitations of Current Research and Future Directions

The research we have presented here shows that gossip may be a beneficial intrasexual competition strategy for both men and women to employ when competing for desirable mates. However, some global limitations were identified that may limit interpretation or suggest alternative explanations for the findings discussed throughout this chapter. First, the majority of studies investigating reputation-based gossip base their experimental methodologies on hypothetical scenarios (e.g., Massar et al., 2011; Sutton & Oaten, 2014). Accordingly, the research presented throughout this chapter may be low in external validity, leading to questions about the applicability of these findings to real-world contexts. Cooper and Sheldon (2002) have noted that more than half of the studies investigating close relationships in the past 70 years have utilized hypothetical scenarios. In addition, a number of benefits are gained from employing hypothetical scenarios when exploring gossip. Because gossip can be a subtle and confidential behavior, it can be difficult to study empirically (Wert & Salovey, 2004), and gossip studied in naturalistic settings may face ethical concerns (Foster, 2004). Finally, there is some evidence that participants do respond to hypothetical attraction and relationship scenarios similarly to those in real-life contexts (Kurzban & Weeden, 2005, 2007). As such, whereas future researchers may benefit from utilizing more naturalistic methodologies when studying gossip, the current approach does not devalue the findings presented throughout this chapter.

Second, and relatedly, the majority of research findings discussed throughout this chapter came from self-report questionnaires (e.g., De Backer et al., 2007, Nevo et al., 1993; Sutton & Oaten, 2014). This may be problematic because people might be reluctant to accurately report on such socially undesirable activities as gossip, competitor derogation, and mate poaching (Davies, Shackelford, & Hass, 2010; Fisher et al., 2009; Nevo & Nevo, 1993). Many of the gossip questionnaires utilized by researchers investigating gossip aim to bypass or minimize this problem by avoiding mention of gossip in their methodologies (e.g., the *Tendency to Gossip Questionnaire* does not use the word "gossip" throughout; Nevo et al., 1993). In addition, many gossip studies are conducted online (e.g., Sutton & Oaten, 2014), meaning that participants are able to answer surveys privately and anonymously, thus decreasing social desirability concerns. Nevertheless, on the basis of the research findings discussed throughout this chapter, it may be useful for future researchers to utilize more objective methodologies when investigating the role of gossip in mate competition.

Third, one of the aims of this chapter was to investigate sex differences in a gossip-based poaching strategy. The research presented here indicates that men have a higher likelihood than women of sharing gossip about a competitor, terminating their relationships after hearing gossip about their relationship partners, and engaging in mate retention after hearing gossip being spread about their reputations (Sutton & Oaten, 2014). In considering an overarching explanation for these sex differences, it may be that the results were influenced by the specific type of gossip investigated: namely, sexual reputation gossip (and particularly, gossip pertaining to sexual infidelity). Sexual reputation is an element of reputation than can be difficult to verify and should be especially pertinent in mate poaching contexts (Bringle & Buunk, 1991; Hess & Hagen, 2002). However,

researchers investigating sex differences in relational jealousy have contended that men are more distressed at the thought of a partner's sexual infidelity, and women, conversely, are more distressed at the notion of emotional infidelity (Buss, Larsen, Westen, & Semmelroth, 1992). Thus, this may offer an explanation for why men were found to have heightened reactions for sexual infidelity gossip relative to women. In addition, it also suggests that the sex differences reported in this chapter may be specific to sexual infidelity gossip and will not be found with other gossip content. Researchers including DeSteno and Salovey (1996) and Harris and Christenfeld (1996) have suggested that sex differences in relational jealousy may be a methodological artifact only occurring when forced-choice measures are used in studies. Regardless, in future, it might be useful for researchers to investigate how gossip based on alternative content, particularly gossip that manipulates emotional infidelity, influences men and women's responses to gossip scenarios.

It would also be useful for future researchers to investigate reputation-based gossip in online contexts. There are numerous reasons why reputation-based gossip may be ideally suited to an online context. First, when communicating via the Internet, many important cues that are exchanged in face-to-face conversations (including voice tone, hand gestures, and facial expressions) are lost (Bargh & McKenna, 2004). This lack of a direct response from another individual following an exchange can have depersonalizing consequences for the initiator of the aggression (Smith et al., 2008). Such depersonalizing effects can include reduced feelings of guilt, shame, and empathy in addition to a lack of responsibility for behaviors and actions (Smith et al., 2008; Solove, 2007). In line with this, the anonymity that the Internet offers is also a significant advantage when communicating sensitive material (Buchanan, Joinson, Paine, & Reips, 2007). Second, the Internet makes gossip more permanent and widespread but less discriminating in the appropriateness of the audience (Smith et al., 2008). Furthermore, information that is shared on the Internet is both retrievable and archival, with details becoming stored as personal digital baggage (Piazza & Bering, 2009). As a result of this, derogating a competitor online may cause more widespread, long-lasting damage to the competitor's reputation than derogating him or her in an offline exchange.

However, these unique advantages associated with derogating competitors online may also, in turn, discourage men and women from engaging in reputation-based gossip over the Internet. First, whereas information shared online may cause sustained damage to a competitor's reputation, doing so may lead to increased risks for the individual. For example, because Internet-based gossip is archival and retrievable, it is more easily traced back to the derogator than is offline gossip (Solove, 2007). As a consequence, this may shift gossip from a low-risk to a high-risk strategy. Indeed, as McAndrew outlines in his chapter, information presented on Facebook can trigger feelings of rage and jealousy, particularly for women. The individual may therefore be disinclined to gossip online for fear of facing negative repercussions from the victims of her gossip (Campbell, 2004). This may be particularly the case when the individual is sharing derogatory gossip about a competitor with the aim of poaching the competitor's partner. From an evolutionary perspective, as a result of the additional risks associated with both mate poaching and Internet-based communications, it might be hypothesized that women (being risk-avoidant) will be disinclined to participate in reputation-based gossip online. Conversely, men (being risk-accepting) may remain willing to engage in a gossip-based derogation strategy in online contexts. Additional research needs to be conducted to investigate such hypotheses.

Implications and Concluding Thoughts

At the start of this chapter, we initially considered the notion that "the gossip is a woman" (Rysman, 1977, p. 178). Yet, on the basis of the research that we have presented throughout, gossip appears to be a non-sex-specific strategy for intrasexual competition. In both traditional and poaching attraction contexts, research investigating gossip usage indicates that both men and women are willing to be "the gossip." Although sex differences in gossip usage do exist, from an evolutionary perspective, these differences can be explained as a result of men and women strategically engaging in gossip in order to achieve the most desirable mating outcome. Furthermore, research from the perspective of both the target and the competitor is suggestive of gossip being a low-risk and effective intrasexual competition strategy for individuals to employ when competing for mates. In conclusion, it appears that classifying gossip as "women's talk" is far too simplistic. Rather, research suggests that reputation-based gossip is both men's and women's talk, and that, regardless of their sex, individuals

may benefit from engaging in the strategy when involved in mate competition.

References

Bargh, J. A., & McKenna, K. Y. A. (2004). The Internet and social life. *Annual Review Psychology, 55*, 573–590.

Basow, S. A., Cahill, K. F., Phelan, J. E., & Longshore, K. (2007). Perceptions of relational and physical aggression among college students: Effects of gender of perpetrator, target, and perceiver. *Psychology of Women Quarterly, 31*, 85–95.

Baumeister, R. F., Zhang, L., & Vohs, K. D. (2004). Gossip as cultural learning. *Review of General Psychology, 8*, 111–121.

Bergmann, J. R. (1993). *Discreet indiscretions: The social organization of gossip.* New York: Aldine de Gruyter.

Bjorklund, D. F., & Shackelford, T. K. (1999). Differences in parental investment contribute to important differences between men and women. *Current Directions in Psychological Science, 8*, 86–89.

Bloom, P. (2004). Postscript to the special issue on gossip. *Review of General Psychology, 8*, 138–140.

Bringle, R. G., & Buunk, B. P. (1991). Extradyadic relationships and sexual jealousy. In K. McKinney & S. Sprecher (Eds.), *Sexuality in close relationships* (pp. 135–153). Hillsdale, NJ: Erlbaum.

Bromley, D. B. (1993). *Reputation, image, and impression management.* New York: John Wiley & Sons.

Buchanan, T., Joinson, A. N., Paine, C., & Reips, U. D. (2007). Looking for medical information on the Internet. Self-disclosure, privacy and trust. *Health Information on the Internet, 58*, 8–9.

Buss, D. (1988). The evolution of human intrasexual competition: Tactics of mate attraction. *Journal of Personality and Social Psychology, 54*, 616–628.

Buss, D. M., Abbott, M., Angleitner, A., Biaggio, A., Blanco-Villasenor, A., BruchonSchweitzer, M., et al. (1990). International preferences in selecting mates: A study of 37 societies. *Journal of Cross Cultural Psychology, 21*, 5–47.

Buss, D., & Dedden, L. (1990). Derogation of competitors. *Journal of Social and Personal Relationships, 7*, 395–422.

Buss, D. M., Larsen, R. J., Westen, D., & Semmelroth, J. (1992). Sex differences in jealousy: Evolution, physiology, and psychology. *Psychological Science, 3*, 251–255.

Buss, D. M., Shackelford, T. K., Choe, J., Buunk, B. P., & Dijkstra, P. (2000). Distress about mating rivals. *Personal Relationships, 7*, 235–243.

Buss, D. M., Shackelford, T. K., & LeBlanc, G. J. (2000). Number of children desired and preferred spousal age difference: Context-specific mate preference patterns across 37 cultures. *Evolution and Human Behavior, 21*, 323–331.

Campbell, A. (1986). Self-report of fighting by females. *British Journal of Criminology, 26*, 28–46.

Campbell, A. (1999). Staying alive: Evolution, culture, and women's intrasexual aggression. *Behavioral and Brain Sciences, 22*, 203–252.

Campbell, A. (2001). Women and crime an evolutionary approach. *Aggression and Violent Behavior, 6*, 481–497

Campbell, A. (2004). Female competition: Causes, constraints, content, and contexts. *Journal of Sex Research, 41*, 16–26.

Coates, J. (1998). *Language and gender: A reader.* Oxford: Blackwell.

Cooper, M. L., & Sheldon, M. S. (2002). Seventy years of research on personality and close relationships: Substantive and methodological trends over time. *Journal of Personality*, *70*, 783–812.

Cox, A., & Fisher, M. (2008). A framework for exploring intrasexual competition. *Journal of Social, Evolutionary, and Cultural Psychology*, *2*, 144–155.

Daly, M., & Wilson, M. (2001). Risk-taking, intrasexual competition, and homicide. *Nebraska Symposium on Motivation*, *47*, 1–36.

Darwin, C. (1859). *On the origin of species by means of natural selection, or the preservation of favoured races in the struggle for life.* London: John Murray.

Davies, A. P., Shackelford, T. K., & Hass, R. G. (2010). Sex differences in perceptions of benefits and costs of mate poaching. *Personality and Individual Differences*, *49*, 441–445.

De Backer, C. J. (2005). *Like Belgian chocolate for the universal mind: Interpersonal and media gossip from an evolutionary perspective* (Unpublished doctoral dissertation). Universiteit Gent, Ghent, Belgium. Retrieved from http://www.ethesis. net/gossip/gossip_contence.htm

De Backer, C. J., & Fisher, M. L. (2012). Tabloids as a window into our interpersonal relationships: A content analysis of mass media gossip from an evolutionary perspective. *Journal of Social, Evolutionary, and Cultural Psychology*, *6*, 404–424.

De Backer, C. J., Nelissen, M., & Fisher, M. L. (2007). Let's talk about sex: A study on the recall of gossip about potential mates and sexual rivals. *Sex Roles*, *56*, 781–791.

DeSteno, D. A., & Salovey, P. (1996). Evolutionary origins of sex differences in jealousy? Questioning the "fitness" of the model. *Psychological Science*, *7*, 367–372.

de Vries, B. (1996). The understanding of friendship: An adult life course perspective. In C. Malatesta-Magai & S. McFadden (Eds.), *Handbook of emotion, adult development, and aging* (pp. 249–268). New York: Academic.

DiFonzo, N., & Bordia, P. (2007). Rumor, gossip and urban legends. *Diogenes*, *54*, 19–35.

Dunbar, R. I. M. (2010). *How many friends does one person need? Dunbar's number and other evolutionary quirks.* Cambridge, MA: Harvard University Press.

Emler, N. (1994). Gossip, reputation, and social adaptation. In Goodman, B. F. & Ben-Ze'ev, A. (Eds.), *Good gossip* (pp. 117–138). Lawrence: University of Kansas Press.

Fisher, M., & Cox, A. (2009). The influence of female attractiveness on competitor derogation. *Journal of Evolutionary Psychology*, *7*, 141–155.

Fisher, M., Cox, A., & Gordon, F. (2009). Deciding between competition derogation and self-promotion. *Journal of Evolutionary Psychology*, *7*, 287–308.

Fisher, M., Shaw, S., Worth, K., Smith, L., & Reeve, C. (2010). How we view those who derogate: Perceptions of female competitor derogators. *Journal of Social, Evolutionary, and Cultural Psychology*, *4*, 265–276.

Foster, E. K. (2004). Research on gossip: Taxonomy, methods, and future directions. *Review of General Psychology*, *8*, 78–99.

Geary, D. C. (2000). Evolution and proximate expression of human paternal investment. *Psychological Bulletin*, *126*, 55–77.

Gilligan, C. (1982). *In a different voice: Psychological theory and women's development.* Cambridge, MA: Harvard University Press.

Gluckman, M. (1963). Gossip and scandal. *Current Anthropology*, *4*, 307–315.

Gluckman, M. (1968). Psychological, sociological, and anthropological explanations of witchcraft and gossip: A clarification. *Man*, *3*, 20–34.

Golombok, S., & Hines, M. (2002). Sex differences in social behavior. In P. K. Smith & C. H. Hart (Eds.), *Blackwell handbook of childhood social development* (pp. 117–136). Malden, MA: Blackwell.

Goodwin, M. (1980). He-said-she-said: Formal cultural procedures for the construction of a gossip dispute activity. *American Ethnologist*, *7*, 674–694.

Graziano, W. G., Jensen-Campbell, L. A., Todd, M., & Finch, J. F. (1997). Interpersonal attraction from an evolutionary perspective: Women's reactions to dominant and prosocial men. In J. A. Simpson and D. T. Kenrick (Eds.), *Evolutionary social psychology* (pp. 141–168). Mahwah, NJ: Lawrence Erlbaum.

Harris, C. R., & Christenfeld, N. (1996). Gender, jealousy, and reason. *Psychological Science*, *7*, 364–366.

Hess, N. C., & Hagen, E. H. (2002). Informational warfare. *Cogprints*. Retrieved from http://cogprints.ecs.soton.ac.uk/ archive/00002112/

Hoppe, H. C., Moldovanu, B., & Sela, A. (2009). The theory of assortative matching based on costly signals. *Review of Economic Studies*, *76*, 253–281.

Hrdy, S. B. (1981). *The woman that never evolved.* Cambridge, MA: Harvard University Press.

Kaighobadi, F., & Shackelford, T. K. (2012). Vigilance, violence, and murder in mateships. In M. DeLisi & P. Conis (Eds.), *Violent offenders: Theory, research, policy, and practice* (pp. 125–142). Boston: Jones and Bartlett.

Kaplan, H. S., & Lancaster, J. B. (2003). An evolutionary and ecological analysis of human fertility, mating patterns, and parental investment. In K. W. Wachter & R. A. Bulatao (Eds.), *Offspring: Human fertility behavior in biodemographic perspective* (pp. 170–223). Washington, DC: National Academies.

Kurzban, R., & Weeden, J. (2005). HurryDate: Mate preferences in action. *Evolution and Human Behavior*, *26*, 227–244.

Kurzban, R., & Weeden, J. (2007). Do advertised preferences predict the behavior of speed daters? *Personal Relationships*, *14*, 623–632.

Leaper, C., & Holliday, H. (1995). Gossip in same-gender and cross-gender friends' conversations. *Personal Relationships*, *2*, 237–246.

Levin, J., & Arluke, A. (1985). An exploratory analysis of sex differences in gossip. *Sex Roles*, *12*, 281–286.

Lukaszewski, A. W., & Roney, J. R. (2010). Kind toward whom? Mate preferences for personality traits are target specific. *Evolution and Human Behavior*, *31*, 29–38.

Massar, K., Buunk, A. P., & Rempt, S. (2011). Age differences in women's tendency to gossip are mediated by their mate value. *Personality and Individual Differences*, *52*, 106–109.

McAndrew, F., & Milenkovic, M. (2002). Of tabloids and family secrets: The evolutionary psychology of gossip. *Journal of Applied Social Psychology*, *32*, 1064–1082.

Miller, G. (2000). *The mating mind. How sexual choice shaped the evolution of human nature.* London: William Heinemann.

Nevo, O., & Nevo, B. (1993). The tendency to gossip and its relation to vocational interests. *Counselling Psychology Quarterly*, *6*, 229–238.

Nevo, O., Nevo, B., & Derech Zehavi, A. (1993). The development of the Tendency to Gossip Questionnaire: Construct and concurrent validation for a sample of Israeli college students. *Educational and Psychological Measurement*, *53*, 973–981.

Owens, L., Shute, R., & Slee, P. (2000). "Guess what I just heard … " Indirect aggression among teenage girls in Australia. *Aggressive Behavior*, *26*, 67–83.

Paquette, J. A., & Underwood, M. K. (1999). Gender differences in young adolescents' experiences of peer victimization: Social and physical aggression. *Merrill-Palmer Quarterly, 45*, 242–266.

Piazza, J., & Bering, J. M. (2009). Evolutionary cyberpsychology: Applying an evolutionary framework to Internet behavior. *Computers in Human Behavior, 25*, 1258–1269.

Pinker, S. (1995). *The language instinct*. London: Penguin Books.

Power, C. (1998). Old wives' tales: The gossip hypothesis and the reliability of cheap signals. In J. R. Hurford, M. Studdert-Kennedy, & C. Knight (Eds.), *Approaches to the evolution of language* (pp. 111–129). Cambridge, UK: Cambridge University Press.

Rodseth, L. R., Wrangham, R. W., Harrigan, A. M., & Smuts, B. B. (1991). The human community as a primate society. *Current Anthropology, 32*, 221–254.

Rysman, A. (1977). How the "gossip" became a woman. *Journal of Communication, 27*, 176–180.

Schmitt, D. P. (2002). A meta-analysis of sex differences in romantic attraction: Do rating contexts moderate tactic effectiveness judgments. *British Journal of Social Psychology, 41*, 387–402.

Schmitt, D. P., & Buss, D. M. (1996). Strategic self-promotion and competitor derogation: Sex and context effects on the perceived effectiveness of mate attraction tactics. *Journal of Personality and Social Psychology, 70*, 1185–1204.

Schmitt, D. P., & Buss, D. M. (2001). Human mate poaching: Tactics and temptations for infiltrating existing mateships. *Journal of Personality and Social Psychology, 80*, 894–917.

Schmitt, D. P., & members of the International Sexuality Description Project. (2004). Patterns and universals of mate poaching across 53 nations: The effect of sex, culture, and personality on romantically attracting another person's partner. *Journal of Personality and Social Psychology, 86*, 560–584.

Schmitt, D. P., & Shackelford, T. K. (2003). Nifty ways to leave your lover: The tactics people use to entice and disguise the process of human mate poaching. *Personality and Social Psychology Bulletin, 29*, 1018–1035.

Smith, P. K., Mahdavi, K., Carvalho, M., Fisher, S., Russell, S., & Tippett, N. (2008). Cyberbullying: It's nature and impact in secondary school pupils. *Journal of Child Psychology and Psychiatry, 49*, 376–385.

Solove, D. J. (2007). *The future of reputation: Gossip, rumor and privacy on the internet*. New Haven, CT: Yale University Press.

Spacks, P. M. (1982). In praise of gossip. *Hudson Review*, 19–38.

Suls, J. M. (1977). Gossip as social comparison. *Journal of Communication, 27*, 164–168.

Sutton, K. A., & Oaten, M. (2014). *An exploration of gossip as an intrasexual competition strategy* (Unpublished doctoral dissertation). Macquarie University, Sydney, Australia.

Trivers, R. L. (1972). Parental investment and sexual selection. In B. Campbell (Ed.), *Sexual selection and the descent of man, 1871–1971* (pp. 136–179). Chicago: Aldine-Atherton.

Underwood, M. K. (2003). *Social aggression among girls*. New York, NY: Guilford.

Walters, S., & Crawford, C. B. (1994). The importance of mate attraction for intrasexual competition in men and women. *Ethology and Sociobiology, 15*, 5–30.

Watson, D. C. (2012). Gender differences in gossip and friendship. *Sex Roles, 67*, 494–502.

Wert, S. R., & Salovey, P. (2004). A social comparison account of gossip. *Review of General Psychology, 8*, 122–137.

Wilson, M., & Daly, M. (1985). Competitiveness, risk taking, and violence: The young male syndrome. *Ethology and Sociobiology, 6*, 59–73.

Informational Warfare: Coalitional Gossiping as a Strategy for Within-Group Aggression

Nicole H. Hess

Abstract

Evolutionary scholars often emphasize the strategic benefits of coalitions in male aggression and warfare. Evolutionary theories of human female coalitions, however, have not recognized any competitive function for coalitional behavior and instead emphasize mutual nurturing and help with child care. This focus is despite the fact that a significant body of research has shown that coalitions in nonhuman female primates do serve competitive functions. This essay argues that coalitional relationships among human females—like those among human males and those among female nonhuman primates—serve aggressive functions in reputational competition. It further argues that, for either sex, competition via gossip and coalitional gossip is usually a better strategy than physical aggression when it comes to within-group competition. Finally, the essay proposes that, because human females might face more within-group competition than human males, women and girls might engage in more gossip than men and boys.

Key Words: evolutionary, coalitions, aggression, warfare, coalitional behavior, reputational competition, gossip, coalitional gossip, within-group competition

Resource Competition and the Evolution of Coalitions

Evolutionary accounts of coalitional relationships among human males emphasize the role of physical aggression in obtaining valued, limited resources (Chagnon, 1988; Kurzban, 2001; Tiger, 1969; Tooby & Cosmides, 1988; Wrangham & Peterson, 1996). When physical force determines access to important resources like food, territory, and mates, alliances and coalitions provide a distinct advantage to their members because larger groups will almost always outcompete smaller groups or individuals for the valued resource.

Most evolutionary theories of coalitional aggression ignore, or even deny, that women's relationships are used in female–female aggression. For example, the influential "tend and befriend" account of women's relationships proposed by Taylor and colleagues (2000) emphasizes the evolutionary benefits

of women's mutual nurturing, caregiving, and emotional support under stressful conditions. Whether or not this account is correct (see Hess, 2006, pp. 134–142 for a detailed critique), it misleadingly suggests that women's friendships play little role in competition with other women. Another account of coalitional aggression among women suggests that women form coalitions to protect themselves from physical aggression by men (Smuts, 1992, 1993). Smuts points out that, whereas in patrilocal societies women typically live with the husband's female relatives who share *his* interests in asserting control over his wife, in matrilocal societies, the wife's female relatives are nearby and can intervene to protect her from spousal abuse (Smuts, 1992, pp. 13–14; Smuts & Smuts, 1993, especially pp. 34–35). These evolutionary theories leave the impression that women's coalitions serve benign or defensive functions but not competitive, offensive functions.

Here I develop a theory of coalitional aggression in which groups collect, analyze, and disseminate information to harm the reputations of competitors. I term this form of coalitional aggression *informational warfare* and argue that human females are more inclined to compete with informational warfare, whereas males compete using either physical warfare or informational warfare.

The Socioecological Model

The view that the coalitional tactics of human females are intrinsically benevolent is inconsistent with well-established findings that female nonhuman primates often form alliances and coalitions to better physically compete with other females for limited resources. Female primates fight against other females, often in coalitions, and whether and how they do so varies across and within species.

Primate sociality probably evolved as a defense against predators (van Schaik, 1983) and/or to enhance abilities in competition with conspecifics over resources (Wrangham, 1980). Not all primates live in groups, but studies of primates who are social have revealed substantial variation in the patterns of relationships that form among group members. In primates, and many other taxa, female fitness is primarily constrained by access to resources and male fitness is primarily constrained by access to females (Lindenfors, Froeberg, & Nunn, 2004; Trivers, 1972; Wrangham, 1980). Under the *socioecological model*, ecological conditions predict the degree to which females directly compete for resources, which, in turn, predicts the nature of female relationships (e.g., Isbell & Young, 2002; Silk, 2002a, 2002b; Sterck, Watts, & van Schaik, 1997; van Schaik, 1989; cf. Wrangham, 1980).

With regard to within-group competition only, resources that are valuable, clumped, and easily monopolized by one or more group members lead to strong within-group contest competition, involving intimidation and physical displacement of competitors. The overt, within-group agonistic interactions inherent to contest competition drive selection for alliances and coalitions to enhance physical competitiveness, as well as the dominance hierarchies that decrease the costs of fighting for all (Schjelderup-Ebbe, 1922). Frugivorous primates, whose food resources are high-value, clumped, and therefore monopolizable, tend to display these social patterns.

In contrast, ecological conditions in which resources are low-value, dispersed, and abundant—and therefore need not or cannot be monopolized—select for within-group scramble competition. Displacement efforts and aggression rates are low (because one animal's access to food is not limited by the efforts of another), as are the benefits of alliances/coalitions and dominance hierarchies. Folivores, for example, tend toward scramble competition rather than contest competition because leaves are usually abundant and nonmonopolizable. Data from several primate taxa generally support these and other predictions about female within-group competition derived from the socioecological model, as well as many other predictions about relationships between ecological and social variables, such as between-group competition, predator avoidance, sex, and infanticide (e.g., Barrett & Henzi, 2002; Boinski et al., 2002; Isbell & Young, 2002; Kappeler & van Schaik, 2002; Koenig, 2002; Silk, 2002a; Sterck et al., 1997; but see Janson, 2000).

Tufted capuchin monkeys (genus *Sapajus*) nicely illustrate the socioecological model. The bearded capuchin monkey (*S. libidinosus*) and the black-horned capuchin monkey (*S. nigritus*) are closely related Brazilian species that resemble each other in many respects: group sizes are similar, sex ratios are similar, and both have the same polygynous mating system. The environments of each species differ substantially, however. *S. libidinosus* lives in a seasonally dry open woodland with high availability of fruit, whereas *S. nigritus* lives in an area covered by dense evergreen trees with no dry season and lower availability of fruit but abundant access to leaves. As predicted by the socioecological model, within-group food competition is higher in *S. libidinosus* and lower in *S. nigritus*. Accordingly, *S. libidinosus* females stay in their natal groups and form linear dominance hierarchies and coalitionary grooming relationships. *S. nigritus* females, on the other hand, tend to transfer between groups and form egalitarian relationships with no hierarchies or coalitionary relationships (Izar et al., 2012).

The socioecological model is meant to explain the evolution of relationships among female nonhuman primates, but, applied to humans, it may be useful in understanding coalitional relationships in both sexes. Chapais (1996, pp. 19–20) makes the point that because "competing through cooperation" (i.e., via alliances and coalitions) is so widespread in primates, it was probably present in an early primate ancestor. Humans might therefore have inherited the basic psychological architecture for seeking allies and forming coalitions to increase success in contests over resources and dominance.

Humans, however, have unique cognitive abilities such as language and are highly prosocial compared to most primates, widely sharing food and other valuable resources. For instance, food sharing is ubiquitous among contemporary human hunter-gatherers (Kaplan & Gurven, 2005). Consequently, Chapais argues, humans appear to have extended their primate legacy well beyond simply pooling physical power to also pool, for example, services, goods, and information in order to better compete with other groups. The key, distilled insight of the model that I argue is particularly relevant to the human case is that alliances and coalitions are useful in contest competition. Under the socioecological model, a human ecology that involved valuable, monopolizable resources should have selected for psychological adaptations to form coalitions and alliances because these would have dramatically enhanced competitive formidability.

How monopolizable were food and other valuable resources in human groups over evolutionary time? Although evidence for central place foraging (repeatedly bringing food to the same location) by early Pleistocene Homo is controversial (O'Connell, Hawkes, Lupo, & Blurton-Jones, 2002), there is clear archaeological evidence from the late middle Pleistocene and later that Homo hunted big game, returning large packages of meat to caves and other central sites where it was processed and consumed by multiple individuals (Stiner, 2002). Most theorists of food sharing agree that, although contemporary foragers share meat widely, meat distribution is usually controlled by the hunter or other individuals and can be directed to, for example, offspring and other kin, spouses, sex partners, or reciprocal partners (for a review, see Kaplan & Gurven, 2005; the tolerated theft model is an exception; see Blurton Jones, 1984, 1987).

In addition to meat, contemporary small-scale societies, including foragers, rely heavily on other kinds of resources that are valuable, limited, and monopolizable. Examples of such resources include scarce nutrients like salt (personal observation), artifacts like weapons and tools (Kelly, 1995), drug plants (Roulette, Hagen, & Hewlett, 2016), or territories (Dyson-Hudson & Smith, 1978). Social partners, such as mates and friends, are also monopolizable (e.g., Barclay & Willer, 2007; Buss, 1988a, 1988b; Noe & Hammerstein, 1994). With regard to mating partners, men can benefit by competing for fertile and sometimes multiple mates (Symons, 1979), and, because human fathers (unlike most mammalian fathers) often invest significant material and social resources in offspring (e.g., Hewlett, 1992), women can benefit by competing for monopolizable mates who are able to provide many resources (e.g., Buss, 1988a, 1988b; Campbell, 1995). Like meat, most of these valuable, limited, monopolizable resources are obtained by cooperating with other members of one's group.

Hunter-gatherer societies have a hierarchical structure, and material, social, informational, and genetic resources are exchanged among all levels. In one scheme, individuals are nested within nuclear families, which are nested within dispersed mobile residential groups, which are nested within annually aggregated residential groups, which are nested within larger socioeconomic groups that aggregate every few years, which are nested within a regional ethnic group (Binford, 2001; Hamilton, Milne, Walker, Burger, & Brown, 2007). For the purposes of this essay, "group" refers to the local residence group.

Humans engage in contest competition for limited material and social resources with other humans both within and between groups (e.g., Hawley, 1999; Hawley et al., 2008). It follows from the socioecological model that both sexes should exhibit the aggression, alliances, coalitions, and dominance hierarchies that are associated with contest competition (in primatology, alliances are long-lasting relationships; coalitions are the temporally delimited groups of two or more allies that form to attack one or more individuals; Pandit & van Schaik, 2003). At the between-group level, human males commonly aggress in coalitions, often kin, for the kinds of limited resources described previously—in other words, men engage in warfare and raiding (e.g., Chagnon, 1988; Tooby & Cosmides, 1988; Wrangham & Peterson, 1996).

Human males physically contest over social and material resources within groups as well (Barker, Barclay, & Reeve, 2012), often forming within-group coalitions and dominance hierarchies, where age, kinship, and descent play large roles (e.g., Hawley, 1999). Among !Kung hunter-gatherers of Southern Africa, between 1920 and 1955, for instance, poisoned arrow fights occurred on average once every two years, typically over a woman (Lee, 1984). Lee recounts an incident in which a young woman was promised to one man but another man wanted to take her as a second wife. The second man attacked the first, whose father came to his aid; other men supported the second man, and more relatives were drawn in on both sides. None of the four wounded in the ensuing melee were principals in the original argument over the woman. Chagnon (1968) relates a similar incident among the Yanomamö, hunter-horticulturalists from South America, in which a young woman was promised to her older sister's husband but instead started an affair with another young man. The husband challenged the young man and his father to a club fight, and the latter two backed down.

Among women, there appears to be little, if any, evidence for physical coalitional aggression, either between or within groups. That is, women do not form groups to physically attack other women. As Rodseth, Wrangham, Harrigan, and Smuts (1991) point out, unlike female bonds in other primates, the close, affiliative bonds women form with other women are not used aggressively in physical competition. Indeed, though some evidence indicates individual women do occasionally aggress physically against each other (Burbank, 1994), there is no evidence that women regularly form alliances or coalitions to physically compete for contestable resources. Rodseth et al. concluded that relationships among women

> seem to be characterized by high degrees of noninterference mutualism, i.e., cooperation that does not impose a cost on any "third party." This varies little with residence pattern, so that even unrelated women in the most extreme patriarchal societies. . .regularly engage in peaceful cooperation toward common goals with close and enduring friendships (e.g., Abu-Lughod 1986). Such an observation would seem mundane if it were not for the striking contrast with dispersing females in other primates. (p. 232)

We are thus left with an apparent contradiction. When resources are clumped and monopolizable, females in nonhuman primates form coalitions and alliances to better compete for, and defend, these resources. Ancestral human groups were characterized by clumped, monopolizable resources. Yet, although men form coalitions and alliances to physically compete for these resources, consistent with patterns seen in nonhuman primates, women do not. Either the assumption about ancestral human groups is incorrect or the socioecological model is incomplete or incorrect.

Despite the apparent lack of coalitional aggression in human females, I now argue that, just like females in other primates, coalitional relationships among women and girls do function to facilitate aggressive within-group competition for valuable, monopolizable resources. I argue, however, that

this aggression relies not on physical but informational capabilities and that it can be used strategically by either males or females. This perspective also explains why women tend to avoid physical aggression.

Evolutionary Models of Cooperation Emphasize Reputation

Unlike in most nonhuman primate societies, many of the valuable and monopolizable social and material resources that are important to human fitness, such as food, mates, protection, and care, must be obtained from others. Empirical studies in small, kin-based societies indicate that reputation is an important mediator of access to the social and material resources that are provided by others. Among the Yanomamö, for instance, a reputation for fierceness appears to increase access to wives (Chagnon, 1988). Among the Ache of Paraguay, a reputation for generosity increases donations of food when one is sick (Gurven, Allen-Arave, Hill, & Hurtado, 2000; see also Sugiyama & Chacon, 2000). Sugiyama and Scalise Sugiyama (2003) similarly find, across a broad range of societies, that individuals cultivate reputations as providers of difficult-to-replace benefits, which motivate others to help them should they become injured or sick. Among the Hadza, hunter-gatherers in Tanzania, men with better reputations as hunters have harder-working wives and more children (Hawkes, O'Connell, & Blurton Jones, 2001; Marlowe, 1999). Among the Meriam, indigenous foragers in Australia, men with reputations as successful hunters had an earlier onset of reproduction, higher age-specific reproductive success, and more and higher-quality mates. Women with better reputations as hard workers, in turn, were preferentially chosen by the best hunters (Smith & Bliege Bird, 2000; Smith, Bliege Bird, & Bird, 2003).

In experimental economics experiments, in which typically anonymous subjects have the option of sharing real money with other subjects or keeping it for themselves, sharing can be sustained if players are allowed to develop reputations as donors; otherwise it collapses (e.g., Milinski, Semmann, Bakker, & Krambeck, 2001; Milinski, Semmann, & Krambeck, 2002; Wedekind & Milinski, 2000).

Reputation also plays a central role in recent evolutionary models of human cooperation. In the indirect reciprocity theories (Alexander, 1987; Leimar & Hammerstein, 2001; Mohtashemi & Mui, 2003; Nowak & Sigmund, 1998; Panchanathan & Boyd, 2003), benefits are provided to an individual based on information about his or her past contributions to others in the group—generous individuals are rewarded by receiving benefits from group members. In the "health-insurance" theories (Gurven et al., 2000; Sugiyama & Chacon, 2000), individuals increase the likelihood that they will be taken care of when ill or injured by generously providing benefits to group members when they are well. In the "show-off" or "costly signaling" theories (Gintis et al., 2001; Hawkes, 1991; Smith & Bliege Bird, 2000), individuals engage in behavior, such as big-game hunting, that signals their quality as mates or social partners and consequently reap valuable mating or social benefits (see Smith & Bliege Bird, 2000, for a discussion of the similarities and differences between their "costly signaling" model and Hawkes's "show-off" model).

Reputation can also play an important role in reciprocal altruism models (e.g., Cox, Sluckin, & Steele, 1999; Enquist & Leimar, 1993; Pollock & Dugatkin, 1992). In these models, individuals benefit from learning whether future social partners previously defected or cooperated with other social partners. In more sophisticated versions of these reciprocal altruism models, if the values of benefits that individuals provide vary, then individuals should attempt to cooperate with those who can provide the greatest benefits at the lowest cost. Due to the fact that cooperation with one individual may necessarily preclude cooperation with another, individuals may have to compete for cooperative partners, resulting in a market for cooperators (Bull & Rice, 1991; Nöe, 1992; Nöe & Hammerstein, 1994; Nöe, Van Schaik, & Van Hoof, 1991); these markets have been argued to be particularly important in humans (e.g., Dugatkin, 1995; Gilbert, 1997; Hagen, 1995; Henrich & Gil-White, 2001; Tooby & Cosmides, 1996). Thus, providers of valuable benefits can themselves be commodities over which individuals compete. Note that individuals may have different reputations in different markets. For example, a woman may be avoided as a foraging partner but sought after as a political partner, which indicates that reputation is multidimensional.

In each of these models, as several authors have noted (e.g., Enquist & Leimar, 1993; Leimar & Hammerstein, 2001), *information* about key behaviors (such as generosity to others or a successful hunting expedition) must be reliably transmitted to group members. Although direct observations are obviously informative in the indirect reciprocity models, key behaviors may also be communicated to other group members by the few observers of individual acts of generosity. The show-off/costly

signaling and health insurance models assume that the key behaviors will be directly observed by those who ultimately provide benefits. However, with these models too, most group members will not directly observe who killed the elephant but instead will have to rely on reports (as well as seeing the dead elephant) to properly assign credit to the successful hunter or hunters. Further, although the health insurance models posit that beneficiaries of past generosity will have a fitness interest in caring for providers when they are injured, it would be reasonable to extend this model. For example, it would be in the fitness interests of all *potential* beneficiaries to care for an injured provider (even if some had not been personal beneficiaries in the past), because they could benefit from the future generosity of the provider when he or she is well. In this extended version, information about individual acts of generosity must be transmitted to other group members by observers of these acts.

These empirical and theoretical results suggest that in order to maximize the benefits one acquires from others, one must achieve and maintain a reputation for being able to provide valuable benefits to others. One's reputation is based on information about one's traits, behaviors, intentions, abilities, and culturally specific competencies. Direct observations of key characteristics and actions are informative, but because it is impossible to observe everyone all of the time, information relevant to an individual's reputation is often obtained via reports from others rather than eyewitness accounts.

Gossip as the Manipulation of Reputational Information

If reputation did regularly mediate access to contested social partners and the resources they provided in ancestral environments, there would have been a selection pressure for adaptations to manipulate reputations to one's own benefit—to attack and defend reputations with information. This would involve providing information to resource providers that impugned the reputations of competitors or enhanced one's own reputation (or the reputations of one's kin and allies) and withholding information that enhanced the reputation of competitors or damaged one's own.

"Gossip" is a construct that captures the notion of information exchange about the doings of others. One definition of gossip states

> Gossip is informal, private communication between an individual and a small, selected audience

concerning the conduct of absent persons or events. Gossip thrives when the facts are uncertain, neither publicly known nor easily discovered. Gossip generally contains some element of evaluation or interpretation of the event or person, but it may be implicit or unstated.

(Merry, 1984, p. 275)

Several evolutionary psychologists (Barkow, 1992; Buss & Dedden, 1990; DeBacker, 2005; Hess & Hagen, 2006a; McAndrew & Milenkovic, 2002) and nonevolutionary social scientists (e.g., Emler, 1990, Paine, 1967; Radin, 1927) have offered reasons for why people gossip. Some researchers have taken an individual-centered approach, arguing that individuals compete for scarce resources by using information to damage their opponents' reputations and improve their own (Barkow, 1989, 1992; Buss & Dedden, 1990; Emler, 1990; Leimar & Hammerstein, 2001; McAndrew & Milenkovic, 2002; Paine,1967; Radin, 1927). The empirical evidence that gossip is self-serving and competitive includes the wide body of research on nonphysical aggression, variously termed relational, social, or indirect aggression (e.g., Björkqvist, Osterman, & Kaukianian, 1992; Galen & Underwood, 1997; Crick & Grotpeter, 1995; Owens et al., 2000a, 2000b; Underwood, Galen, & Paquette, 2001). In each of these forms of aggression, individuals aggress against others using gossip and other nonphysical tactics. These forms of aggression have been documented in more than sixty studies on four continents (see Archer, 2004, and Archer & Coyne, 2005 for reviews; see Goodwin, 1990a, 1990b, for a detailed ethnographic account of gossip in conflicts among children). In a study of college women, for example, Holland and Eisenhart (1990, p. 114) present "Rosalind's" account of what one woman did in order to attract Rosalind's boyfriend. This account clearly illustrates the use of apparently false gossip to attack a competitor's reputation in order to obtain a valued resource—a mate:

That girl would do anything in her power to spite me. . . . She's always trying to get something against me. . . . [the authors ask what the woman would do] Well, to start off she likes [my boyfriend]. And she'll tell him things [lies] about me. . . . And she'll come over to [my neighbor's] room. You can hear right through the walls. She'll even open the door . . . and she'll strike up a conversation about me. She calls me every name in the book . . . trying to provoke me into fighting her . . . and trying to make [my

boyfriend] think that I'm lying to him. . . . [She'll be] telling him that some [other] man paged me . . . or came and picked me up . . . [when] no guy called me that morning . . . or picked me up. (brackets and omissions in the original)

Similarly, McAndrew and Milenkovic (2002) found that participants were more likely to pass on negative information than positive information about potential adversaries and that subjects were quite likely to share positive, but not negative, information about friends and relatives.

Gossip, broadly construed, probably has many other functions, some of which have been explained using evolutionary principles. Barkow (1992) views gossip as information that had important implications for individuals' fitness-relevant social strategies in the ancestral environment (also known as the environment of evolutionary adaptedness). Gossip has been argued to be: "cultural learning" (e.g., Baumeister, Vohs, & Zhang, 2004); "social learning," such as learning norms or one's place in a group (e.g., Eckert, 1990; Fine, 1977; Fine & Rosnow, 1978; Gottman & Mettetal, 1986; Suls, 1977) or acquiring new and important knowledge (e.g., Watkins & Danzi, 1995); strategy learning (DeBacker, 2005); social "bonding" (e.g., Dunbar, 1996, 2004); social comparison (e.g., Wert & Salovey, 2004); a mechanism for showing off one's social skill and connections and therefore one's mate value (Miller, 2000); norm learning and enforcement or "policing" (e.g., Wilson, Wilczynski, Wells, & Weisner, 2000); a means to maintain the good reputations of allies (e.g., Brenneis, 1984); and a means to maintain the unity, morals, and values of social groups (e.g., Gluckman, 1963).

Language can be used to communicate on a variety of topics, so it is not surprising that there are a number of theories for the function of "gossip." What is surprising is the degree to which different definitions and theories of gossip overlap with one another—even those developed from the study of a range of diverse cultures, such as the Native American Makah and Hopi (Colson, 1953; Cox, 1970), rural Spanish (Gilmore, 1978), urban African Americans (Goodwin, 1990a, 1990b), Caribbean peasants (Abrahams, 1970), Polynesian Nukulaeae (Besnier, 1989), Fijians and the Caribbeans (Brenneis, 1984, 1987), and the Zinacantan of Chiapas, Mexico (Haviland, 1977). Most researchers agree that gossip is intimately related to reputation and the doings of others and plays a central role in community dynamics.

One major disagreement, vetted in a brief flurry of articles in the late 1960s, was whether gossip functions primarily at the group level (e.g., Gluckman, 1963, 1968) or individual level (e.g., Cox, 1970; Haviland, 1977; Paine, 1967; Szwed, 1966). The debate "came to an abrupt halt as it appeared obvious that we were riding the old warhorses—psychology or sociology: the individual or the group" (Wilson, 1974, p. 93). To briefly recap, Gluckman (1963, 1968) typified those who viewed gossip functioning primarily at the group level. Though recognizing a within-group competitive aspect to gossip, he argued that gossip functions primarily to "maintain the unity, morals, and values of social groups" and to promote within-group solidarity and between-group separation (Gluckman, 1963, p. 308; also see Colson, 1953). This idea has recently been promoted by evolutionary scholars who favor various forms of group selection (e.g., Wilson et al., 2000).

Paine (1967) conceived of gossip as strategic "information-management" and typified those who viewed gossip as functioning primarily at the individual level. Paine responded to Gluckman (1963) by offering an analysis of gossip as competition-oriented "information-management," arguing that "discussion of the values of gossipers is best related to what we can find out about their self-interests; I would hypothesize that gossipers also have rival interests; that they gossip, and also regulate their gossip, to forward and protect their own interests" (p. 280). Similarly, Brenneis (1984), a linguistic anthropologist, discusses reputation manipulation in conflicts via gossip among the Hindi-speaking Fijian Indians in the rural village of Bhatgaon (Brenneis, 1984):

> [I]ndividual reputation is central to one's actual social position. A man's reputation is subject to constant renegotiation through his own words and deeds and through those of others. Villagers are quite sensitive to perceived attempts by others to lower their reputations; the fear of reprisal by the subject of a gossip session has an important constraining effect upon the form of those sessions. Reputation management is a constant concern in disputes, for conflict often arises from apparent insult, and the remedy lies in the public rebalancing of one's reputation with that of one's opponent. (p. 489)

Bloom (2004) suggests that gossip is probably not a natural kind; for example, there is no neurophysiologically or psychologically distinct mechanism that produces only gossip statements, nor are there any linguistic features that uniquely characterize all gossip statements. Therefore, it has no single function, and thus both camps could be correct. Gossip as strategic reputation management is consistent with evolutionary arguments for methodological individualism—that social facts can be explained by reference to individual actions and motivations (e.g., Smith & Winterhalder, 1992). As such, the view of gossip as self-serving reputation management aligns more closely with Paine's view than with Gluckman's. The Paine–Gluckman debate was really a debate about whether (group-level) functionalism is correct; that is, are there institutions that serve some function for the group that is independent of individual motivation? If functionalism is correct (e.g., Richerson & Boyd, 1998, 1999), some form of socially sanctioned negative "gossip" should play an important role (Wilson et al., 2000). Whether or not it is correct, it is clear that gossip is used competitively between individuals and factions within groups.

One category of hypothesis garnering increasing attention attempts to link gossip to the evolution of human cooperation (e.g., Sommerfeld et al., 2007; Dunbar, 2004). Humans have language, and humans cooperate extensively with nonkin, so it is hypothesized that there is a causal relationship between these phenomena. Dunbar (1993, 1996, 2004) advocates a theory of gossip that occupies a middle ground between the individual competition view and the group functional view. Dunbar proposed that language and gossiping evolved to replace grooming as a facilitator of social bonding among primates. If our ancestors, whose group size Dunbar estimates at 150 individuals, followed nonhuman primate patterns, they would have spent an inordinate 40% of their time grooming one another to maintain cohesion in such large groups. According to Dunbar, an alternative mechanism to grooming had to evolve to allow people to maintain the bonds among individuals necessary to live in large groups; Dunbar suggests that this alternative might have been language. Language can be used to address multiple individuals, reducing effort, and it allows people to communicate information about their own and others' behaviors and mental states (i.e., to gossip). Given socially relevant topics are important to social bonding, language may have evolved to allow social bonding in larger group sizes. However, see Grueter et al, 2013.

More recent versions of the idea that gossip allowed for the evolution of cooperation in humans explore gossip as a mechanism for indirect reciprocity. Gossip, defined as information obtained via communication rather than direct observation, has been demonstrated to influence cooperation in various experimental economic games (e.g., Beersma & van Kleef, 2011; Mollerman, van den Broek, & Egas, 2013; Sommerfeld, Krambeck, & Milinski, 2008; Sommerfeld, Krambeck, Semmann, & Milinski, 2007). Sommerfeld et al. (2007), for example, found that gossip about cooperative individuals was more positive than gossip about uncooperative individuals, and cooperation levels were higher when people encountered positive gossip compared with negative gossip.

Gossip clearly serves multiple functions. As we have seen, however, the evidence strongly suggests that gossip is, at least in part, an aggressive, exclusionary, and competitive strategy that serves the needs of individuals of both sexes who may or may not be cooperating in small groups. Gossip researchers have yet to design studies that explicitly test any one of these theories pitted against any other.

Informational Warfare: The Coalitional Manipulation of Reputations

I propose that alliances and coalitions are valuable in contests over monopolizable resources where the "weapon" is not just physical aggression but reputational manipulation, via gossip. Just as cooperating men are more powerful than individuals in using combat and intimidation in physical warfare, cooperating individuals of either sex are more powerful than individuals in using information to attack, and threatening to attack, the reputations of their competitor(s) in informational warfare. An important implication is that, whereas most other theories of coalitional aggression explicitly deny that women aggress in coalitions, this perspective holds that women aggress in coalitions at least as frequently as men.

There are several reasons why coalitional relationships can be beneficial in reputational contests. Some analogies are helpful. Coalitions that engage in reputational contests function somewhat like a team of detectives trying to piece together the doings of others. They also function somewhat like a supercomputer cluster that can solve more complex problems than can a single computer.

1. Improved information collection
   Coalitions provide more eyes and ears through which to collect accurate information about competitors. Information can be difficult to obtain because people try to actively conceal certain behaviors (e.g., extramarital affairs),

because key behaviors or demonstrations of abilities occur infrequently (e.g., reaction to enemy attack), or because cues to the occurrence of key behaviors or traits are too subtle to notice without careful attention (e.g., disease resistance). The more individuals there are who are trying to collect information that is rare and difficult to obtain, the more likely that information is to be found.

2. Improved information analysis
   Coalitions can more thoroughly analyze information than individuals working alone. Multiple members can provide additional, relevant information; offer different perspectives on the same piece of information; and bring a more diverse array of past experiences to bear on the interpretation of the available evidence. Together, these would substantially enhance the analysis of new gossip.

3. Improved information dissemination
   Coalitions can provide more vectors (mouths) through which to strategically disseminate information. Further, some coalition members may have network ties to target recipients of certain information. Some members would also be able to identify costs and/or benefits of disseminating particular details or could offer especially effective interpretations of these details and thus, together, could craft a version of the gossip that would have the maximum influence.

4. Greater believability for information recipients
   Information reported by coalitions may be more believable than that reported by an individual. Random error (noise) can degrade information as it is communicated among different parties, but the probability that multiple accounts contain the same random error decreases rapidly as the number of parties transmitting the information increases. Information reported by multiple parties is also more believable, as lying entails different costs and benefits for different people. That is, the benefits of lying might outweigh the costs of lying for one party, but the benefits of lying are less likely to outweigh the costs of lying for additional parties. Thus, information reliability increases when multiple, independent sources attest to the same story. Hess and Hagen (2006a) showed that gossip believability decreased with the addition of noise and information that gossipers may have ulterior motives. Gossip believability

increased with reiteration of the gossip, and with source multiplicity (i.e., gossip being reiterated by the same source or by a different source or sources). Gossip believability also increased with source independence in that gossip relayed by multiple sources who had independently seen and reported the event was more believed than gossip from multiple sources where one source had heard of the event from the other source.

5. Improved defense against attacks

   Defensive manipulation of the reputations of oneself, one's kin, and one's allies can be just as important as offensive manipulation of the reputations of one's competitors. For the reasons outlined here, coalitions may protect members' reputations by providing alibis and evidence against harmful accusations.

The distinction between collecting and analyzing information on the one hand and disseminating information on the other is important and can be illustrated by drawing on an analogy with physical warfare. In physical warfare, group violence can be extremely costly to both sides. However, a well-prepared group can effectively deter attacks, thereby avoiding the costs of fighting. Groups spend a considerable amount of time preparing for physical warfare by building weapons, patrolling boundaries, solidifying coalitional ties, sharing information about enemies, and reviewing past battles. In informational warfare, a coalition that invests effort in collecting and analyzing information is more likely to damage the reputations of competitors and is better able to defend the reputations of its members by providing effective alibis and evidence against accusations. Trading reputational attacks can be costly to all competing factions, so coalition members should not engage in unrestrained dissemination of harmful information about competitors. Rather, coalitions should spend considerable time readying themselves for informational warfare by collecting and analyzing relevant information. As with physical warfare, effective threats and deterrence of attacks are a major goal of a coalition's activity.

The costs of collecting and analyzing information, like the costs of preparing for war, are not trivial. Information that occurs infrequently or that is concealed or subtle can take a significant amount time to acquire, as can learning background information that is relevant to its processing. Sorting through and synthesizing combinations of fragmentary information into a complete account that might matter to current or future reputational contests of oneself or one's allies, and then deciding what to do with that information based on the current competitive climate, is also time consuming. The effort and concentration devoted to the collective analysis of reputational information could be spent on alternative tasks, such as processing fitness-relevant information that is not of a social nature.

There is an interesting sex difference that might be related to potential differences in informational versus physical warfare. Researchers have found that girls' play groups are smaller than boys' play groups (Goodwin, 1990a, pp. 38–39; Laosa & Brophy, 1972; Lever, 1974, cited in Eder & Hallinan, 1978; Omark & Edelman, 1973; Waldrop & Halverson, 1975). Girls also more often view outsiders as threats to existing close friendships rather than as contributors to a larger coalition. In a study of children, Eder and Hallihan (1978) found that, because of the exclusivity of dyadic female friendships, newcomers had a hard time making friends. Eder and Hallihan also reported that girls' triadic friendships were more exclusive than boys' triadic friendships and that girls had more exclusive triadic friendships than they did nonexclusive triadic friendships. Benenson, Hodgson, Heath, and Welch (2008) reported that 10-year-old girls were more likely than boys to ostracize a same-sex peer. Similarly, Feshbach and Sones (1971) reported that adolescent girls made less favorable judgments of newcomers than did adolescent boys. Owens et al. (2000b) reported that jealousy over female friends was particularly intense, and they described the phenomenon of "a girl 'poaching' [stealing] another's best friend," sometimes using negative gossip, as was suspected by one informant in their study: "I reckon that Brooke and her were good friends and very close and probably somebody, another girl in the group, wants to be very close to Brooke and she goes and spreads something about Jo" (p. 36).

When it comes to conflicts specifically, Xie, Cairns, and Cairns (2002) found that in a US school population, whereas 97% of physically aggressive conflicts (characteristic of boys) involved dyads, 70% of socially aggressive conflicts (characteristic of girls) involved at least triads.

To the extent that girls tend to play at informational warfare, whereas boys tend to play at physical warfare, these differences in girls' versus boys' coalitions might reflect some important differences in informational versus physical warfare. If informational warfare occurs primarily within groups, then the sizes of competing cliques within groups would obviously be smaller than the size of the group as a whole.

The informational warfare model also resembles modern-day computer clusters that can solve more complex problems than single computers. To do so, computers must be connected via high-speed communication channels. A "cluster" of human brains, however, is "connected" by a relatively slow communication channel (language), and typically only one person can talk at a time. Thus, cliques would increase efficiency by allowing one person to inform several other people by telling the story once. However, if, as seems likely, information processing is enhanced by *conversation*, and not simply storytelling by one person, then the potential complexity of the conversation could increase rapidly with group size, as each person might need to respond to *every other person*; thus the potential complexity grows as $n(n-1)/2$, or quadradically with group size. This might serve to limit the number of participants in groups engaging in informational warfare, much as it does the number of central processing units in computing clusters that tackle nonparallelizable problems (Martin, Vahdat, Culler, & Anderson, 1997.)

In informational warfare, in order for every member to contribute to, and benefit from, membership in the coalition, each member must process collected information and recent events with respect to the life circumstances of every other coalition member. This information-processing load cannot easily be divided among coalition members—everyone has to have the full story in order to make a worthwhile contribution. Despite the improved ability of larger coalitions to collect and disseminate information, the substantial amount of time it takes to process new information from, and about, each coalition member places a severe constraint on coalition size. This constraint would be relaxed if cooperation were not based on reciprocity but instead on, for instance, a single mutual threat. For example, modern political campaigns employ large teams to dig up dirt on a small number of opponents.

In contrast, in physical warfare against a common enemy, there is no fixed resource like time that must be divided among each and every coalition member. If the potential benefits of warfare and the local resource base are large enough, the advantages of large coalitions will outweigh the disadvantages. Coalitions taking part in informational warfare should be considerably smaller than those used in physical warfare and are perhaps better referred to as "cliques."

Empirical Support for Informational Warfare

Although informational warfare theory as outlined here has not yet been tested explicitly in published research, some examples from the literature provide partial, indirect support. Ethnographic and psychological studies of gossip and conflict show that people gossip in groups and that a primary objective of such gossiping is to diminish others' reputations. Goodwin (1980, 1982, 1988, 1990a, 1990b) studied the phenomenon of the "he-said-she-said" gossip dispute. In ethnographic studies of play, communication, and group formation in inner-city children, Goodwin (1980) found that the conflicts of female neighborhood play groups took the form of coalitional, verbal confrontations, often in the form of small groups against individuals. Girls presented their stories such that hearers became aligned with speakers, then formed consensus against absent parties (Goodwin, 1990b). Goodwin described how girls strategically distributed gossip and recruited allies against a third party:

> [The] storyteller skillfully works to align hearer with teller against an absent third party. A coalition of what the girls call "two against one" (storyteller and hearer against absent third party) is established in the immediate interaction. From the teller's perspective, the offended party's alignment is important for bringing forth a future confrontation. From the recipient's perspective the fact that at least two parties agree on a particular version of an event provides a warrant for bringing action against a third party.
> *(Goodwin, 1990b, p. 128)*

Goodwin (1982) also suggests that when verbal confrontations among girls occur, the accuser usually wins, due, in part, to the accuser's alliances. In contrast to the general assumption that girls tend to avoid conflict, Goodwin (1990b) suggested that they in fact compete fiercely with other girls and that the competition reveals a coalition structure among girls:

> Girls affirm the organization of their social group through assessing the behavior of absent parties. The alliances formed in the process of discussing others mark who is included and excluded from the social group of the moment, rather than relative rank.
>
> . . .
>
> As the data presented here vividly show, within the he-said-she-said storytelling event, girls react with righteous indignation when they find that their character has been maligned. They display an

intense interest in initiating and elaborating disputes about their rights (not to be talked about behind their backs) that differentiate offending and offended parties. *Alignments* taken up during such disputes clearly demarcate who stands within the bounds of an inner circle of friends, as well as who is regulated to that circle's periphery.

(Goodwin, 1990b, p. 129; emphasis added)

Leaper and Holliday (1995) similarly showed that adult females use gossip to promote solidarity in an "us versus them" manner. Proveda (1975) suggested that gossip is the weapon by which girls manipulate information, and that this manipulation of social information appears to explain how girls' coalitions differ from boys' coalitions:

> Gossip, of course, is the major weapon which girls use to regulate information about each other. This method of informal social control accounts for the tighter clique structure among girls than boys, as well as the nature of peer group solidarity among girls. Girls frequently describe other girls as friendly and well-liked within their own group, but unfriendly to outsiders. It is apparent that the clique is crucial in the regulation of information about peers. What is known to one member of a clique is known to all; therefore, it is important to control and limit the association patterns of the clique. The vulnerability of girls to revealing or not revealing information about the self makes girls much more sensitive to social criticism than boys. In this sense, the girl's fate rests with the fate of the clique. (p. 133)

Work by Owens et al. (2000a, 2000b) on indirect aggression showed that "intimacy" was achieved within groups of female friends when nonmembers were derogated and that derogating others was often needed to gain acceptance into (or maintain a position in) a particular group, suggesting the group nature of female competition. Other aggressive tactics identified by Owens et al., such as ostracism, breaking confidences, and discussing victims, are all inherently cooperative forms of competition (i.e., at least two aggressors are required). Supporting the idea that coalitions facilitate the dissemination of information, Owens et al. (2000b) found that "the girls in the present study revealed that the act of revenge often involves utilizing other members of the group through the spreading of a rumour or organizing to ignore or exclude the other" (p. 43).

Research by Adler and Adler (1998) on peer power relations shows that sociologically popular children use bullying (coercion, intimidation, ridicule, and assault) specifically to increase group solidarity and strength, "turning people against an outsider served to solidify the group and asserting power of the strong over the vulnerability of the weak" (p. 65). Adler and Adler continue

> Getting picked on instilled outsiders with fear, grinding them down to accept their inferior status and discouraging them from rallying together to challenge the power hierarchy. In a confrontation between a clique member and an outsider, most people sided with the clique member. They knew that clique members banded together against outsiders, and that they could easily become the next target of attack if they challenged them. Clique members picked on outsiders with little worry about confrontation or repercussion. They also knew that their victims would never carry the tale to teachers or administrators (as they might against other targets...) for fear of reprisal. As Mike, a fifth-grade clique follower, observed, "They know if they tell on you, then you'll 'beat them up,' and so they won't tell on you, they just kind of take it in, walk away."

Adler and Adler (1998) describe an act of ostracism among some fourth-graders, where individuals actually left their school due to effective coalitional exclusion:

> Diane recalled the way she turned all the members of her class, boys as well as girls, against an outsider: "I was always mean to people outside my group like Crystal and Sally Jones; they both moved schools.... I had this gummy bear necklace, with pearls around it and gummy bears. She [Crystal] came up to me one day and pulled my necklace off. I'm like, 'It was my favorite necklace,' and I got all of my friends, and all the guys even in the class, to revolt against her. No one liked her. That's why she moved schools, because she tore my gummy bear necklace off and everyone hated her. They were like, 'That was mean. She didn't deserve that. We hate you.'" (p. 64)

Most of the research just described focuses on children and teenagers in Western school populations. The large number of psychological studies looking at indirect, relational, and social aggression (discussed in the next section; also see Archer, 2004) also includes mostly young Western subjects. One example among somewhat older females, still in a Western population, comes from Laidler and Hunt (2001), who observed of female gangs in the San Francisco Bay Area:

> As in Lees' study of English girls (1997), we find gang girls spending a great deal of energy "bitching" or casting doubt on others' reputations. This cross-cultural process operates not only as a mechanism of social control, but also of distancing and confirming one's own reputation. (p. 668)

Describing gossip among adult members of a small community in the Central Pacific who speak a dialect of Polynesian Tuvaluan called Nukulaelae, Besnier (1989) wrote, "In order to create a successful gossip session, gossips must ensure that their audience shares their own feelings and attitudes toward the specific topic of the gossip" (p. 320). Besnier points out that gossip among the Nukulaelae is more commonly a female than male activity, argues that collusion is a main feature of gossip among the Nukulaelae, and discusses how gossipers delayed the introduction of key elements of a story so that their listeners took an active role in the co-production of gossip. The coalitional, strategic use of gossip requires that coalition members agree on their interpretations of, and attitudes toward, reputation-relevant information. This shared co-production strategy might help the main gossiper avoid retribution for gossiping by diffusing the responsibility of the information transference to others (i.e., "I didn't damage so-and-so's reputation; everyone did"). Along these lines, research among Western adolescents by Eder and Enke (1991) found that a supporting response to an initial negative gossip statement about another caused other conversation participants to subsequently make only negative comments that were in agreement with this evaluation (early challenges to the evaluation, which were relatively infrequent, led to less conformity). Gottman and Mettetal (1986) similarly found that four- and five-year-olds gossip in a process leading to extremes in opinions against the discussed party, creating an atmosphere of "we against others."

Human Dominance Hierarchies Are Based on More than Just Physical Fights

The socioecological model emphasizes that monopolizable resources select for coalitions and also for dominance hierarchies. Dominance hierarchies (Schjelderup-Ebbe, 1922), found in a wide range of group-living primates and other taxa (Bernstein, 1981a, 1981b; Silk, 2007a, 2007b), are characterized by a consistent outcome in agonistic relations (Drews, 1993); that is, when two animals contest a resource, the one with higher rank in the hierarchy almost always obtains the resource without a fight. Dominance hierarchies are thought to have evolved for the mutual benefit of avoiding the cost of a fight (Maynard Smith & Parker, 1976). In some cases, dominance rank is determined by observable qualities, such as age, sex, and body size. In others, however, it might be determined by the outcomes of previous interactions—in other words, by the animal equivalent of individual reputation (e.g., Drews, 1993). Maintaining or increasing rank in primate societies often requires allies (Chapais, 1996; Harcourt & de Waal, 1992; Silk, 2007a). In a typical example, allies will intervene on behalf of kin in a conflict against an unrelated, lower-ranked group member.

Female dominance hierarchies are common in animals, including nonhuman primates (van Schaik, 1989), elephants (Archie, Morrison, Foley, Moss, & Alberts, 2006), hyenas (Holekamp et al., 1997; Owens & Owens, 1996), and mongooses (Creel & Waser, 1997), yet the study of dominance in humans has focused on males, perhaps as an artifact of a focus on physical coercion (Hawley et al. 2008). When indirect aggression and prosocial behavior are considered, however, dominant females and males appear remarkably similar. Based on recent studies, Hawley et al. (2008) conclude that despite some sex differences in dominance, across all age groups the most dominant members of a social group are both female and male and that the aim of achieving dominance is resource control. They further conclude that high-dominance females and males are attractive to others, typically have high centrality in social networks, and are often bistrategic, using both indirect aggression and prosocial behavior to attain and defend dominance (see also Henrich & Gil-White, 2001).

Turning to the ethnographic record, high-ranked individuals in small-scale societies, such as headmen and chiefs, often obtain their (limited) authority, in part, on the basis of their munificence (e.g., Lowie, 1948). Such prosocial behavior is probably important in achieving dominance among humans because many of the valuable and monopolizable social and material resources that are important to individual fitness must be obtained from other people.

In summary, whereas animal dominance hierarchies are usually grounded in fighting abilities, human dominance hierarchies are grounded in both aggressive abilities and a reputation for being able to provide valuable benefits to others. To maintain or increase rank in human societies, it is therefore often necessary to increase one's reputation for providing valuable benefits or to decrease the reputations of one's competitors. Importantly, highly dominant females and males both appear to have numerous allies insofar as they are often the most popular, most liked, and most central members of their social networks (Hawley et al., 2008, and references therein).

Sex Differences in Physical Aggression

Archer's (2004) meta-analysis looked at sex differences in aggression types in a large number of studies. With regard to physical aggression, 124 studies yielded a very consistent, large male bias in physical aggression across cultures. This bias appears at or before the age of two and does not increase with age during childhood. He also found that the maximum sex differences in physical aggression occur well after puberty, between 18 and 30 years of age. Physical aggression appears to be linked to upper body strength, which is highly sexually dimorphic, probably due to sexual selection in males (Sell, Hone, & Pound, 2012).

Archer (2004) also looked at indirect aggression in sixty-one studies. He found that the female bias increases with age from 6 to 17 years, reaching a peak between 11 and 17 years. He found little evidence of a behavioral sex bias among adults, and in the few cross-cultural studies of indirect aggression reviewed, there was no sex bias or female bias. One limitation of Archer's meta-analysis is that it only reported sex differences in aggression, not absolute levels of aggression, so it is not clear if absolute levels of indirect aggression peak during this age range.

The sex difference in indirect aggression peaks at puberty, suggesting the role of sexual selection (Campbell, 1995; see also Geary, 1998). Why should female aggression peak earlier than male aggression? I argue that, just as physically aggressive behavior in males should peak at the ages at which males would have been competing for mates in the ancestral environment, indirect aggressive behavior should peak in females at the ages at which females would have been competing for mates in the ancestral environment (Hess & Hagen, 2006b). Worldwide, women tend to marry at younger ages than men—in less well-developed regions, the

average age at first marriage for men is 24.9, and for women, 21.4. In the 15- to 19-year-old age category, over five times as many women are married (14.7%) as men (2.6%) (unweighted averages across 199 and 191 countries and regions, respectively; data from United Nations, 2000). It is conceivable that, in the ancestral environment, an even greater fraction of women and an even smaller fraction of men in the 15- to 19-year-old age category would have been married. Female intrasexual aggression, if related to mating, should therefore peak earlier than male intrasexual aggression. In addition, girls begin and complete puberty earlier than boys (Mouritsen et al., 2013). Further, many first marriages in the ancestral environment would have been arranged by parents and other senior family members. In order to influence the decision-making of these parties, young women might have had to spread negative gossip about competitors. Consistent with this, the female bias in indirect aggression is greatest among 11- to 17-year-olds, and the male bias in physical aggression is greatest among 18- to 30-year-olds (Archer, 2004). Nonetheless, most women compete for mates into their 20s and beyond to retain mates or in order to switch to new mates.

The conclusion of most studies, then, is that men physically aggress much more than women across all ages, but the sexes indirectly aggress equally often, with a possible female bias only in adolescence. Given that females in many nonhuman animals, including nonhuman primates, frequently engage in physical aggression, the evolutionary conundrum is why women rarely engage in physical aggression. Several hypotheses have been advanced.

Campbell (1999) argues that physical aggression is less common among women than men because maternal care is more crucial to female inclusive fitness than paternal care is to male inclusive fitness. When conflicts arise, women cannot afford the high costs of physical aggression and instead engage in indirect or low-level direct combat such as negative gossip (Archer, 2009; Campbell, 1999). However, nonhuman female mammals all face the same high costs yet often engage in physical aggression.

Gossip Is Better than Physical Aggression for Within-Group Competition

Another potential explanation for women's avoidance of physical aggression is that, whereas between-group competition emphasizes physical formidability and is arguably more important for males, within-group competition emphasizes reputation and is arguably equally important to females and males. For within-group competition, indirect aggression is superior to physical aggression. Within-group physical aggression entails the risk of injuring a fellow group member. Although physically harming a competitor might increase one's access to a resource, injuring a competitor also reduces the benefits that competitor can provide to other group members, such as goods and services, protection from predators, and military strength. Physical aggression also puts the aggressor at risk of injury, similarly reducing the benefits he or she can provide to other group members. Further, physical aggression within groups can undermine a group's ability to compete with other groups. Aka hunter-gatherers, for instance, view physical aggression as one of the worst acts an Aka can do (Hess, Helfrecht, Hagen, Sell, & Hewlett, 2010). Knauft (1991, p. 13) notes that in hunter-gatherer groups, "interpersonal aggression and violence tend to be unrewarded if not actively devalued by men and women alike." Thus, women and men would be discouraged from physically aggressing against fellow group members.

In contrast, gossip can be important information that is sought after by group members. People want to know about people that they are or will be in exchange relationships with, and, importantly, they are going to want to know both positive and negative attributes about those people. Gossip, whether it reflects negatively or positively on its subject, can *benefit* other group members—people *want* to know accurate information about members of their group. Thus, gossip about community members, even negative gossip, should be discouraged much less than physical aggression toward community members and when the competition is within groups.

In addition, whereas physical aggression would harm an individual's ability to provide benefits to others in multiple domains (e.g., one's ability to forage *and* one's ability to engage in intergroup conflict), gossip can be more specifically tailored to serve a targeted, strategic, competitive end. Gossip allows an individual to harm a competitor in one domain (e.g., his or her mate status) while sparing that person's well-being in other domains (e.g., his or her ability to care for a sick family member, to gather water). With gossip, one can limit a competitor's *access* to desired resources, thereby increasing one's own access to those resources, without limiting that competitor's ability to *provide* resources to other community members; this makes gossip a good weapon for within-community competition.

A final potential account of why women engage in less physical aggression than men is related to human pair-bonding: most adult females have close ties to an adult male. In humans, men are physically much more physically formidable than women (Pheasant, 1983). If a woman physically aggressed against another woman, this might bring her into conflict with that woman's spouse, who would almost certainly prevail in a physical conflict. Hence, female–female physical aggression might quickly become a fight between the husbands.

Sex Differences in Indirect Aggression

Most studies have not found a sex difference in self-reported indirectly aggressive behavior, with perhaps a small female bias in late adolescence and none in adults (Archer, 2004). However, in a scenario study involving conflict with a same-sex competitor and employing both forced choices and Likert scale ratings of desires to retaliate, Hess and Hagen (2006b) found clear evidence of sex differences. In the forced-choice paradigm, significantly more women expressed a *desire* to retaliate with gossip (90%) than with physical aggression (10%), whereas men were about evenly divided in their desire to retaliate with gossip (55%) versus physical aggression (45%); controlling for social norms and approval, the odds of a woman retaliating with gossip was 14.22 times higher than that of a man. In the Likert scale ratings, women expressed significantly stronger desire to retaliate with gossip than did men (moderately large effect, Cohen's $d = -0.39$).

In addition, men's desire to retaliate with gossip was more strongly influenced by perceived social norms against gossip than was women's: even women who thought it was wrong to gossip had a strong desire to gossip, whereas men who thought it was wrong to gossip did not desire to retaliate with gossip. Finally, these differences could not be explained by sex differences in social norms against gossiping or physical aggression because, although social norms did have a strong influence on women's and men's retaliation strategies, there were minimal sex differences in perceived social norms against gossiping. Thus, even though there does not appear to be much of a sex difference in gossiping behavior (if any), there does appear to be a clear sex difference in gossiping psychology.

Another limitation of most studies of adult aggression is that they utilize self-reports and are often conducted in Western populations. In a study of physical and indirect aggression in Aka hunter-gatherers of the Central African Republic that used peer ratings of aggression, Hess et al. (2010) found that, after controlling for peer-rated anger, Aka women had higher peer ratings of indirect aggression than men. Most studies of sex differences in aggression do not control for anger.

The foregoing results need to be replicated in other populations. Nevertheless, they indicate that sex differences in indirect aggression among adults might be important. If so, it is worth speculating about possible explanations. Indirect aggression is a strategy that is used by both sexes. Sex differences in the use of this strategy could occur for a number of reasons, including that the benefits of the strategy are higher for one sex, or the costs lower; that one sex more frequently finds itself in situations that evoke indirect aggression; or that competitors of one sex are more easily harmed by indirect aggression.

As discussed earlier, women may engage in less physical aggression than men for several reasons. A separate question is: "Why might women use more indirect aggression than men?" Campbell (1999) suggests that women engage in more indirect aggression because it is a safer alternative to using physical aggression. Moreover, the "indirectness" of tactics like gossip separates the aggressors from their harm, meaning the possibility of the aggressors being detected is lower, and so the possibility of the aggressors being retaliated against is lower. In contrast, with physical aggression the identity of the aggressor is known, so harm from retaliation is more likely. This safety is especially important for vulnerable pregnant women and women with dependent offspring. This hypothesis for why women use indirect aggression is reasonable, but it does have shortcomings. First, the argument should also apply to males: in female–female competition, the danger is that the victim is vulnerable because she cannot incur the fitness costs of injury inflicted by another female. However, in male–male competition, a male is also particularly vulnerable because of the fact that his *male* opponent is well-equipped to inflict severe physical harm. Losing a fight to a male might not harm dependent offspring, but it is more likely to inflict substantial damage. Second, the absence alone of one strategic option is not necessarily an argument in favor of one particular argument among multiple potential alternative arguments. Why use indirect aggression rather than physically harming or doing away with a competitor

in a secretive or long-distance manner, such as using slow-acting poison or setting dangerous traps? Third, indirect aggression does not guarantee the aggressor will go undetected. Gossips can be identified and punished. For example, among the Ashanti, gossiping against powerful individuals was punished by cutting off the perpetrator's lips (Stirling, 1956, cited in Fine & Rosnow, 1978). Fourth, as discussed earlier, among female nonhuman primates, whose physical welfare is crucial to reproductive success, physical contests are in fact common, evidenced in in part by the prevalence of female dominance hierarchies. A recent example from the popular press describes the fights and injuries that erupted among female baboons at the Toronto zoo, prompting a brief closure of the zoo's exhibit: "Brutal baboon battle erupts for throne at Toronto Zoo after matriarch dies. . . . Medical records show injuries ranging from deep lacerations near their eyes to hair ripped out and tail injuries" (Casey, 2015.)

Perhaps, then, women and girls engage in indirect aggression not because it is a safer alternative to physical aggression, but *because it is particularly effective at harming a female competitor*. One way in which gossip, ostracism, and other forms of indirect aggression might be more harmful to women than men was proposed by Geary (1998, p. 250), who suggested that indirect forms of aggression "disrupt" the reciprocal relationships of unrelated female competitors. Disrupting social relationships and inducing stress has been shown to reduce fertility in other primates (Abbott, 1993; Smuts & Nicolson, 1989, cited in Geary, 1998), and it may be the case that women disrupt social relationships and induce stress in other women as a form of reproductive competition (Geary, 1998, pp. 137–138). Geary's proximate account for why women use more indirect aggression involves hormonal attributes that women possess and men do not.

Another reason why women and girls use indirect aggression more than men and boys was suggested by Proveda (1975), who pointed out that reputation has different meanings for males and females:

> Reputation may be regarded as a function of both a person's actual behavior and of the information distribution about the person. It is suggested that in the girl's social system, reputation is achieved (or lost) largely through the manipulation of information about people. In the boy's social system, earning a reputation is much more a function of actual behavior. (p. 133)

Proveda continues

[T]he boys are not so vulnerable to this secret and sometimes vicious manipulation of information about persons since their behavior may be *publicly* tested. The behavior and social identities that are rooted in being a good athlete, a good fighter, or a good student may be relatively easily confirmed or refuted. On the other hand, how is it possible to test whether one is a "slut" or a "whore"? (p. 133)

This reasoning was also alluded to in a quote by Campbell (1995):

One teenage girl . . . remarked that "a girl that's been called a slag is the same as a boy that's been called a chicken," and indeed from the viewpoint of future reproductive success their impact is similar. A male can demonstrate that he is not a chicken by fighting anyone who impugns him. A girl, however, is unable to demonstrate in any convincing and public way that the accusation is false. Her best hope is to successfully repel anyone who so accuses her and thus minimize the chance of anyone else repeating such a reputational attack. (p. 115)

The following is a breakdown of the logic under-lying Proveda and Campbell's observations that female reputations are more vulnerable to misinformation:

1. It is difficult to disprove false gossip when relevant information is hard to come by.

2. Information about some dimensions of reputation can be hard to come by because

    a. collecting relevant information can be time-consuming (assessing someone's relative vulnerability to infectious disease, for example, would require observations over months or years);

    b. collecting relevant information can be risky (e.g., "spies," if caught, are often subject to punishment, and "nosey" people are often avoided and/or disliked);

    c. relevant information can often be actively concealed; extramarital affairs, for example, are difficult to investigate;

    d. relevant information may be available only to certain individuals who are unwilling to share it; and

    e. once obtained, it is often necessary to process relevant information in order to determine how it impacts on a person's reputation; this processing can be time-consuming and may require considerable additional background information.

3. Dimensions of reputation that are difficult to confirm are therefore more vulnerable to false gossip than dimensions that are easy to confirm.

4. Compared to men, a greater fraction of female reputation depends on difficult-to-confirm dimensions of reputation.

5. Women are therefore more vulnerable to false gossip than are men.

6. Gossip is therefore a more effective competitive strategy for women than men.

The key premise of this sex difference argument is step 4. Although many aspects of male and female reputation are equally important and equally easy or difficult to confirm (such as political abilities, medical abilities, kinship ties, etc.), in ancestral environments, some important but difficult-to-confirm dimensions of male and female reputation arguably constituted a greater fraction of female reputation than male reputation: fertility, fidelity, child-care ability, and ability or intent to cooperate with affines (relatives by marriage rather than shared biological descent).

There is a large sex difference in the minimum level of parental investment. Due to the fact that women get pregnant and men do not, women's reproductive capacity is a valuable and limited resource over which men compete. In addition, especially in societies characterized by alliance by marriage, parents and other authority figures also seek to influence and control women's reproductive choices. Consequently, if a woman's reproductive ability is reduced (e.g., premature infertility), or if she uses it in socially disapproved ways (e.g., infidelity), these could have imposed substantial fitness costs on her husband, family, in-laws (likely a significant fraction of the community she married into), and any other community members benefiting from any alliances that were solidified by her socially approved marriage.

In contrast, although a man's infertility is costly to him, his wife could have often married another group member—perhaps a brother—and no one *else* would have suffered a fitness cost (there is little competition over men's sperm). Philandering by a man would also not necessarily impose a cost on his wife and family members unless he also expended resources to obtain extra-pair mating opportunities and/or invested in the socially disapproved offspring. Sex differences in parental investment, then, might explain why fertility and fidelity are more important dimensions of female reputation than male reputation.

Compared to men, women's willingness and ability to invest in offspring, including gestation, lactation, and other critical forms of direct care, also have a larger impact on offspring survivorship. Men may have had a greater variance in their willingness and ability to invest in offspring than women (see La Cerra, 1995), but it is not the amount of variance in child investment that matters. What matters is the effect that variance has on the outcome, which is child survivorship. Whereas mothers might have an ability to buffer unpredictability in male parental investment, fathers simply could not buffer variance in, for example, a mate's willingness to nurse a child. Consequently, ability and willingness to parent should be a more important determinant of female reputation than male reputation.

Female exogamy—the practice of women marrying outside the tribe, family, clan, community, or other social unit or group—is much more common than male exogamy in contemporary small-scale societies, including hunter-gatherer societies (cf. Marlowe, 1999). Data from the Ethnographic Atlas show that 69% of societies studied practice female exogamy (Rodseth et al., 1991, p. 230; see also Murdock, 1967), a pattern supported by genetic data (Lippold et al., 2014; Seielstad, Minch, & Cavalli-Sforza, 1998). Female exogamy puts exogamous women in the position of being expected to make costly economic and political contributions to group members to whom they are not biologically related. Absent kinship, exogamous women may feel disinclined to do so. Moreover, they may be unable to do so for various reasons, such as lacking sufficient resources, lacking relevant cultural knowledge or important skills, or physical limitations. When community members have not observed a new woman's history of providing valuable contributions and benefits, the woman can be vulnerable to a competitor's misrepresentations of her willingness and ability to do so. Ethnographic evidence indicates that young women marrying into a new group often face considerable social hardships and competition from resident women (e.g., Sudanese women (Kenyon, 1994); Zincanteco women (Haviland, 1977, 1988); Yanomamö women (Peters, 1998; Valero, 1965); and women in gangs (Campbell, 1995)). For example, Haviland (1977, p. 188) described gossip among Zincanteco Indians from highland Chiapas as a form of within-group competition, "[a] new bride, introduced to her husband's household, represents a serious potential

breach of confidentiality; her in-laws begrudge her to even occasional visits to her own mother, where she can leak out family secrets and gossip about her new household to an outsider." Haviland later discusses how a newly married woman's unmarried, coresiding sisters-in-law can "make life unbearable for a young woman who has never before lived away from her own hearth," a young woman whom they view as "incompetent and an intolerable spy in their midst" (Haviland, 1988, p. 417). Female "exogamy" can also result from raiding. Peters (1998, pp. 116–117) described the experiences of recently kidnapped Yanomamö women in their captors' village: "Other women will belittle her for non-Xilixana behavior or her peculiar accent. Her status improves with time, after she integrates and bears children." Helena Valero, a Spanish woman kidnapped by a Yanomamö group when she was a child, provided a firsthand account of the conflict engendered by wife capture (Valero, 1965):

> Every woman of the shapuno said to her husband's female prisoner: "Now you'll do as I say. You'll have to go gather wood for me, and water in the igarape for me. If you don't do it, I'll beat you.' One woman replied, "I came because your husband brought me; I should have run away at once." The husband said: "Stop talking, else I'll give you both a beating." The wife went on: 'No, I will kill her and then you will burn her by yourself; I will run off with other men. (p. 44)

When female exogamy and polygyny—the marrying of one man to multiple wives—occur in concert, female–female competition and conflict among affines is compounded. Young women entering groups with polygynous mating systems can face especially strong competition with unrelated co-wives, their children, sisters-in-law, and others. For example, Shostak (1981, p. 170) writes of tension among Ju/'hoansi co-wives, "Many become furious when their husband suggests [polygyny]. They claim that sexual jealousy, rivalry, subtle (and not so subtle) favoritism, and disputes over chores and other responsibilities make the polygynous life a very unpleasant one." Senior wives appear to have the upper hand in these competitions. Shostak quotes a Ju/'hoansi woman discussing her position in a polygynous marriage, "I am in the stronger position because I am older and because I married our husband first.... I can tell my sister to get water, but she never tells that to me" (p. 170). Shostak reports that senior wives had the power to make the lives of a new co-wife and the husband miserable to the point that the new wife opted to leave the marriage. Senior wives also appear to have more children and healthier children than junior wives in small-scale, polygynous societies (e.g., Daly & Wilson, 1983, as cited in Geary, 1998, p. 250; Hagen, Hames, Craig, Lauer, & Price, 2001; Sellen, 1999; Strassman, 1997). The benefits of seniority may result from demonstrated success in providing one's affines and other community members with reproductive, economic, and other benefits. I would posit that senior wives also reap benefits from memberships in well-established coalitions with other women, perhaps in the domain of informational warfare.

To summarize, fertility, fidelity, child-care ability, and ability or intent to cooperate with affines were probably equally difficult to ascertain for both sexes. However, these qualities in women were arguably more important to most other community members than the same qualities in men because male reproductive capacity (i.e., sperm) was cheap and easily replaced, because male childcare was less important to offspring survivorship than female childcare, and because male–male cooperation was probably facilitated by within-group kinship (due to males less commonly leaving their natal communities at marriage). Fighting and hunting ability might have been more important determinants of male reputation than female reputation. However, fighting and hunting were relatively easy to assess and thus less vulnerable to inaccurate gossip. When challenged, a man fights and wins or he loses; a man regularly comes home with game or he does not. Of course, information about fighting and hunting ability will be gossiped about, but inaccurate gossip can be easily corrected. The unequivocal evidence that would be needed to disconfirm false accusations about a female's fertility, fidelity, child-care ability, and intent to cooperate with new in-laws can be difficult or impossible to acquire.

I suggest one final reason for why women and girls might use indirect aggression more than men and boys: women and girls might have faced more within-group competition than men and boys because women were more often exogamous than men (Lippold et al., 2014) and thus had the challenge of integrating into new groups of nonkin (Hess, 2006). As argued earlier, gossip is a better within-group competitive strategy than physical aggression. If gossip were a better within-community competitive strategy than physical aggression, and if female exogamy (*or anything else*) caused

women to face more within-community competition than men, then ancestral women may have been under stronger selection than ancestral men to aggress against same-sex others with gossip.

Within-Coalition Dynamics: The Role of Reciprocity in "Friendship"

In critiquing evolutionary accounts of human friendship that have assumed reciprocity explains much of human "friendship" among nonkin, Silk (2003) discusses evidence distinguishing between exchange relationships and communal relationships. In exchange relationships, individuals give benefits to strangers or casual acquaintances with an expectation that comparable benefits will be returned. In communal relationships, which tend to occur in close friendships and among kin, benefits are given when needed, and there is no obligation for reciprocity. Studies show that immediate, short-term, tit-for-tat-style exchanges are more characteristic of exchange relationships than communal relationships. These findings call into question the role of reciprocity in deeper, communal relationships. Shackelford and Buss (1996) defend the role of reciprocity in close friendships. Silk (2003) summarizes their argument, but then dismisses it:

> Shackelford and Buss (1996) suggest that the difference in the dynamics of reciprocity in communal and exchange relationships reflects differences in the timescale over which accounting is done. According to their view, in coalitions and exchange relationships, the shadow of the future is short, and immediate reciprocity is required to prevent exploitation and cheating. In communal relationships (such as close friendships), the shadow of the future is extended, and there is more tolerance of short-term imbalances in relationship accounts. In such cases, insistence on immediate reciprocity signals uncertainty about the continuation of the relationship, and thus elicits feelings of concern, distress, or betrayal. They hypothesize that the difference in responses to requests for immediate reciprocation by close friends and coalition partners . . . arises because a demand for immediate reciprocity implies that future interactions are unlikely to occur. This is more disturbing for close friends, and elicits stronger feelings of betrayal, than for coalition partners. Although this explanation might explain why friends avoid Tit-for-Tat reciprocity, it does not explain why they obscure their contributions to joint tasks with friends. (p. 47)

Silk concludes that the function of close, cooperative relationships with nonkin, such as close friend, remains an unsolved puzzle.

What is interesting about Shackelford and Buss's (1996) study, and Silk's (2003) take on it, is that "coalitions" are viewed as more similar to exchange relationships than communal (or "close friend") relationships. I believe that an alternative view of "close friends" *as coalitions* may help to elucidate the friendship puzzle: relationships that fit the "friends" construct function to cooperatively analyze information, particularly social and reputational information. On this view, friendships serve the goal of understanding and manipulating the social environment via the cooperative collection, analysis, and dissemination of information. One might ask, however, why close or enduring friendships serve this goal better than acquaintances or temporary allies. The answer is that close, long-term friends are able to make better use of relevant information. They are more likely to know the intentions, history, and characteristics of the people involved, the relevant background information, and the details of the current predicament as they relate to various parties. As one college sorority informant said of her closest sorority friends in an interview (Hess, 2006, p. 353): "They know the people; they know the situation."

Conclusion

Humans might be a supporting data point for one general and powerful claim of the socioecological model: that, for both sexes, coalitions are useful in within-group contest competition to maintain or improve rank or reputation. I have proposed that the value of coalitions is not limited to the domain of physically aggressive competition. The coalitional manipulation of reputations might be more effective than reputational manipulation by individuals because coalitions have improved abilities to strategically collect, analyze, and disseminate information. Coalitions can do this offensively by harming the reputations of competitors and defensively by protecting the reputations of coalition members. In addition, information from multiple individuals may be more believable. Further, I have proposed that the benefits of coalitions are not limited to male competition. In contrast to nonagonistic theories of women's friendship (e.g., Taylor et al., 2000), female alliances and coalitions may be beneficial in contest competition for resources when the "weapon" is not physical aggression but reputational manipulation and other forms of indirect aggression.

Alliances and coalitions are clearly useful in alternative forms of competition not addressed here, such as ostracism, enforcement of costly group norms, and punishment. Wilson (1997) and Wilson et al. (2004) argue that in addition to activities such as hunting and warfare, cooperation can also evolve in the context of cognitive activities, such as perception, memory, attention, and decision-making; for cognitively difficult tasks, two (or more) minds are better than one. I have applied and extended this idea to reputational competition, where one "difficult task" is discovering the objectionable acts committed, or the undesirable traits possessed, by one's opponent. This task can be difficult because it requires observing rare events, or acts or traits that are usually concealed (e.g., few readily admit to cheating on a spouse, failing to help others in need, or lacking some essential skill). In this sense, two "detectives" are better than one.

Coalitions can be useful for noncompetitive goals that do not involve violence or the exchange of reputation-relevant information—goals that improve manipulating the environment (such as cooperative net hunting) and goals that involve understanding the nonsocial environment (such as exchanges of hard-to-acquire information about rare food resources or medicinal plants; see, e.g., Kaplan & Gurven, 2005). Often, inferences of social and ecological conditions must be made based on fragmentary, ambiguous, and perhaps contradictory information. Coalition members can make use of social and ecological data structures that have been processed, or partially processed, by others. Further, coalitions are likely quite valuable for improved collection and analysis of many kinds of nonsocial information, such as how to assemble different data collection components of a Mars lander. For additional benefits of enduring, cooperative relationships, see, for example, Smuts (1992), Tooby and Cosmides (1996), Hawley (1999), and Henrich and Gil-White (2001). These benefits notwithstanding, improved information collection and processing is an important benefit of belonging to within-group cliques or coalitions (Wilson et al., 2004), regardless of the ultimate use to which the processed information is allocated.

References

Abott, D. H. (1993). Social conflict and reproductive suppression in marmoset and tamarin monkeys. In W. A. Mason &

S. P. Mendoza (Eds.), *Primate social conflict* (pp. 331–372). Albany: State University of New York Press.

Abrahams, R. D. (1970). A performance-centered approach to gossip. *Man, 5,* 290–301.

Abu-Lughod, L. (1986). *Veiled sentiments.* Berkeley: University of California Press.

Adler, P. A., & Adler. P. (1998). *Peer power: Preadolescent culture and identity.* New Brunswick, NJ: Rutgers University Press.

Alexander, R. D. (1987). *The biology of moral systems.* New York: Aldine de Gruyter.

Archer, J. (2004). Sex differences in aggression in real-world settings: A meta-analytic review. *Review of General Psychology, 8,* 291–322.

Archer, J. (2009). Does sexual selection explain human sex differences in aggression? *Behavioral and Brain Sciences, 32,* 249–266.

Archer, J., & Coyne, S. M. (2005). An integrated review of indirect, relational, and social aggression. *Personality and Social Psychology Review, 9,* 212–230.

Archie, E. A., Morrison, T. A., Foley, C. A. H., Moss, C. J., & Alberts, S. C. (2006). Dominance rank relationships among wild female African elephants, *Loxodonta Africana. Animal Behaviour, 71,* 117–127.

Barclay, P., & Willer, R. (2007). Partner choice creates competitive altruism in humans. *Proceedings of the Royal Society B: Biological Sciences, 274*(1610), 749–753.

Barker, J. L., Barclay, P., & Reeve, H. K. (2012). Within-group competition reduces cooperation and payoffs in human groups. *Behavioral Ecology, 23,* 735–741.

Barkow, J. H. (1989). *Darwin, sex, and status: Biological perspectives on mind and culture.* Toronto: University of Toronto Press.

Barkow, J. H. (1992). Beneath new culture is old psychology: Gossip and social stratification. In J. H. Barkow, L. Cosmides, & J. Tooby (Eds.), *The adapted mind: Evolutionary psychology and the generation of culture* (pp. 627–637). New York: Oxford University Press.

Barrett, L., & Henzi, S. P. (2002). Constraints on relationship formation among female primates. *Behaviour, 139,* 263–289.

Baumeister, R. F., Vohs, K. D., & Zhang, L. (2004). Gossip as cultural learning. *Review of General Psychology, 8,* 111–121.

Beersma, B., & van Kleef, G. A. (2011). How the grapevine keeps you in line: Gossip increases contributions to the group. *Social Psychological and Personality Science, 2,* 642–649.

Beisner, N. (1989). Information withholding as a manipulative and collusive strategy in Nukulaelae gossip. *Language in Society, 18,* 315–341.

Benenson, J. B., Hodgson, L., Heath, S., & Welch, P. J. (2008). Human sexual differences in the use of social ostracism as a competitive tactic. *International Journal of Primatology, 29,* 1019–1035.

Bernstein, I. S. (1981a). Dominance relationships and ranks: Explanations, correlations, and empirical challenges. *Behavioral and Brain Sciences, 4*(3), 449–457.

Bernstein, I. S. (1981b). Dominance: The baby and the bathwater. *Behavioral and Brain Sciences, 4,* 419–429.

Binford, L. R. (2001). *Constructing frames of reference: An analytical method for archaeological theory building using ethnographic and environmental data sets.* Berkeley: University of California Press.

Björkqvist, K., Österman, K., & Kaukiainen, A. (1992). The myth of the nonaggressive female. In K. Björkqvist & P. Niemela (Eds.), *Of mice and women: Aspects of female aggression* (pp. 3–16). San Diego: Academic Press.

Bloom, P. (2004). Postscript to the special issue on gossip. *Review of General Psychology, 8,* 138–140.

Blurton-Jones, N. B. (1984). A selfish origin for food sharing: Tolerated theft. *Ethology and Sociobiology, 5,* 1–3.

Blurton-Jones, N. B. (1987). Tolerated theft: Suggestions about the ecology and evolution of sharing, hoarding, and scrounging. *Social Science Information, 26,* 31–54.

Boinski, S., Sughrue, K., Selvaggi, L., Quatrone, R. Henry, M., & Cropp, S. (2002). An expanded test of the ecological model of primate social evolution: Competitive regimes and female bonding in three species of squirrel monkeys (*Saimiri oerstedii, S. boliviensis,* and *S. sciureus*). *Behaviour, 139,* 227–261.

Brenneis, D. (1984). Grog and gossip in Bhatgaon: Style and substance in Fiji Indian conversation. *American Ethnologist, 11,* 487–506.

Brenneis, D. (1987). Talk and transformation. *Man, 22,* 499–510.

Bull, J. J., & Rice, W. R. (1991). Distinguishing mechanisms for the evolution of co-operation. *Journal of Theoretical Biology, 149,* 63–74.

Burbank, V. K. (1994). Cross-cultural perspectives on aggression in women and girls: An introduction. *Sex Roles, 30,* 169–176.

Buss, D. M. (1988a). The evolution of human intrasexual competition: Tactics of mate attraction. *Journal of Personality and Social Psychology, 54*(4), 616–628.

Buss, D. M. (1988b). From vigilance to violence: Tactics of mate retention in American undergraduates. *Ethology and Sociobiology, 9*(5), 291–317.

Buss, D. M., & Dedden, L. (1990). Derogation of competitors. *Journal of Social and Personal Relationships, 7,* 395–422.

Campbell, A. (1995). A few good men: Evolutionary psychology and female adolescent aggression. *Ethology and Sociobiology, 16,* 99–123.

Campbell, A. (1999). Staying alive: Evolution, culture, and women's intra-sexual aggression. *Behavioral and Brain Sciences, 22,* 203–252.

Casey, L. (2015, November 29). Brutal baboon battle erupts for throne at Toronto Zoo after matriarch dies. *The Toronto Star.*

Changon, N. A. (1968). *Yąnomamö, the fierce people: Case studies in cultural anthropology.* New York: Holt, Rinehart & Winston.

Chapais, B. (1996). Competing through co-operation in non-human primates: Developmental aspects of matrilineal dominance. *International Journal of Behavioral Development, 19,* 7–23.

Colson, E. (1953). *The Makah Indians.* Manchester, UK: Manchester University Press.

Cox, B. A. (1970). What is Hopi gossip about? Information management and Hopi factions. *Man, 5,* 88–98.

Cox, S. J., Sluckin, T. J., & Steele, J. (1999). Group size, memory, and interaction rate in the evolution of cooperation. *Current Anthropology, 40,* 369–377.

Creel, S. R., & Waser, P. M. (1997). Variation in reproductive suppression among dwarf mongooses: Interplay between mechanisms and evolution. In N. G. Solomon & J. A. French (Eds.), *Cooperative breeding in mammals* (pp. 150–170). Cambridge, UK: Cambridge University Press.

Crick, N. R., & Grotpeter, J. K. (1995). Relational aggression, gender, and social-psychological adjustment. *Child Development, 66,* 710–722.

Daly, M., & Wilson, M. (1983). *Sex, evolution, and behavior.* Boston: Willard Grant.

De Backer, C. J. (2005). *Like Belgian chocolate for the universal mind: Interpersonal and media gossip from an evolutionary perspective* (Unpublished doctoral dissertation). Universiteit Gent, Gent, Belgium. Retrieved from http://www.ethesis.net/gossip/gossip_contence.htm

Drews, C. (1993). The concept and definition of dominance in animal behaviour. *Behaviour, 125,* 283–313.

Dugatkin, L. A. (1995). Partner choice, game theory and social behavior. *Journal of Quantitative Anthropology, 5,* 3–14.

Dunbar, R. I. M. (1993). Co-evolution of neocortex size, group size and language in humans. *Behavioral and Brain Sciences, 16,* 681–735.

Dunbar, R. I. M. (1996). *Grooming, gossip, and the evolution of language.* London: Faber & Faber.

Dunbar, R. I. M. (2004). Gossip in evolutionary perspective. *Review of General Psychology, 8,* 100–110.

Dyson-Hudson, R., & Smith, E. A. (1978). Human territoriality: An ecological reassessment. *American Anthropologist, 80,* 21–41.

Eckert, P. (1990). Cooperative competition in adolescent "girl talk." *Discourse Processes, 13,* 91–122.

Eder, D., & Enke, J. L. (1991). The structure of gossip: Opportunities and constraints on collective expression among adolescents. *American Sociological Review, 56,* 494–508.

Eder, D., & Hallinan, M. T. (1978). Sex differences in children's friendships. *American Sociological Review, 43,* 237–250.

Emler, N. (1990). A social psychology of reputation. In W. Stroebe & M. Hewstone (Eds.), *European Review of Social Psychology* (Vol. 1, pp. 171–193). Chichester, England: John Wiley.

Enquist, M., & Leimar, O. (1993). The evolution of cooperation in mobile organisms. *Animal Behaviour, 45,* 747–757.

Feshbach, N., & Sones, G. (1971). Sex differences in adolescent reactions toward newcomers. *Developmental Psychology, 4,* 381–386.

Fine, G. A. (1977). Social components of children's gossip. *Journal of Communication, 27,* 181–185.

Fine, G. A., & Rosnow, R. L. (1978). Gossip, gossipers, gossiping. *Personality and Social Psychology Bulletin, 4,* 161–168.

Galen, B. R., & Underwood, M. K. (1997). A developmental investigation of social aggression among children. *Developmental Psychology, 33,* 589–600.

Geary, D. C. (1998). *Male, female: The evolution of human sex differences.* Washington, DC: American Psychological Association.

Gilbert, P. (1997). The evolution of social attractiveness and its role in shame, humiliation, guilt and therapy. *British Journal of Medical Psychology, 70,* 113–147.

Gilmore, D. (1978). Varieties of gossip in a Spanish rural community. *Ethnology, 17,* 89–99.

Gintis, H., Smith, E. A., & Bowles, S. (2001). Costly signaling and cooperation. *Journal of Theoretical Biology, 213,* 103–119.

Gluckman, M. (1963). Gossip and scandal. *Current Anthropology, 4,* 307–316.

Gluckman, M. (1968). Psychological, sociological, and anthropological explanations of witchcraft and gossip: Clarification. *Man, 3,* 2–124.

Goodwin, M. H. (1980). He-said-she-said: Formal cultural procedures for the construction of a gossip dispute activity. *American Ethnologist, 7,* 674–695.

Goodwin, M. H. (1982). "Instigating": Storytelling as social process. *American Ethnologist, 7,* 799–819.

Goodwin, M. H. (1988). Cooperation and competition across girls' play activities. In A. D. Todd & S. Fisher (Eds.), *Gender and discourse: The power of talk* (pp. 55–96). Norwood, NJ: Ablex.

Goodwin, M. H. (1990a). *He-said-she-said: Talk as social organization among black children.* Bloomington: Indiana University Press.

Goodwin, M. H. (1990b). Tactical uses of stories—participation frameworks within the girls' and boys' disputes. *Discourse Processes, 13,* 52–71.

Gottman, J. M., & Mettetal, G. (1986). Speculations about social and affective development: Friendship and acquaintance through adolescence. In J. M. Gottman & J. G. Parker (Eds.), *Conversations of friends: Speculations on affective development* (pp. 192–237). Cambridge, UK: Cambridge University Press.

Grueter, C. C., Bissonnette, A., Isler, K., & van Schaik, C. P. (2013). Grooming and group cohesion in primates: implications for the evolution of language. Evolution and Human Behavior, 34(1), 61-68.

Gurven, M., Allen-Arave, W., Hill, K., & Hurtado, M. (2000). "It's a wonderful life": Signaling generosity among the Ache of Paraguay. *Evolution and Human Behavior, 21,* 263–282.

Hagen, E. H. (1995). *Intraspecific exploitative mimicry in humans.* Paper presented at the Human Behavior and Evolution Society annual meeting. Santa Barbara, CA, June.

Hagen, E. H., Hames, R. B. Craig, N. M., Lauer, M. T., & Price, M. E. (2001). Parental investment and child health in a Yanomamö village suffering short-term food stress. *Journal of Biosocial Science, 33,* 503–528.

Hamilton, M. J., Milne, B. T., Walker, R. S., Burger, O., & Brown, J. H. (2007). The complex structure of hunter-gatherer social networks. *Proceedings of the Royal Society B: Biological Sciences, 274,* 2195–2202.

Harcourt, A. H., & de Waal, F. (1992). *Coalitions and alliances in humans and other animals.* Oxford: Oxford University Press.

Haviland, J. B. (1977). Gossip as competition in Zincantan. *Journal of Communication, 27,* 185–191.

Haviland, J. B. (1988). We want to borrow your mouth: Tzotzil marital squabbles. *Anthropological Linguistics, 30,* 395–447.

Hawkes, K. (1991). Showing off: Tests of an hypothesis about men's foraging goals. *Ethology and Sociobiology, 12,* 29–54.

Hawkes, K., O'Connell, J. F., & Blurton-Jones, N. G. (2001). Hadza meat sharing. *Evolution and Human Behavior, 22,* 113–142.

Hawley, P. H. (1999). The ontogenesis of social dominance: A strategy-based evolutionary perspective. *Developmental Review, 19,* 97–132.

Hawley, P. H., Little, T. D., & Card, N. A. (2008). The myth of the alpha male: A new look at dominance-related beliefs and behaviors among adolescent males and females. *International Journal of Behavioral Development, 32,* 76–88.

Henrich, J., & Gil-White, F. J. (2001). The evolution of prestige. *Evolution and Human Behavior, 22,* 165–196.

Hess, N. H. (2006). *Informational warfare: Female friendship and coalitional manipulation of reputation* (Unpublished doctoral dissertation). University of California, Santa Barbara.

Hess, N. H., & Hagen, E. H. (2006a). Psychological adaptations for assessing gossip believability. *Human Nature, 17,* 337–354.

Hess, N. H., & Hagen, E. H. (2006b). Sex differences in indirect aggression: Psychological evidence from young adults. *Evolution and Human Behavior, 27*, 231–245.

Hess, N. H., Helfrecht, C., Hagen, E. H., Sell, A., & Hewlett, B. S. (2010). Interpersonal aggression among Aka hunter-gatherers of the Central African Republic: Assessing the effects of sex, strength, and anger. *Human Nature, 21*, 337–354.

Hewlett, B. S. (1992). *Father–child relations: Cultural and biosocial contexts.* New York: Aldine de Gruyter.

Holekamp. K. E., Cooper, S. M., Katona, C. I., Berry, N. A., Frank, L. G., & Smale, L. (1997). Patterns of association among female spotted hyenas (*Crocuta crocuta*). *Journal of Mammalogy, 78*, 55–64.

Holland, D. C., & Eisenhart, M. A. (1990). *Educated in romance: Women, achievement, and college culture.* Chicago: University of Chicago Press.

Isbell, L. A., & Young, T. P. (2002). Ecological models of female social relationships in primates: Similarities, disparities, and some directions for future clarity. *Behaviour, 139*, 177–202.

Izar, P., Verderane, M. P., Peternelli-Dos-Santos, L., Mendonça-Furtado, O., Presotto, A., Tokuda, M., & Fragaszy, D. (2012). Flexible and conservative features of social systems in tufted capuchin monkeys: Comparing the socioecology of Sapajus libidinosus and Sapajus nigritus. *American Journal of Primatology, 74*, 315–331.

Janson, C. H. (2000). Primate socio-ecology: The end of a golden age. *Evolutionary Anthropology, 9*, 73–86.

Kaplan, H., & Gurven, M. (2005). The natural history of human food sharing and cooperation: A review and a new multi-individual approach to the negotiation of norms. In H. Gintis, S. Bowles, R. Boyd, & E. Fehr (Eds.), *Moral sentiments and material interests: The foundations of cooperation in economic life* (pp. 75–113). Cambridge, MA: MIT Press.

Kappeler, P. M., & van Schaik, C. P. (2002). Evolution of primate social systems. *International Journal of Primatology, 23*, 707–740.

Kelly, R. L. (1995). *The foraging spectrum.* Washington, DC: Smithsonian Institution Press.

Kenyon, S. (1994). Gender and alliance in central Sudan. In J. Dickerson-Putman & J. K. Brown (Eds.), *Women among women: Anthropological perspectives on female age hierarchies* (pp. 15–29). Urbana: University of Illinois Press.

Koenig, A. (2002). Competition for resources and its behavioral consequences among female primates. *International Journal of Primatology, 23*, 759–783.

Knauft, B. (1991). Violence and sociality in human evolution. *Current Anthropology, 32*, 391–428.

Kurzban, R. (2001). The social psychophysics of cooperation: Nonverbal communication in a public goods game. *Journal of Nonverbal Behavior, 25*, 241–259.

Laidler, K. J., & Hunt, G. (2001). Accomplishing femininity among the girls in the gang. *British Journal of Criminology, 41*, 656–678.

Laosa, L. M., & Brophy, J. E. (1972). Effects of sex and birth order on sex-role development and intelligence among kindergarten children. *Development Psychology, 6*, 409–415.

La Cerra, M. M. (1995). *Evolved mate preferences in women: Psychological adaptations for assessing a man's willingness to invest in offspring* (Unpublished doctoral dissertation). University of California, Santa Barbara.

Leaper, C., & Holliday, H. (1995). Gossip in same-gender and cross-gender friends' conversations. *Personal Relationships, 2*, 237–246.

Lee, R. B. (1984). *The Dobe! Kung.* New York: Holt, Rinehart & Winston.

Leimar, O., & Hammerstein, P. (2001). Evolution of cooperation through indirect reciprocity. *Proceedings of the Royal Society B: Biological Sciences, 268*, 745–753.

Lever, J. (1974). *Games children play: Sex differences and the development of role skills* (Unpublished doctoral dissertation). Yale University, New Haven.

Lindenfors, P., Froberg, L., & Nunn, C. L. (2004). Females drive primate social evolution. *Proceedings of the Royal Society B: Biological Sciences, 271(Suppl. 3)*, S101–S103.

Lippold, S., Xu, H., Ko, A., Li, M., Renaud, G., Butthof, A., & Stoneking, M. (2014). Human paternal and maternal demographic histories: Insights from high-resolution Y chromosome and mtDNA sequences. *Investigative Genetics, 5*, 1–17.

Lowie, R. H. (1948). *Social organization.* New York: Rinehart.

Marlowe, F. (1999). Showoffs or providers: The parenting effort of Hadza men. *Evolution and Human Behavior, 20*, 391–404.

Martin, R. P., Vahdat, A. M., Culler, D. E., & Anderson, T. E. (1997). Effects of communication latency, overhead, and bandwidth in a cluster architecture. In *Proceedings of the 24th Annual International Symposium on Computer Architecture:* (Vol. 25, No. 2, pp. 85–97). New York: Association for Computing Machinery.

Maynard-Smith, J. A., & Parker, G. A. (1976). The logic of asymmetric contests. *Animal Behaviour, 24*, 159–175.

McAndrew, F. T., & Milenkovic, M. A. (2002). Of tabloids and family secrets: The evolutionary psychology of gossip. *Journal of Applied Social Psychology, 32*, 1064–1082.

Merry, S. E. (1984). Rethinking gossip and scandal. In D. Black (Ed.), *Toward a general theory of social control, Vol. 1: Fundamentals.* Orlando, FL: Academic Press, pp. 47–74.

Milinski, M., Semmann, D., Bakker, T. C. M., & Krambeck, H.-J. (2001). Cooperation through indirect reciprocity: Image scoring or standing strategy? *Proceedings of the Royal Society B: Biological Sciences, 268*, 2495–2501.

Milinski, M., Semmann, D., & Krambeck, H.-J. (2002). Reputation helps solve the "tragedy of the commons." *Nature, 415*, 424–426.

Miller, G. (2000). *The mating mind: How sexual choice shaped the evolution of human nature.* New York: Anchor Books.

Mohtashemi, L., & Mui, M. (2003). Evolution of indirect reciprocity by social information: The role of trust and reputation in evolution of altruism. *Journal of Theoretical Biology, 223*, 523–531.

Molleman, L., van den Broek, E., & Egas, M. (2013). Personal experience and reputation interact in human decisions to help reciprocally. *Proceedings of the Royal Society of London B: Biological Sciences, 280*(1757). doi:10.1098/rspb.2012.3044

Mouritsen, A., Aksglaede, L., Soerensen, K., Hagen, C. P., Petersen, J. H., Main, K. M., & Juul, A. (2013). The pubertal transition in 179 healthy Danish children: Associations between pubarche, adrenarche, gonadarche, and body composition. *European Journal of Endocrinology, 168*(2), 129–136.

Murdock, G. P. (1967). *Ethnographic atlas.* Pittsburgh, PA: University of Pittsburgh Press.

Noë, R. (1992). Alliance formation among male baboons: Shopping for profitable partners. In A. H. Harcourt & F. B. M. de Waal (Eds.), *Coalitions and alliances in humans and other animals* (pp. 285–322). Oxford: Oxford University Press.

Noë, R., & Hammerstein, P. (1994). Biological markets: Supply and demand determine the effect of partner choice in cooperation, mutualism and mating. *Behavioral Ecology and Sociobiology*, *35*(1), 1–11.

Nöe, R., van Schaik, C. P., & van Hoof, J. A. (1991). The market effect: An explanation for pay-off asymmetries among collaborating animals. *Ethology*, *87*, 97–118.

Nowak, N. A., & Sigmund, K. (1998). Evolution of indirect reciprocity by image scoring. *Nature*, *393*, 573–577.

O'Connell, J. F., Hawkes, K., Lupo, D., & Blurton-Jones, N. G. (2002). Male strategies and Plio-Pleistocene archaeology. *Journal of Human Evolution*, *43*, 831–872.

Omark, D. R., & Edelman, M. (1973). *Peer group social interactions from an evolutionary perspective*. Paper presented at the Society for Research in Child Development Conference, Philadelphia, March.

Owens, D., & Owens, M. (1996). Social dominance and reproductive patterns in brown hyaenas, Hyaena brunnea, of the central Kalahari desert. *Animal Behaviour*, *51*, 535–551.

Owens, L., Shute, R., & Slee, P. (2000a). "Guess what I just heard!": Indirect aggression among teenage girls in Australia. *Aggressive Behavior*, *26*, 67–83.

Owens, L., Shute, R., & Slee. P. (2000b). "I'm in and you're out &": Explanations for teenage girls' indirect aggression. *Psychology, Evolution, and Gender*, *2*, 19–46.

Panchanathan, K., & Boyd, R. (2003). A tale of two defectors: The importance of standing for evolution of indirect reciprocity. *Journal of Theoretical Biology*, *224*, 115–126.

Paine, R. (1967). What is gossip about? An alternative hypothesis. *Man*, *2*, 278–285.

Pandit, S. S., & van Schaik, C. P. (2003). A model for leveling coalitions among primate males: Toward a theory of egalitarianism. *Behavioral Ecology and Sociobiology*, *55*, 161–168.

Peters, J. F. (1998). *Life among the Yanomami*. Ontario: Broadview Press.

Pheasant, S. T. (1983). Sex differences in strength: Some observations on their variability. *Applied Ergonomics*, *14*, 205–211.

Pollock, G., & Dugatkin, L. A. (1992). Reciprocity and the emergence of reputation. *Journal of Theoretical Biology*, *159*, 25–37.

Proveda, T. G. (1975). Reputation and the adolescent girl. *Adolescence*, *10*, 127–136.

Radin, P. (1927). *Primitive man as philosopher*. New York: Appleton.

Richerson, P., & Boyd. R. (1998). The evolution of human ultra-sociality. In I. Eibl-Eibesfeldt & F. K. Salter (Eds.), *Indoctrinability, ideology and warfare* (pp. 71–96). New York: Berghahn Books.

Richerson, P., & Boyd, R. (1999). Complex societies: The evolutionary origins of a crude superorganism. *Human Nature*, *10*, 253–289.

Rodseth, L., Wrangham, R. W., Harrigan, A. M., & Smuts, B. B. (1991). The human community as a primate society. *Current Anthropology*, *32*, 221–254.

Roulette, C. J., Hagen, E. H., & Hewlett, B. S. (2016). A biocultural investigation of gender differences in tobacco use in an egalitarian hunter-gatherer population. *Human Nature*, *27*(2), 105–129.

Schjelderup-Ebbe, T. (1922). Beiträge zur Sozialpsychologie des Haushuhns. *Zeitschrift fur Psychologie*, *88*, 225–252.

Seielstad, M. T., Minch, E., & Cavalli-Sforza. L. L. (1998). Genetic evidence for a higher female migration rate in humans. *Nature Genetics*, *20*, 278–280.

Sell, A., Hone, L., & Pound, N. (2012). The importance of physical strength to human males. *Human Nature*, *23*, 30–44.

Sellen, D. W. (1999). Polygyny and child growth in a traditional pastoral society. *Human Nature*, *10*, 329–371.

Shackelford, T. K., & Buss, D. M. (1996). Betrayal in mateships, friendships, and coalitions. *Personality and Social Psychology Bulletin*, *22*, 1151–1164.

Shostak, M. (1981). *Nisa: The life and words of a !Kung woman*. New York: Vintage Books.

Silk, J. B. (2002a). Females, food, family, and friendship. *Evolutionary Anthropology*, *11*, 85–87.

Silk, J. B. (2002b). Using the "F"-word in primatology. *Behaviour*, *139*, 421–446.

Silk, J. B. (2003). Cooperation without counting: The puzzle of friendship. In P. Hammerstein (Ed.), *Genetic and cultural evolution of cooperation* (pp. 36–53). Cambridge, MA: MIT Press.

Silk, J. B. (2007a). The adaptive value of sociality in mammalian groups. *Philosophical Transactions of the Royal Society B*, *362*, 539–559.

Silk, J. B. (2007b). The strategic dynamics of cooperation in primate groups. *Advances in the Study of Behaviour*, *37*, 1–42.

Smith, E. A., Bird, R. B., & Bird, D. W. (2003). The benefits of costly signaling: Meriam turtle hunters. *Behavioral Ecology*, *14*(1), 116–126.

Smith, E. A., & Bliege Bird, R. L. (2000). Turtle hunting and tombstone opening: Public generosity as costly signaling. *Evolution and Human Behavior*, *21*, 245–261.

Smith, E. A., & Winterhalder, B. (Eds.). (1992). *Evolutionary ecology and human behavior*. Hawthorne, NY: Aldine de Gruyter.

Smuts, B. B. (1992). Male aggression against women: An evolutionary perspective. *Human Nature*, *3*, 1–44.

Smuts, B. B., & Nicholson, N. (1989). Dominance rank and reproduction in female baboons. *American Journal of Primatology*, *19*, 229–246.

Smuts, B. B., & Smuts, R. W. (1993). Male aggression and sexual coercion of females in nonhuman primates and other mammals: Evidence and theoretical implications. *Advances in the Study of Behavior*, *22*, 1–63.

Sommerfeld, R. D., Krambeck, H. J., & Milinski, M. (2008). Multiple gossip statements and their effect on reputation and trustworthiness. *Proceedings of the Royal Society B: Biological Sciences*, *275*, 2529–2536.

Sommerfeld, R. D., Krambeck, H. J., Semmann, D., & Milinski, M. (2007). Gossip as an alternative for direct observation in games of indirect reciprocity. *Proceedings of the National Academy of Sciences*, *104*(44), 17435–17440.

Sterck, E. H. M., Watts, D. P., & Van Schaik, C. P. (1997). The evolution of female social relationships in nonhuman primates. *Behavioral Ecology and Sociobiology*, *41*, 291–309.

Stiner, M. C. (2002). Carnivory, coevolution, and the geographic spread of the genus Homo. *Journal of Archaeological Research*, *10*, 1–63.

Stirling, R. B. (1956). Some psychological mechanisms operative in gossip. *Social Forces*, *34*, 262–267.

Strassman, B. I. (1997). Polygyny as a risk factor for child mortality among the Dogon. *Current Anthropology*, *38*, 688–695.

Sugiyama, L. S., & Chacon, R. (2000). Effects of illness and injury among the Yora and Shiwiar. In N. A. Chagnon, L. Cronk, & W. Irons (Eds.), *Human behavior and adaptation: An anthropological perspective* (pp. 371–395). New York: Aldine de Gruyter.

Sugiyama, L. S., & Sugiyama, M. S. (2003). Social roles, prestige, and health risk. *Human Nature, 14*(2), 165–190.

Suls, J. M. (1977). Gossip as social comparison. *Journal of Communication, 27*, 164–168.

Symons, D. (1979). *The evolution of human sexuality*. Oxford: Oxford University Press.

Szwed, J. F. (1966). Gossip, drinking, and social control: Consensus and communication in a Newfoundland parish. *Ethnology, 5*, 434–444.

Taylor, S. E., Klein, L. C., Lewis, B. P., Gruenewald, T. L., Gurung, R. A. R., & Updegraff, J. A. (2000). Biobehavioral responses to stress in females: Tend-and-befriend, not fight-or-flight. *Psychological Review, 107*, 411–429.

Tiger, L. (1969). *Men in groups*. New York: Random House.

Tooby, J., & Cosmides, L. (1988). *The evolution of war and its cognitive foundations*. Technical Report 888–1. Palo Alto, CA: Institute for Evolutionary Studies.

Tooby, J., & Cosmides, L. (1996). Friendship and the banker's paradox. *Proceedings of the Royal British Academy, 88*, 119–143.

Trivers, R. L. (1972). Parental investment and sexual selection. In B. Campbell (Ed.), *Sexual selection and the descent of man, 1871–1971* (pp. 136–179). Chicago: Aldine de Gruyter.

Underwood, M. K., Galen, B. R., & Paquette, J. A. (2001). Top ten challenges for understanding gender and aggression in children: Why can't we all just get along? *Social Development, 10*, 248–266.

United Nations. (2000). World marriage patterns 2000. Retrieved from http://www.un.org/esa/population/publications/worldmarriage/worldmarriage.htm.

Valero, H. (1965). *Yanoama*. New York: E. P. Dutton.

van Schaik, C. P. (1983). Why are diurnal primates living in groups? *Behaviour, 87*, 120–144.

van Schaik, C. P. (1989). The ecology of social relationships amongst female primates. In V. Standen & R. A. Foley (Eds.), *Comparative socioecology: The behavioural ecology of humans and other mammals* (pp 195–218). Oxford: Blackwell.

Waldrop, M. F., & Halverson, C. F. Jr. (1975). Intensive and extensive peer behavior: Longitudinal and cross-sectional analyses. *Child Development, 46*, 19–26.

Watkins, S. C., & Danzi, A. D. (1995). Women's gossip and social change: Childbirth and fertility control among Italian and Jewish women in the United States, 1920–1940. *Gender & Society, 9*, 469–490.

Wedekind, C., & Milinski, M. (2000). Cooperation through image scoring in humans. *Science, 288*, 850–852.

Wert, S. R., & Salovey, P. (2004). A social comparison account of gossip. *Review of General Psychology, 8*, 122–137.

Wilson, D. S. (1997). Incorporating group selection into the adaptationist program: A case study involving human decision making. In J. Simpson & D. Kenrick (Eds.), *Evolutionary social psychology* (pp. 345–386). Mahwah, NJ: Erlbaum.

Wilson, D. S., Timmel, J. J., & Miller, R. R. (2004). Cognitive cooperation. *Human Nature, 15*, 225–250.

Wilson, D. S., Wilczynski, C., Wells, A., & Weiser, L. (2000). Gossip and other aspects of language as group-level adaptations. In C. Heyes & L. Huber (Eds.), *The evolution of cognition* (pp. 347–365). Cambridge, MA: MIT Press.

Wilson, P. J. (1974). Filcher of good names: An enquiry into anthropology and gossip. *Man, 9*, 93–102.

Wrangham, R. W. (1980). An ecological model of female-bonded primate groups. *Behaviour, 75*, 262–300.

Wrangham, R. W., & Peterson, D. (1996). *Demonic males: Apes and the origins of human violence*. New York: Houghton Mifflin.

Xie, H., Cairns, R. B., & Cairns, B. D. (2002). The development of social aggression and physical aggression: A narrative analysis of interpersonal conflicts. *Aggressive Behavior, 28*, 341–355.

Mate Availability and Mating Relationships

Do Women Compete for Mates When Men Are Scarce? Sex Ratio Imbalances and Women's Mate Competition Cross-Culturally

Emily A. Stone

Abstract

This review explores whether and how imbalances in the number of men and women—the sex ratio—affects mating competition. I evaluate the available evidence against two hypotheses: a mating supply and demand hypothesis, which predicts mate competition to increase when mates are scarce, and predictions from a 'faithful as your options' hypothesis, which suggests mate competition should increase with a surplus of mates because the returns to mating effort are greatest. Men's mating effort consistently increased with a surplus of mates, supporting the 'faithful as your options' hypothesis, but results for women's mating effort were mixed. Some measures supported the mating supply and demand hypothesis, some supported the 'faithful as your options' hypothesis, and some found no relationship with the sex ratio. Socioeconomic development may explain variation in sex ratio effects for women if men are better able to constrain women's mating effort in traditional societies, or other variables, like variation in mate quality, may better explain women's mate competition.

Key Words: mating effort, sex ratio, parental investment, sexual selection, mate choice, aggression, mate preferences, cross-cultural, sociosexuality

Introduction

The goal of this chapter is to explore whether, and how, women compete over mates as a function of one variable hypothesized to intensify women's competition: the sex ratio. In the social sciences, the sex ratio has been measured as the number of reproductive-aged men per 100 women (e.g., Guttentag & Secord, 1983), and researchers studying mating have used it as a window into men's and women's mate preferences and competition strategies (Pedersen, 1991; Schmitt, 2005). The reasoning has been—*sensu* supply and demand—a scarcity of mating opportunities should increase the intensity of competition among the surplus sex (Emlen & Oring, 1977). Also, it should reveal the preferences of the scarce sex because they have

more alternative potential mates available to them and may be in good position to exert their preferences (Guttentag & Secord, 1983; Pedersen, 1991). Newer theoretical models in biology follow the old adage that men are as faithful as their options and predict the opposite relationship between a scarcity of mates and the intensity of competition, however. These models predict increased competition when returns to mating effort are greatest—when there is a surplus of mates.

I review evidence from sociology, psychology, and anthropology to evaluate the evidence for two hypotheses about how sex ratio imbalances impact women's mate competition: the mating supply and demand hypothesis and the 'faithful as your options' hypothesis. Throughout, I emphasize data from small-scale societies and cross-cultural samples in an effort to provide as representative an account of women's behavior as possible (e.g., Henrich, Heine, & Norenzayan, 2010).

Sex Ratio in Sociology

The consequences of imbalances in the sex ratio were first popularized by Guttentag and Secord (1983) in their book *Too Many Women? The Sex Ratio Question*. They examine the demographic and social consequences of sex ratio imbalances in historical and contemporary datasets using a social exchange perspective, which emphasizes power and dependency as a result of market forces to understand romantic relationships (Cameron, Oskamp, & Sparks, 1977). This perspective proposes that the amount one person depends on his or her partner for satisfaction indicates the amount of power wielded by that partner, and this should be affected by the sex ratio. A member of the sex in short supply should be less dependent on his or her partner because that person has more alternative potential mates available to him or her. Guttentag and Secord call this *dyadic power* and propose that it allows members of the sex in short supply to negotiate more favorable outcomes from their partners than they might otherwise be able to negotiate. However, Guttentag and Secord note that a second concept also applies: most, if not all, societies are patriarchal, and thus women's ideal options—when potential husbands are plentiful and women have greater dyadic power—are yet constrained by men's greater *structural power*. Thus, they attempt to explain the effects of imbalanced sex ratios across contemporary and historical societies as the result of an interaction between men's and women's dyadic and structural power.

Although pervasive in the sociology literature, this perspective makes many of the same predictions as the mating supply and demand hypothesis, which I introduce next. The available data do not allow for distinguishing between them, but I reviewed it here due to its historical importance.

Sex Ratio and the Mating Supply and Demand Hypothesis

Pedersen (1991) combined concepts from Guttentag and Secord's (1983) social exchange perspective with sexual selection theory; namely, he added the concept of mate choice and mate preferences to predict mating success in societies with an imbalanced sex ratio. He suggested, similar to previous researchers, that the sex in excess should

compete intensely for members of the scarce sex, but he added that this competition should take the form of the preferred marital traits of the scarce sex. For example, men tend to place greater emphasis on physical attractiveness in a long-term mate than women do (e.g., Buss, 1989); thus, Pedersen hypothesized that women compete to improve their physical appearance when men are scarce. This is similar to Guttentag and Secord's prediction regarding dyadic power because it presumes that the scarce sex has the power to drive mate competition toward their preferred domains (e.g., men's preference for attractiveness should increase women's competition to display it when men are scarce). It differs from the Guttentag and Secord perspective, however, by arguing that the resulting patterns reveal evolved sex differences in men's and women's mate preferences and corresponding competition tactics, rather than resulting from an interaction between dyadic and structural power. Thus, from this perspective, sex ratio imbalances are a powerful tool to reveal underlying mate preferences and, to the extent a shortage of mates intensifies mating effort, reveal tactics in mate competition.

Explaining Variation in Sex Roles and Mating Effort

The term "sex roles" is shorthand for the amount of reproductive effort allocated to mating versus parenting, which tends to vary between the sexes. Because this chapter reviews one variable hypothesized to affect the amount of effort women devote to mating competition—the sex ratio—it's important to note the other variable that has historically received the most attention to explain sex roles and mating effort: sex differences in parental investment. This argument begins by considering the consequences of sex differences in primary sexual traits. In humans, these sex differences include a difference in minimal obligatory parental investment required to reproduce (Trivers, 1972). For men, this is as brief as a few minutes, whereas for women, reproduction entails a minimum of months, and likely longer, for gestation and subsequent breastfeeding. These sex differences in the potential reproductive rates of males and females result in what are considered to be conventional sex roles (Clutton-Brock & Vincent, 1991)—namely, that males tend to be ardent in competing over choosy, discriminating females, who provide most of the parental care (Darwin, 1871).

Explaining sex roles as a consequence of sex differences in parental investment has been criticized in evolutionary biology as a logical fallacy, however, because "sunk costs" in initial parental investment (e.g., expensive ovum) do not predict optimal allocation toward additional parental investment (e.g., gestation, lactation, and subsequent care, instead of competing for mating opportunities; Dawkins & Carlisle, 1976). Newer theoretical models have identified several variables that might instead explain the origin of sex roles—one of which is the sex ratio (Kokko & Jennions, 2008).

Sex Ratio and the 'Faithful as Your Options' Hypothesis

New biological models hypothesize the sex ratio should have important consequences for mating and parenting effort because it creates frequency-dependent costs and benefits to competing and caring if there are different numbers of males and females in a population (Kokko & Jennions, 2008). That is, imbalances in the sex ratio should affect the costs and benefits of competition, such that if men are the scarce sex (a low sex ratio), the benefits of competition (additional mating opportunities among a surplus of women) increase faster than the costs (the risk of injury or death). The logic underlying this hypothesis is the old adage that 'men are as faithful as their options,' and these new biological models have essentially mathematically formalized it. In addition, these models remind us that every baby requires one mother and one father, and although men have a faster *potential* reproductive rate, their actual reproductive rate must, on average, be the same as women's—but only if the adult sex ratio is equal (Queller, 1997).

To illustrate—in a population where women are scarce (a high sex ratio), there are few benefits for a man leaving his mate to compete for new mating opportunities if a new wife is hard to find. Contrary to older perspectives (e.g., Emlen & Oring, 1977; Pedersen, 1991) that argue that a scarcity of mates increases demand, these models indicate that if mates are scarce, competing is not necessarily the best option, especially if everyone else is competing, too. The abundant sex, rather than increasing the intensity of competition over the scarce sex, should *avoid* competition, because new mates are hard to find, and increase their parenting effort instead (Kokko & Jennions, 2008). One caveat in applying this model to humans is that it was designed to explain the origin of sex roles and may not apply to shorter time scales; feedback about frequency-dependent costs and benefits may require longer periods, like generations, rather than the time scales

under investigation by most social scientists. There is evidence, however, that human populations adjust to the frequency-dependent benefits of imbalanced sex ratios in brief time scales, insofar as the sex of people's offspring (termed "sex allocation") adjusts to the sex ratio of the population: in a preindustrial Finnish society, there were significantly more boys born in low sex ratio parishes, where the reproductive benefits of being among the rare baby boys are greater than being one of the relatively plentiful baby girls (Lummaa, Merilä, & Kause, 1998).

An additional qualification is that the sex ratio is not the only variable the models indicate should affect sex roles—variation in paternity certainty and sexual selection on males should, too (Kokko & Jennions, 2008). However, those literatures are beyond the scope of this review, and I focus only on the sex ratio for the remainder of this chapter.

Whither Sex Ratio? A Note on Sex Ratio in Biology

Social scientists were not the first to predict that imbalances in the number of males and females in a population might affect mating dynamics. Emlen and Oring, in 1977, introduced the term *operational sex ratio* (OSR) as a measure of the intensity of competition over mates. The OSR consists of two components: the ratio of reproductive-aged men to women that we have been discussing here—termed the *adult sex ratio* in biology—and an additional term for receptivity, which is the availability to mate and reproduce (e.g., Kvarnemo & Ahnesjö, 1996). That is, in humans, a woman is not "available to mate" during her pregnancy—a new mating opportunity could not result in an additional pregnancy—but her husband's could. Including this term for "availability to mate" in the OSR captures additional information about parental investment and reproductive rates that vary between the sexes and between species and may provide a more precise measure of the reproductive resources at stake.

The new biological models explaining the origins of sex roles, and which motivate the 'faithful as your options' hypothesis, highlight important distinctions between the adult sex ratio and the OSR. First, the potential reproductive rate that is included in the calculation of the OSR—that second term—may not be as informative as the actual reproductive rate (Kokko & Jennions, 2008). In addition, biologists have until recently used the OSR and the adult sex ratio almost interchangeably in their experiments. Many studies manipulated the numbers of males and females in an effort to manipulate the OSR (e.g., Chipman & Morrison, 2013; Dreiss, Cote, Richard, Federici, & Clobert, 2010; Owens & Thompson, 1994). The discussion over the importance of the OSR relative to the adult sex ratio continues (e.g., Kokko, Klug, & Jennions, 2012; see also Dillon, Adair, & Brase [this volume] for additional discussion on the OSR and the adult sex ratio in humans). This chapter will focus on the adult sex ratio to allow for testing predictions from the 'faithful as your options' hypothesis, but also for pragmatic reasons. There are few studies examining the OSR in humans (e.g., Blurton Jones, Marlowe, Hawkes, & O'Connell, 2000; Hurtado & Hill, 1992; see also Marlowe & Berbesque, 2012) compared to a great many reporting relationships with the adult sex ratio.

Hypotheses

Following Emlen and Oring (1977), the *mating supply and demand hypothesis* (Pedersen, 1991; Campbell, 2013) predicts that a shortage of mates will increase the intensity of women's mate competition—in particular, competition to display traits attractive to men (Pedersen, 1991). Thus, given men's greater interest in short-term, casual relationships (e.g., Buss & Schmitt, 1993; Schmitt, 2003), this hypothesis predicts that women should be more interested and willing to engage in these relationships when men are scarce (low sex ratio societies). Women should also increase their intensity of competition in additional domains preferred by men, including physical attractiveness (e.g., Buss, 1989) and perhaps resource competition (e.g., South, 1991). Additionally, women should compete using aggression when mates are scarce (Campbell, 2013).

In contrast, the *'faithful as your options' hypothesis* (Kokko & Jennions, 2008) predicts the opposite relationship between a shortage of mates and competition: men and women each should compete most intensely when the returns to mating effort are greatest—when there is a surplus of mates. If everyone else is competing over scarce husbands in low sex ratio societies, it might pay women to devote more effort to parenting; if men are plentiful in high sex ratio societies, then the benefits that may accrue to women of mating effort (e.g., Brown, Laland, & Borgerhoff Mulder, 2009; Hrdy, 2000) should be relatively larger. According to this hypothesis, a shortage of mates should lead to *less* mate competition; whereas, according to the mating supply and demand hypothesis, a shortage of mates should lead to *more* mate competition.

Ironically, although the two hypotheses predict opposite relationships between the sex ratio and the intensity of competition, they predict similar patterns for marriage rates and marital stability. This is because they place different emphasis on evaluating mate competition as a function of mate preferences versus tradeoffs. The mating supply and demand hypothesis tests for the sex ratio to interact with marriage patterns, which should reveal sex differences in preferred amounts of parental investment (e.g., Buss & Schmitt, 1993) among the scarce sex. The 'faithful as your options' hypothesis is interested in these same patterns of parental investment because it should trade off with levels of mating effort if human reproductive effort reflects either mating or parenting effort (e.g., Betzig, 1988). Thus, in high sex ratio societies where women are scarce, both hypotheses expect men to devote more effort to caring (which might also manifest as mate guarding), reflected by early and stable marriages. From a mating supply and demand perspective, this occurs because women's scarcity allows them to exert their preferences for paternal investment (e.g., Buss & Schmitt, 1993); this also supports the 'faithful as your options' hypothesis, however, which predicts the same outcome as a consequence of the reduced payoff to mating effort if new mating opportunities are rare in high sex ratio societies.

A Note on the Causes of Sex Ratio Imbalances

Population variation is ultimately due to three factors: births, deaths, and migration (Guttentag & Secord, 1983). The emphasis in this chapter is on the potential *consequences* of imbalances in the sex ratio, but across the world, there appear to be different *causes* of imbalanced sex ratios. For example, the Amazonian region in Brazil contains large deposits of natural resources, drawing a fast-growing number of men to work the mines to extract them (Roberts & Dodoo, 1995). In contrast, Chinese sex ratio imbalances are primarily due to sex-specific infanticide favoring boys, which is exacerbated by the country's one-child policy (Hudson & den Boer, 2004). In a cross-national sample, Schmitt and Rohde (2013) found sex ratio imbalances to be highly correlated with sex differences in mortality rates. This is likely the case in Colombia, where the very low sex ratios in some states are driven by excess male mortality due to violence rather than male migration (Jones & Ferguson, 2006).

Most of the research reviewed here is correlational, rather than experimental. As a result, we cannot conclusively determine if those findings are caused by sex ratio imbalances. Where available, I will highlight the results of experiments. For the remainder, there are two reasons we might suppose them to be linked. First, there are distinct causes of sex ratio imbalances across the world, and despite this, many variables show fairly consistent patterns. Second, all studies include a number of control variables, although these vary by study. Until we have a larger body of experimental work—and it is growing in psychology (e.g., Griskevicius et al., 2012; Watkins, Jones, Little, DeBruine, & Feinberg, 2012)—this will remain a limitation of much sex ratio research.

Thus, I examine whether the available evidence supports the mating supply and demand hypothesis or the 'faithful as your options' hypothesis to understand how imbalances in the sex ratio relate to women's mate competition.

Analysis

There are several ways we might measure mating competition to test if it increases when mates are scarce (the mating supply and demand hypothesis) or if it increases with a surplus of mates (the 'faithful as your options' hypothesis). First, I review measures that may indicate an overall intensity of mating effort, including the marital patterns (such as marital stability) discussed previously, but also sociosexuality, mate poaching, and marriage systems. Then, I review specific tactics of mate competition, including aggression and mate choice competition, which should vary in frequency according to the intensity of women's mating competition and thus provide a test of our hypotheses.

The Sex Ratio and General Measures of Mating Effort

MARRIAGE AND REPRODUCTION

A great deal of research in sociology examines the consequences of sex ratio imbalances for marriage and reproduction. They find a consistent general pattern using a variety of measures: high sex ratio societies are associated with a greater proportion of the population marrying (Albrecht, Fossett, Cready, & Kiecolt, 1997; Angrist, 2002; Cox, 1940; Lichter, McLaughlin, Kephard, & Landry, 1992; South & Trent, 1988), marriage at earlier ages (Kruger, Fitzgerald, & Peterson, 2010; South, 1988; Trent & South, 2011; Trovato, 1988), fewer divorces (Albrecht & Albrecht, 2001; Blurton Jones, et al., 2000; South & Trent, 1988; Trent & South, 1989, 2003), higher fertility rates (Fu,

1992; Schmitt & Rohde, 2013; South, 1988), and fewer births out of wedlock (Barber, 2001, 2003; Fossett & Kiecolt, 1990, 1991). Thus, the general pattern is one of early, stable, and fertile marriages in high sex ratio societies where men outnumber women, and unstable, lower-investing relationships in low sex ratio societies where there is a surplus of women.

As mentioned earlier, this is consistent with predictions from both perspectives. The mating supply and demand hypothesis predicts that men can exert their preferences for short-term, low-investing relationships in low sex ratio societies because they have an excess of mating options—and women thus compete to display these traits to attract mates (Pedersen, 1991; Schmitt, 2005). The 'faithful as your options' hypothesis also predicts less paternal care and lower-investing relationships in low sex ratio societies because the returns to men's mating effort are higher compared to when women are scarce (Kokko & Jennions, 2008). For these patterns, it is difficult to distinguish the role of women's mating effort from men's, however, so perhaps additional measures provide a better test.

SOCIOSEXUALITY AND MATE "POACHING"

Some studies have attempted to capture men's and women's mating effort more directly than marriage measures by using the Sociosexuality Orientation Inventory (SOI). Sociosexuality includes self-reported attitudes and behaviors that endorse casual sex (e.g., "Sex without love is OK," "Number of sexual partners within the past year"), and sex differences in this measure are considered to represent men's greater exertion of mating effort compared to women (e.g., Schmitt, 2005). People who are interested in sex without commitment, thereby possessing an "unrestricted SOI," are more likely to have sex earlier in their relationships, maintain sexual relationships with multiple partners concurrently, and be in relationships that are less committed and investing (Simpson & Gangestad, 1991). They are also less attracted to people with good parenting qualities, preferring instead mates who are physically attractive, and are indeed more likely to be dating an attractive partner (Simpson & Gangestad, 1992). Ethological and self-report investigations provide behavioral evidence that sociosexually unrestricted people engage in more mating effort as measured by flirting behaviors (Bleske-Rechek & Buss, 2006; Simpson, Gangestad, & Biek, 1993) and by a greater number of lifetime sexual partners (Yost & Zurbriggen, 2006).

Thus, variation in sociosexuality is thought to reflect variation in mating effort (e.g., Schmitt, 2005) and likely captures some indication of the time and intensity a person expends attracting mates and mating opportunities. As such, women should report relatively unrestricted sociosexuality when men are scarce, according to the mating supply and demand hypothesis, whereas the 'faithful as your options' hypothesis predicts the opposite—that women should have an unrestricted sociosexuality when mates are abundant and the returns to mating effort are great.

An analysis of men's and women's combined average SOI scores across 48 countries found SOI was negatively related to a country's sex ratio, meaning that men and women in low sex ratio countries reported they were comfortable with and engaged in more short-term relationships (Schmitt, 2005). Because men's and women's sociosexuality measures were combined, however, it's difficult to test predictions regarding women's mating effort. Additional evidence comes from an online survey replicating that study, which sampled over 200,000 people from 53 countries and analyzed men's and women's SOI scores separately (Lippa, 2007). There was a marginally significant trend for men's and women's SOI scores to negatively correlate with the national sex ratio, thus providing suggestive support for the mating supply and demand hypothesis. A more recent study replicated these two, analyzing participants' SOI scores by US state (Kandrik, Jones, & DeBruine, 2015). They found SOI scores were negatively related to the sex ratio for *both* men and women. This provides the first substantive evidence to distinguish between the hypotheses. However, to the extent that sociosexuality captures general mating effort, it indicates conflicting support: variation in women's sociosexuality is consistent with the mating supply and demand hypothesis; men's is consistent with the 'faithful as your options'. Both men and women may compete more when there is a surplus of women.

Additional support for this pattern comes from a related measure analyzed by US county. Among a representative sample of 12,571 people in 2002, both men and women were more likely to report having concurrent, overlapping sexual partners if they lived in a low sex ratio county relative to those living in a balanced sex ratio county (Adimora et al., 2013). There is evidence, for men, that this pattern holds at the behavioral level: among the Hadza, when there

were relatively more reproductive-aged women in camp compared to when there were fewer reproductive-aged women in camp, men spent significantly less time with their kids (Marlowe, 1999). Notably, they did not appear to spend their time directly courting women; they were instead in discussion with other men, indicating perhaps that their competition took the form of negotiating alliances. Thus, although the data are weak but suggestive at the cross-national level, there is strong reason to believe that a surplus of women is associated with increased mating effort among men.

For women, the negative relationship between sociosexuality and the sex ratio may be limited to developed societies. Schacht and Borgerhoff Mulder (2015) tested this among the Makushi, who practice slash-and-burn horticulture in southwestern Guyana. They administered the SOI to 301 people across eight Makushi villages that varied in the sex ratio and found men's (but not women's) responses to again be consistent with previous work. As the sex ratio decreased—fewer men relative to women—men's SOI scores increased while women's SOI scores remained stable across all eight villages. Thus, low sex ratios are consistently associated with mating effort among men, supporting the 'faithful as your options' hypothesis, but it is less clear how broadly sex ratio effects apply to women's mating effort.

Another window into mating effort is investigations of mate "poaching." These studies provide a more targeted measure of mating effort by examining the self-reported frequency and circumstances of consciously attempting to attract someone else's mate (Schmitt & Buss, 2001). In his study of 53 nations, Schmitt (2004) asked nearly 17,000 participants about how frequently they had tried to attract someone already in a relationship. Analyzing men and women separately, he found support for the mating supply and demand hypothesis among women: women's mate poaching was more frequent when mates were scarce. Men's mate poaching was also more frequent in low sex ratio countries, providing additional evidence that men's mating effort increases with a surplus of mates. Thus, these data are consistent with the sociosexuality measures: women's mating effort appears to support the mating supply and demand hypothesis and men's appears to support the 'faithful as your options' hypothesis. Again, however, these data derive from primarily developed nations, and it appears we need additional data from women in small-scale societies.

MARRIAGE SYSTEMS AS INDICATORS

Marriage systems are a cultural institution that can vary by society (e.g., whether polygyny is permitted or not) and may provide additional insight into mating effort from non-Western societies. Marriage systems can affect the variance in reproductive success—meaning variance in the number of offspring surviving to adulthood—which should indicate the intensity of competition over access to mates (Bateman, 1948; Brown et al., 2009). This is because if a few men are able to monopolize a large number of women, leading other men to be shut out from reproduction entirely, the intensity of competition should be higher than if mating opportunities were more evenly distributed (Betzig, 1982).

Marriage systems do correspond to variance in reproductive success in humans: men have significantly higher variance in reproductive success than do women in polygynous societies, relative to monogamous societies where the variance in men's and women's reproductive success is similar (Brown et al., 2009). Because the focus of this chapter is women's competition, polyandry might provide the converse for women, but because polyandry is rare, Brown et al. (2009) were not able to report on whether women's reproductive success differs in polyandrous societies. However, this analysis will suppose that it may be associated with greater variance in women's reproductive success than other marriage systems and is thus possibly linked to a greater intensity of mating competition among women.

Do imbalances in the sex ratio relate to marriage systems, which may serve as a society-level indicator of the intensity of competition? Consistent with the sociosexuality studies suggesting that men exert more mating effort in low sex ratio societies, a random sample of cultures drawn from the Human Relations Area Files (HRAF) indicates that polygynous societies are significantly more likely to have low sex ratios than are nonpolygynous societies (Ember, 1974). In contrast, using the Standard Cross-Cultural Sample—which consists of a representative sample of the world's cultures—Quinlan (2008) found no relationship. Additional evidence supports a relationship between polygyny and a low sex ratio, however. Pollet and Nettle (2009) investigated whether the proportion of the population polygynously married varied by the sex ratio in the 2002 Ugandan census. Using a representative sample, they found that low sex ratio districts had more polygynous marriages. Thus, if polygyny is associated with greater variance in reproductive success,

men in low sex ratio districts are likely competing more intensely than men in high sex ratio districts where women are scarce. This, too, suggests that men's mating effort supports the 'faithful as your options' hypothesis.

Starkweather and Hames (2012) examined whether this pattern extended to women. Using the HRAF, they found polyandrous societies, which may be associated with higher variance in women's reproductive success and therefore more intense mate competition, were more likely to have a high sex ratio and an excess of men. In contradiction to the sociosexuality studies, this raises the possibility that some non-Western societies—those that practice polyandry—exhibit a positive relationship between the sex ratio and women's mating effort. This relationship is reinforced by one other study (Trent & South, 2011). Using a nationally representative sample in China, although on average infrequent, women in counties with relatively higher sex ratios reported being more likely to have had premarital sex and extramarital affairs (Trent & South, 2011; see also Trent & South, 2012). Thus, these two studies provide initial support for women's mating effort increasing with a surplus of mates in some non-Western societies.

In sum, across the various general measures of mating effort, there is a consistent pattern for men in low sex ratio societies to engage in more short-term casual relationships, to engage in more mate poaching, and to marry polygynously. This pattern is consistent for cross-national, individual-level, and behavioral analyses—among developed and traditional societies alike. These measures provide strong support for men's mating effort conforming to predictions of the 'faithful as your options' hypothesis. The picture is more complicated for women. Studies of sociosexuality and mate poaching among developed populations suggest that women increase their mating effort when men are scarce (e.g., Adimora et al., 2013; Kandrik et al., 2015; Schmitt, 2004, 2005), consistent with the mating supply and demand hypothesis. In contrast, evidence from non-Western samples, including China (Trent & South, 2011) and polyandrous societies (Starkweather & Hames, 2012), suggests that women may engage in more multiple mating, and thus likely more mating effort, in high sex ratio societies. This pattern does not extend to women in all traditional societies, though, given that sex ratio variation was unrelated to women's sociosexuality among the Makushi (Schacht & Borgerhoff Mulder, 2015).

These measures are approximations of mating effort, however. Perhaps a clear pattern for women will emerge by examining the frequency of specific mate competition tactics.

Mating competition can take several forms. Darwin (1871) popularized two primary means of competition over mating opportunities: the tendency for males to compete with other males using physical aggression—what is often called *male–male competition* or *contest competition*— as well as competition to display traits attractive to females, known as *female choice* or *mate choice* (Cronin, 1991). In humans, both sexes appear to compete in both ways in some societies: qualitative evidence suggests that women compete aggressively over men (Burbank, 1987; Campbell, 1986; Lepowsky, 1994; but see Ainsworth & Maner, 2012, 2014) and vice versa (Benson & Archer, 2002; Chagnon, 1988; Wilson & Daly, 1985), but also that men and women compete to display traits attractive to the opposite sex (Buss & Dedden, 1990; Walters & Crawford, 1994) and that they both exhibit choosiness (Kenrick, Sadalla, Groth, & Trost, 1990; Stulp, Buunk, Kurzban, & Verhulst, 2013; Todd, Penke, Fasolo, & Lenton, 2007). Next, I review what we know about how imbalances in the sex ratio relate to the specific tactics women use in mate competition.

PHYSICAL AGGRESSION

Most research on physical aggression has studied men, and for good reason—they are overwhelmingly more aggressive than women, at least as far as homicides go (see Daly & Wilson, 1990, for a comparison of same-sex homicides across a number of societies). Without a doubt, women can be aggressive, too, however. It is often directed toward men (Burbank, 1992; Hines & Fry, 1994; Pizarro, DeJong, & McGarrell, 2010), but when it is directed toward other women, the causes range from jealousy over a man (Schuster, 1983; Lepowsky, 1994), to defending her own or a friend's reputation (e.g., against accusations of promiscuity; Campbell, 1986), or protecting the honor of their neighborhood (Harris, 1994).

A number of studies have investigated whether sex ratio imbalances are associated with women's physical aggression, and none find a relationship.

Campbell, Muncer, and Bibel (1998) examined women's same-sex assault rates across 34 criminal jurisdictions in Massachusetts and found a small but nonsignificant trend for there to be more assaults in lower sex ratio districts. However, their measure of sex ratio incorporated the entire population, and including people of nonreproductive ages (i.e., children or postreproductive women) might explain this weak correlation. Thus, Stone (2015) conducted a carefully matched comparison of how sex ratio imbalances relate to aggression on two small island populations. Two outer islands of Yap, in the Federated States of Micronesia, had similar population sizes, spoke the same language, and shared the same general culture but differed in the sex ratio—one had more men than women and the other had more women than men. Rates of women's reported physical aggression toward other women within the past year were nearly identical on the two islands, however, meaning that women's physical aggression was unrelated to the sex ratio. In addition, Schwartz (2006) examined 1,618 counties in the 2000 US census matched with FBI homicide data and found no relationship between imbalances in the sex ratio and women's perpetration of homicide, which also suggests that sex ratio imbalances are unrelated to women's aggressive competition. Note, however, that her dependent variable did not isolate women's same-sex homicide from aggression toward men.

The only studies that find any relationship between women's physical aggression and the sex ratio are two that have investigated women's involvement in crime, which includes assaults (Hitchell, 2004; South & Messner, 1987). They report a negative relationship between the sex ratio across nations and women-perpetrated crime rates, which would support the mating supply and demand hypothesis. Crime measures include a number of extraneous variables, like property crimes, however, and thus are not a suitable test for this analysis.

Additional support for a null effect comes from an experiment examining men's and women's competitive responses to a hypothetical scenario wherein they witnessed an attractive rival flirt with their mate. Women who had been primed to believe that mates were scarce, relative to women who were primed to think that members of the opposite sex were abundant, were no more likely to say they would behave physically aggressively toward the rival (Arnocky, Ribout, Mirza, & Knack, 2014).

Thus, there is as yet no evidence to suggest that women become more physically aggressive when there is a scarcity *or* a surplus of men.

INDIRECT AGGRESSION

As many other chapters in this volume show, physical aggression is but one way to harm another person. Indirect aggression harms a competitor circuitously, potentially allowing for the aggressor to remain anonymous. Examples of indirect aggression include spreading vicious rumors about the other person or making negative comments about their appearance to someone else (Green, Richardson, & Lago, 1996). Some researchers have found that women—in particular, adolescent girls—use indirect aggression more than do boys (e.g., Lagerspetz, Björkqvist, & Peltonen, 1988), but a number of studies show that men and women report using a similar frequency of indirect aggression (e.g., Archer & Coyne, 2005; Hess, Helfrecht, Hagen, Sell, & Hewlett, 2010). Studies do find a sex difference in adults' *relative* frequency of use, however, indicating that a larger percentage of women's aggressive behavior is indirect (e.g., Österman et al., 1998; Vaillancourt, 2013).

Does women's indirect aggression vary with the sex ratio? To my knowledge, only two studies have investigated this issue and with mixed results. Stone (2015) analyzed self-reported indirect aggression, in addition to physical aggression, on the two Micronesian islands that varied in the sex ratio and found no difference between the islands. Single women did report a higher frequency of indirect aggression than did married women, suggesting it is indeed likely related to competition for access to mates. The other study experimentally induced a perceived scarcity or surplus of mates by priming participants using fictitious magazine articles and measured their response to a scenario in which they witnessed a highly attractive rival flirting with their partner (Arnocky et al., 2014). In this case, women did report being significantly more likely to be indirectly aggressive toward the rival (e.g., make a joke about how ugly she was to her friends; tell her friends the rival was a jerk) when they believed mates were scarce relative to abundant. This finding provides experimental support for women increasing indirect aggression when mates are scarce. It may be that a shortage of men incites indirect aggression only in the case of mate guarding, thus explaining the contrasting results between the experiment and data from Micronesia. It may also be similar to the

pattern for sociosexuality, which indicated a negative relationship with the sex ratio among samples from developed nations but was unrelated to sex ratio among the Makushi. Clearly, we need additional research to understand if there is a pattern between women's indirect aggression and a shortage of mates.

MATE CHOICE COMPETITION TO DISPLAY PHYSICAL ATTRACTIVENESS

Men find a number of traits attractive in a long-term mate, including mutual attraction/love, dependable character, and emotional stability (Buss et al., 1990). Relative to women, men place greater importance on a partner's physical attractiveness (Buss, 1989). As a result, many studies have examined whether women use physical attractiveness to attract and retain mates. They do so by examining whether women find a highly attractive peer threatening or intolerable (e.g., Buss & Dedden, 1990; Vaillancourt & Sharma, 2011) or by examining self- and peer-reports of the kinds of resources and traits over which women compete, wherein they identify trying to increase one's physical attractiveness (e.g., Buss, 1988; Cashdan, 1998). That this is a primary arena of women's competition makes sense because good looks appear to be a salient feature for attracting men (e.g., Li, Bailey, Kenrick, & Linsenmeier, 2002; Marlowe, 2004).

Only a handful of studies have addressed whether women's competition to display attractiveness varies with the sex ratio (Barber, 1998a, 1998b; Pedersen, 1991), and these investigate societal trends as opposed to individual behavior. Pedersen (1991) presented a qualitative argument that the low sex ratios in the United States during the 1970s were associated with an increased emphasis on women's athletic fitness, as well as on weight loss. He argued that athletic fitness represents a more accurate indication of a woman's "reproductive efficacy" than does a proxy like beauty, and he argued that the proliferation of this fitness trend when men were scarce indicates support for increased competition in a low sex ratio society. Pedersen notes also that this 1970s trend was associated with feminist psychologies promoting women feeling in control of their bodies and less like they were catering to men's fashion whims; this logic is contradictory to an increase in the intensity of mate choice competition, however, because the nature of this competition is to increase attractiveness in the domains that men find appealing.

Another analysis examined the waist-to-hip ratios of *Playboy* centerfolds from 1959 to 1978 and found quantitative support for Pedersen's (1991) assertion: models had fewer curves in years when men were scarce (Barber, 1998a). Similar data come from an analysis of the bust-to-waist ratio of *Vogue* models from 1949 to 1993: models were curvier when there was a surplus of men (Barber, 1998b). Thus, there appears to be a historical pattern for low sex ratios to be associated with idealized figures that are less feminine. Again, although this is congruent with Pedersen's interpretation, it contradicts the mating supply and demand hypothesis that women in low sex ratio societies are competing to display traits men find attractive (as men find feminine waist-to-hip ratios; Singh, Dixson, Jessop, Morgan, & Dixson, 2010). This pattern appears to be more consistent with the 'faithful as your options' hypothesis, given that women perceive high-quality feminine traits, like feminine faces, curvier busts, and lower waist-to-hip ratios, to be greater competitive threats than low-quality feminine traits (Fink, Klappauf, Brewer, & Shackelford, 2014).

This pattern for low sex ratios to be associated with ideal physiques that are less feminine might instead be consistent with increased competition by women over other things, like resources, given that variation in women's waist-to-hip ratios reflects a tradeoff between estrogenic and androgenic hormones (Cashdan, 2008). This interpretation—that low sex ratios are related to increased competition by women over resources and not necessarily over physical attractiveness—is supported by an analysis of 117 countries that found that low sex ratio societies were associated with a greater proportion of women participating in the labor force (South & Trent, 1988; see Durante, Griskevicius, Simpson, Cantú, & Tybur, 2012, for similar experimental results) and might also explain the negative correlation between the sex ratio and women's crime, which includes theft (Hitchell, 2004; South & Messner, 1987).

In sum, although not a direct test of individual behavior, these studies suggest that women might compete to display attractiveness in high sex ratio societies when there is a surplus of men, which is consistent with predictions from the 'faithful as your options' hypothesis. Given how salient competition to increase attractiveness is for women (e.g., Cashdan, 1998), future research should examine whether this positive correlation between the sex ratio and women's attractiveness competition exists at the individual level, as well as investigate how sex ratio imbalances relate to women's resource competition.

MATE CHOICE COMPETITION TO DISPLAY RESOURCES

Although most mate selection research emphasizes women's greater interest in resources relative to men's, women's economic productivity is not irrelevant for men (e.g., South, 1991). For example, in response to the open-ended question "If you were looking for a wife, what kind of woman would you want?" more Hadza men said they look for a hard-working forager than all other traits mentioned, except for her character and her physical attractiveness (Marlowe, 2004). In addition, among the Shuar of Ecuador, men placed the same emphasis on a mate's resources as women did (Pillsworth, 2008). As such, perhaps women in some societies compete to attract high-quality mates using resources.

Dowry may represent one such cultural practice, in which a woman's family accumulates goods and resources to give to her and her husband on their marriage. Gaulin and Boster (1990) argue that in some societies—in particular, those with high social stratification and a prohibition on polygyny—dowry represents female–female economic competition over well-resourced men. Without polygyny to dilute a husband's resources, women and their families may benefit reproductively by economically competing for men who control disproportionately large resources (Gaulin & Boster, 1997). If dowry represents female competition to attract high-quality husbands, perhaps dowry prices reflect the intensity of competition and provide a test of our hypotheses.

Two studies have investigated this question. In India, Rao (1993) sampled 141 households from three southern districts and found that as the ratio of women to men who were of marriageable age increased, so did the average dowry payment. Thus, an increase in female competitors was associated with an increase in a woman's dowry, supporting the mating supply and demand hypothesis. In Taiwan, Francis (2011) examined the consequences of the influx of mainlander Chinese to Taiwan after the government was overthrown by Mao Zedong in the Communist Revolution of 1949. Seventy-one percent of marriages in Taiwan involved payments on the part of both the bride's family (dowry) and the groom's family (called bride-price). He found a similar relationship: as the number of men decreased, the ratio of bride-price to dowry payment decreased. Thus, there was a higher relative dowry payment by the bride's family when husbands were scarce. He found that this extended to highly educated men, arguably high-quality husbands, as predicted by the hypothesis: the more educated the husband, the lower the ratio of bride-price to dowry, indicating that her family was willing to pay more relative to his family.

As Dickemann (1991) notes, payment on behalf of one's family is not identical to female–female competition engaged in by the woman herself. However, in societies where women have little autonomy, dowry may represent a plausible expression of the intensity of competition over husbands, especially considering that kin contribute to marriage contracts in many societies (Gaulin & Boster, 1997). One experiment aimed to test whether a perceived shortage of mates was associated with economic competition in the West (Griskevicius et al., 2012). In a college and community sample in the United States, men, when primed to believe that their campus and community had a high sex ratio, were more likely to report that they would take economic risks by saving less and incurring more debt, whereas women's spending was unrelated to a perceived scarcity or a surplus of mates (Griskevicius et al., 2012). Risk may underlie the null effect for women's economic competition in this study, compared to the dowry analyses, which would be consistent with the null effects for another risky form of competition reviewed earlier—women's physical aggression (e.g., Arnocky et al., 2014; Campbell et al., 1998; Stone, 2015).

In conclusion, although qualitative evidence indicates that women at times use physical aggression to compete for access to mates and in mate guarding, there is no evidence that a scarcity or a surplus of mates affects the frequency of this form of competition. Support for women's indirect aggression responding to sex ratio imbalances is mixed, with one experiment supporting the mating supply and demand hypothesis (e.g., Arnocky et al., 2014) and another study reporting no relationship (Stone, 2015). However, a surplus of men may be associated with an increase in competition to attract men via feminine physiques—at least, there is evidence that cultural ideals follow this pattern—providing suggestive support for the 'faithful as your options' hypothesis. Last, although it doesn't extend to American women's likelihood of engaging in risky spending, dowry prices do appear to reflect an increasing intensity of competition when husbands are scarce, supporting the mating supply and demand hypothesis.

Conclusion and Future Directions

Both hypotheses to explain how sex ratio imbalances affect women's mating effort received some support, but neither was the clear winner. Corroborating mating supply and demand hypothesis, three measures indicated that women's mating effort increases when mates are scarce: sociosexuality (Adimora et al., 2013; Kandrik et al., 2015), albeit not among the Makushi (Schacht & Borgerhoff Mulder, 2015), mate poaching measures (Schmitt, 2004), and dowry payments (Francis, 2011; Rao, 1993). Attractiveness competition, as measured by figures in magazines, and polyandrous marriage systems provided the only consistent support for the 'faithful as your options' hypothesis (Barber, 1998a, 1998b; Starkweather & Hames, 2012). Four studies (e.g., Campbell et al., 1998; Schwartz, 2006), including one in a small-scale, traditional Micronesian society (Stone, 2015) and another an experiment (Arnocky et al., 2014), suggest that imbalances in the sex ratio are unrelated to an increase in women's physical aggression. Only two studies investigated sex ratio imbalances and indirect aggression, and these found mixed support for either the mating supply and demand hypothesis (Arnocky et al., 2014) or for no effect (Stone, 2015).

Two measures of women's mating effort were related with the sex ratio in developed nations but unrelated when tested in small-scale, traditional societies. Neither Makushi women's SOI scores (Schacht & Borgerhoff Mulder, 2015) nor Micronesian women's indirect aggression (Stone, 2015) varied by the sex ratio, in contrast to evolutionary psychological support from developed nations (e.g., Arnocky et al., 2014; Kandrik et al., 2015). This may be consistent with other research that indicates that sex ratio "effects" are stronger in developed nations than in less-developed nations (South & Trent, 1988). More specifically, Lippa (2007) found women's variability in sociosexuality decreased as gender egalitarianism decreased. Perhaps variation in women's mating effort is sensitive to men's ability to constrain women's behavior. It may be that developed societies provide an opportunity to witness women's mating effort with fewer constraints imposed by men; however, these societies are the least representative of human populations, including, most likely, ancestral human populations (Henrich et al., 2010).

Indeed, women's behavior in small-scale societies may be comparatively constrained, but they do compete over men. Among the Tsimane, for example, conflicts over men (both adulterous husbands and single men) were named as the second-most frequent type of conflict women have with other women; the most frequent same-sex conflicts were social, involving conflicts over reciprocal contract defections and friendships, and the least frequent regarded food, including food theft and meat theft (Rucas, Gurven, Winking, & Kaplan, 2012). Future research should explore what *does* consistently predict variation in women's mating effort in traditional societies, if not the sex ratio, as well as how women's mating effort interacts with men's efforts to constrain it. Additionally, it may be that other predictors of women's mating competition apply consistently across developed and undeveloped societies alike (although Lippa's 2007 analysis suggests it may not). Whether this "development effect" applies to women's mating effort more broadly than the sex ratio is another avenue for future research.

Only one pattern indicated unanimous support: men's mating effort—measured as unrestricted sociosexuality (e.g., Kandrik et al., 2015), concurrent sexual partners (e.g., Adimora et al., 2013), mate poaching (Schmitt, 2004), and likelihood of marrying polygynously (e.g., Pollet & Nettle, 2009)—increased with a surplus of mates. Importantly, this pattern held for small-scale, non-Western societies (e.g., the Makushi; Schacht & Borgerhoff Mulder, 2015), including a behavioral analysis among the Hadza that indicated men spent less time with their children when there were more women in camp (Marlowe, 1999). This increase in men's mating effort when there is a surplus of mates supports the 'faithful as your options' hypothesis.

However, as mentioned previously, this pattern has been interpreted as support for the mating supply and demand hypothesis (e.g., Kandrik, et al., 2015; Schmitt, 2005), due to evolutionary psychology's emphasis on mate preferences and on competing for mates in ways that the scarce sex finds attractive. Specifically, it supports the hypothesis that men prefer low-investing relationships and that women compete to offer these preferences when men are scarce and in demand. There are a number of reasons why this pattern is more consistent with an increase of mating effort by men, however.

First, as is evident in this review, we do not yet have a clear sense of how sex ratio imbalances impact women's competition. It remains a presumption that women's mate competition facilitates this pattern, especially if low sex ratio societies are associated with an increase in women's resource competition, rather than mating competition, as suggested earlier. Second, if sex differences in sociosexuality are interpreted to reflect sex differences in mating effort (e.g., Lippa, 2007; Schmitt, 2005), then variation in men's sociosexuality is an indicator of men's mating effort. Using that logic, this review reinterpreted results that had previously been argued as supportive of the mating supply and demand hypothesis, noting that men's data in those studies instead indicated support for the 'faithful as your options' hypothesis. This may be an incorrect interpretation of the sociosexuality measure, however, which is ultimately designed to measure willingness to have sex without commitment. Nevertheless, the remaining measures of men's mating effort (i.e., concurrent sexual partners, mate poaching, polygynous marriage, and behavioral tradeoffs with direct paternal care) indicated consistent support at all levels of analysis for a negative relationship with the sex ratio. Third, *strategic pluralism theory*, a primary evolutionary psychological hypothesis for explaining variation in men's and women's mating effort (Gangestad & Simpson, 2000), shares the same underlying logic as the 'faithful as your options' hypothesis. Although Gangestad and Simpson emphasize the role of men's symmetry and its attractiveness to women, their argument is that symmetrical men, relative to less symmetrical men, should engage in more mating effort (and less symmetrical men in more parenting effort) because the returns to symmetrical men's mating effort are greater. The 'faithful as your options' hypothesis extends this argument to all men in low sex ratio societies, where the returns to mating effort are greater than in high sex ratio societies.

This review has raised several additional issues for future investigation. One outstanding issue remains conflicting measures of mate competition. Evolutionary psychologists place great emphasis on two factors in studies of mating: mate preferences and understanding relationships on a temporal spectrum—i.e., explaining short-term, casual relationships versus long-term, committed relationships. Mate preferences are fundamental to understanding mate choice, but mate choice is only one way that men and women compete for mates (see, e.g., Andersson & Iwasa, 1996). In this case, measuring the intensity of competition as a function of preferences for temporal relationships (e.g., men's preferences for short-term relationships in low sex ratio societies vs. women's preferences for long-term relationships in high sex ratio societies), although informative, appears to have obscured the nature of the competition. One way forward is to unify the language of evolutionary psychology with that of evolutionary biology and anthropology. Presumably, the underlying variable of interest in studying relationships on a temporal spectrum is parental investment. Adopting this language, along with the concept of reproductive effort as a behavioral tradeoff between mating effort and parenting effort (e.g., Betzig, 1988), might also bring clarity and consistency between the evolutionary disciplines. This is not a panacea, however—it remains difficult at times to distinguish whether a particular behavior represents mating effort or parenting effort (e.g., marriage and paternal care; Blurton Jones, et al., 2000; Marlowe, 1999; Winking, Gurven, Kaplan, & Stieglitz, 2009). Even so, the fact that the mating supply and demand hypothesis and the 'faithful as your options' hypothesis predict the opposite relationship for the intensity of mating effort, but predict the same pattern for marriage, demands a reformulation.

Another issue raised by this review is the need for additional research on women's mating effort. It is obviously more complicated than men's mating effort. The only measure indicating a consistent pattern across developed and traditional societies alike was the null result for women's physical aggression. This suggests two avenues for future research: whether general measures of women's mating effort (like sociosexuality, mate poaching, and marriage systems) relate to specific tactics of women's mate competition (like aggression or mate choice competition to enhance attractiveness), as they logically should, but did not, in this review; and whether variables other than the sex ratio are instead important in women's mate competition. Variation in male mate quality has received attention in the biology literature (e.g., Rosvall, 2011) and is predicted to affect the intensity of women's competition in evolutionary psychology as well (e.g., Campbell, 1995, 2013).

In sum, this review found mixed results for how sex ratio imbalances affect women's mating competition. Some studies found it increased with a shortage of mates, as predicted by the mating supply and demand hypothesis; some found it increased with a surplus of mates, as predicted by the 'faithful as your options' hypothesis; others found no relationship. This review raises important avenues for future research, including linking measures of women's general mating effort to the frequency of mate competition tactics, as well as whether sex ratio effects

among women apply only to developed societies due to men's greater constraints on women's mating effort in traditional societies. Given the relevance of small-scale, traditional societies to understanding past human environments, understanding variables that *do* predict women's mating effort in these societies is of great interest. Also, given the conflicting pattern of results for women, we need additional research to clarify whether a shortage or a surplus of mates affects women's mating effort at all. It may be that other variables, like variation in male quality, are more important. Last, men's mating effort is consistently associated with a surplus of mates—indicating strong support for the 'faithful as your options' hypothesis to explain men's mating effort—and future research should clarify how men's and women's mating effort interacts to produce this pattern.

Acknowledgment

I am grateful to Ryan Schacht for pointing out this interpretation of the sociosexuality literature.

References

Adimora, A. A., Schoenbach, V. J., Taylor, E. M., Khan, M. R., Schwartz, R. J., & Miller, W. C. (2013). Sex ratio, poverty, and concurrent partnerships among men and women in the United States: A multilevel analysis. *Annals of Epidemiology*, *23*, 716–719.

Ainsworth, S. E., & Maner, J. K. (2012). Sex begets violence: Mating motives, social dominance, and physical aggression in men. *Journal of Personality and Social Psychology*, *103*, 819–829.

Ainsworth, S. E., & Maner, J. K. (2014). Assailing the competition: Sexual selection, proximate mating motives, and aggressive behavior in men. *Personality and Social Psychology Bulletin, 40*, 1648–1658.

Albrecht, C. M., & Albrecht, D. E. (2001). Sex ratio and family structure in the nonmetropolitan United States. *Sociological Inquiry, 71*, 67–84.

Albrecht, C. M., Fossett, M. A., Cready, C. M., & Kiecolt, K. J. (1997). Mate availability, women's marriage prevalence, and husband's education. *Journal of Family Issues, 18*, 429–452.

Andersson, M., & Iwasa, Y. (1996). Sexual selection. *Trends in Ecology and Evolution, 11*, 53–58.

Angrist, J. (2002). How do sex ratios affect marriage and labor markets? Evidence from America's second generation. *Quarterly Journal of Economics, 117*, 997–1038.

Archer, J., & Coyne, S. M. (2005). An integrated review of indirect, relational, and social aggression. *Personality and Social Psychology Review, 9*, 212–230.

Arnocky, S., Ribout, A., Mirza, R. S., & Knack, J. M. (2014). Perceived mate availability influences intrasexual competition, jealousy and mate-guarding behavior. *Journal of Evolutionary Psychology, 12*, 45–64.

Barber, N. (1998a). The slender ideal and eating disorders: An interdisciplinary "telescope" model. *International Journal of Eating Disorders, 23*, 295–307.

Barber, N. (1998b). Secular changes in standards of bodily attractiveness in women: Tests of a reproductive model. *International Journal of Eating Disorders, 23*, 449–453.

Barber, N. (2001). Mustache fashion covaries with a good marriage market for women. *Journal of Nonverbal Behavior, 25*, 261–272.

Barber, N. (2003). Paternal investment prospects and cross-national differences in single parenthood. *Cross-Cultural Research, 37*, 163–177.

Bateman, A. J. (1948). Intra-sexual selection in Drosophila. *Heredity, 2*, 349–368.

Benson, D., & Archer, J. (2002). An ethnographic study of sources of conflict between young men in the context of a night out. *Psychology, Evolution, and Gender, 4*, 3–30.

Betzig, L. L. (1982). Despotism and differential reproduction: A cross-cultural correlation of conflict asymmetry, hierarchy, and degree of polygyny. *Ethology and Sociobiology, 3*, 209–221.

Betzig, L. (1988). Mating and parenting in Darwinian perspective. In L. Betzig, M. Borgerhoff-Mulder, P. Turke (Eds.), *Human reproductive behavior* (pp. 3–20). Cambridge, UK: Cambridge University Press.

Bleske-Rechek, A., & Buss, D. M. (2006). Sexual strategies pursued and mate attraction tactics deployed. *Personality and Individual Differences, 40*, 1299–1311.

Blurton Jones, N. G., Marlowe, F. W., Hawkes, K., & O'Connell, J. F. (2000). Paternal investment and hunter-gatherer divorce rates. In L. Cronk, N. Chagnon, & W. Irons (Eds.), *Adaptation and human behavior: An anthropological perspective* (pp. 69–90). Hawthorne, NY: Aldine de Gruyter.

Brown, G. R., Laland, K. N., & Borgerhoff Mulder, M. (2009). Bateman's principles and human sex roles. *Trends in Ecology and Evolution, 24*, 297–304.

Burbank, V. K. (1987). Female aggression in cross-cultural perspective. *Cross-Cultural Research, 21*, 70–100.

Burbank, V. K. (1992). Sex, gender, and difference: Dimensions of aggression in an Australian Aboriginal community. *Human Nature, 3*, 251–278.

Buss, D. M. (1988). The evolution of human intrasexual competition: Tactics of mate attraction. *Journal of Personality and Social Psychology, 54*, 616–628.

Buss, D. M. (1989). Sex differences in human mate preferences: Evolutionary hypotheses tested in 37 cultures. *Behavioral and Brain Sciences, 12*, 1–49.

Buss, D. M., Abbott, M., Angleitner, A., Asherian, A., Biaggio, A., Blanco-Villasenor, A., . . . Yang, K. (1990). International preferences in selecting mates: A study of 37 cultures. *Journal of Cross-Cultural Psychology, 21*, 5–47.

Buss, D. M., & Dedden, L. A. (1990). Derogation of competitors. *Journal of Social and Personal Relationships, 7*, 395–422.

Buss, D. M., & Schmitt, D. P. (1993). Sexual strategies theory: An evolutionary perspective on human mating. *Psychological Review, 100*, 204–232.

Cameron, C., Oskamp, S., & Sparks, W. (1977). Courtship American style: Newspaper ads. *Family Coordinator, 26*, 27–30.

Campbell, A. (1986). Self-report of fighting by females: A preliminary study. *British Journal of Criminology, 26*, 28–46.

Campbell, A. (1995). A few good men: Evolutionary psychology and female adolescent aggression. *Ethology and Sociobiology, 16*, 99–123.

Campbell, A. (2013). The evolutionary psychology of women's aggression. *Philosophical Transactions of the Royal Society B, 368*, 20130078.

Campbell, A., Muncer, S., & Bibel, D. (1998). Female-female criminal assault: An evolutionary perspective. *Journal of Research in Crime and Delinquency, 35*, 413–428.

Cashdan, E. (1998). Are men more competitive than women? *British Journal of Social Psychology, 37*, 213–229.

Cashdan, E. (2008). Waist-to-hip ratio across cultures: Trade-offs between androgen- and estrogen-dependent traits. *Current Anthropology, 49*, 1099–1107.

Chagnon, N. A. (1988). Life histories, blood revenge, and warfare in a tribal population. *Science, 239*, 985–992.

Chipman, A., & Morrison, E. (2013). The impact of sex ratio and economic status on local birth rates. *Biology Letters, 9*, 20130027.

Clutton-Brock, T. H., & Vincent, A. C. J. (1991). Sexual selection and the potential reproductive rates of males and females. *Nature, 351*, 58–60.

Cox, O. C. (1940). Sex ratio and marital status among Negroes. *American Sociological Review, 5*, 937–947.

Cronin, H. (1991). *The ant and the peacock: Altruism and sexual selection from Darwin to today.* New York: Cambridge University Press.

Daly, M., & Wilson, M. (1990). Killing the competition: Female/female and male/male homicide. *Human Nature, 1*, 81–107.

Darwin, C. (1871). *The descent of man, and selection in relation to sex.* London: John Murray.

Dawkins, R., & Carlisle, T. R. (1976). Parental investment, mate desertion and a fallacy. *Nature, 262*, 131–133.

Dickemann, M. (1991). Woman, class, and dowry. *American Anthropologist, 93*, 944–946.

Dreiss, A. N., Cote, J., Richard, M., Federici, P., & Clobert, J. (2010). Age- and sex-specific response to population density and sex ratio. *Behavioral Ecology, 21*, 356–364.

Durante, K. M., Griskevicius, V., Simpson, J. A., Cantú, S. M., & Tybur, J. M. (2012). Sex ratio and women's career choice: Does a scarcity of men lead women to choose briefcase over baby? *Journal of Personality and Social Psychology, 103*, 121–134.

Ember, M. (1974). Warfare, sex ratio, and polygyny. *Ethnology, 13*, 197–206.

Emlen, S. T., & Oring, L. W. (1977). Ecology, sexual selection, and the evolution of mating systems. *Science, 197*, 215–223.

Fink, B., Klappauf, D., Brewer, G., & Shackelford, T. K. (2014). Female physical characteristics and intra-sexual competition in women. *Personality and Individual Differences, 58*, 138–141.

Fossett, M. A., & Kiecolt, K. J. (1990). Mate availability, family formation, and family structure among black Americans in non–metropolitan Louisiana 1970-1980. *Rural Sociology, 55*, 305–327.

Fossett, M. A., & Kiecolt, K. J. (1991). A methodological review of the sex ratio: Alternatives for comparative research. *Journal of Marriage and the Family, 53*, 941–957.

Francis, A. M. (2011). Sex ratios and the red dragon: Using the Chinese Communist Revolution to explore the effect of the sex ratio on women and children in Taiwan. *Journal of Population Economics, 24*, 813–837.

Fu, X. (1992). A cross-national analysis of the world divorce rate. *Encyclia, 69*, 125–144.

Gangestad, S. W., & Simpson, J. A. (2000). The evolution of human mating: Trade-offs and strategic pluralism. *Behavioral and Brain Sciences, 23*, 573–587.

Gaulin, S. J. C., & Boster, J. S. (1990). Dowry as female competition. *American Anthropologist, 92*, 994–1005.

Gaulin, S. J. C., & Boster, J. S. (1997). When are husbands worth fighting for? In Betzig, L. (Ed.), *Human nature: A critical reader* (pp. 372–374). Oxford: Oxford University Press.

Green, L. R., Richardson, D. R., & Lago, T. (1996). How do friendship, indirect, and direct aggression relate? *Aggressive Behavior, 22*, 81–86.

Griskevicius, V., Tybur, J. M., Ackerman, J. M., Delton, A. W., Robertson, T. E., & White, A. E. (2012). The financial consequences of too many men: Sex ratio effects on saving, borrowing, and spending. *Journal of Personality and Social Psychology, 102*, 69–80.

Guttentag, M., & Secord, P. (1983). *Too many women?* Beverly Hills, CA: Sage.

Harris, M. G. (1994). Cholas, Mexican-American girls, and gangs. *Sex Roles, 30*, 289–301.

Henrich, J., Heine, S. J., & Norenzayan, A. (2010). The weirdest people in the world? *Behavioral and Brain Sciences, 33*, 61–83.

Hess, N., Helfrecht, C., Hagen, E., Sell, A., & Hewlett, B. (2010). Interpersonal aggression among Aka hunter-gatherers of the Central African Republic. *Human Nature, 21*, 330–354.

Hines, N. J., & Fry, D. P. (1994). Indirect modes of aggression among women of Buenos Aires, Argentina. *Sex Roles, 30*, 213–236.

Hitchell, A. R. (2004). *Sex ratio and crime: A cross-cultural investigation* (Master's thesis). Retrieved from ProQuest Dissertation Services (Accession No. 1423414).

Hrdy, S. B. (2000). The optimal number of fathers: Evolution, demography, and history in the shaping of female mate preferences. *Annals of the New York Academy of Sciences, 907*, 75–96.

Hudson, V. M., & den Boer, A. M. (2004). *Bare branches: The security implications of Asia's surplus male population.* Cambridge, MA: MIT Press.

Hurtado, A. M., & Hill, K. R. (1992). Paternal effect on offspring survivorship among Ache and Hiwi hunter-gatherers: Implications for modeling pair-bond stability. In B. S. Hewlett (Ed.), *Father-child relations: Cultural and biosocial contexts* (pp. 31–55). Hawthorne, NY: Aldine de Gruyter.

Jones, J. H., & Ferguson, B. (2006). The marriage squeeze in Colombia, 1973–2005: The role of excess male death. *Biodemography and Social Biology, 53*, 140–151.

Kandrik, M., Jones, B. C., & DeBruine, L. M. (2015). Scarcity of female mates predicts regional variation in men's and women's sociosexual orientation across US states. *Evolution and Human Behavior, 36*, 206–210.

Kenrick, D. T., Sadalla, E. K., Groth, G., & Trost, M. R. (1990). Evolution, traits, and the stages of human courtship: Qualifying the parental investment model. *Journal of Personality, 58*, 97–116.

Kokko, H., & Jennions, M. D. (2008). Parental investment, sexual selection, and sex ratios. *Journal of Evolutionary Biology, 21*, 919–948.

Kokko, H., Klug, H., & Jennions, M. D. (2012). Unifying cornerstones of sexual selection: operational sex ratio, Bateman gradient and the scope for competitive investment. *Ecology Letters, 15*, 1340–1351.

Kruger, D. J., Fitzgerald, C. J., & Peterson, T. (2010). Female scarcity reduces women's marital ages and increases variance in men's marital ages. *Evolutionary Psychology, 8*, 420–431.

Kvarnemo, C., & Ahnesjö, I. (1996). The dynamics of operational sex ratios and competition for mates. *Trends in Ecology & Evolution, 11*, 404–408.

Lagerspetz, K. M. J., Björkqvist, K., & Peltonen, T. (1988). Is indirect aggression typical of females? Gender differences in aggressiveness in 11- to 12-year-old children. *Aggressive Behavior, 14*, 403–414.

Lepowsky, M. (1994). Women, men, and aggression in an egalitarian society. *Sex Roles, 30*, 199–211.

Li, N. P., Bailey, J. M., Kenrick, D. T., & Linsenmeier, J. A. W. (2002). The necessities and luxuries of mate preferences: Testing the tradeoffs. *Journal of Personality and Social Psychology, 82*, 947–955.

Lichter, D. T., McLaughlin, D. K., Kephard, G., & Landry, D. J. (1992). Race and the retreat from marriage: A shortage of marriageable men? *American Sociological Review, 57*, 781–799.

Lippa, R. A. (2007). Sex differences in sex drive, sociosexuality, and height across 53 nations: Testing evolutionary and social structural theories. *Archives of Sexual Behavior, 38*, 631–651.

Lummaa, V., Merilä, J., & Kause, A. (1998). Adaptive sex ratio variation in pre-industrial human (*Homo sapiens*) populations? *Proceedings of the Royal Society B, 265*, 563–568.

Marlowe, F. (1999). Male care and mating effort among Hadza foragers. *Behavioral Ecology and Sociobiology, 46*, 57–64.

Marlowe, F. W. (2004). Mate preferences among Hadza hunter-gatherers. *Human Nature, 15*, 365–376.

Marlowe, F. W., & Berbesque, J. C. (2012). The human operational sex ratio: Effects of marriage, concealed ovulation, and menopause on mate competition. *Journal of Human Evolution, 63*, 834–842.

Österman, K., Björkqvist, K., Lagerspetz, K., Kaukiainen, A., Landau, S. F., Frączek, A., & Caprara, G. V. (1998). Cross-cultural evidence of female indirect aggression. *Aggressive Behavior, 24*, 1–8.

Owens, I. P. F., & Thompson, D. B. A. (1994). Sex differences, sex ratios, and sex roles. *Proceedings of the Royal Society B, 258*, 93–99.

Pedersen, F. A. (1991). Secular trends in human sex ratios: Their influence on individual and family behavior. *Human Nature, 2*, 271–291.

Pillsworth, E. (2008). Mate preferences among the Shuar of Ecuador: Trait rankings and peer evaluations. *Evolution and Human Behavior, 29*, 256–267.

Pizarro, J. M., DeJong, C., & McGarrell, E. G. (2010). An examination of the covariates of female homicide victimization and offending. *Feminist Criminology, 5*, 51–72.

Pollet, T. V., & Nettle, D. (2009). Market forces affect patterns of polygyny in Uganda. *Proceedings of the National Academy of Science, 106*, 2114–2117.

Queller, D. C. (1997). Why do females care more than males? *Proceedings of the Royal Society B, 264*, 1555–1557.

Quinlan, R. J. (2008). Human pair-bonds: Evolutionary functions, ecological variation, and adaptive development. *Evolutionary Anthropology, 17*, 227–238.

Rao, V. (1993). The rising price of husbands: A hedonic analysis of dowry increases in rural India. *Journal of Political Economy, 101*, 666–677.

Roberts, J. T., & Dodoo, F. N. (1995). Population growth, sex ratios, and women's work on the contemporary Amazon frontier. *Yearbook: Conference of Latin American Geographers, 21*, 91–105.

Rosvall, K. A. (2011). Intrasexual competition in females: Evidence for sexual selection? *Behavioral Ecology, 22*, 1131–1140.

Rucas, S. L., Gurven, M., Winking, J., & Kaplan, H. (2012). Social aggression and resource conflict across the female life-course in the Bolivian Amazon. *Aggressive Behavior, 38*, 194–207.

Schacht, R., & Borgerhoff Mulder, M. (2015). Sex ratio effects on reproductive strategies in humans. *Royal Society Open Science, 2*, 140402.

Schmitt, D. P. (2003). Universal sex differences in the desire for sexual variety: Tests from 52 nations, 6 continents, and 13 islands. *Journal of Personality and Social Psychology, 85*, 85–104.

Schmitt, D. P. (2004). Patterns and universals of mate poaching across 53 nations: The effects of sex, culture, and personality on romantically attracting another person's partner. *Journal of Personality and Social Psychology, 86*, 560–584.

Schmitt, D. P. (2005). Sociosexuality from Argentina to Zimbabwe: A 48-nation study of sex, culture, and strategies of human mating. *Behavioral and Brain Sciences, 28*, 247–275.

Schmitt, D. P., & Buss, D. M. (2001). Human mate poaching: Tactics and temptations for infiltrating existing mateships. *Journal of Personality and Social Psychology, 80*, 894–917.

Schmitt, D. P., & Rohde, P. A. (2013). The human polygyny index and its ecological correlates: Testing sexual selection and life history theory at the cross-national level: Human polygyny index. *Social Science Quarterly, 94*, 1159–1184.

Schuster, I. (1983). Women's aggression: An African case study. *Aggressive Behavior, 9*, 319–331.

Schwartz, J. (2006). Effects of diverse forms of family structure on female and male homicide. *Journal of Marriage and Family, 68*, 1291–1312.

Simpson, J. A., & Gangestad, S. W. (1991). Individual differences in sociosexuality: Evidence for convergent and discriminant validity. *Journal of Personality and Social Psychology, 60*, 870–883.

Simpson, J. A., & Gangestad, S. W. (1992). Sociosexuality and romantic partner choice. *Journal of Personality, 60*, 31–51.

Simpson, J. A., Gangestad, S. W., & Biek, M. (1993). Personality and nonverbal social behavior: An ethological perspective of relationship initiation. *Journal of Experimental Social Psychology, 29*, 434–461.

Singh, D., Dixson, B. J., Jessop, T. S., Morgan, B., & Dixson, A. F. (2010). Cross-cultural consensus for waist-hip ratio and women's attractiveness. *Evolution and Human Behavior, 31*, 176–181.

South, S. J. (1988). Sex ratios, economic power, and women's roles: A theoretical extension and empirical test. *Journal of Marriage and the Family, 50*, 19–31.

South, S. J. (1991). Sociodemographic differentials in mate selection preferences. *Journal of the Marriage and the Family, 53*, 928–940.

South, S. J., & Messner, S. F. (1987). The sex ratio and women's involvement in crime: A cross-national analysis. *Sociological Quarterly, 28*, 171–188.

South, S. J., & Trent, K. (1988). Sex ratios and women's roles: A cross-national analysis. *American Journal of Sociology, 93*, 1096–1115.

Starkweather, K. E., & Hames, R. (2012). A survey of non-classical polyandry. *Human Nature, 23*, 149–172.

Stone, E. A. (2015). *Do women use aggression in matecompetition? Evidence from Micronesia.* Manuscript in preparation.

Stulp, G., Buunk, A. P., Kurzban, R., & Verhulst, S. (2013). The height of choosiness: Mutual mate choice for stature results in suboptimal pair formation for both sexes. *Animal Behaviour, 86*, 37–46.

Todd, P. M., Penke, L., Fasolo, B., & Lenton, A. P. (2007). Different cognitive processes underlie human mate choices and mate preferences. *Proceedings of the National Academy of Sciences, 104*, 15011–15016.

Trent, K., & South, S. J. (1989). Structural determinants of the divorce rate: A cross-societal analysis. *Journal of Marriage and the Family, 51*, 391–404.

Trent, K., & South, S. J. (2003). Spousal alternatives and marital relations. *Journal of Family Issues, 24*, 787–810.

Trent, K., & South, S. J. (2011). Too many men? Sex ratios and partnering behavior in China. *Social Forces, 90*, 247–268.

Trent, K., & South, S. J. (2012). Mate availability and women's sexual experiences in China. *Journal of Marriage and Family, 74*, 201–214.

Trivers, R. (1972). Parental investment and sexual selection. In B. Campbell (Ed.), *Sexual selection and the descent of man* (pp. 136–179). Chicago: Aldine-Atherton.

Trovato, F. (1988). A macrosocial analysis of change in the marriage rate: Canadian women, 1921–25 to 1981–85. *Journal of Marriage and the Family, 50*, 507–521.

Vaillancourt, T. (2013). Do human females use indirect aggression as an intrasexual competition strategy? *Philosophical Transactions of the Royal Society B, 368*, 20130080.

Vaillancourt, T., & Sharma, A. (2011). Intolerance of sexy peers: Intrasexual competition among women. *Aggressive Behavior, 37*, 569–577.

Walters, S., & Crawford, C. B. (1994). The importance of mate attraction for intrasexual competition in men and women. *Ethology and Sociobiology, 15*, 5–30.

Watkins, C. D., Jones, B. C., Little, A. C., DeBruine, L. M., & Feinberg, D. R. (2012). Cues to the sex ratio of the local population influence women's preferences for facial symmetry. *Animal Behaviour, 83*, 545–553.

Wilson, M., & Daly, M. (1985). Competitiveness, risk taking, and violence: The young male syndrome. *Ethology and Sociobiology, 6*, 59–73.

Winking, J., Gurven, M., Kaplan, H., & Stieglitz, J. (2009). The goals of direct paternal care among a South Amerindian population. *American Journal of Physical Anthropology, 139*, 295–304.

Yost, M. R., & Zurbriggen, E. L. (2006). Gender differences in the enactment of sociosexuality: An examination of implicit social motives, sexual fantasies, coercive sexual attitudes, and aggressive sexual behavior. *Journal of Sex Research, 43*, 163–173.

Operational Sex Ratio and Female Competition: Scarcity Breeds Intensity

Haley M. Dillon, Lora E. Adair, *and* Gary L. Brase

Abstract

When there is a surplus of one sex in a population, members of that sex often compete against each other for access to the scarcer sex. This chapter reviews the theoretical foundations for this phenomenon, focusing on the concept of operational sex ratio (OSR; the ratio of viable and available males to females in a given mating market) versus overall sex ratio, as well as the phylogenetic evidence of sex ratios as an important factor influencing mating behaviors. Research on human OSR and its effects is a fairly recent development but has already led to findings that are generally coherent and consistent with the nonhuman evidence. The evidence to date indicates that people who find themselves in female-disadvantaged mating markets show systematic and adaptive changes in their behaviors, including increased female intrasexual competition. The chapter concludes with discussions of additional issues and future directions for research on OSR.

Key Words: competition, operational sex ratio, sex ratio, intrasexual competition, mating markets

Introduction

Imagine two spaceships have been sent out to colonize new worlds. One spaceship has ten men on board and one woman, whereas the other spaceship has ten women on board and one man. Interplanetary travel takes a while, so suppose the trip takes about a year and also suppose that fairly soon after liftoff all the astronauts get to work on their goal of creating a population for their new world. As the spaceships reach their destinations, what is the largest number of new baby colonists that could be living on the first and second spaceships? The first spaceship, with a ten to one male/female ratio clearly is at a reproductive disadvantage (yet, incidentally, is more faithful to the three to one ratio in the 1968 movie *Planet of the Apes* that was supposed to colonize a new world). The one to ten male/female ratio spaceship, on the other hand, could have nearly doubled its population before even reaching the new world. In short, sex ratios are very important. This story about the importance of sex ratios is used sometimes to help students understand the ideas of (mammalian) females as a limiting factor in reproduction and the related concept of differential parental investment (Trivers, 1972).

The sex ratio within a population has many other consequences beyond potential number of offspring, though, and this chapter aims to incorporate sex ratio into our understanding of certain types of human behavior, particularly competition among females. This chapter starts with a review of the theoretical reasons to expect sex ratio to be an important ecological variable that influences behaviors, then examines the empirical evidence that sex ratio actually influences behaviors in nonhuman species. These background sections lead us to our goal, which is to address ways in which sex ratio can affect a variety of human relationship perceptions, judgments, and behaviors. A recurrent focus is the issue of how sex ratio may affect female intrasexual competition. The chapter concludes with some open questions regarding the conceptualization, measurement, and use of sex ratio, particularly operational sex ratio (OSR).

The Theoretical Foundations of Sex Ratios

The equitable production of males and females within most species has been intriguing biologists since the days of Darwin. In 1930, R. A. Fisher proposed an evolutionary model to explain why so many species seem to produce approximately equal numbers of male and female offspring at birth (cited in Wilson & Colwell, 1981). Fisher's basic explanation was that, because each offspring has a male and female parent, whichever sex is in short supply would have greater fecundity. More technically, Fisher pointed out that, because each offspring born through sexual reproduction must have both a mother and a father, the total reproductive value of male parents must equal that of the total reproductive value of female parents. Thus, if the population begins to deviate from this 1:1 ratio, pairs producing the *rarer* and therefore more greatly valued sex will have a selective advantage until the population sex ratio restores to 1:1 (Myers, 1978).

Fisher's theory is based on the concept that a genotype that produces an excessive number of the minority sex within its own offspring would be favored by natural selection until there is an equilibrium of the sexes (Wilson & Colwell, 1981). In other words, evolutionarily, there will be a constant homeostatic selection pressure for an equal number of each sex; whenever an unequal sex ratio somehow arises it will be unstable and the population will tend to restabilize at equality. This model favoring equal numbers of males and females is quite robust, and Fisher's hypothesis has been mathematically proven multiple times (for a review, see Werren, 1983).

If there is an equal ratio of the sexes, it is assumed that there will be an equal number of males looking for female mates and vice versa (considering just heterosexual relationships, of course). In fact, the human sex ratio in Western cultures generally is about 1:1, but it does on occasion deviate substantially. There are three basic sex ratio states that are usually distinguished: (a) *equitable mating markets*, wherein there is an approximately equal number of available males and females; (b) *disadvantaged mating markets*, wherein the focal individual is part of the relatively larger population of their sex and thus has fewer mating opportunities; and (c) *advantaged mating markets*, wherein the focal individual is part of the relatively smaller population of his or her sex and thus has more mating opportunities.

As one might expect, the situation of a disadvantaged mating market tends to elicit competition among the members of the disadvantaged sex. The phenomenon of intrasexual competition, in which there is a relatively small number of reproductively viable opposite-sex mates, can be reduced to a general rule: *relative scarcity incites competition* (Cox & Le Boeuf, 1977). This scarcity can be either because of objective scarcity (an unequal sex ratio in the overall population) or an effective scarcity (such as, for example, when a single or several powerful males monopolize larger numbers of females, which creates scarcity for all other males). In fact, the scarcity-incites-competition rule works across several contexts as a general tenet of economics (e.g., if there is less food available, there will be increased competition for access to food).

Equitable mating markets are typically dominated by assortative mating patterns, which means that people tend to end up with partners who are similar to themselves, rather than someone significantly higher or lower than themselves on traits such as attractiveness, status, and relative mate value (see Buss & Barnes, 1986). The result of assortative mating is the nonrandom coupling of individuals based on similarity for one or more genotypic or phenotypic attributes (Buss & Barnes, 1986). If there is an equal sex ratio, individuals can seek mates that fit their own characteristics and attributes and can afford to be moderately choosy, selectively pursuing similarly valued mates and rejecting those of lesser value. However, if the sex ratio is unequal, assortative mating takes a back seat to mating as a whole—individuals in a disadvantaged mating market are focused more on finding any suitable mate with which to reproduce, rather than finding a mate with similar characteristics. In these disadvantaged mating markets, individuals cannot afford to be as choosy by demanding a mate of similar value. On the other hand, individuals in an advantaged mating market are able to be exceptionally choosy and demand mates that exceed their own mate value, rather than aiming for assortative equity.

One scenario in which it seems clear that sex ratio may influence the level of female competition is in populations where females are the disadvantaged sex—a *female disadvantaged mating market* refers to an ecology characterized by many females and a relatively small number of males. In such situations, intrasexual competition among females is expected to be higher compared to populations in which there are a relatively equal number of males and females. In ecologies where the ratio of males to females is unequal, the "advantaged" sex is afforded the opportunity to be choosy; in other words, the sex with lesser representation in a particular mating market has a greater number of available suitors to choose from and can therefore dismiss potential mates of lesser quality for the opportunity to pursue higher-quality mates (Berglund, 1994). However, the disadvantaged sex that is overrepresented in a particular mating market is forced to compete with members of the same sex for access to a smaller number of mates who are of equal quality as themselves. They perhaps will need to settle for an available mate of lower quality than themselves in order to avoid the risk of rejecting this mate and losing him or her to a same-sex rival.

Parental Investment and Sex Ratios

Parental investment theory (Trivers, 1972) states that whichever sex provides more resources to offspring (i.e., more parental investment) is inherently the "sought-after" sex and is thus choosier in picking a mate, which consequently creates intrasexual competition within the opposite sex. This could, and does, generate female intrasexual competition in species within which males are responsible for the majority of the care of offspring (e.g., in pipefish, males care for broods), but in the majority of species (all mammals, for example), the female provides more parental investment to the offspring. As a result, females tend to be choosier in picking a mate. Thus, parental investment theory has often been used to explain the phenomenon of male intrasexual competition (see Alexander & Sherman, 1977; Wade, 1979).

Trivers and Willard (1973) expanded on Fisher's ideas about sex ratios, beyond the adaptive forces that favor the production of a particular sex, to include patterns of parental investment. The Trivers–Willard hypothesis posits that parents will exhibit a sensitivity to and awareness of their status in the social hierarchy when choosing whether or not to invest in sons versus daughters. Male reproductive success, in particular, is more greatly affected by differences in social standing. In principle, males can produce a very large number of offspring when provisioned with ample resources, whereas males with little or no resources often have few or no offspring. Female reproductive success, in contrast, is less influenced by variability in access to resources. The implication, therefore, is that parents will tend to experience greater inclusive fitness (i.e., the survival and propagation of their genes) if they invest more in their sons while at the top of a social hierarchy and invest more in their daughters when

their social standing is less prestigious. Trivers and Willard (1973) hypothesized that

> If the model is correct, natural selection favors deviations away from 50/50 investment in the sexes, rather than deviations in sex ratios per se. In species with a long period of PI [parental investment] after birth of young, one might expect biases in parental behavior toward offspring of different sex, according to parental condition; parents in better condition would be expected to show a bias toward male offspring. (p. 91)

This proposed contextual sensitivity, in theory, optimizes the differential reproductive success of male and female offspring. The Trivers–Willard hypothesis has been subsequently extended to encompass the idea that social status or context can influence sex ratios even as early as conception or birth. However, the results of empirical studies on this hypothesis have been inconsistent, sometimes finding little or no support of this hypothesis (e.g., Freese & Powell, 1999; Keller, Nesse, & Hofferth, 2001) and sometimes finding indications of imbalanced sex ratios consistent with the hypothesis (e.g., Cameron & Dalerum, 2009).

Many of the theories that suggest a tendency for parents to invest more heavily in male offspring originate from the idea that males of many species (particularly mammals) have a greater variance in reproductive success and can produce more offspring than their female counterparts (Queller, 1997). What is of particular interest in terms of female intrasexual competition is that, in species that are able to selectively change the sex ratio of their offspring (observed in female lizards, wasps, and callitrichines [a type of monkey]), the ratio tends to be toward a male bias (Robert & Thompson, 2001). Producing a sex ratio with more males leads to a male-disadvantaged mating market and less female competition in the long run. In other words, intrasexual competition becomes a more distinctly male behavior (i.e., males compete for access to females, and females are given the opportunity to be more choosy in selecting a mate). Thus, available theoretical evidence seems to suggest that females who can selectively change the sex ratio of their offspring should create a male-biased brood as a method of optimizing their reproductive success and in a few species appear to do exactly that.

Of course, having more male offspring is better for an individual's reproductive success (because those males can usually reproduce faster and in greater numbers than females), but this is not necessarily better for the overall population. Two consequences of a male-biased reproductive pattern will be more intense competition between males and less competition between females. If there are more males in a population, females are the advantaged sex and thus are able to choose rather than compete when they are searching for mates.

According to Silk and Brown (2008), sex ratio theory represents one of the triumphs of evolutionary theory in that it provides researchers an accepted source of testable predictions about sex allocation strategies and is critically important to one of the major foci of current research: competition. Patterns of selective investment in, and production of, females and males have tremendous consequences for the dynamics of the mating market. Depending on what the sex ratio is for a population, males and females within that population have differing opportunities to be scrupulously selective or to assortatively mate, and to be focused on evaluating the fitness of opposite-sex suitors or to be aggressively competing with members of their own sex.

Computational Modeling

Computational modeling is another avenue to understand the dynamics and implications of sex ratios within species. With this tool, one can create a simplified model "world" that includes specific biological constraints that explain reproductive success and the implications of different sex ratios as a consequence of those constraints (Kamimura, Abe, & Ito, 2008). By definition, females are the sex that invests more in offspring. For instance, the reproductive success of female mammals is limited by their number of ova (and gestation and nursing constraints), whereas male mammals can potentially inseminate all females available to them and thus have a potentially higher rate of reproductive success. This seems to suggest that the very common 1:1 sex ratio results in the production of "redundant males"; there are more males in an equal sex ratio population than are actually *needed* to inseminate the female population. (Recall the two spaceships in the introduction, which demonstrated this point.)

So why do populations continue to overproduce males? The idea of local mate competition (Kamimura et al., 2008) attempts to explain certain aspects of sex ratios, including overproduction of males, especially within species that are capable of choosing the sex ratio of their offspring. Kamimura and colleagues propose that "Redundant production of males is reduced in cases of local mate competition (LMC) in which the sons of only two

to several females (foundresses) compete to mate with their daughters. [...] In such a situation, theory predicts that foundresses will bias the sex ratio toward females, depending on the number of foundresses, to reduce unnecessary competition among their own sons" (p. 277). They conclude that, as the number of foundresses increases, the sex ratio begins to approximate a more balanced sex ratio. That is, with multiple females producing offspring, there is intrasexual competition for *their* sons to be the fathers of the next generation, and this leads to a more equitable sex ratio (as in the traditional Fisherian model).

A game theoretic model of parental care under various sex ratio situations (Ramsey, 2010) suggests that there are two states for males: either searching for a mate or breeding. Females, on the other hand, can be in one of three states: receptive (searching for a mate), nonreceptive, or breeding. According to Ramsey, when in a searching state, individuals find partners at a rate dependent on the proportion of opposite-sex individuals who are in the state of searching. In other words, males and females must match up: one must be searching while the other is in the receptive state in order to pair up.

Taken together, the implications of these computational models suggest that sex ratio is determined not only by the number of available females and males in a given population but the compatibility of the reproductive states of these females and males. Within single generations there can also be an effect of reproductive states on competition. If, for example, more males were breeding than receptive, the females not currently breeding with those males should theoretically compete with one another for access to the remaining receptive males. (We come back to this issue later as the idea of OSR.)

Costs and Benefits

A basic underlying idea in Fisher's early work on sex ratio is the importance of the accurate assessment of expected costs and benefits when it comes to the sex ratio of offspring. There are costs and benefits to having offspring in and of itself, and some of these costs and benefits are unequally distributed for male and female offspring. Consequently, the overall sex ratio of offspring adds complexity to the topic of potential inclusive fitness costs and benefits. According to Williams (1979), it is often assumed that offspring of both sexes are important to parents' reproductive success, and the best general strategy is to devote resources equally to the rearing of both male and female offspring. However, given situation variability, there are some situations in which this general strategy is not optimal and the production of more offspring of a certain sex (or investing more in offspring of a certain sex) is more beneficial with regard to fitness. That is, in some situations having more sons or focusing resources on sons is more likely to result in a higher quantity of future offspring, thus increasing reproductive fitness. Furthermore, in real-world dynamic environments, there can be various times at which the costs and benefits of raising off-spring of a particular sex change (see Boucher, 1977). These changes should, in theory, lead to parental investment adjustments (e.g., as proposed by Trivers & Willard, 1973), and those adjustments, in turn, can create changes in intrasexual competition.

One powerful environmental variable is the avail-ability of food resources. If sex ratio adjustments do occur in environmentally stressed populations, Myers (1978) argues that, for many species, the best reproductive strategy in terms of offspring sex ratio would be to produce relatively more females than males. The basis of this argument is that males are larger than females in most sexually dimorphic spe-cies. Therefore, producing male offspring is more costly to parents in terms of required resources (i.e., larger males will be larger during pregnancy; they will require more food from parents, etc.). If resources are particularly limited in a given environ-ment, it makes more sense for parents to have (lower resource demanding) female offspring rather than (more resource demanding, possibly unsuccessful) male offspring. In contexts characterized by signifi-cant environmental stress, females who differentially produced and cared for more female than male off-spring, to put it in layman's terms, would get "more bang for their buck." Based on this reasoning, Myers (1978) predicted that, for a sexually dimorphic spe-cies, resource limitation over a number of genera-tions can select for sex ratio adjustments in favor of the less expensive sex. Oksanen (1981) generalizes this idea as: "Whenever the risks and rewards of being a male are unevenly distributed in time, there are periods when bearing all-female litters is the optimal strategy" (p. 110). Further, Oksanen argues that the optimal allocation of any differential effort between male and female offspring depends on the individual costs of raising the offspring and on the ability to compete with those born in times of resource and reproductive surplus. Taken together, this work suggests that female-biased sex ratios, and therefore female-disadvantaged mating markets and increased female competition, are a likely outcome of environments characterized by stress and resource

scarcity. Consider for a moment human popula-tions in which there are particularly high levels of stress and resource scarcity (e.g., war zones, inner cities, collapsing rural communities); this model suggests that these groups should start experienc-ing fewer male offspring and thus increased female competition.

A contrasting model to Myers' (1978) work, however, suggests a possible pathway for female-biased sex ratio among resource-poor organisms. McGinley's model (1984) starts by assuming a hypothetical distribution of reproductive effort (RE) in a polygamous species wherein each off-spring "costs" one unit of RE to be produced. Within such a model, females with large amounts of available RE can produce multiple offspring at once, but those with low RE can only produce one offspring at a time. McGinley suggests that moth-ers who are stressed to the point of having low amounts of available RE, and can therefore only produce single offspring, may be able to invest any remaining residual RE into their single offspring and ensure that it has all the investment possible (i.e., any fractional RE of less than one unit can be invested in this single offspring, without being diluted by distribution across multiple offspring). McGinley thus conjectures that these stressed mothers should bias the sex ratio of their offspring in favor of males to increase the reproductive suc-cess of their offspring in their stressed environment, thereby increasing their own inclusive fitness. This is a gamble, however, because male reproductive success is highly variable. However, it is less of a gamble than favoring females, as females repro-ductive success is also varied. This work presents an alternate sex ratio outcome in environments characterized by stress: a reproductive strategy that favors a male-biased sex ratio and therefore male-disadvantaged mating markets and increased male competition.

Looking only at the general costs of breeding for females, Bleu, Bessa-Gomes, and Laloi (2012) discuss how change in costs and benefits can shape female mate choice. There is competition among females related to how choosy they are actually able to be; if they are not choosy enough, there is the *cost* of producing or investing in lower-quality off-spring due to a poor mate choice, whereas females who are *too* choosy may remain unmated due to a lack of available males who meet their requirements. As a result, Bleu et al. predict that choosiness should evolve toward a balanced cost-benefit analysis. The existing sex ratio of a population, however, also plays a role in this analysis. Females who are in a disadvantaged mating market—filled with many females and few available males—are not able to be as choosy as those female counterparts in advantaged mating markets with relatively few competitors and many available mates. Understanding the ways in which a disadvantaged mating market changes female mate choice is fundamental for understanding female competition.

The incorporation of a cost-benefit analysis from the male perspective, alongside that of the female cost-benefit analysis, serves to complicate calculations further. According to Wild and Taylor (2005), conflict exists between pair-bonded mates over the sex ratio of offspring. Wild and Taylor's model for the evolution of sex ratio assumes local resource competition among females within two basic scenarios. One possibility is the *simultaneous allocation scenario*, in which parents make simultaneous sex ratio decisions. This assumes a fair sex determination mechanism, which would produce equal numbers of male and female offspring. The second possibility is the *sequential allocation scenario*, in which parental sex ratio decisions occur one after the other. In the sequential allocation scenario, sex ratio of offspring is not decided through a mechanism but through the behavioral patterns of the mother and father—this scenario, then, is more likely to lead to unequal numbers of male and female offspring. This model was founded on the basic idea that there exists local competition for reproductive resources—which, as previously discussed, can lead to a male-biased sex ratio. Wild and Taylor discuss the resolution of the sex ratio conflict between mates under local resource competition and explain that this resolution depends on how parental efforts may be combined to determine the realized sex ratio of a brood. When parents make simultaneous sex ratio decisions, the weights assigned to sex-specific levels of care play a major part in conflict resolution. In other words, if the weight assigned to *paternal* care is sufficiently large, the sex ratio of the brood is more greatly determined by the interests of the father. If the weight assigned to *maternal* care is sufficiently large, the sex ratio of the brood is determined more by the interests of the mother. In contrast, when parents make sequential allocation decisions, offspring survival is low (high rates of infant mortality and predation), and the parent responsible for providing more parental care (usually the mother) has a greater control over the sex ratio of the brood. Thus, when offspring survival is high, the parent who invests less (typically the father) has more control over the sex ratio of the brood (Wild & Taylor, 2005). This ability of certain species to potentially determine the sex ratio of their brood is discussed more later in this chapter.

In sum, sex ratios tend to have a constant selection pressure toward equality, but several additional pressures can push the ratio one way or the other to create either disadvantaged or advantaged mating markets. Female-disadvantaged mating markets are particularly relevant for creating the potential for female competition and conflict, and such situations certainly can occur. How prevalent they are in the world, though, depends on a number of factors, probably including patterns of differential parental investment, local resource availability, and relative costs and benefits of producing and sustaining male and female offspring. Finally, it is important to note that once circumstances conspire to create female competition, this becomes part of the mating environment for males. As female competition changes, males can be expected to adapt and incorporate those changes into their own reproductive behaviors.

Operational Sex Ratios Versus Overall Sex Ratios

Both the theoretical and computational modeling results point toward an important refinement in the conceptualization of sex ratios and their effects on organisms' behaviors. From the perspective of an individual who is evaluating an environment and making decisions about behaviors based on the surrounding ratio of males and females, the overall sex ratio—the inclusion of everybody—is not always the best measure. One can, and should, be more attuned to the ratio of reproductively viable and available males and females in a given mating market: the operational sex ratio (OSR).

This seemingly subtle distinction, between overall sex ratio and OSR, can make a tremendous difference in how people experience reproductively relevant implications. Consider all the subgroups within the human population who are, by default, counted within the overall sex ratio but excluded from the OSR: all males and females who are juveniles, all females who are postreproductive age, and close kin. (Kin constitute a relatively small group to exclude from OSR, but it is an important exclusion because they are typically very frequently interacted with and could therefore be an otherwise influential part of one's experienced sex ratio.) Also included in the overall sex ratio but excluded from the OSR are people who are otherwise reproductively viable but are currently nonreceptive (e.g., pregnant or otherwise not available at this particular time; Ramsey, 2010). It is possible that individuals may even eliminate people from their perceived OSR if they are too low or too high in overall mate value, defined here in relation to the person who is making the observation and therefore his or her own subjective experience of OSR. This caveat in reference to assortative mate value explains the relative way in which assortative mating may affect OSR, rather than the previously mentioned way in which overall OSR may affect assortative mating. The influence of subjective valuations of OSR is demonstrated by a short story about three upper-middle-class women going out to lunch together in New York City and complaining that "there are no men in this city!" Meanwhile, there are men all around them: the waiter, the busboy, the bartender, the maitre de, and so on (Ellis, 1992; see Figure 15.1). These working-class males are below some subjective threshold of these particular women in terms of mate value (specifically, social and economic status) and therefore apparently excluded from their OSR calculations.

This story also illustrates a potentially game-changing implication of the shift to considering OSR rather than just overall sex ratio. It is quite possible for a population that has an overall sex ratio of 1:1 to nevertheless also have a dramatically *different* OSR. Male-advantaged markets, female-advantaged markets, relatively impoverished markets (i.e., many people but few reproductively viable), and relatively rich markets (i.e., disproportionately large numbers of potential mates, such as on college campuses) all become possible without actually changing the overall 1:1 sex ratio for the total population. These variations in OSR, rather than changes in overall sex ratio, may be important as a cause of mate competition in populations that are seemingly equal. This is an important factor to keep in mind when researching OSR. OSR has typically been assessed via census data, which may not account for the possible nuances of OSR that can exist within the 1:1 sex ratio population. These nuances provide important insight for those interested in researching the implications of OSR, as we must first determine if we are successfully assessing the mating market when we operationally define OSR.

Phylogenetic Evidence

One of the avenues by which we can gain some insight into the effects of different sex ratios is to look across animal species with the hope of finding a broader range of sex ratios than those that occur in human populations. When we see a similar phenomenon across multiple species, associated with particular sex ratio patterns, it can suggest general principles about that phenomenon, such as the

"There are just no men in this city."

Figure 15.1 Female OSR perception may be influenced by subjective standards of what defines a reproductively viable male. (Original artwork created by Matthew Alan Cahill, 2013.)

effects of differential selection pressures, ecologies, and contexts. Such systematic patterns also help lead us to converging lines of evidence for a particular phenomenon being recognized as an adaptation, and absences of patterns can lead us to consider alternative or additional factors.

For instance, Hamilton (1967) noted that biased sex ratios could be adaptations to the populations from which they are manifested. In other words, the adaptation is the evolutionary ability to capitalize on the population structure in order to produce the most offspring. Across polygynous species, he noted, a nonbreeding surplus of males is commonly observed during the breeding season; not all males are able to mate with females. One might expect this to produce an imbalanced sex ratio of more females relative to males. Yet, even given this unbalanced ratio for mating adults, the sex ratio at birth for these species tends to stay at about 1:1. Hamilton accounted for this observation by noting that outbreeding across populations could restore balance between overall male and female reproductive successes.

As the preceding sections suggest, different OSRs are associated with several systematic variations in mating behaviors across species. Within nonhuman research, differences in OSR have been found to have consistent relationships with physical dimorphism between the sexes, male intrasexual competition for mates, and degrees of parental investment by males and females (Kokko & Johnstone, 2002). According to Kokko and Johnstone, "sex roles— i.e., competitiveness for matings—are assumed to depend solely on the OSR" (p. 319). Whereas male intrasexual competition has been a particular focus of OSR-based hypotheses due to the prevalence of male-disadvantaged mating markets in many mammalian species (and differential parental investment), the behaviors and strategies of *females* within various OSR states is understudied. Such work is particularly important because, although competition is widely studied, the information available is almost entirely composed of data on males and thus may be inadvertently biased.

Some accounts of relatively stable female-disadvantaged mating markets have been proposed. For instance, Smith and Stenseth (1978) observed a systematically maintained female-biased sex ratio in wood lemmings and suggested that this female-biased sex ratio may be evolutionarily stable due to recurrent inbreeding. Specifically, simulated mating environments indicate that brother–sister and father–daughter pairs produce recurrent female-biased sex ratios, because only half as many males were "needed" for reproduction.

Female Selective Sex Ratios of Broods

A sizeable amount of the nonhuman research on sex ratios has focused on the question of whether, and if so, when, mothers are able to determine the sex ratio of their offspring. The strongest version of the Trivers–Willard hypothesis suggests that mothers should choose which offspring (males or females) will receive greater investment, and biasing sex at birth (or, actually, at conception) would be the most effective and efficient mechanism to accomplish this. Are there situations in which mothers produce female-biased sex ratios? And, if so, is there a corresponding increase in female intrasexual conflict?

One possible example of producing more females and the likely increase of female intrasexual competition is discussed by Rapaport, Kloc, Warneke, Mickelberg, and Ballou (2013), who found that female captive callitrichines could have a bias for female offspring who are helpful in raising subsequent offspring. This hypothesis goes against many theories of female competition in mating contexts, in that Rapaport et al.'s underlying assumption is that having more females allows them to help one another to optimize benefits to their inclusive fitness, as opposed to having more females leads to increased female competition. Although this particular situation is possibly due to shared kinship, it is interesting to note as a factor that may tip the scales in favor of more female offspring.

The wasp species analyzed by Werren (1983), *Nasonia vitripennis*, was chosen for research due to its relatively useful attributes as a subject for studying local mate competition. These wasps lay batches of eggs, which typically produce an extremely female-biased sex ratio (only 5% to 25% of offspring tend to be male). For this type of wasp, fertilized eggs develop into females and unfertilized eggs develop into males, thus giving the female of the species the opportunity to control the brood sex ratio. One particular type of population of the *Nasonia virtripennis* that Werren studied was those in a *superparasitism model*, which occurs when a second wasp lays eggs in a previously parasitized host—that is, on a host that has already been chosen as an egg-laying site by another female conspecific. Werren found that the optimal sex ratio of the superparasite was strongly dependent on her brood size relative to the brood size of the primary parasite (i.e., the female parasite that chose this egg-laying site first). When her brood size was relatively small compared to that of the primary parasite, an "all-son" brood tended to be produced. As this superparasite's relative brood size increases, her optimal sex ratio shifted toward the customary female bias. Suzuki and Iwasa (1980) came to a similar conclusion regarding sex ratios in superparasitic populations.

Of specific interest about this particular sex-ratio research is the relative control the female of the species has over the sex ratio in her offspring. Further, the specific area of studying the sex ratio of offspring in a superparasitic model is the epitome of female competition. Multiple females are sharing a host in this ecology, and as a result one female must change her particular reproductive strategy, through the offspring sex ratio, based on the reproductive behavior of another female.

Sex Ratio and Local Resource Competition

Competition within both sexes exists in many species. As previously mentioned, much of the available research focuses on male–male mating competition, which is characterized by the competition between males over more highly valued and sought-after females. Another aspect of intrasexual competition that is relatively understudied is local resource competition, which is the competition over resources available to the given population, within its limited ecology. Clark (1978) first suggested local resource competition as a way to designate competition among kin for limited breeding resources. Like local mate competition, local resource competition was a concept developed in the context of sex ratio theory. That is, patterns of female intrasexual competition for mates, as well as for breeding resources, are intimately connected with and affected by existing sex ratios.

In its essence, local resource competition is a more general version of local mate competition; both are intrasexual competitions that favor an opposite-sex-biased sex ratio. In other words, the competition among female conspecifics for access to important resources tends to produce selection pressures in favor of the production of more male offspring. Unlike the Trivers–Willard hypothesis, however, the local resource competition theory focuses on processes that affect all members of a species within the location and therefore might generate a uniform bias across individuals rather than selectively impacting individuals with differential access to resources (Silk & Brown, 2008).

There is some empirical evidence that local resource competition may affect sex ratios among primates. Clark (1978) noticed a male bias in off-spring of the *G. crassicaudatus umbrosus* primate species in North Transvaal and noted that it was associated with females who tended to share areas of food resources with other females. Clark surmised that, beyond sharing areas with high food resources (areas that are more than capable of supplying to multiple females), individual females were in fact in a position to gain from sharing these areas. After initial competition, these females groom each other as well as help with parenting of offspring that are not their own. Clark believed these were bonds between females who were kin (mothers and daughters, mostly) and that finding an area to share with other females is essential to a given female's reproductive success.

Though the behaviors of these females do seem to promote cooperation in general, there is an initial competition for land and resources, displaying a type of female intrasexual competition that, while related to mating overall, is not focused entirely on mating opportunities and behaviors. Because of this female competition over local food resources, Clark (1978) claims that these female primates can enhance their own, as well as their daughters', fitness by producing more sons. This ties in with another finding of Clark's; that within several captive primate populations, including the nocturnal, arboreal prosimian primates *Galago crassicaudatus*, there was a sex ratio skewed toward males. In these examples, a bias toward the production of male off-spring is associated with a social structure characterized by both female intrasexual competition for, and sharing of, local resources.

Human Evidence

The abundance of theoretical and phylogenetic evidence suggesting that OSR can influence mating strategies and behaviors stands in contrast to the relatively small and recent body of work on OSR influences on human behaviors. Inferential logic says that a factor—such as OSR—that has clear influences on behaviors across a wide array of other species should similarly play a role in human behavior. Indeed, most of the research that looks at this topic does find such support. Much more work, though, is clearly needed.

Demographic Research

An early study by Pedersen (1991) used archival demographic data to document that couples who married during periods of male-disadvantaged sex ratios (i.e., more males than females) had lower divorce rates, more male commitment to both good careers and helping with child care, and higher fertility. More recently, an impressive collection of findings have been amassed by Daniel Kruger and colleagues (Garcia & Kruger, 2010; Kruger, 2009; Kruger & Fitzgerald, 2012; Kruger, Fitzgerald, & Peterson, 2010; Kruger & Schlemmer, 2009; see also Pollet & Nettle, 2008), leading to the general conclusion that OSR is related to changes in marriage patterns and marriage ages (as markers for selectivity, competition, and mating strategies). Although useful as a foundation from which further work on OSR in humans can proceed, they are limited by the fact that the data are generally drawn from large surveys, such as the US Census, that were collected for other purposes. As such, we have little insight into the psychological processes underlying the perception and use of OSR, and these studies have (so far) been restricted to comparisons of different areas within the United States. Furthermore, as previously mentioned in this chapter, census data may reveal variations in the overall sex ratio in a given area, but due to various factors the OSR of that area may in fact be quite different.

Cross-Cultural Research

There has been one non-US study that used data from a computer dating service to look at mate preferences in Tel Aviv, Israel, which has a very imbalanced sex ratio of 1:.656 (Bokek-Cohen, Peres, & Kanazawa, 2008). This study, though, found that even in this female-disadvantaged mating market, the women expressed more selective mating preferences than men (at least within the computer dating service). Because this research did not involve a comparison with other cultures, it is unclear if women in Tel Aviv were more or less selective than women in other locations (e.g., locations with equitable sex ratios).

The results of the Bokek-Cohen et al. (2008) study are inconsistent with two other, much more extensive, cross-cultural research efforts on sex ratios across different cultures. Stone, Shackelford, and Buss (2007) found that male and female mating behaviors changed in systematic ways across 36 cultures according to the sex ratios within those cultures. When the sex ratio was imbalanced, there was more intrasexual competition within the more plentiful sex to acquire a mate of the less plentiful sex. The nature of these competitions were sex specific; both men and women shifted their competitive efforts according to the typical mating behaviors of

each sex. For example, in humans, men are more interested in casual sex than are women (Buss & Schmitt, 1993), so in populations with women competing more than men for mates, there were higher rates of female promiscuity. The disadvantaged sex thus behaves in a way that the advantaged sex prefers in order to procure a mate. This is akin to the sexually selected mating displays of nonhuman animals, where individuals of one sex display traits or behaviors that are highly sought after by the opposite sex. Similarly, in populations in which men are competing more than women for access to mates, males adopt mating strategies that females prefer, usually more monogamy and displays of possible future parental investment. An even larger study (Schmitt, 2005) found that sociosexuality— relative preference for monogamous versus promiscuous mating strategies—was related to both OSR and reproductively demanding environments across 48 cultures. In particular, cultures in which there were more women than men tended to have higher sociosexuality scores overall (i.e., more promiscuity), whereas cultures in which there were more men than women tended to have lower sociosexuality scores (i.e., more monogamy).

Laboratory Research

One way of demonstrating sex ratio's effect on human female competition is to look at situations in which there is a female-disadvantaged mating market in an existing human population, focusing on outcomes such as mating tactics and achieved behaviors in these environments. For instance, Dillon (2011) found that monogamous female college students who were in disadvantaged local mating markets had significantly higher ratings of the attractiveness of their male partners than did females in more equitable or advantaged mating markets. In particular, women in disadvantaged mating markets assessed their mates more favorably on scales such as the Mate Value Inventory (Kirsner, Figueredo, & Jacobs, 2003). Dillon proposed that these female-disadvantaged mating contexts are characterized by relatively higher levels of female intrasexual competition for mates, and women may therefore adjust their goals, expectations, and perceptions of potential mates when faced with mating markets that necessitate their settling for available mates who may not be of particularly high quality. Dillon further proposed that those women who had successfully obtained mates would maintain relatively higher evaluations of their partners, which could function to increase their relationship satisfaction and decrease the likelihood of female defection or rejection of mates in these disadvantaged ecologies.

Existing populations with female-disadvantaged mating markets, however, are ultimately limited for research because they lack control; there could be any number of other factors that are systematically covarying across populations along with the sex ratio difference. Laboratory research has the potential to systematically manipulate OSR, if only briefly, to study changes in behavior that are more clearly a function of the OSR and not other variables. As it turns out, manipulating people's perceived OSR is possible, and there are currently a couple different methods that have been developed.

Wilson and Daly (2004) had participants view a series of 12 photographs showing either very attractive or nonattractive opposite-sex people. After men (but not women) rated how appealing they found the very attractive people (but not the unattractive people), they showed higher discounting rates. Discounting rate refers to the relative preference for a smaller reward immediately, versus a larger reward after some delay; thus a higher discount rate indicates relative "impatience." This finding is consistent with an adaptive shift toward more short-term strategies when there is a mating market that is perceived as male advantaged, as found also in the demographic sex-ratio-based research (e.g., Schmitt, 2005).

Importantly, experimentally altering the perceived sex ratio of the local environment allows researchers to much more easily investigate the psychological changes that occur as a result. Whereas long-term behavioral consequences such as marriage patterns and offspring produced are important eventual results, they are also difficult to disentangle from a myriad of other influencing factors. The more immediate changes in perceptions (Dillon, 2011) and decisions can provide more responsive and illuminating details about how individuals ultimately achieve their particular behavioral outcomes.

More recent research has extended the finding that perceptions of different OSR can influence various financial decisions in men (Griskevicius, Simpson, Durante, Kim, & Cantu, 2012), with multiple results all generally in the direction of males spending more, sooner, when they were induced to perceive a male-disadvantaged mating market. In contrast, when women were induced to perceive that they were in a female-disadvantaged mating market, they were more likely to orient toward lucrative careers and to orient away from

starting a family (Durante, Griskevicius, Simpson, Cantú, & Tybur, 2012). Both of these findings were replicated using three different methods of varying OSR: by demographic measures of actual sex ratios, by manipulating perceived local OSR through viewing photographs (e.g., rating 18 photographs that included either 12–14 of one sex, equal number of both sexes, or 12–14 of the other sex), and by having participants read fictitious local or regional newspaper articles about biased sex ratios on college campuses.

Additional research has adopted the use of images as a means for priming a particular local OSR and has found that men (but not women) are more sensitive to intrasexual dominance cues (facial masculinity) when primed with photographs indicating a male-disadvantaged mating market (Watkins, Debruine, Feinberg, & Jones, 2013). Additionally, women show a stronger preference for more facially symmetrical (i.e., higher mate quality) men when induced to perceive a female-advantaged mating market, and men showed a preference for more facial symmetry when they were induced to perceive a male-advantaged mating market (Watkins, Jones, Little, DeBruine, & Feinberg, 2012). In other words, both men and women pay more attention to cues of potential mate quality when they have some expectation of being able to be more selective.

Open and Ongoing Issues Regarding Operational Sex Ratios in Humans

It is a truism that good research not only answers questions but also raises a host of new questions. The following section describes a few of the directions in which human OSR research, speculatively, can go in the future based on questions the existing research has raised.

The Cognitive Mechanism Tracking Operational Sex Ratios

For any organism to take into account the OSR in its environment, there must be some type of mental mechanism that tracks the frequency with which males and females are being encountered. As yet, though, very little is understood about how the human mind (or, for that matter, any animal mind) attends to, remembers, and processes the OSR of its species.

Research on many nonhuman species can largely continue without too much concern about this issue, instead using the researcher-calculated actual sex ratio as a measure of the OSR (with perhaps some small adjustments). Indeed, even in humans, many studies use demographic sex ratio information as a measure of OSR (e.g., Garcia & Kruger, 2010; Kruger, 2009; Kruger, et al., 2009, 2010, 2012; Pedersen, 1991; Pollet & Nettle, 2008; Schmitt, 2005; Stone, Shackelford, & Buss, 2007). There are several reasons to be cautious about using overall sex ratios for human OSR, however. Humans are a particularly long-lived and social species that has a much larger proportions of nonreproductive individuals. Nonreproductive-status individuals among humans include juveniles, and because of the greatly extended juvenile period for humans, this is a sizeable group.

Humans also live in an environment that is, in some ways, radically different from the environment under which the cognitive mechanisms that track OSR would have evolved. We live in cities made up of thousands, hundreds of thousands, and millions of other people. These population sizes dwarf what humans would have normally experienced over most of evolutionary history and are nothing like the population sizes that were common during the Environment of Evolutionary Adaptedness. At what level do individuals judge their environment's OSR? Do they attend to the OSR of their nation, their state, their city, or even their neighborhood? (We suspect that directly experienced, local information is more influential.) Do people calculate OSR based on their larger community, their immediate neighborhood, their street? What is the time window within which a person maintains a record of experienced males and females for the purpose of determining OSR? (Some of the research reviewed in the previous section, such as by Griskevicius and colleagues [2012], suggests surprisingly strong influences of very recent experiences.)

Modern society also does some very (evolutionarily) unusual things with people in terms of age segregation, putting people into narrow bands of similarly aged individuals in schools, workplaces, and retirement. Finally, it is not clear how the cognitive mechanisms that track human OSR are responsive to exposures to people (both real and fictional) via traditional media (e.g., television and movies) and via social media. It is possible, for example, that women who watch reality dating shows (e.g., *The Bachelor* or *Flavor of Love*) would become increasingly competitive with other women in real life because of their perceptions of the highly imbalanced sex ratios in these shows.

A number of psychological experiments now indicate that the mechanism that tracks OSR may actually be quite sensitive, responding to even small samplings of photographs within a laboratory setting (Durante, et al., 2012; Griskevicius, et al., 2012). Although this is a convenient tool for researchers, it raises a number of questions about the malleability of perceived OSR—and therefore human behavior—in everyday life (Griskevicius et al., 2012).

Emotional Responses to Operational Sex Ratios

Within the comparative literature it is customary to discuss the direct effects of OSR on mating behaviors, without consideration of the subjective experiences, thoughts, or feelings associated those behaviors. In the human case, though, we have both access to this inner phenomenology and an interest in better understanding these phenomena. For example, there has been a long-running literature on the different reactions men and women have to types of relationship infidelities. (On average, men are more upset by sexual infidelity than by emotional infidelity, as compared to women; see Buss, Larsen, Westen, & Semmelroth, 1992.) While this finding has proven to be controversial (Harris, 2003), it also is well established (e.g., Sagarin, et al., 2012).

We can anticipate that a male-disadvantaged OSR (many males, competing for fewer females) would be likely to exacerbate reactions such as the male experience of being upset and distressed by the idea of his partner's sexual infidelity. Males experience jealousy at the notion of a partner's sexual infidelity for numerous reasons, a primary reason being paternal uncertainty (i.e., if a male believes his female partner to be engaging in intercourse with other males, he is less sure of his paternity for any offspring that female bears; Daly, Wilson & Weghorst, 1982). In a male-disadvantaged OSR situation, there is greater risk of such an occurrence (either through the greater number of temptations or the greater number of outside attempts to gain sexual access). In fact, D'Alessio and Stolzenberg (2010) found that a male-disadvantaged sex ratio (defined by census records) was associated with higher rates of men committing intimate partner violence. Similarly, a female-disadvantaged OSR (more females than males) would be likely to exacerbate female reactions of being upset and distressed by the idea of a partner's emotional infidelity. With more opportunities for a male partner to divert resources to a different female, a directly implied hypothesis is that an existing female partner would up-regulate her monitoring for and reactions to such a possibility.

China's One-Child Policy

Large parts of Asia and North Africa are currently in the middle of, effectively, a massive sex ratio experiment. There is a strong cultural preference for male children (sons), and, in combination with increasingly lower fertility rates (i.e., fewer children per family), this has led to strongly male-biased childhood sex ratios. This phenomenon is most striking in China where a one-child policy, enacted in order to decrease population size, has exacerbated this trend. There are currently 118 male births for every 100 female births, rising as high as 135 to 100 in some rural areas, and this translates to somewhere between 20 million to 80 million excess males (or "missing females") of reproductive age (Hesketh & Xing, 2006; Zhou, Li, Yan, & Hesketh, 2013).

Based on the existing models and research findings on male-disadvantaged OSRs, we can expect various consequences from this situation. For our current purposes, some of these consequences are that females in China will experience a decrease of intrasexual competition due to the excess of available mates (and, of course, males in China will have increased intrasexual competition based on the lack of available mates). What the studies have found so far is that women in China are more likely to have earlier, premarital sex and are more likely to contract sexually transmitted diseases (South & Trent, 2010; Trent & South, 2012). At the same time, however, the value of females—at least by some measures—is beginning to sharply increase in Asia. The costs paid by potential husbands for a wife, sometimes called "bride price," has been increasing in China and can now easily reach over $10,000 and also include the expectation of an apartment from the groom's family (Lim, 2013). The preceding two findings are somewhat paradoxical in juxtaposition. We would suggest that what may be occurring is both a higher demand for wives (hence the bride price increases) and a higher demand for sexual access (hence the increases in sexual activity). In other words, these may be two somewhat different emerging sets of experiences occurring for women within China.

What is clearly needed is more research on the effects of changing sex ratios in Asian countries, including the predicted potential decrease of female intrasexual competition. It may be that female intrasexual competition is not changing at all, or it may be a matter of it not having been looked for yet. (The absence of evidence is not evidence of absence.)

Last, the imbalanced sex ratios in China and elsewhere appear to have been accomplished primarily via sex-specific abortions, abandonment of unwanted female infants, and other post-conception manipulations. This is notable in that the cultural pressures do not appear to have any direct influence on sex ratios at conception. It remains to be seen, however, if future Asian generations show compensating sex ratio biases as would be predicted by Fisherian selection pressures. In other words, will future generations be female-biased in order to counteract the current male-biased population and regain homeostasis?

Future Directions

There is a logical connection between initial offspring sex ratios and eventual OSRs; offspring eventually grow up to be part of the mating pool. In some senses, then, the sex ratio for a generational cohort is largely established about 15 to 20 years before the actual mating strategies, potentially influenced by that ratio, are implemented. As mentioned before, this raises a question about the sensitive window for human tracking of population sex ratios. Are there effects of population sex ratios at times and contexts other than mating? For example, do cohort sex ratios influence children's development as they begin to develop social interaction styles? Do changes in experienced sex ratios (e.g., from differential mortality of one sex, or simply individuals relocating to different populations) change developmental, behavioral, and strategic trajectories? We have seen, for example, that superparasite wasps are able to adjust the sex ratio of their brood deposits based on the initial parasites' brood sex ratio (a behavior change based on a very local and specific sex ratio; Werren, 1983). In humans, the sex ratio effects found by Pedersen (1991)—documenting changes in divorce rates, male relationship behaviors, fertility, and sexual violence—were based specifically on the sex ratios that existed at the time of his subjects' marriages.

It is possible that OSR influences not only mating strategies but also other behaviors relating to social interactions. Some of these behaviors may entail female intrasexual competition and aggression, particularly when there are contexts that include a female-disadvantaged sex ratio. In conjunction with the open questions about the window of sensitivity for mentally registering OSR, understanding the ways in which we register OSR information from the environment could be tremendously useful in both research and our understanding of human behavior.

Conclusion

OSRs appear to be a potentially important and powerful factor in explaining variation in human mating behaviors, including variations across social groups, across cultures, and across time periods. Some of those variations include clear implications for female intrasexual competition, the most general being environments of female-disadvantaged mating markets. Female-disadvantaged markets appear to be less common than male-disadvantaged markets (Bleu, Bessa-Gomes, & Laoli, 2012), perhaps because differential parental investment exerts a continuous pressure to assess females more highly in terms of mating value. There are some places, though, where females substantially outnumber males (e.g., Tel Aviv, Israel; Bokek-Cohen, Peres, & Kanazawa, 2008). Female competition exists to some extent in all mating markets, but female-disadvantaged mating markets appear to increase this competition. Women are at their most competitive, regarding mating behaviors, when males are scarce.

Given the experimental results on inducing different perceptions of local OSRs, the focus on large-scale OSR measures such as cities or counties may be too coarse of a methodology. Local, directly experienced OSRs may be more cognitively relevant and therefore better measures of OSR as a mechanism for understanding behavioral changes. If that is correct, then a number of real-world situations emerge that can plausibly provide clearly female-disadvantaged mating markets. These include, for instance, single-sex educational institutions (e.g., women's colleges), college students who are in strongly sex-biased majors (e.g., women's studies, nursing, and psychology), occupations that similarly have skewed sex ratios, and elderly populations (in which higher rates of male mortality create imbalanced sex ratios). Across all these situations, which can be thought of as micro-populations with female-biased OSRs, we may see effects on general mating strategies that can include changes in female intrasexual competition.

References

Alexander, R. D., & Sherman, P. W. (1977). Local mate competition and parental investment in social insects. *Science, 196*(4289), 494–500.

Berglund, A. (1994). The operational sex ratio influences choosiness in a pipefish. *Behavioral Ecology, 5*, 254–258.

Bleu, J., Bessa-Gomes, C., & Laloi, D. (2012). Evolution of female choosiness and mating frequency: Effects of mating cost, density and sex ratio. *Animal Behavior, 83*, 131–136.

Bokek-Cohen, Y., Peres, Y., & Kanazawa, S. (2008). Rational choice and evolutionary psychology as explanations for mate selectivity. *Journal of Social, Evolutionary, and Cultural Psychology, 2*, 42–55.

Boucher, D. H. (1977). On wasting parental investment. *American Naturalist, 111*(980), 786–788.

Buss, D., & Barnes, M. (1986). Preferences in human mate selection. *Journal of Personality and Social Psychology, 50*, 559–570.

Buss, D. M., Larsen, R. J., Westen, D., & Semmelroth, J. (1992). Sex differences in jealousy: Evolution, physiology, and psychology. *Psychological Science, 3*, 251.

Buss, D. M., & Schmitt, D. P. (1993). Sexual strategies theory: an evolutionary perspective on human mating. *Psychological Review, 100*, 204–232.

Cahill, M. A. (2013). There are no men in this city [Original artwork].

Cameron, E. Z., & Dalerum, F. (2009). A Trivers-Willard effect in contemporary humans: male-biased sex ratios among billionaires. *PLoS ONE, 4*, e4195.

Clark, A. B. (1978). Sex ratio and local resource competition in a prosimian primate. *Science, 201*, 163–165.

Cox, C. R., & Le Boeuf, B. J. (1977). Female incitation of male competition: A mechanism in sexual selection. *American Naturalist, 111*, 317–335.

D'Alessio, S. J., & Stolzenberg, L. (2010). The sex ratio and male-on-female intimate partner violence. *Journal of Criminal Justice, 38*, 555–561.

Daly, M., Wilson, M., & Weghorst, S. J. (1982). Male sexual jealousy. *Ethology and Sociobiology, 3*, 11–27.

Dillon, H. M. (2011). An *evolutionary analysis of partner perceptions within mateships: The beauty and the beast effect, the role of trait factors, and the nature of mate settling* (Unpublished master's thesis). State University of New York-New Paltz, New Paltz, NY.

Durante, K. M., Griskevicius, V., Simpson, J. A., Cantú, S. M., & Tybur, J. M. (2012). Sex ratio and women's career choice: Does a scarcity of men lead women to choose briefcase over baby? *Journal of Personality and Social Psychology, 103*, 121–134.

Ellis, B. J. (1992). The evolution of sexual attraction: Evaluative mechanisms in women. In J. Barkow, L. Cosmides, & J. Tooby (Eds.), *The adapted mind: Evolutionary psychology and the generation of culture* (pp. 267–288). New York: Oxford University Press.

Freese, J., & Powell, B. (1999). Sociobiology, status, and parental investment in sons and daughters: Testing the Trivers–Willard hypothesis. *American Journal of Sociology, 6*, 1704–1743.

Garcia, J. R., & Kruger, D. J. (2010). Unbuckling in the Bible Belt: Conservative sexual norms lower age at marriage. *Journal of Social, Evolutionary, and Cultural Psychology, 4*, 206–214.

Griskevicius, V., Simpson, J. A., Durante, K. M., Kim, J., & Cantu, S. (2012). Evolution, social influence, and sex ratio. In D. Kenrick, N. Goldstein, & S. Braver (Eds.), *Six degrees of social influence: Science, application, and the psychology of Robert Cialdini*. (pp. 79–89) New York: Oxford University Press.

Griskevicius, V., Tybur, J. M., Ackerman, J. M., Delton, A. W., Robertson, T. E., & White, A. E. (2012). The financial consequences of too many men: Sex ratio effects on saving, borrowing, and spending. *Journal of Personality and Social Psychology, 102*, 69–80.

Hamilton, W. D. (1967). Extraordinary sex ratios. *Science, 156*, 477–488.

Harris, C. R. (2003). A review of sex differences in sexual jealousy, including self-report data, psychophysiological responses, interpersonal violence, and morbid jealousy. *Personality and Social Psychology Review, 7*, 102–128.

Hesketh, T., & Xing, Z. W. (2006). Abnormal sex ratios in human populations: Causes and consequences. *Proceedings of the National Academy of Sciences, USA, 103*, 13271–13275.

Kamimura, Y., Abe, J., & Ito, H. (2008) The continuous public goods game and the evolution of cooperative sex ratios. *Journal of Theoretical Biology, 252*, 277–287.

Keller, M. C., Nesse, R. M., & Hofferth, S. (2001). The Trivers–Willard hypothesis of parental investment: No effect in the contemporary United States. *Evolution and Human Behavior, 22*(5), 343–360.

Kirsner, B. R., Figueredo, A. J., & Jacobs, W. J. (2003). Self, friends, and lovers: Structural relations among beck depression inventory scores and perceived mate values. *Journal of Affective Disorders, 75*, 131–148.

Kokko, H., & Johnstone, R. A. (2002). Why is mutual mate choice not the norm? Operational sex ratios, sex roles, and the evolution of sexually dimorphic and monomorphic signalling. *Philosophical Transactions of the Royal Society B, 357*, 319–330.

Kruger, D. J. (2009). When men are scarce, good men are even harder to find: Life history, the sex ratio, and the proportion of men married. *Journal of Social, Evolutionary, and Cultural Psychology, 3*, 93–104.

Kruger, D. J., & Fitzgerald, C. J. (2012). Sexual conflict and the operational sex ratio. In T. K. Shackelford & A. Goetz (Eds.) *The Oxford handbook of sexual conflict in humans* (pp. 283–294). New York: Oxford University Press.

Kruger, D. J., Fitzgerald, C. J., & Peterson, T. (2010). Female scarcity reduces women's marital ages and increases variance in men's marital ages. *Evolutionary Psychology, 8*, 420–431.

Kruger, D. J., & Schlemmer, E. (2009). Male scarcity is differentially related to male marital likelihood across the life course. *Evolutionary Psychology, 7*, 280–287.

Lim, L. (Producer). (2013, April 23). *For Chinese women, marriage depends on right "bride price."* [Special series: The changing lives of women broadcast] Washington, DC: National Public Radio. Retrieved from http://www.npr.org/2013/04/23/176326713/for-chinese-women-marriage-depends-on-right-bride-price]

Maynard Smith, J., & Stenseth, N. C. (1978). On the evolutionary stability of the female-biased sex ratio in the wood lemming (*Myopus schisticolor*): The effect of inbreeding. *Heredity, 41*, 205–214.

McGinley, M. A. (1984). The adaptive value of male-biased sex ratios among stressed animals. *American Naturalist, 124*, 597–599.

Myers, J. H. (1978). Sex ratio adjustment under foodstress: Maximization of quality or numbers of offspring? *American Naturalist, 112*, 381–388.

Oksanen, L. (1981). All-female litters as a reproductive strategy: Defense and generalization of the Trivers–Willard hypothesis. *American Naturalist, 117*, 109–111.

Pedersen, F. A. (1991). Secular trends in human sex ratios: Their influence on individual and family behavior. *Human Nature, 2*, 271–291.

Pollet, T. V., & Nettle, D. (2008). Driving a hard bargain: Sex ratio and male marriage success in a historical US population. *Biology Letters, 4*, 31–33.

Queller, D. C. (1997). Why do females care more than males? *Proceedings of the Royal Society of London, Series B: Biological Sciences, 264*, 1555–1557.

Ramsey, D. M. (2010). A large population parental care game: Polymorphisms and feedback between patterns of care and the operational sex ratio. *Journal of Theoretical Biology, 266*, 675–690.

Rapaport, L. G., Kloc, B., Warneke, M., Mickelberg, J. L., & Ballou, J. D. (2013). Do mothers prefer helpers? Birth sex ratio adjustment in captive callitrichines. *Animal Behaviour, 85*, 1295–1302.

Robert, K. A., & Thompson, M. B. (2001). Sex determination: Viviparous lizard selects sex of embryos. *Nature, 412*, 698–699.

Sagarin, B. J., Martin, A. L., Coutinho, S. A., Edlund, J. E., Patel, L., Skowronski, J. J., & Zengel, B. (2012). Sex differences in jealousy: A meta-analytic examination. *Evolution and Human Behavior, 33*, 595–614.

Schmitt, D. P. (2005). Sociosexuality from Argentina to Zimbabwe: A 48-nation study of sex, culture, and strategies of human mating. *Behavioral and Brain Sciences, 28*, 247–311.

Silk, J. B., & Brown, G. R. (2008) Local resource competition and local resource enhancement shape primate birth sex ratios. *Proceedings of the Royal Society, 275*, 1761–1765.

South, S. J., & Trent, K. (2010). Imbalanced sex ratios, men's sexual behavior, and risk of sexually transmitted infection in china. *Journal of Health and Social Behavior, 51*, 376–390.

Stone, E. A., Shackelford, T. K. & Buss, D. M. (2007) Sex ratio and mate preferences: A cross-cultural investigation. *European Journal of Social Psychology, 37*, 288–296.

Suzuki, Y., & Iwasa, Y. (1980). A sex ratio theory of gregarious parasitoids. *Research on Population Ecology, 22*, 366–382.

Trent, K., & South, S. J. (2012). Mate availability and women's sexual experiences in China. *Journal of Marriage and Family, 74*, 201–214.

Trivers, R. L. (1972). Parental investment and sexual selection. In B. Campbell (Ed.), *Sexual selection and the descent of man, 1871–1971* (pp. 136–179). Chicago: Aldine.

Trivers, R. L., & Willard, D. E. (1973). Natural selection of parental ability to vary the sex ratio of offspring. *Science, 179*, 90–92.

Wade, M. J. (1979). Sexual selection and variance in reproductive success. *American Naturalist, 114*(5), 742–747.

Watkins, C. D., Debruine, L. M., Feinberg, D. R., & Jones, B. C. (2013). A sex difference in the context-sensitivity of dominance perceptions. *Evolution and Human Behavior, 35*(3), 366–372.

Watkins, C. D., Jones, B. C., Little, A. C., DeBruine, L. M., & Feinberg, D. R. (2012). Cues to the sex ratio of the local population influence women's preferences for facial symmetry. *Animal Behaviour, 83*, 545–553.

Werren, J. H. (1983). Sex ratio evolution under local mate competition in a parasitic wasp. *Evolution, 37*, 116–124.

Wild, G., & Taylor, P. D. (2005). A kin-selection approach to the resolution of sex-ratio conflict between mates. *Journal of Theoretical Biology, 236*, 126–136.

Williams, G. C. (1979). The question of adaptive sex ratio in outcrossed vertebrates. *Proceedings of the Royal Society of London, Series B: Biological Sciences, 205*, 567–580.

Wilson, D. S., & Colwell, R. K. (1981). Evolution of sex ratios in structured demes. *Evolution, 5*, 882–897.

Wilson, M., & Daly, M. (2004). Do pretty women inspire men to discount the future? *Proceedings of the Royal Society of London, Series B: Biological Sciences, 271*, 177–179.

Zhou, X. D., Li, L., Yan, Z., & Hesketh, T. (2013). High sex ratio as a correlate of depression in Chinese men. *Journal of Affective Disorders, 114*, 79–86.

The Influence of Women's Mate Value on Intrasexual Competition

Maryanne L. Fisher *and* Ana María Fernández

Abstract

In order to engage in assortative mating, people must be accurate in self-assessments of their current worth on the mating market. We argue that people intrinsically know their worth (i.e., mate value), and that this knowledge has far-reaching implications on a variety of behaviors and decisions. Here our focus is on women's mate value and how it relates to their intrasexual competition for access to, and retention of, romantic partners. We start with a review of definitions and the components of female mate value, discuss mate preferences in relation to assessment of mate value, and then briefly provide a sample of some auxiliary issues, such as how feelings of control over mate value influence one's well-being. We then turn to female intrasexual competition and specifically review competitive strategy use in relation to mate value. In the last section, we provide areas for further investigation.

Key Words: women, mate value, competition, rivalry, sociometric theory

Introduction

When seeking potential mates, the majority of people are fairly reasonable in their expectations. For example, the man living in the small bungalow next door does not truly believe that he will be able to secure a romantic or sexual relationship with a famous and attractive celebrity. Likewise, an older aunt does not genuinely think that she will be able to secure the romantic affection of a wealthy, superstar hockey player. Instead, our neighbor and aunt aim their dating attention at more tangible targets—individuals possessing similar worth on the mating market to themselves. That is, if our neighbor judges his worth or desirability to women to be about a "7" out of 10 (with "10" indicating he is of extremely high worth), he should seek a mate who is likewise about a "7" in order to have an attainable chance of forming a stable, long-term relationship. If he instead selects someone who has lower value, he is undercutting himself, as he would be able to obtain a mate with more desirable features. Alternatively, if he selects someone who has

a higher mate value, he may have difficulty gaining her interest, and if he does start dating her, he may lose her to a man of higher quality down the road. There are other considerations, though; he may decide that he would be willing to date someone of lower value simply to avoid being alone (i.e., date until someone better comes along), or that although the chances of maintaining a long-term relationship with someone of higher value are low, a short-term relationship is better than no relationship at all. Research suggests that men generally decrease their standards for many characteristics, including physical attractiveness, as the anticipated length of the relationship decreases. In contrast, women pursuing a short-term sexual relationship, especially a one-night stand, increase their standards for physical attractiveness (Kenrick, Groth, Trost, & Sadalla 1993). We will return to these issues.

The core topic here, though, is mate value. One's mate value generally refers to one's self-perceived worth on the current mating market, or how desirable one is to members of the opposite sex (assuming heterosexuality), and in comparison to other people of the same sex who may be potential rivals. As a side note, although presumably we could define mate value in terms of nonheterosexual relationships given this definition, the lack of research on mate value and nonheterosexual individuals necessitates that the current chapter focus on individuals who are primarily heterosexual.

Thus, in general, theoretical terms "mate value" can be boiled down to a simple number, reflecting one's worth to potential mates, and should depend on the local environment, such as the ratio of how many mates are available versus potential rivals (see Dillon, Adair, & Brase, and Adair, Dillon, & Brase, this volume), as well as internally dynamic characteristics, such as one's current hormonal or fertility status (e.g., Beaulieu, 2007) or feelings of state-based self-esteem (e.g., Brase & Guy, 2004). We review these identified factors, and others, to provide evidence that mate value is not stable or context-free. What is novel about this chapter, though, is our exploration of the relationship between mate value and intrasexual (i.e., within-sex) competition for access to, and retention of, mates. We argue that one's mate value must be relative to the potential alternatives a mate could instead select from in the surrounding market, and consequently, there exists an intimate link between mate value and intrasexual competition to access or retain mates.

The key factor in this hypothesized relationship between mate value and intrasexual competition for mates is mate preference. Theory suggests that mate value should have a strong coupling with the mate preferences of the opposite sex. Thus, women in Western cultures typically express a preference for slightly older men who are athletic, wealthy, kind, and honest, with a low to moderate number of former sexual partners, and hence, men who possess these features should perceive themselves as having fairly high value on the current mating market for this culture (e.g., Buss, 1989). Wealth and status have been particularly studied, given sex differences in parental investment that have historically (and potentially contemporarily) rendered women dependent on men. That is, given women's relatively larger investment in children than men, in terms of pregnancy, lactation, postnatal care, and onward, women may have limited opportunities to accrue necessary resources for themselves and their children. Thus, evidence suggests that men may attempt to show off or display resource-related features (e.g., material wealth) in order to draw more attention from women. This advertisement of one's

traits is considered a competitive strategy termed "self-promotion" (Buss, 1988; Fisher & Cox, 2009). Moreover, men may try to conceal these features in other men, which would fall under the competitive strategy of competitor derogation (Buss & Dedden, 1990; Fisher & Cox, 2009).

Likewise, men in Western cultures generally express a preference for younger yet fecund women who are healthy, kind, and caring, and are not sexually promiscuous (Buss, 1989). As a result, women with these traits will be in demand and will thus possess a higher mate value relative to mating rivals. Presented this way, it is easy to see a direct conceptual link between mate preferences, mate value, and within-sex competition for mates.

Due to the enormous attention of researchers to the topic of mate preferences, this aspect will be discussed only in brief terms in the current chapter, and only in relation to mate value. The focus of this chapter is instead solely on the relationship between mate value and intrasexual competition. We spend the majority of the chapter focused on women, partly because men's intrasexual competition for mates has received considerably greater attention (see Fisher, 2013, for a review).

The chapter begins with a review of definitions of mate value; the traits that underlie mate value; the assortative aspect of these features in mating; and a sample of some secondary topics, such as how feelings of control over mate value influence one's well-being, and the role of mate value in feelings of romantic relationship satisfaction. Then we turn to the primary topic of the chapter, which is women's mate value and how it relates to female intrasexual competition for access to, and retention of, romantic partners. Given that an individual's conceptualization of her own mate value must be relative to the potential alternatives a mate faces in the surrounding environment, we argue that mate value and intrasexual competition are closely connected. We will also discuss some of the issues surrounding self-assessment versus others' assessments of mate value, as the selective pressures of successful mating competition suggests that one should be very accurate in one's own mate-value appraisal. Mate value in relation to competitive strategy use will then be presented, and the chapter will close with directions for future research.

What Is Mate Value?
Penke, Todd, Lenton, and Fasolo (2007) review that most decisions related to mating rely on two types of behavior. One type of behavior is mate choice,

which encapsulates all factors related to the selection of an appropriate target for one's mating effort. The other is mating tactics, referring to how one decides to allocate one's resources, such as time and energy, for the purposes of mating. Previously, Fisher, Cox, Bennett, & Gavric (2008) argued that both aspects relate to mate value, as "researchers could focus on the value of a mate and how to successfully obtain that person, or they could examine how individuals influence their own mate value to obtain the best mate possible" (p. 14). We first begin with a review of mate choice, and orient the discussion to focus on how people seem to select those who possess approximately the same mate value as oneself. Later in the chapter, we turn the discussion to mating tactics, as related to mate value.

Homogamy in Romantic Relationships

For decades, social psychologists have dedicated impressive effort trying to comprehend the underlying causes that lead individuals to be attracted to each other. One popular theory is that people are attracted to those who are similar to themselves in some way. That is, assortative mating occurs when individuals exhibit preferences for those who are similar to themselves (i.e., homogamy), which is in keeping with the cliché that "birds of a feather flock together." In marked contrast is the theory that people are instead attracted to those who are dissimilar to themselves (i.e., heterogamy), which is aligned with the idea that "opposites attract."

When it comes to long-term romantic relationships, homogamy rather than heterogamy seems to be the general pattern and leads to increased relationship satisfaction (see Hromatko, Bajoghli, Rebernjak, Joshaghani, & Tadinac 2015, for a review). Previous research has documented that individuals tend to be more similar to their spouses than they are to other individuals. For example, people tend to marry those from the same social group or those who have similar status (for a review, see Kalmijn, 1998). Watson, Beer, and McDade-Montez (2014) showed that individuals tend to actively seek particular mate preferences, which then result in similarity within couples. That is, people tend to place importance on particular traits mirroring characteristics that they themselves possess. Similarly, people who like themselves tend to consider an ideal romantic partner as having many similar traits to themselves (Brown & Brown, 2015). Homogamy may be key for relationship happiness and satisfaction, as well as relationship stability, and may be more likely to lead to children (see Hromatko et al., 2015, for a review).

Moreover, the similarity seems to extend to genetics; Domingue and colleagues (2014) reported that among a national sample of Caucasian individuals living in the United States, genome-wide genetic similarity is greater between spouses than it is between individuals chosen at random. However, it is at best about a third of the magnitude of educational similarity; similarity in the level of education is an important predictor. Thus, the authors conclude that an approximately one standard deviation increase in genetic similarity increases the probability of marriage by about 15%.

When it comes to understanding homogamy, one underlying feature of note is mate value. Individuals who are of approximately the same mate value should pair together, as their mate represents the best (i.e., highest-quality) mate that they are able to attain and retain. In other words, the mating market is highly similar to a business marketplace, and assortative mating is equivalent to people exchanging goods of approximately equal worth (see Dillon, Adair, Geher, Wang, & Strouts 2015, for a review). Pairings become the outcome of social exchanges, whereby access to socially and sexually desired attributes in an individual is bartered over (see Kirsner, Figueredo, & Jacobs, 2003). Access to desired mates involves an opportunity cost in terms of the constraints it introduces with respect to one's time, money, and energy, which may become depleted or unavailable to use on other activities or on alternative mates. That is, people expend mating effort, in which they devote their resources to pursuing a selected mate. The quality of their investment may reflect the quality of the individual making the offer; high-quality resources and significant time spent on relationship formation and maintenance may indicate not only one's fitness as a potential partner but also the fitness of any children (see Kirsner, Figueredo, & Jacobs 2003, for a review). Therefore, the value of the investments of time and resources one receives depends partially on one's mate value. Moreover, one may at least incrementally rise in mate value by increasing mating effort to compensate for any imbalances in mate value (Kirsner, Figueredo, & Jacobs 2009). For example, one could dedicate more time and attention to a potential mate than one typically would, given that one's mate value is lower than same-sex others in the local environment.

The issue, though, becomes more complex when considering mating effort as distinct from genetic fitness. That is, mating effort is a separate but related feature to one's physical mate value, or heritable fitness. Theoretically, if both partners are devoting equivalent mating effort to each other, their perceived heritable mate value must be approximately matched for both to stay in the relationship. If instead one is investing far more mating effort, then the other must have a much higher heritable mate value (Kirsner et al., 2003, 2009). In this manner, mate value becomes equivalent to formidability in social exchange. The more valuable individual will feel entitled to better treatment, such as in the recalibrational theory of anger (e.g., thinking he or she deserves an increased share of the welfare tradeoff ratio to the self from the partner; see Sell, Tooby, & Cosmides, 2009). As we review, considering mate value in terms of heritable fitness allows for cues related to attractiveness, but also personality, to impact on one's mate value.

It is important to note that assortative mating patterns are not necessarily reflective of people's desires; individuals may want mates of much higher mate value than they themselves are worth on the mating market. However, market pressures act upon individuals such that there are restrictions on who one can afford (Kalick & Hamilton, 1986). Indeed, higher mate value results in attaining higher-quality mates (e.g., Buss & Shackelford, 2008). Individuals with high mate value generally have higher expectations from partners, which impacts on their satisfaction with the relationship (see Hromatko et al., 2015). While mating with someone with a higher mate value than oneself could hold potential benefits (e.g., higher social status, children of a higher genetic quality), one may also be concerned that the partner would leave the relationship once a better alternative becomes available (i.e., someone with a higher mate value). Mate desertion can involve a high cost, particularly for women, given that women tend to invest more in children than men (see Buss, 1995, for a review). Moreover, relationship satisfaction may be hindered by mate value discrepancies, leading the less valuable partner to impose costs on the other person, instead of providing benefits in terms of mate retention strategies (Salkicevic, Stanic, & Grabovac, 2014).

How Is Mate Value Defined?

The question then becomes: What exactly is mate value and how is it determined? While evolutionary psychologists (and those working in similar fields) have turned their attention to interpersonal attraction, with the area of mate preferences in particular being well explored, mate value has remained rather neglected or reduced to simply being about physical attractiveness (see Fisher, Cox, et al., 2008). In theory, in the mating marketplace, each individual has a value associated with his or her worth, relative to others in the local mating environment. This value, which represents a concept loosely referred to as "mate value," is dependent on many factors. To date, there is no unified definition of mate value in the literature, and hence, no agreement about the factors used by individuals to arrive at this value.

Within evolutionary psychology, there have been several definitions proposed. For example, Waynforth (2001, p. 207) defined mate value as "the total value of the characteristics that an individual possesses in terms of the potential contribution to his or her mate's reproductive success." Likewise, Kirsner et al. (2003) suggested mate value is the genetic quality or fitness of oneself as a potential sexual partner, as displayed through observable characteristics or cost/benefit analysis of weighing relevant characteristics that may exist outside of conscious awareness. Using a different focus, one that zeroes in on the outcome, Sugiyama (2005, p. 324) posited that "people differ in mate value, defined as the degree to which an individual would promote the reproductive success of another individual by mating with him or her." Alternatively, Fisher, Cox, et al. (2008) noted the dynamic nature of mate value, defining it as "the total sum of characteristics an individual possesses at a given moment and within a particular context that impacts on their ability to successfully find, attract, and retain a mate" (p. 14). Some of these definitions hint at the issue of self-perceived mate value and other-perceived mate value; this issue will be addressed more fully later in this chapter.

As aforementioned, the attributes that are central to mate value vary according to sex, with status key for men and physical attractiveness key for women. Campbell and Wilbur (2009) conducted six studies to test the hypothesis that the self-concepts of men and women match the preferences of their potential mates. The results of the first three studies showed that traits resembling status were a critical aspect of men's self-concepts, whereas traits related to physical attractiveness were a crucial aspect of women's self-concepts. The last three studies found that men were more distressed when derogated on traits related to status, whereas women were more distressed when derogated on their physical attractiveness. The researchers interpret these findings as showing that status for men and attractiveness for women are important factors for self-concept and mate value. This pattern is sensible, given that, cross-culturally, men place a premium on women's appearance and consider it important in a potential mate relative to women, while women place relatively more importance on men's status and ability to accrue resources (Buss & Schmitt, 1993).

However, attractiveness and status cannot be the sole determinants of mate value, given that the research on mate preferences suggests that both men and women select their mates based on a variety of characteristics, including aptitude, personality, self-esteem, intelligence, and social skills (Hatfield, Aronson, Abrahams, & Rottman, 1966); having a pleasing disposition; and emotional stability (Buss, 1989). Said another way, the collection of attributes that form mate value is not random, and the characteristics that underlie mate preferences reflect evolutionary adaptations that increased the fitness of those who preferred these traits (Sugiyama, 2005). That is, by preferring mates who are healthy and display characteristics that show they may be loyal and physically attractive (such that they do not carry genetic abnormalities or faced problems during their development that could have led to genetic weaknesses), these "preference mechanisms motivate us to engage in behaviors that tended to increase fitness under the environmental conditions in which they were selected" (Sugiyama, 2005, p. 293). Moreover, a meta-analysis revealed that physical attractiveness and earning potential predicted evaluations of current romantic partners similarly among both sexes (Eastwick, Luchies, Finkel, & Hunt, 2014). One reason for the incongruent findings may be that earlier work has examined ideal preferences involved in mate choice (e.g., Buss, 1989), and while preferences seem to influence the initial stages of mate selection (Li et al., 2013), once a relationship is formed, other features such as communication patterns (Stanley, Markman, & Whitton, 2002), equity (Van Yperen & Buunk, 1990), and the presence of children (Singh & Williams, 1981) may play an increasingly important role.

Furthermore, one must remember that the current state of affairs is distinct from future potentials. Thus, mate value must include not only one's current fertility and fecundity, but also one's future reproductive value, which can be estimated in part by one's age and sex (see Singh, Dixson, Jessop, Morgan, & Dixson, 2010). For example, older women presumably have lower mate value than young women due to the former's decreased reproductive potential. Signals of age in women, such as gray hair, wrinkles, and increased fat deposits, may consequently act as indicators of decreased reproductive potential. In contrast, older men may not experience the same decline in mate value (although sperm quality does decline; Johnson, Dunleavy, Gemmel, & Nakagawa 2015), because age is often related to an increase in income and status (De Sousa Campos, Otta, & de Oliveira Siqueira, 2002). Therefore, as Sugiyama (2005, p. 296) writes, "over time, selection would spread genes that organized developmental properties motivating individuals to be attracted to conspecifics exhibiting cues of high mate value because these preferences likely led to more successful reproduction than alternative designs that may have arisen." Indeed, Sugiyama (2005) proposed that mate value is composed of factors such as one's sex, age, degree of relatedness, health, status, fertility, fecundity, intelligence, status, parenting skill, kindness, and willingness and ability to invest in offspring, all of which vary between individuals. He further argued, "Our mate-selection psychology must assess a potential mate for cues associated with each of these components, weigh their relative importance under current and probable future conditions, and then integrate these inputs to arrive at a comprehensive estimation of mate value" (p. 325).

One commonality among the majority of definitions of mate value is that they emphasize mate value as a composite construct, rather than clearly elucidating the individual factors; Sugiyama's (2005) list is unusual in this regard. This multi-dimensional perspective is not always the case, though; mate value for women has often been synonymous with physical attractiveness in the literature (e.g., waist-to-hip ratio, Singh, 2002, Sugiyama, 2004), and has likewise been narrowly defined for men (e.g., physical fitness, Hönekopp, Rudolph, Beier, Liebert, & Müller 2007; physical condition and ability to provide resources, Penke et al., 2007). More recently, Lu, Zhu, and Chang (2015) defined men's mate value (at least in terms of consideration for long-term relationships) as composed of three factors: genetic quality (i.e., being physically attractive, athletic, and possessing a sense of humor), ability to provide for a family (as evidenced by education, career, and wealth), and fathering ability (being kind, loving, and staying at home). As Kirsner et al. (2003) suggest, earlier researchers considered mate value in terms of specific traits while later researchers (e.g., after 2000) tended to regard it as a composite variable, with the lack of one preferred trait compensated by the presence of another (see also Fisher, Cox, et al., 2008, for a review).

In general, more recent views, especially by those working directly on the topic, tend to consider mate value as a representation of one's *overall* desirability as a potential mate. This composite theme is echoed by Edlund and Sagarin (2014); while constructing a short inventory to determine mate value, they propose that mate value is a holistic, all-encompassing construct. They base their conceptualization on Brase and Guy's (2004) idea that people seem to have an accurate sense of their own value, and the value of others, although they may be unable to clarify the factors underpinning this evaluation. While this conjecture may be accurate, people engage in behavior that allows them to outcompete potential mating rivals (see Fisher, 2013, for a review), suggesting that individuals have some awareness of how their mate value is determined. That is, they presumably know which traits to emphasize or deemphasize in themselves, and when interacting with potential rivals and mates, in order to appear at their best.

When considering how mate value is assessed by oneself and others, it is critical to recall that genetic quality is often difficult for people to observe. As a result, people rely on proxies that are thought to reliably act as honest signals, indicating a potential partner's genetic quality. One direct example in men links self-perceived mate value (as measured by dominance and attractiveness, as well as across the dimensions of sociality, parenting, looks, wealth, views of the opposite sex, relationship history, and fear of failure; Fisher, Cox, et al., 2008) to ejaculate quality. Leivers, Rhodes, and Simmons (2014) found sperm motility and concentration increased with mate value but was context-dependent, such that this relationship was only apparent when men viewed photographs of highly attractive women.

Assessing Mate Value

Self-assessment of one's own mate value can take many forms. One may concentrate on self-perceived mate value, and which qualities are linked to its determination (e.g., Fisher, Cox, et al., 2008; Landolt, Lalumiere, & Quinsey, 1995). This process is largely thought to be context-dependent, such that the contrast effect assists individuals in assessing the local mating-market economy and then fine-tuning their self-assessment (Strout et al., 2008). Some surveys incorporate a variety of attributes (e.g., attractiveness, health, intelligence, Kirsner et al., 2003; personality and parenting qualities, Fisher, Cox, et al., 2008). These researchers propose that, presumably, people consider how much they possess these attributes relative to others in the local environment.

A second approach is to examine the sociometric properties of self-perception, which typically includes factors related to self-esteem (Brase & Guy,

2004; Wyckoff & Kirkpatrick, 2016). According to Leary (1999), individuals are generally highly motivated to protect their self-esteem and to increase it through their thoughts and actions. Therefore, a sociometer is a measure of how desirable one would be to other individuals, which is influenced by one's self-esteem. However, desirability also relates to other variables that influence social adjustment or the formation and maintenance of adult relationships. For example, Fernández and Dufey (2015) found that mate value is positively correlated with interpersonal closeness and dependence, and negatively related to anxiety in close relationships. These results strongly indicate that having a positive model of oneself, which is used in many studies as a synonym of self-esteem, and how others react (i.e., a secure model of others), provides a cue of relational mate value, beyond physical attractiveness or dominance.

Self-esteem is a gauge that serves to monitor interactions between individuals, after which it sends signals back to the individuals to help them assess the social acceptability of their behaviors. This feedback is key, since humans' sociality and drive for successful interpersonal relationships are critical aspects of our evolutionary history, and lead to a higher probability of individuals' survival and reproduction (Leary, 1999). Indeed, mate value and self-esteem are tightly linked; Goodwin and colleagues (2012) examined self-perceived mate value and self-esteem in eight cultures, including a total of 1,066 participants. Overall, in all eight samples, there was a significant moderate correlation (overall $r = .38$). Interestingly, they also found that men generally had higher self-esteem than women. In contrast, Fernández, Muñoz-Reyes, Dufey, Buccioni, and Cid (2015) observed in a Chilean sample of college students that there was no sex difference in self-esteem. However, two components used in a mate-value scale by Fisher, Cox, et al. (2008), views from the opposite sex and parenting, were significantly higher in women, while men accrued higher scores in the component of sociality. Interestingly, Fernández and colleagues found that these last two features of mate value (parenting and sociality) were the only ones that correlated significantly, but to a low degree, with women's and men's self-esteem.

Third, one could investigate people's intuitive knowledge of their mate value, via examining how they attain mates and compete with rivals (e.g., Cox & Fisher, 2008). This third aspect is the conceptual link to the current chapter. We propose that individuals rely on indicators from the local mating market to provide them with an accurate self-assessment of their mate value, which in turn influences the competitive strategy they use to attain and retain mates. Cox and Fisher (2008) argue that theory suggests people can assess potential rivals' mate value, relative to their own, to determine who is more desirable to a potential mate, and then decide whether competition is a worthy pursuit. According to their model of intrasexual competition for mates, individuals are required to know their ability to compete (i.e., their own mate value), the ability of their competitors (i.e., competitor's mate value), and the value of the targeted resource (i.e., the target's mate value). To date, this model has not been developed further nor subjected to empirical investigation. However, there is evidence that women's self-perceived mate value does positively influence their direct aggression toward their same-sex peers (with no effect on indirect aggression), while for men the effect of a higher mate value decreased indirect aggression with their same-sex peers (with no effect for direct aggression; Wyckoff & Kirkpatrick, 2016). Interestingly, Wyckoff and Kirkpatrick (2016) found that, generally, individuals who reported high levels of mate value and dominance, which they linked to self-esteem, are less likely to rely on indirect aggression, and to favor direct aggression, than those low in mate value and dominance.

Self- versus Other-Perceived Mate Value

It is becoming more evident, according to recent studies, that the way individuals perceive themselves in the context of mating is directly related to the perceptions the partners have of them, and how each person behaves in their relationship (Sela, Mogilski, Shackelford, Zeigler-Hill, & Fink, in press). In a study of college students and community samples, Sela et al. (in press) reported that if one possesses low mate value relative to a romantic partner, there is a decrease in the delivery of benefits toward oneself. Further, Hromatko et al. (2015) found that across two samples of adults from Croatia and Iraq, how one views the value of one's partner is a strong predictor of relationship satisfaction.

As part of a study on negative affect and mating effort, Kirsner et al. (2009) used the Mate Value Inventory (Kirsner et al., 2003) to examine personal assessment of mate value, but also attainable short-term versus long-term mate value of a partner, and ideal short-term versus long-term mate value of a partner. While they did not report the results for the various mate values, they did find that negative affect increased mating effort by indirectly reducing expected partner mate value. Similarly, Holden et al. (2014) found that husbands' self-esteem is negatively associated with their direct guarding behavior, implying that less self-esteem in the men increases their reported mate-retention strategies.

Looking at actual similarities of mate value within couples, Fernández, Muñoz-Reyes, and Pavez (2016) found that self-perceived and partner's perceived mate value in dating and committed couples is significantly correlated among men and women. In their first study of 65 to 67 dating couples of young adults, they found that women's self-perceived physical attractiveness was positively and moderately associated with their perception of their partner being physically attractive ($r = .35$, $p = .004$). There was also a positive correlation among partners' perception of self-attractiveness ($r = .25$, $p = .042$), satisfaction ($r = .32$, $p = .010$), and commitment to their partner ($r = .37$, $p = .002$). Similarly, assessing the specific mate-value components (see Fisher, Cox, et al., 2008) for both partners (i.e., how related the two partners were to each other) yielded a positive correlation among all the facets ($r = .34$, $p = .006$), and in particular, the dimensions of sociality ($r = .27$, $p = .030$) and parenting ($r = .26$, $p = .034$) were significantly correlated among both individuals within the dating couples. In a second study of cohabiting couples (n = 112), the researchers similarly observed positive correlations among the mate-value components ($r = .19$, $p = .028$), BMI ($r = .22$, $p = .022$), and relationship satisfaction ($r = .35$, $p < .000$). However, they suggest that one's mate value relative to the local mating market may have a reduced influence over time, as relationship satisfaction may increase its importance over the course of the relationship. In other words, similarity in mate value may help to establish positive feelings at the start of a romantic relationship, but its importance may decrease over time in favor of other variables related to relationship satisfaction.

Other Issues to Consider: Control and Context

One's perception of control over the traits that lead to mate-value assessments also seems to matter. Women tend to find it difficult to control the characteristics related to mate value, such as age, which can lead to increased negative feelings, lowered self-esteem, and increased motivation to change their physical attractiveness. In general, Hamida, Mineka, and Bailey (1998) hypothesized that women feel as if they have less control over traits signaling their desirability, compared to men's perceived control. Their findings show men of various ages self-report selecting partners based on traits that are relatively uncontrollable such as youth, or attractiveness, whereas women chose partners based on traits that are more controllable, such as status. The perceived uncontrollability of traits relevant to female mate value may cause women to have negative symptoms, such as depression and low self-esteem, as compared to men.

Another important issue is the perceived duration of the expected relationship: Is one considering their mate value as a short-term versus long-term partner? For example, Landolt et al. (1995) examined sex differences in the effects of physical attractiveness and earning potential on short-term versus long-term mating strategies. Their findings indicated that romantic interest was influenced by a person's physical attractiveness and earning potential; however, these characteristics interacted only in women's ratings. Self-assessed mating success was observed in men's mating tactics, such that men who perceived themselves as successful, compared to men who perceived themselves as less successful, preferred short-term mating strategies rather than long-term.

One possible explanation for this result is that men may generally try to maximize the number of mating opportunities they may have, given they typically invest less in children than women (i.e., seek a strategy of quantity of mates, rather than a quality relationship). This strategy of seeking quantity may offset the potential costs associated with a lack of paternity certainty; if there is a 25% chance of being cuckolded by a female mate, then having four mates rather than one increases the probability of having at least one genetic offspring. Likewise, a mate could be infertile, or have genetic abnormalities, and seeking multiple mates may increase the odds of having a genetically related healthy child. Meanwhile, women are generally theorized as being more concerned about quality mates, rather than engaging in a high quantity of short-term mating relationships, presumably due to the differential in parental investment, as well as social risks (e.g., being labeled as sexually promiscuous). Thus, women may express a preference for long-term relationships but may be willing to consider a short-term relationship if the mate value of the male is particularly high. Partial support for this contention is provided by Kenrick et al (1993), who found that women place higher importance on physical attractiveness in a potential mate when seeking a one-night stand, versus longer relationships. It could be that if these

women conceive in such a situation, and have a son, their son will inherit the traits that lead the male to have high mate value (i.e., the sexy son hypothesis). However, the fitness benefits of having a sexy son seem to be minor (Huk & Winkel, 2007).

Mate Value and Intrasexual Competition
Why Is Mate Value Important to Female Intrasexual Competition?

Charles Darwin's (1871) work on sexual selection, which he saw as the selective force caused by this competition, led to his identification of two types of selection. First, there is intrasexual selection, which is the process whereby traits are selected to enable individuals to compete with members of the same sex for sexual access to the opposite sex. The second form is intersexual selection, which is the process whereby individuals with a given trait are preferred by the opposite sex as mating partners. Due to this preference, that trait becomes more prevalent within the population. Recall that the rules of assortative mating indicate that people generally do not form lasting relationships with those with too low a mate value, and yet are unlikely to attract a vastly superior partner with a much higher value (for review, see Penke et al., 2007).

Thus, people vary in the degree to which they possess the characteristics associated with mate value. Consequently, individuals compete for access to those with high mate value, given that they are relatively scarce in a local environment. Individual choice and preferences play an important role, though, as individuals show variation in their mate preferences (Sefcek, Brumbach, Vasquez, & Miller 2006), meaning that values assigned to potential mates and rivals are somewhat subjective due to individual preferences. In addition, mate value is relative to the type of relationship one is seeking. For example, as mentioned, standards shift for various traits according to whether one is seeking a brief, sexual relationship versus marriage (Kenrick et al., 1993), and thus, there are varied standards for both potential mates and assessments of potential rivals.

There is a tight, multifaceted relationship between mate value and intrasexual competition for mates. Sugiyama (2005) proposes, at least for males, that the costs of mating competition could be reduced or avoided if individuals assessed the relative mate value of potential rivals before competing with them. Thus, males (although we argue females as well) may benefit by saving time, resources, and effort by avoiding competition with rivals they are unlikely to win against (i.e., who possess a significantly higher mate value). Therefore, if individuals can accurately assess their own mate value, as well as the mate value of local rivals, they are able to decide whether a competition would be worthwhile, or if it would imminently lead to loss. If one's mate value is much lower than that of a rival, then the competition would likely result in a loss. If instead one's mate value is much higher than a rival, a win is almost guaranteed, and competition will likely be unnecessary. Deduction suggests that the majority of competition for mates should occur with those with whom one has the most similar mate value. In other words, one must engage in a comparison of the rivals, relative to one's own and the target mate's value. This said, when there is a choice of potential mates within an attainable range, one should select the individual with this highest value, at least in theory (Cox & Fisher, 2008; but see Fawcett & Johnstone, 2003).

Theoretically, then, there are definite advantages to being able to accurately assess one's own mate value relative to potential mating rivals, as a woman can then predict whether she will win the competition and plan her actions accordingly. This assessment of oneself and rivals must also consider the mate value of a potential partner, to determine whether or not he is actually worth competing over. As Cox and Fisher (2008, p. 5) propose, "each participant forms perceptions of their own, the target's, and all rivals' mate values." Along the same lines, Kirsner et al. (2003) mention that one's upper and lower limits for an attainable partner should inherently include an assessment of one's own mate value, the range of mate values of available partners within the environment, and the range of mate values of sexual competitiors in the environment (see p. 133). They mention this model only in passing, and it warrants further examination by future researchers.

We predict that intrasexual competition will likely be the most intense among rivals of similar mate value. Given that one presumably has the best chance to mate with opposite-sex others who are of similar value to oneself, due to assortative mating, rivalry is probably the most intense with those who are similar in value to oneself because they have the highest chance of attaining the desired mate compared to all other members of the same sex. Said another way, competition should be strongest among those who are most likely to end up with the same potential mate, which also suggests competition should be the most intense among those with similar mate values. It seems that this prediction has remained untested to date.

Among those who are highly attractive, though, evidence suggests that there might be a reliance on indirect aggression, or at least less reliance on directly aggressive behavior. Muñoz-Reyes, Gil-Burmann, Fink, and Turiegano (2012) found that attractiveness is negatively related to the use of anger and verbal aggression in adolescent men and women, which is quite compelling since adolescence is a developmental period in which mate competition is particularly exacerbated in both sexes. Hence, those with higher mate value (as indicated by attractiveness) may compete with rivals in a different manner than those with lower mate value. Fisher and Cox (2009) provide some support for this possibility, as they found that derogations made by an attractive woman were far more effective in changing men's views of potential mates, as compared to a woman who was less attractive.

There are some promising lines of evidence that suggests competition and mate value are linked. First, Fawcett and Johnstone (2003) used game theory to create a model for competition and mate preferences, arguing that the perceived costs of competition are an important consideration. They argue that the weakest competitors prefer mates with lower value, as they do not provoke strong competition and, by association, heavy costs. Specifically, their model leads to the prediction that males with high mate quality have a preference for high-quality females that is far greater than the preferences from males of less quality. They propose that their model applies equally well for females, although it was created to test male competition for mates. As an aside, their model shows that for animals where there is a fixed breeding time-frame, as the period for mate acquisition ends, male choosiness declines to the extent that they become indifferent to mate quality. They propose that this pattern is due to the increased probability of ending up with no mate at all. In a similar vein, women's age is a good predictor of their use of competitive mating strategies (Fernández, Muñoz-Reyes, & Dufey, 2014), with younger women at their peak fertility (18–26 years of age) being much more competitive than their older counterparts (over 26 years of age). That is, younger women possess the highest mate value (given that female fertility declines with age), and compete the most; they also have the strongest demands for high-quality mates (Waynforth & Dunbar, 1995). Another study provides a similar result; Buunk, Stulp, and Ormel (2014) report daughters of parents with higher socioeconomic status are more intrasexually competitive than those of parents with lower socioeconomic status. They propose that in contemporary society, young women are often more highly educated than young men, which leads to intense competition for those men who are as highly educated (or even more highly educated) than themselves. Although resources are not an integral part of female mate value, it is nearly impossible to tease apart attractiveness from wealth, although often wealthy individuals are considered to be the most physically attractive (see McClintock, 2014, for a review).

Second, among humans, preliminary data suggest that the way that women use verbal aggression does differ according to the relative attractiveness of rivals, although not in the expected direction. Anderson, Reid, and Gaulin (2012) found women direct more unprovoked verbal aggression to rivals who are less physically attractive than themselves. They propose that "women seem to aggress towards unattractive rivals when unprovoked, and perhaps cautiously avoid competition when provocation is high. It may be the case that the women interpret provocation as a signal that a rival is more likely to retaliate and that competition may be more risky" (p. 24). These intriguing results fit well with some of the arguments concerning women's use of indirect aggression (Campbell, 2004). However, this finding is limited to verbal aggression, in situations involving provocation.

The findings of Anderson and colleagues (2012) support the idea that being attractive, and thereby potentially dominant, seems to have advantages. Further, but more convoluted, evidence is provided by Frankel (1990), who found the most popular and the most ignored girls reported lower levels of stress. The highest levels of stress were reported by girls who were average in popularity, mostly likely the result of having to actively compete for status. Those high in status seem secure in their position, while those lowest in status may avoid competing so as not to become the focus of aggression from others. Put into terms of mate value, it may be that those below and above an individual's mate value are less likely to be competitive.

It is worth noting that mate value assessments are not made in isolation of other factors, including intelligence. As Dillon et al. (2015) point out, one may not necessarily have to select mates dependent upon their mate value alone. Instead, those who are intelligent decision-makers might

be able to get more for less in the mating market by using strategies via mating intelligence. Mating intelligence refers to cognitive processes within the mating domain, linked to displays and detection of signals related to genetic fitness (see Dillon et al. for a review). They found that those with higher mating intelligence reported higher levels of self-perceived mate value, higher partner mate value, and less mate-settling for partners of lower mate value.

Accuracy in Self-Assessment Is Key

In order for self-perceived mate value to be useful in helping one determine whom to seek out as a potential mate, or identify who might be mating rivals, self-assessment needs to be highly accurate. Indeed, as Kirsner, Figueredo, and Jacobs (2009) point out, self-perceived mate value must closely match the value others perceive, at least on particular attributes, in order for social exchange to occur. Recent studies suggest that this match is very important for relationship equality and satisfaction. For example, individuals who perceive themselves to be higher in mate value than their partners typically spend less in providing benefits to their partner and resort to more negative inducements to retain their partner (Sela et al., in press).

There are individual differences in levels of accuracy. Using the context of speed-dating, Back and colleagues (2011) found that sociosexually unrestricted (i.e., showing willingness to engage in sexual activity) men and more agreeable women were more accurate in self-assessed mate-value compared to sociosexually restricted men and less agreeable women. Accuracy was determined by asking participants after each date whom they would choose, and who would choose them. Then, two scores were calculated: actual mate value (i.e., the number of times the person was chosen divided by the number of potential dates with whom the person interacted) and expected mate value (i.e., the number of times the person expected to be chosen divided by the number of potential dates with whom the person interacted). The closer the relationship between actual and expected values, the more accurate the person was at self-assessing their mate value. The authors propose that when individuals match sex-typical mating styles, their mate value increases; hence, "men with an unrestricted sociosexuality have a personality more supportive of typical male mating tactics than do men with a restricted sociosexuality, and women with higher agreeableness have a personality more supportive of typical female mating tactics than do less agreeable women" (p. 985). Interestingly, tactics used in intrasexual competition do not mirror these findings; while women report that they try to act kind and friendly toward men in an effort to self-promote, men do not report on their willingness to engage in uncommitted sexual relationships (see Fisher & Cox, 2009). It may be useful in future research for speed daters to be asked to assess their mate value, and then to assess the values of those around them garnering for dating attention. Although Back et al.'s (2011) formulation of mate value is ecologically valid, in that the outcome variable is a direct gauge of one's market worth, there are many potentially confounding factors (e.g., women scoring high on agreeableness may simply be perceived as more approachable). Moreover, the authors state, "Our results show that, on average, individuals seem to have difficulty judging their own mate value, at least when it comes to real-life mating decisions" (p. 986), which undermines the argument that accuracy is key to mating, both in terms of mate acquisition and also in competition with rivals.

Using a different approach, Gutierres and associates (1999) documented that self-assessments are highly dependent on perceptions of competitors. They investigated men's and women's self-assessments of mate value (i.e., desirability as a marriage partner) when exposed to socially dominant and physically attractive others. They found that women's self-assessment of their own mate value was lowered by exposure to physically attractive women, and was unaffected by exposure to socially dominant women. In contrast, a man's self-perceived mate value was more influenced by social dominance, rather than physical attractiveness of the men he was shown. Interestingly, they argue that it may be the case that these effects are attributable to an individual's perception of the population of potential rivals, rather than a shift in the individual's own self-assessments of their appearance or dominance.

Supporting evidence shows a general trend whereby women perceive themselves in more negative ways when exposed to more attractive women, compared to unattractive women. DelPriore and colleagues (this volume) review that women often feel more negatively about themselves when exposed to attractive same-sex others, and that this negativity includes feeling less attractive and more self-conscious, decreased self-reported desirability as a marriage partner, and decreased body satisfaction and mood. Indeed, exposure to attractive women can cause aversion and feelings of being threatened,

as it typically causes women to feel more negatively about themselves.

Said another way, self-assessment seems very finely tuned to the local population of same-sex others who may represent potential mating rivals. Congruent with DelPriore et al. [this volume], a woman may perceive her own attractiveness more negatively when faced with other women's superior attractiveness (Kenrick et al., 1993), and this effect may also lead to perceived lowered feelings of relationship satisfaction with one's romantic partner (Kenrick, Neuberg, Zierk, & Krones, 1994). Men were generally found to decrease their attractiveness ratings of average-looking women, and reported lower relationship satisfaction, after being exposed to highly attractive women.

The fact that self-perceived attractiveness is at least partly dependent on others in the local environment may explain why evidence is mixed as to whether women generally overestimate (Brewer, Archer, & Manning, 2007) or underestimate their own attractiveness (Price, Dunn, Hopkins, & Kang 2012). In future research, it may be advantageous to examine how the attractiveness of potential rivals within the local mating market influences self-assessed attractiveness with respect to more objective criteria (such as known markers for facial attractiveness; see Abend et al., 2015).

It is also possible that one could examine an individual's mate value by using their partner's views. Salkicevic, Stanic, and Grabovac (2014) report that people who have partners with high mate value have more frequent use of positive inducements (e.g., compliment on appearance), and public signals of possession (e.g., hand-holding in public). Thus, people may indirectly infer their own mate value partially based on how their partner treats them, specifically as to whether they engage in these sorts of positive signals.

Mate Value and Competitive Strategy Use
How Is Mate Value Manipulated?

Cox and Fisher (2008) conjecture that people involved in intrasexual competition for mates can perform acts to alter perceptions of their mate value. They can either modify their own mate value, relative to rivals via self-promotion, or they can attempt to decrease a rival's mate value relative to oneself via competitor derogation (see Fisher, 2013, for a discussion of women and competition). One strategy, self-promotion, entails trying to make oneself appear more desirable relative to rivals. Women may, therefore, attempt to appear more attractive by wearing cosmetics, and altering their personality in an effort to be flirty, kind, and friendly. Alternatively, women may engage in a strategy involving competitor derogation, in which they attempt to make the potential rival seem less desirable than themselves. To do so, they may say that the rival is unattractive, unintelligent, or immature (Fisher & Cox, 2011). There are other strategies used for intrasexual competition, such as competitor manipulation, which involves the manipulation of one's rivals to reduce the need for competition. For example, an individual may tell a rival that the potential mate is not worth her attention, thus turning the rival's attention away from him, thereby decreasing the competition. Another identified strategy is mate manipulation, which refers to removing the mate so no competition is necessary, such as by creating a screen that hides the presence or actions of rivals. In this case, one may try to sequester the mate or take up his time so that he is unable to spend time with rivals (see Fisher & Cox, 2011 for a review).

These four strategies for intrasexual competition may be used in distinct ways in reference to the developmental stage of a romantic relationship (Fisher & Cox, 2011). Self-promotion may be most effective at the start of a relationship, in order to draw attention from a potential mate and away from potential rivals. Moreover, one only needs minimal information about potential rivals in order to effectively self-promote. Thus, it is not surprising that self-promotion is reported to be the most used strategy for intrasexual competition. However, to effectively self-promote, one must have an awareness of the local mating market; what quality of mate should one reasonably be able to attain? What is the mate value of the local competitors, who may also be interested in the same partner?

Mate manipulation may occur as soon as a potential mate has been identified. That is, a woman might immediately, upon relationship formation, attempt to circumvent any time or attention the mate would otherwise dedicate to her potential rivals. The remaining strategies, competitor derogation and competitor manipulation, may be used once a potential rival has been identified and they may be most frequently directed toward those of similar mate value. Moreover, though, individuals take into account their strengths and weaknesses, from the perspective of the preferences of potential mates, and shapes their strategy use accordingly. For example, women who are relatively unattractive and have low mate value may not be able to effectively derogate the appearance of potential rivals. Fisher and Cox (2009) found that derogations of potential rivals made by unattractive women had little effect on men, while derogations made by attractive women caused men to significantly alter their evaluations of other women. Thus, unattractive women with low mate value likely use alternative strategies. This possibility remains untested to date.

Apparently the length of the expected romantic relationship also plays a role in women's strategy use. As DelPriore et al. (this volume) review, there are shifts in appearance enhancement when women's competition for long-term mates is explicitly activated. For example, Hill and Durante (2011) show that there is a relationship between priming women for goals related to mating, competition for mates, and desire to enhance their appearance. When women are primed with photographs of attractive men or attractive women, or asked to report an instance when they competed for a mate, they increased their willingness to engage in relatively risky strategies to increase their attractiveness (e.g., tanning, using diet pills), while also simultaneously decreasing how risky they associated these behaviors to be toward health (Hill & Durante, 2011). Relating these findings to mate value, we argue that women may attempt to improve their mate value via self-promotion when thinking about long-term mates who possess high mate value, as well as the local rivals.

Gossip is also frequently used to decrease rivals' mate value. Fisher and Cox (2011) found women self-report that they use gossip to compete for attention from potential dates via spreading rumors, telling a potential rival's secrets, or saying bad things about rivals to a potential mate. However, age is an important consideration, as younger women generally gossip more than older women, which is mediated by women's self-perceived mate value (Massar, Buunk, & Rempt, 2012). Women's mate value generally declines with age, particularly at menopause. Thus, although there are age differences in women's tendency to gossip, the difference disappears when mate value is controlled for statistically. Regardless, it would be informative to know if the content of the gossip itself changes over a woman's lifespan, due to decreasing mate value with female age. Do older women engage in gossip for the purposes of competitor and mate manipulation, for example, while younger women engage in more competitor derogation and self-promotion? We propose that age causes this pattern, as older women typically have lower mate value; their ability to self-promote positive attributes may be diminished relative to younger women. Likewise, derogating a rival's characteristics relative to oneself may also not be as effective for older than younger women. However, manipulation is likely a worthy strategy for older women, as they can shape the attention of rivals and mates without necessarily drawing too much attention to their own lowered mate value, relative to younger women.

Targeting Mate Value Characteristics

As Gallup (this volume) reviews, mating competition by adult women, as well as girls and adolescents in middle and high school, is a frequent motive behind aggression, with aggressors preferentially targeting the mate value of rivals. He documents that the qualities used by aggressors for derogation are those that are most preferred by potential mates, for example fidelity and physical appearance. This derogation may also involve derogating a potential rival's social standing or reputation, particularly among adolescents.

Interestingly, there is a high correlation between comparing one's appearance with others and body dissatisfaction, which Gallup posits leads women who perceive themselves as having relatively low mate value to be more inclined to engage in aggression for the purposes of mating competition. That is, in terms of mating competition, the most physically attractive girls and women are the greatest threat, and may be specifically targeted by those with similar or lower attractiveness. If correct, then it is not surprising that people may perceive attractive women as having negative personality traits such as vanity, egotism, and being unsympathetic and materialistic (Dermer & Thiel, 1975). Moreover, though, it might not be that attractiveness is the key variable for potential rivals, but rather the interaction of attractiveness with self-confidence. Campbell (2013) argues that while attractive girls and women represent the strongest competitors for male attention and hence are highly threatening, adding self-confidence to physical attractiveness is significant. This combination seems to place these women at a much higher advantage than those with physical attractiveness alone.

According to this perspective, physically attractive women are often the targets of intrasexual competition, but not necessarily the primary aggressors. This conjecture is plausible, given that in most instances women with high mate value (for which attractiveness is a proxy) do not need to compete with those of lower value, as they will likely win

by default. However, as reviewed elsewhere in this chapter, women from households with high levels of resources compete intensely for mates with resources. Hence, by extension it is plausible that physically attractive women dismiss those with less attractiveness and compete mostly with those who have equivalent or higher attractiveness than themselves. This possibility remains to be tested; likewise, how men view women according to more global definitions of mate value (i.e., in addition to just attractiveness), and how women interact with those whom men perceive as having higher, similar, or lower mate value, needs to be examined.

Gallup (this volume) further clarifies that using competitive tactics may serve to produce a negative reputation in potential rivals, and also make them less willing to compete or capable of competing for high-quality mates due to their heightened social anxiety and depression from peer victimization. He elucidates that hostility between adolescent girls can be motivated by, and is effective in, disrupting dating relationships of rivals, as well as gaining access to desired dating partners. Put together, this evidence suggests that females derogate potential rivals using characteristics related to mate value, which is successful at eliminating competitors. This promising idea warrants closer scrutiny, as the issue is far from clearcut. Fisher and Cox (2009) propose that women use derogation to lower the perceived mate value of rivals in the hopes of tangentially increasing their own mate value and, consequently, the likelihood that they will attain or retain a high-quality mate. If so, then women who believe they are unlikely to win via only self-promotion (e.g., those who are less attractive or in a romantic relationship) should be the ones most likely to use competitor derogation. However, while Fisher, Tran, and Voracek (2008) found negligible effects due to relationship status on competitive derogation, Fisher, Cox, and Gordon (2009) found women who were not involved in a romantic relationship (as well as those in casual dating relationships), along with more attractive women, engage in more derogation of same-sex others than mated women and less attractive women. These findings oppose work by Buss and Dedden (1990) and Fisher and Cox (2011) where women involved in romantic relationships were the most likely to use competitor derogation.

One way that these discrepant findings may be interpreted is that the issue is not the relative mate value between the women that matters per se but, instead, the difference in the mate value between women and their romantic partners (as suggested by DelPriore et al., this volume). DelPriore and colleagues rely on the findings of Buss and Shackelford (1997), in which women who were evaluated to be less attractive than their husbands were more likely to use competitor derogation than women who were evaluated to be more attractive than their husbands. Further, it seems to be the woman's perception that is key, as wives' evaluations of their husbands' attractiveness were negatively related to the use of competitor derogation. Future research must address not only the role of attractiveness but also self-perceived mate value, partner mate value, and strategy use to determine if the difference between romantic partners indeed drives the use of competitor derogation.

Future Work and Limitations

There are many areas pertaining to the relationship between mate value and intrasexual competition that remain to be explored. Here we explicitly outline four promising directions for future research.

First, given that mate value changes across the lifespan for women, are there concurrent changes in intrasexual competition? Based on the reviewed literature, young adult women may engage in a high degree of competition, given that their mate value is high. Older women, with lower mate value, likely compete less. However, what is more intriguing is the possibility of how age (and hence mate value) relates to strategy use. For example, self-promotion draws attention to one's own positive attributes, including attractiveness. Older women may be less likely to use self-promotion, and instead favor strategies that are less likely to draw attention to their age. Likewise, if a woman becomes a mother and is competing to retain her mate, she might use her status as the biological mother (as well as use the child) to help keep her mate's attention on her and her children, and away from potential rivals. For example, she might advertise (i.e., self-promote) her skills as a successful mother and caregiver, and derogate those skills in potential rivals. How mate value changes across women's lives, as well as their roles within their lives (e.g., motherhood) in relation to intrasexual mating competition, remains to be examined.

Second, are women who are more competitive more accurate in assessing their own mate value, and are they more concerned about mate value generally, than those who are less competitive? Likewise, are narcissists accurate at self-assessed mate value? Buunk and Fisher (2009) created and validated a measure of individual differences in intrasexual

competition (albeit in terms of personality, and less so in the context of mating competition). It could be the case that those who are generally more competitive, according to this measure, are more accurate in their mate-value assessments, given that "wanting to be the best" is likely tied to one's mate value. However, perhaps there is domain specificity at play, and instead, only attitudes and behaviors specifically oriented toward mating competition are aligned with mate value. Those who are most concerned with their mate value are likely more competitive; people who invest heavily in their appearance and in trying to make themselves have the highest value on the mating market likely self-promote this value. Narcissists enhance their self-esteem using the admiration of others, while general measures of competitiveness tend to focus on winning contests and retaining respect from others (Luchner, Houston, Walker, & Houston, 2011). Luchner et al. (2011) documented that narcissism is correlated with competitiveness; however, their preliminary data revealed that covert narcissists (i.e., people who internalize behaviors, feel vulnerable, have deflated self-esteem, and are hypersensitive) show a negative correlation with general competitiveness. They posit that covert narcissists "do not consciously desire competitive situations since they are invested in protecting a view of themselves as empathic, responsive, selfless, and helpful" (p. 781). Overt narcissists, meanwhile, are arrogant, have inflated self-esteem, and are often aggressive and grandiose, and it is sensible that these behaviors would align with competitiveness. Therefore, extending this work to mating competition, those with overt narcissism may show the highest level of mating competition, and report that they have high mate value. However, those with covert narcissism would rely on particular strategies or tactics (see Fisher & Cox, 2009) that allow them to still appear helpful and kind, while drawing attention to themselves. Self-promotion is one such strategy, and many individuals report that they actively try to appear kind and nice to outcompete mating rivals.

A third issue involves the characteristics of the potential rivals, and the interpersonal dynamics of the women involved in the competition. Anderson (this volume) points out that most of the work on intrasexual competition does not take into account the attractiveness of a potential rival. There are some exceptions, though; Buunk and Massar (2014) found women generally prefer same-sex friends who are less attractive than themselves. Likewise, Colyn and Gordon (2012) report women experience more schadenfreude when an envied same-sex friend experienced a hypothetical misfortune that decreased her physical attractiveness versus social status. Aside from these studies, though, the interpersonal dynamics of those involved are widely overlooked, and one potential lead for future direction is a recalibration model. Anderson, Reid, and Gaulin (2012) propose that such a model provides a mechanism that leads people to become angry and/or aggressive. According to the model, there are a set of inputs to a neurocognitive mechanism that calculates a welfare trade off ratio between one's own welfare relative to others involved in a social exchange (see, for example, Sell, Cosmides, Tooby, Sznycer, von Rueden, & Gurven, 2009; Sell, Tooby, & Cosmides, 2009). Anderson et al. (2012) review that during competition for resources or mates, one's actions impact on the welfare of another person, and those who are more formidable (e.g., physically strong), or who are better able to acquire benefits (e.g., physically attractive), feel entitled and value their own welfare more than that of others. It has been documented that these entitled individuals express greater anger and report greater success in conflict (Sell et al., 2009). Thus, the mating advantage that being attractive may confer on women leads us to predict that high-mate-value women who feel they are not receiving their just share of rewards from less attractive rivals should become angry, whereas women who are less attractive should acquiesce. Anger and aggression can be thought of as communicative processes that aid in negotiating a balanced welfare tradeoff ratio between competitors as well as cooperative partners. People who are of high status should aggress when they feel that their position is not being given appropriate welfare from those who are lower status; similarly, people who are low status may aggress if they feel that their position is being overly compromised. By extension, then, within romantic relationships, women of high mate value relative to their partners may be more aggressive as they feel entitled in their relationships, as well as in other relationships (see Wyckoff & Kirkpatrick, 2016, for partial support).

A fourth issue that is worthy of future consideration pertains to the role of the ovulatory cycle on self-assessed mate value. Hormonal fluctuations during the ovulatory cycle lead to shifting probabilities of conception, with the highest probability being around the time of ovulation. Fisher (2004) documented that women's intrasexual competition seems to increase during this time, which may be due to this window representing when women are most fertile. A similar study revealed these findings extend directly to mate value, via social comparison of potential rivals. In a novel study pertaining to costs associated with poor mating decisions (e.g., choosing a mate below one's value), Beaulieu (2007) proposed women's social comparisons provide a foundation from which to avoid poor decisions. He argued that poor mating decisions are most costly during peak windows for conception (given that they may result in pregnancy), and hence, that social comparisons should be strongest during this time. His findings revealed that, compared with women at less fertile phases of their cycle, women with high fertility reported more frequent social comparisons involving physical attractiveness and placed greater emphasis on their own attractiveness. Whether these results are consistent regardless of the type of relationship one is considering has not yet been tested. However, Beaulieu and Havens (2015), using the same framework of costs assessment, have documented that women in a phase of maximum fertility exhibit a general increase in their mate preference criteria across a wide variety of characteristics and relationships. To summarize, then, women's assessments of mate value for themselves, as well as mates and potential rivals, are seemingly not constant but rather dynamic, in accordance with fluctuating ovulatory hormones. Further research on the role of fertility would be informative.

One limitation to this chapter is the exclusion of social structural theory, in favor of exploring an evolutionary psychological perspective. Unlike an evolutionary perspective wherein the focus lies on issues such as evolved mate preferences and women's advertisement of characteristics related to successful mating, social structural theories emphasize the role of cultural divisions of labor. Both theories suggest that individuals adjust their mating strategies in relation to environmental contexts. For example, in the evolutionary perspective, pathogen prevalence, economic stress, and resource scarcity may drive individuals to alter the qualities they seek in mates or the length of the relationship they seek (see Goodwin et al., 2012 for a review). The social structuralist perspective instead views issues such as earning differentials and divisions of labor as key (Eagly & Wood, 2013). Previously, Goodwin et al. (2012) have explored self-perceived mate value in relation to these theories and found that gender-role equality plays a large role in mating strategy. They suggest that self-perceived mate value is likely composed of personality traits that show similarity between men and women when societies are highly gender unequal, as well as mating strategies wherein sex differences generally increase in more gender-unequal societies. Together, then, self-perceived mate value may be difficult to examine unless one tears apart mating strategies from personality, and then examines gender-role equality.

A second limitation is that the vast majority of research on mating competition and mate value relies on contexts where individuals have the ability to choose their mates, rather than in societies where parents or local governance choose one's mate. Indeed, the influences of others on mate choice remain rather understudied, given that it presumably impacts on a wide assortment of mating behaviors, including competitive strategy use. In situations involving arranged marriages, do parents advertise the same traits that individuals would self-promote? Casual observation of advertisements indicates there is a general correlation, with advertisements in the *Times of India* referencing education, appearance, and familial resources. However, reporters also state that there is a shift whereby individuals, particularly women, have started to be more selective in what they seek in a partner in an arranged marriage (e.g., Sridharani, 2016).

Conclusion

In this chapter, we reviewed how assortative mating creates a situation where people must be accurate in self-assessments of their current worth on the local mating market. This awareness of one's mate value is relative not only to the possible mates in the area, thereby allowing one to find the best mate possible given one's own worth, but also to assess who may be a potential rival for a selected mate. We contend that individuals have an unconscious knowledge of their mate value, which has far-reaching implications on a variety of behaviors and decisions.

We focused our chapter on women's mate value and how it relates to female intrasexual competition for access to, and retention of, romantic partners. We reviewed several pertinent issues (e.g., the components of female mate value, mate preferences in relation to assessment of mate value, and the role of mate value in relationship satisfaction). We then turned to the primary issue of the chapter, which was to address the relationship between women's intrasexual competition and mate value. We argued mate value may be manipulated or

altered by potential rivals for the purposes of mating competition.

Furthermore, we conclude that mate value seems to be a central influence on women's intrasexual competition, and that it opens numerous, different possibilities for understanding women's mating behavior more deeply. For example, we have reviewed throughout this chapter how self-perceived mate value, relative to potential rivals, drives different behavioral strategies that very likely involved strong emotional reactions to the assessment of mate value in the local context. When women are single and looking for a potential partner, their temporal mating orientation, their competition with potential rivals, and their own self-perceived mate value are affected by their context very differently than if they were instead involved in a committed relationship and trying to retain a valuable partner.

It is not surprising, then, that women's intrasexual competition is closely linked to their mate value, given that mate value is highly connected to theories stemming from sexual selection. Research on evolutionary psychology has accumulated important evidence of strong intrasexual competition in women, contrary to the passive role that women were thought to initially play in the realm of mating. Recent evidence suggests that women's intrasexual competition is strategically attuned to the mate value of other women in the local mating market, and exchanges with potential rivals (as well as romantic partners) attest to the importance of understanding reciprocity that underlies most social interactions.

References

Abend, P., Pflüger, L. S., Koppensteiner, M., Coquerelle, M. & Grammer, K. (2015). The sound of female shape: A redundant signal of vocal and facial attractiveness. *Evolution and Human Behavior*, 36(3), 174–181.

Anderson, G. L., Reid, S. A., & Gaulin, S. (2012, May). *How aggression among women is calibrated by physical attractiveness: An experimental test of the recalibration theory of anger*. Presented at the International Communication Association, Phoenix, AZ.

Back, M., Penke, L., Schmukle, S., & Asendorpf, J. (2011). Knowing your own mate value: Sex-specific personality effects on the accuracy of expected mate choices. *Psychological Science*, 22(8), 984–989.

Beaulieu, D. (2007). Avoiding costly mating mistakes: Ovulatory shifts in personal mate value assessment. *Journal of Social and Personal Relationships*, 24, 441–455.

Beaulieu, D., & Havens, K. (2015). Fertile women are more demanding: Ovulatory increases in minimum mate preference criteria across a wide range of characteristics and relationship contexts. *Personality and Individual Differences*, 72, 200–207.

Brase, G., & Guy, E. (2004). The demographics of mate value and self-esteem. *Personality and Individual Differences, 36,* 471–484.

Brewer, G., Archer, J., & Manning, J. (2007). Physical attractiveness: The objective ornament and subjective self-ratings. *Journal of Evolutionary Psychology, 5*(1), 29–38.

Brown, M. A., & Brown, J. D. (2015). Self-enhancement biases, self-esteem, and ideal mate preferences. *Personality and Individual Differences, 74,* 61–65.

Buss, D. M. (1988). The evolution of human intrasexual competition: Tactics of mate attraction. *Journal of Personality and Social Psychology, 54,* 616–628.

Buss, D. M. (1989). Sex differences in human mate preferences: Evolutionary hypotheses tested in 37 cultures. *Behavioral and Brain Sciences, 12,* 1–49.

Buss, D. M. (1995). Psychological sex differences: Origins through sexual selection. *American Psychologist, 50*(3), 164–168.

Buss, D., & Dedden, L. (1990). Derogation of competitors. *Journal of Social and Personal Relationships, 7,* 395–422.

Buss, D. M., & Schmitt, D. P. (1993). Sexual strategies theory: An evolutionary perspective on human mating. *Psychological Review, 100,* 204–232.

Buss, D. M., & Shackelford, T. K. (1997). From vigilance to violence: Mate retention tactics in married couples. *Journal of Personality and Social Psychology, 72*(2), 346–361.

Buss, D. M., & Shackelford, T. K. (2008). Attractive women want it all: Good genes, economic investment, parenting proclivities, and emotional commitment. *Evolutionary Psychology, 6*(1), 134–146.

Buunk, A. P., & Fisher, M. L. (2009). Individual differences in intrasexual competition. *Journal of Evolutionary Psychology, 7,* 37–48.

Buunk, A. P., & Massar, K. (2014). A night on the town: When the importance of mate acquisition overrides intrasexual competition. *Anthropological Review, 77*(3), 273–385.

Buunk, A. P., Stulp, G., & Ormel, J. (2014). Parental social status and intrasexual competitiveness among adolescents. *Evolutionary Psychology, 12,* 1022–1037.

Campbell, A. (2004). Female competition: Causes, constraints, content, and contexts. *Journal of Sex Research, 41*(1), 16–26.

Campbell, A. (2013). The evolutionary psychology of women's aggression. *Philosophical Transactions of the Royal Society B, 368*(1631), 20130078.

Campbell, L., & Wilbur, C. J. (2009). Are the traits we prefer in potential mates the traits they value in themselves? An analysis of sex differences in the self-concept. *Self and Identity, 8*(4), 418–446.

Colyn, L. A., & Gordon, A. K. (2012). Schadenfreude as a mate-value-tracking mechanism. *Personal Relationships, 20*(3), 524–545.

Cox, A., & Fisher, M. (2008). A framework for exploring intrasexual competition. *Journal of Social, Evolutionary, and Cultural Psychology, 2*(4), 144–155.

Darwin, C. (1871). *The descent of man and selection in relation to sex.* London: John Murray.

De Sousa Campos, L., Otta, E., & de Oliveira Siqueira, J. (2002). Sex differences in mate selection strategies: Content analyses and responses to personal advertisements in Brazil. *Evolution and Human Behavior, 23*(5), 395–406.

Dermer, M., & Thiel, D. L. (1975). When beauty may fail. *Journal of Personality and Social Psychology, 31*(6), 1168–1176.

Dillon, H. M., Adair, L. E., Geher, G., Wang, Z., & Strouts, P. H. (2015). Playing smart: The mating game and mating intelligence. *Current Psychology, 35,* 414–420.

Domingue, B. W., Fletcher, J., Conley, D., & Boardman, J. D. (2014). Genetic and educational assortative mating among US adults. *Proceedings of the National Academy of Science, 111*(2).

Eagly, A. H., & Wood, W. (2013). The nature-nurture debates: 25 years of challenges in the psychology of gender. *Perspectives on Psychological Science, 8,* 340–357.

Eastwick, P. W., Luchies, L. B., Finkel, E. J., & Hunt, L. L. (2014). The predictive validity of ideal partner preferences: A review and meta-analysis. *Psychological Bulletin, 140,* 623–665.

Edlund, J. E., & Sagarin, B. J. (2014). The mate value scale. *Personality and Individual Differences, 64,* 72–77.

Fawcett, T. W., & Johnstone, R. A. (2003). Mate choice in the face of costly competition. *Behavioral Ecology, 14*(6), 771–779.

Fernández, A. M., & Dufey, M. (2015). Adaptation of Collins' dimensional adult attachment scale revised to the Chilean context. *Psicologia Reflexão e Crítica, 28,* 213–223.

Fernández, A. M., Muñoz-Reyes, J. A., & Dufey, M. (2014). BMI, age, mate value, and intrasexual competition in Chilean women. *Current Psychology, 33,* 435–450.

Fernández, A. M., Muñoz-Reyes, J. A., Dufey, M., Buccioni, G., & Cid, V. (2015). Adaptación del Cuestionario de Componentes del Valor de Pareja al Contexto Chileno (Adaptation of the Mate Value Components Questionnaire to the Chilean context, trans.). *Revista Iberoamericana de Diagnostico y Evaluacion Psicologica, 1*(40), 94–102.

Fernández, A. M., Muñoz-Reyes, J. A., & Pavez, P. (2016, August). *The reciprocal nature of romantic relationship.* Oral presentation at the XXIII biennial congress of the International Society of Human Ethology, Stirling, Scotland.

Fisher, M. (2013). Women's intrasexual competition for mates. In M. L. Fisher, J. R. Garcia, & R. S. Chang (Eds.), *Evolution's empress: Darwinian perspectives on the nature of women* (19–42). New York: Oxford University Press.

Fisher, M. (2004). Female intrasexual competition decreases female facial attractiveness. *Proceedings of the Royal Society of London, Series B (Supplemental), 271,* S283–S285.

Fisher, M. & Cox, A. (2009). The influence of female attractiveness on competitor derogation. *Journal of Evolutionary Psychology, 7,* 141–155.

Fisher, M., & Cox, A. (2011). Four strategies used during intrasexual competition for mates. *Personal Relationships, 18*(1), 20–38.

Fisher, M., Cox, A., Bennett, S., & Gavric, D. (2008). Components of self-perceived mate value. *Journal of Social, Evolutionary, and Cultural Psychology, 2,* 156–168.

Fisher, M., Cox, A., & Gordon, F. (2009). Self-promotion versus competitor derogation: The influence of sex and romantic relationship status on intrasexual competition strategy selections. *Journal of Evolutionary Psychology, 7*(4), 287–308.

Fisher, M., Tran, U., & Voracek, M. (2008). The influence of relationship status, mate seeking and sex on intrasexual competition. *Journal of Social Psychology, 148,* 493–508.

Frankel, K. A. (1990). Girls' perceptions of peer relationship support and stress. *Journal of Early Adolescence, 10*(1), 69–88.

Goodwin, R., Marshall, T., Fülöp, M., Adonu, J., Spiewak, S., Neto, F., & Plaza, S. H. (2012). Mate value and self-esteem: Evidence from eight cultural groups. *PLoS One, 7*(4), e36106.

Gutierres, S. E., Kenrick, D. T., & Partch, J. J. (1999). Beauty, dominance, and the mating game: Contrast effects in self-assessment reflect gender differences in mate selection. *Personality and Social Psychology Bulletin, 25*(9), 1126–1134.

Hamida, S. B., Mineka, S., & Bailey, J. M. (1998). Sex differences in perceived controllability of mate value: An evolutionary perspective. *Journal of Personality and Social Psychology, 75*(4), 954–966.

Hatfield, E., Aronson, V., Abrahams, D., & Rottman, L. (1966). The importance of physical attractiveness in dating behavior. *Journal of Personality and Social Psychology, 4*, 508–516.

Hill, S. E., & Durante, K. M. (2011). Courtship, competition, and the pursuit of attractiveness: Mating goals facilitate health-related risk taking and strategic risk suppression in women. *Personality and Social Psychology Bulletin, 37*(1), 383–394.

Holden, C. J., Shackelford, T. K., Zeigler-Hill, V., Starratt, V. G., Miner, E. J., Kaighobadi, F., Jeffrey, A. J., & Buss, D. M. (2014). Husband's esteem predicts their mate retention tactics. *Evolutionary Psychology, 12*, 655–672.

Hönekopp, J., Rudolph, U., Beier, L., Liebert, A., & Müller, C. (2007). Physical attractiveness of face and body as indicators of physical fitness in men. *Evolution and Human Behavior, 28*(2), 106–111.

Hromatko, I., Bajoghli, H., Rebernjak, B., Joshaghani, N., & Tadinac, M. (2015). Relationship satisfaction as a function of mate value. *Evolutionary Behavioral Sciences, 9*(4), 242–256.

Huk, T., & Winkel, W. (2007). Testing the sexy-son hypothesis: A research framework for empirical approaches. *Behavioral Ecology, 19*(2), 456–461.

Johnson, S. L., Dunleavy, J., Gemmell, N. J., & Nakagawa, S. (2015). Consistent age-dependent declines in human semen quality: A systematic review and meta-analysis. *Ageing Research Reviews, 19*, 22–33.

Kalick, S. M., & Hamilton, T. E. (1986). The matching hypothesis reexamined. *Journal of Personality and Social Psychology, 51*, 673–682.

Kalmijn, M. (1998). Intermarriage and homogamy: Causes, patterns, trends. *Annual Review of Sociology, 24*, 395–421.

Kenrick, D., Groth, G., Trost, M. & Sadalla, E. (1993). Integrating evolutionary and social exchange perspectives on relationships: Effects of gender, self-appraisal, and involvement level on mate selection criteria. *Journal of Personality and Social Psychology, 64*, 951–969.

Kenrick, D. T., Montello, D. R., Gutierres, S. E., & Trost, M. R. (1993). Effects of physical attractiveness on affect and perceptual judgments: When social comparison overrides social reinforcement. *Personality and Social Psychology Bulletin, 19*, 195–199.

Kenrick, D. T., Neuberg, S. L., Zierk, K. L., & Krones, J. M. (1994). Evolution and social cognition: Contrast effects as a function of sex, dominance, and physical attractiveness. *Personality and Social Psychology Bulletin, 20*(2), 210–217.

Kirsner, B., Figueredo, A. J., & Jacobs, W. (2003). Self, friends, and lovers: Structural relations among Beck Depression Inventory scores and perceived mate values. *Journal of Affective Disorders, 75*, 131–148.

Kirsner, B., Figueredo, A. J., & Jacobs, W. (2009). Structural relations among negative affect, mate value, and mating effort. *Evolutionary Psychology, 7*(3), 374–397.

Landolt, M. A., Lalumiere, M. L., & Quinsey, V. L. (1995). Sex differences in intra-sex variations in human mating tactics: An evolutionary approach. *Ethology and Sociobiology, 16*, 3–23.

Leary, M. R. (1999). Making sense of self-esteem. *Current Directions in Psychological Science, 8*(1), 32–35.

Leivers, S., Rhodes, G., & Simmons, L. W. (2014). Context-dependent relationship between a composite measures of men's mate value and ejaculate quality. *Behavioral Ecology, 25*(5), 1115–1122.

Li, N. P., Yong, J. C., Tov, W., Sng, O., Fletcher, G. J., Valentine, K. A., . . . Balliet, D. (2013). Mate preferences do predict attraction and choices in the early stages of mate selection. *Journal of Personality and Social Psychology, 105*(5), 757–776.

Lu, H. J., Zhu, Z. Q., & Chang, L. (2015). Good genes, good providers, and good fathers: Economic development involved in how women select a mate. *Evolutionary Behavioral Sciences, 9*(4), 215–228.

Luchner, A. F., Houston, J. M., Walker, C., & Houston, M. A. (2011). Exploring the relationship between two forms of narcissism and competitiveness. *Personality and Individual Differences, 51*, 779–782.

Massar, K., Buunk, A. P., & Rempt, S. (2012). Age differences in women's tendency to gossip are mediated by their mate value. *Personality and Individual Differences, 52*(1), 106–109.

McClintock, E. (2014). Beauty and status: The illusion of exchange in partner selection? *American Sociological Review, 79*, 575–604.

Muñoz-Reyes, J. A., Gil-Burmann, C., Fink, B., & Turiegano, E. (2012). Physical strength, fighting ability and aggressiveness in adolescents. *American Journal of Human Biology, 24*, 611–617.

Penke, L., Todd, P., Lenton, A. & Fasolo, B. (2007). How self-assessments can guide human mating decisions. In G. Geher & G. Miller (Eds.), *Mating intelligence: New insights into intimate relationships, human sexuality, and the mind's reproductive system* (pp. 37–75). Mahwah, NJ: Lawrence Erlbaum.

Price, M. E., Dunn, J., Hopkins, S., & Kang, J. (2012). Anthropometric correlates of human anger. *Evolution and Human Behavior, 33*(3), 174–181.

Salkicevic, S., Stanic, A. L., & Grabovac, M. T. (2014). Good mates retain us right: Investigating the relationship between mate retention strategies, male value, and relationship satisfaction. *Evolutionary Psychology, 12*(5), 1038–1052.

Sefcek, J., Brumbach, B., Vasquez, G., & Miller, G. (2006). The evolutionary psychology of human mate choice: How ecology, genes, fertility, and fashion influence mating strategies. *Journal of Psychology and Human Sexuality, 18*, 125–182.

Sela, Y., Mogilski, J. K., Shackelford, T. K., Zeigler-Hill, V., & Fink, B. (in press). Mate value discrepancy and mate retention behaviors of self and partner. *Journal of Personality*.

Sell, A., Cosmides, L., Tooby, J., Sznycer, D., von Rueden, C., & Gurven, M. (2009). Human adaptations for the visual assessment of strength and fighting ability from the body and face. *Proceedings of the Royal Society of London B: Biological Sciences, 276*(1656), 575–584.

Sell, A., Tooby, J., & Cosmides, L. (2009). Formidability and the logic of human anger. *Proceedings of the National Academy of Sciences, 106*, 15073–15078.

Singh, D. (2002). Female mate value at a glance: Relationship of waist-to-hip ratio to health, fecundity, and attractiveness. *Neuroendocrinology Letters, 23*(4), 81–91.

Singh, B. L., & Williams, J. S. (1981). Childlessness and family satisfaction. *Research on Aging, 3,* 218–227.

Singh, D., Dixson, B. J., Jessop, T. S., Morgan, B., & Dixson, A. F. (2010). Cross-cultural consensus for waist-to hip ratio and women's attractiveness. *Evolution and Human Behavior, 31,* 176–181.

Stanley, S. M., Markman, H. J., & Whitton, S. W. (2002). Communication, conflict, and commitment: Insights on the foundations of relationship success from a national survey. *Family Process, 41,* 659–675.

Sridharani, S. (2016). In today's well-arranged marriages, women are upfront with their needs. *Times of India.* Retrieved October 2, 2016 from http://timesofindia.indiatimes.com/india/In-todays-well-arranged-marriages-women-are-upfront-with-their-needs/articleshow/54597108.cms.

Strout, S., Dutton, E., Crooker, E., Hudanish, A., & Jones, S. (2008, May). *Am I hot or not? The effects of social comparison on self-perception of mate value.* Paper presented at the annual conference of the NorthEastern Evolutionary Psychology Society, Manchester, New Hampshire.

Sugiyama, L. S. (2004). Is beauty in the context-sensitive adaptations of the beholder?: Shiwiar use of waist-to-hip ratio in assessments of female mate value. *Evolution and Human Behavior, 25*(1), 51–62.

Sugiyama, L. S. (2005). Physical attractiveness in adaptationist perspective. In D. M. Buss (Ed.), *The handbook of evolutionary psychology* (pp. 292–343). Hoboken, NJ: Wiley.

Van Yperen, N. W., & Buunk, A. P. (1990). A longitudinal study of equity and satisfaction in intimate relationships. *European Journal of Social Psychology, 20,* 287–309.

Watson, D., Beer, A., & McDade-Montez, E. (2014). The role of active assortment in spousal similarity. *Journal of Personality, 82*(2), 116–129.

Waynforth, D. (2001). Mate choice trade-offs and women's preference for physically attractive men. *Human Nature, 12,* 207–219.

Waynforth, D., & Dunbar, R. I. M. (1995). Conditional mate choice strategies in humans: Evidence from "Lonely Hearts" advertisements. *Behaviour, 132*(9), 755–779.

Wyckoff, J. P., & Kirkpatrick, L. A. (2016). Direct and indirect aggression tactics as a function of domain-specific self-esteem. *Personality and Individual Differences, 92,* 135–142.

Single and Partnered Women: Competing to Obtain and Retain High-Quality Men

Gayle Brewer

Abstract

The form, function, and prevalence of intrasexual competition is expected to differ for single and partnered women. For single women focused on the identification and recruitment of desirable mates, competition increases access to potential partners. For partnered women focused on the maintenance of current relationships, competition reduces the risk of infidelity and relationship dissolution. This chapter considers the specific threats experienced by single and partnered women, the extent to which these threats may impact on willingness to engage in intrasexual competition, and the competitive tactics employed. Additional factors influencing women's engagement in intrasexual competition such as age and mating system type are also discussed.

Key Words: age, single, partnered, relationship status, infidelity, mating system

"It is because of men that women dislike one another."

—*Jean de la Bruyere,* Characters, *1688*

Female intrasexual competition serves a range of adaptive functions, each of which influences reproductive success. The primary function of intrasexual competition is expected to differ for single and partnered women. For single women focused on the identification and recruitment of desirable mates, competition increases access to potential partners. For partnered women focused on the maintenance of current relationships, competition reduces the risk of infidelity and relationship dissolution. Relationship status should also influence the selection of specific competitive tactics. For example, partnered women may recruit support from family members. These people have a personal interest in the success of the relationship as the withdrawal of male investment increases the support that they are required to provide. This chapter considers the specific threats experienced by single and partnered

women, the extent to which these threats may impact on willingness to engage in intrasexual competition, and the competitive tactics employed.

Single Women and the Search for a Suitable Mate

"All women are basically in competition with each other for a handful of eligible men."

—*Mignon McLaughlin,* The Second Neurotics Notebook, *1966*

In many species, including humans, females provide the majority of parental investment in infant care. This investment serves to both reduce the number of offspring that the female can rear and increase her vulnerability as she attempts to source sufficient resources and protect the infant from potential danger. As a consequence, many species requiring extensive paternal investment are pair bonded—a mating system that increases the level of the investment available and increases the likelihood of offspring survival. There are therefore clear advantages to long-term committed relationships. As explained by one vaudeville song "I think we would all prefer marriage with strife; than to be on the shelf and nobody's wife" (Nicholson, 2008, p. 64). In species with greater female investment in offspring, the theory of parental investment (Trivers, 1972) predicts male intrasexual competition for desirable mates and female selection of male partners. Recent research indicates that while male intrasexual competition is typically greater than female intrasexual competition in species with high levels of female investment, female intrasexual competition also occurs.

The acquisition of a mate per se is not sufficient for women to successfully reproduce. Potential mates vary across a range of physical and nonphysical traits such as health, intelligence, and reliability (Buss, 1989). Women selecting diseased or weak men are less likely to receive protection or valued resources. In addition, offspring fathered by poor-quality men may inherit his poor-quality genes, increasing the level of investment required by infants and reducing the likelihood that they will survive to sexual maturity and obtain a mate. Women selecting unreliable, selfish mates are also unlikely to receive consistent access to essential resources. Therefore, competition between women provides access to the most desirable high-quality mates (i.e., those possessing valued physical and nonphysical resources), which increases the likelihood of subsequent reproductive success.

"Women dress alike all over the world: They dress to be annoying to other women."

—*Elsa Schiaparelli*

Women employ a range of strategies to increase their own attractiveness and decrease the attractiveness of rivals who are competing for the same men. Men place a greater importance on the physical attractiveness of a partner than women and cross-culturally prefer attractive women as romantic or sexual partners (Buss & Schmitt, 1993). Consequently, physical attractiveness forms the basis for a large component of female competition (Symons, 1979), influencing both the level and type of intrasexual competition in which women engage. Improving physical appearance is a relatively frequent form of intrasexual competition reported by women (Buss, 1988), and derogation of a rival's appearance is a strategy used more frequently by women than by men (Buss & Dedden, 1990). Indeed, women may also use luxury items such as handbags and shoes to compete with rivals and are more likely to seek and display these items when motivated to guard their partner (Wang & Griskevicius, 2014). It appears that women use luxury products to signal the devotion of their partner in order to deter those intending to disrupt the relationship. In this context, it is also argued that restricted eating and the pursuit of thinness are associated with intrasexual competition and access to suitable mates as women seek to display signals of youth to potential partners (Abed, 1998; Faer, Hendricks, Abed, & Figueredo, 2005).

Women selectively attend to attractive female faces (Maner, Gailliot & DeWall, 2007), a tendency that facilitates the identification and monitoring of the most threatening rivals. A number of traits signaling female mate quality are attended to, such as vocal femininity and waist-to-hip ratio, and women report greater distress when a rival possesses a more attractive face or body (Buss, Shackelford, Choe, Buunk, & Dijkstra, 2000). When assessing the appearance of potential rivals, women overestimate the extent to which men find other women desirable (Hill, 2007). This overestimation encourages vigilance and ensures that women are not complacent to the threat posed by women, particularly if other factors (such as willingness to engage in sexual behavior) increase the desirability of moderately attractive women.

Women do not therefore evaluate their physical attractiveness in isolation, and relative attractiveness (i.e., comparison between a woman's attractiveness and the attractiveness of her rival) is particularly important. This forms an important aspect of rival derogation (Schmitt, 1988), and, compared to men, women's jealousy is more related to comparisons between the rival and self (Dijkstra & Buunk, 2001). Furthermore, while there are a number of universally attractive physical traits, such as a clear complexion, when evaluating the threat posed by potential rivals it is important to consider the preferences of a particular man. Partnered women place a considerable importance on the preferences of their partner (DeSteno & Salovey, 1996) and those traits or qualities most valued by a partner may be especially important when evaluating or derogating a potential rival (Schmitt, 1988). Though this form of comparison and evaluation of specific traits may be less available to single women, some knowledge of their target partner's preferences may help identify the most threatening rivals.

The Importance of Age

"Age to women is like Kryptonite to Superman."

—*Kathy Lette*

The experience of being single or in a relationship (and the related advantages or disadvantages of being single or partnered) varies substantially across the life cycle. For women, reproduction is limited by menarche and menopause, restricting (compared to men) opportunities to reproduce and subsequent reproductive output (i.e., number of children). Therefore the intensity of competition for long-term partners may also vary across the lifespan. Younger, postpubertal women have a relatively greater period of time in which to search for and attract suitable men. In contrast, older women (intending to reproduce) for whom "time is of the essence" may feel under pressure to enter into a long-term relationship. This pressure may be exacerbated by competition with younger single women who are, as a consequence of their age, physical attractiveness, and reproductive value, often more desirable to potential partners. Older single women in this situation may of course elect to become single parents, a decision that reduces available investment in the child and may influence a range of outcomes for the child such as educational attainment (Krein, 1986). Hence, this form of less desirable nonmarital reproduction is described by Clarke (2011) as "the only game in town fertility" (p. 100).

"I've been dating since I was fifteen. I'm exhausted. Where is he?"

—Sex and the City

There may not, of course, be a specific age at which a woman becomes conscious of her declining fertility and thus increases her efforts to obtain a suitable partner. Increased motivation to secure a long-term mate may in part reflect the availability of desirable men and factors such as the average age of marriage. Though most women in Western societies are married by their mid-thirties (as shown in Figure 17.1), this is influenced by a range of individual and environmental factors. These include the presence of conservative sexual values (Garcia & Kruger, 2010). As shown in Figure 17.2, the number of women of the same age that are married or single varies substantially between cultures. Competition for mates between women across the lifespan should reflect these social norms. In addition, the age at which a woman marries has a number of important consequences. Teenage marriages are less likely to survive, and whereas later marriages are less likely to end in divorce or for partners to contemplate divorce, they are relatively poor in quality (Amato, Booth, Johnson, & Rogers, 2007; Glenn, Uecker, & Love, 2010). Therefore, competition between single women for access to suitable mates should reflect these trends.

In some circumstances, the competition among single women for a desirable mate may be particularly intense. For example, following the First World War, few men in Britain were available to marry. Approximately 1 million men from the British Army were killed in action, missing in action, or died as a consequence of disease or injury (www.1914-18.net/army). As the senior mistress of one school announced to her female pupils: "I have come to tell you a terrible fact. Only one out of

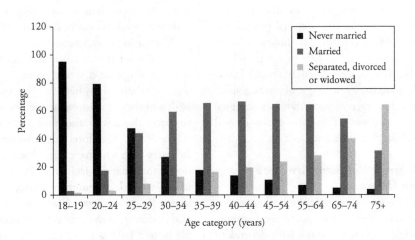

Figure 17.1 Marital status of American women by age (U.S. Census Bureau, 2010).

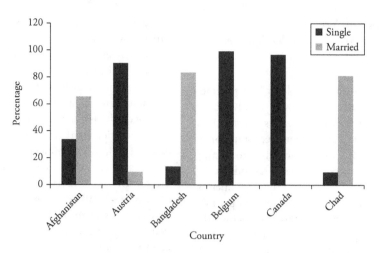

Figure 17.2 Percentage of single and married women ages 20 to 24 years in a range of countries (United Nations, Department of Economic and Social Affairs, Population Division, 2013).

ten of you girls can ever hope to marry. This is not a guess of mine. It is statistical fact. Nearly all the men who might have married you have been killed" (Nicholson, 2008, p. 20).

Age and fertility are clearly issues that influence the reproductive decisions of all women. Important differences between cultural groups may, however, influence the availability of potential mates, relationship status, and subsequent intrasexual competition. A range of studies have highlighted the decline in marriage rates among minority and low-income populations, hypothesized to reflect the availability of economically acceptable mates. Indeed, there is a high percentage of Black women who are unmarried at each age category, and Black women spend a lower proportion of their reproductive career (compared to other ethnic groups) married (Clarke, 2011). Clarke also highlights the importance of educational attainment, as women with college degrees (in each ethnic group) are more likely to have delayed parenthood (or remained childless) compared to those with lower levels of educational success such as a high school diploma. Therefore, future research should investigate the importance of a range of demographic variables including age, ethnicity, and educational attainment for strategic relationship decisions and the use of female intrasexual competition.

We Are All Single But Some Are More Single Than Others

Relationship status extends beyond the distinction between single and partnered women. Divorced single women and those with dependent children find it more difficult to attract a romantic partner than women who have never been married (Vaillant & Harrant, 2008). The importance of dependent children for woman's desirability may of course reflect men's unwillingness to enter relationships with women who must invest a substantial amount of time and energy raising those children or men's unwillingness to contribute to investment in the children themselves. The difficulty childless divorced single women have in attracting a mate may suggest that men are reluctant to enter relationships with women who have been in committed relationships with another man (i.e., potential conflict for affection) or have been in an unsuccessful relationship (i.e., lack of conflict-resolution strategies). Indeed, common sources of jealousy involve talking to or about previous partners (Knox, Zusman, Mabon & Shriver, 1999), and renewed relationships with former partners are viewed as a greater threat than relationships with previously unknown rivals (Cann & Baucom, 2004).

Alternatively, differences between single and divorced women may reflect the tendency for those who are single or divorced to marry those with a similar relationship history. For example, those with a history of divorce themselves are more likely to marry those who also have a history of divorce (Ono, 2006). Therefore, single women are expected to marry men who have never been married, a tendency that may be facilitated by access to a wide social network of potential mates from which to select. In this context, cities have been characterized as densely populated areas in which single people benefit from a wider choice of potential mates (Gautier, Svarer, & Teulings, 2010). It is argued that single women are willing to pay a premium for the greater opportunities to attract a partner, but after the formation of a long-term relationship (when the opportunity to meet potential partners is less important), women leave the cities. Therefore, divorced women (particularly those with dependent children) who relocated when married are more likely to live in rural areas with limited opportunities for socializing and meeting potential partners.

Partnered Women and the Importance of Retaining a Mate

"No rose without a thorn, or a love without a rival."

—*Turkish proverb*

As previously outlined, there are clear advantages to the acquisition of a suitable (i.e., high-quality) partner. However, while fairy tales, romance novels, and movies encourage women to believe that finding and attracting "the one" leads to a life of "happily ever after," this is far from a foregone conclusion. For women in a romantic relationship, the potential dissolution of the relationship and infidelity represent important threats.

Mate poaching refers to attracting a person who is in a current romantic relationship (Schmitt & Buss, 2001). This is a relatively common mating strategy that occurs cross-culturally. Mate poaching is often successful, with almost half of men and women who have received a previous poaching attempt reporting succumbing to the poacher and approximately 15% of current relationships resulting directly from mate poaching (Schmitt & Buss, 2001). Further highlighting the potential threat that this strategy poses to partnered women, research indicates that approximately 40% of women report that they have attempted to poach a mate for either a short- or long-term relationship (Schmitt et al., 2004). Mate poaching is particularly successful for female poachers, as men are more likely than women to succumb to a short-term mate-poaching attempt.

The prevalence of mate poaching is consistent with the existence of mate copying whereby women are more likely to select mates who have been chosen by other women. Research indicates that men are rated as more desirable when surrounded by other women compared to alone or surrounded by other men (Hill & Buss, 2008). It appears that women searching for a partner may infer that partnered status indicates the possession of a range of desirable qualities that cannot be directly observed, such as

socioeconomic status or reliability (Little, Burriss, Jones, DeBruine, & Caldwell, 2008). Hence, this form of copying is particularly valuable for rivals with little sexual experience (Waynforth, 2007).

Infidelity that does not lead to the dissolution of the relationship may lead to the temporary withdrawal of valued resources and protection and therefore also poses a threat. For example, male Ache hunters in Paraguay divert resources such as food from their primary mate and offspring to extra-pair partners (Hill & Hurtado, 1996). However, though both temporary infidelity and relationship dissolution may impact on a woman's survival and the survival of her offspring, it is the permanent removal of support associated with relationship dissolution that constitutes the greatest threat. Exacerbating this threat, involuntary dissolution of the relationship impairs the ability to attract another partner. Learning that a person was rejected by his or her previous mate reduces desirability as a romantic partner (Stanik, Kurzban, & Ellsworth, 2010), suggesting that the resources and protection offered by the previous partner are not easily replaced.

Women are sensitive to those rivals and situations that present the greatest threat. In this context, jealousy serves an important adaptive function, alerting partnered women of threats to a valued relationship. This distress prompts a number of behaviors intended to maintain the current relationship, referred to as mate-retention behaviors (Buss, 1988). These include a range of strategies, such as monitoring partners (e.g., they have started to change the way they dress) and potential rivals (e.g., flirting with one's partner). Whereas some behaviors are employed as a "last resort" attempt to retain a partner, others are adopted as a form of routine relationship maintenance (Shackelford, Goetz, & Buss, 2005). A number of factors may influence the type and frequency of mate-retention behaviors that are employed, including the relationship status of the rival.

Single Rivals

Partnered women are expected to perceive single women as more threatening than rivals in a current romantic relationship. As previously mentioned, the vast majority of single women have desires to marry or enter into long-term relationships (Sugiura-Ogasawara, Ozaki, Kaneko, Kitaori, & Kumagai, 2010), and these unpartnered women appear to take active steps to increase their opportunities to meet potential mates (Gautier, Svarer, & Teulings, 2010). While a range of single men may be available, single women may choose to pursue partnered men if those men are thought to be of a higher mate value (e.g., higher socioeconomic status or more physically attractive). Consistent with the suggestion that single women present the greatest threat, Parker and Burkley (2009) report that single, but not partnered, women are more interested in obtaining a partnered man as opposed to a currently single man. Of the behaviors employed by partnered women to deter single rivals, derogation may be particularly effective if it is suggested that her single status signals low mate quality.

In this context, women who are not married by an appropriate age may be deemed unmarriageable and typecast, often referred to using insulting terms such as "spinster" or "old maid" (Taylor, 2011). Single women are also sometimes viewed as low quality or in some manner undesirable. For example, single women are often portrayed as susceptible to mental illness (Holden, 2007). This type of depiction serves to lower the single woman's mate value and her attractiveness to partnered men, effectively reducing the likelihood that she will form an extra-pair relationship with the target man (Fisher & Cox, 2009). In recent years, one frequent form of labeling is to describe women who are not married by a particular age as "overly selective." This implies that these women are detached, uncompromising, and thus lacking in the type of emotional warmth and social skills (cooperation and forgiveness, etc.) required for successful long-term relationships (Lahad, 2013). As outlined by one relationship advisor:

> He is too short, too fat, too thin, too stupid, and too sweaty . . . We are so judgmental, so quick to call it off and not give it a chance . . . Tell me the truth [addressing the single woman]: would it be so bad to try to get to know him? . . . But no way! She [the single woman] says: I won't go out and be seen in public with a man that dresses like him . . . Over my dead body; I would rather remain an old maid and not humiliate myself.
>
> (Holzman-Bismut, 2007, cited in Lahad, 2013)

In this manner, older single women are urged to "settle" (Gotlieb, 2008) and "be reasonable about their expectations" (Ng & Ng, 2009, p. 111). The pressure to "settle" for less desirable mates clearly encourages single women to form stable long-term relationships without further delay and to accept lower-quality mates. This strategy is more compatible with the immediate selection of available

(i.e., single) men rather than the riskier strategy of attempting to poach a man in a current relationship, which may impact on her reputation and ability to secure a long-term partner. This strategy reduces the threat to women in current romantic relationships, which is strengthened further by the greater value placed by society on the lives of partnered women. The separation between single and married women can be particularly harsh. As one person recalled: "And the smug wives turned a blind eye when their children played evil tricks on the single women and taunted them" (Nicholson, 2008, pp. 29–30). The status afforded to married women encourages those who are not married to avoid delay and enter stable long-term relationships, which may be further exacerbated by the frequent expectation that single women should become the primary caregiver for elderly relatives and to relinquish their social relationships or live with those requiring care (Burnley, 1987).

Partnered Rivals

A wealth of research demonstrates that women are more reluctant than men to enter sexual relationships and are less likely to engage in the extra-dyadic behaviors deemed to be acceptable only within the primary relationship (Luo, Cartun, & Snider, 2010). Women do engage in extra-pair sexual relationships, however, and female infidelity has been reported in a number of traditional societies such as the Ache in Paraguay (Hill & Hurtado, 1996) and Yanomamo of Venezuela (Chagnon, 1983), which suggests that this is not a Western phenomenon. Extra-pair relationships may offer women a number of advantages. These include the opportunity to acquire resources, which reduces the resources that a man may provide to his original partner, and mate switching, which may lead to a man abandoning his original mate (Greiling & Buss, 2000). Consequently, partnered rivals also present an important threat to women in a relationship.

In comparison to single women, the risk posed by partnered women may be less or more controllable. Women who engage in extra-pair relationships must be cautious to avoid discovery by their primary partner. The discovery of an extra-pair relationship may result in a range of consequences such as relationship dissolution or domestic violence (Blumstein & Schwartz, 1983), which impact on her survival and reproductive success. Therefore, women willing to engage in extra-pair relationships must be careful that they do not arouse suspicion in order to protect themselves and any offspring that benefit from male investment. The restraint exercised by partnered women (e.g., greater time before deciding that she wishes to become involved with a man or fewer advances toward him) provides women who are concerned about the threat of mate poaching by a rival female with a number of opportunities to monitor the situation and act accordingly. For example, a range of expressions, gestures, and postures are employed by women as courtship signals to encourage male advances, and observation of these expressions and gestures may alert a woman to specific threats. Where required, women may then employ appropriate mate-retention behaviors that prevent a mate from abandoning the relationship or being unfaithful.

It may be more difficult for women to monitor some interactions (e.g., between her partner and his female colleagues), and the assessment of the threat may be less accurate for strangers (for whom no additional personal information is available) than acquaintances (Biesanz, West, & Millevoi, 2007). In this situation, partnered women may recruit the support of kin. A woman's relatives have a strong interest in the success of her relationship. In particular, any loss of resources or protection increases the support that they must provide to the woman and her child. Relatives may therefore be encouraged to monitor her partner's behavior in order to reduce the likelihood of his infidelity, and a number of mate-retention behaviors (such as intimidation of potential rivals) may be effective when employed by relatives. A woman may also enlist the support of her partner's relatives, who may fear separation from her children or stigma if the couple are to separate. This support from a partner's kin may be particularly effective and easy to solicit if a woman is able to portray the rival female as undesirable (e.g., promiscuous), a trait that increases the risk of cuckoldry (i.e., a man investing in an infant which he believes to be his own biological child) and may lower their own reproductive success.

Friends and "Frenemies": The Importance of Same-Sex Relationships

"If you haven't got anything nice to say about anybody, come sit next to me."

—Alice Roosevelt Longworth

Self-disclosure of personal information and gossip about others form an important part of female friendships. Indeed, those who do not disclose often arouse suspicion and may in consequence threaten the intimacy of the relationship. Therefore, the individuals who comprise a woman's (same-sex) social network have important implications for her ability to compete with others. Specifically, these friendships both increase the availability of information about rivals or potential mates via gossip and provide potential rivals (i.e., same-sex friends) with personal information, through self-disclosure, which may be used against her during competition. Indeed, increased competition for potential mates is an established disadvantage of same-sex friendships (Bleske & Shackelford, 2001).

"To a friend who asked him how to find out a girl's faults, he gave the sage advice to praise her to her girl friends."

(*Edwin Lille Miller*, Explorations in Literature, about Benjamin Franklin, *1938*)

Social networks vary, and when asked to name members of their social network, married women are most likely to name friends who are also married while single women are most likely to identify single friends. Research indicates that while age accounts in part for these differences in social network composition, the social boundaries that exist between single and married women persist when controlling for age (Kalmijn & Vermunt, 2007). This may to some extent reflect the manner in which people meet potential friends; for example, married women with children may meet other married mothers through their children's school activities. For married women, the romantic partner may fulfil many of the functions (e.g., provision of emotional support) previously performed by same-sex friends, thus reducing reliance on external social networks. The influence of cohabitation on withdrawal from same-sex friendships appears less marked, however, than the impact of marriage (Kalmijn & Bernasco, 2001), suggesting that women require the formal commitment of marriage before relinquishing the support of their same-sex friends. Therefore, women who are cohabiting may experience greater intrasexual competition from friends than married women but may also draw on the support of same-sex friends in the presence of a rival.

"The only thing worse than a smug married couple; lots of smug married couples."

(*Bridget Jones*)

Relationships with others of the same relationship status are more rewarding, due to common interests and opportunities for shared activities.

However, the preference for friends of a similar relationship status may also reflect the tendency for people to view their current relationship status as the universal ideal. This tendency is particularly strong for those who believe their current relationship status will continue (Laurin, Kille, & Eibach, 2013). The tendency for partnered women to form friendships with other partnered women may also reflect negative societal stereotypes that portray single women as immature and self-centered, particularly if older than the average age of marriage (Morris, DePaulo, Hertel & Ritter, 2006, cited in DePaulo & Morris, 2006). Indeed, single women experience considerable discrimination, which is largely viewed as legitimate (Morris, Sinclair, & DePaulo, 2007).

As highlighted, communication—and gossip in particular—forms an important part of friendship. The tendency for women to be friends with those of the same relationship status may increase the value of this information. Romantic relationships form the basis for most gossip, and reputation gossip, which especially contains important details about a specific individual (Bromley, 1993), provides valuable information that may enhance reproductive success. Single women may exchange information about the availability of desirable mates (or help friends avoid undesirable men). In contrast, the gossip of partnered women may focus on the romantic histories of other women, raising awareness about sexual rivals and potentially lowering their attractiveness through targeted comments. As described by Hess and Hagen (2002): "because gossip is an excellent strategy for within-group competition, and because it is effective in attacking and defending difficult-to-assess aspects of reputation, gossip may have been a more effective weapon in female intrasexual competition than it was in male intrasexual competition, increasing selection for psychological adaptations for informational aggression in females" (p. 12). Therefore, while friendships among single women may increase the likelihood of intrasexual competition, friendships with those of a similar relationship status afford important benefits for both single and partnered women.

Mating Systems

"When one woman strikes at the heart of another, she seldom misses, and the wound is invariably fatal."

—*Pierre Choderlos de Laclos,* Dangerous Liaisons

A review of the literature provides readers with a biased account of heterosexual personal relationships, implying in particular that all relationships are romantic in nature and exist only between one man and one woman. Indeed this chapter also focuses on romantic, sexually exclusive relationships. It is important to note, however, that a range of relationship types exist. As shown in Figure 17.3, data from the Standard Cross-Cultural Sample (Murdock & White, 1980), which provides information on the world's most ethnographically described societies ($N = 186$), reveals that monogamy is not the most common mating system. Furthermore, societies may feature more than one mating system type. For example, among the Yanamamo in Venezuela, a minority of married men are in polygynous relationships (Hames, 1996). The frequency, form and intensity of female intrasexual competition that is experienced are expected to vary for each mating system and relationship type.

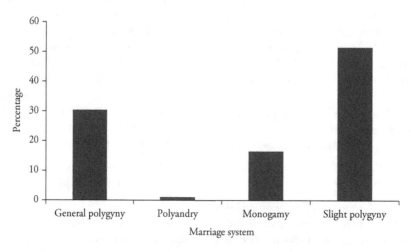

Figure 17.3 Percentage of mating system types in the standard cross-cultural sample (Murdock, 1967).

Arranged Marriages

Women do not date or marry in isolation, and families often have a strong interest in the partner she selects. In industrialized Western countries, differences between parent and child preferences for a "suitable" partner may lead to a certain level of conflict, as any teenager will testify. However, women are typically expected (for better or worse) to select a partner themselves. These are often termed "love" marriages. In many cultures, such as India and the Middle East, women's families are much more involved in the selection of a marriage partner, and a substantial number of marriages are arranged by family members (Goode, 1963). The arrangement of the marriage by older family members is thought to address the fact that younger people are not able to make the correct selection themselves, for example favoring characteristics such as physical attractiveness rather than other factors such as the reputation of the extended family. Furthermore, the meaning of marriage varies cross-culturally, and whereas in Western countries there is an emphasis on romance, sexual maturity, and emotional support, in other cultures the strengthening of the family unit and wider social relationships are of greater importance.

Cultures practicing arranged marriage are often collectivist cultures, and the mate chosen may have a greater impact on the social and economic success of the wider family unit in these environments than in individualistic cultures (Buunk, Park, & Duncan, 2010). In these circumstances, factors other than sexual attraction and romantic love may determine partner selection. For example, approximately half of those in India and Pakistan report that they would marry a mate whom they do not love if the mate has the qualities that they value, compared to less than 5% of those asked in North America (Levine, Sato, Hashimoto, & Verma, 1995). Previous research has considered a range of differences between "love" and arranged marriages, such as marital outcomes (Myers, 2010), though to date there is little consideration of female intrasexual competition in arranged marriages, which may involve signals directed at a potential partner's family rather to the man himself or the display of qualities that are of particular value to the wider family group.

Future research is required to investigate the extent to which parental selection of the marital partner and expectations of romantic love influence female intrasexual competition. There is some suggestion that the role of women within many societies practicing arranged marriage may influence intrasexual competition between single women. In particular, the lower social status afforded to unmarried women may heighten the importance of securing a marriage partner. As described in Strier and Zidan (2013), "Being unmarried is a life on hold, a suspended existence. The dependent nature of the unmarried women's social status has detrimental consequences for their self-image, as they see themselves as almost certainly having some imperfection that explains their unmarriability" (p. 206). Of course the distinction between the status of single and married women is not necessarily restricted to those societies in which arranged marriages occur. In Jane Austen's famous novel *Pride and Prejudice*, the younger Lydia clearly delights in announcing to her elder sister, "Ah, Jane, I take your place now, and you must go lower, because I am a married woman!" (p. 243).

Intrasexual competition between female members of the wider family unit (e.g., women selecting potential partners for their children) would be a particularly interesting area of research, and future studies may compare women's competitive behavior when selecting or retaining their own partner with competition to secure a husband for their daughter. Again, the involvement of the wider family unit, while expected to be particularly strong when arranged marriages take place, may not be restricted to these cultures. Also noted in *Pride and Prejudice*, "It is a truth universally acknowledged, that a single man in possession of a good fortune must be in want of a wife. However little known the feelings or views of such a man may be on first entering a neighbourhood, the truth is so well fixed in the minds of the surrounding families, that he is considered as the rightful property of some one or other of their daughters" (p. 5).

Polyandry

Polyandry, in which one woman is married to more than one man, is a relatively rare marriage system (Marlowe, 2000). It almost always involves fraternal polyandry whereby brothers share a wife. This system has been studied in a number of populations, including Tibetans in Nepal, the Khasas and Lahul in northern India, and the Kandyans in Sri Lanka. This mating system may be particularly advantageous if it allows the brothers to retain lands that would otherwise become fragmented or to ensure that sufficient labor is present to support the household. Polyandry may also increase investment in each child, resulting in lower child mortality.

However, these fraternally polyandrous relationships may not be permanent, and brothers (particularly younger brothers) appear to regularly leave polyandrous relationships, often motivated by fraternal friction or the desire to develop independent family units (Levine & Silk, 1997). By reducing the number of available men in a population, polyandry increases the number of women within the group who are unable to marry. Hence, in polyandrous societies, female intrasexual competition to attract long-term partners is of particular importance and may provide a number of reproductive advantages (e.g., opportunities to mate and likelihood of offspring survival) to successful competitors. It is essential for future research to investigate the role of female intrasexual competition in partner selection and acquisition in polyandrous societies and the female strategies that have developed to address this form of reproductive threat.

Polygyny

Compared to polyandry, polygyny, whereby one man is married to more than one woman, is relatively common. Indeed, it is a normative mating system within many societies (van de Walle, 2005). There is, of course, an important distinction between societies in which polygyny is accepted and societies in which it is widely practiced, as in many cultures accepting polygyny, most marriages are monogamous (Murdock, 1967). There is also a distinction between a system in which the wives create wealth or the sororal polygyny in which wealth provides the opportunity for a man to obtain more than one wife. In polygynous societies, relatively few women remain unmarried. However, all wives may not receive equal treatment, and factors such as position within the marriage (e.g., first or second wife) and male preference may affect the ability to obtain resources or to influence strategic family decisions. Therefore, women in polygynous societies should compete for position, particularly to be the first wife, which often confers an element of seniority within the household.

Wives may live together, though it is most common for each wife to have an independent household (Broude, 1994). Women within a polygynous marriage share many objectives, and cooperation during domestic or child-care activities is an important element of polygynous marriages. Though often dependent on close proximity, this cooperation may allow women to pursue paid work outside the home and is particularly important during periods of illness or pregnancy. Indeed, the cooperation that wives display toward each other may have a positive impact on child survival (Chisholm & Burbank, 1991). Relationships between polygynous wives also involve conflict, particularly for the attention and investment of their husband. Recalling the arrival of the sixth wife in a polygynous marriage, the fifth wife stated, "I felt rotten, I was angry, I didn't understand. My little boy was only eight months old and he was getting married? Who would look after me? Why did he marry me if he wanted another?" (Al-Krenawi & Graham, 1999, p. 503).

Therefore, successful negotiation of these intrasexual relationships (i.e., increasing cooperation while ensuring male investment) has an important impact on the women's own welfare and that of their children. The importance of relationships with co-wives may be further exacerbated by the emotional detachment and relatively low social support provided by polygynous compared to monogamous husbands (Orubuloye, Caldwell, & Caldwell, 1997), and future research may consider the influence of husband–wife relationship quality on interactions between wives. A range of factors such as age and rank influence the level of cooperation or conflict between wives (Jankowiak, Sudakov, & Wilreker, 2005), and the level of conflict or jealousy that is experienced presumably influences women's marital satisfaction and stress. In part, these factors may account for the varied advantages experienced by wives, such as the greater status and reproductive success of senior compared to junior wives (Gibson & Mace, 2006). Relationships with their husband's family, particularly his mother, may also influence status within the family unit and subsequent investment from the husband. Future research should consider the importance of these wider familial relationships for competition between wives.

Duolocal Residence and Competition Between Sisters

"Sisters, as you know, also have a unique relationship. This is the person who has known you your entire life, who should love you and stand by you no matter what, and yet it's your sister who knows exactly where to drive the knife to hurt you the most."

—Lisa See

In a small number of societies, such as the Mosuo of Southwestern China, men and women live separately, each remaining in their mother's home after marriage. Women therefore live in a communal household containing three generations, with men visiting only at night. Women typically cooperate with domestic tasks, agricultural labor, and child care, though the presence of multiple women of reproductive age in the same household creates competition. Ji et al. (2013) showed that women's reproductive success is negatively affected by this competition, with the presence of sisters related to later age of having a first child. Older, dominant sisters achieve the greatest success and have a greater number of children than their lower-ranking siblings.

The Presence of Male Observers

"My biggest challenge will be to play the totally submissive woman. It takes a toll on you when you play someone who's so far removed from your personality."

—*Regina King*

When faced with a partner's infidelity or the threat of infidelity, the partner rather than the rival is often the target of anger and blame (Mathes & Verstraete, 1993). The romantic rival is, however, more salient for women faced with their partner's infidelity than for men in this situation. Specifically, the emotional and behavioral reactions of women toward a rival are greater than those of men (Paul, Foss, & Galloway, 1993). Directly addressing the threat posed by female rivals (rather than focusing on behavior directed toward the partner) offers a number of advantages, such as deterring those rivals and demonstrating commitment to a current relationship. There are, however, a number of disadvantages for women displaying jealous or competitive reactions. These behaviors are typically inconsistent with societal norms that depict men and women as assertive and passive, respectively (though some cultural variation exists; Mead, 1935), and aggressive women are evaluated more negatively than aggressive men, particularly if physical rather than verbal aggression is involved (Barber, Foley & Jones, 1999).

Men observing female intrasexual competition may reject women whom they perceive to be acting in an aggressive or dominant manner. For example, Flinn (1988) highlights the embarrassment experienced by men in response to female intrasexual competition and explicit mate-guarding behavior, which may reduce opportunities for men to develop polygynous relationships. Therefore, while women may prefer to engage in indirect rather than direct intrasexual competition, even nonphysical forms of competition such as derogation lower desirability as a romantic partner. Hence, women should be cautious when competing with rivals, particularly when they are being directly observed by men, in order to protect their own reputation and desirability. While the presence of male observers is expected to influence the behavior of both single and partnered women, it may be of greatest importance for those in a romantic relationship. Single women who appear to be excessively jealous or aggressive (thus alienating the man they seek to attract) have the option to refocus their attention on other men who have not observed their undesirable behavior. Partnered women, however, cannot avoid the consequences of their competitive actions by directing their attention to a different mate; therefore, competition with rivals may lead to conflict with their partner and increase the likelihood of relationship dissolution.

Previous research suggests that women are aware of the influence that female competitiveness may have on their attractiveness as a romantic partner and adapt their behavior accordingly. In particular, women are less competitive when faced with opposite-sex opponents, a phenomenon that is more frequent during naturalistic compared to experimental studies (Weisfeld, 1986). Their discomfort during these competitions is clearly observable through their adoption of defensive postures and submissive behavior, though they may not be consciously aware that they change their behavior when competing (Weisfeld, Weisfeld, & Callaghan, 1982). Females who do not depress their performance when competing with males display signs of anxiety (Morgan & Mausner, 1973), perhaps in anticipation of the negative reactions to their competitive behavior and subsequent success. This reduction of competitive behavior when women are in the presence of men has been observed cross-culturally, suggesting that it may not be dependent on societal reactions to female dominance. At present, few studies have considered the effect of male observation on female (relationship-oriented) intrasexual competition or the manner in which this is influenced by relationship status, and additional research in this area is required.

Hormonal Mechanisms Influencing Intrasexual Competition of Single and Partnered Women

"Love is indeed, at root, the product of the firings of neurons and release of hormones."

—Julian Baggini

This chapter focuses on the functions served by intrasexual competition for single and partnered women. It is also important to consider potential physiological differences between single and partnered women that may facilitate competition. This section outlines the hormonal mechanisms influencing intrasexual competition by single and partnered women and changes in competitive behavior across the menstrual cycle.

Hormones are chemicals that are secreted into the bloodstream. They produce specific physiological effects and may influence or be influenced by a range of behaviors. Hormonal influence is typically characterized by altering the likelihood or intensity of a behavior rather than as switching behavior on or off (see Cobey and Hahn in this handbook for a detailed account of the endocrinology of female competition). Of particular importance for aggressive and competitive behavior is the sex steroid testosterone. Research often investigates testosterone in the context of male competition or differences between men and women. However, while circulating testosterone levels are higher in men than in women (leading to the common assumption that testosterone is a "male hormone"), testosterone also influences female aggression and competition. A number of studies indicate that the testosterone levels of single and partnered women differ (van Anders & Goldey, 2010). In addition, testosterone levels are lower in women with children than those without, suggesting that a reduction in circulating testosterone levels may serve to reduce conflict and promote cohesion in women in romantic relationships or those with caring responsibilities. The relationship between relationship status and testosterone levels is, however, influenced by a range of factors, such as interest in new or additional partners. In particular, partnered women who engage in frequent uncommitted sexual activity display similar testosterone levels to single women (Edelstein, Chopik, & Kean, 2011).

These results suggest that testosterone levels may, to an extent, account for some of the behavioral differences between single and partnered women. In particular, hormonal differences between women

of different relationship status may influence the propensity to engage in intrasexual competition and the specific competitive behaviors employed. Consistent with this suggestion, research conducted in nonhuman species indicates that testosterone increases female aggression, and, in women, testosterone has been related to dominance and violent behavior (Dabbs & Hargrove, 1997). Furthermore, testosterone is associated with a number of related traits such as impulsivity, sensitivity to punishment and reward, empathetic behavior, and cooperation (e.g., Mehta, Wuehrmann, & Josephs, 2009) that are expected to influence competition with rival females. Together, these findings indicate that future research should consider the manner in which testosterone may contribute to the prevalence and intensity of intrasexual competition experienced by single and partnered women.

Premenopausal sexually mature women experience regular hormonal fluctuations across the reproductive or menstrual cycle. The length of the cycle varies considerably between women and between cycles, though the average cycle lasts for approximately twenty-eight days. A range of studies demonstrate that women's sexual behavior and partner preferences vary across the menstrual cycle, indicating a greater sexual interest (especially in men who are not their regular partner) during the most fertile phase. A range of cognitive abilities differ across the menstrual cycle, and women's ability to categorize male faces increases during the fertile phase (Macrae Alnwick, Milne, & Schloerscheidt, 2002). Provocative dress during the high fertile phase and attendance at situations (such as parties) in which they are more likely to attract mates (Haselton & Gangestad, 2006) further suggests a greater sexual motivation at this time. Women's preferences for specific physical and nonphysical traits also vary across the menstrual cycle, including the preference for face and voice type, height, social status, and dominance (e.g., Pawlowski & Jasienska, 2005). These findings suggest that competition for mates may be most frequent or most intense during the fertile phase. Future research investigating intrasexual competition across the menstrual cycle is required.

Importantly, behavioral fluctuation across the menstrual cycle appears to differ among single and partnered women. For example, Bressan and Stranieri (2008) showed that partnered women were more attracted to partnered men compared to single men but only during the low fertile phase. During the high fertile phase, partnered women were more attracted to single men compared to partnered men. The responses of single women did not vary across the menstrual cycle. Furthermore, the attentional bias for courtship language during the fertile phase exists for partnered but not single women (Rosen & Lopez, 2009). Together, these findings suggest that cyclical changes in hormone levels may influence female mate preferences and sexual behavior differently according to relationship status. Further research investigating the interaction between hormone levels and relationship status, and subsequent impact on female intrasexual competition, is required.

Future Directions

As outlined, the form, frequency, and intensity of intrasexual competition differs for single and partnered women. Important differences exist between individuals, however, and the factors influencing this variation are expected to vary for single and partnered women. For example, future research investigating sociosexual orientation for single women and relationship quality for partnered women is of particular interest.

"Sex without love is an empty experience, but as empty experiences go it's one of the best."
—Woody Allen

Sociosexual orientation refers to the willingness to engage in short-term uncommitted relationships. Those with a restricted sociosexual orientation prefer long-term relationships with a high level of commitment, whereas those with an unrestricted sociosexual orientation favor short-term relationships with low levels of commitment (Simpson & Gangestad, 1991). Previous research (e.g., Lewis, Al-Shawaf, Conroy-Beam, Asao, & Buss, 2012) indicates that the adoption of a restricted or unrestricted sexual strategy is related to mate preference and the use of mate-retention tactics. Sociosexual orientation may therefore also influence a woman's willingness to engage in intrasexual competition or the perceived threat that she poses to other women. Research suggests that higher mating effort (i.e., greater desire for sex and higher levels of sexual activity) is associated with greater aggressiveness (Rowe, Vazsonyi, & Figueredo, 1997), and (in men) orientation toward short-term uncommitted relationships is associated with the use of direct intrasexual competition, which may reflect a higher mate quality and more favorable comparisons with potential rivals (Simpson, Gangestad, Christensen,

& Leck, 1999). Furthermore, experimental studies demonstrate that priming with sexual stimuli (i.e., words such as "sex" and "passion") is related to intrasexual competition (Massar & Buunk, 2009). The greater levels of intrasexual competition displayed by those with a more unrestricted sociosexual orientation may reflect both a willingness to obtain mates without concern for the social consequences or a more distrustful and competitive reaction from potential rivals who appear able to accurately detect sociosexual orientation from facial cues (Boothroyd, Burt, DeBruine, & Perrett, 2008), which escalates the competition.

Same-sex friendships with unrestricted women may be particularly difficult. Women avoid friendships with sexually available rivals and are reluctant to befriend women described as sexually promiscuous (Bleske & Shackelford, 2001). Hence unrestricted individuals report lower-quality same-sex friendships than those with a restricted strategy (Hebl & Klashy, 1995). The lower quality of these friendships may reflect the widespread competition between same-sex friends to attract sexual partners and the fact that women can accurately report their friend's sociosexual orientation and mate-attraction tactics (Bleske-Rechek & Buss, 2006). Unrestricted women may detect the distrust of their female friends. Sacco, Hugenberg, and Sefcek (2009) demonstrate that unrestricted men and women are better able to discriminate between women's real and deceptive facial signals (i.e., smiles). Sensitivity to facial signals provides a competitive advantage via identification and avoidance of the most threatening or distrustful rivals. These women may conclude that close same-sex friendships are not viable, instead focusing on competition rather than cooperation with other women.

Relationship Quality

"Before marriage, a man declares that he would lay down his life to serve you; after marriage, he won't even lay down his newspaper to talk to you."
—Helen Rowland

It may be assumed that women in romantic relationships wish to protect those relationships against same-sex rivals and potential relationship dissolution. However, relationships vary widely, from abusive and destructive relationships to those that are loving and rewarding. Therefore, the motivation to protect relationships against the threat of infidelity or dissolution and willingness to engage in intrasexual competitive behavior may also vary. Important factors influencing relationship satisfaction or quality may include the value of the partner (e.g., attractiveness, wealth, kindness) and the level of investment made in the relationship (e.g., length of relationship, integration with partner's social network; Acitelli, Kenny, & Weiner, 2001; Simpson, 1987). Women in long-term relationships with a high-quality partner, characterized by shared responsibilities such as childrearing, should be more willing to engage in intrasexual competition when required than women in comparatively short-term relationships with less desirable mates.

Although previous experience with infidelity may weaken the quality of the relationship, it may heighten awareness of potential threats to the relationship and increase jealousy or intrasexual competition (Buss, Larsen, Westen, & Semmelroth, 1992). Future studies may therefore investigate the influence of this experience on the frequency and intensity of intrasexual competition and whether women in this situation are most likely to direct mate-retention behaviors toward their partner or female rival. The quality of viable alternatives and the level of nonspousal support available to women should also influence the importance women place on their current relationships and hence their willingness to protect those relationships from potential rivals (Miller, 1997). Women who receive valued support from family, friends, or other agencies, or who believe there to be a range of high-quality mates available, should be less dependent on their current relationship than other women and so less likely to compete with rivals who threaten the survival of this relationship (South, 2001). Future research should consider the quality of the threatened relationship, relationship history, and the wider context in which the relationship is situated.

Conclusion

In sum, relationship status influences the frequency, form, and intensity of female intrasexual competition. Single women are most likely to compete for access to desirable partners, and competitive strategies center on those attributes most valued by potential partners such as physical attractiveness. For partnered women, the retention of a mate is most important. Jealousy alerts women to the most threatening rivals or situation, prompting her to employ a range of mate-retention techniques targeted either at the strengthening of the current relationship or toward the rival. Single rivals, who present the greatest threat, may be most vulnerable to derogation of relationship status and association with negative stereotypes of single women. Partnered women, while also threatening, provide greater opportunities for observation of sexual interest and deployment of appropriate mate-retention behaviors. Differences between the intrasexual competition of single women may in part be facilitated by hormonal mechanisms. Present findings focus on female intrasexual competition in the context of romantic sexually exclusive relationships, and additional research investigating intrasexual competition in nonmonogamous mating systems is required. Research assessing those factors such as sociosexual orientation and relationship quality that may influence the competitive behaviors employed by single and partnered women respectively is also recommended.

References

Abed, R. T. (1998). The sexual competition hypothesis for eating disorders. *British Journal of Medical Psychology, 71*, 525–547.

Acitelli, L. K., Kenny, D. A., & Weiner, D. (2001). The importance of similarity and understanding of partners' marital ideals to relationship satisfaction. *Personal Relationships, 8*, 167–185. doi: 10.1111/j.1475-6811.2001.tb00034.x

Al-Krenawi, A., & Graham, J. R. (1999). The story of Bedouin-Arab women in a polygamous marriage. *Women's Studies International Forum, 22*, 497–509. doi: 10.1016/S0277-5395(99)

Amato, P. R., Booth, A., Johnson, D. R., & Rogers, S. J. (2007). *Alone together: How marriage in America is changing*. Cambridge, MA: Harvard University Press.

Barber, M. E., Foley, L. A., & Jones, R. (1999). Evaluations of aggressive women: The effects of gender, socioeconomic status and level of aggression. *Violence and Victims, 14*, 353–363.

Biesanz, J. C., West, S. G., & Millevoi, A. (2007). What do you learn about someone over time? The relationship between length of acquaintance and consensus and self–other agreement in judgments of personality. *Journal of Personality and Social Psychology, 92*, 119–135. doi: 10.1037/0022-3514.92.1.119

Bleske, A. L., & Shackelford, T. K. (2001). Poaching, promiscuity, and deceit: Combatting mating rivalry in same-sex friendships. *Personal Relationships, 8*, 407–424. doi: 10.1111/j.1475-6811.2001.tb00048.x

Bleske-Rechek, A., & Buss, D. M. (2006). Sexual strategies pursued and mate attraction tactics deployed. *Personality and Individual Differences, 40*, 1299–1311.

Blumstein, P., & Schwartz, P. (1983). *American couples*. New York: Simon & Schuster.

Boothroyd, L. G., Jones, B. C., Burt, D. M., DeBruine, L. M., & Perrett, D. I. (2008). Facial correlates of sociosexuality. *Evolution and Human Behavior, 29*, 211–218. doi: 10.1016/j.evolhumbehav.2007.12.009

Bressan, P., & Stranieri, D. (2008). The best men are (not always) already taken: Female preference for single versus attached males depends on conception risk. *Psychological Science, 19*, 145–151. doi: 10.1111/j.1467-9280.2008.02060.x

Bromley, D. B. (1993). *Reputation, image and impression management*. Oxford: John Wiley & Sons.

Broude, G. J. (1994). *Marriage, family, and relationships: A cross-cultural encyclopaedia*. Denver, CO: ABC–CLIO.

Burnley, C. S. (1987). Caregiving: The impact of emotional support for single women. *Journal of Aging Studies, 1*, 253–264. doi: 10.1016/0890-4065(87)90017-X

Buss, D. M. (1988). The evolution of human intrasexual competition: Tactics of mate attraction. *Journal of Personality and Social Psychology, 54*, 616–628. doi: 10.1037/0022-3514.54.4.616

Buss, D. M. (1989). Sex differences in human mate preferences: Evolutionary hypotheses tested in 37 cultures. *Behavioral and Brain Sciences, 12*, 1–14. doi: 10.1017/S0140525X00023992

Buss, D. M., & Dedden, L. A. (1990). Derogation of competitors. *Journal of Social and Personal Relationships, 7*, 395–422. doi: 10.1177/0265407590073006

Buss, D. M., Larsen, R. J., Westen, D., & Semmelroth, J. (1992). Sex differences in jealousy: Evolution, physiology, and psychology. *Psychological Science, 3*, 251–255. doi: 10.1111/j.1467-9280.1992.tb00038.x

Buss, D. M., & Schmitt, D. P. (1993). Sexual Strategies Theory: An evolutionary perspective on human mating. *Psychological Review, 100*, 204–232. doi: 10.1037/0033-295X.100.2.204

Buss, D. M., Shackelford, T. K., Choe, J., Buunk, B. P., & Dijkstra, P. (2000). Distress about mating rivals. *Personal Relationships, 7*, 235–243. doi: 10.1111/j.1475-6811.2000.tb00014.x

Buunk, A. P., Park, J. H., & Duncan, L. A. (2010). Cultural variation in parental influence on mate choice. *Cross-Cultural Research, 44*, 23–40. doi: 10.1177/1069397109337711

Cann, A., & Baucom, T. R. (2004). Former partners and new rivals as threats to a relationship: Infidelity type, gender, and commitment as factors related to distress and forgiveness. *Personal Relationships, 11*, 305–318. doi: 10.1111/j.1475-6811.2004.00084.x

Chagnon, N. (1983). *Yanomamo: The fierce people* (3rd ed). New York: Holt, Rinehart & Winston.

Chisholm, J. S., & Burbank, V. K. (1991). Monogamy and polygyny in Southeast Amhem land: Male coercion and female choice. *Ethology and Sociobiology, 12*, 291–313. doi: 10.1016/0162-3095(91)90022-I

Clarke, A. Y. (2011). *Inequalities of love: College-educated Black women and the barriers to romance and family*. London: Duke University Press.

Dabbs, J. M., & Hargrove, M. F. (1997). Age, testosterone, and behavior among female prison inmates. *Psychosomatic Medicine, 59*, 477–480.

DePaulo, B. M., & Morris, W. I. (2006). The unrecognized stereotyping and discrimination against singles. *Current Directions in Psychological Science, 15*, 251–254. doi: 10.1111/j.1467-8721.2006.00446.x

DeSteno, D. A., & Salovey, P. (1996). Jealousy and the characteristics of one's rival: A self-evaluation maintenance perspective. *Personality and Social Psychology Bulletin, 22*, 920–932. doi: 10.1177/0146167296229006

Dijkstra, P., & Buunk, B. P. (2001). Sex differences in the jealousy-evoking nature of a rival's body build. *Evolution and Human Behavior, 22*, 335–341. doi: 10.1016/S1090-5138(01)00070-8

Edelstein, R. S., Chopik, W. J., & Kean, E. L. (2011). Sociosexuality moderates the association between testosterone and relationship status in men and women. *Hormones and Behavior, 60*, 248–255. doi: 10.1016/j.yhbeh.2011.05.007

Faer, L. M., Hendriks, A., Abed, R. T., & Figueredo, A. J. (2005). The evolutionary psychology of eating disorders: Female competition for mates or for status? *Psychology and Psychotherapy: Theory, Research and Practice, 78*, 397–417.

Fisher, M. L., & Cox, A. (2009). The influence of female attractiveness on competitor derogation. *Journal of Evolutionary Psychology, 7*, 141–155.

Flinn, M. V. (1988). Mate guarding in a Caribbean village. *Ethology and Sociobiology, 9*, 1–28. doi: 10.1016/0162-3095(88)90002-7

Garcia, J. R., & Kruger, D. J. (2010). Unbuckling in the Bible Belt: Conservative sexual norms lower age at marriage. *Journal of Social, Evolutionary and Cultural Psychology, 4*, 206–214.

Gautier, P. A., Svarer, M., & Teulings, C. N. (2010). Marriage and the city: Search frictions and the sorting of singles. *Journal of Urban Economics, 67*, 206–218.

Gibson, M., & Mace, R. (2006). Polygyny, reproductive success and child health in rural Ethiopia: Why marry a married man? *Journal of Biological Science, 39*, 287–300.

Glenn, N. D., Uecker, J. E., & Love, R. W. B. (2010). Later first marriage and marital success. *Social Science Research, 5*, 787–800. doi: 10.1016/j.ssresearch.2010.06.002

Goode, W. J. (1963). *World revolution and family patterns*. New York: Free Press.

Gotlieb, L. (2008, March 1). Marry him: The case for settling for Mr good enough. *The Atlantic*. Retrieved from http://www.theatlantic.com/magazine/archive/2008/03/marry-him/306651

Greiling, H., & Buss, D. M. (2000). Women's sexual strategies: The hidden dimension of extra-pair mating. *Personality and Individual Differences, 28*, 929–963. doi: 10.1016/S0191-8869(99)00151-8

Hames, R. (1996). Costs and benefits of monogamy and polygyny for Yanomamo women. *Ethology and Sociobiology, 17*, 181–199. doi: 10.1016/0162-3095(96)00003-9

Haselton, M. G., & Gangestad, S. W. (2006). Conditional expression of women's desires and men's mate guarding across the ovulatory cycle. *Hormones and Behavior, 49*, 509–518. doi: 10.1016/j.yhbeh.2005.10.006

Hebl, M. R., & Kashy, D. A. (1995). Sociosexuality and everyday social interaction. *Personal Relationships, 2*, 371–383. doi: 10.1111/j.1475-6811.1995.tb00099.x

Hess, N. C., & Hagen, E. H. (2002). Informational warfare, *Cogprints*. Retrieved from http://cogprints.org/2112/.

Hill, S. E. (2007). Overestimation bias in mate competition. *Evolution and Human Behavior, 28*, 118–123. doi: 10.1016/j.evolhumbehav.2006.08.006

Hill, S. E., & Buss, D. M. (2008). The mere presence of opposite-sex others on judgements of sexual and romantic desirability: Opposite effects for men and women. *Personality and Social Psychology Bulletin, 34*, 635–647. doi: 10.1177/0146167207313728

Hill, K., & Hurtado, A. M. (1996). *Ache life history: The ecology and demography of a foraging people*. Hawthorne, NY: Aldine de Gruyter.

Holden, K. (2007). *The shadow of marriage: Singleness in England, 1914–1960*. Manchester: Manchester University Press.

Jankowiak, W., Sudakov, M., & Wilreker, B. C. (2005). Co-wife conflict and co-operation. *Ethnology, 44*, 81–98.

Ji, T., Wu, J.-J., He, Q.-Q., Xu, J.-J., Mace, R., & Tao, Y. (2013). Reproductive competition between females in the matrilineal Mosuo of southwestern China. *Philosophical Transactions of the Royal Society B, 368*, 20130081, doi: 10.108/rstb.2013.0081

Kalmijn, M., & Bernasco, W. (2001). Joint and separated lifestyles in couple relationships. *Journal of Marriage and the Family, 63*, 639–654. doi: 10.1111/j.1741-3737.2001.00639.x

Kalmijn, M., & Vermunt, J. K. (2007). Homogeneity of social networks by age and marital status: A multilevel analysis of ego-centered networks. *Social Networks, 29*, 25–43. doi: 10.1016/j.socnet.2005.11.008

Knox, D., Zusman, M. E., Mabon, L., & Shriver, L. (1999). Jealousy in college student relationships. *College Student Journal, 33*, 328–329.

Krein, S. F. (1986). Growing up in a single parent family: The effect on education and earnings of young men. *Family Relations, 35*, 161–168.

Lahad, K. (2013). "Am I asking for too much?" The selective single woman as a new social problem. *Women's Studies International Forum, 40*, 23–32. doi: 10.1016/j.wsif.2013.04.009

Laurin, K., Kille, D. R., & Eibach, R. P. (2013). "The way I am is the way you ought to be": Perceiving one's relational status as unchangeable motivates normative idealization of that status. *Psychological Science, 24*, 1523–1532. doi: 10.1177/0956797612475095

Levine, N., & Silk, J. B. (1997). Why polyandry fails: Sources of instability in polyandrous marriages. *Current Anthropology, 38*, 375–398.

Levine, R., Sato, S., Hashimoto, T., & Verma, J. (1995). Love and marriage in eleven cultures. *Journal of Cross-Cultural Psychology, 26*, 554–571. doi: 10.1177/0022022195265007

Lewis, D. M. G., Al-Shawaf, L., Conroy-Beam, D., Asao, K., & Buss, D. M. (2012). Friends with benefits II: Mating activation in opposite-sex friendships as a function of sociosexual orientation and relationship status. *Personality and Individual Differences, 53*, 622–628. doi: 10.1016/j.paid.2012.04.040

Little, A. C., Burriss, R. P., Jones, B. C. DeBruine, L. M., & Caldwell, C. A. (2008). Social influence in human face preference: Men and women are influenced more for long-term than short-term attractiveness decisions. *Evolution and Human Behavior, 29*, 140–146. doi: 10.1016/j.evolhumbehav.2007.11.007

Luo, S., Cartun, M. A., & Snider, A. G. (2010). Assessing extradyadic behavior: A review, a new measure, and two new models. *Personality and Individual Differences, 49*, 155–163. doi: 10.1016/j.paid.2010.03.033

Macrae, C. N., Alnwick, K. A., Milne, A. B., & Schloerscheidt, A. M. (2002). Person perception across the menstrual cycle: Hormonal influences on social-cognitive functioning. *Psychological Science, 13*, 532–536. doi: 10.1111/1467-9280.00493

Maner, J. K., Galliot, M. T., & DeWall, C. N. (2007). Adaptive attentional attunement: Evidence for mating-related perceptual bias. *Evolution and Human Behavior, 28*, 28–36. doi: 10.1016/j.evolhumbehav.2006.05.006

Marlowe, F. (2000). Paternal investment and the human mating system. *Behavioural Processes, 51*, 45–61. doi: 10.1016/S0376-6357(00)00118-2

Massar, K., & Buunk, A. P. (2009). The effect of a subliminally primed context on intrasexual competition depends on individual differences in sex drive. *Journal of Research in Personality, 43*, 691–694. doi: 10.1016/j.jrp.2009.02.004

Mathes, E. W., & Verstraete, C. (1993). Jealous aggression: Who is the target, the beloved or the rival? *Psychological Reports, 72*, 1071–1074. doi 10.2466/pr0.1993.72.3c.1071

Mead, M. (1935). *Sex and temperament in three primitive societies.* New York: Morrow.

Mehta, P. H., Wuehrmann, E. V., & Josephs, R. A. (2009). When are low testosterone levels advantageous? The moderating role of individual versus intergroup competition. *Hormones and Behavior, 56*, 158–162. doi: 10.1016/j.yhbeh.2009.04.001

Miller, R. S. (1997). Inattentive and contented: Relationship commitment and attention to alternatives. *Journal of Personality and Social Psychology, 73*, 758–766. doi: 10.1037/0022-3514.73.4.758

Morgan, S. W., & Mausner, B. (1973). Behavioral and fantasied indicators of avoidance of success in men and women. *Journal of Personality, 41*, 457–470. doi: 10.1111/j.1467-6494.1973.tb00106.x

Morris, W. L., Sinclair, S., & DePaulo, B. M. (2007). No shelter for singles: The perceived legitimacy of marital status discrimination. *Group Processes & Intergroup Relations, 10*, 457–470. doi: 10.1177/1368430207081535

Murdock, G. P. (1967). *Ethnographic atlas.* Pittsburgh: University of Pittsburgh Press.

Murdock, G. P., & White, D. R. (1980). Standard cross-cultural sample. In H. Barry & A. Schlegel (Eds.), *Cross-cultural samples and codes* (pp. 3–43). Pittsburgh: University of Pittsburgh Press.

Myers, J. E. (2010). Marriage satisfaction and wellness in India and the United States: A preliminary comparison of arranged marriages and marriages of choice. *Journal of Counseling and Development, 83*, 183–190.

Ng, G. H. E., & Ng, C. W. (2009). Single working women in Hong Kong: A case study of "normal deviance". In C. Kwok-bun, A. S. Ku, & C. Yin-wah (Eds.), *Doing families in Hong Kong* (pp. 111–134). Leiden: Brill.

Nicholson, V. (2008). *Singled out: How two million women survived without men after the First World War.* London: Penguin.

Ono, H. (2006). Homogamy among the divorced and the never married on marital history in recent decades: Evidence from vital statistics data. *Social Science Research, 35*, 356–383. doi: 10.1016/j.ssresearch.2005.02.001

Orubuloye, I. O., Caldwell, J. C., & Caldwell, P. (1997). Perceived male sexual needs and male sexual behaviour in southwest Nigeria. *Social Science & Medicine, 44*, 1195–1207. doi: 10.1016/S0277-9536(96)

Parker, J., & Burkley, M. (2009). Who's chasing whom? The impact of gender and relationship status on mate poaching. *Journal of Experimental Social Psychology, 45*, 1016–1019. doi: 10.1016/j.jesp.2009.04.022

Paul, L., Foss, M. A., & Galloway, J. (1993). Sexual jealousy in young women and men: Aggressive responsiveness to partner and rival. *Aggressive Behavior, 19*, 401–420. doi: 10.1002/1098-2337

Pawlowski, B., & Jasienska, G. (2005). Women's preferences for sexual dimorphism in height depend on menstrual cycle phase and expected duration of relationship. *Biological Psychology, 70*, 38–43. doi: 10.1016/j.biopsycho.2005.02.002

Rosen, M. L., & Lopez, H. H. (2009). Menstrual cycle shifts in attentional bias for courtship language. *Evolution* and Human Behavior, 30, 131–140. doi: 10.1016/j.evolhumbehav.2008.09.007

Rowe, D. C., Vazsonyi, A. T., & Figueredo, A. J. (1997). Mating-effort in adolescence: A conditional or alternative strategy. Personality and Individual Differences, 23, 103–115. doi: 10.1016/S0191-8869(97)00005-6

Sacco, D. F., Hugenberg, K., & Sefcek, J. A. (2009). Sociosexuality and face perception: Unrestricted sexual orientation facilitates sensitivity to female facial cues. Personality and Individual Differences, 47, 777–782. doi: 10.1016/j.paid.2009.06.021

Schmitt, B. H. (1988). Social comparison in romantic jealousy. Personality and Social Psychology Bulletin, 14, 374–387. doi: 10.1177/0146167288142015

Schmitt, D. P., & Buss, D. M. (2001). Human mate poaching: Tactics and temptations for infiltrating existing mateships. Journal of Personality and Social Psychology, 80, 894–917. doi: 10.1037/0022-3514.80.6.894

Schmitt, D. P. and 121 members of the International Sexuality Description Project (2004). Patterns and universals of mate poaching across 53 nations: The effects of sex, culture and personality on romantically attracting another person's partner. Journal of Personality and Social Psychology, 86, 560–584. doi: 10.1037/0022-3514.86.4.560

Shackelford, T. K., Goetz, A. T., & Buss, D. M. (2005). Mate retention in marriage: Further evidence of the reliability of the Mate Retention Inventory. Personality and Individual Differences, 39, 415–425. doi: 10.1016/j.paid.2005.01.018

Simpson, J. A. (1987). The dissolution of romantic relationships: Factors involved in relationship stability and emotional distress. Journal of Personality and Social Psychology, 53, 683–692. doi: 10.1037/0022-3514.53.4.683

Simpson, J. A., & Gangestad, S. W. (1991). Individual differences in sociosexuality: Evidence for convergent and discriminant validity. Journal of Personality and Social Psychology, 60, 870–883.

Simpson, J. A., Gangestad, S. W., Christensen, P. N., & Leck, K. (1999). Fluctuating asymmetry, sociosexuality, and intrasexual competitive tactics. Journal of Personality and Social Psychology, 76, 159–172. doi: 10.1037/0022-3514.76.1.159

South, S. J. (2001). Time-dependent effects of wives' employment on marital dissolution. American Sociological Review, 66, 226–245.

Stanik, C., Kurzban, R., & Ellsworth, P. (2010). Rejection hurts: The effect of being dumped on subsequent mating efforts. Evolutionary Psychology, 8, 682–694.

Strier, R., & Zidan, I. (2013). Arranged marriages: An oppressed emancipation? Women's Studies International Forum, 40, 203–211. doi: 10.1016/j.wsif.2013.07.005

Sugiura-Ogasawara, M., Ozaki, Y., Kaneko, S., Kitaori, T., & Kumagai, K. (2010). Japanese single women have limited knowledge of age-related reproductive time limits. International Journal of Gynecology & Obstetrics, 109, 75–76.

Symons, D. (1979). The evolution of human sexuality. New York: Oxford University Press.

Taylor, A. (2011). Blogging solo: New media, "old" politics. Feminist Review, 99, 79–97. doi: 10.1057/fr.2011.33

Trivers, R. (1972). Parental investment and sexual selection. Chicago: Aldine.

United Nations, Department of Economic and Social Affairs, Population Division. (2013). World Marriage Data 2012 (POP/DB/Marr/Rev2012). New York: Author.

U.S. Census Bureau. (2010). America's Families and Living Arrangements. Table 1A, Marital Status of People 15 Years and Over, by Age, Sex, Personal Earnings, Race, and Hispanic Origin: 2010. Washington, DC: Author.

Vaillant, N. G., & Harrant, V. (2008). Determinants of the likelihood of finding the right partner in an arranged marriage: Evidence from a French matchmaking agency. Journal of Socio-Economics, 37, 657–671. doi: 10.1016/j.socec.2006.12.055

van Anders, S. M., & Goldey, K. L. (2010). Testosterone and partnering are linked via relationship status for women and "relationship orientation" for men. Hormones and Behavior, 58, 820–826. doi: 10.1016/j.yhbeh.2010.08.005

Van de Walle, E. (2005). African households: Censuses and surveys. General Demography of Africa series. Armonk: M. E. Sharpe.

Wang, Y., & Griskevicius, V. (2014). Conspicuous consumption, relationships, and rivals: Women's luxury products as signals to other women. Journal of Consumer Research, 40, 834–854. doi: 10.1086/673256

Waynforth, D. (2007). Mate choice copying in humans. Human Nature, 18, 264–271. doi: 10.1007/s12110-007-9004-2

Weisfeld, C. C. (1986). Female behavior in mixed-sex competition: A review of the literature. Developmental Review, 6, 278–299. doi: 10.1016/0273-2297(86)90015-8

Weisfeld, C. C., Weisfeld, G. E., & Callaghan, J. W. (1982). Female inhibition in mixed-sex competition among young adolescents. Ethology and Sociobiology, 3, 29–42. doi: 10.1016/0162-3095(82)90028-0

I'll Have Who She's Having: Mate Copying, Mate Poaching, and Mate Retention

Lora E. Adair, Haley M. Dillon, *and* Gary L. Brase

Abstract

Women, as with men, are in competition with one another to identify, attract, and retain quality mates. Identifying quality mates can be a difficult, risky, and costly endeavor; however, women can usefully draw on the mating preference of other women to inform their own choices. After reviewing theoretical foundations of the benefits of using female conspecifics as sources of information about potential mates, this chapter discusses evidence of mate copying, poaching, and retention behaviors across multiple species and then the parallel evidence emerging for these behaviors in humans. Of particular interest is identifying why women compete with one another for mates and under what ecological conditions such behaviors are more likely to emerge. Understanding these contextual issues leads to suggestions about the psychological mechanisms that enable women to acquire information about other women's preferences, when that information is utilized, and the strength of social information in shifting women's mating preferences.

Key Words: mating, mate copying, mate poaching, mate retention, mating preferences, competition

"All women are basically in competition with each other for a handful of eligible men."
—*Mignon McLaughlin*

Introduction

In March of 1962, Marilyn Monroe and John F. Kennedy allegedly met for a tryst in Palm Beach, Florida. These two lovers enjoyed nearly inestimable mate value, both in terms of the youth and physical attractiveness of Monroe and the social status of Kennedy. These traits, women's youth and beauty and men's social power and wealth, are among the most important traits evaluated in potential mates (Li, Bailey, Kenrick, & Linsenmeier, 2002; Sprecher, Sullivan, & Hatfield, 1994). With plenty of these mating commodities, both of these individuals displayed similar appeal and demand on the mating market, so their pairing is perhaps not too psychologically, or historically, surprising. According to

a phenomenon known as *assortative mating*, individuals are more likely to mate with those of similar prestige and wealth (Warren, 1966) as well as attractiveness (Buss, 1985) or overall value on the mating market (Dillon, Adair, Wang, & Johnson, 2013; Little, Burt, Penton-Voak, & Perrett, 2001; Price & Vandenberg, 1979). Using a market analogy to describe mate choice helps to explain a typical consequence—while we would all love to take an actress or a president for a romantic getaway, the quality of mate we can attract is constrained by our own value as a mate (Feingold, 1988).

The mating interest that John F. Kennedy and Marilyn Monroe had for one another can be, at least in part, explained by their similarly high value on the mating market. However, their (albeit brief) pairing raises another mating question—can these tremendously desirable mates be tied down? By 1962, Monroe had been successfully courted by three high-quality men (one of whom was Joe DiMaggio) and had left them all. John F. Kennedy was already committed to a high-quality partner at the time of this affair: the daughter of Wall Street's wealthy John Bouvier, Jacqueline Kennedy. But neither Marilyn Monroe nor John F. Kennedy were successfully retained by their partners, likely because as high-quality mates they were both highly desired on the mating market and therefore tended to attract additional potential mates (Goetz et al., 2005). The interest shown by these additional potential mates is, in subtext, communicating, "I want a mate *like him*" (something we refer to as *mate copying*; Kirkpatrick & Dugatkin, 1994) or "I want *him*" (what we call *mate poaching*; Schmitt & Buss, 2001). In other words, extra-pair admirers of high-quality mates might be interested in the borrowing of social information about what a good mate is like, or perhaps simply taking this (already chosen) mate. Indeed, attractive individuals are more likely to have had rivals (relative to their current partner) try to take them from their current partner (Schmitt & Buss, 2001) and are more likely to actually follow through and engage in sexual infidelity (Gangestad & Thornhill, 1997; Hughes & Gallup, 2003).

During their meeting at a dinner party in New York City, the extra-pair admirer Marilyn Monroe drew John F. Kennedy's attention, her mate poaching behaviors ultimately creating an opportunity for the two to engage in (allegedly) sexual and romantic contact in the future. Although the first lady was not invited, sources close to her report that Jackie Kennedy was aware of John F. Kennedy's chronic absence of sexual exclusivity. According to biographer J. Randy Taraborrelli, Jackie Kennedy confessed the following at a White House ball: "Don't think I'm naive about what you and Jack are doing with all those pretty girls, like Marilyn, sailing on the Potomac under the moonlight" (Taraborrelli, 2009, p. 416). Jackie was facing one of the most frequently cited reasons for relationship dissolution (Betzig, 1989)—how should one respond to the presence of threats to one's current mateship? Her situation is generally reduced to two basic options: stay, by engaging in efforts to retain one's current mate (i.e., mate retention), or leave (i.e., dissolve the relationship). Given a partner of sufficient mate quality, leaving might not be her most advantageous option. For example, the genetic benefits imparted to any potential children resulting from a pairing, particularly high when a woman of low mate quality is paired with a high-quality mate, decrease the likelihood that a woman will seek divorce after a partner's

bout of infidelity (Shackelford, 1998). Although most women are vehemently intolerant of partner infidelity (Shackelford, Buss, & Bennett, 2002), high-quality males who can contribute high-quality genes and resources to their children are likely able to pursue more diverse sexual opportunities without compromising their overall positive appeal.

Instead of dissolving their relationship, Jackie Kennedy might have tried to constrain J. F. K.'s opportunities to pursue extra-pair mates by monopolizing his time, acting affectionately, investing effort into her own appearance and attractiveness, or even threatening rival females (Buss & Shackelford, 1997). These mate retention efforts would be particularly important for individuals such as Jackie Kennedy to employ, given the value of her partner on the mating market and the attention that he therefore attracted. Whereas in most species females are so highly sought after on the mating market that they rarely have to compete with other females for high-quality mating opportunities (Gwynne, 1991), human females (a species with tremendous, biparental, long-term offspring investment) face a phylogenetically unusual set of challenges. Human mate choice is bidirectional, meaning that mateships are the result of evaluation, scrutiny, and discrimination by both potential partners. Therefore, women—like Marilyn Monroe—select high-quality mates by acquiring considerable information about the characteristics (i.e., quality) of their prospects. When this information gathering includes not only direct experience with potential partners but also the assessments and decisions of other women, copying the decisions of other women or poaching their mates can result. In this context, other women—like Jackie Kennedy—must then react by employing a toolbox of retention strategies for keeping their high-quality mates for themselves. Human females are likely to respond defensively to mating rivals, rather than simply sharing their partners, given the typically high levels of parental investment made in children by both mothers and fathers. Emlen and Oring (1977) were among the first to identify conditions where monogamy is likely to be created and maintained, concluding that in species (like humans) where offspring require high time and energetic investment from both parents, little resources are left to take advantage of "polygamy potential" (p. 197).

This chapter explores this phenomenon of female competition for "taken" mates, reviewing theoretical explanations of female competition within the domain of mating as well as empirical investigations of human and nonhuman female competition for mates. Particularly, we focus on mate copying, mate poaching, and mate retention behaviors. Overall, the goals of this chapter are to review the topic of female competition for mates through an evolutionary lens and address why females compete for mates, how females engage in competition with other females in the mating market, under what conditions females compete for mates, and what consequences emerge as a result of female intrasexual competition for mates.

Theoretical Evidence

As our historical example illustrates, high-demand, high-quality males attract evaluative attention from rival females for the purpose of finding a mate *like him* for themselves or poaching *that* man from his current partner. In the presence of this attention from rivals, females who have successfully paired with high-quality mates must engage in mate retention efforts in order to avoid their mate's resources being diverted away from them to rival females (as well as any offspring they might produce). This particular mating market climate, characterized by female competition for access to and retention of mates, is produced due to the high investment provided by both parents to human offspring over a relatively long developmental period.

Why Women Compete for Mates

There are several noteworthy theoretical explanations elucidating *why* females should compete with one another for access to fit mates through mate copying and poaching mechanisms. First and foremost, parental investment theory and sexual selection explain the evolutionary forces that can shape female competition, and both game theory and other forms of computational analyses have been used to isolate specific parameters in an environment that might favor female competition and the use of social resources to make mating decisions (Pruett-Jones, 1992; Rasmusen, 1989; Sirot, 2001; Stoehr, 1998). These lines of theoretical evidence suggest ultimate-level explanations as to *why* female competition might be observed in mating contexts and can ultimately provide insight into the questions: why do women compete for mates, and why should women use one another as sources of information when making mating decisions?

Parental investment theory accounts for a general pattern in mammalian species (including humans) in which male intrasexual competition is likely to dominate the mating market. This theory has been used to explain prevalent nonhuman animal mating exchanges, which are often characterized by male ornamentation (e.g., male peacock trains) and male–male competition (e.g., the antlers of deer). According to parental investment theory, male competition prevails due to differences in obligatory investment in offspring (Trivers, 1972); as Parker (1983) puts it, "intrasexual competition will be most intense in the sex that invests least in a given pairing. Usually, therefore, it will be the male that experiences the most intense direct competition" (p. 160). While mammalian males need only invest a single copulatory act in order to produce an offspring, females must invest not only the copulation effort but the internal gestation time as well as the time and energy required for nursing. This differential obligate parental investment produces a higher demand and value for females on the mating market (thus facilitating male competition for reproductive access to females) due to the potential costs associated with mating. The mandatory consequences of a poor choice on the mating market involve, for males, the time lost from a brief sexual encounter, whereas the consequences of a poor choice for females might be years of trying to provide for an offspring. This higher potential cost incurred by mammalian females tends to produce greater choosiness in females and intrasexual competition and fitness displays by male conspecifics to attract females (Andersson, 1994). In other words, the forces of sexual selection have shaped male traits to advertise one's genetic fitness to choosy females in unidirectional mating contexts (i.e., contexts where mate choice is in one direction, such as females evaluating and choosing males to mate with regardless of male preference), such as costly physical ornamentation or bouts of intrasexual aggression that are difficult to fake (Kodric-Brown & Brown, 1984). While unidirectional mate choice in mating markets characterized by higher female obligatory investment in offspring results in greater *male* intrasexual competition, *female* competition with one another for access to high-quality mates may also be observed where bidirectional mate choice is present (i.e., contexts where mate choice is in both directions, where males and females evaluate one another and act on shared preferences).

Unlike many other animals, human mate choice is almost always bidirectional; both females and males must invest efforts into attracting potential mates and compete with members of the same sex for access to those mates. Bidirectional mate choice is a product of the high investment (both obligate and facultative) typically provided by both mothers *and* fathers to human offspring. In other words, because successfully raising human offspring usually involves investment from both the sexes, there is a higher level of bidirectional mate choice than in species where offspring investment is typically provided by just one sex. For example, female black grouse (Beehler & Foster, 1988) and bullfrogs (Emlen, 1976) engage in unidirectional evaluation of potential mates, and their chosen mates typically do not invest more in their offspring than fertilization. To optimize the survival and success of human offspring, high levels of investment—and costs associated with poor mate choice—are experienced by both males and females. These similar costs incurred by both sexes, associated with mate choice, have shaped choosiness on the part of both human males and females. In sum, in mating markets where mate choice is bidirectional (like that of humans), we can expect to also observe female competition for high-demand, fit mates (Parker, 1983).

Game Theory Simulations

Game theory has been used in many scientific disciplines (including biology, psychology, and economics) to determine, under extremely simplified and controlled conditions, the outcomes associated with systematically varied parameters in a given environment. In this simulated environment, one can manipulate the information and behaviors available to actors and observe the outcomes (sometimes referred to as "payoffs") contingent on the actors' chosen behavioral strategies (Rasmusen, 1989). A theoretical rationale for female competition for mates—through mate copying, poaching, and retention strategies—can be strengthened through the use of simulation techniques. That is, game theory can provide much-needed insight into the types of environmental constraints that might shape female intrasexual competition in mating contexts. In such an application, the development of female nonindependent mate choice, or females' use of one another as sources of mating-relevant information, was found to rest on the relative costs associated with a female's active mate choice (Pruett-Jones, 1992), the honesty of male signals of genetic fitness (Sirot, 2001), and differential age and mating experience of the females in the population (Stoehr, 1998). Below we explore simulated mating environments wherein females are more likely to engage in mate copying and poaching when evaluating potential mates is a particularly costly endeavor (Pruett-Jones, 1992), when it is possible for males to "fake" their genetic fitness (Sirot, 2001), and when other

females with more mating experience are present in the mating environment (Stoehr, 1998).

In some species (including humans, Guianan cock-of-the-rock birds, pied flycatchers, and sticklebacks) it is advantageous for females to engage in active mate choice, where a mate is not chosen based on attraction in a single encounter but instead multiple possible mates are encountered, compared, and females "actively" dismiss some candidates in favor of others based on their quality relative to the available pool of possible mates (Parker, 1983). Active mate choice—spending valuable time and resources to acquire information about the fitness of available mates in one's environment—is particularly advantageous when mate quality is highly variable (Parker, 1983). In environments where there is considerable variation in quality from one mate to another, the benefits of being choosy (e.g., evaluating and comparing suitors) begin to outweigh the costs (e.g., the time, energy, and potential mates lost to same-sex competitors; Reynolds & Gross, 1990) that are incurred when engaging in this comparative and discriminatory mate choice process. Therefore, active mate choice is favored in human contexts as human mate quality varies greatly from individual to individual, in heritable ways (Gangestad & Buss, 1993). Females in these mating contexts can enjoy genetic benefits, such as greater overall health in any potential offspring produced by a pairing, by engaging in costly active mate choice—even going so far as to sacrifice certain mate preferences, such as a preference for monogamy, in order to acquire a genetically fit mate (Low, 1990). The benefits enjoyed by offspring produced by genetically fit parents, such as an improved ability to fight off pathogens or disease-causing organisms, may justify incurring the costs of active mate choice and polygyny. This strategy of sacrifice for genetic benefits to offspring may very well have contributed to Jackie Kennedy's continued commitment to her ever-unfaithful, presidential partner.

Pruett-Jones (1992) found that an alternative to this direct and active mate search strategy might be favored if actors can utilize some indirect measures of mate qualities, such as the informed choices of other actors. Independent information acquisition for potential mate traits can be quite costly—judging the fitness of mates on the mating market requires an investment of energetic resources, time, a risk of losing a potential mate to a rival, and (in some cases) an increased risk of predation to the actor engaging in independent search (Parker, 1983; Pomiankowski, 1987; Reynolds & Gross,

1990). Pruett-Jones' model illustrates that these cost parameters in a mating environment encourage mate copying: "the greater the costs relative to the benefits of active choice, the greater the proportion of copiers in the population" (p. 1006). Women, relative to men, face a particularly higher cost schedule potential mate assessment because some of the traits in which they are most interested (e.g., social status, access to resources, willingness to devote resources) are more difficult to directly and rapidly assess, as compared to male's differential focus on physical attractiveness. Therefore, women are more likely to engage in mate copying and poaching behavior compared to men, to enjoy the benefits associated with selecting a high-quality mate through genetic and resource contributions, without having to pay the costs associated with direct searching for such a mate.

Sirot (2001) observed what he termed "prudence" in an application of game theory to mate selection and female intrasexual competition. The prudence he observed in a simulated mating environment was female mate copying; finding, surprisingly, that females were more likely to copy the mating choices of other females in the environment even when other, more attractive but *not previously mated* males were available. Potential mates in the environment that have not had any previous partners are a risky choice, given that evidence of their suitability as a partner is limited. Specifically, these potential mates have not emerged as preferred in their mating market. When a female chooses a male as a mate, this indicates to other females that this particular male is desirable enough to have been chosen. The prevalence of female mate copying behavior here can be thought of as a pattern of risk avoidance, wherein females are less likely to select the riskier choice of an unmated partner (Sirot, 2001). The avoidance of this unmated partner in favor of males that have already been chosen by other females might be indicative of a mating strategy that attempts to account for the presence of dishonest or "faked" fitness indicators. If fitness indicators can indeed be faked, then the apparent attractiveness of this unmated male might not be genuinely associated with any direct (i.e., genetic quality such as pathogen resistance) or indirect (i.e., the provision of support and resources to potential offspring) fitness benefits for the female. In this case, the unmated male is the riskier choice, given that he has not successfully courted (or been courted by) other females and his apparent attractiveness might be dishonest. Importantly, when we refer to the attractiveness or appeal of males we are referring to more than just traits that are directly observable, such as physical attractiveness. In fact, women report that other attributes such as a man's ambition and earning potential tend to emerge as more important characteristics than physical attractiveness when evaluating potential mates; men are far more likely to place a premium on their mate's physical attractiveness (Buss, 1989; Buss & Barnes, 1986; Feingold, 1990).

The coevolutionary struggle between males and females, adapting and changing the traits that they prefer in potential mates as well as the traits that they develop to advertise their fitness/desirability to potential mates through sexual selection, has produced both a female preference for traits that are honest signals of genetic fitness and a male penchant for displaying these desired traits *with or without* the associated genetic advantages. According to Trivers (2011), such evolutionary patterns of deceit (e.g., the faking of fitness) and deceit-detection (e.g., the preference for hard-to-fake traits such as facial symmetry) are present when any two organisms have different goals. In the context of human mating, males can feasibly increase their inclusive fitness by pursuing more short-term mating opportunities, whereas females' larger obligatory parental investment impels them to pursue long-term investment. Within this evolutionary conflict, sexual selection can favor the ability of males to develop desired traits *even without* superior genetic fitness. However, it is worth noting that both men and women can facultatively adjust their mating strategies, pursuing long-term and short-term investment opportunities (Buss & Schmitt, 1993).

Specifically, some have posited that certain traits associated with increased attractiveness (such as female breasts and buttocks) are dishonest signals, which exaggerate an individual's fitness to potential mates (in this example, the female's fecundity; Jones, 1996; Low, Alexander, & Noonan, 1987). Faking fitness in human mating markets can arguably be done with increasing ease; for example, beauty-enhancing treatments such as plastic surgery allow human males and females to increase their attractiveness to potential mates while leaving their underlying genetic fitness unchanged (Gallup & Frederick, 2010). (For a more in-depth discussion of female competitive physical enhancement, see chapters in this volume by DelPriore, Prokosch, and Hill and by Johnsen & Geher.)

Importantly, direct physical challenges between same-sex conspecifics competing for access to mates are relatively infrequent in modern human mating markets—compared to the mating markets such as those of ram and deer (Candolin, 2000)—so "faking" is less likely to be punished. As these mechanisms for discouraging social dishonesty are compromised in human mating markets, the cost-benefit evaluation scales of faking genetic fitness are tipped, allowing for the presence of attractive mates who will provide relatively little direct and/or indirect fitness benefits to potential partners. Taken together, human mating markets seem particularly vulnerable to the presence of fakers or cheaters. Due to this vulnerability, female copying and poaching of mates from other females is favored over independent mate choice, which might lead actors to choose deceptively attractive unmated males with low fitness contributing potential. Our conjecture that this vulnerability to faking increases the benefits and likelihood of mate copying and poaching is consistent with Sirot's (2001) findings that female mate copying behavior increases as the reliability of male sexual signals decreases.

Several decision-making models in other domains have found that relying on the behavior of others to make decisions can be favored by evolutionary forces. For example, decisions about where one should forage for food (Boyd & Richerson, 1988), whom one should trust in a social exchange (Valone & Templeton, 2002), whom one can (and cannot) safely challenge to rise in a social hierarchy (Johnsson & Akerman, 1998), and—our current focus—with whom one should mate (Dugatkin, 1996) can benefit from the use of social information (i.e., copying) when individual judgments are inaccurate or it is costly and difficult to improve those judgments. As illustrated above, mate choice judgments can be error-prone due to dishonesty in advertising, and acquiring accurate fitness information about a potential mate can be costly and difficult, given that many fitness cues are not directly observable.

Further, complex mate choice judgments can be made more quickly and accurately when young females can rely on the choices and preferences of older, more experienced and knowledgeable females in the population. By monopolizing on the experiences of other females in the population, "copiers" improve the accuracy of their mate choice judgments by avoiding mating with unfit, low-quality partners. The use of other females in this way is particularly important if a given female decision maker is inexperienced in the "mating game" (Stoehr, 1998). In a simulated environment, Stoehr observed that female intrasexual competition in the form of copying increased as more experienced, older females entered the population and the importance of shortening mate search time increased. Although capitalizing on the experience and careful appraisal processes of others can often be generally advantageous for decision makers in a variety of contexts, this advantage seems to be particularly pronounced when one can rely on the judgment of a more experienced individual. In the mating market, these more experienced females are likely to make better mate choices that are worthy of copying, given the additional time and resources they have invested in sampling, evaluating, and comparing.

How Women Compete for Mates

Theoretical models have provided various contexts in which female intrasexual competition for mates might occur; however, these models do not provide insight into *how* these females might initiate and complete these various competitive tactics. Applications of Bayesian models (Castellano, Cadeddu, & Cermelli, 2012) suggest ways in which females might use socially acquired information to make decisions such as with whom to pursue mating opportunities via mate copying and poaching behaviors.

Suppose that this mating-relevant social information comes in two varieties: (a) information about male status and fitness garnered from observing male intrasexual competition and (b) information about male attractiveness and fitness garnered from observing his interactions with other females. A Bayesian modeling approach to mate assessment and choice suggests that females who engage in mate copying or poaching—therefore acquiring and using information about a prospective mate from his interactions with other receptive females—do not simply use this information in lieu of their own assessments of mate attractiveness (Castellano et al., 2012). In their model expressing how a female might conclude that a given male is "appropriate" as a mate (i.e., $p[A]$), it is suggested that females use their own previous information about the quality of a particular male (i.e., $p[H]$), as well as information about the honesty or value of male sexual signals of fitness (i.e., $p[A|H]$). In sum, this model dictates the probability that a given male is an "appropriate" mate choice based on (a) the amount of evidence about this potential mate available to a female and (b) the perceived value of that evidence.

Importantly, when social information is integrated into this mathematical model, it does not seem to affect a given female's information about that mate *acquired on her own* (i.e., $p[H]$). Instead, information about other females' preferences in a given ecology affects a female's estimated probability that a male is "appropriate." This application of Bayesian modeling suggests that when females engage in intrasexual competitive strategies, such as copying or poaching, they use information gathered from other females to complement—rather than replace—their own, individual judgments (Castellano et al., 2012). This prediction regarding *how* females compete for mates complements the findings of previous models suggesting *when* females compete for mates. For instance, Stoehr's (1998) conclusion that inexperienced decision makers particularly favor mate copying strategies indicates that females continue to collect and use their own information about mates while facultatively supplementing it with information from other females based on the quality of their assessments.

In summary, parental investment theory, sexual selection, and several applications of game theory create a theoretical rationale and a fairly well-defined set of circumstances in which women can experience selection pressures for mate copying, poaching, and retention or guarding behaviors. These phenomena are likely to occur when (a) males and females both contribute high levels of parental investment, creating selection pressures for bidirectional mate choice; (b) there are high costs associated with acquiring fitness information about a potential mate, which can include the information being not directly observable; (c) there is dishonest sexual signaling, which increases the likelihood that an individual might make a mistake when judging a potential mate's fitness on her own; and (d) conspecifics in the population differ in age and mating experience, allowing younger individuals to improve their mating choices by copying or stealing from experienced assessors.

Phylogenetic Evidence

The importance of an evolved mechanism's ability to help solve an adaptive problem can be established, in part, through phylogenetic evidence. In other words, to determine the importance of the use of social information in mating, we can look at the existence of certain problem-solving mechanisms across multiple species. Evolved mechanisms are psychological tools shaped by evolutionary forces (Buss, 1995); here we review evidence suggesting that organisms' capacity to engage in mate copying, poaching, and retention has been advantageous for

several species. Such evidence supports the proliferation of evolved mechanisms through sometimes millions of years of selection pressures and can help to identify sets of similar environmental circumstances that produced parallel behaviors. Female competition through mate copying/poaching and retention efforts is associated with lines of evidence suggesting that these behaviors are indeed the outputs of evolved psychological mechanisms (see Buss, 1995). The significance of female competition for mates is explored through examples of female mate copying, poaching, and retention or guarding behaviors across multiple species, as well as a proposal that these behaviors exhibit certain common characteristics.

Species that exhibit female mate copying behavior include guppies (Dugatkin, 1996; Dugatkin & Godin, 1993), birds (Hoglund, Alatalo, & Lundberg, 1990; Stoehr, 1998), bats (Parker, 1983), rats (Galef, Lim, & Gilbert, 2008), and even some species of invertebrates (Mery et al., 2009). This cross-species evidence of female mate copying indicates that competitive female behavior likely has been a feature of the environment for a large part of evolutionary history and has been a long-standing selection pressure. It should be noted that in the available animal behavior literature, there is little distinction between mate copying and mate poaching. It is likely that this lack of a distinction is due to the fact that mate copying in these species generally involves sequential mating with a male who had previously mated with another individual. This pattern is almost entirely seen in low paternal investment species where poaching and copying are essentially the same, because the males do not stay "mated" past conception.

In one of the first demonstrations of female mate copying behavior in the laboratory, Dugatkin and Godin (1992) observed female guppies' preference for males they had observed courting other females over males that had not courted other females in their environment. In general, female guppies prefer brightly colored males—an indication of genetic fitness. When placed in a container and allowed to observe courting behavior between a male and female, and to also observe a slightly brighter colored male but without any female sexual interest, observer females later spent much more time with the less brightly colored, previously chosen male. This preference for mated males was observed even when the locations of the chosen and not-chosen males were reversed, indicating that female guppies attend to, and remember, the mating choices of other females in their environment (as opposed to remembering preferred locations). By systematically varying the male that was courting the female, Dugatkin (1996) demonstrated that these females were not simply making the same mate choices on their own. In these cases, the observing female demonstrated a preference for the courted male in 85% of pairings (Dugatkin, 1996).

Further investigations of female intrasexual competition via mate copying behavior in the guppy (Dugatkin, 1996, 1998) found that when sufficient social information is available to a female, these observed preferences will outweigh other traits that have been found to signal male fitness. Specifically, when female guppies observe courting behavior between a single female and a 40% more dully colored male (less attractive, by guppy standards), observers will ignore the preferences of this female and elect to spend more time with the brighter, unmated male. However, when *multiple* females are courted by a less attractive male, observers will ignore brighter, more attractive males to pursue mating opportunities with mated males (Dugatkin, 1998). Applications of game theory (Sirot, 2001) have similarly demonstrated how powerful the preferences of other females can be in mating contexts, finding that female actors in simulated environments will still copy the mating choices of other females even when doing so necessitates passing over more attractive but not previously mated males. Dugatkin's work suggests that the strength of the social information contributes to how likely females are to ignore direct male sexual signals of fitness.

The fundamental adaptive nature of female mate copying behavior is exemplified by evidence of this intrasexually competitive behavior in a relatively simple invertebrate organism. When young, inexperienced female flies were allowed to observe interactions between male and female flies, they later used this information to inform mating decisions (Mery et al., 2009). Female observers were found to spend more time near males who were previously paired with females than those who were presented alone, even if these previously mated males were of poorer quality (Mery et al., 2009). Specifically, the quality and attractiveness of the males was manipulated across two independent experiments by varying the quality of the food and nutrients provided to the males as well as their coloring. Female flies were observed spending more time near the males they had seen other females with, even when these males were provided poorer nutrition or were dusted with a less attractive color (Mery et al., 2009).

It seems that socially acquired information about mates—through the behaviors of other females—can affect the preferences of female flies (Mery et al., 2009) as well as guppies (Dugatkin, 1998) more strongly than direct male signals of fitness that can be assessed independently, such as the size and color of the potential mate. It is likely that the ability of males to fake, or dishonestly display, signals of fitness has driven females of multiple species to rely more heavily on other females as a source of information about male quality than on an individual male's apparent attractiveness. This apparent attractiveness assessed by the individual female can be operationalized as physical attractiveness or as other mating-relevant traits, such as dominance and wealth. As Sirot's (2001) application of game theory demonstrated, female mate copying might be a solution to (and therefore should increase with) the unreliability of male sexual signals. Copying or poaching the choices of other females, even if these choices appear to be flawed based on low apparent male attractiveness, enables females to avoid making the costly mistake of mating with a male that will provide little direct or indirect fitness benefits to her and any offspring that they might produce.

In field research, Hoglund et al. (1990) observed female mate copying behavior in black grouse leks. Leks are a mating market that occurs in many species of animals that are characterized by unidirectional mate choice and are composed of several males that aggregate to engage in mating displays and intrasexual competition for access to females. Hoglund et al. recorded the patterns of female arrival and copulation at a lek in Finland, finding that females visited the lek, made mate choice decisions, and were physically dispersed in nonrandom ways. Natural female mate copying in birds was observed, showing that females were likely to land close to one another on their multiple visits to the lek, apparently to better observe the mating preferences of one another. Specifically, young, inexperienced females were more likely to mate copy and poach—making an average of three days of additional observations of other females' mating choices compared to females that were one year old or older (Hoglund et al., 1990). These observations of female intrasexual competition from natural bird mating behaviors mirror the conclusions of Stoehr's (1998) simulated mating environment. In Stoehr's simulation, female mate copying increased along with the number of older, more experienced females in the environment. Taken together, it appears that using the costly acquired preferences of other females in a mating market is particularly advantageous for relatively inexperienced females. When older, more experienced females are present, younger females have much more to gain by copying, and even poaching, chosen mates; this time and effort that older females have invested in actively evaluating, comparing, and selectively dismissing available males has likely improved their ability to identify higher-quality mates.

In some mating contexts, females might be able to copy the mate choices of other females without directly observing their courting behaviors. For example, female hammer-headed bats display preferences for males who have been previously chosen by other females, but these females do not travel together to visit leks of advertising males. This mate copying behavior suggests that these female bats—unlike the female black grouses—are not acquiring social information about mates from close physical proximity and visual observations. Parker (1983) suggests that these females are instead attending to the vocal emissions of recently mated females. Since female hammer-headed bats do not visit leks together, it is likely that mate copying in these contexts is facilitated through the use of the calls of other females emitted after copulation to gather information relevant to male mate quality (Parker, 1983). This auditory information can then be used to preferentially seek out males that have been recently chosen by other females.

Another example of female mate choice copying without an opportunity to directly observe the mate choices of other females is in the Norwegian rat. Galef et al. (2008) found that female rats use chemosignaling (rather than vocalizations like that of the female hammer-headed bat) to acquire social information regarding the mate choices of other females. When placed in a cage with a male that had recently mated with another female and a male that had not recently mated, female rats spent significantly more time on the side of the cage where the recently mated male was placed and were more likely to allow a recently mated male to copulate with them. However, this preference for recently mated males was not observed when these males were kept behind Plexiglas or when these males were recently paired with nonreceptive females (Galef et al., 2008). This lack of preference for mated males when the transmission of scent is prevented or manipulated suggests that chemical (rather than visual) signals are used in female rat mate copying

behavior—and that *sexual* contact with another female, rather than nonsexual contact and proximity to another female, is necessary for females to exhibit a preference for previously chosen males. In some similar ways, human females have opportunities to acquire socially learned mate preferences through different mediums; women display greater attraction to men who are visually pictured with other (physically attractive) women (Waynforth, 2007) or men who are simply described as having a significant other (Eva & Wood, 2006). Evidence of human mate copying in the form of women's preference for men who have already been chosen as mates has been termed the "wedding ring effect" (Knight, 2000) and has received mixed support (Uller & Johansson, 2003). It is possible that mixed findings regarding the appeal of men associated with other women reflects somewhat diminishing returns; men who have had previous partners and are seen with attractive women are likely to possess desirable traits that attract them; however, men who are engaged or married may pose too great a risk to pursue (Uller & Johansson, 2003). Indeed, when presented with men described as "dating" (Waynforth, 2007) or featured with other women in the absence of relationship commitment information (Graziano, Jensen-Campbell, Shebilske, & Lundgren, 1993), women have been found to exhibit mate copying behavior.

Given these demonstrations of females' marked attraction to previously mated males, it is thus advantageous for females of various species to respond defensively with mate retention or guarding efforts if there is any risk of the dispersal of male fitness contributions to other females and offspring. For some of the above species (e.g., guppies, flies), there is no male investment after copulation, so the issue of mate retention (as well as the distinction between mate copying and mate poaching, as noted earlier in this section) is moot. Some species of mammals and birds, though, do have significant male postcopulatory investment and have been studied with regard to females' behaviors that might decrease the likelihood that other interested parties will poach their chosen mates. Although the majority of empirical work relevant to mate retention behaviors focuses on male mate guarding of females (as the sex with higher obligatory parental investment), females have a toolbox of strategies to dissuade their mates from straying. Females of several species, including certain birds (such as the starling; Eens & Pinxten, 1995) and humans (Buss, 2002), have been found to use sexual contact to keep their mates from other females. Females' use of "sexual inducement" (Buss, 2002) to retain their mates actually helps to resolve the apparent puzzle posed by observed copulation initiated by starling females even after male fertilization and egg laying. Eens and Pinxten observed that females were likely to court males—who often refused their sexual advances—who were signaling to attract other females. Similar to the starling, women are more likely than men to use their own attractiveness and solicitations to retain their mates in the presence of jealousy-inducing cues (Buss, 2002). Observed (Eens & Pinxten, 1995) and reported (Buss, 2002) use of sexual contact to protect one's relationship from same-sex competitors suggests that these females are engaging in copulation solicitation, not for copulation's sake but to disrupt their mate's efforts to attract other females.

Psychological Evidence

According to Buss (1995), a claim that a behavior is the result of an evolved psychological mechanism can be supported if the behavior solved a problem related to survival and/or reproduction in the environment of evolutionary adaptedness, a behavior and its underlying mechanism are specific to that situation, and it is only expressed in response to certain input from the environment. Our proposed psychological mechanism driving mate copying and poaching behaviors—attraction to mated or previously mated males—does alleviate certain adaptive problems associated with costly mate search such as the considerable investment of time and resources as well as an increased risk of predation. Further, attraction to mated or previously mated males alleviates some problems associated with bad mating choices such as choosing a mate that provides little direct or indirect fitness benefits (Pruett-Jones, 1992; Sirot, 2001). The psychological evidence, then, needs to clearly delineate the specificity of the eliciting environmental situations and resulting behaviors associated with mate copying, mate poaching, and mate retention.

Emotions as Regulators

The fitness advantages for an individual demonstrating mate copying (and, we presume, mate poaching) can produce empirically observed patterns of preference for males simply pictured with other females (Eva & Wood, 2006), for males who have had multiple previous mates, as well as for males with a current partner (e.g., candidates for mate poaching tactics; Place, Todd, Penke, & Asendorpf, 2010) without any conscious deliberation as to

the underlying logic of this preference. It is worth noting, however, that the relationship between a man's number of previous mates and his attractiveness appears to be nonlinear; specifically, having had more romantic partners only *initially* increases men's reported appeal (Kenrick, Sundie, Nicastle, & Stone, 2001). In the above theoretical arguments, the proposed aspects of the environment that favor mate copying behavior can operate through the psychological force of *attraction*. Thus, it is not necessary to propose that actors are explicitly aware of the process or logic of copying the mating decisions of other females to avoid costly searches/mistakes or to monopolize on expertise—even though it seems clear that these are reasons that mate copying has been propagated through generations and across species. Like other mating behaviors, such as increased sexual activity during times of peak fertility, conscious awareness of the adaptively significant forces at work is not necessary to produce the sexually selected behaviors. Mate copying and mate poaching can simply be experienced as the up-regulation and down-regulation of attraction to particular target groups or target individuals. In other words, changes in feelings of attraction to mated or preferred types of mates are proposed to underlie both mate copying and mate poaching behaviors.

Mate retention and guarding may also be regulated to some extent by feelings of not only attraction but also jealousy. The experience of jealousy within relationships has been an active topic of research for several years (e.g., Buss, Larsen, Westen, & Semelroth, 1992, and resulting follow-up research). Given that feelings of attraction and jealousy are specifically cued by adaptively relevant stimuli that would have been present in the environment of evolutionary adaptedness, such as the presence of other females (Waynforth, 2007) and a mate spending additional time away from his current partner (Schützwohl, 2005), there is a well-developed framework to support our proposal that mate copying, poaching (via attraction), and retention efforts (via jealousy) are the products of evolved psychological mechanisms that exert their influence, at least in part, through emotional reactions.

Mate Copying Versus Mate Poaching

As noted previously, the distinction between mate copying and mate poaching is not useful in species that have little or no male parental investment. Poaching of a male mate is immaterial when the male's reproductive job is done after copulation (leaving aside the narrow window of interference with the actual copulation). With the high level of facultative paternal investment in humans, though, the copying/poaching distinction becomes much more important. Information is free, and since mate copying involves only the use of information from others, we should expect copying to be tolerated—perhaps even appreciated—by other females. Mate poaching, though, entails very real and significant costs to the female being poached, and so we should expect to see a sharp demarcation between copying and poaching within female intrasexual competition. Thus, although many of the theoretical factors that have shaped mate copying behaviors logically extend to mate poaching behaviors, we can expect them to be psychologically treated very differently.

Under what circumstances would we expect human mate poaching rather than copying? Generally, copying is useful if there are alternative males of similar quality and easily identifiable as such (e.g., perhaps they are in the same family, company, or fraternity as the template male, and signaling of mate quality is fairly honest). Copying can also occur if the male in question was previously mated but no longer is in that earlier relationship. Poaching becomes more likely as the evaluating female does not perceive that there are any other additional mates of similar quality, either because they are not easily perceivable or because they do not exist. And, of course, as the circumstances that promote mate poaching become more prevalent, we should also expect that reactionary mate retention and mate guarding behaviors will increase as well, to the extent that the already mated female similarly perceives these circumstances.

Mate Copying Versus Normative Influence

Another distinction is merited here, specifically delineating female *mate copying* and *social conformity* mechanisms. One could argue that the present claims regarding female intrasexual competition, via mate copying and poaching as a mate choice strategy, could instead be regarded as simply a behavioral outcome of normative influence. In other words, how can we be certain that the mate copying behaviors we observe are not mate copying but merely a specific example of a more general tendency toward social conformity? Fortunately, experimental evidence exists that enables us to distinguish mate copying from general conformity.

Dunn and Doria (2010) were able to, across two experiments, demonstrate both mate copying and conformity behaviors as evidenced in attractiveness ratings of opposite-sex targets. In their first experiment, females, but not males, perceived opposite-sex targets as more attractive when they were featured with other same-sex models feigning sexual interest. That is, in humans, as is the case in many other species with higher obligatory female parental investment, mate copying seems to be a specifically female mate choice tactic. However, normative influence on attractiveness ratings demonstrated no such sex specificity. In their second experiment, Dunn and Doria found that both male and female attractiveness ratings were inflated by verbal accounts of model attractiveness supposedly made by other participants. When told that other participants perceived a given model as attractive, both males and females tended to conform (by increasing their own attractiveness ratings of the model). Thus, although more research is certainly needed to better establish the specificity of mate copying as a psychological process, the existing evidence supports the claim of mate copying as a specific mechanism rather than part of a larger norm of conformity.

Summary

Several immediately testable hypotheses about the nature of human mate copying and mate poaching remain to be evaluated. We would expect that female mate copying and poaching will be more common in situations where there are males producing unreliable and/or dishonest signals of valued traits (e.g., status, resources). We also expect that the value and utilization of this social information—for copying and poaching purposes—should be highest for young, inexperienced females that are of reproductive age. Although it is clearly the case in other animals (e.g., Dugatkin, 1996, 1998), it remains to be seen if strong social information can override other, direct cues within a mate copying context. In fact, mathematical models suggest that social information is not used as an alternative but instead as a supplement to direct cues of attractiveness.

Both mate poaching and—to a lesser extent—mate copying have been studied in humans, but there has been little integration of the two research streams beyond a common evolutionary focus. We expect that mate poaching will occur in more circumscribed contexts, where fewer reproductively viable mates are available. Further, we predict that mate poaching will be associated with more anxiety on the part of the perpetrator given the social disapproval associated with this particular mating strategy (Schmitt, 2004). We also expect that mate poaching will elicit much stronger and more negative reactions from the partner of the person being targeted, compared to reactions elicited by the use of mate copying strategies. Indeed, the relevant research indicates that people tend to *not* engage in mate poaching if there is an available alternative mate of similar quality (Davies, Schackelford, & Hass, 2010) and if they are already in a relationship (Parker & Burkley, 2009).

Research on mate retention and mate guarding enjoys a somewhat larger research foundation; there is even an instrument for assessing the occurrence of various common mate retention behaviors (Buss, Shackelford, & McKibbin, 2008). This literature is almost entirely focused on male retention and guarding behaviors regarding their female partners. It is possible that this bias reflects patterns of parental investment in mammals, in which females are more likely to provide more offspring care, are therefore regarded as the more valuable sex on the mating market, and are therefore more likely to be guarded once "acquired." We believe that some of these findings, however, may generalize across both men and women. For example, Starratt, Shackelford, Goetz, and McKibbin (2007) found that men adjust their mate retention behaviors in response to their perceived risk of partner infidelity, so it is possible that women make a similar adjustment. The actual evidence on this has not been collected, however. What we do know about women's mate retention behaviors is that, relative to men's behaviors, they tend to be calibrated with their partner's income and status striving and that the retention tactics used tend to focus more (relative to male tactics) on enhancing their own physical appearance (Buss & Shackelford, 1997). Last, the emotions associated with mate retention and mate guarding (as well as with mate copying and mate poaching) are underresearched. If the lyrics of popular music are any indication, there are some rich and powerful emotional concomitants of these situations (Fisher & Candea, 2012).

Cross-cultural Evidence

Cross-cultural examinations of female intrasexual competitive behaviors can help us to identify candidate aspects of human ecology that might make mate copying, poaching, or retention behaviors more (or less) likely to occur. It is possible, for example, that these social strategies of mate choice might depend on the amount of independent mate choice (compared to kin-based arrangements of relationships) that exists within a particular cultural

setting. We predict that less female intrasexual competition for mates might be observed in cultures where arranged marriages dominate the mating marketplace, and therefore mate choice has been transferred from the individual to his/her kin. Various social norms might also constrain the incidence of mate poaching behaviors to human ecologies that are more tolerant of divorce and polygyny. Indeed, certain general mate preferences have been demonstrated to vary culturally. For example, culture likely influences waist-to-hip ratio preferences (Yu & Shepard, 1998), and resource scarcity seems to influence male preferences for female body size (Swami & Tovée, 2005, 2006). In response to relative resource scarcity or unreliability, males and females shift their mate preferences to accept larger body sizes, as more plentiful fat deposits signal an improved ability to survive and reproduce in harsh environments.

Like many adaptations, mate copying, poaching, and retention strategies more effectively increase reproductive success to the extent that they are sensitive to the demands, constraints, and aspects of the environment in which they occur. Female guppies demonstrate such sensitivity to ecological constraints in their use of mate copying tactics, with well-fed female guppies being significantly more likely to copy the mate choices of other females compared to hungry female guppies (Dugatkin & Godin, 1998. However, some invariance of mate copying behavior in female guppies has also been demonstrated, such as the finding that the presence of a predator had no affect on the frequency of female mate choice copying (Briggs et al., 1996). These mixed findings suggest that women might differentially employ mate copying strategies based on the availability of resources and the presence of stressors or threats in the environment. To understand the extent that women engage differentially in these mating tactics as a result of their cultural and ecological environment, evidence will need to be collected.

Surprisingly, evidence for cultural variation (or invariance) in the incidence of female mate copying has not yet been gathered in human populations, to our knowledge. Certain possibilities for cultural variance in female mate copying exist to the extent that there are cultural differences in the amount of independent mate choice that is allowed; indeed, in many contemporary cultures, gender roles are likely maintained by kin choice of female marriage partners (Talbani & Hasanali, 2000). Further, female mate copying has been proposed as a powerful avenue of cultural transmission, and therefore possible cultural variation, in mating preferences and practices (Yu & Shepard, 1998). Copying the mating preferences and choices of women in one's environment, therefore within a particular culture and extrapolated across several generations, might produce overall cultural differences in mating behaviors. However, since human females have faced specific challenges across their adaptive history regarding the securing of male resource and fitness contributions, female mate choice copying might simply serve as a low-cost opportunity to select for similar, culturally invariant indicators of male fitness (Waynforth, 2007). As Waynforth postulates, "copying patterns may reflect female mate-choice requirements that transcend cultures, such as the need for male investment in offspring. In other words, there is no need to invoke culture or cultural transmission to explain some aspects of mate choice copying in human females" (p. 269). The common needs that women share on the mating market might foster cultural invariance in some dimensions of mate preferences and mate choice tactics, such as those that implicate female intrasexual competition. It is possible that similar preferences for mates observed across females from different cultures, such as a preference for social status and earning potential (Buss, 1989), have been passed down not through similar cultural and social standards but rather based on similar needs in a romantic relationship that are shared by all women.

Fairly comprehensive evidence shows that mate poaching occurs across a wide array of cultures (Schmitt, 2004; Schmitt & Shackelford, 2008). The levels of mate poaching vary across regions, as do the relative prevalence rates of poaching for men and for women (women are more likely to engage in mate poaching behavior in more gender-egalitarian cultures; Schmitt, 2004). In addition, certain personality traits are significantly associated with both perpetrating mate poaching and being successfully poached, with extraversion being one of the stronger correlates (Schmitt & Buss, 2001). Schmitt points out that sensitivity of mate poaching tactics to ecological constraints is predicted by *sexual pluralism theory* (Gangestad & Simpson, 2000), which explains that humans shift their mating behaviors and preferences in a way that optimally fits with their environment.

An ecological factor that has been previously demonstrated to orchestrate reliable differences in mate preferences, *resource scarcity* or *environment harshness* (Swami & Tovée, 2005, 2006), might facilitate differential patterns of female mate poaching. Schmitt's (2004) findings suggest that, consistent with sexual pluralism theory, females in environments characterized by greater resource scarcity and harshness were less likely to poach males from other females. In these contexts, the importance of male (and female) investment in offspring survival and success is prioritized; therefore mating tactics that favor the dispersal of male resources among several females and their offspring are abandoned. In harsh and unpredictable environments, individuals cannot "afford" to adopt mating strategies that disperse already-scarce resources among multiple mates and families. Females' mate poaching tactics appear to be particularly sensitive to resource scarcity compared to males; females' attempts and experiences with mate poaching decrease dramatically in harsh environments, whereas female and male mate poaching frequency is quite similar in resource-rich environments (Schmitt, 2004).

Another ecological factor that might affect females' willingness to poach mates from other females is the *operational sex ratio*, which refers to the proportion of males and females of reproductive age in a given mating environment. In a female-disadvantaged mating market, where males are scarce, it would be advantageous for females to increase their willingness to poach fit mates from other females; doing so will increase their likelihood of securing a desirable male mate in an environment with a high proportion of females. (For more information on the operational, see chapters in this volume by Dillon, Adair, & Brase and by Stone.) Schmitt (2004) found that women's mate poaching strategies were sensitive to the sex ratio of their ecology. In female-disadvantaged mating markets, women were more likely to attempt to poach men from their female romantic partners. Surprisingly, this increased willingness to poach when members of the opposite sex are scarce was observed only in women (Schmitt, 2004). Taken together, it seems that women's use of mate poaching tactics is contextually, or culturally, sensitive. For example, women might be less likely to engage in mate poaching within cultures in which marriages are arranged by an individual's kin, as well as cultures characterized by greater gender inequality (Schmitt, 2004). Further, resource scarcity and the relative number of males in a given ecology seem to be important forces in shaping women's use of mate poaching strategies (Schmitt, 2004).

Jealousy Across Cultures

The emotional component of the evolved psychological mechanism proposed to produce mate retention behaviors—jealousy—has been found to exhibit culturally stable patterns. Given that, per parental investment theory, females have more to lose when males form emotional commitments to rival females (which increases the likelihood that these males will divert and distribute their resources from their primary mate), females are expected to be particularly sensitive and averse to male cues of emotional infidelity and more likely to respond with the adoption of mate retention tactics. It is possible that cultural variations in acceptance of extra-pair sexual encounters (i.e., cheating) might produce shifts in female jealousy and mate retention. In other words, cultural norms relevant to mating might affect female's feelings of jealousy when confronted with infidelity, as well as their willingness to adopt mate retention strategies and discourage extra-pair relationships. However, accounts of distress women report regarding emotional and sexual commitments to rival females in more strictly monogamous cultures (such as American culture) and more sexually "relaxed" and extra-pair affair-tolerant cultures (such as German and Dutch) were strikingly similar (Buunk et al., 1996). Regardless of their culture's tolerance of extra-pair commitments, women consistently reported greater distress when confronted with a male partner's emotional commitment to, compared to sexual involvement with, a rival female (Buunk et al., 1996).

Demonstrations of cultural invariance in behaviors, and thereby indications of species-typical psychological mechanisms, have been evidence in support of the importance of evolutionary forces (selection pressures along with advantages in survival and reproduction), rather than social, proximate influences, in producing phenomena. However, such "nature versus nurture" divisions often obscure the complex, interactive, and inseparable relationship that ultimate (i.e., evolutionary) and proximate mechanisms have with one another when producing behavioral and psychological mechanisms. Therefore, cross-cultural investigations of female intrasexual competitive behaviors might provide insight into the specific ways that adaptations for female mate poaching efforts are context specific and even suggest aspects of an individual's ecology that influence female use of mate poaching efforts. Whereas preliminary evidence suggests that female jealousy and mate retention are somewhat culturally invariant, female mate poaching seems to shift in order to produce optimal mating strategies in response to environment harshness and operational sex ratio. The flexibility of women's intrasexually competitive strategies offers an advantage to women on the mating market—an ability to acquire and use information about one's environment to produce more optimal mating strategies.

Developmental Evidence

Some evidence for context-specificity in human mating strategies indicates that female mate poaching behaviors are sensitive to environment harshness and operational sex ratio (Schmitt, 2004). Life history theory can be applied to explain such context-specific adjustment of mating strategies in response to cues of environment harshness and resource availability.

According to life history theory, organisms can adjust their allocation of limited resources to somatic, reproductive, and parenting efforts, and an accumulating body of evidence indicates that this adjustment is calibrated by the level of harshness and instability of an organism's early environment (Kaplan & Gangestad, 2005). Specifically, organisms in resource-rich environments can adopt "slow" life history strategies, in which they produce fewer offspring and invest more resources in their success. In such situations, parenthood can often be delayed in order to increase one's social standing and resources for family care. Alternatively, in harsh environments characterized by variable availability of resources and high mortality, a "fast" life history strategy is favored; in this case, organisms invest heavily into reproductive efforts, producing many offspring and investing relatively little in their individual success (Kaplan & Gangestad, 2005). Indeed, experiences in early development, such as the presence or absence of paternal investment and socioeconomic status, have been found to affect sexual debut, onset of menstruation (Ellis & Essex, 2007), and age of first birth in human females (Brumbach, Figueredo, & Ellis, 2009; Miller, Benson, & Galbraith, 2001). These observed differences based on parental investment and resource abundance suggest that aspects of one's environment in *early development* might set certain competitive strategies in motion.

Some phenotypic evidence suggests that life history strategy might affect females' ability and willingness to use mate copying and poaching strategies; specifically, female guppies tend to rely on mate copying tactics when resources are abundant

(Dugatkin & Godin, 1998). Contrary to their predictions, Dugatkin and Godin found that it was the well-fed guppies that were using same-sex conspecifics for mate quality information, compared to hungry guppies. This finding indicates that the use of socially acquired information to make mate choice decisions might not be a fast and frugal strategy preferentially employed by those with little resources and minimal time to spare (i.e., those with fast life history strategies). One possible way to accommodate this surprising finding is that it might be due to the computational use of social information described by Bayesian modeling, that is, that females are not relying on other females' judgments *in lieu* of their own, but in *addition to* their own assessments of male attractiveness (Castellano et al., 2012). Although the relationship between early environment harshness and the incidence of female mate copying has yet to be explored in the human mating literature, phenotypic and mathematical modeling evidence suggests that mate copying behaviors might be used by those employing slow life history strategies, who have the time and resources to integrate both socially and personally acquired information to inform their mating decisions.

Other Potential Lines of Evidence

Schmitt and Pilcher (2004) suggest that the existence of an evolved trait can be supported by multiple lines of evidence, and several such lines—theoretical, phylogenetic, psychological, and cross-cultural—have been discussed in the preceding sections. Other types of evidence could potentially be brought to bear, but they have not yet been explored. For instance, are there neurological foundations for the psychological mechanisms that enable mate copying, mate poaching, and mate retention? This type of evidence could be revealed via studies of functional neuroanatomy (e.g., fMRI, PET scans), by documenting lesion case studies that are theoretically possible (e.g., individuals who are unable to use social information as part of their mate evaluations), or by identifying hormonal influences on mate copying, mate poaching, and mate retention behaviors. This is an area ripe for future work. Hormonal shifts have already been linked to several mating-relevant behaviors, such as an individual's willingness to engage in extra-pair relationships (Pillsworth & Haselton, 2006), an individual's preferences for certain mating-relevant traits (Gangestad, Thornhill, & Garver-Apgar, 2005), as well as the likelihood of employing mate retention strategies, including affirmations of love and commitment (Pillsworth & Haselton, 2006).

Although more research in this area is needed, recent work does suggest that hormonal states are a potentially viable avenue for proximate mechanisms that regulate mating strategies. Welling, Puts, Roberts, Little, and Burriss (2012) found that the use of hormonal contraceptives altered, among other things, mate retention behaviors. Heterosexual women who were using hormonal contraceptives reported using mate retention tactics more frequently than nonhormonal-contraceptive-using women. Interestingly, this result was specific to partner-directed behaviors (i.e., intersexual competition) rather than intrasexual competition, and the strength of the effect was related to the dosage level of synthetic estradiol. Among noncontraceptive-using women (i.e., free cycling), being near ovulation produced subtle but reliable changes in feelings and behaviors (e.g., feeling more attractive, being more interested in going out to social gatherings; Haselton & Gangestad, 2006). These ovulatory phase-related changes were also attended by, among other things, increases in mate guarding by male partners (Haselton & Gangestad, 2006).

Summary

From the infamous love triangle between Jackie Kennedy, John F. Kennedy, and Marilyn Monroe, to guppies, birds, bats, and flies, we have explored the prevalence and incidence of female intrasexual competition, specifically proposing *why* females compete with one another for access to fit mates, *under what conditions* female intrasexual competition is particularly likely to occur, and *how* females compete with one another on the mating market. Like Marilyn Monroe, we found that females—of species where both maternal and paternal investment is costly—are likely to compete with other females for access to high-quality mates. When considerable male and female investment in offspring is necessary for offspring survival and success, it is advantageous for both sexes to actively assess and compare multiple suitors when making a mate choice decision. In these contexts, females are impelled to compete with one another to win the affections of highly sought-after mates.

This female intrasexual competition for mates is one of the key components that sets the stage for phenomena such as mate copying, mate poaching, and mate retention/guarding behaviors in reaction to the presence of perceived relationship threats. Mate copying and poaching is particularly advantageous when information about potential mates is costly to acquire or potentially unreliable, or when females have not had much experience making such assessments. When these particular environmental attributes are present, females can decrease the costs of acquiring difficult-to-assess fitness information, as well as the risks of making a "bad" choice, by relying on the information manifested by the behaviors of other females. Indeed, the affect of other females' mating preferences can be so strong that some females will display a preference for *less attractive* males given that a sufficient amount of attention from other females is present. This reliance on the judgments of other females can extend even to attempts to steal spoken-for mates, a phenomenon that seems to be associated with harsh environments and environments in which relatively few high-quality, available males are present.

Taken together, a fairly clear picture is developing in the literature that shows how female intrasexual competition in mating contexts, as observed in an array of species, has produced psychological adaptations for using the mating behaviors of conspecific females as information that feeds into individual female mating decisions. Under particular conditions (e.g., expensive search, deceptive signals, lack of knowledge), females can improve their mate choice decisions by using one another as sources of information. Female decision makers can use such information from their social environment to determine if they should copy the preferences of other females, attempt to steal mated males, and/or aggressively defend their chosen partners.

References

Andersson, M. (1994). *Sexual selection*. Princeton, NJ: Princeton University Press.

Beehler, B. M., & Foster, M. S. (1988). Hotshots, hotspots, and female preference in the organization of lek mating systems. *American Naturalist, 131*, 203–219.

Betzig, L. (1989). Causes of conjugal dissolution: A cross-cultural study. *Current Anthropology, 30*, 654–676.

Boyd, R., & Richerson, P. J. (1988). An evolutionary model of social learning: The effects of spatial and temporal variation. In T. Zentall & B. G. Galef Jr. (Eds.) *Social learning: Psychological and biological perspectives* (pp. 29–43). Hillsdale, NJ: Erlbaum.

Briggs, S. E., Godin, J. G. J., & Dugatkin, L. A. (1996). Mate-choice copying under predation risk in the Trinidadian guppy (*Poecilia reticulata*). *Behavioral Ecology, 7*, 151–157.

Brumbach, B. H., Figueredo, A. J., & Ellis, B. J. (2009). Effects of harsh and unpredictable environments in adolescence on development of life history strategies. *Human Nature, 20*, 25–51.

Buss, D. M. (1985). Human mate selection: Opposites are sometimes said to attract, but in fact we are likely to marry someone who is similar to us in almost every variable. *American Scientist, 73*, 47–51.

Buss, D. M. (1989). Sex differences in human mate preferences: Evolutionary hypotheses tested in 37 cultures. *Behavioral and Brain Sciences, 12*, 1–49.

Buss, D. M. (1995). Evolutionary psychology: A new paradigm for psychological science. *Psychological Inquiry, 6*, 1–30.

Buss, D. M. (2002). Human mate guarding. *Neuroendocrinology Letters, 23*, 23–29.

Buss, D. M., & Barnes, M. (1986). Preferences in human mate selection. *Journal of Personality and Social Psychology, 50*, 559–570.

Buss, D. M., Larsen, R. J., Westen, D., & Semmelroth, J. (1992). Sex differences in jealousy: Evolution physiology, and psychology. *Psychological Science, 3*, 251–255.

Buss, D. M., & Schmitt, D. P. (1993). Sexual strategies theory: an evolutionary perspective on human mating. *Psychological Review, 100*, 204–232.

Buss, D. M., & Shackelford, T. K. (1997). From vigilance to violence: mate retention tactics in married couples. *Journal of Personality and Social Psychology, 72*, 346.

Buss, D. M., Shackelford, T. K., & McKibbin, W. F. (2008). The Mate Retention Inventory–Short Form (MRI-SF). *Personality and Individual Differences, 44*, 322–334.

Buunk, B. P., Angleitner, A., Oubaid, V., & Buss, D. M. (1996). Sex differences in jealousy in evolutionary and cultural perspective: Tests from the Netherlands, Germany, and the United States. *Psychological Science, 7*, 359–363.

Candolin, U. (2000). Increased signaling effort when survival prospects decrease: male–male competition ensures honesty. *Animal Behavior, 60*, 417–422.

Castellano, S., Cadeddu, G., & Cermelli, P. (2012). Computational mate choice: Theory and empirical evidence. *Behavioural Processes, 90*, 261–277.

Davies, A. P. C., Shackelford, T. K., & Hass, R. G. (2010). Sex differences in perceptions of benefits and costs of mate poaching. *Personality and Individual Differences, 49*, 441–445.

DelPriore, D., Hill, S., & Prokosch, M. (in press). The causes and consequences of women's competitive beautification. In M. L. Fisher (Eds.), *Oxford handbook of women and competition*. New York: Oxford University Press.

Dillon, H. M., Adair, L. E., Wang, Z., & Johnson, Z. (2013). Slow and steady wins the race: Life history, mate value, and mate settling. *Personality and Individual Differences, 55*, 612–618.

Dugatkin, L. A. (1996). Copying and mate choice. In C. M. Heyes & B. G. Galef (Eds.), *Social learning in animals: The roots of culture* (pp. 85–105). San Diego, CA: Academic Press.

Dugatkin, L. A. (1998). Genes, copying, and female mate choice: shifting thresholds. *Behavioral Ecology, 9*, 323–327.

Dugatkin, L. A., & Godin, J. G. J. (1992). Reversal of female mate choice by copying in the guppy (*Poecilia reticulata*). *Proceedings of the Royal Society of London, Series B: Biological Sciences, 249*, 179–184.

Dugatkin, L. A., & Godin, J. G. J. (1993). Female mate copying in the guppy (Poecilia reticulata): Age-dependent effects. *Behavioral Ecology, 4*, 289–292.

Dugatkin, L. A., & Godin, J. G. J. (1998). Effects of hunger on mate-choice copying in the guppy. *Ethology, 104*, 194–202.

Dunn, M. J., & Doria, M. V. (2010). Simulated attraction increases opposite sex attractiveness ratings in females but not males. *Journal of Social, Evolutionary, and Cultural Psychology, 4*, 1–17.

Eens, M., & Pinxten, R. (1995). Inter-sexual conflicts over copulations in the European starling: Evidence for the female mate-guarding hypothesis. *Behavioral Ecology and Sociobiology, 36*, 71–81.

Ellis, B. J., & Essex, M. J. (2007). Family environments, adrenarche, and sexual maturation: A longitudinal test of a life history model. *Child Development, 78*, 1799–1817.

Emlen, S. T. (1976). Lek organization and mating strategies in the bullfrog. *Behavioral Ecology and Sociobiology, 1*, 283–313.

Emlen, S. T., & Oring, L. W. (1977). Ecology, sexual selection, and the evolution of mating systems. *Science, 197*, 215–223.

Eva, K. W., & Wood, T. J. (2006). Are all the taken men good? An indirect examination of mate-choice copying in humans. *Canadian Medical Association Journal, 175*, 1573–1574.

Feingold, A. (1988). Matching for attractiveness in romantic partners and same-sex friends: A meta-analysis and theoretical critique. *Psychological Bulletin, 104*, 226–235.

Feingold, A. (1990). Gender differences in effects of physical attractiveness on romantic attraction: A comparison across five research paradigms. *Journal of Personality and Social Psychology, 59*, 981–993.

Fisher, M. L., & Candea, C. (2012). You ain't woman enough to take my man: Female intrasexual competition as portrayed in songs. *Journal of Social, Evolutionary, and Cultural Psychology, 6*, 480–493.

Gallup G. G. Jr., & Frederick, D. A. (2010). The science of sex appeal: An evolutionary perspective. *Review of General Psychology, 14*(3), 240.

Gangestad, S. W., & Buss, D. M. (1993). Pathogen prevalence and human mate preferences. *Ethology and Sociobiology, 14*, 89–96.

Gangestad, S. W., & Simpson, J. A. (2000). The evolution of human mating: Trade-offs and strategic pluralism. *Behavioral and Brain Sciences, 23*, 573–587.

Gangestad, S. W., & Thornhill, R. (1997). The evolutionary psychology of extrapair sex: The role of fluctuating asymmetry. *Evolution and Human Behavior, 18*, 69–88.

Gangestad, S. W., Thornhill, R., & Garver-Apgar, C. E. (2005). Adaptations to ovulation implications for sexual and social behavior. *Current Directions in Psychological Science, 14*, 312–316.

Galef, B. G., Lim, T. C. W., & Gilbert, G. S. (2008). Evidence of mate choice copying in Norway rats, Rattus norvegicus. *Animal Behavior, 75*, 1117–1123.

Goetz, A. T., Shackelford, T. K., Weekes-Shackelford, V. A., Euler, H. A., Hoier, S. Schmitt, D. P., & LaMunyon, C. W. (2005). Mate retention, semen displacement, and human sperm competition: A preliminary investigation of tactics to prevent and correct female infidelity. *Personality and Individual Differences, 38*, 749–763.

Graziano, W., Jensen-Campbell, L., Shebilske, L., & Lundgren, S. (1993). Social influence, sex differences, and judgments of beauty: Putting the interpersonal back in interpersonal attraction. *Journal of Personality and Social Psychology, 65*, 522–531.

Gwynne, D. T. (1991). Sexual competition among females: What causes courtship-role reversal? *Trends in Ecology & Evolution, 6*, 118–121.

Haselton, M. G., & Gangestad, S. W. (2006). Conditional expression of women's desires and men's mate guarding across the ovulatory cycle. *Hormones and Behavior, 49*, 509–518.

Höglund, J., Alatalo, R. V., & Lundberg, A. (1990). Copying the mate choice of others? Observations on female black grouse. *Behaviour, 114*, 221–231.

Hughes, S. M., & Gallup, G. G. (2003). Sex differences in morphological predictors of sexual behavior: Shoulder to hip and waist to hip ratios. *Evolution and Human Behavior, 24*, 173–178.

Johnsson, J. J., & Akerman, A. (1998). Watch and learn: Preview of the fighting ability of opponents alters contest behaviour in rainbow trout. *Animal Behavior, 56*, 771–776.

Jones, D. (1996). An evolutionary perspective on physical attractiveness. *Evolutionary Anthropology, 5*, 97–109.

Kaplan, H. S., & Gangestad, S. W. (2005). Life history theory and evolutionary psychology. In D. M. Buss (Ed.), *The handbook of evolutionary psychology* (pp. 68–95). Hoboken, NJ: Wiley.

Kenrick, D. T., Sundie, J. M., Nicastle, L. D., & Stone, G. O. (2001). Can one ever be too wealthy or too chaste? Searching for nonlinearities in mate judgment. *Journal of Personality and Social Psychology, 80*, 462–471.

Kirkpatrick, M., & Dugatkin, L. A. (1994). Sexual selection and the evolutionary effects of copying mate choice. *Behavioral Ecology and Sociobiology, 34*, 443–449.

Kodric-Brown, A., & Brown, J. H. (1984). Truth in advertising: The kinds of traits favored by sexual selection. *American Naturalist, 124*, 309–323.

Li, N. P., Bailey, J. M., Kenrick, D. T., & Linsenmeier, J. A. (2002). The necessities and luxuries of mate preferences: Testing the tradeoffs. *Journal of Personality and Social Psychology, 82*, 947–955.

Little, A. C., Burt, D. M., Penton-Voak, I. S., & Perrett, D. I. (2001). Self-perceived attractiveness influences human female preferences for sexual dimorphism and symmetry in male faces. *Proceedings of the Royal Society of London, Series B: Biological Sciences, 268*, 39–44.

Low, B. S. (1990). Marriage systems and pathogen stress in human societies. *American Zoologist, 30*, 325–339.

Low, B. S., Alexander, R. D., & Noonan, K. M. (1987) Human hips, breasts, and buttocks: Is fat deceptive? *Ethology and Sociobiology, 8*, 249–257.

Mery, F., Varela, S. A., Danchin, É., Blanchet, S., Parejo, D., Coolen, I., & Wagner, R. H. (2009). Public versus personal information for mate copying in an invertebrate. *Current Biology, 19*, 730–734.

Miller, B. C., Benson, B., & Galbraith, K. A. (2001). Family relationships and adolescent pregnancy risk: A research synthesis. *Developmental Review, 21*, 1–38.

Parker, G. A. (1983). Mate quality and mating decisions. In P. Bateson (Ed.), *Mate choice* (pp. 141–164). New York: Cambridge University Press.

Parker, J., & Burkley, M. (2009). Who's chasing whom? The impact of gender and relationship status on mate poaching. *Journal of Experimental Social Psychology, 45*, 1016–1019.

Pillsworth, E. G., & Haselton, M. G. (2006). Male sexual attractiveness predicts differential ovulatory shifts in female extra-pair attraction and male mate retention. *Evolution and Human Behavior, 27*, 247–258.

Place, S. S., Todd, P. M., Penke, L., & Asendorpf, J. B. (2010). Humans show mate copying after observing real mate choices. *Evolution and Human Behavior, 31*, 320–325.

Pomiankowski, A. (1987). The costs of choice in sexual selection. *Journal of Theoretical Biology, 128*, 195–218.

Price, R. A., & Vandenberg, S. G. (1979). Matching for physical attractiveness in married couples. *Personality and Social Psychology Bulletin, 5*, 398–400.

Pruett-Jones, S. (1992). Independent versus nonindependent mate choice: Do females copy each other? *American Naturalist, 140*(6), 1000–1009.

Rasmusen, E. (1989). *Games and information: An introduction to game theory.* Cambridge, MA: Blackwell.

Reynolds, J. D., & Gross, M. R. (1990). Costs and benefits of female mate choice: Is there a lek paradox? *American Naturalist, 136*, 230–243.

Schmitt, D. P. (2004). Patterns and universals of mate poaching across 53 nations: The effects of sex, culture, and personality on romantically attracting another person's partner. *Journal of Personality and Social Psychology, 86*, 560–584.

Schmitt, D. P., & Buss, D. M. (2001). Human mate poaching: tactics and temptations for infiltrating existing mateships. *Journal of Personality and Social Psychology, 80*, 894–917.

Schmitt, D. P., & Pilcher, J. J. (2004) Evaluating evidence of psychological adaptation: How do we know one when we see one? *Psychological Science, 15*, 643–649.

Schmitt, D. P., & Shackelford, T. K. (2008). Big five traits related to short-term mating: From personality to promiscuity across 46 nations. *Evolutionary Psychology, 6*, 246–282.

Schützwohl, A. (2005). Sex differences in jealousy: The processing of cues to infidelity. *Evolution and Human Behavior, 26*, 288–299.

Shackelford, T. (1998). Divorce as a consequence of spousal infidelity. In V. De Munck (Ed.), *Romantic love and sexual behavior* (pp. 135–153). Westport, CT: Praeger.

Shackelford, T. K., Buss, D. M., & Bennett, K. (2002). Forgiveness or breakup: Sex differences in responses to a partner's infidelity. *Cognition and Emotion, 16*, 299–307.

Sirot, E. (2001). Mate-choice copying by females: The advantages of a prudent strategy. *Journal of Evolutionary Biology, 14*, 418–423.

Sprecher, S., Sullivan, Q., & Hatfield, E. (1994). Mate selection preferences: Gender differences examined in a national sample. *Journal of Personality and Social Psychology, 66*, 1074–1080.

Starratt, V. G., Shackelford, T. K., Goetz, A. T., & McKibbin, W. F. (2007). Male mate retention behaviors vary with risk of partner infidelity and sperm competition. *Acta Psychologica Sinica, 39*, 523–527.

Stoehr, S. (1998). Evolution of mate-choice copying: A dynamic model. *Animal Behavior, 55*, 893–903.

Swami, V., & Tovée, M. J. (2005). Male physical attractiveness in Britain and Malaysia: A cross-cultural study. *Body Image, 2*, 383–393.

Swami, V., & Tovée, M. J. (2006). Does hunger influence judgments of female physical attractiveness? *British Journal of Psychology, 97*, 353–363.

Talbani, A., & Hasanali, P. (2000). Adolescent females between tradition and modernity: Gender role socialization in South Asian immigrant culture. *Journal of Adolescence, 23*, 615–627.

Taraborrelli, J. R. (2009). *The secret life of Marilyn Monroe.* New York: Rose Books.

Trivers, R. L. (1972). Parental investment and sexual selection. In B. Campbell (Ed.), *Sexual selection and the descent of man, 1871–1971* (pp. 136–179). Chicago: Aldine.

Trivers, R. L. (2011). *The folly of fools: The logic of deceit and self-deception in human life.* Philadelphia: Basic Books.

Uller, T., & Johansson, L. C. (2003). Human mate choice and the wedding ring effect. *Human Nature, 14*, 267–276.

Valone, T. J., & Templeton, J. J. (2002). Public information for the assessment of quality: A widespread social phenomenon. *Philosophical Transactions of the Royal Society B, 357*, 1549–1557.

Warren, B. L. (1966). A multiple variable approach to the assortative mating phenomenon. *Eugenics Quarterly, 13*, 285–290.

Waynforth, D. (2007). Mate choice copying in humans. *Human Nature, 18*, 264–271.

Welling, L. L. M., Puts, D. A., Roberts, S. C., Little, A. C., & Burriss, R. P. (2012). Hormonal contraceptive use and mate retention behavior in women and their male partners. *Hormones and Behavior, 61*, 114–120.

Yu, D., & Shepard, G. (1998). Is beauty in the eye of the beholder? *Nature, 396*, 321–322.

Intrasexual Mate Competition and Breakups: Who Really Wins?

Craig Morris, Melanie L. Beaussart, Chris Reiber, *and* Linda S. Krajewski

Abstract

Female competition for male attention is multifaceted. Typically psychological and relational in nature, this competition may be no less damaging than physical violence more commonly used between males. Research on female–female mate competition has examined short-term effects, yet how women cope with long-term effects of romantic relationship dissolution has been little explored. If negative emotions exist because they provide an evolutionary advantage (attuning physiological processes, thoughts, and behaviors to deal with situations that have frequently incurred high fitness costs), then emotions arising from the loss of a mate to a sexual rival may potentially motivate actions that could make one avoid this scenario in the future. This essay argues that there are consequences of female intrasexual mate competition that may be both evolutionarily adaptive and also beneficial in terms of personal growth and that may expand beyond mating and into other realms of personal development.

Key Words: female competition, mate competition, intrasexual competition, romantic relationships, relationship dissolution

Introduction

Imagine that you are a woman and your best friend calls you in the middle of the night to say that she has discovered that her man has left her for another woman. She is distraught and crying. What do you say? What do you do? You may offer her emotional support: "I'm here for you, girl!" You could make self-esteem-enhancing affirmations: "You were too good for him anyway!" You might even give her advice: "Divorce him and take everything!" You may make some colorful and slanderous comments about the other woman. And, if you are a good friend, you may become the arbiter of some, perhaps ill-advised, social justice: "Let's go out, get drunk, and then burn all his clothes!" These are, of course, only some of the many ways a woman may react when faced with this situation, and although a bit tongue in cheek, it exemplifies the immediate and dramatic effect that an infidelity-fueled breakup can have on a woman.

There is as much variability in how one might respond to a friend's late-night call as there is variability in how a woman would be affected by the loss of a significant romantic relationship (Frazier & Cook, 1993; Frazier, Port, & Hoff, 1996). Although there are several key factors (e.g., social support, emotionality, personality, cognitive manifestations) that determine the outcome, good or bad, for a woman who has endured a breakup (Frazier & Cook, 1993), research on the effects of mate loss has focused on a breakup's short-term consequences, such as emotional distress. However, it has been argued that humans have evolved emotions and behaviors that deal with fitness-reducing environmental challenges. Therefore, it is possible that, in addition to the immediate negative results of female intrasexual mate competition, there may be long-term effects to mate loss that have not been previously explored. This essay examines several key aspects of the long-term consequences of mate loss precipitated by intrasexual competition. After the initial emotional and physical traumas have dissipated, how do personal and social factors in the latter stages of relationship dissolution—such as the affective response after a breakup, cognitive changes, and even social mechanisms—function to increase the future fitness of a woman who has just lost her mate to another woman?

Sexual Strategies Theory and Mate Loss

Men and women have divergent reproductive challenges that, during the course of evolutionary history, have led to sex differences in mating strategies. In 1989 David Buss published *Sex Differences in Human Mate Preferences: Evolutionary Hypotheses Tested in 37 Cultures*, a study that is still considered a benchmark for cross-cultural sex surveys. Since its publication, Buss has expanded his theoretical model (Buss, 2003) to include a myriad of behaviors that explore the full range of human mating interactions from an evolutionary perspective. This model, called sexual strategies theory (Buss, 1989), has framed much of the investigation into the biological foundations of human sexual behavior for the past 20 years.

Buss (2003) parses the term "strategy" carefully; he uses the example of sweating as a "strategy" to avoid overheating. In many ways, it is equivalent to "adaptation." In no instance in these readings has "strategy" been used in the conventional sense—as a consciously preplanned series of actions designed to elicit some sort of reproductive benefit. Therefore, sexual strategies are, in their original iteration, simply adaptive solutions to mating problems, as those who failed to reproduce failed to become our ancestors. Each strategy is tailored to a specific adaptive problem—such as attracting a mate or besting a competitor. Underlying each strategy are evolved emotional mechanisms such as jealousy, lust, and love. These mechanisms are sensitive to environmental cues such as physical attractiveness or displays of fidelity. They are also self-reflexive and sensitive to individual mating attributes such as perceived attractiveness or the amount of resources an individual controls.

Again, sexual strategies do not require conscious thought: "Just as a piano player's sudden awareness of her hands may impede performance, most human sexual strategies are best carried out without the awareness of the actor" (Buss, 2003, p. 3). Critically, different strategies are available and employed, often resulting in emotional conflict, by males and females. Sexual strategies theory emphasizes that both men and women have evolved tactics

for obtaining long-term mates and investing in children, but short-term mating will occur when reproductive benefits outweigh costs. Other theories such as social role/biosocial theory contend that sex differences in sexual behavior are also shaped by the formation of gender roles, expectancy confirmation, and self-regulation (Eagly & Wood, 1999).

Regardless, humans today are all descendants of many generations of ancestors who reproduced successfully. The genotypes of those whose phenotype caused them to reproduce sparingly, or not at all, were statistically overwhelmed by the genotypes of those who reproduced prolifically. As an example, there is a (likely apocryphal) tale of an old rancher being laboriously questioned about his livestock by a potential buyer. Exasperated, the rancher finally says, "Son, my family has owned this ranch for generations; all I can assure you with certainty is that these animals all come from good breeding stock." Evolutionarily, the same logic applies to humans. We are all descendants of ancestors, going back hundreds of generations, who reproduced successfully. Behaviors like romantic-relationship formation and biparental care of children are argued to be evolutionarily adaptive—leading to increased reproductive success. Therefore those ancestors who possessed some suite of behaviors that allowed them to continue successful mating behavior after the termination of one or more relationships are the ones whose biological predispositions we possess today.

Of course breaking up with a romantic partner can be one of the most traumatic experiences in a woman's life (Morris & Reiber, 2011). From a biological perspective, women bear the larger minimum parental investment—nine months of gestation as well as the metabolic costs of lactation—and therefore are more "selective" in their mate choice (Trivers, 1972). That is to say that women are argued to have higher standards for a potential long-term mate (wealth, status, good looks) than men. The dissolution of an active romantic relationship (as opposed to being widowed) is an experience that almost 85% of all women will face during their lifetimes (Morris & Reiber, 2011). The adaptive problems such as loss of protection, status, and resources a woman—and her children—face if her partner leaves or is expelled from the relationship are considerable due to the aforementioned biological cost a woman inherently invests versus the man. In addition to the resource and fitness benefits of long-term mate retention for a woman, there are benefits to intimate relationships (e.g., support, companionship, love, and sexual activity), which are often all met only by a long-term romantic partner (Laumann, 1994). Thus, relationship breakup often comes at great emotional and physical cost to a woman.

We realize that the word "breakup" is a colloquialism; however, it is used for clarity to indicate the termination of a romantic relationship via social or legal dissolution as opposed the physical loss (death) of a mate. It is important to reiterate this point because, as seen throughout this essay, the wide variety of relationship styles, particularly among young women, precludes a rigid definition of a breakup. However, most women have little difficulty identifying the end of a relationship, even if the relationship itself was very different from one she, or her cohort, had participated in previously (Morris & Reiber, 2011). A man who is already in a committed romantic relationship is often viewed as more desirable to women than an unattached man (Dugatkin, 1992; Uller & Johansson, 2003). This may be because he has been prescreened by another woman for resources and a willingness to commit to a romantic relationship or because of some other heuristic (Gigerenzer & Goldstein, 1996). One study (Parker & Burkley, 2009) found that a man's relationship status directly affected his attractiveness to women; when women thought a man was single, 59% found him attractive, but when they thought he was in a committed relationship, 90% found him attractive. Hence one form of competition between women is to attract the highest-quality mate, even if it means "poaching" him from a monogamous relationship. In one study (Schmitt et al., 2004), 53% of women confessed to having attempted to lure someone else's mate into a long-term relationship, 80% of men reported that someone had attempted to lure them out of a romantic relationship, and roughly 30% of women said they lost a partner to a mate poacher (Schmitt et al., 2004).

Since women have faced recurrent fitness costs associated with romantic breakups, it follows that natural selection would favor adaptations to cope with these costs—adaptations expected to differ from men's (i.e., sex-specific strategies formulated to help offset the costs of mate loss). Indeed, there is some indication that, as a result of a potential mate loss from a partner's affair, men and women are predisposed to respond to counteract the sex-specific costs. For example, men may have to address lost mating opportunities or a decrease in social status, whereas women may face a more tangible loss (e.g., protection, resources; Miller & Maner, 2008). As a result, men report more feelings of anger and engage in more violent and self-destructive behaviors than women (e.g., substance abuse; Morris & Reiber, 2011). Women, in comparison, frequently feel more depressed and participate in more social, affiliative behaviors than men (Miller & Maner, 2008). Women's behaviors could be argued to be more constructive strategies as a result of their tendency to preserve the relationship, whereas men choose destructive strategies for maintaining their own self-esteem (Bryson, 1991).

Reactions to Mate Loss

Breakups can be tremendously distressing. Research has shown that romantic-relationship dissolution is recognized as a significant lifetime event (Kendler, Hettema, Butera, Gardner, & Prescott, 2003). Moreover, relationship dissolution can result in major psychological difficulties (Amato, 2000), which can manifest as a perseveration or fixation with the lost mate, hyperbolic effort to resume the relationship, as well as physical and emotional distress. Though the most intense symptoms of distress often appear immediately after the breakup and diminish over time (Knox, Zusman, Kaluzny, & Cooper, 2000; Moller, Fouladi, McCarthy, & Hatch, 2003), breaking up with a loved one can have profound long-lasting effects (Chung et al., 2003). It should be noted that our ongoing research suggests that explicit or perceived infidelity tends to produce the most extreme negative short-term effects, both emotional and physical, for most women. Research on mate loss has concentrated on the psychological responses and emotional discomfort of the experience (Fine & Sacher, 1997; Sbarra & Ferrer, 2006). The loss of a mate can have several adverse results; for instance, it can trigger the onset of a major mental health condition (Kendler et al., 2003; Mearns, 1991). Research has shown that serious mental health problems such as anxiety, anger, and feeling hopeless often follow a breakup (Davis, Shaver, & Vernon, 2003; Monroe, Rohde, Seeley, & Lewinsohn, 1999). Some studies have addressed the emotional costs of a breakup but without any explicit theoretical framework (Jankowiak & Fischer, 1992; Jankowiak & Paladino, 2008). One such study found that those who had pre-existing issues with depression and anxiety expressed stronger emotional problems following a breakup. Additionally, self-blame and "catastrophic" misperception were the most robustly correlated cognitive variables associated with mate loss (Boelen & Reijntjes, 2009). A similar longitudinal study on relationship-specific forecasting errors (e.g., how severe and long-lasting individuals assumed that their breakup experience would be initially as compared to how they evaluated the experience after time) found that those who were more in love with their partners, who thought it was unlikely they would soon enter a new relationship, and who did not initiate the breakup made especially inaccurate predictions about the specifics of the breakup (Eastwick et al., 2008).

Aversive mental health symptoms do not seem to be correlated with the "formality" of a romantic relationship. Married couples, cohabitating couples, couples with plans to marry, and those simply "in a relationship" all experience the same spectrum of emotional distress following a breakup (Rhoades, Kamp Dush, Atkins, Stanley, & Markman, 2011). Regardless of which partner initiated the breakup and regardless of whether the desire to break up was one-sided or mutual, it is clear that the dissolution of romantic relationships is often intensely stressful, and stressful interpersonal contexts are among the most reliable precipitants of depressed states (Kendler et al., 2003; Monroe et al., 1999). The degree of a woman's physical and emotional response to a breakup can be predicted by numerous variables, including the length of the relationship (Tashiro & Frazier, 2003), the time since the loss (Sprecher, Felmlee, Metts, Fehr, & Vanni, 1998), or who initiated the breakup (Perilloux & Buss, 2008). Interestingly, psychological distress and lowered life satisfaction are expressed even by those individuals who wanted the relationship to end (Rhoades et al., 2011).

Grief

Bowlby (1980) posited a multiple-stage theory of grief that applies to coping with the loss of an important relationship, such as a romantic relationship. It structures the stages of coping following a breakup. The first phase involves protest against the breakup. The next phase is despair, in which the reality of the loss becomes more immediate and the emotional and psychological responses shift to sorrow, depression, withdrawal, and disorganization. The third and final phase is reorganization, wherein the internal representations of the self and the absent partner are altered to reflect the new circumstances of the relationship. While this three-stage hypothesis has been challenged—the periods of specific grief reactions differ considerably, both

across individuals and with respect to the varying causes of grief (Archer, 1999)—it nonetheless serves as a starting reference for visualizing the possible adaptive value of grief (i.e., "a time out" that may facilitate introspection and prevent repetition of costly behaviors).

Archer (1999) has also suggested that grief is a universal human experience, derived from observable (but less complex) forms in the animal world. In its base form, the experience involves two processes: active distress (i.e., search and anger) and an inactive, depressed state. In human grief, a complex set of reactions is added involving a radical change in the personal identity of the afflicted. Grief is thus produced as a result of a "tradeoff" between physiological costs and benefits. Thus, humans establish bonds that have multiple advantages and great adaptive value. However, these bonds can and do break. When they do, there is a cost to pay; Archer calls it the cost of commitment, which consists of all the physical and emotional benefits of the bond. Per the adaptive value of these bonds, their severance (in most instances) proves maladaptive. As we have argued, it is likely that a strong negative emotion, such as grief, accompanies maladaptive behavior. Put simply, the greater the loss, the more intense the grieving process, and the more likely (in most instances) an individual will engage in future bond formation with an eye toward avoiding past experiences. Importantly, Archer's model shows that grief is not a homogenous entity. The mental processes involved in grieving can include intrusive thoughts, hallucinations, distraction, self-blame, and anxiety. Importantly, these processes are often magnified by extant mental and physical conditions (e.g., anxiety, addictions, chronic depression; Fisher, 2004a). Archer concludes that there is little doubt that the intensity of grief reflects the lost relationship's cost of commitment.

Depression

Depression is a mental health condition marked by a persistent low mood or sadness and is often associated with low self-esteem and lack of interest or enjoyment in previously pleasurable activities. This cluster of symptoms is collectively classified as a mood disorder (Karp, 1997). However, the term "depression" is vague since it may be used to suggest both a chronic disabling condition that negatively influences a person's entire life and a transitory lower mood state that does not have any clinical significance. In this essay, when talking about a person being depressed or sad, we are referring to subclinical (i.e., not medically diagnosed and treated) depression.

Nesse (2000) has argued that low mood and depression are historically difficult to distinguish from related states such as sadness, grief, demoralization (i.e., severe loss of self-esteem with concomitant loss of motivation), and guilt (Keller & Nesse, 2005). This "fuzziness" may reflect the nature of natural selection: gradual differentiation from a generic state of inhibition into subtypes specialized to cope with particular kinds of situations. Sadness, depression, and grief may be partially differentiated members of a behavioral suite explained partially by phylogeny and partially by the benefits certain responses offer in any potentially harmful situation. For example, Nesse has suggested that functions of depression may include communicating a need for help, signaling yielding in a hierarchy conflict, fostering disengagement from commitments to unreachable goals, and regulating patterns of investment (Keller & Nesse, 2005).

Although sex differences in emotional distress after a breakup are rarely identified in the research (Perilloux & Buss, 2008), women have historically reported more severe initial depression and hopelessness than men (Kuehner, 2003). When vulnerability factors (e.g., existing psychiatric conditions, life history variation) interact with life stressors, the risk of depression increases. In fact, women 18 to 45 years of age are at a markedly heightened risk of depression compared to older women and men of all ages (Culbertson, 1997). One study found that after losing a mate, young women are inclined to experience more emotional distress; have more invasive thoughts about the former partner; and experience higher rates of unhappiness, anxiety, and adverse emotions than men (Field, Diego, Pelaez, Deeds, & Delgado, 2010). In a case where a woman has lost her mate to a rival, it is likely that the "suite" of emotions and behaviors would be more far-reaching than in a case in which the relationship was terminated for some other reason. For example, a breakup caused by a man leaving the relationship for another woman is more likely to incorporate the loss of self-esteem, demoralization, jealousy, and anger than a breakup caused by physical distance.

Therefore there is an additional level of psychological toxicity to cope with when the situation is complicated by having been outcompeted for a mate by another female. Even the effects of simply competing for mates and losing can take an emotional toll, since feelings of defeat are shown to be significantly correlated with depression (Gilbert & Allan, 1998). Some evolutionary models such as the social risk hypothesis claim that the accessibility of resources that will greatly enhance one's overall fitness is related to an individual's social status within a particular group. Loss of access to such resources could trigger in-group conflict. A lowered mood or more submissive attitude by individuals losing resource control might be a lesser evil than losing access to the group itself. Furthermore, it is argued that adaptations to the affective systems enable an individual to negotiate social relationships that are crucial for his or her survival, since the affective systems are the trigger for adaptive behaviors to evade threats to a person's well-being (Lennox, Jacob, Calder, Lupson, & Bullmore, 2004). Thus, the social risk hypothesis implies that depression serves an adaptive function after a threat to one's status within a group by reducing behaviors that would cause a person to lose any further reproductive opportunities (Nesse, 2000). Other members of the social group can put each other at risk and may harm one another. Hence individuals should be cautious of those who can hurt them and coordinate their responses accordingly. If an individual cannot command greater resource control, low mood may signal a level "acquiescence" that prevents further harm to his or her social status.

Those who do not follow these social rules tend to be at risk of serious injury or death (Higley et al., 1996). Most certainly within the environment of evolutionary adaptedness, the environment in which the brain and its adaptations evolved (Bowlby, 1969; Buss, 2004), a considerable effect on fitness was incurred by social exclusion via lack of in-group protections and foraging but also because low-status individuals receive fewer acts of altruism, fewer exchanges of resources, and less access to sexual partners (Baumeister & Leary, 1995; Buss, 1990). Furthermore, this hypothesis predicts that low mood would interrupt the evaluation mechanism that determines the value of future outcomes and instead becomes sensitive to stimuli that would provide immediate reward (e.g., after a breakup, women are likely to increase their alcohol consumption; Allen & Badcock, 2003). However, this is only a temporary artifact during the emotional transition to normality; after a few months, women's alcohol use tends to return to pre-breakup levels (Fleming et al., 2010).

After a breakup, many women suffer an extreme loss of self-esteem and a concurrent questioning of "what they did wrong" (Morris & Reiber, 2011). Women often doubt their self-worth, their physical appearance, and whether they themselves are responsible for "losing" their mate. For these reasons, social withdrawal ("subordination" in non-human animals) can be a response to a situation in which it is vital for an animal to have an internal, inhibitory, regulating process that confines acquisition and seeking behavior (Gilbert, 2006). Sapolsky (1990) notes that subordinate baboons are sensitive to stress-induced hypercortisolism, which in part is caused by the harassment and threat signals presented by the more dominant animals but also because the less dominant animals do not possess the ability to overpower their adversaries. Applying this theory to humans, then, as part of this recalibration, women must also face the need to adjust their self-perceived mate value—the degree to which an opposite-sex partner's reproductive fitness is increased by mating with them (Sugiyama, 2005)— in light of events that led to their mate loss. The self-evaluative psychological mechanisms that track one's status within a group or, more commonly, a woman's self-esteem, can be severely diminished by failing to win a mate after competition with a rival. Moreover, low self-esteem is expected to be a prominent part of depression that arises from the inability to yield in a status competition. It may also be the case that the more intimate the rival is socially, the more intense the response to the breakup, as this scenario allows for a greater loss of standing within the social circle in additional to possibly magnifying the feelings of anger, distrust, and betrayal that frequently accompany loss of a mate to "another woman."

The Utility of Emotional Response

Like a fever, grief is something that may initially appear to be maladaptive. With moderate fever there is discomfort, restlessness, dehydration, and other unpleasant sensations. With grief, the situation is much the same—strong negative feelings that can lead to unhealthy behavior (e.g., poor diet, decreased performance at school or work; Keller & Nesse, 2005; Nesse, 1996). It has proven difficult to offer an evolutionary theory of grief; how could grief be considered the product of evolution when it seems so maladaptive for survival and procreation? Evolutionary medicine has shown us that non-life-threatening fever serves an adaptive purpose (i.e., it "cooks out" pathogens). Perhaps a moderate level of grief also serves an adaptive purpose (e.g., avoidance of repeating a risky behavior, a recalibration of personal values, and a mechanism to discourage "bad evolutionary investments")? Nesse (2000) has

suggested that the pursuit of substantive life goals requires the construction of social enterprises that are resource intensive, emotionally costly, and difficult to replace (e.g., marriages, friendships, careers, status). A major setback or loss in one of these enterprises precipitates life crises. Nesse (2005) further argues that this dilemma is frequently resolved by changing or accepting the current situation or by moving on.

Perhaps a more broad evolutionary account arises from an attempt to ascertain in what ways the characteristics of depression increase an individual's ability to handle the adaptive challenges that could result in harm or lost resources. For example, the loss of a romantic partner tends to be associated with external expressions of grief, as well as internal emotions that may serve an instructive purpose to prevent future occurrences of the aversive event (i.e., a possible increase in overall mating intelligence). As troubles increase and energies tend to be exhausted, a melancholy state helps individuals to separate from their hopeless situation, with the result of seeking other ways to deal with their sadness. Women experiencing depression following a breakup may initially withdraw from social contact—avoiding rivals, friends, and family alike— but tend to acquire much more social support (over time) than do men (Morris & Reiber, 2011). This initial social withdrawal may prevent or limit activities that might create additional losses. An example might involve the aforementioned trend of women increasing alcohol consumption following a breakup. In men, this seems to often be an act of self-destructive isolation (Morris & Reiber, 2011). In women, the consumption seems to accompany other prosocial behavior. However, drinking to excess, perhaps publicly and in a highly emotional state, carries risks for women that it does not for men. In such situations, caution and lack of motivation may yield a fitness advantage by inhibiting certain actions, especially futile or dangerous challenges to dominant figures, actions in the absence of a crucial resource or a viable plan, efforts that would damage the body, and actions that could lead from an unsatisfactory social enterprise to a worse alternative (Nesse, 2005).

There is some support for the idea that these non-clinical levels of depression might have evolved as defenses that also serve fitness-enhancing functions. One of those functions is to solve fitness-reducing problems. Depressed individuals, especially those saddened by a mate loss, often think intensely about their problems (Saffrey & Ehrenberg, 2007).

Called ruminations, these thoughts are persistent, and depressed individuals have difficulty thinking about anything else. For example, say a woman is depressed because the man she was interested in pursuing a serious relationship with has picked another woman instead of her. This situation, for many women, could lead to self-doubting ruminations over factors that are mating related. For instance, since a woman's physical attractiveness and sexual chastity are highly valued by opposite-sex mates (Buss, 1989), it is likely that women would fret over their physical attributes ("What if I was prettier?") or past behaviors ("Why did I sleep with him on the first date?"; Morris & Reiber, 2011).

Though self-analysis may seem on the surface to only reinforce low self-esteem, it may also elucidate personal insights that are useful for attracting and keeping future mates. After a breakup, rejectees must first ascertain the key behaviors that triggered the breakup and reassess their mate value. Such self-analysis, however, requires a concerted effort, and subclinical levels of depression may help direct neurochemical fluctuations in the brain toward an unadulterated state ideal for introspection (Andrews & Thomson, 2009). These physiological changes, such as lower overall energy levels, may aid individuals in analyzing their problems without distraction. Therefore there may be a tentative relationship between why women, who in general report more depressive symptoms after a breakup, also report more personal growth than men (Bevvino & Sharkin, 2003; Mearns, 1991). This was demonstrated by Morris and Reiber (2011) who, in a campus-based pilot study, found that women (mostly ages 18–24) brought up this painful loss of self-esteem twice as often as men. In many cases, this loss precluded women's ability to form deep romantic relationships for quite some time. Many women also questioned their body shape, weight, and choice of clothing following a breakup. Self-doubt related to judgment and perceived personality flaws that were brought to light as part of the breakup (e.g., tolerance of poor mate behavior, regret at the pace of sexual activity) were also frequently mentioned. Nonetheless, virtually every comment identifying a "silver lining" of increased personal awareness and greater perceptivity regarding future relationships was submitted by a woman.

Emotional response to mate loss has been studied from the neurological perspective as well as the psychological. Helen Fisher (e.g., 2006) has written extensively on the neurochemical activity associated with mate rejection and relationship termination.

She concludes that breakups are metabolically expensive and time-consuming, yet are likely an evolutionary adaptation. Fisher (2004a) states, "We humans are soft-wired to suffer terribly when we are rejected by someone we adore" (p. 1). Using the same functional magnetic resonance imaging techniques she employed when studying people in love (2004b), Fisher studied those who had recently suffered a breakup. She found (a) being rejected in love is among the most painful experiences a human being can endure; (b) deserted lovers often become obsessed with winning back their former mate; (c) separation anxiety is expected; and (d) "abandonment rage"(i.e., a propensity for self-destruction vs. self-reflection) is likely, particularly in men. She concludes that this suite of responses "developed to enable jilted lovers to extricate themselves from dead-end love affairs and start again" (2004a, p. 4).

Personal Growth Following Trauma

If some degree of emotional trauma following a breakup is adaptive, then it follows that there must be some fitness-enhancing benefit of the experience. Researchers have examined some of these ways in which the experience of a breakup can lead to positive life changes. For example, individuals may come out of a breakup with an improved sense of self-reliance and valuable experience in managing relationships that they did not have previously. To explore potential positive outcomes following romantic relationship breakups, Tashiro and Frazier (2003) surveyed 92 undergraduate university students on their post-breakup experiences. Participants were asked to "Briefly describe what positive changes, if any, have happened as a result of your breakup that might serve to improve your future romantic relationships" (p. 118). Following a breakup, participants reported a number of positive changes related to personal growth that they felt may assist with future relationships. The most common types of changes reported by participants were related to how they had changed as a person (e.g., feeling stronger, more independent, and better off emotionally). It was also common for participants to report that they had gained wisdom that would help them with future relationships. Anecdotally, there seems to be an argument that divorced women are in better shape, more groomed, and better dressed than when they were married—perhaps as a way to compete more effectively. However, to date, no systematic data bear this out. What is often seen is that virtually all the "improvements" relayed directly by women fall under the umbrella of higher mating intelligence. An improvement in physical health and appearance can be inferred, but it is rarely (if ever) made explicit. In another study (Clark & Georgellis, 2013), 10,000 people in the UK were asked to rank how happy they were before and after certain major life milestones; while both men and women said that they felt happier after they were divorced than during their marriage, the effect was more pronounced for women.

Positive Rumination

In addition to the possible fitness-enhancing aspects of depression, there is another line of evidence that suggests that people in depressed mood states are better at solving social dilemmas. It has been shown that when low mood is experimentally induced, participants show a reduction in making fundamental attribution errors (i.e., the error of explaining someone else's behavior as an internal characteristic with very little external mitigating influences; Forgas, 1998) and likewise the halo error (i.e., the cognitive bias in which one judges a person's character by his or her physical appeal; Sinclair, 1988). Schaller and Cialdini (1990) state that sad people are less likely to rely on heuristic shortcuts to process social cues and instead utilize more systematic processing strategies that invoke a cost-benefit analysis. Furthermore, a woman with depression who is feeling as though she has lost control over her current social environment is more sensitive to cues that allow her to interpret social situations more accurately (Weary, Elbin, & Hill, 1987). For example, consider a woman who is pregnant and discovers that her partner is having an affair with another woman. Is her "best" strategy to ignore the affair and continue receiving benefits from her mate, or should she risk abandonment by forcing him to choose between her and the other woman? Her eventual actions are contingent on multiple relationship-specific factors (e.g., the nature of the affair [Shackelford, LeBlanc, & Drass, 2000], socioeconomics [Sayer, England, Allison, & Kangas, 2011], and the wife's mate value [Shackelford & Buss, 1997]). The motivations of these actions are complicated by the misattribution errors related to low mood (e.g., unnecessary self-blame, misunderstanding the mate's motivations, skewed evaluation of the rival's "sex appeal"). However, the level of depression that would naturally occur in such a woman, caused by female–female competition, would be beneficial overall because it would afford her the temporal and psychological resources to choose the "best" strategy.

Social Support and Female Competition After Mate Loss

For women, the general competition for male attention, and specifically attention from high-quality mates, is multifaceted. There are four themes of female mate competition: self-promotion, competitor derogation, mate manipulation, and competitor manipulation (Fisher & Cox, 2011). Although the tactics employed in this competition are typically psychological and relational in nature, it is no less damaging to the competitors than the physical forms of competition more commonly seen in men (Miller & Maner, 2008). Interestingly, direct aggression (i.e., physical) toward other women is not typically an expected means of competition (Björkqvist, Lagerspetz, & Österman, 1992). Instead, for the purpose of competing, women engage in various forms of indirect aggression (Björkqvist, 1994; Björkqvist, Österman, & Lagerspetz, 1994), which are commonly referred to as relational aggression. A very simple example is that a man is far more likely to "call out" a competitor publicly and engage in a physical altercation over an attempted mate poach, whereas a woman is more likely to start or spread rumors about her rival, engage in social exclusion, or otherwise impair a rival's social network in the heat of female–female mate competition.

Regardless of whether it is less risky socially, more effective, or both, women cross-culturally are more likely to use subtle forms of aggression, such as starting rumors or otherwise trying to manipulate their social circle, rather than using more direct confrontations or competitions (Barkow, 1992; Björkqvist et al., 1994). In other words, competitor derogation, which involves the direct or indirect attack of a sexual rival (e.g., indirectly insulting a rival, gossiping about her, or insinuating that she is promiscuous) is one of the most likely aggressive tactics a woman will employ (Fisher & Cox, 2011). In the case of female–female mate competition, this competitor derogation is often expressed in the language used by women to describe "the other woman" (e.g., bitch, whore, slut; Morris & Reiber, 2011).

Whether it is an intentional or unintentional artifact of seeking the support and consolation of one's friends—indeed, the woman does not necessarily need to be conscious about the purpose (Trivers, 1972)—great harm can be incurred when a woman impugns another woman's reputation. A positive social status is imperative in communal groups since a woman's social standing can mediate her access to resources (Gurven, Allen-Arave, Hill, & Hurtado, 2000; Kaplan, Gurven, Hill, & Hurtado, 2005), govern reciprocal partners (Brown & Moore, 2002; Gurven, Hill, Kaplan, Hurtado, & Lyles, 2000), and provide valuable information to prospective mates about potential mate attributes such as parental investment strategies (Campbell, 2004) and sexual fidelity (Hess & Hagen, 2006). Sexually permissive women are often socially stigmatized and rejected as potential friends or partners (Crawford & Popp, 2003; Vrangalova, Bukberg, & Rieger, 2014).

In general, women's perceived undesirability of others' sexual permissiveness can place the latter at elevated risk for social rejection and peer aggression. Therefore, if a woman can successfully label another as being sexually permissive, this derision can have a powerful impact on the other woman's social status and overall reproductive fitness. While this can be a risky strategy that may entice men to seek the more sexually available rival, it is nonetheless commonly used (Arnocky et al., 2013; Buss & Dedden, 1990). Evolutionarily, sexual promiscuity is often a short-term strategy, for while at that moment a woman may have "won the battle" by accessing additional resources, building future intersexual alliances, or successfully poaching a mate, she could be "losing the war" by engaging in reputation-damaging behavior that will reduce her ability to acquire a long-term mate of high quality in the future.

Avoiding Similar Situations
Avoiding Mate Loss Through Mate-Retention Tactics

Inclusive fitness demonstrates that relatedness is often important for human altruism (i.e., humans are inclined to behave more altruistically toward kin than toward unrelated individuals). An effective way to avoid the inclusive fitness risks of resource loss is to prevent a mate from ever getting to the point of engaging in sexual or emotional infidelity. Preventing a mate from engaging in extra-pair relationships is a major challenge faced by many sexually reproducing species. Even a single romantic infidelity can lead to large reproductive and social costs. For instance, if a man impregnates his mistress, resources may be permanently diverted from his wife and her offspring to support the offspring of the mistress (Marlowe, 2003). As a result, adaptive psychological and behavioral processes may have

evolved to guard against possible rivals and to reduce the likelihood of infidelity (Buss & Shackelford, 1997; Buss, Shackelford, & McKibbin, 2008; Starratt, Shackelford, Goetz, & McKibbin, 2007). Precisely how much effort an individual allocates to mate guarding is a function of the value of the mate being guarded. Men who view themselves as married to young and physically attractive mates invest more effort in mate guarding compared to men married to older and "less attractive" women (Buss, 2002). Similarly, women married to men with high income and ambition put more effort into guarding their partners than do women married to men who earn less or strive less for status (Buss, 2002). These patterns presumably reflect the fact that physically attractive women and high-status men are higher in mate value than same-sex others lacking these qualities. As a consequence, high-value mates experience more frequent sexual or romantic interest from others and hence have more potential mating options—requiring a higher allocation of mate guarding by their current partner (Buss, 1988; Buss & Shackelford, 1997).

Relationship jealousy can be defined as thoughts, emotions, or behaviors that occur as a result of the perceived threat of losing a potential mate to an actual or imagined rival (Buunk & Dijkstra, 2004). Evolutionarily, the costs of repeated mate loss may have been severe. It would be of likely benefit for rejectees to be more vigilant in their mate-guarding efforts, including experiencing frequent and intense feelings of jealousy, increasing their sensitivity to cues of partner infidelity, and behaving accordingly to prevent partner infidelity. In men, it has been suggested that the "master mechanism" for maintaining pair bonds is their almost pathological sexual jealousy that stems, evolutionarily, from the fear of cuckoldry (Buss, 2007). This threat of uncertain genetic parentage is not only what "keeps us together" but is also the root cause of much dangerous male behavior, from the boorish to the brutal (Buss & Shackelford, 1997). An example would be that of an ancestral male supplying his mate with adaptively relevant resources (food and shelter), keeping competitors at bay via mate guarding and shows of social/physical dominance, and using destructive measures (e.g., physical or emotional abuse) when needed to ensure mate retention (Buss, 2003).

For women, jealously could be adaptive if it has encouraged careful scrutiny of partners to forestall any potential threats to a woman's monopolization of a man's resources or direct paternal care.

The more dependent the individual is on the relationship, the more likely he or she will be jealous, since he or she has more to lose (Buunk & Bringle, 1987). Jealous women may monitor their partners' whereabouts by calling them incessantly, follow their partners everywhere, spy on their partners, and/or show up unexpectedly at their partners' workplace or home (Breitner & Anderson, 1994; Mullins, 2010). Women employ nonphysical mate-retention strategies more so than men (e.g., monopolization of time, sexual inducements, derogation of competitors; Buss, 2002), but in some women these intense and persistent feelings of jealousy can and do lead to morbid jealousy that can include substance abuse, harm to self, and physical assaults on the partner (Buss, 2000; Kingham & Gordon, 2004).

Women Who Stop Competing

Nonetheless, even the most vigorous mate-guarding tactics are unlikely to totally prevent infidelity, desertion, or loss of a mate to another woman. If sexual selection shapes female–female competition over mating opportunities, one question worth asking is: Are particular females able to competitively exclude others from mating altogether? There has been some research that suggests that females do have the intention to oust others from the mating game by using competitor manipulation (Fisher & Cox, 2011). For example, women have been known to deliberately manipulate competitors by deceiving them as to the target's sexual orientation or keeping the opponent busy with other tasks. However, even without the deliberate goal of a competitor to eliminate a rival, a woman could withdraw from competition rather than remain vulnerable to the stressors that accompany the mating game.

Low-ranking animals frequently engage in submissive behavior, experience social anxiety, feel inferior to others, and generally are subject to higher stress than their higher-ranking companions (Gilbert, 2001; Sloman, Gilbert, & Hasey, 2003). However, even within the most homogeneous population, differences exist in how an individual copes with social defeat and rejection. In a study of tree shrew behavior, Von Holst (1986) found that those that experienced social adversity and lost out on resources employed either a strategy of continuing activities in a hesitant and tentative manner or a strategy of "shutting down" almost entirely, perhaps due to learned helplessness.

This behavior may be a method of demobilization designed to promote the safety of the defeated animal. Expressing subdued behavior indicates a subordinate status, thereby letting the animal's competitors know it yields defeat, it is "out of the game," and it is not worthy of further attacks (Price, Gardner, & Erickson, 2004). These tactics allow the animal to withdraw for a time, hopefully to recover its energies and resources to compete more successfully in the future (Price et al., 1994). However, this behavior has immediate biological costs. Levitan, Vaccarino, Brown, and Kennedy (2002) found chronic stress with increased hypothalamic-pituitary-adrenal axis activity in subordinates that are defeated and/or harassed after they maintain these submissive behaviors (Abbott et al., 2003; Ray & Sapolsky, 1992). Studies on defeated rodents show physiological and behavioral changes, such as reduced exploratory behavior, increased defensiveness, and decreased offensive aggression (Gilbert, 2001).

While food resources or group dominance are often the focus of animal models of defeat behavior, there is also support for their application to human mating and reproductive behaviors. Wasser and Barash (1983) found that women with impaired self-esteem and poor social support from family and friends often had more reproductive complications during and following birth and were more likely to abandon or abuse their children. Psychological stress, including the stress from mate loss and female competition, can serve as a powerful force in altering a woman's reproductive potential. For example, active competition may cause lowered reproductive fitness by mating interruption, ovulation disruptions, or increased stress (Hohmann & Fruth, 2003; Wasser & Starling, 1988). The reproductive suppression model states that when a woman is in a situation that is, at that time, unfavorable to reproduction, her lifetime reproductive success may be increased by waiting to reproduce until conditions become more favorable (e.g., lower levels of financial and social stress are frequent indicators of "improved" conditions). This down-regulation of reproductive effort may prevent her from incurring steep reproductive costs that would be better utilized in more favorable conditions (Wasser & Barash, 1983). Thus, a woman who experiences a temporary delay in reproduction through rejection by her mate may find it prudent to wait until environmental factors are improved and the pressure of intrasexual competition is reduced; evolutionarily, her short-term loss may not preclude her from long-term success.

Conclusion and Future Directions

Despite the short-term pain of a breakup, findings indicate that most women are resilient and recover (Morris & Reiber, 2011). Furthermore, most women also report feeling significantly less distressed about the breakup than they did initially in as little as two months (Eastwick, Finkel, Krishnamurti, & Loewenstein, 2008). Ongoing research suggests that life history variation in relationship length, number of previous other relationships, and time since breakup significantly influence a woman's initial reaction as well as future recollection of the events.

Lucas et al. (2003) and Stutzer and Frey (2006) explored patterns of change in marital status and concluded that any positive well-being effect does not last beyond the early years of marriage. That is to say, after the first few years of marriage, people return to a baseline level of happiness set before they were married. Lucas (2005) also found approximately 50% of the initial decline in happiness following divorce is recovered after a few years, but individuals do not seem to return to their predivorce levels of happiness. Interestingly, men derive fewer benefits from divorce compared with women (Kitson & Holmes, 1992; Marks & Lambert, 1998). Moreover, the lowest point of happiness is found to be one year before the actual breakup takes place. We would argue that this is analogous to the process of recovery from alcohol or substance abuse, where individuals must frequently "hit bottom" before becoming motivated to extricate themselves from their painful and destructive life situations. Given the costly investment individuals make in romantic relationships, it is understandable that if conscious of the relationship "hitting bottom," an individual may need time to contemplate what action is the best to take. Future research regarding who initiated the relationship end, its timing, and its cause will provide insight into this hypothesis.

As previously noted, depression and low self-esteem may modify a person's behavior in a manner that reduces the likelihood of any further social devaluation. However, a byproduct of this reduction in self-esteem might serve as a motivational mechanism by which a woman increases the frequency of actions that lead to a rise in the respect she feels from others. As one would expect, success in romantic relationships raises self-esteem (Brase & Guy, 2004; Locker, McIntosh, Hackney, Wilson, & Wiegand, 2010). Recent research suggests that women who had higher levels of depression had more short-term sexual encounters than nondepressed women

(Beaussart, Kaufman, & Kaufman, 2012). Ancestral women may have used extra-pair sex to acquire resources during lean times and to form alliances with men during times of strife. This behavior may be a conscious one motivated by a cost-benefit analysis or spurred by depression and anxiety caused by environmental cues. However, a temporary increase in uncommitted sexual activity after a mate loss is a double-edged sword: short-term promiscuity may be a way for a woman to recover her self-esteem and gain access to intersexual social status, but she may at the same time run the risks of being labeled as promiscuous and experience intrasexual ostracism. Researchers have also begun conducting studies to identify factors that may be associated with a speedier recovery from a breakup. For both men and women, the sooner they began dating someone new, the sooner they recovered from the previous breakup (Locker et al., 2010).

We have also argued that reputational difficulties after a mate poaching can reduce a poacher's inclusive fitness by labeling her as promiscuous and therefore less likely to benefit from strategic social alliances. However, what has yet to be explored is how a woman combats the negative effects of being labeled a "home-wrecker." For instance, how effective is it to challenge this title by making one's own allegations that justify her mate poaching? Can a woman improve her reputation by leveling her own allegations that the rejected woman was abusive, neglectful, or perhaps infertile? For example, we know that in many cultures infertility is justifiable cause to demand return of brideprice and send a woman back to her family; so if "infertility" can be "advertised," it may devalue a woman. Are the women within a social group more inclined to forgive a mate poacher if she can effectively reduce the social status of the rejected woman (e.g., if there is a social cost for being labeled "the other woman," can that cost be mitigated within the social group by reducing the social "value" of the mate's prior partner)? Furthermore, what counterattacks are the most effective for "saving face"?

Though many aspire to a love that lasts a lifetime, there are factors outside of any relationship that influence its health and longevity. Breakups, initially, can bring storms of negative and stressful emotions upon both parties. However, among the debris, positive emotional experiences and beneficial personal transformations can be found. Nonclinical depression symptoms, whether precipitated by mate loss through a breakup or failure to compete successfully with another woman for a potential mate, can provide fertile ground for self-reflection from which fruitful changes in self-confidence and mate-seeking and mate-retaining strategies can grow.

While the concept of rumination is often associated with negative aspects of low mood states, it may also provide a period of intense self-analysis in which a woman can better examine and evaluate what went wrong in her lost relationship and make plans for avoiding these same issues in future relationships. This rumination, coupled with regret over what she could or could not have done to retain her mate, may allow a woman to do a comprehensive inventory of her own relational strengths and weaknesses as compared to potential rivals. While this process is not without pain and grief, the knowledge gained could potentially help a woman rise above the failed relationship and move on as a stronger and more competitive woman in search of a better mate.

Women have been shown to shun other women who are labeled as promiscuous by employing relational aggression to wreak havoc on their social value in hopes of reducing their mate value. Therefore, social support is perhaps the most powerful tool women have to combat intrasexual competition and mate loss. From the direct support given in the immediate aftermath of a breakup, to friends who actively derogate the defected mate and his new partner, friends and family members provide a social means to restore the "defeated" woman to a position of emotional power, perhaps at the expense of the supposed "winner" of the competition.

Breakups happen to virtually all women at some point in their life, usually more than once, and have the potential to be one of the most traumatic experiences a woman ever faces. These breakups happen for varied and complex reasons (e.g., lack of communication, geographical distance, incompatible goals; Morris & Reiber, 2011). However, we have argued that, relative to other causes of relationship termination, losing one's mate to another woman creates unique and difficult challenges. If the force of differential parental investments is coupled with the risk of subpar male parental investment, females are likely to be more discriminating and may actively avoid mating with poor-quality males. Since women are then competing for a few high-quality men, this would eventually lead women to have zero-sum benefits from competing. But there is an important real-life feature of the game—the game changes in very significant ways when repeated, or if the players interact with each other in the future. That is, a person who fails to

win the first time will likely not use the same strategy again (Engle-Warnick & Slonim, 2004, 2006).

Therefore mate loss via intrasexual competition can result in significant psychological distress and decreased life satisfaction in the short term while also providing "the loser" with opportunities for long-term personal growth. Women seem to recover from breakups faster than men and report an overall "silver lining" of increased self-awareness and "relationship intelligence" that men do not (Morris & Reiber, 2011). Therefore women may emerge from breakups stronger, wiser, and better equipped to succeed in their next romantic relationship. Future research may demonstrate that there are real opportunities for learning, personal growth, and an evaluation of relationship experience to be had from heartbreak. Taking advantage of these opportunities may help a woman reduce the likelihood that the next broken heart will be hers.

References

Abbott, D., Keverne, E., Bercovitch, F., Shively, C., Mendoza, S. P., Saltzman, W., . . . Garland, T. (2003). Are subordinates always stressed? A comparative analysis of rank differences in cortisol levels among primates. *Hormones and Behavior*, *43*(1), 67–82.

Allen, N. B., & Badcock, P. B. (2003). The social risk hypothesis of depressed mood: Evolutionary, psychosocial, and neurobiological perspectives. *Psychological Bulletin*, *129*(6), 887.

Amato, P. R. (2000). The consequences of divorce for adults and children. *Journal of Marriage and Family*, *62*(4), 1269–1287.

Andrews, P. W., & Thomson, J. A. (2009). The bright side of being blue: Depression as an adaptation for analyzing complex problems. *Psychological Review*, *116*(3), 620–654.

Archer, J. (1999). *The nature of grief: The evolution and psychology of reactions to loss*. New York: Routledge.

Arnocky, S., Sunderani, S., & Vaillancourt, T. (2013). Mate-poaching and mating success in humans. *Journal of Evolutionary Psychology*, *11*(2), 65–83.

Barkow, J. H. (1992). Beneath new culture is old psychology: Gossip and social stratification. In J. H. Barkow, L. Cosmides & J. Tooby (Eds.), *The adapted mind: Evolutionary psychology and the generation of culture* (pp. 627–637). New York: Oxford University Press.

Baumeister, R. F., & Leary, M. R. (1995). The need to belong: Desire for interpersonal attachments as a fundamental human motivation. *Psychological Bulletin*, *117*(3), 497.

Beaussart, M. L., Kaufman, S. B., & Kaufman, J. C. (2012). Creative activity, personality, mental illness, and short-term mating success. *Journal of Creative Behavior*, *46*(3), 151–167.

Bevvino, D. L., & Sharkin, B. S. (2003). Divorce adjustment as a function of finding meaning and gender differences. *Journal of Divorce & Remarriage*, *39*(3–4), 81–97.

Björkqvist, K., Lagerspetz, K. M. J., & Österman, K. (1992). Direct and indirect aggression scales (DIAS). Vasa, Findland: Abo Academi University, Department of Social Sciences.

Björkqvist, K. (1994). Sex differences in physical, verbal, and indirect aggression: A review of recent research. *Sex Roles*, *30*(3–4), 177–188.

Björkqvist, K., Österman, K., & Lagerspetz, K. M. (1994). Sex differences in covert aggression among adults. *Aggressive Behavior, 20*(1), 27–33.

Boelen, P. A., & Reijntjes, A. (2009). Negative cognitions in emotional problems following romantic relationship break ups. *Stress and Health, 25*(1), 11–19.

Bowlby, J. (1969). *Attachment and loss: Vol 1. Attachment.* New York: Basic Books.

Bowlby, J. (1980). *Attachment and loss: Vol. 3. Loss; sadness and depression.* New York: Basic Books.

Brase, G. L., & Guy, E. C. (2004). The demographics of mate value and self-esteem. *Personality and Individual Differences, 36*(2), 471–484.

Breitner, B. C., & Anderson, D. N. (1994). The organic and psychological antecedents of delusional jealousy in old age. *International Journal of Geriatric Psychiatry, 9*(9), 703–707.

Brown, W. M., & Moore, C. (2002). Smile asymmetries and reputation as reliable indicators of likelihood to cooperate: An evolutionary analysis. In S. P. Shohov (Ed.), *Advances in psychology research* (pp. 59–78). New York: Nova Science.

Bryson, J. B. (1991). *Modes of response to jealousy-evoking situations.* New York: Guilford Press.

Buss, D. M. (1988). From vigilance to violence: Tactics of mate retention in American undergraduates. *Ethology and Sociobiology, 9*(5), 291–317.

Buss, D. M. (1989). Sex differences in human mate preferences: Evolutionary hypotheses tested in 37 cultures. *Behavioral and Brain Sciences, 12*(1), 1–14.

Buss, D. M. (1990). The evolution of anxiety and social exclusion. *Journal of Social and Clinical Psychology, 9*(2), 196–201.

Buss, D. M. (2000). The evolution of happiness. *American Psychologist, 55*(1), 15.

Buss, D. M. (2002). Human mate guarding. *Neuroendocrinology Letters, 23*(4), 23–29.

Buss, D. M. (2003). *The evolution of desire: Strategies of human mating.* New York: Basic Books.

Buss, D. M. (2004). *Evolutionary psychology: The new science of the mind.* Boston: Pearson Education.

Buss, D. M. (2007). The evolution of human mating. *Acta Psychologica Sinica, 39*(3), 502–512.

Buss, D. M., & Dedden, L. A. (1990). Derogation of competitors. *Journal of Social and Personal Relationships, 7*(3), 395–422.

Buss, D. M., & Shackelford, T. K. (1997). Human aggression in evolutionary psychological perspective. *Clinical Psychology Review, 17*(6), 605–619.

Buss, D. M., Shackelford, T. K., & McKibbin, W. F. (2008). The Mate Retention Inventory–Short Form (MRI–SF). *Personality and Individual Differences, 44*(1), 322–334.

Buunk, B. P., & Bringle, R. G. (1987). Jealousy in love relationships. In D. Perlman & S. Duck (Eds.), *Intimate relationships: Development, dynamics, and deterioration* (pp. 13–42). Thousand Oaks, CA: SAGE.

Buunk, B. P., & Dijkstra, P. (2004). Gender differences in rival characteristics that evoke jealousy in response to emotional versus sexual infidelity. *Personal Relationships, 11*(4), 395–408.

Campbell, A. (2004). Female competition: Causes, constraints, content, and contexts. *Journal of Sex Research, 41*(1), 16–26.

Chung, M. C., Farmer, S., Grant, K., Newton, R., Payne, S., Perry, M., . . . Stone, N. (2003). Coping with post-traumatic stress symptoms following relationship dissolution. *Stress and Health, 19*(1), 27–36.

Clark, A. E., & Georgellis, Y. (2013). Back to baseline in Britain: Adaptation in the British Household Panel Survey. *Economica, 80*(319), 496–512.

Crawford, M., & Popp, D. (2003). Sexual double standards: A review and methodological critique of two decades of research. *Journal of Sex Research, 40*(1), 13–26.

Culbertson, F. M. (1997). Depression and gender: an international review. *American Psychologist, 52*(1), 25.

Davis, D., Shaver, P. R., & Vernon, M. L. (2003). Physical, emotional, and behavioral reactions to breaking up: The roles of gender, age, emotional involvement, and attachment style. *Personality and Social Psychology Bulletin, 29*(7), 871–884.

Dugatkin, L. A. (1992). Sexual selection and imitation: Females copy the mate choice of others. *American Naturalist, 139*, 1384–1389.

Eagly, A. H., & Wood, W. (1999). The origins of sex differences in human behavior: Evolved dispositions versus social roles. *American Psychologist, 54*(6), 408–423.

Eastwick, P. W., Finkel, E. J., Krishnamurti, T., & Loewenstein, G. (2008). Mispredicting distress following romantic breakup: Revealing the time course of the affective forecasting error. *Journal of Experimental Social Psychology, 44*(3), 800–807.

Engle-Warnick, J., & Slonim, R. L. (2004). The evolution of strategies in a repeated trust game. *Journal of Economic Behavior & Organization, 55*(4), 553–573.

Engle-Warnick, J., & Slonim, R. L. (2006). Inferring repeated-game strategies from actions: Evidence from trust game experiments. *Economic Theory, 28*(3), 603–632.

Field, T., Diego, M., Pelaez, M., Deeds, O., & Delgado, J. (2010). Breakup distress and loss of intimacy in university students. *Psychology, 1*(3), 173–177.

Fine, M. A., & Sacher, J. A. (1997). Predictors of distress following relationship termination among dating couples. *Journal of Social and Clinical Psychology, 16*(4), 381–388.

Fisher, H. (2004a). Dumped! *New Scientist, 2434*, 40–43.

Fisher, H. (2004b). *Why we love: The nature and chemistry of romantic love.* New York: Henry Holt.

Fisher, H. (2006). The drive to love: The neural mechanism for mate selection. In R. Sternberg & K. Weis (Eds.), *The new psychology of love* (pp. 87–115). New Haven, CT: Yale University Press.

Fisher, M., & Cox, A. (2011). Four strategies used during intrasexual competition for mates. *Personal Relationships, 18*(1), 20–38.

Fleming, C. B., White, H. R., Oesterle, S., Haggerty, K. P., & Catalano, R. F. (2010). Romantic relationship status changes and substance use among 18- to 20-year-olds. *Journal of Studies on Alcohol and Drugs, 71*(6), 847–856.

Forgas, J. P. (1998). On being happy and mistaken: Mood effects on the fundamental attribution error. *Journal of Personality and Social Psychology, 75*(2), 318–331.

Frazier, P. A., & Cook, S. W. (1993). Correlates of distress following heterosexual relationship dissolution. *Journal of Social and Personal Relationships, 10*(1), 55–67.

Frazier, P. A., Port, C. L., & Hoff, P. (1996). Social support: The provider's experience. *Journal of Loss & Trauma, 1*(1), 109–128.

Gigerenzer, G., & Goldstein, D. G. (1996). Reasoning the fast and frugal way: Models of bounded rationality. *Psychological Review, 103*(4), 650–669.

Gilbert, P. (2001). Depression and stress: A biopsychosocial exploration of evolved functions and mechanisms. *Stress: The International Journal on the Biology of Stress, 4*(2), 121–135.

Gilbert, P. (2006). Evolution and depression: Issues and implications. *Psychological Medicine, 36*(3), 287–297.

Gilbert, P., & Allan, S. (1998). The role of defeat and entrapment (arrested flight) in depression: An exploration of an evolutionary view. *Psychological Medicine, 28*(3), 585–598.

Gurven, M., Allen-Arave, W., Hill, K., & Hurtado, M. (2000). "It's a wonderful life": Signaling generosity among the Ache of Paraguay. *Evolution and Human Behavior, 21*(4), 263–282.

Gurven, M., Hill, K., Kaplan, H., Hurtado, A., & Lyles, R. (2000). Food transfers among Hiwi foragers of Venezuela: Tests of reciprocity. *Human Ecology, 28*(2), 171–218.

Hess, N. H., & Hagen, E. H. (2006). Sex differences in indirect aggression: Psychological evidence from young adults. *Evolution and Human Behavior, 27*(3), 231–245.

Higley, J. D., King, S. T., Jr., Hasert, M. F., Champoux, M., Suomi, S. J., & Linnoila, M. (1996). Stability of interindividual differences in serotonin function and its relationship to severe aggression and competent social behavior in rhesus macaque females. *Neuropsychopharmacology, 14*(1), 67–76.

Hohmann, G., & Fruth, B. (2003). Intra- and inter-sexual aggression by bonobos in the context of mating. *Behaviour, 140*(11), 1389–1414.

Jankowiak, W. R., & Fischer, E. F. (1992). A cross-cultural perspective on romantic love. *Ethnology, 31*, 149–155.

Jankowiak, W. R., & Paladino, T. (2008). Desiring sex, longing for love: A tripartite conundrum. In W. R. Jankowiak (Ed.), *Intimacies: Love and sex across cultures* (pp. 1–36). New York: Columbia University Press.

Kaplan, H., Gurven, M., Hill, K., & Hurtado, A. M. (2005). The natural history of human food sharing and cooperation: A review and a new multi-individual approach to the negotiation of norms. In H. Gintis, S. Bowles, R. Boyd, & E. Fehrs (Eds.), *Moral sentiments and material interests: The foundations of cooperation in economic life* (pp. 75–113). Cambridge, MA: MIT Press.

Karp, D. A. (1997). *Speaking of sadness: Depression, disconnection, and the meanings of illness.* New York: Oxford University Press.

Keller, M. C., & Nesse, R. M. (2005). Is low mood an adaptation? Evidence for subtypes with symptoms that match precipitants. *Journal of Affective Disorders, 86*(1), 27–35.

Kendler, K. S., Hettema, J. M., Butera, F., Gardner, C. O., & Prescott, C. A. (2003). Life event dimensions of loss, humiliation, entrapment, and danger in the prediction of onsets of major depression and generalized anxiety. *Archives of General Psychiatry, 60*(8), 789–796.

Kingham, M., & Gordon, H. (2004). Aspects of morbid jealousy. *Advances in Psychiatric Treatment, 10*(3), 207–215.

Kitson, G. C., & Holmes, W. M. (1992). *Portrait of divorce: Adjustment to marital breakdown.* Guilford Press.

Knox, D., Zusman, M. E., Kaluzny, M., & Cooper, C. (2000). College student recovery from a broken heart. *College Student Journal, 34*(3), 322–324.

Kuehner, C. (2003). Gender differences in unipolar depression: An update of epidemiological findings and possible explanations. *Acta Psychiatrica Scandinavica, 108*(3), 163–174.

Laumann, E. O. (1994). *The social organization of sexuality: Sexual practices in the United States.* Chicago: University of Chicago Press.

Lennox, B. R., Jacob, R., Calder, A. J., Lupson, V., & Bullmore, E. T. (2004). Behavioural and neurocognitive responses to sad facial affect are attenuated in patients with mania. *Psychological Medicine, 34*(5), 795–802.

Levitan, R. D., Vaccarino, F. J., Brown, G. M., & Kennedy, S. H. (2002). Low-dose dexamethasone challenge in women with atypical major depression: Pilot study. *Journal of Psychiatry and Neuroscience, 27*(1), 47–51.

Locker, L., McIntosh, W., Hackney, A., Wilson, J., & Wiegand, K. (2010). The breakup of romantic relationships: Situational predictors of perception of recovery. *North American Journal of Psychology, 12*(3), 565–578.

Lucas, R. E. (2005). Time does not heal all wounds: A longitudinal study of reaction and adaptation to divorce. *Psychological Science, 16*(12), 945–950.

Lucas, R. E., Clark, A. E., Georgellis, Y., & Diener, E. (2003). Reexamining adaptation and the set point model of happiness: Reactions to changes in marital status. *Journal of Personality and Social Psychology, 84*(3), 527–539.

Marks, N. F., & Lambert, J. D. (1998). Marital status continuity and change among young and midlife adults longitudinal effects on psychological well-being. *Journal of Family Issues, 19*(6), 652–686.

Marlowe, F. W. (2003). A critical period for provisioning by Hadza men: Implications for pair bonding. *Evolution and Human Behavior, 24*(3), 217–229.

Mearns, J. (1991). Coping with a breakup: Negative mood regulation expectancies and depression following the end of a romantic relationship. *Journal of Personality and Social Psychology, 60*(2), 327–334.

Miller, S. L., & Maner, J. K. (2008). Coping with romantic betrayal: Sex differences in responses to partner infidelity. *Evolutionary Psychology, 6*(3), 413–426.

Moller, N. P., Fouladi, R. T., McCarthy, C. J., & Hatch, K. D. (2003). Relationship of attachment and social support to college students' adjustment following a relationship breakup. *Journal of Counseling & Development, 81*(3), 354–369.

Monroe, S. M., Rohde, P., Seeley, J. R., & Lewinsohn, P. M. (1999). Life events and depression in adolescence: Relationship loss as a prospective risk factor for first onset of major depressive disorder. *Journal of Abnormal Psychology, 108*(4), 606–614.

Morris, C. E., & Reiber, C. (2011). Frequency, intensity and expression of post-relationship grief. *EvoS Journal: The Journal of the Evolutionary Studies Consortium, 3*(1), 1–11.

Mullins, D. (2010). Morbid jealousy: The green-eyed monster. *Irish Journal of Psychological Medicine, 27*(2), i–vii.

Nesse, R. (1996). *Why we get sick : The new science of Darwinian medicine* (1st ed.). New York: Vintage Books.

Nesse, R. M. (2000). Is depression an adaptation? *Archives of General Psychiatry, 57*(1), 14–20.

Nesse, R. M. (2005). Evolutionary psychology and mental health. In D. M. Buss (Ed.), *Handbook of evolutionary psychology* (pp. 903–927). Hoboken, NJ: Wiley.

Parker, J., & Burkley, M. (2009). Who's chasing whom? The impact of gender and relationship status on mate poaching. *Journal of Experimental Social Psychology, 45*(4), 1016–1019.

Perilloux, C., & Buss, D. M. (2008). Breaking up romantic relationships: Costs experienced and coping strategies deployed. *Evolutionary Psychology, 6*(1), 164–181.

Price, J. S., Gardner, R., & Erickson, M. (2004). Can depression, anxiety and somatization be understood as appeasement displays? *Journal of Affective Disorders, 79*(1), 1–11.

Price, J. S., Sloman, L., Gardner, R., Gilbert, P., & Rohde, P. (1994). The social competition hypothesis of depression. *British Journal of Psychiatry, 164*(3), 309–315.

Ray, J. C., & Sapolsky, R. M. (1992). Styles of male social behavior and their endocrine correlates among high-ranking wild baboons. *American Journal of Primatology, 28*(4), 231–250.

Rhoades, G. K., Kamp Dush, C. M., Atkins, D. C., Stanley, S. M., & Markman, H. J. (2011). Breaking up is hard to do: The impact of unmarried relationship dissolution on mental health and life satisfaction. *Journal of Family Psychology, 25*(3), 366–374.

Saffrey, C., & Ehrenberg, M. (2007). When thinking hurts: Attachment, rumination, and postrelationship adjustment. *Personal Relationships, 14*(3), 351–368.

Sapolsky, R. M. (1990). Adrenocortical function, social rank, and personality among wild baboons. *Biological Psychiatry, 28*(10), 862–878.

Sayer, L. C., England, P., Allison, P., & Kangas, N. (2011). She left, he left: How employment and satisfaction affect men's and women's decisions to leave marriages. *AJS; American Journal of Sociology, 116*(6), 1982.

Sbarra, D. A., & Ferrer, E. (2006). The structure and process of emotional experience following nonmarital relationship dissolution: Dynamic factor analyses of love, anger, and sadness. *Emotion, 6*(2), 224–238.

Shackelford, T. K., & Buss, D. M. (1997). Anticipation of marital dissolution as a consequence of spousal infidelity. *Journal of Social and Personal Relationships, 14*(6), 793–808.

Shackelford, T. K., LeBlanc, G. J., & Drass, E. (2000). Emotional reactions to infidelity. *Cognition & Emotion, 14*(5), 643–659.

Schaller, M., & Cialdini, R. B. (Eds.). (1990). *Happiness, sadness, and helping: A motivational integration.* Vol. 18. New York: Guilford Press.

Schmitt, D. P., Alcalay, L., Allik, J., Angleitner, A., Ault, L., Austers, I., . . . Cunen, B. (2004). Patterns and universals of mate poaching across 53 nations: The effects of sex, culture, and personality on romantically attracting another person's partner. *Journal of Personality and Social Psychology, 86*(4), 560–584.

Sinclair, R. C. (1988). Mood, categorization breadth, and performance appraisal: The effects of order of information acquisition and affective state on halo, accuracy, information retrieval, and evaluations. *Organizational Behavior and Human Decision Processes, 42*(1), 22–46.

Sloman, L., Gilbert, P., & Hasey, G. (2003). Evolved mechanisms in depression: The role and interaction of attachment and social rank in depression. *Journal of Affective Disorders, 74*(2), 107–121.

Sprecher, S., Felmlee, D., Metts, S., Fehr, B., & Vanni, D. (1998). Factors associated with distress following the breakup of a close relationship. *Journal of Social and Personal Relationships, 15*(6), 791–809.

Starratt, V. G., Shackelford, T. K., Goetz, A. T., & McKibbin, W. F. (2007). Male mate retention behaviors vary with risk of partner infidelity and sperm competition. *Acta Psychologica Sinica, 39*(3), 523–527.

Stutzer, A., & Frey, B. S. (2006). Does marriage make people happy, or do happy people get married? *Journal of Socio-Economics, 35*(2), 326–347.

Sugiyama, L. S. (2005). Physical attractiveness in adaptationist perspective. In D. M. Buss (Ed.), *Handbook of evolutionary psychology* (pp. 292–342). Hoboken, NJ: Wiley.

Tashiro, T., & Frazier, P. A. (2003). "I'll never be in a relationship like that again": Personal growth following romantic relationship breakups. *Personal Relationships, 10*(1), 113–128.

Trivers, R. (1972). *Parental investment and sexual selection.* Cambridge, MA: Biological Laboratories, Harvard University.

Uller, T., & Johansson, L. C. (2003). Human mate choice and the wedding ring effect. *Human Nature, 14*(3), 267–276.

Von Holst, D. (1986). Psychosocial stress and its pathophysiological effects in tree shrews (Tupaia belangeri). *Biological and Psychological Factors in Cardiovascular Disease, 4,* 476–490.

Vrangalova, Z., Bukberg, R. E., & Rieger, G. (2014). Birds of a feather? Not when it comes to sexual permissiveness. *Journal of Social and Personal Relationships, 31*(1), 93–113.

Wasser, S. K., & Barash, D. P. (1983). Reproductive suppression among female mammals: Implications for biomedicine and sexual selection theory. *Quarterly Review of Biology, 58*(4), 513–538.

Wasser, S. K., & Starling, A. K. (1988). Proximate and ultimate causes of reproductive suppression among female yellow baboons at Mikumi National Park, Tanzania. *American Journal of Primatology, 16*(2), 97–121.

Weary, G., Elbin, S., & Hill, M. G. (1987). Attributional and social comparison processes in depression. *Journal of Personality and Social Psychology, 52*(3), 605–610.

Endocrinology and Psychobiological Considerations

Psychobiological Responses to Competition in Women

Raquel Costa, Miguel A. Serrano, *and* Alicia Salvador

Abstract

From an evolutionary perspective, questions have been raised about whether women have a psychobiological pattern similar to that of men. In humans, hormonal effects of competition and its outcome have been investigated under the biosocial status hypothesis, which proposes that, after a competition, winners would show increases in testosterone whereas losers would show reductions, and the challenge hypothesis, which emphasizes the functional role of testosterone increases in the spring to promote agonistic behavior related to territoriality and access to females. Subsequently, the coping competition model has defended the study of competition within a more general stress model, considering the psychobiological responses as part of the coping response. This chapter shows that women investigations are increasing in number in recent years and that, in competitive situations, they present coping strategies with a psychobiological response pattern that can be enlightened by the coping competition model.

Key Words: women, competition, psychobiological responses, variables, coping competition model

Introduction

In 1987 . . . it was still acceptable to exclude women from research because of the "noise" that might be introduced in the data due to their menstrual cycle and associated hormones. In 1993, . . . the policy . . . became that women must be included . . . the noise turned into orchestrated notes of independent variables that have spurred entire areas of inquiry in the field of women's health. . . . Thus, the noise crescendos into a melody of hope that the next decade of women's health research will provide as much information about improving the lives of women as the previous decade has provided about the causes our illnesses.

—*Girdler, 2005, p. 1*

In 2005, Girdler emphasized the lack of studies on women's health, mainly due to female hormonal changes, and the importance of including women in research. She also indicated that there was a need for studies, so that "the noise crescendos into

a melody of hope that the next decade of women's health research will provide as much information about improving the lives of women" (p. 1). This objective includes a wider range of variables in order to understand the complete picture of women's health. The psychobiological basis of competitive behavior in women is one of the topics that has been omitted. When this type of research began in humans, it was carried out mainly in men, with only a few exceptions in recent decades. Studies on human competition have shown very complex scenarios because hormones and behavior interact in a direct and simple way, while other factors, such as cognitive and personality variables or the situation appraisal, mediate these relationships (Salvador, 2005; Salvador & Costa, 2009). Currently there are data available from sports and laboratory contests that allow us to conclude that women also compete, although at least some characteristics of their competitive behavior tend to be different from that of men.

In this chapter we explain the importance of competition for women and its main characteristics from an evolutionist approach. In the first part, basic concepts and definitions related to competition and sex differences are introduced from this perspective. In the second part, we present and compare the main explanatory hypotheses proposed in the literature, leading to the third part, where the main results obtained from the empirical research are introduced and interpreted. Based on the previous points, the final section is dedicated to a general discussion about the psychobiology of competition in women.

Competition as a Form of Stress

Briefly, competition involves the confrontation between two or more individuals to obtain a goal in order to achieve or maintain status. In this situation, one opponent (person or group) ends up winning, whereas the other is defeated. Therefore, one or several individuals carry out actions leading to an objective that is not possible for everyone to achieve. In addition, competition plays an important social role not only to gain primary reinforcements like food or mating but also to obtain other secondary resources (i.e., employment, promotion) that make it possible to attain the best primary resources (Salvador & Costa, 2009). The outcome can have short- or long-term consequences for the individual or individuals. This situation is clearly present in nature, where the resources are usually limited. For example, a mouse strives for food, and its motivation is primarily to avoid dying of starvation, but agonistic encounters are also motivated by the possibility of rising in the hierarchy in order to obtain better food (primary resources) or social relationships. The short-term consequences of defeat can be worse or insufficient food, whereas the long-term consequences can be immunological impairment and premature death.

Thus, agonistic behavior is an adaptive behavior that is used to reach goals because the outcome, winning or losing, affects the achievement of significant aims in the daily lives of these individuals (e.g., obtaining territory, mates, or food). From an evolutionary point of view, the importance of competitive behavior that leads to maintaining and/or rising to a higher status is clear, and it has strong repercussions for the organization of social species (Blanchard, McKittrick, & Blanchard, 2001; Koolhaas, de Boer, Buwalda, & van Reenen, 2007). In humans, men's physiological and particularly

hormonal responses associated with competition have been studied since the 1980s. Specifically, sports competition has some special characteristics that are not present in other competitive situations in humans, which make it an ideal situation to investigate psychobiological responses to competition. The most important characteristics are that the outcome is not established, the main criterion for success is merit or ability, the duration of the sports competition is limited, and, finally, the result has clear consequences because there is a winner and a loser (Salvador, 2005).

However, competition is also a social stressor (Suay et al., 1999), which means that a wide range of literature must be considered (Salvador, 2005; Salvador & Costa, 2009), and researchers must take into account competition's potential strength and frequency in a social species. In other words, stress implies an imbalance between demands and resources, so there is a loss of homeostasis. Moreover, an individual must perceive the situation as threatening, new, or uncontrollable, which involves psychophysiological and hormonal changes. The fight-or-flight response described by Cannon (1932) immediately prepares the individual by activating the autonomic nervous system (ANS), especially the sympathetic adreno-medullar system (SAM), with increases in blood pressure, heart rate, and secretion of catecholamines into the bloodstream, among other responses, in order to mobilize energy. In addition, the hypothalamus–pituitary–adrenal (HPA) is activated, increasing the levels of cortisol (C), a catabolic hormone that supports the SAM to increase the available energy. This is essentially the basic physiological response to stress. However, in this chapter we focus on social stress, which has a more complex pattern because the social stimuli that are capable of being sources of stress require processing and depend on many contextual and experiential cues. In this sense, Huether (1996) highlighted the value of psychosocial stress as a trigger for adaptive behavioral modifications. The primitive stress response is elicited by an external stimulus, such as a predator, and the responses are limited, stereotyped, and stable. However, the most frequent source of stress in humans comes from psychosocial conflict, such as a public speech, rather than a real threat to life (i.e., a public speech is a high psychosocial stressor accompanied by HPA and SAM activation, but the repetition of a speech can diminish the anxiety and physiological activation). Both sexes share behavioral and hormonal components to compete, but proximate evolutionary mechanisms suggest a sex-specific adaptation (Rosvall, 2013; Salvador, 2012), as we review in the following section.

Biological Differences Between the Sexes and Main Theoretical Explanations

In this section, we offer a concise synopsis of biological differences between men and women, focusing on the differences related to competition as a social stressor.

Are There Biological Differences That Could Affect the Way the Sexes Cope With Competition?

Competitive and aggressive behavior has predominantly been associated with males (Clutton-Brock & Huchard, 2013) who were placed by evolution into the main flight-or-fight settings. This idea is developed and explained in this section. It is assumed that the male brain is shaped to compete and that morphological (e.g., higher muscle mass) and physiological differences (e.g., testosterone [T] levels) could help males to be more effective competitors than females. This does not mean that women do not compete, but, based on evolutionary theories, men would be more prone to competing than women. However, in today's Western societies, women compete at the same levels as men because social competition depends more on psychosocial resources than on biological resources.

But are women really less competitive than men? Can we state that female brains are not adapted to competition, relative to male brains? In this section we briefly explain that men and women have developed competitive behaviors differently, depending on androgen exposure, and that we have to be cautious about extrapolating results from studies conducted with men to draw conclusions about women.

Obviously men and women are biologically different. Sexual selection operates on males and females through many morphological components (Clutton-Brock & Huchard, 2013). Specifically, the brain development of the sexes is different starting in the embryonic period. Throughout life, women have a different biological development from men, basically, although not solely, due to the influence of steroid hormones. This influence results in brain dimorphism, which complements the other effects of the steroid hormones in the development of male or female bodies. Furthermore, during adolescence, males are exposed to surges of gonadal T, while this does not occur in adolescent female bodies, where other hormones, such as estrogens, are at work. Most of these differences are explained by the so-called organizational–activational hypothesis (Arnold, 2009). In this context, we can understand that there are sex- and individual-specific behavioral and neural responses depending on the effect of T throughout the lifespan. Thus, fetal T levels are significantly responsible for the maturation of the neural circuitry of the brain (Arnold & Breedlove, 1985; Phoenix, Goy, Gerall, & Young, 1959), making the brain more sensitive to T throughout one's life. Taking into account that in early studies T was found to be involved in aggressive and dominant behavior (Mazur & Booth, 1998), and later related to social status hierarchies (Eisenegger, Haushofer, & Fehr, 2011), and that in male mice T has rewarding properties (Arnedo, Salvador, Martínez-Sanchís, & Pellicer, 2002), this hormone must leave a trace that shapes men's behavior differently from women's.

If we look further, most brain regions related to the stress response circuitry are sexually dimorphic in animals and in humans. Subcortical areas, such as the central amygdala, hypothalamus and hippocampus, and cortical areas, such as the orbitofrontal cortex or prefrontal cortex, are directly related to physiological arousal (McEwen & Magarinos, 1997; Price, 1999). Moreover, these dimorphic regions regulate the HPA and hypothalamic–pituitary–gonadal axes (Bao, Hestiantoro, Van Someren, Swaab, & Zhou, 2005; Goldstein, Jerram, Abbs, Whitfield-Gabrieli, & Makris, 2010; Keverne, 1988; Ostlund, Keller, & Hurd, 2003; Swaab, 2004), suggesting hormonal regulation of stress response circuitry (Goldstein et al., 2010). Therefore, sex differences in the stress response circuitry are hormonally regulated via the influence of subcortical brain activity on the cortical control of arousal, which also demonstrates that females have been endowed with a natural hormonal capacity to regulate the stress response that differs from males (Goldstein et al., 2010). Apart from the differences in the brain and hormones, there is relatively consistent evidence that men are more risk-taking than women on most tasks (i.e., in economic games) and that, on average, women prefer less competitive situations than men in objective probability lotteries or high-stakes decisions (in laboratory and field situations). Moreover, these differences are stable when comparing single and married people. One possible explanation is that women experience stronger emotions than men, which affects decisions involving risk (Croson & Gneezy, 2009). Specifically, women report more anxiety and fear in anticipation of negative outcomes (Brody, 1993), and they have a greater fear of losing, because they are less confident in uncertain situations than men (Croson & Gneezy, 2009). However, this decision-making is also affected by the menstrual cycle (Chen, Katuščák, & Ozdenoren, 2013). During the menstrual cycle, levels of estradiol, progesterone, the luteinizing hormone, and the follicle-stimulating hormone change. It has been suggested that women change their decision-making according to their menstrual cycle phase. Thus, naturally cycling women bid (on the lottery) significantly higher in the first part of the menstrual cycle, when estrogen levels are high, than in the second part of the cycle, when estrogen levels are lower and progesterone levels are higher (Chen et al., 2013). Furthermore, women are more predisposed to engage in risky behavior during their fecund phase, around the ovulatory period. Thus, from an evolutionary point of view, Pearson and Schipper (2013) have interpreted these risky behaviors as a way to increase the probability of conception during this specific menstrual phase. Consequently, sex differences in risky decision-making would depend on the phase of the menstrual cycle.

Therefore, there are some neuroendocrine differences between men and women that may predispose them to behave differently. We next address the issue of whether morphological and physiological factors could modify the way the sexes cope with life events, including competition for resources.

Main Theoretical Frameworks in Competition Research: Why Men and Women Respond Differently to Competition

In social neuroscience, two hypotheses analyze how sex differences influence adaptive behavior: the fight-or-flight and tend-and-befriend strategies. As Taylor et al. (2000) point out, "Survival depends upon the ability to mount a successful response to threat. The human stress response has been characterized as fight-or-flight (Cannon, 1932), and has been represented as an essential mechanism in the survival process" (p. 411). This type of response has mainly been studied in males, particularly in male rats. In our species, it has been studied in men but less so in women. However, natural selection has caused both men and women to be effective competitors, although the paths they use may be different due to sex-specific reproductive strategies (Benenson, 2013). Male mammals typically invest less in their offspring than females do, and they can potentially have more offspring (Bateman, 1948). Female mammals, however, must invest more time and energy in caring for their offspring, be more

selective about their partners, and compete for the resources they need for their offspring to mature (Lancaster & Lancaster, 1983). Thus, Taylor et al., from a meta-theoretical perspective, assume that successful responses pass through generations, according to the principles of natural selection, and what is most adaptive for men might not necessarily be adaptive for women. Specifically, they propose that the female human response is not characterized by fight-or-flight, as assumed in the literature, but by tend-and-befriend, suggesting that protection and care of offspring and a desire for membership (i.e., creating and maintaining relationships with other women in a small group) are adaptive behaviors for females.

Next we introduce a more detailed explanation of differences between sexes in response to stress. In males, the fight-or-flight strategy is linked to sympathetic activation and to an organized pattern of behavior, due in part to activating androgens. The female response is not as clearly related to androgens but rather to another hormone (oxytocin), at least partially, and it is more associated with protective behavior (Archer, 1991). In this sense, the fight response can be maladaptive for females (i.e., females are usually not as strong as males) and, although the flight response in females may seem more appropriate than the fight, it is not a dominant response; if a female is caring for her offspring, flight would mean abandoning them (Taylor et al., 2000). In a complementary way, both sexes have androgen receptors in the nervous system and in peripheral tissues exhibiting behavioral or physiological responses to T (Rosvall, 2013). Thus, androgens could have effects on both males and females. Nonetheless, Taylor et al. sustained that in females, tend-and-befriend behavior could be more adaptive than the fight-or-flight response to reach their vital objectives, such as the care of their offspring. They argue that it is more adaptive for women to look for protection in safe contexts (e.g., look for affiliation with other female groups to protect themselves and their offspring from predators), as it is not necessary to compete when females can take advantage of other alternatives (in the previous example, the group would reduce the probability of confrontation with the predator). Research in humans concludes that the desire to affiliate with others is more pronounced in women than in men, and it is one of the most robust sexually dimorphic behaviors (Taylor et al., 2000). Moreover, women's tendency to engage in affiliative behavior while under stress causes them to bond with other women (Schachter,

1959). Although Taylor et al. (2000, 2002) do not deny that women are competitive, they support the idea that there is no basis for direct aggression between females from an evolutionary perspective. However, this argument allows that competition is in the behavioral repertoire of women; according to Geary and Flinn (2002), women compete for social and material resources by showing another type of aggression (i.e., relational). In fact, Campbell (2013) states that women compete, and it has been asserted that in women, relatively low-risk competitive strategies are favored by means of indirect aggression, which is a low-cost but effective form of competition (Stockey & Campbell, 2013).

These approaches to understanding the causes of behavior are based on attempts to explain the evolutionary, adaptive strategies employed by men and women. However, they need to be accompanied by other approaches that make it possible to analyze the proximate causes (how a mechanism interacts with environment), which depict the biological process that contributes to a response, such as to maintain one's status. From an empirical point of view, it is difficult to transfer critical concepts like survival to routine investigation. Thus, from a theoretical perspective, several hypotheses have been proposed to test how competition exerts its effects in humans and how these hypotheses can help to explain evolutionary adaptive strategies (Salvador, 2012).

Hypotheses Used to Frame Empirical Studies in Competition Research

In the 1970s and 1980s, important research on agonistic behavior in rodents and nonhuman primates was carried out by studying how T was involved in changes in hierarchical status. One study with rats showed increases in T after winning and decreases in T after losing an encounter (Schuurman, 1980). Moreover, when T levels were exogenously manipulated, the same results were found. These studies, along with others in nonhuman primates (Bernstein, Gordon, & Rose, 1983), pointed to T as the most important factor related to social status, and they delineated the way hierarchies were constructed in several species. These findings were also used to try to explain human hierarchies. In this context, the biosocial status hypothesis was formulated by Mazur (1985). According to this hypothesis, victory would induce T elevations in subjects, making them more likely to engage in future agonistic encounters in order to maintain or increase dominance, whereas T decreases were expected in losers, who would develop submissive behavior (see Figure 20.1). Moreover, winners must experience less stress and losers must experience more, which would be reflected in stress hormones, such as C in the case of humans.

In the 1990s, another important hypothesis was formulated in relation to T and behavior: the challenge hypothesis (Wingfield, Hegner, Dufty, & Ball, 1990). It emerged from the observation of behavior in monogamous birds and highlighted the role of T changes to favor aggressive behaviors related to territoriality, dominant behavior, or protection of offspring. According to this hypothesis, T increases occurring in the spring are responsible for the behavior of these birds (i.e., 20 species of captive and free-living populations) at this time of year. Thus, social interaction affects androgen levels in males, which should be high when they have to fight for resources (e.g., family, territory, or status). The pattern could be the same in females, depending on the species (Wingfield et al., 1990).

The challenge hypothesis has also been used to explain the relationship between T and some behaviors in humans (van Anders & Watson, 2006). In specific situations, the functional value of T would favor aggressive behaviors that serve to compete for territory or mating and are considered positive or adaptive. Archer (2006) explained that T in humans could also be involved in situations where honor or personal merits are important. However, having high levels of T for long periods

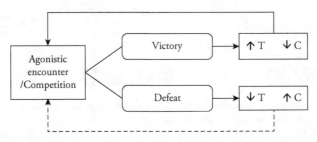

Figure 20.1 Mazur's biosocial status hypothesis. The victory from agonistic encounters or competitions between males promotes increases in T and diminutions in C. In contrast, defeat leads to a diminution in T and increase in C. The outcome influences future competitions.

of time could become negative for the individual. After the administration of exogenous T, subjects are less sensitive to punishment and more sensitive to reinforcement, favoring risky behaviors in both men (Archer, 2006) and women (Van Honk et al., 2004).

Both of these hypotheses focus on the role of T in competition or dominance, mainly based on observations from nature and studies in different contexts and species. However, as stated earlier, other attempts have also been made to explain competition as a social stress response, including, apart from hormones, psychological and autonomic responses. There is a lack of clear, consistent findings regarding the T response to competition and its outcome in humans. For example, some studies found increases in T after winning, others found no differences between winners and losers, and still others found increases in losers (Salvador, 2005; Salvador & Costa, 2009). This inconsistency led to Salvador's proposal to integrate competition within a more general stress model.

This model (see Figure 20.2) incorporates subjective processes, especially appraisal, based on the consideration that previous results on this topic can

be better explained as a part of the coping response to competition (see Salvador & Costa, 2009). Based on this coping competition model, it is necessary to consider not only the outcome obtained but also the way the individual copes with competition. The model considers the initial step of appraisal, which begins before the competition and includes some distant factors that influence the analysis of the situation, such as status, previous experience, personality, and generic skills. These characteristics affect the specific situation in which other cognitive variables, such as expectancies, motivation, ego involvement, or self-efficacy, lead to a specific appraisal. In sum, if the individual appraises the competitive situation as important, controllable, and dependent on his or her own effort (i.e., as a challenge), an active coping response pattern is more likely to be adopted. This pattern would be characterized by increases in T, sympathetic nervous system activation, and positive mood, with no clear effects on C. All these responses would increase the probability of victory, depending on the nature of the competition. By contrast, a threat appraisal would drive an individual into a passive coping response pattern, characterized by insufficient T and sympathetic

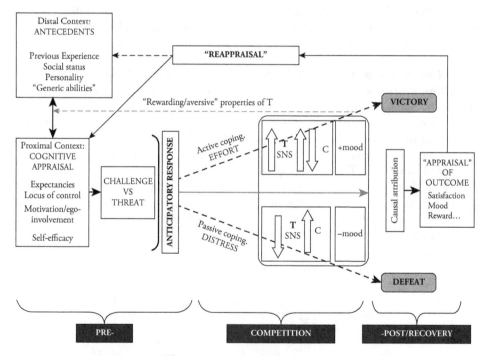

Figure 20.2 Salvador and Costa's coping competition model. Competition begins before the event with cognitive appraisal, whereby a situation can be viewed as a challenge or threat. A challenge appraisal is related to an active coping response with increases in T, in sympathetic nervous system, and in positive mood, increasing the probability of victory. A threat appraisal leads to a passive coping response with diminutions or insufficient increases in T and sympathetic nervous system, increases in C and in negative mood, which increases the probability of defeat. After competition, the appraisal influences future competitions, in proximal contest and even in distal ones.

nervous system activation and increases in negative affect and C levels, and these responses would increase the probability of defeat (Salvador, 2005). This model emphasizes the cognitive appraisal of the specific situation, which begins before the competitive situation, at a conscious or preconscious level. Subsequently, the outcome of the situation also involves cognitive appraisal, which influences future competitions. In other words, a cognitive reappraisal emerges from the causal attribution, the satisfaction with the outcome or the reward, complementary to the real outcome, and these variables have an influence on the individual (Salvador, 2005; Salvador & Costa, 2009).

Both the biosocial status hypothesis and the challenge hypothesis are applicable to females. However, sex differences in the competitive stress response have been found, related to different evolutionary functions (Troisi, 2001), which means that, in general, women invest more time and energy in attracting partners, developing social networks, and taking care of offspring than men, who are more likely to engage in competition to reach or maintain status. Competitive contexts are not exclusive to men, although they are probably somewhat different in women. Furthermore, competition for limited resources drives both natural and sexual selection; even though both men and women can compete, the nature of their competition may differ, especially in response to environmental variations (van Anders & Watson, 2006). However, some contests are common to both sexes, especially in Western societies, where men and women share academic or intellectual tasks, or even sporting events, so that competition on these tasks could be fairly similar for both (Cashdan, 1998).

Psychobiological Responses to Competition in Women

Important studies on competition in women, as well as those that include comparisons with men, exist. Since the 1990s, several studies about women and competition have been carried out in sports and laboratory settings. This section presents an explanation and interpretation of the main results in light of the theoretical explanations: the biosocial status hypotheses, the challenge hypotheses, and the coping competition model, described earlier.

Initially, the main theories on competition defended the possibility of being applicable to females as well as males (Mazur, 1985; Wingfield et al., 1990). However, as mentioned, research on competition was mainly carried out on men, with only a few studies addressing women. Those that mentioned women mostly did so in the context of sports (see Table 20.1).

Women's endocrine response to competition has been studied, measuring T and C in saliva, in several sports such as rugby (Bateup, Booth, Shirtcliff, & Granger, 2002), soccer (Edwards, Wetzel, & Wyner, 2006; Oliveira, Gouveia, & Oliveira, 2009), and volleyball (Edwards & Kurlander, 2010). Generally, competition heightens T levels, regardless of the outcome (Bateup et al., 2002; Edwards & Kurlander, 2010; Edwards & O'Neal, 2009; Edwards et al., 2006; Hamilton, van Anders, Cox, & Watson, 2009). These results do not support the biosocial hypothesis, but they are compatible with the challenge hypothesis. The latter defends the functional significance of the T increases, as it is linked to competitive and aggressive behaviors. In a few studies, higher T levels were found in winners compared to losers (Jiménez, Aguilar, & Alvero-Cruz, 2012; Oliveira et al., 2009).

Bateup et al. (2002) were the first to confirm T changes in real competitive situations involving five rugby league matches with high physical and psychological implications. These changes were not related to the outcome or to performance self-assessments (labeled the "competition effect," i.e., competition elicits more of a hormonal response than the final outcome does). Later, Edwards et al. (2006) explained the T increases in competition based on their functional significance, relating them to dominant behavior, physical risks, and better reaction time and spatial memory. Hamilton et al. (2009) reported significant T increases, unrelated to outcome, in wrestling, an individual sports competition, pointing to a link between individual head-to-head competition and T in women.

Soon after, the "winner effect" (a hormonal response only for winners) was found in a competitive situation with high personal involvement, where the outcome had clear and especially important consequences. The situation involved a change of status in a final soccer competition (Oliveira et al., 2009). However, the same effect was found in a competition without these relevant implications (Jiménez et al., 2012).

The importance of the type of event has been emphasized in the T anticipatory response. Increases in T during the warm-up period before competition have been reported in several competitions, in comparison with another, more neutral day, although the increase appeared only in women who believed that they were actually going to compete and not

Table 20.1. Summary of Studies on the Influence of Competition on Hormonal Response in Women.

	Studies	N and Sex	Experimental Situation	Variables and Measures	Results
SPORTS	Bateup et al., 2002	17 ♀	Rugby (in 5 meets)	Tsal, Csal: 15 min before, after match	↑T and C after match
	Kivlighan et al., 2005	23 ♂, 23 ♀	Rowing ergometer	Tsal, Csal: before, 20 min after, 40 min after	♀: ↓T, ↑C
	Edwards et al., 2006	22 ♂, 18 ♀	Soccer competition	Tsal, Csal: 1 h before, 20 min after	♀: ↑T and C after match
	Filaire et al., 2009	8 ♂, 8 ♀	Tennis competition	Csal:Resting day: 08:00 h, 20:00 h Compete: 08:00 h, 1 h before, 10 min before, 10 min after, 1 h after, 20:00	C: ↑L, ♂ and ♀ C: ↑ competition day
	Oliveira et al., 2009	33 ♀	Soccer competition (final)	Tsal, Csal: 30 min before, 30 min after	T↑ W: ↓L: C: ↑ marginal L
	Hamilton et al., 2009	13 ♀	Wrestler (2 meets with different result)	Tsal: 20 min before, 10 min after	↑T after match
	Edwards & O'Neal, 2009	80 ♀	Soccer, volleyball, softball, roller derby	Tsal: Before and after competition, winners and losers	↑T after match
	Edwards & Kurlander, 2010	(a) 15 ♀ (b) 8 ♀	(a) Volleyball: competition and practice (b) Tennis: match and practice	(a) Tsal, Csal: before warm-up, mid-warm-up, after competition (b) Tsal, Csal: prior warm-up, after warm-up, prior doubles competition, after single competition Booth: Tsal, Csal: before and after a practice session	(a) W: ↑T and C after match↑T and C after practice (b) L: ↑T after warm-up, doubles, and singles, ↑C after doubles ↑T after practice
	Jimenez et al., 2012	27 ♂, 23 ♀	Badminton elite competition	Tsal, Csal: 40 min before and 40 min after competition	W: ↑T in ♂ and ♀ L: ↓C in ♂ and ♀

Table 20.1. Continued.

	Studies	N and Sex	Experimental Situation	Variables and Measures	Results
LABORATORY	Mazur et al., 1997	28 ♂, 32 ♀	Tennis video game	Tsal, Csal: 20 min before, 8 min after explanation, half a task, 10 min after, 20 min after	♀: T and C n.s.
	van Anders & Watson, 2006	(a) 37 ♂, 38 ♀ (b) 31 ♂, 43 ♀	Computed vocabulary Outcome (a) real, (b) random (manipulated)	Tsal before and after	(a) ♀: T n.s.
	Costa & Salvador, 2012	40 ♀	Face-to-face paper-and-pencil competition	Tsal, Csal 45 min before, just before and after task, 15 min after, 30 min after HR before, during, and after task BP 45 min before, just before, after task, 5 min after	W: ↑T, HR, SBP

Note. Studies are divided in sport and laboratory settings, with characteristics of each investigation detailed to include sample size, experimental situation, variables and measures, and outcome results.

♀ = female; ♂ = male; Tsal = salivary testosterone; Csal = salivary cortisol; T = testosterone; C = cortisol; min = minutes; h = hours; W = win; L = loss; n.s. = not significant; HR = heart rate; BP = blood pressure; SBP = systolic blood pressure.

in those who did not go on to play (Edwards & Kurlander, 2010). These anticipatory increases may stem from physical exertion or from the psychological effect of preparing for competition. Kivlighan, Granger, and Booth (2005) reported a more complex response pattern, depending on previous experience. They found that precompetition T was lower than baseline (collected on a nonexercise, noncompetition day, at the same hour as the competition) and that T levels and rises predicted lower performance in novice women but not in varsity women.

To analyze the function of the T changes, some studies have measured several psychological variables in real-life competitions and in the laboratory. T levels have been related to the expression of competitive and aggressive interactions (Cashdan, 2003), to dominant behavior (Edwards et al., 2006), and to the need to dominate or influence others, reinforcing competitive and aggressive behaviors (Schultheiss, Dargel, & Rohde, 2003; Schultheiss, Wirth, & Stanton, 2004). Likewise, T administration promotes a motivational balance, with a reduction in punishment sensitivity and heightened sensitivity to reward dependency (van Honk

et al., 2004). Moreover, an association between T, mood changes, and performance has been found in sports (Oliveira et al., 2009) and laboratory (Costa & Salvador, 2012) competitions, pointing out that mood changes may play a role as modulators of this response. Additionally, precompetition T levels have been related to connectedness or bonding with teammates in rugby (Bateup et al., 2002), volleyball (Edwards & Waters, 2003), softball (Edwards & Weiss, 2005), and soccer (Edwards et al., 2006), providing evidence of a relationship between status or dominance and T in female team sports.

The vast majority of studies on female sports competitions have included C, along with T. Initially, the role of C was investigated under the assumption that losers should experience more stress and, therefore, C increases would be expected, as predicted by Mazur's (1985) biosocial hypothesis. On the other hand, the functional significance of elevated C levels has been related to the availability of energy, activating and maintaining increases in blood pressure and glucose in the blood (Suay & Salvador, 2012). C participates in the physiological and behavioral response to physical challenges and physiological stressors, altering mood, memory, and behavior (Erickson, Drevets, & Schulkin, 2003). In this sense, C increases would prepare individuals to facilitate the response to competition. For example, Salvador et al. reported that a subgroup of judo players who displayed higher C levels, along with T increases and higher motivation to win scores, also obtained the best outcome (Salvador, Suay, González-Bono, & Serrano, 2003). However, extreme elevations of C may lead to poor performance because they interfere with cognitive processes (Erickson et al., 2003).

During sports competitions, C levels usually increase, although these increases are not significantly related to outcome (Edwards et al., 2006; Filaire, Alix, Ferrand, & Verger, 2009; Kivlighan et al., 2005). Findings are inconsistent and show C increases in winners and losers but more so in losers (Bateup et al., 2002), increases only in losers (Filaire et al., 2009; Jiménez et al., 2012; Oliveira et al., 2009), and increases only in winners (Edwards & Kurlander, 2010). These inconsistent results are difficult to interpret; therefore, the assessment of other psychological variables may be beneficial in helping to explain these C changes.

One such variable could be experience. Anticipatory C responses unrelated to outcome are higher in novices than in veterans (Filaire et al., 2009; Kivlighan et al., 2005). Filaire et al., while studying C and anxiety as a sensitive index of stress, found an increase in C prior to competition, which they explained is an indicator of a high stress level. Thus, a greater increase in C during the game has been related to the players' impression that the opponent is challenging (Bateup et al., 2002).

Therefore, C seems to have paradoxical effects on competition. On the one hand, positive responses to competition may increase C levels in order to mobilize energetic resources; on the other hand, appraisal of the situation with high anxiety, unpredictability, or negative mood also increases C levels. Furthermore, the dual imbalance hypothesis proposes that T increases in competition only when C levels are low, pointing out the relationship between the two hormones (Mehta & Josephs, 2010). In fact, in a large sample of soccer, volleyball, softball, and tennis athletes, women with low C levels before competition showed higher T responses to competition, although outcome was not included in the study (Edwards & Castro, 2015).

In sum, a number of studies on different sport competitions have found a competition effect, with increases in T and C in women. In all of these cases,

women belonged to a fairly specific group; they were young and usually varsity sportswomen, with considerable previous experience and an enhanced physical condition. These factors have been shown to influence the hormonal response to stress (Salvador, Simón, Suay, & Llorens, 1987). Furthermore, some of these sports require considerable physical effort and a high level of fitness (e.g., rugby, soccer, and wrestling). It remains to be determined whether these findings can be extended to other groups of women with different characteristics.

Although the sports context allows a high degree of ecological validity, because athletes are usually measured in real competitions where the outcome has short-term consequences, researchers in the laboratory have greater control over all the variables and can take a larger number of measurements (although competition is usually promoted through task instructions and/or a monetary reward). We agree with Kivlighan and Granger (2006) about the importance of recording complete hormonal measures, along with ANS responses. In the next section, we describe the results on the role of hormones and the ANS in laboratory competitions and their outcomes.

A few studies have been carried out in the laboratory with female university students, employing different competitive tasks in order to analyze hormonal responses to competition. For example, in competitions employing computer games, no changes in T or C responses were found to be linked to the outcome (Mazur, Susman, & Edelbrock, 1997; van Anders & Watson, 2006).

In a similar vein, we measured T, C, heart rate, blood pressure, and mood responses to competition via a paper-and-pencil task completed by young female university students. The results showed two response patterns: one related to passive coping, which combined state anxiety, negative mood, and blood pressure, and another representing active coping, which included T, heart rate, positive mood, and better performance. This second pattern was associated with winning; additionally, the women who became winners felt higher efficacy and less frustration than the losers. In sum, we found different patterns of psychobiological responses to laboratory competition in young women in a situation requiring no physical effort (Costa & Salvador, 2012). Thus, our findings support the model described previously, in which appraisal of the situation explains the psychobiological response to competition (see Figure 20.2; Salvador, 2005; Salvador & Costa, 2009).

It is worth noting that there has been previous laboratory research on cardiovascular (CV) measurement. The main results revealed that CV activation is required in competitive situations and that competition could be an important factor in the etiology of CV disease (Manuck, 1994; Newton, 2009; Obrist, 1981). Competitive situations included an active coping response (e.g., arithmetic tasks), compared to other stressors where the individual had no control over the task and presented a passive coping response (e.g., the cold pressor test). Obrist (1981) reported that an active coping task elicited higher systolic blood pressure and heart rate, but less diastolic blood pressure than passive coping tasks. The former responses were a result of the influence of the beta-adrenergic receptors on the myocardium, which shortened the cardiac cycle, whereas diastolic blood pressure is less related to sympathetic influences on the myocardium. Active stressors, such as arithmetic, public speaking, video games, or time-reaction tasks, predominantly elicit these responses. However, surprisingly, there are few published studies on the CV influence on competitive stress (Harrison et al., 2001), and most of them use mixed-sex samples, which makes it more difficult to draw clear conclusions about CV responses to competition in women. There is evidence that jobs with competitive elements cause heart rate and blood pressure increases, along with a decrease in the pre-ejection period (an index of myocardial contractility and beta-adrenergic influences on myocardium; Sherwood, Light, & Blumental, 1989). On grammatical reasoning tasks, increases in heart rate and better performance were reported when subjects were told that they would be compared to others, thus introducing a competitive element into the task. On a reaction-time task in competitive (i.e., against another player) and noncompetitive (i.e., alone) conditions, an increase in heart rate was found during the task and recovery, as well as better performance, in the competitive situation (Beh, 1998). Moreover, Kivlighan and Granger (2006) emphasized that the increased activation of the sympathetic system could facilitate performance. Ritcher and Gendolla (2007) concluded that the task incentive (i.e., the reward) directly influenced CV responses to a laboratory task in young men and women. In addition to the effort required, when the incentive is important and the goal is attainable, higher reactivity appears (Costa & Salvador, 2012), as previously predicted by Obrist (1981) for moderately difficult tasks but not for very easy or difficult ones.

Along these lines, Ricarte, Salvador, Costa, Torres, and Subirats (2001) analyzed the CV response of men and women who participated in a competitive task involving a group negotiation, finding a different pattern in heart rate pattern associated with performance. Heart rate increased in subjects who adequately performed the negotiation and became winners, followed by decreases after the task once they realized they had won. By contrast, losers showed decreases in heart rate during the task. In addition, winners made more internal attributions (i.e., reporting more control over the situation) than losers. Regarding blood pressure, no significant differences based on the outcome were found. Therefore, the CV response pattern to competition was indicative of beta-adrenergic activation. Other studies found that in the noncompetitive (i.e., performing the task alone, not against another player) condition, the CV response was lower than in the competitive condition (Harrison et al., 2001; van Zanten et al., 2002). A study with women found that the effort required was related to heart rate and systolic blood pressure responses; however, no differences were found in the diastolic blood pressure (Wright, Killebrew & Pimpalapure, 2002).

Finally, Peretti (1971) found that women responded faster under competitive conditions, while men did not show differences in performance. Peretti concluded that women felt more anxious in the competitive situation and, consequently, increased their surveillance and performance, although no sex differences were found in another study (Palmer & Folds-Bennett, 1998).

In sum, competition to reach goals or obtain resources requires CV activation, but this adaptive response could become a health threat when activated continuously. For example, dominance has been related to greater vulnerability to developing CV disease (Newton, 2009; Shapiro, Goldstein, & Jamner, 1995), and evaluations of personal resources and situational demands are associated with different autonomic and endocrine patterns (Seery, 2011). Few studies have addressed the influence of competitive stress on CV measures, and they are limited to laboratory studies. In general, higher heart rate and blood pressure responses on competitive tasks than on noncompetitive tasks have been described (Beh, 1998; Harrison et al., 2001; Sherwood et al., 1989; van Zanten et al., 2002; Wright et al., 2002). Furthermore, laboratory studies have introduced parameters that need to be considered when measuring the CV system, suggesting that beta-adrenergic activation is associated with performance and outcome.

Several moderating variables may help to explain the response to competition and its outcome in women. First, *motivation*, measured directly, as in the study by Costa and Salvador (2012), or indirectly, as the result of an objective situation like a final league game (Oliveira et al., 2009), is a necessary factor in obtaining involvement and, consequently, a response to competition. Other factors evaluated in the literature are the *emotional changes* in competition, as increases in positive mood have been described in real competitions and in laboratory settings, or *bonding and relationship with others* in team sports. Moreover, *self-efficacy*, seldom measured, is another variable that could help explain these results. Recent data indicate that self-efficacy is positively related to T levels, positive mood, and performance in a laboratory competition in women (Costa, Serrano & Salvador, 2016).

Conclusion

After reviewing the scientific literature on the psychobiology of competition in women, it is clear that there is an increasing interest in studying women's responses in these types of situations. In our opinion, this increase is related to the awareness and recognition of sex differences in the variables that must be controlled in order to draw valid conclusions about women. Social neuroscience has used all these advances to create a more comprehensive vision of the role of both sexes in our complex contexts. Decades of studies on sex differences have produced a clearer scenario in which to study both men and women in social interactions. Thus, women's psychobiological responses to competition could be different from men's, although a similar pattern has also been reported, probably related to the different contexts where the competitions took place. Moreover, although no clear differences in ANS have been found, a slightly different response patterns seems to exist between the sexes.

In spite of the minor role of androgens in the female brain, it seems that, at a physiological and behavioral level, they activate similar responses to those of men, depending on the amount and the vital moment when they are activated. Androgens produce similar effects in both sexes, although in women they are modulated by female hormones and conditions (Ketterson, Nolan, & Sandell, 2005; Rosvall, 2013). When men and women compete, similar hormones are involved, although dimorphic structures and their physiological products modify the degree of influence of these hormones. In addition, cognitive processes should be included in the analyses in order to correctly interpret the behavioral responses and their physiological correlates. In this regard, Rosvall (2013) argued that greater attention should be paid to multiple analyses (i.e., from hormones to genes or intra-individual variations) in trying to understand the complex mechanisms underlying intersexual coevolution and, therefore, competition.

It is worth noting that age is also a very important variable that needs further study in relation to responses to competition. The studies described here have mainly employed samples of young adults. It is possible that these women are at a point in life that involves high competitiveness in terms of their careers, the search for a partner, and the formation and reaffirmation of social and family links. Therefore the existence of differences in other life-cycle periods is plausible.

Overall, three main hypotheses have been defended in the field of the psychobiology of competition. The first and most predominant is the biosocial status hypothesis, although most research results do not support it. Another is the challenge hypothesis, which emphasizes the functional changes in T. Several studies in women have reported increases in T after competition, although it would be an a posteriori explanation. A third position has adopted a broader approach from human stress theories; it does not deny the previous models but instead tries to complement them. Thus, the coping competition model contextualizes the different results and points to the importance of cognitive appraisal in understanding the psychobiological responses to human competition. In this sense, competition begins when the individual anticipates a contest, activating cognitive mechanisms that can be conscious or preconscious. His or her appraisal depends on proximal factors (such as who the opponent is or how important the competition is) and on indirectly related factors (such as characteristics of personality, social abilities, or previous history of successes and failures). Finally, these cognitive processes lead to a biological and emotional response that ultimately may help or impair performance. In general, it is plausible to suppose that an active coping strategy related to increases in T and positive mood would increase the probability of victory. However, the opponent is an uncontrollable variable in the equation, and, therefore, victory is not always achieved. Furthermore, the competition does not end with the outcome because the attributions and satisfaction with the outcome obtained could also influence and affect future competitions. This model has found support in some recent studies in men and women.

In conclusion, more studies are needed to achieve a more complete understanding of which hormones influence female competition and in what way. In this regard, we suggest a comprehensive model that includes hormones, autonomic responses, and, especially, cognitive variables that would explain how women (and men) cope with competition. It should include motives and expectations (and their associated emotional responses) about future competitions and the appraisal of past competitions, in order to obtain a broader view of the complex response pattern involved in competition. Moreover, the attempt to understand the evolutionary development of social status among individuals, and its proximal and distal factors, should be taken into account. Many of the studies presented here focus on variables that affect a single competition (proximal context). However, we also have to consider how the outcome of a single competition (and its cognitive and emotional interpretations) affects future competitions, because experience is fundamental in human behavior. Studying this question would make it easier to discover whether men and women have different response patterns to competition and whether this response is motivated by different evolutionary cues.

Acknowledgments

We thank Ms. Cindy DePoy for the revision of the English text and the funding sources that supported the investigations on the psychobiology of stress and competition: the Spanish Education and Science Ministry (Grants BSO2000-12068, SEJ2007-62019/PSIC, PSI201021343) and the Generalitat Valenciana (Grants PROMETEO2011-048 and ISIC2013/001).

References

Archer, J. (1991). The influence of testosterone on human aggression. *British Journal of Psychology, 82*, 1–28.

Archer, J. (2006). Testosterone and human aggression: An evaluation of the challenge hypothesis. *Neuroscience and Biobehavioral Reviews, 30*, 319–345.

Arnedo, M. T., Salvador, A., Martínez-Sanchís, S., & Pellicer, O. (2002). Similar rewarding effects of testosterone in mice rated as short and long attack latency individuals. *Addiction Biology, 7*, 373–379.

Arnold, A. P. (2009). The organizational-activational hypothesis as the foundation for a unified theory of sexual differentiation of all mammalian tissues. *Hormones and Behavior, 55*(5), 570–579.

Arnold, A. P., & Breedlove, S. M. (1985). Organizational and activational effects of sex steroids on brain and behavior: a reanalysis. *Hormones and Behavior, 19*, 469–498.

Bao, A. M., Hestiantoro, A., Van Someren, E. J., Swaab, D. F., & Zhou, J. N. (2005). Colocalization of corticotropin-releasing hormone and oestrogen receptor α in the paraventricular nucleus of the hypothalamus in mood disorders. *Brain, 128*, 1301–1313.

Bateman, A. J. (1948). Intrasexual selection in Drosophila. *Heredity, 2*, 349–368.

Bateup, H. S., Booth, A., Shirtcliff, E. A., & Granger, D. (2002). Testosterone, cortisol, and women's competition. *Evolution and Human Behavior, 23*, 181–192.

Beh, H. C. (1998). Cardiovascular reactivity to psychological stressors. *Australian Journal of Psychology, 50*(1), 49–54.

Benenson, J. F. (2013). The development of human female competition: Allies and adversaries. *Philosophical Transactions of the Royal Society B, 368*, 20130079.

Bernstein, I., Gordon, T. P., & Rose, R. M. (1983). The interaction of hormones, behavior and social context in nonhuman primates. In B. B. Svare (Ed.), *Hormones and aggressive behavior* (pp. 535–561). New York: Plenum.

Blanchard, R. J., McKittrick, C. R., & Blanchard, D. C. (2001). Animal models of social stress: Effects on behavior and brain neurochemical systems. *Physiology and Behavior, 73*, 261–271.

Brody, L. R. (1993). On understanding gender differences in the expression of emotion. In S. L. Ablon, D. Brown, E. J. Khantzian, & J. E. Mack (Eds.), *Human feelings: Explorations in affect development and meaning* (pp. 87–121). Hillsdale, NJ: Analytic Press.

Campbell, A. (2013). The evolutionary psychology of women's aggression. *Philosophical Transactions of the Royal Society B, 368*, 20130078.

Cannon, W. B. (1932). *The wisdom of the body*. New York: Norton.

Cashdan, E. (1998). Are men more competitive than women? *British Journal of Social Psychology, 37*, 213–229.

Cashdan, E. (2003). Hormones and competitive aggression in women. *Aggressive Behavior, 29*, 107–115.

Chen, Y., Katuščák, P., & Ozdenoren, E. (2013). Why can't a woman bid more like a man? *Games and Economic Behavior, 77*, 181–213.

Clutton-Brock, T., & Huchard, E. (2013). Social competition and its consequences in female mammals. *Journal of Zoology, 289*, 151–171.

Costa, R., & Salvador, A. (2012). Associations between success and failure in a face-to-face competition and psychobiological parameters in young women. *Psychoneuroendocrinology, 37*, 1780–1790.

Costa, R., Serrano, M. A., & Salvador, A. (2016). Importance of self-efficacy in psychoendocrine responses to competition and performance in women. *Psicothema, 28*, 66–70.

Croson, R., & Gneezy, U. (2009). Gender differences in preferences. *Journal of Economic Literature, 47*, 1–27.

Edwards, D. A., & Castro, K. V. (2015). Baseline cortisol moderates testosterone reactivity to women's intercollegiate athletic competition. *Physiology & Behavior, 142*, 48–51.

Edwards, D. A., & Kurlander, L. S. (2010). Women's intercollegiate volleyball and tennis: Effects of warm-up, competition, and practice on saliva levels of cortisol and testosterone. *Hormones and Behavior, 58*, 606–613.

Edwards, D. A., & O'Neal, J. L. (2009). Oral contraceptives decrease saliva testosterone but do not affect the rise in testosterone associated with athletic competition. *Hormones and Behavior, 56*(2), 193, 195–198.

Edwards, D. A., & Waters, J. (2003). Women's intercollegiate volleyball: Saliva testosterone and cortisol are elevated during competition and before match testosterone is related to team mate ratings of playing ability. *Hormones and Behavior, 44,* 47.

Edwards, D. A., & Weiss, A. (2005). Women's intercollegiate softball: Saliva testosterone is elevated during competition and before-game testosterone is related to team mate ratings of playing ability. *Hormones and Behavior, 48,* 99.

Edwards, D. A., Wetzel, K., & Wyner, D. R. (2006). Intercollegiate soccer: Saliva cortisol and testosterone are elevated during competition, and testosterone is related to status and social connectedness with team mates. *Physiology and Behavior, 87,* 135–143.

Eisenegger, C., Haushofer, J., & Fehr, E. (2011). The role of testosterone in social interaction. *Trends in Cognitive Sciences, 15*(6), 263–271.

Erickson, K., Drevets, W., & Schulkin, J. (2003). Glucocorticoid regulation of diverse cognitive functions in normal and pathological emotional states. *Neuroscience & Biobehavioral Reviews, 27,* 233–246.

Filaire, E., Alix, D., Ferrand, C., & Verger, M. (2009). Psychophysiological stress in tennis players during the first single match of a tournament. *Psychoneuroendocrinology, 34,* 150–157.

Geary, D. C., & Flinn, M. V. (2002). Sex differences in behavioral and hormonal response to threat: Commentary on Taylor et al. (2000). *Psychological Review, 109*(4), 745–750.

Girdler, S. (2005). Current trends in women's health research: It is time to strike up the band as we march forward into the 21st century. *Biological Psychology, 69,* 1–3.

Goldstein, J. M., Jerram, M., Abbs, B., Whitfield-Gabrieli, S., & Makris, N. (2010). Sex differences in stress response circuitry activation dependent on female hormonal cycle. *Journal of Neuroscience, 30*(2), 431–438.

Hamilton, L. D., van Anders, S. M., Cox, D. N., & Watson, N. V. (2009). The effect of competition on salivary testosterone in elite female athletes. *International Journal of Sports and Physiology Performance, 4,* 538–542.

Harrison, L. K., Denning, S., Easton, H. L., Hall, J. C., Burns, V. E., Ring, C., & Carroll, D. (2001). The effects of competition and competitiveness on cardiovascular activity. *Psychophysiology, 38,* 601–606.

Huether, G. (1996). The central adaptation syndrome: Psychosocial stress as a trigger for adaptive modifications of brain structure and brain function. *Progress in Neurobiology, 48,* 569–612.

Jiménez, M., Aguilar, R., & Alvero-Cruz, J. R. (2012). Effects of victory and defeat on testosterone and cortisol response to competition: Evidence for the same response patterns in men and women. *Psychoneuroendocrinology, 37,* 1577–1581.

Ketterson, E. D., Nolan, V., & Sandell, M. (2005). Testosterone in females: Mediator of adaptive traits, constraint on the evolution of sexual dimorphism, or both? *American Naturalist, 166,* S85–S98.

Keverne, E. B. (1988). Central mechanisms underlying the neural and neuroendocrine determinants of maternal behaviour. *Psychoneuroendocrinology, 13,* 127–141.

Kivlighan, K. T., & Granger, D. A. (2006). Salivary alpha-amylase response to competition: Relation to gender, previous experience, and attitudes. *Psychoneuroendocrinology, 31,* 703–714.

Kivlighan, K. T., Granger, D. A., & Booth, A. (2005). Gender differences in testosterone and cortisol response to competition. *Psychoneuroendocrinology, 30,* 58–71.

Koolhaas, J. M., de Boer, S. F., Buwalda, B., & van Reenen, K. (2007). Individual variation in coping with stress: A multidimensional approach of ultimate and proximate mechanisms. *Brain Behavior and Evolution, 70,* 218–226.

Lancaster, J. B., & Lancaster, C. S. (1983). Parental investment: the hominid adaptation. In D. Ornter (Ed.), *How humans adapt: A biocultural odyssey* (pp. 33–66). New York: Smithsonian.

Manuck, S. B. (1994). Cardiovascular reactivity and cardiovascular disease: "Once more unto the breach." *International Journal of Behavioral Medicine, 1,* 4–31.

Mazur, A. (1985). A biosocial model of status in face-to-face primate groups. *Social Forces, 64,* 377–402.

Mazur, A., & Booth, A. (1998). Testosterone and dominance in men. *Behavioral and Brain Sciences, 21,* 353–397.

Mazur, A., Susman, E. J., & Edelbrock, S. (1997). Sex difference in testosterone response to a video game contest. *Evolution and Human Behavior, 18,* 317–326.

McEwen, B. S., & Magarinos, A. M. (1997). Stress effects on morphology and function of the hippocampus. *Annals of the New York Academy of Sciences, 821,* 271–284.

Mehta, P. H., & Josephs, R. A. (2010). Testosterone and cortisol jointly regulate dominance: Evidence for a dual-hormone hypothesis. *Hormones and Behavior, 58,* 898–906.

Newton, T. L. (2009). Cardiovascular functioning, personality, and the social world: The domain of hierarchical power. *Neuroscience and Biobehavioral Reviews, 33,* 145–159.

Obrist, P. (1981). *Cardiovascular psychophysiology: A perspective.* New York: Plenum Press.

Oliveira, T., Gouveia, M. J., & Oliveira, R. F. (2009). Testosterone responsiveness to winning and losing experiences in female soccer players. *Psychoneuroendocrinology, 34*(7), 1056–1064.

Ostlund, H., Keller, E., & Hurd, Y. L. (2003). Estrogen receptor gene expression in relation to neuropsychiatric disorders. *Annals of the New York Academy of Sciences, 1007,* 54–63.

Palmer, D. L., & Folds-Bennet, T. (1998). Performance on two attention tasks as a function of sex and competition. *Perceptual and Motor Skills, 86,* 363–370.

Pearson, M., & Schipper, B. C. (2013). Menstrual cycle and competitive bidding. *Games and Economic Behavior, 78,* 1–20.

Peretti, P. (1971). Effects of competitive, non-competitive instructions and sex on performance in a color-word interference task. *Journal of Psychology, 79,* 67–70.

Phoenix, C. H., Goy, R. W., Gerall, A. A., & Young, W. C. (1959). Organizing action of prenatally administered testosterone propionate on the tissues mediating mating behavior in the female guinea pig. *Endocrinology, 65,* 369–382.

Price, J. L. (1999). Prefrontal cortical networks related to visceral function and mood. *Annals of the New York Academy of Sciences, 877,* 383–396.

Ricarte, J., Salvador, A., Costa, R., Torres, M. J., & Subirats, M. (2001). Heart rate and blood pressure responses to a competitive role-playing game. *Aggressive Behavior, 27,* 351–359.

Ritcher, M., & Gendolla, G. H. E. (2007). Incentive value, unclear task difficulty, and cardiovascular reactivity in active coping. *International Journal of Psychophysiology, 63*, 294–301.

Rosvall, K. A. (2013). Proximate perspectives on the evolution of female aggression: Good for the gander, good for the goose? *Philosophical Transactions of the Royal Society B, 368*, 20130083.

Salvador, A. (2005). Coping with competitive situations in humans. *Neuroscience and Biobehavioral Reviews, 29*, 195–205.

Salvador, A. (2012). Steroid hormones and some evolutionary-relevant social interactions. *Motivation and Emotion, 36*, 74–83.

Salvador, A., & Costa, R. (2009). Coping with competition: Neuroendocrine responses and cognitive variables. *Neurosciences Biobehavioral Reviews, 33*, 160–170.

Salvador, A., Simón, V., Suay, F., & Llorens, L. (1987). Testosterone and cortisol responses to competitive fighting in human males: A pilot study. *Aggressive Behavior, 13*, 9–13.

Salvador, A., Suay, F., González-Bono, E., & Serrano, M. A. (2003). Anticipatory cortisol, testosterone and psychological responses to judo competition in young men. *Psychoneuroendocrinology, 28*, 364–375.

Schachter, S. (1959). *The psychology of affiliation*. Stanford, CA: Stanford University Press.

Schultheiss, O. C., Dargel, A., & Rohde, W. (2003). Implicit motives and gonadal steroid hormones: Effects of menstrual cycle phase, oral contraceptive use, and relationship status. *Hormones and Behavior, 43*, 293–301.

Schultheiss, O. C., Wirth, M. M., & Stanton, S. J. (2004). Effects of affiliation and power motivation arousal on salivary progesterone and testosterone. *Hormones and Behavior, 46*, 592–599.

Schuurman, T. (1980). Hormonal correlates of agonistic behavior in adult male rats. *Progress in Brain Research, 53*, 415–420.

Seery, M. D. (2011). Challenge or threat? Cardiovascular indexes of resilience and vulnerability to potential stress in humans. *Neuroscience and Biobehavioral Reviews, 35*, 1603–1610.

Shapiro, D., Goldstein, I. B., & Jamner, L. D. (1995). Effects of anger/hostility, defensiveness, gender and family history of hypertension on cardiovascular reactivity. *Psychophysiology, 32*, 425–435.

Sherwood, A., Light, K. C., & Blumental, J. A. (1989). Effects of aerobic exercise training on hemodynamic responses during psychosocial stress in normotensive and borderline hypertensive Type A men: A preliminary report. *Psychosomatic Medicine, 51*, 123–136.

Stockey, P., & Campbell, A. (2013). Female competition and aggression: Interdisciplinary perspectives. *Philosophical Transactions of the Royal Society B, 368*, 20130073.

Suay, F., & Salvador, A. (2012). Cortisol. In F. Ehrlenspiel & K. Strahler (Eds.), *Psychoneuroendocrinology of sport and exercise* (pp. 63–90). London: Routledge.

Suay, F., Salvador, A., González-Bono, E., Sanchis, C., Martínez, M., Martínez-Sanchis, S., ... Montoro, J. B. (1999). Effects of competition and its outcome on serum testosterone, cortisol and prolactin. *Psychoneuroendocrinology, 24*, 551–566.

Swaab, D. F. (2004). The human hypothalamus. Basic and clinical aspects. Part II: Neuropathology of the hypothalamus and adjacent brain structures. In M. J. Aminoff, F. Boller, & D. F. Swaab (Eds.), *Handbook of clinical neurology* (pp. 193–231). Amsterdam: Elsevier.

Taylor, S. E., Klein, L. C., Lewis, B. P., Gruenewald, T. L., Gurung, R. A. R., & Updegraff, J. A. (2000). Biobehavioral responses to stress in females: Tend-and-befriend, not fight-or-flight. *Psychological Review, 107*(3), 411–429.

Taylor, S. E., Lewis, B. P., Gruenewald, T. L., Gurung, R. A. R., Updegraff, J. A., & Klein, L. C. (2002). Sex differences in biobehavioral responses to threat: Reply to Geary and Flinn (2002). *Psychological Review, 109*(4), 751–754.

Troisi, A., (2001). Gender differences in vulnerability to social stress. A Darwinian perspective. *Physiology and Behavior, 73*, 443–449.

van Anders, S. M., & Watson, N. V. (2006). Social neuroendocrinology: Effects of social contexts and behaviors on sex steroids in humans. *Human Nature, 17*, 212–237.

Van Honk, J., Schutter, D. J., Hermans, E. J., Putman, P., Tuiten, A., & Koppeschaar, H. (2004). Testosterone shifts the balance between sensitivity to punishment and reward in healthy young women. *Psychoneuroendocrinology, 29*, 937–943.

van Zanten, J. J., De Boer, D., Harrison, L. K., Ring, C., Carroll, D., Willemsen, G., & De Geus, E. J. (2002). Competitiveness and hemodynamic reactions to competition. *Psychophysiology, 39*, 759–766.

Wingfield, J. C., Hegner, R. E., Dufty, A. M., & Ball, G. F. (1990). The challenge hypothesis: "Theoretical implications" for patterns of testosterone secretion, mating systems, and breeding strategies. *American Naturalist, 136*, 829–846.

Wright, R. A., Killebrew, K., & Pimpalapure, D. (2002). Cardiovascular incentive effects where a challenge is unfixed: Demonstrations involving social evaluation, evaluator status, and monetary reward. *Psychophysiology, 39*, 188–197.

The Endocrinology of Female Competition

Kelly Cobey *and* Amanda Hahn

Abstract

This chapter takes a broad look at women's competitive behavior and the hormonal mechanisms that contribute to it, beginning with a comparative discussion of competition in female, males, and nonhumans. Here we hope to illustrate how hormonal trade-offs impact women's competition similarly in some respects but distinctively in others when compared to men and nonhumans. We then discuss naturally occurring hormonal variation across the female lifespan, from birth to menarche, during the reproductive years, and after menopause, and what impact such fluctuation has on women's competition. This section highlights how knowledge of the impact of hormonal variation on women's competition at one stage of life may be extended to inform knowledge at others. Through utilizing both a comparative and lifespan approach we hope to provide a broad scope for how hormones regulate competitive behavior in women. We conclude with a discussion of avenues for future research in this area.

Key Words: hormones hormonal variation, women's competitive behavior lifespan

In order to enhance the understanding of female competition, as this handbook seeks to do, it is imperative that we appreciate the underlying physiological mechanisms that contribute to the maintenance of competitive behavior. Discussion of the role of hormones in female competition promotes a long-overdue look at how the unique female biology generates a distinct set of representations of competitive behavior. In women, as in men (and a range of other species), the maintenance of competition is thought to be achieved via hormonal trade-offs. Trade-offs, in the context of life history theory, refer to variation in the allocation of energy between to two opposing functions (Stearns, 1992); that is, a trade-off occurs when a benefit in one trait is associated with a subsequent disadvantage in another trait. In the absence of trade-offs, natural selection would drive traits linked to positive fitness outcomes toward their limits. That selection of this sort has not occurred extensively suggests that many existing traits operate via the limits of their impact on other related traits (Stearns, 1989).

Evidence for the centrality of hormones in regulating trade-offs is long established, with this notion having been best recognized through studies that manipulate hormone levels directly. In keeping with the theme of this handbook, this chapter focuses on how hormonal variation and hormonal trade-offs are used to arbitrate female competitive behavior. The chapter begins with a brief outline of two central theoretical frameworks for the role of hormones in competition: the Challenge Hypothesis and the Dual-Hormone Hypothesis. The majority of the endocrinological evidence for these frameworks comes from animal studies or studies of human males. As such, in what follows we first briefly review this evidence to gain a more complete scope of how hormones might regulate competitive behavior in women.

While sex differences, and certainly species differences, in the hormonal underpinnings of competition do exist, we argue that this broader research can be used as a platform to inform hypotheses about the hormonal mechanisms of competition in women. We do, of course, additionally acknowledge that competition itself may be displayed differently between the sexes. For example, much research, some of which has already been outlined in this handbook (see, e.g., chapters by Anderson, Sutton, or McAndrew), provides evidence that women are far less likely than men to compete overtly or physically but rather make use of indirect subtle behavioral tactics such as gossip, competitor derogation, or stigmatization (e.g., Campbell, 2004). What's more, the object of competition may also differ between the sexes, with women being more likely to compete in the arena of physical attractiveness than men (e.g., Buss & Barnes, 1986). Sex differences in competition may even prevail when the function of competition is the same in males and females (e.g., to secure a high-quality partner). We are therefore cognizant of the fact that competition among women may be more subtle, and thus more difficult to quantify, meaning careful consideration in terms of how studies in men can best be extrapolated to inform research in women is needed.

Following onward from our overview of competition we delve deeper into the precise physiology of female competition across a continuum of female life events. Here we draw specific reference to competitive behavior in girls prior to menarche, across the female reproductive cycle, and during hormonal contraceptive use, as well as in menopause. We end by summarizing the implications of hormones as mediators of female competition and outline some suggestions for further research. The goal of this chapter is to provide an understanding of how hormonal variation impacts competition in women and how these findings can be understood relative to research in men and animals. We hope to illustrate how hormonal trade-offs impact women's competition similarly in some respects but distinctively in others when compared to men and animals.

Endocrine Theories for Competitive Behavior: The Challenge Hypothesis

Testosterone is an androgen steroid hormone that is controlled by the hypothalamic-pituitary-gonadal (HPG) axis and is secreted by the male testes and, in reduced quantities, by the female ovaries. It is generally thought that testosterone controls masculinization, and folk wisdom has long implicated testosterone in the management and maintenance of aggressive competitive behavior. However, testosterone is also known to have a number of immune-compromising costs; high testosterone levels are associated with lower health and

survivorship (Folstad & Karter, 1992; Muehlenbein & Bribiescas, 2005). For example, in a meta-analysis that included data from a range of species, immune activation was shown to suppress testosterone levels (Boonekamp, Ros, & Verhulst, 2008). This suggests that testosterone does not act to suppress immune function (which is also a commonly held belief; see, e.g., Roberts, Buchanan, & Evans, 2004) but that immune activation itself drives changes in testosterone. Regardless of the path of action, decreases in immune function negatively impact survivorship. Some researchers even propose that sex differences in testosterone may contribute to differences observed in average lifespans among men and women (e.g., Klein, 2000). The idea that testosterone is costly also provides insight into the existence of population-level differences in testosterone between individuals living in industrialized populations and nonindustrialized populations: across the lifetime individuals from industrialized populations, where pathogen threat is low and energy expenditure tends to be moderate, have higher levels of baseline testosterone than individuals from nonindustrialized societies (Bribiescas & Hill, 2010; Ellison et al., 2002). The Challenge Hypothesis argues that the immune-compromising costs of high testosterone generate a "double-edged sword," so to speak, wherein levels of testosterone must be carefully balanced such that they are high enough for an individual to compete successfully but low enough that they do not impair overall function.

The Challenge Hypothesis: Evidence from Nonhuman Species

The initial studies on the link between competitive aggression and testosterone were conducted on birds; this research led to the development of what is termed the Challenge Hypothesis (Wingfield, Hegner, Dufty, & Ball, 1990). The Challenge Hypothesis, as it was originally conceived, predicted that particular mating systems in birds would contribute to specific hormonal changes associated with response to a territorial threat. For example, it was predicted that a larger increase in testosterone would occur among monogamous male birds when they were exposed to a territorial threat as compared to polygynously mated male birds. This hypothesis was based on the idea that polygynous species have higher levels of general competition (i.e., for mates) and should therefore possess higher baseline testosterone levels. In this sense, birds in polygynous mating systems can be viewed as having testosterone levels that are closer to their maximum possible values, since competition is a recurring pressure. By contrast, monogamous breeders, who are likely to be pair-bonded, can benefit from down-regulating testosterone levels to manage against immune-compromising effects since they face lower levels of competition for mates (Wingfield et al., 1990). Secondary to reducing physical health risks, the down-regulation of testosterone levels has been shown to promote parenting behaviors. Together, these processes could function in tandem to enhance reproductive fitness; a trade-off exists wherein upon exposure to a territorial threat, a selective and rapid increase in testosterone levels among monogamous birds could be advantageous to enhance competitive ability, so long as testosterone then swiftly subsides in the absence of the threat to facilitate investment and parenting (Wingfield et al., 1990). An analogous increase among polygamously breeding birds is thought to have less of an impact on enhancing competitive ability since baseline testosterone levels, and therefore levels of competition, are already greater. From this theorizing, the Challenge Hypothesis (i.e., the idea that testosterone can be understood to increase [only] in situations when there is a need to compete for mates or resources) was born.

Compelling evidence now exists in support of the Challenge Hypothesis. For example, it is known that testosterone rises during the breeding season when mating competition is high and that testosterone implants can induce polygyny in species of birds that are typically monogamous (e.g., De Ridder, Pinxten, & Eens, 2000). Experimentally manipulating testosterone (via implants) has similarly been shown to promote aggressive behavior while at the same time decreasing paternal reactions. While there is much research supporting the idea that high testosterone inhibits parenting behavior in male birds (e.g., De Ridder et al., 2000; Stoehr & Hill, 2000), this relationship has not always been observed (e.g., Lynn, Hayward, Benowitz-Fredericks, & Wingfield, 2002; Lynn, Walker, & Wingfield, 2005). Consistent with the idea that testosterone controls a trade-off between mating competition and parenting behavior, high concentrations of testosterone are absent in bird species where there is little competition for mates and few territorial threats (e.g., Goymann et al., 2004; Lormée, Jouventin, Lacroix, Lallemand, & Chastel, 2000). In light of this evidence, testosterone levels can be viewed as very plastic and responsive to the social environment. While it is important to stress

that baseline hormone levels and hormonal changes do not prompt a specific behavioral response or action, testosterone clearly appears to increase the probability of particular competitive behaviors in bird species. In this way, testosterone can be seen as both effecting and responding to social behavior to regulate reproductive strategy in allocating between competitive mating behavior and parenting effort.

While much research purporting to support the Challenge Hypothesis has focused on nonhuman *males*, a considerable sum of research on testosterone and competition exists specifically within *females* of various animal species. Similar breeding-season-dependent aggressive behaviors have been associated with higher testosterone levels in female birds, such as the red-winged blackbird (Hurly & Robertson, 1984; Cristol & Johnsen, 1994), spotted sandpipers (Fivizzani & Oring, 1986) European robins (Schwabl, 1992) moorhens (Eens & Pinxten, 2000), and other species such as lizards (Moore, 1986). Langmore, Cockrem, and Candy (2002) have likewise shown that testosterone increases when males are removed from the environment to stimulate greater levels of mating competition and that this increase in testosterone regulates a facultative increase in bird song.

In addition, female mammals that acquire dominant status have been shown to have higher levels of circulating testosterone during pregnancy, as well as higher rates of aggression than do subordinate females (e.g., meerkats, Clutton-Brock et al., 2006; baboons, Beehner, Phillips-Conroy, & Whitten, 2005). This is relevant since dominance rank in some female mammal species has also been directly tied to reproductive success (e.g., chimpanzees, Pusey, 1997). In line with these findings, long-term administration of testosterone in female rats has been shown to induce competitive behavior; however, it is noteworthy that similar findings were not observed among male rats, in which aggressive behavior best related to the down-regulation of neurosteroid synthesis within the brain (Pinna, Costa, & Guidotti, 2005). Other interesting research based on studies conducted using pregnant nonhuman females indicates that hormonal changes during gestation contribute to levels of offspring competitive behavior via maternal effects. For example, among spotted hyenas, late gestation is associated with higher levels of testosterone in dominant as compared to subordinate females, and the subsequent offspring born to these more dominant mothers display relatively higher rates of aggressive behavior (Dloniak, French, & Holekamp, 2005).

Together, these findings indicate that testosterone modulates competitive behavior in females of a number of species, providing strong theoretical grounds for exploring the link between this hormone and intrasexual competition in humans.

Endocrine Theories for Competitive Behavior: The Dual-Hormone Hypothesis

More recent to the Challenge Hypothesis, the Dual-Hormone Hypothesis has been proposed. This theory suggests that socially aggressive competitive behavior in humans might be better explained through considering changes in testosterone and cortisol in tandem (Mehta & Josephs, 2010). Cortisol is a glucocorticoid that is typically released in response to stress. Unlike testosterone release, which is controlled by the HPG axis, cortisol release is under the control of the hypothalamic-pituitary-adrenal (HPA) axis, which is activated during periods of stress or threat. Cortisol helps to maintain homeostasis, and high endogenous levels can thus be considered a sign of stress or trauma (Brown et al., 1996). Since testosterone inhibits the HPA axis, and cortisol is the end product of the HPA axis, the Dual-Hormone Hypothesis proposes that the HPA and HPG function in concert to regulate aggressive and competitive behavior. That is, the interaction between testosterone and cortisol levels is proposed to reveal a more nuanced measure of competitive behavior (i.e., testosterone is positively related to competitive behavior only in instances where the corresponding levels of cortisol are low). In this way, testosterone, which is associated with motivation and has previously been shown to down-regulate cognitive control (Schutter & van Honk, 2004), and cortisol, which is associated with avoidance and subsequent threat response, are thought to interact to best predict competitive reactivity. Evidence for this possibility lies in the fact that both hormones have been shown to bind to steroid hormone regions in the amygdala, the brain area most centrally involved in emotion processing. It has been proposed that the lack of association in some previous studies that consider testosterone levels and competitive behavior in isolation may therefore be explained by a failure to consider the potential for additional hormonal relationships. In some respects, tests of the Dual Hormone Hypothesis are in their infancy, and research measuring larger ranges of hormones is just beginning to more completely illustrate the potential for cortisol and testosterone, and a suite of other hormones, to contextually

moderate competitive behavior. In this way, the Dual Hormone Hypothesis can also be considered a more general concept to allow us to move away from the idea that testosterone is the sole hormone underpinning competitive behavior.

The Dual-Hormone Hypothesis: Evidence from Nonhuman Species

When one considers the evidence for the Dual Hormone Hypothesis in nonhumans relative to the evidence for the Challenge Hypothesis in nonhumans, it is apparent that support for the former is relatively sparse. Of course, recall that the Challenge Hypothesis originated from research on birds while, in contrast, the Dual Hormone Hypothesis was originally used to explain aggressive socially competitive behavior in humans. In spite of this, there is no fundamental reason why the hypothesis should not be supported in animals. Indeed, a large number of studies have measured cortisol, sometimes even in combination with testosterone, when examining competition. Though they may not have explicitly predicted an interaction or relationship between the hormones, this nonetheless allows us to consider indirect evidence for the idea that the HPA and HPG axis work together to prompt competitive behavior in nonhuman species. In this section we do exactly that by providing a brief outline of studies in nonhumans, examining cortisol either in isolation or in conjunction with testosterone. The aim of this section is to briefly illustrate the variety of findings for relationships between cortisol and competition in nonhumans in the context of the predictions of the Dual-Hormone Hypothesis.

Research in baboons has shown that corticosterone (the nonhuman version of cortisol) release inhibits the production of testosterone (Sapolsky, 1985). Corticosterone has further been shown to relate to behaviors linked to inhibition, leading to the possibility that it may contribute to avoidance-motivated behaviors and hence therefore be negatively related to testosterone and competitive inclinations. Work by Haller, Halász, Mikics, and Kruk (2004) conceptually supports this idea; they showed that chronic corticosterone deficiency led rats to display lessened response to social challenges in spite of the fact that this deficiency did not interfere with actual locomotor activity (i.e., the ability to respond physically). These findings can all be interpreted as supporting premises of the Dual-Hormone Hypothesis.

However, corticosterone levels are also known to increase after sex in animals (e.g., bull and boars,

Borg, Esbenshade, & Johnson, 1991), which is consistent with the pattern observed for testosterone, but appears not to support the idea that the two hormones interact to contribute to mating competition. Muehlenbein and Watts (2010) have recently shown that testosterone, but not corticosterone, relates to dominance rank in wild male chimps, suggesting that corticosterone may not contribute to achieving status, at least in this species.

Together these studies paint a somewhat inconsistent pattern of results for the contribution of corticosterone in competitive interactions. Future research on competition in nonhumans could benefit from analyzing both corticosterone and testosterone and testing for a relationship between these variables more explicitly. It is imperative that factors like type of competition (e.g., physical task, cognitive task) and organism (e.g., species, mating system, reproductive value) are controlled in these studies to make clearer relative comparisons of findings possible. Importantly, the mixed animal evidence does not render the hypothesis invalid but rather suggests more empirical work on this possibility is needed. More broadly, measuring a wider range of hormones when examining the hormonal underpinnings of competition is certainly a much-needed approach to improve understanding of how isolated findings (e.g., single hormone tests) may relate.

Testing the Challenge Hypothesis and Dual-Hormones Hypothesis in Humans

In the previous sections we have described the two main theoretical concepts that attempt to explain the endocrinology of competitive behavior. We have seen evidence from nonhuman species in support of both the Challenge Hypothesis and the Dual-Hormone Hypothesis. However, we have also acknowledged a number of studies failing to conceptually support these ideas and briefly discussed the possibility that a larger range of hormones interact more complexly to generate competitive behavior. We expand on this idea further later in the chapter. In the subsequent section we first review a series of studies that have attempted to extend the principals of the Challenge Hypothesis and Dual Hormone Hypothesis to humans. As stated in the introduction, we include a significant section on male competition because discussion of this literature allows us to illustrate how hormonal trade-offs impact women's competition similarly in some respects but distinctively in others when compared to men.

Evidence from Men

There is accumulating evidence that the fundamental principles of the Challenge Hypothesis also extend to humans. This possibility has been studied most extensively among human males, perhaps because they have substantially higher levels of testosterone than females. Consistent with nonhuman literature, it appears that human males also regulate the trade-off between mating effort (i.e., competing for mating opportunities) and parenting effort (i.e., maintaining existing romantic relationship and caring for dependent offspring) through variation in testosterone. Indeed, regardless of baseline testosterone levels, men can obtain a selective advantage from enhancing testosterone levels in situations of competition, since high testosterone promotes muscle performance and can prepare the body for potential injuries (e.g., Bhasin et al., 2001). In this section, we provide a brief overview of how testosterone relates to human male competition. Note this section is not exhaustive but provides a comparative context for the human female literature subsequently outlined.

Evidence supporting the idea that high testosterone levels may contribute to male willingness to compete aggressively is widespread. For example, testosterone has been shown to relate to particular male behaviors or personality styles, including decreased neuroticism, increased antisocial personality, and higher levels of mania—all of which may be more likely to be associated with competition (Dabbs, Hopper, & Jurkovic, 1990). Harris, Rushton, Hampson, and Jackson (1996) reported that testosterone levels positively relate to aggression and negatively relate to prosocial personality traits, while others have explicitly shown that a rise in testosterone positively predicts aggressive behavior (Carré, McCormick, & Hariri, 2011; Klinesmith, Kasser, & McAndrew, 2006). Popma et al. (2007) extended these results by showing that testosterone related to aggressive behavior in delinquent boys. Interestingly, however, this finding was true only in specific groups of boys who had low cortisol levels and not in those with relatively higher cortisol levels. This finding is in line with other work by Dabbs, Jurkovic, and Frady (1991), who studied adult male offenders and found a stronger relationship between testosterone and aggressive behavior, as assessed by the degree of crime violence among male offenders who had low as opposed to relatively high cortisol levels. Together, these studies support the idea that testosterone trade-offs are used to regulate competitive aggressive behavior. However, the last two studies in particular appear to additionally support the interaction of cortisol and testosterone in predicting competitive mating behavior, in line with the Dual-Hormone Hypothesis.

A broader view of the literature on this topic, unfortunately, muddies this conclusion. For example, research examining mating competition by van der Meij, Buunk, and Salvador (2010) showed that after a brief social interaction with men or women, levels of cortisol decreased consistent with the diurnal rhythm, but that this decrease was relatively lower after interacting with a woman. Prior to this, Roney and colleagues (2007) showed that men waiting in a room with female confederates had higher cortisol levels as compared to men waiting in a room alone, thereby suggesting that social contact with a woman facilitates a cortisol response. These authors then showed that men approached by a flirtatious woman in a waiting room experienced (nonsignificant) increases in cortisol while men approached by a friendly man in a waiting room experienced (significant) decreases in cortisol levels. Further research, which examined cortisol response to viewing erotic videos, has provided additional contradicting evidence for the role of cortisol in the down-regulation of competitive mating behavior. Uckert and colleagues (2003) found a decrease in cortisol after viewing erotic videos, while a series of other researchers found no change in cortisol after viewing erotic videos (e.g., Carani et al., 1990). Together, these studies suggest that testosterone tends to reliably predict aggressive competitive behavior among men, but the impact of cortisol levels on competitive behavior is less consistent.

Testosterone is also known to increase during competitive contexts outside of the realm of mating. For example, when a man is in a competitive situation and "wins," a series of studies have provided evidence that a surge in testosterone follows. For example, testosterone has been shown to peak among men prior to athletic competition and then again when they subsequently "win" the contest (e.g., Booth, Shelley, Mazur, Tharp, & Kittok, 1989). This pattern of results has similarly been documented in nonphysical competitive contexts such as playing a match of chess (Mazur, Booth, & Dabbs, 1992). Pregame rises in testosterone suggest that testosterone may be up-regulated in preparation for competition. Indeed, pregame increases in testosterone have been documented in a variety of sporting contexts (e.g., Booth et al., 1989), and even among men who are playing video games (Mazur et al., 1997). Even men who are not physically taking part in sporting competition but rather supporting a competitive match as a spectator have been shown to experience increased levels of testosterone (Bernhardt, Dabbs, Fielden, & Lutter, 1998). At first glance, the relationship between testosterone and competition appears to be reciprocal among men. However, it must be acknowledged that a number of studies have failed to document the association between "winning" and testosterone variation (e.g., Suay et al., 1999). Interestingly, this pattern of results has also been demonstrated for cortisol, which would go against the predictions asserted by the Dual-Hormone Hypothesis that these two hormones interact to generate competitive socially aggressive behaviors.

Support for the other side of the Challenge Hypothesis, namely that low testosterone is associated with instances wherein competitive mating behavior is not adaptive, extends from research examining human male social investment. For example, men who are in a committed relationship have lower testosterone levels than their single counterparts (Burnham et al., 2003; Gray et al., 2004; Pollet, Cobey, & van der Meij, 2013; Sakaguchi, Oki, Honma, & Hasegawa, 2006). Unsurprisingly, marital status is also associated with differences in testosterone levels, with married men having lower levels of testosterone than nonmarried men (Booth & Dabbs, 1993; Gray, Kahlenberg, Barrett, Lipson, & Ellison, 2002; Mazur & Michalek, 1998). These results also appear to replicate within nonindustrialized societies, since Ariaal men of Kenya who are partnered also have lower levels of testosterone than men within their society who are single (Gray, Ellison, & Campbell, 2007). Men who are already partnered have less to compete for (with respect to mating) than their single conspecifics and can therefore afford to reduce testosterone levels and invest less heavily in mating competition. This explanation is consistent with other research carried out among societies with mixed mating structures wherein polygamously married men have been found to have higher testosterone levels on average than monogamously married men and single men (Alvergne et al., 2009; Van Anders, Hamilton, & Watson, 2007).

Evidence from Women

Evidence providing support for the utility of the Challenge Hypothesis or Dual-Hormone Hypothesis among human females is scarcer when compared to the available literature in human males. Moreover, findings tend to be somewhat less robust. It is not entirely surprising that testosterone responses in men and women do not precisely mimic one another, for several reasons. First, testosterone levels in men far exceed levels in women, with research suggesting values three to seven times higher among men (e.g., Dabbs, 1990). Second, the source of most testosterone production in men is via the testes while principal testosterone production in women occurs within the adrenal glands and to a lesser extent in the ovaries. Based on differing sources of testosterone production, parallel testosterone responses in social situations may be unlikely to occur. In spite of these differences, some research in women has indeed shown that testosterone positively relates to competitive behavior. In this section, this evidence is outlined as it relates to female aggressive behavior, sexual behavior, mating effort, and maternal investment.

In addition to their work on male competition, Harris, Rushton, Hampson, and Jackson (1996) have shown that testosterone levels are positively related to aggression and negatively related to prosocial personality traits among women. Further evidence supporting the idea that testosterone contributes to increased aggression proneness is evidenced by work in a moderate size group of female-to-male transsexuals who reported increased aggression proneness after the administration of androgens (Van Goozen, Frijda, & van de Poll, 1994). In contrast, male-to-female transsexuals, who typically are administered anti-androgens, reported lower levels of anger and lessened aggression (Van Goozen, Cohen-Kettenis, Gooren, Frijda, & van de Poll, 1995). These studies support the idea that testosterone contributes to aggressive behavior and personality characteristics in women in a way that is similar to what has been observed among men. Testosterone has likewise been linked to female sexual arousal or libido (Alexander & Sherwin, 1993; Braunstein et al., 2005; Tuiten et al., 2000). Van Anders, Hamilton, Schmidt, and Watson (2007) showed that female testosterone levels were higher after intercourse and that there was a positive association between testosterone and orgasm.

In spite of the aforementioned evidence for the role of testosterone in female libido and aggressive behavior, it remains largely unclear if, and how, these behaviors are relevant to actual mating behavior. A series of studies have documented positive relationships between testosterone levels and number of sex partners among women, thereby suggesting a relevant consequence for this hormonal variation. For example, in a study on college women, Cashdan

(2003) reported a positive association with number of sex partners and testosterone; however, among these same women levels of testosterone negatively predicted levels of status or rank. This finding is in contrast to much of the nonhuman and human male literature (outlined in the previous sections), which has tended to document positive associations between testosterone and rank. In spite of this, some evidence supporting the idea that testosterone may relate to dominance in women was reported by Cashdan (2003): testosterone levels were positively related to high self-regard and infrequent smiling, which can be considered a form of nonverbal dominance behavior. Nevertheless, other research has failed to conceptually replicate the finding that testosterone levels positively relate to women's motivation to seek out and competitively acquire mating opportunities. For instance, when controlling for a number of relevant variables, using a sample of elderly Americans, Pollet et al. (2011) failed to find a relationship between testosterone and lifetime sex partners in women. From a theoretical perspective, it is likely that increasing numbers of sex partners may have a greater impact on male than female reproductive success (Trivers, 1972). For this reason, additional sex partners in women may not reflect higher levels of libido or mating effort in the same way that they do among men. However, it is important to acknowledge that the women studied in Pollet et al. (2011) were close to the end of their lifespan, likely having undergone menopause and the hormonal changes associated with it. It may therefore be that the association between testosterone and reported number of sex partners is only present among younger women.

Evidence from López, Hay, and Conklin (2009) provides some further indication that female mating competition and sexual motivation are underpinned by hormonal trade-offs. In their study, López and colleagues had women view a video that portrayed one of the following: an attractive man courting a woman, an unattractive man courting a woman, a control video portraying a nature documentary, or a control video portraying an attractive woman. These researchers found that testosterone and cortisol increased in women after viewing the video of the attractive man courting the woman but not after viewing any of the other videos. Note that the premises of the Dual-Hormone Hypothesis would have predicted high testosterone and low cortisol when viewing the video of the attractive male attempting to court the woman. Future research remains necessary to test this interaction more closely; however, given that testosterone levels are much lower in women, and the lack of interaction between testosterone and cortisol in many of the female studies outlined in this section, the hypotheses may simply not ring true.

Apart from contributing to sexual motivation and function, testosterone in women, much like in men, is known to fluctuate prior to, and after, overt physical competition. For example, Oliveira, Gouveia, and Oliveira (2009) found a pregame rise in testosterone, but also cortisol, levels among female soccer players. These authors also found that performance outcomes were related to mood changes and postgame testosterone but not to pregame testosterone levels, therefore suggesting that changes in mood may contribute directly to increases in testosterone in "winners." This is in line with other findings that similarly report an increase in both testosterone and cortisol in response to competition among female rugby players (Bateup, Booth, Shirtcliff, & Granger, 2002) and female soccer players (Edwards, Wetzel, & Wyner, 2006). However, in the latter of these studies this increase was not related to winning or losing. A number of other studies examining female competitive behavior and testosterone response have nevertheless found divergent results. For example, no association between testosterone or cortisol levels and competition was found among women's competition as it relates to playing video games, rowing, or taking part in a competitive vocabulary task (e.g., Kivlighan, Granger, & Booth, 2005; Allan Mazur, Susman, & Edelbrock, 1997; Van Anders & Watson, 2007).

Previous research has also shown that women in relationships have lower levels of testosterone than single women, which parallels the link between testosterone and partner status in men (Van Anders & Goldey, 2010). Interestingly, however, these researchers showed that among partnered women, the frequency of sexual activity mediated this effect, while in men, interest in new partners mediated this effect. This points toward differing psychosocial actors contributing to this hormonal variation. This variation is further demonstrate in another study by (Van Anders & Watson, 2007), which showed that women in long-distance relationships had higher testosterone levels than women in same-city relationships, thereby suggesting that physical partner presence is important for female investment levels. Interestingly, this was not the case for male participants, in which levels of testosterone were the same among men in long-distance and same-city relationships, suggesting that investment may

be relatively less dependent on partner presence in men than women. This finding may be explained best by the partners' physical presence since, unlike findings in men, levels of relationship commitment do not consistently relate to testosterone levels in women (Caldwell Hooper, Gangestad, Thompson, & Bryan, 2011).

Beyond Testosterone: The Potential Role of Additional Peptide and Steroid Hormones in Competition

Thus far we have stressed the role of testosterone and, to a lesser extent, cortisol in governing competitive behavior. While accumulating evidence clearly suggests a role for these hormones in competitive behavior, there is additional evidence that "female sex hormones" (i.e., oestrogen and progesterone) may also influence female competitive behavior, although the mechanisms by which these hormones are involved in the regulation of competition are far less well understood. At the outset of this discussion it is therefore of value to comment on the fact that, in contrast to the previous section wherein we described the role of testosterone and then cortisol in competition with respect to two theoretically driven hypotheses, literature testing the role of other hormones in competition tends not to be as theoretically guided. That is, the articulation of a strong theoretical basis for the role of oestrogen and progesterone in general competitive behavior is not necessarily present for these additional hormones. For example, high levels of circulating oestrogen, unlike testosterone, are not associated with negative immunological effects; indeed, just the opposite appears to be true, as oestrogen has been shown to reduce the risk of cardiovascular disease (Mendelsohn & Karas, 1999) and limit skeletal degeneration (Turner, Riggs, & Spelsberg, 1994), among other health benefits. Additionally, high levels of oestrogen are associated with higher fertility (e.g., Lipson & Ellison, 1993) and a more feminine physical appearance (Jasieńska, Lipson, Ellison, Thune, & Ziomkiewicz, 2006; Jasieńska, Ziomkiewicz, Ellison, Lipson, & Thune, 2004), which may actually increase women's mate value, thus making them the object of male competition and reducing their need to compete. For this reason, it is unlikely that oestrogen would underpin a trade-off in competitive behavior and maternal activity.

One possible theory for the involvement of "female sex hormones" in the regulation of competitive behavior is that their effects on competitive behavior are a by-product of individual differences in levels of hormones or, alternatively, changes in hormone levels that are associated with pregnancy and function to increase reproductive success by protecting the mother and fetus from threat (e.g., Jones et al., 2005) or increase infant survival postpartum via bond formation, protection, or resource provisioning (Fleming, Ruble, Krieger, & Wong, 1997; Ramirez, Bardi, French, & Brent, 2004; Stockley & Bro-Jørgensen, 2011; Swain, Lorberbaum, Kose, & Strathearn, 2007). Hormonal effects of estrogen and progesterone on maternal aggression could, therefore, impact on female competition during times when the woman is neither pregnant nor caring for an infant simply as a by-product. As such, hormones linked to female fertility and reproduction may influence competitive behavior across the lifespan. This section draws on evidence from animal studies exploring the link between estrogen and progesterone and competitive behavior.

"Female Sex Hormones": Estrogens and Progestogens

Female sexual development and fertility are largely controlled by the HPG axis. Estrogen and progesterone, the primary female sex hormones, are both gonadal steroid hormones and are synthesized from cholesterol (note that both hormones also exist in men, in lesser amounts).

In women, the ovaries are the primary site of production for both hormones (except during pregnancy, when the placenta becomes the primary source of production, at least in humans), although production also occurs in the adrenal cortex and some peripheral tissues. Progesterone is the main progestogen involved in female reproductive functioning and plays a key role in preparation for and maintenance of pregnancy (i.e., progestational). Estrogens are important for the development of secondary sexual characteristics as well as regulation of the menstrual cycle. There are three major forms of naturally occurring estrogens: estrone, estradiol, and estriol. Estradiol is the predominant form of estrogen during a female's natural reproductive window (i.e., from menarche to menopause), while estrone is the primary form of estrogen synthesized postmenopause and estriol acts as the primary estrogen source during pregnancy, when it is produced by the placenta (see Cui, Shen, & Li, 2013, for a recent review of estrogen synthesis and function). For the duration of this chapter, the term *estrogen* reflects estradiol,

the predominant form of estrogen produced during the majority of the lifespan, unless otherwise specified.

Estrogen, Progesterone, and Competition: Evidence from Nonhuman Species

Estrogen has been linked to dominance and aggression in a number of animal species (for a brief review see Trainor, Kyomen, & Marler, 2006). For example, treating subordinate ovariectomized female cows with exogenous estrogen can result in dominance reversals within a pairing, with the subordinate female becoming dominant over the originally dominant female posttreatment (Bouissou, 1990). Similarly, in female chimpanzees dominance status is enhanced with raised estrogen levels (Birch & Clark, 1948). Indeed, the link between estrogen and dominance or aggressive behaviors appears to be especially prevalent among primate species. Endogenous estrogen levels have been linked to aggression in female rhesus macaques (Michael & Zumpe, 1970), especially noncontact aggression toward other group members (Mallow, 1981; Walker, Wilson, Gordon, & Regional, 1983). However, not all studies have found evidence for a link between estrogen and competitive behavior. For example, although castrated male rats given exogenous testosterone outperformed those not treated with testosterone in a food competition task, estrogen treatment had no effects on competitive performance (Work & Rogers, 1972). Similar studies in ovariectomized female rats have demonstrated no effect of exogenous estrogen treatment on aggression toward unfamiliar conspecifics (van de Poll, van Zanten, & de Jonge, 1986), although evidence for increased performance on the food competition task is mixed (see Albert, Jonik, & Walsh, 1992).

Estrogen may be a critical modulator of indirect aggression and more subtle forms of competition among females, such as proceptive behaviors (i.e., any behavior the female engages in that attempts to attract a male). In several rodent species, scent-marking behaviors and other proceptive behaviors are increased following administration of exogenous estrogen (see Takahashi, 1990). This behavior may reflect a more subtle form of intrasexual competition compared to direct aggression in that females compete by attempting to make themselves more attractive (than other females) to male conspecifics rather than engaging in direct, aggressive combat for access to a male.

Importantly, there is evidence that estrogen alone may not influence competitive behaviors; rather, it may be a suite of hormones acting in concert that influence such behavior. Van de Poll et al. (1986) demonstrated that estrogen treatment activates aggressive intrasexual behaviors in female rats but only when dihydrotestosterone propionate is administered alongside the estrogen treatment. Similarly, Albert et al. (1990) found that combined implants of estrogen and testosterone are best at restoring competitive functioning measured using food competition tasks. Further evidence that estrogen and testosterone may function together to influence female competition comes from studies of lizards. Female lizards have elevated levels of estrogen and testosterone at times of the year when they most strongly demonstrate aggression; however, neither hormone appears to be associated with aggression directly. Rather, the interaction between hormones and/or other factors, such as receptor levels, appear to mediate aggression and other intrasexual behaviors (Woodley & Moore, 1999).

Evidence for a role of progesterone in the maintenance and expression of competitive behaviors is somewhat mixed. In general, progesterone has been shown to decrease aggressive behaviors (e.g., Erpino & Chappelle, 1971; Fraile, McEwen, & Pfaff, 1988). Progesterone levels in mice during a resident-intruder test have been shown to be lower than those of control mice not interacting with a conspecific (Davis & Marler, 2003), and in rats administration of exogenous progesterone inhibits aggressive responses typically seen following treatment with estrogen and testosterone (Albert et al., 1992). Similarly in hamsters, progesterone has been shown to reduce aggressive behavior. Importantly, this inhibition of aggression does not appear to be the result of a general reduction in locomotor activity (Fraile, McEwen, & Pfaff, 1987; Fraile et al., 1988).

Although a number of studies have provided support for the inhibitory role of progesterone in aggressive behavior, it is important to note that some have demonstrated a positive link between progesterone and aggressive intrasexual behaviors (e.g., in voles, Kapusta, 1998; and hamsters, Meisel & Sterner, 1990), while others have demonstrated no link between progesterone and aggression (Mayer, Monroy, & Rosenblatt, 1990; Svare & Gandelman, 1975). There is some evidence that estrogen and progesterone may function together to influence aggression. When given a prolonged treatment of exogenous estrogen along with daily injections of

progesterone in an attempt to mimic high levels of these hormones seen during pregnancy, the concurrent hormonal treatment increases the aggressive behavior of female rats toward unfamiliar conspecifics (Tamada & Ichikawa, 1980). Similarly, prolonged treatment with this pregnancy-like pattern of hormones raises aggression in ovariectomized females (Mayer et al., 1990).

In humans, much of the research to date has involved studying behavior across the lifespan, or throughout the menstrual cycle, when levels of estrogen and progesterone vary. In the following section, we outline the evidence for a role of these hormones in the maintenance and expression of competitive behavior in humans.

Hormonal Influences on Competition Across the Human Female Lifespan

In the previous sections, we outlined the evidence for endocrinological theories of intrasexual competition, from the role of testosterone in competition to the potential role of additional hormones, or a suite of hormones, in female competition among humans and nonhumans. In the following section we expand this discussion as it specifically relates to variation in competitive behavior across the female lifespan. Although competition across the lifespan has been discussed previously in this handbook, here we seek to use knowledge of the hormonal changes across the lifespan to educate the discussion of the endocrinological basis of female competition. The female lifespan is characterized by distinct reproductive states, including: premenarchal (from birth), puberty and menarche (average age of menarche in the UK = 12.9; Dratva et al., 2009), the reproductive years (peak fertility in the mid-20s; Dunson, Colombo, & Baird, 2002), and menopause (average age of menopause in the UK = 51.1 years; Dratva et al., 2009). Each of these time periods involves a specific and unique endocrinological profile, which may distinctively influence competitive behavior. It is essential to understand how key hormones fluctuate across the lifespan in order to discuss their potential effects on female competitive behavior at various stages. Here we provide a brief overview of the typical patterns seen for the gonadotrophic hormones (follicle stimulating hormone [FSH], luteinizing hormone [LH]) and the steroid hormones (estrogen, progesterone, and androgens) governing sexual development and fertility. In what follows we outline the evidence for competition at various stages of the female reproductive lifespan and discuss the potential hormonal mechanisms underpinning these behaviors. A general representation of fluctuating levels of these relevant hormone levels across the female lifespan can be seen in Figure 21.1.

Hormonal Profile: Birth to Menarche

Female sexual development and fertility are largely controlled by the HPG axis. Each component of this axis—the hypothalamus, pituitary gland, and ovaries (i.e., female gonads)—is present from birth. Placental hormones during development suppress hormonal secretion by the fetus; shortly after birth, in the absence of placental endocrine regulation, gonadotropin levels begin to rise during a transient activation of the HPG axis that typically begins shortly after birth (Forest, Sizonenko, & Cathard, 1974) and ends within the first two to three years of life (Winter & Faiman, 1972). FSH levels peak near the end of the newborn period while LH levels tend to peak near 1 month (Schmidt & Schwarz, 2000). Levels of estrogen, LH, and FSH tend to decline by 10 months (Burger, Yamada, Bangah, Mccloud, & Warne, 1991). By age 12 to 20 months, the HPG axis is suppressed, and a period of reproductive quiescence persists until the start of puberty.

At the onset of puberty, pulsatile secretion of gonadotropin releasing hormone induces pituitary gonadotropin hormone production (i.e., FSH and LH; Sisk & Zehr, 2005; Sisk, Lonstein, & Gore, 2013). LH and FSH act together to stimulate the production of gonadal steroid hormones (i.e., estrogens, progesterone, androgens). Early in puberty, these gonadotrophic secretions happen only during sleep, but, as puberty progresses, pulsatile secretion occurs throughout the day (Forbes & Dahl, 2010) and this gonadal activation leads to ovarian secretion of estradiol, progesterone, and ovarian androgens (i.e., DHEA, DHEAS, androstenedione, testosterone). Both estrogen and progesterone play critical roles in the expression of secondary sexual characteristics in women. Estrogen promotes development of secondary sex characteristics in peripheral tissues (i.e., breast development), whereas progesterone is responsible for glandular development. The hormonal changes during puberty eventually lead to the development of ovulatory menstrual cycles, menarche (i.e., the onset of menstruation), and, thus, reproductive potential in females (for a detailed review of pubertal development, see Buck Louis et al., 2008).

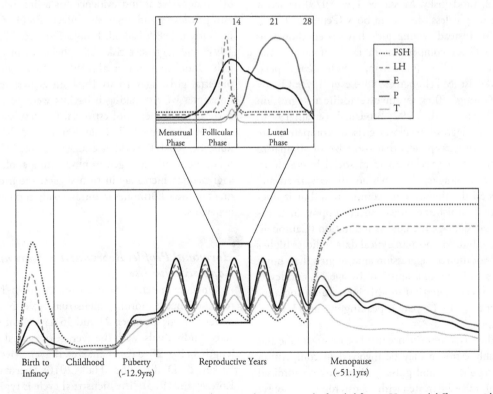

Figure 21.1 Schematic overview of approximate ovarian hormone changes across the female lifespan. Hormonal differences within or between various reproductive life stages may relate to behavioral differences in competition.

Competition in Girls Prior to Menarche and During Puberty

Earlier in this chapter we presented evidence for a possible link between testosterone and intrasexual competition among humans (i.e., the Challenge Hypothesis). Testosterone is the most widely studied hormonal correlate of aggressive behavior in children. During childhood, androgen levels in children are relatively stable and are lowest in preschool-age children (age five and under; Forest, 1989). The majority of studies among this age group have focused on aggressive behavior in boys, although some have also investigated this link in girls, with mixed results. In one study, testosterone levels were negatively correlated with social interactions in young girls, indicating a possible relationship between testosterone and antisocial behavior; however, there was no relationship between testosterone and aggressive behaviors (preschool-age; Sánchez-Martín et al., 2000). A potential explanation for the apparent lack of a testosterone–competition relationship among girls is that girls may not compete via direct aggression in the same way that boys do. Some studies have indicated that girls use less direct physical aggression than boys (Bjökqvist, Lagerspetz, & Kaukiainen, 1992; Brodzinsky, Messa, & Tew, 1979) or are at least caught less often than boys (Pepler & Craig, 1995). Instead, young girls have been shown to avoid direct competition in favor of tactics that diffuse conflict (Goodwin, 1980; Lagerspetz, Björkqvist, & Peltonen, 1988; Lever, 1976; Ostrov & Keating, 2004) or involve indirect aggression (Bjökqvist et al., 1992; Brodzinsky et al., 1979). Indirect aggression allows girls to compete more subtly via gossip, acts that ostracize or stigmatize others, and/or exclusion from social interactions. This type of aggression does not directly assert any physical dominance over competitors, but it does act to diminish the target's social support or status and can damage the target's reputation (Campbell, 2004). Indeed, meta-analytical data indicate higher levels of indirect aggression among girls than boys; this sex difference is apparent by age 11, and levels of indirect aggression in girls increase during adolescence (6 to 17 years), peaking at age 11 to 17 (Archer, 2004).

There is some evidence that both testosterone and possibly estrogen may be involved in competition among girls around puberty. When ovariectomized female mice are treated with testosterone at the onset of puberty (30 days old), they show increased levels of aggression toward other females as compared to control mice (Edwards, 1970). Similarly, development of a stereotypical food-protecting behavior has been shown to be contingent on the presence of ovarian hormones in mice (Sisk & Zehr, 2005). In humans, experimental manipulation of exposure to gonadal steroid hormones during pubertal development is not possible, for obvious ethical reasons. However, some studies have indicated that gonadal hormones may influence indirect aggression and risk-taking behaviors. Testosterone levels in adolescent girls (age 14) have been found to correlate with behavioral measures of "nastiness," which may reflect a tendency toward indirect aggression (Susman et al., 1987). Indeed, adolescent girls (age 15 to 17) suffering from conduct disorder, and particularly aggressive conduct disorder, have been shown to have higher levels of free testosterone but lower cortisol to testosterone levels as compared to control adolescents (Pajer et al., 2006). In complementary research on hypogonadal adolescents, Finkelstein et al. (1997) has demonstrated that administration of exogenous estrogen and testosterone treatments increases aggression in both boys and girls (assessed via self-report). Interestingly, the effects of these exogenous hormones on aggressive behavior were stronger in girls than boys. Similarly, a number of studies have found evidence for a link between estrogen levels and aggressive affect (Brooks-Gunn & Warren, 1989; Paikoff, Brooks-Funn, & Warren, 1991) and aggressive risk-taking behavior in young girls (Inoff-Germain et al., 1988). In a study of pubertal girls, ages 14 to 15, both aggressive and nonaggressive risk-taking behaviors were positively correlated with levels of estrogen, free testosterone, and LH (Vermeersch, T'Sjoen, Kaufman, & Vincke, 2008). Overall, the evidence suggests a role for both testosterone and estrogen in modulating adolescent aggression, which may in turn suggest the involvement of these hormones in intrasexually competitive behaviors.

Hormonal Profile: Reproductive Years and Contraceptive Use

Once menarche has occurred, women begin to experience a monthly menstrual cycle. Normal cycles can vary between 21 and 35 days within and across individuals, with the average or typical cycle length being 28 days (Chiazze, Brayer, Macisco, Parker, & Duffy, 1968; Hall, 2010; Sherman & Korenman, 1975). The menstrual cycle is typically divided into three stages: the menstrual phase (or menses, day 1 to 5), the follicular phase (or proliferative stage, day 6 to 14), and the luteal phase (or secretory stage, day 15 to 28). After menstruation, pituitary release of FSH and LH stimulates follicular development in the ovary. The developing follicle produces estrogen, which causes proliferation of the endometrial tissue and generates positive feedback on the pituitary leading to an LH surge. This LH surge triggers ovulation, which typically occurs 24 to 48 hours later and signifies the end of the follicular phase. Near ovulation, women have high levels of estrogen, have a high estrogen-to-progesterone (E:P) ratio, and experience a small surge in testosterone (Bao et al., 2003; Gandara, Leresche, & Mancl, 2007; Lu, Bentley, Gann, Hodges, & Chatterton, 1999; Wong et al., 1990). At the start of the luteal phase, the ruptured follicle forms the corpus luteum, which secretes progesterone. This progesterone functions to maintain the lining of the uterus to prepare for implantation of a fertilized egg if conception occurs. High estrogen and progesterone levels provide a negative feedback signal to the pituitary, which halts the release of FSH and LH. Consequently, the corpus luteum atrophies. During the luteal phase, women experience rising levels of progesterone, a decrease in estrogen as compared to the follicular phase (notably, estrogen levels are still much higher during the luteal phase than during the menstrual phase), and a relatively low E:P ratio (as a consequence of the estrogen decrease and simultaneous rise in progesterone). In the absence of implantation (and subsequent human chorionic gonadotropin production), estrogen and progesterone levels drop rapidly at the end of the luteal phase. This sudden drop triggers the shedding of the endometrial lining (i.e., menstruation; levels of both estrogen and progesterone are relatively low), and the cycle begins again (Jabbour, Kelly, Fraser, & Critchley, 2006). Women continue to cycle throughout their lives until reaching menopause. See Figure 21.1 for a visual representation of relative hormonal levels across the menstrual cycle.

Since becoming publicly available in the 1960s, hormonal contraceptives have become a widely used method of birth control among reproductive-age women. Recent survey data indicate that 41% of women in the UK between the ages of 16 and 49 reported current use of hormonal contraception, the most popular form being the oral contraceptive pill ("the pill"; 28% of women report current use; United Nations, 2012). From 2006 to 2008 over 80% of women surveyed in the United States

reported having ever used the pill (Mosher & Jones, 2010). The pill provides exogenous estrogens and progestins, which act to inhibit the natural action of the HPG axis. The continuous supply of synthetic estrogen and progesterone acts to suppress ovulation, as well as change the cervical mucus (which impacts sperm mobility) and alter endometrial development (which discourages implantation should an egg be released). This means that the cyclical fluctuation in hormones described in the previous section is blunted and that users do not experience mid-cycle fertility. The synthetic estrogen component of the pill is ethinyl estradiol (although some formulations use mestranol, which is metabolized to ethinyl estradiol), and most formulations use 20 to 50 micrograms per pill (Hall, 2010), while multiple synthetic progestins are used and the dosage and specific progestin can vary widely based on pill brand (Frye, 2006). Notably, these progestin components vary in terms of their androgenic profile (Hall, 2010). Use of the pill provides a unique opportunity to study the psychological effects of exogenous hormone treatment in humans.

Competition Across the Menstrual Cycle and During Hormonal Contraceptive Use

A sexual encounter will act to increase a female's reproductive success only if it occurs when she is fertile. As such, it is during times of high conception risk in the menstrual cycle that intrasexual competition for access to high-quality mates is most pertinent. In light of this fact, evolutionary hypotheses posit that increased intrasexual competition among females should parallel their fertility status. However, please see our commentary (Havlicek et al., 2015) for an alternative explanation that is not consistent with this mainstream evolutionary theory for menstrual cycle effects. Fertility is determined by cyclical variations in the hormones described in the previous section. As such, studies that directly assess hormone levels as well as studies that use diary data or LH-surge measures to predict (or directly assess) fertility may inform our understanding of the endocrinological mechanisms underpinning female competition.

It is important to keep in mind the relative concentrations of the female sex hormones during the course of the menstrual cycle (see Figure 21.1). Levels of estrogen and progesterone are low during the menstrual phase of the cycle. Estrogen levels steadily rise during the follicular phase, peaking around ovulation, while progesterone levels remain low during this phase of the cycle (and therefore the

E:P ratio is high). Estrogen levels decline during the luteal phase (but still remain moderately high as compared to the menstrual phase), while progesterone levels steadily rise. The resultant E:P ratio is much lower during this phase of the cycle (see Bao et al., 2003; Gandara et al., 2007; Lu et al., 1999; Sherman & Korenman, 1975; Wong et al., 1990). An understanding of these hormone levels across the cycle, and their relative concentrations, is crucial if we are to draw inferences regarding potential hormonal mechanisms of intrasexual behaviors observed across the menstrual cycle in the absence of direct hormonal assessment.

There is evidence from nonhuman primates that aggressive intrasexual behaviors fluctuate with fertility. For example, female macaque monkeys and chimpanzees display increased agonistic responses toward other females when they are in estrus (i.e., when fertile; Lacreuse & Herndon, 2003; Lacreuse, Martin-Malivel, Lange, & Herndon, 2007). Female bonobos in estrus tend to engage in more interruption of the mating attempts made by other females (Hohmann & Fruth, 2003) and harassment of mating pairs (Niemeyer & Anderson, 1983). These behaviors and female–female aggression appear to correlate with the number of other females currently in estrus, not the number of available males in the group. This would indicate that females compete for higher-quality males when other females are also seeking mating opportunities. Similarly, in yellow baboons, harassment of subordinate females occurs more often when the subordinate females are fertile (Wasser & Starling, 1988). Interestingly, these attacks are often made by pregnant or nonsexually receptive females who are not competing for access to a mate. Rather, these females may be engaging in reproductive suppression as a form of intrasexual competition, which will allow their offspring access to more resources.

Mid-cycle, or fertile, aggression has also been demonstrated in humans. Ellis (1972) found that aggressive responses in female inmates tend to be higher than average near ovulation (although, surprisingly, they peaked near menstruation). This aggressive response near fertility may be related to elevated testosterone levels mid-cycle. Indeed, an additional study demonstrated a link between age, testosterone, and inmate aggression independent of cycle (Dabbs & Hargrove, 1997). Similar links between testosterone levels and aggressive responses have been seen during the early follicular phase (Persky, Smith, & Basu, 1971) and

mid-follicular phase (Dougherty, Bjork, Moeller, & Swann, 1997) in nonincarcerated women.

Although there is evidence that cyclical shifts in testosterone may be the underlying mechanism for observable cyclical shifts in competitive behavior or aggression, it may also be that cyclical changes in estrogen drive, or at least contribute to, cyclical changes in these behaviors. Indeed, work by Dabbs (1990) suggests that within-day variation in testosterone (due, for example, to circadian rhythm) may be greater than within-month shifts and that changes in testosterone across the cycle can therefore largely be considered negligible. Cashdan (2003) found that women with low levels of circulating estrogen were less likely to report engaging in athletic competition than women with higher levels (although, notably, there was no link observed between estrogen levels and aggressive tactics employed in this study). Similarly, estrogen levels have been shown to positively correlate with implicit desire for power (Schultheiss, Dargel, & Rohde, 2003; Stanton & Schultheiss, 2007), which may reflect a drive to achieve social dominance and could be linked to aggressive behaviors (although these were not directly assessed).

In spite of the aforementioned studies, other research has failed to document increases in overt female intrasexual competitive behavior during the fertile phase of the menstrual cycle. In previous work we have conducted, women were followed longitudinally across the menstrual cycle, and self-reported levels of intrasexual competition did not differ when fertile as compared to nonfertile (Cobey, Klipping, & Buunk, 2013). The results from this study, while certainly not definitive, are powerful in the sense that we utilized strong methods wherein the same women were tracked within-subjects and transvaginal ultrasonography was used to confirm fertility. This is interesting for two reasons. First, it suggests that if cyclical shifts in intrasexual competition are occurring across the cycle, women are not conscious of them. Second, it raises the possibility that testosterone levels across the menstrual cycle may not increase during high conception risk (Liening, Stanton, Saini, & Schultheiss, 2010; Pearlman, Crepy, & Murphy, 1967; Schultheiss, Dargel, & Rohde, 2003). This being the case, if testosterone is the underlying mechanism behind shifts in competitive behavior, as predicted by the Challenge Hypothesis, then fertility-related cyclical shifts in competitive behavior would not necessarily have been anticipated.

This then begs the question: how can the findings outlined earlier, which appear to document shifting female competitive behavior across the menstrual cycle, be understood in context of the Challenge Hypothesis? We propose that cyclical shifts in behavior, such as attention to female faces and consumer products, may be best explained via variation in estrogen, which may impact lower-level cognitive processes such as attention processing and spatial relations. Thus, intrasexual competition in the context of these studies may relate to shifts in salience of stimuli and cognitive processes rather than conscious awareness or overt competitive drive. The scale we employed to assess intrasexual competition examines competition more broadly, encompassing a wider range of competitive behaviors than other studies that tend to explore intrasexual competition in the specific domain of physical attractiveness. It may therefore be that testosterone governs these sorts of overt behavioral responses, while estrogen (or other hormonal factors) may be implicated in the more subtle forms of competition. Indeed, women's jealousy responses (potentially a more subtle form of aggression or competitive drive) have been shown to track estrogen levels across the menstrual cycle (e.g., Geary, DeSoto, Hoard, Sheldon, & Cooper, 2001), and the use of oral contraceptives with a higher dose of synthetic estrogen is linked to greater increases in jealousy as compared to low-dose contraceptives (Cobey et al., 2012).

The tendency to engage in indirect forms of aggression such as the social manipulation seen in adolescent girls is also prevalent in adulthood, indicating a tendency among women to engage in more subtle forms of competition (Björkqvist, Österman, & Lagerspetz, 1994; Hess & Hagen, 2006). One such form of subtle competition is effort to outdo rivals. Men place a high premium on physical appearance when assessing a potential partner (Buss & Barnes, 1986; Buss, 1988). Given that men prefer physically attractive women and mate preferences are the underlying force driving intrasexual competition (see Darwin, 1871), it follows that women should compete with one another in terms of physical appearance (Campbell, 2004). Indeed, Buss (1988) found that one of the primary ways women report engaging in intrasexual competition tactics is by alteration of their physical appearance. Behavioral studies have provided evidence that this effort to outdo rivals fluctuates cyclically, suggesting an underlying hormonal basis. Haselton et al. (2007) found that, near ovulation, women report greater levels

of self-grooming and ornamentation (via attractive clothing choice). Naive judges even indicated, at above-chance levels, that they perceived the photographs of these women taken in the fertile phase as having invested more effort to look attractive as compared to photographs of the same women during the luteal phase of the cycle. Interestingly, Cashdan (1995) found that estrogen levels are positively correlated with enhanced perception of one's own status or popularity in a group of same-sex individuals. The magnitude of this overestimation of one's rank correlated positively with estrogen levels (although also with testosterone). Further examples of cyclical shifts in women's dress and consumer behavior near ovulation are discussed elsewhere in this book (see chapter by Nikiforidis, Arsena & Durante).

Based on the animal literature demonstrating a link between estrogen and proceptive behaviors, it is likely that heightened estrogen levels at mid-cycle may influence this ornamentation behavior among women. Indeed, a study of real-world female dress choice across the menstrual cycle demonstrated that when out for the night at a club, estrogen levels were positively correlated with amount of skin displayed and clothing tightness (although this effect was present only in partnered women; Grammer, Renninger, & Fischer, 2004). Additionally, a relationship between testosterone levels and clothing sheerness was found among both single and partnered women. Because testosterone is linked to sex drive, it is perhaps unsurprising that women with higher testosterone levels wore sexier clothing. Interestingly, women who self-described their dress style as bold or sexy also tended to report flirting or sex as their motivation for attending the club.

In addition to subtle efforts to outshine rivals, previous work we have conducted provides evidence that women may exert effort to view attractive peers in an effort to "check out the competition" during peak fertility (Hahn, 2013). This behavior could potentially increase mating success. Gathering relevant information about competitors may aid women in determining when it is worthwhile to invest effort in potential mating opportunities. When there is high competition (i.e., attractive rivals), women may waste energy pursuing high-quality potential mates who are likely to choose an alternative female. Attractive women pose a threat (with regard to mating attempts) and are, therefore, relevant social stimuli. Primate studies have shown that social stimuli may act as rewards or reinforcers (Andrews & Rosenblum, 1993;

Fujita & Matsuzawa, 1986; Fujita, 1987; Swartz & Rosenblum, 1980) and that status impacts the salience of these social stimuli (Deaner, Khera, & Platt, 2005; McNelis & Boatright-Horowitz, 1998). Additionally, the most attractive peer faces can be a source of aspiration and fashion tips. By attending to attractive peers, women can realize their own mate value and be informed in decisions about competition for a mate.

Another way in which women may engage in subtle intrasexual competition is through competitor derogation. According to Buss and Dedden (1990), women can manipulate other's impressions of them by either elevating their own status or derogating others (i.e., diminishing other's status). As previously discussed, there is evidence that women invest more effort and financial resources in self-elevation during periods of heightened competition (Durante, Griskevicius, Hill, Perilloux, & Li, 2011; Durante, Li, & Haselton, 2008; Haselton et al., 2007). Fisher (2004) has found that women are more likely to derogate rivals by providing lower evaluations of their attractiveness around ovulation (i.e., peak fertility) as compared to menstruation (i.e., low fertility). Interestingly, in the Cashdan (1995) study where estrogen levels were shown to correlate with overestimation of one's rank within the social group, this overestimation may have been driven by derogation, as women with high estrogen levels (remember that estrogen is associated with femininity and attractiveness) were ranked as less popular with other women by the same-sex peers in their group (as compared to women with lower estrogen). Fisher and Cox (2009) have provided evidence that such derogation can cause potential mates (i.e., men) as well as other rivals (i.e., women) to decrease their own assessment of the individual in question. Interestingly, derogatory statements from highly attractive women have a greater effect than those from unattractive women. The cyclical variation in derogatory responses has been suggested to be the result of high estrogen levels near ovulation as compared to relatively low levels of estrogen at periods of low fertility. In light of the potential link between aggression and estrogen discussed previously, this explanation seems plausible. However, it may also be that testosterone influences derogatory behaviors or that heightened progesterone later in the cycle inhibits aggression, resulting in decreased derogation.

Support for the idea that testosterone may govern overt female intrasexual competition comes from the fact that within our research we found that when our regularly cycling participants initiated use of hormonal contraceptives, they self-reported significantly lower levels of intrasexual competition, at least if they had a romantic partner (Cobey et al., 2013). The novel finding that hormonal contraceptive use influences self-reported intrasexual competition raises the possibility that modern-day use of hormonal contraception may be negatively impacting psychosocial behavior (Alvergne & Lummaa, 2010; Roberts, Gosling, Carter, & Petrie, 2008; Cobey & Buunk, 2012). This pattern of results is also consistent with the Challenge Hypothesis since hormonal contraceptives vastly suppress levels of female androgens, including testosterone (Alexander, Sherwin, Bancroft, & Davidson, 1990; Bancroft, Sherwin, Alexander, Davidson, & Walker, 1991). Therefore, testosterone suppression during use of the pill appears to result in lower levels of female competition, but the absence of shifts in testosterone across the cycle means intrasexual competition remains constant at this time.

It is important to acknowledge here that other research provides evidence for a subtle increase in testosterone near ovulation (e.g., Welling et al., 2007). If this is true, then our results may be explained by the fact that the relative shift in testosterone levels across the cycle is much smaller than on the transition to hormonal contraceptive use. Indeed, during hormonal contraceptive use total testosterone levels decrease by upward of 31% (Zimmerman, Wouters, & Coelingh Bennink, 2013). This would explain our finding that women's self-reported intrasexual competition did not vary across the cycle (Cobey et al., 2013).

Other research exploring the effects of hormonal contraceptive use on female behavior provides further evidence for changes in competitive behavior among pill users. For example, Welling, Puts, Roberts, Little, and Burriss (2012) have previously shown that women using hormonal contraceptives report increased levels of mate guarding behavior. Furthermore, they documented a contraceptive pill dose relationship with mate guarding behavior, namely that women on combined oral contraceptives containing higher doses of synthetic estrogen reported higher levels of mate guarding. This is consistent with other research that documents a contraceptive pill ethlnyl estradiol dose dependency with jealousy response, wherein higher doses are associated with higher levels of self-reported jealousy (Cobey, Pollet, Roberts, & Buunk, 2011). Together these studies prompt the intriguing possibility that hormonal contraceptive use is lowering female competitive behavior, which subsequently may alter relationship functioning and generate changes in emotional reactivity. It is known, for example, that ethinyl estradiol stimulates hepatic sex hormone binding globulin production in a dose-dependent manner. What this means is that the suppression of free testosterone is even more pronounced (61%) than total testosterone levels since sex hormone binding globulin binds and inactivates testosterone, suggesting that bioavailable testosterone is thus greatly reduced (Coenen, Thomas, Borm, Hollanders, & Rolland, 1996; Zimmerman et al., 2013). This may mean that the relatively lower levels of bioavailable testosterone among women using higher estrogenic doses in their contraceptives result in changes in emotional reactivity to competition (e.g., being more jealousy and displaying greater degrees of mate guarding).

While the studies reviewed here suggest that cyclical changes in hormone levels may influence competitive behavior, without directly assessing hormone levels it is impossible to make any causal links between specific hormones and behavior. This initial evidence for a hormonal effect on intrasexual behavior is promising; however, we hope to emphasize the importance of future research measuring actual hormone levels in relation to female behavior and specifically intrasexual competition.

Hormonal Profile: Menopause

Menopause, from the Greek *pausis* and the root *men-* (month), refers to the cessation of monthly menstrual cycles and marks the end of a woman's reproductive years. Menopause typically occurs in women between the age of 45 and 55, with the average age of menopause in the UK at 51.1 years (Dratva et al., 2009). Dramatic hormonal changes occur during this time; most notably, estrogen and progesterone levels decrease significantly. During the menopausal transition, ovarian production of estrogen and progesterone halts (Gilbert, 2000). Peripheral conversion of androstenedione into estrone becomes the prominent source of estrogen, with approximately 5% of this estrone being further converted into estradiol. Similarly, the adrenal glands become the primary source of progesterone (Al-Azzawi & Palacios, 2009). Circulating androgen levels (i.e., testosterone) have been shown to have an age-related decline that may not be linked to the menopausal transition specifically (Davis, Davison, Donath, & Bell, 2005). Notably, although overall levels of these hormones decrease dramatically with menopause, there can be massive fluctuations in absolute levels of estrogen and progesterone, as well as relative levels of these hormones, during the menopausal transition, which can take several years (Al-Azzawi & Palacios, 2009; Burger, Dudley, Robertson, & Dennerstein, 2002).

Effects of Menopause on Female Competition

Once thought to be unique to humans, there is now evidence that other species, such as some nonhuman primates (Atsalis & Margulis, 2006; Emery Thompson et al., 2007; Nishida et al., 2003), orcas (Foote, 2008; McAuliffe & Whitehead, 2005; Ward, Parsons, Holmes, Balcomb, & Ford, 2009), and pilot whales (Kasuya & Marsh, 1984; Marsh & Kasuya, 1984) also experience menopause. Notably, these species all have relatively long lifespans and produce offspring that are heavily reliant on maternal care, often for a large portion of the lifespan (Foote, 2008; Johnstone & Cant, 2010). A number of hypotheses as to the evolutionary function of menopause have been proposed. Most notably are the Grandmother Hypothesis and the Reproductive Conflict Hypothesis. According to the Grandmother Hypothesis, the elimination of reproductive potential with menopause allows females to focus their resources on survival, rather than reproduction (O'Connell, Hawkes, & Jones, 1999). They can then redirect effort to caring for their offsprings' offspring (i.e., grandchildren), rather than competing for additional reproductive opportunities themselves, and ensure genetic propagation in this fashion. Alternatively, the Reproductive Conflict Hypothesis posits that menopause might, in part, have evolved in order to decrease competition between generations of reproducing women within a given family or social unit and increase child survival in times when resources for childrearing were scarce (Cant, Johnstone, & Russell, 2009). A common theme in both of these arguments is a decline in the need for intrasexual competition with the loss of one's own reproductive potential (i.e., menopause). Indeed, menopause is associated with decreased fertility (Burger et al., 2002; Burger, Hale, Dennerstein, & Robertson, 2008), and some have argued that this decrease in fertility is accompanied by a shift away from a mating-oriented psychology toward a more prosocial-oriented psychology (Hawkes, O'Connell, Jones, Alvarez, & Charnov, 1998).

The psychological impact of menopause has been widely studied with regard to mood (e.g.,

Baker, Simpson, & Dawson, 1997; Dennerstein, Lehert, Burger, & Dudley, 1999; Dennerstein, Randolph, Taffe, Dudley, & Burger, 2002; Pearlstein, Rosen, & Stone, 1997), sleep (e.g., Baker et al., 1997; Eichling & Sahni, 2005; Young, Finn, Austin, & Peterson, 2003), cognitive functioning (e.g., Manning, Gengo, & Joe, 1995; Meyer et al., 2003; Sherwin, 1997), and sexual function (e.g., Dennerstein et al., 2002; Dennerstein, Alexander, & Kotz, 2003; Nappi & Lachowsky, 2009). Conversely, very little work has been done exploring the effects of menopause on mating psychology. We know of only two studies exploring intrasexual behaviors among menopausal women. Additional studies have explored *inter*sexual preferences and behaviors among women near menopause (e.g., Little et al., 2010); however, only those studies that also provide data on *intra*sexual behavior are presented here. In the first of these studies, Vukovic et al. (2009) tested the impact of manipulated facial femininity on attractiveness judgments in a set of young same-sex and opposite-sex faces among premenopausal and postmenopausal women, all ages 40 to 64 years. Premenopausal women demonstrated diminished femininity preferences compared to postmenopausal women, and this effect was present for judgments of the attractiveness of same-sex faces only. These data support the argument that fertility impacts derogation of attractive same-sex competitors, as premenopausal women (who have higher fertility than postmenopausal women) were less willing to assess feminized female faces as attractive. This refusal to acknowledge increased attractiveness in same-sex faces may reflect derogation of potential competitors among premenopausal women that is reduced among postmenopausal women. Notably, these effects were independent of participant age, and both groups of women indicated that femininity was attractive in female faces, but this preference was stronger in the postmenopausal group than the premenopausal group. The facial stimuli used in this study depicted individuals in the late teens to early 20s. Attractive young females likely pose a strong threat to menopausal-age women as circum-menopausal women's romantic relationships are typically with men their own age and men in this age group are known to demonstrate strong preferences for young adult women (Buss, 1989). An additional study utilizing peer-age faces as stimuli again demonstrated that premenopausal women show diminished femininity preferences as compared to postmenopausal women (Jones, Vukovic, Little,

Roberts, & Debruine, 2011). Here the effect was present for both same-sex and opposite-sex faces. Although men have demonstrated preferences for youthful women, attractive peer-age females may also pose a threat to an existing relationship or future prospects. As such, these females may be viewed as competitors worthy of derogation.

Although it is difficult to ascertain the specific hormonal mechanism underpinning these circum-menopausal changes in intrasexual behavior, it is likely that changes in estrogen levels play a dominant role in circum-menopausal variation in perceptions, given the dramatic changes in estrogen level that accompany menopause (Burger et al., 2002) and the previously detailed effects estrogen has been shown to have on female intrasexual behavior. The limited evidence presented here highlights the need for future work among women in this circum-menopausal age group. The hormonal profiles associated with menopause (and the transitional period) offer a unique opportunity to explore the link between female sex hormones and mating psychology.

Summary

Throughout this chapter, we have explored the animal and human evidence for hormonal regulation of competitive behavior. We began with a discussion of the role of testosterone and cortisol in context to the Challenge Hypothesis and the Dual-Hormone Hypothesis and then moved on to discuss the potential role of estrogen and progesterone in competitive behavior. Following this, we outlined the specific variation in hormones across the female lifespan and discussed how each of these phases of unique hormonal transition may impact competitive behavior. The two overarching themes that we have communicated in this chapter are, first, how a suite of hormones appear to influence competition and that the relative understanding of the interactions between sets of these hormones is quite poor. While there is strong support for a role of testosterone in competitive behavior, even among women, it is also clear from our discussion that testosterone alone does not underpin competitive behavior. While we acknowledge financial constraints in hormone research, future studies that assay a larger range of hormones in tandem will be necessary to build models of competition in which we can test the relative impact of several hormones on competitive behavior in a single test. Only once these sorts of decisive studies have been conducted will we be able to understand the fundamental influence of different hormones on competitive behavior. Second, we have emphasized the idea that the maintenance of competition in nonhumans, human males, and human females occurs similarly in some respects but distinctively in others. For instance, in the second half of this chapter, by outlining the stage of hormonal variation across the female lifespan, we intended to stress that both within women (e.g., across the cycle) and across women (e.g., at different ages) there is a great deal of variation in hormone levels that needs to be considered and accounted for in research. This is without doubt essential information to consider when conducting cross-species comparisons. While we have largely focused on a general understanding of the potential hormonal control of competitive behavior, it is important to stress that individual variation may also occur. This is a vastly understudied topic and would be a fruitful area for future research.

It is also important to stress that the varied means of assessing competition across, and even within, species presents significant challenges in terms of drawing parallels and conclusive deductions. Although we have drawn on evidence from both men and women here, the ways in which evidence from men can inform our understanding of competition among women may be limited. This means that in order to continue to examine the hormonal basis of female competition we may first benefit from establishing a firmer grip on what female competition actually is and then determining how best to measure it. With an improved understanding of this basic sex difference, we may then be more aware of which specific indirect or subtle female competitive behaviors we would hypothesize to be subject to hormonal variation.

We hope to emphasize the need to investigate the hormonal mechanisms of behavior (and not just competition) using direct assessments of hormone levels. With these explicit measures, we can begin to understand the influence of individual hormones as well as their concerted effects on behavior. This knowledge may have broad societal implications in areas including the development and use of hormonal contraceptives, as well as hormone therapies for women during the postpartum and menopausal transition. Such research may likewise speak toward and enable a better understanding of a variety of (aggressive) psychiatric mood and personality disorders. Notably, in these areas a better understanding of receptor function is also critical to understand how circulating levels of these hormones relate to actual uptake and the impact on brain chemistry.

To conclude, women, like men and other nonhuman species, manage the need to compete and behave aggressively via underlying physiological changes in hormones. A better understanding of this hormonal underpinnings is necessary to fully appreciate and understand competitive behavior.

References

Al-Azzawi, F., & Palacios, S. (2009). Hormonal changes during menopause. *Maturitas, 63*(2), 135–137.

Albert, D. J., Jonik, R. H., & Walsh, M. L. (1990). Aggression by ovariectomized female rats: Combined testosterone/estrogen implants support the development of hormone-dependent aggression. *Physiology & Behavior, 47*(5), 825–830.

Albert, D. J., Jonik, R. H., & Walsh, M. L. (1992). Hormone-dependent aggression in male and female rats: Experiential, hormonal, and neural foundations. *Neuroscience and Biobehavioral Reviews, 16*(2), 177–192.

Alexander, G. M., & Sherwin, B. B. (1993). Sex steroids, sexual behavior, and selection attention for erotic stimuli in women using oral contraceptives. *Psychoneuroendocrinology, 18*(2), 91–102.

Alexander, G. M., Sherwin, B. B., Bancroft, J., & Davidson, D. W. (1990). Testosterone and sexual behavior in oral contraceptive users and nonusers: A prospective study. *Hormones and Behavior, 24*(3), 388–402.

Alvergne, A., Faurie, C., & Raymond, M. (2009). Variation in testosterone levels and male reproductive effort: Insight from a polygynous human population. *Hormones and Behavior, 56*(5), 491–497.

Alvergne, A., & Lummaa, V. (2010). Does the contraceptive pill alter mate choice in humans? *Trends in Ecology & Evolution, 25*(3), 171–179.

Andrews, M. W., & Rosenblum, L. A. (1993). Live-social-video reward maintains joystick task performance in bonnet macaques. *Perceptual Motor Skills, 77,* 755–763.

Archer, J. (2004). Sex differences in aggression in real-world settings: A meta-analytic review. *Review of General Psychology, 8*(4), 291–322.

Atsalis, S., & Margulis, S. W. (2006). Sexual and hormonal cycles in geriatric *Gorilla gorilla gorilla. International Journal of Primatology, 27*(6), 1663–1687.

Baker, A., Simpson, S., & Dawson, D. (1997). Sleep disruption and mood changes associated with menopause. *Journal of Psychosomatic Research, 43*(4), 359–369.

Bancroft, J., Sherwin, B. B., Alexander, G. M., Davidson, D. W., & Walker, A. (1991). Oral contraceptives, androgens, and the sexuality of young women: II. The role of androgens. *Archives of Sexual Behavior, 20*(2), 121–135.

Bao, A., Liu, R., Someren, E. J. W. Van, Hofman, M. A., Cao, Y., & Zhou, J. (2003). Diurnal rhythm of free estradiol during the menstrual cycle. *European Journal of Endocrinology, 148,* 227–232.

Bateup, H. S., Booth, A., Shirtcliff, E. A., & Granger, D. A. (2002). Testosterone, cortisol, and women's competition. *Evolution and Human Behavior, 23*(3), 181–192.

Beehner, J. C., Phillips-Conroy, J. E., & Whitten, P. L. (2005). Female testosterone, dominance rank, and aggression in an

Ethiopian population of hybrid baboons. *American Journal of Primatology*, *67*(1), 101–119.

Bernhardt, P. C., Dabbs, J. M., Fielden, J. A, & Lutter, C. D. (1998). Testosterone changes during vicarious experiences of winning and losing among fans at sporting events. *Physiology & Behavior*, *65*(1), 59–62.

Bhasin, S., Woodhouse, L., Casaburi, R., Singh, A. B., Bhasin, D., Berman, N., . . . Storer, T. W. (2001). Testosterone dose-response relationships in healthy young men. *American Journal of Physiology, Endocrinology and Metabolism*, *281*(6), E1172–1181.

Birch, H. G., & Clark, G. (1948). Hormonal modification of social behavior: II. The effects of sex-hormone administration on the social status of the female-castrate chimpanzee. *Psychosomatic Medicine*, *8*, 320–331.

Björkqvist, K., Österman, K., & Lagerspetz, K. M. (1994). Sex differences in covert aggression sex differences among adults. *Aggressive Behavior*, *20*(194), 27–33.

Björkqvist, K., Lagerspetz, K. M., & Kaukiainen, A. (1992). Do girls manipulate and boys fight? Developmental trends in regard to direct and indirect aggression. *Aggressive Behavior*, *18*, 117–127.

Boonekamp, J. J., Ros, A. H. F., & Verhulst, S. (2008). Immune activation suppresses plasma testosterone level: A meta-analysis. *Biology Letters*, *4*(6), 741–744.

Booth, A., & Dabbs J. M. Jr. (1993). Testosterone and men's marriages. *Social Forces*, *72*(2), 463–477.

Booth, A, Shelley, G., Mazur, A., Tharp, G., & Kittok, R. (1989). Testosterone, and winning and losing in human competition. *Hormones and Behavior*, *23*(4), 556–571.

Borg, K. E., Esbenshade, K. L., & Johnson, B. H. (1991). Cortisol, growth hormone, and testosterone concentrations during mating behavior in the bull and boar. *Journal of Animal Science*, *69*, 3230–3240.

Bouissou, M. F. (1990). Effects of estrogen treatment on dominance relationships in cows. *Hormones and Behavior*, *24*(3), 376–387.

Braunstein, G. D., Sundwall, D. A., Katz, M., Shifren, J. L., Buster, J. E., Simon, J. A., . . . Rodenberg, C. (2005). Safety and efficacy of a testosterone patch for the treatment of hypoactive sexual desire disorder in surgically menopausal women, *Archives of Internal Medicine*, *165*, 1582–1589.

Bribiescas, R. G., & Hill, K. R. (2010). Circadian variation in salivary testosterone across age classes in Ache Amerindian males of Paraguay. *American Journal of Human Biology*, *22*(2), 216–220.

Brodzinsky, D. M., Messa, S. B., & Tew, J. D. (1979). Sex differences in children's expression and control of fantasy and overt aggression. *Child Development*, *50*, 372–379.

Brooks-Gunn, J., & Warren, M. P. (1989). Biological and social contributions to negative affect in young adolescent girls. *Child Development*, *60*(1), 40–55.

Brown, L. L., Tomarken, A. J., Orth, D. N., Loosen, P. T., Kalin, N. H., & Davidson, R. J. (1996). Individual differences in repressive-defensiveness predict basal salivary cortisol levels. *Journal of Personality and Social Psychology*, *70*(2), 326–371.

Buck Louis, G. M., Gray, L. E., Marcus, M., Ojeda, S. R., Pescovitz, O. H., Witchel, S. F., . . . Euling, S. Y. (2008). Environmental factors and puberty timing: Expert panel research needs. *Pediatrics*, *121*(Suppl. 3), S192–S207.

Burger, H. G., Dudley, E. C., Robertson, D. M., & Dennerstein, L. (2002). Hormonal changes in the menopause transition. *Recent Progress in Hormone Research*, *57*, 257–275.

Burger, H. G., Hale, G. E., Dennerstein, L., & Robertson, D. M. (2008). Cycle and hormone changes during perimenopause: The key role of ovarian function. *Menopause*, *15*(4 Pt 1), 603–612.

Burger, H. G., Yamada, Y., Bangah, M. L., Mccloud, P. I., & Warne, G. L. (1991). Serum gonadotropin, sex steroid, and immunoreactive inhibin levels in the first two years of life. *Journal of Clinical Endocrinology and Metabolism*, *72*(3), 682–686.

Burnham, T. C., Chapman, J. F., Gray, P. B., McIntyre, M. H., Lipson, S. F., & Ellison, P. T. (2003). Men in committed, romantic relationships have lower testosterone. *Hormones and Behavior*, *44*(2), 119–122.

Buss, D. M. (1988). The evolution of human intrasexual competition: Tactics of mate attraction. *Journal of Personality and Social Psychology*, *54*(4), 616–628.

Buss, D. M. (1989). Sex differences in human mate preferences: Evolutionary hypotheses tested in 37 cultures. *Behavioral and Brain Sciences*, *12*, 1–49.

Buss, D. M., & Barnes, M. (1986). Preferences in human mate selection. *Journal of Personality and Social Psychology*, *50*(3), 559–570.

Buss, D. M., & Dedden, L. A. (1990). Derogation of competitors. *Journal of Social and Personal Relationships*, *7*, 395–422.

Caldwell Hooper, A. E., Gangestad, S. W., Thompson, M. E., & Bryan, A. D. (2011). Testosterone and romance: The association of testosterone with relationship commitment and satisfaction in heterosexual men and women. *American Journal of Human Biology*, *23*(4), 553–555.

Campbell, A. (2004). Female competition: Causes, constraints, content, and contexts. *Journal of Sex Research*, *41*(1), 16–26.

Cant, M. A., Johnstone, R. A., & Russell, A. F. (2009). Reproductive conflict and the evolution of menopause. In R. Hager & C. B. Jones (Eds.), *Reproductive skew in vertebrates: Proximate and ultimate causes* (pp. 24–50). Cambridge, UK: Cambridge University Press.

Carani, C., Bancroft, J., Del Rio, G., Granata, A. R. M., Facchinetti, F., & Marrama, P. (1990). The endocrine effects of visual erotic stimuli in normal men. *Psychoneuroendocrinology*, *15*(3), 207–216.

Carré, J. M., McCormick, C. M., & Hariri, A. R. (2011). The social neuroendocrinology of human aggression. *Psychoneuroendocrinology*, *36*(7), 935–944.

Cashdan, E. (1995). Hormones, sex and staus in women. *Hormones and Behaviour*, *29*, 354–366.

Cashdan, E. (2003). Hormones and competitive aggression in women. *Aggressive Behavior*, *29*(2), 107–115.

Chiazze, L. Jr, Brayer, F. T., Macisco, J. J., Parker, M. P., & Duffy, B. J. (1968). The length and variability of the human menstrual cycle. *Journal of the American Medical Association*, *203*(6), 377–380.

Clutton-Brock, T. H., Hodge, S. J., Spong, G., Russell, A. F., Jordan, N. R., Bennett, N. C., . . . Manser, M. B. (2006). Intrasexual competition and sexual selection in cooperative mammals. *Nature*, *444*(7122), 1065–1068.

Cobey, K. D., & Buunk, A. P. (2012). Conducting high-quality research on the psychological impact of oral contraceptive use. *Contraception*, *86*(4), 330–1.

Cobey, K. D., Buunk, A. P., Roberts, S. C., Klipping, C., Appels, N., Zimmerman, Y., . . . Pollet, T. V. (2012). Reported jealousy differs as a function of menstrual cycle stage and contraceptive pill use: A within-subjects investigation. *Evolution and Human Behavior*, *33*(4), 395–401.

Cobey, K. D., Klipping, C., & Buunk, A. P. (2013). Evolution and human behavior: Hormonal contraceptive use lowers female intrasexual competition in pair-bonded women. *Evolution and Human Behavior, 34*, 294–298.

Cobey, K. D., Pollet, T. V., Roberts, S. C., & Buunk, A. P. (2011). Hormonal birth control use and relationship jealousy: Evidence for estrogen dosage effects. *Personality and Individual Differences, 50*(2), 315–317.

Coenen, C. M. H., Thomas, C. M. G., Borm, G. F., Hollanders, J. M. G., & Rolland, R. (1996). Changes in androgens during treatment with four low-dose contraceptives. *Contraception, 53*, 171–176.

Cristol, D. A., & Johnsen, T. S. (1994). Spring arrival, aggression and testosterone in female red-winged blackbirds (Agelaius phoeniceus). *The Auk, 111*(1), 210–214.

Cui, J., Shen, Y., & Li, R. (2013). Estrogen synthesis and signaling pathways during aging: From periphery to brain. *Trends in Molecular Medicine, 19*(3), 197–209.

Dabbs, J. M. (1990). Salivary testosterone measurements: Reliability across hours, days, and weeks. *Physiology & Behavior, 48*(1), 83–86.

Dabbs, J. M., & Hargrove, M. F. (1997). Age, testosterone, and behavior among female prison inmates. *Psychosomatic Medicine, 59*(5), 477–480.

Dabbs, J. M., Hopper, C. H., & Jurkovic, G. J. (1990). Testosterone and personality among college students and military veterans. *Personality and Individual Differences, 11*(12), 1263–1269.

Dabbs, J. M., Jurkovic, G. J., & Frady, R. L. (1991). Salivary testosterone and cortisol among late adolescent male offenders. *Journal of Abnormal Child Psychology, 19*, 469–478.

Darwin, C. (1871). *The descent of man, and selection in relation to sex* (1st ed.). London: John Murray.

Davis, E. S., & Marler, C. A. (2003). The progesterone challenge: Steroid hormone changes following a simulated territorial intrusion in female Peromyscus californicus. *Hormones and Behavior, 44*(3), 185–198.

Davis, S. R., Davison, S. L., Donath, S., & Bell, R. J. (2005). Circulating androgen levels and self-reported sexual function in women. *Journal of the American Medical Association, 294*(1), 91–96.

Deaner, R. O., Khera, A. V., & Platt, M. L. (2005). Monkeys pay per view: Adaptive valuation of social images by rhesus macaques. *Current Biology, 15*(6), 543–548.

Dennerstein, L., Alexander, J. L., & Kotz, K. (2003). The menopause and sexual functioning: A review of the population-based studies. *Annual Review of Sex Research, 14*(1), 64–82.

Dennerstein, L., Lehert, P., Burger, H. G., & Dudley, E. (1999). Mood and the menopausal transition. *Journal of Nervous & Mental Disease, 187*(11), 685–691.

Dennerstein, L., Randolph, J., Taffe, J., Dudley, E., & Burger, H. (2002). Hormones, mood, sexuality, and the menopausal transition. *Fertility and Sterility, 77*(4), S42–S48.

De Ridder, E., Pinxten, R., & Eens, M. (2000). Experimental evidence of a testosterone-induced shift from paternal to mating behaviour in a facultatively polygynous songbird. *Behavioral Ecology and Sociobiology, 49*(1), 24–30.

Dloniak, S. M., French, J. A., & Holekamp, K. E. (2005). Rank-related maternal effects of androgens on behaviour in wild spotted hyenas. *Nature, 440*, 1190–1193.

Dougherty, D. M., Bjork, J. M., Moeller, F. G., & Swann, A.C. (1997). The influence of menstrual-cycle phase on the relationship between testosterone and aggression. *Physiology & Behavior, 62*(2), 431–435.

Dratva, J., Gómez Real, F., Schindler, C., Ackermann-Liebrich, U., Gerbase, M. W., Probst-Hensch, N. M., ... Zemp, E. (2009). Is age at menopause increasing across Europe? Results on age at menopause and determinants from two population-based studies. *Menopause, 16*(2), 385–394.

Dunson, D. B., Colombo, B., & Baird, D. D. (2002). Changes with age in the level and duration of fertility in the menstrual cycle. *Human Reproduction, 17*(5), 1399–1403.

Durante, K. M., Griskevicius, V., Hill, S. E., Perilloux, C., & Li, N. P. (2011). Ovulation, female competition, and product choice: Hormonal influences on consumer behavior. *Journal of Consumer Research, 37*(6), 921–934.

Durante, K. M., Li, N. P., & Haselton, M. G. (2008). Changes in women's choice of dress across the ovulatory cycle: Naturalistic and laboratory task-based evidence. *Personality & Social Psychology Bulletin, 34*(11), 1451–1460.

Edwards, D. A. (1970). Post-neonatal androgenization and adult aggressive behavior in female mice. *Physiology & Behavior, 5*, 465–467.

Edwards, D. A., Wetzel, K., & Wyner, D. R. (2006). Intercollegiate soccer: Saliva cortisol and testosterone are elevated during competition, and testosterone is related to status and social connectedness with team mates. *Physiology & Behavior, 87*(1), 135–143.

Eens, M., & Pinxten, R. (2000). Sex-role reversal in vertebrates: Behavioural and endocrinological accounts. *Behavioural Processes, 51*(1–3), 135–147.

Eichling, P. S., & Sahni, J. (2005). Menopause related sleep disorders. *Journal of Clinical Sleep Medicine, 1*(3), 291–300.

Ellis, D. P. (1972). Menstruation and aggressive behavior in a correctional center for women. *Journal of Criminal Law and Criminology, 62*(3), 288–395.

Ellison, P. T., Bribiescas, R. G., Bentley, G. R., Campbell, B. C., Lipson, S. F., Panter-Brick, C., & Hill, K. (2002). Population variation in age-related decline in male salivary testosterone. *Human Reproduction, 17*(12), 3251–3253.

Emery Thompson, M., Jones, J. H., Pusey, A. E., Brewer-Marsden, S., Goodall, J., Marsden, D., ... Wrangham, R. W. (2007). Aging and fertility patterns in wild chimpanzees provide insights into the evolution of menopause. *Current Biology, 17*(24), 2150–2156.

Erpino, M. J., & Chappelle, T. C. (1971). Interactions between androgens and progesterone in mediation of aggression in the mouse. *Hormones and Behavior, 2*(3), 265–272.

Finkelstein, J. W., Susman, E. J., Chinchilli, V. M., Kunselman, S. J., D'Arcangelo, M. R., Schwab, J., ... Kulin, H. E. (1997). Estrogen or testosterone increases self-reported aggressive behaviors in hypogonadal adolescents. *Journal of Clinical Endocrinology & Metabolism, 82*(8), 2433–2438.

Fisher, M., & Cox, A. (2009). The influence of female attractiveness on competitor derogation. *Journal of Evolutionary Psychology, 7*(2), 141–155.

Fisher, M. L. (2004). Female intrasexual competition decreases female facial attractiveness. *Proceedings of the Royal Society B, 271*(Suppl.), S283–S285.

Fivizzani, A. J., & Oring, W. (1986). Plasma steroid hormones in relation reversal in the spotted sandpiper, *Actitis macularia*. *Biology of Reproduction,* (35), 1195–1201.

Fleming, A. S., Ruble, D., Krieger, H., & Wong, P. Y. (1997). Hormonal and experiential correlates of maternal responsiveness during pregnancy and the puerperium in human mothers. *Hormones and Behavior, 31*(2), 145–158.

Folstad, I., & Karter, A. J. (1992). Parasites, bright males, and the immunocompetence handicap. *The American Naturalist, 139*(3), 603–622.

Foote, A. D. (2008). Mortality rate acceleration and post-reproductive lifespan in matrilineal whale species. *Biology Letters, 4*(2), 189–191.

Forbes, E. E., & Dahl, R. E. (2010). Pubertal development and behavior: Hormonal activation of social and motivational tendencies. *Brain and Cognition, 72*(1), 66–72.

Forest, G. (1989). Physiological changes in circulating androgens. *Pediatric Adolescent Endocrinology, 19*, 104–129.

Forest, M. G., Sizonenko, P. C., & Cathard, A. M. (1974). Hypophyso-gonadal function in humans during the first year of life. *Journal of Clinical Investigation, 53*(7), 819–828.

Fraile, I. G., McEwen, B. S., & Pfaff, D. W. (1987). Progesterone inhibition of aggressive behaviors in hamsters. *Physiology & Behavior, 39*(2), 225–229.

Fraile, I. G., McEwen, B. S., & Pfaff, D. W. (1988). Comparative effects of progesterone and alphaxalone on aggressive, reproductive and locomotor behaviors. *Pharmacology, Biochemistry, and Behavior, 30*(3), 729–735.

Frye, C. A. (2006). An overview of oral contraceptives: Mechanism of action and clinical use. *Neurology, 66*, S29–S36.

Fujita, K. (1987). Species recognition by five macaque monkeys. *Primates, 28*(3), 353–366.

Fujita, K., & Matsuzawa, T. (1986). A new procedure to study the perceptual world of animals with sensory reinforcement: Recognition of humans by a chimpanzee. *Primates, 27*(3), 283–291.

Gandara, B. K., Leresche, L., & Mancl, L. (2007). Patterns of salivary estradiol and progesterone across the menstrual cycle. *Annals of the New York Academy of Sciences, 1098*, 446–450.

Geary, David C., DeSoto, M. C., Hoard, M. K., Sheldon, M. S., & Cooper, M. L. (2001). Estrogens and relationship jealousy. *Human Nature, 12*(4), 299–320.

Gilbert, S. F. (2000). *Developmental biology*. Sunderland, MA: Sinauer.

Goodwin, M. H. (1980). He-said-she-said: Formal cultural procedures for the construction of a gossip dispute activity. *American Ethnologist, 7*(4), 647–695.

Goymann, W., Moore, I. T., Scheuerlein, A., Hirschenhauser, K., Grafen, A., & Wingfield, J. C. (2004). Testosterone in tropical birds: Effects of environmental and social factors. *The American Naturalist, 164*(3), 327–334.

Grammer, K., Renninger, L., & Fischer, B. (2004). Disco clothing, female sexual motivation, and relationship status: Is she dressed to impress? *Journal of Sex Research, 41*(1), 66–74.

Gray, P. B., Chapman, J. F., Burnham, T. C., McIntyre, M. H., Lipson, S. F., & Ellison, P. T. (2004). Human male pair bonding and testosterone. *Human Nature, 15*(2), 119–131.

Gray, P. B., Ellison, P. T., & Campbell, B. C. (2007). Testosterone and marriage among Ariaal men of northern Kenya. *Current Anthropology, 48*(5), 750–755.

Gray, P. B., Kahlenberg, S. M., Barrett, E. S., Lipson, S. F., & Ellison, P. T. (2002). Marriage and fatherhood are associated with lower testosterone in males. *Evolution and Human Behavior, 23*(3), 193–201.

Hahn, A. C. (2013). Variations in motivation across the menstrual cycle. In A. C. Hahn, *Factors influencing the motivational salience of faces* (pp. 135–151). St. Andrews: University of St. Andrews.

Hall, J. E. (2010). The female reproductive system: Infertility and contraception. In J. L. Jameson (Ed.), *Harrison's endocrinology* (2nd ed., pp. 186–200). Chicago: McGraw-Hill Medical.

Haller, J., Halász, J., Mikics, E., & Kruk, M. R. (2004). Chronic glucocorticoid deficiency-induced abnormal aggression, autonomic hypoarousal, and social deficit in rats. *Journal of Neuroendocrinology, 16*(6), 550–557.

Harris, J. A., Rushton, J. P., Hampson, E., & Jackson, D. N. (1996). Salivary testosterone and self-report aggressive and pro-social personality characteristics in men and women. *Aggressive Behavior, 22*(5), 321–331.

Haselton, M. G., Mortezaie, M., Pillsworth, E. G., Bleske-Rechek, A., & Frederick, D. A. (2007). Ovulatory shifts in human female ornamentation: Near ovulation, women dress to impress. *Hormones and Behavior, 51*(1), 40–45.

Havlíček, J., Cobey, K. D., Barrett, L., Klapilová, K., & Craig Roberts, S. (2015). The spandrels of Santa Barbara? A new perspective on the peri-ovulation paradigm. *Behavioral Ecology 26*(5), 1249–1260. doi: https://doi.org/10.1093/beheco/arv064

Hawkes, K., O'Connell, J. F., Jones, N. G. B., Alvarez, H., & Charnov, E. L. (1998). Grandmothering, menopause, and the evolution of human. *Proceedings of the National Academy of Sciences, 95*, 1336–1339.

Hess, N. H., & Hagen, E. H. (2006). Sex differences in indirect aggression. *Evolution and Human Behavior, 27*(3), 231–245.

Hohmann, G., & Fruth, B. (2003). Intra- and inter-sexual aggression by bonobos in the context of mating. *Behaviour, 140*(11), 1389–1413.

Hurly, A. T., & Robertson, R. J. (1984). Aggressive and territorial behaviour in female red-winged blackbirds. *Canadian Journal of Zoology, 62*(2), 148–153.

Inoff-Germain, G., Arnold, G. S., Nottelmann, E. D., Susman, E. J., Cutler, G. B., Jr & Chrousos, G. P. (1988). Relations between hormone levels and observational measures of aggressive behavior of young adolescents in family interactions. *Developmental Psychology, 24*, 129–139.

Jabbour, H. N., Kelly, R. W., Fraser, H. M., & Critchley, H. O. D. (2006). Endocrine regulation of menstruation. *Endocrine Reviews, 27*(1), 17–46.

Jasieńska, G., Lipson, S. F., Ellison, P. T., Thune, I., & Ziomkiewicz, A. (2006). Symmetrical women have higher potential fertility. *Evolution and Human Behavior, 27*(5), 390–400.

Jasieńska, G., Ziomkiewicz, A., Ellison, P. T., Lipson, S. F., & Thune, I. (2004). Large breasts and narrow waists indicate high reproductive potential in women. *Proceedings of the Royal Society B, 271*(1545), 1213–1217.

Johnstone, R. A., & Cant, M. A. (2010). The evolution of menopause in cetaceans and humans: The role of demography. *Proceedings of the Royal Society B, 277*(1701), 3765–3771.

Jones, B. C., Perrett, D. I., Little, A. C., Boothroyd, L., Cornwell, R. E., Feinberg, D. R., ... Moore, F. R. (2005). Menstrual cycle, pregnancy and oral contraceptive use alter attraction to apparent health in faces. *Proceedings of the Royal Society B, 272*(1561), 347–354.

Jones, B. C., Vukovic, J., Little, A. C., Roberts, S. C., & Debruine, L. M. (2011). Circum-menopausal changes in women's preferences for sexually dimorphic shape cues in peer-aged faces. *Biological Psychology, 87*(3), 453–455.

Kapusta, J. (1998). Gonadal hormones and intrasexual aggressive behavior in female bank voles (*Clethrionomys glareolus*). *Aggressive Behavior, 24*(1), 63–70.

Kasuya, T., & Marsh, H. (1984). Life history and reproductive biology of the short-finned pilot whale, *Globicephala macrorhynchus*, off the Pacific Coast of Japan. *Reports of the International Whaling Commission, 6,* 259–310.

Kivlighan, K. T., Granger, D. A., & Booth, A. (2005). Gender differences in testosterone and cortisol response to competition. *Psychoneuroendocrinology, 30*(1), 58–71.

Klein, S. L. (2000). The effects of hormones on sex differences in infection: From genes to behavior. *Neuroscience and Biobehavioral Reviews, 24*(6), 627–638.

Klinesmith, J., Kasser, T., & McAndrew, F. T. (2006). Guns, testosterone, and aggression: An experimental test of a mediational hypothesis. *Psychological Science, 17*(7), 568–571.

Lacreuse, A., & Herndon, J. G. (2003). Estradiol selectively affects processing of conspecifics' faces in female rhesus monkeys. *Psychoneuroendocrinology, 28*(7), 885–905.

Lacreuse, A., Martin-Malivel, J., Lange, H. S., & Herndon, J. G. (2007). Effects of the menstrual cycle on looking preferences for faces in female rhesus monkeys. *Animal Cognition, 10*(2), 105–115.

Lagerspetz, K. M. J., Björkqvist, K., & Peltonen, T. (1988). Is indirect aggression typical of females? Gender differences in aggressiveness in 11- to 12-year-old children, *Aggressive Behavior, 14,* 403–414.

Langmore, N. E., Cockrem, J. F., & Candy, E. J. (2002). Competition for male reproductive investment elevates testosterone levels in female dunnocks, *Prunella modularis. Proceedings of the Royal Society B, 269*(1508), 2473–2478.

Lever, J. (1976). Sex differences in the games children play. *Social Problems, 23*(4), 478–487.

Liening, S. H., Stanton, S. J., Saini, E. K., & Schultheiss, O. C. (2010). Salivary testosterone, cortisol, and progesterone: Two-week stability, interhormone correlations, and effects of time of day, menstrual cycle, and oral contraceptive use on steroid hormone levels. *Physiology & Behavior, 99*(1), 8–16.

Lipson, S. F., & Ellison, P. T. (1993). Comparison of salivary steroid profiles in naturally occurring conception and non-conception cycles. *Human Reproduction, 11*(10), 2090–2096.

Little, A. C., Saxton, T. K., Roberts, S. C., Jones, B. C., DeBruine, L. M., Vukovic, J., ... Chenore, T. (2010). Women's preferences for masculinity in male faces are highest during reproductive age range and lower around puberty and post-menopause. *Psychoneuroendocrinology, 35*(6), 912–920.

López, H. H., Hay, A. C., & Conklin, P. H. (2009). Attractive men induce testosterone and cortisol release in women. *Hormones and Behavior, 56*(1), 84–92.

Lormée, H., Jouventin, P., Lacroix, A., Lallemand, J., & Chastel, O. (2000). Reproductive endocrinology of tropical seabirds: Sex-specific patterns in LH, steroids, and prolactin secretion in relation to parental care. *General and Comparative Endocrinology, 117*(3), 413–426.

Lu, Y., Bentley, G. R., Gann, P. H., Hodges, K. R., & Chatterton, R. T. (1999). Salivary estradiol and progesterone levels in conception and nonconception cycles in women: Evaluation of a new assay for salivary estradiol. *Fertility and Sterility, 71*(5), 863–868.

Lynn, S. E., Hayward, L. S., Benowitz-Fredericks, Z. M., & Wingfield, J. C. (2002). Behavioural insensitivity to supplementary testosterone during the parental phase in the chestnut-collared longspur, Calcarius ornatus. *Animal Behaviour, 63*(4), 795–803.

Lynn, S. E., Walker, B. G., & Wingfield, J. C. (2005). A phylogenetically controlled test of hypotheses for behavioral insensitivity to testosterone in birds. *Hormones and Behavior, 47*(2), 170–177.

Mallow, G. K. (1981). The relationship between aggressive behavior and menstrual cycle stage in female rhesus monkeys (Macaca mulatta). *Hormones and Behavior, 15*(3), 259–269.

Manning, C., Gengo, F., & Joe, S. (1995). Pergamon possible acceleration of age effects on cognition. *Journal of Psychiatric Research, 29*(3), 153–163.

Marsh, H., & Kasuya, T. (1984). Changes in the ovaries of the short-finned pilot whale, *Globicephalu macrorhynchus*, with age and reproductive activity. *Report of the International Whaling Commission, 6,* 311–355.

Mayer, A.D., Monroy, M. A., & Rosenblatt, J. S. (1990). Prolonged estrogen-progesterone treatment of nonpregnant ovariectomized rats: Factors stimulating home-cage and maternal aggression and short-latency maternal behavior. *Hormones and Behavior, 24*(3), 342–364.

Mazur, A., Booth, A. J., & Dabbs, J. M. (1992). Testosterone and chess competition. *Social Psychology Quarterly, 55*(1), 70–77.

Mazur, A., & Michalek, J. (1998). Marriage, divorce, and male testosterone. *Social Forces, 77*(1), 315–330. doi: 10.1093/sf/77.1.315

Mazur, A., Susman, E. J., & Edelbrock, S. (1997). Sex difference in testosterone response to a video game contest. *Evolution and Human Behavior, 18*(5), 317–326.

McAuliffe, K., & Whitehead, H. (2005). Eusociality, menopause and information in matrilineal whales. *Trends in Ecology & Evolution, 20*(12), 650.

McNelis, N. L., & Boatright-Horowitz, S. L. (1998). Social monitoring in a primate group: The relationship between visual attention and hierarchical ranks. *Animal Cognition, 1,* 65–69.

Mehta, P. H., & Josephs, R. A. (2010). Testosterone and cortisol jointly regulate dominance: Evidence for a dual-hormone hypothesis. *Hormones and Behavior, 58*(5), 898–906.

Meisel, R. L., & Sterner, M. R. (1990). Progesterone inhibition of sexual behavior is accompanied by an activation of aggression in female Syrian hamsters. *Physiology & Behavior, 47*(3), 415–417.

Mendelsohn, M. E., & Karas, R. H. (1999). The protective effects of estrogen on the cardiovascular system. *Mechanisms of Disease, 340*(23), 1801–1811.

Meyer, P. M., Powell, L. H., Wilson, R. S., Everson-Rose, S. A., Kravitz, H. M., Luborsky, J. L., ... Evans, D. A. (2003). A population-based longitudinal study of cognitive functioning in the menopausal transition. *Neurology, 61*(6), 801–806.

Michael, R. P., & Zumpe, D. (1970). Aggression and gonadal hormones in captive Rhesus monkeys (*Macaca mulatta*). *Animal Behaviour, 18*(1), 1–10.

Moore, M. C. (1986). Elevated testosterone levels during nonbreeding-season territoriality in a fall-breeding lizard, *Sceloporus jarrovi. Journal of Comparative Physiology A, 158*(2), 159–163.

Mosher, W. D., & Jones, J. (2010). Use of contraception in the United States: 1982–2008: Data from the National Survey of Family Growth. *Vital and Health Statistics, Series 23*, 1–44.

Muehlenbein, M. P., & Bribiescas, R. G. (2005). Testosterone-mediated immune functions and male life histories. *American Journal of Human Biology, 17*(5), 527–558.

Muehlenbein, M. P., & Watts, D. P. (2010). The costs of dominance: Testosterone, cortisol and intestinal parasites in wild male chimpanzees. *BioPsychoSocial Medicine, 4*(1), 21.

Nappi, R. E., & Lachowsky, M. (2009). Menopause and sexuality: Prevalence of symptoms and impact on quality of life. *Maturitas, 63*(2), 138–141.

Niemeyer, C. L., & Anderson, J. R. (1983). Primate harassment of matings. *Ethology and Sociobiology, 4*(4), 205–220.

Nishida, T., Corp, N., Hamai, M., Hasegawa, T., Hiraiwa-Hasegawa, M., Hosaka, K., ... Zamma, K. (2003). Demography, female life history, and reproductive profiles among the chimpanzees of Mahale. *American Journal of Primatology, 59*(3), 99–121.

O'Connell, J. F., Hawkes, K., & Jones, N. G. B. (1999). Grandmothering and the evolution of *Homo erectus. Journal of Human Evolution, 36*, 461–485.

Oliveira, T., Gouveia, M. J., & Oliveira, R. F. (2009). Testosterone responsiveness to winning and losing experiences in female soccer players. *Psychoneuroendocrinology, 34*(7), 1056–1064.

Ostrov, J. M., & Keating, C. F. (2004). Gender differences in preschool aggression during free play and structured interactions: An observational study. *Social Development, 13*(2), 255–277.

Paikoff, R. L., Brooks-Funn, J., & Warren, M. P. (1991). Effects of girls' hormonal status on depressive and aggressive symptoms over the course of one year. *Journal of Youth and Adolescence, 20*(2), 191–215.

Pajer, K., Tabbah, R., Gardner, W., Rubin, R. T., Czambel, R. K., & Wang, Y. (2006). Adrenal androgen and gonadal hormone levels in adolescent girls with conduct disorder. *Psychoneuroendocrinology, 31*(10), 1245–1256.

Pearlman, W. H., Crepy, O., & Murphy, M. (1967). Testosterone-binding levels in the serum of women during the normal menstrual cycle, pregnancy, and the post-partum period. *Journal of Clinical Endocrinology and Metabolism, 27*, 1012–1018.

Pearlstein, T., Rosen, K., & Stone, A. B. (1997). Mood disorders and menopause. *Endocrinology and Metabolism Clinics of North America, 26*(2), 279–294.

Pepler, D. J., & Craig, W. M. (1995). A peek behind the fence: Naturalistic observations of aggressive children with remote audiovisual recording. *Developmental Psychology, 31*, 548–553.

Persky, H., Smith, K. D., & Basu, G. K. (1971). Relation of psychologic measures of aggression and hostility to testosterone production in man. *Psychosomatic Medicine, 33*(3), 265–277.

Pinna, G., Costa, E., & Guidotti, A. (2005). Changes in brain testosterone and allopregnanolone biosynthesis elicit aggressive behavior. *Proceedings of the National Academy of Sciences of the United States of America, 102*(6), 2135–2140.

Pollet, T. V., Cobey, K. D., & van der Meij, L. (2013). Testosterone levels are negatively associated with childlessness in males, but positively related to offspring count in fathers. *PLoS One, 8*(4), e60018.

Pollet, T. V., van der Meij, L., Cobey, K. D., & Buunk, A. P. (2011). Testosterone levels and their associations with lifetime number of opposite sex partners and remarriage in a large sample of American elderly men and women. *Hormones and Behavior, 60*(1), 72–77.

Popma, A., Vermeiren, R., Geluk, C. A.M. L., Rinne, T., van den Brink, W., Knol, D. L., ... Doreleijers, T. A. H. (2007). Cortisol moderates the relationship between testosterone and aggression in delinquent male adolescents. *Biological Psychiatry, 61*(3), 405–411.

Pusey, A. (1997). The influence of dominance rank on the reproductive success of female chimpanzees. *Science, 277*(5327), 828–831.

Ramirez, S. M., Bardi, M., French, J. A., & Brent, L. (2004). Hormonal correlates of changes in interest in unrelated infants across the peripartum period in female baboons (*Papio hamadryas anubis sp.*). *Hormones and Behavior, 46*(5), 520–528.

Roberts, M. L., Buchanan, K. L., & Evans, M. R. (2004). Testing the immunocompetence handicap hypothesis: A review of the evidence. *Animal Behaviour, 68*(2), 227–239.

Roberts, S. C., Gosling, L. M., Carter, V., & Petrie, M. (2008). MHC-correlated odour preferences in humans and the use of oral contraceptives. *Proceedings of the Royal Society B, 275*(1652), 2715–2722.

Roney, J. R., Lukaszewski, A. W., & Simmons, Z. L. (2007). Rapid endocrine responses of young men to social interactions with young women. *Hormones and Behavior, 52*(3), 326–333.

Sakaguchi, K., Oki, M., Honma, S., & Hasegawa, T. (2006). Influence of relationship status and personality traits on salivary testosterone among Japanese men. *Personality and Individual Differences, 41*(6), 1077–1087.

Sánchez-Martín, J. R., Fano, E., Ahedo, L., Cardas, J., Brain, P. F., & Azpíroz, A. (2000). Relating testosterone levels and free play social behavior in male and female preschool children. *Psychoneuroendocrinology, 25*(8), 773–783.

Sapolsky, R. M. (1985). Stress-induced suppression of testicular function in the wild baboon: Role of glucocorticoids. *Endocrinology, 116*, 2273–2278.

Schmidt, H., & Schwarz, H. P. (2000). Serum concentrations of LH and FSH in the healthy newborn. *European Journal of Endocrinology, 143*(2), 213–215.

Schultheiss, O. C., Dargel, A., & Rohde, W. (2003). Implicit motives and gonadal steroid hormones: Effects of menstrual cycle phase, oral contraceptive use, and relationship status. *Hormones and Behavior, 43*(2), 293–301.

Schutter, D. J. L. G., & van Honk, J. (2004). Decoupling of midfrontal delta-beta oscillations after testosterone administration. *International Journal of Psychophysiology, 53*(1), 71–73.

Schwabl, H. (1992). Winter and breeding territorial behaviour and levels of reproductive hormones of migratory European Robins. *Ornis Scandinavica, 23*(3), 271–276.

Sherman, B. M., & Korenman, S. G. (1975). Hormonal characteristics of the human menstrual cycle throughout reproductive life. *Journal of Clinical Investigation, 55*, 699–706.

Sherwin, B. B. (1997). Estrogen effects on cognition in menopausal women. *Neurology, 48*, S21–S26.

Sisk, C., Lonstein, J. S., & Gore, A. C. (2013). Critical periods during development: Hormonal influences on neurobehavioral transitions across the lifespan. In D. W. Pfaff (Ed.), *Neuroscience in the 21st century* (pp. 1715–1752). New York: Springer.

Sisk, C. L., & Zehr, J. L. (2005). Pubertal hormones organize the adolescent brain and behavior. *Frontiers in Neuroendocrinology*, *26*(3–4), 163–174.

Stanton, S. J., & Schultheiss, O. C. (2007). Basal and dynamic relationships between implicit power motivation and estradiol in women. *Hormones and Behavior*, *52*(5), 571–580. doi: 10.1016/j.yhbeh.2007.07.002

Stearns, S. C. (1989). Trade-offs in life-history evolution. *Functional Ethology*, *3*(3), 259–268.

Stearns, S. C. (1992). *The evolution of life histories*. Oxford: Oxford University Press.

Stockley, P., & Bro-Jørgensen, J. (2011). Female competition and its evolutionary consequences in mammals. *Biological Reviews of the Cambridge Philosophical Society*, *86*(2), 341–366.

Stoehr, A. M., & Hill, G. E. (2000). Testosterone and the allocation of reproductive effort in male house finches (*Carpodacus mexicanus*). *Behavioral Ecology and Sociobiology*, *48*(5), 407–411.

Suay, F., Salvador, A, González-Bono, E., Sanchís, C., Martínez, M., Martínez-Sanchis, S., . . . Montoro, J. B. (1999). Effects of competition and its outcome on serum testosterone, cortisol and prolactin. *Psychoneuroendocrinology*, *24*(5), 551–66.

Susman, E., Inoff-Germain, G., Nottelmann, E., Loriaux, D., Cutler, G. J., & Chruso, G. (1987). Hormones, emotional dispositions, and aggressive attributes in young adolescents. *Child Development*, *58*, 1114–1134.

Svare, B., & Gandelman, R. (1975). Postpartum aggression in mice: Inhibitory effect of estrogen. *Physiology & Behavior*, *14*(1), 31–35.

Swain, J. E., Lorberbaum, J. P., Kose, S., & Strathearn, L. (2007). Brain basis of early parent–infant interactions: Psychology, physiology, and in vivo functional neuroimaging studies. *Journal of Child Psychology and Psychiatry and Allied Disciplines*, *48*(3–4), 262–287.

Swartz, K. B., & Rosenblum, L. A. (1980). Operant responding by bonnet macaques for color videotape recordings of social stimuli. *Animal Learning and Behavior*, *8*(2), 311–321. doi: 10.3758/BF03199611

Takahashi, L. K. (1990). Hormonal regulation of sociosexual behavior in female mammals. *Neuroscience and Biobehavioral Reviews*, *14*(4), 403–413.

Tamada, H., & Ichikawa, S. (1980). The effect of estrogen on fetal survival in ovariectomized rats. *Endocrinology Japan*, *27*(2), 163–167.

Trainor, B. C., Kyomen, H. H., & Marler, C. A. (2006). Estrogenic encounters: How interactions between aromatase and the environment modulate aggression. *Frontiers in Neuroendocrinology*, *27*(2), 170–179.

Trivers, R. (1972). Parental investment and sexual selection. In B. Campbell (Ed.), *Sexual selection and the descent of man, 1871–1971* (pp. 136–179). Chicago: Aldine.

Tuiten, A., Van Honk, J., Koppeschaar, H., Bernaards, C., Thijssen, J., & Verbaten, R. (2000). Time course of effects of testosterone administration on sexual arousal in women. *Archives of General Psychiatry*, *57*(2), 149–153.

Turner, R. T., Riggs, B. L., & Spelsberg, T. C. (1994). Skeletal effects of estrogen. *Endocrine Reviews*, *15*(3), 275–300.

Uckert, S., Fuhlenriede, M. H., Becker, A. J., Stief, C. G., Scheller, F., Knapp, W. H., & Jonas, U. (2003). Is there an inhibitory role of cortisol in the mechanism of male sexual arousal and penile erection? *Urology Research*, *31*(6), 402–406.

United Nations. (2012). *World Contraceptive Use 2012* (No. POP/DB/CP/Rev2012). New York: Author.

Van Anders, S. M., & Goldey, K. L. (2010). Testosterone and partnering are linked via relationship status for women and "relationship orientation" for men. *Hormones and Behavior*, *58*(5), 820–826.

Van Anders, S. M., Hamilton, L. D., Schmidt, N., & Watson, N. V. (2007). Associations between testosterone secretion and sexual activity in women. *Hormones and Behavior*, *51*(4), 477–482.

Van Anders, S. M., Hamilton, L. D., & Watson, N. V. (2007). Multiple partners are associated with higher testosterone in North American men and women. *Hormones and Behavior*, *51*(3), 454–459.

Van Anders, S. M., & Watson, N. V. (2007). Testosterone levels in women and men who are single, in long-distance relationships, or same-city relationships. *Hormones and Behavior*, *51*(2), 286–291.

Van de Poll, N. E., van Zanten, S., & de Jonge, F. H. (1986). Effects of testosterone, estrogen, and dihydrotestosterone upon aggressive and sexual behavior of female rats. *Hormones and Behavior*, *20*(4), 418–431.

Van der Meij, L., Buunk, A. P., & Salvador, A. (2010). Contact with attractive women affects the release of cortisol in men. *Hormones and Behavior*, *58*(3), 501–505.

Van Goozen, S., Cohen-Kettenis, P. T., Gooren, L. J. G., Frijda, N., & van de Poll, N. (1995). Gender differences in behaviour: Activating effects of cross-sex hormones. *Psychoneuroendocrinology*, *20*(4), 343–363.

Van Goozen, S., Frijda, N., & van de Poll, N. (1994). Anger and aggression in women: Influence of sports choice and testosterone administration. *Aggressive Behavior*, *20*(3), 213–222.

Vermeersch, H., T'Sjoen, G., Kaufman, J.-M., & Vincke, J. (2008). Estradiol, testosterone, differential association and aggressive and non-aggressive risk-taking in adolescent girls. *Psychoneuroendocrinology*, *33*(7), 897–908.

Vukovic, J., Jones, B. C., DeBruine, L. M., Little, A. C., Feinberg, D. R., & Welling, L. L. M. (2009). Circum-menopausal effects on women's judgements of facial attractiveness. *Biology Letters*, *5*(1), 62–4.

Walker, B. Y. M. L., Wilson, M. E., Gordon, T. P., & Regional, Y. (1983). Female rhesus monkey aggression during the menstrual cycle. *Animal Behavior*, *31*, 1047–1054.

Ward, E. J., Parsons, K., Holmes, E. E., Balcomb, K. C., & Ford, J. K. (2009). The role of menopause and reproductive senescence in a long-lived social mammal. *Frontiers in Zoology*, *6*, 4.

Wasser, S. K., & Starling, A. K. (1988). Proximate and ultimate causes of reproductive suppression among female yellow baboons at Mikumi National Park, Tanzania. *American Journal of Primatology*, *16*, 97–121.

Welling, L. L. M., Jones, B. C., DeBruine, L. M., Conway, C. A., Law Smith, M. J., Little, A. C., . . . Al-Dujaili, E. A. S. (2007). Raised salivary testosterone in women is associated with increased attraction to masculine faces. *Hormones and Behavior*, *52*(2), 156–161.

Welling, L. L. M., Puts, D. A., Roberts, S. C., Little, A. C., & Burriss, R. P. (2012). Hormonal contraceptive use and mate retention behavior in women and their male partners. *Hormones and Behavior*, *61*(1), 114–120.

Wingfield, J. C., Hegner, R. E., Dufty, A. M. Jr., & Ball, G. F. (1990). The "challenge hypothesis": Theoretical implications for patterns of testosterone secretion, mating systems, and breeding strategies. *American Naturalist, 136,* 829–846.

Winter, J. S., & Faiman, C. (1972). Serum gonadotropin in concentrations in agonadal children and adults. *Journal of Clinical Endocrinology & Metabolism, 35*(4), 561–564.

Wong, Y. F., Mao, K., Panesar, N. S., Loong, E. P. L., Chang, A. M. Z., & Mi, Z. J. (1990). Salivary estradiol and progesterone during the normal ovulatory menstrual cycle in Chinese women. *European Journal of Obstetrics & Gynecology and Reproductive Biology, 34*(1–2), 129–135.

Woodley, S., & Moore, M. (1999). Female territorial aggression and steroid hormones in mountain spiny lizards. *Animal Behaviour, 57*(5), 1083–1089.

Work, M. S., & Rogers, H. (1972). Effect of estrogen level on food-seeking among male rats. *Journal of Comparative and Physiological Psychology, 79*(3), 414–418.

Young, T., Finn, L., Austin, D., & Peterson, A. (2003). Menopausal status and sleep-disordered breathing in the Wisconsin Sleep Cohort Study. *American Journal of Respiratory and Critical Care Medicine, 167*(9), 1181–1185.

Zimmerman, Y., Wouters, W., & Coelingh Bennink, H. J. T. (2013). The bioequivalence of the contraceptive steroids ethinylestradiol and drospirenone is not affected by co-administration of dehydroepiandrosterone. *European Journal of Contraception & Reproductive Health Care, 18*(3), 206–214.

The Effect of Fertility on Women's Intrasexual Competition

Lambrianos Nikiforidis, Ashley Rae Arsena, *and* Kristina M. Durante

Abstract

This chapter examines how the ovulatory cycle affects the tactics women use to compete with one another. As fertility increases near ovulation, women's mating psychology changes, with implications for intersexual courtship (i.e., attracting opposite-sex mates) and intrasexual competition (i.e., outshining same-sex rivals) which is the primary focus of this chapter. The ovulatory competition hypothesis refers to the effect of fertility on women's competition, manifested mainly in the domains of physical attractiveness and relative status. Previous research shows that women's tendency to enhance their appearance near ovulation is driven not by a desire to impress men, but by a motivation to outcompete other women, when those women are perceived as potential rivals. Moreover, the effect of fertility on women's consumption and financial decision making stems from a desire to surpass other women in status and resources. Implications for women's materialism, consumption of luxury items, and financial decision making are discussed.

Key Words: intrasexual competition, fertility, menstrual cycle, hormones, ovulatory competition hypothesis, relative status, physical attractiveness, consumer behavior, financial decision making

As dawn breaks at the Yerkes National Primate Center in Atlanta, Georgia, a group of female monkeys sit together quietly, alternating between grooming each other and watching the sun rise. After a couple of hours, the group heads out to grab a bite to eat and later retreats to the top of a favorite rock to soak up some afternoon sun. The females repeat this daily routine over the course of a month's time—with one small exception. For a few days mid-month, the tide changes and these normally placid females become increasingly aggressive, using threatening gestures and sometimes physically attacking other females in the group. What might be the source of this increased female–female aggression? It is not due to a dwindling supply of food or a drastic change in the weather pattern but rather to the increase in the ovarian hormone estrogen that accompanies estrus—the time each month when females are ovulating and are most likely to become pregnant. When the female monkeys are

fertile, they are more aggressive. Fertile females use threatening gestures and sometimes even physically attack other females in their group with whom they are competing for male attention (Walker, Wilson, & Gordon, 1983; Wallen, 2000; Wallen & Tannenbaum, 1997). This aggression serves to intimidate female rivals and allows the dominant females to assert their status. High-ranking (or dominant) females are able to gain better access to mates (e.g., increased time spent with males). Eventually, as estrogen levels decrease and fertility wanes, the gaggle of females returns once again to a quiet perch upon their favorite rock—at least until the middle of the next month.

What about human females? Do the hormones that regulate fertility increase intrasexual aggression in women? We do not often hear about or witness fisticuffs between women for the attention of the neighborhood cad; however, fertility-induced shifts in intrasexual aggression may take a different, less direct form in women. In this chapter, we examine the tactics women use to compete with one another through the lens of the ovulatory cycle. Whereas a large body of research has examined the relation between hormones and men's competition (e.g., Anderson, Bancroft, & Wu, 1992; O'Connor, Archer, & Wu, 2004), much less research has examined the role hormones play in women's competition. For example, research on men has found a direct relationship between men's testosterone levels and dominant behavior, including overt physical aggression, nonaggressive dominant behavior, and even antisocial behavior (Mazur & Booth, 1998). Focusing on women's competition and drawing on research on nonhuman primates, we propose that estrus (henceforth ovulation)—the phase of the menstrual cycle when the probability of conception is highest—should amplify women's intrasexual competitive tendencies. We call this idea the *ovulatory competition hypothesis*. Here, we develop this hypothesis and discuss the current state of knowledge on how the hormones associated with ovulation influence women's mating psychology, including women's desire to outcompete rivals. We consider the various competitive tactics that shift near ovulation, and we highlight avenues for future research. In the next section, we discuss the broader implications for understanding how ovulatory hormones influence women's competition.

The Ovulatory Cycle: A Window into Mechanism

The ovulatory cycle spans, on average, 28 days. A woman is most fertile and has a substantial probability of becoming pregnant on only about 6–7 days of each cycle, which is known as the *ovulatory phase* (Jones, 1997; Wilcox, Weinberg, & Baird,

1995). On the remaining days of the cycle, the probability of conception is very low. Ovulation, or estrus, in other animals is known to influence female behavior. Shifts in behavior near ovulation are driven by the sex hormones estrogen (an ovarian hormone) and luteinizing hormone (LH; a pituitary hormone), which fluctuate in specific ways across the cycle (Lipson & Ellison, 1996). It is the rise in estrogen levels that is responsible for triggering the surge in LH that initiates ovulation. Levels of these sex hormones peak in the week of the ovulatory phase each month when women are most fertile (Jones, 1997; see Figure 22.1). In contrast, progesterone (an ovarian hormone) reaches its peak levels somewhat later, during the luteal (i.e., premenstrual) phase of the cycle (Fleischman, Navarrete, & Fessler, 2010). If pregnancy does not occur, hormone levels drop back to baseline after ovulation (Venners et al., 2006). Consistent with these hormonal drivers, the behavioral effects of the ovulatory phase are suppressed when women are using hormonal contraception (e.g., the pill, the patch, hormonal intrauterine device [IUD], vaginal ring; Fleischman et al., 2010; Miller, Tybur, & Jordan, 2007). Hormonal contraceptives introduce synthetic estrogen and progesterone into the body, thus suppressing the body's production of these hormones, which results in lower total levels of estrogen and progesterone (Fleischman et al., 2010). Thus, oral contraception disrupts the normal fluctuation of female sex hormones across the cycle, and therefore it erases the behavioral effects associated with ovulation. The use of hormonal contraceptives can even influence women's mate preferences and actual partner choice; women who choose their partners while on the pill tend to experience lower sexual satisfaction with and attraction toward their partners

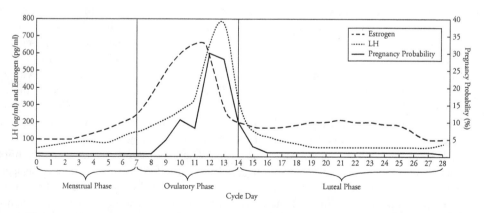

Figure 22.1 The phases of the female monthly ovulatory cycle and fertility based on Wilcox et al. (1995) and Jones (1997). Note that probability of conception and the associated levels of estrogen and luteinizing hormone (LH) peak in the ovulatory phase of the cycle.

but tend to be more satisfied with their partners' paternal qualities and have longer, more stable relationships (Roberts et al., 2012).

Despite the fact that the fertile phase of the ovulatory cycle lasts only about one week, it can provide an important window into the underlying mechanisms that drive women's motivations and behaviors. Unlike men, women are likely to reproduce only during ovulation. Although this period is brief, women's behavior tends to shift near ovulation in ways that are designed to optimize reproductive outcomes (e.g., Thornhill & Gangestad, 2008). This means that women should be particularly motivated to engage in behaviors that serve both direct courtship and intrasexual competitive goals at peak fertility. The distinction between intersexual courtship and intrasexual competition relates primarily to the intended audience. During intersexual courtship, the intended audience is men (i.e., attracting male attention), whereas during intrasexual competition, the intended audience is other women who constitute potential rivals (i.e., competing with rivals for male attention).

The tactics women use to attract mates and compete with other women for access to mates should be particularly evident near ovulation (e.g., enhancing attractiveness compared to other local women or motivation to gain status relative to other women; Durante, Griskevicius, Cantú, & Simpson, 2014; Durante, Griskevicius, Hill, Perilloux, & Li, 2011). For example, near ovulation, the attractiveness of other women who constitute potential rivals in the mating pool serves as a proximate-level cue about the need to enhance one's own attractiveness to stand out. Given that ovulation is accompanied by a specific hormonal profile, researchers are able to confirm this period of peak fertility in the laboratory and examine shifts in behaviors that are predicted to be motivated by direct courtship or intrasexual competition (e.g., Durante et al., 2011; Durante, Li, & Haselton, 2008; Haselton, Mortezaie, Pillsworth, Bleske-Rechek, & Frederick, 2007).

Although women may still desire to be attractive to mates and outcompete rival women outside of the high fertility point within the cycle, the indirect (genetic) benefits of attracting and mating with the highest-quality mate available are maximized during the ovulatory phase, when women have a substantial probability of conception. Across human evolution, those women who successfully attracted high-quality men and outshined female rivals for men's attention during the high-fertility phase of their cycle tended to enjoy greater reproductive success compared to women who exhibited the same behaviors during the low-fertility phase, when conception is very unlikely. The potential evolutionary benefits of optimizing mating outcomes are lower when women are not ovulating. Hence, women who experienced an increase in motivation to compete with rival women specifically when fertile in their cycles were more likely to secure a mate who possessed markers of genetic fitness (e.g., traits purported to be a reliable cue to genes that were beneficial in ancestral environments such as masculinity, social dominance; Gangestad, Garver-Apgar, Simpson, & Cousins, 2007; Penton-Voak & Perrett, 2000). That is, ancestral women who became more intrasexually competitive near ovulation would subsequently be more likely to attract high-quality mates and produce offspring who were also relatively high in genetic quality. It is important to note that this motivational shift is nonconscious, especially since women in general are unaware of exactly when they ovulate. Nevertheless, documenting shifts in women's behavior near ovulation can have important implications for our understanding of how mating goals influence women's behavior.

Existing Research on Ovulatory Shifts in Women's Behavior

Ovulation is known to influence reproductive behavior, and therefore the majority of human research on ovulation has examined how ovulation affects women's mating psychology. This body of work lends support to the conclusion that ovulation leads women to be more interested in mating than they are during the rest of their cycle. For example, women during their ovulatory phase have greater interest in meeting men (Haselton & Gangestad, 2006), pay more attention to men (Anderson et al., 2010), and are more likely to cheat on their current romantic partner than during any other time of the month (Garver-Apgar, Gangestad, Thornhill, Miller, & Olp, 2006). Near ovulation, women also exhibit an increased preference specifically for men who display markers of genetic fitness (e.g., facial symmetry and attractiveness: Gangestad & Thornhill, 1998; Gangestad, Thornhill, & Garver-Apgar, 2005; Pillsworth & Haselton, 2006a; masculinity: Penton-Voak & Perrett, 2000; Puts, 2005, 2006; social dominance: Durante, Griskevicius, Simpson, Cantú, & Li, 2012; Gangestad et al., 2007; and major histocompatibility complex gene compatibility: Garver-Apgar et al., 2006). As the probability of conception across the ovulatory cycle increases, even women's preferences for men's body scent change; specifically, women tend to prefer the scent of men with higher testosterone levels (Thornhill, Chapman, & Gangestad, 2013).

Research finds that a woman's ovulation-induced sexual attraction to indicators of genetic fitness is often targeted toward men other than her primary partner (Gangestad, Simpson, Cousins, Garver-Apgar, & Christensen, 2004; Haselton & Gangestad, 2006; Pillsworth & Haselton, 2006b). Near ovulation, women have more fantasies about other men and are more likely to have extramarital affairs (Baker & Bellis, 1995; Bellis & Baker, 1990; Sheldon, Cooper, Geary, Hoard, & DeSoto, 2006). For example, Gangestad and colleagues (2002) found that partnered women's sexual attractions, interests, and fantasies toward their partner did not differ across the cycle. In contrast, the same women experienced a significant increase in sexual attraction to and fantasies about men other than their primary partner near ovulation (Gangestad, Thornhill, & Garver, 2002). Furthermore, women near ovulation evaluate men high in genetic fitness more positively as short-term sexual partners but not necessarily as long-term partners (Durante et al., 2012; Gangestad et al., 2007). Research also finds that the hormones associated with ovulation lead women to report an increased probability that they will date and have a brief affair with a man other than their current partner (Durante & Li, 2009; Gangestad, Thornhill, & Garver-Apgar, 2010). This increased sexual attraction to different men is particularly strong if a woman's current partner lacks indicators of genetic fitness, such as physical attractiveness or facial symmetry (for a review, see Larson, Pillsworth, & Haselton, 2012). This shift in preference makes sense from an evolutionary perspective because the benefits of mating with men high in genetic fitness can be actualized only near ovulation.

In sum, a body of research that spans nearly 15 years demonstrates that women's mate preferences change in the aforementioned ways across the ovulatory cycle. However, enhancing reproductive fitness involves more than direct courtship; it also involves successfully outcompeting same-sex individuals for status and access to mates (Campbell, 2004; Kenrick, Griskevicius, Neuberg, & Schaller, 2010). Higher social status can offer greater access to high-quality mates, and the first hurdle to successfully attracting and retaining a desired mate is to be as desirable as one's same-sex rivals in the same vicinity.

The Ovulatory Competition Hypothesis

For any social animal, including *Homo sapiens*, reproductive fitness involves much more than intersexual attraction and mating—it also involves outcompeting same-sex conspecifics for opposite-sex attention. At the outset of this chapter, we discussed how ovulation affects intrasexual competition in nonhuman primates, whereby female primates become more aggressive and competitive toward other females during the ovulatory phase (Walker et al., 1983; Wallen, 2000). This suggests that ovulation might not only alter women's mate preferences, but it might also influence their competitive tendencies.

We refer to the idea that ovulation should amplify women's intrasexual competition as the *ovulatory competition hypothesis*. Relatively little research has considered how the ovulatory cycle affects outcomes not directly related to mating. Successfully attracting a mate also involves outcompeting other women for access to mates, which implies that women should become more competitive with other women near ovulation. However, unlike nonhuman female primates who use threatening gestures and direct attacks to compete with rivals (Walker et al., 1983), human females are predicted to use more indirect tactics to compete with other women near ovulation.

Men more than women use overt aggression to gain status and access to mates (Li & Kenrick, 2006; Maner, DeWall, & Gailliot, 2008; Mealey, 1985; Turke & Betzig, 1985), and the sex hormone testosterone—the hormone that regulates male fertility—has been linked to overt forms of aggression and displays of dominance in men, such as verbally challenging or attacking rivals in the form of a fistfight (Anderson et al., 1992; Archer, 1988; O'Connor et al., 2004). However, the ovulatory hormone estrogen—the dominant sex hormone that regulates fertility in women—should drive women's indirect (but not direct) aggressive tendencies because overt aggression tends to be less effective and more costly for women than for men (Campbell, 2004).

For men, aggression enhances status, which can indirectly augment a man's ability to attract a mate (Betzig, 1986; Buss, 1989). In contrast, women generally do not enhance their ability to attract a mate through overt aggression. As Campbell (2004) argues, women usually compete for mates by advertising their youth, beauty, or fidelity, which is a more effective strategy than aggression for women. Physical aggression among women is less frequent and tends to take place only when intrasexual competition escalates due to a paucity of quality men or a skewed sex ratio in the local environment (Campbell, 2004). The costs of physical aggression are also very different for men and women. Maternal investment has been more crucial than paternal investment for offspring survival; thus, women evolved to place a higher premium on self-protection by developing a more cautious approach—compared to men—when faced with the possibility of physical harm (Campbell, 1999). This is consistent with the fact that men tend to engage in more physical aggression than women do because the benefits of status gained via aggression can lead to greater reproductive success for men, which can outweigh the risks. This is not the case for women, whose larger parental investment places an upper limit to their number of offspring and makes offspring survival a primary concern. Thus, the risks of direct aggression tend to outweigh the benefits for women, making indirect aggression and competition a more viable tactic.

Given that, from an evolutionary perspective, engaging in direct, physical attacks (e.g., fistfights) on rivals was much more costly for women than for men in terms of reputational damage, serious injury, or death, and because women's overt aggression is not directly linked to reproductive success as it is in men, women are more likely to use tactics to circuitously aggress against same-sex rivals (Archer & Coyne, 2005; Campbell, 1999, 2004). One domain of female–female competition that is most likely to shift near ovulation is women's desire to appear more physically attractive than rival women.

Physical Attractiveness

Ancestral women likely varied in their ability to produce offspring; variations in fertility and reproductive value may have been due to age, health, adiposity, and other factors that affect fecundity (Ellison, 2001). Therefore, men may have evolved to be physically attracted to romantic partners who have outward indicators of fertility (Symons, 1979). One of these indicators is physical beauty, which is a predictor of health and fertility in women (Durante & Li, 2009; Law Smith et al., 2006). Research finds that men place a high premium on physical attractiveness when selecting a mate (Buss & Schmitt, 1993; Li, Bailey, Kenrick, & Linsenmeier, 2002; Li et al., 2013), with men high in genetic fitness valuing attractiveness in prospective mates the most. There is empirical evidence that the most attractive men (whose physical attractiveness acts as an overt

cue of genetic fitness) have the highest expectations and standards when judging female attractiveness as well (Montoya, 2008). Moreover, there tends to be positive assortative matching across attractiveness levels in the early stages of male-to-female social interaction. That is, researchers have found that men invest more time and effort and show more interest in interacting with women at approximately the same level of attractiveness as themselves (van Straaten, Engels, Finkenauer, & Holland, 2009). Therefore, insofar as women aim for attractive (and by extension genetically fit) men, one domain in which women should compete is physical attractiveness (Cashdan, 1998; Etcoff, 2000), and this tendency should be especially enhanced when the reproductive payoff of attracting a high-quality mate is highest—near ovulation.

In a landmark study, women rated photographs of other women as lower in attractiveness when their estrogen levels were particularly high, which suggests that women are derogating competitors in the domain of physical attractiveness when fertility within their cycle is highest (Fisher, 2004). Building on this finding, a recent study found that, near ovulation, women dehumanized other women but not other target groups (e.g., men, the elderly; Piccoli, Foroni, & Carnaghi, 2013). As conception probability within the cycle increased, women used more animal-related words (e.g., paw, snout) to describe other women and reported more agreement with statements like "I tend to look for negative characteristics in attractive women" than they did during other points in the cycle. If women are derogating the attractiveness of other women near ovulation, this suggests that women may subsequently attempt to enhance their own attractiveness near ovulation.

Research has found that women in photographs taken in the high-fertility phase of their cycle (near ovulation) were consistently rated by both men and women as wearing "more fashionable clothes" or "nicer clothes" compared to women at low-fertility points in the cycle (Haselton et al., 2007, p. 43). Photographs of women during the high-fertility phase were especially likely to be chosen as more fashionable if the women completed their high-fertility laboratory session on one of the days closest to ovulation.

Women also wear outfits that are more revealing and sexy near ovulation, particularly when preparing for a social event (Durante et al., 2008). In this study, women posed for full-body photographs once near ovulation and again at a low-fertility point in the cycle. In addition, during both high- and low-fertility sessions, participants were told to imagine they are attending a party at a friend's apartment in the evening. They were further instructed to think about what they would wear to the party. Participants were then given a sheet of paper containing an outline of a woman's figure, upon which they sketched an outfit using colored pencils. The amount of skin revealed on the outfit sketch was then calculated in square millimeters, and outside raters judged the photographs and outfit sketches for how revealing and sexy the outfit looked. Not only were the outfits that women wore to the lab near ovulation rated as more revealing and sexy, but women who were near ovulation sketched outfits that revealed more skin and were rated as more revealing and sexy compared to the outfit sketches drawn by women at a low-fertility point in the cycle (see Figure 22.2).

Another study found not only that women had a greater desire for products that enhanced attractiveness (e.g., high heels, makeup) near ovulation, but they actually spent more money on sexy and revealing clothes near ovulation (Saad & Stenstrom, 2012). Taken together, these studies lend support

to the conclusion that women enhance their own attractiveness more near ovulation; however, none of these studies tested the specific *function* of the increased desire near ovulation to appear more attractive. Although it is possible that women increase their attractiveness at ovulation to impress men directly, it is also possible that women increase their attractiveness at ovulation to enhance their ability to compete with other women for access to mates. A third possibility is that both direct courtship and intrasexual competitive motivations are at play, which we consider next.

The question of intended audience is particularly important from an evolutionary perspective. An understanding of the intended audience would provide insight into the evolutionary function of the ovulatory-regulated shift. For example, consider three different evolved animal traits: the peacock's train, the red deer's antlers, and the lion's mane. Although all three traits evolved because they ultimately serve to enhance reproduction, each one has evolved for a different function and via different selection pressures (see Alcock, 2005; Anderson, 1994; Griskevicius et al., 2009). Specifically,

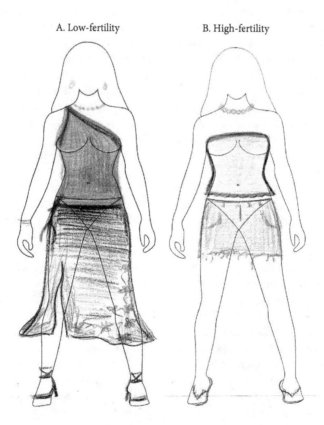

A. Low-fertility   B. High-fertility

Figure 22.2 Example of an outfit illustration drawn by the same participant at low-fertility (A) and high-fertility (B) phases (Durante, Li, & Haselton, 2008).

whereas the peacock uses its train exclusively to display to the opposite sex in courtship, the red deer uses its antlers exclusively to compete with same-sex rivals for status, whereby the highest-status male earns access to females. The lion's mane, on the other hand, serves a function both in courtship and in same-sex competition, meaning that both types of selection pressures contributed to the evolution of this trait.

Although at first glance it may seem that the ovulation effect on women's choice of sexy clothing is most akin to the example of a deer's antlers, it should be tested as an empirical question whether the function of this ovulatory effect is most analogous to the function of a peacock's train (courtship function), a deer's antlers (same-sex competition function), or a lion's mane (both courtship and same-sex competition function). To answer this question, Durante and colleagues (2011) experimentally led women to think about attractive local women versus attractive local men and examined the kinds of clothing women selected when they were ovulating versus not ovulating. In this study, *local* meant that the people depicted in the stimuli purportedly attended the same university as the participants. This is important because it implies that these attractive women and men constituted potential rivals and targets (respectively) in the participants' local mating pool. The dependent measure was choice of sexy clothing, operationalized as follows: participants were presented with a shopping website that contained photographs of 128 clothing and accessory (e.g., purses, shoes) items. No price or brand information was given, and the order of the items was randomized. Half the items were pretested to be sexy (without being too provocative), whereas the other half were pretested to be more conservative. The participants were instructed to choose 10 items from this website, and the dependent measure was the percentage of those 10 items that were pretested as *sexy*. Ovulation had the largest effect on women's desire to dress in sexier outfits specifically when they were led to believe there were many attractive female rivals nearby. There was no effect of ovulation on clothing choice when women were led to believe there were many attractive men in the local neighborhood or when led to believe that the local women were not particularly attractive relative to the average woman on campus. It should be noted that the difference in attractiveness across conditions was substantial. The participants in each experimental condition were asked (under the guise of a cover story) to rate the people in the

photographs shown to them for attractiveness on a 1–9 scale. The photographs in the attractive prime were rated more than 2 standard deviations (SD) above the midpoint, whereas the photographs in the less attractive prime were rated more than 1 SD below the midpoint, on average.

Additional findings showed that the ovulatory effect on the choice of sexy clothing is driven by women's perceptions of the attractiveness of local women, not women who live in far-away cities and thus do not represent direct competitors. A comparison condition where the prime was attractive *distant* women (i.e., women who purportedly attended a university more than 1,000 miles away) found no effect of ovulation on the choice of clothing. Together, these findings support the prediction that the effect of ovulation on women's desire to enhance their attractiveness is driven by a desire to outdo attractive rival women, and thus it is most akin to the deer's antlers. Minimizing the presence of attractive women who are potential rivals (by telling participants that these women are far away) suppressed the ovulatory effect on the desire for sexy clothes and other fashion accessories.

Might ovulation also have broader effects on women's competitive tactics? Given the fact that men place a premium on women's physical attractiveness, it follows that women compete with one another on the dimension of physical attractiveness. This raises the question: what about other dimensions—even dimensions that, on the surface, appear to have little to do with mating? Recall the aggressive tendencies of female monkeys that arise at estrus. Threatening and attacking female rivals is unlikely a tactic that is used to increase one's attractiveness compared to other females. Rather, it is most likely a tactic that is used to intimidate other females and increase one's status relative to others in the group. Therefore, it is possible that jockeying for relative status is another dimension of female competition. If so, women's concern for status relative to other women should be enhanced at ovulation.

Relative Status

What is meant by relative status? Consider the following situations drawn from both history books and recent news. In 1615, Queen of France Marie de Medici commissioned the building of Luxembourg Palace, an extravagant 60-acre estate with custom-made sculptures, specialized ponds for sailing model boats, and a private marionette theater. Just one year later, in 1616, her English rival, Queen Anne of Denmark, embarked on erecting her own palatial retreat in Greenwich. Not to be outdone by her rival, de Medici soon enlisted eminent painter Peter Paul Rubens to paint 24 canvases to adorn her newly gilded study (Ayers, 2004; Bold, 2000).

Modern women continue to feel the urge to outspend rivals. In 2008, after prominent hotel heiress Paris Hilton purchased a $200,000 Bentley, her friend-turned-rival Kim Kardashian bought a $220,000 Bentley and a $250,000 Rolls Royce. Shortly afterward, Ms. Hilton acquired her own custom-built $300,000 Rolls Royce (Silverman, 2008). The fact that the aforementioned behaviors seem so invariant across time and across different cultures lends support to the conclusion that fundamental motives underlie these behaviors, deepseated in human evolution.

Conspicuous consumption battles such as those just described are often considered to be a tactic that men use to attract mates. These tactics function as costly signals of men's ability and willingness to provide material resources (Griskevicius et al., 2007; Sundie et al., 2011), which are qualities that women tend to value in prospective mates (Buss & Schmitt, 1993). At the same time, though, women account for more than half of the spending on lavish goods such as luxury cars and jewelry in the United States (D'Arpizio, 2011; Mintel Report, 2011). Men are unlikely to be more attracted to a woman because of the size of her home or her custom Bentley. Across human evolution, the minimal parental investment required of women (i.e., nine months of gestation plus several months of lactation) has always been larger than the parental investment required of men (Trivers, 1972). Hence, women's fertility and reproductive value have been more important concerns for men than women's ability to invest material resources (Buss & Schmitt, 1993). Thus, women's conspicuous consumption may be a tactic women use not to attract men but to outcompete rival women for status and access to mates. Is women's desire to outspend one another related to intrasexual competition? To test this question, researchers have examined how ovulatory hormones influence women's desire to acquire resources (e.g., Durante et al., 2014).

An initial investigation into fertility and desire for relative status found that women closest to the expected day of ovulation were less likely to share a monetary award and more likely to reject a low offer to share in a monetary stake with another woman (Lucas, Koff, & Skeath, 2007). The authors proposed that, near ovulation, women may be prone to competing for material resources—suggesting that

women's desire to acquire resources is motivated by intrasexual competition. If this is the case, women's materialism and their motivation to outspend rivals should be influenced by ovulation—a time when gaining a relative advantage over other women by intimidating them or by inducing deference has the highest potential payoff. The reason is that only during ovulation can more resources or higher status (relative to other women in the local mating pool) translate into better reproductive outcomes by helping women secure or retain a high-quality mate.

Materialism is a set of beliefs about the importance of possessions, with materialistic individuals being especially driven to acquire material goods (Richins & Dawson, 1992). At its core, materialism is strongly linked to the desire for prestigious goods (Prendergast & Wong, 2003; Rindfleisch, Burroughs, & Denton, 1997; Tatzel, 2002; Watson, 2003; Wong, 1997; Wong & Ahuvia, 1998). Materialistic individuals not only seek products that are associated with status, but they also desire products that are visible among their peers (Richins, 1994a, 1994b). An individual's materialism can be defined and measured across three separate dimensions: success, centrality, and happiness (Richins & Dawson, 1992). The *success* dimension reflects an individual's belief that the acquisition of material possessions is a measure of one's own success relative to others (e.g., "I like to own things that impress people"). The *centrality* dimension refers to the extent to which acquiring material possessions constitutes a crucial aspect of one's life, and the *happiness* dimension refers to the extent to which one thinks that material possessions can make one happier. According to the ovulatory competition hypothesis, ovulation should amplify women's success materialism. In a test of this prediction, it was found that, as fertility in the cycle increased, so did success materialism (but not centrality or happiness materialism; Kim, Durante, & Griskevicius, 2015). Ovulation increased women's desire to acquire material goods (e.g., jewelry) as a means to get ahead of one's peers but not as a means to enhance well-being or happiness.

Although the ovulatory cycle appears to systematically alter women's success materialism, the target for women's displays of materialism is unclear. It is also unclear whether ovulating women simply want more possessions, or if the possessions they are interested in depend on what their peers already own. The ovulatory competition hypothesis suggests that ovulation should boost women's tendency to maximize relative gains rather than absolute gains specifically as compared to other women. In one study, ovulating and nonovulating women made product choices that could either maximize absolute gains or maximize relative gains (Durante et al., 2014). For example, based on Frank (2005), women chose which option they preferred between two states of the world: State A—You get a $7,000 diamond ring; other women get $15,000 diamond rings, or State B—You get a $5,000 diamond ring; other women get $1,000 diamond rings. State B represents the relative gain option. As fertility in the cycle increased, so did the probability of selecting the choice that maximized a woman's relative standing. Near ovulation, women were willing to accept lesser versions of a product as long as they had better products than other women. When women made the same choices but the relative advantage was over men, there was no effect of ovulation. That is, women did not want relatively more than men when they approached the phase of ovulation. In fact, women did not desire relative status over men regardless of cycle phase. Near ovulation, women's desire to acquire resources was limited to outspending rival women.

Based on the ovulatory competition hypothesis, one might posit that the effect of the ovulatory cycle should manifest itself not only in women's consumer choices, but also in their financial decisions that have a bearing on other women versus men. For example, ovulation should affect women's actual behavior in an incentive-compatible Dictator Game (Durante et al., 2014). In the Dictator Game, a player is given a fixed amount of money and is tasked with dividing it between herself and another person. The player can give as much or as little of the money to the other person as she dictates. The more the player gives, however, the less money she gets to keep for herself. A meta-analysis of more than 100 Dictator Game studies found that people tend to give about 25–50% of the money to the other person when playing against a stranger (Engel, 2011).

In this study (Durante et al., 2014), female participants in two phases (once near ovulation and again at a low-fertility point in the cycle) were randomly assigned to play the Dictator Game against either a man or a woman. Participants were led to believe that their partner was a student at the same university and was participating in the study in an adjoining room. Before the game began, participants saw a webcam photograph of the other player, along with his or her name and year of study. The photograph depicted either an attractive man or

an attractive woman, rated in a pre-test as above average in attractiveness (with a mean attractiveness rating of slightly more than 6 on a 1–9 scale). Participants were given $5.00 in cash. The participants' task was to allocate $5.00 between themselves and the other player. The dependent measure was the portion of the $5.00 participants gave to the other person (participants kept the remainder of the money for themselves).

Consistent with the ovulatory competition hypothesis, Durante and colleagues (2014) found that ovulating women kept more money for themselves rather than give it to another woman ($M_{ovulating}$ = gave 27.5% of endowment to other woman vs. $M_{not-ovulating}$ = gave 50.6% of endowment to other woman). However, ovulation did not have the same effect when the woman played with a man. In fact, women gave significantly more money to a man when they were ovulating versus not ovulating ($M_{ovulating}$ = gave 61.3% of endowment to man vs. $M_{not-ovulating}$ = gave 40.5% of endowment to man). Unlike with other women, ovulating women became more generous to men, giving men more than 50% of the endowment, which is consistent with previous findings showing that ovulating women are more attracted to desirable men near ovulation (Anderson et al., 2010; Durante et al., 2012; Haselton & Gangestad, 2006), although this study did not explicitly lead women to believe the men were high quality. Research using the Ultimatum Game found a similar pattern (Lucas & Koff, 2013). Near ovulation, women's offers to other women—but not men—were significantly lower than at a low-fertility point in the cycle. This sex-specific pattern of findings supports the ovulatory competition hypothesis; namely, that ovulation leads women to become more competitive against other women but not men.

Another recent experimental study found that women in general tend to bid significantly higher than men do during auctions, which results in lower profits for women. The only exception is during the ovulatory phase, when women tend to bid more aggressively and place lower bids (Pearson & Schipper, 2013). This change in bidding behavior during mid-cycle was observed for naturally cycling women, but not for women on hormonal contraceptives. The authors argued that this more aggressive bidding resulted from women's higher tolerance for risk during ovulation (Pearson & Schipper, 2013). This makes sense, insofar as the ovulatory phase is the time when risk-taking can translate into higher genetic benefits. Increased risk-taking near ovulation (to the extent that all sexual activity carries some inherent risk) can result in a higher probability of conception. Perhaps more importantly, risk-taking (e.g., in the form of extrapair mating, which can come with significant costs if discovered) can give a woman access to higher-quality genes (Pearson & Schipper, 2013).

Overall, emerging research supports the conclusion that women's intrasexual competition is influenced by ovulation, particularly in the domains of physical attractiveness and relative status. Research on the influences of the ovulatory cycle—and of hormones more generally—on intrasexual competition is in its infancy because many hypotheses are waiting to be tested. Given that the ovulatory cycle provides a window into women's competitive psychology, we discuss the implications of the current findings for future research programs.

Directions for Future Research

Researchers have identified a variety of tactics used in intrasexual mate competition and have found that women compete with one another just as much as men do (e.g., Buss, 1988). For example, women tend to flaunt luxury products not to impress men, but to intimidate or outdo other women who are seen as a threat; that is, female rivals who may poach one's current romantic relationship (Wang & Griskevicius, 2014). Yet overall, women's intrasexual competition has received much less attention than men's (Fisher, 2013). The benefits of successfully outcompeting rivals for male attention are highest near ovulation, and hence the ovulatory cycle is likely to have important effects on additional female competition tactics, other than appearance enhancement and resource display or acquisition. Some of these possible tactics are outlined below.

Existing research suggests that women derogate other women more near ovulation (e.g., Fisher, 2004; Piccoli et al., 2013), which can have serious implications for how women interact with one another in the workplace. Women may be more likely to gossip about and criticize female colleagues during their high-fertility phase (Piccoli et al., 2013), and this tendency can impact on the way women manage other women. Near ovulation, female supervisors may become overly critical of the job performance, choice of dress, hair style, and etiquette of the women who report to them. Conversely, if a woman views a female supervisor as a competitor, she may spread rumors or negative gossip about her (for more details, see chapter by McAndrew and chapter by Sutton & Oaten,

this volume). It is also possible that intrasexual competitive motives may impinge on hiring decisions. For example, ovulating women may be less likely to hire another woman, particularly if that woman is attractive. Ovulation may also influence how women negotiate. Recent attention has been placed on why women do not perform as well as men in negotiation and are less likely to ask for more money (e.g., Stuhlmacher & Walters, 1999; Walters, Stuhlmacher, & Meyer, 1998). Ovulating women may become better at negotiation when they are negotiating with other women, in that women may be less likely to accept initial offers near ovulation if that offer comes from another woman.

The ovulatory cycle, and ovulation more specifically, might also influence charitable giving and ethical decisions (e.g., Galak, Small, & Stephen, 2011; Irwin & Naylor, 2009; Small & Verrochi, 2009). For instance, given that women become more competitive during the ovulatory phase, ovulating women may be less sensitive to others' needs and more willing to take unethical routes to gain status. By the same token, ovulation may also influence women's morality. Near ovulation, women may be more likely to lie or cheat to get ahead of other women. Given that ovulating women became stingier when playing against other women in the Dictator Game (Durante et al., 2014), they might also be more or less responsive to salespersons' persuasive efforts to complete the sale depending on the sex of the salesperson.

Another interesting question that has received much less attention than questions focused on behavioral shifts near ovulation is what behaviors might be expected to shift at a low-fertility point in the cycle. In the second half of the ovulatory cycle (i.e., the luteal phase), the hormone progesterone increases to prepare a woman's body for pregnancy (e.g., Jones, 1997). Progesterone begins to increase relative to estrogen immediately after women ovulate (Lipson & Ellison, 1996; Roney & Simmons, 2012). Research on ovulatory effects often treats the luteal phase as a "baseline" condition against which the fertile phase is contrasted (e.g., Durante et al., 2011, 2014; Haselton et al., 2007), with little attention paid to the function of progesterone effects (with some notable exceptions: DeBruine, Jones, & Perrett, 2005; Fessler & Navarrete, 2003; Jones et al., 2005). An interesting question, then, is whether progesterone dampens women's motivation to compete with one another or whether progesterone leads women to compete in ways that are different from competitive tactics used near ovulation. An unanticipated finding in the research on women's desire to dress sexier at ovulation is that nonovulating women who viewed photographs of attractive local women chose fewer sexy items compared to nonovulating women who were primed with photographs of men or less attractive women (Durante et al., 2011). It is possible that the salience of female rivals leads women in the low-fertility phase of the cycle (when progesterone levels are high) to distance themselves from competition. The evolutionary benefit of winning costly status competitions, in terms of access to high-quality mates, is lower when women are not ovulating. Thus, instead of competing at this time, women might save the risks and costs associated with competition for when ovulation is approaching—the time when the potential evolutionary benefits of winning status competitions are highest.

The risks and costs of intrasexual competition involve physical violence less often for women than for men (Campbell, 1999); however, competition among women can lead to other hurtful, indirect tactics, "such as shunning, stigmatizing, and gossiping" (Campbell, 1999, p. 209). Women may thus avoid competition with other women at low-fertility points in the cycle. Of course, it is also possible that the tactics of women's competition change given the key roles the luteal phase and the hormone progesterone play in pregnancy and implantation. For example, women may participate in more relational aggression while in a phase of low fertility, such as manipulating social relationships through disseminating information, entertaining, and trying to set social norms and enhance social bonding (Fine & Rosnow, 1978; Leaper & Holliday, 1995). For example, women may desire to socialize more with other women at low-fertility points in the cycle, provide advice, or lend a hand. Enhancing reciprocity can be one low-cost way to indirectly compete because it may decrease the likelihood that the women one befriends would double-cross one. It is plausible that some level of competition among women (such as the tactic just described) would be present even during the low-fertility phase; for instance, so that women maintain their current relationship, guard their partner, and prevent mate poaching from female rivals.

Future research is poised to examine these and other predictions that stem from a consideration of women's competitive tactics. The hormones associated with ovulation increase women's sensitivity toward intrasexual competitors, and thus researchers can examine behavior that is predicted to serve intrasexual competitive goals as a function of fertility status. Examining women's behavior through the lens of the ovulatory cycle can give researchers a bird's-eye view into women's competitive psychology.

Conclusion

The study of how ovulation affects women's intrasexual competition has vast implications not only for research and application, but also for linking theory and research in social psychology with theory and research in biology and animal behavior. In this chapter, we considered women's competition across the ovulatory cycle. We discussed why examining intrasexual competition across the cycle is important—namely, because it gives a window into the psychological mechanism that underlies women's motivations, behaviors, attitudes, and preferences. We focused on how women's competitive motivations might be affected by ovulation. Bridging a concept studied in evolutionary biological approaches to animal behavior with human outcomes, we showed that ovulation has theoretically consistent effects on human behavior. These effects, however, are not limited to mating outcomes; they extend to other important domains, such as financial decision making, consumer choice, and beyond. Questions of how and why ovulation influences different types of competitive behaviors have myriad implications, especially for an understanding of behaviors that serve mating goals versus other fundamental goals (e.g., parenting, self-protection; Kenrick et al., 2010).

References

Alcock, J. (2005). *Animal behavior: An evolutionary approach* (8th ed.). Sunderland, MA: Sinauer Associates.

Anderson, M. (1994). *Sexual selection*. Princeton, NJ: Princeton University Press.

Anderson, R. A., Bancroft, J., & Wu, F. C. (1992). The effects of exogenous testosterone on sexuality and mood of normal men. *Journal of Clinical Endocrinology & Metabolism, 75*(6), 1503–1507.

Anderson, U. S., Perea, E. F., Vaughn Becker, D., Ackerman, J. M., Shapiro, J. R., Neuberg, S. L., & Kenrick, D. T. (2010). I only have eyes for you: Ovulation redirects attention (but not memory) to attractive men. *Journal of Experimental Social Psychology, 46*(5), 804–808.

Archer, J. (1988). *The behavioural biology of aggression*. Cambridge, UK: Cambridge University Press.

Archer, J., & Coyne, S. M. (2005). An integrated review of indirect, relational, and social aggression. *Personality and Social Psychology Review, 9*(3), 212–230.

Ayers, A. (2004). *The architecture of Paris: An architectural guide.* London, England: Edition Axel Menges.

Baker, R. R., & Bellis, M. A. (1995. *Human sperm competition: Copulation, masturbation and infidelity.* London, England: Chapman & Hall.

Bellis, M. A., & Baker, R. R. (1990). Do females promote sperm competition? Data for humans. *Animal Behaviour, 40*(5), 997–999.

Betzig, L. L. (1986). *Despotism and differential reproduction: A Darwinian view of history.* New York: Aldine.

Bold, J. (2000). *Greenwich: An architectural history of the royal hospital for seamen and the queen's house.* New Haven, CT: Yale University Press.

Buss, D. M. (1988). The evolution of human intrasexual competition: Tactics of mate attraction. *Journal of Personality and Social Psychology, 54*(4), 616–628.

Buss, D. M. (1989). Conflict between the sexes: Strategic interference and the evocation of anger and upset. *Journal of Personality and Social Psychology, 56*(5), 735–747.

Buss, D. M., & Schmitt, D. P. (1993). Sexual strategies theory: An evolutionary perspective on human mating. *Psychological Review, 100*(2), 204-232.

Campbell, A. (1999). Staying alive: Evolution, culture, and women's intrasexual aggression. *Behavioral and Brain Sciences, 22*(2), 203–214.

Campbell, A. (2004). Female competition: Causes, constraints, content, and contexts. *Journal of Sex Research, 41*(1), 16–26.

Cashdan, E. (1998). Smiles, speech, and body posture: How women and men display sociometric status and power. *Journal of Nonverbal Behavior, 22*(4), 209–228.

D'Arpizio, C. (2011). *Spring 2011 update: Luxury goods worldwide market study.* Retrieved from http://www.bain.com/bainweb/about/press_release_detail.asp?id=28459&menu_url=for_the_media.asp

DeBruine, L. M., Jones, B. C., & Perrett, D. I. (2005). Women's attractiveness judgments of self-resembling faces change across the menstrual cycle. *Hormones and Behavior, 47*(4), 379–383.

Durante, K. M., Griskevicius, V., Cantú, S. M., & Simpson. J. A. (2014). Money, status, and the ovulatory cycle. *Journal of Marketing Research, 51*(1), 27–39.

Durante, K. M., Griskevicius, V., Hill, S. E., Perilloux, C., & Li, N. P. (2011). Ovulation, female competition, and product choice: Hormonal influences on consumer behavior. *Journal of Consumer Research, 37*(6), 921–934.

Durante, K. M., Griskevicius, V., Simpson, J. A., Cantú, S. M., & Li, N. P. (2012). Ovulation leads women to perceive sexy cads as good dads. *Journal of Personality and Social Psychology, 103*(2), 292–305.

Durante, K. M., & Li, N. P. (2009). Oestradiol level and opportunistic mating in women. *Biology Letters, 5*(2), 179–182.

Durante, K. M., Li, N. P., & Haselton, M. G. (2008). Changes in women's choice of dress across the ovulatory cycle: Naturalistic and laboratory task-based evidence. *Personality and Social Psychology Bulletin, 34*(11), 1451–1460.

Ellison, P. T. (2001). *On fertile ground: A natural history of human reproduction.* Cambridge, MA: Harvard University Press.

Engel, C. (2011). Dictator games: A meta-study. *Experimental Economics, 14*(4), 583–610.

Etcoff, N. (2000). *Survival of the prettiest: The science of beauty.* New York: Anchor Books.

Fessler, D. M. T., & Navarrete, C. D. (2003). Domain-specific variation in disgust sensitivity across the menstrual cycle. *Evolution and Human Behavior, 24*(6), 406–417.

Fine, G. A., & Rosnow, R. L. (1978). Gossip, gossipers, gossiping. *Personality and Social Psychology Bulletin, 4*(1), 161–168.

Fisher, M. L. (2004). Female intra-sexual competition decreases female facial attractiveness. *Proceedings of the Royal Society B, 271*, S283–S285.

Fisher, M. L. (2013). Women's intrasexual competition for mates. In M. L. Fisher, J. R. Garcia, & R. Sokol Chang (Eds.), *Evolution's empress: Darwinian perspectives on the nature of women* (pp. 19–42). New York: Oxford University Press.

Fleischman, D. S., Navarrete, C. D., & Fessler, D. M. (2010). Oral contraceptives suppress ovarian hormone production. *Psychological Science, 21*(5), 750–752.

Frank, R. H. (2005). Positional externalities cause large and preventable welfare losses. *American Economic Review, 95*(2), 137–141.

Galak, J., Small, D., & Stephen, A. T. (2011). Micro-finance decision making: A field study of prosocial lending. *Journal of Marketing Research, 48*, 130–137.

Gangestad, S. W., Garver-Apgar, C. E., Simpson, J. A., & Cousins, A. J. (2007). Changes in women's mate preferences across the ovulatory cycle. *Journal of Personality and Social Psychology, 92*(1), 151.

Gangestad, S. W., Simpson J. A., Cousins A. J., Garver-Apgar, C. E., & Christensen, P. N. (2004). Women's preferences for male behavioral displays across the menstrual cycle. *Psychological Science, 15*(3), 203–207.

Gangestad, S. W., & Thornhill, R. (1998). Menstrual cycle variation in women's preferences for the scent of symmetrical men. *Proceedings of the Royal Society B, 265*(1399), 927–933.

Gangestad, S. W., Thornhill, R., & Garver, C. E. (2002). Changes in women's sexual interests and their partners' mate-retention tactics across the menstrual cycle: Evidence for shifting conflicts of interest. *Proceedings of the Royal Society B, 269*(1494), 975–982.

Gangestad, S. W., Thornhill, R., & Garver-Apgar, C. E. (2005). Women's sexual interests across the ovulatory cycle depend on primary partner developmental instability. *Proceedings of the Royal Society B, 272*(1576), 2023-2027.

Gangestad, S. W., Thornhill, R., & Garver-Apgar, C. E. (2010). Fertility in the cycle predicts women's interest in sexual opportunism. *Evolution and Human Behavior, 31*(6), 400–411.

Garver-Apgar, C. E., Gangestad, S. W., Thornhill, R., Miller, R. D., & Olp, J. J. (2006). Major histocompatibility complex alleles, sexual responsivity, and unfaithfulness in romantic couples. *Psychological Science, 17*(10), 830–835.

Griskevicius, V., Tybur, J. M., Gangestad, S. W., Perea, E. F., Shapiro, J. R., & Kenrick, D. T. (2009). Aggress to impress: Hostility as an evolved context-dependent strategy. *Journal of Personality and Social Psychology, 96*(5), 980–994.

Griskevicius, V., Tybur, J. M., Sundie, J. M., Cialdini, R. B., Miller, G. F., & Kenrick, D. T. (2007). Blatant benevolence and conspicuous consumption: When romantic motives elicit strategic costly signals. *Journal of Personality and Social Psychology, 93*(1), 85–102.

Haselton, M. G., & Gangestad, S. W. (2006). Conditional expression of women's desires and men's mate guarding across the ovulatory cycle. *Hormones and Behavior, 49*(4), 509–518.

Haselton, M. G., Mortezaie, M., Pillsworth, E. G., Bleske-Rechek, A., & Frederick, D. A. (2007). Ovulatory shifts in human female ornamentation: Near ovulation, women dress to impress. *Hormones and Behavior, 51*(1), 40–45.

Irwin, J. R., & Naylor, R. W. (2009). Ethical decisions and response mode compatibility: Weighting of ethical attributes in consideration sets formed by excluding versus including product alternatives. *Journal of Marketing Research, 46*(2), 234–246.

Jones, B. C., Little, A. C., Boothroyd, L., DeBruine, L. M., Feinberg, D. R., Smith, M. J., ... Perrett, D. I. (2005). Commitment to relationships and preferences for femininity and apparent health in faces are strongest on days of the menstrual cycle when progesterone level is high. *Hormones and Behavior, 48*(3), 283–290.

Jones, R. E. (1997). *Human reproductive biology* (2nd ed.). New York: Academic Press.

Kenrick, D. T., Griskevicius, V., Neuberg, S. L., & Schaller, M. (2010). Renovating the pyramid of needs: Contemporary extensions built upon ancient foundations. *Perspectives on Psychological Science, 5*(3), 292–314.

Kim, A., Durante, K. M., & Griskevicius, V. (2015). Fertility and women's luxury spending. Manuscript in preparation.

Larson, C. M., Pillsworth, E. G., & Haselton, M. G. (2012). Ovulatory shifts in women's attractions to primary partners and other men: Further evidence of the importance of primary partner sexual attractiveness. *PLoS One, 7*(9), e44456. doi:10.1371/journal.pone.0044456

Law Smith, M. J., Perrett, D. I., Jones, B. C., Cornwell, R. E., Moore, F. R., Feinberg, D. R., ... Hillier, S. G. (2006). Facial appearance is a cue to oestrogen levels in women. *Proceedings of the Royal Society B, 273*(1583), 135-140.

Leaper, C., & Holliday, H. (1995). Gossip in same gender and cross-gender friends' conversations. *Personal Relationships, 2*(3), 237–246.

Li, N. P., Bailey, J. M., Kenrick, D. T., & Linsenmeier, J. A. (2002). The necessities and luxuries of mate preferences: Testing the tradeoffs. *Journal of Personality and Social Psychology, 82*(6), 947–955.

Li, N. P., & Kenrick, D. T. (2006). Sex similarities and differences in preferences for short-term mates: What, whether, and why. *Journal of Personality and Social Psychology, 90*(3), 468–489.

Li, N. P., Yong, J. C., Tov, W., Sng, O., Fletcher, G. J., Valentine, K. A., ... Balliet, D. (2013). Mate preferences do predict attraction and choices in the early stages of mate selection. *Journal of Personality and Social Psychology, 105*(5), 757–776.

Lipson, S. F., & Ellison, P. T. (1996). Endocrinology comparison of salivary steroid profiles in naturally occurring conception and non-conception cycles. *Human Reproduction, 11*(10), 2090–2096.

Lucas, M., & Koff, E. (2013). How conception risk affects competition and cooperation with attractive women and men. *Evolution and Human Behavior, 34*(1), 16–22.

Lucas, M. M., Koff, E., & Skeath, S. (2007). Pilot study of relationship between fertility risk and bargaining. *Psychological Reports, 101*(1), 302–310.

Maner, J. K., DeWall, C. N., & Gailliot, M. T. (2008). Selective attention to signs of success: Social dominance and early stage interpersonal perception. *Personality and Social Psychology Bulletin, 34*(4), 488–501.

Mazur, A., & Booth, A. (1998). Testosterone and dominance in men. *Behavioral and Brain Sciences, 21*(3), 353–363.

Mealey, L. (1985). The relationship between social status and biological success: A case study of the Mormon religious hierarchy. *Ethology and Sociobiology, 6*(4), 249–257.

Miller, G., Tybur, J. M., & Jordan, B. D. (2007). Ovulatory cycle effects on tip earnings by lap dancers: Economic evidence for human estrus. *Evolution and Human Behavior, 28*(6), 375–381.

Mintel Report. (2011). *Consumer attitudes toward luxury goods.* Retrieved from http://academic.mintel.com.ezp2.lib.umn.edu/sinatra/oxygen_academic/search_results/show&/display/id=543136

Montoya, R. M. (2008). I'm hot, so I'd say you're not: The influence of objective physical attractiveness on mate selection. *Personality and Social Psychology Bulletin, 34*(10), 1315–1331.

O'Connor, D. B., Archer, J., & Wu, F. C. (2004). Effects of testosterone on mood, aggression, and sexual behavior in young men: A double-blind, placebo-controlled, cross-over study. *Journal of Clinical Endocrinology and Metabolism, 89*(6), 2837–2845.

Pearson, M., & Schipper, B. C. (2013). Menstrual cycle and competitive bidding. *Games and Economic Behavior, 78*, 1–20.

Penton-Voak, I. S., & Perrett, D. I. (2000). Female preference for male faces changes cyclically: Further evidence. *Evolution and Human Behavior, 21*(1), 39–48.

Piccoli, V., Foroni, F., & Carnaghi, A. (2013). Comparing group dehumanization and intrasexual competition among normally ovulating women and hormonal contraceptive users. *Personality and Social Psychology Bulletin, 39*(12), 1600–1609.

Pillsworth, E. G., & Haselton, M. G. (2006a). Women's sexual strategies: The evolution of long-term bonds and extrapair sex. *Annual Review of Sex Research, 17*(1), 59–100.

Pillsworth, E. G., & Haselton, M. G. (2006b). Male sexual attractiveness predicts differential ovulatory shifts in female extra-pair attraction and male mate retention. *Evolution and Human Behavior, 27*(4), 247–258.

Prendergast, G., & Wong, C. (2003). Parental influence on the purchase of luxury brands of infant apparel: An exploratory study in Hong Kong. *Journal of Consumer Marketing, 20*(2), 157–169.

Puts, D. A. (2005). Mating context and menstrual phase affect women's preferences for male voice pitch. *Evolution and Human Behavior, 26*(5), 388–397.

Puts, D. A. (2006). Cyclic variation in women's preferences for masculine traits. *Human Nature, 17*(1), 114–127.

Richins, M. L. (1994a). Special possessions and the expression of material values. *Journal of Consumer Research, 21*(3), 522–533.

Richins, M. L. (1994b). Valuing things: The public and private meanings of possessions. *Journal of Consumer Research, 21*(3), 504–521.

Richins, M. L., & Dawson, S. (1992). A consumer values orientation for materialism and its measurement: Scale development and validation. *Journal of Consumer Research, 19*(3), 303–316.

Rindfleisch, A., Burroughs, J. E., & Denton, F. (1997). Family structure, materialism, and compulsive consumption. *Journal of Consumer Research, 23*(4), 312–325.

Roberts, S. C., Klapilová, K., Little, A. C., Burriss, R. P., Jones, B. C., DeBruine, L. M., . . . Havlicek, J. (2012). Relationship satisfaction and outcome in women who meet their partner while using oral contraception. *Proceedings of the Royal Society B, 279*(1732), 1430–1436.

Roney, J. R., & Simmons, Z. L. (2012). Men smelling women: Null effects of exposure to ovulatory sweat on men's testosterone. *Evolutionary Psychology, 10*(4), 703–713.

Saad, G., & Stenstrom, E. (2012). Calories, beauty, and ovulation: The effects of the menstrual cycle on food and appearance-related consumption. *Journal of Consumer Psychology, 22*(1), 102–113.

Sheldon, M. S., Cooper, M. L., Geary, D. C., Hoard, M., & DeSoto, M. C. (2006). Fertility cycle patterns in motives for sexual behavior. *Personality and Social Psychology Bulletin, 32*(12), 1659–1673.

Silverman, S. M. (2008, December 24). *Paris Hilton picks up a hot pink Bentley.* Retrieved from http://www.people.com/people/article/0,,20248920,00.html

Small, D. A., & Verrochi, N. M. (2009). The face of need: Facial emotion expression on charity advertisements. *Journal of Marketing Research, 46*(6), 777–787.

Stuhlmacher, A. F., & Walters, A. E. (1999). Gender differences in negotiation outcome: A meta-analysis. *Personnel Psychology, 52*(3), 653–677.

Sundie, J. M., Kenrick, D. T., Griskevicius, V., Tybur, J. M., Vohs, K. D., & Beal, D. J. (2011). Peacocks, Porsches, and Thorstein Veblen: Conspicuous consumption as a sexual signaling system. *Journal of Personality and Social Psychology, 100*(4), 664–680.

Symons, D. (1979). *The evolution of human sexuality.* New York: Oxford University Press.

Tatzel, M. (2002). "Money worlds" and well-being: An integration of money dispositions, materialism, and price-related behavior. *Journal of Economic Psychology, 23*(1), 103–126.

Thornhill, R., Chapman, J. F., & Gangestad, S. W. (2013). Women's preferences for men's scents associated with testosterone and cortisol levels: Patterns across the ovulatory cycle. *Evolution and Human Behavior, 34*(3), 216–221.

Thornhill, R., & Gangestad, S. W. (2008). *The evolutionary biology of human female sexuality.* New York: Oxford University Press.

Trivers, R. L. (1972). Parental investment and sexual selection. In B. G. Campbell (Ed.), *Sexual selection and the descent of man: 1871–1971* (pp. 136–179). Chicago, IL: Aldine.

Turke, P. W., & Betzig, L. L. (1985). Those who can do: Wealth, status, and reproductive success on Ifaluk. *Ethology and Sociobiology, 6*(2), 79–87.

van Straaten, I., Engels, R. C. M. E., Finkenauer, C., & Holland, R. W. (2009). Meeting your match: How attractiveness similarity affects approach behavior in mixed-sex dyads. *Personality and Social Psychology Bulletin, 35*(6), 685–697.

Venners, S. A., Liu, X., Perry, M. J., Korrick, S. A., Li, Z., Yang, F., & Wang, X. (2006). Urinary estrogen and progesterone metabolite concentrations in menstrual cycles of fertile women with non-conception, early pregnancy loss or clinical pregnancy. *Human Reproduction, 21*(9), 2272–2280.

Walker, M. L., Wilson, M. E., & Gordon, T. P. (1983). Female rhesus monkey aggression during the menstrual cycle. *Animal Behaviour, 31*(4), 1047–1054.

Wallen, K. (2000). Risky business: Social context and hormonal modulation of primate sexual desire. In K. Wallen & J. E. Schneider (Eds.), *Reproduction in context* (pp. 289–323). Cambridge, MA: MIT Press.

Wallen, K., & Tannenbaum, P. L. (1997). Hormonal modulation of sexual behavior and affiliation in rhesus monkeys. *Annals of the New York Academy of Sciences, 807*(1), 185–202.

Walters, A. E., Stuhlmacher, A. F., & Meyer, L. L. (1998). Gender and negotiator competitiveness: A meta-analysis. *Organizational Behavior and Human Decision Processes, 76*(1), 1–29.

Wang, Y., & Griskevicius, V. (2014). Conspicuous consumption, relationships, and rivals: Women's luxury products as signals to other women. *Journal of Consumer Research, 40*(5), 834–854.

Watson, J. J. (2003). The relationship of materialism to spending tendencies, saving, and debt. *Journal of Economic Psychology, 24*(6), 723–739.

Wilcox, A. J., Weinberg, C. R., & Baird, D. D. (1995). Timing of sexual intercourse in relation to ovulation: Effects on the probability of conception, survival of pregnancy, and sex of the baby. *New England Journal of Medicine, 333*, 1517–1521.

Wong, N. Y. (1997). Suppose you own the world and no one knows? Conspicuous consumption, materialism, and self. *Advances in Consumer Research, 24*(1), 197–203.

Wong, N. Y., & Ahuvia, A. C. (1998). Personal taste and family face: Luxury consumption in Confucian and Western societies. *Psychology and Marketing, 15*(5), 423–441.

Health and Aging

Social Aggression, Sleep, and Well-Being among Sidama Women of Rural Southwestern Ethiopia

Alissa A. Miller *and* Stacey L. Rucas

Abstract

Many researchers have studied how social competition and aggression affect health and well-being. However, few have made significant theoretical contributions to the understanding of how competition and aggression specific to women's same-sex social networks may alter their health and well-being. Indeed, several lines of research indicate that positive interpersonal relationships between women are correlated to improved health, and, as a corollary, stressful and competitive interpersonal relationships result in significant health costs. Using evolutionary ecological theory and supporting data from Sidama pastoralist women in rural southwestern Ethiopia, this essay proposes that sleep quality and trade-offs between time spent sleeping for more waking time may be one of the pathways through which women's health is affected by competition and aggression with other women. Sleep is gained or lost due to ruminations and investments over immediate social situations with other women, and this in turn can affect women's health and well-being.

Key Words: aggression, Sidama, Ethiopia, competition, women's health, sleep, evolutional ecological theory, pastoralist

Introduction

"Make sure you never, never argue at night. You just lose a good night's sleep, and you can't settle anything until morning anyway."

—*Rose Kennedy*

"Never go to bed mad. Stay up and fight."

—*Phyllis Diller*

The majority of essays in this volume lay bare the many ways and reasons that women compete with one another throughout their lives. By contrast, we explore the effect that female–female competition exhibits upon health and well-being via intermediary pathways and illuminate how different types of social resources exhibit independent effects on inclusive fitness. In particular, we focus on how sleep operates as a major pathway through which

loss of social capital due to circumstances such as intrasexual conflict, friendship deficits, co-wife competitions, and other negative social behaviors that are experienced during waking time compromise the immune system and psychological well-being through their negative effects on sleep quality via increased insomnia. We examine and connect promising literature among diverse fields along with supporting data collected from interviews among pastoralist Sidama women of southwestern Ethiopia for insights into these tantalizing associations. An evolutionary ecological perspective is employed to better predict and explain the seemingly disparate links between women's same-sex social aggression, nightly sleep acquisition, and general health and well-being.

Several evolutionary ecologists have documented competition and aggression between women cross-culturally and across the life course in the life histories of women (Low, this volume). Evolutionary theory presupposes that aggressive behavioral strategies specific to women's same-sex interpersonal relationships are the result of evolved sex differences in mate preferences due to same-sex competition for access to quality mates driven mainly via intrasexual selection (Fisher & Cox, 2009; Fisher & Moule, 2013; Fisher, Tran, & Voracek, 2008). This competition for mates is due to the fact that the reproductive success of women is limited by access to the variable quantity and quality of resources provided by their ecologies (Kaplan, 1996; Kaplan & Lancaster, 2003). Indeed, in a recent line of cross-cultural research, Rucas and colleagues (2012) demonstrated that while the topics of women's social disputes are widely varied among Tsimane women, they tend to revolve around resources central to the evolutionary goals of production and reproduction, such as access to food and mates. The authors further discovered that the predominance of specific resource-related social disputes shifts across the life course, reflecting life history timing concerns about quantity and quality of mates and trade-offs between current versus future reproduction. For example, life history theory proposes that time and energy spent on one life activity cannot be spent on another. In this way, focusing on quantity of children forces a trade-off in quality of children. Also, in order to optimize overall lifetime fertility, women's time and energy is better spent on achieving certain goals at specific points in the life course. For example, the Tsimane research team discovered that women compete more via social aggression and quarreling for mate acquisition when they are younger and mate retention when they are older, a life history pattern that produces more and better offspring. Similar findings have also been reported in other cross-cultural literature about competition between co-wives (Jankowiak, Sudakov, & Wilreker, 2005). A large ethnographic survey, for instance, found an absence of co-wife relationship harmony outside of pragmatic cooperation. In other words, the interaction of co-wives across societies where they exist is most commonly frictional or dissonant and merely cooperative in matters requiring domestic practicality, and even then, helpfulness is not always assured. Also, the degree of competition among these women varies greatly across age, rank, and individual household socioeconomics. Their manifestations of competition primarily arise from instances of jealousy of preferential treatment, access to parental investment in offspring, or access

to other household capital resources (Borgerhoff-Mulder, 1992; Jankowiak et al., 2005; Madhavan, 2002). Taken together, these findings indicate that conflicts among women are not merely caused by competition over men but in fact encompass a variety of other topics, and these disputes remain central to the interpersonal relations between women across the life course.

Throughout the broad span of human evolution, women's competitive strategies have ultimately been shaped by inclusive fitness goals, or the innate drive to increase genetic success at the level of the individual. Ecological factors that prompt life history strategies by signaling cues about the differential need for investment into the timing and pace of reproduction (see, e.g., Quinlan, 2007) also motivate competitiveness between women to secure fitness opportunities. For example, environments with many women competing for the best mates trigger higher levels of relational aggression in women (Rharbite, 2012), and resource-poor environments drive up criminal physical aggression among women in addition to contributing to greater economic dependence upon men (Campbell, Muncer, & Bibel, 1998). Such behavior is also well documented among girls, where competition for resource-rich mates has been cited as a strong motive for physical aggression (Campbell, 1995).

While conflict driven by access to mates and resources may be at the heart of female–female competition across the life course, other trends also speak to the methods of women's aggression. Due to the potential risks associated with physical aggression on the health of current and future children, women tend to avoid physically fighting with each other (Campbell, 2004). Research among Aka hunter-gatherers, for instance, has shown a male bias favoring physical aggression and a female bias toward indirect social aggression (Hess, Helfrecht, Hagen, Sell, & Hewlett, 2010). Similar sex differences in aggression have been observed among college students (Hess & Hagen, 2006b). To avoid reproductive costs from risks posed by physical aggression, women specialize in using social intelligence and manipulation to impose interpersonal damages on others whereby women's strategies overall tend to favor social, relational, and indirect forms of social aggression via quarreling, gossiping, and reputational damages (Campbell, 2004; Hess & Hagen, 2006a; Rucas et al., 2006). In fact, thematic content analysis of qualitative data from interviews with women in college has shown the most common forms of relational aggression occur within small groups by order of name-calling, gossiping, criticism, ridicule, "the silent treatment," and ostracism (Miller-Ott & Kelly, 2013). Outside of the documented interpersonal damages suffered by perceived rivals and competitors ensuing from aggression by women, other lines of evidence suppose that these forms of social aggression and conflict also correlate with mild to severe detriments in health and well-being.

Social Relationships, Women's Same-Sex Aggression, and Well-Being

"I love the friendships that you see in Nancy Meyers' movies, but for me, that kind of friendship is elusive. I feel like a lot of the female relationships I see on TV or in movies are in some way free of the kind of jealousy and anxiety and posturing that has been such a huge part of my female friendships, which I hope lessens a little bit with age."

—Lena Dunham

The extent to which social relationships influence well-being spans multiple interrelated physiological, behavioral, and psychosocial domains in both positive and negative directions. Generally, positive social relationships improve well-being, while negative social relations pose health costs. As a corollary to this pattern, and in the broadest sense, positive and plentiful peer relations have been shown to extend longevity in both men and women, even after controlling for other socioeconomic and health factors that are known to influence mortality risk (Brummett et al., 2001; House, Landis, & Umberson, 1988). General health ratings also correlate to more positive peer relations beginning in childhood (Molcho, Nic Gabhainn, & Kelleher, 2007). These findings are in line with others that show how poor social support in interpersonal relationships correlates negatively with multiple markers of underlying morbidity (see Uchino, 2006, for review), including reducing allostatic loads, or the wear and tear on the body due to constant and repeated stressors (Seeman, Singer, Ryff, Love, & Levy-Storms, 2002). Researchers have similarly discovered that having more diverse social ties minimizes susceptibility to common colds (Cohen, Doyle, Skoner, Rabin, & Gwaltney, 1997). Improvements in psychological wellness are also correlated to positive social interactions with others, higher-status group affiliations, and better friendships. Meanwhile, negative social interactions, poor peer affiliations, and low friendship quality result in poor wellness outcomes (La Greca & Harrison, 2005; Preddy & Fite, 2012; Schuster, Kessler, & Aseltine, 1990). Similarly, costs of poor personal relationships from debilitating feelings of social isolation, loneliness, and relational victimization have harmful psychological effects that instigate deterioration in other aspects of physiological health and recovery and more experiences of somatic complaints (Cacioppo & Hawkley, 2003; Nixon, Linkie, Coleman, & Fitch, 2011). While both plainly have consequences, psychological well-being appears to react more strongly to perceptions of negative rather than positive peer interactions (Pagel, Erdly, & Becker, 1987; Schuster et al., 1990). Unfortunately, while many studies have discovered a relationship between social capital and health and well-being for both men and women, most have focused on marital relationships, the sizes and quality of friendships, or social networks in general, making outcomes relevant to same-sex interpersonal relationships between women less documented.

Women appear to experience positive and negative peer relations differently than men, and thus the effects of social capital on health and well-being may be sex-specific. For example, conflicts and stress with one's parents, lovers, and friends are more detrimental for women than they are for men (Darling, McWey, Howard, & Olmstead, 2007). Among low-income women, disputes with family and friends are differentially associated with greater anxiety, depression, hostility, somatization, and an overall greater severity of adverse psychological symptoms (Bassuk, Perloff, Mickelson, & Bisseil, 2002). On the flip side, support from friends and family buffers the repercussions on well-being resulting from social conflict more strongly for women (Walen & Lachman, 2000). As well, although marital strains are harmful to both men and women, they are costlier for women, who tend to experience greater psychological detriments due to marital discord than men (Bolger, DeLongis, Kessler, & Schilling, 1989; Gove, Hughes, & Style, 1983).

When considering interpersonal conflict as a major source of daily stress, multiple lines of evidence by Almeida and colleagues (2002) suggest sex differences in how well-being is impacted on by social aggression. For both men and women reporting in a daily diary, interpersonal stressors and concerns about events being experienced by others in their social networks were key types of daily stress that correlated positively to psychological and physiological complaints (Almeida, 2005).

Women, however, were more stressed by the events being experienced by others in their social networks than men, indicating that women are comparatively more concerned about general social stressors involving people (Almeida, Wethington, & Kessler, 2002). Moreover, while over the course of several daily interviews men and women listed interpersonal arguments and tensions as the most commonly experienced type of daily stress (Almeida et al., 2002), women by comparison were more disturbed by interpersonal arguments (Almeida & Kessler, 1998). The corollary outcomes on health and well-being from social stress were also greater for women, as outcomes from interpersonal conflict on daily mood and social network stressors on physical health are stronger in women (Almeida et al., 2002).

Observing social conflict among others also results in psychological and physical markers of distress. Women who witnessed simulated videotaped disputes among couples exhibited stronger reactions than men of anger in the scenarios that involved unresolved disputes, and they reported more happiness than men in the simulated scenarios in which the couples resolved their conflict (El-Sheikh, Buckhalt, & Reiter, 2000). In a related experiment, women who watched their close friends being harassed while performing math tasks reported feelings of anger, annoyance, and irritation, which were some of the same feelings felt by those performing the task (Lavoie, Miller, Conway, & Fleet, 2001). In other words, women shared the same emotional reaction to viewing harassment as those who were actually being harassed.

Similarly, being the target of relational aggression, a hallmark of women's social aggression beginning in childhood, can result in peer rejection, feelings of loneliness, depression, and social isolation (Crick & Grotpeter, 1995). By way of gossip and rumors, these outcomes incrementally harm well-being, especially because females appear to be more sensitive to, and devastated by, the effects of indirect aggression than are males (Galen & Underwood, 1997). Indeed, one study by McAndrew, Bell, and Garcia (2007) found that gossip about damaging information related to rivals is especially likely to be passed on by both men and women and that both sexes prefer same-sex gossip over opposite-sex gossip. The authors further found that women prefer to share gossip more widely than men, including with both their lovers and their friends (McAndrew et al., 2007). Unlike men, women seem to share gossip with friends regardless of the quality of their friendships (Watson, 2012), which further indicates that they share gossip more widely than men.

The impacts of social aggression via gossip have been reportedly experienced as early as young adolescence. While gossip can also be positive and can therefore offer health, well-being, and prosocial benefits (Feinberg, Willer, Stellar, & Keltner, 2012; Thomas & Rozell, 2007), much of gossip is negative in content and used for Machiavellian purposes (e.g., to manipulate social situations in one's favor). Paquette and Underwood (1999) found that, among juveniles, being the victim of gossip was the most commonly experienced form of social aggression. It was further discovered that most aggressors were the same sex and that girls were more negatively affected by the social aggression than boys. Being the victims of gossip for girls is tied to more domains of negative self-concepts such as appearance, athletic abilities, friendship qualities, romantic appeal, and overall self-worth, and girls are also more able to recall specific instances of attacks from rivals, confirming that social aggression is a larger source of worry for girls than for boys (Paquette & Underwood, 1999). When used with manipulative mal-intent, gossip can operate as a form of bullying, such as when one uses information about another to harm the person's reputation or relationships with others. This results in damage to psychological and physical well-being and social status for women (see Crothers, Lipinski, & Minutolo, 2009, for review). Bullying via gossip impairs health and well-being in multiple ways for young girls by damaging mental health, and victims report increased somatic complaints, which further parallels increased school absences and poorer academic performances (see review in Raskauskas & Stoltz, 2004). Primary school-aged victims of this form of social aggression report higher incidences of stomachaches, headaches, and depression (Williams, Chambers, Logan, & Robinson, 1996). Additional investigations have discovered that bullying via gossip also impairs sleep in primary school-aged children, including complaints of not sleeping well, bedwetting, and insomnia (Abdirahman, Bah, Shrestha, & Jacobsen, 2012; Williams et al., 1996). Such injuries are especially costly since sleep is a core component of health that regulates nearly all biological systems and behavioral aspects of optimal functioning for humans.

When women are motivated by aggression and competition, their gossip is intentionally and strategically aimed at imposing costs onto perceived competitors in order to improve one's relative access to mates and resources. Women not only have more competitive interactions over appearing physically attractive than men (Cashdan, 1998), but physical appearance gossip is more common by women than men (Watson, 2012), which highlights the importance of physical attractiveness in female competition. Additionally, women are known to use relational aggression to derogate other physically attractive women (Vaillancourt & Sharma, 2011). In some of these instances, relational aggression toward attractive female peers may be motivated by jealousy over physical appearance (Arnocky, Sunderani, Miller, & Vaillancourt, 2012).

Instances of female competition driven by appearance, however, pose a multitude of costs to well-being. In fact, Hill and Durante (2011) found competitive inclinations to secure mates increase women's willingness to enhance cultural-specific perceptions of attractiveness by taking diet pills and tanning. When primed with mating goals, these women underestimate the health costs associated with their risky behaviors. Furthermore, female competition is the main causal force in modern trends of extreme dieting, such as anorexia and bulimia (Faer, Hendriks, Abed, & Figueredo, 2005), starting in adolescence (Salmon, Crawford, & Walters, 2008). Moreover, while no studies provide evidence of the specific effects of stress from female competition on adolescent well-being (Salmon et al., 2008), stress is known to have detrimental effects on health and well-being across the lifespan.

It is likely that multiple proximate pathways, or closely related causes, are operating to produce the wide array of trends and outcomes connecting social capital to women's health and well-being. We propose that one key issue that has been vastly overlooked is sleep or, more accurately, interrupted or loss of sleep. In fact, we contend that sleep may be one of the most important and unexplored avenues for connecting women's same-sex relationships to health through the lens of evolutionary theory. Of the evidence that does exist about how sleep is influenced by other types and sources of interpersonal conflict, sleep loss has been shown to ensue as both a cause and consequence of heightened social aggression (Gunn, Troxel, Hall, & Buysse, 2013; Hasler & Troxel, 2010; Rogojanski, Carney, & Monson, 2013), suggesting that sleep has circular associations with interpersonal relationship functioning. In effect, sleeping well is central to psychological and physical well-being, and it fluctuates in response to socioecological challenges such as social aggression, friendships, and social support.

Sleep

"What probing deep has ever solved the mystery of sleep?"
—Thomas Bailey Aldrich

Sleeping occupies nearly one-third of the time and energy budget of humans across the life course. Recent theoretical and empirical research contributions about the evolutionary ecology of human sleep have grown, albeit modestly (McKenna, Ball, & Gettler, 2007; McNamara, 2004; McNamara, Dowdall, & Auerbach, 2002; Worthman, 2008; Worthman & Brown, 2007; Worthman & Melby, 2002). Further, while some have shown that human sleeping behaviors are related to components of our life history strategies, such as familial circumstances that alter REM sleep and produce later alterations in reproductive behaviors, or lack of sleep that increases risk-taking propensities (McNamara et al., 2002; Miller & Rucas, 2012; Rucas & Miller, 2013a, 2013b), or parenting and co-sleeping behaviors (Gettler, McKenna, McDade, Agustin, & Kuzawa, 2012; Haig, 2014), overall little research exists about human sleep in evolutionary ecological perspectives. Accordingly, the relationships between women's competition, sleep loss, and well-being have not yet been explored together in this perspective. Sleep quantity and quality among women, however, is known to be influenced by many evolutionarily significant life history themes such as nighttime caregiving to children (Burgard, 2011), attachment styles (Troxel, Cyranowski, Hall, Frank, & Buysse, 2007), reproductive status (Lee, Baker, Newton, & Ancoli-Israel, 2008), pregnancy (Chang, Pien, Duntley, & Macones, 2010), and marital stability (Rauer, Kelly, Buckhalt, & El-Sheikh, 2010).

"That we are not much sicker and much madder than we are is due exclusively to that most blessed and blessing of all natural graces, sleep."
—Aldous Huxley

Achieving and maintaining adequate sleep is essential to optimal health and well-being in humans. The states of "awake" and "asleep" are two mutually exclusive activities in which the individual is either engaged in catabolic (awake) or anabolic (asleep) activities. Specifically, sleep serves to repair, rejuvenate, and grow bodily systems, organs, and tissues that are broken down for energy during daily wakeful activities of production and reproduction (Rodéhn, 1999; Shneerson, 2005). While many hypotheses exist about the functions of sleep, the homeostatic drive to maintain and optimize biological and neurological systems appears to remain an overarching principle central to the purpose of sleep (Benington, 2000). Sleeplessness as a result of sleeping too little or from poor—quality sleep, therefore, poses significant behavioral and physiological costs (Banks & Dinges, 2007) including impaired immunological functioning (Bryant, Trinder, & Curtis, 2004; Opp, 2009), deregulated inflammatory responses (Frey, Fleshner, & Wright, 2007), delayed recovery from illness (Haack & Mullington, 2005), proliferation of somatic complaints (Haack & Mullington, 2005; Kahn-Greene, Killgore, Kamimori, Balkin, & Killgore, 2007), and heightened depression and anxiety (Kahn-Greene et al., 2007). These are coincidentally some of the *same* costs ensuing from negative social interactions and social aggression, manifestations that similarly detract from health via a multitude of direct and indirect pathways.

Other lines of evidence highlight the critical role of maintaining adequate sleep in relation to numerous aspects of daily living that are also negatively affected by social conflict. These include academic performance (Kelly, Kelly, & Clanton, 2001), job satisfaction (Scott & Judge, 2006), and overall well-being and psychological mood (Totterdell, Reynolds, Parkinson, & Briner, 1994). In other words, social interactions affect mood and promote compulsive mental ruminating about interpersonal relationships that in turn disrupts sleep and ultimately injures health and well-being.

"Life is something that happens when you can't get to sleep."
—*Fran Lebowitz*

Using comparative insight derived from what is known about human sleep ecologies in evolutionary, historical, and cross-cultural perspectives (Worthman & Melby, 2002), Worthman (2008) proposed the sources of sleep loss can be understood in behavioral, ecological, psychological, and endogamous domains. Routes of sleep loss within these domains occur in response to time and energy budget demands and other cognitive-emotional or physiological arousals. In other words, sleep patterns, sleep–wake ratios (total sleep time), and sleep architecture are plastic, shifting according to individual circumstances and signals about local ecological and sociocultural contexts. While the relationship between individual differences and sleep parameters is well documented, comparatively less is known about the social contexts of sleep, although research interests are growing.

Troxel (2010), for instance, notes the need for understanding the influence of interpersonal relationships on sleeping behaviors and offers a conceptual model of how sleep mediates the pathway between these social relationships and health and well-being. Central to her argument about women is their keen awareness of social environments, which, in some instances, give rise to sleep loss, possibly via sensitivities to relational stressors stemming from recurring challenges faced by women throughout evolutionary history. Essentially, women must closely monitor other women who are perceived as rivals and competitors since they may pose fitness threats in shared reproductive ecologies. That is to say that women dip from the same pool of resources as their friends and enemies, except that where the former will cooperate and share, the latter will compete, obstruct, and oppose women's access to everything from mates to social status. Moreover, throughout the evolutionary trajectory of humans, it makes logical sense that female–female competition, often taking the form of social relational aggression, would similarly impact on sleep such that sleep loss ensuing from current conflicts with other women may be adaptive, as it may allow for more waking time to solve social challenges that are ultimately related to successful production and reproduction via accumulation and execution of various forms of social capital.

"In its early stages, insomnia is almost an oasis in which those who have to think or suffer darkly take refuge."
—*Sidonie-Gabrielle Colette*

Insomnia is regarded as the most commonly experienced sleep disorder by adults, marked by acute or chronic problems associated with falling and staying asleep. Stress from work, school, family, and health status are exceptionally well known to cause insomnia. As well, the sleep loss experienced from stressful events during the day, as measured by polysomnography, a diagnostic tool that measures nightly biophysiological changes, indicate a rapid flexible response of sleep to immediate ecological cues (Bastien, Vallieres, & Morin, 2004; Bernert, Merrill, Braithwaite, Van Orden, & Joiner, 2007; Drake, Richardson, Roehrs, Scofield, & Roth, 2004). In other words, what happens to someone during the day can immediately impact his or her sleep, causing him or her to take longer to fall asleep or experience the inability to fall back asleep upon waking in the middle of the night, typically due to rumination of the previous day's or next day's anticipated social events. In another example, stresses specific to the severity of interpersonal conflict or disagreement experienced in a day are correlated to negative emotions, which further result in subsequent increases in self-reported sleep disturbances the same night (Brissette & Cohen, 2002). Yet women more commonly than men experience feelings and severity of overall daily stress as a cause of sleep loss (Lund, Reider, Whiting, & Prichard, 2010), and cross-cultural meta-analysis confirms insomnia to be more prevalent among women than men (Zhang & Wing, 2006).

Maume (2013) has recently shown that social ties are more important than other biological factors in explaining some aspects of total sleep time during adolescence. Additionally, for both girls and boys, increases in positive peer relations tend to lengthen sleep duration. Adolescent girls, however, report more overall sleep disruptions than boys, including nighttime wakings; nighttime worrying about friends, family, and home; and not being able to fall back to sleep. As a corollary, longer sleep time averages predict fewer frequencies of common illness during adolescence (Orzech, Acebo, Seifer, Barker, & Carskadon, 2013), and because females have more insomnia, the health costs of sleeplessness are more expensive for them. These costs are not limited to adolescence, however, since adult women who perceive poor social relationships have more resultant sleep complaints (Ravan, Bengtsson, Lissner, Lapidus, & Bjorkelund, 2010). However, as mentioned before, social support buffers the impact of interpersonal aggression on sleep loss more for women than men (Takaki et al., 2010).

Certain aspects of sleeplessness are clearly functional for problem-solving. For instance, in a unique line of research, Wicklow and Espie (2000) asked participants (66.7% female) to voice-record their spontaneous thoughts during times of sleeplessness, known as sleep onset insomnia. Principal components analysis specifically indicated that active problem-solving, including rehearsing and planning, was the most prominent factor influencing sleep loss in the sample and was further predictive of longer actigraphy-measured sleep onset insomnia in minutes. Other delays in sleep onset and overall measures of disturbed sleep also parallel these findings, indicating that the presleep period is often full of both thoughts and imagery that allow for both rumination on past events and time to worry about present and future events related to psychosocial stressors and interpersonal transgressions (Harvey, 2000; Stoia-Caraballo et al., 2008;

Zoccola, Dickerson, & Lam, 2009). In fact, suppressing presleep arousal cognition results in poorer overall subjective sleep for both good sleepers and insomnia sufferers than for those individuals who do not suppress (Harvey, 2003). Overall, however, insomnia sufferers experience longer bouts of presleep cognitive arousal, with increased presleep heart rates and more unpleasant cognitive content (Nelson & Harvey, 2003a, 2003b).

Sleep is so essential to optimal health and well-being that time allocated for sleep should not be traded off for more waking time unless local socioecological circumstances proximally signal the need for more waking time to resolve challenges related to immediate fitness goals and outcomes. Sleep quantity and quality throughout the evolutionary trajectory would have been a reflection of local environmental circumstances, such that impaired sleep represented environments requiring more waking time for solving challenges and uncertainties related to vigilance, production, and reproduction. For example, in a series of papers, Miller and Rucas (2012), Rucas and Miller (2013a), and Rucas and Miller (2013b) have shown that sleep loss resulting from environmental unpredictability is correlated to alterations in behavioral strategies and psychology of individuals that are more geared toward immediate survival and to secure immediate fertility opportunities. Similarly, evolutionary ecological theory predicts that increased social stress arising from aggression between women is a cue of local levels of female–female competition for resources. During such bouts more waking time is required to invest in the resolution of daytime problems with other women that may otherwise hinder or pose threats to other productive and reproductive time and energy investments, even at the risk of immediate health and well-being which results from the sleep loss.

To test whether women's social relationships with other women affect their health and well-being by altering their sleep patterns, we needed a natural fertility cultural group, absent the pressures unique to modern ecologies, and more similar to those of our evolutionary past. Rural highland Sidama women in Ethiopia were chosen to test this research question since their social ecology lacks modern sleep medicines and household electronic technologies that may interfere with sleep, they exhibit high levels of natural fertility, and they have occasional polygyny, providing situations of multihouse heads, which was common in cross-cultural small-scale societies of the past.

Interpersonal Relationships, Sleep, and Health Outcomes: A Case Study from Pastoralist Sidama Women in Rural Southwestern Ethiopia

"Anga itoommana anga it."
(My hands have received what my hands have given.)

—*Sidama women's proverb*

The Sidama are one of the largest ethnic groups in Ethiopia and mostly live in the southwestern region of the country. Some Sidama reside in an urban center in the Southern Nations, Nationalities, and People's Region, while others reside in rural villages across highly variable lowland and highland environments. Hawule, a *kebele*, or neighborhood administrative political unit, is an approximate 30-minute walk from the nearest town and capital of Arbegona, Yaye, in the highlands of southwestern Ethiopia. The fieldsite for the study was established, and its location was contained between two streams in a large valley with some elevations reaching over 8,600 feet. Approximately 50 individual families reside in Hawule, a majority of whom report that they practice monogamous marriage unions. This finding is interesting, as Sidama have traditionally practiced both monogamous and polygynous forms of marriage (Hamer, 1987). Recent surveys of rural Sidama villages document current polygynous marriage rates somewhere between 11.9% and 15.3% (Hailu & Regassa, 2007; Regassa & Stoecker, 2011), significantly lower rates than practiced in past generations.

Interviews were conducted with women living in Hawule to provide evidence about women's sleep, health, and social environments. The questions inquired about women's life histories, sleep environments, sleep disorder symptom complaints, sleep quality, psychological well-being, overall health, and social relationships with other women. Some variables were gathered from questions in preexisting instruments, including the Pittsburgh Sleep Quality Index and the Harvard Sleep Disorder Screening Survey.

As seen and recorded among many rural Sidama agropastoralist groups (Hailu & Regassa, 2008; Hamer, 1987), there is a clear sexual division of labor between men and women in Hawule. Women provide the bulk of parental care and manage many aspects of the household, including food preparation and cleaning. Interview data also suggest that women sleep less than men in Hawule due to working more hours on average than men, and a recent study indicates that this pattern is also the case for other rural Sidama populations, describing that women work between 16 and 18 hours per day (Hailu & Regassa, 2008). Investigations with Hawule women about daily time budget allocation reveal they sleep on average fewer hours per night than men because of their extra domestic labor and child-care duties. Women additionally allocate part of their daily time budget to caring for and looking after household cattle and other animals.

Outside of household routine daily work, it is common to see Hawule women either working or socializing together in small groups. Friendship bonds among younger Sidama women appear to be maintained, at least partially, by close physical contact and tactile interaction. While walking along paths in rural areas or on busy streets in the urban center, it is common to see two or three young, unmarried women with their arms linked together or holding hands. When sitting or standing in casual daytime discussion, often one friend will have her arm loosely rested around the top of her friend's shoulders.

More detailed results from interviews showed that Sidama women's same-sex social networks are made up of kin, nonkin, friends, and enemies. Hawule women in this study report a breadth of between one and ten best friends, with an average of 3.68. Best friends are reportedly a mixture of both kin and nonkin. Most women (*n* = 53, or 88.33% of the sample) have no enemies, but those who had enemies had either 1 (*n* = 4) or 2 (*n* = 3) enemies. The number of enemies a woman reported having was positively correlated to the number of women she was currently arguing with (*r* = .857). In times of social conflict with other women, Hawule women nearly universally report that they argue and gossip with one another primarily concerning the production and reproduction issues relating to cattle, which as pastoralists are their most valuable material resources, and children (whether their own biological children or their younger siblings). And while the sources of gossip may also relate to issues about cattle and children, the behavior of *heme*, or gossip (the more literal translation is "back-biting"), is itself an additional source of disagreements between women, because they are attuned to and anxious over the concern that others are producing harmful *heme* about them behind their backs.

The interviews about women's daily lives, social relationships, nighttime activities, and sleeping behaviors elucidated cultural insight into the interpersonal relationships of Sidama women. Specifically, they revealed information about their friendships and social capital stressors, or proxies of social competition, such as enemies, jealousy, gossip, and arguing. Using this information, we tested two hypotheses:

1. Women's interpersonal relationships impact on their well-being such that women trade off sleep quality in favor of more waking time when their social environment with other women is more competitive and stressful; and

2. Women exposed to more female competitive aggression during their childhood and adolescent development will have increased insomnia complaints and poorer health and well-being outcomes in adulthood.

To understand the relationships of social competition with outcomes of sleep among Sidama women, we used independent variables relating to health and well-being and predictor variables relating to social aggression and social capital. Table 23.1 describes these variables.

Socially Rich Sidama Women Sleep Better and Feel Better

"A ruffled mind makes a restless pillow."

—*Charlotte Brontë*

Table 23.1. Independent and Predictor Variables.

	Composite Variables[a]	Yes or No Questions
Independent variables	Insomnia-related sleep quality	Do you wake up at night and have trouble falling back to sleep?
		Do you take a long time to fall asleep?
		Do you wake up early and have trouble being able to fall back to sleep?
		Do you have difficulty staying asleep?
		Do you feel irritable when you can't sleep?
	Overall health and well-being status	Do you have poor overall health?
		Do you get sick more often than other women your age?
		Do you have bodily pain?
		Do you feel sad sometimes?
		Do you feel nervous sometimes?
		Do you sometimes feel sick because other women are gossiping about you behind your back?
Predictor variables	Social aggression and stress	Are you currently arguing with other women?
		Are your girlfriends arguing with one another? Do you have enemies?
		Are other women gossiping about you behind your back?
		Do you frequently argue with other women about issues regarding kids?
	Social support capital	Do you have plenty of other women to talk to?
		Do you get plenty of help from other women?
		Do you have plenty of friends?

[a] Independent and dependent composite variables were measured using the scores from additive dummy scores from yes/no response questions.

Is it true that social richness, as measured through more and better friendships, improves sleep, mood, and health? If so, is it equally true that social stressors detract from health and well-being via sleep detriments? Nighttime provides an often quiet space to ruminate on the day's events and make plans for the future. On days in which activities have been stressful and negative, one might rehearse and practice social events in one's mind in order to craft alternative possible outcomes resulting from different choices and actions, or one might replay the day's social situations with poor outcomes in order to discover the cause of events so that similar mistakes are not made in the future. In these ways, women with richer and more positive social worlds will end up with better, more restful sleep. This will ultimately improve their health and well-being. Figure 23.1 illustrates a general linear regression model showing the negative relationship of insomnia and general health and well-being among fifty-eight Sidama women. Women reporting more insomnia complaints experienced significantly poorer health and well-being ($\beta = -.888$, $p < .001$). The intensity of experienced insomnia accounted for a generous 30.8% of the variance in Sidama women's reported general health and well-being, highlighting an important and critical link between sleep quality, health, and fitness. Women who reported having lower social capital and more social aggression slept poorly, which appears to lead to poor health.

Hypothesis 1 Outcomes: Women's Interpersonal Relationships, Sleep, and Health

Women with the most social stress and social aggression, as measured by how many arguments they are having with other women and how many enemies they report in their lives, are expected to complain more about the quality of their sleep. Likewise, women with more friends and social companions should be buffered against nighttime insomnia complaints. Figure 23.2 illustrates a general linear model regression test of Hypothesis 1 and depicts the effects of social support capital and social stress and aggression on insomnia intensity among forty-four Sidama women. Women reporting higher social support capital exhibited marginally fewer insomnia complaints ($\beta = -.507$, $p = .082$). In contrast, women reporting higher amounts of social stress and aggression exhibited significantly more insomnia complaints ($\beta = .352$, $p = .015$). Together, these results are significant and indicate that Sidama women with more friends, better-quality friendships, less social stress, and less social aggression tend to report the fewest problems sleeping and higher-quality sleeping episodes.

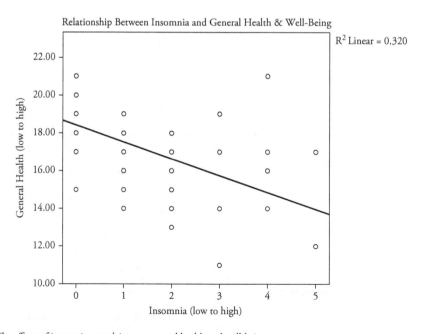

Figure 23.1 The effects of insomnia complaints on general health and well-being.

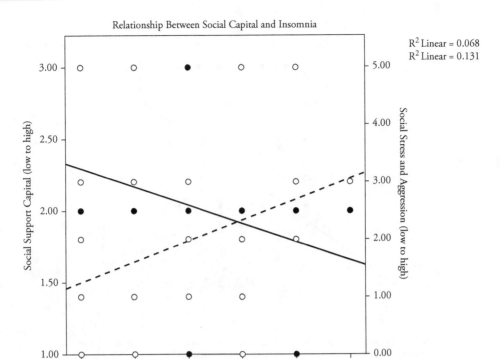

Figure 23.2 Social capital effects on insomnia outcomes.

Similar to previous results, but following through the pathway toward health, it was predicted that women experiencing more arguments with friends and more enemies should show diminished health and well-being. Likewise, women's health should be buffered by having friends and sufficient companionship. Figure 23.3 illustrates the general linear model regression test of Hypothesis 1 and depicts the positive effects of social support capital and the negative effects of social stress and aggression on general health status among forty-four Sidama women. Women reporting higher social support capital exhibited significantly higher health and well-being outcomes (β = 1.234, p = .009). Contrariwise, women reporting more social stress and aggression exhibited significantly poorer health and well-being (β = −.523, p = .021). The adjusted variance accounted for by both predictors in the social capital and health status model explains approximately 21.3% of the variance in general health among women in the sample. In effect, Sidama women with fewer friends and more social stress from other women tend to report not only more insomnia but also poorer general health via added specific health and wellness complaints.

Hypothesis 2 Outcomes: The Impacts of Polygyny and Competition among Co-Wives on the Adult Insomnia Complaints and Health Status of Their Daughters

Figure 23.4 depicts the general linear regression model of Hypothesis 2 and shows insomnia complaints among fifty-nine Sidama adult women as influenced by having a father's co-wives present during one's childhood and adolescent development. Women who had polygynously married fathers during growth and development, as measured by a "no" or "yes" dummy variable, experienced significantly more insomnia complaints in adulthood (β = .957, p = .019). The adjusted variance accounted for by the predictor variable in the polygyny and adulthood insomnia model explains approximately 7.6% of the variance in women's insomnia complaints.

Likewise, Figure 23.5 depicts the general linear regression model of Hypothesis 2 and illustrates the influence of having a father's co-wives present during one's growth and development on one's later (i.e., adult) general health and well-being status. Women reporting their father was polygynously married experienced a marginally poorer general health and well-being status in adulthood (β = −1.044, p = .102). The adjusted variance accounted

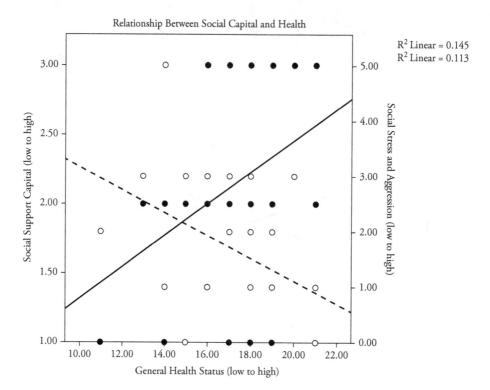

Figure 23.3 Social capital effects on general health and well-being status.

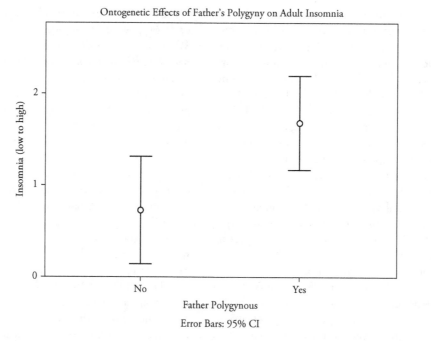

Figure 23.4 Father's marital arrangement effects on adult insomnia.

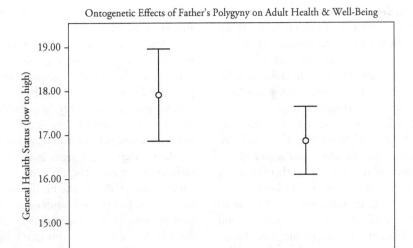

Figure 23.5 Father's marital arrangement effects on adult general health and well-being.

for by the predictor in the polygyny and general health and well-being status model explains approximately 3% of the variance in adulthood general health and well-being status among the fifty-eight Sidama women in the sample.

Traumatic Co-Wife Rivalries Injure the Sleep, Health, and Well-Being of Children

"One wife, you're happy, two and you're tired, three and they'll hate each other, four and they'll hate you."

—*Patrick Rothfuss*, The Name of the Wind

Possible sources of conflict in the household could arise from a variety of causes, but co-wife social dynamics and their ensuing effects on husbands, children, and other household members are one likely contributor to household stress specific to polygynous unions that may give rise to sleep disturbances and corollary negative health outcomes. Co-wives across cultures regularly engage in intense reproductive competition via avenues of rivalry for youth, beauty, seniority status, and access to the time and influence of their shared husband. There is often a struggle to have as many children as possible in order to claim larger portions of limited paternal resources and to increase the quality of their children through education and inheritance. This

struggle may also extend to competitions to have more male children in societies where maleness confers greater social status as adults and where the possibility of greater numbers of grandchildren is achievable via polygynously married sons. Co-wife households mirror the struggles between monogamously mated women in small-scale societies within villages but occur instead at the household level (Zeitzen, 2008). Outside of pragmatic cooperation, cross-culturally it has been claimed that no co-wife relationship is harmonious (Jankowiak et al., 2005). Co-wife competition is driven by emotional and sexual jealousies derived from the limited pool of paternal time and energy (Borgerhoff-Mulder, 1992; Madhavan, 2002). Evidence confirms that, indeed, the reproductive success of one wife can negatively impact on the total fertility of another, likely through the diminished resource pool that one wife ends up with relative to another (Anderton & Emigh, 1989). This competition is so intense that some cultures have invented words for the practice. For example, in Kenya, the Gusii have a word that means "hatred between co-wives," and the Luo have one that translates co-wife to "my partner in jealousy" (Burbank, 1994). Occasionally children are direct victims of this competition via severe forms of mistreatment by their mother's rival co-wives (Zeitzen, 2008). While aggression among co-wives may not always be so direct or deliberate toward other wives' children, the exposure to strained situations still poses a substantial risk factor for childhood illness susceptibility (Strassmann, 1997). Such traumatic family circumstance can lead to risky or chronically high cortisol levels in children, ultimately suppressing immune function and heightening illness vulnerability (Flinn & England, 1995). Among the Sidama, households with insecure food statuses also have an elevated risk of spousal violence (Regassa, 2012), an additional source of tremendous household stress, a finding that is true for both monogamous and polygynous unions.

Although little is known about sleep environments and the predictors of sleep quantity and quality for children of polygynous households, other studies indicate that many aspects of childhood sleep ecologies predict later adult sleep health. Further, while there is no existing literature that shows that female–female conflict arising from competition causes sleep loss, many of the sources of sleep loss during childhood that have long-term effects arise from exposure to interpersonal conflict between adults within the household. Recent research specifies that the effects of interpersonal conflict begin to disturb children's development as early as infancy. Even while sleeping, for example, heightened neural responses to angry tones of voice are easily detectable by infants (Graham, Fisher, & Pfeifer, 2013). Therefore, environmental stress arising from interpersonal conflict, at least among parents, begins to adversely alter brain function such as emotional regulation during infancy and childhood (Crockenberg, Leerkes, & Lekka, 2007).

Traumatic childhood environments marked by poor-quality parent–child relationships (Koskenvuo, Hublin, Partinen, Paunio, & Koskenvuo, 2010), poorer quality of care as a child (Sansone, Edwards, & Forbis, 2010), and adverse childhood experiences relating to exposure to abuse in the household or being the victim of abuse (Anda et al., 2006) are all predictive of lower self-reported sleep quality in adulthood. Insomnia experienced in early adulthood is associated with family conflict during childhood and adolescence (Gregory, Caspi, Moffitt, & Poulton, 2006). Some propose this relationship may be because stress responses change physiology and consequently sleep, or because of poor sleep hygiene (e.g., noise, lack of sleep ritual behaviors) resulting from a disorganized or chaotic family structure and sleeping environment (Gregory et al., 2006). Such a poor socioecological environment has long-lasting impacts on sleep patterns that persist into adulthood (Dregan & Armstrong, 2010) and carry with

them the corollary and potential for cumulative detriments to health and well-being.

While the interviews involve only a small number of women, the aforementioned empirical evidence generally supports a proposition that the extra potential for social conflict and social stress within Sidama polygynous family households could have long-lasting impacts on sleep quality and health status of children. Sidama women report that co-wives regularly compete and argue most often over their children and cattle. The effect sizes are predictably small, however, due to the likelihood of confounding factors. For example, among the Sidama, as is true in most polygynous cultures, only wealthier, more powerful men—in this case those with more land and cattle—are best able to secure extra wives. Thus, the additional food, material goods, and social status of these families may help offset some of the costs of social aggression and tension among co-wives. Additionally, some co-wife relationships may be more harmonious, and therefore cooperative, than others, therefore plausibly adding to social capital through greater instances of reciprocal sharing. Still, these data imply that the added social stress of polygyny is on the whole costlier to children's sleep and health in adulthood rather than beneficial. Therefore, there is overall less polygyny worldwide compared to monogamous marriages, since a detriment in the fitness to one spouse affects both parents and because women's slower fertility rates act as the controlling agent in the population size of all cultures worldwide. While polygynously mated males may gain in quantity over quality of offspring, improving their reproductive success relative to polygynous-mated females and spectacularly more than monogamously mated males, it is still possible that high levels of co-wife conflict could act as a strong deterrent to male mating decisions.

A Complex Ending

"In adolescence when everyone is a riot of hormones and insecurities a group of close girlfriends is fertile breeding ground for resentments, unspoken competition, simmering jealousies. Your best friend can send your spirits soaring one moment and crush you with a word or gesture the next ... What I realise now in hindsight is that there is a natural ebb and flow to friendships."

—Colette McBeth, Telegraph

"There are worse things than having behaved foolishly in public. There are worse things than

these miniature betrayals, committed or endured or suspected; there are worse things than not being able to sleep for thinking about them. It is 5 a.m. All the worse things come stalking in and stand icily about the bed looking worse and worse and worse."

—*Fleur Adcock*

Medical research has, for decades, been compiling evidence that connects the social world to health and well-being. In an ultimate evolutionary sense, a clear explanation for the connection between the two is that the social world provides valuable resources via broadly defined prosocial sharing and cooperative pathways and thus affords positive fitness outcomes for women. What is not always clear, however, is exactly what proximate pathways are most responsible for securing the health benefits that sociality produces. This work, among the first of its kind, makes the bold prediction that same-sex relationships are central and crucial components of the social world of women, the quality of which greatly impacts on their sleep and consequently their health and happiness.

"Sleep is the interest we have to pay on the capital which is called in at death; and the higher the rate of interest and the more regularly it is paid, the further the date of redemption is postponed."

—*Arthur Schopenhauer*

Regrettably, the significance of sleep has been largely neglected as a topic of importance by evolutionary ecological researchers working with either a biological or a cultural emphasis. Perhaps this oversight is because in so many ways sleep is still a mysterious state of unconsciousness, making methods of scientific inquiry rather difficult. This should not, however, excuse the dearth of evolutionary research and theory that has ensued across the decades regarding a state of existence that represents an entire third of the time budget of humans across the life course. Due to this fact, one must rely more on medical health research to conclude that sleep is a basic biological drive, the function of which is not production or reproduction directly but rather to regulate and protect the psychological and biological systems needed to expertly execute the byzantine waking activities of production and reproduction (e.g., seek resources, find mates, and care for offspring). In effect, when waking production and reproduction activities require more time and energy, there is only one place to take it from in this 24-hour cycle of life,

and that is sleep. Due to the fact that sleep protects and rebuilds all bodily systems, subsequent daily functions are impaired when it declines. Sleep tries desperately to make up this debt in the intervening sleep bouts, but it cannot do so completely, and repeated trade-offs that fail to go in sleep's favor further compound health and wellness complaints by women (Balkin, Rupp, Picchioni, & Wesensten, 2008; Banks, Van Dongen, Maislin, & Dinges, 2010; Belenky et al., 2003; Dinges et al., 1997; Pejovic et al., 2013).

One theoretical perspective might conclude that sociality should always be beneficial, because it provides social capital in the form of support for productive activities, reciprocal sharing, and social status. However, sociality comes with extensive costs. For example, individuals can choose the wrong companions who instead of sharing will compete with them for food, mates, or social positions. These socially stressful partnerships can have profound effects on biology such as raising stress hormones like cortisol (Maestripieri & Georgiev, 2016) and impairing sleep quality and quantity. The latter can ultimately shift a multitude of physiological systems and outcomes. The social condition variables that are expected to negatively impact on women's sleep and subsequent fitness and well-being are as multifaceted as human sociality itself and include considerations such as descent on the social ladder, shifting social groups, violence from others, encountering new companions, social ostricization, aggressive gossip, loss of friendships, too few sharing partners, Machiavellianism from the socially astute, and reputation damage that impairs mating chances.

Coincidentally, the same social capital losses that deter sleep (Hyyppä, Kronholm, & Mattlar, 1991) are also clearly destructive to health and well-being (Benson & Beckmeyer, 2013), and these defeats may be more difficult for women to overcome than for men (Burke & Weir, 1978). In an emotional sense, these costs can include depression, loneliness, lower life satisfaction, emotional exhaustion, impaired self-esteem, and anxiety (Einarsen & Mikkelsen, 2003; Trompetter, Scholte, & Westerhof, 2011).

There are many causes of impaired sleep, and impoverished sleep in turn can make one more aggressive, violent, and anxiety-prone through alterations in neurotransmitters and hormones (Kamphuis, Meerlo, Koolhaas, & Lancel, 2012). One perspective is that these are nonadaptive responses by a 24-hour sleep–wake system that has gone woefully awry. However, evolutionary ecological theory posits that when environmental circumstances are stressful and current opportunities poor, excessive wakefulness may take precedence in order to secure the resources needed for production and reproduction, even at the expense of critical biological drives such as sleep. This trade-off optimizes finite fitness resources in stressed environments. In this way, the biological and psychological outcomes resulting from poor sleep quantity and quality may not always be considered maladaptive. In fact, social stressors that cause sleep loss may do so because of an individual's unconscious perceived need to restore valuable social resources, requiring more awake time, and exhibiting profound, indirect impacts on wellness and, ultimately, fitness.

Evolutionary theory offers great potential for better understanding the mechanisms by which loss of social capital affects health and well-being via impaired sleep among women. Most especially, this theory could help illuminate reasons for interactions and outcomes that appear maladaptive on the face but are at least sometimes optimal in reality. Future work might look more directly at how social influences shift sleep parameters such as insomnia, sleep architecture, and total sleep time and where there is a circular feedback mechanism, as some emerging work has found (Zohar, Tzischinsky, Epstein, & Lavie, 2005). Overall, sociality has benefitted individuals, which is why it has evolved to such a sensational degree in humans; however, this does not mean that every incidence of sociality offers pleasant outcomes. Therefore, we expect humans to flexibly alter behaviors in ways that mitigate costs in order to maximize fitness outcomes in variable environmental contexts—those environments that produce heightened aggression and competition among women. Our investigation into this matter indicates that more work needs to be done cross-culturally and experimentally using solid theory in order to better understand how sleep, a foundation of Maslow's (1943) hierarchy of needs, interacts with the social world of wakefulness. Additionally, the proximate potential of a single socially aggressive event to impair the same night's sleep indicates the need to tailor future studies to capture event-level relationships to understand their possible cumulative effects on well-being and health.

Evolutionary ecologists have argued that other aspects of sleep may be adaptive for problem-solving, including problems of the social realm. Dreaming, for example, offers a safe virtual environment to solve challenges and practice strategies related to survival and reproduction threats (Franklin & Zyphur,

2005; Valli & Revonsuo, 2009; Valli et al., 2005). Interpersonal conflicts have been documented as a common theme of bad dream content, and recent research on nighttime unpleasantries of nightmares shows that thematic content and frequency patterns vary by sex. The frequency of interpersonal conflict in nightmares, for example, is nearly two times higher for women than for men (Robert & Zadra, 2014). Further, women's nightly sleep is interrupted more often by nightmares (Ohayon, Morselli, & Guilleminault, 1997). Together this evidence indicates that threats to social capital resulting from social aggression may show up more often in the dream content of women as an unconscious way for the brain to work out or rehearse potential scenarios and outcomes of their social dynamics. Therefore, social stresses may tax sleeping quality in ways that go beyond simple insomnia and offer an additional avenue of evolutionary investigation.

Another direction of potential investigation involves whether or not social capital increases bear positively on sleep quantity and quality, just as social detriments produce harm. This is especially interesting in light of the fact that overall sociality is more beneficial than it is detrimental to individual fitness. In this respect, just as one might expect social tensions to reduce health and well-being via sleep, one might also propose that increases in social capital through friendship gains, reputational boosts from positive gossip, social status, and more pleasant reciprocal relationships with other women might increase survivorship and longevity through proximate enhancements to sleep quantity and quality. Therefore, future researchers might examine the relative effects of social costs to social benefits on sleep outcomes.

Conclusion

A good night's sleep is required for optimal physiological functioning and maintenance of the body and brain. Sleep interacts with virtually every bodily process as part of the daily circadian rhythm of hormones and systems. Sleep trades off against waking activities, and when more time and mental energy are needed for such productive and social actions, sleep inevitably loses out. Women's relationships with other women can be both cooperative and helpful or competitive and detracting. The latter type requires substantial time and energy reinvestments to resolve them to a null status or bring them back to a positive cooperative framework, if possible. When sleep is used to solve these social problems with other women, the protecting, anabolic physiological processes of the night cannot work to properly function and maintain the brain and body in optimal working order. The result is diminished health and well-being, and chronic social stress with other women should produce chronically poor health outcomes and psychological well-being.

The wealth of recent work on women's behaviors with other women has elucidated one glaring and notable fact: their social relationships are unendingly complex. One woman's behavior with another is contingent on an endless array of current, past, and future variables, many of which are social and therefore dynamic themselves. The social intelligence required to successfully navigate these relationships is vast and colossal. The social world is so important that, at times, it trumps the very basis of hierarchical needs such as food, sex, and even sleep.

References

Abdirahman, H. A., Bah, T., Shrestha, H., & Jacobsen, K. (2012). Bullying, mental health, and parental involvement among adolescents in the Caribbean. *West Indian Medical Journal, 61*(5), 504–508.

Almeida, D. M. (2005). Resilience and vulnerability to daily stressors assessed via diary methods. *Current Directions in Psychological Science, 14*(2), 64–68.

Almeida, D. M., & Kessler, R. C. (1998). Everyday stressors and gender differences in daily distress. *Journal of Personality and Social Psychology, 75*(3), 670–680.

Almeida, D. M., Wethington, E., & Kessler, R. C. (2002). The daily inventory of stressful events an interview-based approach for measuring daily stressors. *Assessment, 9*(1), 41–55.

Anda, R. F., Felitti, V. J., Bremner, J. D., Walker, J. D., Whitfield, C. H., Perry, B. D., ... Giles, W. H. (2006). The enduring effects of abuse and related adverse experiences in childhood. *European Archives of Psychiatry and Clinical Neuroscience, 256*(3), 174–186.

Anderton, D. L., & Emigh, R. J. (1989). Polygynous fertility: Sexual competition versus progeny. *American Journal of Sociology, 94*(4), 832–855.

Arnocky, S., Sunderani, S., Miller, J. L., & Vaillancourt, T. (2012). Jealousy mediates the relationship between attractiveness comparison and females' indirect aggression. *Personal Relationships, 19*(2), 290–303.

Balkin, T. J., Rupp, T., Picchioni, D., & Wesensten, N. J. (2008). Sleep loss and sleepiness: Current issues. *CHEST Journal, 134*(3), 653–660.

Banks, S., & Dinges, D. F. (2007). Behavioral and physiological consequences of sleep restriction. *Journal of Clinical Sleep Medicine, 3*(5), 519–528.

Banks, S., Van Dongen, H. P., Maislin, G., & Dinges, D. F. (2010). Neurobehavioral dynamics following chronic sleep restriction: Dose-response effects of one night for recovery. *Sleep, 33*(8), 1013–1026.

Bassuk, E. L., Perloff, J. N., Mickelson, K. D., & Bisseil, H. D. (2002). Role of kin and nonkin support in the mental health of low income women. *American Journal of Orthopsychiatry, 72*(1), 39–49.

Bastien, C. H., Vallieres, A., & Morin, C. M. (2004). Precipitating factors of insomnia. *Behavioral Sleep Medicine, 2*(1), 50–62.

Belenky, G., Wesensten, N. J., Thorne, D. R., Thomas, M. L., Sing, H. C., Redmond, D. P., ... Balkin, T. J. (2003). Patterns of performance degradation and restoration during sleep restriction and subsequent recovery: A sleep-dose-response study. *Journal of Sleep Research, 12*(1), 1–12.

Benington, J. H. (2000). Sleep homeostasis and the function of sleep. *Sleep, 23*(7), 959–966.

Benson, J., & Beckmeyer, J. (2013, November). Relational aggression and subjective well-being in independent senior living communities. Paper presented at the meeting of the Gerontological Society of America, New Orleans, LA.

Bernert, R. A., Merrill, K. A., Braithwaite, S. R., Van Orden, K. A., & Joiner, T. E. Jr. (2007). Family life stress and insomnia symptoms in a prospective evaluation of young adults. *Journal of Family Psychology, 21*(1), 58–66.

Bolger, N., DeLongis, A., Kessler, R. C., & Schilling, E. A. (1989). Effects of daily stress on negative mood. *Journal of Personality and Social Psychology, 57*(5), 808–818.

Borgerhoff-Mulder, M. (1992). Women's strategies in polygynous marriage. *Human Nature, 3*(1), 45–70.

Brissette, I., & Cohen, S. (2002). The contribution of individual differences in hostility to the associations between daily interpersonal conflict, affect, and sleep. *Personality and Social Psychology Bulletin, 28*(9), 1265–1274.

Brummett, B. H., Barefoot, J. C., Siegler, I. C., Clapp-Channing, N. E., Lytle, B. L., Bosworth, H. B., ... Mark, D. B. (2001). Characteristics of socially isolated patients with coronary artery disease who are at elevated risk for mortality. *Psychosomatic Medicine, 63*(2), 267–272.

Bryant, P. A., Trinder, J., & Curtis, N. (2004). Sick and tired: Does sleep have a vital role in the immune system? *Nature Reviews Immunology, 4*(6), 457–467.

Burbank, V. K. (1994). *Fighting women: Anger and aggression in Aboriginal Australia.* Berkeley: University of California Press.

Burgard, S. A. (2011). The needs of others: Gender and sleep interruptions for caregivers. *Social Forces, 89*(4), 1189–1215.

Burke, R. J., & Weir, T. (1978). Sex differences in adolescent life stress, social support, and well-being. *Journal of Psychology, 98*(2), 277–288.

Cacioppo, J. T., & Hawkley, L. C. (2003). Social isolation and health, with an emphasis on underlying mechanisms. *Perspectives in Biology and Medicine, 46*(3), 39–52.

Campbell, A. (1995). A few good men: Evolutionary psychology and female adolescent aggression. *Ethology and Sociobiology, 16*(2), 99–123.

Campbell, A. (2004). Female competition: Causes, constraints, content, and contexts. *Journal of Sex Research, 41*(1), 16–26.

Campbell, A., Muncer, S., & Bibel, D. (1998). Female–female criminal assault: An evolutionary perspective. *Journal of Research in Crime and Delinquency, 35*(4), 413–428.

Cashdan, E. (1998). Are men more competitive than women? *British Journal of Social Psychology, 37*(2), 213–229.

Chang, J. J., Pien, G. W., Duntley, S. P., & Macones, G. A. (2010). Sleep deprivation during pregnancy and maternal and fetal outcomes: Is there a relationship? *Sleep Medicine Reviews, 14*(2), 107–114.

Cohen, S., Doyle, W. J., Skoner, D. P., Rabin, B. S., & Gwaltney, J. M. (1997). Social ties and susceptibility to the common cold. *Journal of the American Medical Association, 277*(24), 1940–1944.

Crick, N. R., & Grotpeter, J. K. (1995). Relational aggression, gender, and social-psychological adjustment. *Child Development, 66*(3), 710–722.

Crockenberg, S. C., Leerkes, E. M., & Lekka, S. K. (2007). Pathways from marital aggression to infant emotion regulation: The development of withdrawal in infancy. *Infant Behavior and Development, 30*(1), 97–113.

Crothers, L. M., Lipinski, J., & Minutolo, M. C. (2009). Cliques, rumors, and gossip by the water cooler: Female bullying in the workplace. *The Psychologist-Manager Journal, 12*(2), 97–110.

Darling, C. A., McWey, L. M., Howard, S. N., & Olmstead, S. B. (2007). College student stress: The influence of interpersonal relationships on sense of coherence. *Stress and Health, 23*(4), 215–229.

Dinges, D. F., Pack, F., Williams, K., Gillen, K. A., Powell, J. W., Ott, G. E., . . . Park, A. I. (1997). Cumulative sleepiness, mood disturbance and psychomotor vigilance performance decrements during a week of sleep restricted to 4–5 hours per night. *Sleep, 20*(4), 267–277.

Drake, C., Richardson, G., Roehrs, T., Scofield, H., & Roth, T. (2004). Vulnerability to stress-related sleep disturbance and hyperarousal. *Sleep, 27*(2), 285–292.

Dregan, A., & Armstrong, D. (2010). Adolescence sleep disturbances as predictors of adulthood sleep disturbances—A cohort study. *Journal of Adolescent Health, 46*(5), 482–487.

Einarsen, S., & Mikkelsen, E. G. (2003). Individual effects of exposure to bullying at work. In S. Einarsen, H. Hoel, D. Zapf, & G. Cooper (Eds.), *Bullying and emotional abuse in the workplace: International perspectives in research and practice* (pp. 127–144). London: Taylor & Francis.

El-Sheikh, M., Buckhalt, J. A., & Reiter, S. L. (2000). Gender-related effects in emotional responding to resolved and unresolved interpersonal conflict. *Sex Roles, 43*(9–10), 719–734.

Faer, L. M., Hendriks, A., Abed, R. T., & Figueredo, A. J. (2005). The evolutionary psychology of eating disorders: Female competition for mates or for status? *Psychology and Psychotherapy: Theory, Research and Practice, 78*(3), 397–417.

Feinberg, M., Willer, R., Stellar, J., & Keltner, D. (2012). The virtues of gossip: Reputational information sharing as prosocial behavior. *Journal of Personality and Social Psychology, 102*(5), 1015–1030.

Fisher, M., & Cox, A. (2009). The influence of female attractiveness on competitor derogation. *Journal of Evolutionary Psychology, 7*(2), 141–155.

Fisher, M. L., & Moule, K. R. (2013). A new direction for intrasexual competition research: Cooperative versus competitive motherhood. *Journal of Social, Evolutionary, and Cultural Psychology, 7*(4), 318–325.

Fisher, M. L., Tran, U. S., & Voracek, M. (2008). The influence of relationship status, mate seeking, and sex on intrasexual competition. *Journal of Social Psychology, 148*(4), 493–512.

Flinn, M. V., & England, B. G. (1995). Childhood stress and family environment. *Current Anthropology, 36*(5), 854–866.

Franklin, M. S., & Zyphur, M. J. (2005). The role of dreams in the evolution of the human mind. *Evolutionary Psychology, 3*, 59–78.

Frey, D. J., Fleshner, M., & Wright, K. P. (2007). The effects of 40 hours of total sleep deprivation on inflammatory markers in healthy young adults. *Brain, Behavior, and Immunity, 21*(8), 1050–1057.

Galen, B. R., & Underwood, M. K. (1997). A developmental investigation of social aggression among children. *Developmental Psychology, 33*(4), 589–600.

Gettler, L. T., McKenna, J. J., McDade, T. W., Agustin, S. S., & Kuzawa, C. W. (2012). Does cosleeping contribute to lower testosterone levels in fathers? Evidence from the Philippines. *PLoS One, 7*(9), e41559.

Gove, W. R., Hughes, M., & Style, C. B. (1983). Does marriage have positive effects on the psychological well-being of the individual? *Journal of Health and Social Behavior, 24*(2), 122–131.

Graham, A. M., Fisher, P. A., & Pfeifer, J. H. (2013). What sleeping babies hear: A functional MRI study of interparental conflict and infants' emotion processing. *Psychological Science, 24*(5), 782–789.

Gregory, A. M., Caspi, A., Moffitt, T. E., & Poulton, R. (2006). Family conflict in childhood: A predictor of later insomnia. *Sleep, 29*(8), 1063–1067.

Gunn, H. E., Troxel, W. M., Hall, M. H., & Buysse, D. J. (2013). Interpersonal distress is associated with sleep and arousal in insomnia and good sleepers. *Journal of Psychosomatic Research, 76*(3), 242–248.

Haack, M., & Mullington, J. M. (2005). Sustained sleep restriction reduces emotional and physical well-being. *Pain, 119*(1), 56–64.

Haig, D. (2014). Troubled sleep: Night waking, breastfeeding, and parent-offspring conflict. *Evolution, Medicine, and Public Health, 2014*(1), 32–39.

Hailu, A., & Regassa, N. (2007). Correlates of household food security in densely populated areas of southern Ethiopia: Does the household structure matter? *Studies on Home and Community Science, 1*(2), 85–91.

Hailu, A., & Regassa, N. (2008). Characterization of women under polygamous marital union in selected communities in southern Ethiopia. *Journal of Oriental Anthropologists, 8*(1–2), 169–179.

Hamer, J. H. (1987). *Humane development: Participation and change among the Sadama of Ethiopia.* Tuscaloosa: University of Alabama Press.

Harvey, A. G. (2000). Pre-sleep cognitive activity: A comparison of sleep-onset insomniacs and good sleepers. *British Journal of Clinical Psychology, 39*(3), 275–286.

Harvey, A. G. (2003). The attempted suppression of presleep cognitive activity in insomnia. *Cognitive Therapy and Research, 27*(6), 593–602.

Hasler, B. P., & Troxel, W. M. (2010). Couples' nighttime sleep efficiency and concordance: Evidence for bidirectional associations with daytime relationship functioning. *Psychosomatic Medicine, 72*(8), 794–801.

Hess, N., Helfrecht, C., Hagen, E., Sell, A., & Hewlett, B. (2010). Interpersonal aggression among Aka hunter-gatherers of the Central African Republic. *Human Nature, 21*(3), 330–354.

Hess, N. H., & Hagen, E. H. (2006a). Psychological adaptations for assessing gossip veracity. *Human Nature, 17*(3), 337–354.

Hess, N. H., & Hagen, E. H. (2006b). Sex differences in indirect aggression: Psychological evidence from young adults. *Evolution and Human Behavior, 27*(3), 231–245.

Hill, S. E., & Durante, K. M. (2011). Courtship, competition, and the pursuit of attractiveness: Mating goals facilitate health-related risk taking and strategic risk suppression in women. *Personality and Social Psychology Bulletin, 37*(3), 383–394.

House, J. S., Landis, K. R., & Umberson, D. (1988). Social relationships and health. *Science, 241*(4865), 540–545.

Hyyppä, M. T., Kronholm, E., & Mattlar, C. E. (1991). Mental well-being of good sleepers in a random population sample. *British Journal of Medical Psychology, 64*(1), 25–34.

Jankowiak, W., Sudakov, M., & Wilreker, B. C. (2005). Co-wife conflict and co-operation. *Ethnology, 44*(1), 81–98.

Kahn-Greene, E. T., Killgore, D. B., Kamimori, G. H., Balkin, T. J., & Killgore, W. D. (2007). The effects of sleep deprivation on symptoms of psychopathology in healthy adults. *Sleep Medicine, 8*(3), 215–221.

Kamphuis, J., Meerlo, P., Koolhaas, J. M., & Lancel, M. (2012). Poor sleep as a potential causal factor in aggression and violence. *Sleep Medicine, 13*(4), 327–334.

Kaplan, H. S. (1996). A theory of fertility and parental investment in traditional and modern human societies. *American Journal of Physical Anthropology, 39*, 91–135.

Kaplan, H. S., & Lancaster, J. B. (2003). An evolutionary and ecological analysis of human fertility, mating patterns, and parental investment. In K. W. Wachter & R. A. Bulatao (Eds.), *Offspring: Human fertility behavior in biodemographic perspective* (pp. 170–223). Washington, DC: National Academies Press.

Kelly, W. E., Kelly, K. E., & Clanton, R. C. (2001). The relationship between sleep length and grade-point average among college students. *College Student Journal, 35*(1), 84–86.

Koskenvuo, K., Hublin, C., Partinen, M., Paunio, T., & Koskenvuo, M. (2010). Childhood adversities and quality of sleep in adulthood: A population-based study of 26,000 Finns. *Sleep Medicine, 11*(1), 17–21.

La Greca, A. M., & Harrison, H. M. (2005). Adolescent peer relations, friendships, and romantic relationships: Do they predict social anxiety and depression? *Journal of Clinical Child and Adolescent Psychology, 34*(1), 49–61.

Lavoie, K. L., Miller, S. B., Conway, M., & Fleet, R. P. (2001). Anger, negative emotions, and cardiovascular reactivity during interpersonal conflict in women. *Journal of Psychosomatic Research, 51*(3), 503–512.

Lee, K. A., Baker, F. C., Newton, K. M., & Ancoli-Israel, S. (2008). The influence of reproductive status and age on women's sleep. *Journal of Women's Health, 17*(7), 1209–1214.

Lund, H. G., Reider, B. D., Whiting, A. B., & Prichard, J. R. (2010). Sleep patterns and predictors of disturbed sleep in a large population of college students. *Journal of Adolescent Health, 46*(2), 124–132.

Madhavan, S. (2002). Best of friends and worst of enemies: competition and collaboration in polygyny. *Ethnology, 41*, 69–84.

Maestripieri, D., & Georgiev, A. V. (2016). What cortisol can tell us about the costs of sociality and reproduction among free-ranging rhesus macaque females on Cayo Santiago. *American Journal of Primatology, 78*(1), 92–105.

Maslow, A. H. (1943). A theory of human motivation. *Psychological Review, 50*(4), 370–396.

Maume, D. J. (2013). Social ties and adolescent sleep disruption. *Journal of Health and Social Behavior, 54*(4), 498–515.

McAndrew, F. T., Bell, E. K., & Garcia, C. M. (2007). Who do we tell and whom do we tell on? Gossip as a strategy for status enhancement." *Journal of Applied Social Psychology, 37*(7), 1562–1577.

McKenna, J. J., Ball, H. L., & Gettler, L. T. (2007). Mother–infant cosleeping, breastfeeding and sudden infant death syndrome: What biological anthropology has discovered about normal infant sleep and pediatric sleep medicine.

American Journal of Physical Anthropology, 134(Suppl. 45), 133–161.

McNamara, P. (2004). *An evolutionary psychology of sleep and dreams.* Westport, CT: Praeger.

McNamara, P., Dowdall, J., & Auerbach, S. (2002). REM sleep, early experience, and the development of reproductive strategies. *Human Nature, 13*(4), 405–435.

Miller, A. A., & Rucas, S. L. (2012). Sleep–wake state tradeoffs, impulsivity and life history theory. *Evolutionary Psychology, 10*(2), 173–186.

Miller-Ott, A. E., & Kelly, L. (2013). Communication of female relational aggression in the college environment. *Qualitative Research Reports in Communication, 14*(1), 19–27.

Molcho, M., Nic Gabhainn, S., & Kelleher, C. C. (2007). Interpersonal relationships as predictors of positive health among Irish youth: The more the merrier. *Irish Medical Journal, 100*(8), 33–36.

Nelson, J., & Harvey, A. G. (2003a). An exploration of pre-sleep cognitive activity in insomnia: Imagery and verbal thought. *British Journal of Clinical Psychology, 42*(3), 271–288.

Nelson, J., & Harvey, A. G. (2003b). Pre-sleep imagery under the microscope: A comparison of patients with insomnia and good sleepers. *Behaviour Research and Therapy, 41*(3), 273–284.

Nixon, C. L., Linkie, C. A., Coleman, P. K., & Fitch, C. (2011). Peer relational victimization and somatic complaints during adolescence. *Journal of Adolescent Health, 49*(3), 294–299.

Ohayon, M. M., Morselli, P., & Guilleminault, C. (1997). Prevalence of nightmares and their relationship to psychopathology and daytime functioning in insomnia subjects. *Sleep, 20*(5), 340–348.

Opp, M. R. (2009). Sleeping to fuel the immune system: Mammalian sleep and resistance to parasites. *BMC Evolutionary Biology, 9*(8), 1–3.

Orzech, K. M., Acebo, C., Seifer, R., Barker, D., & Carskadon, M. A. (2013). Sleep patterns are associated with common illness in adolescents. *Journal of Sleep Research, 23*(2), 133–142.

Pagel, M. D., Erdly, W. W., & Becker, J. (1987). Social networks: We get by with (and in spite of) a little help from our friends. *Journal of Personality and Social Psychology, 53*(4), 793–804.

Paquette, J. A., & Underwood, M. K. (1999). Gender differences in young adolescents' experiences of peer victimization: Social and physical aggression. *Merrill–Palmer Quarterly, 45*(2), 242–266.

Pejovic, S., Basta, M., Vgontzas, A. N., Kritikou, I., Shaffer, M. L., Tsaoussoglou, M., … Chrousos, G. P. (2013). Effects of recovery sleep after one work week of mild sleep restriction on interleukin-6 and cortisol secretion and daytime sleepiness and performance. *American Journal of Physiology-Endocrinology and Metabolism, 305*(7), E890–E896.

Preddy, T. M., & Fite, P. J. (2012). The impact of aggression subtypes and friendship quality on child symptoms of depression. *Child Indicators Research, 5*(4), 705–718.

Quinlan, R. (2007). Human parental effort and environmental risk. *Proceedings of the Royal Society B, 274*(1606), 121–125.

Raskauskas, J., & Stoltz, A. D. (2004). Identifying and intervening in relational aggression. *Journal of School Nursing, 20*(4), 209–215.

Rauer, A. J., Kelly, R. J., Buckhalt, J. A., & El-Sheikh, M. (2010). Sleeping with one eye open: Marital abuse as an antecedent of poor sleep. *Journal of Family Psychology, 24*(6), 667–677.

Ravan, A. R., Bengtsson, C., Lissner, L., Lapidus, L., & Bjorkelund, C. (2010). Thirty-six-year secular trends in sleep duration and sleep satisfaction, and associations with mental stress and socioeconomic factors: Results of the Population Study of Women in Gothenburg, Sweden. *Journal of Sleep Research, 19*(3), 496–503.

Regassa, N. (2012). Intimate partners' violence in southern Ethiopia: Examining the prevalence and risk factors in the Sidama Zone. *Journal of Humanities and Social Sciences, 3*(2), 101–110.

Regassa, N., & Stoecker, B. J. (2011). Household food insecurity and hunger among households in Sidama district, southern Ethiopia. *Public Health Nutrition, 15*(7), 1276.

Rharbite, S. N. (2012). *Relational aggression in university women: Comparing sorority members and their peers.* Philadelphia: Drexel University.

Robert, G., & Zadra, A. (2014). Thematic and content analysis of idiopathic nightmares and bad dreams. *Sleep, 37*(2), 409–417.

Rodéhn, M. (1999). The importance of sleep. *Nursing Standard 13*(24), 44–47.

Rogojanski, J., Carney, C. E., & Monson, C. M. (2013). Interpersonal factors in insomnia: A model for integrating bed partners into cognitive behavioral therapy for insomnia. *Sleep Medicine Reviews, 17*(1), 55–64.

Rucas, S. L., Gurven, M., Kaplan, H., Winking, J., Gangestad, S., & Crespo, M. (2006). Female intrasexual competition and reputational effects on attractiveness among the Tsimane of Bolivia. *Evolution and Human Behavior, 27*(1), 40–52.

Rucas, S. L., Gurven, M., Winking, J., & Kaplan, H. S. (2012). Social aggression and resource conflict across the female life course in the Bolivian Amazon. *Aggressive Behavior, 38*(3), 194–207.

Rucas, S. L., & Miller, A. A. (2013a). Locus of control and sleep in evolutionary perspective. *Journal of Social, Evolutionary, and Cultural Psychology, 7*(2), 79–96.

Rucas, S. L., & Miller, A. A. (2013b). Sleep and risk-taking propensity in life history and evolutionary perspectives. *Structure and Dynamics: eJournal of Anthropological and Related Sciences, 6*(3), 1–19.

Salmon, C., Crawford, C. B., & Walters, S. (2008). Anorexic behavior, female competition and stress: Developing the Female Competition Stress Test. *Evolutionary Psychology, 6*(1), 96–112.

Sansone, R. A., Edwards, H. C., & Forbis, J. S. (2010). The relationship between caretaking experiences in childhood and sleep disturbances in adulthood. *Psychiatry, 7*(5), 33–36.

Schuster, T. L., Kessler, R. C., & Aseltine, R. H. Jr. (1990). Supportive interactions, negative interactions, and depressed mood. *American Journal of Community Psychology, 18*(3), 423–438.

Scott, B. A., & Judge, T. A. (2006). Insomnia, emotions, and job satisfaction: A multilevel study. *Journal of Management, 32*(5), 622–645.

Seeman, T. E., Singer, B. H., Ryff, C. D., Love, G. D., & Levy-Storms, L. (2002). Social relationships, gender, and allostatic load across two age cohorts. *Psychosomatic Medicine, 64*(3), 395–406.

Shneerson, J. M. (2005). Physiological basis of sleep and wakefulness. In J. M. Shneerson, *Sleep medicine: A guide to sleep and its disorders* (pp. 22–53). Malden, MA: Wiley-Blackwell.

Stoia-Caraballo, R., Rye, M. S., Pan, W., Kirschman, K. J. B., Lutz-Zois, C., & Lyons, A. M. (2008). Negative affect and anger rumination as mediators between forgiveness and sleep quality. *Journal of Behavioral Medicine, 31*(6), 478–488.

Strassmann, B. I. (1997). Polygyny as a risk factor for child mortality among the Dogon. *Current Anthropology, 38*(4), 688–695.

Takaki, J., Taniguchi, T., Fukuoka, E., Fujii, Y., Tsutsumi, A., Nakajima, K., & Hirokawa K. (2010). Workplace bullying could play important roles in the relationships between job strain and symptoms of depression and sleep disturbance. *Journal of Occupational Health, 52*(6), 367–374.

Thomas, S. A., & Rozell, E. J. (2007). Gossip and nurses: Malady or remedy? *Health Care Manager, 26*(2), 111–115.

Totterdell, P., Reynolds, S., Parkinson, B., & Briner, R. B. (1994). Associations of sleep with everyday mood, minor symptoms and social interaction experience. *Sleep, 17*(5), 466–475.

Trompetter, H., Scholte, R., & Westerhof, G. (2011). Resident-to-resident relational aggression and subjective well-being in assisted living facilities. *Aging & Mental Health, 15*(1), 59–67.

Troxel, W. M. (2010). It's more than sex: Exploring the dyadic nature of sleep and implications for health. *Psychosomatic Medicine, 72*(6), 578–586.

Troxel, W. M., Cyranowski, J. M., Hall, M., Frank, E., & Buysse, D. J. (2007). Attachment anxiety, relationship context, and sleep in women with recurrent major depression. *Psychosomatic Medicine, 69*(7), 692–699.

Uchino, B. N. (2006). Social support and health: A review of physiological processes potentially underlying links to disease outcomes. *Journal of Behavioral Medicine, 29*(4), 377–387.

Vaillancourt, T., & Sharma, A. (2011). Intolerance of sexy peers: Intrasexual competition among women. *Aggressive Behavior, 37*(6), 569–577.

Valli, K., & Revonsuo, A. (2009). The threat simulation theory in light of recent empirical evidence: A review. *American Journal of Psychology, 122*(1), 17–38.

Valli, K., Revonsuo, A., Pälkäs, O., Ismail, K. H., Ali, K. J., & Punamäki, R.-L. (2005). The threat simulation theory of the evolutionary function of dreaming: Evidence from dreams of traumatized children. *Consciousness and Cognition, 14*(1), 188–218.

Walen, H. R., & Lachman, M. E. (2000). Social support and strain from partner, family, and friends: Costs and benefits for men and women in adulthood. *Journal of Social and Personal Relationships, 17*(1), 5–30.

Watson, D. C. (2012). Gender differences in gossip and friendship. *Sex Roles, 67*(9–10), 494–502.

Wicklow, A., & Espie, C. A. (2000). Intrusive thoughts and their relationship to actigraphic measurement of sleep: Towards a cognitive model of insomnia. *Behaviour Research and Therapy, 38*(7), 679–693.

Williams, K., Chambers, M., Logan, S., & Robinson, D. (1996). Association of common health symptoms with bullying in primary school children. *British Medical Journal, 313*, 17–19.

Worthman, C. M. (2008). After dark: The evolutionary ecology of human sleep. In W. R. Trevathan, E. O. Smith, & J. J. McKenna (Eds.), *Evolutionary medicine and health* (pp. 291–313). Oxford: Oxford University Press.

Worthman, C. M., & Brown, R. A. (2007). Companionable sleep: Social regulation of sleeping and cosleeping in Egyptian families. *Journal of Family Psychology, 21*(1), 124–135.

Worthman, C. M., & Melby, M. K. (2002). Toward a comparative developmental ecology of human sleep. In M. A. Carskadon (Ed.), *Adolescent sleep patterns: Biological, social, and psychological influences* (pp. 69–117). New York: Cambridge University Press.

Zeitzen, M. K. (2008). *Polygamy: A cross-cultural analysis.* New York: Berg.

Zhang, B., & Wing, Y. (2006). Sex differences in insomnia: A meta-analysis. *Sleep, 29*(1), 85–93.

Zoccola, P. M., Dickerson, S. S., & Lam, S. (2009). Rumination predicts longer sleep onset latency after an acute psychosocial stressor. *Psychosomatic Medicine, 71*(7), 771–775.

Zohar, D., Tzischinsky, O., Epstein, R., & Lavie, P. (2005). The effects of sleep loss on medical residents' emotional reactions to work events: A cognitive-energy model. *Sleep, 28*(1), 47–54.

Is Female Competition at the Heart of Reproductive Suppression and Eating Disorders?

Catherine Salmon

Abstract

This chapter examines the role of female competition in reproductive suppression in humans and other species. Most research on same-sex competition has focused on the showy, often violent aggression typically seen in male–male competition. Competition between females has been less studied for a variety of reasons, from the fact that many researchers have been male and focused on their own competitive arena to the fact that female competition is often more subtle, difficult to observe, and thus more challenging to study. Two aspects of female competition, competition for status or dominance and competition for mates, are part of the focus of this chapter. The other focus is the possible role that female competition plays in reproductive suppression, whether that suppression is self-induced or imposed by others. One modern outcome of the mismatch between a once-adaptive response to female competition and the modern environment is extreme dieting behavior.

Key Words: reproductive suppression, dieting, female competition, status, dominance, mismatch

Introduction

At the heart of sexual selection is competition for mates. Males compete physically for access to females and to advertise their status and health or genetic quality (Gangestad & Thornhill, 1997) to prospective mates. Such competition between males has been well articulated in a number of articles such as Puts (2010), which focuses on mechanisms of sexual selection and how male traits are better designed for contest competition than other mechanisms of sexual selection, and Miller (2000), which highlights the importance of advertising genetic quality through a variety of methods, including art and music, as well as physical appearance and symmetry. However, the recent focus on competition between males and the preferences of choosy females has often left neglected the issue of competition between females. Females also compete for access to quality mates and to display traits desirable to males. Under some circumstances, female competition can take a physical form as when inner-city female gang members join forces to attack female newcomers who, partially due to male preferences for novelty, are seen as a threat to existing male–female relationships (Campbell, 1991, 2013). More typically, female competition occurs through more subtle means, including gossip (McAndrew, this volume; Sutton & Oaten this volume), derogation of competitors (Buss & Dedden, 1990), as well as dominant females inflicting higher levels of stress on subordinates and reproductive suppression, as a result of stress responses (Salmon, Figueredo, & Woodburn, 2009).

Much attention has been given to issues of body image in women in Western societies, and while some have argued that male desires drive female concerns over body image, others have blamed the media more generally, claiming that the thinness of women seen on television and film convinces women that they need to be as thin as possible and that thin is what is attractive (Botta, 2003; Groesz, Levine, & Murnen, 2002; Polivy & Herman, 2002). A few researchers have also suggested that it is women themselves who are responsible for the drive for thinness. Donohoe, van Hippel, and Brooks (2009) report that men actually prefer the body size of "normal" women with their multivariate analysis indicating that the torsos of women of average weight are most attractive to men, suggesting that men prefer a heavier standard of beauty than women prefer. In addition, Ferguson, Winegard, and Winegard (2011) suggest that the correlation between media exposure and body dissatisfaction is actually quite low, accounting for only 3% of the variation in such dissatisfaction in their meta-analysis, indicating that media exposure in itself is not responsible for the desire of some women for extreme thinness. So what could possibly be motivating this concern about weight among Western women in particular, as this focus on thinness is less common in many other cultures (Anderson, Crawford, Nadeau, & Lindberg, 1992)? While some have suggested that a culture of thinness prevalent in industrialized affluent societies has been marketed by the fashion industry and other media outlets such that women feel they must conform (Gordon, 1988), a more likely candidate for the concern with thinness is competition between women, not over who can be the thinnest but for social status, dominance, and mates.

Female Competition in Mammals

The majority of research on same-sex aggression and competition has focused on competition between males (Boesch, Kohou, Nene, & Vigilant, 2006; Craig, Herman, & Pack, 2002; Robinson, Pilkington, Clutton-Brock, Pemberton, & Kruuk, 2006; Scott, Mann, Watson-Capps, Sargeant, & Connor, 2005). There are a number of reasons for this focus; for one, male–male competition is often very showy, such as in elephant seals where it is accompanied by loud noises and bloody injuries. It is also often very intense due to the greater variation in male reproductive success, compared to female reproductive success, whereby some males may be big winners at the reproductive game while others are totally shut out. While females do compete with other females, that competition tends to look somewhat different from that which occurs between males, as it is often less noisy and rarely physically violent (Campbell, 2013). Female fitness is less often limited by access to mates than male fitness. Male fitness is mainly limited by access to

fertile females, while females are limited by their own bodies' ability to gestate and breastfeed typically one offspring at a time. A man could conceivably impregnate several women in one day, while a woman is not able to produce multiple pregnancies in the same time frame. As a result, female competition for mates tends to be less frequent and intense, although a high-quality male can be worth fighting for in species in which males invest parentally or if the male is of especially good genetic quality. While in some species males do not invest anything other than sperm in the production and care of offspring, paternal investment in humans is quite valuable and comes in many forms (Clutton-Brock, 1991). Human fathers typically provide food, shelter, and other resources, as well as protection and their time, whether that be in the form of taking children to hockey practice, reading books, playing video games, or spending time on social skills. Such resources can also include social contacts and support in species that engage in co-operative offspring care. Good genetic quality in a father can translate to healthier and more successful offspring. Access to resources that can be converted into offspring or offspring support is a more frequent limiting factor for female fitness than access to high-genetic-quality males, since good genes can be obtained from short-term mating, but the resources to raise offspring are usually only found consistently when females have a long-term mate. Not all females will have the same access to high-resource men for long-term mateships due to their own variable mate value. The point here is that females do vary in reproductive success (even if the variance in reproductive success is typically larger for males) and that female competitive ability is related to reproductive skew. Reproductive skew refers to the distribution of reproduction among individuals in a population. Populations with high skew are those in which a few dominant individuals monopolize reproduction, while in low-skew populations, reproduction is more equitably distributed. High reproductive skew within a society indicates that some women experience greater reproductive success than others. Stockley and Bro-Jørgenson's (2011) review of female competition in mammals describes a range of female adaptations for competition from aggressive behavior and conspicuous sexual signaling to olfactory signaling (Stockley, Bottell, & Hurst, 2013), social alliances, derogation of competitors (Fisher, Cox, & Gordon, 2009), and reproductive suppression.

Female competition for limited resources can be direct or relatively indirect. Female rodents may defend feeding territories, aggressively excluding other females (Daly & Daly, 1974; Koskela, Mappes, & Ylonen, 1997; Vessey, 1987). A territory may also be taken over by a larger female who appears on the territory and cannot be displaced. Wolves, lionesses, and other carnivores also defend feeding territories, as do many other female mammals. For some species, group-living mammals in particular, a delicate balance must be found between competition and cooperation. A number of researchers have documented this problem for wild dogs. For wild dogs, communal activities include hunting and defense of the territory. However, the dominant female typically prevents lower-ranking females from breeding. If subordinate females do manage to breed, the dominant one will typically kill their pups (Creel & Creel, 1995, 1998; Frame, Malcolm, Frame, & Van Lawick, 1979). Rank is related to foraging time and diet in some wild chimpanzee populations. Females with high rank spend less time foraging and have a higher-quality diet than low-ranking females, which can be seen as evidence of food competition between females resulting in lower-rank females being pushed into poorer-quality environments (Murray, Eberly, & Pusey, 2006; Murray, Mane & Pusey, 2007). Dominant females also appear to experience better access to preferred food resources in Arctic barnacle geese (Stahl, Tolsma, Loonen, & Drent, 2002), as well as solitary foraging hedgehogs (Cassini & Foger, 1995) and brown bears (Gende & Quinn, 2004), as subordinates avoid foraging in areas where dominants do so.

Female ground squirrels compete very aggressively with other females to the point that infanticide is not uncommon. Female ground squirrels who lose a litter of pups to predation move on to a different territory. Once there, unable to reproduce again in the remaining season, they raid burrows of unrelated females and kill their pups, though they do not use the pups as a food source (Sherman, 1981). If such a female is successful, she will breed in the new territory during the next season. Typically, female ground squirrels live near their female kin and cooperate in defending their burrows against such intruders as well as other predators (Sherman, 1977). In cooperatively breeding meerkats, dominant females may kill subordinate females' pups. The subordinate females then often allonurse the dominant female's own litter (MacLeod, Nielsen, & Clutton-Brock, 2013). Similarly, killing and consuming unrelated infants has been reported in a number of primates, including chimpanzees and gorillas (Goodall, 1986; Jolly, 1985). While

in cooperative breeders preventing other females from breeding may result in extra adult care for the dominant female's offspring, as well as less competition from other litters for food or other resources in general, in species without cooperative breeding, like gorillas, the absence of unrelated infants mainly means more food available for an individual female and her own offspring. Therefore, some female aggression that has historically been attributed to the protection of food resources may actually be designed to protect pups from infanticidal female intruders (Wolff, 1993).

Female competition can also occur indirectly in mammals. Rival females can compete for scarce resources, such as food, without direct aggression by using more subtle routes such as social coercion or manipulation. In mice, young females delay puberty when exposed to an environment with odor cues produced by older adult females (Massey & Vandenbergh, 1980). In a sparsely populated habitat, young females mature quickly and reproduce. However, if the habitat is crowded and there are too many adult females in the area, a reproductively ready young female will be targeted for attack by established breeding females. If she is not able to compete successfully and repel their attacks, the young female would benefit by remaining reproductively immature (i.e., no longer a target of aggression for more dominant females) until the breeding situation in her habitat changes.

Reproductive Suppression in Mammals

Mammalian female reproductive success can be influenced by female dominance in a variety of ways, including via direct and indirect effects on resource accessibility, offspring defense, infanticide, and the behavioral or physiological suppression of subordinate's reproduction (King & Allaine, 2002; Wasser & Barash, 1983). Social group-living mammals are often subject to reproductive synchrony and reproductive suppression. Reproductive synchrony, where female ovulation and offspring births are clustered around the same time, can make it difficult for any one male to monopolize female matings, as many females will be fertile at the same time and one dominant male cannot mate with them all at the same time or guard access to all of them successfully. Other males will have the opportunity to get mating access. As a result, females should synchronize when there is a benefit to having access to multiple males. Group-living females may experience reproductive suppression when dominant females can increase their reproductive success by suppressing the reproduction of less dominant females. Under these kinds of systems, certain individuals, particularly younger, philopatric females, who remain in their natal group and have reached sexual maturity, may delay reproduction due to suppression by older, more dominant individuals. Such suppression may be externally imposed by the dominants or may be a strategy adopted by subordinates, as is discussed in a later section.

Some studies have suggested a role for stress-induced hormonal changes in triggering reproductive suppression, arguing that elevated levels of stress are an indicator of conditions that are not optimal to successful reproduction. Under such conditions, reproduction should be postponed until conditions improve with a lower stress level indicator; however, the relationship between specific hormones and dominance is not clear-cut (Creel, 2001, 2005). Creel has summarized the results of field studies on the dwarf mongoose, the African wild dog, and the gray wolf. Subordinates rarely breed in these three social group-living species; however, in these species, there is no evidence that stress hormones drive the suppression. On the other hand, cooperatively breeding meerkats do show evidence of a role for elevated stress hormones, resulting from aggression perpetrated by dominants, in the reproductive suppression of subordinates (Young et al., 2006). One might imagine that if individuals can suppress the reproduction of competitors, they should; however, there are costs and benefits to suppressing subordinate reproduction. There is a cost experienced by dominant meerkats when subordinates breed in terms of lower-weight pups that experience less survival and breeding success of their own. As a result, dominant meerkat females often suppress the reproduction of subordinates, but it is modulated by the cost and their own reproductive state (Clutton-Brock, Hodge, Flower, Sprang, & Young, 2010). In addition, studies of Mongolian gerbils indicate that ovulation and hormone secretion may be suppressed in young female gerbils due to cues of the presence of the natal family (Saltzman, Ahmed, Fahimi, Wittwer, & Wegner, 2006). These gerbils engage in alloparental care in which additional parental care is performed by individuals other than parents, such as siblings or older offspring. For these gerbils, cues of the presence of kin serve to delay the start of reproduction when conditions for reproduction are not optimal and when both generations would experience greater fitness benefits if the younger females engage in alloparental care rather than reproduce themselves.

Brown bears sometimes display an unusual example of reproductive suppression in that, unlike most species with reproductive suppression that are group living, brown bears are solitary carnivores. Reproductive suppression (by other adult females) has been used to explain delayed first births (Stoen, Zedrosser, Wegge, & Swenson, 2006) in brown bear populations. The presence of an adult female with cubs on a nearby territory also reduces an adult female's probability of having cubs in a given year (Ordiz, Stoen, Swenson, Kojola, & Bischof, 2008). In this case maturity is not being delayed, but individual reproductive seasons occur in already reproducing bears. The explanation offered is that this adult reproductive suppression is caused by resource competition between the neighboring female bears. Some studies (Clarke, Miethe, & Bennett, 2001) have attempted to distinguish between reproductive suppression as the result of control by dominant females—that is, imposed through mechanisms of aggression, pheromones, or interference with copulation—and suppression that is really self-imposed in currently resource-poor environments that are likely to improve in the future. Clarke et al.'s study of Damaraland mole-rats found no evidence for the effects of pheromones, stress resulting from aggression by dominants, or interference by dominants in copulations in subordinate reproductive suppression (which did occur). As a result, they attributed the suppression that was observed to self-suppression and suggested it could possibly reduce the chances of inbreeding.

In a number of nonhuman mammals, dominants are not subject to the same levels of harassment experienced by subordinates. Rather, high-status females harass subordinates to induce reproductive suppression, through physical attacks or threat displays as well as social intimidation or commandeering food. Such harassment can be direct and involve coalitions of females or can largely come from one more dominant individual. The result is that subordinate stress levels rise and reproduction shuts down in response with an absence of estrus (Ellis, 1995), resulting in increased reproductive success for the dominant females. The dominant females will be the only ones coming into estrus and producing offspring.

Resource competition among female primates frequently leads dominants to out-reproduce subordinates (Bercovitch & Strum, 1993; Harcourt, 1987). This greater reproductive success on the part of dominant primate females can happen as a result of the reproductive suppression of subordinates

(Barrett et al. 1993; Saltzman, Prudom, Schultz-Darken, Wittwer, & Abbott, 2004; Ziegler & Sousa, 2002), but it can also occur through infanticide committed against the offspring of subordinates and other postreproductive tactics that could impair the survivorship of competitors' offspring and might also include self-suppression in response to resource availability (Thompson, Kahlenberg, Gilby, & Wrangham, 2007). Garcia, Lee, and Rosetta's (2008) work on captive olive baboons suggests that the social environment does affect menstrual cycle regularity, with dominance rank being related to fertility. Low-ranking females go through more cycles before conception, as well as having longer cycles and displaying smaller sexual swellings when compared to high-ranking females. Variation in menstrual cycle length and menstrual disruptions were also related to social stress, as has been reported in other primates, including humans (Abbott, 1992; Bethea et al. 2008; Fenster et al. 1999; Sanders & Bruce, 1999).

It seems clear that in many species status and reproductive dominance are linked. Females with greater social status or position in the dominance hierarchy out-reproduce lower-ranked or subordinate females. In species where social rank is passed from mother to daughter, several generations of one lineage may dominate the breeding pool. Intrasexual competition can be played out through dominant individuals monopolizing food resources, imposing social stress on subordinates, or commiting infanticide, with the result that subordinates are less successful reproductively than dominant females.

Female–Female Competition in Humans

In the earlier section on mammals, a number of examples of female–female competition from the animal literature were discussed, highlighting competition for status and reproductive dominance, reproductive suppression of subordinates, as well as access to males. The fact that female competition has figured prominently in other mammalian species suggests the likelihood that it has been a significant selective pressure on human female evolution as well. In primate species generally, researchers suggest that females compete with each other to maximize their own reproductive success at the expense of other females (Campbell, 2004; Hrdy, 1981). In the case of talapoin monkeys, for example, the presence of dominant females is associated with an alteration in hormone levels in subordinate monkeys. The result is the suppression of ovulation (Bowman, Dilley, & Keverne, 1978), a form of reproductive

suppression that we return to later in this section on female competition in humans.

Hrdy (1981) and others (Campbell, 2004; Cashdan, 1999) have characterized female–female competition as more subtle and covert, in comparison to the loud and overly aggressive displays seen frequently when males compete. Research focused on competition between human females (e.g., Campbell, 2004, Fisher, 2013; Walters, 1990) depicts aspects of such competition as adaptive, suggesting that ancestral women who were good intrasexual competitors experienced greater reproductive success when compared to women who were less accomplished competitors.

Within-sex competitiveness plays an important role in the lives of women and girls. Adolescent girls must begin the process of acquiring the necessary resources, status, power, and self-respect for successful adult life. The peer relationships of higher-status individuals provide social resources that can result in the kind of influence that leads to greater access to resources (Volk, Camilleri, Dane, & Marini, 2012). Having high status for female adolescents is associated with greater male acceptance (Dijkstra, Lindenberg, & Veenstra, 2008) and access to desirable males (Benenson, 2009; Geary, 2010). Adolescent peer relationships, while extremely important sources of support, intimacy, and acceptance (Frankel, 1990; Merten, 2004), are also potential sources of great stress as the main sources of support are also competitors. Teenage girls who are not high in peer status are at greater risk of anxiety and depression when compared to those of high or average status, even as adults (Modin, Ostberg, & Almquist, 2011). While features such as status are highly valued, they are not equally available to all members of a specific peer group (Adler & Adler, 1996; Byrne, Davenport, & Mazanov, 2007). Competition between peer-group members may be overt or subtle, encompassing both physical fighting and subtle verbal put-downs. The majority consists of indirect aggression, which allows the aggressor to appear to not have any harmful intentions (Barash, 2006; Björkqvist, Lagerspetz, & Kaukiainen, 1992). Examples of such indirect aggression in human females includes breaking confidences, being critical of clothing or other aspects of appearance or personality, exclusion from the group, gossip, or spreading rumors (Björkqvist, 1994; Owens, Shute, & Slee, 2000; Simmons, 2002).

Relatively little research has focused on the precise nature of competition for status among adolescent girls. The majority of studies have instead focused on adolescent stress more generally and its negative impact on health (Bryne et al., 2007), coping skills and optimism (Finkelstein, Kubzabsky, Capitman, & Goodman, 2007), and depression (Hankin, Mermelstein, & Roesch, 2007), though White, Gallup, and Gallup (2010) report specifically on earlier onset of sexual behavior in aggressive girls, suggesting that competition for mates may be driving some degree of aggression. One aspect of female competition that has attracted substantial attention is the importance young girls place on having an attractive and fashionable appearance and its possible connection to status (Toro et al., 2006). It may be that fashion is an arena where young women compete to display clothes associated with high-status brands, as well as emphasizing the attractiveness of their own bodies (see Johnsen & Geher, this volume, for a discussion of fashion and women's competition). Weisfeld, Bloch, and Ivers (1984) reported that, among midadolescent girls, being seen as fashionable, attractive, and well groomed was correlated with being seen as more dominant by their peers. Lott (1981) asserts that adolescent girls are acutely aware of how important their appearance is and that, in turn, they spend a significant amount of time trying to perfect it as much as possible. Physical attractiveness and a fashionable appearance in adolescent girls appear to be assays of status (De Bruyn & van den Boom, 2005). Several studies have reported that a major source of competition among female undergraduates surrounds the optimization of physical appearance (Buss, 1988; Walters & Crawford, 1994), while other studies of undergraduate females have also indicated that the derogation of sexual rivals is often focused on physical appearance and promiscuity (Buss & Dedden, 1990; Fisher, 2004; Fisher et al., 2009). The importance of physical attractiveness and promiscuity to female intrasexual competition is not surprising considering the premium males place on attractiveness in their partners, which serves as an indicator of health and fertility (Etcoff, 1999). Men also value a lack of promiscuity in a partner, as it is viewed as an indicator that she will be sexually faithful in the future.

While direct physical assertiveness is often seen as a signal of dominance in boys, it may provide fewer benefits to girls and entail more costs, hence the greater frequency of indirect aggression. For girls, popularity among peers is often viewed as an indicator of dominance (Cronin, 1980; Savin-Williams, 1987). While popularity indexes general success in resource acquisition in social contexts

(ancestrally essential to child-raising) and attracting the attention of others, attractiveness is the best single predictor of popularity among girls in the United States (Adams, 1977; Kennedy, 1990; Luthar & Latendresse, 2005; Rankin, Lane, Gibbons, & Gerrard, 2004; Weisfeld & Weisfeld, 1984). Interestingly, women in romantic relationships who make frequent social comparisons in terms of attractiveness are more likely to engage in indirect aggression designed to reduce the social status of their target via false rumors, for example. The result is often increased depression and anxiety in the target (Arnocky et al., 2011). Adolescent boys and girls perceived by their peers as popular, leading, and dominant exhibit more displays of dominance, such as erect posture, direct gaze, and relaxation, than their peers (Weisfeld & Weisfeld, 1984). Similar findings have been reported in UK adolescents (Boardway & Weisfeld, 1994).

During the transition from childhood to adolescence, the concern with social standing expressed by young girls and boys increases (Weisfeld, 1999) and continues as they transition into adulthood. Within-sex competition intensifies at reproductive maturity (Trivers, 1985), as successful competition for mates and social resources becomes a biological necessity. For primates, female competition is focused on rearing young successfully. One way in which they compete to do that is to be attractive to males. Those females who are able to attract high-quality males with a willingness to invest will experience greater reproductive success, as do those females high in social dominance, which leads to the opportunity to monopolize available resources. In addition, support from other females has also played a significant role in successful childrearing, particularly in humans, where children need significant amounts of care over an extended period of time. Such support often comes from female kin, but same-sex friends often share childcare tasks, which is one reason there is tension between female competition and cooperation (Essock-Vitale & McGuire, 1985; Geary, 2000).

Girls' and women's social relationships, whether they be among same-sex adolescents at school, young adults at university or the workplace, or involving relationships with boys and young men, seem to be significant sources of competition. A number of researchers have documented the relevance of sexual jealousy to indirectly aggressive acts, including gossip, ridicule, and derogation of appearance/personality, reporting that greater levels of sexual jealousy or prompting cues of infidelity are associated with a greater willingness to engage in competitive acts (Arnocky et al., 2011; Campbell, 1995; Hines & Fry, 1994; Lepowsky, 1994). It is likely that a certain amount of dominance among their peer group will be valuable to most girls in reducing acts of indirect aggression directed toward themselves due to fears of retaliation from a more dominant individual and her allies. Achieving such dominance likely involves learning to use assertiveness, tact, and humor, as well as indirect aggression to achieve one's goals while remaining well liked and respected by other girls. As Fisher and colleagues (2009) have noted, self-promotion can at times be a more successful strategy than competitor derogation. Frankel (1990) reported that the most popular and the most ignored girls reported lower levels of stress. The highest levels of stress were reported by girls who were average in popularity, mostly likely the result of having to actively compete for status. Those high in status seem secure in their position, while those lowest in status may avoid competing so as not to become the focus of aggression from others. Young women must also become adept at starting and maintaining relationships with men, as well as women, and skilled at terminating relationships with undesirable friends and lovers. In Western societies where marriage and childrearing are often postponed (Schmidt, Sobotka, Bentzen, & Nyboe Anderson, 2011), these balancing acts begin early, as the age of menarche has decreased (Parent et al., 2003), and go on longer, as the age at first marriage has increased (Payne, Brown, & Manning, 2013). Western society has created an extended adolescence in which same- and opposite-sex competition are attenuated. As a result, it is not surprising that several studies have linked stress in adolescents and young adults (from same-sex competition as well as between-sex) to the development of disordered eating behavior (Salmon, Crawford, Dane, & Zuberbier, 2008; Salmon, Crawford, & Walters, 2008).

Reproductive Suppression in Humans

Several researchers have suggested an adaptive role for reproductive suppression in human females. The reproductive suppression hypothesis (RSH; Crawford, 1989; Surbey, 1987; Voland & Voland, 1989) suggests that selection has shaped an adaptive mechanism that adjusts female reproduction to local environmental (social and ecological) conditions by adjusting levels of body fat. When social and ecological cues, ones that ancestrally would have reliably signaled the need to temporarily postpone reproduction, are now experienced at extreme levels of intensity and duration, fears of fatness and negative body image may result, resulting in anorexic-like dieting behavior. The resulting drop in body fat leads to suppression of ovulation, postponing reproduction.

The RSH is based on two basic biological concepts: adaptive reproductive suppression and the critical fat hypothesis. Adaptive reproductive suppression (previously discussed in the nonhuman mammals section) suggests that, due to the high reproductive costs experienced by female mammals, women will do better (in terms of lifetime reproductive success) to delay reproduction until conditions improve (Becker, Breedlove, & Crews, 1993; Wasser & Barash, 1983; Williams, 1966). Research on juveniles often focuses on risk-taking and discounting the future on the part of young males in high-mortality environments where conditions are unlikely to improve in the future (Wilson & Daly, 1997). In these circumstances, for males and females, the best solution fitness-wise may be to compete and reproduce now while the opportunity exists (Daly & Wilson, 2005). However, if conditions are likely to change, refraining from competition and reproduction may provide a better lifetime reproductive success outcome. In this light, reproductive suppression is seen as an environmentally contingent response.

The critical fat hypothesis (Boyne et al., 2010; Frisch, 1985, 1990, 2002; Lash & Armstrong, 2009) states that there is a positive relationship between female body fat and the processes of ovulation and menstruation. Adjusting levels of body fat in response to environmental conditions (including social stress) is an effective mechanism for altering female reproduction because female body fat stores significant amounts of estrogen and converts androgens to estrogen (Becker et al., 1993; Frisch, 1990). The relationship between fertility and weight is largely curvilinear (Caro & Sellen, 1990; Frisch, 2002), and a majority of women require 17% to 22% of body weight to be adipose tissue to commence menstruation and maintain their ovulatory cycle (Frisch, 1985; Frisch & Barbieri, 2002). This threshold for ovulation varies between women, and in female athletes, for example, who are often close to this threshold, losing a few pounds can stop menstruation (Frisch, 2002; Frisch et al., 1981). Similarly, a decrease in typical adolescent weight gain or increasing weight loss in lean adult women (Rippon, Nash, Myburgh, & Noakes, 1988) could have been an efficient mechanism for adjusting ancestral reproductive effort in response to environmental conditions, either to slow down reproductive development or temporarily suspend reproductive capacity. There are limitations to this theory, particularly with regard to the specific threshold argument (see Scott & Johnston, 1982), but the premise that energy intake and energy expenditure influence ovarian functioning as a response to energetic stress has been the focus of work by Ellison (1990, 2003) suggesting that increases in energetic imbalance are associated with reductions in ovarian steroid levels. Vitzthum (2008) has recently proposed a flexible response model that has been used to account for the fact that while the ovarian cycles of healthy American women appear easily disrupted by dieting and exercise, women in nonindustrialized countries have high fertility despite low fat levels and high physical expenditures. In this model, the focus is on the fact that the conditions that might trigger ovarian suppression in the United States, for example, are likely to be temporary with conditions likely to improve in future, while in the nonindustrialized countries such conditions are chronic and there would be no adaptive advantage to delaying reproduction.

Based on the mammalian literature, as well as our understanding of reproduction in modern hunter-gatherers (Betzig, Borgerhoff-Mulder, & Turke, 1988), including how investment in partners and offspring is allocated within a life-history framework (Cronk, 2000; Kaplan, Hill, Hurtado, & Lancaster, 2001; Lancaster & Kaplan, 2000), there are a number of socioecological pressures that could have selected for mechanisms of reproductive suppression in humans. Such pressures include intense female social competition, stressful sexual attention from undesirable males, and overt pressure to reproduce (kin or male based) when it is not in the female's best interests to do so. Early maturing girls often lack the psychological maturity (and social capital) for successful reproduction (see Ellis, 2004, for a comprehensive discussion of the relationship between timing of female pubertal maturation and the environment). While early maturing in boys is often associated with social dominance, in girls it is more often associated with social stress and anxiety on the part of the individual and often from other family members (Blumenthal et al., 2011; Ge, Conger, & Elder, 1996; Jones & Mussen, 1958; Tobin-Richards, Boxer, & Petersen, 1983), especially if dating starts early as well (Simmons et al., 1983). Many girls in industrialized countries reach sexual maturity long before they are ready to be a mother. As a result, they experience greater vulnerability to reproductive stresses and are more likely to experience activation of ancestral mechanisms for reproductive suppression. Adolescence and young adulthood are a time in which females are particularly susceptible to developing excessive dieting, as a form of self-imposed reproductive suppression in response to competition, since this is a life stage that covers prime fertility as well as high levels of same-sex competition. Data on eating disorders suggest that adolescence is a time of increased competition and excessive dieting (Polivy & Herman, 2002; Smink, van Hoeken, & Hoek, 2012; Stice, Marti, Shaw, & Jaconis, 2009; Striegel-Moore & Bulik, 2007). Anorexics and others obsessed with thinness and dieting share characteristic attitudes and behaviors that can be seen as manifestations of a mechanism for reproductive suppression. These include body-image distortions, desire for thinness, negative attitudes toward food, amenorrhea, and reduced interest in sexual relationships, all of which have been associated in a number of studies with various eating-disordered behavior (Friedrichs, 1988; Haimes & Katz, 1988; Mintz & Betz, 1986; Stewart, 1992; Vaz-Leal & Salcedo-Salcedo, 1992). Garfinkel and Garner (1982) pioneered measuring such attitudes and behaviors to diagnose eating disorders such as anorexia nervosa. From this perspective, the media's use of thin women in advertising/fashion and on television and movies is its response to the preferences for thinness exhibited by women under conditions of high stress and female competition.

Self-Imposed Reproductive Suppression

A number of researchers have concentrated their attention on adolescent girls and the possibility that their desire in Western societies to significantly limit their food intake may be the reflection of a mechanism designed to slow sexual maturation and delay first reproduction in response to cues indicating poor conditions for reproduction in the current environment (Anderson et al., 1992; Salmon, Crawford, & Walters, 2008; Surbey, 1987). Anderson and colleagues examined this aspect of reproductive suppression in terms of cross-cultural standards of female beauty, pointing out that when women's reproductive work, having and raising children, is more highly valued than their work outside the home, as it can be in modern Western countries, a heavier standard of beauty prevails. Salmon, Crawford, and Walters (2008) developed a test of female competition to be used on adolescent girls based on high levels of female competition indicating an environment that is not ideal for reproduction. Responses to the items on the test collapsed into two main factors: dissatisfaction with physical appearance and female social competition. Surbey (1987) suggests that the activation of this suppression mechanism may explain anorexia in adolescent girls and documents a range of supporting evidence that highlights the psychological and demographic features shared by the early maturing girls in her sample and anorexics, such as high socioeconomic status, urban backgrounds, body dissatisfaction, emotional distress at puberty, and a fear of sexual maturation. Among high-socioeconomic status females, for example, intrasexual competition may be exaggerated if there are not enough high-status males to go around as mates, since females, and their families, prefer to marry within or up in social status (Schwartz, 2013).

Voland and Voland (1989) have also documented clinical patterns in anorexics that are uniquely predicted by the RSH. Anorexia is more common in countries with low adult mortality across the sexes. First sexual experiences are often associated with onset, and anorexics often experience conditions in which reproduction is currently unfavorable but likely to change in the future, such as a lack of committed relationship or low social support from family (Voland & Voland, 1989).

The very low frequency of clinical anorexia in nonindustrialized countries (Bemporad, 1997; Pate, Pumariega, Hester, & Garner, 1992; Voland & Voland, 1989), suggests that the ancestral mechanism might not have involved weight loss so much; rather, the intent was an altered weight-gain trajectory. The onset of menarche entails rapid physical growth (in height, weight, and proportion of body fat) even in populations where there is substantial nutritional stress (Frisch, 1985; Johnson, 1981). The onset of menstruation can be significantly delayed (without a corresponding decrease in final height/weight) simply by lowering the rate of prepubertal weight gain (Ellison, 1982; Whissell-Buechy & Willis, 1989). The value of the RSH depends on its ability to predict the environmental cues that could have elicited these changes in weight gain and their reproductive consequences. From this view, anorexia is a problem of the modern world, caused by the socioecological conditions faced by adolescent girls in industrialized societies in which cues to suppress reproduction (such as female competition, stress, quality of available males) may be present at much higher and more consistent levels than would have been found ancestrally. This suggests that increased competition for mates, for example, would result in a greater incidence of anorexia, and, while this is difficult to test directly, several researchers have reported supportive indirect evidence (Abed, 2011; Faer, Hendricks, Abed, & Figueredo, 2005).

Adaptation or Mismatch for Adolescent Girls

The pathway to adulthood in humans entails cognitive, social, physical, and sexual maturation. For hunter-gatherers living in ecological conditions closer to those of ancestral populations than urban Westerners, these maturation milestones are usually synchronized (Short, 1976). While hunter-gatherer girls may become sexually active around menarche, there are typically several years of adolescent sterility before their first births (Howell, 1979; Matthews & Hamilton, 2009). By the time of first birth, their cognitive and social development has reached the stage where they are capable of caring for a child.

Because the coordination of areas of maturation is important, an ancestral girl would have been disadvantaged if her sexual development (particularly first reproduction) preceded social and cognitive competence or occurred in an unfavorable environment because social variables, such as competition between females or local mate quality, are key factors in female reproductive success. Socially subordinate females, measured most commonly by behavioral observation and/or peer assessment in humans, have poorer reproductive outcomes in many primate species, including humans, as measured by pregnancy outcome and growth/survival of offspring. This occurs despite the efforts expended by the mother (Hardy, Welcher, Stanley, & Dallas, 1978; Peyser, Ayalon, Harell, Toaff, & Cordova, 1973; Smith & Kunz, 1976; Wasser & Barash, 1983; Wasser & Isenberg, 1986).

Ancestrally, a number of cues could have signaled an unfavorable social environment for reproduction. As puberty approached, a girl would have perceived insufficient support from kin or other allies. There could be a shortage of quality males available. A delay in her sexual maturation via modification of her weight-gain trajectory (in the absence of modern tools like the birth control pill) could result in improved success of her first pregnancy if the delay extended until her social resources or the external social conditions improved. This motivation to slow down the accumulation of body fat would be mild to moderate when she could expect to quickly improve her skills or the environment was likely to improve in the very near future. But in modern industrial societies, the intensity and duration of courtship and the sheer numbers of peers (or competitors) in school, sports, or other social settings expose girls to cues of competition and stress at levels likely never experienced by ancestral populations. In this light, anorexia can be seen as the result of supernormal stimuli, or exaggerated cues of poor reproductive environments, switching an ancestrally adaptive weight-control mechanism on and leaving it on, leading to extreme levels of weight loss in some cases. Juda, Campbell, and Crawford (2004) found that women who perceived themselves as having relatively low levels of social support (particularly from their romantic partner or family) report increased dieting behavior and lower perceptions of parental readiness. This echoes Turke's suggestion (1989) that the breakdown of extended kin networks is related to decreased fertility (whether that decrease occurs through reproductive suppression or failure to implant).

Anderson and Crawford (1992) modeled the types of conditions in which this kind of mechanism for adolescent weight control would be adaptive. Their results suggest that a reproductive-suppression mechanism that responds to social stress would have been most likely to evolve when females had relatively few surviving offspring, typically over the lifespan and when first reproduction under poor conditions would produce substantial decreases in future reproductive success or survival. Evidence suggests that such conditions were probably common ancestrally (Kruger & Nesse, 2005; Tooby & Cosmides, 1990).

Relevant Factors Influencing the Mechanism

What conditions would render self-suppression an adaptive choice for young women? And how widespread are such conditions now? Anderson and Crawford's (1992) model, as mentioned previously, would predict that psychological states leading to weight control could be relatively easily produced in girls experiencing unfavorable social conditions in a population where reproductive success is high under optimal conditions, socially disadvantaged girls receive little help when pregnant, and maximum reproductive value is relatively low. These conditions are frequently found in industrialized countries and, unsurprisingly, so is dieting in young women (Garfinkel & Garner, 1982; Polivy & Herman, 2002; Striegal-Moore & Bulik, 2007).

Several studies have examined the relationship between dieting in Western societies, perception of social support, and female competition (Faer et al., 2005; Juda et al., 2004; Salmon, Crawford, Dane, et al., 2008). Female competition has been of special interest because human females are unique in the extent to which female social support is necessary for successful reproduction, including assistance during birth, help with infant care, and care of older siblings (Trevathan, 1987). However, supporters are also often primary competitors for individual access to the resources required for successful reproduction (Hrdy, 1981). As a result, environments characterized by intense female social competition (in the modern world, think all-girl school; ancestrally think local shortage of males, high number of females) would have been unfavorable for reproduction to many women and more likely to trigger reproductive suppression.

The role of intrasexual competition on eating disorders has been explored from an evolutionary perspective with several different specific stressors as the focus, though most see a mismatch between the modern social environment and female adaptations for intrasexual competition for mates and status. Salmon, Crawford, Dane, et al. (2008) examined the relative influence of female competition, male attention, media influence, and parental pressure on eating-disordered behavior and reported a larger effect for high versus low female competition-based stress as opposed to other stressors. In other words, high levels of social competition resulted in higher disordered-eating scores than did high levels of exposure to media images of women, undesirable male attention, or parental pressure. Abed et al. (2012) examined what they refer to as the sexual competition hypothesis (SCH), that female intrasexual competition is the cause at the heart of eating disorders. They, like Faer et al. (2005) and Salmon et al. (2009), reported results that suggest that high levels of such competition are highly predictive of eating-disordered behavior, especially in women following a fast life history strategy that entails reproducing early and often. Slow life history strategy, having fewer offspring but investing more in them, seems to be associated with lower levels of, or lower responsiveness to, female intrasexual competition, resulting in less eating-disordered behavior.

Li, Smith, Griskevicius, Cason, and Bryan (2010) focused on the role of status competition in eating restriction and found that exposure to high-status and competitive same-sex individuals who were not thin or highly attractive led to greater body dissatisfaction and restrictive eating attitudes for women and not for men. Smith, Li, and Joiner

(2011) also looked at the relationship between status seeking and disordered eating. Exposure to thin, successful career women increased body dissatisfaction and feelings of ineffectiveness but more so in women who were high in status-seeking than in women with lower status aspirations. Intrasexual competition for status was related to body dissatisfaction in high status-seeking women. Additionally, there is some evidence that developmental environment can influence adult women's responses to environmental cues that might trigger reproductive suppression. Hill, Rodeheffer, DelPriore, and Butterfield (2013) report that when women grow up in a low-socioeconomic-status environment, harshness cues in the adult environment result in an increased desire for food. However, for women who grow up in high socioeconomic environments, harshness cues result in less of a desire for food and increased concern with dieting. This is most likely due to the fact that such cues may be more likely seen as temporary based on their early environment, in which case suppression of reproduction would be adaptive if conditions are likely to improve.

Suppression of Other Women

The majority of research on humans discussed so far has focused on self-suppression in response to environmental conditions. Linda Mealey (1999, 2000) was one of the first to suggest that too narrow a focus on self-suppression and the RSH can result in overlooking the role that manipulation of subordinate females by dominant females may have in reproductive suppression. She suggested that extreme dieting or anorexia could be better explained as the product of dominant women co-opting an adaptive mechanism for self-regulation of reproduction in order to reduce the reproductive value of other women, decreasing competition for limited resources for the benefit of the more dominant women. While male competition often plays out in physical confrontations, female competition typically does not (Campbell, 2004). Intrasexual signaling of social status, advertising attractiveness, and male choosiness are more often the vehicle for female competitiveness (Cashdan, 1996), as well as verbal attacks and indirect social aggression (Cashdan, 1999; Schmitt & Buss, 1996; Vaillancourt, Miller, & Sharma, 2010). Female competition more often specializes in rumors and manipulation of social reputations (Buss & Dedden, 1990; Österman et al., 1998). And the target of such innuendo is typically a sexual rival—the strategy derogation and suggestions that decrease her desirability as a mate.

This type of competition can have a significant impact on female psychology (Wiederman & Hurst, 1998) and reproductive physiology. Low self-esteem and poor perception of social support from family and friends has been associated with increased rates of reproductive problems, including infertility, ovulatory delay, and spontaneous abortion (Laukaran & Van Den Berg, 1980; Nuckolls, 1975), similar to other mammals experiencing high levels of female aggression. Wasser and Barash (1983) report studies of noncontracepting populations in which, over a 10-year span, less than 50% of fertile women had two or more children while over 40% had none. They interpret this finding as indicative of the reproductive suppression of subordinate women by dominant ones. Vaillancourt (2013) has also suggested that dieters engage in more indirect aggression, such as verbal derogation, toward and are more competitive with other females than those who do not diet and that this is part of their mate-competition strategy. In addition, the indirect (verbal) aggression is targeted toward the weight and food intake of their competitors.

Conclusions

Research in other mammalian species suggests that one outcome of female competition is reproductive suppression of subordinate individuals by socially dominant ones. Evidence indicates this happens through tactics like social harassment, which results in an increased stress response and corresponding hormonal changes that reduce the likelihood of reproduction. Other tactics, such as monopolizing food resources, can lead to reproductive suppression through insufficient nutrient supply. The suggestion has been made that a similar phenomenon can occur in human females in response to high levels of female competition over social status and/or access to mates, though in the case of humans there is debate over whether suppression is imposed by others or is self-selected in response to socioecological cues, though the mechanism is suggested to involve excessive dieting or exercise designed to suppress ovulation under conditions of high competition and insufficient resources required for reproduction. More work needs to be done examining mechanisms by which reproductive suppression or delay occurs in humans. Are changes in steroid hormones, as a result of dieting or excessive exercise, shutting down ovulation in response to high levels of female competition?

Are other chemical signals involved? Some studies have suggested a role for odor cues or vocal signals in female competition in other species. Could there be scent or verbal cues given off by human females that indicate success, or a lack of success, in social competition and might therefore result in suppression of others?

If we accept that reproductive suppression occurs in human females as a result of female competition, one relevant question is whether most reproductive suppression is imposed on subordinates by dominants or whether it is it a strategic choice on the part of subordinate females. Subordinates might, for example, try to avoid the high costs of current competition in order to compete more effectively at a later date when their own status may have improved. What kinds of methodologies will allow us to distinguish between these two possibilities? Assessing this question will likely require longitudinal studies of women of varying social status. It would also be relevant to know how much success in female competition can be attributed to dominants raising the cost of competition experienced by subordinates. Are the actions of dominants, or the threats of actions such as social exclusion, enough to make subordinates bow out of the competition entirely? Subordinates may be more likely to switch social environments when competition is high, perhaps even by moving from one city or job site to the next in the Western world, hoping to be in a better position than their current one.

This suppression mechanism has been used as part of an evolutionary approach to the understanding of eating disorders such as anorexia, which are associated with low body weight and amenorrhea. These evolutionary approaches to dieting suggest that women experiencing environments with abundant cues of intrasexual competition will be most at risk of developing an eating disorder. However, many studies examining the relationship between adaptive reproductive suppression and eating disorders have used nonclinical populations and focused on undergraduates or adolescents in Western societies. More work needs to be done in this area using clinical and nonclinical populations, as well as populations varying naturally (as well as experimentally) on various dimensions of female competition and factors such as social support and other measures of resilience. It would also be helpful to have a better understanding of what happens as nonindustrialized societies transition in terms of levels and cues of female competition, as well as any development of dieting-based eating disorders.

In addition, if the modern consequences of the ancestral mechanism for reproductive suppression, such as eating disorders, are undesirable, what can be done to alter the mechanism's functioning? If cues to suppress are present, are there factors that can be determined and influenced that would reduce susceptibility to female competition? Some previously suggested preventative factors include social support from friends and family. In a similar vein, are there individual differences in susceptibility to develop excessive dieting in response to female competition? Salmon, Crawford, Dane, et al. (2008) suggested that there were individual differences in susceptibility to experimental manipulations of competition cues in terms of increasing disordered eating, but this question awaits further exploration in order to develop successful interventions.

Overall, interest in research on female intrasexual competition appears to be at an all-time high, and attention has started to shift from showy male displays of competition to the often subtler forms of competition seen between females. These forms typically include gossip and the derogation of competitors, relatively low-risk competitive tactics, though under some socioecological conditions, such as high variance in male quality and resource acquisition and poverty, the benefits of more aggressive, risky competition may outweigh the risks. The fact that variance in reproductive success, measured by offspring birth and survival, occurs between women is an indicator that competition is occurring. Based on the nonhuman animal literature and the growing human reproductive suppression literature, it seems likely that reproductive suppression is another tactic in the female competition arsenal. A better understanding of how this ancestral suppressive mechanism functions will also be useful for managing the dangerous effects it can have in a modern environment, with frequent cues of exaggerated levels of competition.

References

Abbott, D. H. (1992). Social conflict and reproductive suppression in marmoset and tamarin monkeys. In W. A. Mason & S. P. Mendoza (Eds.), *Primate social conflict* (pp. 331–373). New York: SUNY Press.

Abed, R. T. (2011). The sexual competition hypothesis for eating disorders. *British Journal of Medical Psychology, 71*, 525–547.

Abed, R. T., Mehta, S., Figuerdo, A. J., Aldridge, S., Balson, H., Meyer, C., & Palmer, R. (2012). Eating disorders and intrasexual competition: Testing an evolutionary hypothesis among young women. *Scientific World Journal, 1*, 1–8.

Adams, G. R. (1977). Physical attractiveness research: Toward a developmental social psychology of beauty. *Human Development, 28*, 217–239.

Adler, P. A., & Adler, P. (1996). Preadolescent clique stratification and the hierarchy of identity. *Sociological Inquiry, 66,* 111–142.

Anderson, J. L., & Crawford, C. B. (1992). Modeling costs and benefits of adolescent weight control as a mechanism for reproductive suppression. *Human Nature, 3,* 299–334.

Anderson, J. L., Crawford, C. B., Nadeau, J., & Lindberg, T. (1992). Was the Duchess of Windsor right? A cross-cultural analysis of attitudes toward fatness in women. *Ethology and Sociobiology, 13,* 197–227.

Arnocky, S., Sunderani, S., Miller, J., & Vaillancourt, T. (2011). Jealousy mediates the relationship between attractiveness comparisons and females' indirect aggression. *Personal Relationships, 19,* 290–303.

Barash, S. S. (2006). *Tripping the prom queen: The truth about women and rivalry.* New York: St. Martin's Griffen.

Barrett, J., Abbott, D. H., & George, L. M. (1993). Sensory cues and the suppression of reproduction in subordinate female marmoset monkeys, *Callithrix jacchus. Journal of Reproduction and Fertility, 97,* 301–310.

Becker, J. B., Breedlove, S. M., & Crews, D. (1993). *Behavioral endocrinology.* Cambridge, MA: MIT Press.

Bemporad, J. R. (1997). Cultural and historical aspects of eating disorders. *Theoretical Medicine, 18,* 401–420.

Benenson, J. F. (2009). Dominating versus eliminating the competition: Sex differences in human intrasexual aggression. *Behavior and Brain Sciences, 32,* 268–269.

Bercovitch, F. B., & Strum, S. C. (1993). Dominance rank, resource availability, and reproductive maturation in female savanna baboons. *Behavioral Ecology and Sociobiology, 33,* 313–318.

Bethea, C. L., Centeno, M. L., & Cameron, J. L. (2008). Neurobiology of stress-induced reproductive dysfunction in female macaques. *Molecular Neurobiology, 38,* 199–230.

Betzig, L. L., Borgerhoff Mulder, M. B., & Turke P. W. (1988). *Human reproductive behavior: A Darwinian perspective.* Cambridge, UK: Cambridge University Press.

Björkqvist, K. (1994). Sex differences in physical, verbal, and indirect aggression: A review of recent research. *Sex Roles, 30,* 177–188.

Björkqvist, K., Lagerspetz, K. M., & Kaukiainen, A. (1992). Do girls manipulate and boys fight? Developmental trends in regard to direct and indirect aggression. *Aggressive Behavior, 18,* 117–127.

Blumenthal, H., Leen-Feldner, E. W., Babson, K. A., Gahr, J. L., Trainor, C. D., & Frala, J. L. (2011). Elevated social anxiety among early maturing girls. *Developmental Psychology, 47,* 1133–1140.

Boardway, R. H., & Weisfeld, G. E. (1994). Social dominance among English adolescents. Poster presented at International Society for Human Ethology Congress, Toronto, August.

Boesch, C., Kohou, G., Nene, H., & Vigilant, L. (2006). Male competition and paternity in wild chimpanzees of the Tai Forest. *American Journal of Physical Anthropology, 130,* 103–115.

Botta, R. A. (2003). For your health? The relationship between magazine reading and adolescents' body image and eating disturbances. *Sex Roles, 48,* 389–399.

Bowman, L. A., Dilley, S. R., & Keverne, E. B. (1978). Suppression of oestrogen-induced LH surges by social subordination in talapoin monkeys. *Nature, 275,* 56–58.

Boyne, M. S., Thame, M., Osmond, C., Fraser, R. A., Gabay, L., Reid, M., & Forrester, T. E. (2010). Growth, body composition, and the onset of puberty: Longitudinal observations in Afro-Caribbean children. *Journal of Clinical Endocrinology and Metabolism, 95,* 3194–3200.

Buss, D. M. (1988). The evolution of human intrasexual competition: Tactics of mate attraction. *Journal of Personality and Social Psychology, 54,* 616–628.

Buss, D. M., & Dedden, L. A. (1990). Derogation of competitors. *Journal of Social and Personal Relationships, 7,* 395–422.

Byrne, D. G., Davenport, S. C., & Mazanov, J. (2007). Profiles of adolescent stress: The development of the Adolescent Stress Questionnaire (ASQ). *Journal of Adolescence, 30,* 393–416.

Campbell, A. (1991). *The girls in the gang.* Oxford: Blackwell.

Campbell, A. (1995). A few good men: Evolutionary psychology and female adolescent aggression. *Ethology and Sociobiology, 16,* 99–123.

Campbell, A. (2004). Female competition: Causes, constraints, content, and contexts. *Journal of Sex Research, 41,* 16–26.

Campbell, A. (2013). The evolutionary psychology of women's aggression. *Philosophical Transactions of the Royal Society B, 368,* 20130078.

Caro, T. M., & Sellen, D. W. (1990). The reproductive advantages of fat in women. *Ethology and Sociobiology, 11,* 51–66.

Cashdan, E. (1996). Women's mating strategies. *Evolutionary Anthropology, 5,* 134–143.

Cashdan, E. (1999). How women compute. *Behavioural and Brain Sciences, 22,* 221.

Cassini, M. H., & Foger, B. (1995). The effect of food distribution on habitat use of foraging hedgehogs and the ideal non-territorial despotic distribution. *Acta Oecologica, 16,* 657–669.

Clarke, F. M., Miethe, G. H., & Bennett, N. C. (2001). Reproductive suppression in female Damaraland mole-rats *Cryptomys damarensis:* Dominant control or self-restraint. *Proceedings of the Royal Society B, 268,* 899–909.

Clutton-Brock, T. H. (1991). *The evolution of parental care.* Princeton, NJ: Princeton University Press.

Clutton-Brock, T. H., Hodge, S. J., Flower, T. P., Sprang, G. F., & Young, A. J. (2010). Adaptive suppression of subordinate reproduction in cooperative mammals. *American Naturalist, 176,* 664–673.

Craig, A. S., Herman, L. M., & Pack, A. A. (2002). Male mate choice and male–male competition coexist in the humpback whale (*Megaptera novaeangliae*). *Canadian Journal of Zoolology, 80,* 745–755.

Crawford, C. B. (1989). Sex differences in life histories: The role of sexual selection and mate choice. *Behavioral and Brain Sciences, 12,* 18.

Creel, S. (2001). Social dominance and stress hormones. *Trends in Ecology and Evolution, 16,* 491–497.

Creel, S. (2005). Dominance, aggression, and glucocorticoid levels in social carnivores. *Journal of Mammology, 86,* 255–264.

Creel, S., & Creel, N. M. (1995). Communal hunting and pack size in African wild dogs, *Lycaon pictus. Animal Behaviour, 50,* 1325–1339.

Creel, S., & Creel, N. M. (1998). Six ecological factors that may limit African wild dogs, *Lycaon pictus. Animal Conservation, 1,* 1–9.

Creel, S., Creel, N. M., Mills, M. G. L., & Monfort, S. L. (1997). Rank and reproduction in cooperatively breeding African wild dogs: bevaioral and endocrine correlates. *Behavioral Ecology, 8,* 298-306.

Cronin, C. L. (1980). Dominance relations and females. In D. R. Omark, F. F. Strayer, & D. G. Freedman (Eds.), *Dominance* relations: An ethological view of human conflict and social interaction (pp. 299–318). New York: Garland.

Cronk, L. (2000). Female-biased parental investment and growth performance among the Mukogodo. In L. Cronk, N. Chagnon, & W. Irons (Eds.), Adaptation and human behavior: An anthropological perspective (pp. 203–222). New York: Aldine de Gruyter.

Daly, M., & Daly, S. (1974). Spatial distribution of a leaf-eating Saharan gerbil (Psammomys obesus) in relation to its food. Mammalia, 38, 591–603.

Daly, M., & Wilson, M. (2005). Carpe diem: Adaptation and devaluing the future. Quarterly Review of Biology, 80, 55–61.

De Bruyn, E. H., & van den Boom, D. C. (2005). Interpersonal behavior, peer popularity, and self- esteem in early adolescence. Social Development, 14, 555–573.

Dijkstra, J. K., Lindenberg, S., & Veenstra, R. (2008). Beyond the class norm: Bullying behavior of popular adolescents and its relation to peer acceptance and rejection. Journal of Abnormal Child Psychology, 36, 1289–1299.

Donohoe, M. L., van Hippel, W., & Brooks, R. C. (2009). Beyond waist-hip ratio: Experimental multivariate evidence that average women's torsos are most attractive. Behavioral Ecology, 20, 716–721.

Ellis, B. J. (2004). Timing of pubertal maturation in girls: An integrated life history approach. Psychological Bulletin, 130, 920-958.

Ellis, L. (1995). Dominance and reproductive success among nonhuman animals: A cross-species comparison. Ethology & Sociobiology, 16, 257–333.

Ellison, P. T. (1982). Skeletal growth, fatness, and menarcheal age: A comparison of two hypotheses. Human Biology, 54, 269–281.

Ellison, P. T. (1990). Human ovarian function and reproductive ecology: New hypotheses. American Anthropologist, 92, 933–952.

Ellison, P. T. (2003). Energetics and reproductive effort. American Journal of Human Biology, 15, 342–351.

Essock-Vitale, S. M., & McGuire, M. T. (1985). Women's lives viewed from an evolutionary perspective. II. Patterns of helping. Ethology and Sociobiology, 6, 155–173.

Etcoff, N. (1999). The survival of the prettiest: The science of beauty. New York: Doubleday.

Faer, L. M., Hendricks, A., Abed, R. T., & Figueredo, A. J. (2005). The evolutionary psychology of eating disorders: Female competition for mates or for status. Psychological Psychotherapy, 78, 397–417.

Fenster, L., Waller, K., Chen, J., Hubbard, A. E., Windham, G. C., Elkin, E., & Swan, S. (1999). Psychological stress in the workplace and menstrual function. American Journal of Epidemiology, 149, 127–134.

Ferguson, C. J., Winegard, B., & Winegard, B. M. (2011). Who is the fairest one of all? How evolution guides peer and media influences on female body dissatisfaction. Review of General Psychology, 15, 11–28.

Finkelstein, D. M., Kubzansky, L. D., Capitman, J., & Goodman, E. (2007). Socioeconomic differences in adolescent stress: The role of psychological resources. Journal of Adolescent Health, 40, 127–134.

Fisher, M. L. (2004). Female intrasexual competition decreases female facial attractiveness. Proceedings of the Royal Society B, 271(Suppl. 5): S283–S285.

Fisher, M. L. (2013). Women's intrasexual competition for mates. In M. L. Fisher, J. R. Garcia, & R. Sokol Chang (Eds.), Evolution's empress: Darwinian perspectives on the nature of women (pp. 19–42). New York: Oxford University Press.

Fisher, M. L., Cox, A., & Gordon, F. (2009). Deciding between competition, derogation, and self- promotion. Journal of Evolutionary Psychology, 7, 287–308.

Frame, L. H., Malcolm, J. R., Frame, G. W., & Van Lawick, H. (1979). Social organization of African wild dogs (Lycaon pictus) on the Serengeti Plains, Tanzania 1967–1978. Zeitschrift für Tierpsychologie, 50, 225–249.

Frankel, K. A. (1990). Girls' perceptions of peer relationship support and stress. Journal of Early Adolescence, 10, 69–88.

Friedrichs, M. (1988). The dependent solution: Anorexia and bulimia as defenses against danger. Women and Therapy, 7(4), 53–73.

Frisch, R. E. (1985). Fatness, menarche, and female fertility. Perspectives in Biology and Medicine, 28, 611–633.

Frisch, R. E. (1990). The right weight: Body fat, menarche, and ovulation. Bailliere's Clinical Obstetrics and Gynaecology, 4, 419–439.

Frisch, R. E. (2002). Female fertility and the body fat connection. Chicago: University of Chicago Press.

Frisch, R. E., & Barbieri, R. L. (2002). Female fertility and the body fat connection. Chicago: University of Chicago Press.

Frisch, R. E., von Gotz-Welbergen, A., McArthur, S., Albright, T., Witschi, J., Bullen, B., . . . Hermann, H. (1981). Delayed menarche and amenorrhea of college athletes in relation to age of onset of training. Journal of the American Medical Association, 246, 1559–1563.

Gangestad, S. W., & Thornhill, R. (1997). Human sexual selection and developmental stability. In J. A. Simpson & D. T. Kenrick (Eds.), Evolutionary social psychology (pp. 169–195). Mahwah, NJ: Erlbaum.

Garcia, C., Lee, P. C., & Rosetta, L. (2008). Impact of social environment on variation in menstrual cycle length in captive female olive baboons (Papio anubis). Reproduction, 135, 89–97.

Garfinkel, P. E., & Garner, D. M. (1982). Anorexia nervosa: A multidimensional perspective. New York: Bruner-Mazel.

Ge, X., Conger, R. D., & Elder G. H. Jr. (1996). Coming of age too early: Pubertal influences on girls' vulnerability to psychological distress. Child Development, 67, 3386–3400.

Geary, D. C. (2000). Evolution and proximate expression of human parental investment. Psychological Bulletin, 126, 55-77.

Geary, D. C. (2010). Male, female: The evolution of sex differences. (2nd ed.) Washington, DC: American Psychological Association.

Gende, S. M., & Quinn, T. P. (2004). The relative importance of prey density and social dominance in determining energy intake by bears feeding on Pacific salmon. Canadian Journal of Zoology, 82, 75–85.

Goodall, J. (1986). The chimpanzees of Gombe. Cambridge, MA: Harvard University Press.

Gordon, R. A. (1988). A sociocultural interpretation of the current epidemic of eating disorders. In B. J. Blinder, B. F. Chaitin, & R. S. Goldstein (Eds.), The eating disorders: Medical and psychological bases of diagnosis and treatment. (pp. 285–293). New York: PMA.

Groesz, L. M., Levine, M. P., & Murnen, S. K. (2002). The effects of experimental presentation of thin media images on body satisfaction: A meta-analytic review. *International Journal of Eating Disorders, 31,* 1–16.

Hankin, B. L., Mermelstein, R., & Roesch, L. (2007). Sex differences in adolescent depression: Stress exposure and reactivity models. *Child Development, 78,* 279–295.

Harcourt, A. H. (1987). Dominance and fertility among female primates. *Journal of Zoology, 213,* 471–487.

Hardy, J. B., Welcher, D. W., Stanley, J., & Dallas, J. R. (1978). Long-range outcomes of adolescent pregnancy. *Clinical Obstetrics and Gynecology, 21,* 1215–1232.

Haimes, A. L., & Katz, J. L. (1988). Sexual and social maturity versus social conformity in restricting anorectic, bulimic, and borderline women. *International Journal of Eating Disorders, 3,* 331–341.

Hill, S. E., Rodeheffer, C. D., DelPriore, D. J., & Butterfield, M. E. (2013). Ecological contingencies in women's calories regulation psychology: A life history approach. *Journal of Experimental Social Psychology, 49,* 888–897.

Hines, N. J., & Fry, D. P. (1994). Indirect modes of aggression among women of Buenos Aires, Argentina. *Sex Roles, 30,* 213–236.

Hrdy, S. B. (1981). *The woman that never evolved.* Cambridge, MA: Harvard University Press.

Howell, N. (1979). *Demography of the Dobe!Kung.* New York: Academic Press.

Johnson, P. L. (1981). When dying is better than living: Female suicide among the Gainj of Papua New Guinea. *Ethnology, 20,* 325–335.

Jolly, A. (1985). *The evolution of primate behavior* (2nd ed.). New York: Macmillan.

Jones, M. C., & Mussen, P. H. (1958). The later careers of boys who were early- or late maturing. *Child Development, 28,* 113–128.

Juda, M. N., Campbell, L., & Crawford, C. B. (2004). Dieting symptomatology in women and perceptions of social support: An evolutionary approach. *Evolution and Human Behavior, 25,* 200–208.

Kaplan, H., Hill, K., Hurtado, A. M., & Lancaster, J. (2001). The embodied capital theory of human evolution. In P. T. Ellison (Ed.), *Reproductive ecology and human evolution* (pp. 293–318). New York: Aldine de Gruyter.

Kennedy, J. H. (1990). Determinants of peer social status: Contributions of physical appearance, reputation, and behavior. *Journal of Youth and Adolescence, 19,* 233–244.

King, W. J., & Allaine, D. (2002). Social, maternal, and environmental influences on reproductive success in female Alpine marmots (*Marmota marmota*). *Canadian Journal of Zoology, 80,* 2137–2143.

Koskela, E., Mappes, T., & Ylonen, H. (1997). Territorial behavior and reproductive success of bank vole *Clethrionomys glareolus* females. *Journal of Animal Ecology, 66,* 314–349.

Kruger, D. L., & Nesse, R. M. (2005). An evolutionary life-history framework for understanding sex differences in human mortality rates. *Human Nature, 17,* 74–97.

Lancaster, J., & Kaplan, H. (2000). Parenting other men's children: Costs, benefits, and consequences. In L. Cronk, N. Chagnon, & W. Irons (Eds.), *Adaptation and human behavior: An anthropological perspective* (pp. 179–202). New York: Aldine de Gruyter.

Lash, M. M., & Armstrong, A. (2009). Impact of obesity on women's health. *Fertility and Sterility, 91,* 1712–1716.

Laukaran, V. H., & Van Den Berg, B. J. (1980). The relationship of maternal attitude to pregnancy outcomes and obstetric complications. *American Journal of Obstetrics and Gynecology, 136,* 374–379.

Lepowsky, M. (1994). Women, men and aggression in an egalitarian society. *Sex Roles, 30,* 199–211.

Li, N. P., Smith, A. R., Griskevicius, V., Cason, M. J., & Bryan, A. (2010). Intrasexual competition and eating restriction in heterosexual and homosexual individuals. *Evolution and Human Behavior, 31,* 365–372.

Lott, B. (1981). *Becoming a woman: The socialization of gender.* Springfield, IL: Charles C. Thomas.

Luthar, S. S., & Latendresse, S. J. (2005). Children of the affluent: Challenges to well-being. *Current Directions on Psychological Science, 14,* 49–53.

MacLeod, K. J., Nielsen, J. F., & Clutton-Brock, T. H. (2013). Factors predicting the frequency, likelihood, and duration of allonursing in the cooperatively breeding meerkat. *Animal Behaviour, 86,* 1059–1067.

Massey, A., & Vandenbergh, J. G. (1980). Puberty delay by a urinary cue from female house mice in feral populations. *Science, 209,* 821–822.

Matthews, T. J., & Hamilton, B. E. (2009). Delayed childbearing: More women are having their first child later in life. *NCHS Data Brief, 21,* 1–8.

Mealey, L. (1999). Evolutionary models of female intrasexual competition. *Behavioral and Brain Sciences, 22,* 234.

Mealey, L. (2000). Anorexia: A "losing" strategy? *Human Nature, 11,* 105–116.

Merten, D. E. (2004). The best of friends: The politics of girls' friendships: I. Securing her experience: Friendship versus popularity. *Feminism and Psychology, 14,* 361–365.

Miller, G. F. (2000). *The mating mind.* New York: Doubleday.

Mintz, L. & Betz, N. (1986). Sex differences in the nature, realism, and correlates of body image. *Sex Roles, 15,* 185–195.

Modin, B., Ostberg, V., & Almquist, Y. (2011). Childhood peer status and adult susceptibility to anxiety and depression. A 30-year hospital follow-up. *Journal of Abnormal Child Psychology, 39,* 187–199.

Murray, C. M., Eberly, L. E., & Pusey, A.E. (2006). Foraging strategies as a function of season and rank among wild female chimpanzees (*Pan troglodytes*). *Behavioral Ecology, 17,* 1020–1028.

Murray, C. M., Mane, S. V., & Pusey, A. E. (2007). Dominance rank influences female space use in wild chimpanzees, *Pan troglodytes*: Towards an ideal despotic distribution. *Animal Behaviour, 74,* 1795–1804.

Nuckolls, K. (1975). Life crisis and psychological assets: Some clinical implications. In B. H. Kaplan & J.C. Cassell (Eds.), *Family and health: An epidemiological approach,* (pp. 108–124). Chapel Hill, NC: Institute for Research in Social Sciences.

Ordiz, A., Stoen, O. G., Swenson, J. E., Kojola, I., & Bischof, R. (2008). Distance-dependent effect of the nearest neighbor: Spatiotemporal patterns in brown bear reproduction. *Ecology, 89,* 3327–3335.

Österman, K., Björkqvist, K., Lagerspetz, K. M. J., Kaukiainen, A., Landau, S. F., Fraczek, A., & Caprara, G. V. (1998). Cross-cultural evidence of female indirect aggression. *Aggressive Behavior, 24,* 1–8.

Owens, L., Shute, R., & Slee, P. (2000). "Guess what I just heard!" Indirect aggression among teenage girls in Australia. *Aggressive Behaviour, 26,* 67–83.

Parent, A., Teilmann, G., Jual, A., Skakkeback, N. E., Toppari, J., & Bourguignon, J. (2003). The timing of normal puberty and the age limits of sexual precocity: Variations around the world, secular trends, and changes after migration. *Endocrine Reviews, 24,* 668–693.

Pate, J. E., Pumariega, A. J., Hester, C., & Garner, D. M. (1992). Cross-cultural patterns in eating disorders: A review. *Journal of the American Academy of Child and Adolescent Psychiatry, 31,* 802–808.

Payne, K. K., Brown, S. L., & Manning, W. D. (2013). *Crossover in median age at first marriage and first birth: Thirty years of change.* Bowling Green, OH: National Center for Family & Marriage Research.

Peyser, M. R., Ayalon, D., Harell, J., Toaff, R., & Cordova, T. (1973). Stress-induced delay of ovulation. *Obstetrics and Gynecology, 42,* 667–670.

Polivy, J., & Herman, C. P. (2002). Causes of eating disorders. *Annual Review of Psychology, 53,* 187–213.

Puts, D. (2010). Beauty and the beast: Mechanisms of sexual selection in humans. *Evolution and Human Behavior, 31,* 157–175.

Rankin, J. L., Lane, D. J., Gibbons, F. X., & Gerrard, M. (2004). Adolescent self-consciousness: Longitudinal age changes and gender differences in two cohorts. *Journal of Research on Adolescence, 14,* 1–21.

Rippon, C., Nash, J., Myburgh, K. H., & Noakes, T. D. (1988). Abnormal eating attitude test scores predict menstrual dysfunction in lean females. *International Journal of Eating Disorders, 7,* 617–624.

Robinson, M. R., Pilkington, J. G., Clutton-Brock, T. H., Pemberton, J. M., & Kruuk, L. E.B. (2006). Live fast, die young: Trade-offs between fitness components and sexually antagonistic selection on weaponry in Soay sheep. *Evolution, 60,* 2168–2181.

Salmon, C., Crawford, C., Dane, L., & Zuberbier, O. (2008). Ancestral mechanisms in modern environments: Impact of competition and stressors on body image and dieting behavior. *Human Nature, 19,* 103–117.

Salmon, C., Crawford, C. B., & Walters, S. (2008). Anorexic behaviour, female competition, and stress: Developing the Female Competition Stress Test. *Evolutionary Psychology, 6,* 96–112.

Salmon, C., Figueredo, A. J., & Woodburn, L. (2009). Life history strategy and disordered eating behavior. *Evolutionary Psychology, 7,* 585–600.

Sanders, K. A., & Bruce, N. W. (1999). Psychosocial stress and the menstrual cycle. *Journal of Biosocial Science, 31,* 393–402.

Saltzman, W., Ahmed, S., Fahimi, A., Wittwer, D. J., & Wegner, F. H. (2006). Social suppression of female reproductive maturation and infanticidal behavior in cooperatively breeding Mongolian gerbils. *Hormones and Behavior, 49,* 527–537.

Saltzman, W., Prudom, S. L., Schultz-Darken, N. J., Wittwer, D. J., & Abbott, D. H. (2004). Social suppression of cortisol in female marmoset monkeys: Role of circulating ACTH levels and glucocorticoid negative feedback. *Psychoneuroendocrinology, 29,* 141–161.

Savin-Williams, R. C. (1987). *Adolescence: An ethological perspective.* New York: Springer-Verlag.

Schmidt, L., Sobotka, T., Bentzen, J. G., & Nyboe Anderson, A. (2011). Demographic and medical consequences of the postponement of parenthood. *Human Reproduction Update, 18,* 29–43.

Schmitt, D. P., & Buss, D. M. (1996). Strategic self-promotion and competitor derogation: Sex and context effects on the perceived effectiveness of mate attraction tactics. *Journal of Personality and Social Psychology, 70,* 1185–1204.

Schwartz, C. R. (2013). Trends and variation in assortative mating: Causes and consequences. *Annual Review of Sociology, 39,* 451–470.

Scott, E. C., & Johnston, F. E. (1982). Critical fat, menarche, and the maintenance of menstrual cycles: A critical review. *Journal of Adolescent Health Care, 2,* 249–260.

Scott, E. M., Mann, J., Watson-Capps, J. J., Sargeant, B. L., & Connor, R. C. (2005). Aggression in bottlenose dolphins: Evidence for sexual coercion, male–ale competition, and female tolerance through analysis of tooth-rake marks and behavior. *Behaviour, 142,* 21–44.

Sherman, P. W. (1977). Nepotism and the evolution of alarm calls. *Science, 197,* 1246–1253.

Sherman, P. W. (1981). Reproductive competition and infanticide in Belding's ground squirrels and other animals. In R. D. Alexander & D. W. Tinkle, (Eds.), *Natural selection and social behavior* (pp. 311–331). New York: Chiron Press.

Short, R. V. (1976). The evolution of human reproduction. *Proceedings of the Royal Society of London B, 195,* 3–24.

Simmons, R. (2002). *Odd girl out: The hidden culture of aggression in girls.* New York: Harcourt.

Simmons, R. G., Blyth, D. A., & McKinney, K. L. (1983). The social and psychological effects of puberty on white females. In J. Brooks-Gunn & A.C. Petersen (Eds.), *Girls at puberty: Biological and psychological perspectives* (pp. 229–272). New York: Plenum.

Smink, F. R. E., van Hoeken, D., & Hoek, H. W. (2012). Epidemiology of eating disorders: Incidence, prevalence and mortality rates. *Current Psychiatry Reports, 14,* 406–414.

Smith, A. R., Li, N., & Joiner, T. E. (2011). The pursuit of success: Can status aspirations negatively affect body satisfaction? *Journal of Social and Clinical Psychology, 30,* 531–547.

Smith, J. E., & Kunz, P. R. (1976). Polygyny and fertility in nineteenth-century America. *Population Studies, 30,* 465–480.

Stahl, J., Tolsma, P. H., Loonen, M. J. J. E., & Drent, R. H. (2002). Subordinates explore but dominants profit: Resource competition in high Arctic barnacle goose flocks. *Animal Behaviour, 61,* 257–264.

Stewart, D. E. (1992). Reproductive functions in eating disorders. *Annals of Medicine, 24,* 287–291.

Stice, E., Marti, C., Shaw, H., & Jaconis, M. (2009). An 8-year longitudinal study of the natural history of threshold, subthreshold, and partial eating disorders from a community sample of adolescents. *Journal of Abnormal Psychology, 118,* 587–597.

Stockley P., Bottell L., Hurst J.L. (2013). Wake up and smell the conflict: Odour signals in female competition. *Philosophical Transactions of the Royal Society of London. Series B: Biological Sciences, 368,* 20130082.

Stockley, P., & Bro-Jørgensen, J. (2011). Female competition and its evolutionary consequences in mammals. *Biological Reviews, 86,* 341–366.

Stoen, O. G., Zedrosser, A., Wegge, P., & Swenson, J. E. (2006). Socially induced delayed primiparity in brown bears *Ursus arctos. Behavioural Ecology and Sociobiology, 61,* 1–8.

Striegel-Moore, R. H., & Bulik, C. M. (2007). Risk factors for eating disorders. *American Psychologist, 62,* 181–198.

Surbey, M. K. (1987). Anorexia nervosa, amenorrhea, and adaptation. *Ethology and Sociobiology, 8*(Suppl.), 47S-61S.

Thompson, M. E., Kahlenberg, S. M., Gilby, I. C., & Wrangham, R. W. (2007). Core area quality is associated with variance in reproductive success among female chimpanzees at Kibale National Park. *Animal Behavior, 73,* 501–512.

Tobin-Richards, M. H., Boxer, A. M., & Petersen, A. C. (1983). The psychological significance of pubertal change: Sex differences in perception of self during adolescence. In J. Brooks-Gunn & A. C. Petersen (Eds.), *Girls at puberty* (pp. 127–154). New York: Plenum.

Toro, J., Gomez-Peresmitre, G., Sentis, J., Valles, A., Casula, V., Castro, J., . . . Rodriguez, R. (2006). Eating disorders and body image in Spanish and Mexican female adolescents. *Social Psychiatry and Psychiatric Epidemiology, 41,* 556–565.

Tooby, J., & Cosmides, L. (1990). The past explains the present: Emotional adaptations and the structure of ancestral environments. *Ethology and Sociobiology, 11,* 375–424.

Trevathan, W. R. (1987). *Human birth: An evolutionary perspective.* New York: Aldine de Gruyter.

Trivers, R. L. (1985). *Social evolution.* Menlo Park, CA: Benjamin/Cummings.

Turke, P. W. (1989). Evolution and the demand for children. *Population and Development Review, 15,* 61–90.

Vaillancourt, T. (2013). Do human females use indirect aggression as an intrasexual competition strategy? *Philosophical Transactions of the Royal Society B, 368,* 20130080.

Vaillancourt, T., Miller, J. L., & Sharma, S. (2010). "Tripping the prom queen": female intrasexual competition and indirect aggression. In K. Österman (Ed.), *Indirect and direct aggression* (pp. 17–32). Frankfurt: Peter Lang.

Vaz-Leal, F. J., & Salcedo-Salcedo, M. S. (1992). Sexual adjustment and eating disorders: Differences between typical and atypical anorexic adolescent females. *International Journal of Eating Disorders, 12*(1), 11–19.

Vessey, S. H. (1987). Long-term population trends in white-footed mice and the impact of supplemental food and shelter. *American Zoologist, 27,* 879–890.

Vitzthum, V. J. (2008). Evolutionary models of women's reproductive functioning. *Annual Review of Anthropology, 37,* 53–73.

Voland, E., & Voland, R. (1989). Evolutionary biology and psychiatry: The case of anorexia nervosa. *Ethology and Sociobiology, 10,* 223–240.

Volk, A. A., Camilleri, J. A., Dane, A. V., & Marini, Z. A. (2012). Is adolescent bullying an evolutionary adaptation? *Aggressive Behavior, 38,* 222–238.

Walters, S. (1990). *Tactics of intrasexual competition: An exploratory investigation of sex differences* (Unpublished master's thesis). Simon Fraser University, Burnaby, BC, Canada.

Walters, S., & Crawford, C. (1994). The importance of mate attraction for intrasexual competition in men and women. *Ethology and Sociobiology, 15,* 5–30.

Wasser, S. K., & Barash, D. P. (1983). Reproductive suppression among female mammals: Implications for biomedicine and sexual selection theory. *Quarterly Review of Biology, 58,* 513–538.

Wasser, S. K., & Isenberg, D. Y. (1986). Reproductive failure among women: Pathology or adaptation? *Journal of Psychosomatic Obstetrics and Gynaecology, 5,* 153–175.

Weisfeld, G. C. (1999). *Evolutionary principles of human adolescence.* New York: Basic Books.

Weisfeld, G. E., Bloch, S. A., & Ivers, J. W. (1984). Possible determinants of social dominance among adolescent girls. *Journal of Genetic Psychology, 144,* 115–129.

Weisfeld, G. E., & Weisfeld, C. C. (1984). An observational study of social evaluation: An application of the dominance hierarchy model. *Journal of Genetic Psychology, 145,* 89–99.

Whissell-Buechy, D., & Wills, C. (1989). Male and female correlations for taster (PTC) phenotypes and rate of adolescent development. *Annals of Human Biology, 16,* 131–146.

White, D. D., Gallup, A. C., & Gallup, G. G. (2010). Indirect peer aggression in adolescence and reproductive behavior. *Journal of Evolutionary Psychology, 8,* 49–65.

Wiederman, M. W., & Hurst, S. R. (1998). Body size, physical attractiveness, and body image among young adult women: Relationships to sexual experience and sexual esteem. *Journal of Sex Research, 35,* 272–281.

Williams, C. G. (1966). Natural selection, the costs of reproduction, and a refinement of Lack's principle. *American Naturalist, 100,* 687–690.

Wilson, M., & Daly, M. (1997). Life expectancy, economic inequality, homicide, and reproductive timing in Chicago neighbourhoods. *BMJ: British Medical Journal, 314,* 1271–1274.

Wolff, J. O. (1993). Why are female small mammals territorial? *Oikos, 68,* 364–370.

Young, A. J., Carolson, A. A., Monfort, S. L., Russell, A. F., Bennett, N.C., & Clutton-Brock, T. (2006). Stress and the suppression of subordinate reproduction in cooperatively breeding meerkats. *Proceedings of the National Academy of Sciences, 103,* 12005-12010.

Ziegler, T. E., & Sousa, M. B. C. (2002). Parent–daughter relationships and social controls on fertility in female common marmosets, *Callithrix jacchus. Hormones and Behavior, 37,* 618–627.

Moderation of Female–Female Competition for Matings by Competitors' Age and Parity

Melanie MacEacheron *and* Lorne Campbell

Abstract

Previous research on female intrasexual competition, especially but not only for matings or mateships, has largely been conducted using convenience samples of women of undergraduate status and therefore generally between the ages of 17 and 22. Even among such articles including women over 25, the majority do not focus on mate competition. There is a priori reason, however, to believe that intrasexual competition for matings and mateships would extend and change beyond this life stage. This chapter provides an overview of the literature on female intrasexual competition over women's reproductive careers, discusses factors that should result in predictable changes in female intrasexual competition as women age, and proposes testable hypotheses that should help guide future research in this area of research. Based on this analysis, new theories concerning reproductive advantage derivable from acquiring the status of successful mother are proposed.

Key Words: female intrasexual competition, mating, parity, motherhood, age

For women, the average age of first menarche, signaling the beginning of puberty and fertility, is approximately 13 years of age (e.g., Anderson, Dallal, & Must, 2003). The average age of menopause, signaling the cessation of fertility, is approximately 50 to 51 years of age (Harlow & Signorello, 2000). Women therefore spend on average 38 years of their lives within their reproductive career. Several physical and psychological changes can occur over such a long time frame. Some of these changes include wrinkling of skin, changes in fat depositions, and emotional maturation. Many of these changes result from life experiences possible only with aging, such as becoming a mother and having additional children, losing one's partner, and acquiring access to resources such as social standing. All of these likely influence how women compete with each other for mates (see e.g., Hrdy, 2000). For example, a 20-year-old childless woman may enact mate competition tactics that differ in predictable ways from a single 35-year-old mother of four: only the latter may have lesser attractiveness and greater experience and has preexisting investment in offspring.

The extant literature on human female–female competition for mates does not seem to us, however, to focus on similarities and differences within women at different points across their reproductive careers. It therefore misses, for example, competition by mothers for mates. To develop a better sense of the sampling used to test hypotheses regarding human female–female competition for mates, and the likely undersampling of women over 22 years of age, we first conducted a survey of the literature. We wanted to know the age range of female participants typically included in research in this area and the degree to which differences in female–female competition for mates over time (and other related female–female competition) was directly assessed in this body of research.

Following this analysis of the extant literature, we provide rationale for broadening the study of female intrasexual competition for mates to consider potential differences across women's reproductive careers. The goal of our chapter is to discuss how differences between premenopausal women of different ages and circumstances may influence patterns of female competition for mates. Special focus is given to parity as opposed to nulliparity (i.e., the number of live births a woman has had versus the state of having never had any live births) as such a circumstance. With greater parity comes decreased residual reproductive capacity (see Thornhill & Gangestad, 2008), or the number of future children a woman may be expected to bear. Focus is also directed on the anticipated role of residual reproductive capacity on competitive strategy. Women past the point of maximal residual reproductive capacity but premenopausal are referred to as "older women" in this chapter. We provide new perspective regarding older women's mateship competitions, as well as on women's mateship and other competitions generally as suggested by this preliminary look into older women's mateship competition. We then proffer several testable predictions to encourage and stimulate research on this topic.

State of Research on Female–Female Competition for Mates

At the time of writing, we conducted a literature search on PsycINFO as well as Summon (the University of Western Ontario's database covering every discipline but not including some content due to licensing arrangements), AnthropologyPlus, and AnthroSource to identify published research broadly on the topic of human female–female competition using the search terms "female–female competition" and "human." We then reviewed the listed articles. Using this approach, we identified a total of 44 articles presenting research involving humans and at least arguably involving female–female competition, over a mate or not. We carefully read these articles and noted, when indicated, the age range of the female participants in each of the study samples.

In 33, or 75%, of the 44 identified articles focusing on female–female competition, the age of female participants was in the 18 to 25 range. This is largely due to the use of convenience samples on college/university campuses and in a few instances of restricting the range of eligible participants for samples obtained via the Internet. Eleven, or 25%, of the articles reported using a fairly wide age range of female participants (e.g., 18–70), but this seems to be a result of the research methodologies employed rather than the intentional targeting of older and younger women for the purposes of testing age-related differences. For example, Campbell, Muncer, and Bibel (2001) utilized archival crime data from around the world, with ages of offenders ranging from 15 to over 65 years, to show that competition among women for males who would provide provisioning more often results in greater rates of property compared to violent crime (see also Campbell, Muncer, & Bibel, 1998). In a study on dyadic conversational styles, Grainger and Dunbar (2009) had a research assistant unobtrusively code conversations of naturally occurring dyads. These dyads were of same and mixed sex who appeared to be between 18 and 50 years of age. The coding took place in social settings. The researchers found that cooperation between two interacting women decreased, and nonverbal competition increased, when males were nearby. Additionally, Elliot and Pazda (2012) recruited women between the ages of 18 and 45 from the Internet (Study 1) and surveyed actual online dating profiles of women ages 18 to 35 (Studies 2 and 3) to demonstrate that women who were more interested in casual sex were more likely to use the color red on their profile web page. In the studies described, and in the other eight articles not discussed, however, the focus of the research was not on age-related differences in the outcomes measured. Nor was the focus of research on other factors potentially influenced by age (e.g., attractiveness) that, based on other research, might influence female–female competition for mates.

A large majority of all previous research on female intrasexual competition, especially but not only for matings or mateships, has therefore been conducted with convenience samples: women of undergraduate status and therefore generally between the ages of 17 and 22. There is a priori reason, however, to believe that intrasexual matings and mateship competition would extend and change beyond this life stage. Such matings/mateship formations following youngest adulthood, additionally, are not expected to have been rare over our evolutionary history. Evidence for this comes, for example, from the fact that modern foragers often change mates over the life-course (e.g., Hrdy, 2000). Though data are sparse, the divorce rate during the first 5 years of marriage among the !Kung, a foraging society of Angola, Namibia, and Botswana, for example, has been reported to be 37% (Howell, 2000). The similar figure for the Hadza, a foraging society from Tanzania, is 37% (Blurton Jones, Marlowe, Hawkes,

& O'Connell, 2000). In the modern United States, mates are also often changed during adulthood (see, e.g., review in Sassler, 2010). Changes in mateship competition in the modern United States following youngest adulthood have been reported. Sassler notes, for example, that

> ... Emerging adults who desire marriage in their early 20s engage in different relationship patterns than do those whose marital horizons are later; not only do they express more conservative sexual attitudes ... but they are less likely to engage in premarital sexual activity ... (B)ecause the marriage market changes with age, preferences for desired partner attributes and methods of finding romantic partners shift. Adults who are parents or previously married are more tolerant of prospective mates who are divorced or have children. (2010, p. 561)

The current literature on female–female competition for mateships has covered up to only 5 out of a woman's approximately 38 years (Harlow & Signorello, 2000) of reproductive career. This reproductive career stage, additionally, has been primarily associated with initial mate selection only (Hudson & Henze, 1969). Finally, in the Western countries in which most of these studies occurred, little or no reproduction (based on average age at first reproduction of females: see e.g., Copen, Daniels, & Vespa, 2012) is predicted for the participants. Thus, this research is predicted to miss *most* of the variability in female intrasexual competition for matings/mateships, including any associated with childbearing. There is ample evidence (e.g., from marriage statistics by age) that a woman's "mate value" (defined as, e.g., the amount by which she would increase a male partner's reproductive success: Singh, 2002) and other of women's resources relevant to gaining them matings/mateships change over a woman's reproductive career. Some of these elements of mate value and other relevant resources to be discussed include physical attractiveness, social standing, and proven ability to mother. There are many possible, testable predictions concerning changes to women's evolved mating psychology (and men's, in response to it, as well as offsprings'), as evidenced by women's intrasexual competition, changing over the lifecourse sensitively to changes in such resources. The absence of research on why and how older women enter into some matings/mateships and not others renders it impossible to even know the identities of all of these "resources."

Rationale for Examining the Entire Reproductive Career Course

What are the consequences of focusing almost all research attention on women's competition for mateships on nulliparous women of maximal attractiveness? What are the implications of using only convenience sampling (i.e., usually undergraduates during their first year: see, e.g., Kam, Wilking, & Zechmeister, 2007), regarding understanding behavior that likely changes over time, especially when that time frame is about 38 years (see, e.g., Harlow & Signorello, 2000)? It is impossible to know. What is known is that women of convenience sample age (approximately 17–18 years of age) in the Western cultures in which they are almost uniformly studied almost never have children yet (see, e.g., Copen et al., 2012). Given that a vital, ultimate unit of analysis in evolutionary psychology is the unit of reproductive success, this is problematic.

Strong preference for postadolescent females as sexual partners was the case in all primate species (with one possible exception), including our own, in Anderson's (1986) review of the topic. She notes that !Kung females only attain "prime" reproductive value at 22.5 years of age. Anderson also found that postadolescent women had greater reproductive success (e.g., greater infant survival rate) and that multiparous (i.e., having had more than one birth) non-human primate females were preferred as mates over not just the nulliparous but also over those having had one birth (primiparas). Male chimpanzees, members of one of the two species comprising our closest relatives, prefer the oldest (still-fertile) females as mates (Muller, Thompson, & Wrangham, 2006). In chimpanzees and most of the other primates that were the subject of Anderson's review, there is no paternal care (but see exceptions among primates in Hrdy, 2009), so males generally experience no loss by having a *mate* (i.e., this is just a mat*ing*) who may produce no more offspring following her next, attendant on preferring the oldest still-fertile females. Hrdy (1999) hypothesizes that human males may tend to prefer the youngest women as mates due to the fact that such men "are in a position to monopolize access to their mate and to literally *possess* her long-term. The mate he acquires may end up living in his social unit for a long time, whereas a male chimpanzee is merely seeking to fertilize a female and have done" (p. 186, emphasis in original).

From the anthropological literature, we know that women at the age of 19 are likely to have had their first child, if part of a foraging society such as the !Kung (Howell, 2000). The lifetime prevalence of women dying due to birthing is 1 in 30 in the Gabbra, a natural fertility and mortality pastoral society of Kenya and Ethiopia (Mace & Sear, 1996): it is generally high wherever modern medicine is unavailable (Khan, Wojdyla, Say, Gulmezoglu, & Van Look, 2006). !Kung women who survived first childbirth would have had perhaps four more children on average (with a variance of 4.88: Howell, 2000). There is a priori reason, moreover, to believe that intrasexual competition for matings and mateships extends and changes beyond the age at which women are at maximal residual reproductive capacity (and, necessarily, nulliparity). For women, this tends to occur prior to menopause (see, e.g., Copen et al., 2012). Menopause is defined as early if occurring before age 45 in the modern West (e.g., Harlow & Signorello, 2000). This is also at least roughly the case in modern foraging cultures (Hill & Hurtado, 1996).

Women's body shape, even after any postpartum weight loss, changes with parity (with respect to waist-to-hip ratio [WHR], e.g., Singh, 1993; see, e.g., Dugdale & Eaton-Evans, 1989; with respect to breast shape, see Larsson & Andersson-Ellström, 2003; Pisacane & Continisio, 2004; see also Anderson, 1986, regarding change in nipple length with parity in chimpanzees), and overall weight may increase with increasing parity (see discussion in Neville, McKinley, Holmes, Spence, & Woodside, 2014). Changes to female body shape are theorized to reflect women's decreased residual reproductive capacity or number of future children she is able to bear (see generally Thornhill & Gangestad, 2008; and see Buss, 1989; Thornhill & Palmer, 2000). Women's overall attractiveness as rated by males also diminishes with age (Buss & Schmitt, 1993; see generally Buss, 1989). Given only these facts, we argue it becomes clear that women would be expected to compete differently with each other for mateships once maximal reproductive capacity and nulliparity have passed. Put simply, female reproductive strategy should change after age 22.5 and nulliparity, meaning that women's reproductive strategies, including competition, need to be investigated after this age and state.

It is understandable to have only studied the youngest, likely almost exclusively nulliparous women well, as social and evolutionary psychology are not the only areas of research that oversample first-year university undergraduates. By doing so, however, research is neglecting to examine a very

important outcome of mateships: children. We also, in failing to study female–female competition in other than the youngest, nulliparous women (but see Rucas, Gurven, Winking, & Kaplan, 2012), necessarily fail to study many other crucial life events/decisions influencing human development. This includes, by necessary implication, first, the youngest *men's* successful mateship competitions (to the extent women take older men as mates: see, e.g., Buss, 1989). Second, this includes outcomes of children born to older versus younger mothers. A third crucial life event/decision impacting on human development that is missed is the contributions of extended family and community to women's mateship competition after choice of first partner. This list will likely be lengthened once we have studied more than just the youngest women's mateship competitions.

This chapter focuses on factors likely to change over the course of a woman's reproductive career and how these changes may influence patterns of competitions for mates and mateships. In performing this task we make some speculative hypotheses but attempt to ground these in existing theory and data when possible. Our discussion is broken down into three primary sections. The first focuses on age-related changes in women. The second section focuses on motherhood and associated cues of fertility. The third focuses on competitive mothering. In these sections we discuss how these factors/actions may be expected to influence competition between women for mates.

In the first section, factors that vary with a woman's age that may influence her intrasexual competition for mateships are divided into two general types. Presented first are changes related simply to the aging process. These would include, for example, reduced physical attractiveness and fertility. Some potential attempts to reduce the advantages of good looks in young women by older women are also discussed.

In the second section, we discuss changes due to motherhood and advancing parity and present hypotheses regarding competition for mates associated with these changes. In the environment of evolutionary adaptedness (EEA), human mothers' surviving children could be expected to remain around them until maturity and perhaps longer. Thus, an opportunity for a fitness display for a woman via her children existed over evolutionary time (Miller, 2000). That is, it would have been obvious which women could and could not successfully complete tasks requisite to successful reproduction, that only they as the mother could perform. Given the woman's age, it would further have been obvious *how* successful she had been in these tasks—how many healthy children she had, given her age. These possibilities are discussed in the third section.

Age-Related Changes across the Reproductive Career That May Influence Women's Competition for Mates
Reduced Attractiveness as a Mate

Cross-culturally, men rate attractiveness in an opposite-sex partner as more important than do women (e.g., Buss, 1989). The average decline in women's perceived attractiveness may coincide with their marked decline in sex hormone production and fertility preceding menopause (Schmitt et al., 2002). Women are therefore predicted to be in more of a race against time, as it affects their attractiveness, in attracting mates, than are men. This means changes in attractiveness should generally be of key importance in aging women's mateship competitions. This would be predicted to be the case especially during women's most intense period of intrasexual competition for mates: from initial maturity to menopause.

Females' ability to choose mates, as well as their competitiveness in struggles for optimal mates, have both been expected to decrease markedly as they age beyond maximal residual reproductive capacity due to being perceived as less physically attractive by potential mates (e.g., Buss, 1989, and see Rucas, Gurven, Winking, & Kaplan, 2012, for evidence from women from Tsimane society). According to Rucas and collaborators,

> A woman's reproductive value, need for a long-term partner, and the number of child dependents she has are expected to vary over a woman's life-course, and hence the type and quantity of resources needed throughout her life should vary accordingly. . . . [E]xpect mate-retention conflicts to be generally focused at younger ages, (in part) because . . . women's reproductive value decreases with age. (p. 195)

Let us say for the sake of argument that occurrences of older women competing for mateships are indeed rare. Such rare competitions could, in theory, result in one more surviving child for a mother. This would render such competition highly evolutionarily relevant. Of course all of a woman's children may be the ultimate culmination of a partnership competed for and established, with no subsequent competition on her part to sustain it, when the woman was

young. As noted, however, there is evidence from foraging and other societies of changes in spouses over the reproductive career for many women. As such, it makes sense to at least scrutinize whether there might exist female–female competition for mateships post-initial competition.

Life History Theory and Potential Change in Sexual Strategy and Ornament Concealment with Age

Time and energetic resources required to reproduce and/or sustain life are inherently limited. Where time and energy are expended in any one of the important biological tasks of sustaining life, growth, reproduction, or investing in one's children, they cannot also be expended in any of the others. Life history theory provides an explanation of individuals' allocations of time and energy selectively to each of the given important biological tasks. Under this theory, trade-offs in investment in one's own body (survival and growth) versus reproduction, including parental investment, must be made. These trade-offs are systematic and represent either a slow life history strategy (basically, greater investment in survival and growth, delayed reproduction, greater investment in each offspring, and longer lifespan) or a fast life history strategy (basically, hastened reproduction, lesser investment in one's own body, lesser investment in each offspring including less time between births, and shorter lifespan: Hill, 1993; see also discussion in Belsky, Steinberg, & Draper, 1991). Note that individuals may sometimes, however, switch from long-term (representing slower life history) to short-term (representing faster life history) mating strategy under certain conditions (Fletcher, Simpson, Campbell, & Overall, 2015).

Either a fast or slow life history strategy is advantageous to each individual's reproductive success, depending on the effect of his or her environment on his or her genes and phenotype (Hill, 1993). For example, individuals in a semistressful, somewhat amenable, somewhat predictable environment but possessing health- and reproduction-promoting genes would be predicted to generally follow a slower life history than individuals in the same environment who do not possess health- and reproduction-promoting genes. Women who have consistently utilized a slow life history strategy would thus be expected to be more likely to remain living, and perhaps to still look attractive, at each point in time after the start of their reproductive careers compared to women utilizing a fast life history strategy. The former are also more likely to possess health- and reproduction-promoting genes and therefore higher value as a mate.

Women having pursued a slow life history strategy compared to those of the same age having pursued a fast life history strategy may tend to be more attractive. This is hypothesized in part due to the former women's lesser total parity and thus lesser total experienced stress associated with childbearing and breastfeeding. Additionally, as noted, women pursuing a slower life history strategy would tend to live in environments richer in nutritional resources. (Interestingly, such women might even have better fertility at an older age: see results and review of the literature in Sun et al., 2015.)

Childbearing, even after any postpartum weight loss, tends to produce telling decrements to women's attractiveness (see generally, e.g., Dugdale & Eaton-Evans, 1989). It might, however, have less pronounced effects on the appearances of women in environments containing relatively more nutritional resources. Having greater nutritional resources during pregnancy and lactation can prevent tooth and bone loss (Black et al., 2008), presumably affecting attractiveness. Successive childbearing, speculatively, might also have less pronounced negative effects on the appearances of women possessing more health-promoting genes. This conjecture is based on the finding of increases in variance of facial asymmetry with advancing age (Kobylianski & Livshits, 1989; Penke et al., 2009), suggesting that an *accumulation* of stresses over time may lead to greater such asymmetry. Such stresses, according to the developmental instability hypothesis (see, e.g., Polak et al., 2003), are buffered for some individuals by their less stressful and more predictable and resource-rich environments, as well as by their health-promoting genes. To the extent that repeated pregnancy, birthing, breastfeeding, and associated weight changes constitute such stresses, it is possible that women for whom such stresses are buffered by more health-promoting genes would have greater facial symmetry, and therefore attractiveness, compared to other women of the same parity. Any lesser attractiveness on the part of older women having pursued a fast life history strategy could also be due to greater levels of stress from the environment associated with the pursuit of such life history unrelated to childbearing, which due to the individual's personal attributes are not well-buffered (see Hoffman & Parsons, 1989, for evidence of such buffering among longer-lived *Drosophila melanogaster*: see also Polak et al., 2003; Sun et al., 2015).

Thus, we tentatively propose that women possessing more health-promoting genes may tend to be more attractive than female parity mates, controlling for age (see, e.g., Jones, 1996). If this is actually the case, then advertisable proof of possession of health-promoting genes is possible for such women as they age (for a potential example of advertisement of relative attractiveness by parous women citing maternal age in the modern West, see, e.g., People.com, 2013).

Lesser parity, it should be noted, need not be associated with fewer surviving children: with greater investment in each child, better maternal health, and the inheritance of a mother's health-promoting genes, a greater survival rate of children is predicted. For example, with more closely spaced births there is an increased risk of miscarriage, congenital deformity, and death in infancy (see review in Wynn, 1987).

As noted, phenotypic changes with parity may occur, for example, to breast size or shape or WHR. Such shape and ratio may be fitness indicators—ornaments—on the part of women, indicating residual reproductive capacity. If so, and if these body parts lose their maximally attractive shape with successive childbearing, a competitive strategy that might be pursued by older multiparous women versus the younger nulliparous could be dressing to conceal especially these body parts more than they did when they were younger. Another such strategy might consist of using their better social standing to insist that young women do the same and thus not be able to reap the advantage from advertising these particular features while they are at maximal attractiveness for them. Older multiparous women who remain attractive might not take part in greater concealment of these body parts with age given the continuing competitive advantage of being able to advertise fitness via exhibiting them.

Our prediction is that men and other women will tend to take notice when an older woman is particularly attractive (see, e.g., Hodapp & Luciani, 2013). We also predict that such attractiveness will predict males' willingness to engage in short-term but not long-term relationships with such women and other women's competitive behavior against such women. The short- versus long-term relationship prediction distinction here is made based on male chimpanzees' and other nonhuman primates' preference for the oldest still-fertile females as mates and these species' absence of paternal care (Anderson, 1986). (For theory concerning this phenomenon in human short-term versus long-term relationships resulting in offspring, see generally Buss & Schmitt, 1993.)

Older Women's Desire to Have a Child

Having time on one's reproductive clock to bear only one more child may mean that the criteria for choosing a partner may strategically change. Schmitt et al. (2002) found evidence consistent with a sexual peak, or increased interest in having sexual relations, in women in their early 30s. These women, they suggested, may be (unconsciously) seeking to reproduce at the last time in their reproductive careers at which it is safe for them and their offspring to do so. Easton, Confer, Goetz, and Buss (2010) used a between-subjects design to compare women predicted to be "expediting" reproduction due to decreasing time in which to reproduce (i.e., women in their late 20s to early 40s) with younger ones. The older women were found to spend more time thinking about sex, to think about sex more frequently with such thoughts having greater intensity, to fantasize more about someone other than their current partner, to report having sex more frequently, and to report more willingness to engage in sex after knowing a potential partner for one month. If such self-reports of greater interest and more frequent sex map onto actual sexual behavior, this would be evidence of a change in average sexual strategy, from longer term to shorter term, with increasing female premenopausal age.

The child of a woman who has only him or her left to bear will receive the benefit of her great experience (see discussion in Flinn, Ward, & Noone, 2005, regarding older mothers' value to children as experienced navigators of social and political environments) and resources. Such a child would, additionally, have no younger siblings as competitors and should tend to receive the most investment from older siblings. Given these facts, the mother of such a child especially benefits from him or her surviving—she has no opportunity for another child within the lengthy period of life ahead of her, and none of her other children should fare so well (assuming the child does not possess a deleterious genetic abnormality—a greater possibility with greater maternal age: see discussion in Schmitt et al., 2002). That is, she experiences a nonrecoupable lost opportunity to reproduce should her last child not survive, and this child may be the one with the greatest expected fitness. The loss of such a child being particularly bad for female primates' reproductive success may be reflected in the findings, discussed by Hrdy (1999), of increased altruism toward offspring of some primate mothers of greater age.

A mother facing having her last child, therefore, might be predicted to especially value health-promoting genes in a mateship producing him or her (see also Easton et al., 2010). Good resources on the part of the father would be predicted to be less relevant due to the woman's own resources, accumulated over time. Additionally, she may be quite willing to have or tolerate a suitor being a short-term partner (see analysis in "Potential Resource Accumulation over Time"). She would thus be freer to choose a sire possessing the most health-promoting genes and to not accept a mate who possesses fewer such genes but who would be willing to assist in provisioning offspring. Taken together, this means that reproduction with such a woman would be relatively low cost to a male in terms of the resources he would need to expend to derive a reproductive benefit. It is predicted that men have evolved to pay attention to such a competitive position.

Older, Mated Women's Competition with Younger Mate Poachers

Rucas et al. (2012) found that intrasexual arguments in the Tsimane women studied tended to occur between age-mates. Indeed, the very youngest women would be expected to directly compete most between themselves, as they are at peak desirability and their greatest competition is from members of their own age range.

Women, however, may be expected to compete not just with their age-mates, we contend, but also with younger/older rivals. Only older women will have mothered and will likely be mothering the children of their current husbands. An older woman with children faces the threat of losing resources from a partner if he is mate-poached, something that should provide a strong incentive to protect her mateship. This incentive would seem much stronger than that of a young woman contemplating mate-poaching a given husband. After all, such a young woman is at the peak of her attractiveness and may have multiple mateship opportunities. Rucas et al. (2012) found that married women in their 20s and 30s "harassed" the youngest, single women, possibly representing a unilateral form of female–female aggression initiated by the older women in an attempt to retain their husbands. Indeed, these younger victims were not coded by the authors as engaging in much competition with older, married women. Just because these younger women were not coded as engaging in much such competition, however, might not indicate the absence of such behaviors. A young woman has much to offer a potential mate reproductively and would therefore be predicted to be accorded much attention by the husbands of other women. This means that any attempted poaching on her part might be more efficiently perpetrated casually towards the desired male, and thus be less noticeable, than a married woman's defense of her partnership against it.

Such harassment, additionally, may be an intrasexually competitive tactic "designed" to reduce the victim's fertility. Thus, to the extent fertility is detectable by and attractive to men, these older women may be reducing these younger women's attractiveness. Hrdy (1999) reports findings across several nonhuman primates showing more dominant females' better reproductive success due in large part to the harassment by these of subordinate females. Pusey, Williams, and Goodall (1997) provide evidence of significantly earlier menarche of daughters and greater survival past infancy of offspring of more dominant chimpanzee females. Though dominance can occur in young chimpanzee females (e.g., via "inheritance" from their dominant mothers), it is generally the product of multiple interactions over time and therefore more often the province of older females (see generally de Waal, 2007). Older female geladas and chimpanzees (i.e., of "prime" fertility, as opposed to adolescent fertility or the decreased fertility associated with old age) have been documented to harass female adolescents and to thereby decrease their reproductive success (see review by Anderson, 1986).

Darwin (1871) spoke about intrasexual selection as consisting of "conquering" same-sex reproductive competitors, for example, by vanquishment. He pointed out eminently noticeable vanquishment of rivals in various species in males particularly in making his point that such intrasexual competition was the province of (almost only) males. Human competition, however, may also be indirect (Campbell, 1999; Vaillancourt, 2005) and even concealed (Benenson, 2013). Indirect and therefore less detectable competition may be expected to be more commonly engaged in by women generally as compared to men (see, e.g., discussion in Geary, 2010; Merten, 1997; Vaillancourt, 2013; also see Campbell, 1999, 2004). The reason for this, ultimately, is theorized to be that while in most species, among individuals surviving to maturity, most females reproduce at least minimally, males often do not. Some males, due to the possibility of polygyny,

can have immense reproductive success: This success, however, necessarily results in other males having much less or none. There is, thus, much to gain and little or nothing to lose reproductively on the part of male contestants from engaging in highly aggressive—and therefore obvious—competition with other males (Darwin, 1871). Women, on the other hand, are usually able to reproduce at least minimally and thus are not so advantaged by the sort of highly aggressive—and noticeable—intrasexual competition engaged in by men that may produce a complete loss of reproductive success for losers (Campbell, 1999, 2004). The younger women being harassed in the Rucas et al. (2012) study may not have been observed as attempting to mate-poach their older female harassers' husbands but may nevertheless have been attempting to, or at least perceived by the older women to have been attempting to. *Preemptive* reduction of a potential competitor's attractiveness could instead be the "goal" of such harassment and would still constitute intrasexual competition for mateships on the part of older women against younger women.

Potential Resource Accumulation over Time

All else being equal, women of greater age will have increased opportunity to accumulate both physical and social resources, than will women of lesser age. Holding physical resources is not necessarily predictive of positive outcome for females in intrasexual interactions in the nonhuman animal literature (as discussed by Rosvall, 2011), whereas it is for males (Parker, 1974). Since men and women attain or increase reproductive success via different means (e.g., primarily for men only, increasing it by increasing his number of mates), however, they would be expected to compete differently, especially intrasexually. Resources do tend to be more desired by women in a male partner than by men in a female partner, and this almost certainly affects the type of competitions men tend to engage in among themselves, versus those entered into by women among themselves, for mates (see, e.g., Buss, 1989). Could our species be special, however, perhaps due to its unusually high amount of paternal care compared with other mammal species', in the holding of resources being helpful in female–female competition for mates (see, e.g., Wang & Griskevicius, 2014)?

Gowaty (1996, 1997) hypothesizes that internal fertilization necessitates a suboptimal relationship deal for some female mammals, whereby they need and/or are benefitted by choosing resource-holding males (who may not possess health- and reproduction-promoting genes) as sires, due to difficulties in making a living especially during pregnancy and lactation. She hypothesizes that where resources are not an issue for an individual female (perhaps a woman at a later stage of reproductive career), she need not choose a male with resources and so is less likely to do so. Assuming some older women at a later stage of reproductive career may only expect short-term relationships, they would be free to choose partners whose reproductive contribution to the relationship would only or primarily be health- and reproduction-promoting genes. Perhaps older women with resources are able to negotiate either long- or short-term relationships with physically more attractive men than are less wealthy women their age. Their wealth might give them a competitive advantage to attracting mates, whether by making them more attractive as partners or freeing them from the need to insist on a long-term relationship.

Role of Extended Family

Lengthy periods of dependency and short inter-birth intervals of human children are generally viewed as absolutely requiring provision of assistance to mothers, in order to meet energetic needs of children (Sear & Mace, 2008). Hrdy (2009) notes that, among foraging groups studied, maternal grandmothers tend to preferentially help their neediest daughter (often, the one with the least mothering experience) care for her own offspring. An older mother's own mother is more likely to have another daughter with less mothering experience, whom she may be busy helping (see generally Leonetti, Nath, Heman, & Neill, 2005). An older woman's mother is also more likely to be too frail to assist her. Thus, the older the mother with a new baby, the less likely she may be to receive her own mother's assistance. A woman's own mother's assistance with a child significantly increases that child's survival prospects (Sear & Mace, 2008). A significant disadvantage relative to younger mothers is associated with greater maternal age.

Also relevant to the amount of help received from an extended family is the mate's age. If his family (a woman's affines) are old enough or deceased, they may assist less. Since women generally choose mates older than themselves (Kenrick & Keefe, 1992), older women should generally expect less help from affines. A woman's own natal family and affines, however, may also constitute less of a brake on a woman's interests where they are too old

to interfere effectively in them (see, e.g., Apostolou, 2007). Lesser interference may be experienced by women in the context of initiating relationships (e.g., in the !Kung [Howell, 2000] and the Kanuri of Bornu [Cohen, 1967]), in maintaining relationships, and as to where the woman may direct the fruits of her labor. This minimal interference would be expected to result in the woman generally being able to act so as to maximize her own reproductive success by seeking out preferred mates and retaining the resources she accrues or directing them to her offspring. This is a competitive advantage over young women, whose sexual and marital access may often be guarded by parents and others within her natal family, often with the side effect of limiting the resources she is able to generate (see, e.g., discussions in Daly, Wilson, & Weghorst, 1982; Dickemann, 1981; Thornhill & Palmer, 2000; Voland & Beise, 2005).

Motherhood and Cues to Fertility
Proof of Fertility and Ability to Perform Motherly Tasks Required for Child Survival

Rosenthal (1985) provides the likelihood of becoming pregnant with 12 months of unprotected intercourse for otherwise healthy women by age bracket, as follows: 20–24 years old, 86%; 25–29 years old, 78%; 30–34 years old, 63%; 35–39 years old, 52%; 40–44 years old, 36%; 45–49 years old, 5%; and 50 years or older, 0%. Thus, this probability decreases approximately linearly after about age 20 and then markedly after about age 40 (Rosenthal, 1985).

If the relationship between current parity and total lifetime number of children expected to survive to weaning, however, is considered, a different picture emerges of which women would be most likely to produce surviving children in the future (and, on that basis at least, make good mates). Assuming a population of stable size and therefore with an average of two children surviving to adulthood per woman, each woman at nulliparity (i.e., mostly the youngest women) would have less than two lifetime number of children expected to survive. Why would that be? Some such women would have a complete inability to conceive (primary sterility). Others would have a complete inability to successfully gestate, birth a live infant, survive the perinatal period herself, and breastfeed adequately. There can be no proof that the nulliparous (or women having just birthed their first child) possess the ability and willingness to learn how to care for their own children in a way that would have kept them alive in the

EEA. Presumably some did not or at least possessed lesser such ability and willingness than others. Child mortality may be greater for mothers of lesser parity (see Srivastava & Saksena, 1981; also see generally Leonetti et al., 2005, but see Atkinson & Volk, 2013): it is plausible that mothers of low parity whose children die go on to have fewer total surviving children. Finally, lesser ability or willingness on the part of some women to breastfeed, which would be undetectable among the nulliparous and newly primiparous, would be expected to further decrease their total expected number of surviving children.

Primiparous women, though faring better in terms of total expected number of children surviving due to at least minimally adequate ability to conceive, gestate, and birth a live baby, would still be expected to have fewer than two children survive, perhaps even to weaning. In addition to the previously cited reasons concerning child mortality and breastfeeding, primiparas are more likely to die in childbirth (e.g., Anderson, 1986: see also that author's discussion of preference for multiparas as mates among primates generally). Such women could have no more than one surviving child. Young children whose mothers die have also been shown to have lower survival rates (see, e.g., Sear & Mace, 2008). Where maternal death occurred during childbirth, death rate of infants may have approached 100% in the EEA. At multiparity of two, the total number of children expected to survive should increase, though it would still not reach two. This would be due to the possibility that the mother could or would not adequately breastfeed (but see evidence for increased lactation in several mammal species with multiparity: Hastings & Testa, 1998; Hejcmanova et al., 2011) or act so as to prevent child mortality where possible, and the possibility that her firstborn did not survive long enough to allow her to accrue mothering experience, assuming this impacts second-borns' survival. The total number of children expected to survive to weaning, however, increases compared to the primiparous (who may be incapable of surviving the perinatal period and therefore who die following their first), due to every multiparous woman's proven ability to survive birthing herself.

With increasing parity, if the children survive to weaning, and especially if the parity is achieved at a lower maternal age, there is increasing proof of ability to more optimally perform each of the tasks requisite to child survival that only a mother can perform, as well as delegable tasks that help ensure child survival that mothers usually perform. Parous women, when nearing menopause, would have a lower infertility rate than that reflected for their age range by Rosenthal (1985), since none of them suffer from primary infertility. They would also be capable of gestation and of birthing an infant in a live state. Finally, these women, assuming their first birth did not happen very recently, would also have the demonstrated ability to survive the perinatal period. Parous women would be more likely than women not having achieved parity to successfully perform all the tasks requisite on the part of a mother to enable a child to survive. The truth of this last statement does, indeed, diminish with age due to associated lesser fertility and, presumably, associated lesser ability to gestate, birth, and survive the perinatal period. As argued, however, the truth of this statement also *increases* with age up to menopause-associated infertility for the parous, to the extent of their successful parity.

An alternate way to consider this is offered for illustrative purposes. This illustration incorporates consideration of the theoretical advantage to male reproductive success of mating with a multiparous woman within a relationship of one year's duration. Consider separately each of the tasks requisite to producing a child over evolutionary time that only its mother can perform ("requisite mothering tasks"): conception, then gestation, then birthing an infant in a live state, then surviving the birth herself, and finally breastfeeding. None of these tasks is (fully) delegable to someone other than the mother, and each is required for the child to survive and the father's reproductive success to be augmented.

Women who can successfully conceive comprise a subset of all women, women who can successfully gestate comprise a subset of women who can conceive, women who can birth a baby in a live state comprise a subset of women who can successfully gestate, and so on. The proportion of women succeeding at all of these tasks may be represented by the product of the proportions of women succeeding at each, who have successfully completed all preceding requisite mothering tasks (Figure 25.1).

Here we consider the multiple "nestedness" of women represented by those having successfully weaned an offspring. To do so, we use the proportion p of women failing to successfully perform each requisite mothering task per attempt at it (who have successfully completed all preceding ones), as reported in the literature; $1 - p$ equals the proportion successful at each such task per attempt at it. The product of each of these values of $(1 - p)$ provides a broad approximation of the proportion of

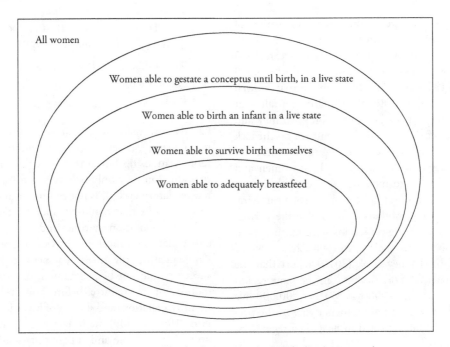

Figure 25.1. Illustration of nesting of women capable of each requisite task of motherhood. Not to scale.

women able to successfully bring a child to weaning per attempted conception (defined in this section as one year of unprotected intercourse: see Rosenthal, 1985). Note that it was not possible to obtain data on proportion of failure at each of the requisite tasks of motherhood due solely to maternal factors (i.e., the proportion of miscarriages due neither to paternal nor environmental factors, nor to an interaction of one of these with the other, nor to an interaction of one or both with maternal factors). To the extent these proportions do not represent failure due solely to maternal factors, they thus underrepresent women's ability to successfully perform requisite mothering tasks.

Half of the values of p used here to approximate the proportion of women unsuccessful at each requisite mothering task per attempt were the most conservative (lowest) of those found in the literature. By choosing solely these, a "best case" percentage of women expected to be successful at each such task would be obtained. Where proportions of women unsuccessful at requisite mothering tasks, however, were obtainable from reviews of foraging societies and societies without modern health care (thus better approximating EEA conditions), as well as large-scale studies, they were used herein.

The first "nest" is ability to conceive: $p = 0.14$ of otherwise-healthy 20- to 24-year-old women in a study in the United States with modern, Western

levels of health care and nutrition did not conceive following one year of unprotected intercourse (Rosenthal, 1985). This age group of women had the highest conception rate of any within the study. Nested within women conceiving would be those able to bring a conceptus to the time of birth in a live state. Proportion miscarrying has been estimated in women in the modern West in multiple studies to be approximately $p = 0.134$ (see discussion and results in Goldstein, 1994). Note that these studies' designs, however, often necessarily miss occult miscarriage (i.e., those occurring after initial human chorionic gonadotropin rise associated with implantation but before pregnancy is normally detected by the pregnant woman: Edmonds, Lindsay, Miller, Williamson, & Wood, 1983). Proportion of conceptions resulting in a miscarriage when occult pregnancies are included was found to be 0.62 in one study (as reported by Edmonds et al., 1983). Thus, the proportion miscarrying that we use is conservative. Average proportion of stillbirths in the nations studied in a large sample of Latin American countries was $p = 0.02$. (Note that this proportion also declines almost monotonically with number of pregnancies the mother has experienced and thus likely also declines with parity: Gadow, Castilla, Lopez Camelo, & Queenan, 1991).

Next we turn to neonatal mortality, including that associated with birthing difficulties and other maternal factors. The lowest proportion of births resulting in neonatal mortality (i.e., death of the newborn within 28 days) between 1995 and 2008 in sub-Saharan Africa was $p = 0.039$ in 2008 (Kinney et al., 2010). Note that Howell (2000), however, estimated infant mortality at 20% of live births among the !Kung. Kinney and collaborators, in their article, comment on the lack of appropriate health care among the mothers and infants they studied—a reality these women and children share with most others over evolutionary time. Nested within mothers who birth a surviving infant are those mothers who survive the perinatal period, assuming no infants with mothers who died so soon after their birth themselves survived in the EEA. Kinney et al. (2010) report that the lowest maternal mortality ratio in the same region between 1990 and 2008 was 571 per 100,000 live births (or proportion of mothers dying in the perinatal period not expected to have died regardless, of $p = 0.006$).

Finally, among this (multiply nested) group, only those who were able to adequately breastfeed their infant (with those mothers only inadequately doing so presumably losing him or her) could be counted. In one study, 13% of otherwise healthy, motivated women were incapable of adequately breastfeeding, for reasons other than modern manipulations such as breast surgery (based on Neifert et al., 1990; but see Volk, 2009, stating that almost all women can learn to breastfeed).

Thus, a rough estimate of the proportion of women in this multiply nested group who would be expected to perform all the tasks only they, as mothers, could perform over evolutionary time, in order to conceive a child within one year of unprotected intercourse and keep it alive until weaning, can be calculated. It would be the product of all values of $(1 - p)$, where p in each case equals the proportion of nonsuccess at each requisite task of motherhood, given an attempt at each. This figure, based on this section's review of the literature, is as follows:

$$(1 - \text{proportion failing to conceive}) \times$$
$$(1 - \text{proportion miscarrying}) \times$$
$$(1 - \text{proportion stillborn}) \times$$
$$(1 - \text{proportion neonatal mortality}) \times$$
$$(1 - \text{proportion perinatal maternal mortality}) \times$$
$$(1 - \text{proportion unable to adequatly breastfeed})$$

$$= (1 - 0.14) \times (1 - 0.134) \times (1 - 0.02) \times$$
$$(1 - 0.039) \times (1 - 0.006) \times (1 - 0.13)$$
$$= 0.86 \times 0.866 \times 0.98 \times 0.961 \times$$
$$0.994 \times 0.87$$
$$\approx 0.61$$

Clearly, a woman's success at augmenting a man's reproductive success, especially within a short-term relationship (given that in such relationships reproduction may only be attempted for one or a few ovulatory cycles), is not assured. Failure in any of these tasks that could be done by the mother only, over evolutionary time, and the child would either not be conceived or would not survive. Consequently, the male partner's reproductive success would not be augmented. Assuming three months of intercourse before conception, nine months' gestation, and 4 years of breastfeeding (see Hrdy 1999, p. 409), he in fact might have wasted up to 5 years' time and energy provisioning a lost reproductive cause. The facts that none of the requisite tasks of motherhood is delegable and that a substantial proportion of women will fail at each are key. These facts mean that men's reproductive success, assuming they must forsake some potential partners in order to attract others, would be increased if they had proof that potential partners could perform all these tasks. Such proof is only available from having successfully performed all these tasks in the past.

Assuming just 2% of women in each "nested subset" were *absolutely* incapable of each of the requisite mothering tasks (i.e., conception, successful gestation until birth, live birthing, surviving the birth herself, and adequate breastfeeding), about 10% of nulliparous women at maximal reproductive capacity were absolutely incapable of augmenting a male partner's reproductive success. Not counting women who died while of reproductive age (and whose health, and thus ability to conceive, gestate, or birth, may have been poorer), it has been estimated that 10% of natural fertility !Kung women studied never experienced a live birth. This was despite universal marriage for women in that society (see discussion in Howell, 2000). What greater percentage of such women might have then failed to survive such a birth or to breastfeed adequately cannot be known.

Over evolutionary time, moreover, *variation* in fertility, ability to bring a conceptus to term, birth it in a live state, survive the birth, and adequately breastfeed would have been easily detectable by the number and health of children given the mother's age. As such, there has been an opportunity for male psychology to evolve to notice and value such information and for female psychology to evolve to promote it to competitive advantage. Proof of ability to perform requisite mothering tasks would have been greatest among the oldest still-fertile multiparous mothers. As noted, such women often would have spent a portion of their adult lives either with no male partner (due to widowhood or divorce) or an unsatisfactory one, and thus perhaps have sought (a) mate(s). They would, additionally, have been in the best possible position among females to provide reassurance of success to any reproduction attempted with them, even if involving limited male investment.

Potential Traits of Males Who Might Value Proven Success at Requisite Mothering Tasks

Having successfully conceived, gestated, given birth to, survived the birth of, and breastfed a baby would have been the only proof of ability to perform these tasks over evolutionary time. These were all, of course, requisite abilities on the part of any woman who would increase a male's reproductive success. That a nonhuman primate female has successfully performed these tasks is weighted, via some mechanism, significantly favorably by some nonhuman primate males in their choices regarding with which females to attempt to mate (see review in Anderson, 1986). As noted, male chimpanzees prefer the oldest still-fertile female chimps as mates. The theorized reason is these females provide the greatest proof of ability to successfully rear offspring (Muller et al., 2006). Additionally, the youngest of a chimpanzee mother's offspring might also benefit from investment from its older siblings (see generally Anderson, 1986). Even the offspring of multiparous primate females have greater reproductive success in their lifetimes than do the offspring of females having only one offspring (Anderson, 1986).

As noted, primiparous women are more likely to die in childbirth, and young children whose mothers die show lower rates of survival: this may have approached 100% in the EEA. Nulliparous women are also more likely to give birth to children with congenital abnormalities, who would be expected to have survived less often than children without such difficulties in the EEA. Thus, forming a (especially monogamous) pair bond with a nulliparous woman, especially if she was still in adolescence

and thus would not be at full fertility for some years (Anderson, 1986), would have, for a male, represented the risk of losing several of his prime fathering (provisioning, etc.) years or even having no (surviving) children at all (see Anderson, 1986).

As briefly discussed here and expounded on elsewhere (e.g., Buss, 1989), men typically greatly value youth in a female partner. The characteristics of men who do *not* partner with the very youngest (and therefore nulliparous) women, therefore, may not only cast light on why the youngest, nulliparous women are generally preferred but also on arenas of potential mateship competition for older women. Up until the age of about 50 (England & McClintock, 2009), US men choose probably still-fertile (younger) women as partners. A groom in his 20s, for example, is on average about a year older than his bride. A groom in his 30s is on average about 3 years older than his bride. A groom in his 40s is on average about 7 years older than his bride. Why do men, at least starting at the age of 30, tend to not marry the youngest women—does the reasoning as to men's reproductive success benefiting from partnering with the youngest women stop applying? Men beyond their 20s may have decreased attractiveness and perhaps also decreased ability to provision a partner due to, for example, preexisting children and a shorter time horizon before old age. With less to offer a woman in such domains, a man—perhaps of any age—may not be able to attract the youngest women as wives. Thus, if they partner at all, it may tend to be with a woman past youngest adulthood.

It would be odd if human males, somewhat uniquely among primates and especially given their unusually high levels of paternal investment, would not have evolved to at least sometimes choose female mates partially on the basis of proven ability to perform requisite mothering tasks. A man, X, who took such information into account as part of his calculus of mate selection would *not* have reaped as great a reproductive return as a man, Y, who committed to marrying only nulliparous young women at the peak of residual reproductive capacity *and who was able to realize this ambition*. X, however, would have been more likely to experience at least some reproductive success, assuming Y could not replace a wife who could not perform all requisite mothering tasks with another who could (but see generally Betzig, 1989). This makes such mate-selection strategy on the part of males a viable reproductive niche strategy. Such strategy may have been the optimal one for many males, including those with lesser reproductive value of their own for various reasons, including being older, having fewer resources, and/or being less attractive. Generally, selection should favor those males, where there is reproductive capacity available, with the trait of taking advantage of it, rather than eschewing it in favor of lesser reproductive success. Still-fertile women past maximal reproductive value and likely with at least one surviving child could have advertised their proven ability to perform the requisite tasks of motherhood to compete with one another and with nulliparous women for such mateships and investment by these mates.

Women having proven themselves to have non-deleterious reproductive outcomes (e.g., no children born with a deformity or stillborn) might have been desired on this basis as mates. Such outcomes would have dampened ancestral humans' reproductive success (see, e.g., Shepher, 1983), and the physiology of a woman who did have such an outcome might have contributed to it. Here, age and parity are especially relevant: primiparous mothers have a higher rate of congenital deformities (in at least one culture) and stillbirths (in at least two: see discussion in Anderson, 1986). It is possible that one reason primiparas have such negative outcomes more often than other mothers is that males are less likely to choose such women as partners after the unfortunate event. A prediction here regarding female–female competition is that mothers of healthy and perhaps attractive children might advertise these facts as an attempt to induce epigamic selection by observing males (see Fisher & Moule, 2013). They might also advertise that other mothers' children are less healthy/attractive as a means of reducing these other women's competitiveness on the mating market, especially if these other women or the woman advertising became single.

For analogous reasons, women miscarrying early enough to be able to hide it are predicted to do so, in order to not attain a reputation of not being able to successfully carry a pregnancy. Teenage (and thus, likely, nulliparous) women, as well as those over 35, have the greatest risk of miscarriage: women in their mid-20s are at the least risk (Hrdy, 1999, citing Wood, 1994). Thus, the maternal age range at which miscarriage is of least risk is also that at which ability to conceive is greatest. This means that having miscarried may come to be associated by onlookers with relatively low fertility. Howell (2000) noted

that !Kung women do not acknowledge pregnancy until it becomes visible, at approximately the third or fourth month. In this population, marriages are contracted by pregnant women, almost always to the sire. Based on this population's pregnant women's marriages contracted past the time of conception but before pregnancy becomes visible, Howell comments the women seem to be aware that they are pregnant before their pregnancies become visible and they announce them. We predict that women will tend to not publicize pregnancies until they become detectable anyway, in part at least to avoid incurring a reputation as unable to carry a pregnancy, and thus lesser ability to perform a requisite task of motherhood or lower fertility, should they miscarry.

As discussed, primiparous mothers are also more likely to die in the perinatal period, thus making themselves no longer available as romantic partners and likely leading to the death of the offspring (see, e.g., Campbell, 2010, but see Sear & Mace, 2008). Thus, "successful" (perhaps especially, multiparous) mothers are predicted to have been one type of desirable woman (in addition to the desirable younger woman at her maximal reproductive value), by virtue of having proven ability to conceive, gestate, birth in a live state, survive the birth herself, and breastfeed.

"Desirable Mother" as a Possible Mateship Competitive Strategy Niche

An informal pornography study sampling 10,000 porn actors' standard profiles as well as pornography film titles available on the Internet found that the second-most-common title after those indicating "teen" or similar was "MILF" (roughly, "Mother I'd like to have sexual relations with"). Ten percent of all titles used this latter such reference or one similar (Millward, 2013). The average age of the female actors in such films was 33, while the average age for a woman to initiate her career as a pornography actor was only 22. The average number of years for such a female actor to engage in this work was 3 (Millward, 2013). Searches involving the word "MILF," "mom," or similar are reported to comprise a total of 2.7% of all "sexual searches" on Dogpile, an Internet search engine (behind "sexual searches" for "teen," "young," or similar, at 7.8%: Ogas & Gaddam, 2011). Vannier, Currie, and O'Sullivan (2014) performed a content analysis of free "teen" and MILF offerings on the Internet. O'Sullivan, in a newspaper interview regarding this article (Brean,

2013), commented that the MILF film female lead "never looks older than her 30s. . . . (and) it's understood that she is a mother." Thus, it appears that the MILF designation for a pornography film indicates both a more aged than average female lead and one who portrays specifically a mother.

Another informal study of data from "millions" of hits to the reportedly largest pornography website in the world found that out of the 47 US states for which data were available, 20 had MILF as one of their top three terms searched. (Note that MILF search terms were differentiated from "wife" search terms in this study: Pornhub Insights, 2013.) Although the results of only four studies, three of which were informal, should be viewed only as suggestive, they raise a question. Why do so many men show enough interest in watching *mothers* have sexual relations that they are willing to pay for the privilege? Why, furthermore, is the average age of female leads in such films 33, while the average age of a woman entering the pornography acting field is 22 (on average, quitting after 3 years)? If just the "mother" designation within the film was what was attracting viewers, a much younger woman could be used to play the role and is the more popular choice in the genre generally. It is possible that still-fertile successful mothers, old enough to be multiparous and even to be nearing the end of their reproductive careers, may be attractive to men on those bases, at least for the purposes of a short-term mateship or extra-pair copulation (EPC)—those mateships presumably portrayed in pornographic films.

We hypothesize that proven mother status confers some attractiveness to a woman among *some* men, at least for the purposes of a short-term mateship or EPC. If our hypothesis is correct, however, why has a womanly or motherly as opposed to postadolescent female figure not been found in the literature to be considered particularly attractive?

Anderson (1986), within her review of the primate literature (including that on humans) on mate preferences among males based on female age, speculates on appearance cues that could be relied on by males to allow them to preferentially choose the oldest, still-fertile females as mates. She states that "males could discriminate between (female) adults and adolescents on the basis of size, body fat, or the ratio between the two and between nulliparous and multiparous adults on the basis of elongated nipples" (p. 320). Certainly the nonhuman primate males of species she reviews who are attempting more copulations with older, still-fertile females are

somehow detecting which females fall into both of these categories. If nonhuman primate males can do so by appearance, presumably so too could human males over evolutionary time. Thus, the opportunity for preference for such appearance to evolve has existed.

We speculate that any preference for a more motherly figure in women on the part of some men might be obscured in non-EEA type (i.e., nonforaging, controlled fertility) cultures by the availability of technology allowing women to make their appearances more youthful and to delay first births. Why might this be the case? Such a preference on the part of a man might only be advantageous to him in the circumstance of there being so few of the *youngest* women available compared with the number of men that such an individual man, given his mate value, could not reasonably expect to obtain one as a mate. Thus, such a preference might be sensitive to the social environment and ratio of the youngest women to all men. What happens, however, when there is *apparently* a higher ratio of the "youngest" women to men than was observed in the EEA? That is, what happens when there are many nulliparous women past their late teens who look as attractive as late teenage women due to excellent nutrition, health care, appearance-improving technologies, and delay of first birth? Speculatively, Western birth-delaying, youth-mimicking culture, in which images of and actual "youthful" women abound, might be mimicking a condition of apparent plenty of the youngest women in the minds of its men (see also Kenrick, 2011, chapter 2).

This might be part of the reason why there have been few findings consistent with preference or liking for a later age and parity as opposed to a just-postadolescent female figure in the literature, which is largely derived from work on Western populations. In the minds of its women, such "plenty" might lead them to go to extremes of youth mimicry in order to be competitive on the mating market with the maximally attractive youngest women (see, e.g., Dubbs, Kelly, & Barlow in this volume for discussion of increased reported willingness to opt for cosmetic surgery among women following a female–female competition prime). Hill and Durante (2011; and see elsewhere in this volume), perhaps relatedly, found that after women viewed images of attractive women, they expressed more willingness to engage in the risky, appearance-enhancing, and likely youth-mimicking activity of taking diet pills.

There is limited cross-cultural evidence of societies from the anthropological literature in which older women are at least sometimes preferred as mates (e.g., the Kanuri, Cohen, 1967, and the Tiwi, Hart & Pilling, 1979). Anderson (1986) notes that men may be "forced to *marry* adolescents because, with virtually universal marriage for females in most tribal societies, the only unmarried females available are widows and adolescents" (emphasis in original, p. 318). This begs the question: Why not marry a widow or a divorcée? These women might have children whom a new husband would likely be expected to help provision, thus inhibiting any remarriage. In the !Kung women studied by Howell (2000) between 1967 and 1969, however, widows generally remarried within 5 years and divorcées within 1 year of the dissolution of their marriages. Regardless of these facts, it would seem that the youngest, nulliparous woman in the EEA was indeed the best choice as a long-term partner for men, and thus she had a great advantage in competition with other women. This might be less the case where the environment was worse and better mothering was required for infant survival, however, or where a given young woman was not sufficiently attractive to appear fertile enough to yield as many children as would be predicted by partnership with a proven though still young mother. Preferred and actual age of mates among males of varying levels of attractiveness, age, and wealth might be measured to assess whether among those men with lesser values on these traits (i.e., lower mate value), attractive young mothers may actually be preferred to and/or partnered with more often than less attractive nulliparous, younger women.

WHR in women of 0.7 has been rated most attractive by men in one Western culture (Singh, 1993). There is limited evidence of this also being the case in Japan (Swami, Caprario, Tovée, & Furnham, 2006) and in urban but not rural populations in Britain and Malaysia (Swami & Tovée, 2005). WHR increases with pregnancy and childbearing and is a reliable indicator, along with body mass index (BMI), of female fertility (e.g., Singh, 1993, 2002). Female fat, and its position, is clearly related to fertility (e.g., Frisch, 1987; Singh, 1993). As noted, we speculate that a high population ratio of women apparently at maximal reproductive value to men may lead to lesser or no preference on average among men for a more motherly female figure. If this speculation is correct, then this preference should be less observed in natural fertility, foraging societies in which the youngest/apparently youngest

females are not more frequent than they were in EEA communities. It has been found in small-scale, subsistence-based societies generally that women's WHR of 0.7 is not preferred on average by men at least compared to WHRs of up to 0.9 (see discussion in Sugiyama, 2004). This is thought to be due to these cultures existing in environments in which nutrition is uncertain (see also Swami & Tovée, 2005; and see Yu & Shephard, 1998) and thus higher fat stores in women reproductively beneficial.

Women 1 year postpartum have been shown to have increased fat storage particularly in their abdomens, as compared to pre-pregnancy (Sohlström & Forsum, 1995). Parity would seem to increase WHR (Lewis et al., 1994; Rodin, Radke-Sharpe, Rebuffé-Scrive, & Greenwood, 1990; Singh, 2002: but see Koch et al., 2008, in which women in the developing country of Chile did not show greater WHR with increasing parity). Perhaps in those environments in which nutrition is relatively uncertain the proven ability to mother—in addition to its correlate of greater WHR—may be preferred at a higher rate than elsewhere. The putative portion of men's evolved psychology regarding female figure beauty might be sensitive to the physical environment, with men in the worst environments generally showing greater attraction to female figures usually compatible with previous motherhood.

Why else might a higher WHR (at least compared to the local average: see Sugiyama, 2004) figure not have been more frequently found in the literature to be perceived as more or even as equally attractive by men, as the figures of women with WHR of 0.7? Singh (1993) found older (ages 30–86) US men rated a female figure of normal BMI and 0.7 WHR as more attractive than an otherwise similar figure of underweight BMI, while college-aged US men did not. These findings could merely constitute a cohort effect, with the older cohort not being as subject to the then recently changed (Abed, 1998) and perhaps faddish cultural norm that underweight females are attractive. In the same study, however, college students estimated the former figure as approximately 23 to 26 years old and the latter as approximately 17 to 19 years old. Even though college-aged male participants are generally too young to wish to partner with women younger than themselves (Kenrick, Keefe, Gabrielidis, & Cornelius, 1996), they would not tend to be preferred as partners by women older than themselves (see, e.g., Buss, 1989). Thus, they may be expressing heightened interest in women they can actually attain as mates—the youngest and thinnest ones. They still most prefer, however, along with the rest of the men in the study, a fuller though still fertile-appearing (based on WHR) female figure. Such a figure can occur with multiparity and was rated in the study as being of an age at which multiparity would have been likely among women in the EEA.

Preference for Mothers as Sexual Partners May Be Limited to Short-Term and EPC Partnerships

Any preference for a mother as a sexual partner could also be dependent on the particular type of relationship sought by the man and woman. Men seeking a short-term partnership, perhaps especially an EPC, may prefer a woman of proven fertility over a nulliparous woman of maximal residual reproductive capacity. Why might that be? Not only would the latter woman be more benefited by and in a better position to insist upon a long-term and monogamous partnership, but for a short-term relationship to have the reproductive success–impacting consequence of pregnancy, given that it may take on average six months of *regular* sexual intercourse to conceive (see generally Potter & Parker, 1964), conception would be more assured with a proven mother. This would make a woman of proven fertility a better (reproductive success–enhancing) choice for relatively infrequent (e.g., because it is clandestine) sexual intercourse or that confined to a short time frame. Additionally, if she was mated, as one might expect ancestrally most mothers still within the reproductive career would be (see e.g., Howell, 2000), the advantage to a male of having another man provision his offspring might be obtained via an EPC with her.

Possible Relationships with Children's Evolved Psychology

Konner (2010) notes that language development in children coincides with weaning age in hunter-gatherer societies, perhaps allowing for earlier weaning. That is, such language development may have allowed children to more widely elicit provisioning. Assuming a breastfeeding woman experiences lactation-induced amenorrhea, once she ceases breastfeeding she will recommence ovulating and, on average, start experiencing its associated effects. One such effect is increased libido in women in partnered relationships, though where these are of longer duration interest may not be for the mate (Pillsworth, Haselton, & Buss, 2004: see also Fisher, 1992, regarding the prevalence of

divorce occurring when the child of a marriage reaches approximately 4 years of age). Another such effect is greater competitiveness with other women, at least insofar as how highly they rate these others' facial attractiveness (Fisher, 2004). Thus, the mother of a child who just stopped breastfeeding him or her might reacquire or undergo an intensification of interest in intrasexual competition and/or mating and even conceive again immediately. From a child's perspective, this could prove to be a distraction from the mother's attention and provisioning of him or her and a threat to his or her survival or future reproductive success (Blurton Jones & da Costa, 1987). A mother who no longer needs to breastfeed her child should be capable of provisioning him or her with a greater number of calories, given that conversion of food into breast milk necessarily entails energy loss. Speech may indeed assist in eliciting provisioning from a mother no longer so frequently in close contact with a child due to cessation of breastfeeding, as well as by others in the community. Perhaps, however, children's language development or other new behaviors following weaning could additionally be a response to their mothers' renewed interest in intrasexual competition and/or mating.

In the EEA, any woman interested in having only one child would not have contributed as much to our modern genome as would a woman who had greater reproductive success. This suggests that there should be a psychological mechanism leading to women continuing to desire sexual intercourse, despite already having a child in whose interest it is, if the child is very young, to delay her in its pursuit. Blurton Jones and da Costa (1987) discuss unweaned children's extension of the period of anovulation in their mothers via nighttime breastfeeding as adaptive for the children, in that it delays the arrival of competitor siblings. Haig and Wharton (2003) and Smit (2009) discuss instances of communicative behaviors of children putatively designed to delay new births on the part of their mothers. These behaviors would occur both before and after the time of weaning. We suggest that where such behaviors occur after weaning and cessation of the mother's lactation-induced amenorrhea, they may constitute a counteradaptation on the part of the child to his or her mother seeking out new mateships and thus, potentially, her next child being only a half- rather than a full sibling. Alternately, these tactics may constitute a counteradaptation to her reestablishment of regular sexual relations with her partner, performed by the child to delay attendant decreased attention to and investment in himself or herself.

Higher levels of testosterone are correlated with greater competitiveness in women (Cashdan, 1995; and see Bateup, Booth, Shirtcliff, & Granger, 2002) as well as libido, and have been found in mothers of children slightly older than 2 years compared with mothers of younger children (Kuzawa, Gettler, Huang, & McDade, 2010). Perhaps this former group of mothers are experiencing a return to greater competitiveness and libido at the very time it would fit their interests to start a new pregnancy. We predict that mothers will recommence engagement in greatest female–female competition for mateships or engage in a resurgence in sexual interest for an existing partner when her current, youngest child reaches the age at which her reproductive success would be optimized by starting a new pregnancy. If true, one implication is that female–female competition for new mateships by mothers would be predicted to be somewhat cyclical, starting with each conception and lasting until the next pregnancy. Within such a cycle, the greatest such competition would occur with the recommencement of ovulation (e.g., following lactation) and last until the next pregnancy. Thus, assuming each of her children survives to weaning, a mother's intrasexual mateship competition should recommence with greatest intensity somewhat less than about every 4 years. This length of time is posited based on the !Kung (Howell, 2000) average interbirth interval for mothers being approximately every 4 years. If this 4-year interval is assumed to represent a *compromise* between the interests of a mother and her current child in interbirth interval, then the optimum for the mother should be less than this amount of time (see, e.g., Haig, 2014).

Competitive Mothering

The idea that mothers might compete with one another for mateships is not new. Miller (2000) posits that very few of the mates available in the EEA would have been young and childless. Competition for mateships among them would have been *between parents* (thus, if female–female, between mothers), and the most competent would have stood favorably over others:

> Before contraception, our female ancestors would have produced their first child by around age 20, within a few years of reaching sexual maturity. . . . Before legally imposed monogamous marriage,

individuals probably passed through several sexual relationships during their reproductive years. . . . (the children of which) would have been hanging around their mothers almost all the time. . . . Female hominids must have juggled their courtship efforts with their mothering. Some of their courtship displays may have originated by turning normal motherly duties into better fitness indicators. (pp. 192–194)

Assuming Miller is right, one implication is that "competitive mothering" as reported in modern media (e.g., FoxNews.com, 2013, in which a physically fit mother of three young children asks other mothers what their excuse is for not being fit; Pickert, 2012, in which a mother engaged in breastfeeding is pictured with the caption "Are you mom enough?"; Y! OMG! Blog, 2013, in which celebrities' children's attractiveness and number, primarily, is commented on) may not be just a modern or Western phenomenon and may serve, in part, as a fitness advertisement on the part of the mother. One study of modern foragers, the Tsimane, did indeed find that gossip about mothers' mothering abilities and the unkemptness of their children had a large effect on these mothers' reputations as attractive, among other women only (Rucas et al., 2006). We would predict that searches of other societies' cultural output as well as historical records would reveal displays by mothers as to the quality and quantity of their offspring, primarily to other women, which would be attended to by these others.

Despite the existence of Rucas et al. (2006), our searches for articles using the search string "female–female competition" revealed not a single hit concerning competitive mothering. Fisher and Moule (2013) comment that though there exists some sociological literature concerning the phenomenon, there is none from an evolutionary perspective. The fact that our "female–female competition" searches revealed no hits concerning competitive mothering and, generally, the dearth of articles concerning this phenomenon from an evolutionary perspective may have several causes. These might include the difficulty inherent in moving beyond convenience sampling and in sampling, especially, new mothers—a group one would expect to be extremely busy and therefore less available to participate. It may also, however, indicate that many evolutionary researchers simply have not yet examined such displays from women under the lens of their possible competitiveness regarding reproductive success–impacting resources.

A novel idea here is that the health, attractiveness, or other indicator of being well brought up on the part of women's children might have served as a fitness advertisement for the mother (especially since mothers rather than fathers tend to be primarily responsible for children's health and upbringing: see, e.g., Hrdy, 1999). Anderson (1986) has hypothesized that the state of being successfully multiparous (and therefore, necessarily, also having postmaximal reproductive value) might have been maximally attractive to males due to greater survivorship of offspring born to the multiparous. We posit that being a woman who had proven herself successful at conceiving, gestating, birthing, breastfeeding, and other mothering tasks would have occupied a separate competitive niche to that of the young woman of maximal residual reproductive capacity. We further posit that such proven success at mothering may have been particularly effective when advertised to men alongside the mother's own good looks (see also Fisher & Moule, 2013).

Potentially, no group of men on average prefers a motherly as opposed to a youthful, nulliparous female figure. Men, additionally, may only generally prefer older women (and, perhaps, among these, the multiparous) for short-term mateships and EPCs. So then why would women competitively mother and thus disclaim their mother status in a way men might notice, in any society in which the fact one is a mother may be largely hidden to strangers and in which nulliparous appearance can be mimicked (e.g., Western society)? Advertising how attractive or healthy their children are, and thus the magnitude of these children's expected fitness, is a possible answer. If, however, competitive mothering is not a fitness display of the woman herself, and only, for example, a display of her children's expected fitness, might we not see "competitive fathering" more often? If competitive mothering, additionally, occurs primarily among mothers of children too young to reproduce (see previously cited popular media examples, in which competing mothers' children by and large were years from puberty), how reasonably is it explained as a display of these children's expected fitness? The answer to this puzzle may lie in the possibility that this is a form of female intrasexual competition detectable preferentially by other women (for increased detectability by women of female intrasexual competition in general, see discussion in Geary, 2010; Merten, 1997; Vaillancourt, 2013; and see Campbell, 1999, 2004), designed to "vanquish" them to depression, anxiety, or lowered

fertility (see "Older, Mated Women's Competition with Younger Mate Poachers").

In competitively mothering, women may be competitively showing off their own (perhaps in addition to their children's) fitness to other women. They may especially be doing so to older women like themselves, whether non-mothers or mothers (their primary competition, once nulliparity and youngest womanhood have passed). Men may not engage in competitive parenting themselves for the same reasons they may not engage in as much subtle relational aggression of the type preferred by women (see, e.g., Buss & Dedden, 1990, Vaillancourt & Sharma, 2011).

Discussion

This chapter has attempted to assess the possible effect of the relative dearth of research on still-fertile women past nulliparity and maximal residual reproductive capacity ("older women") on the literature concerning female intrasexual mateship competition. As discussed, 75% of the literature we sampled concerning female–female competition for mateships sampled only women ages 18 to 25. The remaining articles, additionally, did not compare women's competitive mateship acquisition/retention tactics across the reproductive career. Given that the former set of studies were performed in Western cultures and very little reproduction in such cultures occurs at these ages among women, only nulliparous women by and large were likely sampled. Given that reproductive success, perhaps *the* vital metric in evolutionary psychology, cannot be directly assessed in studies involving only the nulliparous, this is a problem. In this chapter we have also attempted to provide specific hypotheses regarding the ways and areas in which older, still-fertile women, when studied, would compete differently for mateships as compared to the youngest, fertile women.

One such way they are hypothesized to compete differently relates to their loss of mate value in some domains and their gain of it in others. The main loss in mate value for older women, and therefore an important focus of this section of the chapter, was argued to be in physical attractiveness. Evidence from the literature was provided that the maximally attractive shape of female ornaments or attributes indicating residual reproductive capacity would diminish with increasing parity and age. Theory was provided that such losses in the EEA would on average have been tellingly greater for women having pursued a faster life history strategy at a younger age. Evidence from the literature on WHR was reviewed and arguably showed that motherhood, at least for younger mothers, was not incompatible with possession of a female figure that would be rated as attractive. The apparent extreme plentifulness of the youngest, most attractive women in Western societies was discussed as possibly contributing to Western women's greater preference for their figures to approximate those of the youngest, nulliparous women, as opposed to a fuller figure not incompatible with motherhood.

Women may experience a sexual peak of desire in their early 30s or later. This finding was discussed as a basis for positing that older women may be competing for mateships differently than younger women. The main *gain* in mate value possible with age, separate from any experienced by virtue of attaining the status of proven mother, was posited to be increased resources (in the EEA, these could have primarily been social in nature). The extremely limited evidence and theory available on women's differing mateship acquisition strategies with greater age and wealth was reviewed to show the plausibility of such strategy changing to one of greater choosiness for health- and reproduction-promoting genes in and lesser choosiness for investment from a mate.

Competitive mothering was one type of intrasexual competition posited to be utilized among older, still-fertile women. We hypothesized that competitive mothering is a personal fitness display on the part of the mother. Though primarily targeted to other older women (co-competitors) as a means of demonstrating degree of personal fertility and mothering ability, and of thereby vanquishing other females into subordinate status, it was hypothesized to additionally perhaps serve to advertise fertility to men.

Important to our discussion and analysis was consideration of the underestimated importance of each of the nondelegable tasks of mothering requisite to every offspring's survival over evolutionary time. These tasks are conceiving, gestating, birthing a live infant, surviving the birth herself (assuming the children of women dying in childbirth themselves died in the EEA), and adequately breastfeeding. We hypothesized that such abilities, being requisite to augmenting a man's reproductive success and providable only by his female mate, would not have gone unnoticed and unappreciated over evolutionary time in mate selection, at least by men of a certain status. As such, men's evolved psychologies are predicted to be sensitively attuned to cues of mothering ability where that man was engaged in short-term mating, infant survival was less certain due to harsh environment, or his own anticipated ability to provision was decreased (e.g., due to advancing age) or his mate value low enough such that he could maximize his reproductive success by partnering with a nonnulliparous widow or divorcée. Also as such, we agree with Fisher and Moule (2013) in hypothesizing that mothers would advertise their successful motherhood, especially alongside their relative youth and beauty given their parity, to men in an effort to induce epigamic selection. Supporting these hypotheses, we reviewed the available data regarding the incidence of viewing pornography depicting older women specifically portrayed as mothers and provided examples from current, popular media of competitive mothering.

We hypothesized that since ovulation temporarily ceases with pregnancy and postpartum, as well as with any lactation-induced amenorrhea, mothers' most intense competition for any new mateships may be cyclical, occurring roughly every 3 to 4 years given her latest child's survival during that period and natural fertility. We reviewed children's possible responses to their mothers exiting the period of lactation-induced anovulation, given these children's interest in delaying the birth of the next child and/or ensuring maximum provisioning for themselves and the mother's interest in expediting her next birth relative to this point.

In one of our two nearest species relatives, the common chimpanzee, and in a number of other primates in which paternal investment can also be considered nil, the oldest still-fertile females (likely of greatest parity) are preferentially approached for mating. The posited reason is that these females are most likely to give birth to offspring that will survive and themselves have greater reproductive success relative to earlier-borns (Anderson, 1986). We echoed the hypothesis of Hrdy (1999) that since men, unlike male chimpanzees, can "possess" women as mates, they tend cross-culturally to prefer the very youngest women as wives, rather than either those at maximum fertility (a few years older) or older. Thus, we hypothesize that where men are pursuing a short-term, nonpaternally investing mating strategy, and thus have as little to lose and as much to gain as do male chimpanzees by mating with a more fertile (older) female, they will, more often than when not pursuing such a strategy, seek older, fertile women as mates. We further hypothesize and argue that the female participants in EPCs ancestrally may have tended to *already* have been mothers and that the reproductive interests of men pursuing short-term mating strategies may have been especially served by attempting to cuckold the husband of a proven mother.

Conclusions

Women's competition among themselves for greatest personal reproductive success, over evolutionary time, would seem to have been an individual endurance test of up to approximately 38 years, up to nine pregnancies and births, and perhaps 14 years of breastfeeding. There is every reason to suppose that personal reproductive success is so worthy a prize that it would have been competed for in each of these 38 years. With such long duration of reproductive "race" and attendant significant physical, social resource, and physical resource changes occurring over it, there is no reason to suppose utilized tactics would not change over a woman's reproductive career. A slow competition for reproductive success is still a competition, and its winners are not known until it is complete. Perhaps we currently only know about the starting line of the race.

References

Abed, R. T. (1998). The sexual competition hypothesis for eating disorders. *British Journal of Medical Psychology, 71*, 525–547.

Anderson, C. M. (1986). Female age: Male preference and reproductive success in primates. *International Journal of Primatology, 7*, 305–326.

Anderson, S. E., Dallal, G. E., & Must, A. (2003). Relative weight and race influence average age at menarche: Results from two nationally representative surveys of US girls studied 25 years apart. *Pediatrics, 111*, 844–850.

Apostolou, M. (2007). Sexual selection under parental choice: the role of parents in the evolution of mating. *Evolution and Human Behavior, 28*, 403–409.

Atkinson, J., & Volk, A. (2013). Infant and child death in the human environment of evolutionary adaptedness. *Evolution and Human Behavior, 34*, 182–192.

Bateup, H. S., Booth, A., Shirtcliff, E. A., & Granger, D. A. (2002). Testosterone, cortisol, and women's competition. *Evolution and Human Behavior, 23*, 181–192.

Belsky, J., Steinberg, L., & Draper, P. (1991). Childhood experience, interpersonal development, and reproductive strategy: An evolutionary theory of socialization. *Child Development, 62*, 647–670.

Benenson, J. F. (2013). The development of human female competition: Allies and adversaries. *Philosophical Transactions of the Royal Society B, 368*, 20130079.

Betzig, L. (1989). Causes of conjugal dissolution: A cross-cultural study. *Current Anthropology, 30*, 654–676.

Black, R. E., Allen, L. H., Bhutta, Z. A., Caulfield, L. E., de Onis, M., Ezzati, M., ... Rivera, J. (2008). Maternal and child undernutrition: global and regional exposures and health consequences. *Lancet, 371*, 243–260.

Blurton Jones, N. G., & da Costa, E. D. (1987). A suggested adaptive value of toddler night waking: Delaying the birth of the next sibling. *Ethology and Sociobiology, 8*(2), 135–142.

Blurton Jones, N. G., Marlowe, F. W., Hawkes, K., & O'Connell, J. F. (2000). Paternal investment and hunter-gatherer divorce rates. In L. Cronk, N. Chagnon, & W. Irons (Eds.), *Adaptation in human behaviour: An anthropological perspective* (pp. 69–90). Chicago: Aldine.

Brean, J. (2013, November 19). Porn study finds that "teens" and "moms" rule the online sex world. *National Post*. http://news.nationalpost.com/2013/11/19/porn-study-finds-that-teens-and-moms-rule-the-online-sex-world/

Buss, D. M. (1989). Sex differences in human mate preferences: Evolutionary hypotheses tested in 37 cultures. *Behavioral and Brain Sciences, 12*, 1–14.

Buss, D. M., & Dedden, L. A. (1990). Derogation of competitor. *Journal of Social and Personal Relationships, 7*, 395–422.

Buss, D. M., & Schmitt, D. P. (1993). Sexual strategies theory: An evolutionary perspective on human mating. *Psychological Review, 100*, 204–232.

Campbell, A. (1999). Staying alive: Evolution, culture, and women's intrasexual competition. *Behavioral and Brain Sciences, 22*, 203–252.

Campbell, A. (2004). Female competition: Causes, constraints, content, and contexts. *Journal of Sex Research, 41*, 16–26.

Campbell, A. (2010). Oxytocin and human social behavior. *Personality and Social Psychology Review, 14*, 281–295.

Campbell, A., Muncer, S., & Bibel, D. (1998). Female–female criminal assault: An evolutionary perspective. *Journal of Research in Crime and Delinquency, 35*, 413–428.

Campbell, A., Muncer, S., & Bibel, D. (2001). Women and crime: An evolutionary approach. *Aggression and Violent Behavior, 6*, 481–497.

Cashdan, E. (1995). Hormones, sex, and status in women. *Hormones and Behavior, 29*, 354–366.

Cohen, R. (1967). *The Kanuri of Bornu*. New York: Holt, Rinehart & Winston.

Copen, C. E., Daniels, K. & Vespa, J. (2012, March 22). *First marriages in the United States: Data from the 2006–2010 National Survey of Family Growth*. National Health Statistics Reports 49. Washington, DC: US Department of Health and Human Services. http://www.cdc.gov/nchs/data/nhsr/nhsr049.pdf

Daly, M., Wilson, M., & Weghorst, S. J. (1982). Male sexual jealousy. *Evolution and Human Behavior, 3*, 11–27.

Darwin, C. (1871). *The descent of man and selection in relation to sex*, 2nd ed. London: John Murray.

de Waal, F. (2007). *Chimpanzee politics: Power and sex among apes*. Rev. ed. Baltimore, MD: Johns Hopkins University Press.

Dickemann, M. (1981). Paternal confidence and dowry competition: A biocultural analysis of purdah. In R. D. Alexander & D. W. Tinkle (Eds.), *Natural selection and social behavior: Recent research and new theory* (pp. 417–438). New York: Chiron Press.

Dugdale, A. E., & Eaton-Evans, J. (1989). The effect of lactation and other factors on post-partum changes in body-weight and triceps skinfold thickness. *British Journal of Nutrition, 61*, 149–153.

Easton, J. A., Confer, J. C., Goetz, C. D., & Buss D. M. (2010). Reproduction expediting: Sexual motivations, fantasies, and the ticking biological clock. *Personality and Individual Differences, 49,* 516–520.

Edmonds, D. K., Lindsay, K. S., Miller, J. F., Williamson, E., & Wood, P. J. (1983). Early embryonic mortality in women. *Obstetrical and Gynecological Survey, 38*(7), 433–434.

Elliot, A. J., & Pazda, A. D. (2012). Dressed for sex: Red as a female sexual signal in humans. *PLoS One, 7*(4), e34607.

England, P., & McClintock, E. A. (2009). The gendered double standard of aging in US marriage markets. *Population and Development Review, 35,* 797–816.

Fisher, H. E. (1992). *Anatomy of love: A natural history of mating, marriage, and why we stray.* New York: Fawcett Columbine.

Fisher, M. L. (2004). Female intrasexual competition decreases female facial attractiveness. *Proceedings of the Royal Society B, 271*(Suppl. 5), S283–S285.

Fisher, M. L., & Moule, K. R. (2013). A new direction for intrasexual competition research: Cooperative versus competitive motherhood. *Journal of Social, Evolutionary, and Cultural Psychology, 7,* 318–325.

Fletcher, G. J. O., Simpson, J. A., Campbell, L., & Overall, N. C. (2015). Pair-bonding, romantic love, and evolution: The curious case of *Homo sapiens. Perspectives on Psychological Science, 10,* 20–36.

Flinn, M. V., Ward, C. V., & Noone, R. (2005). Hormones and the human family. In D. M. Buss (Ed.), *The handbook of evolutionary psychology* (pp. 552–580). Hoboken, NJ: Wiley.

FoxNews.com. (2013). "What's your excuse?": Fit mother's Facebook post ignites controversy. http://www.foxnews.com/health/2013/10/16/what-your-excuse-fit-mother-facebook-post-ignites-controversy/print

Frisch, R. E. (1987). Body fat, menarche, fitness and fertility. *Human Reproduction, 2,* 521–533.

Gadow, E. C., Castilla, E. E., Lopez Camelo J., & Queenan, J. T. (1991). Stillbirth rate and associated risk factors among 869,750 Latin American hospital births 1982–1986. *International Journal of Gynecology and Obstetrics, 35,* 209–214.

Geary, D. C. (2010). *Male, female: The evolution of human sex differences,* 2nd ed. Washington, DC: American Psychological Association.

Goldstein, S. R. (1994). Embryonic death in early pregnancy: A new look at the first trimester. *Obstetrics & Gynecology, 84*(2), 294–297.

Gowaty, P. A. (1996). Battles of the sexes and origins of monogamy. In J. M. Black (Ed.), *Partnerships in birds: The study of monogamy.* New York: Oxford University Press.

Gowaty, P. A. (1997). Sexual dialectics, sexual selection, and variation in reproductive behavior. In P. A. Gowaty, *Feminism and evolutionary biology* (pp. 351–384). Boston: Springer.

Grainger, A. S., & Dunbar, R. I. (2009). The structure of dyadic conversations and sex differences in social style. *Journal of Evolutionary Psychology, 7*(1), 83–93.

Haig, D. (2014). Interbirth intervals: Intrafamilial, intragenomic and intrasomatic conflict. *Evolution, Medicine, and Public Health, 2014*(1), 12–17.

Haig, D., & Wharton, R. (2003). Prader-Willi syndrome and the evolution of human childhood. *American Journal of Human Biology, 15*(3), 320–329.

Harlow, B. L., & Signorello, L. B. (2000). Factors associated with early menopause. *Maturitas, 35,* 3–9.

Hart, C. W. M., & Pilling, A. R. (1979). *Tiwi of North Australia.* New York: Hold, Rinehart & Winston.

Hastings, K. K., & Testa, J. W. (1998). Maternal and birth colony effects on survival of Weddell seal offspring from McMurdo Sound, Antarctica. *Journal of Animal Ecology, 67,* 722–740.

Hejcmanova, P., Vymyslicka, P., Kolockova, K., Antoninova, M., Havlikova, B., Stepkalova, ... Hejcman, M. (2011). Suckling behavior of eland antelopes (*Taurotragus* spp.) under semi-captive and farm conditions. *Journal of Ethology, 29,* 161–168.

Hill, K. (1993). Life history theory and evolutionary anthropology. *Evolutionary Anthropology. 2,* 78–88.

Hill, S. E., & Durante, K. M. (2011). Courtship, competition, and the pursuit of attractiveness: Mating goals facilitate health-related risks taking and strategic risk suppression in women. *Personality and Social Psychology Bulletin, 37,* 383–394.

Hill, K., & Hurtado, A. M. (1996). *Ache life history.* New York: Aldine de Gruyter.

Hodapp, P., & Luciani, J. (2013, August 1). 16 female celebs who have aged gracefully and 16 others who don't have time on their side. *Shape.* http://www.shape.com/celebrities/celebrity-photos/16-female-celebs-who-have-aged-gracefully/

Hoffman, A. A., & Parsons, P. A. (1989). Selection for increased dessication resistance in *Drosophila melanogaster*: Additive genetic control and correlated responses for other stresses. *Genetics, 122,* 837–845.

Howell, N. (2000). *Demography of the Dobe!Kung,* 2nd ed. New York: Walter de Gruyter.

Hrdy, S. (1999). *Mother nature: A history of mothers, infants, and natural selection.* New York: Pantheon Books.

Hrdy, S. (2000). The optimal number of fathers: Evolution, demography and history in the shaping of female mate preferences. *Evolutionary Perspectives on Human Reproductive Behavior, 907,* 75–96.

Hrdy, S. (2009). *Mothers and others: The evolutionary origins of mutual understanding.* Cambridge, MA: Harvard University Press.

Hudson, J. W., & Henze, L. F. (1969). Campus values in mate selection: A replication. *Journal of Marriage and Family, 31,* 772–775.

Jones, D. (1996). An evolutionary perspective on physical attractiveness. *Evolutionary Anthropology, 5,* 97–109.

Kam, C. D., Wilking, J. R., & Zechmeister, E. J. (2007). Beyond the "narrow data base": Another convenience sample for experimental research. *Political Behavior, 29,* 415–440.

Kenrick, D. T., & Keefe, R. C. (1992). Age preferences in mates reflect sex differences in human reproductive strategies. *Behavioral and Brain Sciences, 15,* 75–133.

Kenrick, D. T., Keefe, R. C., Gabrielidis, C., & Cornelius, J. S. (1996). Adolescents` age preferences for dating partners: Support for an evolutionary model of life-history strategies. *Child Development, 67,* 1499–1511.

Kenrick, D. T. (2011). *Sex, murder and the meaning of life.* New York: Perseus Books.

Khan, K. S., Wojdyla, D., Say, L., Gulmezoglu, A. M., & Van Look, P. F. A. (2006). WHO analysis of causes of maternal death: A systematic review. *Lancet, 367,* 1066–1074.

Kinney, M. V., Kerber, K. J., Black, R. E., Cohen, B., Nkrumah, F., Coovadia, H., ... Lawn, J. E. (2010). Sub-Saharan

Africa's mothers, newborns, and children: Where and why do they die? *PLoS Medicine, 7*(6), e1000294.

Kobylianski, E., & Livshits, G. (1989). Age dependent changes in morphometric and biochemical traits. *Annals of Human Biology, 16,* 237–247.

Koch, E., Bogado, M., Araya, F., Romero, T., Diaz, C., Manriquez, L., ... Kirschbaum, A. (2008). Impact of parity on anthropometric measures of obesity controlling by multiple confounders: A cross-sectional study in Chilean women. *Journal of Epidemiology and Community Health, 62*(5), 461–470.

Konner, M. (2010). *The evolution of childhood.* Cambridge, MA: Harvard University Press.

Kuzawa, C. W., Gettler, L. T., Huang, Y. Y., & McDade, T. W. (2010). Mothers have lower testosterone than nonmothers: Evidence from the Philippines. *Hormones and Behavior, 57*(4), 441–447.

Larsson, G., & Andersson-Ellström, A. (2003). Experiences of pregnancy-related body shape changes and of breast-feeding in women with a history of eating disorders. *European Eating Disorders Review, 11,* 116–124.

Leonetti, D. L., Nath, D. C., Heman, N. S., & Neill, D. B. (2005). Kinship organization and the impact of grandmothers on reproductive success among the matrilineal Khasi and patrilineal Bengali of northeast India. In E. Voland, A. Chasiotis, & W. Schiefenhovel (Eds.), *Grandmotherhood: The evolutionary significance of the second half of female life* (pp. 194–214). New Brunswick, NJ: Rutgers University Press.

Lewis, C. E., Smith, D. E., Caveny, J. L., Perkins, L. L., Burke, G. L., & Bild, D. E. (1994). Associations of body mass and body fat distribution with parity among African-American and Caucasian women: The CARDIA Study. *Obesity Research, 2,* 517–525.

Mace, R., & Sear, R. (1996). Maternal mortality in a Kenyan pastoralist population. London: LSE Research Online. http://eprints.lse.ac.uk/archive/00000686

Merten, D. E. (1997). The meaning of meanness: Popularity, competition, and conflict among junior high school girls. *Sociology of Education,* 175–191.

Miller, G. (2000). *The mating mind.* New York: Random House.

Millward, J. (2013, February 14). Deep inside: A study of 10,000 porn stars and their careers, http://jonmillward.com/blog/studies/deep-inside-a-study-of-10000-porn-stars/

Muller, M. N., Thompson, M. E., & Wrangham, R. W. (2006). Male chimpanzees prefer mating with old females. *Current Biology, 16*(22), 2234–2238.

Neifert, M., DeMarzo, S., Seacat, J., Young, D., Leff, M., & Orleans, M. (1990). The influence of breast surgery, breast appearance, and pregnancy-induced breast changes on lactation sufficiency as measured by infant weight gain. *Birth, 17,* 31–38.

Neville, C. E., McKinley, M. C., Holmes, V. A., Spence, D., & Woodside, J. V. (2014). The relationship between breast-feeding and postpartum weight change—a systematic review and critical evaluation. *International Journal of Obesity, 38,* 577–590.

Ogas, O., & Gaddam, S. (2011). *A billion wicked thoughts.* New York: Penguin.

Parker, G. A. (1974). Assessment strategy and evolution of fighting behavior. *Journal of Theoretical Biology, 47,* 223–243.

Penke, L., Bates, T. C., Gow, A. J., Pattie, A., Starr, J. M., Jones, B. C., ... Deary, I. J. (2009). Symmetric faces are a sign of successful cognitive aging. *Evolution and Human Behavior, 30,* 429–437.

People.com. (2013). Body after baby: Celebrity moms show off shockingly svelte figures after giving birth. http://www.people.com/people/archive/topic/0,,20230194,00.html

Pickert, K. (2012, May 21). Are you mom enough? *Time Magazine.*

Pillsworth, E. G., Haselton, M. G., & Buss, D. M. (2004). Ovulatory shifts in female sexual desire. *Journal of Sex Research, 41,* 55–65.

Pisacane, A., & Continisio, C. (2004). Breastfeeding and perceived changes in the appearance of the breasts: A retrospective study. *Acta Paediatrics, 93,* 1346–1348.

Polak, M., Møller, A. P., Gangestad, S. W., Kroeger, D. E., Manning, J. T., & Thornhill, R. (2003). Does an individual asymmetry parameter exist? A meta-analysis. In M. Polak (Ed.), *Developmental instability: Causes and consequences* (pp. 81–96). Oxford: Oxford University Press.

Pornhub Insights, Pornhub.com. (2013, October 3). What are Americans searching for on Pornhub? http://pornhub.com/insights/what-do-people-in-the-us-search-for-in-pornhub-and-how-long-they-last-in-each-visit

Potter, R. G., & Parker, M. P. (1964). Predicting the time required to conceive. *Population Studies, 18,* 99–116.

Pusey, A., Williams, J., & Goodall, J. (1997). The influence of dominance rank on the reproductive success of female chimpanzees. *Science, 277*(5327), 828–831.

Rodin, J., Radke-Sharpe, N., Rebuffé-Scrive, M., & Greenwood, M. R. C. (1990). Weight cycling and fat distribution. *International Journal of Obesity, 14,* 303–310.

Rosenthal, M. S. (1985). *The fertility sourcebook,* 1st ed. New York: McGraw-Hill.

Rosvall, K. A. (2011). Intrasexual competition in females: Evidence for sexual selection? *Behavioral Ecology, 22,* 1131–1140.

Rucas, S. L., Gurven, M., Kaplan, H., Winking, J., Gangestad, S., & Crespo, M. (2006). Female intrasexual competition and reputational effects on attractiveness among the Tsimane of Bolivia. *Evolution and Human Behavior, 27,* 40–52.

Rucas, S. L., Gurven, M., Winking, J., & Kaplan, H. (2012). Social aggression and resource conflict across the female life-course in the Bolivian Amazon. *Aggressive Behavior, 38*(3), 194–207.

Sassler, S. (2010). Partnering across the life course: Sex, relationships, and mate selection. *Journal of Marriage and Family, 72,* 557–575.

Schmitt, D. P., Shackelford, T. K., Duntley, J., Tooke, W., Buss, D. M., Fisher, M. L., ... Vasey, P. (2002). Is there an early-30s peak in female sexual desire? Cross-sectional evidence from the United States and Canada. *Canadian Journal of Human Sexuality, 11,* 1–18.

Sear, R., & Mace, R. (2008). Who keeps children alive? A review of the effects of kin on child survival. *Evolution and Human Behavior, 29,* 1–18.

Shepher, J. (1983). *Incest: A biosocial view.* New York: Academic Press.

Singh, D. (1993). Body shape and women's attractiveness: The critical role of waist-to-hip ratio. *Human Nature, 4,* 297–321.

Singh, D. (2002). Female mate value at a glance: Relationship of waist-to-hip ratio to health, fecundity and attractiveness. *Neuroendocrinology Letters, 23*(Suppl. 4), 81–91.

Smit, H. (2009). Genomic imprinting and communicative behaviour: Prader-Willi and Angelman syndrome. *Netherlands Journal of Psychology*, *65*(3), 78–88.

Sohlström, A., & Forsum, E. (1995). Changes in adipose tissue volume and distribution during reproduction in Swedish women as assessed by magnetic resonance imaging. *American Journal of Clinical Nutrition*, *61*(2), 287–295.

Srivastava, J. N., & Saksena, D. M. (1981). Infant mortality differentials in an Indian setting: Follow-up of hospital deliveries. *Journal of Biosocial Science*, *13*, 467–478.

Sugiyama, L. S. (2004). Is beauty in the context-sensitive adaptations of the beholder? Shiwiar use of waist-to-hip ratio in assessments of female mate value. *Evolution and Human Behavior*, *25*, 51–62.

Sun, F., Sebastiani, P., Schupf, N., Bae, H., Andersen, S. L., McIntosh, A., . . . Perls, T. T. (2015). Extended maternal age at birth of last child and women's longevity in the Long Life Family Study. *Menopause: The Journal of the North American Menopause Society*, *22*(1), 26–31.

Swami, V., Caprario, C., Tovée, M. J., & Furnham, A. (2006). Female physical attractiveness in Britain and Japan: A cross-cultural study. *European Journal of Personality*, *20*, 69–81.

Swami, V., & Tovée, M. J. (2005). Female physical attractiveness in Britain and Malaysia: A cross-cultural study. *Body Image*, *2*, 115–128.

Thornhill, R., & Gangestad, S. W. (2008). *The evolutionary biology of human female sexuality*. New York: Oxford University Press.

Thornhill, R., & Palmer, C. T. (2000). *A natural history of rape: Biological bases of sexual coercion*. Cambridge, MA: MIT Press.

Vaillancourt, T. (2005). Indirect aggression among humans: Social construct or evolutionary adaptation? In R. E. Tremblay, W. W. Hartup, & J. Archer (Eds.), *Developmental origins of aggression* (pp. 158–177). New York: Guilford.

Vaillancourt, T. (2013). Do human females use indirect aggression as an intrasexual competition strategy? *Philosophical Transactions of the Royal Society B*, *368*(1631), 20130080.

Vaillancourt, T., & Sharma, A. (2011). Intolerance of sexy peers: Intrasexual competition among women. *Aggressive Behavior*, *37*, 569–577.

Vannier, S. A., Currie, A. B., & O'Sullivan, L. F. (2014). Schoolgirls and soccer moms: A content analysis of free "teen" and "MILF" online pornography. *Journal of Sex Research*, *51*, 253–264.

Voland, E., & Beise, J. (2005). The husband's mother is the devil in the house. Data on the impact of the mother-in-law on stillbirth mortality in historical Krummhörn (1750–1874) and some thoughts on the evolution of the postgenerative female life. In E. Voland, A. Chasiotis, & W. Schiefenhövel (Eds.), *Grandmotherhood. The evolutionary significance of the second half of female life* (pp. 239–255). New Brunswick, NJ: Rutgers University Press.

Volk, A. A. (2009). Human breastfeeding is not automatic: Why that's so and what it means for human evolution. *Journal of Social, Evolutionary, and Cultural Psychology*, *3*, 305–314.

Wang, Y., & Griskevicius, V. (2014). Conspicuous consumption, relationships, and rivals: women's luxury products as signals to other women. *Journal of Consumer Research*, *40*(5), 834–854.

Wood, J. (1994). *Dynamics of human reproduction: Biology, biometry, demography*. New York: Aldine de Gruyter.

Wynn, A. (1987). Nutrition before conception and the outcome of pregnancy. *Nutrition and Health*, *5*, 31–43.

Y! OMG! Blog. (2013). Celebrity Broods. http://ca.omg.yahoo.com/blogs/celebrity-broods/

Yu, D. W., & Shephard, G. H. (1998). Is beauty in the eye of the beholder? *Nature*, *396*, 321–322.

Motherhood and Family

Competitive Motherhood from a Comparative Perspective

Katherine A. Valentine, Norman P. Li, *and* Jose C. Yong

Abstract

Mothers play an important role in helping their children achieve maximal reproductive success. We explore how mothers across species manipulate birth sex ratios favoring the sex that will be best suited to their environments and how maternal competition affects offspring reproductive success in nonhuman mammals as well as humans. The Trivers-Willard hypothesis, resource competition hypothesis, resource enhancement hypothesis, and maternal dominance hypothesis are considered with respect to maternal birth sex ratio manipulation. Next, the primate literature is reviewed as inspiration for hypotheses on maternal competition for positive offspring outcomes. Nonhuman primates as well as humans are argued to compete for status, breeding opportunities, and allomothers (i.e., caregivers apart from the mother), and these factors have an impact on their reproductive success. Status is passed on from mother to offspring, amplifying the effects of competition for status. Future directions are delineated to fill in gaps in the existing literature.

Key Words: reproductive success, Trivers-Willard hypothesis, birth sex ratio, maternal dominance, female status striving, paternal care, allomothers, alloparents

Obviously the grain of truth in the stereotype remains the universal commitment of female primates to reproduction. But they clearly have an equally powerful and universal commitment to compete, and in particular to quest for high status. Access to resources—the key to successful gestation and lactation—and the ability to protect one's family from members of one's own species are so nearly correlated with status that female status has become very nearly an end in itself.

—*Hrdy, 1999, p. 128*

Mothers matter. Great ape mothers nurse their babies for 4 to 7 years, and chimpanzees keep them in constant contact throughout night and day for a minimum of 3.5 months (van Noordwijk & van Schaik, 2005). Aka hunter-gatherer mothers breastfeed their infants 4.02 times per hour, Ngandu agrarian mothers 2.01 times per hour, and city-dwelling Euro-American mothers breast- or bottle-feed 1.61 times per hour (Hewlett, Lamb, Leyendecker, & Schölmerich, 2000). Hunter-gatherers' lives embody the closest proxy we have to an estimation of the lives of our ancestors throughout our evolution until 10,000 years ago. Hunter-gatherer mothers allow other people (mostly kin) to hold their babies sooner and more often than nonhuman ape mothers but are still in contact with their babies around 70% of the time (Hrdy, 2009). Maternal death severely decreases child survivorship (to a greater extent than paternal death; e.g., Penn & Smith, 2007). Without their mothers, children are much less likely to survive and thrive.

Mothers not only provide nurturance but also compete for better outcomes for their offspring (Low, 2005). In this chapter, we examine how mothers across species compete before the birth of their offspring, around conception, in their offspring's infancy, and throughout their offspring's adult lives. It will begin with an examination of birth sex ratio biasing. Then, the competitive behaviors of female independent breeders (i.e., species in which females raise offspring on their own) and the result of such behaviors on their offspring's reproductive success are examined. Women's similarities to independent breeders are analyzed. After that, the competitive behaviors of female cooperative breeders (i.e., species in which females raise offspring with the help of others) are explored. Subsequently, the literature on women's competition for investing mates, breeding opportunities, and allomothers is reviewed and future directions discussed.

Competition from Conception

Evidence from hundreds of species, including humans, suggests that mothers can and do manipulate birth sex ratios (i.e., the ratio of males to females to whom a mother gives birth) to give their offspring a head start in an environmentally adaptive manner (Thogerson et al., 2013). We review the three main models that have been explored: (1) the Trivers-Willard (1973) hypothesis; (2) the local resource competition hypothesis (Hamilton, 1967); and (3) the local resource enhancement hypothesis (Gowaty & Lennartz, 1985). In this section, we also investigate the maternal dominance hypothesis (Grant, 1996), which is a more recent, but highly relevant, birth sex ratio model. By manipulating their birth sex ratios, mothers are able to compete for the best outcomes for their offspring even before birth.

Fisher (1999) set the stage for sex ratio manipulation theory by showing that natural selection favors a 50:50 ratio of males to females when parents invest equally in an average son or daughter. A 50:50 ratio of daughters to sons is quickly favored in response to random deviations from this rate, as deviations cancel each other out. That is, if there are too many males in a population, females will be more reproductively successful than males and vice versa. However, evidence has been accumulating to suggest that while a relatively balanced ratio will tend to be displayed at the population level over time, at the

individual level, it can be beneficial to bias the sex ratio in one direction or the other depending on specific contextual factors. As an example, Helle, Helama, and Jokela (2008) found that an increase in 1°C annual mean temperature in northern Finland was associated with a 1% increase in the number of boys born that year in a historical sample. Across several years, the birth sex ratio for northern Finland was sometimes male biased and sometimes female biased, depending on the temperature each year, so the proportion of males to females would be approximately 50:50 over many years.

Hamilton (1967) argued that an individual who was able to bias her birth sex ratio in a manner that allowed her offspring to successfully reproduce and outcompete peers would benefit by producing more grandchildren than those who did not bias the sex ratio. For example, female pigs' fallopian tubes are capable of distinguishing between X and Y sperm and respond by encouraging or discouraging the sperm from reaching the egg using local immune responses (Almiñana et al., 2014). If a female pig was in an environment wherein there were few male pigs and plenty of female pigs, she would benefit from giving birth to more male piglets than female piglets. To better understand why, let us say that every male pig can impregnate three female pigs, and every female pig has 80 piglets in her reproductive years. A sow who gives birth to 40 male piglets and 40 female piglets will have 12,800 grand piglets. A sow who gives birth to 80 male piglets and 0 female piglets will have 19,200 grand piglets. Thus, a sow could have 50% more grand piglets by killing off X-chromosome (i.e., female) sperm in her fallopian tubes in this scenario.

Recently, Thogerson and colleagues (2013) demonstrated that the offspring of individuals who bias their own birth sex ratios do indeed have higher reproductive success. The authors examined data from 678 mammalian species, consisting of 38,075 individuals across three generations from the breeding records of the San Diego Zoo in California. Across species, granddams and grandsires who biased their own birth sex ratios toward either males or females produced more grandoffspring than those who did not skew their birth sex ratios, with the strongest skew predicting the highest reproductive success. Sons of granddams who primarily gave birth to males sired 2.7 times as many offspring as sons of granddams who gave birth to an equal number of males and females. Daughters of granddams who primarily gave birth to females had 1.2 times as many offspring as daughters of granddams who gave birth to an equal number of males and females. These findings suggest that being able to adjust one's birth sex ratio in response to ecological cues can result in large fitness gains. The next question, then, is which contexts favor bearing males and which favor bearing females?

The Trivers-Willard Hypothesis

Trivers and Willard (1973) argued that a female's reproductive success is limited by how many offspring she can have, and a male's reproductive success is limited by how many females with whom he can mate. Females in good condition (e.g., heavier, more dominant, less stressed during pregnancy, higher socioeconomic status) should give birth to more males, while those in poor condition should give birth to more females. For example, a female wild horse is more likely to have a male foal when gaining body fat around conception, is more likely to have a female foal when losing body fat around conception, and has an equal chance of having a male or female foal when maintaining the same body fat percentage around conception (Cameron & Linklater, 2007).

The underlying logic is that the offspring's condition reflects the mother's condition around conception, and the offspring's condition affects its reproductive success on reaching adulthood. A female in poor condition will still outperform a male in poor condition (i.e., she is likely to still attract mates and have offspring, while the male will have difficulty doing either), and a male in good condition will outperform a female in good condition (i.e., he will be able to sire offspring by multiple females, while she can only bear as many offspring as is possible for one female of her species).

Trivers and Willard (1973) hypothesized that this bias would vary with environmental conditions rather than being genetically set because females in good condition would always outperform females in poor condition, so sex-biased genes could not accumulate dichotomously in two types of female. This hypothesis can also extend to parental investment beyond birth, but this section focuses on its application to birth sex ratios in humans and nonhuman animals. The Trivers-Willard hypothesis has been tested in hundreds of species across several taxa

in around 1,000 papers, but results remain inconsistent (Cameron, 2004).

MIXED EVIDENCE FOR THE TRIVERS-WILLARD HYPOTHESIS

Many studies have shown support for the idea that females of good condition are more likely to produce sons while those of poor condition are more likely to produce daughters. For example, dominant red-deer mothers are more likely to have sons, and reproductively successful red-deer males are more likely to have high-dominance mothers (Clutton-Brock, Albon, & Guinness, 1984). In nonhuman primates, Meikle, Tilford, and Vessey (1984) found that more dominant rhesus macaque females gave birth to more sons than less dominant females. In humans, a study looking into the birth sex ratios of monogamous and polygynous women in Rwanda found that third or lower-ranking co-wives had more daughters and fewer children overall than first or second wives or monogamously married women (Pollet, Fawcett, Buunk, & Nettle, 2009). The authors found that while monogamously married women had 99 daughters for every 100 sons, third or lower-ranking co-wives had 106 daughters for every 100 sons. Thus, in a polygynous society wherein male reproductive success is more variable than female reproductive success, daughters are overrepresented among low-ranking women, and high-ranking women have approximately equal numbers of sons and daughters. Similarly, a study performed in a rural, food-stressed community in Ethiopia found that women with higher body mass indices (BMIs; weight scaled for height) or more mid–upper arm muscle (which were correlated) were more likely to have sons than those in poorer condition (Gibson & Mace, 2003). Taken together, these studies suggest that good maternal condition might make females more likely to bear sons than daughters while poor maternal condition might make females more likely to bear daughters than sons in species and societies in which male reproductive success is more variable than female reproductive success.

Several reviews and meta-analyses, however, indicated that many studies testing the Trivers-Willard hypothesis have shown null or opposite-than-expected findings. Cameron (2004) reviewed 422 tests of the Trivers-Willard hypothesis among nonhuman mammals and found that only 34% supported the hypothesis. Similarly, Brown and

Silk (2002) examined thirty-five data sets across fifteen nonhuman primate species from twenty-three populations and found no overall difference in the proportion of males produced by high- versus low-ranking females. Furthermore, they found that effect size was negatively correlated with sample size, suggesting that significant findings were due to random variation. Similar inconsistencies have been found in humans. Lazarus (2002) revealed that only twenty-six of fifty-four studies (48%) of status and birth sex ratio among humans have reported results consistent with the Trivers-Willard hypothesis. Although these inconsistencies do not appear to bode well for sex ratio biasing, they may be due to differences in the way maternal condition is measured across studies.

MECHANISMS FOR BIASING SEX RATIOS

Initial tests of the Trivers-Willard hypothesis did not propose a mechanism through which the birth sex ratio bias could occur, but Cameron's (2004) meta-analysis suggested one. She demonstrated that among tests of the Trivers-Willard hypothesis in nonhuman mammals, only those that measured body condition (i.e., measured or estimated body fat percentage) significantly supported the hypothesis (other measures outside body condition included age, dominance, territory quality, time of season, etc.). Furthermore, tests using indicators of maternal body condition conducted around conception were more likely to support the hypothesis (74%) than tests performed during gestation (41%) or at birth (5%). So, it is possible that the Trivers-Willard hypothesis is valid but only manifests itself through specific pathways; that is, the mixed findings are due to the results being clouded by irrelevant measures of maternal condition, such as dominance or age.

Cameron (2004) further suggested that higher glucose levels could lead to a higher rate of male births. Expanding blastocysts (i.e., embryos about 5 days after fertilization) show sexual dimorphism and signal pregnancy to the mother (Larson, Kimura, Kubisch, & Roberts, 2001). Increased glucose levels have been found to prevent expanding blastocysts from forming female structures (Larson et al., 2001). In support of the hypothesis that glucose levels around conception affect sex determination, a recent study found that mouse mothers fed a high-fat diet at conception produced more males than those fed a low-fat diet, despite the fact that the diets were matched in total calories (Rosenfeld,

Grimm, Livingston, Lamberson, & Roberts, 2003). High fat can lead to high glucose levels (Folmer, Soares, Gabriel, & Rocha, 2003), thus supporting the hypothesis that glucose levels at conception mediate the relationship between maternal condition and birth sex ratio. No similar meta-analysis to Cameron's (2004) has been performed in humans, but it is likely that one of the reasons results in humans have been so inconsistent is because of their focus on socioeconomic status rather than key physiological mechanisms, such as body condition indicators around the time of conception.

Local Resource Competition

Competition for access to resources such as mates, territories, food, and shelter typically occurs more fiercely among community members in a local ecology. When one sex in a species tends to disperse or range more widely while the other tends to stay in their natal community or remain closer to their mothers the nontraversing sex competes more intensely with community members; thus, birth sex ratios favor the traversing sex (Hamilton, 1967). This phenomenon is called *local resource competition*. Each additional offspring of the remaining sex stands to decrease the reproductive success of the mother, as well as existing offspring of that sex. This type of birth sex ratio bias was first discovered among the galagos (i.e., a small, nocturnal African primate). Galagos males range freely, while galagos females range in close proximity to their mothers. The benefit of having more males then increases (or, conversely, the cost of having more females increases), as the birth of more females increases competition for the same scarce resources, such as mates and food, which results in a male-biased birth sex ratio (Cronk, 2007).

Silk and Brown (2008) examined 217 samples across 102 species and 45 genera to determine whether local resource competition affected birth sex ratios. They found that birth sex ratios were indeed biased toward males when males dispersed, females when females dispersed, and no bias was present when both sexes dispersed. When the data were restricted to wild populations, these findings still held. It seems that birth sex ratios can be subject to uniform ecological factors, such as the scarcity of local resources, as well as to maternal condition. No studies that the authors are aware of have addressed local resource competition birth sex ratio biases in humans. This is an area ripe for future research.

Local Resource Enhancement

When offspring of one sex are less costly or more beneficial to their parents' or siblings' reproductive success than the other sex, the enhancing sex will experience a favorable birth sex ratio bias; this phenomenon is called *local resource enhancement* (Cronk, 2007). Local resource enhancement often occurs in cooperatively breeding species when male and female helpers differ in their helping effectiveness and this difference remains constant across breeding pairs (Silk & Brown, 2008). In alpine marmots and wild dogs, both of which breed cooperatively, males are better helpers than females and are favored in the birth sex ratios of their respective species (Allainé, 2004; Griffin, Sheldon, & West, 2005). Silk and Brown (2008) investigated ten species of cooperatively breeding primates and found they had a male-biased birth sex ratio, which was higher than the birth sex ratio of a noncooperatively breeding species within the same subfamily.

Cooperatively breeding mammals seem to favor a male-biased birth sex ratio. Despite the fact that humans are cooperative breeders, local resource enhancement has been minimally explored in humans. However, the global human birth sex ratio is slightly male biased (107 males for every 100 females), while the sex ratios in developed countries, where teenaged boys rarely provide extra food for their families, are female biased (Central Intelligence Agency, 2013). These facts suggest that the resource enhancement hypothesis warrants further investigation in humans.

Some studies have looked at whether human parents invest more after birth in the sex that is more helpful. Margulis, Altmann, and Ober (1993) found that daughters were nursed longer than sons in the North American Hutterite community, and this was attributed to Hutterite daughters being less costly to raise due to the help they subsequently provide in the household. Similarly, a study investigating Hungarian Gypsies found that daughters were nursed longer than sons because of the household assistance they provide later in life (Bereczkei & Dunbar, 1997). However, among Hiwi foragers (who do not store food), female infants are killed four times more often than male infants because males provide more food than females (Hill & Hurtado, 2009; Hill, Hurtado, & Walker, 2007). However, girls are often more helpful than boys at a young age in pastoral and agricultural societies and thus receive more nursing, care, and investment as detailed previously (Hames & Draper, 2004). Therefore, the utility of sons versus daughters in humans seems to depend on local ecological and economic factors. Issues such as local resource competition and enhancement have been neglected in the human literature and offer a fertile field for future studies.

Maternal Dominance Hypothesis

The maternal dominance hypothesis was conceived by Grant (1994) when she discovered that women who scored higher on a psychometric dominance test were more likely to give birth to sons. She went on to show that dominant personalities in women are correlated with elevated testosterone levels (Grant & France, 2001; mirroring the same finding for men, Mazur & Booth, 1998), and that high-achieving women have a male-biased birth sex ratio (Grant & Yang, 2003). Thus, dominant women are more likely to have high serum testosterone levels and give birth to boys. Grant (2003) hypothesized that it is specifically testosterone levels during the period around conception to early pregnancy that cause a male-biased birth sex ratio. Recent research in other mammals supports the hypothesis that females with high testosterone levels preferentially give birth to males (Grant, Irwin, Standley, Shelling, & Chamley, 2008; Helle, Laaksonen, Adamsson, Paranko, & Huitu, 2008). Grant (2003) proposed that the ultimate reason for this bias could be that dominant females are better able to raise reproductively successful males while less dominant females are more likely to be able to raise reproductively successful females.

Brown and Silk's (2002) aforementioned meta-analysis seems to contradict this hypothesis, given that their findings suggest that, across primates, there is no effect of maternal rank on birth sex ratio. Grant (2003), however, countered this argument with the assertion that it is behavioral dominance, not rank, that matters because rank can be influenced by factors such as age, while behavioral dominance is postulated to be more closely related to testosterone levels. Support for this assertion is found in Sheldon and West's (2004) meta-analysis of hoofed mammals; they found that maternal behavioral dominance predicted male-biased birth sex ratios around four times more strongly than physiological measures of maternal condition.

Cameron and Dalerum's (2009) findings present another problem: Billionaire women who contributed to their own fortunes are less likely to have boys (~45% sons) than billionaire women who inherited their wealth (56% sons) or women who had children with billionaire men (65% sons). These results contradict both the maternal dominance hypothesis and the Trivers-Willard hypothesis. According to the maternal dominance hypothesis, we should see the opposite pattern because more dominant and high-achieving women (i.e., women who would be expected to create their own fortune) are predicted to have more sons. According to the Trivers-Willard hypothesis, all three of these groups should have male-biased birth sex ratios because all three sets of mothers should be in good condition as they have more money to acquire adequate food and other resources.

Leimar (1996) offered a potential explanation using his mathematical model to suggest that high-quality females might actually benefit from having girls instead of boys because while a high-quality mother can be reasonably certain that her daughter's children will also be of high quality, she cannot be so sure that her son's children will be high quality (particularly if he is mating with several different women). Thus, over several generations, offspring quality is more likely to be maintained by favoring girls rather than boys. In the long run, this can lead to higher reproductive success.

The maternal dominance hypothesis offers an alternative to the Trivers-Willard hypothesis but needs further work to be truly convincing. While there is a fair amount of support for the association between maternal testosterone and male-biased birth sex ratios (see Grant, 2003, for a review), there is less evidence that women with more dominant personalities are more likely to have sons. The dearth of available evidence for dominant women having more sons may indicate a correlation between testosterone and having sons rather than high dominance leading to high testosterone leading to more sons, but only further research can provide definitive answers.

Conclusion

It seems that mothers can, and do, influence birth sex ratios to allow their offspring to be maximally competitive in their environment (Cameron, 2004). Doing so allows parents, particularly females, to gain reproductive success across several generations (Thogerson et al., 2013). It is still somewhat unclear under which circumstances females should favor male versus female offspring, but tests of the Trivers-Willard hypothesis, the local resource competition hypothesis, the local resource enhancement hypothesis, and the maternal dominance hypothesis have given us some clues. A mother in good physical condition around the time of conception tends

to give birth to more males than females, in support of the Trivers-Willard hypothesis (Cameron, 2004). When there are high levels of competition for local resources, nonhuman mammal mothers seem to give birth to the dispersing sex more than the remaining sex; this model should be further explored in humans (Silk & Brown, 2008). When local resources are enhanced by one sex but not the other in nonhuman mammals, which tends to happen in cooperatively breeding species, the enhancing sex is favored in birth rates; this model should also be further explored in humans (Cronk, 2007). Finally, when a mother's testosterone levels around conception are high, she is more likely to give birth to a male than a female, in support of the maternal dominance hypothesis (Grant, 2003). These manipulations that occur before a child is even born are a means for mothers around the world to compete with other mothers to create children who will carry their genes across the generations.

Competitive Motherhood in Independently Breeding Primates and Humans

It may be unclear whether maternal dominance affects birth sex ratios, but in nonhuman primates rank clearly influences a mother's lifetime reproductive success and that of her offspring. While in humans female dominance and intrasexual competition are rarely discussed, in nonhuman primates dominance rank has been shown across many species to be predictive of access to food, social partners, mates, and male protection, all of which contribute to the chances that a mother's offspring will survive and reproduce (Cheney, Silk, & Seyfarth, 2012). By examining the effects of female intrasexual competition and rank in these species of nonhuman primates, it is possible to make predictions about the effects of maternal competition in the lives of women and their children.

This section details the ways independently breeding primate mothers (i.e., primate mothers in species typified by a lack of assistance from fathers or other family in rearing offspring) compete for the benefit of their offspring and the ways that women similarly compete. Humans are not independent breeders (Hrdy, 2009). While there are many single mothers, human mothers typically have at least one allomother (i.e., individual other than the mother who helps the mother raise offspring) helping them with the day-to-day tasks of parenting, whether that be their husbands, their mothers, their older children, or their in-laws (Sear & Mace, 2008). However, unlike other cooperative breeders (i.e., species in which mothers typically rely on the assistance of allomothers), humans live in multifamily communities with distantly related and unrelated individuals. This aspect of human sociality is more similar to independent breeders than cooperative breeders; thus, both must be examined as potential models of human maternal competition. This section reviews the ways that (1) mothers in female philopatric (i.e., females stay in the communities in which they were born, while males relocate around puberty) species compete for their offspring's rank and mating success and protect their infants from infanticide; (2) mothers in male philopatric (i.e., males stay in the communities in which they were born, while females relocate around puberty) species compete for the best territories in order to feed their offspring and compete for offspring rank and mating opportunities; and (3) human mothers pursue status, pass that status to their children, and help their children find the best mates.

Female Philopatric Primate Species

Maternal dominance is particularly important in female philopatric primate species, which include all macaques, savanna baboons, and vervet monkeys. Silk (2009) reviewed the effects of maternal kin biases among these species. She found that strong, stable matrilineal dominance hierarchies develop with mothers often supporting their daughters in agonistic interactions; daughters assume the rank just below their mothers at maturity, and younger daughters are favored over older daughters. High-ranking females of these species mature earlier, grow faster, produce healthier infants, experience shorter interbirth intervals, live longer, and thus achieve higher lifetime reproductive success than lower-ranking females. Since a mother's rank is passed on to her youngest daughter, when a mother competes for status she potentially increases not only her own reproductive success, but also that of her kin in the next generation.

While the clearest benefits are passed from mother to daughter in female philopatric species, maternal rank affects sons as well. Maternal rank at a male infant's conception has been found to predict the son's chronic fecal glucocorticoid concentrations as a subadult better than age and dominance rank in yellow baboons (Onyango, Gesquiere, Wango, Alberts, & Altmann, 2008). The significance of this finding is that chronically elevated glucocorticoids in feces are indicative of consistent stress, which is predictive of compromised reproductive functioning, immune system functioning, and growth. Subadult males are no longer dependent on their mothers, and in some cases their mothers have already died, so the link is not due to continuity of maternal care. These findings suggest that low-ranking females give birth to anxious males, and this anxiety lasts beyond the period of maternal care.

Maternal effects on son's reproductive success have also been found in a group of wild long-tailed macaques. Van Noordwijk and van Schaik (1999) found that male offspring of high-ranking females are more likely to become alpha males after they relocate to a new group. In macaques, the alpha male sires most of the offspring in the group, so a male's lifetime reproductive success is dependent on how long he can remain the alpha. Males who never become the alpha produce few offspring, so the association between mothers' rank and alpha achievement is significant.

Female baboons benefit offspring of both sexes by competing for paternal protection from infanticide during lactation by forming friendships with their mating partners (Palombit, Cheney, & Seyfarth, 2001). Baboon males evolved an adaptation to kill the infants of any females living in a community of which they have just become the alpha male: Infanticide accounts for at least 37% of infant deaths (Palombit, 2000). Killing the infants ends the lack of ovulation that occurs while females are lactating and enables new alpha males to impregnate females in the group sooner (van Schaik & Janson, 2000). These friendships, typified by spending more time in close proximity, increased grooming, and increased infant handling, only occur during lactation (Palombit, 2000). Females who fail to acquire a special male friend experience elevated glucocorticoid levels in response to an immigrant male entering the group (i.e., when infanticide is most likely; Engh et al., 2006), indicating a higher level of stress. High female rank is associated with having a greater number of male friends (Lemasson, Palombit, & Jubin, 2008). Thus, by attaining high rank, baboon females can acquire several male friends who will protect their offspring from infanticide if a new male joins the group. Thus, it seems that both male and female offspring of high-ranking females in female philopatric species benefit reproductively from their mothers' dominance rank.

Male Philopatric Primate Species

Overall, these studies suggest that maternal dominance has a large impact on offspring's reproductive success in female philopatric primates, but what about male philopatric primates? Bonobos, also known as pygmy chimpanzees, are more closely related to humans (sharing 99.4% of our functionally important DNA; Wildman, Uddin, Liu, Grossman, & Goodman, 2003) than any other primate except the common chimpanzee and are male philopatric (like the majority of human societies; Rodseth et al., 1991). The mating success of male bonobos, which are more likely to be in contact with their mothers after reaching maturity than females, is influenced by their mothers' dominance status. Among bonobos, more dominant males have higher mating success (Surbeck, Mundry, & Hohmann, 2011), and having a more dominant mother helps a male achieve a higher rank in the dominance hierarchy (Furuichi, 1997).

Furuichi (1997) found that a mother who is the alpha female will help her son become the alpha male through supporting him in agonistic male–male interactions. This support could include aggressive, dominant behaviors such as a running approach, raising arms, display vocalization, physical attack, or chasing (Furuichi, 1997). The author noted that in chimpanzees a male will usually assume alpha status while in the prime of his life, whereas in bonobos, females assume alpha status in their prime, with their sons achieving alpha status at a younger age. So, in bonobos, male rank seems to have little to do with fighting prowess because if so males would achieve alpha status in their physical prime.

Surbeck and colleagues (2011) found that when a non–alpha male's mother is present, she can help prevent the alpha male from monopolizing estrus females: In a bonobo party with no mothers, the alpha male was able to achieve 40.8% of all matings with the most fertile females, while in parties with all mothers present, the alpha male only achieved 25% of matings with the most fertile females. Thus, even in a male philopatric society, a bonobo mother's assistance, intervention, and rank can help her son be more reproductively successful.

The common chimpanzee is also male philopatric, and while female chimpanzees' dominance hierarchies are less clearly defined, females tend to compete for territories with higher-quality food resources, which have long-term consequences on offspring. Pusey, Williams, and Goodall (1997) used data from a 35-year field study to establish that high-ranking female chimpanzees do have higher infant survival, shorter interbirth intervals, and faster-maturing daughters, leading to higher lifetime reproductive success. They suggested that this advantage in reproductive success was because

of better access to areas with more berries, nuts, and fruits. A subsequent study seems to confirm this hypothesis: High-ranking female chimpanzees have smaller territories that they retain across time, and immigrant females avoid these areas by staying closer to lower-ranking females (Murray, Mane, & Pusey, 2007). This pattern suggests that these feeding areas are of higher quality, and dominant females are able to defend their territories from lower-ranking females.

Further support comes from a study of wild chimpanzees that revealed that mothers with superior feeding areas had elevated ovarian hormone production, shorter interbirth intervals, and higher infant survivorship (Thompson, Kahlenberg, Gilby, & Wrangham, 2007). Over their lifespan, mothers with higher-quality feeding areas have twice as many offspring surviving to reproductive age (Thompson et al., 2007). Furthermore, while as a general rule female chimpanzees migrate at maturity, a female occasionally stays in her natal group when her mother has a particularly good feeding patch, thus securing fitness benefits in the next generation (Hrdy, 2009). Across both male and female philopatric nonhuman primates, it seems that a mother's dominance is associated with positive effects for her own lifetime reproductive success, as well as that of her offspring.

Women Pursuing Rank in Multifamily Communities

The independent breeders discussed previously tend to live in multifamily communities and thus can contribute to our predictions about the causes and consequences of human mothers pursuing rank. Primates living in multifamily communities compete for access to food and higher-quality feeding areas (van Noordwijk & van Schaik, 1999; Pusey et al., 1997); offspring's rank (Furuichi, 1997); and offspring's mating opportunities (Surbeck et al. 2011), all of which lead to higher reproductive success for their offspring. Human mothers are also expected to pursue higher rank for the increased access to resources it brings, to attempt to pass that rank on to their children, and to help their children find the best mate.

Among humans, rank or status can be defined as how influential a person is when it comes to allocating resources, resolving conflicts, and making group decisions (Berger, Rosenholtz, & Zelditch, 1980). Henrich and Gil-White (2001) proposed that dominance is one route to high rank in humans, as in other mammals, but that humans uniquely have another route to high rank: prestige. Prestige, the authors argued, evolved to facilitate rank-dependent social learning, is possessed by those who are highly skilled in a valuable domain, and prestigious individuals are granted an asymmetrical flow of resources and influence in exchange for learning opportunities. Dominance, on the other hand, is achieved by winning aggressive interactions, is based on fear, and is a strategy to obtain deference, respect, and access to resources through coercion and intimidation. Cheng, Tracy, Foulsham, Kingstone, and Henrich (2013) demonstrated that dominance and prestige are independent, similarly effective tactics used by both sexes to influence others' thoughts and behaviors. The use of both dominance and prestige is associated with gaining people's attention and other-perceived assertiveness, but only people who use prestige are well liked (Cheng et al., 2013).

Women favor using prestige over dominance to achieve higher rank (Hays, 2013), which may explain why some researchers (e.g., Buss & Schmitt, 1993) have failed to recognize that women do strive for status, not just resources. Hays (2013) found that women prefer occupations in which they would be "respected and admired within the organization" (p. 1132) more than men, while men preferred jobs that would give them a "powerful position within the organization" (p. 1132) more than women. Johnson, Burk, and Kirkpatrick (2007) found that self-rated dominance was correlated with hostility, physical aggression, anger, and verbal aggression in both men and women, while self-rated prestige was only correlated with verbal aggression in women. Given that women are more likely to use verbal over physical aggression due to the greater reproductive costs involved in physical aggression (Campbell, 2004), this finding further suggests that women use prestige as a route to status.

Unfortunately, researchers have not directly examined the extent to which women strive to achieve high status in foraging societies; however, two studies lend some indirect supportive evidence. Lee (1982) described leadership among the !Kung San hunter-gatherers and indicated that while men are more likely than women to become leaders, there are female leaders as well. The !Kung leaders have no formal authority but are listened to more than others because of their skills as speakers, ritual specialists, or hunters. Being overbearing or arrogant makes someone less likely to be a leader. These descriptions are similar to the prestige route to status, which suggests

that hunter-gatherer societies may have provided a relatively friendly environment for female status seeking.

Further evidence for female status seeking among hunter-gatherers comes from Rucas and colleagues (2006), who investigated the effects of personal attributes on attractiveness among Tsimane forager-horticulturalist women. Women's rankings of other women's wealth, power, speaking ability, and work effort were the strongest positive predictors of their rankings on attractiveness to men. Future researchers should investigate women's status striving in forager societies more directly, but it seems that status may be pursued by women across cultures.

WOMEN'S STATUS IMPROVES CHILD QUALITY

Status can have a real impact on reproductive success. Valentine, Li, Penke, and Perrett (2014) found that women find dominance, one route to status, attractive for short-term relationships in a live-interactive dating context. Von Rueden, Gurven, and Kaplan (2010) demonstrated that both dominant and prestigious men among the Tsimane forager-horticulturalists have higher in-pair fertility and more extramarital affairs, and prestigious men have higher offspring survival. Unfortunately, the effects of women's dominance and prestige were not tested; however, prestigious women might similarly be expected to have more surviving offspring because of their ability to attain resources and caregiving mates.

No researchers have tested this last idea directly in a foraging population; however, Apicella and Dreber (2015) did find an association between women's competitiveness at a female-centric task and reproductive success among Hadza foragers. Participants collected as many red beads as possible in 30 seconds from a bucket of beads of several different colors. This was female-centric because women usually make the beaded accessories that the Hadza often wear. Competitiveness was measured by how participants chose to be compensated: receiving a quarter cup of maize for each red bead retrieved (noncompetitive) or receiving a half cup of maize for each red bead found, but only if they found more red beads than a paired same-sex community member (competitive). Women were just as competitive as men on this task (though were less competitive than men on a gender-neutral and male-centric task), and women who were more competitive on this task (as well as the male-centric task) had more surviving children. This offers some tentative support for the hypothesis that women who pursue higher status have either more children or more healthy children among hunter-gatherers.

Child health and survivorship across cultures is enhanced by mothers' wealth (Low, Simon, & Anderson, 2002). Women in Guatemala with higher incomes have taller and heavier children for their age, and women who make more relative to their husband have heavier children for their age (Engle, 1991). In a representative sample of India, short-for-age children were less likely to be malnourished if they had working mothers (Diiro, Sam, & Kraybill, 2014). Developing countries with a higher proportion of women in politics and the workforce are characterized by more rapidly decreasing child mortality rates than similar countries with fewer women in high-status positions (Kuruvilla et al., 2014). Among mothers in the United States, higher educational levels, income levels, and occupational status are predictive of breastfeeding, which protects against infant illness and infection (Heck, Braveman, Cubbin, Chávez, & Kiely, 2006). In addition, even though infant mortality is low in the United States, it is most common among low-income families (Olson, Diekema, Elliott, & Renier, 2010). Higher maternal status contributes to offspring health across nations.

A population-based study of modern Finnish people has similarly demonstrated that women who have status-pursuing personalities have higher reproductive success (Jokela & Keltikangas-Jarvinen, 2009). Women who endorsed more status-perusing statements about themselves as teenagers (e.g., "My peers always choose me to be a leader in various activities," "I always want to win," "I always take charge of things") have children later than women less interested in status but still have 19% more children by the time they are 39. Women higher in these status-related qualities were more likely to have three children than those low in status-related qualities. This positive relationship between women's status and number of surviving children may depend on the high level of allomaternal care that children receive from their fathers in Finland. This is discussed further in the section on women's similarities to cooperative breeders.

WOMEN PASS THEIR STATUS ON TO THEIR CHILDREN

Research suggests that women can and do pass their status on to their children, particularly in cultures with higher levels of female contribution to subsistence, and thus more control of resources (Low, 2005). In preindustrial societies in which women can pass on wealth, women often transfer some resources to their sons, and their sons are then able to have more children (Low, 2005). When women control more resources, they also train their daughters to be more dominant: Across preindustrial societies, when women have more power, girls are less likely to be instructed in submissiveness and obedience, particularly when women can inherit property (Low, 2005). Similarly, a study conducted with nationally representative samples in twenty-four industrialized countries across the world found that when mothers work during their daughters' childhoods, their daughters are more likely to be employed, to have higher-status jobs, and to earn higher wages when they grow up (McGinn, Castro, & Lingo, 2015). As family sizes have fallen with the demographic transition, women's status has become even more important because, as the costs of raising competitive children increase and everyone has fewer children (one to three instead of eight to ten), women's resource-garnering value can become similarly important to their reproductive value (Low, 2005).

WOMEN HELP THEIR CHILDREN ATTAIN MATES

Women pass resources on to their children in ways that help their children attract mates. Judge and Hrdy (1992) looked into how deceased people with wills divided their incomes and found that parents distributed their wealth equally among children, ignoring sex. Wealth makes men more attractive as mates across societies (Nettle & Pollet, 2008) and can make women more attractive as mates in certain ecological conditions (Valentine, 2015). In some contexts, competition is high, and parents must essentially pay to obtain the best mates for their daughters. Gaulin and Boster (1990) found that dowry is a competitive tactic used in societies that are stratified and monogamous. Because there are wealthy men who provide resources for only one woman, parents of eligible women compete for these men by offering a dowry, with poorer families offering larger dowries than wealthier families. The authors proposed that, in monogamous societies without a dowry system (i.e., like much of the Western world), females may be competing through income generation for paternal investment (both direct and indirect). Sweeney and Cancian's (2004) finding that wealthy men are increasingly selecting wealthier women in the United States lends some support to this hypothesis. Valentine's (2015) finding that high-income women are willing to marry men who make less than them if those men are willing to do 50% or more of the housework and child care also suggests that intergenerational wealth transfers could enable women to select men who are willing to invest directly in child care. Women's competition for men prepared to do child care is discussed further subsequently in the chapter.

Conclusion

This section explained how macaque, baboon, vervet monkey, bonobo, chimpanzee, and human females compete for the good of their young. Among female philopatric primate species, mothers actively help their daughters assume the rank just below their own (Silk, 2009), hormonally help their sons achieve mating success (Onyango et al., 2008), and secure protection from infanticide by establishing male friends during lactation (Palombit et al., 2001). Among male philopatric primate species, mothers try to secure the best territory to provide the most plentiful food for their offspring (Thompson et al., 2007), alpha female mothers help their sons reach alpha status (Furuichi, 1997), and mothers of subalpha males help ensure mating opportunities with females in estrus (Surbeck et al., 2011). Among humans, similar to these independent breeders in multifamily communities, mothers pursue higher rank for the increased access to resources it brings, attempt to pass that rank on to their children, and help their children find the best mate. The next section explores how cooperative breeders, who mostly compete within extended families rather than with individuals from other families, engage in competitive motherhood.

Competitive Motherhood in Cooperatively Breeding Mammals

Cooperatively breeding females have distinct patterns of maternal competition from female independent breeders. Female independent breeders compete for protection by mates from infanticide (Palombit et al., 2001), offspring's rank and mating opportunities (Silk, 2009; Surbeck et al. 2011; van Noordwijk & van Schaik, 1999), and higher-quality feeding areas (Pusey et al., 1997), all of which lead to higher reproductive success for their offspring. However, female–female competition among cooperative breeding mammals is even more intense because cooperative breeding is typified by a single female monopolizing reproduction within each group, with other group members helping her raise her offspring (Clutton-Brock et al., 2006). By engaging in competitive interactions to establish dominance, females in cooperatively breeding species are determining who will be allowed to mate, who will be allowed to rear offspring, who will gain paternal care, and who will gain alloparental care (i.e., care from individuals apart from the parents) in one fell swoop (Rosvall, 2011). This section uses the competitive maternal behaviors of cooperatively breeding mammals as a lens through which to view women's competitive maternal behaviors. We review the ways (1) female wild dogs, (2) callitrichid females (i.e., marmosets and tamarins), and (3) women compete to gain or retain investing mates, breeding opportunities, and alloparents.

Wild Dogs

Creel, Creel, Mills, and Monfort (1997) studied the effects of rank on reproductive success in a population of 153 wild dogs (*Lycaon pictus*) in the Selous Game Reserve, Tanzania, over a period of 5 years. In many ways, hunter-gatherers (i.e., humans who live the way all humans lived during the time in which humans became distinct from hominoid ancestors) are more similar to wild dogs than to chimpanzees, bonobos, and gorillas: Humans and wild dogs have social monogamy, have provisioning and protection by alloparents, travel great distances in search of food, and have large areas in which they live throughout the year (Marlowe, 2005).

Dominance ranks in the Tanzanian sample of wild dogs were determined by who won aggressive interactions most consistently. Alpha males were replaced as often as three times per year, but alpha females retained their positions longer, and when they were replaced, it was usually by immigrant females. Alpha females were more aggressive than subordinate females during the mating period (but not during nonmating periods). It should be noted that, as in humans, males engaged in direct intrasexual aggression (i.e., physical fights with same-sex competitors) more often than females. Alpha females mated over ten times as often as beta females and over thirty times as often as subordinate females. The dogs' hormonal profiles suggested that only more dominant female dogs ovulate. Unlike independent breeders, dominant individuals of both sexes had elevated corticosterone levels.

The probability that alpha females would give birth was 81.5% each year, but 100% for stable packs, while the probability for subordinate individuals was only 6.4%. Of the seven litters that subordinates produced, one was safely raised separately from the dominant's litter, one was killed immediately, and five were raised with the dominants' litters, which leaves the fate of the pups uncertain.

Thus, in wild dogs, climbing the dominance ranks gains a female access to mating opportunities, freedom from infanticide, and allomaternal care in the form of pup feeding, retrieving, and guarding by all group members. Because the rank of relatives often influences the rank of pups in social carnivores, a wild dog mother has much to gain for her offspring by competing to be the alpha (Frank, 1986).

Callitrichids

Similar patterns of competition and offspring success are found in callitrichids (i.e., marmoset and tamarin monkey species). Most callitrichids are monogamous, with one breeding female, but polygynous groups do form when conditions (e.g., more steady food supply) support two breeding females (Digby, Ferrari, & Saltzman, 2006). Callitrichid fathers, similar to human fathers and unlike all non-human great ape fathers, play a substantial role in directly caring for infants (Gray & Anderson, 2010). There is a higher cost of infant care in callitrichids compared to other primate species due to the fact that twinning is typical, a high infant to maternal weight ratio is common (i.e., it would be physically challenging for mothers to carry both infants), and lactation and pregnancy often overlap; this necessitates the cooperative care of young (Digby et al., 2006). Both parents, older siblings, extended family members, and even unrelated individuals engage in babysitting, food sharing, resource and territory defense, infant carrying, and occasional allonursing (Garber, 1997). Because only one female in each group typically benefits from all of this allomaternal care, competition for dominant status is intense.

Common marmosets offer a typical example of callitrichid female–female competition. Dominant females produce two sets of twins each year, while subordinate females typically have no offspring (Saltzman, 2003). It is unknown as of yet whether most subordinate females eventually become dominant or whether they typically fail to reproduce entirely (Saltzman, 2003). Breeding females behave more aggressively towards extragroup (i.e., outside-of-the-group) females than extragroup males, suggesting that they compete to defend their breeding status (Lazaro-Perea, 2001). An experimental study of golden lion tamarins (*Leontopithecus rosalia*) suggests that callatrichids also compete for alloparents: A dominant female is more aggressive toward extragroup females when there are more alloparents in the existing group (French & Inglett, 1989). Among stable groups of common marmosets, vocal threats are much more typical than physical aggression,

but when new groups are being formed, ovulating females will often physically wound each other to establish dominance (Saltzman, 2003; Saltzman, Liedl, Salper, Pick, & Abbott, 2008).

Emergent subordinate females in new peer groups undergo a lowering of luteinizing hormone (LH) within a few days and soon stop ovulating, meaning that they lose the ability to conceive; however, a minority (~25%) continue ovulating, but with shortened luteal phases and thus a reduced chance of conception (Abbott & George, 1991; Abbott, Saltzman, Schultz-Darken, & Tannenbaum, 1998). The likelihood of ovulation is rank related: The second most dominant female is more likely to be ovulating than the third most dominant female (Abbott & George, 1991). As in wild dogs, subordinate female marmosets have *lower* levels of cortisol than dominant females, suggesting that stress is not the factor that causes the cessation of ovulation (Saltzman, 2003). Dominant female marmosets also have much higher mating rates than subordinate females, with subordinate females typically abstaining from mating even when in groups of unrelated adults (Rothe, 1975; Abbott, 1984). Subordinate females do sometimes mate with extragroup males, but this mating does not usually lead to conception, probably because they are unlikely to be ovulating (Digby, 1999; Lazaro-Perea, 2001).

The cause of anovulation and sexual restraint among subordinate common marmosets may be the increased risk of infanticide when subordinate females do manage to conceive (Saltzman et al., 2008). Among many mammalian species, it is males who tend to commit infanticide to halt mothers' investments into offspring sired by other males and to end the temporary infertility that accompanies exclusive breastfeeding in most species (van Schaik & Janson, 2000). Marmoset females do not stop ovulating when breastfeeding, and adult male marmosets have not been observed committing infanticide; they help take care of infants regardless of parentage (Saltzman, 2003).

Cooperatively breeding species, however, are more likely to demonstrate infanticide committed by females as a form of reproductive competition; by killing rival females' offspring, they gain more alloparental investment for their own new infants (Digby, 2000). Infanticide has been implicated in at least twelve captive groups and at least six free-ranging groups and typically occurs when an unfamiliar adult male joins the group and mates with two of the group members instead of the usual one dominant female (reviewed in Saltzman, 2003).

Infanticide can be committed by the dominant female against the subordinate female's offspring or vice versa (Saltzman et al., 2008) but seems to be committed by dominant individuals more frequently (Saltzman, 2003). The timing of this event is usually several weeks into the aggressor's pregnancy: Seventy-five percent of live-born infants were killed if they were born when another female was at least 26 days' pregnant (of a 144-day gestational period; Saltzman et al., 2008). Cooperatively breeding females sometimes viciously compete for alloparental investment and other resources for their infants, taking extreme measures like infanticide of other breeding females' newborns when necessary (Clutton-Brock et al., 2006).

Humans as Cooperative Breeders

Chimpanzees and bonobos are the mammals most genetically similar to humans, but in terms of mating and breeding systems, provisioning, and food sharing, cooperatively breeding callitrichids and wild dogs have more in common with humans and thus might offer a better model for human behavior (Burkart, Hrdy, & van Schaik, 2009; Marlowe, 2005). First, callitrichids and African wild dogs (*Lycaon pictus*) tend to be socially monogamous, like humans, which seems to be a precondition of cooperative breeding (Lukas & Clutton-Brock, 2012). Due to the absence of pair bonds, chimpanzee, bonobo, and macaque mothers raise their offspring independently, with the only assistance from others coming in the form of protection by potential sires against infanticide by unfamiliar males (Palombit et al., 2001). Humans, callitrichids, and wild dogs all share parenting responsibilities among multiple group members, including carrying, food sharing, provisioning, and protection (Burkart et al., 2009; Marlowe, 2005).

Hill and Hurtado (2009) demonstrated that women in modern South American forager groups consumed more food than they produced during their reproductive years and suggested that children would be unable to survive without provisioning by fathers and other adult male helpers. In natural fertility populations, grandmothers, elder sisters, and fathers help keep children alive (Sear & Mace, 2008). While it may not seem like humans have the same degree of reproductive skew as cooperative breeders (i.e., usually only one breeding pair at a time), consider the fact that cooperative breeders usually live in family groups, and the mating systems become more similar (Emlen, 1995). In preindustrial societies, a breeding pair often receives alloparental care from a maternal grandmother who is past the age of reproduction or from prereproductive sisters (Mace & Sear, 2005). Humans live in groups consisting of multiple (breeding) families, unlike many cooperatively breeding species, which tend to contain one extended family. This arrangement is probably because of our uniquely large neocortex, which allows for more complex social arrangements and reciprocal exchanges and does not negate the fact that most alloparental care still comes from kin (Dunbar, 1992; Hrdy, 2006). In short, throughout our evolutionary history, humans tended to live in cooperatively breeding groups (i.e., extended families helping to raise the offspring of one breeding pair) nested within multifamily communities.

Cooperative breeding has facilitated the higher total fertility rate seen in humans as compared to nonhuman great ape mothers (Kramer, 2010). Human mothers cease breastfeeding earlier and have subsequent children sooner than any other great ape, and yet their offspring are much more likely to survive because resources and parental care are coming not only from the mother, but also from allomothers (i.e., caregivers other than the mother; Hrdy, 2006). Among nonhuman primates, species with allomaternal care experience faster postnatal growth and shorter interbirth intervals than species in which the mother is the sole caregiver (Isler & van Schaik, 2012; Mitani & Watts, 1997). Similarly, within humans, interbirth intervals decrease with the presence of allomothers without having to sacrifice child quality (Kramer, 2010; Lahdenperä, Lummaa, Helle, Tremblay, & Russell, 2004).

Given the competitive behaviors seen in nonhuman cooperative breeders for the benefit of their offspring, what behaviors might we expect to see in women? Rosvall (2011) argued that when males vary in quality and willingness to provide direct benefits (e.g., nutrients, territory, parental care) females would be expected to compete over investing fathers for monogamous pair bonds and aggress when secondary females attempt to mate or settle with primary females' mates. This pattern has been demonstrated in common marmosets (Saltzman, 2003) and is predicted to occur in women as well, as discussed further subsequently in this chapter. Furthermore, cooperatively breeding females compete for status because it gives them access to breeding opportunities and alloparents for their offspring; if status confers the same benefits among women, then women would be expected to pursue status, as detailed in the material that follows (Clutton-Brock et al., 2006; Creel et al., 1997;

Digby et al., 2006). So, women are expected to pursue status and resources for the increased access to investing mates, breeding opportunities, and alloparents it brings.

WOMEN COMPETE FOR MEN WITH RESOURCES

One means women have of gaining status and resources is by marrying men with status and resources. Buss and Schmitt (1993) hypothesized that women have recurrently faced the problem of determining which men are willing and able to invest resources in women's children throughout human evolutionary history, and many studies bolstered this hypothesis. Among foragers, good hunters have higher fertility and more surviving offspring with their long-term partners than poor hunters (Gurven & von Rueden, 2006). Wealthy fathers in historical preindustrial societies enabled their children to marry at younger ages, and thus both male and female children could have greater lifetime reproductive success (Low, 2005). Even in industrialized societies, household wealth, to which fathers often contribute substantially, decreases child mortality (Olson et al., 2010), and wealthy sons are more likely to avoid childlessness (Hopcroft, 2006). Men with resources should be valued by women because of the indirect benefits they provide for shared offspring in natural fertility populations: lower child mortality, younger age at first marriage, and higher fertility.

Women seem to find men's ability to provide resources attractive (Valentine, 2016). Marlowe (2004) asked Hadza foragers about their mate preferences and found that women named foraging as the most important trait in a partner. Pillsworth (2008) found that Shuar forager-horticulturalist young women's assessment of young men's provider qualities predicted which men were most romantically desirable. Another study, performed in an industrialized society, found that women preferred men with above-average earning capacity for steady dating and marriage (Kenrick, Groth, Trost, & Sadalla, 1993). These studies are consistent with research indicating that women prioritize social status when considering qualities of long-term mates on surveys (Li, 2007; Li, Bailey, Kenrick, & Linsenmeier, 2002; Li & Kenrick, 2006; Li, Valentine, & Patel, 2011) and in live-interactive contexts (Li et al., 2013). Women, overall, seem to prefer men who are capable of providing resources.

Women compete for men capable of provisioning by enhancing their physical attractiveness. Men across cultures value fertility and therefore find the physical indicators that signal fertility, such as lower waist-to-hip ratios, larger breasts, and more feminine faces, attractive (Li et al., 2013; Lippa, 2007; Marlowe, 2004). As a direct consequence of these evolved mate preferences, women compete intrasexually on the trait that men value: physical attractiveness (Buss, 1988; Walters & Crawford, 1994). Buss (1988) found that the tactics women most commonly use to attract men are related to looks (e.g., wearing cosmetics). Indeed, "she keeps herself well-groomed" was seen as one of the most effective ways to attract men. These kinds of tactics are classified as self-promotion in the literature (Fisher, 2013).

Given that women compete on traits related to physical attractiveness, women who are more physically attractive to men are thus also seen as greater competition to other women (Fink, Klappauf, Brewer, & Shackelford, 2014). Furthermore, women are more likely to derogate intrasexual competitors based on their looks, while men are more likely to derogate intrasexual competitors based on their resources or physical prowess (Buss & Dedden, 1990). Self-promotion is more commonly used than competitor derogation by both men and women when competing for mates (Fisher & Cox, 2011) because derogating competitors makes an individual less desirable as a mate (Fisher, Shaw, Worth, Smith, & Reeve, 2010). Finally, being exposed to attractive women in an experimental prime makes women more likely to report a desire to engage in risky, appearance-enhancing behaviors like tanning and taking diet pills (Hill & Durante, 2011). Women compete for men using attractiveness enhancement methods.

WOMEN MAY COMPETE FOR CAREGIVING MEN

The mate value of men who are capable of providing resources has long been acknowledged (e.g., Symons, 1979), but more recently researchers are recognizing the value of men as caregivers. Humans are the only great ape with fathers who carry, clean, teach, feed, and play with their offspring, suggesting that direct paternal care independently evolved in humans (Valentine, 2015). Children are less likely to survive in foraging societies when they do not have an investing father (e.g., Dwyer & Minnegal, 1993; Hill & Hurtado, 1996). Furthermore, a longitudinal study conducted in a Caribbean village found that father absence or living with a stepfather causes higher cortisol levels (indicating stress), illness, and immunosuppression, as compared to living with one's biological father, suggesting that an absence of paternal care might leave children more vulnerable to disease and stress (Flinn & England, 1997; Kentner, Abizaid, & Bielajew, 2010).

Father care has positive effects in postindustrial societies as well. Sarkadi, Kristiansson, Oberklaid, and Bremberg (2008) reviewed eighteen studies of the effects of father engagement (defined as play, reading, outings, or caregiving activities) and found positive effects in seventeen of the eighteen articles. They found that father engagement was particularly important for children of low socioeconomic status. Some of the positive effects that could have an impact on reproductive success include avoiding homelessness or becoming a welfare recipient when the children grew up, higher IQ scores, higher educational attainment, lower emotional distress, and lower mental illness rates among children with more father engagement. Men's care can help offspring survive and thrive just as their provisioning can and may become more valuable when the local ecology enables women to provide resources themselves.

If paternal care helps women create higher-quality children, then women would find cues to men's interest in paternal care attractive. Several studies have found that women do find cues to men's interest in children appealing. Roney, Hanson, Durante, and Maestripieri (2006) measured men's interest in infants using an implicit choice task and then investigated women's attraction to these men for short- and long-term relationships. They found that women were able to accurately deduce from photographs which men were interested in infants and preferred these men as long-term mates even when controlling for physical attractiveness, kindness, and masculinity (physical attractiveness and kindness also predicted attractiveness for a long-term relationship; masculinity did not). Similarly, researchers asked men explicitly whether they liked children and then had their photographs rated for long- and short-term attractiveness; the results indicated that women prefer the faces of men who like children for both types of relationship (Penton-Voak et al., 2007). Furthermore, women found photographs of the same man more attractive for a long-term relationship and more sexually attractive when the man was playing with a smiling baby rather than ignoring the baby in an experiment (Brase, 2006). Finally, a field experiment staged a confederate meeting with his "sister" and her baby and either interacting with the baby or ignoring him (Gueguen, 2014). Eventually, the sister and her baby left, and the confederate asked a young woman seated nearby for her phone number. The confederate was given the woman's phone number more often, and was rated as more attractive, fatherly, desirable for a long-term relationship, kind, and loving when he interacted with the baby. These studies show that women are attracted to signs of direct child care capability in men, not just signals indicating the ability to provide resources.

Unfortunately, researchers have not looked into preferences for mates who are willing and able to engage in direct child care among preindustrial societies. However, divorce rates across societies may indicate which attributes are valued in a long-term partner. A study performed by Hendrix and Pearson (1995) examined the relationship between female food production, father–infant proximity, and divorce in 186 preindustrial societies. Across cultures, fathers spending more time in direct contact with their children was associated with lower divorce rates. This pattern was particularly strong among societies in which females contributed substantially to food production: When fathers spent little time near their children, the divorce rate was 57%, but when fathers spent a significant amount of time with their children, the divorce rate was 19%. As the author concluded, "Marriage is stabilized if women are heavily involved in productive labor and men are involved in reproductive labor" (Hendrix & Pearson, 1995, p. 226).

The only other type of society with a similarly low divorce rate (17%) was agricultural societies with low female economic and political power, which also limit women's access to divorce (Hendrix & Pearson, 1995). Thus, when women have full access to divorce in preindustrial societies, the best way to stabilize marriages is for women's contribution to subsistence and men's contribution to parenting to approach equality. This finding suggests that women who are capable of provisioning their families might have increased preferences for paternal caregiving characteristics and vice versa.

Men who are particularly capable caregivers might prefer women with more resources. Kenrick et al. (1993) found that men's self-ratings on family orientation were more strongly related to their preference for dominance in a potential long-term mate than women's self-ratings on family orientation. Similarly, Valentine (unpublished data, 2015) found that the more time off men want to take when their children are born, the more willing they are to marry a woman who makes much more than them. This area of research still needs further support, but initial findings suggest that men inclined toward direct care prefer dominant women capable of providing resources.

If this is indeed the case, women may compete for resources in part to attract men who are willing to engage in a substantial amount of direct child care. In support of the idea that women might use resource displays to attract men, newlywed women were as likely to say that they had bragged about their resources to attract their husbands when they were dating as men were to say they displayed resources to attract their wives (Buss, 1988). Similarly, buying a date dinner at a nice restaurant is seen as an equally effective tactic to attract both men and women (Buss, 1988). Among the Hadza foragers of Tanzania, while women value foraging more than men, foraging was still among the top three most important traits to Hadza men (Marlowe, 2004). Furthermore, Pillsworth (2008) found no sex differences in the importance of a potential long-term mate possessing resource-related traits among adult Shuar forager-horticulturalists. Thus, it seems that women might use resource displays to compete for men who are willing to provide child care.

There is evidence that women are trading their resources and status for their partners' caregiving, and that doing so positively affects women's reproductive success. Valentine (2015) found that the more money women made, the more housework and child care they expected potential husbands to do. Furthermore, fathers in Finland are more likely to take parental leave if their wife is in a high-status job (i.e., expert or managerial position; Lammi-Taskula, 2008). Time use surveys across twenty countries between 1965 and 2003 indicated that men's unpaid work increased when national levels of women's employment increased, parental leave was available to men, and women worked longer hours (Hook, 2006). While income, a signal of status (Cheng & Tracy, 2013), generally decreases women's fertility in industrialized societies (e.g., Nettle & Pollet, 2008), this trend can be offset by high levels of allomaternal care. There is a positive relationship between a woman's earnings and her likelihood of having a second child in Finland, Norway, and Sweden, which all have high levels of paternal as well as state-funded child care (Vikat, 2004). Furthermore, moderately long paternal leave-taking is associated with third-birth propensity in Sweden (Duvander & Andersson, 2006). Sear and Coall (2011) suggested that the demographic transition may have occurred because industrial, wage-based economies moved people away from kin. Within those industrialized economies, having paternal care, state-funded child care, and a high maternal income might offset some of the costs of lost kin networks.

WOMEN COMPETE FOR BREEDING OPPORTUNITIES

The closest instances of cooperative breeders to humans from a genetic perspective, callatrichids, live in extended family groups with occasional immigration of extragroup individuals into a breeding position (Digby et al., 2006). Females are generally not very directly aggressive, but dominant females become hostile when a new fertile female enters the group (Saltzman, 2003). Aggression subsides when all other females become anovulatory (Saltzman, 2003). When two females bear offspring around the same time (usually a mother and her daughter), there is intense reproductive competition, and it is not uncommon for infanticide to occur by a mother against her daughter's children or by a daughter against her mother's children (Saltzman et al., 2008). Similar patterns might be expected to occur in human extended families; that is, a woman would be expected to avoid direct aggression under most circumstances, but become directly aggressive when a co-wife joins the family or when mother and daughter reproduce simultaneously.

Based on a callitrichid model, women would be expected to generally be quite peaceful, but aggress when co-wives try to join preexisting unions because they represent a threat to breeding opportunities, resources, and alloparents. Indeed, this is the case. Women are less directly aggressive than men (Daly & Wilson, 1988), but when women do directly aggress, it tends to be against co-wives or other sexual rivals across preindustrial and postindustrial societies (Burbank, 1987; Campbell, 2004). In the preindustrial societies with instances of co-wife interactions, conflict between co-wives was found to be high in 88% of those societies (Jankowiak, Sudakov, & Wilreker, 2005), and it was not unheard of for a woman to physically attack another woman when she tried to join the family as a co-wife (Burbank, 1987). As Jankowiak and colleagues (2005) described, "Among the Iatmul, it is not uncommon for a co-wife to attack a newly arrived wife with knives, shovels, spears, sticks, or anything at hand" (p. 89). Among the Tonga, women even reportedly kill co-wives and their children on occasion (Jankowiak et al., 2005). However, usually physical fights are unarmed and lead to few lasting injuries, and verbal aggression is more common than physical aggression (Burbank, 1987). Aggression between co-wives is reduced when polygyny is sororal (i.e., co-wives are sisters, so their children are also kin) or when one co-wife is postmenopausal (Jankowiak et al., 2005). In industrialized societies, jealousy about a romantic partner is one of the most common reasons for physical aggression between young women (Campbell, 2004). As in marmosets, aggression by females seems to reliably occur when there is reproductive competition.

Women fight to retain the upper hand in polygynous households because doing so benefits their children. In polygynous societies, women from wealthy families are more likely to marry wealthier men at younger ages and as first wives (Gibson & Mace, 2007; Matz, 2012). First wives seem to be able to funnel resources toward themselves and their children: Their own BMI (weight scaled for height) is highest, and their children are less likely to be malnourished and attend school more often (Gibson & Mace, 2007; Matz, 2012). First-ranked wives also have more surviving children (two more on average) than lower-ranked wives, suggesting lower infant mortality (Gibson & Mace, 2007). By becoming the first wife, a woman can produce higher-quality children who will be more competitive in the next generation.

As in marmosets, mothers and daughters, as well as mothers-in-law and daughters-in-law, are in reproductive competition when their reproductive years overlap; this may help explain the evolution of menopause in humans (Mace, 2013). Lahdenperä, Gillespie, Lummaa, and Russell (2012) used a 200-year data set of preindustrial, natural fertility Finns to demonstrate that there were negative consequences of reproductive competition between mothers-in-law and daughters-in-law for children. Mothers-in-law's children were 50% less likely to survive to the age of 15 when born within 4 years of daughters-in-law's children, while daughters-in-law's children were 66% less likely to survive to the age of 15 when born within 4 years of mothers-in-law's children. It is possible that some of this lowered survival was due to infanticide, although it is also conceivable that decreased survival rates were due to competition for necessary resources, such as food. This finding suggests that reproductive competition does occur when female in-laws reproduce around the same time. Mothers' and daughters' offspring were unaffected by reproductive overlap (cf. Mace & Alvergne, 2012).

The authors modeled the inclusive fitness benefits of an older mean age of last reproduction when wives lived with their husbands' families and found that the benefits significantly decreased beginning at age 41 (the actual mean age at last reproduction

in preindustrial Finland) and decreased further with age. These decreases were best explained by a combination of the negative consequences of reproductive competition and the benefits of grandmaternal care (Lahdenperä et al., 2012). Thus, cooperation is the other side of the coin to competition: Grandmothers would not be so helpful if there was not such fierce reproductive competition (Mace, 2013). Mace and Alvergne (2012) suggested that it is the intense reproductive competition between daughters-in-law and mothers-in-law that has led to the cultural evolution of older ages at first marriage for men than women in patrilocal societies, the end result being an absence of reproductive overlap between the two generations. In a sense, grandmothers have been coerced into helping over evolutionary time through persistent competition for resources needed for children to survive and thrive.

WOMEN COMPETE FOR ALLOPARENTS

Alloparenting does not come for free; more productive mothers are more likely to receive alloparenting. Exchanges of maternal work for allomaternal care are observed in hunter-gatherer societies. Ivey (2000) investigated cooperative care among Efe foragers and found that mothers spent more time working when not taking care of an infant, and the number of allomothers taking care of mothers' children predicted around half of the variance in the time mothers spent in child care. Similarly, marmoset mothers reduce the amount of time they carry infants not only when resources are low, but also when resources are sufficient and they have multiple experienced alloparents (Fite et al., 2005). Allomothers have positive effects on child survival in hunter-gatherers: The number of allomothers at age 1 predicts survivorship at age 3 (Ivey, 2000). Thus, among hunter-gatherers, mothers who work more have more allomothers and higher child survivorship.

Women also compete for allomothers in developing and industrialized societies. Snopkowski and Sear (2015) found that grandparents in Indonesia were more likely to provide household help if their daughters worked outside of the home. Similarly, a study of over 1,000 children in the United States found that maternal income had a positive relationship with the likelihood of receiving nonmaternal care (NICHD Early Childhood Research Network, 1997). Similarly, a Dutch study found that grandparental child care was more likely when mothers were employed (Geurts, Van Tilburg, Poortman, & Dykstra, 2015).

Children reap several benefits from this alloparental care (reviewed in Coall & Hertwig, 2010). Children with more grandparental contact mentally develop more quickly (Tinsley & Parke, 1987), have higher language and mathematics test scores (Falbo, 1991), and are less likely to become depressive if their mothers were depressive (Silverstein & Ruiz, 2006). Thus, even in industrialized countries with lower rates of grandparental care and high child survival, women compete for alloparents, and alloparental care positively affects their children in ways that could lead to higher reproductive success.

Conclusion

This section explored the maternal competition that occurs in cooperatively breeding mammals (including humans). It revealed that high-ranking wild dog females mate more often, have more offspring, have higher offspring survivorship, and receive more allomaternal care than low-ranking dogs (Creel et al., 1997). Then, we showed that dominant callitrichid females also mate more often (Rothe, 1975); have more offspring (Saltzman, 2003); have higher offspring survivorship (Saltzman, 2003); guard their investing mates from other females (Lazaro-Perea, 2001); and compete for alloparental care (French & Inglett, 1989). Finally, we demonstrated that women also compete for investing mates (e.g., Buss & Schmitt, 1993; Valentine, 2015); breeding opportunities (e.g., Gibson & Mace, 2007; Lahdenperä et al., 2012); and alloparents (e.g., Geurts et al., 2015; Ivey, 2000). Given the similarities between these other cooperatively breeding mammals and humans, the literature on cooperative breeders has been underutilized for hypothesis generation. The next section gives a summary overview of this entire chapter and proposes some areas for future study to rectify this gap.

General Discussion and Future Directions

This chapter has described the ways human and nonhuman mothers compete to give their offspring the best chance to successfully thrive and mate in the next generation. Birth sex ratio biasing allows mothers to manipulate the sex of their offspring to best suit the current situation. A range of competitive behaviors occur after the birth of offspring. Independently breeding primates compete for food, territory, protection by mates from infanticide, and offspring's rank and mating opportunities. Women similarly compete for mates, resources, status, and mating opportunities for their children. Doing so

positively affects offspring's reproductive success in humans and nonhuman primates. Cooperative breeders compete for the chance to rear offspring, alloparental care, and mates who are willing to invest in children by providing food and care. Women do the same. Examining animal models of competitive motherhood has revealed more diverse ways that women compete than is often recognized in the literature and highlights areas that need further research.

Sex Ratio Biasing

Birth sex ratio biasing was the first way that mothers compete examined in this chapter. An exploration of the Trivers-Willard hypothesis showed that mothers do have more male offspring when the mothers are in good physical condition (i.e., well-fed, higher body fat percentage; Cameron, 2004). Trivers and Willard (1973) suggested that the reason for this sex ratio bias is that mothers' good condition would be more helpful to males than females. The most reproductively successful males across many species can have multiple offspring by multiple females, while the least successful males have no offspring. Meanwhile, the most reproductively successful females are still limited by the number of offspring one female can have in a lifetime, and the least successful females still tend to have *some* offspring. Thus, when a mother is in good condition, it is more beneficial to have a male than a female offspring to maximize the number of grandoffspring she will have. Cameron's (2004) meta-analysis demonstrated that the Trivers-Willard hypothesis only seems to consistently apply in nonhuman animals when maternal body condition is used as the measure of maternal status rather than age, dominance, parity, range quality, or other variables. A similar meta-analysis should be performed in humans to see if the same pattern can be found.

Other, less well-known, forms of sex ratio biasing were also examined. Local resource competition sex ratio biasing, wherein the sex that typically disperses is born at a rate greater than chance, was found to be common in a meta-analysis of 217 samples across 102 species and 45 genera (Silk & Brown, 2008). Local resource competition sex ratio biasing is thought to occur because it leaves more mates, territories, and food for the parents and siblings of the dispersing sex (Cronk, 2007). A study should be conducted to test for local resource competition birth sex ratio biasing in human preindustrial societies. The local resource competition model would be confirmed if societies in which men disperse have more boys and societies in which women disperse have more girls.

Local resource enhancement sex ratio biasing, wherein the sex that is more helpful to their parents' and siblings' reproductive success is more common, was also explored. Cooperatively breeding species seem to have a male-biased sex ratio because males are better helpers than females (Silk & Brown, 2008). The local resource enhancement model should also be tested with respect to birth sex ratio in humans, although it will be somewhat more difficult to test because in each society researchers would have to determine whether prereproductive boys or girls were more useful to their parents' reproductive success. This research could begin looking at individual societies to determine whether the more useful sex experiences a birth sex ratio bias. From existing work, it seems that boys may be more useful in foraging societies for the surplus food they provide (Hill et al., 2007; Hill & Hurtado, 2009), and girls may be more useful in agricultural societies because of the household assistance they give (Bereczkei & Dunbar, 1997).

Finally, the maternal dominance hypothesis was examined. Grant (2003) argued that women's behavioral dominance leads to higher testosterone levels, which leads to having more boys than girls because dominant women may be better able to raise reproductively successful sons, while submissive women may be better able to raise reproductively successful daughters. The link between testosterone and having more males is consistent across species (Grant, 2003). However, the link between maternal dominance and giving birth to more males is more tenuous. Sheldon and West (2004) found that hoofed mammals do display a strong association between maternal behavioral dominance and a male-biased birth sex ratio. Furthermore, Grant (1994) found that women who scored higher on a dominance inventory were more likely to have boys. However, Brown and Silk (2002) showed that there was no link between maternal rank and birth sex ratio among primates. In addition, Cameron and Dalerum (2009) demonstrated that billionaire women who make their own fortunes, who should be high in behavioral dominance, had a slight female-biased sex ratio.

One way to obtain persuasive evidence for the maternal dominance hypothesis would be to assign women who were trying to have children to a behaviorally dominant condition or a control condition, and if the result was higher testosterone levels and

more boys born in the former than the latter condition, the hypothesis would be supported. Another issue is determining what behavioral dominance means in humans; it could be as simple as playing a sport (i.e., engaging in competitive behavior; Bateup, Booth, Shirtcliff, & Granger, 2002) but may require asserting control over valued resources (Henrich & Gil-White, 2001). Further work needs to be done to specify what qualifies as behavioral dominance for women, what the hormonal correlates of behavioral dominance are in women, and whether both cause a male-biased sex ratio.

Maternal Competition Among Independent Breeders and Humans

Independently breeding primate females and women have to compete with unrelated females for the benefit of their offspring. Independent breeders compete for rank; protection by mates from infanticide (Palombit et al., 2001); offspring's rank and mating opportunities (Silk, 2009; Surbeck et al. 2011; van Noordwijk & van Schaik, 1999); and higher-quality feeding areas (Pusey et al., 1997). Competing in these ways yields higher reproductive success for their offspring.

Women display many similar behaviors. More competitive, wealthy, and high-status women have higher-quality children. Among hunter-gatherers, women who compete for food when experimentally given the opportunity have more surviving children (Apicella & Dreber, 2015). Across societies, higher levels of maternal wealth are associated with higher child health and survivorship (Low et al., 2002). Furthermore, in an industrialized society, women with more status-pursuing personalities have 19% more surviving children by age 39 (Jokela & Keltikangas-Jarvinen, 2009). Women compete to positively affect their children's status. In preindustrial societies in which women can accumulate and control wealth, they pass on resources to their sons and train their daughters to be more dominant (Low, 2005). Furthermore, in industrialized societies women's working during their daughters' childhoods is associated with a higher likelihood that their daughters will have high-status, high-income jobs (McGinn et al., 2015). Finally, women compete for mating opportunities for their children. Women pass money on to their children in their wills (Judge & Hrdy, 1992), and through dowries (Gaulin & Boster, 1990), both of which make their children more attractive as mates. Women bear many similarities to independently breeding primate females in the ways they compete; however, female status hierarchies have been more thoroughly explored in nonhuman primates.

Determinants of intrasexual status among hunter-gatherer women should be assessed. A probable indicator of status would be gathering ability acknowledged by same-sex peers; other possibilities include quality of foraging areas or talent for any valued skill because it is possessing useful knowledge that leads to prestige (Henrich & Gil-White, 2001). A similar study to von Rueden and colleagues' (2010), wherein the effect of men's prestige and dominance on their total number of surviving children was examined, should be conducted with women. Women might be predicted to benefit more through prestige than dominance due to the greater threat direct aggression poses to women's reproductive success (Campbell, 2004).

Maternal Competition Among Cooperative Breeders

Cooperatively breeding mammalian females compete with same-sex extended family members to determine who will be allowed to mate, who will be allowed to rear offspring, who will gain paternal care, and who will gain alloparental care (Rosvall, 2011). Among wild dogs, a breed of social carnivore in which alloparents engage in pup feeding, retrieving, and guarding, female dominance matters. Alpha females mate thirty times more often than subordinate females, suppress the ovulation of subordinate females, have an 81.5% probability of giving birth in a given year compared to subordinate females' 6.4%, and sometimes kill what pups subordinate females manage to have (Creel et al., 1997). Successfully achieving alpha status profoundly affects female wild dogs' reproductive success.

Callitrichid females also see enormous gains in offspring quantity and survival when they achieve dominant status. Both parents, older siblings, and extended family members engage in babysitting, food sharing, resource and territory defense, infant carrying, and occasional allonursing, but only for the dominant female's offspring (Garber, 1997). Dominant females typically have four offspring per year, while subordinates typically have none (Saltzman, 2003). Breeding females behave aggressively toward extragroup females to protect their breeding status (Lazaro-Perea, 2001) and to maintain the support of allomothers (French & Inglett, 1989). Ovulation likelihood is related to rank: The most dominant females tend to ovulate, and the second most dominant female is more likely to ovulate than the third in line (Abbott & George, 1991).

Dominant females also mate more often than subordinates: Subordinate females tend to abstain (Abbott, 1984; Rothe, 1975). When a subordinate female does manage to give birth, infanticide is relatively common (Saltzman, 2003). Callitrichid females intensely compete to have the chance to ovulate, mate, breed, and maintain a group of caring allomothers.

Women also compete for investing mates, breeding opportunities, and alloparents. Just as in other cooperatively breeding species, grandmothers', elder sisters', and fathers' presence decreases the chance that children will die (Sear & Mace, 2008). Women compete for men who can provide resources for mutual offspring by enhancing their looks (Buss, 1988) and seek to exchange resources they have earned for child care from a partner (Valentine, 2015). Women are less directly aggressive than men (Daly & Wilson, 1988), but when women do directly aggress, it tends to be against co-wives or other sexual rivals across preindustrial and postindustrial societies (Burbank, 1987; Campbell, 2004). First-ranked wives have two more surviving offspring than lower-ranked wives, suggesting that there are real consequences to a woman's standing within the family hierarchy (Gibson & Mace, 2007).

It is not just co-wives with whom women compete. Just as callitrichid females are in reproductive competition with their mothers, women are in reproductive competition with their mothers-in-law. Reproductive overlap between mothers-in-law and daughters-in-law decreased child survivorship by 50% or more in a historic sample of natural fertility Finnish women (Lahdenperä et al., 2012). Just as subordinate callitrichid females stop ovulating when another female ascends to dominance, menopause in women is partly explained by the reproductive competition between mothers-in-law and daughters-in-law (Lahdenperä et al., 2012). However, the inclusive fitness benefits of grandmaternal care also play a role (Lahdenperä et al., 2012). Women trade work for allomaternal care in industrialized societies (Lammi-Taskula, 2008) and in hunter-gatherer societies (Ivey, 2000). The more allomothers a child has at age 1, the more likely that child is to survive to age 3, so it makes sense that women would compete for them (Ivey, 2000). Women have much in common with cooperative breeders when it comes to competing for mates, breeding opportunities, and allomothers.

More work needs to be done investigating competitive women, caring men, and their preference for each other. Men who are interested in children are attractive to women (Brase, 2006; Gueguen, 2014; Penton-Voak et al., 2007; Roney et al., 2006), and men with high self-rated family orientation are looking for dominant women (Kenrick et al., 1993). Both men and women are willing to trade resources for child care when selecting a long-term mate, such that high-income women and low-income men expect an egalitarian division of paid and unpaid labor, while low-income women and high-income men expect to have a male breadwinner–female homemaker household model (Valentine, 2015). Future studies should examine whether the faces of men who are interested in participating directly in child care are more attractive to high-status women. Reciprocally, it could be predicted that men interested in providing child care would be most interested in the faces of high-status women. Women may be using status to compete for men who are prepared to invest directly through child care and vice versa. Several studies have begun to look into female intrasexual mate competition in the physical attractiveness domain, but none has examined female intrasexual mate competition in the status acquisition domain. This should be rectified.

Humans are now being recognized as cooperative breeders (e.g., Hrdy, 2009), but there are still many unexplored implications of this classification. How extensive is reproductive skew in human families? Studies should test whether onset of mothers' menopause predicts onset of daughters' menses and whether there is less conflict between mother and daughter when there is no overlap of reproductive years. It would also be predicted that sisters closer in age, who would thus be in their reproductive years at the same time, would experience higher levels of competition than sisters more distant in age. In addition, twinning in callitrichids is attributed to allomaternal care (Digby et al., 2006); it could be hypothesized that women with more allomaternal support might be more likely to have twins. There are many avenues of research suggested by using cooperative breeders as models of human behavior that have yet to be explored.

Conclusion

Women, like female nonhuman mammals, are competitive mothers. The animal literature was reviewed and used as a basis for examining human competitive motherhood. Different forms of birth sex ratio biasing were explored as a means of competing to give offspring the best chance of maximal reproductive success before they are even born. The contexts and content of intrasexual competition in independent and cooperative breeders were investigated. Women, like independently breeding primate mothers, compete for access to food for their children, children's status, and mating opportunities for their children. Women, like cooperatively breeding mammalian mothers, compete for investing mates, breeding opportunities, and alloparents. Finally, several lines of research that still need attention were highlighted. Women's competition is beginning to be considered in earnest, but there is still much to be learned.

References

Abbott, D. G. (1984). Behavioral and physiological suppression of fertility in subordinate marmoset monkeys. *American Journal of Primatology, 6*, 169–186.

Abbott, D. H., & George, L. M. (1991). Reproductive consequences of changing social status in female common marmosets. In H. O. Box (Ed.), *Primate responses to environmental change* (pp. 295–309). London: Chapman & Hall.

Abbott, D. H., Saltzman, W., Schultz-Darken, N. J., & Tannenbaum, P. L. (1998). Adaptations to subordinate status in female marmoset monkeys. *Comparative Biochemistry and Physiology Part C, 119*, 261–274.

Allainé, D. (2004). Sex ratio variation in the cooperatively breeding alpine marmot *Marmota marmota. Behavioral Ecology, 15*(6), 997–1002.

Almiñana, C., Caballero, I., Heath, P. R., Maleki-Dizaji, S., Parrilla, I., Cuello, C., ... Martinez, E. A. (2014). The battle of the sexes starts in the oviduct: modulation of oviductal transcriptome by X and Y-bearing spermatozoa. *BMC Genomics, 15*, 1.

Apicella, C. L., & Dreber, A. (2015). Sex differences in competitiveness: Hunter-gatherer women and girls compete less in gender-neutral and male-centric tasks. *Adaptive Human Behavior and Physiology, 1*(3), 247–269.

Bateup, H. S., Booth, A., Shirtcliff, E. A., & Granger, D. A. (2002). Testosterone, cortisol, and women's competition. *Evolution and Human Behavior, 23*(3), 181–192.

Bereczkei, T., & Dunbar, R. I. M. (1997). Female-biased reproductive strategies in a ethnic Hungarian Gypsy population. *Proceedings of the Royal Society B, 264*, 17–22.

Berger, J., Rosenholtz, S. J., & Zelditch, M. (1980). Status organizing processes. *Annual Review of Sociology, 6*, 479–508. doi:10.1146/annurev.so.06.080180.002403

Brase, G. L. (2006). Cues of parental investment as a factor in attractiveness. *Evolution and Human Behavior, 27*(2), 145–157.

Brown, G. R., & Silk, J. B. (2002). Reconsidering the null hypothesis: Is maternal rank associated with birth sex ratios in primate groups? *Proceedings of the National Academy of Sciences of the United States of America, 99*, 11252–11255.

Burbank, V. K. (1987). Female aggression in cross-cultural perspective. *Cross-Cultural Research, 21*(1–4), 70–100.

Burkart, J. M., Hrdy, S. B., & van Shaik, C. P. (2009). Cooperative breeding and human cognitive evolution. *Evolutionary Anthropology, 18*, 175–186.

Buss, D. M. (1988). The evolution of human intrasexual competition: Tactics of mate attraction. *Journal of Personality and Social Psychology, 54*(4), 616.

Buss, D. M., & Dedden, L. A. (1990). Derogation of competitors. *Journal of Social and Personal Relationships, 7,* 395–422.

Buss, D. M., & Schmitt, D. P. (1993). Sexual strategies theory: An evolutionary perspective on human mating. *Psychological Review, 100*(2), 204–232.

Cameron, E. Z. (2004). Facultative adjustment of mammalian sex ratios in support of the Trivers-Willard hypothesis: Evidence for a mechanism. *Proceedings of the Royal Society B, 271,* 1723–1728.

Cameron, E. Z., & Dalerum, F. (2009). A Trivers-Willard effect in contemporary humans: Male-biased sex ratios among billionaires. *PLoS ONE, 4,* e4195.

Cameron, E. Z., & Linklater, W. (2007). Extreme sex ratio variation in relation to change in condition around conception. *Biology Letters, 3,* 395–397.

Campbell, A. (2004). Female competition: Causes, constraints, content, and contexts. *Journal of Sex Research, 41*(1), 16–26.

Central Intelligence Agency. (2013). *The world factbook.* Retrieved from https://www.cia.gov/library/publications/the-world-factbook/fields/2018.html

Cheney, D. L., Silk, J. B., & Seyfarth, R. M. (2012). Evidence for intrasexual selection in wild female baboons. *Animal Behaviour, 21,* 21–27.

Cheng, J. T., & Tracy, J. L. (2013). The impact of wealth on prestige and dominance rank relationships. *Psychological Inquiry, 24,* 102–108.

Cheng, J. T., Tracy, J. L., Foulsham, T., Kingstone, A., & Henrich, J. (2013). Two ways to the top: Evidence that dominance and prestige are distinct yet viable avenues to social rank and influence. *Journal of Personality and Social Psychology, 104*(1), 103–125.

Clutton-Brock, T. H., Albon, S. D., & Guinness, F. E. (1984). Maternal dominance, breeding success and birth sex ratios in red deer. *Nature, 308*(5957), 358–360.

Clutton-Brock, T. H., Hodge, S. J., Spong, G., Russell, A. F., Jordan, N. R., Bennett, N. C., ... Manser, M. B. (2006). Intrasexual competition and sexual selection in cooperative mammals. *Nature, 444*(7122), 1065–1068.

Coall, D. A., & Hertwig, R. (2010). Grandparental investment: Past, present, and future. *Behavioral and Brain Sciences, 33,* 1–59.

Creel, S., Creel, N. M., Mills, M. G., & Monfort, S. L. (1997). Rank and reproduction in cooperatively breeding African wild dogs: Behavioral and endocrine correlates. *Behavioral Ecology, 8*(3), 298–306.

Cronk, L. (2007). Boy or girl: Gender preferences from a Darwinian point of view. *Ethics, Bioscience and Life, 2,* 23–32.

Daly, M., & Wilson, M. (1988). *Homicide.* Piscataway, NJ: Transaction Books.

Digby, L. J. (1999). Sexual behavior and extra group copulations in a wild population of common marmosets (*Callithrix jacchus*). *Folia Primatologica, 70,* 136–145.

Digby, L. J. (2000). Infanticide by female marmosets: Implications for the evolution of social systems. In C. P. van Schaik & C. H. Janson (Eds.), *Infanticide by males and its implications* (pp. 423–446). Cambridge: Cambridge University Press.

Digby, L. J., Ferrari, S. F., & Saltzman, W. (2006). The role of competition in cooperatively breeding species. In C. Campbell, A. Fuentes, K. MacKinnon, S. Bearder, & R. Stumpf (Eds.), *Primates in perspective* (pp. 85–106). New York: Oxford University Press.

Diiro, G. M., Sam, A. G., & Kraybill, D. S. (2014). *Heterogeneous effects of maternal labor market participation on nutritional status of children: Empirical evidence from rural India* (SSRN 2445011). Retrieved from http://papers.ssrn.com/sol3/Papers.cfm?abstract_id=2445011

Dunbar, R. I. (1992). Neocortex size as a constraint on group size in primates. *Journal of Human Evolution, 22*(6), 469–493.

Duvander, A. Z., & Andersson, G. (2006). Gender equality and fertility in Sweden: A study on the impact of the father's uptake of parental leave on continued childbearing. *Marriage & Family Review, 39*(1–2), 121–142.

Dwyer, P. D., & Minnegal, M. (1993). Are Kubo hunters "show-offs"? *Ethology and Sociobiology, 14,* 53–70.

Emlen, S. (1995). An evolutionary theory of the family. *Proceedings of the National Academy of Sciences of the United States of America, 92,* 8092–8099.

Engh, A. L., Beehner, J. C., Bergman, T. J., Whitten, P. L., Hoffmeier, R. R., Seyfarth, R. M., & Cheney, D. L. (2006). Female hierarchy instability, male immigration and infanticide increase glucocorticoid levels in female chacma baboons. *Animal Behaviour, 71*(5), 1227–1237.

Engle, P. L. (1991). Maternal work and childcare strategies in peri-urban Guatemala: Nutritional effects. *Child Development, 62*(5), 954–965.

Falbo, T. (1991). The impact of grandparents on children's outcomes in China. *Marriage and Family Review, 16,* 369–76.

Fink, B., Klappauf, D., Brewer, G., & Shackelford, T. K. (2014). Female physical characteristics and intra-sexual competition in women. *Personality and Individual Differences, 58,* 138–141.

Fisher, M. (2013). Women's intrasexual competition for mates. In M. L. Fisher, J. R. Garcia, & R. S. Chang (Eds.), *Evolution's empress* (pp. 19–42). New York: Oxford University Press.

Fisher, M., & Cox, A. (2011). Four strategies used during intrasexual competition for mates. *Personal Relationships, 18,* 20–38.

Fisher, M. Shaw, S., Worth, K., Smith, L., & Reeve, C. (2010). How we view those who derogate: Perceptions of female competitor derogators. *Journal of Social, Evolutionary, and Cultural Psychology, 4,* 265–276.

Fisher, R. A. (1999). *The genetical theory of natural selection: A complete variorum edition.* New York: Oxford University Press.

Fite, J. E., Patera, K. J., French, J. A., Rukstalis, M., Hopkins, E., & Ross, C. N. (2005). Opportunistic mothers: Female marmosets (*Callithrix kuhlii*) reduce their investment in offspring when they have to, and when they can. *Journal of Human Evolution, 49*(1), 122–142.

Flinn, M. V., & England, B. G. (1997). Social economics of childhood glucocorticoid stress response and health. *American Journal of Physical Anthropology, 102*(1), 33–53.

Folmer, V., Soares, J. C. M., Gabriel, D., & Rocha, J. B. T. (2003). A high-fat diet inhibits delta-aminolevulinate dehydratase and increases lipid peroxidation in mice (*Mus musculus*). *Journal of Nutrition, 133,* 2165–2170.

Frank, S. A. (1986). The genetic value of sons and daughters. *Heredity, 56,* 351–354.

French, J. A., & Inglett, B. J. (1989). Female-female aggression and male indifference in response to unfamiliar intruders in lion tamarins. *Animal Behavior, 37,* 487–497.

Furuichi, T. (1997). Agonistic interactions and matrifocal dominance rank of wild bonobos (*Pan paniscus*) at Wamba. *International Journal of Primatology, 18,* 855–875.

Garber, P. A. (1997). One for all and breeding for one: Cooperation and competition as a tamarin reproductive strategy. *Evolutionary Anthropology, 5*, 187–199.

Gaulin, S. J., & Boster, J. S. (1990). Dowry as female competition. *American Anthropologist, 92*(4), 994–1005.

Geurts, T., Van Tilburg, T., Poortman, A. R., & Dykstra, P. A. (2015). Child care by grandparents: Changes between 1992 and 2006. *Ageing and Society, 35*, 1318–1334.

Gibson, M. A., & Mace, R. (2003). Strong mothers bear more sons in rural Ethiopia. *Proceedings of the Royal Society B, 270*, S108–S109.

Gibson, M. A., & Mace, R. (2007). Polygyny, reproductive success and child health in rural Ethiopia: Why marry a married man? *Journal of Biosocial Science, 39*(02), 287–300.

Gowaty, P. A., & Lennartz, M. R. (1985). Sex ratios of nestling and fledgling red-cockaded woodpeckers (*Picoides borealis*) favor males. *American Naturalist, 347*–353.

Grant, V. G. (1994). Maternal dominance and the conception of sons. *British Journal of Medical Psychology, 67*, 343–351.

Grant, V. J. (1996). Sex determination and the maternal dominance hypothesis. *Human Reproduction, 11*(11), 2371–2375.

Grant, V. J. (2003). The maternal dominance hypothesis: Questioning Trivers and Willard. *Evolutionary Psychology, 1*, 96–107.

Grant, V. J., & France, J. T. (2001). Dominance and testosterone in women. *Biological Psychology, 58*, 41–47.

Grant, V. J., Irwin, R. J., Standley, N. T. Shelling, A. N., & Chamley, L. W. (2008). Sex of bovine embryos may be related to mothers' preovulatory follicular testosterone. *Biology of Reproduction, 78*, 812–818.

Grant, V. J., & Yang, S. (2003). Achieving women and declining sex ratios. *Human Biology, 75*, 917–927.

Gray, P. B., & Anderson, K. G. (2010). *Fatherhood: Evolution and human paternal behavior.* Cambridge, MA: Harvard University Press.

Griffin, A. S., Sheldon, B. C., & West, S. A. (2005). Cooperative breeders adjust offspring sex ratios to produce helpful helpers. *The American Naturalist, 166*(5), 628–632.

Gueguen, N. (2014). Cues of men's parental investment and attractiveness for women: A field experiment. *Journal of Human Behavior in the Social Environment, 24*(3), 296–300.

Gurven, M., & von Rueden, C. (2006). Hunting, social status and biological fitness. *Social Biology, 53*(1–2), 81–99.

Hames, R., & Draper, P. (2004). Women's work, childcare, and helpers-at-the-nest in a hunter-gatherer society. *Human Nature, 15*, 319–341.

Hamilton, W. D. (1967). Extraordinary sex ratios. A sex-ratio theory for sex linkage and inbreeding has new implications in cytogenetics and entomology. *Science, 156*, 477–488.

Hays, N. A. (2013). Fear and loving in social hierarchy: Sex differences in preferences for power versus status. *Journal of Experimental Social Psychology, 49*, 1130–1136.

Heck, K. E., Braveman, P., Cubbin, C., Chávez, G. F., & Kiely, J. L. (2006). Socioeconomic status and breastfeeding initiation among California mothers. *Public Health Reports, 121*(1), 51.

Helle, S., Helama, S., & Jokela, J. (2008). Temperature-related birth sex ratio bias in historical Sami: Warm years bring more sons. *Biology Letters, 4*, 60–62.

Helle, S., Laaksonen, T., Adamsson, A., Paranko, J., & Huitu, O. (2008). Female field voles with high testosterone and glucose levels produce male-biased litters. *Animal Behaviour, 75*(3), 1031–1039.

Hendrix, L., & Pearson, W. (1995). Spousal interdependence, female power and divorce: A cross-cultural examination. *Journal of Comparative Family Studies, 26*(2), 217–232.

Henrich, J., & Gil-White, F. J. (2001). The evolution of prestige: Freely conferred deference as a mechanism for enhancing the benefits of cultural transmission. *Evolution and Human Behavior, 22*, 165–169.

Hewlett, B. S., Lamb, M. E., Leyendecker, B., & Schölmerich, A. (2000). Parental investment strategies among Aka foragers, Ngandu farmers, and Euro-American urban-industrialists. In L. Cronk, N. Chagnon, & W. Irons (Eds.), *Adaptation and human behavior: An anthropological perspective* (pp. 155–178). Hawthorne, NY: Aldine de Gruyter.

Hill, K. R., & Hurtado, A. M. (1996). *Ache life history: The ecology and demography of a foraging people.* Livingston, NJ: Transaction.

Hill, K., & Hurtado, A. M. (2009). Cooperative breeding in South American hunter-gatherers. *Proceedings of the Royal Society B, 276*, 3863–3870.

Hill, K., Hurtado, A. M., & Walker, R. (2007). High adult mortality among Hiwi hunter-gatherers: Implications for human evolution. *Journal of Human Evolution, 52*, 443–454.

Hill, S., & Durante, K. (2011). Courtship, competition, and the pursuit of attractiveness: Mating goals facilitate health-related risk-taking and strategic risk suppression in women. *Personality and Social Psychology Bulletin, 37*, 383–394.

Hook, J. L. (2006). Care in context: Men's unpaid work in 20 countries, 1965–2003. *American Sociological Review, 71*(4), 639–660.

Hopcroft, R. L. (2006). Sex, status, and reproductive success in the contemporary United States. *Evolution and Human Behavior, 27*(2), 104–120.

Hrdy, S. B. (1999). *The woman that never evolved.* Cambridge, MA: Harvard University Press.

Hrdy, S. B. (2006). Evolutionary context of human development: The cooperative breeding model. In C. S. Carter, L. Ahnert, K. E. Grossman, S. B. Hrdy, M. E. Lamb, S. W. Porges, & N. Sachser (Eds.), *Attachment and bonding: A new synthesis* (pp. 9–32). Cambridge, MA: MIT Press.

Hrdy, S. B. (2009). *Mothers and others.* Cambridge, MA: Harvard University Press.

Isler, K., & van Schaik, C. P. (2012). Allomaternal care, life history and brain size evolution in mammals. *Journal of Human Evolution, 63*(1), 52–63.

Ivey, P. K. (2000). Cooperative reproduction in Ituri Forest hunter-gatherers: Who cares for Efe infants? *Current Anthropology, 41*(5), 856–866.

Jankowiak, W., Sudakov, M., & Wilreker, B. C. (2005). Co-wife conflict and co-operation. *Ethnology, 81*–98.

Johnson, R. T., Burk, J. A., & Kirkpatrick, L. A. (2007). Dominance and prestige as differential predictors of aggression and testosterone levels in men. *Evolution and Human Behavior, 28*(5), 345–351.

Jokela, M., & Keltikangas-Jarvinen, L. (2009). Adolescent leadership and adulthood fertility: Revisiting the "central theoretical problem of human sociobiology." *Journal of Personality, 77*(1), 213–229.

Judge, D. S., & Hrdy, S. B. (1992). Allocation of accumulated resources among close kin: Inheritance in Sacramento, California, 1890–1984. *Ethology and Sociobiology, 13*(5), 495–522.

Kenrick, D. T., Groth, G. E., Trost, M. R., & Sadalla, E. K. (1993). Integrating evolutionary and social exchange perspectives on relationships: Effects of gender, self-appraisal, and involvement level on mate selection criteria. *Journal of Personality and Social Psychology, 64*, 951–969.

Kentner, A. C., Abizaid, A., & Bielajew, C. (2010). Modeling dad: Animal models of paternal behavior. *Neuroscience & Biobehavioral Reviews, 34*(3), 438–451.

Kramer, K. L. (2010). Cooperative breeding and its significance to the demographic success of humans. *Annual Review of Anthropology, 39*, 417–436.

Kuruvilla, S., Schweitzer, J., Bishai, D., Chowdhury, S., Caramani, D., Frost, L., . . . Bustreo, F. (2014). Success factors for reducing maternal and child mortality. *Bulletin of the World Health Organization, 92*, 533–544.

Lahdenperä, M., Gillespie, D. O., Lummaa, V., & Russell, A. F. (2012). Severe intergenerational reproductive conflict and the evolution of menopause. *Ecology Letters, 15*(11), 1283–1290.

Lahdenperä, M., Lummaa, V., Helle, S., Tremblay, M., & Russell, A. F. (2004). Fitness benefits of prolonged post-reproductive lifespan in women. *Nature, 428*(6979), 178–181.

Lammi-Taskula, J. (2008). Doing fatherhood: Understanding the gendered use of parental leave in Finland. *Fathering, 6*(2), 133–148.

Larson, M. A., Kimura, K., Kubisch, H. M., & Roberts, R. M. (2001). Sexual dimorphism among bovine embryos in their ability to make the transition to expanded blastocyst and in the expression of the signaling molecule IFN-tau. *Proceedings of the National Academy of Sciences of the United States of America, 98*, 9677–9682.

Lazaro-Perea, C. (2001). Intergroup interactions in wild common marmosets, *Callathrix jacchus*: Territorial defense and assessment of neighbours. *Animal Behavior, 62*, 11–21.

Lazarus, J. (2002). Human sex ratios: Adaptations and mechanism, problems and prospects. In I. Hardy (Ed.), *Sex ratios and concepts and research methods* (pp. 287–311). Cambridge: Cambridge University Press.

Lee, R. B. (1982). Politics, sexual and non-sexual, in an egalitarian society. In E. Leacock & R. Lee (Eds.), *Politics and history in band societies* (pp. 37–59). Cambridge: Cambridge University Press.

Leimar, O. (1996). Life-history analysis of the Trivers and Willard sex-ratio problem. *Behavioral Ecology, 7*, 316–325.

Lemasson, A., Palombit, R. A., & Jubin, R. (2008). Friendships between males and lactating females in a free-ranging group of olive baboons (*Papio hamadryas anubis*): Evidence from playback experiments. *Behavioral Ecology and Sociobiology, 62*, 1027–1035.

Li, N. P. (2007). Mate preference necessities in long- and short-term mating: People prioritize in themselves what their mates prioritize in them. *Acta Psychologica Sinica, 39*, 528–535.

Li, N. P., Bailey, J. M., Kenrick, D. T., & Linsenmeier, J. A. (2002). The necessities and luxuries of mate preferences: Testing the tradeoffs. *Journal of Personality and Social Psychology, 82*(6), 947.

Li, N. P., & Kenrick, D. T. (2006). Sex similarities and differences in preferences for short-term mates: What, whether, and why. *Journal of Personality and Social Psychology, 90*, 468–489.

Li, N. P., Valentine, K. A., & Patel, L. (2011). Mate preferences in the US and Singapore: A cross-cultural test of the mate-preference priority model. *Personality and Individual Differences, 50*(2), 291–294.

Li, N. P., Yong, J. C., Tov, W., Sng, O., Fletcher, G. J. O., Valentine, K. A., . . . Balliet, D. B. (2013). Mate preferences do predict attraction and choices in the early stages of mate selection. *Journal of Personality and Social Psychology, 105*, 757–776.

Lippa, R. A. (2007). The preferred traits of mates in a cross-national study of heterosexual and homosexual men and women: An examination of biological and cultural influences. *Archives of Sexual Behavior, 36*(2), 193–208.

Low, B. S. (2005). Women's lives there, here, then, now: A review of women's ecological and demographic constraints cross-culturally. *Evolution and Human Behavior, 26*, 64–87.

Low, B. S., Simon, C. P., & Anderson, K. G. (2002). An evolutionary ecological perspective on demographic transitions: Modeling multiple currencies. *American Journal of Human Biology, 14*(2), 149–167.

Lukas, D., & Clutton-Brock, T. (2012). Cooperative breeding and monogamy in mammalian societies. *Proceedings of the Royal Society B, 279*, 2151–2156.

Mace, R. (2013). Cooperation and conflict between women in the family. *Evolutionary Anthropology: Issues, News, and Reviews, 22*(5), 251–258.

Mace, R., & Alvergne, A. (2012). Female reproductive competition within families in rural Gambia. *Proceedings of the Royal Society B, 282*(1810). doi: http://10.1098/rspb.2011.2424

Mace, R., & Sear, R. (2005). Are humans cooperative breeders? In E. Voland, A. Chasiotis, & W. Schiefenhovel (Eds.), *Grandmotherhood: The evolutionary significance of the second half of female life* (pp. 143–159). New Brunswick, NJ: Rutgers University Press.

Margulis, S. W., Altmann, J., & Ober, C. (1993). Sex biased lactational duration in a human population and its reproductive costs. *Behavior, Ecology, and Sociobiology, 32*, 41–45.

Marlowe, F. W. (2004). Mate preferences among Hadza hunter-gatherers. *Human Nature, 15*(4), 365–376.

Marlowe, F. W. (2005). Hunter-gatherers and human evolution. *Evolutionary Anthropology, 14*, 54–67.

Matz, J. A. (2012). *Productivity, rank, and returns in polygyny* (IIS Discussion Paper No. 390). Retrieved from http://www.eea-esem.com/files/papers/eea-esem/2012/746/Matz_Polygamy_IISWP_13feb12.pdf

Mazur, A., & Booth, A. (1998). Dominance and testosterone in men. *Behavioural and Brain Sciences, 21*, 353–397.

McGinn, K. L., Castro, M. R., & Lingo, E. L. (2015). *Mums the word! Cross-national effects of women's employment on gender inequalities at work and at home* (Working Paper No. 15-094). Retrieved from Harvard Business School website http://www.hbs.edu/faculty/Publication%20Files/15-094_4daac072-cfe4-4943-b446-92338c7b493f.pdf

Meikle, D. B., Tilford, B. L., & Vessey, S. G. (1984). Dominance rank, secondary sex ratio, and reproduction of offspring in polygynous primates. *American Naturalist, 124*, 173–188.

Mitani, J. C., & Watts, D. P. (1997). The evolution of non-maternal catering among anthropoid primates: Do helpers help? *Behavioral Ecology and Sociobiology, 40*, 213–220.

Murray, C. M., Mane, S. V., & Pusey, A. E. (2007). Dominance rank influences female space use in wild chimpanzees, *Pan troglodytes*: Towards an ideal despotic distribution, *Animal Behaviour, 74*, 1795–1804.

Nettle, D., & Pollet, T. V. (2008). Natural selection on male wealth in humans. *American Naturalist, 172*(5), 658–666.

NICHD Early Childhood Research Network. (1997). Familial factors associated with the characteristics of nonmaternal care for infants. *Journal of Marriage and Family, 59,* 389–408.

Olson, M. E., Diekema, D., Elliott, B. A., & Renier, C. M. (2010). Impact of income and income inequality on infant health outcomes in the United States. *Pediatrics, 126*(6), 1165–1173.

Onyango, P. O., Gesquiere, L. R., Wango, E. O., Alberts, S. C., & Altmann, J. (2008). Persistence of maternal effects in baboons: Mother's dominance rank at son's conception predicts stress hormone in subadult males. *Hormones and Behavior, 54,* 319–324.

Palombit, R. A. (2000). Infanticide and the evolution of male-female bonds in animals. *Infanticide by males and its implications* (pp. 239–268). Cambridge: Cambridge University Press.

Palombit, R. A., Cheney, D. L., & Seyfarth, R. M. (2001). Female-female competition for male "friends" in wild chacma baboons (*Papio cynocephalus ursinus*). *Animal Behaviour, 61,* 1159–1171.

Penn, D. J., & Smith, K. R. (2007). Differential fitness costs of reproduction between the sexes. *Proceedings of the National Academy of Sciences of the United States of America, 104,* 553–558.

Penton-Voak, I. S., Cahill, S., Pound, N., Kempe, V., Schaeffler, S., & Schaeffler, F. (2007). Male facial attractiveness, perceived personality, and child-directed speech. *Evolution and Human Behavior, 28*(4), 253–259.

Pillsworth, E. G. (2008). Mate preferences among the Shuar of Ecuador: Trait rankings and peer evaluations. *Evolution and Human Behavior, 29*(4), 256–267.

Pollet, T. V., Fawcett, T. W., Buunk, A. P., & Nettle, D. (2009). Sex-ratio biasing towards daughters among lower-ranking co-wives in Rwanda. *Biology Letters, 5,* 765–768.

Pusey, A., Williams, J., & Goodall, J. (1997). The influence of dominance rank on the reproductive success of female chimpanzees. *Science, 277*(5327), 828–831.

Rodseth, L., Wrangham, R. W., Harrigan, A. M., Smuts, B., Dare, R., Fox, R., . . . Wolpoff, M. H. (1991). The human community as a primate society. *Current Anthropology, 32,* 221–254.

Roney, J. R., Hanson, K. M., Durante, K. M., Maestripieri, D. (2006). Reading men's faces: Women's mate attractiveness judgments track men's testosterone and interest in infants. *Proceedings of the Royal Society B, 273*(1598). 2169–2175.

Rosenfeld, C. S., Grimm, K. M., Livingston, K. A., Lamberson, W. E., & Roberts, R. M. (2003). Striking variation in the sex ratio of pups born to mice according to whether maternal diet is high in fat or carbohydrate. *Proceedings of the National Academy of Sciences of the United States of America, 100,* 4628–4632.

Rosvall, K. A. (2011). Intrasexual competition in females: Evidence for sexual selection? *Behavioral Ecology, 22*(6), 1131–1140.

Rothe, H. (1975). Some aspects of sexuality and reproduction in groups of captive marmosets (*Callithrix jacchus*). *Zeitschrift für Tierpsychologie, 37,* 255–273.

Rucas, S. L., Gurven, M., Kaplan, H., Winking, J., Gangestad, S., & Crespo, M. (2006). Female intrasexual competition and reputational effects on attractiveness among the Tsimane of Bolivia. *Evolution and Human Behavior, 27,* 40–52.

Saltzman, W. (2003). Reproductive competition among female common marmosets (*Callithrix jacchus*): Proximate and ultimate causes. In C. B. Jones (Ed.), *Sexual selection and reproductive competition in primates: New perspectives and directions* (pp. 3–35). Norman, OK: American Society of Primatologists.

Saltzman, W., Liedl, K. J., Salper, O. J., Pick, R. R., & Abbott, D. H. (2008). Post-conception reproductive competition in cooperatively breeding common marmosets. *Hormones and Behavior, 53*(1), 274–286.

Sarkadi, A., Kristiansson, R., Oberklaid, F., & Bremberg, S. (2008). Fathers' involvement and children's developmental outcomes: A systematic review of longitudinal studies. *Acta Paediatrica, 97*(2), 153–158.

Sear, R., & Coall, D. (2011). How much does family matter? Cooperative breeding and the demographic transition. *Population and Development Review, 37*(s1), 81–112.

Sear, R., & Mace, R. (2008). Who keeps children alive? A review of the effects of kin on child survival. *Evolution and Human Behavior, 29,* 1–18.

Sheldon, B. C., & West, S. A. (2004). Maternal dominance, maternal condition, and offspring sex ratio in ungulate mammals. *American Naturalist, 163,* 40–54.

Silk, J. B. (2009). Nepotistic cooperation in non-human primate groups. *Philosophical Transactions of the Royal Society B, 364,* 3243–3254.

Silk, J. B., & Brown, G. R. (2008). Local resource competition and local resource enhancement shape primate birth sex ratios. *Proceedings of the Royal Society B, 275,* 1761–1765.

Silverstein, M., & Ruiz, S. (2006). Breaking the chain: How grandparents moderate the transmission of maternal depression to their grandchildren. *Family Relations, 55,* 601–612.

Snopkowski, K., & Sear, R. (2015). Grandparental help in Indonesia is directed preferentially towards needier descendants: A potential confounder when exploring grandparental influences on child health. *Social Science and Medicine, 128,* 105–124.

Surbeck, M., Mundry, R., & Hohmann, G. (2011). Mothers matter! Maternal support, dominance status and mating success in male bonobos (*Pan paniscus*). *Proceedings of the Royal Society B.* doi:10.1098/rspb.2010.1572

Sweeney, M. M., & Cancian, M. (2004). The changing importance of white women's economic prospects for assortative mating. *Journal of Marriage and Family, 66,* 1015–1028.

Symons, D. (1979). *The evolution of human sexuality.* New York.

Thogerson, C. M., Brady, C. M., Howard, R. D., Mason, G. J., Pajor, E. A., Vicino, G. A., & Garner, J. P. (2013). Winning the genetic lottery: Biasing birth sex ratio results in more grandchildren. *PLoS ONE, 8,* e67867.

Thompson, M. E., Kahlenberg, S. M., Gilby, I. C., & Wrangham, R. W. (2007). Core area quality is associated with variance in reproductive success among female chimpanzees at Kibale National Park. *Animal Behaviour, 73,* 501–512.

Tinsley, B. J., & Parke, R. D. (1987). Grandparents as interactive and social support agents for families with young infants. *International Journal of Aging and Human Development, 25,* 259–277.

Trivers, R. L., & Willard, D. E. (1973). Natural-selection of parental ability to vary sex-ratio of offspring. *Science, 179,* 90–92.

Valentine, K. A. (2015). *Bioecological exchange theory: Trading resources for childcare in mate selection* (Unpublished doctoral dissertation). Singapore Management University, Singapore.

Valentine, K. A. (2015). The relationship between men's paternal leave preferences and preferences for social status in long-term mates. Unpublished data.

Valentine, K. A. (2016). Social status and economic resources. In T. K. Shackelford & V. A. Weekes-Shackelford (Eds.), *Encyclopedia of evolutionary psychological science*. New York: Springer.

Valentine, K. A., Li, N. P., Penke, L., & Perrett, D. P. (2014). Judging a man by the width of his face: The role of facial ratios and dominance in mate-choice at speed-dating events. *Psychological Science, 25*(806), 806–811.

van Noordwijk, M. A., & van Schaik, C. P. (1999). The effects of dominance rank and group size on female lifetime reproductive success in wild long-tailed macaques, *Macaca fascicularis. Primates, 40*, 105–130.

van Noordwijk, M. A., & van Schaik, C. P. (2005). Development of ecological competence in Sumatran orangutans. *American Journal of Physical Anthropology, 127*(1), 79–94.

van Schaik, C. P., & Janson, C. H. (2000). *Infanticide by males and its implications.* Cambridge: Cambridge University Press.

Vikat, A. (2004). Women's labor force attachment and childbearing in Finland. *Demographic Research, 3*(8), 175–212.

von Rueden, C., Gurven, M., & Kaplan, H. (2010). Why do men seek high social status? Fitness payoffs to dominance and prestige. *Proceedings of the Royal Society B, 278*, 2223–2232.

Walters, S., & Crawford, C. (1994). The importance of mate attraction for intrasexual competition in men and women. *Ethology and Sociobiology, 15*, 5–30.

Wildman, D. E., Uddin, M., Liu, G., Grossman, L. I., & Goodman, M. (2003). Implications of natural selection in shaping 99.4% nonsynonymous DNA identity between humans and chimpanzees: enlarging genus Homo. *Proceedings of the National Academy of Sciences of the United States of America, 100*(12), 7181–7188.

Cooperative and Competitive Mothering: From Bonding to Rivalry in the Service of Childrearing

Rosemarie I. Sokol-Chang, Rebecca L. Burch, *and* Maryanne L. Fisher

Abstract

Mothers face a novel situation compared to other human roles. While there are benefits in cooperating with others for shared resources, there are simultaneously benefits in competing for one's own gains. Moreover, infants pose unique challenges to mothers, requiring extended provisioning and protection. Women cooperate and support each other to benefit the group and in particular their children; however, mothers may benefit from competing for limited resources that directly impact on them and their children and, hence, engage in indirect reproductive competition. The quandary for mothers becomes whether they should cooperate or compete with other mothers, especially when resources related to reproduction and child care are in limited supply. We review literature on cooperative breeding and allomothering, present literature on women's reproductive competition, and explore limitations on investigating cooperation or competition. We then bring cooperation and competition together and address how mothers follow both strategies, concluding with suggestions for future work.

Key Words: mothers, social support, division of labor, cooperation, competition, child care, human evolution

Female Competition Is Context-Specific

As has been the case throughout the history of the human species (or any species for that matter), flexibility is key to survival and reproduction. Successful individuals shift strategies and levels of cooperative and competitive behaviors to ensure they possess adequate resources and assistance. Human females are no exception, and both competition and cooperation can be of great consequence given the female's weighty parental investment. It can be argued that it is precisely because of the intense pressure parental investment puts on females that both cooperation and competition can become so severe.

Procreation requires a much greater biological investment from women than men (Trivers, 1972). Women invest significantly more in offspring; even at the gametic level, women invest more energy and resources in ova than men invest in sperm. The burden of pregnancy, childbirth, breastfeeding, and childrearing falls primarily on women. Men may participate at each of these stages by providing intermittent aid through resources and protection. This paternal care is unusual considering that in approximately 95% of mammalian species, males provide very little direct investment (e.g., provisioning; see Clutton-Brock, 1991). However, men's investment is typically far less than that of women, and women, unlike men, literally have to live with the consequences of reproduction (Gallup & Suarez, 1983).

Women's significant level of parental investment is coupled with (and partially creates) limited reproductive potential. A woman's reproductive capacity is not only limited to the release of approximately one egg per month but also truncated relative to a man's by virtue of menopause. Given that gestation in humans lasts nine months, and that the likelihood of conception following parturition is reduced by lactational anovulation, the reproductive upper limit for women would be equivalent to about one baby per year (with occasional multiple births) over a period of approximately 25 to 30 years (Gallup & Suarez, 1983). This rate would be the maximum reproductive output for a woman, and this number seems absurdly high. Wyon and Gordon (1971) studied rural women in Punjab, India (i.e., a population without family planning), and found that women typically have only six or seven children over their lives. Other studies have shown intrapopulation variation in fertility (differences in maximum output of offspring), but women in these populations typically reproduce well below any biological maximum (Wood, 1994). In short, the actual limit of women's reproduction is low, and hence there is profound pressure for them to birth healthy children and invest in them heavily so that they will survive and successfully bear their own children.

This intense level of investment with a limited reproductive window has led to sweeping changes in the human species over the course of evolutionary history. For example, the level of parental investment in humans is so high, and women are so particularly burdened, that during human evolution women developed concealed ovulation, effectively forcing men to spend more time with them and invest in their offspring (Alexander & Noonan, 1979). This change resulted in shifting the human mating system to monogamy from one that was more polygynous (Sillen-Tullberg, & Moller, 1993). In short, the level of maternal investment in humans is so significant, and the need for assistance is so strong, that women have shifted the human mating system.

Moreover, women's high level of investment in their children leads to both intense competition and intense cooperation. Women compete because the costs of not obtaining a high-quality, investing mate are extremely high. A mate might exhibit a lack of commitment toward his children, abandon his family, or lack key character traits and skills that enable him to provide sufficient resources or proper paternal care. Women must therefore not only compete against each other to find a suitable mate of reasonable quality but also compete to secure the necessary resources that directly impact on themselves and their children (e.g., food, shelter, status). Further, women compete against each other for resources for their offspring. Simultaneously, women engage in intense cooperation, because without the assistance

of other women when males are absent, noncommittal, unable to help, or abusive, women and their children are in serious danger. In fact, maternal investment and the resources needed to invest in a human child are so great that Cant and Johnstone (2008) argue they are the reason for women's truncated reproductive lifespan; older women cannot successfully compete with younger generations for sufficient resources to raise children. Each of these situations has limitations and exceptions, as women may cooperate as a strategy to obtain mates, and mothers may forgo cooperation in favor of competing for limited resources for themselves and their children.

In this chapter, we examine both sides of the mothering coin. We begin with women as cooperators who engage in allomothering, and include in this examination those who are and are not genetically related. We then examine mothers as competitors for limited resources that directly impinge upon their children, including future children and grandchildren (and so on, along the lineage), as well as themselves (i.e., their reproductive fitness or success). Our review highlights limitations to following either strategy exclusively, and indicates the need for cooperation and competition to be examined together. We propose that mothers demonstrate impressive behavioral flexibility, shifting between cooperation and competition, depending on the social and ecological context.

Patterns of Cooperation and Mothering
Defining Key Terms

We pause here to clarify the term "allomother"; we will use "allomothers" in keeping with Hrdy (2009). We favor this term over "alloparent" because mothers provide the majority of care and, hence, "allomother" may be more appropriate than "alloparent" (see Crittenden & Marlowe, 2008). Allomothering is conceptually tightly linked with the idea of cooperative breeding, which is "a breeding system in which group members other than the genetic parents ... help one or both parents care for and provision their offspring" (Hrdy, 2005, p. 10). Hrdy's (2005) conceptualization of cooperative breeding is that, due to issues surrounding paternity certainty, one typically uses mothers as the frame of reference. Consequently, allomothers are individuals of either sex who are not the mother, such that an allomother may be male or even the genetic father of the child (for more information, see Hrdy, 2005, p, 10). Note that the inclusion of the genetic father violates the cooperative breeding definition, but refines the concept to focus exclusively on assistance provided to the mother. It has also been proposed that humans are a combination of communal breeders (i.e., shared care by those who are mothers) and cooperative breeders (e.g., help provided by postreproductive grandmothers). This pattern is thought to be unique among humans, as none of the three African apes (chimpanzees, bonobos, and gorillas) are communal or cooperative (Lukas & Clutton-Brock, 2012). Finally, humans commonly engage in cooperation with unrelated individuals (i.e., nonbiological kin), and such mutualism may be a cornerstone of maintaining cooperative societies (Clutton-Brock, 2012).

It should be mentioned that Hrdy's arguments regarding allomothering have been controversial (e.g., Strassmann, 2011; Wasser & Barash, 1981). In many cases, it is primarily genetically related individuals who provide child care (especially maternal grandmothers and older siblings), which indicates that it may be simply a case of kin selection. Those who are not having children themselves may therefore be maximizing their inclusive fitness by assisting genetic relatives in the raising of their children (Lukas & Clutton-Brock, 2012). We turn to this issue in the subsequent sections.

Who Raises Children?

The greatest threat to reproduction faced by humans is, most likely, infant and child mortality. Volk and Atkinson (2008) compellingly make this argument with their analysis of modern and historic human groups and modern great apes. Once an individual reaches adulthood, mortality rates are relatively low, with average lifespan ranging between 68 and 78 years among hunter-gatherers (Gurven & Kaplan, 2007). Adults are also likely to find a mate, with virtually 100% of female and at least 90% of male hunter-gatherers doing so (see Volk & Atkinson, 2008, for a brief review). The largest fitness challenges humans face, then, are first surviving their childhood and becoming reproductively successful adults, and then themselves raising children to adulthood. Prior to modern history, infant mortality rates ranged from 25% to 40%, and child mortality rates from 36% to 50%. These rates echo modern hunter-gatherer groups (23% and 46% for infant and child mortality, respectively) (Volk & Atkinson, 2008). Indeed, reporting on the difficulty of raising children, Hrdy (2009) notes that in many hunter-gatherer groups a woman might give birth multiple times and never raise a child to adulthood.

To raise a human infant requires immense levels of skilled care during the child's early years, ideally provided by multiple caregivers. Human infants are born helpless, as they are immobile, unable to sustain a grip, and require provisioning for many years longer than other mammals. Indeed, they are unique among the great apes for having not just a period of infancy and juvenile development but also childhood, during which they have immature features including the absence of a full set of adult teeth and molars (Bjorklund & Pellegrini, 2002). Human mothers are unique when contrasted with other primate mothers in that they continue to share food with immature offspring for years after weaning (Hawkes, O'Connell, & Blurton Jones, 1997; see also Flinn & Ward, 2004). For example, Ueno and Matsuzawa (2004) found that while chimpanzee mothers shared food with young offspring, the majority of "sharing" behaviors were offspring trying to take food from the mother, and 78% of the time the mother rejected the attempt. When mothers voluntarily gave food to offspring (only 16% of the time), they chose unpalatable food. Moreover, this sharing was only for a very short span. It has been proposed that food sharing is a transitioning step for chimpanzees, such that it facilitates the transition from suckling to independent foraging behavior (Silk, 1978). These patterns were also found in orangutans (Jaeggi, van Noordwijk, & van Schaik, 2008). Human mothers not only collect food to provision offspring but also adjust their labor tasks so that older children can collect food in conjunction with adults to maximize the food gathered collectively.

Given the helplessness of infants, it is perhaps not surprising (though only recently acknowledged by scholars) that human mothers require the help of others in raising offspring. Hewlett (1991) found that among many foraging societies, for the 20–50% of the time an infant is held, it is by someone other than the mother, and most often a close female relative or trusted babysitter. Human mothers are notable for their willingness to allow others to interact with infants, often immediately after birth. This behavior contrasts sharply with other great apes, whose members will not allow any non-maternal adult contact with infants until three to six months following birth (Hrdy 2009).

There are conflicting thoughts on the importance of paternal investment, but collectively, these studies show that, in contrast to mothers, fathers have less impact on child survival (Sear & Mace, 2008). It should, however, be noted that Gray and Anderson

(2015) reviewed the influence fathers have on their children, and concluded that paternal investment is typically resource-based (e.g., financial), and may impact on children's survival, health, socio-emotional outcomes, social competence, and educational attainment. Thus, while paternal investment does not seem to affect child mortality rates, Sear and Mace (2008) reported about one-third of the studies they examined that looked at paternal death found that father absence increases the likelihood of child death, but only for a limited time. Mace (2013) argues that humans' unique (compared to other great apes) meat-sharing and pair-bonding led to the "man the hunter" model, which proposed that men provided support for women and children (Lovejoy, 1981). However, she observes that while this behavioral pattern is the case for some societies, in other societies men actually increase, rather than decrease, women's workloads. For example, among Aka forgers, energy expenditure outside of child care increases in the presence of fathers, but decreases in the presence of grandmothers (Meehan, Quinlan, & Malcolm, 2012). One reason may be that child care by Aka fathers simply enables mothers to shift to alternative labors, thus still expending energy but on other tasks. In contrast, grandmothers provision mothers and children, and due to their often widowed status, invest considerable time engaging in provisioning and household responsibilities. Thus, the model transitioned to become less focused on men supporting women, and focused instead on female kin assisting each other. This assistance, primarily in terms of food, underpins humans' relatively fast rate of reproduction.

Hawkes and colleagues (1997) propose that the primary provisioning for children is the result of a mother's foraging effort, and when interrupted during nursing, the decline of provisioning is augmented by the maternal grandmother. In their examination of the Hadza hunter-gatherers, seasonal variations in foraging returns among women predicted variation in child weight for non-nursing mothers. For nursing mothers, the foraging returns of the maternal grandmothers had a positive effect on the child's weight gain. However, Marlowe (2000) proposes that fathers make up for a mother's decreased foraging while nursing. The provisioning by fathers appears to be most critical while a mother is nursing, after which time, the food provisioned by a mother overwhelmingly provides for the child. Fathers' influence on older children's survival typically stems from their reputation as hunters, and not the calories they contribute directly to the family.

Thus, a combination of provisioning during the early neonatal months by the father, accompanied by cooperation of women during this period and extending into childhood, is likely to be an accurate model of human childrearing over the course of human evolutionary history.

Evidence for cooperative child care among humans is found in markers of child development. Children show the largest cognitive and emotional gains when they have three secure attachment partners (see Hrdy, 2009, for a review). If we begin with the assumption that humans have been selected for biparental care, then at least one additional person (i.e., the father, in addition to the mother) had consistent interaction with ancestral human infants. The question of who else keeps children alive then becomes more interesting, and Sear and Mace (2008) had to cast their net wide so as to determine which relatives to consider. Their answer, after examining 45 studies of kin-childrearing patterns among people living in nonindustrialized groups, is that after mothers, maternal grandmothers have the largest effect on child survival. Thus, the likely candidates who most heavily influence child survival are the mother, the maternal grandmother, and the father, in that order.

Following mothers and maternal grandmothers, it is females in the group who invest the most directly in child care. Researchers in the US have found that among kin, the majority of caretakers are single, African American grandmothers (Cuddeback, 2004), while in the United Kingdom it is married white grandmothers who make up the majority (Aldgate & McIntosh, 2006; Farmer & Moyers, 2008; Hunt, 2003). Barry and Paxson (1971), using a controlled sample of 186 societies, found that after mothers, the principal companions and caretakers of children were adult female relatives, then female children, then other females. Crittenden and Marlowe (2008) documented that among the Hadza, while female kin are most likely to engage in allomothering behavior such as holding an infant, female nonkin also assist in these ways to a higher degree than do males. In their review, Weisner et al. (1977) repeatedly state that when care is needed, it is a female more than a male, even if more distantly related, that is preferred.

In both past and present societies, women have had to make choices regarding who cares for their children in their absence. In foraging societies, the need for child care is typically solved by female relatives and close friends. Among hunter-gatherer populations, women engage in food sharing of gathered goods, as well as cooperative child care, which allows mothers to collect resources away from a base camp. Older children in Bwa Mawego in Dominica take on adult domestic tasks, and in some households, girls around 12 years of age spend as much time in domestic activities as adult women (Quinlan, Quinlan, & Flinn, 2003). This activity does not only include child care, and overall relieves mothers' domestic burden, which allows them to spend more time caring for their children. Similarly, among the Abuluyia, females were the caretakers of small children more than twice as often as males (Weisner, 1987). The same trend exists among the Kikuyu of Kenya (Leiderman & Leiderman, 1974). Kikuyu child caretakers are usually 7 to 12 years of age, female, and may be siblings, cousins, or neighbors. They may care for the child for more than half the day, and while they may accompany the mother on various tasks, their primary responsibility is to take care of the child. This care occurs even if the mother is still nursing; the caretakers will take the child to the mother when it is hungry. Therefore, based on the existing evidence from these societies, it seems probable that among humans, there has been selection for food sharing, work sharing, and by extension cooperation, particularly among mothers and grandmothers of young children (Hawkes et al., 1997) and other female group members (Kelly, 1995).

Overwhelmingly, child care is prioritized and performed by women, even during childhood and until they are grandmothers. Due to this preference and the prioritization of the care of the child, women are much more reliant on other women even when they are unrelated—and evidence indicates the model is as much reciprocally cooperative as kin-based. This reliance on a cooperative system has a crucial purpose: the care of one's offspring so as to safeguard their investment, and hence, the continuation of their genetic line. This is not only an important relationship, but a labor-intensive one as well. When examined in its entirety, cooperation among women has been a vital factor in the survival of the species.

Women's Life History and Roles in Group Living

There are many intergroup differences in the roles women perform in their daily lives. Among coastal, temperate, and tropical groups where less than 50% of the diet comes from meat, the variety of gathered foods and the tasks women complete show a greater diversity than among groups

where more than 50% of the diet comes from meat (Keeley, 1995; Waguespack, 2005). Focusing on a sample of the roles women perform within groups, we note some routine tasks women perform, of which mothering is likely the most time-consuming (see Table 27.1). Thus, it is not surprising that women rely on help from allomothers, regardless of whether they are genetically related or not.

Writing about the sexual division of labor in prehistoric groups, Waguespack (2005) notes that, contrasted with men's roles, "women are portrayed in a limited array of roles—primarily as plant gatherers, hide scrapers, and breast feeders, all of which are often presented as secondary to the primary male Clovis occupations—the killing of megafauna" (p. 667). Yet, by looking to the roles presented in Table 27.1, a different picture is painted of the diverse roles women perform in modern-day foraging groups.

In groups with a meat-heavy diet, women mainly gather fruits and roots (Keeley, 1995). In groups where meat is less of a staple, women gather fruit and roots, but spend more time gathering nuts and seeds, which then become more of a staple to the group's diet. The processing costs of these staple plant foods is high, so that even when these foods are present in the environment, they are primarily collected only by groups where less than 50% of their diet consists of meat.

Similarly, the variety of roles a woman performs in a group is related to the amount of meat in the group's diet. The greatest sex difference in division of labor occurs in meat-dependent groups (Murdock, 1981; Waguespack, 2005). Examining 8 roles across 32 foraging societies, Murdock (1981) found that for those in which meat played a less primary role for sustenance, women performed increasingly more of the roles—including house construction and butchering animals.

While in most cultures women do not hunt large game, and only infrequently hunt small game, they are still responsible for many aspects related to hunting. For example, women are responsible for mending equipment associated with hunting, clothing that husbands wear when hunting, and preparing food for storage (Kelly, 1995). These responsibilities can be performed simultaneously with raising offspring, whereas there are no appreciable gains from hunting large game with young children in tow.

As shown in Table 27.1, women do hunt small game and fish in some foraging societies. Compared with men, women tend to hunt and fish in low-risk situations that are likely to be successful, and

Table 27.1. Sample Roles Women Perform in Foraging Societies.

Role	Source*
Child care	Hrdy (1999)
Provisioning children	Bird (1999)
Gathering	Bird (1999)
	Kaplan, Hill, Lancaster, & Hurtado (2000)
	Marlowe (2003)
	Waguespack (2005)
Gardening	Bird (1999)
Fishing**	Bird (1999)
	Bird (2007)
Hunting**	Bird (1999)
	Bird & Bird (2008)
	Noss & Hewlett (2001)
Locating and aggregating prey	Waguespack (2005)
Collecting water and fuel	Halperin (1980)
	Kuhn & Stiner (2006)
	Waguespack (2005)
Preparing food (e.g., pounding palm starch)	Bird (1999)
	Hurtado, Hill, Kaplan, & Hurtado (1992)
Constructing housing	Halperin (1980)
Making tools, clothes, and transportation related to hunting	Halperin (1980)
	Waguespack (2005)
Craft work (weaving, pottery, basketry)	Murdock (1981)
Butchering animals	Murdock (1981)
House building	Murdock (1981)
Burden carrying	Murdock (1981)

* The sources provided in this table are not exhaustive, but rather examples where evidence has been documented.

** Women tend to hunt and fish for low-risk, high-payoff animals, including sea creatures close to the shore and small game, as opportunities arise.

to do so opportunistically (Bird, 1999). In these groups, if women are gathering food and find an opportunity to catch a small animal safely, they will do so. In some groups (e.g., the Agta), women will hunt small game together while a second group of women take care of the children collectively (Kelly, 1995). Men, on the other hand, are more likely to hunt large game, which takes them farther from the group, and yields variable returns. When successful, the food is nutrient-dense and plentiful—and shared across the entire group, rather than within the family unit (see Bird, 1999; Marlowe, 2000).

It is clear that women perform multiple roles in the group, with a real sex difference occurring in the amounts that men and women adjust their labor and work schedules for children. Overall, women adjust their schedules to a much greater extent than men. Gathering is work that can be interrupted, whereas hunting cannot; yet, findings indicate the physical labor involved in either activity is roughly equal (Kelly, 1995). The main benefits, then, of gathering resources as opposed to hunting animals are that: (1) typically individuals do not have to travel as far from the base camp to gather, and therefore children can be left behind with other adults or can keep up with a moving group; (2) older children can accompany a gathering group and can learn to gather more easily and earlier compared to hunting activities; and (3) gathering can more easily be interrupted for nursing or otherwise tending to a child (Kelly, 1995). Women behave opportunistically and flexibly in their labor practices, working it into child-care routines rather than separating the two spheres of labor and child care.

On average, among the Hiwi, Ache, and Hadza, women reach a peak of gathering productivity for skill-intense resources between the ages of 20 and 40 years (Kaplan, Hill, Lancaster, & Hurtado, 2000). Among humans, hunting and gathering are both skill-based activities, and group members must practice for years to learn how to acquire and prepare nutrient-dense but hard-to-obtain food sources. Women are clearly fine-tuning these skills during early child bearing age and contributing the largest amount of food while raising children, yet their productivity declines when nursing infants. Thus, nursing mothers who have to spend a large amount of time caring for infants have to forgo effort into roles they normally perform, such as collecting and preparing food, water, and fuel. Women who provide child care allow nursing mothers to continue performing tasks for other children and relatives.

The Inclusion of Unrelated Individuals as Allomothers

In postindustrialized societies, where groups are much larger and women are less likely to be near kin, as compared with hunter-gatherer and preindustrial societies, women still typically prefer caretakers to be relatives (Uttal, 1999), with particular preference for their spouses. However, these individuals are not usually available, which forces women to look to unrelated caregivers for assistance (Riley & Glass, 2002). Thus, women substitute relatives in ecologically appropriate ways, such as engaging in communal child care (e.g., kibbutzim, day care), or by staying home with a child and seeking other forms of support. Some alternatives developed in the twentieth century include cooperative preschools, where parents volunteer time in the classroom, and therefore get to remain near their children while in a social setting; and what are typically referred to as "mom's groups," or social groups in which mothers (and fathers) of infants and young children meet. This latter faction has been catered to by business models that promote social events that parents and children can participate in together, including "mom and me" athletic programs (e.g., gymnastics, swimming), musical programs, and even events hosted at shopping centers.

When mothers in modern societies must leave their children in the care of a nonrelative, they generally leave them with another woman. This preference occurs in several contexts: women in Western cultures hire nannies to care for their children instead of asking for more parenting from their husbands. As Ehrenreich and Hochschild (2004) state, "the presence of immigrant nannies does not enable affluent women to enter the workforce; it enables affluent men to continue avoiding the second shift" (p. 9). Women who travel to other countries to become nannies prefer to leave their own children in the care of female relatives: "Most mothers try to leave their children in the care of grandmothers, aunts, and fathers, in roughly that order" (Ehrenreich & Hochschild, 2004, p. 21). This pattern is repeated when it comes to control of finances that will keep children fed or enable them to be educated. That is, women generally ensure that the finances of the household are managed by other women, with the expectation that the children will receive sufficient care. Kristof and WuDunn (2010) review how child suffering in impoverished cultures is not just caused by low incomes, but instead may be attributed to men's mismanagement of household finances. When men control the finances, ten times as much money is spent on a combination of alcohol, prostitutes, candy, sugary drinks, and expensive food than is spent on the child's education (Kristof & WuDunn, 2010). The link between

household finances and child development is clear: Duflo (2000) showed that even when the caregivers are grandparents, funds in the hands of grandmothers result in greater physical growth (i.e., height and weight) of the grandchildren. Funds in the hands of grandfathers had no effect on the children. As Duflo (2005) states, "when women command greater power, child health and nutrition improves" (p. 15). These differences lead to an increased importance on reliance and support among women (either related or not), particularly in terms of childrearing.

This preference for female caregivers, even those who are unrelated, can find its roots in a basic biological difference between men and women: due to internal fertilization, women possess genetic assurance. Women endure pregnancy and childbirth, but as a result are certain of their maternal status, but men cannot be certain that their children are actually their own. A man who raises an unrelated child is investing in an individual who will add nothing to his inclusive fitness, or the continuation of his genetic line (referred to as cuckoldry). Due to disadvantages of being cuckolded, men are thought to have developed a variety of tactics for paternal assurance that increase the probability that the children they raise are their own. In contrast, maternity is certain, so women have never needed to use such tactics for this purpose. These tactics include mate guarding (Buss, 2002), sexual jealousy (Daly & Wilson, 1982), and various other techniques (e.g., chastity belts, infibulation) used to discourage or preclude female infidelity, sperm competition (e.g., Shackelford, 2003), semen displacement (Gallup, Burch, Zappieri, Parvez, Stockwell, & Davis, 2003) to reduce the likelihood of conception by the rival male, and pregnancy termination (Burch & Gallup, 2004). Finally, if the pregnancy prevails and a child is born, the remaining class of paternal assurance strategies involves differential investment by the resident male, which can include neglect, abandonment, child abuse, or even infanticide. There is growing evidence, for example, that men are sensitive to paternal resemblance and invest preferentially in infants with whom they share facial features (Burch & Gallup 2000; Platek et al., 2003). Overall, men prefer to invest less and engage in inequitable investment among children. Women have never had this selection pressure, and as a result, do not show these preferences. In fact, Platek, Burch, Panyavin, Wasserman, and Gallup (2002) asked men and women to allocate investment and punishment to computer-generated children's faces that either resembled them or not and found that women tried to spread out investment to all children as equitably as possible, regardless of resemblance. Two women reported distress at having to choose between the children shown on the screen (Burch 2016, personal communication).

The issue of unrelated individuals providing child care has remained relatively unexamined in the literature on human evolution. Generally, nonkin participate in cooperative mothering in a wide variety of species at a rate far less than that for kin. Paul and Kuester (1996) observed that assistance with the rearing of offspring has been documented in a wide variety of birds and mammals, and is typically accepted as an example of altruism or mutualistic behavior. Indeed, there are many articles devoted to the topic of social bonding for the purposes of helping with offspring care among nonhuman (and non–great ape) primates, with most of the findings leading to the conclusion that assistance comes primarily from genetically related individuals. For example, Silk et al. (2009) found females who formed strong bonds with their mothers and adult daughters experienced the highest rates of offspring survival.

At the same time, there is research that speaks to the role of unrelated individuals in support of mothering. For example, social interaction via grooming may be performed in exchange for access to a commodity; in baboons, unrelated females will groom mothers of young infants, possibly to gain access to the infants (the functional purpose remains unknown; Frank & Silk, 2009). Likewise, Cameron, Setsaas, and Linklater (2009) reviewed social bonding between unrelated female feral horses. One benefit of selecting horses was that the group structure of one male (or sometimes more than one male) and one or more unrelated females and their offspring meant researchers could explore the social bonds between females without the confounding factor of kin relatedness. They found that social integration between unrelated females increased foal birth rates and survival, independent of habitat quality, dominance status, and age. Moreover, their results strongly showed that these social bonds decreased rates of male harassment, which can lead to reduced female fecundity. Cameron and colleagues (2009) concluded that social integration improved reproductive success among unrelated females.

Thus, returning to the question of why nonkin may engage in allomothering, it could be that it is observed in situations where there is simply a low number of kin in close proximity, such as seen in the preceding feral horse example. Thus, females rely on nonkin for support because there are no genetic relatives to offer help. It could also be a by-product, though. In their examination of nonhuman primates, Paul and Kuester (1996) suggest infant handling is rarely performed for the manipulation of alliance formation. Instead, it is a nonadaptive by-product of mother–offspring bonding due to kin selection. While nonkin do appear to allomother at least in nonhuman species, there is definitely more room to research *why* they perform this behavior.

Help from Unrelated Women Who Are Friends

Bonds between unrelated individuals in service of childrearing are similar to those between kin, in that these ties promote trust and cooperation, which are two essential characteristics of cooperative care. Women are noted, more so than men, for their tendency to initiate friendships and form close, stable bonds with same-sex relatives and nonkin. In response to stress, rather than exhibiting a strong fight-or-flight autonomic response, women are more likely to display a tend-and-befriend response where they seek interaction and social support (Taylor et al., 2000). Women report loving their same-sex best friend equally as their spouse, and liking their best friend better than their spouse; contrariwise, men report loving and liking their spouse more than their kin or same-sex best friend (Sternberg & Grajek, 1984). Women also display more sexual fluidity, in that they can be sexually aroused by men and women at alternate times, regardless of their sexual orientation; men do not report such fluidity (see Diamond 2009). One evolutionary explanation for this sex difference is that such fluidity cements bonds in the service of allomothering (Kuhle & Radtke, 2013).

Female alliances also form a deep foundation for tending to offspring. Women in most cultures have assistance from other women when giving birth (Rosenberg & Trevathan, 2002). Human morphology causes childbirth to be much more laborious than for other primates. For example, the pelvis is difficult to navigate and is more likely to impose potential problems during childbirth. Once a child is born, breastfeeding—an automatic act in most mammals—is a process that requires ample learning and social support in humans (Volk, 2009). Thus, often immediately before an infant's life begins, a mother's work requires the assistance of other women, and this assistance is sometimes replaced or complemented by male or female professionals in postindustrialized cultures. Indeed, the vast majority of infanticides are committed by young mothers with no social support (Oberman, 2003). These women are not only without partners; they are without the supportive net of relatives and allomothers for their infants.

Following childbirth, once women return to nonparenting roles, the role of other women in their social network becomes clear. Among the Efe, allomothers will on occasion nurse another woman's child if the mother is not available; and when held, infants are held by women in the group upward of 60% of the time (Hewlett, 1989). Ache women cooperate while foraging, such as by holding another woman's child and forging trails to collectible plant foods (Hill, 2002). Likewise, as mentioned, in foraging societies, when a woman's gathering production decreases after the birth of a new child, the slack is most often picked up by friends and female relatives (such as among the Ache; Hill & Hurtado, 1996). This occurs either directly, with the other women supplementing her food production with food they have gathered, or indirectly by their watching her children so she can gather food. Friends would have been critical in women's evolutionary past, due to rates of female exogamy, because women would move into a new group of unrelated individuals once married (e.g., for rates among the Bari, see Lizarralde & Lizarralde, 1991). These alliances may be built upon reciprocal altruism, with a significant exchange of goods, time, and energy, all of which would improve the survival of both mother and child.

Friends are of such importance to women that they may even influence reproductive decisions (see Fisher & Moule, 2013, for a review). They also provide opportunities for new mothers to experience vicarious learning about parenting behavior, which may benefit the mother and her children. Further, friends who already have children provide indirect information about possible social and familial arrangements, such as mating relationships after childbirth or reconciling work and caring responsibilities (Keim, Klärner, & Bernardi, 2009). However, what seems to be overlooked is that these "teacher" friends may also benefit, in that they (presumably unintentionally) have created a context in which their own children may be provided with equivalent care to what they would receive at home, if allomothering were to occur.

The Crucial Role of Female Support and Cooperation

The simplest way to show the importance of female support networks is to examine the damage to the family unit and society when they are lacking. Female support networks are so important that the phrase is interchangeable with "survival networks" in some areas of research (Dominguez & Watkins, 2003; Hognas, 2010). In many cases, this term is coined in low-income groups, but the factors that define these groups could easily apply to normative groups in developing countries; members exchange support through nonbinding agreements and a "sense of fairness" (Hognas, 2010, p. 331). In particular, any extra resources are expected to be shared. This is readily seen in hunter-forager societies, and the importance of female social networks is noted in the anthropological literature (Guyer, 1981).

In these networks, close-knit groups of friends and families exchange support in various ways. Not surprisingly, child care is the primary favor that is exchanged; almost half of the favors are categorized as child care (Hognas, 2010). If this is the case, what is the influence of female social networks on child survival? Adams, Madhavan, and Simon (2002) found that among the Fulbe, social networks correlated with greater infant survival. This correlation may not be due simply to greater support but also to earlier diagnosis and treatment of infant illness. There have been several studies from various cultures that show that societal systems (mostly patriarchal) that are marked by a lack of female support show greater child mortality (Das Gupta, 1995; Dyson & Moore, 1983). One patriarchal structure (Griffiths, Hinde, & Matthews, 2001) showed the opposite effect, but this was because the mother-in-law took special care of her daughter-in-law, particularly in childbirth, in this society. Collins, Dunkel-Schetter, Lobel, and Scrimshaw (1993) found that women who received more support had better labor progress and babies with higher Apgar scores (a measure of neonatal health), and experienced less postpartum depression. Women with larger networks had babies of higher birth weight. Although there are many studies showing confounding factors, for example, larger social groups resulting in easier disease transmission (Aaby, Bukh, Lisse, & Smits, 1983), one theme is abundantly clear: women who are without support networks face higher probabilities of losing their children.

Social support is vital to both survival *in* the human species (longevity) and survival *of* the human species (survival of offspring), and therefore social support has been particularly important to the evolution of human females and would peak during childbearing years. It is difficult to find cases in which women of young children do not have support from other women. Moreover, the evidence clearly suggests that humans have a long tradition of allomothering. One such line of evidence is "motherese" (see Sokol Chang, 2013 for a review). Most primate mothers do not vocalize to their infants, as they remain in constant contact with them. Squirrel monkeys are one exception, where females have a unique, infant-directed call that is used by mothers to infants who are being held by allomothers (Biben, 1992). The allomothers occasionally make the calls to young infants as well. Humans as well have a pervasive infant-directed form of speech, colloquially referred to as "motherese," that is found among virtually every human group (see Falk, 2009 for a review). That this form of speech is used with infants and young children, and they are receptive to this speech by mothers and others, indicates that there has been selection pressure for allomothers in human evolution (Chang & Thompson, 2010).

Women as Competitive Mothers

As reviewed in the first part of this chapter, some researchers (e.g., Hrdy, 1999) suggest that women extensively rely on others, including unrelated individuals, for a variety of resources to assist with childrearing. This view is one of the social group, in that many of the behaviors that women engage in to support each other seem, at face value, to benefit the overall group. However, we must remember that women did not evolve for the betterment of society or the well-being of the group; indeed, mothers did not evolve to benefit the species but rather to translate reproductive effort into progeny who would survive and later reproduce. The focus is not the benefits that the group receives but instead the differential reproductive success of individuals, even at the cost of others in the group (Hrdy, 1999). That is, using the tenets of evolutionary theory, behaviors that enable an individual's genes to be passed throughout future generations are those which should be manifested, and such motivations for behavior do not need to be conscious. In other words, while others in the social group may benefit from a behavior, mothers should be simply concerned with their own genetic offspring, ensuring that those children survive and then themselves reproduce. Thus, the key to understanding mothering is not to examine the benefits that the group receives but instead the differential reproductive

success of individuals, even at the cost of others in the group. Herein lies the interesting dichotomy in women's relationships with other women, as they must decide between providing cooperative support or being competitors to maximize their own reproductive success.

There are many factors that indicate competition between women is particularly intense, compared with other species. Apicella and Dreber (2015) report that females of many species are more likely to compete when there are high levels of maternal investment (including at the biological level, such as during pregnancy and lactation, for access to limited food resources, as well as status and dominance rank; for a review see Stockley & Bro-Jørgensen, 2011); where there are large aggregates of individuals living together, which increases competition for proximal resources; and where paternal investment is needed. All three of these factors apply to humans. First, women invest substantially in their children, in terms of energetic demands of pregnancy and lactation, but also provide infant care. Humans are highly social and, thus, there are plentiful opportunities to be in the same group as other women who are having children. Moreover, men, compared with males of other species, tend to provide high levels of paternal care for children (Clutton-Brock, 1991).

Female Intrasexual Competition

The premise of competition is that there is a limited resource that individuals use strategy or strength to acquire. Thus, competition must be seen as rivalry; two or more individuals are in pursuit of a resource that is perceived to be insufficient in quantity. The individuals do not have to be conscious of the rivalry, or even aware of their competitors, but they must be partaking in an activity that draws them closer to attaining the desired, limited resource (Hrdy, 1999).

As has been reviewed elsewhere (e.g., Fisher, 2013b), female intrasexual competition as a topic of study has been gaining momentum. However, until recently, it remained a relatively understudied area, as compared with male intrasexual competition. This oversight may be attributed to the fact that it is subtle (Hrdy, 1999); that it rarely involves escalating contests or exaggerated secondary sexual characteristics (Clutton-Brock & Huchard, 2013); and that, in humans, women suppress it when men are present in order to avoid seeming undesirable (Cashdan, 1999).

Another potential reason, as reviewed by Apicella and Dreber (2015), is that theoretically, competition among members of the same sex has historically focused on competition for mates. Mating competition is immediately visible among males of most species. That is, when females compete, their competition tends to be of a subtler, covert form without the visible weapons (e.g., antlers) employed by males (Hrdy, 1999). However, female competition is apparent in mammals (for a review see Stockley & Bro-Jørgensen, 2011), including humans (Stockley & Campbell, 2013). Moreover, while the evidence suggests that females compete for access to mates (see Fisher & Moule, 2013 for a review), they also compete for resources that may influence their reproductive fitness outcomes, such as food, nest-sites, protection, territories, and by interfering with the reproduction of other females (Stockley & Bro-Jørgensen, 2011).

Primates, in general, are highly social (Hrdy, 2009). Social species often exhibit competition by group members for the same resources, including food, mates, and social status, which implies the ability to breed. As Clutton-Brock and Huchard (2013) review, within groups, females compete to gain the opportunity to breed; to raise offspring and assist them in gaining necessary resources, as well as social status, so that they can breed; and to protect offspring from harm or eviction. Further, for many species, as group size increases, female fecundity often decreases, and female and infant mortality increases (see Clutton-Brock & Huchard, 2013 for a review). Group composition and mating patterns also matter; female-biased sex ratios, high levels of reproductive synchrony, or females mating with multiple males (who in turn might have sperm depletion) also influence the degree of intrasexual competition (Clutton-Brock & Huchard, 2013).

Competition Outside of a Mating Context

It is undeniable that women compete for mates. Cross-culturally, women compete with other women for high-quality mates who possess phenotypic characteristics that indicate high genetic quality, an interest in (and ability to provide) paternal care (Gray & Anderson, 2010), and an ability to accrue resources (see Fisher, 2013b, for a review). Most of this research pertains to single women, and there has been very little research on competition among women who are already mothers (Fisher & Moule, 2013). If a woman is already a mother, she has found and possibly secured a mate. However, she must ensure the mate continues to provide for her child, and obtains the necessary resources for her and her child. Thus, although the mating has been successful, women must compete among each other after having children. In other words, while locating, obtaining access to, and retaining such a mate is highly critical to a women's reproductive success, in that it will lead to healthy children who may then survive and reproduce, mating is not the only domain in which women compete.

Clutton-Brock (2009) proposes that females in many species may compete more intensely for reproductive resources than for access to mating opportunities. As a consequence, he theorizes that intrasexual competitive behavior between females for reproductive resources be included in reexaminations of Charles Darwin's sexual selection theory. In contrast, Rosvall (2011) suggests traits related to competition for mates be considered in line with sexual selection, while those related to fecundity and offspring survival are congruent with natural selection (there are other domains outside of mating, such as relational status, social dominance, and obtaining sufficient resources for the support of one's children).

One way to explore women's competition is to examine co-wives. In polygynous societies, co-wives intrasexually compete for food and money, for paternal care for their children, and for their children's inheritance (Burbank, 1987). In societies where men generate a family's wealth, nonsororal co-wives compete over household resources or, if living in different households, compete for the husband's time (White, 1988). Importantly, sororal co-wives seem to engage in less overt competition, at least in what appears in the ethnographic records, as compared with unrelated co-wives, perhaps because the rank order established in the natal family carries over into the co-wives context (Jankowiak, Sudakov, & Wilreker, 2005). Competition seems to be particularly noteworthy for nonmaterial resources; material resources may be divided relatively equally among co-wives. However, a husband's emotional affection and sexual attention cannot always be equally divided and tensions rise, particularly in the early stages of plural marriage. Moreover, co-wives may engage in competition to advance the standing of their own children. In 24 (35%) of the 69 cultures studied by Jankowiak et al. (2005), defending or advancing a child's interest was recorded as the source of co-wife conflict. Further, advancing a child's interest was often (23 out of 24 times) reported in conjunction with other motives for co-wife conflict.

The finding that co-wives compete to advance the standing of their own children suggests an awareness that relevant resources may be in limited supply. Aside from paternal care, mothers may also compete for resources that improve child longevity, such as clean drinking water and medicines, given that the most common cause of mortality for children under five years of age is infectious disease (68%; Black et al., 2010).

Trade-Offs in Mothers' Decision-Making

Mothers in all species face competing demands on their energy. For example, young women who are themselves still growing allocate their bodily resources differently than fully matured women. The former tend to have children of lower birth weight, which may indicate that young mothers are reserving some nutrients for their own growth rather than fetal development (Scholl, Hediger, Schall, Khoo, & Fischer, 1994).

Another issue is how much to invest in current versus future children. As Sulloway (2007) reviews, parents may invest in future children at the expense of current children, which the latter often resist. Weaning conflict, and intrauterine conflict between the mother and fetus (as evidenced by gestational diabetes and preeclampsia), are examples of the developing fetus or child trying to acquire more resources than is ideal for the mother (see also Haig, 1993). Likewise, as mothers reach the end of their reproductive years, they tend to allocate more resources to their youngest child than they allocated previously to their children. The argument is that these last-born children cannot be replaced, and thus, resources are provided to as great an extent as possible, especially during infancy and early childhood (see Sulloway, 2007).

Moreover, women carefully (unconsciously) consider the local environment. As reviewed, mothers typically invest more than fathers in varying stages of development, starting with gametes and extending into postpartum child care (Trivers, 1972). Therefore, given that mothers face the larger share of parental investment, their reproductive rate is constrained, and they must consider logical ecological constraints (e.g., food availability, amount of competition), among other issues. For example, Ellison (2008) documents how the fecundity (via variability of ovarian function) of nonpregnant, nonlactating women is sensitive to the energy (i.e., caloric intake) that is available in a local environment. The local ecology, via food, can even influence the sex of the child (see Mathews, Johnson, & Neil 2008).

We previously reviewed that mothers may take into account the level of local support that they have available, particularly the level of allomothering, given that child care is an onerous task. McLanahan, Wedemeyer, and Adelberg (1981) showed that single mothers who had support networks reported greater well-being and work/productivity potential. The networks examined were composed of various combinations of kinship and friendship ties and ranged in structure from close-knit to loose-knit. Yet each network type appeared to provide certain types of support that were adaptive for certain groups of single mothers. Essentially, mothers in this study were able to create networks specifically to address their needs (either to stabilize their roles and families or to help them move on), and when there was a high "goodness of fit," these women adjusted well to single motherhood. We propose that this model indicates that women may engage in allomothering and cooperation in some groups or social networks, and yet compete among other groups of women. For example, single mothers may join together as friends to more easily acquire resources and share care, yet compete against other mothers who possess limited goods.

The Distinct Problem Mothers Face

As reviewed earlier, allomothers may be either genetic relatives or individuals who are not genetically related. In humans, some of these unrelated individuals may be same-sex friends. For women, friends tend to be of approximately the same age (Parker & deVries, 1993), meaning that they share many facets of their life given that they may reach milestones around the same time. Moreover, women may make their reproductive decisions in light of the reproductive context of family and friends in close proximity. Worth and Fisher (2011), using preliminary data on 80 currently or recently pregnant women, showed that many women considered allomothering and shared resources in their reproductive decisions. Thus, in other words, kin and friends represent allies who may provide care, resources, and support for mothers. Moreover, one's friends tend to be highly similar to oneself on a variety of interpersonal characteristics, many of which are linked to mate value (see Bleske & Shackelford, 2001 for a review). One may predict that given the similarities in life stages, and the convergence of high resource needs, these friendships would be strained because of competition for mates, resources for children, and so on. However, women show greater preferences for friends demonstrating traits that indicate a willingness to invest, such as kindness, compassion, and empathy (Sprecher, Sullivan, & Hatfield, 1994; Vigil, 2007).

Along these lines, Taylor et al. (2000) examined the female phenomenon of "tend and befriend" (as opposed to fight or flight) as an adaptive coping strategy to deal with stress. They argued that women forged these beneficial friendships in order to increase the chances not only of their own survival but also, most importantly, that of their children. Their conceptualization of friendship is that women form supportive relationships for coping, rather than viewing these individuals as potential competitors who may engage in indirect aggression when necessary. Others, such as Campbell (2002), have theorized that women's need to ensure the safety of their children is so paramount that it has caused women to pursue indirect strategies for aggression, resulting in a low probability of pursuing physical altercation (Vaillancourt, 2005; but see also Liesen, 2013).

At the same time, similarly aged or younger women represent mating competitors. Same-sex friends may become attracted to the same mate, or try to poach one's current mate. In support of this possibility, Bleske and Shackelford (2001) document that one strategy for women is to avoid becoming friends with women who are described as having a history of sexual promiscuity. According to these researchers, sexually promiscuous women may be more likely to attempt to poach one's mate than women who are less promiscuous. Thus, they show that women are attuned to at least some of the characteristics of potential friends, in conjunction with how desirable those features may be to potential mates.

Said another way, differential parental investment translates into different behaviors postreproduction. Sear and Mace (2008) point out that the most significant person in ensuring infant survival is the mother. Given that women's parental investment is so much higher than men's, mating effort seems to be a much smaller part of women's reproductive strategies overall. Therefore, if women compete for access to mates, they will undoubtedly compete to secure resources for the children in whom they have heavily invested. Further, Sear and Mace (2008) posit that women have far fewer children than men are capable of due to biological constraints. Thus, the loss of any child can have prolonged repercussions on a woman's reproductive success, relative to other women involved in the reproductive competition.

Indirect Aggression Allows for Competitive Mothering

Previous researchers have established that women rely on indirect aggression more so than men. Indirect aggression refers to the behaviors in which a perpetrator attempts to cause harm while simultaneously attempting to make it appear as though there was no harmful intention (Björkqvist, Lagerspetz, & Kaukiainen, 1992). We further this contention and argue that women use indirect ways to establish their "good mothering," thus enhancing their status among other women.

Tangentially, although speculative, we propose that women may want to befriend "good mothers" in the hopes of also being seen as such (i.e., the halo effect), or to directly use them as role models. "Good mothers" are often perceived as having a stable relationship, monogamous, possessing financial security (albeit typically not financial independence or time-intensive employment), and abiding with current cultural practices (e.g., breastfeeding, valuing strong educational opportunities for their children; for a review, see Goodwin & Huppatz, 2010). Moreover, since "good mothers" are valued by society, they may be simply conferred higher social status by their peers. Status is thought to directly translate into access to resources, preferred areas to live, safety, and protection, among other considerations that then impact children (Whyte, 1978). The possibility of whether women who are perceived as "good mothers" are consequently conferred higher social status needs to be examined in the future.

Returning to competition, an auxiliary benefit is that these mothering displays show their mates that they are "good mothers," which may lead to better mate retention and further children. By showing that they are good mothers, women may be signaling their maternal interests to potential or current mates since domestic skills are a known mate preference (Buss, 1989). Simultaneously, these practices are indirect and allow women to disguise their competitiveness, enabling them to remain allies with those they are competing directly against.

The quandary of competing with potential allies poses a particularly strong pressure for mothers. Mothers may gain particular benefits through intrasexual competition (e.g., status, power, dominance, resources, potential mates), but at the cost of their friendships or alliances with other women. Therefore, the issue becomes how do mothers compete against same-sex friends yet remain in strong sharing, dyadic relationships with these individuals?

We propose that the solution is to use indirect aggression, which not only reduces potential physical harm to mothers but also allows for the aggression to be circuitous and thereby reduces retaliation. Whereas men's intrasexual competition tends to be direct and often involves physical aggression, women's intrasexual competition is subtler, covert, and disguised, often relying on indirect aggression (see Fisher, 2013a, for a review).

Competition via indirect aggression allows one to compete but still seem cooperative. Often the victim is attacked circuitously so that the attacker can inflict harm without being correctly identified (Björkqvist, 1994), whereas direct aggression would betray the identity of the attacker. Moreover, one can disguise the intention of an indirectly aggressive act under the ruse of self-improvement. One strategy for female intrasexual competition for mates is self-promotion, whereby one attempts to make herself look better than a rival.

Thus, we propose that women may be using subtle, indirect ways to compete with other mothers to display their maternal skills and to collect status from other women. There are numerous ways in which mothers may indirectly compete; for example, they may strive to have the best-dressed children, to be the most involved in the parent-teacher association, or to post photographs on social media of all the various activities their children perform. These possible venues for indirect mothering competition need to be further examined by future researchers.

For postindustrial societies, we posit that one way in which mothers compete is displaying their abilities via socially sanctioned competitions of domestic skills, such as baking contests. Baking contests originated in the late 1800s, and anecdotal evidence suggests that they were an avenue for young unmarried women to display their cooking skills (BakeLady, 2015). While such contests involve direct competition, in that there is a clear winner, they are of little overall consequence (e.g., a child is not harmed). However, they allow women to display their domestic skills in a manner that does not cause them to seem overtly and directly aggressive. Baking contests still exist, but they seem to have evolved into deft displays of baking prowess as exhibited on Pinterest, an online social network that allows members to virtually "pin" ideas. The majority of Pinterest users are women (for the United States, over 70%; http://searchengineland.com/pinterest-search-now-customized-gender-213486). There are two possibilities for competition via Pinterest. First, women may be engaging in virtual contests with unknown contestants by showing their domestic skills via photographs of their baking (or cooking, do-it-yourself crafts, or gardening) successes. These pinners would gain some prestige and status from having people then repin their ideas. Second, and more of relevance to the current chapter, anecdotal evidence suggests women are using pinned tips and ideas from others' successes to engage in indirect aggression. For example, a woman may go to Pinterest and see tips on making intricate bento box lunches for her child. She arises earlier in the morning than usual to make these lunches, which her child then displays to other children at school. Those children then tell their families about the fancy lunches a peer is eating at school, thereby indirectly allowing their mother to be judged to possess a higher level of domestic skill among those in her community. Although this possibility has not been empirically examined, it is plausible, and could enhance the mothering status of the woman.

Historically, there was a very direct way to examine mothering competition, as women in Canada and the United States competed in terms of their babies' development in a very public manner. From around the 1900s until the 1950s, there were "better baby contests" at national exhibitions, where babies would be weighed and measured, and prizes would be given for the heaviest baby under a particular age (http://www.eugenicsarchive.org/eugenics/topics_fs.pl?theme=43; Thomson, 2000/2001). The outcome of such contests was the development of baby growth charts, and mothers who entered their children into contests would receive charts and their infant's score (http://www.ultimatehistoryproject.com/better-babies.html). This obvious form of maternal competition to see, for example, who had raised the largest, healthiest baby was short-lived, due to issues surrounding judging and fears over the spread of polio (http://www.huffingtonpost.com/hilary-levey/the-evolution-of-american_b_860261.html). One possible avenue for related research is to examine mothers of children involved in beauty pageants (see Shaiber, Johnsen, & Geher, this volume).

Competitive mothering in humans is a totally unexplored issue empirically, despite examples from the primate literature (e.g., bonobos; Surbeck, Mundry, & Hohmann, 2011) and sociological interview data that indicate mothers are acutely aware they are engaged in competition on several levels. For example, Barash (2006) reports that society "considers mothering an integral part of female identity" and "encourages women to compete in regard to children: fertile versus infertile, mothers versus childless women, working mothers versus soccer moms, mothers of high-achieving kids versus mothers whose kids are average or troubled" (p. 133). Some of Barash's interviewees expressed jealousy toward friends who became pregnant easily, feelings of envy toward mothers who work (or do not work), or concerns over who is a "better mother; who does more" (p. 145). Her interviewees talked about rivalry with friends who bragged about their baby sleeping through the night, or that their child had been accepted to a better school than one's own child (p. 145). Each of these themes are important to the lives of contemporary mothers, and warrant future examination.

Problems with Examining Cooperative Behavior

One of the hardest aspects of understanding human behavior is to fully comprehend the motives behind actions. Cooperation highlights this difficulty in a unique way, because what appears to be an example of cooperation is not necessarily individuals intentionally helping each other. In some animal societies, it may be useful for individuals to coordinate activity with other group members simply to achieve their own goals. It could be mutualism, for instance, which is when an individual's behavior maximizes his or her own immediate fitness, and any benefits to others are coincidental. Thus, it is important to note that what may seem like cooperation is not necessarily intentionally cooperative (Clutton-Brock, 2012). For example, as an alternative to cooperation or mutualism, it may be parasitism, whereby individuals exploit others. When an individual joins the group, it reduces the success for group members to find food, but increased membership translates into an increased ability to defend resources.

Allomothering may also not be as positive (i.e., prosocial and helping) as it has been made out by some scholars. Wasser and Barash (1981) propose that even the term "allomothering" is a misnomer, as the behaviors involved are related to reproductive competitive strategies. In their review of the nonhuman literature, they found that newborns are handled more than older infants, possibly because newborns are more susceptible to problems (e.g., dehydration) when separated from the mother. They also review that nulliparous (i.e., has not given birth) and multiparous (i.e., has given birth to more than one offspring) females handle infants and treat them

roughly, and that high-ranking females handle infants more than low-ranking females. In contrast, infants of low-ranking females are handled the most. Reproductive status also matters: those who are reaching ovulation rather than those who are past this phase, and who are not pregnant, handled infants more, as do those currently in the latter stage of pregnancy. Collectively, Wasser and Barash argue that theorists have neglected to explore the possibility that there are benefits the handler receives by harming the infant, or that these theorists have suggested that the handler may be increasing the mother's already strained time budget and thereby cause her to decrease the quality of care she provides to her offspring. There is some agreement in the literature, as Silk (2003) proposed that infant handling by another female in the group is reproductive competition if this interest in an infant causes distress to mothers or harm to infants. In a study of rhesus monkeys, Maestripieri (1999) found that infant harassment (i.e., pulling, dragging, hitting, biting of an infant from a female other than the mother) is not an accidental by-product or result of inexperience, and instead reflects reproductive competition among lactating females. Furthermore, Maestripieri documented that the percentage of harassment episodes increased with the frequency of handling.

Whatever the motivation for allowing others to help rear one's children, trusting another individual incurs risk, especially the possibility of infanticide, which may offset any potential benefits from shared care. Infanticide has been documented in a variety of primate species (including humans). Digby (2000) argues that it indicates the prevalence of female intrasexual reproductive competition, particularly in cases of limited resources. Typically, infanticide is the result of kidnapping, which leads to abuse or neglect (e.g., aunting to death; see, e.g., Nakagawa, 1995). In some species, dominant females kidnap the infant from a subordinate, then restrain the mother until the infant dies from dehydration (see Clutton-Brock & Huchard, 2013, for a review). Note that the issue of dominance hierarchy might not be simple; Silk (2003) reported that females seem equally interested in all infants but have greater access to relatives' and subordinate females' infants.

Returning to humans, it is key to note that we typically follow male philopatry, such that women leave their natal homes and, consequently, spend the majority of their reproductive years among nonkin. As mentioned earlier, human young are particularly vulnerable and dependent on others for a significant duration, meaning the chance of lethal abuse and neglect by others have a longer window than in other species. However, this pattern of male philopatry seems concurrent with the development of agricultural societies and men's ability to monopolize resources. Dunbar (2010) suggests instead that because most modern societies are agricultural, scientists have been led to believe that male philopatry was the trend over evolutionary time. However, he argues that once economic constraints and monopolization are removed, humans show bilateral dispersal or form small, matrilineal social groups of closely related women living closer to the wife's family than the husband's family, meaning that humans are "naturally female-philopatric" (p. 73).

Cooperation and Competition in Human Mothers

Chapais (1996) summarizes the relationship between human cooperation and competition rather well:

> The extent to which our species engages in co-operation (defined as acting with others for mutual benefit) may be the single most original characteristic of human sociality. Such a high degree of interdependence within and between groups, and its associated cognitive complexity, are indeed unprecedented in evolution. But, on the other hand, it is hard to find a single area in human affairs which is not pervaded by inter-individual competition, whether based on physical power (aggression) or the manipulation of the needs of others. This contradiction, however, is only apparent because competition and co-operation are most often interdependent and causally connected. (p. 8)

One of the most important decisions faced by individuals in all social species is when to cooperate and when to compete with others (LaFreniere, 1996). As LaFreniere (1996) reviews, cooperating with others, on the one hand, leads to shared child care, forming alliances to compete with other groups or secure resources. On the other hand, competition leads to individual success and stops others from exploiting oneself. Indeed, a fine balance is needed.

Moreover, competition and cooperation may be interrelated to varying extents. Mace (2013) writes that "communal breeding in animals is generally understood as emerging from competition over the resources needed to breed" (p. 251). Her argument

is that these resources would have been competed for by women, and that one outcome would be to share the goods rather than compete for them, in order to maximize inclusive fitness. Put another way, if one competes with relatives for resources, there is a possibility of inflicting harm. Thus, it is possible that sharing resources, even if the division is not equal, may be the most advantageous solution. If this conjecture is correct, then it leads to the conclusion that competition and cooperation are tightly intertwined. Mace furthers this argument by suggesting that this reproductive competition within and between families may have led to the evolution of some fertility patterns (e.g., menopause), but also to societal marriage and inheritance norms.

This interrelationship of cooperation and competition relies on the fact that women's intrasexual competition is often circuitous, subtle, and indirect. On the one hand, sociocultural norms dictate that mothers be kind, warm, and caring and, ultimately, agreeable and cooperative with others. On the other hand, mothers cannot afford to jeopardize their own fitness and reproductive success, and hence they must compete for limited resources and other issues that relate to child development. Thus, we are left with a puzzle: how do mothers cooperate yet compete?

We suggest that one model that explains this situation for mothers is that of the formation of women's friendships. Friendships are usually a mix of prosocial strategies (e.g., cooperation, assistance, persuasion) and coercive strategies (e.g., aggression, threats, insults). Liesen (2013) posited that this dual-strategy approach allows women to maintain a favorable outward appearance but concurrently control their status in the peer group. Put another way, if a woman has a high perceived popularity or dominance, she may receive increased social support from her peer group yet needs to only minimally reciprocate. Her popularity or dominance may actually allow her to improve her control over resources (e.g., scarce goods, social bonds, and information), which leads her to become even more respected, prominent, and influential. Returning to mothers, perhaps mothers compete against each other (or other fertile women, such as in the case of co-wives) to become socially dominant or popular, because those who are at the top of the hierarchy may receive the most benefits from allomothers.

It is critical to note that indirect aggression, often used by women for the purposes of competition, is not necessarily at odds with prosociality. Hawley and Vaugh (2003) propose that individuals who rely on indirect aggression may actually be socially attractive to peers; some aggressive individuals are able to remain central to their social group and obtain personal gains with minimal cost. Hawley (2003) conjectured that competitive strategies such as those used by women arose over evolutionary time due to the necessity of competing effectively among a social group. Consequently, some individuals are prosocial (i.e., indirect and cooperative with others), while other individuals are coercive (i.e., direct and assertive). Indeed, "social competence may entail a balancing act of the needs to get along (being liked, accepted) and to get ahead (effectiveness, power)" (Hawley, 2003, p. 281). Therefore, one potentially effective competitive strategy is to be "bi-strategic" (or Machiavellian), scoring high on both prosociality and coerciveness (a personality configuration that elsewhere leads these individuals to be referred to as "Machiavellians"; Hawley, 2003). These individuals may show high social competence and can be aggressive without repercussion; at the same time, they maintain their status among their peers. Although Hawley's (2003) work pertains mostly to youth and friendships, the same could be true for adult women dealing with motherhood (see Fisher & Moule, 2013). Thus, bi-strategic mothers would have support from others for allomothering, yet acquire the necessary resources to increase their reproductive success.

Ecological and Social Context Is Important

An alternative perspective to the bi-strategic view is that one may instead choose to be either a cooperator or a competitor. Local ecology, especially in terms of the distribution of resources as well as opportunities for reproduction, likely drives the (unconscious) decision about whether one should cooperate or compete. Across species, if resources are plentiful and distributed, there is little need to compete with others, as there is enough for all individuals. If instead resources are sparse, clumped, and defensible, then females may try to monopolize them and act more singularly. In this case, females may compete with each other to the extent of trying to secure and defend their resources. Another consideration is that decreases in the need for resource competition led to the formation of female groups in many species. However, group size is constrained by the intensity of reproductive competition for specific species (Clutton-Brock & Huchard, 2013). In some species, as group size increases, reproductive suppression, abortion, and infanticide increase. Alternatively, if group size has minimal impact on the intensity of reproductive competition, females may form larger groups that are instead directly limited only by competition for resources that influence fecundity and survival (see Clutton-Brock & Huchard, 2013). What is intriguing, though, is that for some species, including primates, it is actually reproductive competition that leads to the formation of alliances (i.e., cooperative relationships). These alliances help females to establish and maintain their dominance rank. Thus, Clutton-Brock and Huchard (2013) suggest that these supportive relationships and the use of rank systems have led to large, stable groups wherein some females are genetically related, and some are not. Moreover, unlike males who use exaggerated secondary sexual characteristics to engage in direct competition, females often use social strategies to improve their reproductive success. Women are typically more aware of social signals and relationships (Mealey, 2000) than men. Collectively, these findings indicate that it may have been reproductive competition for scarce resources that led to alliances in human mothers, and this form of competition among mothers evolved to become subtle and social in nature as a result.

One caveat is required, though. While it may be the case that some human societies show a high degree of allomothering, the patterns exhibited by one population do not necessarily accurately indicate the patterns of another. In her study of the Dogon of Mali, Strassmann (2011) concludes that cooperative breeding theory is inaccurate for this population. She reports that siblings do not provide assistance, but instead compete for resources. Moreover, children raised within a nuclear family fared just as well as those raised in an extended family. Thus, when drawing conclusions about the cooperative and competitive nature of mothers, one must consider the generalizability of such findings. By way of another example, research on preindustrial groups in Finland shows that elder siblings generally act as "helpers at the nest" and improve the probability of younger siblings' survival until the age of sexual maturity (Nitsch et al., 2013; second page of unnumbered pages). This assistance is in spite of any competition that may occur for parental attention and resources. When the younger sibling reaches sexual maturity, his or her reproductive success was decreased if same-sex elder siblings remained present, but increased if opposite-sex elder siblings remained. These researchers posit that the conclusion of whether elder siblings are cooperators or competitors depends on the sex of those involved, and that a long-term time perspective must be adopted to understand the selection pressures acting on siblings.

Future Work

The literature in this chapter clearly indicates that there has been substantial research into allomothering and cooperation, but far less devoted to competition by mothers. While examining each facet independently is interesting, the key seems to be that cooperative breeders, such as humans, are a good example of cooperation and competition working in tandem. Kin and unrelated individuals in these groups are potentially in conflict in that members would presumably use the same reproductive resources to enhance their fitness. However, for kin, this conflict may be solved by individuals helping genetically related individuals reproduce and share resources, even unequally. A little piece of the cake is better than none at all, so long as the final result is improved fitness overall for all kin involved (Mace, 2013). At the same time, unrelated individuals may also allomother in order to establish a relationship of reciprocal altruism, or to allow younger individuals to gain experience as surrogate mothers, which benefits them later on when they have their own offspring. While we have considered the distinction between kin and nonkin, much work is still needed to examine why individuals engage in allomothering, particularly in humans.

Do kin perform cooperative care only due to kin selection? This issue remains one of the most pervasive problems. If the allomother is a genetic relative who is providing assistance to kin, then it is relatively easy to explain this behavior in terms of inclusive fitness theory. That is, by providing assistance, a related individual might improve the survivability of the child and allow the mother to have subsequent children more quickly, thereby furthering the shared genetic lineage. Indeed, the majority of research indicates that it is kin who are often allomothers (see Fisher & Moule, 2013, for a review), although the issue of competition among kin for selfish reproductive gains has been largely neglected (Wild & Koykka, 2014).

This said, the issue of allomothering by kin versus unrelated individuals is not clear-cut. Even studies on infanticide are mixed in this regard, as whether infanticidal attacks are more likely to be directed at unrelated subordinates than at close relatives remains to be determined (Clutton-Brock & Huchard, 2013). Moreover, allomothering by unrelated individuals is not distinctly human, as it has been documented in a range of species including meerkats (*Surricata surricata*), the common marmoset (*Callithrix jacchus*), Japanese macaques (*Macaca fuscata*), and various species of birds (Chism, 2000; Luhr, 2007; Mota & Sousa, 2000; Raffaella, Bonaventura, Koyama, Hardie, & Schino, 2006). It has also been documented in other great apes (Hrdy, 2009). The underlying reasons for why unrelated individuals engage in allomothering warrant more attention.

Taking this argument one step further, there are limits about the applicability of cooperative breeding as a model for human behavior. Mothers are of extreme importance to infant survival, and cannot be replaced by kin or nonkin (Strassmann, 2011). Thus, future research is needed to determine the precise benefits and costs of allomothering in terms of infant (and future infant) fitness, as compared with simply being mothered. Extending this topic to competition, if such research is performed, it must be noted that the outcomes, and by association the benefits, of women's intrasexual competition may not be able to be determined using a short-term perspective because some benefits may take longer to be accrued (Cain & Rosvall, 2014). These longer-term benefits may include enhanced survival of children, or higher reproductive success of children. Thus, Cain and Rosvall (2014) suggest that we must measure lifetime reproductive success or grand-offspring production.

There is also an issue of cause and effect: how does competition relate to reproductive success, and which one causes the other to occur? Apicella and Dreber (2015) found that Hazda women who competed (marginally so in a bead collection task; significant in a handgrip strength task) had more children than those who did not, which they point out is in keeping with trends found in other mammals, particularly those that are cooperative breeders (Stockey & Bro-Jørgensen, 2011). Apicella and Dreber suggest that having more children could lead women to being more competitive due to the increased need for resources, but competitiveness may also lead to reproductive advantages, such as obtaining higher-quality foods and mates. This finding deserves further research, especially because it may help untangle whether competition leads to greater reproductive success or whether success spurs competition. The decision of when to cooperate versus when to compete is an important one. We have explored some social and ecological factors that may play important roles, but omitted discussion about how change along one's lifespan (i.e., age and associated fecundity) may serve as an influence. For example, among some populations, grandmothers provide much assistance to their daughters, even if they do not live with them on a permanent basis (see Mace, 2013, for a review). In general, paternal grandmothers increase their inclusive fitness when assisting daughters-in-law in reproduction because they are helping their sons. Maternal grandmothers also have much to gain by helping their daughters reproduce. Mace (2013) suggests that after a certain age, the best strategy would be to forgo reproduction and instead help kin reproduce in order to avoid any reproductive overlap and, hence, competition for limited resources. As Mace (2013) writes, "Here, competition is, almost literally, the mother of cooperation" (p. 253). It must be noted that an exception was documented among the Dogon of Mali, where Strassmann (2011) reports that the rate of infant mortality increased twofold if the residential paternal grandmother was alive. She posits that this result might be due to grandmothers being consumers rather than producers within this resource-scarce environment. Therefore, while the decision of whether to cooperate or compete remains itself an intriguing one for additional research, how one's age and reproductive potential affect a woman's strategy should also be considered.

We acknowledge that, up until now, we have not directly disentangled who is competing with whom; that is, we have talked about women competing with women, and mothers competing with mothers. However, nonmothers may compete with mothers for limited food resources, for example, given that food may directly impinge upon future reproduction. Likewise, mothers may compete for mates against nonmothers, in order to engage in hypergamy, for example. That we did not distinguish the identity of competitors was intentional, as the reviewed research often does not make a distinction between mothers and women of reproductive capabilities without children. However, preliminary research suggests that, among women, those who have children are less judgmental toward mothers than women without children (Fisher, 2016). It may therefore be useful to specifically address the ways in which women compete once they are mothers, as compared with women who are capable of being mothers but do not have children. Evolutionarily speaking, being able to have children but choosing not to is a novelty brought by the advent of birth control, although there is evidence that humans have long devised ways to prevent pregnancy (http://time.com/3692001/birth-control-history-djerassi/).

Conclusions

One significant advantage of adopting an evolutionary framework for studying mothering is that it enables a long-term view of the costs and benefits associated with a variety of issues faced by mothers. For example, it enables us to understand that what may appear as mothers' cooperative behavior may be self-serving in the longer term to improve their reproductive success and individual fitness. We have demonstrated in our review of the literature that women have just as many reasons to cooperate as to compete, given that the stakes are so high. We propose that reproductive success, as measured via the number of all genetic offspring in a lineage, is critical to understanding why mothers may cooperate and compete with other women.

The benefits of cooperating for mothers are clear, in that sharing resources and child care removes some of the burden on mothers, thereby providing them with more opportunities to have future children and also to promote higher survival and health in their infant(s). Evidence shows that social bonds are critical to female primates; among female chacma baboons, for example, females who maintain strong bonds with other females have longer lives and higher rates of offspring survival, even independent of dominance rank (see Cheney, Silk, & Seyfarth, 2012, for a review). In humans, a meta-analysis revealed a 50% increased likelihood of survival for participants who possess strong versus weak social relationships. This finding was consistent across many demographic variables and health considerations (e.g., age, sex, cause of death, and initial health status) (Holt-Lunstad, Smith, & Layton, 2010). Indeed, Hrdy (2016) found that, for humans, postpartum maternal responsiveness (i.e., being highly possessive vs. permissive, temporarily distancing, rejecting, or infanticidal) is very sensitive to cues of social support, even compared with other primates.

While there has been debate around different models of human foraging and child care, we believe there is much evidence leading away from the provisioning hypothesis, whereby men provision women and their young infants with meat in exchange for other resources. Rather, there is much evidence regarding the diverse roles of women performed within a group, illustrating that women are largely responsible for the physical provisioning of children as well as their direct care. Despite this responsibility, it is clear that a woman's ability to provision herself and children when caring for a newborn is greatly hindered. During this period, some additional resources are likely provided by the newborn's father; yet, much of the slack appears to be directly and indirectly relieved by female relatives (especially the maternal grandmother) and group members. These individuals both provide food resources when needed and assist in caring for the young so the mother can collect her own resources.

This pattern of social support is echoed in postindustrialized nations, where much of the child care is provided by other women or child-care centers when the mother is unable to provide direct care because of work or other matters. While humans show a heightened amount of paternal investment compared with other mammals and primates, it is clear that women other than the mother also play a large role in raising human infants.

However, intrasexual competition is also an equally important consideration. Women must compete to secure resources (including mates) that directly impinge upon their reproductive success; ultimately, whether they win or lose access to scarce goods will greatly impact on their inclusive fitness. The outcome of such reproductive competition is clear. Pettay, Lahdenperä, Rotkirch, and Lummaa (2016) found that among historic Finnish families, where brothers stayed on the natal farm and unrelated females coresided in the same household, the risk of child mortality (until age 15) was increased 23% if another resident reproduced within a two-year time frame. This result is thought to stem from increased competition for material goods, child care, and grandparental investment. Unlike men's reliance on direct aggression, women tend to use indirect aggression, which allows them to compete but in subtle ways. The evidence we reviewed indicates that social relationships are key and, hence, that covert, indirect aggression related to competition is likely to occur within these social networks. While there exist volumes of research on women's competition for mates, much work remains to be done on the topic of competition by mothers. We fully agree with Pettay and colleagues' (2016) assertion that "studies on evolution of group living and cooperative breeding should investigate the competitive costs as well as the helping benefits within a group" (p. 1). The question then becomes: how do mothers compete for resources yet maintain alliances? One possibility is that mothers who use the highly

effective competitive strategy of being bi-strategic, scoring high on both prosociality and coerciveness, may experience success.

The literature indicates that examining exclusively cooperation or competition is a futile exercise, as the two are deeply intertwined. We agree, like others (e.g., Mace, 2013), that it is highly possible that allomothering by cooperative breeders, such as humans, may have emerged due to the very fact that individuals compete over reproductive resources. One outcome of such competition may have been to share goods that were scarce in the local ecological context, thereby causing the formation of cooperative alliances. Whether cooperation was due to unconscious motivations related to increasing inclusive fitness, vis-à-vis sharing with genetic relatives, or due to establishing reciprocal altruism with unrelated individuals—among other explanations—remains to be determined. Regardless, the overall message is clear: mothers must cooperate and compete in order to promote their reproductive fitness, and as such, future researchers need to examine the two elements together.

References

Aaby, P., Bukh, J., Lisse, I. M., & Smits, A. J. (1983). Measles mortality, state of nutrition, and family structure: A community study from Guinea-Bissau. *Journal of Infectious Diseases, 147*(4), 693–701.

Adams, A. M., Madhavan, S., & Simon, D. (2002). Women's social networks and child survival in Mali. *Social Science and Medicine, 54*(2), 165–178.

Aldgate, J., & McIntosh, M. (2006). *Looking after the family: A study of children looked after in kinship care in Scotland.* Edinburgh: Social Work Inspection Agency.

Alexander, R. D., & Noonan, K. M. (1979). Concealment of ovulation, parental care, and human social evolution. In N. A. Chagnon & W. G. Irons (Eds.), *Evolutionary biology and human social behavior: An anthropological perspective,* 436–453. North Scituate, MA: Duxbury Press.

Apicella, C. L., & Dreber, A. (2015). Sex differences in competitiveness: Hunter-gatherer women and girls compete less in gender-neutral and male-centric tasks. *Adaptive Human Behavior and Physiology, 1*(3), 247–269.

BakeLady (2015). Cooking contests of yesteryear—Early years, history of competitions for home cooks. From Grandma Jam's Retro Baking World blog. Retrieved from http://www.grandmajam.com/2015/01/27/cooking-contests-of-yesteryear-early-years-history-of-competitions-for-home-cooks/.

Barash, S. Shapiro (2006). *Toxic friends: The antidote for women stuck in complicated friendships.* London: St. Martin's Press.

Barry, H. B., & Paxson, L. M. (1971) Infancy and early childhood: Cross-cultural codes 2. *Ethnology, 10*(4), 466.

Biben, M. (1992). Allomaternal vocal behavior in squirrel monkeys. *Developmental Psychobiology, 25,* 79–92.

Bird, R. (1999). Cooperation and conflict: The behavioral ecology of the sexual division of labor. *Evolutionary Anthropology, 8,* 65–75.

Bird, R. B. (2007). Fishing and the sexual division of labor among the Meriam. *American Anthropologist, 109,* 442–451.

Bird, R. B., & Bird, D. W. (2008). Why women hunt: Risk and contemporary foraging in a Western desert Aboriginal community. *Current Anthropology, 49,* 655–693.

Bjorklund, D. F., & Pellegrini, A. D (2002). *The origins of human nature: Evolutionary developmental psychology.* Washington, DC: American Psychological Association.

Björkqvist, K. (1994). Sex differences in physical, verbal, and indirect aggression: A review of recent research. *Sex Roles, 30,* 177–188.

Björkqvist, K., Lagerspetz, K. M., & Kaukiainen, A. (1992). Do girls manipulate and boys fight? Developmental trends in regard to direct and indirect aggression. *Aggressive Behavior, 18,* 117–127.

Black, R. E., Cousens, S., Johnson, H. L., Lawn, J. E., Rudan, I., Bassani, D. G., ... UNICEF. (2010). Global, regional, and national causes of child mortality in 2008: A systematic analysis. *Lancet, 375,* 1969–1987.

Bleske, A. L., & Shackelford, T. K. (2001). Poaching, promiscuity, and deceit: Combatting mating rivalry in same-sex friendships. *Personal Relationships, 8,* 407–424.

Burbank, V. K. (1987). Female aggression in cross-cultural perspective. *Behavior Science Research, 21,* 70–100.

Burch, R. L., & Gallup, G. G. (2000). Perceptions of paternal resemblance predict family violence. *Evolution and Human Behavior, 21*(6), 429–435.

Burch, R. L., & Gallup Jr., G. G. (2004). Pregnancy as a stimulus for domestic violence. *Journal of Family Violence, 19*(4), 243–247.

Buss, D. M. (1989). Sex differences in human mate preferences: Evolutionary hypotheses tested in 37 cultures. *Behavioral and Brain Sciences, 12,* 1–49.

Buss, D. M. (2002). Human mate guarding. *Neuroendocrinology Letters, 23*(4), 23–29.

Cain, K. E., & Rosvall, K. A. (2014). Next steps for understanding the selective relevance of female-female competition. *Frontiers in Ecology and Evolution, 2*(32), 1–3.

Cameron, E. Z., Setsaas, T. H., & Linklater, W. L. (2009). Social bonds between unrelated females increase reproductive success in feral horses. *Proceedings of the National Academy of Sciences, 106*(33), 13850–13853.

Campbell, A. (2002). *A mind of her own: Evolutionary psychology of women.* New York: Oxford University Press.

Cant, M. A., & Johnstone, R. A. (2008). Reproductive conflict and the separation of reproductive generations in humans. *Proceedings of the National Academy of Sciences, 105*(14), 5332–5336.

Cashdan, E. (1999). How women compete. *Behavioral and Brain Sciences, 22,* 221.

Chang, R. S., & Thompson, N. S. (2010). The attention-getting capacity of whines and child-directed speech. *Evolutionary Psychology, 8,* 260–274.

Chapais, B. (1996). Competing through co-operation in non-human primates: developmental aspects of matrilineal dominance. *International Journal of Behavioral Development, 19*(1), 7–23.

Cheney, D. L., Silk, J. B., & Seyfarth, R. M. (2012). Evidence for intrasexual selection in wild female baboons. *Animal Behaviour, 84*(1), 21–27.

Chism, J. (2000). Allocare patterns among Cercopithecines. *Folia Primatologica, 71,* 1/2.

Clutton-Brock, T. H. (1991). *The evolution of parental care.* Princeton, NJ: Princeton University Press.

Clutton-Brock, T. (2009). Sexual selection in females. *Animal Behaviour, 77*(1), 3–11.

Clutton-Brock, T. H. (2012). Status of national guidelines in dictating individual clinical practice and defining negligence: Letter 1. *British Journal of Anaesthesia, 109*(2), 284.

Clutton-Brock, T. H., & Huchard, E. (2013). Social competition and selection in males and females. *Philosophical Transactions of the Royal Society B, 368*(1631), 1–15.

Collins, N. L., Dunkel-Schetter, C., Lobel, M., & Scrimshaw, S. C. (1993). Social support in pregnancy: Psychosocial correlates of birth outcomes and postpartum depression. *Journal of Personality and Social Psychology, 65,* 1243–1258.

Crittenden, A. N., & Marlowe, F. W. (2008). Allomaternal care among the Hazda of Tanzania. *Human Nature, 19,* 249–262.

Cuddeback, G. S. (2004). Kinship family foster care: A methodological and substantive synthesis of research. *Children and Youth Services Review, 26*(7), 623–639.

Daly, M., & Wilson, M. (1982). Homicide and kinship. *American Anthropologist, 84*(2), 372–378.

Dasgupta, P. (1995). *An inquiry into well-being and destitution.* Oxford: Oxford University Press.

Diamond, L. M. (2009). *Sexual fluidity: Understanding women's love and desire.* Cambridge, MA: Harvard University Press.

Digby, L. (2000). Infanticide by female mammals: Implications for the evolution of social systems. In C. P. van Schaik & C. H. Janson (Eds.), *Infanticide by males and its implications* (pp. 423–446). Cambridge, UK: Cambridge University Press.

Dominguez, S., & Watkins, C. (2003). Creating networks for survival and mobility: Social capital among African-American and Latin-American low-income mothers. *Social Problems, 50*(1), 111–135.

Duflo, E. (2000). Child health and household resources in South Africa: Evidence from the old age pension program. *American Economic Review, 90*(2), 393–398.

Duflo, E. (2005). Why political reservations? *Journal of the European Economic Association, 3*(2–3), 668–678.

Dunbar, R. (2010). The social brain and its implications. In U. J. Frey, C. Strömer, & K. P. Willführ (Eds.), *Homo novus: A human without illusions* (pp. 65–78). New York: Springer.

Dyson, T., & Moore, M. (1983). On kinship structure, female autonomy, and demographic behavior in India. *Population and Development Review,* 35–60.

Ehrenreich, B., & Hochschild, A. (Eds.). (2004). *Global woman: Nannies, maids and sex workers in the new economy.* New York: Metropolitan/Owl Books.

Ellison, P. (2008). Energetics, reproductive ecology, and human evolution. *Paleoanthropology,* 172–200. http://www.paleoanthro.org/static/journal/content/PA20080172.pdf.

Falk, D. (2009). *Finding our tongues: Mothers, infants, and the origins of language.* New York: Basic Books.

Farmer, E., & Moyers, S. (2008). *Kinship care: Fostering effective family and friends placements.* London: Jessica Kingsley Publishers.

Fisher, M. (2013a). Tinbergen's influence on advances in female intrasexual competition research. *Human Ethology Bulletin, 28,* 23–30.

Fisher, M. (2013b). Women's intrasexual competition for mates. In M. Fisher, J. Garcia, & R. Sokol-Chang (Eds.), *Evolution's empress: Darwinian perspectives on the nature of women* (pp. 19–42). New York: Oxford University Press.

Fisher, M. (2016). Competitive mothering as explored through judgment. Paper presented at the annual meeting of the North Eastern Evolution Society, Halifax, NS, June.

Fisher, M., & Moule, K. (2013). A new direction for intrasexual competition research: Cooperative versus competitive motherhood. *Journal of Social, Evolutionary, and Cultural Psychology, 7*(4), 318–325.

Flinn, M. V., & Ward, C. V. (2004). Ontogeny and evolution of the social child. In B. J. Ellis & D. F. Bjorklund (Eds.), *Origins of the social mind: Evolutionary psychology and child development* (pp. 19–44). New York: Guilford Press.

Frank, R. & Silk, J. B. (2009). Grooming exchange between mothers and non-mothers: The price of natal attraction in wild baboons (*Papio anubis*). *Behaviour, 136*, 889–906.

Gallup, G. G., & Suarez, S. D. (1983). Optimal reproductive strategies for bipedalism. *Journal of Human Evolution, 12*(2), 193–196.

Gallup, G. G., Burch, R. L., Zappieri, M. L., Parvez, R. A., Stockwell, M. L., & Davis, J. A. (2003). The human penis as a semen displacement device. *Evolution and Human Behavior, 24*(4), 277–289.

Goodwin, S. & Huppatz, K. (Eds.), (2010). *The good mother: Contemporary motherhoods in Australia.* Sydney, Australia: Sydney University Press.

Gray, P. B., & Anderson, K. G. (2010). *Fatherhood: Evolution and human paternal behavior.* Cambridge, MA: Harvard University Press.

Gray, P. B., & Anderson, K. G. (2015). The impact of fathers on children. *Encyclopedia of early childhood development.* Retrieved from http://www.child-encyclopedia.com/sites/default/files/textes-experts/en/4513/the-impact-of-fathers-on-children.pdf.

Griffiths, P., Hinde, A., & Matthews, Z. (2001). Infant and child mortality in three culturally contrasting states of India. *Journal of Biosocial Science, 33*(04), 603–622.

Gurven, M. & Kaplan, H. (2007). Longevity among hunter-gatherers: A cross-cultural examination. *Population and Development Review, 33*(2), 321–365.

Guyer, J. I. (1981). Household and community in African studies. *African Studies Review, 24*, 87–137.

Haig, D. (1993). Genetic conflicts in human pregnancy. *Quarterly Review of Biology, 68*, 495–532.

Halperin, R. H. (1980). Ecology and mode of production: Seasonal variation in the division of labor by sex among hunter-gatherers. *Journal of Anthropological Research, 36*, 379–399.

Hawkes, K., O'Connell, J. F., & Blurton Jones, N. G. (1997). Hadza women's time allocation, offspring provisioning, and the evolution of long postmenopausal life spans. *Current Anthropology, 38*, 551–577.

Hawley, P. H. (2003). Prosocial and coercive configurations of resource control in early adolescence: A case for the well-adapted Machiavellian. *Merrill-Palmer Quarterly, 49*(3), 279–309.

Hawley, P. H., & Vaugh, B. E. (2003). Aggression and adaptive functioning: The bright side to bad behavior. *Merrill-Palmer Quarterly, 49*(3), 239–242.

Hewlett, B. S. (1989). Multiple caretaking among African pygmies. *American Anthropologist, 91*(1), 186–191.

Hewlett, B. S. (1991). Demography and childcare in preindustrial societies. *Journal of Anthropological Research, 47*, 1–37.

Hill, K. (2002). Cooperative food acquisition by Aché foragers. *Human Nature, 13*, 105–128.

Hill, K., & Hurtado, A. M. (1996). *Ache life history: The ecology and demography of a foraging people.* New York: Walter de Gruyter.

Högnas, R. (2010). A mechanism describing how low-income women exchange support in their personal networks. *Sociological Focus, 43*(4), 330–348.

Holt-Lunstad, J., Smith, T. B., & Layton, J. B. (2010). Social relationships and mortality risk: A meta-analytic review. *PLoS Medicine, 7*(7), 1–20.

Hrdy, S. B. (1999). *Mother nature: A history of mothers, infants and natural selection.* New York: Ballantine.

Hrdy, S. B. (2005). Evolutionary context of human development: The cooperative breeding model. In C. S. Cater, L. Ahnert, K. E. Grossmann, S. B. Hrdy, M. E. Lamb, S. W. Porges, & N. Sachser (Eds.), *Attachment and bonding: A new synthesis* (pp. 9–32). Cambridge, MA: MIT Press.

Hrdy, S. B. (2009). *Mothers and others: The evolutionary origins of mutual understanding.* Cambridge, MA: Harvard University Press.

Hrdy, S. B. (2016). Variable postpartum responsiveness among humans and other primates with "cooperative breeding": A comparative and evolutionary perspective. *Hormones and Behavior, 77*, 272–283.

Hunt, C. K. (2003). Concepts in caregiver research. *Journal of Nursing Scholarship, 35*(1), 27–32.

Hurtado, A. M., Hill, K., Kaplan, H., & Hurtado, I. (1992). Tradeoffs between female food acquisition and child care among Hiwi and Ache foragers. *Human Nature, 3*, 185–216.

Jaeggi, A. V., van Noordwijk, M. A., & van Schaik, C. P. (2008). Begging for information: Mother–offspring food sharing among wild Bornean orangutans. *American Journal of Primatology, 70*(6), 533–541.

Jankowiak, W., Sudakov, M., & Wilreker, B. C. (2005). Co-wife conflict and co-operation. *Ethnology, 44*(1), 81–92.

Kaplan, H., Hill, K., Lancaster, J., & Hurtado, A. M. (2000). A theory of human life history evolution: Diet, intelligence, and longevity. *Evolutionary Anthropology, 9*, 156–185.

Keeley, L. H. (1995). Protoagricultural practices among hunter-gatherers: A cross-cultural survey. In T. D. Price & A. B. Gebauer (Eds.), *Last hunters, first farmers: New perspectives on the prehistoric transition to agriculture* (pp. 243–272). Santa Fe, NM: School of American Research Press.

Keim, S., Klärner, A., & Bernardi, L. (2009). Qualifying social influence on fertility intentions composition, structure and meaning of fertility-relevant social networks in Western Germany. *Current Sociology, 57*, 888–907.

Kelly, R. L. (1995). *The foraging spectrum: Diversity in hunter-gatherer lifeways.* Washington, DC: Smithsonian Institution Press.

Kristof, N., & WuDunn, S. (2010). *Half the sky: Turning oppression into opportunity for women worldwide.* New York: Vintage Books.

Kuhle, B. X., & Radtke, S. (2013). Born both ways: The alloparenting hypothesis for sexual fluidity in women. *Evolutionary Psychology, 11*, 304–323.

Kuhn, S. L., & Stiner, M. C. (2006). What's a mother to do? *Current Anthropology, 47*(6), 953–981.

LaFreniere, P. J. (1996). Co-operation as a conditional strategy among peers: Influence of social ecology and kin relations. *International Journal of Behavioral Development, 19*(1), 39–52.

Leiderman, P. H., & Leiderman, G. F. (1974). Affective and cognitive consequences of polymatric infant care in the East African highlands. *Minnesota Symposium on Child Psychology*, 5, 81–109.

Liesen, L. (2013). The tangled web she weaves. In M. Fisher, J. Garcia, & R. Sokol-Chang (Eds.), *Evolution's empress: Darwinian perspectives on the nature of women* (pp. 43–62). New York: Oxford University Press.

Lizarralde, M., & Lizarralde, R. (1991). Bari exogamy among their territorial groups: Choice and/or necessity. *Human Ecology*, 19, 453–67.

Lovejoy, C. O. (1981). The origin of man. *Science*, 211, 341–350.

Luhr, J. (2007). *Earth: The definitive visual guide*. London: Dorling Kindersley Limited.

Lukas, D., & Clutton-Brock, T. (2012). Cooperative breeding and monogamy in mammalian societies. *Proceedings of the Royal Society B*, 279(1736), 2151–2156.

Mace, R. (2013). Cooperation and conflict between women in the family. *Evolutionary Anthropology: Issues, News, and Reviews*, 22(5), 251–258.

Maestripieri, D. (1999). The biology of human parenting: Insights from nonhuman primates. *Neuroscience and Biobehavioral Reviews*, 23(3), 411–422.

Marlowe, F. (2000). Paternal investment and the human mating system. *Behavioural Processes*, 51(1), 45–61.

Marlowe, F. W. (2003). A critical period for provisioning by Hadza men: Implications for pair bonding. *Evolution and Human Behavior*, 24(3), 217–229.

Mathews, F., Johnson, P. J., & Neil, A. (2008). You are what your mother eats: Evidence for maternal preconception diet influencing foetal sex in humans. *Proceedings of the Royal Society B*, 275, doi:10.1098/rspb.2008.0105

McLanahan, S. S., Wedemeyer, N. V., & Adelberg, T. (1981). Network structure, social support, and psychological well-being in the single-parent family. *Journal of Marriage and the Family*, 43(3), 601.

Mealey, L. (2000). *Sex differences: Developmental and evolutionary strategies*. San Diego, CA: Academic Press.

Meehan, C. L., Quinlan, R., & Malcolm, C. D. (2012). Cooperative breeding and maternal energy expenditure among Aka foragers. *American Journal of Human Biology*, 25(1), 42–57.

Mota, T. M., & Sousa, C. B. M. (2000). Prolactin levels of fathers and helpers related to alloparental care in Common Marmosets, *Callithrix jacchus*. *Folia Primatologica*, 71, 1/2.

Murdock, G. P. (1981). *Atlas of world cultures*. Pittsburgh: University of Pittsburgh Press.

Nakagawa, N. (1995). A case of infant kidnapping and allomothering by members of a neighbouring group in patas monkeys. *Folio Primatologia*, 64, 62–68.

Nitsch, A., Faurie, C., & Lummaa, V. (2013). Are elder siblings helpers or competitors? Antagonistic fitness effects of sibling interactions in humans. *Proceedings of the Royal Society B*, 280(1750). doi: 10.1098/rspb.2012.2313

Noss, A. J., & Hewlett, B. S. (2001). The contexts of female hunting in Central Africa. *American Anthropologist*, 103, 1024–1040.

Oberman, M. J. D. (2003). A brief history of infanticide and the law. In M. G. Spinelli (Ed.), *Infanticide: Psychosocial and legal perspectives on mothers who kill* (pp. 3–18). Washington, DC: American Psychiatric Publishing.

Parker, S., & deVries, B. (1993). Patterns of friendship for women and men in same- and cross-sex relationships. *Journal of Social and Personal Relationships*, 10, 617–626.

Paul, A., & Kuester, J. (1996). Infant handling by female Barbary macaques (*Macaca sylvanus*) at Affenberg Salem: Testing functional and evolutionary hypotheses. *Behavioral Ecology and Sociobiology*, 39, 133–145.

Pettay, J. E., Lahdenperä, Rotkirch, A., & Lummaa, V. (2016). Costly reproductive competition between co-resident females in humans. *Behavioral Ecology*. doi: 10.1093/beheco/arw088

Platek, S. M., Burch, R. L., Panyavin, I. S., Wasserman, B. H., & Gallup, G. G. (2002). Reactions to children's faces. *Evolution and Human Behavior*, 23(3), 159–166.

Platek, S. M., Critton, S. R., Burch, R. L., Frederick, D. A., Myers, T. E., & Gallup, G. G. (2003). How much paternal resemblance is enough? Sex differences in hypothetical investment decisions but not in the detection of resemblance. *Evolution and Human Behavior*, 24(2), 81–87.

Quinlan, R. J., Quinlan, M. B., & Flinn, M. V. (2003). Parental investment and age at weaning in a Caribbean village. *Evolution and Human Behavior*, 24(1), 1–16.

Raffaella, V., Bonaventura, M., Koyama, F. N., Hardie, S. & Schino, G. (2006). Reciprocation and interchange in wild Japanese macaques: Grooming, cofeeding and agonistic support. *American Journal of Primatology*, 68, 1138–1149.

Riley, L. A., & Glass, J. L. (2002). You can't always get what you want: Infant care preferences and use among employed mothers. *Journal of Marriage and Family*, 64, 2–15.

Rosenberg, K., & Trevathan, W. (2002). Birth, obstetrics and human evolution. *BJOG: An International Journal of Obstetrics and Gynaecology*, 109, 1199–1206.

Rosvall, K. A. (2011). Intrasexual competition in females: Evidence for sexual selection? *Behavioral Ecology*, 22(6), 1131–1140.

Scholl, T. O., Hediger, M. L., Schall, J. I., Khoo, C. S., & Fischer, R. L. (1994). Maternal growth during pregnancy and the competition for nutrients. *American Journal of Clinical Nutrition*, 60(2), 183–188.

Sear, R., & Mace, R. (2008). Who keeps children alive? A review of the effects of kin on child survival. *Evolution and Human Behavior*, 29, 1–18.

Shackelford, T. K. (2003). Assessing individual differences in death threat: A brief theoretical and psychometric review of the threat index. *OMEGA—Journal of Death and Dying*, 46(4), 323–333.

Silk, J. B. (2003). Cooperation without counting. In P. Hammerstein (Ed.), *Genetic and cultural evolution of cooperation* (pp. 37–54). Cambridge, MA: MIT Press.

Silk, J. B., Beehner, J. C., Bergman, T. J., Crockford, C., Engh, A. L., Moscovice, L. R., ... Cheney, D. L. (2009). The benefits of social capital: Close social bonds among female baboons enhance offspring survival. *Proceedings of the Royal Society B*, 276, 3099–3104.

Silk, J. N. (1978). Patterns of food sharing among mother and infant chimpanzees at Gombe National Park, Tanzania. *Folia Primatologica*, 29, 129–141.

Sillen-Tullberg, B., & Moller, A. P. (1993). The relationship between concealed ovulation and mating systems in anthropoid primates: A phylogenetic analysis. *American Naturalist*, 141(1), 1–25.

Sokol Chang, R. S. (2013). Human attachment vocalizations and the expanding notion of nurture. In M. Fisher, J. R. Garcia, & R. Sokol Chang (Eds.), *Evolution's empress: Darwinian perspectives on the nature of women* (pp. 168–186). New York: Oxford University Press.

Sprecher, S., Sullivan, Q., & Hatfield, E. (1994). Mate selection preferences: Gender differences examined in a national sample. *Journal of Personality and Social Psychology, 66*(6), 1074–1080.

Sternberg, R. J., & Grajek, S. (1984). The nature of love. *Journal of Personality and Social Psychology, 47*, 312–329.

Stockley, P., & Bro-Jørgensen, J. (2011). Female competition and its evolutionary consequences in mammals. *Biological Reviews, 86*, 341–366.

Stockley, P., & Campbell, A. (2013). Female competition and aggression: Interdisciplinary perspectives. *Philosophical Transactions of the Royal Society B, 368*(1631), 1–11.

Strassmann, B. I. (2011). Cooperation and competition in a cliff-dwelling people. *Proceedings of the National Academy of Sciences, 108*(2), 10894–10901.

Sulloway, F. J. (2007). Birth order. In C. A. Salmon & T. K. Shackelford (Eds.), *Family relationships: An evolutionary perspective* (pp. 162–182). New York: Oxford University Press.

Surbeck, M., Mundry, R., & Hohmann, G. (2011). Mothers matter! Maternal support, dominance status and mating success in male bonobos (*Pan paniscus*). *Proceedings of the Royal Society B, 278*(1705), 590–598.

Taylor, S. E., Klein, L. C., Lewis, B. P., Gruenewald, T. L., Gurung, R. A. R., Updegraff, J. A. (2000). Biobehavioral responses to stress in females: Tend-and-befriend, not fight-or-flight. *Psychological Review, 107*, 411–429.

Thomson, G. E. (2000/2001). "A baby show means work in the hardest sense": The better baby contests of the Vancouver and New Westminster local Councils of Women, 1913–1929. *BC Studies, 128*, 5–36.

Trivers, R. L. (1972). Parental investment and sexual selection. In B. Campbell (Ed.), *Sexual selection and the descent of man, 1871–1971* (pp. 136–179). Chicago: Aldine-Atherton.

Ueno, A., & Matsuzawa, T. (2004). Food transfer between chimpanzee mothers and their infants. *Primates, 45*(4), 231–239.

Uttal, L. (1999). Using kin for child care: Embedment in the socioeconomic networks of extended families. *Journal of Marriage and the Family*, 845–857.

Vaillancourt, T. (2005). Indirect aggression among humans: Social construct or evolutionary adaptation. In R. E. Tremblay, W. W. Hartup, & J. Archer (Eds.), *Developmental origins of aggression* (pp. 158–177). New York: Guilford.

Vigil, J. M. (2007). Asymmetries in the friendship preferences and social styles of men and women. *Human Nature, 18*(2), 143–161.

Volk, A. A. (2009). Human breastfeeding is not automatic: Why that is so and what it means for human evolution. *Journal of Social, Evolutionary, and Cultural Psychology, 3*, 305–314.

Volk, T., & Atkinson, J. (2008). Is child death the crucible of human evolution? *Journal of Social, Evolutionary, and Cultural Psychology, 2*, 247–260.

Waguespack, N. M. (2005). The organization of male and female labor in foraging societies: Implications for early Paleoindian archaeology. *American Anthropologist, 107*, 666–676.

Wasser, S. K. & Barash, D. P. (1981). The selfish "allo-mother": A comment on Scollay and DeBold (1980). *Ethology and Sociobiology, 2*, 91–93.

Weisner, T. S. (1987). Socialization for parenthood in sibling caretaking societies. In J. B. Lancaster, J. Altmann, A. S. Rossi, & L. R. Sherrod (Eds.), *Parenting across the life span: Biosocial dimensions* (pp. 237–270). New York: Aldine de Gruyter.

Weisner, T. S., Gallimore, R., Bacon, M. K., Barry, H. III, Bell, C., Novaes, S. C., & Williams, T. R. (1977). My brother's keeper: Child and sibling caretaking [and comments and reply]. *Current Anthropology, 18*(2), 169–190.

White, D. R. (1988). Rethinking polygyny: Co-wives, codes, and cultural systems. *Current Anthropology, 29*(4), 529–572.

Whyte, M. K. (1978). *The status of women in preindustrial societies*. Princeton, NJ: Princeton University Press.

Wild, G., & Koykka, C. (2014). Inclusive-fitness logic of cooperative breeding with benefits of natal philopatry. *Philosophical Transactions of the Royal Society B, 369*(1642), doi: 10.1098/rstb.2013.0361

Wood, J. W. (1994). *Dynamics of human reproduction: Biology, biometry, demography: Evolutionary foundations of human behavior*. Chicago: Aldine Transaction Publishers.

Worth, K., & Fisher, M. L. (2011). An investigation of synchronous pregnancies in women. *Journal of Evolutionary Psychology, 9*, 309–326.

Wyon, J. B., & Gordon, J. E. (1971). The Khanna study: Population problems in the rural Punjab. *Population (French Edition), 26*(5), 976.

Conflicting Tastes: Conflict between Female Family Members in Choice of Romantic Partners

Leif Edward Ottesen Kennair *and* Robert Biegler

Abstract

Shared genes give relatives shared interests in each other's evolutionary success, yet differences in patterns of relatedness can create conflicts. In a monogamous relationship, parents are equally related to all their children and also equally related to all their grandchildren. However, their children are more closely related to their own children and take greater interest in them than in their nieces and nephews. Various types of parent–offspring conflict can be explained in terms of such patterns of genetic relatedness. The authors extend this principle to mother–daughter conflict over choice of the daughter's partner and to competition between sisters by considering how parental influence causes increased competition among same-sex siblings. The authors conclude that females wish family members to choose partners with traits that may provide more direct benefits and potentially improve their fitness, that individuals choose sexier partners for themselves, and that parental influence may theoretically drive sister competition.

Key Words: parent–offspring conflict, genetic conflict, mate choice, mothers, daughters, sisters

Introduction

From classical fiction, such as Shakespeare's *Romeo and Juliet,* to popular stories across cultures from American sitcoms to Bollywood productions, the motif of intergenerational conflict over an offspring's choice of partner entertains us, whether we are from cultures that practice arranged marriages or not. There seems to be a universal fascination with this conflict.

Many cultures have moved from a general acceptance and practice of arranged marriages to a state in which love, romance, and personal choice dominates (Buunk, Park, & Duncan, 2010; Coontz, 2004; Davidson, 2012). Today, in most Western countries, it is considered almost unthinkable that parents should interfere in the process of mate selection. However, parents still attempt to influence children's choice in some cultures, even through rather aggressive or manipulative means

(Apostolou, 2013). Mothers attempt to influence their daughters' sexual behavior both by condoning practices that limit sexual pleasure and promoting behaviors such as female genital mutilation (circumcision). Another example is the practice of "ironing" prepubescent girls' breasts, a practice primarily performed by the girls' mothers (Tapscott, 2012). Breast ironing is usually described as an attempt to protect the girls from male sexual interest and rape predation, despite the pain the girls report and the possible long-term health hazards (Tapscott, 2012). Both of these heinous practices, performed by mothers against their own daughters, may be considered extreme forms of daughter guarding (Perilloux, Fleischman, & Buss, 2008), and examples of intergenerational conflicts between kin due to choice of romantic partners. Many of the tactics reported by Apostolou (2013), such as blackmail, threats of violence, or actual violence, would be illegal and entirely unthinkable in Norway, where the authors of this chapter reside, but we suggest that mothers and daughters differ in their tastes of partners for the daughter, leading to predictable conflicts of interest in one of the world's most gender-egalitarian societies (United Nations Development Programme, 2010).

Although fathers (and other male relatives) often play a major role in deciding who their daughters shall marry in literature, popular culture, and also the scientific literature (e.g., Apostolou, 2010b), the current chapter focuses on conflicts between female family members. Therefore, our primary theoretical focus is on how related women compete or have different interests in the choice of spouse for each other. The original list of traits that we use in this chapter was nominated by women to describe men, which makes comparisons of tastes theoretically possible. It might be that mothers use partner choice mechanisms that they share with their daughters when picking partners for their daughters, which would increase similarity. However, we believe that other evolved mechanisms interplay with these partner choice mechanisms to create strategically relevant differences in choices between female family members for self versus other. This is especially the case in sister–sister conflicts and competition, where one avoids any possible generational effects. We would not hypothesize the same evolved mechanisms for evaluating female partners in men.

Furthermore, we advocate greater research interest in the psychological and social arsenal of influence tools such as strategic misinformation, spreading gossip, or verbally derogating siblings' partner choices (Fisher & Cox, 2010) rather than merely focusing on male societal power and physical strength. We believe that the current volume should improve our understanding of these processes. Where there are stable conflicts of interest and competition, it is predicted that there will evolve methods of influence and strategies for competition. As we shall see, parental influence may also cause a greater need for sister–sister competition.

The current chapter presents a theory of genetic conflict (Trivers, 1974) between female family members, one that drives differences in preferred partner traits between female family members depending on whether the partner is intended for oneself or another female family member and the predictions that follow from this approach. We also present an empirical investigation among mothers and daughters in sexually liberal and gender-egalitarian Norway for the purposes of illustrating and

testing these hypotheses. The chapter also considers how any parental influence over daughters' choice will increase the need or benefits for sisters to compete with each other.

Why Should There Be Any Conflict at All?

Why should a mother and her daughter differ in their choice of an ideal long-term partner for the daughter? It might seem that, in evolutionary terms, parents and offspring would benefit equally from as many healthy offspring in the next generation as possible. Therefore, conflict is unexpected. Despite this, Trivers's (1974) concept of parent–offspring conflict suggests that, due to the fact that parents and offspring only share 50% of their genes, there may indeed be conflict between generations.

We illustrate this genetic argument for parent–offspring conflict in the three scenarios outlined in Figure 28.1, where we present the argument in terms of chromosomes. The genetic basis of parent–offspring conflict is usually presented as an argument involving individual genes based on the assumption that individual genes are inherited entirely independently. For example, although Trivers (1974) does not explicitly state that genes are inherited independently, this is a *necessary* premise for his mathematical approach, which only deals with relatedness without considering linkage among genes. That is true for genes on different chromosomes, as seen in our figure, and for genes far enough apart on the same chromosome that recombination is common. Assume that the first-generation couple, Adam and Betty, has two daughters: Charlotte, who marries Chris, and Debbie, who marries David. Each couple has two children. The number of chromosomes from the first-generation couple has been maintained through the second and third generations. In each generation, there are eight copies of Adam and Betty's chromosomes. Note that because Charlotte and Debbie each receive one set of paternal (P) and one set of maternal (M) chromosomes, they share only half their genetic material (i.e., Charlotte and Debbie share chromosomes P2a and M2b). There are *six* copies of Charlotte's chromosomes in the third generation: four in her own children, and another two in Debbie's children. This model will serve as the baseline for comparison to the other two scenarios, also seen in Figure 28.1.

In our second scenario, a choice has been made that resulted in Charlotte having one child less, but Debbie having three children more than in the first scenario. This change from the first scenario increases the fitness of Adam and Betty because

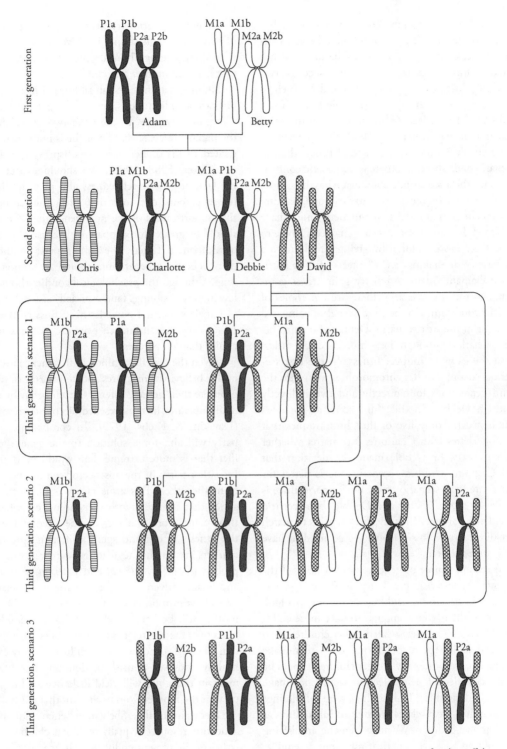

Figure 28.1 Illustration of differential genetic relatedness and the conflict that can arise under some patterns of trading off the reproductive potentials of related individuals. Adam and Betty are equally related to all their grandchildren. Thus, their genetic interests are served by maximizing the total number of grandchildren, regardless of how those children are distributed between their daughters Charlotte and Debbie. In scenario 1, Charlotte and Debbie each have two children. Scenarios 2 and 3 represent different tradeoffs. In scenario 2, Charlotte is reduced to one child, Debbie gains three for a total of five. The increase in the total number of grandchildren benefits Adam and Betty and, of course, Debbie. Genetically, even Charlotte gains. Counting all the chromosomes in the third generation, there are more of Charlotte's genes in that generation in scenario 2 than in scenario 1. Charlotte gained more through the genes she shares with Debbie that were transmitted to Charlotte's nieces and nephews than Charlotte lost through having one fewer child. However, in scenario 3, Charlotte loses more than she gains compared to scenario 1, whereas Adam, Betty, and Debbie still come out ahead. Selection should favor behavior that makes Charlotte resist a tradeoff, resulting in scenario 3.

the third generation now contains not eight, but twelve copies of their chromosomes. Debbie's fitness increases, too, but so does Charlotte's—once inclusive fitness is taken into account—because two of Debbie's children have the P2a and M2b chromosomes that Charlotte and Debbie share. There are seven of Charlotte's chromosomes in the third generation: two in her own child, five in Debbie's children. Everyone has higher total fitness than in scenario one. Therefore, there is no genetic conflict.

In the third scenario, Debbie again has three more children than in the first scenario, but Charlotte has no children at all. Adam and Betty might have obtained the extra resources that enabled Debbie to raise three more children by giving Charlotte to a monastery or making her a vestal virgin or a celibate shaman. Adam and Betty gain fitness compared to the first scenario: there are ten copies of their chromosomes in the third scenario, compared to eight in the first scenario. Debbie also gains fitness. Charlotte, though, loses more in direct fitness than she gains in indirect fitness. In the first scenario, six copies of her chromosomes went into the third generation, four directly and two indirectly through Debbie. In this third scenario, Debbie's children carry only five of the chromosomes that Debbie shares with Charlotte. No matter whether Adam, Betty, or Debbie made the decision that left Charlotte childless, scenario one is better for Charlotte than scenario three, but scenario three is better for Adam, Betty, and Debbie than scenario one. For Charlotte's inclusive fitness gains to match her direct fitness loss, Debbie would need to have four extra children.

A second source of genetic conflict arises if the mother (in our example, Betty, in the first generation) still has young children of her own to look after or if she is young enough to have more children. She is more closely related to her children than her grandchildren, so behavioral traits that make her redirect resources toward her children should be positively selected. Kin selection would not make older children object if all siblings were full siblings because they are as closely related to full siblings as to their own children. We make here the simplifying assumption that we can treat all genes as equivalent. Genomic imprinting makes reality more complicated (Burt & Trivers, 1998), but we have not tried to derive predictions relevant to behavioral traits. Thus, to the extent that the mother redirects resources toward her own reproduction, genetic conflict with her daughter is reduced. However, as explained later, not all siblings were full siblings

throughout evolutionary history, and the selection of behavioral traits should be driven by the average relatedness among siblings, which must be less than that between mother and child.

Siblings may not be full siblings either because of marital indiscretions, one of the parents remarrying, or polygamy. In the latter two cases, one of the parents is aware that he or she is not genetically related to his or her partner's offspring (see Daly & Wilson, 1988, 1998). We should expect that the lack of genetic relatedness also plays itself out in stepparents' decisions that affect the reproductive opportunities of the next generation. Conflict should be greater for stepparents because of genetic unrelatedness. Exactly the same genetic conflict as there is between generations should act among siblings, although the psychological conflict should be less intense if siblings (and especially sisters because of female structural powerlessness; Buss & Barnes, 1986) have less influence over each other's mate choice than do parents.

Given the genetic conflict, both generations will evolve behavioral measures and countermeasures to promote their genetic interests. Each behavior normally operates in the presence of countermeasures (Dawkins & Krebs, 1979). To compensate, each party will aim for a solution to the genetic conflict that is more extreme than would be optimal for either party in the absence of countermeasures from the other. This arms race was discovered in genes that act differently depending on whether they come from the egg or the sperm. During the genesis of egg and sperm, different epigenetic markers are set that regulate gene expression. This process is called *maternal* and *paternal imprinting* and is also driven by different patterns of relatedness between mother and father (Haig, 1997). The mother will be equally related to all her children, but a man may be related to only some of her children. Then, if a mother's first child is already fairly healthy and well-nourished, doubling her investment in this child will yield little benefit but may prevent the mother from having another child while she invests in the first. She would benefit more from allocating resources equally to all her children. The father of the present child, though, may not be the father of the next. The lower the probability that he will father this woman's next child, the less *his* loss from the next child losing fitness. Thus, even a modest gain in fitness for the present child, *his* child, can be better for the father than preserving the mother's resources for her next child. The father gains if the paternally imprinted genes can force a greater allocation of resources to the *present* child, for example by taking more from the placenta. Say that the mother's optimal allocation of resources is to give 100 units, but the father's optimal allocation, given average levels of paternal uncertainty, would be 110. Assume that the actual allocation will be the average of the two values (i.e., 105 units). Then, the maternally imprinted genes should evolve to counter the paternally imprinted genes' demands; for example, by setting a target of 90 units to get the average back to 100. The paternally imprinted genes could counter by setting a target of 130 units and so on. The paternally and maternally imprinted genes active during pregnancy have taken this arms race to the point at which having only maternally or only paternally imprinted genes can be lethal (Cattanach, Beechey, & Peters, 2004).

We must expect the same arms race to amplify the psychological conflict between parents and offspring or among siblings. If such an arms race was the only factor, we would expect severe disagreements between generations. Therefore, we must consider what may moderate the arms race. A potentially moderating factor is lack of power or influence. If women in general (Buss & Barnes, 1986), and daughters especially, have less influence on these social negotiations, then this might dampen the effect of the arms race. Evolution can only act on heritable variation that is expressed in the phenotype. The less a genetic conflict can express itself in the behavioral phenotype for lack of power over another's choices, the less selection pressure there is for countermeasures, counter-countermeasures, and the whole evolutionary arms race. Any strong emotional investment in the absence of power to affect others' choices should be selected against because it would distract from issues one *can* act on. This is a specific example of the general principle that traits that provide no benefits but cost something will be selected against. For example, animals may lose both vision and pigmentation when living in dark environments. Therefore, the extent to which we should expect the genetic conflict between generations and among siblings to express itself behaviorally depends on how much influence parents have over their children, and siblings over each other or over their parents' decisions.

How May the Genetic Conflict Express Itself Behaviorally?

The genetic conflict can express itself in differing mate choice criteria because some of the benefits associated with a partner's traits are easily transferable

whereas others are not. Parents can benefit from wealth, social status, and political alliances that they acquire by marrying off a daughter to a husband of their choice, if their choice has traits that will provide them with direct resources. Within the evolutionary anthropology literature, one differentiates between material, embodied, and relational wealth (Borgerhoff Mulder & Beheim, 2011; Borgerhoff Mulder et al., 2009). Such types of wealth also are transmitted across generations in modern societies. Although material wealth was less relevant in the environment of evolutionary adaptedness (EEA), relational wealth probably was as important then as in societies today (Borgerhoff Mulder et al., 2009), and embodied wealth was probably more important than today. It is therefore the two latter forms that we expect to be most relevant: embodied wealth (e.g., health, skills, knowledge, and strength) and relational wealth (e.g., social ties, social position, trust, kinship, and symbolic goods) (Borgerhoff Mulder & Beheim, 2011). The transmission of these types of wealth improves the fitness of offspring. Parents would benefit only indirectly from any good genes that a daughter's choice of partner may possess. Parents could not transfer those good genes to other members of the family, at least not without either tolerating extramarital affairs or else accepting the costs of polygyny (Henrich, Boyd & Richerson, 2012). Therefore, parents should place greater value on transferable (direct) benefits that a son-in-law might bring into the family than will their daughters. As a result, a daughter should be more interested than either her parents or her sisters in the good genes from which only her children will benefit. Note that some forms of embodied wealth may be markers of good genes, whereas others might be more abilities to convey direct benefits. We therefore suggest that embodied wealth should be considered more specifically depending on which of the two levels of benefits the person represents the most.

Shakespeare's *Romeo and Juliet* illustrates just that pattern. The Lady Capulet of the EEA might want to secure her present survival and reproduction and thus be interested in an ally like Paris of the Pleistocene who has secured resources that can be transferred to Lady Capulet or other children she might have, whether these are material resources, social status, or alliances. Lady Capulet would get less benefit than Juliet from resources that can only go to Juliet's children, such as the good genes indicated by Romeo's sexiness, or from potential that takes a long time to realize (like inherited influence from his social network and family when, for example, his father dies). Prehistoric Juliet might have more to gain from choosing good genes or a male who will live longer and show signs of being a future leader (Young Male Syndrome traits, Wilson & Daly, 1985), picking the more sexy and romantic Romeo than the currently influential but less sexy Paris. Paris has material wealth, but Juliet probably does not have evolved adaptations to consider that sexy, and she probably therefore places less emphasis on this as compared to what her parents wish. Because from an evolutionary perspective material wealth (Borgerhoff Mulder & Beheim, 2011) must be considered mainly as a salient proxy for resource acquisition potential, we also expect parents to be interested in the sort of embodied wealth that conveys mainly resource acquisition potential, rather than good genes.

How Much Influence Do Parents and Siblings Have?

There is a good theoretical basis for expecting that parents and offspring disagree over what makes someone a good partner for the offspring and that siblings apply different criteria to the selection of their own partners than to a sibling's partner. Can parents influence their children's mate choice? And can siblings influence each other's mate choice? We know of relevant data for parents. Apostolou (2007b) reviewed the anthropological literature on mate choice systems in 190 hunter-gatherer societies. He found that parental marital arrangement (i.e., parents choose the spouses of their children) is the primary system in 130 of these societies. In a further 33 societies, spouses are primarily chosen by close kin, in 15 societies the children's choice is usually subject to parental approval, and in only eight societies do children usually choose their own spouses. Most societies feature a mix of mate choice systems, and most of the secondary systems also favor parents' influence. In roughly 96% of societies, parents have at least some influence. In a recent paper, Apostolou (2013) reports a factor analysis of tactics that Cypriot parents use to influence both their children and their children's intended partners, including hardball tactics (e.g., violence and threats), bribing, blackmail, matchmaking, and general advice on who to marry. Many of these tactics are illegal, some are unsavory but, in general, they indicate both the parents' motivation to attempt to influence children's partner choice and the many different ways in which this may be accomplished.

Parental influence will only lead to a behavioral phenotype of conflicting motivations if offspring can also have a say in their own mate selection. This is clearly the case in the 23 societies in which offspring initiate courtship because they are selecting a mate. There are also other options: before being pushed into an unwanted marriage, offspring may appeal to parents' interest in their children's happiness by demonstrating distress at the parents' choice, perhaps going so far as to threaten or attempt suicide. Lee (1984, cited by Apostolou, 2008a) mentions !Kung girls attempting suicide (none successful) to avoid unwanted marriages, which was a successful tactic because the marriages were called off. Furthermore, after an unwanted marriage, offspring may choose to divorce (possible in 125 societies) or seek extra-pair copulations.

Given that parents have influence over their offspring's partner choice, there is one final condition for parents and their offspring to differ over mate choice: the traits that differentially benefit each side should not be highly correlated. If, for example, an indicator of genetic quality that makes a man appear sexy to a young woman were an equally good indicator of social status, which is more important to her parents, then parents and their offspring would not differ over mate choice criteria. Instead, negative correlations have been found, for example, between men's mating effort and parenting effort (Apicella & Marlowe, 2005; Gangestad & Simpson, 2000; Waynforth, 1999). Kokko (1998) argued that it pays for men to trade off mating effort against parenting effort when there is polygyny or extra-pair copulations. Harcourt et al.'s (1981) analysis of the relationship between relative testis size and breeding system suggests moderate promiscuity in humans, which is confirmed by the finding that approximately 1–3% of children are not genetically related to their social fathers (Bellis, Hughes, Hughes, & Ashton, 2005; Larmuseau et al., 2013; Voracek, Haubner, & Fisher, 2008; although these numbers may have been higher in the EEA; e.g., Scelza, 2011).

We would claim that women, here specifically both mothers and sisters, do have influence and have had influence in the EEA. An interest in verbal influence (e.g., gossip, derogation, self-promotion), sibling rivalry (i.e., seeking influence and favor with parents), and other female modes of influence warrants more attention. The current volume has several chapters that consider these different modes of influence.

Differences in Preferences

The conditions for a motivational conflict between parents and offspring over mate choice are present in humans, so what are the data regarding partner trait preferences? There are some empirical findings. Buunk, Park, and Dubbs (2008) found that young adults in several cultures assigned different weights to partner traits than what they expected their parents to give. The young adults judged that they would be more likely than their parents to reject a potential partner for shortcomings in seven out of nine characteristics related to heritable fitness: being physically unattractive or unfit, being fat, bad smell, no sense of humor, and lack of creativity. The young people expected their parents to be more likely than themselves to reject a partner for shortcomings in traits related to parental investment and cooperation: lack of good family background, different ethnic background or religious belief, lower social class, divorced, poor, or poorly educated. Apostolou conversely asked parents to estimate the traits of a possible partner either for themselves or for their children. He found that they rated beauty as more important in a partner for themselves than for their offspring (Apostolou, 2008a) and good family background more important in a partner for their children than for themselves (Apostolou, 2008b). Perilloux et al. (2011) asked both parents and their offspring what traits should be possessed by the ideal partner for the offspring. Offspring found attractiveness and exciting personality more important than did their parents, whereas parents gave greater weight than their offspring to the characteristics of kindness and understanding, earning capacity, being a good housekeeper, good health, and, most importantly, being religious.

What is still missing is a direct comparison of how much parents and their offspring value various traits of the offspring's spouse. To address this question, we performed an empirical investigation on daughters. Perilloux, Fleischman, and Buss (2008) offered both a convincing argument that daughters' reproductive choices should be more important to parents and empirical data that daughters are guarded more closely than sons. Although Apostolou's (2007b) review showed that in most societies fathers had more influence than mothers, we asked for mothers' opinions to avoid a confound with possible sex differences and paternal and grandpaternal uncertainty (Bishop, Meyer, Schmidt, & Gray, 2009). Apostolou also suggests

that the mother's role may have been underestimated (see also Daly & Wilson, 1988).

General Predictions

Despite our focus on differences, let us start by pointing out that we also expect numerous similarities between mothers and daughters. Due to shared genes and shared interest in the daughter's fitness, as well as shared cultural effects, we expect to find similarities between the importance that daughters and mothers place on specific traits. Because both are interested in a long-term relationship for the daughter, given that paternal investment is beneficial for inclusive fitness in humans (Shenk & Scelza, 2011), we expect that both will be interested in signs of commitment. These will probably also be among the most important traits when considering a long-term partner. Other such common traits might include future status or wealth (Buss, 1989), intelligence, and agreeableness (Li, Bailey, Kenrick, & Linsenmeier, 2002).

Where there does seem to be a possible evolved conflict between mothers and daughters is with respect to long- versus short-term partners. This can be interpreted as another consequence of differential relatedness leading to mothers and daughters giving different weights to different partner traits. Mothers have interests in their daughters' choices, and daughters have interest in their own and their siblings' choices. The adaptive problem of partner choice is therefore influenced by the interests of other family members (in this volume, the focus is on competition and conflict between women; thus, in this chapter, between female family members).

One problem in optimal partner choice is to find out the current distribution of partner qualities and how good a partner one can acquire. Social information, which might be gossip or observing interactions between others, can contribute to assessing the distribution of partner qualities. Place et al. (2010) report that humans, like many other species, engage in mate copying: individuals chosen by others as potential mates become more attractive. However, such use of social information can be problematic. When individuals rely more on social than personally acquired information, self-reinforcing fads and fashions can form. Bikhchandani et al. (1992, cited in Giraldeau, Valone, & Templeton, 2002) called this *informational cascades*, and the calculations of Bikhchandani et al. (1998) showed that informational cascades occur only if observers are limited to knowing only the decisions of others, not the cues on which the decisions were based. Giraldeau et al. (2002) proposed that informational cascades could occur through mate copying. We failed to find any empirical research on informational cascades due to mate copying. Rieucau and Giraldeau (2009) did observe informational cascades in the use of social information but that was in foraging nutmeg mannikins, not in humans choosing mates. We know only of merely anecdotal evidence: the phenomena of groupies in general—and of Beatlemania in particular—can be interpreted as examples of informational cascades in human mate choice, which would degrade the value of social information on mate quality. We find it implausible that these four men from Liverpool could have mate values high enough to justify thousands of women screaming for their attention and throwing their underwear onto the stage, and we see this as a plausible case of the positive feedback of witnessing others' enthusiasm creating an informational cascade leading to a vast overestimate of mate value. Alternatively, being male ourselves, we may be engaging in unwitting denigration of competitors, and some competitors need quite extensive denigration for there to be any competition. We leave that judgment as an exercise for the reader.

A second reason why social information may be unreliable is that individuals may benefit from strategic misdirection. Because humans do engage in mate copying, people should benefit from giving the impression of being courted and even from dumping the person who allegedly courted them. The person being dumped would suffer loss of mate value, but mate copying should increase the mate value of the apparently choosy individual (Stanik, Kurzban, & Ellsworth, 2010). Even if a breakup was not planned from the outset, one or both of the people involved may want to mislead others regarding the reasons. Observers would either receive false information on mate value, or else, if they are aware of the problem and discount the reasons they are told, they would be limited to observing decisions and thereby set the stage for an informational cascade. Another strategy would be to reduce competition by hiding interest in or even denigrating an intended mate in order to prevent mate copying. Fisher and Cox (2010) called this *competitor manipulation*. That could even have the indirect effect of making the intended mate feel less desirable and hence bringing a mate within reach who might otherwise seek better choices.

This is an example of *mate manipulation* (Fisher & Cox, 2010).

Personally acquired information should be more relevant than social information to finding out one's own mate value. Social information can tell people about general interest ("he fancies you"), but finding out just how committed one particular individual is to a relationship with oneself should depend more on close-up information gathering.

Another reason to sample information on potential mates close up is to smell them, which provides information on the major histocompatibility complex (MHC) (Havlicek & Roberts, 2009). Mating with an individual whose MHC shows intermediate levels of difference from one's own increases the immunocompetence of offspring (Woelfing, Traulsen, Milinski, & Boehm, 2009) and should be especially relevant when there are cues to a high parasite load in the environment.

Daughters could be as aware as their mothers of the potential costs of close-up sampling (such as possible effective derogation and reputational costs of promiscuity; Bendixen & Kennair, 2014; Fisher, Cox, & Gordon, 2009; Schmitt & Buss, 1996) but may still give greater weight to the benefits of information acquired in this way than do their mothers, who prioritize other information. The crucial feature is not simply that anything that could reduce the daughter's mate value would decrease mother's chance of benefiting from the daughter's partner choice. After all, the daughter also suffers from a loss in mate value in most cultures (Buss & Schmitt, 1993). What significantly creates a conflict of interest is that the mother would benefit less from the kind of information the daughter acquires through close-up sampling and therefore would favor this method less than the daughter would. The function of parents guarding the daughter's sexuality would then be to skew the tradeoff between information gathering and potential loss of mate value toward the balance that parents favor. In a species in which paternal investment greatly enhances fitness (Trivers, 1972), we should also expect that, as Buss and Schmitt (1993) have shown, daughters will also prioritize long-term relationships—a finding we replicated in a Norwegian sample (Kennair, Schmitt, Fjeldavli, & Harlem, 2009). Sampling potential partners through relationships that may last only a short time might serve daughters' choice of a long-term partner, especially if there were no differences in short- and long-term mating psychology (but see Buss & Schmitt, 1993; Kennair et al.,

2009). But she also may have criteria that differ from those of her parents, and they will therefore differ in the preferred sampling method.

Another important perspective is that sex is a fungible resource (Meston & Buss, 2007); it is a resource that someone may offer that others covet and for which they are willing to offer resources in exchange. Historically and cross-culturally, the parents and other family members are also at the negotiation table, not merely the young couple—thus, we believe that there are adaptations for parents to choose mates for their children based on their own self-interest and for children to oppose their parents' choices. It is important to note that parents will attempt to control their interests, whereas the young female may evolve strategies designed to circumvent parental control in an ancestral ecology in which both the potential mates' traits as well as the parents' interests limited her behavior. Modern Western female sexuality might therefore be subject to less control and may not maximize reproductive success in the modern ecology due to a mismatch between our current modern mating environment and her traits that have evolved to counter the influence of kin on her choice.

The main idea behind this research was the prediction that mothers may gain differentially from their daughter's choice of a long-term partner. If the daughter chooses the right partner, then the mother and thus her other younger children and future children may benefit from his provisioning and possible investment by the mother-in-law directly or as an ally by providing social resources here and now (direct traits). If the daughter chooses only short-term partners, or chooses sexy traits/good genes (indirect traits), then the mother will not benefit directly from the choice of partner (see also Dubbs & Buunk, 2010).

All of these differences aside, the genetic, evolutionary nature of the mother–daughter relationship suggests that there also should be a large overlap in interest because their inclusive fitness is, to a large degree, shared. Therefore, to summarize, all general fitness-increasing factors, such as male investment and commitment, ought to be among the most valued traits when considering a long-term mate (following the logic of the Trivers, 1972, parental investment theory and sexual strategies theory, Buss & Schmitt, 1993; see also jealousy literature; e.g., Baumeister & Vohs, 2004; Bendixen et al., 2015; Buss & Haselton, 2005; Kennair et al., 2011). Other such common traits might include future status or wealth (Buss, 1989), intelligence, and agreeableness (Buss, 1989; Li et al., 2002).

An Empirical Investigation: Comparing Mothers and Daughters

To explore the idea of mother–daughter conflict about potential partners for daughters, we had a number of women describe the positive traits of men, resulting in a final list of 133 adjectives. Pairs of questionnaires were handed out to daughters who then recruited their mothers: we received answers from 85 pairs. They were asked to independently rate the importance of these traits. We also asked questions about how important they thought it was for the daughter to have a short-term relationship or a long-term relationship (Buss & Schmitt, 1993).

Considering responses from mothers and the 37 daughters who indicated that they were single or were seeing several people, we found that women in both generations see long-term relationships as far more important for the daughter than short-term relationships ($F_b(1,70) = 64.85$, $p < 10^{-10}$); there was no main effect of generation (F < 1), and the interaction was significant ($F(1,70) = 6.83$, $p = 0.011$). Closer examination of the interaction showed that mothers, more than daughters, thought it was important that the daughters enter a long-term relationship (Mothers, $M = 5.31$, $SD = 1.35$; Daughters, $M = 4.65$, $SD = 1.27$; $t(71) = 2.14$, $p = 0.036$), whereas daughters, more than mothers, felt it was important that daughters have short-term sexual relationships (Mothers, $M = 2.37$, $SD = 1.19$; Daughters, $M = 3.16$, $SD = 1.69$; $t(64.76) = -2.30$, $p = 0.024$); see Figure 28.2.

Rank correlation of the 133 male traits rated by mothers and daughters, Spearman's $rho = 0.79$, $p < 0.001$, suggests that there is a striking similarity between mothers' and daughters' ratings of the different traits; see Figure 28.3. Furthermore, as shown in Table 28.1, 60 (45%) of these traits have a Cohen's d in the range of ~0.2 or smaller (small effect sizes), and 92 (69%) Cohen's d in the range of ~0.5 or smaller (small to medium effect sizes).

These results are consistent with Apostolou's (2009, 2010a) findings that parents prefer to marry later than they think is good for their offspring and that parents find short-term relationships more permissible for themselves than for their offspring. All in all, the mothers obviously have no problem with their daughters leaving home but are simultaneously partaking in something that could look like guarding their daughters' sexual reputation. This fits both with our predictions of the mother wishing the

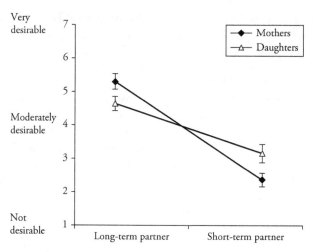

Figure 28.2 Mothers' and daughters' scores indicating how desirable they believe it would be for the daughter to enter a long-term relationship or seek out a short-term, sexual relationship.

Note: Mothers are more interested than their daughters in the daughters entering a long-term relationship, but daughters more than mothers found it desirable for daughters to have short-term relationships. Bars indicate standard error, and all differences are significant.

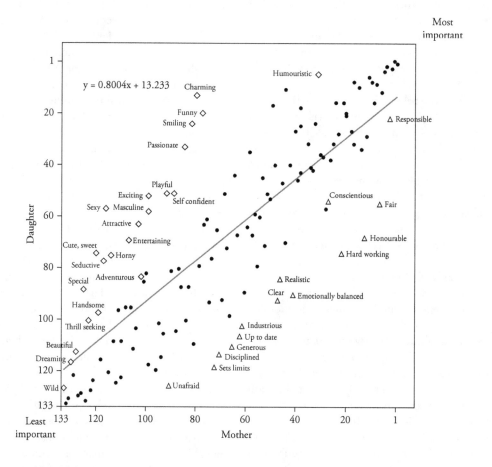

Figure 28.3 Ranking of traits by mother and daughter. The average importance of each trait to mothers and daughters was ranked from 1 (most important) to 133 (least important). The gray circles represent the rankings of traits whose importance does not differ significantly between the generations. The empty triangles indicate those traits that mothers find more important than do daughters, and the empty diamonds indicate those traits that daughters find more important than do mothers. We labeled only those traits on which the generations disagree. The trend line is for all traits.

Table 28.1. Daughters' and mothers' ranking of all of the 133 traits used in this study.

Daughters				Mothers			
Rank	*M*	*SD*	Trait	Rank	*M*	*SD*	*d*
1	4.87	0.43	Faithful	2	4.74	0.51	0.27
2	4.71	0.51	Honest	1	4.77	0.42	−0.14
3	4.54	0.68	Loyal	5	4.43	0.76	0.15
4	4.51	0.68	Trustworthy	3	4.52	0.70	−0.02
5	4.41	0.66	Understanding	6	4.38	0.67	0.04
6	4.35	0.72	Humoristic	32	3.87	0.69	0.68
7	4.34	0.68	Kind	12	4.27	0.81	0.09
8	4.28	0.78	Thoughtful	11	4.27	0.75	0.01
8	4.28	0.73	Cheerful	17	4.08	0.71	0.27
10	4.27	0.89	Sincere	9	4.31	0.85	−0.05
11	4.20	0.72	Joie De Vivre	16	4.12	0.77	0.11
12	4.19	0.88	Loving	44	3.72	0.93	0.52
13	4.15	0.78	Caring	7	4.33	0.77	−0.24
14	4.14	0.80	Charming	81	3.14	0.89	1.18
15	4.13	0.78	Respectful	25	3.99	0.77	0.18
15	4.13	0.77	Nice	22	4.02	0.74	0.14
15	4.13	0.90	Safe	10	4.29	0.72	−0.19
18	4.12	0.78	Sexually Satisfying	50	3.64	0.97	0.55
19	4.07	0.80	Affectionate	37	3.80	0.79	0.34
20	4.05	0.79	Clean	20	4.05	0.85	0.00
20	4.05	0.82	Funny	79	3.15	0.91	1.04
22	4.02	0.77	Supportive	20	4.05	0.68	−0.04
23	4.00	0.76	Responsible	4	4.50	0.61	−0.73
24	3.94	0.81	Smiling	83	3.13	0.91	0.94
24	3.94	0.85	Happy	33	3.87	0.86	0.09
26	3.92	0.66	Independent	37	3.80	0.69	0.18
27	3.88	0.75	Social	41	3.77	0.74	0.15
27	3.88	0.79	Likeable	19	4.07	0.78	−0.25
29	3.86	0.94	Open-Minded	24	3.99	0.69	−0.16
30	3.85	0.78	Considerate	13	4.25	0.67	−0.55

(continued)

Table 28.1 Continued

Daughters Rank	M	SD	Trait	Mothers Rank	M	SD	d
31	3.82	0.73	Friendly	36	3.80	0.67	0.02
31	3.82	0.93	Sociable	26	3.98	0.78	−0.18
31	3.82	0.76	Positive	17	4.08	0.62	−0.38
34	3.82	0.87	Passionate	86	3.08	0.95	0.82
35	3.79	1.01	Empathic	15	4.13	0.80	−0.38
36	3.76	0.92	Cosy	59	3.45	0.78	0.37
37	3.75	0.94	Inclusive	31	3.90	0.76	−0.18
38	3.72	0.72	Sensible	30	3.90	0.82	−0.24
39	3.69	0.72	Helpful	27	3.96	0.70	−0.39
40	3.67	0.94	Polite	43	3.75	0.69	−0.10
40	3.67	0.94	Attentive	49	3.64	0.74	0.03
42	3.65	0.90	Knowledgeable About Self	35	3.83	0.76	−0.59
43	3.64	0.79	Enthusiastic	34	3.86	0.68	−0.29
44	3.62	0.76	Optimistic	37	3.80	0.71	−0.24
45	3.62	0.79	Smart	65	3.32	0.85	0.36
46	3.61	0.82	Warm	54	3.59	0.77	0.03
47	3.60	1.05	Close	40	3.78	0.81	−0.20
48	3.60	0.88	Healthy	46	3.70	0.76	−0.12
49	3.55	0.84	Intelligent	52	3.61	0.84	−0.08
49	3.55	0.73	Playful	93	2.94	0.94	0.72
49	3.55	0.81	Extravert	69	3.27	0.83	0.34
49	3.55	0.76	Self-Confident	90	3.04	0.90	0.62
53	3.51	0.98	Exciting	97	2.72	0.85	0.86
54	3.48	0.87	Patient	51	3.62	0.76	−0.17
55	3.44	0.82	Conscientious	28	3.92	0.79	−0.59
56	3.40	1.03	Fair	8	4.33	0.85	−0.99
57	3.39	0.99	Sexy	116	2.33	1.00	1.07
57	3.39	1.05	Natural	29	3.92	0.83	−0.56
59	3.38	1.06	Masculine	97	2.72	0.85	0.69
60	3.36	0.97	Sensitive	57	3.48	0.80	−0.14

Table 28.1 Continued

Daughters			Trait	Mothers			
Rank	*M*	*SD*		Rank	*M*	*SD*	*d*
61	3.36	0.90	Rich in Initiative	55	3.57	0.74	−0.26
62	3.35	0.95	Romantic	77	3.21	0.85	0.15
63	3.34	0.93	Protective	78	3.17	1.10	0.17
63	3.34	0.81	Attractive	103	2.65	0.86	0.82
65	3.32	0.93	Knowledgeable	60	3.43	0.85	0.25
66	3.31	0.79	Ambitious	72	3.25	0.83	0.08
67	3.29	0.95	Down to Earth	58	3.45	0.79	−0.18
67	3.29	0.86	Active	64	3.34	0.69	−0.07
69	3.29	0.89	Honorable	14	4.24	0.73	−1.16
70	3.28	0.91	Entertaining	107	2.60	0.83	0.78
71	3.27	0.92	Reflective	44	3.72	0.76	−0.53
72	3.26	0.97	Insightful	53	3.60	0.83	−0.38
73	3.25	0.88	Practical	68	3.27	0.84	−0.03
74	3.25	0.87	Cute	120	2.22	1.07	1.06
74	3.25	0.77	Hard Working	23	4.00	0.77	−0.97
76	3.24	1.03	Horny	114	2.53	1.14	0.65
77	3.22	0.86	Humble	74	3.23	0.93	−0.02
78	3.20	0.94	Seductive	117	2.28	1.11	0.89
79	3.20	1.14	Unprejudiced	56	3.57	0.94	−0.35
79	3.20	1.01	Emotional	80	3.15	0.90	0.05
81	3.18	1.10	Sporty	88	3.06	0.87	0.12
82	3.17	0.76	Strong-Willed	91	3.02	0.77	0.19
82	3.16	0.84	Pleasant (both personality and looks)	100	2.71	0.85	0.53
84	3.15	0.88	Adventurous	102	2.66	0.85	0.56
85	3.11	0.91	Realistic	47	3.68	0.70	−0.71
86	3.09	0.84	Talkative	101	2.69	0.76	0.50
87	3.04	0.89	Sensitive	87	3.06	0.88	−0.02
87	3.04	1.09	Fit	84	3.10	0.82	−0.06
89	3.01	1.10	Special	125	2.01	0.94	0.98
90	2.99	0.92	Clever	61	3.41	0.74	−0.51

(continued)

Table 28.1 Continued

Daughters			Trait	Mothers			
Rank	*M*	*SD*		Rank	*M*	*SD*	*d*
91	2.95	0.88	Emotionally Balanced	42	3.76	0.76	−0.98
92	2.94	0.84	Domestic	70	3.26	0.84	−0.38
92	2.94	0.83	Clear	48	3.65	0.78	−0.88
94	2.93	0.90	Tidy	76	3.22	0.90	−0.32
95	2.92	0.89	Sensation-Seeking	108	2.57	0.77	0.42
95	2.92	1.04	Spontaneous	106	2.62	0.95	0.30
97	2.86	1.00	Charismatic	111	2.56	0.82	0.33
98	2.85	0.84	Handsome	119	2.26	0.79	0.73
99	2.83	0.99	Diplomatic	67	3.28	0.85	−0.49
100	2.81	0.88	Curious	85	3.09	0.79	−0.33
100	2.81	0.94	Thrill-Seeking	123	2.07	0.92	0.79
102	2.79	1.02	Imaginative	96	2.83	0.84	−0.04
103	2.76	0.97	Industrious	62	3.41	0.80	−0.73
104	2.75	0.97	Strong	104	2.65	0.96	0.11
105	2.75	0.99	Creative	89	3.06	0.75	−0.35
106	2.73	0.76	Firm	94	2.89	0.80	−0.21
107	2.73	0.94	Up to Date	63	3.35	0.87	−0.68
108	2.72	0.95	Well-Dressed	113	2.54	0.93	0.19
108	2.72	1.03	Muscular	109	2.56	0.85	0.17
110	2.70	0.83	Effective	82	3.14	0.82	−0.53
111	2.69	0.86	Generous	66	3.28	0.79	−0.72
112	2.66	0.82	Eloquent	105	2.63	0.97	0.03
113	2.64	0.87	Beautiful	128	1.99	0.85	0.76
114	2.63	0.85	Disciplined	71	3.25	0.79	−0.76
115	2.61	0.93	Intuitive	95	2.86	0.84	−0.28
116	2.58	0.81	Stylish	118	2.28	0.91	0.35
117	2.56	1.05	Dreaming	130	1.83	0.80	0.78
118	2.55	0.89	Calm	97	2.72	0.90	−0.19
119	2.55	0.86	Sets Limits	73	3.24	0.96	−0.76
120	2.50	1.04	Inventive	75	3.23	4.49	−0.22

Table 28.1 Continued

Daughters				Mothers			
Rank	*M*	*SD*	Trait	Rank	*M*	*SD*	*d*
121	2.49	0.87	Proud	115	2.49	0.98	0.00
122	2.45	1.02	Rugged	129	1.94	0.81	0.56
123	2.44	0.86	Critical	109	2.56	0.90	−0.14
124	2.44	0.88	Tough	121	2.18	0.83	0.30
125	2.41	0.96	Competitive	112	2.54	0.95	−0.14
126	2.40	0.87	Unafraid	92	2.96	0.83	−0.66
127	2.27	0.94	Wild	133	1.49	0.67	0.96
128	2.24	1.21	Musical	122	2.12	0.93	0.11
129	2.21	0.91	Worldly Wise	126	2.01	0.98	0.21
130	2.02	0.75	Stubborn	127	2.00	0.87	0.02
131	1.99	0.94	Cool	131	1.81	0.80	0.21
132	1.94	1.01	Wealthy	124	2.02	0.97	−0.09
133	1.68	0.83	Reckless	132	1.72	0.95	−0.05

Note: These traits were collected by asking 32 women from a wide age range to provide adjectives that positively described men—synonymous words and repetitions were deleted—resulting in this list of 133 traits. Thereafter, they were ranked by the mothers and daughters in our study. Traits are ordered by daughter's ranking.

daughter to enter a long-term relationship for the mother's own benefit and Perilloux et al.'s (2008) daughter-guarding perspective.

Mothers and daughters agree to an extreme degree on which traits are important and which are not. We have no reason to believe that this agreement is primarily due to a lack of independence between results. The majority of daughters handed their answers in by using the drop box at a university, whereas the form was anonymously mailed to us by the mothers.

We find traits such as wealth and musicality, and also many Young Male Syndrome traits (related to competitiveness, risk-taking, and violence; see Wilson & Daly, 1985) at the bottom of both the mothers' and the daughters' lists. The top of both lists is dominated by traits of agreeableness and commitment (see Table 28.1). Although both generations agreed on which traits are most important, when we consider where they disagree on how important a trait is, we find that the traits more important to daughters are typically indirect and markers of either Young Male Syndrome behavior, good genes, or socially and sexually exciting or

stimulating behavior. The daughters thus prioritize indirect traits compared to the mothers, even when the task was explicitly to describe a long-term partner.

In the EEA, there were few resources that could be accumulated. Therefore, a young man could not become an attractive partner by inheriting wealth. Under those conditions, the traits more important to mothers would possibly make up a profile of men who not only acquire more resources than others through diligent hunting, but also share them and follow up on social agreements. From the mother's perspective, living in a world in which wealth cannot buffer against the random vagaries of fate, a good partner for her daughter should be reliable enough so that others will help him when he is unlucky in the confident expectation of future reciprocity. Daughters want that, too, but are willing to trade off some of those traits for others, such as indicators of good genes. Mothers benefit less from good genes and place greater value on what a daughter's partner can provide to the mother. Furthermore, "Sets Limits" and "Clear" are traits that may limit the daughter's behavior, but these may also be interpreted as being desirable for behavior in social deals, too. Thus, they might be relatively more important for mothers.

Theoretically, we are interested in considering direct versus indirect traits. A principal components extraction with Varimax rotation of all 133 traits suggested six components: Agreeableness, Sexy, Conscientiousness, Openness, Physically Fit, and a broad Intelligence component. (Kaiser-Meyer-Olkin's measure of sampling adequacy was only 0.43, although Bartlett's test of sphericity was significant ($p < 0.001$).) The two components with highest explained variance provide the basis for a good test of direct versus indirect traits. The Agreeableness traits indicate a personality characterized by supportive, considerate, and caring behavior. This may affect both daughters and their children, but also mothers, thus contributing positively to all individuals' inclusive fitness. The Sexy traits, on the other hand, suggest good genes and a generally attractive, sexy, and exciting personality, but this will not in any direct way contribute to the present welfare of the daughter, her children, or her mother—instead, these traits might very well predict infidelity, both due to behavioral tendencies and because other females will find these traits sexy. However, they may be indicators of good or sexy genes, which is important because these are traits from which the daughter will benefit more than will her mother.

The two most important factors in the factor analysis of all 133 traits were Agreeableness and Sexy traits. When traits in each of these two factor are ordered by importance to the daughter (see Table 28.2), we found that the top ten sexy traits are all traits significantly more important to daughters, whereas there is no significant disagreement on any of the top ten Agreeableness traits.

The 35 traits ranked significantly differently by mothers and daughters suggested that mothers are seeking a relatively conscientious and hardworking partner for their daughter. The daughters more than the mothers prioritize traits that suggest sexy behavior or physical attractiveness. It should be noted that few of these traits were among the most important for either group, highlighting the fact that mostly mothers and daughters agree on this, as well as on the importance of commitment and agreeableness.

There are obvious surprises in the traits that mothers scored higher than the daughters: mothers prioritized "generous" more than did daughters, which fits our prediction of what motivates mothers. However, at the same time, it is considered that

generosity should be an attractive trait for daughters, too, as a part of general agreeableness. Mothers only rank "generous" in 66th place; daughters on the other hand rank it 112th of 133. "Sets Limits" is also an interesting trait. It might be interpreted that mothers are interested in their daughter finding someone who limits the daughter's behavior and thus providing a link between daughter-guarding (Perilloux et al., 2008) and mate-guarding (e.g., Flinn, 1988); female reproduction is guarded by male partners as well as mothers. Nevertheless, there is a clear image of a hardworking and conscientious ideal in the traits that mothers prioritize.

The top ten traits of each of these Agreeableness and Sexy scales were then used to create two scales of traits by averaging the scores on each of the ten traits that comprise the scale (see Table 28.2). The Agreeableness scale had a Cronbach's $\alpha = 0.908$. The Sexy traits scale had a Cronbach's $\alpha = 0.902$. A mixed design Analysis of Variance model with generations as between-subject factor and agreeable (direct) versus sexy (indirect) traits as within-subject factor showed that agreeableness is generally more important than sexiness ($F(1,158) = 469.93$, $p < 10^{-48}$, $\eta^2 = 0.748$). Generation interacted with the type of trait ($F(1,158) = 71.96$, $p < 10^{-13}$, $\eta^2 = 0.313$). Although we had expected mothers and daughters to differ in their interest in direct traits, they do not. Their scores on the Agreeableness traits scale are practically identical (Mothers, $M = 4.02$, $SD = 0.53$;

Table 28.2. Direct and indirect traits—two scales.

Agreeableness	Sexy traits
Thoughtful	Thrill-seeking
Caring	Seductive
Considerate	Sexy
Understanding	Exciting
Supportive	Handsome
Nice	Passionate
Cosy	Playful
Friendly	Cute
Sociable	Attractive
Likeable	Charming

Note: Traits that make up Agreeableness and Sexy traits scales, identified by selecting the top ten traits in the two components with highest explained variance from a Principal Components Extraction and Varimax Rotation of all of the traits.

Daughters, M = 4.03, SD = 0.55; $t(164)$ = 0.21, p = 0.828, Cohen's d = 0.03). However, daughters prioritize Sexy traits significantly higher than do mothers (Mothers, M = 2.55, SD = 0.66; Daughters, M = 3.39, SD = 0.54; $t(146.49)$ = −8.72, p <10^{-14}, Cohen's d = −1.38); see Figure 28.4.

Agreeableness is one of the typically universally agreed upon traits when considering a romantic partner (Buss, 1989). Some of the traits are also associated with the relational wealth definition given earlier (Borgerhoff Mulder & Beheim, 2011), and it would seem that mothers and daughters agree on the relevance of such traits. There were also clear differences between mothers' and daughters' priorities; daughters were clearly more interested in the more Sexy traits and Young Male Syndrome traits, some of which may represent both good genes and embodied wealth.

The mix of embodied and relational wealth-related traits that mother prioritize are clearly associated with the ability to convey direct benefits—benefits that also may be acquired by the mother and her other children. Some of the traits will increase the likelihood of acquiring resources, others will increase the likelihood of keeping deals and sharing, thus increasing the likelihood of the mother actually benefiting (see Table 28.3).

As reviewed earlier, the traits more important to daughters are typically indirect and markers of either Young Male Syndrome behavior, good genes, or socially and sexually exciting or stimulating behavior. The daughters thus prioritize indirect traits compared to the mothers, even when the task was explicitly to describe a long-term partner. We found strong support for most of our predictions: although

mothers and daughters agree on necessary traits for long-term relationships, daughters focus significantly more on short-term sex and indirect traits, and mothers focus more on traits that may confer direct benefits. This replicates most of the parallel research on this topic (Apostolou, 2007a, 2007b, 2008a, 2008b, Buunk et al., 2008; Dubbs & Buunk, 2010; Perilloux et al., 2011) (see Table 28.4).

We failed to replicate some aspects of previously published research. Both Apostolou (2007a) and Perilloux et al. (2011) found that parents saw "kind and understanding" as more important than did their offspring. In our study, these were two separate items, and mothers and daughters very much agreed on their importance. However, it should be noted that when Buunk et al. (2008) asked young people how unacceptable "unfriendly and unkind" was in a partner and how unacceptable they believed their parents would find that trait, there was no difference in Dutch, Kurdish, and American samples. Buunk and Castro Solano (2010) replicated these results with young Argentineans. Health was more important to parents in Perilloux et al.'s (2011) sample, but not in our study, nor in those of Apostolou (2007a), Buunk et al. (2008), or Buunk and Castro Solano (2010). Cues to parasite load should make indicators of good health more important (Fincher & Thornhill, 2012a, 2012b; Hamilton & Zuk, 1982; DeBruine, Little, & Jones, 2012; Feeley, Saad, Guay, & Traish, 2009; see later discussion), but why health should become more important to parents needs addressing. Health should be one of the indirect traits that are more important to the offspring. But health may be more relevant and a marker of material wealth in the United States versus Norway, whereas

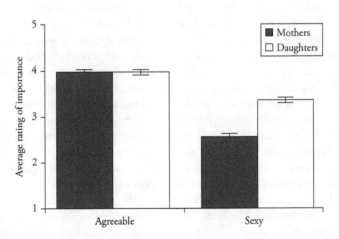

Figure 28.4 Mothers' and daughters' ratings of the Agreeableness vs. Sexy traits scales. Note: Mothers and daughters prioritize traits of agreeableness similarly. They both prioritize sexy traits lower than traits of agreeableness, but daughters prioritize sexy traits higher than mothers. All differences were significant.

Table 28.3. Traits that mothers rate significantly higher than daughters after Bonferroni correction.

| Trait | Daughters | | Mothers | | | |
	M	SD	M	SD	t	df
Clear	2.94	.83	3.65	.78	−5.670	164
Disciplined	2.63	.85	3.25	.79	−4.895	165
Emotionally Balanced	2.95	.88	3.76	.76	−6.262	163
Fair	3.40	1.03	4.33	.85	−6.304	164
Generous	2.69	.86	3.28	.79	−4.586	164
Hard Working	3.25	.77	4.00	.77	−6.368	168
Honourable	3.29	.89	4.24	.73	−7.406	161
Industrious	2.76	.97	3.41	.80	−4.655	160.81
Realistic	3.11	.91	3.68	.70	−4.575	164
Responsible	4.00	.76	4.50	.61	−4.725	167
Sets Limits	2.55	.86	3.24	.96	−4.926	164
Unafraid	2.40	.87	2.96	.83	−4.229	163
Up to Date	2.73	.94	3.35	.87	−4.437	166

Note: All t-tests are significant at $p < 0.05$ after Bonferroni correction for 133 tests.

young women would consider more concrete results of health on skin, appearance, and bodily constitution than an abstract concept of health.

Perilloux et al. (2011) proposed that parents consider religiosity important because parents seek cooperative alliances or social status. We instead suggest that religiosity might be a proxy for trustworthiness because conflicts among religions and denominations mean that parents would need to have more specific preferences than general religiosity if they wish to extend cooperative alliances. In the absence of questions regarding more specific preferences, alternative interpretations must be considered. Perilloux et al. collected their data in the United States, where atheists are distrusted (Edgell, Gerteis, & Hartmann, 2006; Gervais, Shariff, & Norenzayan, 2011). Religiosity in Perilloux et al.'s sample may have been a proxy for trustworthiness. However, our data do not support that speculation because mothers did not see trustworthiness as a more important trait than did their daughters. We have no data that could test Perilloux et al.'s proposal more directly because none of the 133 traits we examined had any clear connection to a man

being able to offer either alliances or status to the parents of his partner. Norway is mainly a secular society with very limited religious conflict (including rather limited conflict between believers and atheists).

On the whole, there is convergence in the different results, which makes it unlikely that selection bias distorted our findings. There is a valid concern that because we needed responses from both mothers and daughters, we sampled only those women with exceptionally good relationships across the generations and that the mothers therefore take a greater interest or apply different criteria than do mothers who are less close to their daughters. That our results converged with those from the other studies mentioned earlier, which only asked for the opinions of one generation and where this selection bias could not occur, speaks against selection bias distorting our results.

There are other potential limitations with the current findings. The return rate was low and may reflect nonrandom self-selection. The other limitation is that the difference between mothers and daughters might not be a behavioral expression of a

Table 28.4. Traits that daughters rate significantly higher than mothers after Bonferroni correction

Trait	Daughters		Mothers			
	M	SD	M	SD	t	df
Adventurous	3.15	.88	2.66	.85	3.675	165
Attractive	3.34	.81	2.65	.86	5.351	167
Beautiful	2.64	.87	1.99	.85	4.851	165
Charming	4.14	.80	3.14	.89	7.642	166
Cute	3.25	.87	2.22	1.07	6.830	165
Dreaming	2.56	1.05	1.83	.80	5.066	155.07
Entertaining	3.28	.91	2.60	.83	5.046	165
Exciting	3.51	.98	2.72	.85	5.511	164
Funny	4.05	.82	3.15	.91	6.762	168
Handsome	2.85	.84	2.26	.79	4.718	167
Horny	3.24	1.03	2.53	1.14	4.084	158
Humoristic	4.35	.72	3.87	.69	4.462	167
Masculine	3.38	1.06	2.71	.85	4.434	159.80
Passionate	3.82	.87	3.08	.95	5.256	162
Playful	3.55	.73	2.94	.94	4.719	166
Seductive	3.20	.94	2.28	1.11	5.724	156.80
Self-Confident	3.55	.76	3.04	.90	3.987	164
Sexy	3.39	.99	2.33	1.00	6.820	161
Smiling	3.94	.81	3.13	.91	6.106	166
Special	3.01	1.10	2.01	.94	6.325	165
Thrill Seeking	2.81	.94	2.07	.92	5.087	163
Wild	2.27	.94	1.49	.67	6.091	149.09

Note: All t-tests are significant at $p < 0.05$ after Bonferroni correction for 133 tests.

genetic conflict but merely a cohort effect in which older generations are, for example, more conservative (see also Perilloux et al., 2011). All previous studies that have considered parents and their children suffer from this same problem. We can exclude cohort effects only by examining the same genetic conflict within generations (Biegler & Kennair, 2016).

In sum, mothers and daughters have many overlapping tastes in partner for the daughter, but differ in predictable ways: the mothers prioritize direct traits—traits that will benefit her more than will indirect traits. The daughters prioritize indirect traits—traits that will benefit her offspring's fitness more than they can benefit her mother's fitness.

How Parent–Offspring Conflict May Drive Sibling Competition

We mentioned that the same genetic conflict that makes a mother favor partner choices that potentially can confer direct benefits to her than to her daughters should also make women nudge their sisters toward more directly beneficial choices (i.e., material wealth, relational wealth, and other traits that suggest potential direct benefits) than those sisters would prefer for themselves. Here, we examine theoretically how generational and sibling conflicts may interact based on the same logic of conflict between mothers and daughters.

The obvious objection would be that the findings reviewed in the preceding section are merely a generational effect. If they are not, though, one might predict that the same principles of choice will be operating for sisters as for mothers–daughters because the same genetic conflict exists. Just like the mothers, sisters will benefit more from their siblings' choosing partners based on direct traits. Furthermore, sisters should choose partners for themselves based on genetic quality and indirect effects, thus expanding the conflict between generations to a competition between sisters. Sisters presumably compete for the same or similar partners and wish to acquire a specific set of traits in their own choice of partner while strategically influencing their sister's choice to benefit their own fitness the most.

Another important effect of parents choosing a spouse for their offspring that we wish to focus on here is that this choice restricts the offspring's choices. If the parents want to cement an alliance by marrying off one of their daughters, they may not care greatly which daughter is involved. On the one hand, if the daughter chosen first resists strongly, it may be more trouble to make her comply to the satisfaction of her husband and his family than to hand over a more compliant daughter. On the other hand, if the husband is desirable, sisters may be competing for him. Intuitively, it would seem that the fewer choices there are, the more important it is to grab a good option or refuse a bad option. If so, then the more parents influence and control mate choice, thereby restricting the pool of potential mates, the more siblings should compete against each other. To be more precise, if parents reduce the choices available to their offspring, we can ask what the value is of making one more choice than the parents intended, regardless of whether that extra choice is snagging a good mate whom the parents intended for a sister or whether it is refusing a bad mate and making a sister take him.

Fortunately, Guttman (1960) already solved the problem as an exercise in probability theory. He phrased the problem as a lottery. Assume one can make n choices in a lottery where numbers are drawn from a normal distribution. Every time a number is presented, one may either accept or reject it and draw again until reaching n choices.

The optimal rule turns out to be to keep drawing new numbers until one of them is at least the value one may expect on average from n choices. The trick is to find that expected value. Guttman argued that refusing to draw gives nothing, and drawing only once gives, on average, the average of the distribution. Then, the more choices one has in reserve, the less likely it is that all future choices will be less than the first, and therefore the expected value will be greater. Guttman's equations indicate that the fewer choices there are, the greater the incremental benefit of an extra choice. That is consistent with our expectation that parental restrictions on their offspring's mate choices increase competition among siblings.

However, Guttman's lottery is analogous to a one-sided choice. If the prospective spouses have any influence at all over whom they will marry, then choice will be partially mutual. If choice has this mutual quality, then one's own mate value matters, too; not only to calibrate aspiration levels, but also to avoid the resentment of someone who feels that he or she could have acquired a better mate. We are not aware of any analysis that would permit us to calculate how much an extra choice is worth in these situations.

There is a possibility that there might be an additional effect of parental control: if the value of an extra choice depends on a woman's own mate value, then it is also possible that the value of an extra choice depends on how precise the information is that a woman has about her own mate value. It would then be in her interest to gather that information and in her parents' interest to prevent her from acquiring that knowledge. That would be an example of daughter-guarding (Perilloux et al., 2008), the increased tendency to prevent daughters from entering into or even considering any relationship but the one approved by her parents. If the value of an extra choice increases with more precise information, then parents can expect offspring's compliance to correlate positively with offspring's ignorance. Furthermore, parents' payoff for controlling their offspring's mate choices should increase the more unequal a society is and the more transferable resources there are that can be accumulated.

It follows from this argument that, despite there not being much evidence of this yet, the more parents influence and control mate choice, the more one should expect the daughters to evolve methods of influencing parental choice—and also compete with siblings via this influence of parental choice. These tactics need to be studied further. In short, if there are conflicting interests in partner choice and possibilities to influence choice, young women should have evolved a mating psychology designed to circumvent parental control or sibling influence.

The Possible Effects of Parasite Load

We already discussed how parental restrictions on mate choice should increase competition among sisters. We also expect that parasite load should have a variety of indirect effects. Recent work suggests that one might find increased intergenerational and intragenerational conflict in societies with higher parasite load than Norway (see Fincher & Thornhill, 2012a, including commentary and authors' responses). Building on Hamilton and Zuk's (1982) seminal work on parasite load and effects on behavior and mate choice, Fincher and Thornhill (2012b) suggested that high parasite stress has a major impact on human sociality because it favors limited dispersal from the natal locale, in-group favoritism, and out-group dislike, all to avoid picking up parasites from others. DeBruine, Little, and Jones (2012) applied these ideas to mate choice. If high testosterone signals resistance to pathogens, then preference for more masculine faces, which are a sign of high testosterone, should pay off when pathogen load is high. Feeley et al. (2009) reported that elevated testosterone is associated with better health, although not in parameters specifically associated with pathogen resistance. DeBruine et al. (2012) reanalyzed earlier research on health measures and preferred facial masculinity using Fincher and Thornhill's (2012a) new measures of parasite stress and found a significant positive relationship between parasite stress and women's preferences for masculine men in Western societies and within the United States. Lee and Zietsch (2011) add a nice bridge between the hypotheses of this chapter and DeBruine et al.'s (2012) findings, providing experimental evidence that women in a forced tradeoff task, after being primed with cues of parasite prevalence, prioritize indirect/genetic quality traits (Thornhill & Gangestad, 2008) rather than direct/parenting traits.

Furthermore, Chang, Lu, and Wu (2012) argue, based on data from the Ethnographic Atlas, that increased parasite stress will lead to a greater likelihood of matrilocality; that is, whether the postmarital residence is typically the female's place of origin, as opposed to patrilocal residence, where the woman moves to her husband's place of origin. If this is the case, mothers in such settings might have even greater interest in daughters' choices, compared to in patrilocal societies, because her daughter's mate will become part of the mother's household or village. An obvious consequence would be that increased matrilocality suggests increased generational conflict over daughters' choices of romantic partners.

The ideas suggested in this chapter ought to be tested across societies with different parasite loads, considering effects of both matrilocality and increased priority on physical attractiveness with increased parasite stress (Gangestad & Buss, 1993; Thornhill & Gangestad, 2008). The recent work on parasite stress suggests that the effects may be stronger in most other countries than Norway, given the low parasite load this far north.

Experimental interventions may also be possible, similar to those in Lee and Zietsch (2011), where priming participants with images of resource limitations or parasite prevalence may increase competition on the relevant dimensions. A more general argument that follows from parasite stress theory is that mate choice strategies have evolved to suit not just an average environment, but a range of environments. Therefore, for the range of environments experienced throughout evolutionary history, we should expect that suitable gene–environment interactions have evolved. Although Lee and Zietsch (2011) focus on plasticity, it is worth noting that they find predictable and systematic variation across the different experimental conditions. One line of theory development must therefore be to discover these gene–environment interactions and how they relate to competition.

Conclusion

Trivers (1974) predicted that genetic conflict driven by differential relatedness should play itself out not only in physiology, but also in behavior, such as parent–offspring and sibling conflict over parental investment. Conflict between parents and offspring over what makes a good mate for the offspring is another behavioral domain in which this conflict plays out. We focused here on the finding that mothers find it more important than do their daughters that the latter should choose a partner who can provide transferable resources. Daughters give greater priority to indicators of good genes, which benefit the daughters more than the mothers. At least, that is true in the more common case of the mother having influence over the daughter's choice. The work of Apostolou (2008a, 2008b) hints at symmetry; if a parent looks for a new partner and the offspring has an influence, then the offspring likewise values the transferable benefits more than the genetic benefits. We expect that indicators of parasite load should increase conflict between those who take a partner and those others who also want to benefit from that partner.

If parents and offspring can come into conflict not only over the parents' investment in their offspring, but also over the offspring's mate choice, then one should expect that sibling conflicts also generalize to the domain of mate choice. We have shown that parent–offspring conflict and sibling conflict should interact in the domain of mate choice: the more parents restrict their offspring's choices, the more intensely the offspring compete against each other for what the offspring consider the best mates from the set of choices that parents permit.

We focused in the introduction on the lack of clear evidence on how mothers influence daughters' choices and how daughters actually influence their parents' choice for them or their sisters. Apostolou (2013) has started considering these, but focuses to a large degree on male interventions. It is necessary for female kin to actually be able to influence their own and their kin's mate selection for these mechanisms to be able to evolve. Further research is needed to see how, for example, a woman may attempt to manipulate her parents, sisters, or other kin to choose the partner that she wants them to choose. Also, the conditions that predict the use of specific interventions remain unknown.

An important and interesting consequence of this area of research, which Apostolou (2007b) pointed out from the start and that is still not fully understood, is that this has consequences for current female mating psychology. Women probably have evolved mechanisms for competing with sisters and avoiding the influence of parents and other kin. How does this influence mainstream mate choice research and modern female mate choice and sexual behavior in societies with limited possibilities for parents or other kin to exert influence on her choice or behavior?

What we have suggested theoretically and reported data on in this chapter may be a general model for conflicts between family members and especially female kin. We expect that patterns similar to those we found between mothers and daughters will be found between sisters. There are several possible ecological features, though, that may drive the relative worth of direct or indirect traits, such as embodied, relational, and material wealth (e.g., Biegler & Kennair, 2016; Borgerhoff Mulder et al., 2009) and that will differ from ecology to ecology.

Acknowledgments

Thanks to Mons Bendixen, Steven Gangestad, Trond Viggo Grøntvedt, Gerit Pfuhl, Ingvild Saksvik-Lehoullier, Gine Skjærvø, and anonymous reviewers for helpful comments to earlier versions of this chapter. Thanks to Håkon Tjelmeland for pointing us in the right direction on the maths.

References

Apicella, C. L., & Marlowe F. W. (2005). Men's reproductive investment decisions. *Human Nature, 18*(1), 22–34.

Apostolou, M. (2007a). Elements of parental choice: The evolution of parental preferences in relation to in-law selection. *Evolutionary Psychology, 5*, 70–83.

Apostolou, M. (2007b). Sexual selection under parental choice: The role of parents in the evolution of human mating. *Evolution and Human Behavior, 28*, 403–409.

Apostolou, M. (2008a). Parent-offspring conflict over mating: The case of beauty. *Evolutionary Psychology, 6*(2), 303–315.

Apostolou, M. (2008b). Parent-offspring conflict over mating: The case of family background. *Evolutionary Psychology, 6*, 456–468.

Apostolou, M. (2009). Parent-offspring conflict over mating: The case of short-term mating strategies. *Personality and Individual Differences, 47*, 895–899.

Apostolou, M. (2010a). Parent-offspring conflict over mating: The case of mating age. *Evolutionary Psychology, 8*(3), 365–375.

Apostolou, M. (2010b). Sexual selection under parental choice in agropastoral societies, *Evolution and Human Behavior, 31*, 39–47.

Apostolou, M. (2013). Do as we wish: Parental tactics of mate choice manipulation. *Evolutionary Psychology, 11*(4), 795–813.

Baumeister, R. F., & Vohs, K. D. (2004). Sexual economics: Sex as female resource for social exchange in heterosexual interactions. *Personality and Social Psychology Review, 8*, 339–363.

Bellis, M. A., Hughes. K., Hughes, S., & Ashton, J. R. (2005). Measuring paternal discrepancy and its public health consequences. *Journal of Epidemiology and Community Health, 59*, 749–754.

Bendixen, M., & Kennair, L. E. O. (2014). Revisiting judgment of strategic self-promotion and competitor derogation tactics. *Journal of Social and Personal Relationships.* doi: 10.1177/0265407514558959

Bendixen, M., Kennair, L. E. O., Ringheim, H. K., Isaksen, L., Pedersen, L., Svangtun, S., & Hagen, K. (2015). In search of moderators of sex differences in forced-choice jealousy responses: Effects of 2D:4D digit ratio and relationship infidelity experiences. *Nordic Psychology,* 1-13. doi: 10.1080/19012276.2015.1013975

Biegler, R., & Kennair, L. E. O. (2016). Sisterly love: Within-generation differences in ideal partner for sister and self. *Evolutionary Behavioral Sciences, 10*(1), 29–42. doi:10.1037/ebs0000060

Bikhchandani, S., Hirshleifer, D., & Welch, I. (1998), Learning from the behavior of others: Conformity, fads, and informational cascades. *Journal of Economic Perspectives, 12*(3), 151–170.

Bishop, D. I., Meyer, B. C., Schmidt, T. M., & Gray, B. R. (2009). Differential investment behaviour between grandparents and grandchildren: The role of paternal uncertainty. *Evolutionary Psychology, 7*(1), 66–77.

Borgerhoff Mulder, M., & Beheim, B. A. (2011). Understanding the nature of wealth and its effects on human fitness. *Philosophical Transactions of the Royal Society B, 366*(1563), 344–356. doi: 10.1098/rstb.2010.0231

Borgerhoff Mulder, M., Bowles, S., Hertz, T., Bell, A., Beise, J., Clark, G., ... Wiessner, P. (2009). Intergenerational wealth transmission and the dynamics of inequality in small-scale societies. *Science, 326*(5953), 682–688. doi: 10.1126/science.1178336

Burt, A., & Trivers, R. (1998). Genetic conflicts in genomic imprinting. *Proceedings of the Royal Society B, 265,* 2393–2397.

Buss, D. M. (1989). Sex differences in human mate preferences: Evolutionary hypotheses tested in 37 cultures. *Behavioral & Brain Sciences, 12,* 1–49.

Buss, D. M., & Barnes, M. L. (1986). Preferences in human mate selection. *Journal of Personality and Social Psychology, 50,* 559–570.

Buss, D. M., & Haselton, M. G. (2005). The evolution of jealousy. *Trends in Cognitive Science, 9,* 506–507.

Buss, D. M., & Schmitt, D. P. (1993). Sexual strategies theory: A contextual evolutionary analysis of human mating. *Psychological Review, 100,* 204–232.

Buunk, A. P., Park, J. H., & Dubbs, S. L. (2008). Parent–offspring conflict in mate preferences. *Review of General Psychology, 12,* 47–62.

Buunk, A. P., Park, J. H., & Duncan, L. A. (2010). Cultural variation in parental influence on mate choice. *Cross-Cultural Research, 44*(1), 23–40. doi: 10.1177/1069397109337711

Buunk, A. P., & Castro Solano, A. (2010). Conflicting preferences of parents and offspring over a mate: A study in Argentina. *Journal of Family Psychology 24*(4), 391–399.

Cattanach, B. M., Beechey, C. V., & Peters, J. (2004). Interactions between imprinting effects in the mouse. *Genetics, 168,* 397–413.

Chang, L., Lu, H. J., & Wu, B. P. (2012). Pathogens promote matrilocal family ties and the copying of foreign religions. *Behavioral and Brain Sciences, 35,* 61–79.

Coontz, S. (2004). The world historical transformation of marriage. *Journal of Marriage and Family, 66*(4), 974–979.

Daly, M., & Wilson, M. (1988). *Homicide.* New York: Aldine de Gruyter.

Daly, M., & Wilson, M. (1998). *The truth about Cinderella: A Darwinian view of parental love.* London: Weidenfeld & Nicolson.

Davidson, D. Z. (2012). "Happy" marriages in early nineteenth-century France. *Journal of Family History, 37*(1), 23–35. doi: 10.1177/0363199011428123

Dawkins, R., & Krebs, J. R. (1979). Arms races between and within species. *Proceedings of the Royal Society B, 205,* 489–511.

DeBruine, L., Little, A. C., & Jones, B. C. (2012). Extending parasite-stress theory to variation in human mate preferences. *Behavioral and Brain Sciences, 35,* 61–79.

Dubbs, S. L., & Buunk, A. P. (2010). Parents just don't understand: Parent-offspring conflict over mate choice. *Evolutionary Psychology, 8,* 586–598.

Edgell, P., Gerteis, J., & Hartmann, D. (2006). Atheists as "other": Moral boundaries and membership in American society. *American Sociological Review, 71,* 211–234.

Feeley, R. J., Saad, F., Guay, A., & Traish A. M. (2009). Testosterone in men's health: A new role for an old hormone. *Journal of Men's Health 6*(3), 169–176.

Fincher, C. L., & Thornhill, R. (2012a). Parasite-stress promotes in-group assortative sociality: The cases of strong family ties and heightened religiosity. *Behavioral and Brain Sciences, 35,* 61–79.

Fincher, C. L., & Thornhill, R. (2012b). The parasite-stress theory may be a general theory of culture and sociality (authors' response to commentators). *Behavioral and Brain Sciences, 35,* 99–119.

Fisher, M., & Cox, A. (2010). Four strategies used during intrasexual competition for mates. *Personal Relationships, 18*(1), 20–38. doi: 10.1111/j.1475-6811.2010.01307.x

Fisher, M., Cox, A., & Gordon, F. (2009). Self-promotion versus competitor derogation: The influence of sex and romantic relationship status on intrasexual competition strategy selection. *Journal of Evolutionary Psychology, 7,* 287–308.

Flinn, M. V. (1988). Mate guarding in a Caribbean village. *Ethology and Sociobiology, 9,* 1–28.

Gangestad, S. W., & Buss, D. M. (1993). Pathogen prevalence and human mate preferences. *Ethology and Sociobiology, 14,* 89–96.

Gangestad, S. W., & Simpson, J. A. (2000). The evolution of human mating: Trade-offs and strategic pluralism. *Behavioral and Brain Sciences, 23,* 573–644.

Gervais, W. M., Shariff, A. F., & Norenzayan, A. (2011). Do you believe in atheists? Distrust is central to anti-atheist prejudice. *Journal of Personality and Social Psychology, 6,* 1189–1206.

Giraldeau, L. A., Valone, T. J., & Templeton, J. J. (2002). Potential disadvantages of using socially acquired information. *Philosophical Transactions of the Royal Society B, 357,* 1559–1566. doi: 10.1098/rstb.2002.1065

Guttman, I. (1960). On a problem of L. Moser. *Canadian Mathematical Bulletin, 3,* 35–39.

Haig, D. (1997). Parental antagonism, relatedness asymmetries, and genomic imprinting. *Proceedings of the Royal Society B, 264,* 1657–1662.

Hamilton, W. D. & Zuk, M. (1982). Heritable true fitness and bright birds: A role for parasites? *Science, 218,* 384-387. doi: 10.1126/science.7123238

Harcourt, A. H., Harvey, P. H., Larson, S. G., & Short, R. V. (1981). Testis weight, body weight and breeding system in primates. *Nature, 293,* 55–57.

Havlicek, J., & Roberts, S. C. (2009). MHC-correlated mate choice in humans: A review. *Psychoneuroendocrinology, 34,* 497–512.

Henrich, J., Boyd, R., & Richerson, P. J. (2012). The puzzle of monogamous marriage. *Philosophical Transactions of the Royal Society B, 367,* 657–669.

Kennair, L. E. O., Nordeide, J., Andreassen, S., Strønen, J., & Pallesen, S. (2011). Sex differences in jealousy: A study from Norway. *Nordic Psychology, 63*(1), 20–34. doi: 10.1027/1901-2276/a000025

Kennair, L. E. O., Schmitt, D., Fjeldavli, Y. L, & Harlem, S. K. (2009). Sex differences in sexual desires and attitudes in Norwegian samples. *Interpersona, 3* (Suppl. 1), 1–32.

Kokko, H. (1998). Should advertising parental care be honest? *Proceedings of the Royal Society B, 265,* 1871–1878.

Larmuseau, M., Vanoverbeke, J., Van Geystelen, A., Defraene, G., Vanderheyden, N., Matthijs, K., ...Decorte, R. (2013).

Low historical rates of cuckoldry in a Western European human population traced by Y-chromosome and genealogical data. *Proceedings of the Royal Society B, 280*, article no. 20132400.

Lee, A. J., & Zietsch, B. P. (2011). Experimental evidence that women's mate preferences are directly influenced by cues of pathogen prevalence and resource scarcity. *Biology Letters, 7*, 892–895.

Li, N. P., Bailey, J. M., Kenrick, D. T., & Linsenmeier, J. A. W. (2002). The necessities and luxuries of mate preferences: Testing the tradeoffs. *Journal of Personality and Social Psychology, 82*, 947–955.

Meston, C., & Buss, D. M. (2007). Why humans have sex. *Archives of Sexual Behavior, 36*, 477–507.

Perilloux, C., Fleischman, D. S., & Buss, D. M. (2008). The daughter-guarding hypothesis: Parental influence on, and emotional reactions to, offspring's mating behavior. *Evolutionary Psychology, 6*, 217–233.

Perilloux, C., Fleischman, D. S., & Buss, D. M. (2011). Meet the parents: Parent-offspring convergence and divergence in mate preferences. *Personality and Individual Differences, 50*, 253–258.

Place, S. S., Todd, P. M., Penke, L., & Asendorpf, J. B. (2010). Humans show mate copying after observing real mate choices. *Evolution and Human Behavior, 31*, 320–325.

Rieucau, G., & Giraldeau, L.-A. (2009). Persuasive companions can be wrong: The use of misleading social information in nutmeg mannikins. *Behavioral Ecology, 20*(6), 1217–1222. doi: 10.1093/beheco/arp121

Scelza B. A. (2011). Female choice and extra-pair paternity in a traditional human population. *Biological Letters, 7*, 889–891.

Schmitt, D. P., & Buss, D. M. (1996). Strategic self-promotion and competitor derogation: Sex and context effects on the perceived effectiveness of mate attraction tactics. *Journal of Personality and Social Psychology, 70*(6), 1185–1204. doi: 10.1037/0022-3514.70.6.1185

Shenk, M. K., & Scelza, B. A. (2011). Paternal investment and status-related child outcomes: Timing of father's death affects offspring success. *Journal of Biosocial Science, 44*(5), 549–569. doi: 10.1017/S0021932012000053

Stanik, C., Kurzban, R., & Ellsworth, P. (2010). Rejection hurts: The effect of being dumped on subsequent mating efforts. *Evolutionary Psychology, 8*(4), 682–694

Tapscott, R. (2012). *Understanding breast "ironing": A study of the methods, motivations, and outcomes of breast flattening practices in Cameroon.* Retrieved from http://fic.tufts.edu/assets/Understanding-breast-flattening.pdf

Thornhill, R., & Gangestad, S. W. (2008). *The evolutionary biology of human female sexuality.* New York: Oxford University Press.

Trivers, R. L. (1972). Parental investment and sexual selection. In B. Campbell (Ed.), *Sexual selection and the descent of man, 1871–1971* (pp. 136–179). Chicago: Aldine.

Trivers, R. L. (1974). Parent-offspring conflict. *American Zoologist, 14*, 249–264.

United Nations Development Programme. (2010). *Human development report 2010.* New York: Palgrave Macmillan.

Voracek, M., Haubner, T., & Fisher, M. L. (2008). Recent decline in nonpaternity rates: A cross-temporal meta-analysis. *Psychological Reports, 103*, 799–811.

Waynforth. D. (1999). Differences in time use for mating and nepotistic effort as a function of male attractiveness in rural Belize. *Evolution and Human Behavior, 20*, 19–28.

Wilson, M., & Daly, M. (1985). Competitiveness, risk-taking and violence: The young male syndrome. *Ethology and Sociobiology, 6*, 59–73.

Woelfing, B., Traulsen, A., Milinski, M., & Boehm, T. (2009). Does intra-individual major histocompatibility complex diversity keep a golden mean? *Philosophical Transactions of the Royal Society B, 364*, 117–128.

Darwinian Perspectives on Women's Progenicide

Alita J. Cousins *and* Theresa Porter

Abstract

Evolutionary perspectives on infanticide suggest that women kill their offspring under specific circumstances: for instance, when children have low fitness, when women are young and unpartnered, when they have older children, and when the birth spacing is too close. Infanticide may also serve as a way to increase women's ability to compete for access to mates, especially when the mating market has a surplus of males. Under these circumstances, to stay intrasexually competitive, unpartnered women are more likely to commit infanticide, indicating that women may sometimes kill their infants as a mechanism to be able to compete for access to better mates. This may be especially true for young women. Stepmothers may also abuse or kill stepchildren to increase access to a mate and increase intrasexual competition. This chapter addresses the circumstances under which mothers abuse, neglect, and kill their offspring, including how intrasexual competition may increase infanticide.

Key Words: infanticide, progenicide, intrasexual competition, women, mothers, evolutionary

Cherlie LaFleur, a 19-year-old high school student, recently gave birth in the girl's bathroom at school. LaFleur reportedly tried to flush the premature child down the toilet; when this failed, she resorted to placing her baby in the bathroom garbage can. Due to the degree of prematurity, the police are unsure if the baby was born alive or if it was stillborn (NYdailymail.com). Regardless, this young mother ensured that her child would not live to see another day by shoving it in a garbage can. Although stories like this are horrifying by most standards, they happen with some degree of regularity. Does killing a child—especially one's own child—ever make sense?

Introduction

From a societal perspective, killing one's own child is unthinkable. In Western society children are usually nurtured and protected as valued members of the family. Yet the single most dangerous day in a person's life—in terms of being

murdered by another individual—is on the day he or she is born, and the most dangerous person to be near on that first day of life is the very person who gave him or her life: the baby's mother (d'Orban, 1979).

On the surface, a Darwinian perspective seems to suggest that parents benefit from investing heavily in children because children bear their parents' genes and thus offspring increase their parents' reproductive success (Trivers, 1972). From this standpoint, mistreatment of offspring, and certainly killing an offspring, seem to be counter to increasing parents' reproductive success. However, we argue that killing one's own offspring may be functional, at least sometimes. While survival and reproduction are paramount in evolution, there are specific circumstances under which killing children (one's own or those of others) could be a viable strategy to increase reproductive success. This chapter outlines those circumstances.

Strictly speaking, neonaticide is the intentional killing of a newborn within 24 hours of birth (Resnick, 1972). This is by far the most common age when children are killed. Research on homicides suggests that 45% of murdered children are less than 24 hours old (d'Orban, 1979). Infanticide is the deliberate killing of a child under the age of one. While infanticide is less prevalent than neonaticide, infants older than 24 hours are more frequently killed by their fathers, while infants younger than 24 hours old are more likely to be killed by their mothers (Marks, 2009). Other research indicates that during the first week of life, mothers are the most likely perpetrator and between 8 days of life and age 12, mothers and fathers are equally likely to be the perpetrators (Kunz & Bahr, 1996). "Filicide" is a more general term for the direct killing of a child by a parent, and it is frequently used when children are over one year old when they are killed (Camperio Ciani & Fontanesi, 2012).

Although there are many cases of parents directly killing their young children, sometimes parents act in a less direct manner to aid in the death of their child. "Deferred infanticide" (sometimes referred to as "delayed infanticide") is a term used to describe behaviors that ultimately lead to the death of offspring, although children are not directly killed. For instance, parents may not adequately supervise their children, which results in the child's death. Other types of delayed infanticide include placing children in danger or failing to provide enough food for a child when there is adequate food available (Brewis, 1992). Relatedly, some researchers use the term "progenicide" to refer to behaviors that reduce the likelihood that offspring will survive (Burgess, Kurland, & Pensky, 1988). Progenicide may not always result in the child's death, but it certainly increases the chance that the child will succumb to accidents or illness (see, e.g, Levine, 1987). We argue that there is a continuum of parental maltreatment of children, from underinvestment in children (e.g., early weaning) to infanticide, and that under some circumstances parents benefit from employing these strategies. For this reason, we use the term "progenicide" because it refers to varying degrees of parental investment that may result in the death of a parent's offspring.

In this chapter we argue that progenicide is an evolutionary adaptation that occurs under specific instances to increase the reproductive success of the mother. For instance, we argue that mothers are more likely to kill their infants when they (a) are young, (b) are unpartnered, (c) do not have family support, (d) have children close in age, and (e) do not have enough resources. We also argue that, in some instances, progenicide may be a means to increase a woman's ability to compete with other women for access to mates. We discuss how a sex ratio in which there are fewer men than women increases women's intrasexual competition. Under these circumstances, when a woman has a child, it decreases her prospects of finding a long-term partner. Some women may commit progenicide to increase their intrasexual competiveness. We end the chapter with suggestions for future research on this topic.

Minimum Investment in Offspring and Progenicide

For mammals, reproduction is a costly investment of time and energy. In humans, gestation takes nine months, which is considerably longer than our fellow primates, whose gestation lasts five to seven months. Unlike men, women can produce a relatively small number of offspring to act as vehicles for their genes, and women must do so during a shorter number of years because of menopause. Lactation is a further demand on the mother's body. One study of women from traditional societies found that the average age for weaning was 30.9 months (Kelly, 1995). Breastfeeding a baby for this length of time is calorically taxing, but long periods of lactation probably increase the child's chances of survival. Not all women are willing to invest this amount of energy into a child, and reducing breastfeeding to a very short period of time may be a form of progenicide.

Together, pregnancy and lactation may use 100,000 calories above a woman's own metabolic needs. Following weaning, there is a protracted period during which human offspring remain vulnerable and dependent, since humans have a late pubertal maturation compared to many other mammals. Historically, women rather than men have been responsible for providing much of the early investment in offspring, and cessation of maternal care in the first two years of a child's life (through maternal death, for instance) significantly increases the likelihood of a child dying. For example, in an analysis of maternal and paternal deaths among the Tsimane of Bolivia, researchers showed that if a child's mother died before the child reached one year of age, there was a 169% increase in the odds that the child would die compared to a child whose mother was living. While the death of a father affected the likelihood that a child would die, it had a much smaller impact than the death of a mother. When a child was between ages one and four, the death of a father increased the odds of the child dying by 3.6%. This was the only time period that the death of a father was important for a child's survival among the Tsimane (Winkling, Gurven, & Kaplan, 2011).

Humans have faced resource scarcity recurrently throughout their evolutionary history. Giving birth when resources are scarce may be detrimental to women, who expend so many calories during pregnancy and lactation. Delayed reproduction may help offset the risk of poor pregnancy timing, and research shows that ovulation suppression occurs when there are circumstances that lead to reduced food intake (Lunn, 1985). For instance, it is well known that ballerinas and long-distance runners, who have very lean body mass, frequently are anovulatory (Lunn, 1985). It is likely that weight loss, both now and throughout our evolutionary history, was a signal to shut down ovulation to reduce the chance of investing in offspring unlikely to survive when conditions are poor. Research indicates that when women lose weight, they may not always ovulate. Nepali women frequently lose weight during monsoon season, and hormonal analysis revealed that only 38% of reproductive-aged women ovulated during monsoon, compared with ovulation rates of 71% during winter (Panter-Brick, Lotstein, & Ellison, 1993). Among the Lese of Zaire, women had seasonal weight fluctuations due to food availability. During the seasons that women lose weight, there were fewer conceptions (Ellison, 2003). Breastfeeding also suppresses ovulation, especially when women are very lean and breastfeed at night (Lunn, 1985). These physiological responses to weight loss reduce the chance of conception but are imperfect, and sometimes pregnancy results even when the timing is poor.

Competition between women for access to resources may be much greater during seasons when there are net imbalances in energy. This may be particularly true for young women, who are in greater conflict for access to mates. One might expect partnered women, especially those whose mates are poor providers, to pursue extra-pair partners when the net payoff is higher—as during seasonal food shortages. Women who are more intrasexually competitive may be able to secure a mate who is a better provider, which would impact their reproductive success. Women whose partners are good providers may need to use more mate-retention strategies to decrease the chance of their partners pursuing an extra-pair partner. These expected results are dampened in Western cultures where food availability is abundant and rarely are there seasonal shortages. We know of no research to date that explores these ideas.

When a poorly timed pregnancy results and women already have older children, parental investment theory suggests that women should focus their investment on older offspring rather than neonates (Trivers, 1972). Older children represent several years of investment in terms of time, food, and energy, and therefore older children have higher parental investment value compared to a newborn, since a newborn represents only nine months of investment. An older offspring who has already survived the most dangerous part of childhood (e.g., illnesses are a frequent cause of death in the first two years of life) has higher fitness relative to a newborn. Newborns must still pass through years of risk and costs to the mother before reaching reproductive age. In some circumstances, when killing a newborn greatly improves an older child's fitness, progenicide may be a functional strategy that enhances a mother's overall reproductive success. For example, during famines, a woman with an infant and at least one older child may kill the infant so that she can provide enough resources for her older child, who is more likely to survive during food scarcity. Although there is no systematic research on this issue, *The Washington Post* recently reported that in North Korea during famines, people not only kill a child but reportedly cannibalize these children as well (Washingtonpost.com). Younger and sicker children are those most likely targeted.

Life History Theory and Progenicide

At its most basic level, evolution is about having more genes represented in future generations. While evolution might seem to indicate that parents should always invest all of their energy and resources into their children, parental investment is about tradeoffs due to the reality of finite resources, time, and energy (Voland, 1998). Effort spent on parenting is not available for somatic effort, including the organism's own growth and maintenance. Throughout their evolutionary history, humans frequently lived with resource scarcity and disease, which indicate that people may—at times— preferentially invest in somatic effort at the cost of investing in offspring. In addition, effort invested in parenting is not available for mating and vice versa (Bjorklund & Shackelford, 1999). For these reasons, all organisms, humans included, develop "strategies" to allocate resources for the optimal outcome of their investment. These strategies must take into account the organism's age, health, and resources, as well as the age, health, and expected resource attainment of potential mates, the health of current offspring, and future reproductive opportunities (Voland, 1998).

Life history theory "generally concerns the evolutionary forces that shape the timing of life events involved in development, growth, reproduction and aging" (Kaplan & Gangestad, 2005, p. 69). The "age schedules" of mortality and fertility are influenced by the local environment, so what is optimal may vary between individuals, across time, or across cultures (Kaplan & Gangestad, 2005, p. 69). Since there is a finite amount of energy available to invest in these activities, tradeoffs occur between present and future reproduction, in the quantity and quality of offspring, and in investment in mating effort versus parenting effort (Kaplan & Gangestad, 2005). These are all relevant in considering child maltreatment and murder.

Current Versus Future Reproduction

The tradeoff between present and future reproduction occurs because reproduction requires energy that cannot be put into other types of maintenance activities. Individuals, therefore, can put effort into tasks like their own growth, repair, and predator reduction, or they can allocate energy to producing offspring. Opportunity costs occur because the time and energy put into one task (e.g., growth) cannot be put into another activity (e.g., reproduction; Kaplan & Gangestad, 2005). What this means is that reproducing *now* incurs the potential cost of *future* reproduction. As an example, a 15-year-old girl can put energy into growth, but if she becomes pregnant, energy must be diverted from her own growth to that of her fetus. Under most circumstances, delaying reproduction until growth is fully realized maximizes fitness (Kramer & Greaves, 2010). Among the Pumé, a hunter-gatherer group in South America, girls generally have their first offspring at a young age (15.5; Kramer & Greaves, 2010). This development is striking when compared to the !Kung, where women reach menarche between 15 and 17 and generally do not have their first birth until they are between 18 and 22 years old due to being subfertile for a number of years (Lee, 1980). Research indicates that starting reproduction early maximizes the reproductive success of Pumé women. What is so interesting here is that Pumé girls expend more energy in skeletal growth

in their early development than girls in other places, which allows them to reach (or almost reach) their full height before beginning reproduction. By growing before they reach sexual maturity, they are able to offset the cost of early reproduction; thus women's life history strategy in this resource-poor area with high infant mortality is modified in ways that mean they do not face the competing demands of growth and reproduction at the same time (Kramer & Greaves, 2010).

Another trait that is affected by life history is age at menarche, which is sensitive to cues that the environment is risky. As Ellis, McFadyen-Ketchum, Dodge, Pettit, and Bates (1999) and Ellis and Garber (2000) show, father absence, presence of a stepfather, conflict within the family, and a poor father–daughter relationship are all associated with earlier menarche.

Another potential problem between investing in current versus future reproduction occurs when women have too many offspring too close together. This may result in maternal depletion, which increases infant and maternal mortality (Conde-Agudelo & Belizán 2000; King 2003). We expect that progenicide is tightly linked with current versus future reproduction: when current reproduction is too costly in terms of future reproduction, we expect progenicide to increase.

Quantity Versus Quality of Children

As Trivers (1972) noted, parents face tradeoffs in their investment in offspring. Many resources cannot be shared by siblings (e.g., food), so investing in one offspring may occur at the cost of investing in other offspring. Total investment must be spread between each additional sibling. Parents face choices, invest more heavily in fewer offspring, and focus on raising high-quality offspring, or focus on producing a higher number of offspring but invest relatively fewer resources in each additional child (Kaplan & Gangestad, 2005). This relationship is often referred to as a quantity versus quality tradeoff. Boone and Kessler (1999) noticed that some families tend to have many children and other families to have just a few children. They hypothesized that status striving, investing resources into attaining status and power, as well as signaling this high status to others, may play a role in increasing reproductive success during catastrophes. They mathematically modeled what happens during bottleneck years (e.g., if there is a famine and many people die) for those families that have few versus many children. They found that, in the short run, large families have higher reproductive success, but after a calamity, small families had higher reproductive success (with the assumption that these calamities happen with relative frequency and that the small families have higher reproductive success during the bottleneck). Based on their mathematical modeling of calamities and the effects on small and large families, Boon and Kessler (1999) noted

> Now, the idea that high-status families might sacrifice numbers of offspring to preserve or increase social status would seem antithetical to the position that the primary fitness benefit of high social status is increased lifetime reproductive success. If, however, the advantage of high rank is more closely tied to a separate component of fitness, that of long-term lineage survival through calamities, as we argued earlier, the effect of "status anxiety" is much easier to understand. (p. 274)

This finding suggests that some women, especially high-status women, may be especially likely to try to reduce the number of offspring in order to maintain their resources and status. There is evidence for this prediction; for example, starting around 1 AD, upper-class Romans limited the number of children through abortion, infanticide, and abandonment. Limiting reproduction appears to be motivated by efforts to maintain power and status (Dixon, 1988, as cited in Boone & Kessler, 1999). In societies with a class structure, women may compete with other women more for access to high-status and wealthy males; women who marry wealthy males may also strive to maintain their status by limiting reproduction through abortion or other means, much like the ancient Romans.

In addition, women are expected to assess the fitness prospects of each child and potentially kill a child who has low fitness. This may include progenicide of children of a particular sex (e.g., killing female children when boys are expected to have higher fitness), progenicide of sickly or premature infants, and progenicide of deformed infants.

Investment in Parenting Versus Mating Effort

Life history theory suggests that the time and energy that must be allocated to parenting occur at a cost in the ability to invest in seeking a mate (Kaplan & Gangestad, 2005). Due to the inherent tradeoff between parenting and mating effort, we predict that women who do not have an established pair bond will be more likely to forego parenting in favor of mating effort; women without a mate should be more intrasexually competitive. Unpartnered women may commit neonaticide to release themselves from parenting effort. This reallocation of effort may be especially true for attractive women, who may be more valued in the mating market and therefore more likely to be able to secure a good-quality mate, one who will invest resources in the woman and her future offspring. For attractive women, there may be more benefits from waiting for a better mate; she may have more offspring, better-quality offspring, or more surviving offspring by waiting for a better partner.

Given the inherent tradeoffs in how energy is used, all of the life history factors listed here must be assessed by women in order to make the best use of finite resources to maximize their reproductive success (Hill & Low, 1992). Women should consider whether reproducing now or in the future will yield a better payoff for them. Women also need to consider whether they should invest more resources in fewer children or invest fewer resources in any one child but have many children. Women also need to decide whether parenting or mating effort will yield a better outcome. The factors involved in the decision to invest in mating effort probably depend on the local mating market and the woman's assessment of her own chances for success in comparison to those of other women.

Summary and Predictions

In sum, based on the theories of parental investment and life history theory, progenicide is predicted to be more likely to occur in specific situations that improve the mother's reproductive success. We propose that progenicide is more likely to occur under the following circumstances:

1. When the cost of current reproduction is higher than delaying reproduction. Specifically

   a. When offspring are spaced too closely together to allow adequate parental investment in both children.

   b. When mothers are young and have more time in the future to reproduce.

   c. When there is a lack of paternal support and investment.

   d. When women lack family support and investment.

   e. When women are poor or lack other essential resources to support a child.

2. When women can expect an increase in reproductive success from putting more effort into mating rather than parenting. This may be especially true for young, attractive women, who are most able to attain a better mate by postponing reproduction—in other words, women who are more intrasexually competitive. These women may benefit by pursuing a mate who will have better genetic quality and thus enhance their reproductive success.

3. When offspring fitness is low. Specifically, sickly, premature, or deformed infants will be most at risk.

Limiting a Costly Investment

Since parenting effort is prolonged and intensive in humans, mothers should limit their investment in unwanted offspring. Research on progenicide provides significant support to parental investment and life history theory predictions. Filicide risk decreases as children age, and children most at risk of death at the hands of their mothers are infants and neonates (Friedman, Cavney, & Resnick, 2012b; Herman-Giddens, Smith, Mittal, Carlson, & Butts, 2003). Children younger than one year old are at four times greater risk of homicide than the general population (Marks & Kumar, 1993). In a study of fatal child neglect, the majority of the victims were under one year old (Creighton, 1985; Margolin, 1990). In support of the idea that neglect is a mechanism to reduce investment in an unwanted child—and that neglect should be more common for younger children—research shows that the incidence of neglect decreases as children grow older (Mraovich & Wilson, 1999). Brookman and Nolan (2006) reviewed records for 298 progenicide cases from England and Wales from 1995 to 2002 and reported that infants under one year old were murdered at a rate of 6.3 per 100,000 (in comparison, 24-year-olds had a homicide rate of 3.3 per 100,000). This pattern of infanticide is not only true in Western cultures. In Japan, infants under the age of one are at the highest risk of being killed compared to all other children ages 15 and younger (Yasumi & Kageyama, 2009).

Newborns are far more at risk of being killed by a mother than by a father or other person (Friedman, Cavney, & Resnick, 2012a; McKee, 2006; Porter & Gavin, 2010). As briefly reviewed already, this finding is not surprising in light of the relatively larger investment mothers must make in comparison to fathers. Mothers, more so than fathers,

should decide early whether to invest in offspring because of the heavy caloric burden of lactation. In a study in Turkey, children under the age of 12 were more likely to be killed by their mother while those between 12 and 18 were more likely to be killed by their father (Karakus, Ince, Ince, Arican, & Sozen, 2003). In addition, as stated before, the first week of life represents the largest risk of maternal progenicide (Kunz & Bahr, 1996).

Progenicide When the Costs of Current Reproduction Are Higher Than Future Reproduction

In this section we provide an overview of the factors that increase progenicide when the costs of current reproduction are higher than the costs of reproducing at some point in the future. Variables such as the interbirth interval, the age of the mother, a lack of support from a partner, the mother's own parents or the community, and resource uncertainty all play a role in increasing progenicide.

Birth Spacing

When births happen in quick succession, life history theory predicts an increased risk of progenicide. Under these circumstances, women may not be able to invest enough resources in an infant if she has another child who still needs heavy investment (e.g., if she has a toddler). In a study involving cases sent to the child abuse registers in the United Kingdom, researchers discovered that abused children had larger numbers of siblings (Creighton, 1985). In a prospective study on child abuse, one factor that increased abuse of premature infants was "inadequate child spacing" (Hunter, Kilstrom, Kraybill, & Loda, 1978, p. 630). Likewise, a Pan American Health Organization study of infant mortality indicated that one of the risk factors for infant mortality was having a mother who already had at least four children (Puffer & Serrano, 1973). Similarly, Overpeck, Brenner, Trumble, Trifiletti, and Berendes (1998) noted that women under the age of 20 who had two children had an elevated risk of progenicide. A recent and widely reported case illustrates this point. Twenty-one-year-olds Justin and Brittany Alston were having a party in their Texas trailer when guests thought they heard a baby crying. Upon investigation, the party-goers found an emaciated, nearly dead infant in the bedroom. Prosecutors claim that the parents did not feed the baby for nearly two months. This couple also had another child (http://www.myfoxdfw.com/story/19990633/couple-gets-60-years-for-starving-baby).

Clearly, parental age and close birth spacing interact to predict filicide. We discuss age more in the next section.

While it is clear that infanticide has been practiced cross-culturally, most likely for thousands of years, there is also evidence that women do not always need to resort to this strategy. In an interesting analysis of !Kung hunter-gatherers, Lee (1980) showed the benefits of long birth intervals, which tend to be approximately four years among the !Kung. !Kung women walk an average of 4200 km per year while foraging and moving camp, and they carry all their children under four years old. Lee figured that women's workload is determined by the total weight of all the children they must carry, the distance they have to travel, and the frequency of births. After calculating the average kg/km per year under different interbirth intervals, he found that the burden (in terms of kg/km) varies greatly depending on the interbirth interval. When the birth interval is five years, a woman's burden is 14,256 kg/km; at four years it is 17,808 kg/km; and at two years it increases to 32,064 kg/km. How do they maintain such long interbirth intervals, despite not using contraceptives? One of the major factors is the length of lactation. Women breastfeed for at least two to three years, and nursing is "vigorous, frequent, given on demand, and ... at night" (Lee, 1980, p. 338). This, coupled with the high energy expenditure on foraging, keeps the intervals between births long. Under conditions such as these, there is less need for infanticide; it is relatively rare among the !Kung, with approximately 2% of births ending in this way (Lee, 1980).

Young Mothers

Life history theory predicts that young mothers have higher rates of progenicide than older mothers because young mothers have more time to reproduce in the future. This prediction is supported, as research indicates that progenicide is more likely to be perpetrated by young mothers than by older ones (Daly & Wilson, 1988; Friedman et al., 2012b; McKee, 2006; Overpeck et al., 1998; Silverman & Kennedy, 1988). Connelly and Straus (1992) reported that the younger the mother was at the time of birth, the greater the risk of child abuse. For example, Luke and Brown (2007) linked birth certificates for all full-term, non-low-birthweight infants born between 1995 and 2000 to their death certificates. For the 356 infants who died due to maternal maltreatment, progenicide risk was associated with the mother's age, with those under

20 years as the highest risk category. Older women with no other children (primiparous women), compared to younger mothers and older mothers with other children, invested more in premature children, as measured by mother's attribution that her child was small and in need of protection (Beaulieu & Bugental, 2008). This finding provides evidence that older mothers with no other children put more effort into *any* child because they have fewer years to produce another child; they cannot wait to invest in a healthy child, unlike younger mothers.

A prospective birth cohort study appears to provide further support for the idea that young mothers are particularly likely to kill their offspring. Data on 4.3 million Californian children indicated that maternal youth was associated with greater risk of intentional fatal child injury (Putnam-Hornstein, 2011). The median age of the progenicidal mothers is young but varies across studies. For example, in a couple of studies the median age was 19 years (Herman-Giddens et al., 2003; Meyer & Oberman, 2001), while in other studies it was the early 20s (e.g., 21 years (D'Orban, 1979; Shelton, Muirhead, & Canning, 2010); and 23 years (Brookman & Nolan, 2006; Spinelli, 2003)). In one of the earliest studies on progenicide, Resnick (1972) reported that 89% of the women in his study were less than 25 years of age. Overpeck et al. (1998) found that the progenicide rate for mothers under the age of 15 was seven times that of mothers over the age of 25.

Since young mothers have higher mate value, they may be better off postponing reproduction and focusing on competing for access to higher-quality mates. Older mothers, on the other hand, are less likely to be able to successfully compete for a mate, and therefore they should be less likely to kill an offspring, particularly when they have no other children that need their investment (i.e., they are childless).

Lack of Paternal Support

Because of the intense investment required to raise offspring, women who do not have paternal support are expected to reduce investment in their offspring and to be more likely to kill their offspring. In one study, the most powerful maternal predictor of child abuse was when the mother did not live with the father of her child (Hunter et al., 1978). Moreover, compared to married women, unmarried women are more likely to kill their offspring (Daly & Wilson, 1988), and termination of the parents' relationship is related to death from child abuse (Lucas et al., 2002). In Turkey, 35% of filicides occurred in couples who were separated (there is no distinction between male and female perpetrators; Karakus et al., 2003). Several studies of progenicide have reported that the triggering event was a significant alteration of domestic status such as a divorce or separation (Alder & Baker, 1997; Loomis, 1986; Messing & Heeren, 2004).

Parental unhappiness and marital instability, which may signal increased risk of male desertion, may also be indicators that reproduction should be delayed. When Tibetan women divorce, having children from their previous union is "an obstacle in the mother's life" (Levine, 1987, p. 294). In other words, it hinders her ability to find another spouse because men are less likely to marry a woman with children from a previous relationship. Not surprisingly, there is evidence that children born to unstable marriages "conveniently" die. Since many children die anyway, it is difficult to determine if these children were actively killed or the victims of progenicide (Levine, 1987). To reiterate, neglect and abuse may function as more "passive" ways to aid in a child's death and may enhance maternal fitness.

Lack of Parental and Community Support

In addition to those who lack paternal support, women who lack family support may be at greater risk of committing progenicide. For example, social isolation and having a poor support system increase the risk of abuse of children (Hunter et al., 1978). When unpartnered women also lack the support of their parents, their children are at greater risk of abuse (Hunter et al., 1978). Unpartnered women likely need extra support from their families in caring and providing for their offspring, so when their parents are not supportive, abuse and progenicide increase.

Resource Uncertainty and Progenicide

Based on life history theory, we predict that mothers who commit progenicide lack resources, which is supported because progenicide is linked with resource scarcity. For instance, in one study of filicide, researchers found that Japanese children were more likely to be killed in years in which unemployment was higher (Yasumi & Kageyama, 2009). In the United States, women were more likely to kill infants in states with lower per capita income and higher numbers of women living in poverty (Gauthier, Chaudoir, & Forsyth, 2003).

In addition to environmental cues of local resource scarcity being important in predicting maternal infanticide, the parent's own poverty increases the risk of progenicide. In Turkey, half of parents who killed children were illiterate and unemployed (this is not broken down by mothers vs. fathers; Karakus et al., 2003). More generally, mistreatment of children (i.e., abuse) is more likely among poor families or those who are unemployed (Straus, 1980). Among Tibetans, parents differentially care for children (i.e., they invest more resources in some children and withhold resources from other children). Unwanted children may be fed less, for instance, and household wealth is one of the frequently cited reasons for differences in parental investment. Among wealthier households, there is more money to support children, and wealthier families may be able to hire help, which allows women to stay home to breastfeed and care for infants, which decreases progenicide (Levine, 1987). Relatedly, when parents reported that they faced a precarious financial situation, they were more likely to abuse their children (Hunter et al., 1978).

Neonaticidal Italian mothers were more likely to be poor compared to infanticidal and filicidal mothers (Camperio Ciani & Fontanesi, 2012), indicating that the youngest children are most at risk of being killed when their mothers are poor. Later we discuss the relevance of these different classifications of homicide by child's age because they may have implications for determining whether killing offspring is an adaptation or whether it is a "slip-up" of a strategy aimed simply at lowering parental investment.

Progenicide and Low-Fitness Offspring

As predicted by parental investment theory, low-fitness offspring are at increased risk of being neglected, abused, and killed (e.g., Ammerman, Van Hasselt, & Hersen, 1988; Lightcap, Kurland, & Burgess, 1982). Apgar scores are used to measure the health of an infant after birth and assess the coloring, respiration, heart rate, and reflexes of the newborn. In one study of low-income families, maltreatment of infants was related to low Apgar scores and prematurity, both markers of reduced fitness (Bugental & Happaney, 2004). In a prospective study on child abuse, children who spent time in neonatal intensive care had high levels of abuse; they had approximately an eightfold increase in the rate of abuse (Hunter et al., 1978). For these children, risk of abuse increased with lower birthweights, younger gestational age at birth, remaining in the hospital for more than 40 days, and congenital defects.

An epidemiological study of 6,532 children in the United Kingdom reported that low-birthweight children were most at risk for violent abuse and failure to thrive, which occurs when children lose weight for no known medical reason (Creighton, 1985). Potentially, failure to thrive may be due to neglect and malnourishment because of reduced investment by the infant's mother. Even when maternal behavior does not rise to full physical abuse or neglect, underinvestment in low-fitness infants may occur. For example, mothers of low-birthweight infants breastfed them for a shorter duration than mothers of infants with normal birthweight (Bereczkei, 2001). Some research shows a more complex relationship between infant quality, maternal resources, and investment. In one study of premature infants, mothers with more resources invested *more* in high-risk infants than low-risk infants, while poor women invested *less* in high-risk infants than low-risk infants (Beaulieu & Bugental, 2008). Wealthier women can afford to support multiple children, including children who have lower fitness; poor women may need to invest their resources more judiciously by supporting only those offspring with high fitness.

Poor women in rural Brazil have very high rates of infant mortality, some of which appears to be attributable to neglect. Women often attribute their infant's death to *doença da crianca* ("sickness of the child"). Sick children who appear to be permanently affected by illness (e.g., they have convulsions or they are emaciated) are often neglected, which virtually ensures their demise. According to Scheper-Hughes (1984), many of these infants are clearly suffering from malnourishment and dehydration (from illness), plus the effects of maternal neglect. One woman who was interviewed about these deaths said,

> "People don't want to take care of such a child. . . .
> There may be a cure that the doctors know of, but we would be afraid to give the medicine, because a child with this kind of sickness is never right again. He could grow up to be twisted and lame or crazy. . . .
> No poor person can take care of a child like that."
> (p. 541)

Children with disabilities have an elevated risk of abuse (Hunter et al., 1978) and filicide by their mothers (Coorg & Tournay, 2013). In Hunter et al.'s prospective study of abuse among premature infants, researchers found that congenital defects increased the rate of abuse. In one study of Japanese progenicide, handicapped or disabled children had

an increased risk of being killed by their parents (Taguchi, 2007). It appears that low-fitness infants face a higher risk of abuse, neglect, and progenicide than high-fitness infants. This is likely to be particularly true for children with obvious congenital defects and for women who have few resources.

Mating Effort, Intrasexual Competition, and Progenicide

Women must make repeated tradeoffs among mating, somatic, and reproductive efforts. What happens if a woman experiences her children as interfering with her mating options?

Women with children are at a significant disadvantage in the mating market. While younger mothers can expect to have more opportunities to reproduce and therefore may choose to engage in mating effort rather than parenting effort, an older mother, with fewer reproductive years, should focus her energy and resources on parental activities (as reviewed earlier). Research supports the idea that older mothers expend less effort on mating compared to younger mothers. Older mothers of young offspring make less mating effort compared to their younger peers. Maternal age and mating effort both affect maternal investment. Younger mothers expend less effort in parenting, and they also expend more effort in mating, as measured by the number of times men moved into and out of their house. This indicates that maternal age has both a direct and indirect effect on parental investment (Schlomer & Belsky, 2012). Research suggests that women with children are less likely to remarry than those without (Koo & Suchindran, 1980; Koo, Suchindran, & Griffith, 1984; Stewart, Manning, & Smock, 2003), indicating that, indeed, women encumbered with children have a reduced ability to find a mate. Buss and Duntley (2011) suggest that when children are perceived as hindering a relationship with a new mate, one who is not biologically related to the child, mothers may invest fewer resources in the child or, with pressure from her new partner, may inflict costs on her child. These costs inflicted by a mother on her child may mean the provisioning of less food, less emotional support, inadequate clothes, or even less money for college.

In extreme cases, mothers may resort to killing their child to secure their relationship with their mate. Support for Buss and Duntley's (2011) hypothesis is found in research on the Ayoreo of South America, who engage in progenicide at the termination or expected termination of the mother's mating partnership, among other reasons (Bugos

& McCarthy, 1984). In another study of domestic murder cases by women, 26 women killed 69 children, and one of the primary reasons was that their offspring interfered with a new relationship (Messing & Heeren, 2004). While several such cases have become notorious in America, such as Diane Downs and Susan Smith, who killed their offspring in part because they believed that being child-free would make them more attractive to a male partner, research in this area remains limited.

Older mothers who commit progenicide, or kill an older child in whom they have invested several years of effort, are more likely to have a mental illness (Dobson & Sales 2000; D'Orban 1979; Haapasalo & Petäjä, 1999; Stone, Steinmeyer, Dreher, & Krischer, 2005), suggesting that this type of progenicide does not have functional utility; rather it is a byproduct of mental illness. We address this issue in more detail later.

Illegitimate Children and Progenicide

Children born to unmarried or unmated women may be at higher risk of being killed by their mothers because unmarried women do not have resources, partner support, or family and community support (Daly & Wilson, 1988). Even in First World countries, single mothers face significantly more economic hardships and other stressors compared to partnered women. In the United States, in comparison with two-parent households and single-father households, households headed by single mothers have the highest poverty rate (31%; National Poverty Center, 2010).

In many places, women who have children outside of marriage are shamed, are rejected, and have reduced marriage prospects (e.g., Immigration and Refugee Board, Canada, 1996; Levine, 1987). For example, while Vietnamese women face no legal repercussions from having illegitimate children, they do face disapproval from their community and family; their parents may punish women who have children outside of marriage (Immigration and Refugee Board, Canada, 1996). Among Tibetan women, having children outside of marriage is frowned upon, and these women lack ways to support themselves. Not surprisingly, among Tibetans, illegitimate children are frequent targets of infanticide and "aggressive neglect" (Levine, 1987).

Not only are unpartnered women more likely to neglect children, but children born to these mothers are at a higher risk of infanticide. One study reported that 77% of the infanticidal women were single (Mendlowicz, Rapaport, Fontenelle, Jean-Louis, & De Moraes, 2002). In another sample of British and Welsh infanticides, *none* of the mothers were married (D'Orban, 1979). These studies show that infanticide is much more likely among unmarried women and show the importance of partner support in raising offspring.

Hidden pregnancies or "pregnancy negation" support the idea that women who become pregnant with illegitimate children are at greater risk for committing neonaticide (Beier, Wille, & Wessel, 2006). In these cases, young mothers, typically still residing with their parents, conceal their pregnancies from the majority of their social networks, give birth in secret, then dispose of the newborns. Overpeck et al. (1999) noted that those women most at risk for this behavior were young, single, and did not obtain prenatal care, such as seeing a doctor regularly. These young women decreased the amount of investment in their offspring prior to birth by hiding their pregnancy. They attempted to prevent people from finding out they were ever pregnant. The case of Cherlie LaFleur discussed at the beginning of the chapter meets these criteria. By all accounts she hid her pregnancy from her disapproving father. She was young, unmarried, and never sought prenatal care. Like other young women in her position, she gave birth in secret, at school, and quickly disposed of her baby. Although this is gruesome, her behavior is understandable when framed in terms of her life history strategy.

Do Mothers Kill Daughters or Sons?

While progenicide of female children in India and China is well publicized (Porter & Gavin, 2010), multiple studies have noted that progenicide of male children appears to be higher in Western societies (Marks & Kumar 1993, 1996; Overpeck et al., 1998; Rougé-Maillart, Jousset, Gaudin, Bouju, & Penneau, 2005). For example, using data from 3,459 cases from 1976 to 1985, Kunz and Bahr (1996) reported that 55% of infants killed were male. In reviewing Finnish cases from 1970 to 1994, 60% of the victims were male (Vanamo, Kauppi, Karkola, Merikanto, & Räsänen, 2001). These data lead to the question of why male infants should be at greater risk of being killed than female infants in Western countries, while in other parts of the world, infanticide is much more likely when women give birth to girls.

The Trivers–Willard model states that parents will invest more in male offspring under "good conditions" and more in female offspring during "bad conditions." This imbalance is because, during good conditions, well-nourished male offspring will have a better chance of outcompeting rivals for access to mates, and hence they will be more likely to have high reproductive success. Under poor conditions, male offspring will not be able to compete and will have low reproductive success. In this context, "poor conditions" appear to correspond to a lack of resources. In general, research supports the idea that poor families invest more in girls while wealthy families invest more in boys. Analyses of Kenyan data comparing the Mukogodo ethnic group to non-Mukogodo showed that the Mukogodo, a relatively low-status and impoverished group, are more likely to bring their daughters to a health clinic, whereas non-Mukogodo are more likely to bring sons to the clinic (Cronk, 1989). Most likely, lack of attention by the Mukogodo to sons often results in their deaths.

Maternal condition, which may indicate resource availability, also supports the Trivers–Willard hypothesis of parental investment. Among Ariaal (a Kenyan traditional group) mothers with high serum vitamin A levels, an indicator of good nutrition, breastfed both daughters and sons equally, while mothers with low serum vitamin A levels breastfed their daughters more frequently (Fujita et al., 2012). In addition, in these same Ariaal mothers, poor mothers had richer breast milk (i.e., fat levels were higher) when they had daughters, and wealthier mothers had richer breast milk when they had sons (Fujita et al., 2012). Interestingly, this society generally favors males, but they faced particularly harsh conditions at the time of the study (there was a drought). So, even when one might expect boys to always be favored, when conditions warrant it, mothers prefer girls.

How does this relate to infanticide? As discussed earlier, we expect that under conditions of resource scarcity, women will be more likely to kill their offspring. The picture is probably more complex, however. When resources are scarce, women may be more likely to kill their sons than their daughters since poor women are less likely to possess the resources necessary to launch a son who will be able to successfully compete with other males, since men frequently require resources (e.g., money) to be successful. However, poor women may be able to successfully launch a daughter. Women are more likely to be able to marry out of their social class, especially if they are attractive. Therefore, poor mothers are sensitive to the ability of their daughters to be able to compete with other women for access to mates. Not surprisingly, progenicide may be one

tactic to increase the chance that a child will be successful, given the family's economic conditions. As stated previously, killing one's child is at the extreme end of a continuum of care (or lack thereof, in the case of killing a child) that parents can invest in offspring. Underinvestment in children could result in their death, especially under ancestral conditions with infectious disease and malnutrition causing many deaths during the first few years of life.

Decreased Parental Investment/Deferred Progenicide

Infanticide is, of course, only one of the multiple ways a woman can lessen her parental investment in a child, and it is in no way to be regarded as "determined" (Low, 2000). Other, nonlethal strategies include abandoning, fostering, or selling offspring, or giving children up for adoption. For example, in 1998, 31,000 American newborns were abandoned by their mothers in hospitals and other public places (McKee, 2006). There is some evidence that Safe Haven laws, which allow mothers to drop off neonates with no questions and no ramifications, have reduced illegal abandonment (Friedman & Resnick, 2009). Another way women may decrease investment is by using a wet nurse. Historically, the ability to use a wet nurse allowed some women to invest fewer resources into their children and thus freed them to perform other tasks (e.g., reproduce again, make money to support their existing children; Hrdy, 1992).

Some researchers argue that pregnancy terminations provide support for evolutionary predictions regarding the factors that promote or reduce parenting effort. As predicted, abortion is more common in younger women (Hill & Low, 1992; Torres & Forrest, 1988) and those with limited resources (Torres & Forrest, 1988). In states with more restrictive abortion laws, more neonates are killed (Friedman & Resnick, 2009). In places where abortion laws are restricted, women who might have terminated a pregnancy may be forced to have a term pregnancy. Therefore, the women in these states kill their newborns at a higher rate. In the United States, societal attitudes toward abortion also appear to correspond to ideas generated by parental investment and life history theory. Those states with the least restrictive abortion policies are also the states with a relatively high proportion of women of reproductive age (Betzig & Lombardo, 1992).

Several researchers have suggested that a percentage of alleged cases of sudden infant death syndrome (SIDS) may be cases of progenicide

(Craft & Hall, 2004). For example, Levene and Bacon (2004) estimate that 30 to 40 cases annually in England and Wales are progenicides misjudged as SIDS, while Stanton and Simpson (2001) estimate that 10% of all SIDS cases may be due to progenicide. In Bajanowski et al.'s (2005) review of 330 alleged SIDS cases from 1998 to 2001, they found 12 cases of progenicide. Determining whether SIDS is actually progenicide is difficult. Whether babies die of heart failure, suffocating due to being unable to move their head, being suffocated purposely is difficult to determine in these cases. Therefore, estimates on progenicide from SIDS deaths should be considered rough estimates.

Stepmothers and Discriminative Parental Solicitude

We have covered the circumstances in which women decrease or completely stop investing in their biological children, but what about women who stepparent children? Discriminative parental solicitude is the idea that parents differentially invest in their biological children and stepchildren (Daly & Wilson, 1980). While biological mothers benefit from investing in their offspring because it usually confers higher inclusive fitness (Harris & Rice, 2012), caring for nongenetic children or stepchildren is a wasted investment, because there are no fitness increases from investing in nonbiological offspring (Hamilton, 1963). In addition, nonrelated children in a household compete for resources with a woman's own genetic offspring (Daly & Wilson, 1980). Discriminative parental solicitude predicts that stepmothers will provide fewer resources to stepchildren, will demonstrate more aggression toward them, and are more likely to kill them than genetic mothers (Friedman et al., 2012a; Harris, Hilton, Rice, & Eke, 2007)

The initial research on discriminative parental solicitude focused on stepfathers and men who live with women and their genetic offspring (regardless of marital status). Multiple studies have demonstrated that the risk of child abuse and death by unrelated, cohabiting men (stepfathers) is considerably higher than by a genetic father (Daly & Wilson, 1994; Herring, 2009; Van IJzendoorn, Euser, Prinzie, Juffer, & Bakermans-Kranenburg, 2009). Cross-cultural studies have demonstrated the same results (Daly & Wilson, 2008). For example, in a study of a South American foraging group, 42% of children raised by a stepfather and biological mother died before reaching age 15, while only

19% of children raised by two biological parents died before age 15 (Daly & Wilson, 1996).

Research on differential investment by stepmothers was initially uncommon, partially due to cultural norms that decreased the likelihood of men having custody of young children. However, stepmotherhood has increased in Western society during the past 40 years and certainly existed further in the past as well (Campbell & Lee, 2002). Research into families with stepmothers is complicated by the fact that some studies use the term "stepmother" only for those homes where the genetic father and nongenetic mother are married. However, Daly and Wilson (2001) point out that a "step" relationship is generally one of cohabitation; if a man dates a woman, she is his "girlfriend," but if he invites her to live with him and his child, she is a "stepmother." If, as Marlowe (2000) suggests, women are motivated to become stepmothers by mating effort rather than by reproductive effort, then stepmothers are women who reside with a child's genetic father, regardless of marital status. By this definition, in 2009, approximately 100,000 US children lived with a genetic father and a nongenetic stepmother (Kreider & Ellis, 2011). The risk of abuse, neglect, and filicide to children living with a stepmother (relative to a genetic mother) is similar to that for children living with a stepfather (relative to a genetic father; Daly & Wilson, 2008).

Killing stepchildren is not the only way to minimize investment in unrelated children. Stepmothers are also expected to provide fewer resources for a stepchild, especially when they have their own genetic children living in the same household. Support for this prediction comes from multiple studies, which support the idea that investment in food, medical care, education, and other expenses is lower for children living with stepmothers. After assessing household food spending in the United States, researchers found that when women lived with biologically unrelated children, they spent less money on food (Case, Lin, & McLanahan, 2000). It did not matter whether those children were stepchildren, foster children, or adopted children. Case et al. also assessed food spending by household type in South Africa. When biological mothers were present, households spent more money on milk, fruits, and vegetables and less money on tobacco and alcohol compared to homes where the genetic mother was not present. When biological mothers were present, more money was spent on clothing for children.

Not only are expenditures on food lower when children live with a stepmother, but children residing in households with a stepmother also face healthcare reductions compared to children who live with a biological mother. Using data from a national health survey of more 17,000 children in the United States, researchers found that children residing with stepmothers were significantly less likely to have routine visits to the doctor or dentist and were less likely to have their own pediatrician or other stable site for medical care, compared to children residing with their genetic mother. This difference could have been due to stepmother concerns regarding her legal options to take a nongenetic child for medical care. However, in the same study, children residing with a stepmother were also less likely to wear seatbelts while riding in a vehicle compared to children who resided with their genetic mother, suggesting that legal concerns were not the primary motivator of the stepmothers' behaviors. Interestingly, children living with stepfathers also had decreased access to health care, but the difference between stepfather investment in health care and biological mothers' investment was half the difference as that between step- and biological mothers' investment (Case, Lin, & McLanahan, 2001). In other words, living with a stepfather reduces the likelihood of good health care for a child but not as much as when a child lives with a stepmother.

As expected by the theory of discriminative parental solicitude, children living with stepmothers receive less money from them and are also less likely to attend college. Among South Africans with school-age children, when the biological mother was present compared to when a nonbiological mother (step, foster, or adoptive) was present, more money was spent on education (Case et al., 2001). Using data from a US national education survey, Zvoch (1999) compared funding for postsecondary education for biological versus stepchildren and found the latter received significantly less financial support. In stepfamily homes, parents decreased the amount of money put aside toward college and started saving for college later. These findings were seen despite controlling for issues such as academic ability, socioeconomic attainment, and number of family members (Zvoch, 1999).

Resource allocation for other opportunities was also lower for children living with stepmothers. In research on parental funding of "the Great Journey" that many Israeli young adults take following their mandatory military service, researchers found that young adults raised in homes with stepmothers received less money for their trip than those young adults raised by genetic mothers or stepfathers. The likely reason why stepfathers give children more money than stepmothers is that stepfathers use their investment in unrelated children to secure their relationship with the child's mother. In other words, stepfather investment of this type is a mating strategy, not a parenting strategy (Tifferet, Jorev, & Nasanovitz, 2010).

In addition to reduced monetary investments in offspring, stepmothers appear to be less emotionally invested in their stepchildren. For instance, one study showed that only 25% of stepmothers claimed to have "parental feelings" toward the nongenetic children in their care. Stepmothers appear to have fewer positive and negative interactions with their stepchildren, indicating that they are relatively disengaged from these nongenetic children (Thomson, McLanahan, & Curtin, 1992). Stepmothers may become even more disengaged from stepchildren once they have a biological child. Stewart (2005) investigated the effect the birth of a new child has on stepparent involvement with stepchildren. She found that stepparent involvement declines significantly after the birth of a biological child. In families that have stepchildren, compared to those without stepchildren, parents have a negative view of how the remarriage affects their family life. For instance, parents who live with stepchildren believe that their children cause them problems, and they state that they would enjoy living apart from their children. They also believe that their remarriage negatively impacted their relationship with their children (White & Booth, 1985), which may be an accurate assessment. Not surprisingly, given all of the perceived problems that having stepchildren causes for those who remarry, children who live with stepparents are more likely to leave their household (White & Booth, 1985).

This disengagement, however, comes at a significant cost to the child. Parenting (step or biological) requires a high degree of monitoring to prevent accidents. Discriminative parental solicitude predicts less consistent oversight of stepchildren and hence more accidental injuries of stepchildren, and this has been supported by several studies. Compared to those residing with both biological parents, children residing in stepfamily homes had higher levels of nonfatal accidental injury. Stepchildren under the age of five were significantly more likely to be accidentally injured compared to children of the same age residing with both biological parents. Residing in stepfamily homes was also linked with an increased risk of hospitalization following nonfatal accidents in preschool children (Wadsworth, Burnell, Taylor, & Butler, 1983). Additionally, fatal accidental injuries are also more common for children raised in stepparent homes. Tooley, Karakis, Stokes, and Ozanne-Smith (2006) used the Australian National Coroner's Information System to analyze 319 unintentional fatal injuries for preschoolers (>5 years) between 2000 and 2003. They reported that stepchildren in this age group had a significantly increased risk of accidental fatal injury, especially drowning, compared to children residing with a single genetic parent.

Early support for differential parental effort by stepparents showed that stepfathers were more aggressive toward their stepchildren. Research also indicates that stepmothers are also more likely to be abusive toward their stepchildren than biological mothers. For instance, data from two-parent homes with documented cases of child abuse indicated that stepparent–stepchild dyads were at higher risk for child abuse than genetic parent–child dyads (Lightcap et al., 1982). In their study, stepparents were much more likely to abuse stepchildren in their care than to abuse their biological offspring, indicating that this was not simply a case of generally abusive adults.

Not only are stepmothers more abusive toward their stepchildren compared to their biological children, but they also are more likely to be abusive toward stepchildren after they have a biological child (Harris et al., 2007). Multiple large-scale US studies have reported similar findings, and, as predicted, children residing with stepmothers experienced far more physical abuse than children residing with biological mothers (Daly & Wilson, 1985, 1996b; Weghorst, 1980). Data from Great Britain and South Korea show a similar trend (Creighton & Noyes, 1989; Kim & Ko, 1990). Given the higher rates of abuse by stepparents, it is not surprising that runaways state that a primary reason for running away was abuse at the hands of a stepmother (Mallett & Rosenthal, 2009).

Stepchildren have an increased risk of death at the hands of a stepmother. Weeks-Shackelford and Shackelford (2004) analyzed child homicide data from 1976 to 1994 and noted that the stepmother homicide rate during that time was 20.6 per million, compared to a rate of 8.6 per million for biological mothers. Similar rates of stepmother-perpetrated child homicide have been found in England, Canada, Mali, Australia, and Wales (Daly & Wilson, 2001; Lancy, 2014), and, as predicted,

stepchildren residing alongside the biological offspring of the stepmother experienced more abuse prior to the murder, compared to those who did not reside with other children (Harris et al., 2007; Stiffman, Schnitzer, Adam, Kruse, & Ewigman, 2002; Willführ & Gagno, 2011).

Not only were stepchildren at an increased risk of being murdered by a stepmother, but the type of death they experience is noteworthy. Studies (Harris et al., 2007; Weekes-Shackelford & Shackelford, 2004) found that stepmothers were more likely to beat a stepchild to death, compared with genetic mothers. Beating a child to death can be viewed as a particularly hostile mode of homicide, compared to faster and less painful methods (Daly & Wilson, 1994).

Killing Offspring as a Mechanism to Outcompete Other Women

While it is clear that reducing investment in, and sometimes killing, offspring has reproductive payoffs (i.e., higher overall reproductive success) for some women, what is less clear is whether progenicide is a strategy to outcompete other women. We have addressed this issue at various points in this chapter, but in this section we address the issue of whether progenicide may be due to intrasexual competition in more detail.

Progenicide as a Mechanism in Young Women to Maintain Their Reproductive Value

Among young, unpartnered women, the ability to secure a good long-term mate is important for lifetime reproductive success. Optimally, women seek mates who are good providers, are willing and able to invest time and energy into the relationship and any associated children, have the potential to be a good dad, and are kind and understanding (Buss & Barnes, 1986). In seeking mates, men prefer attractive women, so when competing for mates, women often use their physical attractiveness to compete against other women. This positions attractive women to be able to exchange their attention and mating access for the resources that men possess.

Baumeister and Vohs (2004) suggest that, for a number of reasons, women exchange sex for resources. There are a variety of factors that underpin the exchange between sexual access by women for resources by men. One factor is that men, more than women, want to have sex. Women are therefore a limiting factor in men's desire for sex.

A second factor regarding why women exchange sex for resources is that men have valuable resources not easily garnered by unpartnered women. Women may need those resources for survival (Baumeister & Vohs, 2004).

According to this idea, there is a "sexual exchange" in which women offer sex and men offer resources. Because of this exchange, and the fact that men seek fertile, physically attractive partners, a woman's reproductive value is dependent on her physical attractiveness and availability as a sex partner. Youth, physical attractiveness, having few prior sex partners, having numerous potential suitors, and dressing in sexy clothing increase women's market value, while being unattractive, having few alternative ways of accessing resources, and having many prior sex partners (or a reputation that suggests this is true) all decrease women's market value (Baumeister & Vohs, 2004).

In addition, environmental factors also influence the sexual exchange between men and women. Under certain conditions, sex is easier to obtain and thus the market value of sex decreases. One example of an important environmental factor is the sex ratio (see Dillon, Adair, & Brase, this volume, for more about sex ratios and intrasexual competition). When there are more women than men, the market value of sex is lower. The market value for sex is also lower when permissive sex is the norm and when men have easy access to "low-cost substitutes" for sex such as prostitutes (Baumeister & Vohs, 2004, p. 340). When the sex ratio is skewed and women are in excess, they compete more for access to mates and teen pregnancy rates increase, despite the relative lack of men. This may be due to the fact that, under these conditions, the best way for women to compete for access to mates is by reducing the commitment they require before having sex. So, when sex ratios favor men, sexual permissiveness increases, as does the teen pregnancy rate (Baumeister & Vohs, 2004).

Importantly, what all this suggests is that there are some circumstances under which women face heightened competition to find an investing long-term partner. So how is all this related to progenicide? We suggest that given the importance of sexual currency, some groups of women face high levels of competition for access to mates. In other words, some women have very high levels of female–female competition. Under these circumstances, if a woman has a child without an investing mate, her market value may be substantially reduced, and because she cannot afford to raise her

child alone, infanticide may be her best tactic. By killing her child, she may put herself in a better position to compete against other women for access to a long-term partner. While not all infanticides may result in an increased ability of women to compete for access to mates, there are some specific circumstances where this may be the case.

First, there is evidence that women with children are disadvantaged in the mating market (Levine, 1987; Lichter & Graefe, 2001). Researchers found that girls who have a child outside of marriage by age 14 are much less likely to be married at 35. Further, the lifetime rate of marriage is also about 20% lower for women who have a child without being married compared to those who did not have a child before marriage (Lichter & Graefe, 2001). Based on findings such as these, women who have a child before they are married must realize they are at a distinct disadvantage in the mating market compared to their childless peers.

Many of these women are also young, uneducated, and poor. These characteristics, coupled with their inability to secure a good long-term partner or even their parents' support, suggests that there may be intense pressure for these women to find a way to compete with other women for access to a good long-term partner. For some of these women, reducing their investment in or killing their offspring could make them more competitive with their female rivals. This possibility may be particularly true when sex ratios are skewed so that there are more women than men and the market value of sex is low (i.e., men have relative control over reproduction and women feel compelled to have uncommitted sex). These types of circumstances appear to occur frequently in inner-city communities where large numbers of young, usually Black men have either been murdered or incarcerated (Newsome & Airhihenbuwa, 2013). African American women are less likely than women of other racial and ethnic groups to use contraception and, when they do use it, they protect against pregnancy (which does not require negotiating with their partner) but not sexually transmitted infections (which does require negotiating with their partner; Wyatt et al., 2000). Men may prefer not to use a condom, so when there are imbalanced sex ratios that favor men, they have more sexual decision-making power. One example of this may be in the inner city, where so many Black men are incarcerated. With an imbalanced sex ratio, Black men have more power in sexual decision-making, so condom use may be out of the question and women may then rely on hormonal contraceptives to prevent pregnancy. These circumstances may also lead to increased levels of infanticide. Cherlie LaFleur, the woman who disposed of her baby in her school trash can, was young, Black, and living in a racially diverse suburb of Philadelphia. It is imaginable that she faced heightened competition for a mate and a mating market that favored male sexual access—and where women must use sex to find a mate (and probably not a long-term one). Indeed, research on sex ratios in different cities suggests that the sex ratio in Philadelphia is particularly low at .87, with many more females than males (Campbell, 2013). That is, in Philadelphia, for every 100 women, there are only 87 men. In poor neighborhoods, the sex ratio is even more unbalanced; in wealthier suburbs, the sex ratios are more even (Campbell, 2013). Research on the link between sex ratio, women's competition, and progenicide is almost nonexistent. The ideas discussed here need further research to elucidate how (and whether) female competition leads to higher levels of infanticide.

Progenicide as an Outcome of Competition Between Ex-Wives and Current Wives

In some ways, maltreatment of a stepchild makes strategic sense. Stepmothers are not genetically related to their stepchildren, and, therefore, parental investment theory suggests that women should limit their investment in these children, particularly when they have their own biological offspring to support. Additionally, childhood maltreatment is associated with later problems such as delinquency, impulsivity, substance abuse, depression, and poor health, all of which are likely to decrease the victim's reproductive success (Harris & Rice, 2012). In turn, these directly decrease the victim's ability to compete with the stepmother's genetic offspring for access to resources and mates.

Although it is clear that stepmothers benefit from reducing or completely divesting in their stepchildren, it may be possible that men's current and former spouses are directly in conflict with each other. We suggest that progenicide by stepmothers may, at least in part, be a result of competition between ex-wives and current wives to secure higher levels of male investment in their biological children. Although it is abundantly clear that current and former spouses are frequently in conflict, there is little actual research on this topic. A search of Google brings up plenty of websites aimed at helping people ameliorate the conflict with their ex's new spouse. Actual research on the potential for conflict and rivalry between current and ex-wives is very rare, but there is general agreement that there may be intense negative feelings between these women (e.g., Warshak, 2000).

There are some similarities between co-wives in polygynous marriages and ex- and current wives: in both cases women must compete for male attention and resources. Research on conflict between co-wives in polygynous marriages suggests that conflict is the norm in these situations (Campbell, 2005). Even language reflects the fact that co-wives are competitors. In the Surinam language, the word for "fight," when literally translated, means "act like a co-wife" (Campbell, 2002, p. 203). However, one might expect that the rivalry between ex-wives and current wives is even more intense than in co-wives, who may benefit from some cooperation. An ex-wife may be in an even worse position (relative to the current spouse) to receive support for her and her offspring than women sharing a spouse.

There is currently no research that directly supports our ideas regarding the influence of conflict between current and ex-wives on progenicide of stepchildren. We encourage researchers to turn their attention to this area. In light of this suggestion, we make several predictions regarding the circumstances when conflict between current and ex-spouses will be high. For each circumstance where conflict is higher, we predict that maltreatment and filicide of stepchildren will also be higher.

First, when the intensity of conflict between current and ex-wives is particularly high, maltreatment of stepchildren will increase and, in some cases, may result in filicide of stepchildren. We expect this because, when conflict is high, women are likely to be competing for access to resources and mating opportunities. To the extent that children hinder this, they may be abused and/or killed. Second, when the sex ratio is imbalanced and there are more women than men available as mates, conflict between current and ex-spouses will be greater and progenicide will be higher. Similar to the logic regarding the first hypothesis, when sex ratios favor males, women have a harder time competing for access to mates; children hinder a woman's ability to receive the benefits of intrasexual competition and may be abused or killed. This prediction is supported, at least in part, by research on sex ratios. Pedersen (1991) suggests that marriage is destabilized when sex ratios are low and that women who divorce are less able to find a new mate; in support of this, divorce rates increased during the 1980s when sex ratios were low and men were able to pursue their reproductive interests. Third, even when the overall sex ratio is balanced, if there is a relative lack of high-status men, women face greater competition over access to these men as mates. Under these circumstances, high-status women may face challenges from lower-status women who seek to "marry up." Interestingly, highly educated women have more negative views toward divorce than less educated women (Martin & Parashar, 2006). This is not surprising, given the fact that high-status women should seek to maintain their status (by remaining married) and low-status women should seek to increase their status through "good" marriages.

Is There an Adaptation for Killing Offspring?

There has been some debate among evolutionary psychologists about whether there are adaptations for homicide. Some evolutionary psychologists posit that there are specific homicide adaptations (Duntley & Buss, 2011). Other evolutionary psychologists believe that selection favored the behaviors that lead up to homicide (like aggression or neglect) but that homicide is essentially an accident (Daly & Wilson, 1988). In the latter explanation, homicide is thought of as a byproduct of selection for other traits, such as aggression (Daly & Wilson, 1988). This theory has been referred to by Duntley and Buss as the "slip-up" explanation for homicide. In the case of infanticide, the slip-up hypothesis suggests that when there are environmental circumstances indicating that investment in a particular child will lower a mother's fitness, there are adaptations for decreased investment by mothers, so that mothers may neglect their children. Under these circumstances, a mother should, in fact, reduce investment in her child but she should not kill her child. According to the slip-up hypothesis, the death of a child is an accidental byproduct of selection for reduced maternal investment. In contrast, homicide adaptation theory suggests that there is a specific adaptation for killing children in addition to adaptations for decreased maternal investment.

It is our view that there is an adaptation for infanticide by biological mothers. We believe the evidence discussed in this chapter supports that view *for the youngest children*. Other researchers concur (e.g., Camperio Ciani & Fontanesi, 2012). In particular, we believe that infanticides that occur in the first few weeks of a child's life are part of a homicide adaptation. The evidence for a homicide

adaptation in older children is less clear, and, in our view, homicide in older children may not be selected for (i.e., it is not an adaptation). In support of this view, mothers who kill older children are more likely to have significant psychological disorders, but neonaticidal mothers rarely have a psychological disorder (Camperio Ciani & Fontanesi, 2012). In fact, in an Italian study of mothers who killed their offspring, researchers found that neonaticidal mothers differed from infanticidal and filicidal mothers in ways that suggest that neonaticide is an evolved strategy, while infanticide and filicide are not (Camperio Ciani & Fontanesi, 2012). In support of this, neonaticidal mothers were young and poor compared to both infanticidal and filicidal mothers (Camperio Ciani & Fontanesi, 2012).

Unlike women who kill newborns, women who kill older children often have a history of previous psychiatric hospitalizations and suicide attempts (Lewis & Bunce, 2003). In one study of filicidal mothers at a psychiatric hospital, 65% of these mothers killed a child older than one year (Krischer, Stone, Sevecke, & Steinmeyer, 2007). While psychosis specifically following childbirth is very rare, occurring at a rate of less than 1 per 1,000 births (Herzog & Detre, 1976; Kendell, Chalmers, & Platz, 1987; O'Hara, Schlechte, Lewis, & Varner, 1991; Terp & Mortensen, 1998), psychosis is a risk for those individuals with an underlying predisposition (Hay, 2009). Long-term follow-up studies of mothers who experienced postpartum psychosis (with or without progenicide) indicate that the majority of the women will go on to have further psychotic episodes, unrelated to childbirth (Robling, Paykel, Dunn, Abbott, & Katona, 2000; Videbech & Gouliaev, 1995).

Conclusion

In this chapter we suggest that infanticide by biological mothers has been selected to mitigate the costs associated with maternal investment in offspring that have a reduced likelihood of survival. In particular, we showed that when mothers are young and lack paternal and parental support, they are more likely to kill their offspring. In addition, mothers are more likely to kill offspring when birth spacing is too close or when children have reduced viability (e.g., they are premature). We believe the weight of the evidence supports the idea of a homicide adaptation for neonaticide by mothers under the specific circumstances stated here. In all of the circumstances we discussed (e.g., poverty), actions, such as early weaning and neglect are part of the suite of behaviors aimed at reducing investment in children who may reduce a mother's reproductive success.

We also addressed filicide by stepmothers. In contrast to biological mothers, stepmothers may be expected to kill older nonbiological children, especially when the stepmother has biological offspring to support. In addition, households that include stepmothers spend less money on food and education and reduce investment in health care for stepchildren. The function of underinvestment and, potentially, murder is to reduce male investment in offspring unrelated to the stepmother and to increase the stepmother's ability to compete intersexually.

We also offered some hypotheses regarding the link between female intrasexual competition and infanticide, suggesting that for young and unpartnered women, especially when there is a skewed sex ratio, infanticide may be an adaptation to compete for access to a mate. In addition, we posited that competition between ex- and current spouses for access to male resources may result in infanticide by stepmothers, and, again, we feel that when the sex ratio is low, infanticide may be a more common result of female intrasexual competition. There is essentially no work in either of these areas, and we encourage research on these topics, especially since they shed light on the unique role of women's intrasexual competition in maternal investment.

It is important not to overlook the reality that divesting in offspring served a real function in the human past and still does today. This is an ugly truth, and we in no way suggest that infanticide and neglect are morally right. We hope that by shedding light on the circumstances that lead to child maltreatment and infanticide, we can discover solutions that reduce the occurrence of these behaviors. We hope that research on this topic translates into policies and social programs that attempt to mitigate those evolved functions. It is plausible that progenicide could be reduced by offering other ways to solve the adaptive problem, such as programs to reduce poverty, increase access to contraception for young women, increase awareness of family conflict in stepfamily households, and increase access to prenatal care to decrease the prevalence of low-fitness offspring.

References

Alder, C. M., & Baker, J. (1997). Maternal filicide: More than one story to be told. *Women & Criminal Justice, 9,* 15–39.

Ammerman, R. T., Van Hasselt, V. B., & Hersen, M. (1988). Maltreatment of handicapped children: A critical review. *Journal of Family Violence, 3,* 53–72.

Bajanowski, T., Vennemann, M., Bohnert, M., Rauch, E., Brinkmann, B., & Mitchell, E. A. (2005). Unnatural causes of sudden unexpected deaths initially thought to be sudden infant death syndrome. *International Journal of Legal Medicine, 119*(4), 213–216.

Baumeister, R. F., & Vohs, K. D. (2004). Sexual economics: Sex as female resource for social exchange in heterosexual interactions. *Personality and Social Psychology Review, 8*(4), 339–363.

Beaulieu, D. A., & Bugental, D. (2008). Contingent parental investment: An evolutionary framework for understanding early interaction between mothers and children. *Evolution and Human Behavior, 29,* 249–255.

Beier, K. M., Wille, R., & Wessel, J. (2006). Denial of pregnancy as a reproductive dysfunction: A proposal for international classification systems. *Journal of Psychosomatic Research, 61,* 723–730.

Bereczkei, T. (2001). Maternal trade-off in treating high-risk children. *Evolution and Human Behavior, 22,* 197–212.

Betzig, L., & Lombardo, L. H. (1992). Who's pro-choice and why. *Ethology and Sociobiology, 13,* 49–71.

Bjorklund, D. F., & Shackelford, T. K. (1999). Differences in parental investment contribute to important differences between men and women. *Current Directions in Psychological Science, 8,* 86–89.

Boone, J. L., & Kessler, K. L. (1999). More status or more children? Social status, fertility reduction, and long-term fitness. *Evolution and Human Behavior, 20,* 257–277.

Brewis, A. A. (1992). Anthropological perspectives on infanticide. *Arizona Anthropologist, 8,* 103–119.

Brookman, F., & Nolan, J. (2006). The dark figure of infanticide in England and Wales complexities of diagnosis. *Journal of Interpersonal Violence, 21,* 869–889.

Bugental, D. B., & Happaney, K. (2004). Predicting infant maltreatment in low-income families: The interactive effects of maternal attributions and child status at birth. *Developmental Psychology, 40,* 234.

Bugos, P. E., & McCarthy, L. M. (1984). Ayoreo infanticide: A case study. In G. Hausfater & S. B. Hrdy (Eds.), *Infanticide: Comparative and evolutionary perspectives* (pp. 503–520). New York: Aldine de Gruyter.

Burgess, R. L., Kurland, J. A., & Pensky, E. E. (1988). Ultimate and proximate determinants of child maltreatment: Natural selection, ecological instability, and coercive interpersonal contingencies. In K. B. MacDonald (Ed.), *Sociobiological perspectives on human development* (pp. 293–319). New York: Springer.

Buss, D. M., & Barnes, M. F. (1986). Preferences in human mate selection. *Journal of Personality and Social Psychology, 50,* 559–570.

Buss, D. M., & Duntley, J. D. (2011). The evolution of intimate partner violence. *Aggression and Violent Behavior, 16,* 411–419.

Campbell, A. (2005). Aggression. In D. Buss (Ed.), *Handbook of evolutionary psychology* (pp. 628–652). New York: Wiley.

Campbell, A. (2013). The evolutionary psychology of women's aggression. *Philosophical Transactions of the Royal Society B, 368,* 1–11.

Campbell, C., & Lee, J. Z. (2002). When husbands and parents die: Widowhood and orphanhood in late Imperial Liaoning,

1789–1909. In R. Derosas & M. Oris (Eds.), *When Dad died: Individuals and families coping with distress in past societies* (pp. 301–322). Bern: Peter Lang.

Camperio Ciani, A. S., & Fontanesi, L. (2012). Mothers who kill their offspring: Testing evolutionary hypothesis in a 110-case Italian sample. *Child Abuse and Neglect, 36,* 519–527.

Case, A., Lin, I. F., & McLanahan, S. (2000). How hungry is the selfish gene? *The Economic Journal, 110,* 781–804.

Case, A., Lin, I. F., & McLanahan, S. (2001). Educational attainment of siblings in stepfamilies. *Evolution and Human Behavior, 22,* 269–289.

Conde-Agudelo, A., & Belizán, J. M. (2000). Maternal morbidity and mortality associated with interpregnancy interval: Cross-sectional study. *British Medical Journal, 321,* 1255–1259.

Connelly, C. D., & Straus, M. A. (1992). Mother's age and risk for physical abuse. *Child Abuse and Neglect, 16,* 709–718.

Coorg, R., & Tournay, A. (2013). Filicide-suicide involving children with disabilities. *Journal of Child Neurology, 28,* 742–748.

Craft, A. W., & Hall, D. M. B. (2004). Munchausen syndrome by proxy and sudden infant death. *British Medical Journal, 328,* 1309.

Creighton, S. J. (1985). An epidemiological study of abused children and their families in the United Kingdom between 1977 and 1982. *Child Abuse and Neglect, 9,* 441–448.

Creighton, S. J., & Noyes, P. (1989). *Child Abuse Trends in England and Wales, 1983–1987.* London: National Society for the Prevention of Cruelty to Children.

Cronk, L. (1989). Low socioeconomic status and female-biased parental investment: The Mukogodo example. *American Anthropologist, 91,* 414–429.

Daly, M., & Wilson, M. (1980). Discriminative parental solicitude: A biological perspective. *Journal of Marriage and the Family, 42,* 277–288.

Daly, M., & Wilson, M. (1985). Child abuse and other risks of not living with both parents. *Ethology and Sociobiology, 6,* 197–210.

Daly, M., & Wilson, M. (1988). *Homicide.* New York: Aldine De Gruyter.

Daly, M., & Wilson, M. (1994). Some differential attributes of lethal assaults on small children by stepfathers versus genetic fathers. *Ethology and Sociobiology, 15,* 207–217.

Daly, M., & Wilson, M. I. (1996). Violence against stepchildren. *Current Directions in Psychological Science, 5,* 77–81.

Daly, M., & Wilson, M. (2001). An assessment of some proposed exceptions to the phenomenon of nepotistic discrimination against stepchildren. *Annales Zoologici Fennici, 38,* 287–296.

Daly, M., & Wilson, M. (2008). Is the "Cinderella Effect" controversial? In C. Crawford & D. Krebs (Eds.), *Foundations of evolutionary psychology* (pp. 383–400). Mahwah, NJ: Erlbaum.

Dixon, S. (1988). *The Roman mother.* Norman: University of Oklahoma Press.

Dobson, V., & Sales, B. D. (2000). The science of infanticide and mental illness. *Psychology, Public Policy, and Law, 6,* 1098.

d'Orban, P. T. (1979). Women who kill their children. *British Journal of Psychiatry, 134,* 560–571.

Duntley, J. D., & Buss, D. M. (2011). Homicide adaptations. *Aggression and Violent Behavior, 16*(5), 399–410.

Ellis, B. J., & Garber, J. (2000). Psychosocial antecedents of variation in girls' pubertal timing: maternal depression, stepfather presence, and marital and family stress. *Child Development, 71*(2), 485–501.

Ellis, B. J., McFadyen-Ketchum, S., Dodge, K. A., Pettit, G. S., & Bates, J. E. (1999). Quality of early family relationships and individual differences in the timing of pubertal maturation in girls: A longitudinal test of an evolutionary model. *Journal of Personality and Social Psychology, 77,* 387–401.

Ellison, P. T. (2003). Natural variation in human fecundity. In C. R. Ember, M. Ember, & P. N. Peregrine (Eds.), *New directions* (pp. 3–19). Saddle River, NJ: Prentice Hall.

Friedman, S. H., Cavney, J., & Resnick, P. J. (2012a). Child murder by parents and evolutionary psychology. *Psychiatric Clinics of North America, 35,* 781–795.

Friedman, S. H., Cavney, J., & Resnick, P. J. (2012b). Mothers who kill: Evolutionary underpinnings and infanticide law. *Behavioral Sciences & the Law, 30,* 585–597.

Friedman, S. H., & Resnick, P. J. (2009). Neonaticide: Phenomenology and considerations for prevention. *International Journal of Law and Psychiatry 32,* 43–47.

Fujita, M., Roth, E. A., Lo, Y. J., Hurst, C., Vollner, J., & Kendell, A. (2012). Low serum vitamin A mothers breastfeed daughters more often than sons in drought-ridden northern Kenya: A test of the Trivers–Willard hypothesis. *Evolution and Human Behavior, 33,* 357–364.

Gauthier, D. K., Chaudoir, N. K., & Forsyth, C. J. (2003). A sociological analysis of maternal infanticide in the United States, 1984–1996. *Deviant Behavior, 24*(4), 393–404.

Haapasalo, J., & Petäjä, S. (1999). Mothers who killed or attempted to kill their child: Life circumstances, childhood abuse, and types of killing. *Violence and Victims, 14*(3), 219–239.

Hamilton, W. D. (1963). The evolution of altruistic behavior. *American Naturalist, 97,* 354–356.

Harris, G. T., Hilton, N. Z., Rice, M. E., & Eke, A. W. (2007). Children killed by genetic parents versus stepparents. *Evolution and Human Behavior, 28,* 85–95.

Harris, G. T., & Rice, M. E. (2012). Filicide and child maltreatment: Prospects for ultimate explanation. In T. K. Shackelford & V. A. Weekes-Shackelford (Eds.), *The Oxford handbook of evolutionary perspectives on violence, homicide, and war* (pp. 91–105). New York: Oxford University Press.

Hay, P. J. (2009). Post-partum psychosis: Which women are at highest risk? *PLoS Medicine, 6,* 130–131.

Herman-Giddens, M. E., Smith, J. B., Mittal, M., Carlson, M., & Butts, J. D. (2003). Newborns killed or left to die by a parent. *Journal of the American Medical Association, 289,* 1425–1429.

Herring, D. J. (2009). Fathers and child maltreatment: A research agenda based on evolutionary theory and behavioral biology research. *Children and Youth Services Review, 31,* 935–945.

Herzog, A., & Detre, T. (1976). Psychotic reactions associated with childbirth. *Diseases of the Nervous System, 37,* 229–235.

Hill, E. M., & Low, B. S. (1992). Contemporary abortion patterns: A life history approach. *Ethology and Sociobiology, 13,* 35–48.

Hrdy, S. B. (1992). Fitness tradeoffs in the history and evolution of delegated mothering with special reference to wet-nursing, abandonment, and infanticide. *Ethology and Sociobiology, 13,* 409–442.

Hunter, R. S., Kilstrom, N., Kraybill, E. N., & Loda, F. (1978). Antecedents of child abuse and neglect in premature infants: A prospective study in a newborn intensive care unit. *Pediatrics, 61,* 629–635.

Immigration and Refugee Board of Canada. (1996, December). *Viet Nam: Information on the societal attitude towards a single mother with an illegitimate child.* Report VNM25543.E. http://www.refworld.org/docid/3ae6ad0c38.html

Kaplan, H. S., & Gangestad, S. W. (2005). Life history theory and evolutionary psychology. In D. M. Buss (Ed.), *The handbook of evolutionary psychology* (pp. 68–95). Hoboken, NJ: Wiley.

Karakus, M., Ince, H., Ince, N., Arican, N., & Sozen, S. (2003). Filicide cases in Turkey, 1995–2000. *Croatian Medical Journal, 44,* 592–595.

Kelly, R. L. (1995). *The foraging spectrum: Diversity in hunter-gatherer lifeways.* Washington: Smithsonian Institution Press.

Kendell, R. E., Chalmers, J. C., & Platz, C. (1987). Epidemiology of puerperal psychoses. *British Journal of Psychiatry, 150,* 662–673.

Kim, K. I., & Ko, B. (1990). An incidence survey of battered children in two elementary schools of Seoul. *Child Abuse and Neglect, 14,* 273–276.

King, J. C. (2003). The risk of maternal nutritional depletion and poor outcomes increases in early or closely spaced pregnancies. *Journal of Nutrition, 133,* 1732S–1736S.

Koo, H. P., & Suchindran, C. M. (1980). Effects of children on women's remarriage prospects. *Journal of Family Issues, 1,* 497–515.

Koo, H. P., Suchindran, C. M., & Griffith, J. D. (1984). The effects of children on divorce and re-marriage: A multivariate analysis of life table probabilities. *Population Studies, 38,* 451–471.

Kramer, K. L., & Greaves, R. D. (2010). Synchrony between growth and reproductive patterns in human females: Early investment in growth among Pumé foragers. *American Journal of Physical Anthropology, 141,* 235–244.

Kreider, R., & Ellis, R. (2011). *Living arrangements of children: 2009.* Current Population Reports. Washington, DC: US Department of Commerce, US Census Bureau.

Krischer, M. K., Stone, M. H., Sevecke, K., & Steinmeyer, E. M. (2007). Motives for maternal filicide: Results from a study with female forensic patients. *International Journal of Law and Psychiatry, 30*(3), 191–200.

Kunz, J., & Bahr, S. J. (1996). A profile of parental homicide against children. *Journal of Family Violence, 11,* 347–362.

Lancy, D. F. (2014). "Babies aren't persons": A survey of delayed personhood. In H. Keller and H. Otto's (Eds.), *Different faces of attachment: Cultural variation of a universal human need* (pp. 66–109). Cambridge: Cambridge University Press.

Lee, R. B. (1980). Lactation, ovulation, infanticide and women's work. In M. N. Cohen R. S. Malpass, & H. G. Klein (Eds.), *Biosocial mechanisms of population regulation* (pp. 321–348). New Haven, CT: Yale University Press.

Levene, S., & Bacon, C. J. (2004). Sudden unexpected death and covert homicide in infancy. *Archives of Disease in Childhood, 89*(5), 443–447.

Levine, N. E. (1987). Differential child care in three Tibetan communities: Beyond son preference. *Population and Development Review, 13,* 281–304.

Lewis, C. F., & Bunce, S. C. (2003). Filicidal mothers and the impact of psychosis on maternal filicide. *Journal of the American Academy of Psychiatry and the Law Online, 31,* 459–470.

Lichter, D. T., & Graefe, D. R. (2001). Finding a mate? The marital and cohabitation histories of unwed mothers. In L. L. Wu & B. L. Wolfe (Eds.), *Out of wedlock: Causes and consequences of nonmarital fertility* (pp. 317–343). New York: Russel Sage Foundation.

Lightcap, J. L., Kurland, J. A., & Burgess, R. L. (1982). Child abuse: A test of some predictions from evolutionary theory. *Ethology and Sociobiology, 3,* 61–67.

Loomis, M. J. (1986). Maternal filicide: A preliminary examination of culture and victim sex. *International Journal of Law and Psychiatry, 9,* 503–506.

Low, B. S. (2000). *Why sex matters: A Darwinian look at human behavior.* Princeton, NJ: Princeton University Press.

Lucas, D. R., Wezner, K. C., Milner, J. S., McCanne, T. R., Harris, I. N., Monroe-Posey, C., & Nelson, J. P. (2002). Victim, perpetrator, family, and incident characteristics of infant and child homicide in the United States Air Force. *Child Abuse and Neglect, 26*(2), 167–186.

Luke, B., & Brown, M. B. (2007). Maternal risk factors for potential maltreatment deaths among healthy singleton and twin infants. *Twin Research and Human Genetics, 10*(5), 778–785.

Lunn, P. G. (1985). Maternal nutrition and lactational infertility: The baby in the driving seat. In J. Dobbing (Ed.), *Maternal nutrition and lactational infertility* (pp. 41–53). Nestle Nutrition workshop series 9. New York: Raven Press.

Mallett, S., & Rosenthal, D. (2009). Physically violent mothers are a reason for young people's leaving home. *Journal of Interpersonal Violence, 24*(7), 1165–1174.

Margolin, L. (1990). Fatal child neglect. *Child Welfare, 69*(4), 309–319.

Marks, M. (2009). Infanticide. *Psychiatry, 8*(1), 10–12.

Marks, M. N., & Kumar, R. (1993). Infanticide in England and Wales. *Medicine, Science, and the Law, 33,* 329–339.

Marks, M. N., & Kumar, R. (1996). Infanticide in Scotland. *Medicine, Science, and the Law, 36,* 299–305.

Marlowe, F. (2000). Paternal investment and the human mating system. *Behavioural Processes, 51,* 45–61.

Martin, S. P., & Parashar, S. (2006). Women's changing attitudes toward divorce, 1974–2002: Evidence for an educational crossover. *Journal of Marriage and Family, 68*(1), 29–40.

McKee, G. R. (2006). *Why mothers kill: A forensic psychologist's casebook.* New York: Oxford University Press.

Mendlowicz, M. V., Rapaport, M. H., Fontenelle, L., Jean-Louis, G., & De Moraes, T. M. (2002). Amnesia and neonaticide. *American Journal of Psychiatry, 159,* 498–499.

Messing, J. T., & Heeren, J. W. (2004). Another side of multiple murder women killers in the domestic context. *Homicide Studies, 8,* 123–158.

Meyer, C. L., & Oberman, M. (2001). *Mothers who kill their children: Understanding the acts of moms from Susan Smith to the prom mom.* New York: New York University Press.

Mraovich, L. R., & Wilson, J. F. (1999). Patterns of child abuse and neglect associated with chronological age of children living in a Midwestern county. *Child Abuse and Neglect, 23,* 899–903.

National Poverty Center. (2010). Poverty in the United States: Frequently asked questions. http://www.npc.umich.edu/poverty/

Newsome, V., & Airhihenbuwa, C. O. (2013). Gender ratio imbalance effects on HIV risk behaviors in African American women. *Health Promotion Practice, 14*(3), 459–463.

O'Hara, M. W., Schlechte, J. A., Lewis, D. A., & Varner, M. W. (1991). Controlled prospective study of postpartum mood disorders: Psychological, environmental, and hormonal variables. *Journal of Abnormal Psychology, 100*, 63–73.

Overpeck, M. D., Brenner, R. A., Trumble, A. C., Smith, G. S., MacDorman, M. F., & Berendes, H. W. (1999). Infant injury deaths with unknown intent: What else do we know? *Injury Prevention, 5*(4), 272–275.

Overpeck, M. D., Brenner, R. A., Trumble, A. C., Trifiletti, L. B., & Berendes, H. W. (1998). Risk factors for infant homicide in the United States. *New England Journal of Medicine, 339*(17), 1211–1216.

Panter-Brick, C., Lotstein, D. S., & Ellison, P. T. (1993). Seasonality of reproductive function and weight loss in rural Nepali women. *Human Reproduction, 8*, 684–690.

Pedersen, F. A. (1991). Secular trends in human sex ratios. *Human Nature, 2* 271–291.

Porter, T., & Gavin, H. (2010). Infanticide and neonaticide: A review of 40 years of research literature on incidence and causes. *Trauma, Violence, and Abuse, 11*, 99–112.

Puffer, R., & Serrano, C. (1973). *Patterns of mortality in childhood.* PAHO/WHO Scientific Publication 262, Washington: Pan American Health Organization.

Putnam-Hornstein, E. (2011). Report of maltreatment as a risk factor for injury death: A prospective birth cohort study. *Child Maltreatment, 16*, 163–174.

Resnick, P. J. (1972). Infanticide. *Infanticide.* In J. G. Howells (Ed.), *Modern perspectives in psycho-obstetrics* (pp. 410–431). Edinburgh: Oliver & Boyd.

Robling, S. A., Paykel, E. S., Dunn, V. J., Abbott, R., & Katona, C. (2000). Long-term outcome of severe puerperal psychiatric illness: A 23-year follow-up study. *Psychological Medicine, 30*, 1263–1271.

Rougé-Maillart, C., Jousset, N., Gaudin, A., Bouju, B., & Penneau, M. (2005). Women who kill their children. *American Journal of Forensic Medicine and Pathology, 26*, 320–326.

Scheper-Hughes, N. (1984). Infant mortality and infant care: Cultural and economic constraints on nurturing in Northeast Brazil. *Social Science Medicine, 19*, 535–546.

Schlomer, G. L., & Belsky, J. (2012). Maternal age, investment, and parent–child conflict: A mediational test of the terminal investment hypothesis. *Journal of Family Psychology, 26*(3), 443.

Shelton, J. L. E., Muirhead, Y., & Canning, K. E. (2010). Ambivalence toward mothers who kill: An examination of 45 US cases of maternal neonaticide. *Behavioral Sciences and the Law, 28*(6), 812–831.

Silverman, R. A., & Kennedy, L. W. (1988). Women who kill their children. *Violence and Victims, 134*, 560–571.

Spinelli, M. G. (2003). *Infanticide: Psychosocial and legal perspectives on mothers who kill.* Arlington, VA: American Psychiatric Publishing.

Stanton, J., & Simpson, A. (2001). Murder misdiagnosed as SIDS: A perpetrator's perspective. *Archives of Disease in Childhood, 85*(6), 454–459.

Stewart, S. D. (2005). How the birth of a child affects involvement with stepchildren. *Journal of Marriage and Family, 67*, 461–473.

Stewart, S. D., Manning, W. D., & Smock, P. J. (2003). Union formation among men in the US: Does having prior children matter? *Journal of Marriage and Family, 65*, 90–104.

Stiffman, M. N., Schnitzer, P. G., Adam, P., Kruse, R. L., & Ewigman, B. G. (2002). Household composition and risk of fatal child maltreatment. *Pediatrics, 109*, 615–621.

Stone, M. H., Steinmeyer, E., Dreher, J., & Krischer, M. (2005). Infanticide in female forensic patients: The view from the evolutionary standpoint. *Journal of Psychiatric Practice, 11*, 35–45.

Straus, M. A. (1980). Wife beating: How common and why. *Victimology, 2, 443–458.*

Taguchi, H. (2007). Maternal filicide in Japan: Analyses of 96 cases and future directions for prevention. *Psychiatria et Neurologia Japonica, 109*(2), 110–127.

Terp, I. M., & Mortensen, P. B. (1998). Post-partum psychoses. Clinical diagnoses and relative risk of admission after parturition. *British Journal of Psychiatry, 172*, 521–526.

Thomson, E., McLanahan, S. S., & Curtin, R. B. (1992). Family structure, gender, and parental socialization. *Journal of Marriage and the Family, 54*, 368–378.

Tifferet, S., Jorev, S., & Nasanovitz, R. (2010). Lower parental investment in stepchildren: The case of the Israeli "Great Journey" *Journal of Social, Evolutionary, and Cultural Psychology, 4*(2), 62–67.

Tooley, G. A., Karakis, M., Stokes, M., & Ozanne-Smith, J. (2006). Generalising the Cinderella effect to unintentional childhood fatalities. *Evolution and Human Behavior, 27*, 224–230.

Torres, A., & Forrest, J. D. (1988). Why do women have abortions? *Family Planning Perspectives, 20*, 169–176.

Trivers, R. L. (1972). Parental investment and sexual selection. In B. Campbell (Ed.), *Sexual selection and the descent of man, 1871–1971* (pp. 136–179). Chicago: Aldine-Atherton.

Vanamo, T., Kauppi, A., Karkola, K., Merikanto, J., & Räsänen, E. (2001). Intra-familial child homicide in Finland 1970–1994: Incidence, causes of death and demographic characteristics. *Forensic Science International, 117*, 199–204.

Van IJzendoorn, M. H., Euser, E. M., Prinzie, P., Juffer, F., & Bakermans-Kranenburg, M. J. (2009). Elevated risk of child maltreatment in families with stepparents but not with adoptive parents. *Child Maltreatment, 14*, 369–375.

Videbech, P., & Gouliaev, G. (1995). First admission with puerperal psychosis: 7–14 years of follow-up. *Acta Psychiatrica Scandinavica, 91*, 167–173.

Voland, E. (1998). Evolutionary ecology of human reproduction. *Annual Review of Anthropology, 27*, 347–374.

Wadsworth, J., Burnell, I., Taylor, B., & Butler, N. (1983). Family type and accidents in preschool children. *Journal of Epidemiology and Community Health, 37*, 100–104.

Warshak, R. A. (2000). Remarriage as a trigger of parental alienation syndrome. *American Journal of Family Therapy, 28*, 229–241.

Weekes-Shackelford, V. A., & Shackelford, T. K. (2004). Methods of filicide: Stepparents and genetic parents kill differently. *Violence and Victims, 19*, 75–81.

Weghorst, S. J. (1980). Household composition and the risk of child abuse and neglect. *Journal of Biosocial Sciences, 12*, 333–340.

White, L. K., & Booth, A. (1985). The quality and stability of remarriages: The role of stepchildren. *American Sociological Review, 50*, 689–698.

Willführ, K., & Gagnon, A. (2011). *Are step-parents always evil? Parental death, remarriage, and child survival in demographically saturated Krummhörn (1720–1859) and expanding Québec (1670–1750).* No. WP-2011-007. Rostock, Germany: Max Planck Institute for Demographic Research.

Winkling, J., Gurven, M., & Kaplan, H. (2011). The impact of parents and self-selection on child survival among the Tsimane of Bolivia. *Current Anthropology, 52*(2), 277–284.

Wyatt, G. E., Carmona, J. V., Loeb, T. B., Guthrie, D., Chin, D., & Gordon, G. (2000). Factors affecting HIV contraceptive decision-making among women. *Sex Roles, 42*, 495–521.

Yasumi, K., & Kageyama, J. (2009). Filicide and fatal abuse in Japan, 1994–2005: Temporal trends and regional distribution. *Journal of Forensic and Legal Medicine, 16*, 70–75.

Zvoch, K. (1999). Family type and investment in education: A comparison of genetic and stepparent families. *Evolution and Human Behavior, 20*, 453–464.

Physical Appearance

The Causes and Consequences of Women's Competitive Beautification

Danielle J. DelPriore, Marjorie L. Prokosch, *and* Sarah E. Hill

Abstract

Much empirical evidence suggests that "what is beautiful is good," particularly for women. Whether in the courtroom or the classroom, attractive females enjoy a variety of benefits not available to their less attractive peers. It is therefore often in a woman's best interest to engage in efforts to enhance her appearance. Women utilize a number of strategies to increase their physical attractiveness (e.g., wearing cosmetics, dieting), particularly when competing for romantic partners. Due to the competitive advantage it provides, however, a woman's beauty can also evoke aversive psychological responses from same-sex competitors. These negative responses—such as decreased self-esteem and increased envy—can have costly consequences for the attractive women who elicit them. In this chapter, we review research suggesting that women strategically enhance their beauty in order to facilitate competitive success. We also address several important questions about the causes and consequences of women's competitive beautification.

Key Words: physical attractiveness, intrasexual competition, human mating, envy, anti-attractiveness bias, appearance enhancement, beautification penalty

Valeria Lukyanova is a real-life Barbie doll. In 2012, the Ukranian model made headlines across cyberspace when photographs of her sporting large breasts, an unrealistically tiny waist, and a smooth, doll-like face surfaced online (for images, see Nemtsova, 2013). Lukyanova is just one of a growing number of women who have gone to unnatural extremes in recent years to achieve a hyperfeminine, doll-like appearance (Soldak, 2012). Although these "human dolls" have gained fame (and likely a number of expensive gifts from interested male suitors) through their efforts, their artificially enhanced looks have also placed these women at the center of a storm of hateful comments, unfair accusations, and inflammatory websites. For example, contributors to one website, "The Dirty," accused Lukyanova of being a fraud—using Photoshop to achieve her doll-like looks—and cast doubt on her sanity (The Dirty, 2012). Website members went so far as to call Lukyanova an ex-mail order bride and touted

her as the "Michael Jackson of Ukraine" due to her alleged plastic surgery. Lukyanova, however, seemed unfazed by the barrage of comments: "[I'm] happy I seem unreal to them. It means I'm doing a good job," she said in response to the plastic surgery accusations. She continued, "This is how they justify not wanting to strive for self-improvement" (Daily Mail, 2012).

Lukyanova and the other "human dolls" have gone to great lengths to achieve what some would consider perfection, altering their appearances much further than most women would dare. Although these women are an extreme example of the potential benefits (e.g., fame and wealth) and sometimes steep costs (e.g., financial cost of the procedures as well as rampant public criticism) associated with extreme appearance enhancement, most women engage in more ordinary forms of appearance enhancement on a daily basis. Some women spend hours at the gym, for example, and count every calorie consumed throughout the day (Cash & Pruzinsky, 1990). Others regularly spend their paychecks on brand-name cosmetics or flattering clothing in order to make themselves feel—and encourage others to perceive them to be—more beautiful (Miller, 2009). This raises a number of important questions: for example, why do women frequently invest time and money (whether great or modest amounts) in an effort to increase their physical attractiveness? What are the potential costs for women who choose to self-beautify? Although there is much empirical evidence suggesting that what is beautiful is perceived to be good (and consequently rewarded), emerging research findings indicate that beauty—particularly beauty resulting from money and effort invested in one's appearance—may actually lead women to be penalized for their attractiveness across various domains, especially at the hands of other women.

What Is Beautiful Is Good, Especially for Women

Is it better to be beautiful? A vast literature documenting the "what is beautiful is good" phenomenon, or the *physical attractiveness stereotype*, suggests that the answer to this question is a decisive "yes" (for a review, see Eagly, Ashmore, Makhijani, & Longo, 1991). The physical attractiveness stereotype refers to the tendency to perceive attractive individuals as possessing more socially desirable traits and being more deserving of—and more likely to attain—positive outcomes than less attractive individuals (Dion, Berscheid, & Walster, 1972). Indeed, from a very young age, attractive males and females receive a number of social benefits not readily available to their less attractive peers. For example, attractive babies (i.e., those possessing relatively wide, open eyes and round heads; Maier, Holmes, Slaymaker, & Reich, 1984) receive more attention and interaction from their parents (Langlois, Ritter, Casey, & Sawin, 1995) and from other caregivers (Ritter, Casey, & Langlois, 1991; Stephan & Langlois, 1984) than less attractive infants. This increased attention and care can lead to more positive outcomes for attractive infants, including better health. One study, for example, found that attractive premature infants spend significantly less time in the hospital post-birth than do their less attractive counterparts (Badr & Abdallah, 2001). Furthermore, physical attractiveness is related to higher ratings of success and popularity for both children and adolescents (Langlois et al., 2000).

The benefits of being attractive continue into adulthood. As adults, beautiful people are perceived as possessing more socially desirable traits than less attractive people (Lucker, Beane, & Helmreich, 1981). Specifically, people believe attractive individuals are more outgoing, socially dominant, confident, sexually responsive and receptive, honest, and mentally stable than less attractive individuals (Cialdini, 1984; Feingold, 1992). In light of these favorable social expectations, it is not surprising that people report a heightened desire to interact with attractive others as romantic partners, as friends, and even as participants in laboratory-based economic games (romantic partners and friends: Lemay, Clark, & Greenberg, 2010; economic game partners: Mulford, Orbell, Shatto, & Stockard, 1998). This increased social desirability can translate into a greater likelihood of receiving anonymous help from strangers than what is offered to less attractive individuals. For instance, one study showed that strangers were more likely to mail a completed graduate school application form that they found in an airport phone booth if the photograph attached to the application depicted a more (vs. less) attractive target (Benson, Karabenick, & Lerner, 1976).

In addition to these social benefits, physical attractiveness also influences people's evaluations of a target's competency, a more objective set of traits that are less directly linked to one's appearance. In general, researchers find that attractive people are perceived to be more competent, although this effect may be reversed when women are oversexualized or objectified (see, e.g., Heflick & Goldenberg, 2009). As early as infancy, both mothers and college students rate attractive babies as more competent cognitively and communicatively (Ritter et al., 1991), smarter (Stephan & Langlois, 1984), and higher functioning (Maier, Holmes, Slaymaker, & Reich, 1984) than less attractive babies of similar ages. In addition, despite cliché jokes portraying attractive individuals (and especially attractive women) as being unintelligent, both teachers and peers actually report having higher expectations regarding the academic motivation (Clifford & Walster, 1973), leadership abilities (Kenealy, Frude, & Shaw, 1988), future educational attainment (Clifford, 1975), and academic potential (i.e., IQ) of attractive versus less attractive students of both sexes (Ritts, Patterson, & Tubbs, 1992). Perhaps as a consequence of these heightened expectations, attractive male and female students receive more favorable evaluations of their work (Bull & Stevens, 1979) and earn higher grades in school than their less attractive peers (male students: Felson, 1980; female students: Hore, 1971; for a meta-analysis of relevant results, see Ritts et al., 1992).

Not surprisingly, attractive men and women also fare better when they leave school and enter the workplace (Hosoda, Stone-Romero, & Coats, 2003). Specifically, attractive people receive higher starting salaries (Frieze, Olson, & Russell, 1991), earn more money across their careers (Umberson & Hughes, 1987), and receive better job suitability ratings and ability rankings (Hosoda et al., 2003) than unattractive individuals. Furthermore, one study found that attractive individuals are terminated less often than unattractive individuals of comparable skill levels (Commisso & Finkelstein, 2012). These favorable evaluations and salary benefits increase even more when the attractive person's job field is gender stereotypic, such as when women are employed as secretaries (Jackson, 1983).

The benefits that attractive individuals reap are not limited to the home, school, and organizational contexts. In addition to the favoritism they receive from their teachers and bosses, attractive people may also benefit from special treatment in a setting where objectivity and impartiality are at an especially high premium: the courtroom. In general, attractive individuals—and particularly attractive females—enjoy more favorable legal outcomes, whether they are the plaintiff or the defendant (for exceptions, see Patry, 2008; Sigall & Ostrove, 1975). For instance, when the plaintiff is an attractive woman, defendants are more likely to be found guilty of sexual harassment and rape and to receive longer sentences (Thornton, 1977). This finding may be due, in part, to attractive female plaintiffs being rated as more sincere, warm, and believable than less attractive plaintiffs (Castellow, Wuensch, & Moore, 1990). Furthermore, attractive female defendants are less likely than their unattractive counterparts to be perceived as guilty of a criminal act (Castellow et al., 1990; Efran, 1974), an effect that generalizes across a range of charges (Mazzella & Feingold, 1994). In the event that they are found guilty, attractive defendants (particularly attractive females) tend to receive lighter sentences than less attractive defendants (DeSantis & Kayson, 1997).

Although attractive people have measurable advantages over their less attractive peers in settings as diverse as the courtroom, the classroom, and the workplace, there are few domains in which the benefits of attractiveness are more pronounced than in the domain of mate attraction (Barber, 1995; Grammer & Thornhill, 1994; Krebs &

Adinolfi, 1975), especially for women (Buss, 1989, 2008; Buss & Schmitt, 1993; Buss, Shackelford, Kirkpatrick, & Larsen, 2001; Kenrick & Keefe, 1992; Li & Kenrick, 2006). Beginning in adolescence, attractive girls are strongly preferred as dating partners by adolescent boys (Ha, Overbeek, & Engels, 2010). As a result, attractive teenage girls (i.e., 14–15 years old) are more likely to be sexually active than their less attractive female peers (de Bruyn, Cillessen, & Weisfeld, 2012). Physical attractiveness remains an invaluable asset for women in adulthood because men across cultures rate this quality as being nearly "indispensable" when selecting a long-term mate (Buss & Schmitt, 1993). As such, attractive women are in the best position to "get what they want" on the mating market. In other words, attractive women have the luxury to preferentially select as mates those men who have high social status/resource access and who are willing to commit to long-term relationships and parenthood—traits that women indicate as being highly desirable in their romantic partners (social status: Regan, 1998; resources: Buss, 2008; Waynforth & Dunbar, 1995; commitment: Buss & Shackelford, 2008). In fact, a woman's attractiveness has been shown to be one of the best predictors of her upward social mobility (Elder, 1969; Krendl, Magoon, Hull, & Heatherton, 2011). For example, one provocative longitudinal study found that attractiveness was a better predictor of a woman's chances of marrying a high-status man than was her intelligence or class origin (Elder, 1969). A later study found similar results, demonstrating that attractive women marry men with more education—and higher income—than do less attractive women (Udry & Eckland, 1984). Taken together, it seems that beauty trumps brains when predicting women's socioeconomic status (or upward mobility) in adulthood.

Although the literature examining the benefits of facial attractiveness—especially for females—is robust, relatively few studies have tested for analogous effects regarding bodily attractiveness. However, the studies that have been conducted provide preliminary evidence that the physical attractiveness stereotype may generalize to bodily attractiveness as well. For instance, a study conducted by Pingitore and colleagues (1994) indicated that participants demonstrated a bias against hiring an overweight (vs. a normal-weight) job applicant in a mock employment interview, an effect that was stronger for female targets. Other studies have examined the importance of bodily attractiveness for women in mating-relevant contexts. In Western societies, a thinner female body is idealized as most attractive by both women and men (although men do not necessarily desire as thin a female body as women think they do; Fallon & Rozin, 1985). This trend is evidenced by the shrinking measurements of *Playboy* centerfolds over recent decades (Garner, Garfinkel, Schwartz, & Thompson, 1980). Accordingly, heterosexual men are more likely than women to indicate that they are seeking a thin partner in their personal ads (Smith, Waldorf, & Trembath, 1990). Results from a recent study of online dating profiles in the United States suggest that this preference for thin women may be strongest among Caucasian men (Glasser, Robnett, & Feliciano, 2009). Although research findings have demonstrated that thinner/normal-weight men receive more favorable social desirability ratings (e.g., rated as friendlier and more trustworthy) relative to heavier/overweight men (Wade, Fuller, Bresnan, Schaefer, & Mlynarski, 2007), future research should examine more extensively whether women perceived to be high in bodily attractiveness (in terms of both their body shape and size) are also perceived to be more socially desirable than women with less attractive bodies.

The Importance of Women's Physical Attractiveness for Successful Mate Competition

Why is physical attractiveness instrumental in shaping many of women's life outcomes? Researchers suggest that the answer to this question has deep evolutionary roots. Women's fertility is inherently limited by various factors, including cyclic ovulation, pregnancy, and menopause (Buss, 1995). Due to these limitations, men have recurrently faced the adaptive problem of identifying and selecting fertile—and rejecting infertile—women as mates (Buss, 2008; Buss & Schmitt, 1993). To help solve this problem, men have evolved preferences for physical features that would have, on average, helped them accurately and reliably distinguish fertile women from those women who are less fertile. Accordingly, men value physical indicators of youth in their female partners, such as full lips, smooth skin, lustrous hair, and femininity, more than they value physical indicators of old age, such as wrinkled skin and graying hair (Buss, 1989, 2008; Symons, 1995). Such youth-linked attractiveness cues, along with certain bodily features (like a low waist-to-hip ratio that results from having full breasts, a small waist, and fat deposited around the hips), are reliable

markers of female fertility (waist-to-hip ratio: Singh & Singh, 2011; breast size: Schaefer et al., 2006; for a review of the association between body shape and youth, see, e.g., Barber, 1995; Symons, 1995). Furthermore, certain traits such as bodily symmetry (Schaefer et al., 2006), facial symmetry (Little, Jones, & Debruine, 2011), average facial features (Gangestad & Thornhill, 1999), and feminine facial features shaped by high estrogen levels (Fink & Penton-Voak, 2002) often signal a stable developmental trajectory free of teratogens (Gangestad & Thornhill, 1997). Thus, these traits typically signal the good health of a potential mate and are consequently perceived to be attractive (Gangestad & Thornhill, 1997).

Men's physical appearance, by contrast, is less diagnostic of their ability to successfully reproduce. This is because men's fertility, unlike women's, is not directly linked to hormonally derived attractiveness indicators, such as facial masculinity (Fink & Penton-Voak, 2002) or height (Jackson, 1992). In other words, a man with a very masculine face would be able to produce a comparable number of offspring as a man with a more feminine face, all else being equal. The same is true with respect to a man whose face exhibits cues associated with age because men's fertility does not decline as sharply with age as does women's fertility. A man's physical attractiveness, therefore, plays a less prominent role in determining his desirability as a mate compared to the role played by a woman's attractiveness (Ellis, 1995; Li & Kenrick, 2006).

Given that men highly value attractiveness in their mates, intrasexual competition among women often manifests itself as a battle to be the most beautiful. Although such competition frequently takes the form of women engaging in activities that will make themselves look *better* (e.g., beautification or self-promotion), it sometimes manifests itself in more sinister ways, such as when women attempt to make their competitors look *worse* (e.g., sabotage or competitor derogation; Buss, 1988; Fisher, Cox, & Gordon, 2009; Schmitt & Buss, 1996). We discuss each of these strategies below.

Women's Appearance Enhancement via Self-Promotion

How attractive a woman is relative to her same-sex competitors is critically important in the mating game. For example, research conducted by Kenrick and colleagues found that another women's superior attractiveness can have negative implications for one's own perceived attractiveness and for how satisfied one's partner feels about the relationship. Specifically, men rated average-looking women as being less attractive and rated themselves as less satisfied with their current relationship partner after viewing videos or images of highly attractive female targets (perceptions of attractiveness: Kenrick & Gutierres, 1980; Kenrick, Montello, Gutierres, & Trost, 1993; relationship partner satisfaction: Kenrick, Neuberg, Zierk, & Krones, 1994). Accordingly, women put a great deal of effort into enhancing their appearance in the service of both attracting and retaining romantic partners (Buss, 1988; Schmitt & Buss, 1996).

One of the most popular routes to appearance enhancement for women is via beauty products or cosmetics, the use of which appears to be tied to women's mate attraction goals. A recent study by Regan (2011), for example, experimentally demonstrated that female participants apply more cosmetics when they expect to interact with an attractive male (and less when they expect to interact with an unattractive male). The use of cosmetics may help women attract a mate by making their faces appear more feminine, younger, and healthier (and ultimately, more attractive). First, it is well established that men tend to prefer more feminine (vs. masculine) women as mates (e.g., Fink & Penton-Voak, 2002; Perrett et al., 1998). Because women tend to have greater facial contrast than men (Russell, 2009), wearing cosmetics can help women further increase their facial contrast—and therefore increase the perceived femininity of their faces (Etcoff, Stock, Haley, Vickery, & House, 2011). This increase in facial contrast can be achieved by shaping and darkening facial features so that they stand out (e.g., by wearing eyeliner or accentuating the lips by wearing lipstick; Russell, 2002, 2009). Cosmetics may also help women appear more feminine by enlarging perceptions of their eyebrow–eye distance with eye shadow (Russell, 2011). In addition to increasing the perceived femininity of women's faces, cosmetics can be used to increase perceptions of facial symmetry (Thornhill & Gangestad, 1994) and to advertise facial cues often associated with youth and health. Specifically, women use cosmetics to make their skin appear more clear (Russell, 2011) and their cheeks more rosy (Low, 1979; Van den Berghe & Frost, 1986), and to accentuate the color in their lips (Stephen & McKeegan, 2010). Thus, women seem to use cosmetics to help themselves appear to adhere to the evolutionarily reinforced mate preferences demonstrated by men across cultures (e.g., good health, facial symmetry, femininity).

Studies confirm that this attractiveness-enhancement strategy is an effective one. Men (and women) consistently rate women wearing cosmetics to be more attractive (Cash, Dawson, Davis, Bowen, & Galumbeck, 1989; Cox & Glick, 1986; Workman & Johnson, 1991), feminine (Cox & Glick, 1986; Workman & Johnson, 1991), and sexy (Cox & Glick, 1986) than women not wearing cosmetics. The benefits of cosmetics use seem to be equally available to women ranging in age and natural attractiveness. For example, Fabricant and Gould (1993) determined that younger women use cosmetics to look older whereas older women use cosmetics to look younger, suggesting that women of any age may be able to use cosmetics to appear more fertile (and, therefore, more attractive) than they actually are based on their age. Furthermore, Osborn (1996) found that participants rated women who were naturally above or below average in attractiveness as being significantly more attractive when wearing cosmetics.

Women's increased attractiveness following cosmetics use has been shown to affect men's approach behavior in more naturalistic settings. For example, Guéguen (2008) demonstrated that women wearing cosmetics were more likely to be approached by men in a bar (and after a shorter period of time) relative to women not wearing cosmetics. Similar effects were found for male drivers stopping to offer a ride to a female confederate posing as a hitchhiker while wearing cosmetics versus when she was not (Guéguen & Lamy, 2013). Women even report feeling better about their bodies when wearing cosmetics (Cash et al., 1989). Although many of these studies are limited in that the effects were obtained in Western (i.e., European and American) samples using primarily Caucasian targets (Mulhern, Fieldman, Hussey, Lévêque, & Pineau, 2003; Nash, Fieldman, Hussey, Lévêque, & Pineau, 2006), Etcoff and colleagues (2011) found that race/ethnicity did not moderate the effects of cosmetics use on perceptions of facial attractiveness.

In addition to wearing cosmetics, women also increase their likelihood of mating success by displaying (or enhancing) their bodily attractiveness. Women list wearing flattering clothing, diet and exercise, and tanning as among the most effective strategies for mate attraction and retention (Buss, 1988). In addition, women report that one of their main reasons for working out at the gym is to improve their body (Garner et al., 1980) in order to become more attractive to the other sex (Mealey, 1997). Specifically, women tend to spend the most time at the gym working out their lower body and abdominal regions to achieve a thinner form (Jonason, 2007) in an attempt to conform to their beliefs about what men find most attractive (Fallon & Rozin, 1985). Women also report that sexualizing their appearance (e.g., by wearing a bust-enhancing bra) is an effective way to attract a mate (Schmitt & Buss, 1996). Women likely place an emphasis on improving their body shape because men prefer women with a low waist-to-hip ratio cross-culturally (Grammer, Fink, Møller, & Thornhill, 2003; Singh, 1994), even in Western cultures where men and women idealize a thinner body size overall (Garner et al., 1980; Harrison, 2003). Interestingly, for both men and women, body shape predicts overall physical attractiveness independent of facial attractiveness (Peters, Rhodes, & Simmons, 2007). In other words, women who enhance the attractiveness of their bodies may enjoy additional fitness benefits above and beyond having just a pretty face. As such, women who engage in efforts to display and/or enhance both their facial *and* bodily attractiveness may be in the best position to successfully attract a desirable romantic partner, although future research is needed to examine this possibility.

Findings suggest that at least some of these body enhancement tactics may help shape men's perceptions of—and behavior toward—women. For example, men rate models wearing revealing clothing (like wet t-shirts and mini-skirts) as being sexier than models wearing more conventional clothing (Williamson & Hewitt, 1986). Men also rate "point-of-light walkers" (i.e., computerized, moving points of light that approximate a moving human body) wearing high heels as being significantly more attractive than those wearing flat-bottomed shoes (Morris, White, Morrison, & Fisher, 2013). Furthermore, a female confederate wearing a special bra to manipulate perceptions of her breast size received an increasing number of offers for a ride when her car was supposedly broken down on the side of the road (Guéguen, 2007a) and was approached by more male suitors at a bar (Guéguen, 2007b) as the cup size of her bra was increased. Although men's evaluations of women's sexy clothing are generally favorable, research findings are mixed for men's evaluation of other forms of bodily enhancements (e.g., women having artificially tanned skin). For example, some studies find that men (and women) rate light-toned women as more attractive (Swami, Furnham, & Joshi, 2008), whereas others find that men are more attracted

to women with darker skin (Fink, Grammer, & Thornhill, 2001). Future research is needed to examine the factors that contribute to these discrepant preferences. Researchers should also assess how women's diet and exercise habits are truly perceived by men when evaluating women's attractiveness as short- and long-term mates. Although men may prefer toned and thin women on average, it is possible that unhealthy weight management tactics that decrease women's fertility might be perceived negatively by men (particularly in long-term mating contexts).

Given that appearance enhancement has been shown to be an effective tactic for mate attraction, it is not surprising that women engage in more of these types of behaviors when competition for mates is especially fierce, salient, or important. One such case is when women are at peak fertility during the ovulatory phase of their monthly menstrual cycle (i.e., when the probability of conception is at its highest). Studies using both diary-tracking and laboratory-based experimental methods provide evidence that during the fertile (vs. infertile) phase of their ovulatory cycle, women report a greater desire to enhance their appearance (Röder, Brewer, & Fink, 2009), perform a greater number of beautification behaviors (Saad & Stenstrom, 2012), spend more money on beauty products (Durante, Griskevicius, Hill, Perilloux, & Li, 2011; Durante, Li, & Haselton, 2008; Hill & Durante, 2009), wear more revealing clothing (Grammer, Renninger, & Fischer, 2004; Schwarz & Hassebrauck, 2008), and apply more cosmetics (Guéguen, 2012). This ramped-up effort to improve one's appearance may be especially pronounced among naturally cycling women who are most likely to be active on the mating market (i.e., "sexually unrestricted" women or women pursuing a short-term mating strategy; Durante et al., 2008). Furthermore, these shifts in self-promoting behaviors are perceptible to third-party observers. For instance, both male and female participants rate photographed targets who are ovulating (i.e., at high fertility) as trying to look more attractive than naturally cycling women who were photographed while they were not ovulating (i.e., at low fertility; Haselton, Mortezaie, Pillsworth, Bleske-Rechek, & Frederick, 2007). Perhaps as a result of this increased effort, women are rated as being more attractive at peak fertility than at other times in their monthly cycle (Roberts et al., 2004).

Women also attempt to enhance their appearance in the service of mate competition when the number of desirable and successful men is limited, such as during an economic recession (Hill, Rodeheffer, Griskevicius, Durante, & White, 2012). Because humans are a biparental species whose offspring experience a prolonged, helpless juvenile period (Trivers, 1972), offspring mortality is significantly reduced for children who receive meaningful levels of paternal investment (Geary, 2005). Accordingly, women greatly prioritize direct benefits from mates—especially the material resources that men may confer upon them and any resulting offspring (Symons, 1979). As a result of women's mate preferences prioritizing resource access (Campos, Otta, & de Oliveira Siqueira, 2002; Dunn, Brinton, & Clark, 2010), the economic climate plays a key role in signaling the availability of high-quality men in a woman's pool of potential mates. During economic recessions, unemployment is typically high and good jobs are scarce. As such, the number of high-quality romantic partners (i.e., men with financial resources) available to women as long-term mates is diminished, too. Because there are fewer desirable men with resources available during a recession for long-term mating, women must compete more fiercely for the attention of those few desirable men (who can now place an even higher premium on a prospective partner's level of physical attractiveness). In response to this heightened level of competition during times of economic recession, women increase their spending on beauty products, ostensibly as a means to successfully compete with other women in the domain of physical attractiveness (Koehn, 2001; Nelson, 2001). This spending shift has been dubbed the "lipstick effect." Evidence for the lipstick effect has been found in both actual consumer spending (Allison & Martinez, 2010) and in the laboratory (Hill et al., 2012). For instance, real-world data show that consumer spending on appearance-enhancing products, including cosmetics and clothing, remains strong during recessions (Hill et al., 2012). Furthermore, women primed with recession cues in the laboratory reported an increased desire to purchase attractiveness-enhancing products but a decreased desire to purchase products that could not be used to enhance their attractiveness relative to women in the control condition (Hill et al., 2012). This effect was driven by an increased desire to attract a man with resources and was strongest for women who were highly motivated to find a long-term mate.

Finally, competitive shifts in appearance enhancement are also observed when women's desire to compete for a long-term mate is explicitly activated. For example, priming mating-relevant goals (by exposing women to photos of attractive men or attractive women or by asking them to write about a time they competed for a romantic partner) increased women's willingness to engage in relatively risky beautification strategies, such as tanning and using diet pills, while simultaneously decreasing the perceived health risks associated with these behaviors (Hill & Durante, 2011). Specifically, women rated tanning and diet pill use as being less risky after mating goals were activated with a writing prime relative to women who wrote about the last time they did their laundry. This strategic risk suppression was specific to behaviors that would increase a woman's attractiveness to the other sex, rather than general risky behaviors that could be detrimental to one's health (such as painting in an unventilated room).

Women's Relative Appearance Enhancement via Derogation

A more sinister tack that women sometimes use to gain a competitive edge is derogation of same-sex rivals. As previously mentioned, physical attractiveness more strongly determines a woman's mate value than it does for men. As such, researchers have found that women are more likely than men to derogate their competitors' appearance when trying to attract a mate (Schmitt & Buss, 1996). Specifically, results reveal sex differences in the degree that derogation and indirect aggression (i.e., aggressive acts intended to harm another that are not easily traced back to the perpetrator; Björkqvist, 1994) are used successfully as mate competition and attraction tactics, with women using them more often than men (Benenson, Markovits, Thompson, & Wrangham, 2011) and enjoying more success from employing these tactics (Buss & Dedden, 1990; Schmitt & Buss, 1996; Walters & Crawford, 1994). For example, Fisher and Cox (2009) found that women's derogation of other women's attractiveness lowered men's perceptions of the targets' attractiveness, especially when the derogator was attractive. However, these negative comments did not influence the judgments of other women (regardless of the derogator's attractiveness). Whereas men are more likely to directly aggress against their same-sex rivals using their fists, women seem to hit each other hardest with the criticism and rumors that they spread behind each other's backs.

Overall, women are more likely to use self-promotion (instead of derogation) tactics when competing for mates. However, there are individual and contextual differences that may increase a woman's likelihood of using derogation to gain an advantage over her same-sex rivals. Researchers posit that women use derogation tactics in order to lower the perceived mate value of rivals and help them increase their own chances of attracting (or retaining) a high-quality mate (Fisher & Cox, 2009; Vaillancourt, 2005). Therefore, it is women who are less able to successfully utilize self-promotion tactics (i.e., mated women) and women who are at a competitive disadvantage (i.e., less attractive women) who might be expected to be the most frequent perpetrators of these aggressive acts. There have been mixed results regarding the effects of relationship status and women's own attractiveness on their use of competitor derogation (see, e.g., Fisher, Tran, & Voracek, 2008). For example, Fisher and colleagues (2009) found that single women (and women in casual dating relationships) and more attractive women engage in more derogation of same-sex others than do mated women and less attractive women, respectively. In contrast, other research findings indicate that women in relationships may be especially likely to use competitor derogation as a successful relationship maintenance tactic (Buss & Dedden, 1990; Fisher & Cox, 2011). In one study, women who were judged as less attractive than their husbands were found to commit more competitor derogation than women who were more attractive than their husbands, although a woman's perceptions of her husband's attractiveness were negatively related to her use of competitor derogation (Buss & Shackelford, 1997). This finding suggests that discrepancies in mate value between women in relationships and their partners, rather than absolute attractiveness, may predict greater use of derogation of other women as a competitive strategy.

Although not much cross-cultural research has been done on this topic, some work has found that competitor derogation is also observed among women in more traditional societies (Cashdan, 1996). For example, research on the mating strategies of Bolivian tribal women found that these women may use reputational derogation tactics to lower the perceived physical attractiveness of other women within the tribe (Rucas et al., 2006). Women in these villages used descriptions such as "keeps a messy house," "is mean," and "is promiscuous" to describe disliked women. When they asked Tsimane women to rank the attractiveness of other female villagers, negative traits predicted lower attractiveness rankings, whereas third-party observers who viewed photos of these women rated them as being more attractive than the same-sex

villagers. This finding suggests that reputation derogation may be an effective means to lower the perceived attractiveness of one's competitors. Further work should be done to clarify why, how, and when women from non-Western cultures derogate potential mating rivals.

Finally, similar to self-promotional strategies, a woman's likelihood of using derogation tactics may vary across contexts. For instance, women have been shown to engage in more frequent acts of derogation (such as spreading rumors about a competitor) when men are scarce (Campbell, 2004; Cashdan, 1996; Schmitt & Buss, 1996). Women also engage in greater derogation of other women, rating their faces as less physically attractive, when the derogator is at peak fertility (Fisher, 2004). Finally, research conducted by Welling and colleagues (2007, 2008) indicates that women may be more likely to engage in a form of derogation (i.e., devaluing feminine faces) when mating motives are activated. Specifically, viewing images of highly attractive men decreased women's preference for femininity (vs. masculinity) in female faces (Welling, Jones, DeBruine, Little, & Smith, 2008). Welling and colleagues (2007) found a similar devaluation of feminine female faces among naturally cycling women when they were near ovulation. Although these studies did not explicitly measure derogation of the female targets with feminine faces, the authors posit that the results may reflect increased derogation of attractive competitors. In all, it seems that the same contexts that promote increased self-promotion (e.g., greater cosmetic use) among women—for example, ovulation and a perceived scarcity of desirable mates—can also lead to increased use of derogation in an attempt to increase one's chances of successfully attracting (or retaining) a desirable mate.

Is What Is Good for the Goose Also Good for Gander When It Comes to Female Beauty?

Given that men preferentially seek out attractive females as romantic partners (e.g., Walster, Aronson, Abrahams, & Rottman, 1966), some women spend much of their time and effort engaged in activities aimed at making themselves appear more attractive than their same-sex competitors. Although these efforts are often rewarded by men (e.g., Guéguen, 2008; Guéguen & Lamy, 2013), is it possible that such behaviors may simultaneously put women in the crosshairs of their same-sex rivals by evoking their envy and ire? That is, although beauty may be an advantage for women when interacting with men, the benefits that beauty brings may be negated (or even reversed) when interacting with other women. In this section, we provide evidence of a beauty paradox and suggest that beauty (although generally rewarded) can, in some situations, inflict cost on those women who possess it.

As noted earlier, although a woman's beauty can inspire the hearts and minds of men, it can also evoke envy and resentment among her same-sex competitors (who may look less attractive by comparison). Being less attractive than one's peers has important implications for a woman's mood (Kenrick et al., 1993; Mathes & Kahn, 1975), as well as for her perceptions of self-worth (e.g., Brase & Guy, 2004; Feingold, 1992). Less attractive women have been shown to have lower self-esteem (Feingold, 1992; Langlois et al., 2000; Mathes & Kahn, 1975) and to be less happy overall (Mathes & Kahn, 1975) than their more attractive peers. In one set of laboratory experiments, for example, women who viewed photographs of attractive same-sex targets subsequently rated themselves as being less attractive and feeling more self-conscious compared to women who viewed relatively unattractive targets (Brown, Novick, Lord, & Richards, 1992; Thornton & Moore, 1993). Others have found comparable causal effects of exposure to attractive female targets on women's self-reported desirability as a marriage partner (Gutierres, Kenrick, & Partch, 1999), body satisfaction (Cattarin, Thompson, Thomas, & Williams, 2000), and mood (Kenrick et al., 1993). Being exposed to attractive same-sex others can thus be aversive and threatening to women because it often has negative implications for how they feel about themselves (Buss, Shackelford, Choe, Buunk, & Dijkstra, 2000).

In addition to (or perhaps because of) women feeling worse about themselves following exposure to attractive same-sex others, these targets have been found to evoke one of the most socially undesirable of the seven deadly sins: envy. Envy is the subjectively unpleasant response that we experience when someone else—often a close competitor—possesses an important social advantage (Smith, 1991; Smith & Kim, 2007) or fitness-relevant resource (Hill & Buss, 2008; Hill, DelPriore, & Vaughan, 2011) that we desire for ourselves. For example, women rate a same-sex peer "becoming noticeably more attractive" as significantly more envy-inducing than do men (Hill & Buss, 2006). In fact, research has shown that women list same-sex peers' superior attractiveness as their most common source of envy (DelPriore, Hill, & Buss, 2012). Undergraduate

men and women were asked to list various times in their lives when they felt envious, detailing who they envied and why. Nearly 18% of all responses provided by women described a peer being more attractive as the source of their envy, and women described this as a source of envy significantly more often than men (who described a peer's attractiveness in approximately 8% of their narratives). Similar results were obtained when men and women were asked to rank the amount of envy that they would experience across 12 scenarios, with women ranking a peer being more attractive as evoking the most envy (the same dimension was ranked number 6 by men, following a peer having "more status and prestige" or a peer having "a more attractive romantic partner").

In addition to experiencing the subjective distress that often accompanies envy, comparing oneself with attractive same-sex others has also been found to evoke another unpleasant (and often related) social emotion: jealousy. Whereas envy refers to the suite of unpleasant psychological states we experience when someone else possesses something that we lack (e.g., a more attractive appearance or a higher paying job), jealousy is the upset that we feel when we fear that we are going to lose something that we already have (e.g., a cherished romantic partner) to another person (Parrott, 1991). Similar to envy, jealous feelings—for example, fear of loss, hurt, suspicion, and anger (Smith, Kim, & Parrott, 1988)—are most often evoked by same-sex rivals in mating contexts (Parrott, 1991). Individuals tend to experience increased romantic jealousy when the mating rival is more advantaged than themselves in fitness-relevant domains. Accordingly, research findings illustrate predictable sex differences in the rival characteristics that most frequently evoke jealous feelings among men and women. Whereas men are most likely to experience jealousy when a mating rival or potential mate poacher is more dominant or has higher status, women's jealousy is most heavily influenced by the same-sex rival's physical attractiveness (Dijkstra & Buunk, 1998, 2002). In other words, women experience greater jealousy when they see their romantic partner interacting with a highly attractive woman than they do when they see their partner interacting with a less attractive woman. Similar effects have been found for brief subliminal presentations of attractive same-sex others, with women experiencing greater jealousy in response to a jealousy-evoking scenario after just a very brief exposure (60 ms) to an attractive (vs. an unattractive) female target (Massar & Buunk,

2010). Among women, feelings of jealousy have been shown to evoke anger and aggression directed at same-sex rivals (Mathes & Verstraete, 1993; Paul & Galloway, 1994).

Due to the negative feelings that attractive competitors can evoke (e.g., decreased self-esteem, increased envy and jealousy), it is not surprising that women may respond negatively and aggressively toward attractive peers. Because physical attractiveness is so closely tied to women's desirability as mates, it is only fitting that attractive women are more often the targets of derogation and aggression than their average-looking counterparts (Campbell, 1995; Vaillancourt, 2005). Evidence for this "prettiness penalty" has been found in the domain of social and economic exchange. Although people are often more willing to enter into play and cooperate with beautiful others (Andreoni & Petrie, 2008; Mulford et al., 1998; Solnick & Schweitzer, 1999; Wilson & Eckel, 2006), some studies provide evidence for the opposite effect, wherein attractive targets are penalized for failing to meet the heightened cooperative expectations established by their appearance (Andreoni & Petrie, 2008; Solnick & Schweitzer, 1999; Wilson & Eckel, 2006). In a public goods game, for example, beautiful women fared better until information about how much they contributed was revealed (Andreoni & Petrie, 2008). People expect attractive individuals to be more generous, and, when they fail to meet these expectations, they are penalized more harshly (and earn less money) than less attractive individuals in economic games. Consistent with this interpretation, researchers found that, in a trust game (Wilson & Eckel, 2006), attractive "trusters" were penalized for not being overly generous in their monetary offers (i.e., violating others' expectations) and therefore received less money back from "trustees" than did less attractive "trusters." Similarly, Solnick and Schweitzer (1999) demonstrated that participants specified higher minimum acceptance levels for attractive women in an ultimatum game, an economic game in which players are able to reject monetary offers that they deem to be too low as a way to penalize the proposer. Naturally cycling women have also been shown to cooperate less with attractive (vs. less attractive) women in an ultimatum game when they are in the fertile phase of their ovulatory cycle (Lucas & Koff, 2013).

Although attractive individuals generally achieve greater overall success in the workplace (as noted earlier), attractive women, specifically, may be at a disadvantage in some professional settings.

According to Luxen and van de Vijver (2006), women rated themselves as more likely to hire an unattractive (vs. an attractive) undergraduate female for a student-assistant job when told they would be working closely with her. Men, however, preferred to hire the attractive female in this situation. Similar results were obtained whether the participants making these assessments were undergraduate students or older, human resource management professionals. Researchers have also found that the professional benefits (or penalties) of female attractiveness may depend on the position type. For example, whereas being attractive seems to benefit men across both managerial and nonmanagerial positions and women in nonmanagerial positions, physical attractiveness becomes a disadvantage for women seeking or holding a managerial position, leading to lower candidacy and performance evaluations (Heilman & Saruwatari, 1979; Heilman & Stopeck, 1985a). This disadvantage becomes even more pronounced when a woman in a managerial position dresses "sexy," so as to accentuate her physical beauty (Glick, Larsen, Johnson, & Branstiter, 2005). Furthermore, high-ranking females who are physically attractive are rated by working men and women as less capable than less attractive females and as less likely to have earned that position due to their ability (Heilman & Stopeck, 1985b). Finally, although beauty may be advantageous for women seeking jobs in traditionally feminine fields (i.e., caretaking), beauty may be disadvantageous for women who are seeking stereotypically masculine jobs (Johnson, Podratz, Dipboye, & Gibbons, 2010). This research has established that there are situations in which men and women penalize attractive females in professional contexts. However, many of these studies did not explicitly test for potential sex differences among the observers who rated these targets. Based on the research reviewed in this chapter, it is possible that the effects obtained in these studies were driven by female participants.

Recent research indicates that the negative responses exhibited toward attractive women in the workplace—and other organizational settings—may indeed be most pronounced among other women. Researchers have revealed a number of biases that could affect individuals' decision making in organizational contexts. The *sexual attribution bias* refers to the tendency to make unfavorable attributions regarding the success of attractive same-sex targets. For instance, one study demonstrated that women wrote off the successes of attractive women as being the product of good luck rather than crediting their ability or hard work (Försterling, Preikschas, & Agthe, 2007). On the other hand, women attributed the success of less attractive females more to ability and less to luck. This pattern was reversed for male targets, with women making more favorable attributions for the success of attractive (versus unattractive) male targets. Analogous effects were revealed for attributions made for targets' failures. Specifically, women were more likely to attribute the failure of attractive same-sex targets to internal, controllable (instead of external, uncontrollable) causes than they did for unattractive same-sex targets (Agthe, Spörrle, & Försterling, 2008). Again, this pattern was reversed for opposite-sex targets.

Being highly attractive can also negatively impact the evaluations given to women by female peers in organizational settings, an effect that may be stronger among women who are disadvantaged in terms of their own physical attractiveness. One study demonstrated that when evaluating potential job candidates and university applicants, women evaluated attractive same-sex targets more negatively than unattractive same-sex targets, although attractiveness increased their desire to hire/admit/interact with opposite-sex targets. This bias was strongest among women with low self-esteem (Agthe, Spörrle, & Maner, 2011). Another set of studies conducted by Agthe and colleagues (2010) demonstrated that participants evaluated attractive same-sex targets more negatively as potential job candidates than unattractive same-sex targets. Again, this effect was reversed for attractive opposite-sex targets and was strongest among participants who were relatively unattractive (Agthe, Spörrle, & Maner, 2010). Complementary results have been found regarding women's bodily attractiveness. For example, a study by Tantleff-Dunn (2002) revealed that women rated a female target with above-average breast size (cup size C) as being significantly less professional than men rated her.

Although attractive women are frequently the target of other women's interpersonal aggression and negative evaluations, women who exert effort to enhance their appearance may be received even more negatively than women who are naturally beautiful. As noted earlier, women tend to experience a suite of negative responses when confronted with attractive same-sex others (see, e.g., Bower, 2001; Joseph, 1985). People also tend to respond negatively when they are confronted with cheaters or any person who uses deception to gain an unfair advantage (Axelrod & Hamilton, 1981; Neuberg, Smith, & Asher, 2000). As such, it is expected that women will react especially negatively toward women who use deceptive means to enhance their physical attractiveness in an attempt to access the rewards of beauty. Vaillancourt and Sharma (2011), for example, found that women reacted in a more "bitchy" manner toward an attractive female confederate, rolling their eyes and laughing at her when she left the room, when she enhanced her appearance by dressing provocatively than when she was conservatively dressed. Women made more disparaging comments about the "sexy" confederate behind her back, were less likely to endorse her as a potential friend, and were less likely to want to introduce her to their boyfriend, relative to the conservatively dressed confederate. The authors reasoned that their effects occurred due to women feeling threatened by this woman's sexual availability (which she advertised by wearing skimpy clothing) and subsequently reacted competitively toward this female, whom they perceived to be a formidable mating rival. Grabe and colleagues (2012) obtained similar results regarding women's derogation of a sexualized female news anchor. Specifically, women were more likely to derogate the appearance, personality, and professional competence of a female news anchor whose appearance was sexualized (i.e., by wearing form-fitting clothing, red lipstick, and a necklace) relative to when the same female anchor's appearance was not sexualized (Grabe, Bas, Pagano, & Samson, 2012).

Research also supports the idea that women who use artificial means to deceptively augment their attractiveness via the use of cosmetics are sometimes penalized in organizational settings. Although cosmetic use had no effects on participants' ratings of the expected performance of averagely attractive female targets applying for a nongender-typed (accounting) position, both perceived and actual cosmetic use had negative effects on ratings made for female targets being evaluated for a gender-typed (secretarial) position (Cox & Glick, 1986). Furthermore, female targets wearing heavy cosmetics were rated by men and women as more likely to provoke sexual harassment than were female targets wearing a moderate amount of or no cosmetics (Workman & Johnson, 1991). Men and women also rate female targets as less capable and assign them lower starting salaries when wearing (vs. not wearing) cosmetics (Kyle & Mahler, 1996).

In accordance with the sexual attribution bias, the negative effects of attempted appearance enhancement via cosmetic use for women may be driven by female observers. For instance, male participants—but not female participants—assign female targets wearing cosmetics to more prestigious jobs (e.g., accountant; Nash et al., 2006). Furthermore, recent research examined the effects of cosmetics use on men's and women's evaluations of female targets in the workplace (DelPriore & Hill, under review). Specifically, female undergraduates were presented with a series of same-sex targets (half wearing cosmetics and half not) and were asked to imagine they worked with these individuals. Results revealed that women evaluated female targets wearing cosmetics as more likely to use their looks to get ahead in the workplace and less likely to achieve success via hard work alone relative to female targets not wearing cosmetics. Although this beautification penalty was found across target attractiveness, the negative response was most pronounced for *attractive* female targets wearing cosmetics. These effects extended to affect individuals' desire to interact with the female targets. Although men expressed a greater desire to affiliate with female targets wearing (vs. not wearing) cosmetics, women indicated a decreased likelihood they would affiliate with these targets in the workplace (an effect that was mediated by decreased perceptions of the targets' trustworthiness in response to their appearance enhancement effort). In summary, whereas female cosmetics use may bolster men's desire to affiliate with women in the workplace, their use can be deleterious when it comes to women's perceptions and evaluations of other women. Although additional research is needed to more rigorously test the differential effects of female attractiveness enhancement strategies on male and female perceivers, the research reviewed here provides preliminary evidence for a beauty paradox wherein a woman's physical attractiveness may be rewarded in some contexts and penalized in others.

Future Directions

Although there is an abundance of research spanning the past four decades demonstrating the "beauty is good" effect, researchers have recently highlighted certain contexts in which prettiness may be penalized, especially in interactions among women. A woman's beauty is often received negatively by same-sex others, and an evolutionary psychological perspective suggests that this unfavorable response is especially likely when these beautiful women are perceived to have an advantage when competing for access to scarce commodities (e.g., men with money during an economic recession). Despite recent advances, there are several potential avenues for future research examining the causes and consequences of women's competitive beautification. Some suggestions include:

1. As noted earlier, there has been much research examining the favorable perceptions made regarding individuals who are conventionally *facially* attractive (e.g., Dion et al., 1972). However, there have been relatively few studies conducted examining whether a similar "halo effect" can be applied to individuals with more attractive bodies. Although it has been established that men tend to prefer certain body types when choosing women as mates (e.g., Singh, 1993; Singh & Young, 1995), little research has looked at whether, in general, people tend to perceive women with attractive bodies as being more socially desirable (for an exception, see Tantleff-Dunn, 2002). For example, would women with relatively attractive bodies be rated as more likeable or fare better in economic game competitions relative to women with less attractive bodies? How would the sex of the rater impact these evaluations? Researchers should examine these effects across a range of body sizes (thin to heavy) as well as bodies ranging in their degree of sexual dimorphism (feminine vs. masculine vs. androgynous).

2. Researchers have established the use of cosmetics to be an effective way for women to increase their perceived attractiveness (e.g., Russell, 2011). However, many of these studies have focused exclusively on the effects of cosmetics use among Caucasian female targets (Mulhern et al., 2003; Nash et al., 2006). Limited research has found that cosmetics may increase attractiveness perceptions of targets of varying ethnicities, although the mechanism by which cosmetics increase attractiveness may vary based on skin pigmentation (e.g., by smoothing of features rather than increasing facial contrast for individuals with darker skin tones) or differences in other physical features that vary across race and ethnicity (Etcoff et al., 2011). Future research should establish whether the effects of cosmetic use—as well as the types of cosmetics used—are comparable for female targets from different racial or ethnic backgrounds.

3. Many of the reported effects were presumably demonstrated in primarily Western, heterosexual samples. Although the "beauty is good" stereotype may hold for at least some non-Western cultures (e.g., Korea; see Wheeler & Kim, 1997), the attributions that individuals

make regarding good-looking people may change based on what social traits are highly valued in their specific culture (Wheeler & Kim, 1997). The specifics of the reviewed "beauty is good" and "prettiness penalty" effects are also likely to vary systematically among females of different sexual orientations. Future research should examine whether attractive female targets are rewarded or penalized by non-heterosexual women and exactly how these responses might vary across contexts.

4. Researchers have demonstrated that another woman's physical attractiveness is a common source of envy for undergraduate women, and, accordingly, women devote a greater amount of cognitive resources to processing attractive (relative to less attractive) targets (Hill et al., 2011). Hill and colleagues posit that this shift in attention and memory serves to increase women's ability to compete with these attractive same-sex others for access to valuable, limited resources (e.g., a desirable mate, a high-paying job). However, researchers have yet to investigate which women are most likely to selectively process this information and precisely how they use this information to their advantage (i.e., to increase their own attractiveness or successfully derogate their attractive same-sex rivals).

5. As noted earlier, extreme (and more innocuous) examples of appearance enhancement via cosmetic surgery are becoming more common in contemporary Western society. Much of the literature reviewed in this chapter, however, focuses on the consequences—both positive and negative—of physical attractiveness for targets who have not undergone such surgical procedures. Many questions need to be addressed regarding the unique consequences of cosmetic surgery: are these women another exception to the "what is beautiful is good" effect? Are women better than men at detecting surgical enhancements in other women? Are beautiful women who have undergone cosmetic procedures more likely to be penalized than naturally beautiful women?

6. Finally, future research should examine the implications of physical attractiveness and female intrasexual competitive processes on marketing strategies. Although many commercials and print advertisements geared toward women seem to feature attractive spokespeople, there is research suggesting that this strategy may inadvertently backfire. For instance, Bower (2001) found that highly attractive models—and the message they were delivering—in a treadmill advertisement were evaluated negatively by women who compared themselves to the model. Researchers should test which targets different women respond to most favorably across social contexts and product types.

Conclusion

This chapter examined how and why women engage in behaviors designed to enhance their physical attractiveness. In accordance with the "beauty is good" phenomenon, women self-beautify in an attempt to gain access to the benefits that are often bestowed upon more naturally attractive individuals across social contexts. From an evolutionary perspective, these efforts will reap the most rewards for women in mating-relevant domains. Men place a high premium on physical attractiveness, and women often compete with one another for access to the highest-quality mates; thus, women can use beautification to gain a competitive edge on their peers, friends, and other same-sex rivals.

Although this self-promotional strategy may give women an advantage when trying to attract potential mates, it may simultaneously create problems with other women. Women can experience aversive psychological states (including envy, jealousy, and heightened sensitivity to mate-poaching cues) when confronted with potential romantic threats due to the presence of more attractive women. These negative emotional states may prompt women to engage in derogatory and aggressive behaviors (such as gossiping and "talking trash" about a competitor's appearance) directed at attractive female rivals. These tactics serve to lower the perceived mate value of rivals and to help eliminate them as serious competition.

Recent research has begun to expand our knowledge of women's intrasexual competition by examining how women treat attractive others in economic, legal, and organizational contexts. Future work should examine other aspects of competitive beautification, including the consequences of extreme forms of self-beautification (such as plastic surgery) in social and professional environments. Regardless, any research done on women's interactions should be careful to consider the powerful role that physical attractiveness plays in shaping women's perceptions of themselves and others, and how these perceptions dually influence both cooperative and competitive behaviors.

References

Agthe, M., Spörrle, M., & Försterling, F. (2008). Success attributions and more: Multidimensional extensions of the sexual attribution bias to failure attributions, social emotions, and the desire for social interaction. *Personality and Social Psychology Bulletin, 34,* 1627–1638.

Agthe, M., Spörrle, M., & Maner, J. K. (2010). Don't hate me because I'm beautiful: Anti-attractiveness bias in organizational evaluation and decision making. *Journal of Experimental Social Psychology, 46,* 1151–1154.

Agthe, M., Spörrle, M., & Maner, J. K. (2011). Does being attractive always help? Positive and negative effects of attractiveness on social decision making. *Personality and Social Psychology Bulletin, 37*(8), 1042–1054. doi:10.1177/0146167211410355

Allison, M., & Martinez, A. (2010, September 9). Beauty-products sales bright spot during recession. *The Seattle Times.* Retrieved from http://seattletimes.com

Andreoni, J., & Petrie, R. (2008). Beauty, gender, and stereotypes: Evidence from laboratory experiments. *Journal of Economic Psychology, 29,* 73–93.

Axelrod, R., & Hamilton, W. D. (1981). The evolution of cooperation. *Science, 211*(4489), 1390–1396.

Badr, L., & Abdallah, B. (2001). Physical attractiveness of premature infants affects outcome at discharge from the NICU. *Infant Behavior & Development, 24*(1), 129–133. doi:10.1016/S0163-6383(01)00068-6

Barber, N. (1995). The evolutionary psychology of physical attractiveness: Sexual selection and human morphology. *Ethology & Sociobiology, 16*(5), 395–424. doi:10.1016/0162-3095(95)00068-2

Benenson, J. F., Markovits, H., Thompson, M. E., & Wrangham, R. W. (2011). Under threat of social exclusion, females exclude more than males. *Psychological Science, 22,* 538–544.

Benson, P. L., Karabenick, S. A., & Lerner, R. M. (1976). Pretty pleases: The effects of physical attractiveness, race, and sex on receiving help. *Journal of Experimental Social Psychology, 12*(5), 409–415.

Björkqvist, K. (1994). Sex differences in physical, verbal, and indirect aggression: A review of recent research. *Sex Roles, 30*(3–4), 177–188.

Bower, A. B. (2001). Highly attractive models in advertising and the women who loathe them: The implications of negative affect for spokesperson effectiveness. *Journal of Advertising, 30*(3), 51–63.

Brase, G. L., & Guy, E. C. (2004). The demographics of mate value and self-esteem. *Personality and Individual Differences, 36,* 471–484.

Brown, J. D., Novick, N. J., Lord, K. A., & Richards, J. M. (1992). When Gulliver travels: Social context, psychological closeness, and self-appraisals. *Journal of Personality and Social Psychology, 62,* 717–727.

Bull, R., & Stevens, J. (1979). The effects of attractiveness of writer and penmanship on essay grades. *Journal of Occupational Psychology, 52*(1), 53–59. doi:10.1111/j.2044-8325.1979.tb00440.x

Buss, D. M. (1988). The evolution of human intrasexual competition: Tactics of mate attraction. *Journal of Personality and Social Psychology, 54,* 616–628.

Buss, D. M. (1989). Sex differences in human mate preferences: Evolutionary hypotheses tested in 37 cultures. *Behavioral & Brain Sciences, 12,* 1–49.

Buss, D. M. (1995). Psychological sex differences: Origins through sexual selection. *American Psychologist, 50*(3), 164–168.

Buss, D. M. (2008). *Evolutionary psychology: The new science of the mind.* Boston, MA: Pearson.

Buss, D. M., & Dedden, L. A. (1990). Derogation of competitors. *Journal of Social and Personal Relationships, 7,* 395–422.

Buss, D. M., & Schmitt, D. P. (1993). Sexual Strategies Theory: An evolutionary perspective on human mating. *Psychological Review, 100,* 204–232.

Buss, D. M., & Shackelford, T. K. (1997). From vigilance to violence: Mate retention tactics in married couples. *Journal of Personality and Social Psychology, 72*(2), 346–361.

Buss, D. M., & Shackelford, T. K. (2008). Attractive women want it all: Good genes, economic investment, parenting proclivities, and emotional commitment. *Evolutionary Psychology, 6*(1), 134–146.

Buss, D. M., Shackelford, T. K., Choe, J., Buunk, B. P., & Dijkstra, P. (2000). Distress about mating rivals. *Personal Relationships, 7,* 235–243.

Buss, D. M., Shackelford, T. K., Kirkpatrick, L. A., & Larsen, R. J. (2001). A half century of mate preferences: The cultural evolution of values. *Journal of Marriage and Family, 63,* 491–503.

Campbell, A. (1995). A few good men: Evolutionary psychology and female adolescent aggression. *Ethology and Sociobiology, 16*(2), 99–123.

Campbell, A. (2004). Female competition: Causes, constraints, content, and contexts. *Journal of Sex Research, 41*(1), 16–26. doi:10.1080/00224490409552210

Campos, L., Otta, E., & de Oliveira Siqueira, J. (2002). Sex differences in mate selection strategies: Content analyses and responses to personal advertisements in Brazil. *Evolution and Human Behavior, 23,* 395–406.

Cash, T. F., Dawson, K., Davis, P., Bowen, M., & Galumbeck, C. (1989). Effects of cosmetic use on the physical attractiveness and body image of American college women. *Journal of Social Psychology, 129,* 349–355.

Cash, T. F., & Pruzinsky, T. E. (1990). *Body images: Development, deviance, and change.* New York: Guilford Press.

Cashdan, E. (1996). Women's mating strategies. *Evolutionary Anthropology, 5,* 134–143. doi:10.1002/(SICI)1520-6505(1996)5:4<134::AID-EVAN3>3.0.CO;2-G

Castellow, W. A., Wuensch, K. L., & Moore, C. H. (1990). Effects of physical attractiveness of the plaintiff and defendant in sexual harassment judgments. *Journal of Social Behavior and Personality, 5,* 547–562.

Cattarin, J. A., Thompson, J., Thomas, C., & Williams, R. (2000). Body image, mood, and televised images of attractiveness: The role of social comparison. *Journal of Social and Clinical Psychology, 19*(2), 220–239. doi:10.1521/jscp.2000.19.2.220

Cialdini, R. B. (1984). *The psychology of persuasion.* New York: Quill William Morrow.

Clifford, M. M. (1975). Physical attractiveness and academic performance. *Child Study Journal, 5*(4), 201–209.

Clifford, M. M., & Walster, E. (1973). The effect of physical attractiveness on teacher expectations. *Sociology of Education, 46,* 248–258.

Commisso, M., & Finkelstein, L. (2012). Physical attractiveness bias in employee termination. *Journal of Applied Social Psychology, 42*(12), 2968–2987. doi:10.1111/j.1559-1816.2012.00970.x

Cox, C. L., & Glick, W. H. (1986). Resume evaluations and cosmetic use: When more is not better. *Sex Roles*, *14*, 51–58.

Daily Mail Reporter. (2012, November). Is the Human Barbie a fake? Video reveals how model who became internet sensation "used Photoshop to create shocking looks." *The Daily Mail*. Retrieved from http://www.dailymail.co.uk

de Bruyn, E. H., Cillessen, A. N., & Weisfeld, G. E. (2012). Dominance-popularity status, behavior, and the emergence of sexual activity in young adolescents. *Evolutionary Psychology*, *10*(2), 296–319.

DelPriore, D. J., Bradshaw, H. K., & Hill, S. E. Appearance enhancement produces a strategic beautification penalty among women. Manuscript submitted for review.

DelPriore, D. J., Hill, S. E., & Buss, D. M. (2012). Envy: Functional specificity and sex- differentiated design features. *Personality and Individual Differences*, *53*, 317–322.

DeSantis, A., & Kayson, W. A. (1997). Defendants' characteristics of attractiveness, race, and sex and sentencing decisions. *Psychological Reports*, *81*, 679–683.

Dijkstra, P., & Buunk, B. P. (1998). Jealousy as a function of rival characteristics: An evolutionary perspective. *Personality and Social Psychology Bulletin*, *24*, 1158–1166.

Dijkstra, P., & Buunk, B. P. (2002). Sex differences in the jealousy-evoking effect of rival characteristics. *European Journal of Social Psychology*, *32*, 829–852.

Dion, K., Berscheid, E., & Walster, E. (1972). What is beautiful is good. *Journal of Personality and Social Psychology*, *24*(3), 285–290.

The Dirty. (2012, November). The world deserves to know Valeria Lukyanova is a fraud (Anonymous web log post). Retrieved March 3, 2014 from http://thedirty.com

Dunn, M. J., Brinton, S., & Clark, L. (2010). Universal sex differences in online advertisers age preferences: Comparing data from 14 cultures and 2 religious groups. *Evolution and Human Behavior*, *31*, 383–393.

Durante, K. M., Griskevicius, V., Hill, S. E., Perilloux, C., & Li, N. P. (2011). Ovulation, female competition, and product choice: Hormonal influences on consumer behavior. *Journal of Consumer Research*, *37*(6), 921–934. doi:10.1086/656575

Durante, K. M., Li, N. P., & Haselton, M. G. (2008). Changes in women's choice of dress across the ovulatory cycle: Naturalistic and laboratory task-based evidence. *Personality and Social Psychology Bulletin*, *34*, 1451–1460.

Eagly, A. H., Ashmore, R. D., Makhijani, M. G., & Longo, L. C. (1991). What is beautiful is good, but . . .: A meta-analytic review of research on the physical attractiveness stereotype. *Psychological Bulletin*, *110*(1), 109–128. doi:10.1037/0033-2909.110.1.109

Efran, M. G. (1974). The effect of physical appearance on the judgment of guilt, interpersonal attraction, and severity of recommended punishment in simulated jury task. *Journal of Research in Personality*, *8*, 45–54.

Elder, G. H. (1969). Appearance and education in marriage mobility. *American Sociological Review*, *34*, 519–533.

Ellis, B. J. (1995). The evolution of sexual attraction: Evaluative mechanisms in women. In J. H. Barkow, L. Cosmides, & J. Tooby (Eds.), *The adapted mind: Evolutionary psychology and the generation of culture* (pp. 267–288). New York: Oxford University Press.

Etcoff, N. L., Stock, S., Haley, L. E., Vickery, S. A., & House, D. M. (2011). Cosmetics as a feature of the extended human phenotype: Modulation of the perception of biologically important facial signals. *PLoS One*, *6*(10), e25656.

Fabricant, S. M., & Gould, S. J. (1993). Women's makeup careers: An interpretive study of color cosmetic use and "face value." *Psychology & Marketing*, *10*, 531–548.

Fallon, A. E., & Rozin, P. (1985). Sex differences in perceptions of the ideal body shape. *Journal of Abnormal Psychology*, *94*, 102–105.

Feingold, A. (1992). Good-looking people are not what we think. *Psychological Bulletin*, *11*, 304–341.

Felson, R. B. (1980). Physical attractiveness, grades and teachers' attributions of ability. *Representative Research in Social Psychology*, *11*(1), 64–71.

Fink, B., Grammer, K., & Thornhill, R. (2001). Human (*Homo sapiens*) facial attractiveness in relation to skin texture and color. *Journal of Comparative Psychology*, *115*(1), 92.

Fink, B., & Penton-Voak, I. (2002). Evolutionary psychology of facial attractiveness. *American Psychological Society*, *11*(5), 154–158.

Fisher, M., & Cox, A. (2009). The influence of female attractiveness on competitor derogation. *Journal of Evolutionary Psychology*, *7*, 141–155.

Fisher, M., & Cox, A. (2011). Four strategies used during intrasexual competition for mates. *Personal Relationships*, *18*(1), 20–38.

Fisher, M., Cox, A., & Gordon, F. (2009). Self-promotion versus competitor derogation: The influence of sex and romantic relationship status on intrasexual competition strategy selection. *Journal of Evolutionary Psychology*, *7*, 287–308.

Fisher, M. L. (2004). Female intrasexual competition decreases female facial attractiveness. *Proceedings of the Royal Society B (Supplemental)*, *271*, S283–S285.

Fisher, M. L., Tran, U. S., & Voracek, M. (2008). The influence of relationship status, mate seeking, and sex, on intrasexual competition. *Journal of Social Psychology*, *148*, 493–508.

Försterling, F., Preikschas, S., & Agthe, M. (2007). Ability, luck, and looks: An evolutionary look at achievement ascriptions and the sexual attribution bias. *Journal of Personality and Social Psychology*, *92*(5), 775–788. doi:10.1037/0022-3514.92.5.775

Frieze, I. H., Olson, J. E., & Russell, J. (1991). Attractiveness and income for men and women in management. *Journal of Applied Social Psychology*, *21*(13), 1039–1057. doi:10.1111/j.1559-1816.1991.tb00458.x

Gangestad, S. W., & Thornhill, R. (1997). Human sexual selection and developmental stability. In J. A. Simpson & D. T. Kenrick (Eds.), *Evolutionary social psychology* (pp. 169–196). Hillsdale, NJ: Lawrence Erlbaum Associates.

Gangestad, S. W., & Thornhill, R. (1999). Facial attractiveness. *Trends in Cognitive Science*, *3*(12), 452–460.

Garner, D. M., Garfinkel, P. E., Schwartz, D., & Thompson, M. (1980). Cultural expectations of thinness in women. *Psychological Reports*, *47*(2), 483–491.

Geary, D. C. (2005). Evolution of paternal investment. In D. M. Buss (Ed.), *The handbook of evolutionary psychology* (pp. 483–505). Hoboken, NJ: John Wiley & Sons.

Glasser, C. L., Robnett, B., & Feliciano, C. (2009). Internet daters' body type preferences: Race–ethnic and gender differences. *Sex Roles*, *61*(1–2), 14–33

Glick, P., Larsen, S., Johnson, C., & Branstiter, H. (2005). Evaluations of sexy women in low- and high-status jobs. *Psychology of Women Quarterly*, *29*(4), 389–395.

Grabe, M. E., Bas, O., Pagano, L. A., & Samson, L. (2012). The architecture of female competition: Derogation of a sexualized female news anchor. *Journal of Evolutionary Psychology, 10,* 107–133.

Grammer, K., Fink, B., Møller, A. P., & Thornhill, R. (2003). Darwinian aesthetics: Sexual selection and the biology of beauty. *Biological Reviews, 78*(3), 385–407.

Grammer, K., Renninger, L., & Fischer, B. (2004). Disco clothing, female sexual motivation, and relationship status: Is she dressed to impress? *Journal of Sex Research, 41,* 66–74.

Grammer, K., & Thornhill, R. (1994). Human (*Homo sapiens*) facial attractiveness and sexual selection: The role of symmetry and averageness. *Journal of Comparative Psychology, 108*(3), 233–242. doi:10.1037/0735-7036.108.3.233

Guéguen, N. (2007a). Bust size and hitchhiking: A field study. *Perceptual and Motor Skills, 105*(3, Pt 2), 1294–1298.

Guéguen, N. (2007b). Women's bust size and men's courtship solicitation. *Body Image, 4*(4), 386–390.

Guéguen, N. (2008). The effects of women's cosmetics on men's approach: An evaluation in a bar. *North American Journal of Psychology, 10,* 221–228.

Guéguen, N. (2012). Makeup and menstrual cycle: Near ovulation, women use more cosmetics. *Psychological Record, 62,* 541–548.

Guéguen, N., & Lamy, L. (2013). The effect of facial makeup on the frequency of drivers stopping for hitchhikers. *Psychological Reports, 113,* 97–101.

Gutierres, S. E., Kenrick, D. T., & Partch, J. J. (1999). Beauty, dominance, and the mating game: Contrast effects in self-assessment reflect gender differences in mate selection. *Personality and Social Psychology Bulletin, 25*(9), 1126–1134. doi:10.1177/01461672992512006

Ha, T., Overbeek, G., & Engels, R. C. (2010). Effects of attractiveness and social status on dating desire in heterosexual adolescents: An experimental study. *Archives of Sexual Behavior, 39*(5), 1063–1071.

Harrison, K. (2003). Television viewers' ideal body proportions: The case of the curvaceously thin woman. *Sex Roles, 48*(5–6), 255–264.

Haselton, M. G., Mortezaie, M., Pillsworth, E. G., Bleske-Rechek, A., & Frederick, D. A. (2007). Ovulatory shifts in human female ornamentation: Near ovulation, women dress to impress. *Hormones and Behavior, 51*(1), 40–45. doi:10.1016/j.yhbeh.2006.07.007

Heflick, N. A., & Goldenberg, J. L. (2009). Objectifying Sarah Palin: Evidence that objectification causes women to be perceived as less competent and less fully human. *Journal of Experimental Social Psychology, 45*(3), 598–601.

Heilman, M. E., & Saruwatari, L. R. (1979). When beauty is beastly: The effects of appearance and sex on evaluations of job applicants for managerial and nonmanagerial jobs. *Organizational Behavior and Human Performance, 23,* 360–372.

Heilman, M. E., & Stopeck, M. H. (1985a). Being attractive, advantage or disadvantage? Performance-based evaluations and recommended personnel actions as a function of appearance, sex, and job type. *Organizational Behavior and Human Decision Processes, 35,* 202–215.

Heilman, M. E., & Stopeck, M. H. (1985b). Attractiveness and corporate success: Different causal attributions for males and females. *Journal of Applied Psychology, 70,* 379–388.

Hill, S. E., & Buss, D. M. (2006). Envy and positional bias in the evolutionary psychology of management. *Managerial and Decision Economics, 27,* 131–143.

Hill, S. E., & Buss, D. M. (2008). The evolutionary psychology of envy. In R. H. Smith (Ed.), *Envy: Theory and research* (pp. 60–70). New York: Oxford University Press.

Hill, S. E., DelPriore, D. J., & Vaughan, P. W. (2011). The cognitive consequences of envy: Attention, memory, and self-regulatory depletion. *Journal of Personality and Social Psychology, 101,* 653–666.

Hill, S. E., & Durante, K. M. (2009). Do women feel worse to look their best? Testing the relationship between self-esteem and fertility status across the menstrual cycle. *Personality and Social Psychology Bulletin, 35,* 1592–1601.

Hill, S. E., & Durante, K. M. (2011). Courtship, competition, and the pursuit of attractiveness: Mating goals facilitate health-related risk taking and strategic risk suppression in women. *Personality and Social Psychology Bulletin, 37*(3), 383–394. doi:10.1177/0146167210395603

Hill, S. E., Rodeheffer, C. D., Griskevicius, V., Durante, K., & White, A. (2012). Boosting beauty in an economic decline: Mating, spending, and the lipstick effect. *Journal of Personality and Social Psychology, 103*(2), 275–291. doi:10.1037/a0028657

Hore, T. (1971). Assessment of teaching practice: An 'attractive' hypothesis. *British Journal of Educational Psychology, 41,* 327–328.

Hosoda, M., Stone-Romero, E. F., & Coats, G. (2003). The effects of physical attractiveness on job related outcomes: A meta-analysis of experimental studies. *Personnel Psychology, 56*(2), 431–462.

Jackson, L. A. (1983). The influence of sex, physical attractiveness, sex role, and occupational sex-linkage on perceptions of occupational suitability. *Journal of Applied Social Psychology, 13*(1), 31–44.

Jackson, L. A. (1992). *Physical appearance and gender: Sociobiological and sociocultural perspectives.* Albany: State University of New York Press.

Johnson, S. K., Podratz, K. E., Dipboye, R. L., & Gibbons, E. (2010). Physical attractiveness biases in ratings of employment suitability: Tracking down the "beauty is beastly" effect. *Journal of Social Psychology, 150*(3), 301–318.

Jonason, P. K. (2007). An evolutionary psychology perspective on sex differences in exercise behaviors and motivations. *Journal of Social Psychology, 147*(1), 5–14.

Joseph, R. R. (1985). Competition between women. *Psychology: A Journal of Human Behavior, 22*(3–4), 1–12.

Kenealy, P., Frude, N., & Shaw, W. (1988). Influence of children's physical attractiveness on teacher expectations. *Journal of Social Psychology, 128,* 373–383.

Kenrick, D. T., & Gutierres, S. E. (1980). Contrast effects and judgments of physical attractiveness: When beauty becomes a social problem. *Journal of Personality and Social Psychology, 38,* 131–140.

Kenrick, D. T., & Keefe, R. C. (1992). Age preferences in mates reflects sex differences in human reproductive strategies. *Behavioral and Brain Sciences, 15,* 75–133.

Kenrick, D. T., Montello, D. R., Gutierres, S. E., & Trost, M. R. (1993). Effects of physical attractiveness on affect and perceptual judgments: When social comparison overrides social reinforcement. *Personality and Social Psychology Bulletin, 19,* 195–199.

Kenrick, D. T., Neuberg, S. L., Zierk, K. L., & Krones, J. M. (1994). Evolution and social cognition: Contrast effects as a function of sex, dominance, and physical attractiveness. *Personality and Social Psychology Bulletin, 20*(2), 210–217.

Koehn, N. F. (2001). Estee Lauder and the market for prestige cosmetics. *Harvard Business School Cases, 801–362*, 1–44.

Krebs, D., & Adinolfi, A. A. (1975). Physical attractiveness, social relations, and personality style. *Journal of Personality and Social Psychology, 31*, 245–253.

Krendl, A. C., Magoon, N. S., Hull, J. G., & Heatherton, T. F. (2011). Judging a book by its cover: The differential impact of attractiveness on predicting one's acceptance to high- or low-status social groups. *Journal of Applied Social Psychology, 41*(10), 2538–2550. doi:10.1111/j.1559-1816.2011.00824.x

Kyle, D. J., & Mahler, H. I. (1996). The effects of hair colour and cosmetic use on perceptions of a female's ability. *Psychology of Women Quarterly, 20*, 447–455.

Langlois, J. H., Kalakanis, L., Rubenstein, A. J., Larson, A., Hallam, M., & Smoot, M. (2000). Maxims or myths of beauty? A meta-analytic and theoretical review. *Psychological Bulletin, 126*(3), 390–423. doi:10.1037/0033-2909.126.3.390

Langlois, J. H., Ritter, J. M., Casey, R. J., & Sawin, D. B. (1995). Infant attractiveness predicts maternal behaviors and attitudes. *Developmental Psychology, 31*(3), 464–472. doi:10.1037/0012-1649.31.3.464

Lemay, E. P., Clark, M. S., & Greenberg, A. (2010). What is beautiful is good because what is beautiful is desired: Physical attractiveness stereotyping as projection of interpersonal goals. *Personality and Social Psychology Bulletin, 36*(3), 339–353. doi:10.1177/0146167209359700

Li, N. P., & Kenrick, D. T. (2006). Sex similarities and differences in preferences for short-term mates: What, whether, and why. *Journal of Personality and Social Psychology, 90*, 468–489.

Little, A. C., Jones, B. C., & Debruine, L. M. (2011). Facial attractiveness: Evolutionary based research. *Philosophical Transactions of the Royal Society B, 366*(1571), 1638–1659. doi:10.1098/rstb.2010.0404

Low, B. S. (1979). Sexual selection and human ornamentation. In N. Chagnon, & W. Irons (Eds.), *Evolutionary biology and human social behavior* (pp. 462–487). North Scituate, MA: Duxbury Press.

Lucas, M., & Koff, E. (2013). How conception risk affects competition and cooperation with attractive women and men. *Evolution and Human Behavior, 34*(1), 16–22. doi:10.1016/j.evolhumbehav.2012.08.001

Lucker, G. W., Beane, W. E., & Helmreich, R. L. (1981). The strength of the halo effect in physical attractiveness research. *Journal of Psychology: Interdisciplinary and Applied, 107*, 69–75.

Luxen, M. F., & van de Vijver, F. J. R. (2006). Facial attractiveness, sexual selection, and personnel selection: When evolved preferences matter. *Journal of Organizational Behavior, 27*, 241–255.

Maier, R. A., Jr., Holmes, D. L., Slaymaker, F. L., & Reich, J. N. (1984). The perceived attractiveness of preterm infants. *Infant Behavior and Development, 7*, 403–414.

Massar, K., & Buunk, A. P. (2010). Judging a book by its cover: Jealousy after subliminal priming with attractive and unattractive faces. *Personality and Individual Differences, 49*, 634–638.

Mathes, E. W., & Kahn, A. (1975). Physical attractiveness, happiness, neuroticism, and self-esteem. *Journal of Psychology: Interdisciplinary and Applied, 90*, 27–30.

Mathes, E. W., & Verstraete, C. (1993). Jealous aggression: Who is the target, the beloved or the rival? *Psychological Reports, 72*, 1071–1074.

Mazzella, R., & Feingold, A. (1994). The effects of physical attractiveness, race, socioeconomic status, and gender of defendants and victims on judgments of mock jurors: A meta-analysis. *Journal of Applied Social Psychology, 24*, 1315–1338. doi:10.1111/j.1559-1816.1994.tb01552.x

Mealey. L. (1997). Bulking up: The roles of gender and sexual orientation on attempts to manipulate physical attractiveness. *Journal of Sex Research, 34*, 223–228.

Miller, G. F. (2009). *Spent: Sex, evolution, and consumer behavior.* New York: Viking.

Morris, P. H., White, J., Morrison, E. R., & Fisher, K. (2013). High heels as supernormal stimuli: How wearing high heels affects judgments of female attractiveness. *Evolution and Human Behavior, 34*(3), 176–181.

Mulford, M., Orbell, J., Shatto, C., & Stockard, J. (1998). Physical attractiveness, opportunity, and success in everyday exchange. *American Journal of Sociology, 103*, 1565–1592.

Mulhern, R., Fieldman, G., Hussey, T., Lévêque, J. -L., & Pineau, P. (2003). Do cosmetics enhance Caucasian female facial attractiveness? *International Journal of Cosmetic Science, 25*, 199–205.

Nash, R., Fieldman, G., Hussey, T., Lévêque, J. -L., & Pineau, P. (2006). Cosmetics: They influence more than Caucasian female facial attractiveness. *Journal of Applied Social Psychology, 36*, 493–504.

Nelson, E. (2001, November 26). Rising lipstick sales may mean pouting economy and few smiles. *The Wall Street Journal*, p. B1.

Nemtsova, A. (2013, August). 16 questions for the real-life Barbie Valerie Lukyanova. *The Daily Beast.* Retrieved from http://www.thedailybeast.com/

Neuberg, S. L., Smith, D. M., & Asher, T. (2000). Why people stigmatize: Toward a biocultural framework. In T. F. Heatherton (Ed.), *The social psychology of stigma* (pp. 31–61). New York: Guilford Press.

Osborn, D. R. (1996). Beauty is as beauty does? Makeup and posture effects on physical attractiveness judgments. *Journal of Applied Social Psychology, 26*, 31–51.

Parrott, W. G. (1991). The emotional experiences of envy and jealousy. In P. Salovey (Ed.), *The psychology of jealousy and envy* (pp. 3–30). New York: The Guilford Press.

Patry, M. W. (2008). Attractive but guilty: Deliberation and the physical attractiveness bias. *Psychological Reports, 102*, 727–733.

Paul, L., & Galloway, J. (1994). Sexual jealousy: Gender differences in response to partner and rival. *Aggressive Behavior, 20*, 203–211.

Perrett, D. I., Lee, K. J., Penton-Voak, I., Rowland, D., Yoshikawa, S., Burt, D. M., et al. (1998). Effects of sexual dimorphism on facial attractiveness. *Nature, 394*, 884–887.

Peters, M., Rhodes, G., & Simmons, L. W. (2007). Contributions of the face and body to overall attractiveness. *Animal Behaviour, 73*(6), 937–942.

Pingitore, R., Dugoni, B. L., Tindale, R. S., & Spring, B. (1994). Bias against overweight job applicants in a simulated employment interview. *Journal of Applied Psychology, 79*(6), 909–917.

Regan, P. C. (1998). Minimum mate selection standards as a function of perceived mate value, relationship context, and gender. *Journal of Psychology and Human Sexuality*, *10*, 53–73.

Regan, P. C. (2011). Cinderella revisited: Women's appearance modification as a function of target audience sex and attractiveness. *Social Behavior and Personality*, *39*, 563–576.

Ritter, J. M., Casey, R. J., & Langlois, J. H. (1991). Adults' responses to infants varying in appearance of age and attractiveness. *Child Development*, *62*(1), 68–82. doi:10.2307/1130705

Ritts, V., Patterson, M. L., & Tubbs, M. E. (1992). Expectations, impressions, and judgments of physically attractive students: A review. *Review of Educational Research*, *62*(4), 413–426. doi:10.2307/1170486

Roberts, S. C., Havlicek, J., Flegr, J., Hruskova, M., Little, A. C., Jones, B. C.,. . . Petrie, M. (2004). Female facial attractiveness increases during the fertile phase of the menstrual cycle. *Proceedings of the Royal Society B*, *271* (Suppl 5), S270–S272.

Röder, S., Brewer, G., & Fink, B. (2009). Menstrual cycle shifts in women's self-perception and motivation: A daily report method. *Personality and Individual Differences*, *47*, 616–619.

Rucas, S. L., Gurven, M., Kaplan, H., Winking, J., Gangestad, S., & Crespo, M. (2006). Female intrasexual competition and reputational effects on attractiveness among the Tsimane of Bolivia. *Evolution and Human Behavior*, *27*(1), 40–52. doi:10.1016/j.evolhumbehav.2005.07.001

Russell, R. (2009). A sex difference in facial contrast and its exaggeration by cosmetics. *Perception*, *38*(8), 1211–1219.

Russell, R. (2011). Why cosmetics work. *Science of Social Vision*, *7*, 186.

Russell, R. P. (2002). Facial coloration, sex, and beauty. *Perception*, *31*, 20.

Saad, G., & Stenstrom, E. (2012). Calories, beauty, and ovulation: The effects of the menstrual cycle on food and appearance-related consumption. *Journal of Consumer Psychology*, *22*(1), 102–113. doi:10.1016/j.jcps.2011.10.001

Schaefer, K., Fink, B., Grammer, K., Mitteroecker, P., Gunz, P., & Bookstein, F. L. (2006). Female appearance: Facial and bodily attractiveness as shape. *Psychology Science*, *48*(2), 187–204.

Schmitt, D. P., & Buss, D. M. (1996). Strategic self-promotion and competitor derogation: Sex and context effects on the perceived effectiveness of mate attraction tactics. *Journal of Personality and Social Psychology*, *70*(6), 1185–1204. doi:10.1037/0022-3514.70.6.1185

Schwarz, S., & Hassebrauck, M. (2008). Self-perceived and observed variations in women's attractiveness throughout the menstrual cycle—A diary study. *Evolution and Human Behavior*, *29*, 282–288.

Sigall, H., & Ostrove, N. (1975). Beautiful but dangerous: Effects of offender attractiveness and nature of the crime on juridic judgment. *Journal of Personality and Social Psychology*, *31*, 410–414.

Singh, D. (1993). Body shape and women's attractiveness. *Human Nature*, *4*(3), 297–321.

Singh, D. (1994). Ideal female body shape: Role of body weight and waist-to-hip ratio. *International Journal of Eating Disorders*, *16*(3), 283–288.

Singh, D., & Singh, D. (2011). Shape and significance of feminine beauty: An evolutionary perspective. *Sex Roles*, *64*(9–10), 723–731. doi:10.1007/s11199-011-9938-z

Singh, D., & Young, R. K. (1995). Body weight, waist-to-hip ratio, breasts, and hips: Role in judgments of female attractiveness and desirability for relationships. *Ethology and Sociobiology*, *16*(6), 483–507.

Smith, J. E., Waldorf, V. A., & Trembath, D. L. (1990). Single white male looking for thin, very attractive. *Sex Roles*, *23*(11–12), 675–685.

Smith, R. H. (1991). Envy and the sense of injustice. In P. Salovey (Ed.), *The psychology of jealousy and envy* (pp. 79–99). New York: The Guilford Press.

Smith, R. H., & Kim, S. H. (2007). Comprehending envy. *Psychological Bulletin*, *133*, 46–64.

Smith, R. H., Kim, S. H., & Parrott, W. G. (1988). Envy and jealousy: Semantic problems and experiential distinctions. *Personality and Social Psychology Bulletin*, *14*, 401–409.

Soldak, K. (2012, October). 'Barbie Flu' spreading in Ukraine. *Forbes Magazine*. Retrieved from http://www.forbes.com

Solnick, S. J., & Schweitzer, M. E. (1999). The influence of physical attractiveness and gender on ultimatum game decisions. *Organizational Behavior and Human Decision Processes*, *79*, 199–215.

Stephan, C. W., & Langlois, J. H. (1984). Baby beautiful: Adult attributions of infant competence as a function of infant attractiveness. *Child Development*, *55*(2), 576–585. doi:10.2307/1129969

Stephen, I. D., & McKeegan, A. M. (2010). Lip colour affects perceived sex typicality and attractiveness of human faces. *Perception*, *39*(8), 1104–1110.

Swami, V., Furnham, A., & Joshi, K. (2008). The influence of skin tone, hair length, and hair colour on ratings of women's physical attractiveness, health and fertility. *Scandinavian Journal of Psychology*, *49*(5), 429–437.

Symons, D. (1979). *The evolution of human sexuality*. New York: Oxford University Press.

Symons, D. (1995). Beauty is in the adaptations of the beholder: The evolutionary psychology of human female sexual attractiveness. In P. R. Abramson & S. D. Pinkerton (Eds.), *Sexual nature, sexual culture* (pp. 80–118). Chicago: University of Chicago Press.

Tantleff-Dunn, S. (2002). Biggest isn't always best: The effect of breast size on perceptions of women. *Journal of Applied Social Psychology*, *32*(11), 2253–2265.

Thornhill, R., & Gangestad, S. W. (1994). Human fluctuating asymmetry and sexual behavior. *Psychological Science*, *5*, 297–302.

Thornton, B. (1977). Effect of rape victim's attractiveness in a jury simulation. *Personality and Social Psychology Bulletin*, *3*(4), 666–669. doi:10.1177/014616727700300422

Thornton, B., & Moore, S. (1993). Physical attractiveness contrast effect: Implications for self-esteem and evaluations of the social self. *Personality and Social Psychology Bulletin*, *19*, 474–480.

Trivers, R. L. (1972). Parental investment and sexual selection. In B. Campbell (Ed.), *Sexual selection and the descent of man: 1871-1971* (pp. 136–179). Chicago, IL: Aldine.

Udry, J. R., & Eckland, B. K. (1984). Benefits of being attractive: Differential payoffs for men and women. *Psychological Reports*, *54*(1), 47–56.

Umberson, D., & Hughes, M. (1987). The impact of physical attractiveness on achievement and psychological well-being. *Social Psychology Quarterly*, *50*, 227–236.

Vaillancourt, T. (2005). Indirect aggression among humans: Social construct or evolutionary adaptation?

In R. E. Tremblay, W. W. Hartup, & J. Archer (Eds.), *Developmental origins of aggression* (pp. 158–177). New York: Guilford Press.

Vaillancourt, T., & Sharma, A. (2011). Intolerance of sexy peers: Intrasexual competition among women. *Aggressive Behavior, 37*(6), 569–577. doi:10.1002/ab.20413

Van den Berghe, P. L., & Frost, P. (1986). Skin color preference, sexual dimorphism and sexual selection: A case of gene culture co-evolution? *Ethnic and Racial Studies, 9*(1), 87–113.

Wade, T. J., Fuller, L., Bresnan, J., Schaefer, S., & Mlynarski, L. (2007). Weight halo effects: Individual differences in personality evaluations and perceived life success of men as a function of weight? *Personality and Individual Differences, 42,* 317–324.

Walster, E., Aronson, V., Abrahams, D., & Rottman, L. (1966). Importance of physical attractiveness in dating behavior. *Journal of Personality and Social Psychology, 4*(5), 508–516.

Walters, S., & Crawford, C. B. (1994). The importance of mate attraction for intrasexual competition in men and women. *Ethology & Sociobiology, 15,* 5–30.

Waynforth, D., & Dunbar, R. I. M. (1995). Conditional mate choice strategies in humans: Evidence from "lonely hearts" advertisements. *Behaviour, 132,* 755–779.

Welling, L. L. M., Jones, B. C., DeBruine, L. M., Conway, C. A., Law Smith, M. J., Little, A. C.,... Al-Dujaili, E. A. S. (2007). Raised salivary testosterone in women is associated with increased attraction to masculine faces. *Hormones and Behavior, 52,* 156–161.

Welling, L. L. M., Jones, B. C., DeBruine, L. M., Little, A. C., & Smith, F. G. (2008). Exposure to sexually attractive men decreases women's preferences for feminine faces. *Journal of Evolutionary Psychology, 6,* 219–230.

Wheeler, L., & Kim, Y. (1997). What is beautiful is culturally good: The physical attractiveness stereotype has different content in collectivistic cultures. *Personality and Social Psychology Bulletin, 23*(8), 795–800.

Williamson, S., & Hewitt, J. (1986). Attire, sexual allure, and attractiveness. *Perceptual and Motor Skills, 63*(2, Pt 2), 981–982.

Wilson, R. K., & Eckel, C. C. (2006). Judging a book by its cover: Beauty and expectations in the trust game. *Political Research Quarterly, 59*(2), 189–202.

Workman, J. E., & Johnson, K. K. (1991). The role of cosmetics in impression formation. *Clothing and Textiles Research Journal, 10,* 63–67.

Ravishing Rivals: Female Intrasexual Competition and Cosmetic Surgery

Shelli L. Dubbs, Ashleigh J. Kelly, *and* Fiona Kate Barlow

Abstract

Intrasexual competition between women is a critically important construct with real implications for women's physical and psychological health. This chapter argues that female competition can cause women to fixate on their appearance and take unnecessary risks in an effort to improve it. Western society sets seemingly impossible criteria for female beauty that few women can naturally—and healthily—achieve. These standards and evolved partner preferences for physical attractiveness in women help to explain why women generally feel enormous pressure to be attractive and are compelled to compete intensely with one another in the realm of physical attractiveness. The authors suggest that intrasexual competition may lead some women to alter their physical appearance through unnecessary, expensive, and ultimately risky medical procedures in order to outdo female mating rivals and attain the best-quality mate. This is may be a dangerous strategy, equivalent to the overt risk-taking behaviors that exemplify male–male intrasexual competition.

Key Words: female intrasexual competition, cosmetic surgery, mate competition, sexual selection, risk taking

Since the early 20th century, modern cosmetic surgery has touted the promise of achieving aesthetic perfection. Specifically, it allows for flawless skin, a brilliant smile, perfect facial and body dimensions, and more. People can be molded like clay; sucked and tucked, tightened and smoothed, injected and implanted. With new innovations and medical advances, an ever-increasing variety of sophisticated cosmetic treatments are available to the public. Unlike in the environments in which our human ancestors survived and evolved, modern humans are able to strongly manipulate their physical appearance. They can choose to maintain their appearance, turn back the hands of time, or even obtain new characteristics that they feel biology has denied them. Through cosmetic procedures, it is possible for people to transform their visible facade and attempt to become closer to the "ideal" human form.

However, modern Western culture sets seemingly impossible criteria for the "ideal" female form that few women can naturally—and healthily—achieve. Furthermore, men typically desire physical attractiveness in women because this may provide them with specific fitness advantages, including fertility and the ability to carry a child to term. In the following sections, we argue that these cultural standards and evolved partner preferences help to explain why women generally feel enormous pressure to be attractive and are compelled to compete intensely with one another in the realm of physical attractiveness. Crucially, we suggest that intrasexual competition may lead some women to alter their physical appearance through unnecessary and ultimately risky medical procedures in order to outdo their female mating rivals. We further discuss how this is can be a dangerous, even life-threatening strategy, one that is rooted in the same fundamental principles of sexual selection that drive men to engage in physical fights over women. First, however, it is important to discuss the practice of cosmetic surgery along with the risks, how these have both changed over time, and why the industry tends to appeal more to women rather than men.

A Brief History of the Cosmetic Surgery Industry

The development of the cosmetic surgery industry is a recent phenomenon; however, altering physical appearance through surgery has its roots in antiquity. For example, Indian Sanskrit texts from more than 2,600 years ago describe skin grafting techniques used on the face and nose, and, likewise, the ancient Romans developed methods for correcting damage to ears, lips, and noses (Hill & Pickart, 2009). These surgeries, however, were intended to restore a "normal" appearance to individuals suffering from either birth defects (e.g., cleft lip) or disfiguring physical injuries (e.g., a severed nose from a sword fight) rather than simply enhancing beauty. Unfortunately, for the recipients of many early surgeries, as well as recipients into the later half of the 19th century, the techniques implemented were not always safe or effective. For example, in Rogers (1971, p. 269), it was cited that Charles Miller (one of several facelift pioneers) implanted a variety of insoluble foreign materials such as silk floss, celluloid, and vegetable ivory into patient's faces to give contour and correct imperfections. Undoubtedly painful, this technique was also dangerous because it posed a high risk of infection. In some instances, poor practice stemmed directly from a lack of knowledge, whereas in others, it was more reflective of bad judgment (Rogers, 1971).

Although advances were occurring, the practice of cosmetic surgery in the early 20th century was largely regarded as a fringe discipline within the medical community. Speaking directly to this point, Miller wrote, "when a woman or man consults the family physician regarding some defect of facial outline or fault of skin, the physician merely laughs and ridicules" (as cited in Rogers, 1971, p. 269). Not only were appearance-based concerns trivialized and reduced to vanity, but many medical professionals perceived cosmetic surgery as illegitimate and unnecessary, and further derogated cosmetic surgeons for interfering with "god's will" (Rogers, 1971, p. 290).

Opposition toward cosmetic surgery gradually declined in the wake of World Wars I and II, when surgeons were tasked with reconstructing the physical features of injured war victims (Hill & Pickart, 2009; Rogers, 1971). Recent advances in medicine included improvements in technology, anesthesia administration, wound care, and the ability to prevent disease and secondary infection and allowed surgeons to increase the safety and effectiveness of many cosmetic procedures (Hill & Pickart, 2009).

Modifying Appearance Is the New Cosmetic Cure-all

With each passing decade, the variety of available cosmetic procedures has increased. For example, in the 1960s, procedures for conducting an abdominoplasty (i.e., the so-called *tummy tuck*, in which loose skin is removed from the lower abdominal region) were refined, and silicone breast augmentation was introduced. In the following decade, liposuction (i.e., where fat is removed from various regions of the body to give a more sculpted appearance) became available. Although the proliferation of newly available procedures gave people the option to manipulate their appearance like never before, the safety of such procedures was still questionable and in need of regulation. Consequently, in 1976, the U.S. Food and Drug Association (FDA) passed the Medical Devices Amendment to the Federal Food, Drug, and Cosmetic Act, which granted the FDA the authority to evaluate the effectiveness of new medical devices used for cosmetic surgical purposes. This act, along with the establishment of the American Society for Aesthetic Plastic Surgery (ASAPS) in 1967, whose primary mission was to educate surgeons and ensure good practice, served to lessen the risks associated with undergoing a cosmetic procedure. As such, the idea of changing one's appearance via a medical, and often surgical, procedure became an increasingly attractive option.

Accordingly, in the past half century, the number of cosmetic procedures performed globally has skyrocketed from 130,000 in 1958 to more than 8 million in 2012 (American Society for Aesthetic Plastic Surgery [ASAPS], 2013). Contributing to this recent influx has been the availability of nonsurgical methods for altering one's face. These procedures are typically used to improve, maintain, or restore a more youthful facial appearance, and range from skin resurfacing techniques (e.g., chemical peels and laser treatments), injectables (e.g., collagen or hyaluronic acid fillers), to toxins (e.g., Botox). The appeal is obvious; these procedures are generally safer and, less expensive, and require less recovery time than the more invasive cosmetic operations. Since 1997, the use of noninvasive techniques has risen by a staggering 461% (ASAPS, 2013). Although nonsurgical options are clearly in vogue, invasive cosmetic surgery has not fallen out of fashion (e.g., liposuction, breast augmentation, facelifts; ASAPS, 2013). Instead, the number of surgical procedures performed has increased by almost 80% over the same time period (ASAPS, 2013). Needless to say, business in this industry is booming, even in the face of the recent global economic hardship. Indeed, for 2012, the ASAPS reported that Americans spent almost US$11 billion on cosmetic procedures, which is an increase of 5.5% on the previous year. Furthermore, this growth is not restricted to the United States. The total number of cosmetic procedures performed has more than doubled between 2010 and 2013 in many countries, including Brazil, Mexico, Germany, Spain, Venezuela, and Argentina (International Society of Aesthetic Plastic Surgery, 2011, 2014).

Attitudes to and Acceptance of Cosmetic Surgery

Coinciding with the heightened demand for both invasive and noninvasive cosmetic procedures, norms and attitudes associated with medically modifying one's appearance have changed over time. Many previously believed the industry itself was preying on people's insecurities, and those who opted for a procedure were commonly labeled "vain" or "self-indulgent." Indeed, recipients frequently hid or denied that they had "work done," even if it was as plain as the nose on their face (Woodstock, 2001). While once condemned as extreme or shallow, cosmetic procedures have entered the mainstream and become increasingly popular and socially acceptable (Brooks, 2004; Woodstock, 2001; for predictors of cosmetic surgery acceptance, see Swami, Chamorro-Premuzic, Bridges, & Furnham, 2009). In 2003, at least a quarter of Americans stated that they would consider getting a cosmetic procedure at some point, and roughly three-quarters of people surveyed claimed that they would not be embarrassed to admit having "work done" (Brooks, 2004).

Increased safety, effectiveness, affordability, and the variety of treatments available may have all contributed to the recent positivity surrounding cosmetic surgery. Perhaps more notably, however, is the visibility of cosmetic surgery in everyday life. Not only are more people opting for it, which increases the probability that a person will know or see someone who has undergone a procedure, but the media

is also awash with commentaries, articles, and programs describing the latest surgical crazes, celebrity fix-ups, and extreme makeovers in which dowdy housewives emerge as beautiful "swans" following multiple, and often extensive, procedures.

Recently, cosmetic surgery in the media has been idealized as a transformative process that delivers spectacular results for both the inner and outer selves (e.g., the ABC television program "Extreme Makeover" touts cosmetic surgery as a life-changing confidence boost). As if overnight, unfortunate-looking souls become the embodiment of beauty while simultaneously exorcising their inner demons (e.g., insecurities, anxieties, and depression). People are portrayed as not only being physically "healed," but also psychologically repaired. Exceptions, though, do exist; for example, botched surgery and criticism toward individuals undergoing multiple procedures are sometimes discussed (Sarwer, Nordmann, & Herbert 2000). The message fostered by the media is, on the face of it, overly positive and perhaps unrealistic. Compared to the benefits, the media focuses little on the financial costs, health risks, and healing process associated with undergoing cosmetic operations (Lazar & Deneuve, 2013). Furthermore, patient outcomes may be either overstated or exceptional. That is, depending on the procedure, the results are typically subtler than those depicted in the media, and, similarly, not all "ducklings" will turn into perfect "swans."

The Changing Face of the Cosmetic Surgical Patient

In addition to the changing norms regarding cosmetic procedures, the face of the typical person seeking such procedures has changed. Once reserved for the famous or the clichéd aging, upper-class white woman desperate to retain her youthful appearance and nubile figure (Woodstock, 2001), today, people of all economic and cultural backgrounds opt for surgery. In the past few years, ethnic and racial minority groups constituted a large portion of the cosmetic surgeon's clientele base (i.e., 21% of all cosmetic procedures in 2011; ASAPS, 2012). Similarly, whereas women between the ages of 35 and 50 are the most widely represented group (accounting for 43% of all procedures in the United States; ASAPS, 2012), an increasing number of men are also choosing to go "under the knife" and needle. In 2012, more than 1 million procedures were performed on men, representing a growth of 130% over the past 15 years and accounting for 10% of the total procedures performed in the United States (ASAPS, 2013). In addition, younger women (18–34), as well as women 65 and over—a demographic that is stereotypically perceived as nonsexual and unconcerned about their appearance (Slevec & Tiggemann, 2010)—are also frequenting the cosmetic surgeon's office (ASAPS, 2012; 2013).

As mentioned, evidence for the popularity of cosmetic surgery is not limited to Western culture. The United States tops the list for the total number of procedures performed; however, several non-Western countries make it into the top 25, including China, Thailand, Mexico, India, Colombia, Turkey, Venezuela, and Romania (International Society of Aesthetic Plastic Surgery, 2011). Taking population size into account, South Korea actually has the greatest number of procedures performed per capita (International Society of Aesthetic Plastic Surgery, 2011). Whereas industries based on cosmetic surgery tourism have, in part, contributed to these statistics in many countries (Bell, Holliday, Jones, Probyn, & Taylor, 2011), the allure of youth and beauty and the associated desire for cosmetic procedures unmistakably transcend cultural boundaries.

Magic Wands and the Fountain of Youth

Being physically attractive has clear benefits, and, indeed, a halo effect exists for attractiveness whereby good-looking individuals are generally evaluated and treated more positively than their less attractive counterparts (Eagly, Ashmore, Makhijani, & Longo, 1991; Feingold, 1992; Langlois et al., 2000; Zebrowitz, Hall, Murphy, & Rhodes, 2002). Some of the perks of attractiveness include earning more money on the job, being perceived as more competent and intelligent, receiving less severe punishments in court, receiving help when needed, and being more popular among peers. Similarly, youthfulness, which is strongly associated with attractiveness, has positive connotations (e.g., energetic, exciting, forward-thinking, cognitively flexible), whereas advanced age evokes many negative stereotypes (e.g., cognitive impairments, incompetency, stubbornness, immobility; Nelson, 2005). Although a person may choose to hide his or her actual age, for many, the signs of aging will be etched into their face in the form of lines, wrinkles, and drooping skin. These features may also inadvertently give the appearance of tiredness or anger (i.e., bags under the eyes, furrows on the forehead, etc.). Given these negative associations, age can often hinder a person (Nelson, 2005), particularly when seeking employment. Even for positions that require experience and leadership that we would expect to be apparent in older individuals, relatively fresher-faced applicants may be favored (Australian Human Rights Commission, 2010).

In light of the social rewards that stand to be gained, it is easy to see why people generally desire attractiveness and the appearance of youth. As expected, most people invest at least some effort into enhancing their appearance or attempting to stave off the aging process. Undoubtedly, if given the opportunity to wave a magic beauty wand or drink from the fountain of youth, the majority of people would probably be tempted to do so. Although such concepts are clearly mythical, medical procedures that can beautify and halt or rewind the hands of time are in existence today. There is, however, a catch. Cosmetic procedures can be financially, physically, and socially risky. In 2012, the average fee per surgery ranged from approximately US$2,000 to $8,000, depending on the procedure (ASAPS, 2013). Patients also risk major complications (related to anesthesia, infection, bleeding, scarring, etc.) and death (Mayo Clinic, 2014), along with the potential social backlash from family and friends for altering their appearance. Consequently, not everyone will be willing to take the chance. For some, though, the allure of beauty and youth eternal may be so strong that the benefits seemingly outweigh the costs. Indeed, it can be predicted that the potential payoff for undergoing a medical cosmetic alteration would be greater for some people than for others. The question then becomes: what factors compel individuals to alter their physical appearance through these drastic and potentially risky methods? Herein, we suggest that sex, culture, and intrasexual competition all play important roles in the pursuit of physical perfection.

Women and the Pursuit of Attractiveness

Although men are not impervious to wanting to change their appearance, women undeniably constitute the core clientele for cosmetic surgeons, outnumbering men approximately 9 to 1 (ASAPS, 2013). Surveys reveal that women, relative to men, hold more positive attitudes toward cosmetic procedures and are more likely to report that they would consider undergoing a cosmetic procedure at present or at some point in the future (ASASP, 2012; Slevec & Tiggemann, 2010). To a large extent, this sex difference is expected from both sociocultural and evolutionary perspectives.

As previously discussed, attractiveness begets many benefits, the most potent of which appears to be in the domain of mating. When it comes to sexual behavior and romance, beautiful people usually have an advantage. They start dating earlier, have more sexual partners, have more long- and short-term relationships, are likely to be more reproductively successful (Jokela, 2009), and may hold more power within their romantic relationships than less attractive individuals (Critelli, Waid, & Schneider, 1979; Zhang, You, Teng, & Chan, 2014). Importantly, however, the sexes do not equally value physical attractiveness in a romantic partner. Across cultures, physical attractiveness is a highly desired trait in women, whereas it is a comparatively less valued trait in men (Buss, 1989; Buss & Shackelford, 2008). Accordingly, although cultures may differ vastly in the overt pressure placed on individuals to be beautiful, women universally appear to bear the burden of this pressure to a much greater extent than men. That is, greater expectations are placed on women to be beautiful, and, in some instances, the very definition of a woman necessitates beauty. Furthermore, individuals, stories, myths, cultural conventions, norms, and the media frequently reproduce this message.

Cultural Influences on Women and Standards of Beauty in the Media

The pressure for women to be beautiful is perhaps most clearly manifested in modern Western culture and increasingly in countries exposed to Western media and ideals (e.g., body dissatisfaction was seen to increase in Fijian girls after prolonged exposure to television, which was previously absent from their region; Becker, Burwell, Herzog, Hamburg, & Gilman, 2002). A culture of beauty seems to exist, wherein obsession with looks, particularly women's appearance, is perpetuated by the media. Indeed, throughout the entire modern era, a standard of female beauty has existed and been exhibited through whatever medium was available at the time: in photographs; on the sides of fighter planes; in calendars, magazines, movies, and television; and in advertisements.

Despite some cultural and temporal differences in what is considered the "ideal" female form (e.g., low vs. high body weight in Westernized vs. some non-Westernized cultures, Furnham & Alibhai, 1983; Swami, Mada, & Tovée, 2012; along with the large breast craze in the 1950s and 1960s and the extreme slenderness trend from the 1980s to today; Mazur, 1986), certain features are seemingly "timeless" and seldom go out of style. That is, female beauty appears to have a formula. Cross-culturally,

beautiful women tend to possess traits indicative of youthfulness and femininity. These include smooth skin; large, bright eyes; a small nose; and a soft, shapely figure, often described as an "hourglass" (Barber, 1995; Cunningham, 1986; Singh, 1993a).

In Westernized societies, however, there is also pressure to maintain a slender figure (Rozin & Fallon, 1988; Stice, Schupak-Neuberg, Shaw, & Stein, 1994). Western media clearly perpetuates this "ideal" standard; flawlessly beautiful women with low body weights are greatly overrepresented in magazines, in advertisements, and on both the large and small screens (Sypeck, Gray, & Ahrens, 2004). One study, for example, found that 94% of magazines aimed at women had an image of a thin model or celebrity on the cover (Malkin, Wornian, & Chrisler, 1999). Similarly, both *Playboy* centerfolds (models who are selected for a male audience) and beauty pageant contestants have decreased in their body mass index (BMI; a marker of weight relative to height) over the past 50 years (Seifert, 2005; Wiseman, Gray, Mosimann, & Ahrens, 1992, using data from 1959 to 1992). Moreover, whereas the quintessential female body has become increasingly slender, a larger-than-average bust size is simultaneously expected and is typically depicted in media images (Goodman & Walsh-Childers, 2004). As a testament to the unrealistic nature of the current beauty standards, models used in modern media are likely to be further perfected by makeup artists and stylists, in addition to expert lighting, camera angles, filters, retouching, and airbrushing. Even those who make their living retouching photographs don't view their work as strictly ethical or as realistic representations of women. Digital photo editor Ken Harris, interviewed for Stacy Malkan's book *Not Just a Pretty Face: The Ugly Side of the Beauty Industry*, stated, "I don't see these photographs as being authentic or real. . . the central point of retouching is to enforce an unrealizable standard of beauty. . . every picture has been worked on some 20 or 30 rounds. . . they're perfected to death" (2007, p. 69).

It is not just the average weight or appearance of young women, however, that is distorted in Western media. Celebrity news and gossip columns often glorify celebrities who have aged "gracefully" and manage to look 10 to 20 years younger than they are while simultaneously berating those who show their age (for an example, see Hodapp & Luciani, 2012). There also seems to be a growing obsession with celebrity women who have regained their svelte, prepregnancy bodies mere weeks after the birth of their child. Sadly, however, there is evidence to suggest that these depictions may further compound the pressure that women face to be physically attractive throughout all stages of their lives (see Slevec & Tiggemann, 2010).

Society has created seemingly impossible criteria for female beauty that few women can naturally—and healthily—achieve. In recent years, even young, healthy (and likely attractive) women consider attempting to alter their appearance through risky and dangerous means, including cosmetic surgery (Swami et al., 2009) and dangerous topical products. Malkan (2007), for example, discusses the popular skin-lightening creams used by great numbers of healthy women in Asian countries, many of which contain a variety of dangerous chemicals, including a "confirmed animal carcinogen that is toxic to the skin, brain, immune system and reproductive system" (pp. 66–67). This same chemical, hydroquinone, deemed "unsafe for use in products left on the skin" and "banned from the European Union," is sold in concentrations of up to 2% in a selection of skin products purchased by women in the United States (Malkan, 2007, p. 67). These women, exposed to Western media, are struggling to attain an unachievable European look through very risky means. Furthermore, such high cultural standards for slimness and beauty seem to reinforce the notion that a woman's value can be determined largely—if not solely—by her physical appearance. This has unquestionably contributed to women's greater experience of appearance-based concerns in comparison to men. Studies show that women's exposure to media images of unrealistically slender and attractive females (e.g., slender models, gossip magazines) leads to increased dissatisfaction with their own physical appearance and body (Groesz, Levine, & Murnen, 2002; Stice, 2002; Stice et al., 1994; Tiggemann & McGill, 2004). Negative evaluations of this nature are not benign and have been directly implicated in the development of low self-esteem, low self-worth, depression, and eating-disordered behaviors (Stice, 2002; Stice et al., 1994), as well as in decreased sexual satisfaction in women (Pujols, Meston, & Seal, 2010). Although cultural ideals of beauty may vary, the fact that women *across* cultures are judged more on their appearance than are men suggests that biology may, in part, underlie our aesthetic preferences. Specifically, evolved partner preferences may help to explain why heterosexual women generally feel more pressure than men to be attractive, as well as why certain features are considered beautiful.

Evolution and Male Mate Preferences

Most people would agree that heterosexual men are highly attuned to women's physical appearance and are particularly attentive to women's bodies. Men are said to be aroused by visual stimuli more so than women (for a review, see Rupp & Wallen, 2008), which coincides with norms surrounding men's tendency to ogle attractive women, frequent strip clubs, and view more pornographic material (see Hald, 2006, for sex differences in pornography consumption). These norms are not completely unfounded in evolutionary psychology. Research reveals that when it comes to selecting a mate, regardless of whether it is for a short-term liaison or a long-term marriage partner, men consistently rate physical attractiveness as a desirable, even indispensable, characteristic (Buss, 1989; Li, Bailey, Kenrick, & Linsenmeier, 2002; Li & Kenrick, 2006); yet women also prefer high levels of physical attractiveness in short-term mates (Li, 2007; Li & Kenrick, 2006). Men's preferences for female faces are clear-cut, with research indicating that men strongly prefer female faces that have been feminized (i.e., faces made shorter and rounder with larger eyes and fuller lips) compared to those that have been masculinized (i.e., a broader jaw line, heavier brow ridge, smaller more closely set eyes, and a wider mouth with thinner lips), for both short- and long-term mates (for a review, see Rhodes, 2006). Research using eye-tracking devices has also demonstrated that men spend more time looking at women's breasts and waistlines relative to their faces, legs, and—perhaps not surprisingly—the background (Dixson, Grimshaw, Linklater, & Dixson, 2011). Studies indicate that, overall, men highly prioritize slenderness (particularly those in Westernized societies; Swami, Caprario, Tovée, & Furnham, 2006; Swami & Tovée, 2005). Additionally, a defined waistline (Singh, 1993a, 1993b) and an average to slightly larger than average bust size (Gallup, 1982; Lynn, 2009) has also been found to increase the perceived attractiveness of a woman's body. Although such an emphasis on a mate's outward appearance may seem shallow, there is sound evolutionary reasoning for why men value physical attractiveness in women.

First, humans tend to form long-term relationships in which women *and* men invest highly in parental effort. Under such circumstances, both men and women will be picky with their mate choices (Edward & Chapman, 2011) because selecting a poor-quality mate will limit both parties' capacity to successfully reproduce. This does not mean, however, that the mate preferences of men and women will be identical. In order to successfully reproduce, men and women face different selective pressures. Men's capacity to reproduce is mostly limited by the woman's fertility. In humans, relative to most other mammals, a female's ability to successfully reproduce is seemingly more variable. Specifically, the rates of fertility sharply decline in women as they age and approach menopause (Hawkes, O'Connell, Blurton Jones, Alvarez, & Charnov, 1998). Further compounding the matter, the large size of the fetus's head and the human's upright body posture make the birthing process especially arduous for humans (Mace, 2000). This would have been an intense selective pressure for our ancestors because maternal mortality due to complications resulting from childbirth is relatively common, particularly in places where Western medical practices are absent (Khan, Wojdyla, Say, Gülmezoglu, & Van Look, 2006). As a result, it is in a man's best interest (genetically speaking) to be attuned to cues that may indicate whether a woman is fertile, is healthy, and has the ability to successfully give birth. Specific visual cues, such as wrinkle-free skin, lustrous hair, a low waist-to-hip ratio (WHR; in which body fat is mostly distributed on the thighs, hips, and buttocks, helping to give the appearance of an "hourglass" figure), full breasts, and full lips, as well as soft and neotenous facial features (including large eyes and a small nose and chin; see Rhodes, 2006), may serve as:

1. A proxy of a woman's age
2. A hormonal profile (high estrogen and low androgens; for a discussion see Barber, 1995; Rhodes, Chan, Zebrowitz, & Simmons, 2003; also large breasts in combination with a low WHR has been related to fecundity and hormonal profiles more suited for conception; Jasienska, Ziomkiewicz, Ellison, Lipson, & Thune, 2004)
3. A signal that she has the necessary fat stores to sustain a pregnancy and postpregnancy lactation (Lassek & Gaulin, 2008)
4. A sign that her hips are wide enough to deliver a newborn (Gallup & Frederick, 2010).
Please see Wheatley et al. (2014) for discussion.

Supporting this evolutionary account, the aforementioned physical features have been found to be attractive to men across several cultures (Cunningham, Roberts, Wu, Barbee, & Druen, 1995). There is, however, a distinct cultural difference in preferences for body size. Whereas a low WHR of approximately 0.7 (whereby the waist is roughly two-thirds the circumference of the hips) appears to be almost universally preferred (Singh, 1993a; although for counter evidence, please see Swami et al., 2006), not all cultures equally value slenderness. In Westernized societies, BMI is a strong predictor of a woman's perceived level of physical attractiveness among both men and women, with thinner frames preferred over larger ones (Swami & Tovée, 2005). By contrast, in less industrialized societies, as well as in those that are less exposed to Western media, heavier female bodies are generally preferred (Swami & Tovée, 2005). Indeed, the strong preference for slender bodies in the West is a relatively recent trend that has occurred since the early to mid-1900s (Abed, 1998) and may be a reaction to the stigma associated with being obese in a society of fast food and abundance.

Women and the Eternal Quest for Beauty

In light of men's focus on women's appearance, it is little wonder that so many women experience concerns about their physical appearance (Garner, Garfinkel, Schwartz, & Thompson, 1980; Stice, 2002). In particular, features most highly indicative of youthfulness and femininity (such as complexion and skin, breasts, buttocks, and body proportions) are those that women seemingly attempt to change, emphasize, or lament over. Supporting this notion, in 2012, injectables constituted the most popular procedure overall for women (with 4,413,675 procedures performed), and skin rejuvenation procedures came in second (1,945,526 procedures); these numbers are in comparison to those for men, who received 467,583 and 160,400 of these procedures, respectively (ASAPS, 2013). Breast augmentation was the most popular invasive surgery for women (330,631 surgeries), followed by liposuction (271,369), abdominoplasty (widely known as the *tummy tuck*; 148,964), and eyelid surgery (129,920, ASAPS, 2013; to correct drooping eyelids as a result of age or for those desiring a more European look). Furthermore, 112,795 breast reductions were performed on women in 2012 (the eighth most popular procedure; ASAPS, 2013), which, although often undertaken to reduce discomfort relating to the weight of the breasts (e.g., neck, back, or skin pain issues; Snodgrass, 2012), can also be used to improve breast appearance and create a perkier look (although this is not typically cited as a common reason for the procedure). Regardless, all plastic surgeries are performed with the goal of creating an attractive result (while resolving any underlying issues), and the major motivation underpinning cosmetic surgery is typically to increase one's attractiveness to others (for a Korean example, see Ja, 2004). While women's appearance-based concerns have been sparking interest in recent decades, their desire to become physically attractive is by no means a recent phenomenon. Indeed, history is replete with examples of contraptions, lotions, potions, and procedures—some of which have proved deadly—that women have sought out in an effort to become more feminine, youthful, beautiful, and desirable to the opposite sex. As an example, in ancient Rome, Egypt, and Persia, women used drops of antimony sulfide to dilate their pupils. Although this action had the desired effect of making the woman's eyes sparkle and dazzle, it often led to blindness and glaucoma later in life. In more recent history, until the early 1900s, women in Western Europe and the United States would frequently wear corsets to create an exaggerated hourglass figure. The corsets, however, were sometimes drawn so tightly and worn so often that they would shift the ribs and internal organs and permanently distort the body shape (see chapter by Johnsen and Geher). Sham products (like "snake-oil"), sworn to enhance women's busts, melt fat, eliminate cellulite, smooth wrinkles, and grow long and shiny hair, are still currently marketed, with each product associated with a varying degree of risk in terms of side effects and financial costs. Luckily, most women today, although certainly not all (see Malkan, 2007), presumably select from a variety of safer options to enhance their physical appearance.

Multi-million-dollar industries specifically target women, promising to help them improve their looks and achieve more youthful and feminine appearances, as well as slender figures. Casual observation suggests that cosmetics, body-shaping undergarments (e.g., padded bras, corsets, shapewear), colorful and stylish clothing, along with diet and exercise plans are used almost ubiquitously by women across cultures that have access to them. Although some of these appearance-changing methods (such as diet and exercise) can result in significant and obvious bodily change, many of the other methods are temporary "quick fixes" or concealments. For example, push-up bras give the appearance of fuller or perkier breasts until the garment is removed, and,

similarly, cosmetics can give the wearer the appearance of fuller lips and a smooth complexion, but it is washed off at the end of each day.

On the other hand, cosmetic procedures, and especially invasive surgical procedures such as liposuction and breast augmentation, offer a near-permanent "solution." Considering that physical attractiveness is an important criterion for mate selection in women and that societal standards for beauty are seemingly unobtainable for the vast majority of women, it is not surprising that women account for approximately 90% of all cosmetic procedures conducted in the United States, as discussed (ASAPS, 2012, 2013). As hinted at earlier, evolutionary theory—based on the mate preferences of men—provides insight into the types of treatments that women would be likely to desire. As discussed, the most frequently obtained surgical cosmetic procedures for women include liposuction, breast augmentation, abdominoplasty, and rhinoplasty (ASASP, 2012, 2013). Notably, in the United States, liposuction and breast augmentation fight for the top spot each year, with more than 300,000 procedures performed for each (ASASP, 2012, 2013). For nonsurgical procedures, Botox (a diluted toxin that paralyzes the muscles and is typically injected in the face to reduce or prevent wrinkles) reigns supreme (ASASP, 2012, 2013). Clearly, these procedures are aimed at restoring the appearance of youthfulness, achieving ideal body portions, and creating a more sexually dimorphic and feminine appearance, which, as mentioned, are the very traits that men find appealing in a mate. Even an early practitioner of cosmetic surgery, Julien Bourguet, emphasized that "men. . . are indifferent to or much less concerned with facial wrinkles than women are" (Rogers, 1971, p. 283). Similarly, Jacques Joseph, who was a major founding figure of modern cosmetic surgery, claimed that the premature appearance of wrinkles could prove to be especially problematic for women looking to earn a living (Rogers, 1971), implying that the sociological costs of aging impact on women more than on men. Accordingly, frequently cited reasons for women wanting cosmetic procedures include the desire to be more attractive to men (e.g., "I want to start dating," "I want my husband to think I'm sexy").

Whereas men's mate preferences for young and fertile women may ultimately be a direct causal factor in women's decisions to seek out cosmetic procedures, we hypothesize that there is an additional variable that also helps to explain women's desire to alter their appearance through medical procedures.

Specifically, we propose that intrasexual competition in women—namely, seeing other women as rivals for the acquisition or retention of mates—further fosters a mindset that drives women to seek and obtain cosmetic procedures.

Intrasexual Selection Theory

It is easy to imagine that if *you* are attracted to someone, *other* people may also be longing for, or even intensely pursuing that person. The characteristics they possess, whether it is being physically attractive, creative, or rich, makes these individuals valuable on the mating market (on average; Buss, 1989; Miller, 2000). Even if such individuals are not actively seeking additional or alternate mates, others might attempt to steal them away, which is a common phenomenon known as *mate poaching* (Schmitt & Buss, 2001). Specifically, in a study by Schmitt and Buss in 2001, approximately half of 236 participants (aged 20–65) reported making mate poaching attempts (either for a short- or long-term encounter), and 85% reported that someone had tried to poach them away from their partner. Therefore, in the mating game, it is not always enough to be attractive to potential mates; individuals may also have to actively compete against members of the same sex for the mates they wish to successfully pursue or retain.

Intrasexual competition is a core tenant of the theory of *sexual selection* (Darwin, 1871), which suggests that it can sometimes benefit an organism to engage in combative and risky behaviors in order to defeat same-sex rivals *even if* such behaviors hinder the organism's ability to survive. Classic examples include stags furiously interlocking antlers, lions ferociously fighting with tooth and claw, and elephant seals combating each other "sumo-style" on the beach. For some, such fights may be their only shot at reproduction and propagating their genes. These fights or displays can serve to either ward off competitors so that the winner can gain access to one or more members of the opposite sex or to show genetic potential to choosy members of the opposite sex who may preferentially pair with the strongest or most intimidating specimen. Those who play it safe may survive to a ripe old age, but they may fail to leave behind any genetic descendants. With stakes this high, it is understandable why (for many species) fights over mating opportunities often escalate into aggressive combats that can result in serious injury or death (e.g., the annual survival of a group of male northern elephant seals was less than 72% per year and likely due to combat and other male risk-taking factors—likely by-products of evolutionary mechanisms designed to push males to take risks to obtain dominance—whereas the annual survival of adult females in the same group was an average of 86% per year; Condit et al., 2014).

Typically, it is the male of the species who engages in fights of this nature. The evolutionary theory of differential parental investment gives insight into why this is the case (Trivers, 1972). Females tend to invest more highly in reproduction than do males, which is exacerbated in mammals since fertilization occurs internally. This means that the number of potential offspring that a female can produce is essentially capped by the time and energy demands of gestation. As a result, females of a given species experience relatively little variance in the total number of offspring they produce over their lifetime. Males, by contrast, are not limited by the energetic demands of reproduction and instead can increase the number of offspring they produce by gaining access to multiple mates. This creates a situation in which, for males, the winner can take all. That is, a single male can potentially monopolize the majority of mates. This leads to a higher degree of variance between males of a given species and the total number of offspring produced in their lifetime. This reproductive skew is precisely why males compete so vigorously with each other: those who cannot intimidate their rivals and gain access to females may fail to reproduce at all. Given that this pattern generally holds across the majority of animal species, intrasexual competition is more frequently discussed in terms of "male–male competition" (because male displays are typically more overt than the more subtle female displays, and, some would argue, most researchers studying intrasexual competition were male). Not surprisingly, then, research on intrasexual competition in humans tends to focus on men.

Male Intrasexual Competition

At first glance, the story of intrasexual competition appears to be the same in humans as in other animals. Men have been found to take physical and financial risks, assert their dominance, and strive for status in the face of intrasexual competition (Daly & Wilson, 1988, 2001; Ronay & von Hippel, 2010). All of these behaviors may serve to increase men's chances of attracting a sexually receptive woman (because women tend to value status, dominance, and resource provision potential in mates), although they may not always aid in their own survival. For example, Daly and Wilson (1988) revealed that men are more likely than women to engage in a variety of risk-taking behaviors, including drag racing, substance abuse, physical fighting, and homicide. Some of these behaviors may be by-products of the evolved tendency for men to risk-take to propagate their genes; but some risks (including fighting and homicide) may serve to gain access to resources, solidify dominance, increase social status, demonstrate strength, or eliminate competitors outright (Buss & Shackelford, 1997; Campbell, 1993). Similarly, a unique behavioral study by Ronay and von Hippel (2010) demonstrated that men are sometimes willing to risk life and limb in order to stand out among other men to attract a potential mate. Their study took place in a skateboard park, where the number of men tends to greatly exceed the number of women. They found that when an attractive female experimenter (a mating cue) was present, male skateboard riders attempted to perform riskier skateboard stunts compared to when a male experimenter was present (no mating signal). Even though skaters' successful performance of difficult tricks increased in front of the beautiful woman, the number of crash landings also increased. Clearly, although risks can pay off (i.e., a man could get noticed by an attractive woman), they are, as the name implies, intrinsically costly (i.e., he may be injured or killed).

As mentioned, not all risks are of the physical nature; men also take risks in order to increase their social status and to acquire resources. Women find these characteristics highly desirable in a potential mate (Buss, 1989), and, therefore, it may benefit men to take risks within these domains. Daly and Wilson (1988) revealed that men are more likely than women to consider taking a job with a high salary even though it may pose a health risk (e.g., it is in a highly populated district). Risk taking in the financial domain may be further exacerbated when men face the prospect of ending up without a mate. Research by Griskevicius and colleagues (2012) revealed that when there are relatively more men than women in a population, which thus intensifies the competition among men for access to women because some men will ultimately end up alone, men tend to become more impulsive with respect to spending (i.e., going into debt, spending money on mating-related goods). This behavior may be particularly evident during an economic crisis, where, intriguingly, some men tend to invest more in luxury goods. The implicit message is that when both the financial and mating markets get tough, it can be beneficial to purchase flashy, luxury products

indicative of status because women may find men who do so more desirable.

Big Girls Don't Cry, They Fight Back Through Female Intrasexual Competition

Theoretically, because women have a higher minimum level of investment in reproduction, and men have a higher degree of variance in reproductive success (i.e., some men have many children, whereas other men might fail to reproduce at all), it follows that men will be more likely to compete and take risks in order to mate. Earlier, we saw that men do in fact compete intensely for mates. Intriguingly, this pattern is also reflected in legends and fairy tales where the damsel in distress typically passively awaits her Prince Charming, who busily overcomes obstacles and foes in order to collect her. Despite this prevalent gendered perspective, however, it is clear from both the literature and other chapters presented in this book that women also compete intrasexually.

As mentioned, unlike the vast majority of other species, human males often invest heavily in their children, contributing to the care and protection of offspring. For this reason, mutual mate choice is the norm in humans, with a body of research demonstrating men's choosiness in long-term mate selection so that they can gain the highest-quality long-term partner (Li et al., 2002). Furthermore, men vary significantly in the benefits they can provide to a mate as well as to their offspring, both in terms of paternal investment (e.g., resources, wealth, willingness to invest in the mother and child) and genetic quality (i.e., heritable qualities such as intelligence, attractiveness). As such, women compete over access to men who have the potential to be "good dads" and those who have "good genes" (for a discussion, see Barber, 1995).

The nature of competition between women, however, tends to take on a different form than it does between men (Stockley & Campbell, 2013). Although women sometimes get into physical confrontations with each other, especially when good men and resources are scarce (Campbell, 1995, 2002), such competitive tactics are not typically the weapons of choice for women. Instead, women appear to employ an arsenal of indirectly aggressive and psychologically damaging tactics to fight their rivals, such as social exclusion, derogation, gossip, and rumor spreading (Stockley & Campbell, 2013; Vaillancourt, 2013). For example, women are frequently found to make disparaging remarks about the physical appearance (e.g., "fat," "ugly"), sexual experience (e.g., "slut," "prude"), and personalities of other women (e.g., "bitch"; see Buss & Dedden, 1990; Campbell, 1995; Fisher, 2004; James, 1998; Vaillancourt & Sharma, 2011). Presumably, the more threatening a woman is to one's relationship in terms of her being highly attractive or sexually promiscuous and thus drawing a mate's attention to her, the more likely she is to be the target of such abuse. Exemplifying this, Vaillancourt and Sharma (2011) used a behavioral study to show that women were more likely to derogate and react negatively toward an attractive woman when she was dressed in a sexy and provocative outfit relative to conservative attire. The authors theorized that revealing outfits cue women to the presence of a threat. That is, women dressed provocatively might succeed in monopolizing men's attention and, furthermore, may signal that they are seeking sex. During Vaillancourt and Sharma's (2011) study, unsuspecting female participants saw an attractive young woman (a confederate) enter the room and ask the experimenter a question. Half of the participants saw her dressed in a tidy polo shirt and jeans, whereas the other half saw her in a skimpy low-cut blouse and short skirt. The female participants were filmed in both situations and their reactions were later coded. As predicted, female participants tended to roll their eyes, gossip about, and generally derogate the attractive woman more when she was dressed in the revealing attire relative to the conservative clothing. In a related study that used photographs of the same woman dressed in either outfit, it was further revealed that women were less trusting of and less willing to befriend the confederate when she was dressed in the provocative, sexy clothing.

Striving to Be a Cut Above the Rest

In addition to indirectly aggressive behaviors, female intrasexual competition has also been linked with attempts to improve one's own appearance. Because men tend to value physical attractiveness in a mate, it can be predicted that women should not only be attuned to the physical appearance of other women (which they are; Fisher, 2004), but also that they should also actively attempt to outcompete other women within this domain. The existing literature supports this premise.

In a study conducted by Buss (1988), women self-reported dressing up in stylish clothing and using cosmetics as a way to out-compete other women. The skilled application of both cosmetics and apparel can clearly enhance the appearance of a woman's face and figure. Consistent with this, "before" and "after" magazine images of women who have undergone makeovers in which professional stylists and cosmetic artists emphasize a woman's best features while simultaneously drawing attention away from "flaws" can be quite dramatic. The beauty-boosting power of cosmetics has even been put through empirical tests. Overall, the results indicate that women are rated as more physically attractive when they wearing cosmetics as opposed to when they do not (Mulhern, Fieldman, Hussey, Lévêque, & Pineau, 2003; Osborn, 1996). Accordingly, US women are greater online consumers of clothing, accessories, and cosmetics than are men (Statista Inc., 2014). However, whereas donning attractive or tight-fitting clothing and glossing one's lips may seem harmless enough, the motivation behind such acts may drive some women to seek much more extreme physical changes.

Deceiving Mother Nature—and Other Nefarious Women

Whereas our species is quite adept at lying and generally deceiving one another, fooling Mother Nature about one's age, fertility, and genetic quality has traditionally proved more challenging—if not impossible—until the modern era. Physical characteristics that are typically deemed attractive in either sex are thought to be costly to produce and thus difficult to fake, which is why they are trusted as "honest" fitness signals that relay important mating information to the opposite sex. Hence, one would obtain a great mating advantage by displaying an attractive "honest" signal that one is not naturally blessed with. In women, characteristics that are associated with beauty, such as a low WHR; full, perky breasts; full lips; neotenous, child-like facial features; and a smooth complexion are thought to be exhibited by individuals who have at least one, if not more, of the following underlying features:

1. Genetic quality (e.g., fewer mutations present in DNA; Thornhill & Gangestad, 1996; for a review see Thornhill & Møller, 1997)

2. High levels of the appropriate sex steroids (e.g., estrogen; Gangestad & Thornhill, 1997; Jasienska et al., 2004)

3. Youthfulness, an indicator of reproductive potential (i.e., the potential number of offspring one may have in the future; Singh, 1993a; for a discussion see Barber, 1995; also Gallup & Frederick, 2010)

4. Phenotypic health, developmental stability, and fertility (Gangestad & Thornhill, 1997; Rantala, 2014; Singh, 1993a; Thornhill & Møller, 1997).

Accordingly, these "honest" characteristics of mate quality serve as a proxy for someone's general health, fertility, and genetic quality (Grammer, Fink, Møller, & Thornhill, 2003; Rhodes et al., 2003; Thornhill & Gangestad, 1996, 2006; Thornhill et al., 2003). As stated, more traditional means of manipulating one's appearance are transient and perhaps typically less efficient at hiding flaws, flaws that are with us from birth or that gradually accumulate over time as we develop and age, decrease in fertility, and get sick and fight infections. In modern times, however, cosmetic procedures allow people to effectively "trick" potential mates—and their rivals—into believing that they are more youthful and more fertile than is actually correct.

In an attempt to win the battle for mates, some women may feel compelled to engage in a variety of potentially harmful behaviors and invasive procedures to improve their appearance. For instance, Hill and Durante (2011) found that women who were exposed to attractive female images reported increased willingness to take risks to improve their appearance. Specifically, they indicated that they would be likely to tan in the sun, which is damaging to skin and increases the risk of developing skin cancer later in life, as well as to take diet pills, many of which can have adverse side effects, such as heart palpitations.

It has also been hypothesized that intrasexual competition may be at least partly responsible for women developing eating disorders such as anorexia and bulimia nervosa (Abed, 1998; Faer, Hendriks, Abed, & Figueredo, 2005; Mealey, 2000). Although studies are only just beginning to explore the exact role that intrasexual competition plays in shaping the dieting and eating behaviors of women, it seems likely that female intrasexual competition is positively related to short-sightedness with respect to health. Women may be attempting to reap short-term gains at the potential expense of long-term, often irreversible damage that is associated with eating-disordered behaviors.

Of course, not all women are the same. Just as people vary in the degree to which they are extraverted, agreeable, or enjoy casual intercourse, women will also vary in the degree to which they view other women as mating rivals. Theoretically, differences between women, such as age, mate value (refer to the chapter by Fisher & Fernández), relationship status (see the chapter by Brewer), and relative number of rivals versus potential mates in one's environment (i.e., operational sex ratio; see the chapter by Dillon, Adair, & Brase) may contribute to intrasexual competition. There are testable predictions that can be made based on the theories presented herein, as well as taking into account individual differences within women and how these affect their attitudes and behaviors toward cosmetic surgery.

Theories, Predictions, and Future Directions

Overall, female intrasexual competition, as measured by the degree to which women tend to compare themselves to other women and want to be more attractive than other women (Buunk & Fisher, 2009), may shape women's desire for cosmetic surgery, their beliefs regarding why other women opt for cosmetic surgery, their beliefs about women who have undergone it, and their perceptions about the difficulty of competing for a mate due to the availability of cosmetic surgery.

Specifically, as discussed, we predict that intrasexual competition may help drive the desire to undergo cosmetic surgery. That is, we expect future research to find that women in more competitive situations (e.g., fewer potential mates within the local mating environment) may indeed display greater desires to obtain both invasive and noninvasive cosmetic procedures. As mentioned, the physical alterations that cosmetics and clothing provide are illusory at best, yet there is evidence to suggest that women routinely use these tactics to compete with rival females (Buss, 1988). At some point, both cosmetics and clothing will be removed, leaving the woman in her natural state, and the way they can modify appearance is limited (e.g., a push-up bra cannot increase breast size to the same extent that breast augmentation could). By contrast, cosmetic procedures allow a woman to change her appearance in a more permanent and convincing matter. Thus, we theorize that the allure of cosmetic surgery will be particularly enticing for women in environments where men are few or have the ability to be choosier. Furthermore, in these environments, women in relationships may be more inclined to opt for cosmetic surgery as a mate retention strategy, especially older women attempting to compete with younger rivals.

Inherent in intrasexual competition is the belief that members of the same sex are the enemy in the mating domain. We suggest intrasexual competition will drive women to attribute competitive motivations to women who decide to undergo cosmetic surgery. Explicitly, we predict that women will be more likely to believe that other women alter their appearance via cosmetic surgery because they are trying to "out-compete" them, in addition to wanting more attention from men. Therefore, they might agree with such statements as, "I think that they are doing it to receive attention from men" and "I think that they are trying to look better than other women."

Intrasexual competition may also compel women to be overtly hostile toward women who receive cosmetic surgery, considering that derogation and gossip are two tactics that women use against their same-sex mating rivals (Schmitt & Buss, 1996) and that women who have undergone cosmetic procedures may have succeeded at improving their attractiveness to men. We predict, then, that women will be more likely than men to derogate the "after" images of women who have undergone cosmetic surgery, perhaps agreeing with statements like "she looks fake" or "she is unattractive." It would also be interesting to see whether these women agree with statements such as, "I think she is shallow/vain," or "If someone wants to get plastic surgery to boost their confidence then I think that they should." Women who undergo cosmetic surgery may also be viewed as aspiring mate poachers. Successful, attractive-looking procedural or surgical outcomes may elicit increased derogation from other women (as compared to derogation levels pre-procedure, with women potentially claiming that the recipient is "slutty" or "dishonest"; see later discussion). It may also elicit reactive appearance-enhancing responses from women attempting to mate guard.

Similarly, women may tend to believe that women who opt for cosmetic surgery are being deceptive and are essentially gaining an unfair competitive advantage in the game of love. That is, they might be likely to think, "Due to women receiving plastic surgery, it is more difficult to compete with women my own age" and, "A woman who has undergone cosmetic surgery is trying to deceive men into thinking she is naturally attractive," especially in conditions where fewer men are available in the mating market. We expect that women may also express noncompetitive motives for their own cosmetic alterations while still attributing competitive intentions to other women who undergo cosmetic procedures.

During this chapter, we have used the terms "attractive," "pretty," and "beautiful" interchangeably to indicate a woman's physical attractiveness; however, it is worth noting that these terms may in fact relate to different aspects of a woman's appeal. Although speculative, in the context of romantic attraction, "attractive" may be taken to mean every attribute of a woman that makes her appeal to others (including traits that are not immediately visually apparent, such as confidence, intelligence, or the way she conducts herself), whereas "beautiful" may mean this to a greater or lesser degree (perhaps with a greater focus on her visual appeal), and "pretty" may refer only to the aesthetically pleasing look of her face or body, or to someone who could not quite be classified as "beautiful." Because of the potential distinctions between these terms in this context, future research aimed at disentangling these notions and, in particular, which classification cosmetic surgery strives for and can achieve, may prove useful. In the current discussion, however, we use them interchangeably as a way to refer to a woman's looks and her immediately apparent physical characteristics that make her visually appealing to others.

Cosmetic Surgery and Female Risk Taking

In addition, future research might benefit from examining the relationship between intrasexual competition and women's perceptions of the risk involved in obtaining cosmetic surgery. Although typically conducted by a board-certified doctor with proper medical credentials, cosmetic surgery *is* inherently risky. In a 2-year, multisite study published in 2008, Sarwer et al. found that approximately 11% of cosmetic surgery patients reported being less than "somewhat satisfied" with their surgical outcome (p. 246; 13% in a previous study, Sarwer et al., 2005). That is, each year, some women report being dissatisfied with the outcome of their procedure and may suffer complications and, in rare, instances, die (see Turner, 2012). To add to this, the potential risks of cosmetic surgery are not limited to physical consequences. The financial cost of the surgery can be exorbitant, with certain surgical procedures costing well over US$7,000 (ASAPS, 2013). Although this expense may be affordable for individuals of the highest socioeconomic classes, as discussed previously, currently an increasing number of people from less wealthy backgrounds are seeking cosmetic surgery (ASAPS, 2012, 2013). Thus, some women may undergo surgery that is well beyond their means (including taking out hefty loans for the procedures), thus leaving them financially unstable and ill equipped to handle any unexpected expenses or even to cover their more basic needs.

In addition, not all women who undergo cosmetic surgery obtain it from a properly qualified surgeon. In order to reduce the cost of surgery, or perhaps obtain it more quickly and conveniently, women might be willing to put themselves at risk by attending "Botox parties" (in which Botox is administered at a health spa or by an uncertified individual) or to travel abroad to receive the procedure of their choice. Although this is not necessarily problematic, not all countries abide by the same standards of medical practice and safety that is typical of the wealthier nations (for an investigation into infection and deaths following cosmetic surgery tourism, see Turner, 2012). Furthermore, this type of arrangement may limit the patient's access to follow-up care, if necessary. No matter where someone lives, it is always recommended that prospective patients do their "homework" before undergoing any surgery by checking the legitimacy and credentials of the practitioner, properly assessing the risks of the surgery, and examining "before" and "after" photos of the doctor's previous patients. Therefore, it would be important for future research to examine whether female intrasexual competition is related to taking excessive medical and financial risks in order to obtain cosmetic surgery or ignoring particular safety information and considerations that would otherwise decrease the likelihood of obtaining certain procedures or using particular practitioners.

If healthy women seem to want plastic surgery more in environments where their desire or need to compete is exacerbated (e.g., more females than males, in older age, when it appears as though many other competitors are altering their appearances) *despite* recognizing the risks, it would be consistent with sexual selection theory. That is, men will often compete in an arena in which they face severe potential consequences if they lose. The logic behind this is simple: finding a mate is critical to passing on one's genes and thus it is better to take a risk that entails the possibility of obtaining a mate than to play it safe alone. When intrasexual competition is primed or elevated, women may see cosmetic surgery similarly. It may be risky, but it may also be necessary in order to outcompete rivals and attract mates. This may be tested experimentally, for example, by presenting women with mating primes and information about potential competitors and then examining whether desires to obtain risky cosmetic surgeries and ignore warnings are affected (potentially extending the findings of Hill & Durante, 2011).

Having said this, there is also evidence that risk-takers are more likely to overestimate their ability to avoid negative consequences and thus see their actions as inherently less risky (Kahneman & Lovallo, 1993). If female intrasexual competition is related to risk taking to improve one's physical appearance, it seems reasonable to hypothesize that women should *underestimate* the risks associated with cosmetic surgery, especially when female competition is primed or elevated (either naturally or ostensibly). Furthermore, certain procedures are clearly more risky than others. Receiving an injection of Botox, which is typically performed in a doctor's office, is undoubtedly safer than liposuction, which requires anesthesia, invasive surgery, and weeks of recovery. In order to disentangle their evaluation of these risks, future investigations may benefit from asking women to estimate the probability that certain negative side effects will occur during or after specific cosmetic procedures (such as breast implants, liposuction, and Botox, as well as traveling abroad to undergo surgery in an attempt to cut costs).

Also, there generally seems to be accepted "healthy" and "unhealthy" motivations for wanting cosmetic surgery (Woodstock, 2001). Healthy motivations include correcting a medical condition or injury or simply to improve one's self-esteem, whereas widely accepted unhealthy reasons include "to look sexy" or "to attract men." We suspect that intrasexual competition may drive women to hold so-called unhealthy motivations for seeking cosmetic surgery, especially when they perceive that other women they must compete with are undertaking such risks. Similarly, a small percentage of women appear to become obsessed with obtaining cosmetic procedures, with some reporting that they have undergone more than 100 procedures (and counting). Their obsessions have cost them hundreds of thousands of dollars and have also imparted social costs (e.g., falling out with family and friends). Whereas other underlying psychological issues are undoubtedly affecting such cases (e.g., body dysmorphic disorder; see Mulkens & Jansen, 2006), we also conjecture that intrasexual competition may play a role.

The Culmination of Competition and Cosmetic Surgery

Throughout this volume, it becomes clear that competition is not just for men. Women, just like men, are frequently pitted against one another in the struggle to obtain a desirable, high-quality mate. In contrast to men, however, we have argued that the most intimidating rival for a woman is not necessarily the one who is the most dominant or physically imposing; instead, it is the most beautiful. Women compete in this realm as a direct consequence of men's mate preferences. Although men are known to sometimes relax their standards for intelligence and kindness in women—particularly for a one-night stand or casual intercourse partner—they show a more consistent preference for physical attractiveness, regardless of whether they are seeking a long- or short-term mate (Li & Kenrick, 2006). More precisely, men desire women who possess the features that are indicative of youthfulness and fertility, such as a slender, hourglass figure; soft and rounded facial features with full lips and large eyes; and smooth, taut skin. In contrast, other traits, including creativity, a sense of humor, and even intelligence, tend to be considered "luxuries" by men, characteristics that are generally desired only once the minimum standard for attractiveness has been met (i.e., good looks appears to be a necessity; Li et al., 2002). Thus, we have argued that intrasexual competition should drive women to indicate a greater willingness to improve their physical appearance through medical or surgical means. That is, unlike men, who might opt to pull a knife on their competitors, we have theorized that female intrasexual competition might compel women to "go under the knife."

We have discussed, however, that intrasexual competition may cause women to feel that people who undergo cosmetic surgery are "cheating nature" and gaining an "unfair advantage" in the mating market. This may drive some people to hide the fact that they have had procedures performed. Indeed, many people do attempt to keep it secret. There are several examples of celebrities who have notoriously and vehemently denied the fact that they have received cosmetic surgery (including Michael Jackson, who—for most of his life—reportedly denied receiving all but two procedures, with his mother later stating that he was embarrassed to admit to the others; *The Sydney Morning Herald*, 2010). Concerns about appearing vain or self-obsessed are likely part of the explanation, but perhaps so too is the fear that others will know that they are "fake." Generally, undergoing cosmetic procedures will typically have a positive impact on appearance. Research indicates that the "after" photos of individuals who have received Botox, liposuction, and breast augmentations are rated as more attractive than their "before" photos, on average. Medical science has progressed significantly, improving the appearance and seamlessness of cosmetic surgical outcomes. Despite this, not all women who undergo cosmetic surgery will look natural or more attractive. Results are highly dependent on the woman's age and physical build, the type of procedure undertaken, the number of procedures that have already been conducted on the area, and the skill of the doctor, as well as the technology and materials used to perform the procedure. As such, cosmetic surgery—particularly if the end result looks unnatural—may not be directly advantageous in securing a mate. Yet, an ever-increasing number of women are choosing to have procedures performed.

It is possible, then, that women may overestimate the degree to which men find cosmetic surgery appealing. That is, men and women perceive the attractiveness of such procedures differently, particularly if the results are not natural-looking. Some evidence suggests that women misperceive the traits men actually desire in romantic partners. Specifically, women tend to believe that men have preferences for slimmer and larger-breasted figures than men report realistically liking (Cohn & Adler, 1992; Rozin & Fallon, 1988). Such a disjunct might also exist for cosmetic surgery. If this is true, then, in spite of the fact that male mate preferences may be an initial driving force for women to attempt to alter their appearance, female intrasexual competition—almost paradoxically—may lead women to strive toward an ideal standard that is less than preferable from a male perspective. Perhaps achieving extreme forms of thinness and femininity (e.g., unrealistically large breast implants) helps women to intimidate their rivals and therefore allows them to gain a mating advantage indirectly (even if men find them a little less attractive).

Conclusion

It is becoming increasingly clear that intrasexual competition has real implications for women's physical and psychological health. Today's society seems to exacerbate female-on-female competition; exposure to images of young, beautiful women is on a scale never seen by our ancestors. Furthermore, the methods available to attempt to change one's appearance are plentiful, ranging from cosmetics and clothing to extreme diets and cosmetic surgery. Whereas previous literature has found that women report that their decisions to receive cosmetic procedures were driven by desires to improve confidence, fix a physical flaw, improve their career prospects, or become more desirable to men, we have argued that a more fundamental—and perhaps less conscious—evolutionary motive may also be driving them. Specifically, we have suggested that female intrasexual competition may lead some women to alter their physical appearance through unnecessary, expensive, and ultimately risky medical procedures.

References

Abed, R. T. (1998). The sexual competition hypothesis for eating disorders. *British Journal of Medical Psychology, 71*(4), 525–547.

American Society for Aesthetic Plastic Surgery (ASAPS). (2012). 15th annual cosmetic surgery national data bank statistics: Expanded data for 2011: Multi-specialty data, multi-year comparisons, 35 cosmetic Procedures. Retrieved from http://www.surgery.org/sites/default/files/ASAPS-Stats2011.pdf

American Society for Aesthetic Plastic Surgery (ASAPS). (2013). *Cosmetic surgery national data bank statistics: Expanded data for 2012, multi-year comparisons, 36 cosmetic procedures, multi-specialty data.* Retrieved from http://www.surgery.org/sites/default/files/ASAPS-2012-Stats.pdf

Australian Human Rights Commission. (2010). *Age discrimination: Exposing the hidden barrier for mature age workers.* Retrieved from http://www.humanrights.gov.au/sites/default/files/document/publication/hiddenbarrier2010.pdf

Barber, N. (1995). The evolutionary psychology of physical attractiveness: Sexual selection and human morphology. *Ethology & Sociobiology, 16*(5), 395–424.

Becker, A. E., Burwell, R. A., Herzog, D. B., Hamburg, P., & Gilman, S. (2002). Eating behaviours and attitudes following prolonged exposure to television among ethnic Fijian adolescent girls. *British Journal of Psychiatry, 180*(6), 509–514.

Bell, D., Holliday, R., Jones, M., Probyn, E., & Taylor, J. S. (2011). Bikinis and bandages: An itinerary for cosmetic surgery tourism. *Tourist Studies, 11*(2), 139–155.

Brooks, A. (2004). "Under the knife and proud of it": An analysis of the normalization of cosmetic surgery. *Critical Sociology, 30*(2), 207–239.

Buss, D. M. (1988). The evolution of human intrasexual competition: Tactics of mate attraction. *Journal of Personality and Social Psychology, 54*(4), 616–628.

Buss, D. M. (1989). Sex differences in human mate preferences: Evolutionary hypotheses tested in 37 cultures. *Behavioral and Brain Sciences, 12*, 1–49.

Buss, D. M., & Dedden, L. A. (1990). Derogation of competitors. *Journal of Social and Personal Relationships, 7*(3), 395–422.

Buss, D. M., & Shackelford, T. K. (1997). Human aggression in evolutionary psychological perspective. *Clinical Psychology Review, 17*(6), 605–619.

Buss, D. M., & Shackelford, T. K. (2008). Attractive women want it all: Good genes, economic investment, parenting proclivities, and emotional commitment. *Evolutionary Psychology, 6*(1), 134–146.

Buunk, A. P., & Fisher, M. (2009). Individual differences in intrasexual competition. *Journal of Evolutionary Psychology, 7*, 37–48.

Campbell, A. (1993). *Men, women, and aggression.* New York: Basic Books.

Campbell, A. (1995). A few good men: Evolutionary psychology and female adolescent aggression. *Ethology and Sociobiology, 16*(2), 99–123.

Campbell, A. (2002). *A mind of her own: The evolutionary psychology of women.* Oxford: Oxford University Press.

Cohn, L. D., & Adler, N. E. (1992). Female and male perceptions of ideal body shapes: Distorted views among Caucasian college students. *Psychology of Women Quarterly, 16*, 69–79.

Condit, R., Reiter, J., Morris, P. A., Berger, R., Allen, S. G., & Le Boeuf, B. J. (2014). Lifetime survival rates and senescence in northern elephant seals. *Marine Mammal Science, 30*(1), 122–138.

Critelli, J. W., Waid, L. R., & Schneider, L. J. (1979). *Inequity in physical attractiveness as a predictor of dominance and romantic love.* Paper presented at the 1979 APA Convention, Texas State University.

Cunningham, M. R. (1986). Measuring the physical in physical attractiveness: Quasi-experiments on the sociobiology of female facial beauty. *Journal of Personality and Social Psychology: Interpersonal Relations and Group Processes, 50*(5), 925–935.

Cunningham, M. R., Roberts, A. R., Wu, C. H., Barbee, A. P., & Druen, P. B. (1995). "Their ideas of beauty are, on the whole, the same as ours": Consistency and variability in the cross-cultural perception of female physical attractiveness. *Journal of Personality and Social Psychology, 68*(2), 261–279.

Daly, M., & Wilson, M. (1988). *Homicide.* Hawthorne, NY: Aldine.

Daly, M., & Wilson, M. (2001). Risk-taking, intrasexual competition, and homicide. *Nebraska Symposium on Motivation, 47*, 1–36.

Darwin, C. R. (1871). *The descent of man and selection in relation to sex.* London, England: Murray.

Dixson, B. J., Grimshaw, G. M., Linklater, W. L., & Dixson, A. F. (2011). Eye-tracking of men's preferences for waist-to-hip ratio and breast size of women. *Archives of Sexual Behavior, 40*(1), 43–50.

Eagly, A. H., Ashmore, R. D., Makhijani, M. G., & Longo, L. C. (1991). What is beautiful is good, but . . .: A meta-analytic review of research on the physical attractiveness stereotype. *Psychological Bulletin, 110*, 109–128.

Edward, D. A., & Chapman, T. (2011). The evolution and significance of male mate choice. *Trends in Ecology and Evolution, 26*(12), 647–654.

Faer, L. M., Hendriks, A., Abed, R. T., & Figueredo, A. J. (2005). The evolutionary psychology of eating disorders: Female competition for mates or for status? *Psychology and Psychotherapy: Theory Research and Practice, 78*(3), 397–417.

Feingold, A. (1992). Gender differences in mate selection preferences: A test of the Parental Investment Model. *Psychological Bulletin, 112*(1), 125–139.

Fisher, M. L. (2004). Female intrasexual competition decreases female facial attractiveness. *Proceedings of the Royal Society B, 271*, S283–S285.

Furnham, A., & Alibhai, N. (1983). Cross-cultural differences in the perception of female body shapes. *Psychological Medicine, 13*, 829–837.

Gangestad, S. W., & Thornhill, R. (1997). Human sexual selection and developmental stability. In J. A. Simpson & D. T. Kendrick (Eds.), *Evolutionary social psychology* (pp. 169–195). Mahwah, NJ: Lawrence Erlbaum.

Garner, D. M., Garfinkel, P. E., Schwartz, D., & Thompson, M. (1980). Cultural expectations of thinness in women. *Psychological Reports, 47*(2), 483–491.

Gallup, G. G. J. (1982). Permanent breast enlargement in human females: A sociobiological analysis. *Journal of Human Evolution, 11*(7), 597–601.

Gallup, G. G. J., & Frederick, D. A. (2010). The science of sex appeal: An evolutionary perspective. *Review of General Psychology, 14*(3), 240–250.

Goodman, J. R., & Walsh-Childers, K. (2004). Sculpting the female breast: How college women negotiate the media's ideal breast image. *Journalism & Mass Communication Quarterly, 81*(3), 657–674.

Grammer, K., Fink, B., Møller, A. P., & Thornhill, R. (2003). Darwinian aesthetics: Sexual selection and the biology of beauty. *Biological Reviews, 78*(3), 385–407.

Griskevicius, V., Tybur, J. M., Ackerman, J. M., Delton, A. W., Robertson, T. E., & White, A. E. (2012). The financial consequences of too many men: Sex ratio effects on saving, borrowing, and spending. *Journal of Personality and Social Psychology, 102*(1), 69–80.

Groesz, L. M., Levine, M. P., & Murnen, S. K. (2002). The effect of experimental presentation of thin media images on body satisfaction: A meta-analytic review. *International Journal of Eating Disorders, 31*, 1–16.

Hald, G. M. (2006). Gender differences in pornography consumption among young heterosexual Danish adults. *Archives of Sexual Behavior, 35*(5), 577–585.

Hawkes, K., O'Connell, J. F., Blurton Jones, N. G., Alvarez, H., & Charnov, E. L. (1998). Grandmothering, menopause, and the evolution of human life histories. *Proceedings of the National Academy of Sciences of the United States of America, 95*(3), 1336–1339.

Hill, P., & Pickart, M. C. (2009). *Cosmetic surgery and the aesthetician.* Clifton Park, NY: Cengage Delmar Learning.

Hill, S. E., & Durante, K. M. (2011). Courtship, competition, and the pursuit of attractiveness: Mating goals facilitate health-related risk taking and strategic risk suppression in women. *Personality and Social Psychology Bulletin, 37*, 383–394.

Hodapp, P., & Luciani, J. (2012). 16 female celebs who have aged gracefully and 16 others who don't have time on their side. *Shape.* Retrieved from http://www.shape.com/celebrities/celebrity-photos/16-female-celebs-who-have-aged-gracefully/slide/all

International Society of Aesthetic Plastic Surgery. (2011). International survey on aesthetic/cosmetic procedures performed in 2010. Retrieved from http://www.isaps.org/Media/Default/global-statistics/ISAPS-Results-Procedures-2010.pdf

International Society of Aesthetic Plastic Surgery. (2014). International survey on aesthetic/cosmetic procedures performed in 2013. Retrieved from http://www.isaps.org/Media/Default/Current%20News/ISAPS%202013%20Statistic%20Release%20FINAL%20(2).pdf

Ja, W. K. (2004). The beauty complex and the cosmetic surgery industry. *Korea Journal, 44*(2), 52–82.

James, D. (1998). Gender-linked derogatory terms and their use by men and women. *American Speech, 73*, 399–420.

Jasienska, G., Ziomkiewicz, A., Ellison, P. T., Lipson, S. F., & Thune, I. (2004). Large breasts and narrow waists indicate high reproductive potential in women. *Proceedings of the Royal Society B, 271*(1545), 1213–1217.

Jokela, M. (2009). Physical attractiveness and reproductive success in humans: Evidence from the late 20th century United States. *Evolution and Human Behavior, 30*, 342–350.

Kahneman, D., & Lovallo, D. (1993). Timid choices and bold forecasts: A cognitive perspective on risk taking, *Management Science, 39*(1), 17–31.

Khan, K. S., Wojdyla, D., Say, L., Gülmezoglu, A. M., & Van Look, P. F. A. (2006). WHO analysis of causes of maternal death: A systematic review. *Lancet, 367*(9516), 1066–1074.

Langlois, J. H., Kalakanis, L., Rubenstein, A. J., Larson, A., Hallam, M., & Smoot, M. (2000). Maxims or myths of beauty? A meta-analytic and the theoretical review. *Psychological Bulletin, 126*, 390–423.

Lassek, W. D., & Gaulin, S. J. C. (2008). Waist-hip ratio and cognitive ability: Is gluteofemoral fat a privileged store of neurodevelopmental resources. *Evolution and Human Behavior, 29*, 26–34.

Lazar, C. C., & Deneuve, S. (2013). Patients' perceptions of cosmetic surgery at a time of globalization, medical consumerism, and mass media culture: A French experience. *Aesthetic Surgery Journal, 33*(6), 878–885.

Li, N. P. (2007). Mate preference necessities in long- and short-term mating: People prioritize in themselves what their mates prioritize in them. *Acta Psychologica Sinica, 39*(3), 528–535.

Li, N. P., Bailey, J. M., Kenrick, D. T., & Linsenmeier, J. A. W. (2002). The necessities and luxuries of mate preferences: Testing the tradeoffs. *Journal of Personality and Social Psychology, 82*(6), 947–955.

Li, N. P., & Kenrick, D. T. (2006). Sex similarities and differences in preferences for short-term mates: What, whether, and why. *Journal of Personality and Social Psychology, 90*(3), 468–489.

Lynn, M. (2009). Determinant and consequences of female attractiveness and sexiness: Realistic tests with restaurant waitresses. *Archives of Sexual Behavior, 38*(5), 737–745.

Mace, R. (2000). Evolutionary ecology of human life history. *Animal Behavior, 59*(1), 1–10.

Malkan, S. (2007). *Not just a pretty face: The ugly side of the beauty industry.* Gabriola Island, Canada: New Society Publishers.

Malkin, A. R., Wornian, K., & Chrisler, J. C. (1999). Women and weight: Gendered messages on magazine covers. *Sex Roles, 40*(7–8), 647–655.

Mayo Clinic. (2014). Cosmetic surgery: Risks. *Tests and Procedures.* Retrieved from http://www.mayoclinic.org/tests-procedures/cosmetic-surgery/basics/risks/prc-20022389

Mazur, A. (1986). U.S. trends in feminine beauty and overadaptation. *Journal of Sex Research, 22*(3), 281–303.

Mealey, L. (2000). Anorexia: A "losing" strategy? *Human Nature, 11*(1), 105–116.

Miller, G. (2000). *The mating mind: How sexual choice shaped the evolution of human nature.* New York: Anchor Books.

Mulhern, R., Fieldman, G., Hussey, T., Lévêque, J. -L., & Pineau, P. (2003). Do cosmetics enhance female Caucasian facial attractiveness? *International Journal of Cosmetic Science, 25*(4), 199–205.

Mulkens, S., & Jansen, A. (2006). Changing appearances: Cosmetic surgery and body dysmorphic disorder. *Netherlands Journal of Psychology, 62*(1), 34–40.

Nelson, T. D. (2005). Ageism: Prejudice against our feared future self. *Journal of Social Issues, 61*(2), 207–221.

Osborn, D. R. (1996). Beauty is as beauty does? Makeup and posture effects on physical attractiveness judgments. *Journal of Applied Social Psychology, 26*(1), 31–51.

Pujols, Y., Meston, C. M., & Seal, B. N. (2010). The association between sexual satisfaction and body image in women. *Journal of Sexual Medicine, 7*(2), 905–916.

Rantala, M. J. (2014). *Physical attractiveness as a signal of biological quality.* (Doctoral Thesis, University of Turku, Turku, Finland). Retrieved from http://www.doria.fi/bitstream/handle/10024/97057/AnnalesB388Rantala.pdf?sequence=2

Rhodes, G. (2006). The evolutionary psychology of facial beauty. *Annual Review of Psychology, 57*(1), 199–226.

Rhodes, G., Chan, J., Zebrowitz, L. A., & Simmons, L. W. (2003). Does sexual dimorphism in human faces signal health? *Proceedings of the Royal Society B, 270,* S93–S95.

Rogers, B. O. (1971). Chronologic history of cosmetic surgery. *Bulletin of the New York Academy of Medicine, 47*(3), 265.

Ronay, R., & von Hippel, W. (2010). The presence of an attractive woman elevates testosterone and physical risk taking in young men. *Social Psychological and Personality Science, 1*(1), 57–64.

Rozin, P., & Fallon, A. (1988). Body-image, attitudes to weight, and misperceptions of figure preferences of the opposite sex: A comparison of men and women in two generations. *Journal of Abnormal Psychology, 97*(3), 342–345.

Rupp, H. A., & Wallen, K. (2008). Sex differences in response to visual sexual stimuli: A review. *Archives of Sexual Behavior, 37*(2), 206–218.

Sarwer, D. B., Nordmann, J. E., & Herbert, J. D. (2000). Cosmetic breast augmentation surgery: A critical overview. *Journal of Women's Health and Gender-Based Medicine, 9,* 843–846.

Sarwer, D. B., Gibbons, L. M., Magee, L., Baker, J. L., Casas, L. A., Glat, P. M.,. . . Young, V. L. (2005). A prospective, multi-site investigation of patient satisfaction and psychosocial status following cosmetic surgery. *Aesthetic Surgery Journal, 25*(3), 263–269.

Sarwer, D. B., Infield, A. L., Baker, J. L., Casas, L. A., Glat, P. M., Gold, A. H.,. . . Young, V. L. (2008). Two-year results of a prospective, multi-site investigation of patient satisfaction and psychosocial status following cosmetic surgery. *Aesthetic Surgery Journal, 28*(3), 245–250.

Schmitt, D. P., & Buss, D. M. (1996). Strategic self-promotion and competitor derogation: Sex and context effects on the perceived effectiveness of mate attraction tactics. *Interpersonal Relations and Group Processes, 70*(6), 1185–1204.

Schmitt, D. P., & Buss, D. M. (2001). Human mate poaching: Tactics and temptations for infiltrating existing mateships. *Journal of Personality and Social Psychology, 80*(6), 894–917.

Seifert, T. (2005). Anthropomorphic characteristics of centerfold models: Trends towards slender figures over time. *International Journal of Eating Disorders, 37,* 271–274.

Singh, D. (1993a). Adaptive significance of female physical attractiveness: Role of waist-to-hip ratio. *Journal of Personality and Social Psychology, 65*(2), 293–307.

Singh, D. (1993b). Body shape and women's attractiveness: The critical role of waist-to-hip ratio. *Human Nature, 4,* 297–321.

Slevec, J., & Tiggemann, M. (2010). Attitudes toward cosmetic surgery in middle-aged women: Body image, aging anxiety, and the media. *Psychology of Women Quarterly, 34*(1), 65–74.

Snodgrass, B. (2012). Female breast reduction: When less is more. *Plastic Surgery Post.* Retrieved from American Society of Plastic Surgeons website: http://www.plasticsurgery.org/news/plastic-surgery-blog/november-2012/female-breast-reduction-when-less-is-more.html

Statista Inc. (2014). Most popular online shopping categories of internet users in the United States as of June 2014, by gender. Retrieved from http://www.statista.com/statistics/311406/us-online-shopping-categories-gender/

Stice, E. (2002). Risk and maintenance factors for eating pathology: A meta-analytic review. *Psychological Bulletin, 128*(5), 825–848.

Stice, E., Schupak-Neuberg, E., Shaw, H. E., & Stein, R. I. (1994). Relation of media exposure to eating disorder symptomatology: An examination of mediating mechanisms. *Journal of Abnormal Psychology, 103*(4), 836–840.

Stockley, P., & Campbell, A. (2013). Female competition and aggression: Interdisciplinary perspectives. *Philosophical Transactions of the Royal Society B, 368*(1631), 20130073.

Swami, V., Caprario, C., Tovée, M. J., & Furnham, A. (2006). Female physical attractiveness in Britain and Japan: A cross-cultural study. *European Journal of Personality, 20*(1), 69–81.

Swami, V., Chamorro-Premuzic, T., Bridges, S., & Furnham, A. (2009). Acceptance of cosmetic surgery: Personality and individual difference predictors. *Body Image, 6*(1), 7–13.

Swami, V., Mada, R., & Tovée, M. J. (2012). Weight discrepancy and body appreciation of Zimbabwean women in Zimbabwe and Britain. *Body Image, 9*(4), 559–562.

Swami, V., & Tovée, M. J. (2005). Female physical attractiveness in Britain and Malaysia: A cross-cultural study. *Body Image, 2*(2), 115–128.

Sypeck, M. F., Gray, J. J., & Ahrens, A. H. (2004). No longer just a pretty face: Fashion magazines' descriptions of ideal female beauty from 1959 to 1999. *International Journal of Eating Disorders, 36*(3), 342–347.

The Sydney Morning Herald (2010). Michael Jackson was addicted to plastic surgery, his mother says. Retrieved from http://www.smh.com.au/lifestyle/celebrity/michael-jackson-was-addicted-to-plastic-surgery-his-mother-says-20101110-17mg1.html

Thornhill, R., & Gangestad, S. W. (1996). The evolution of human sexuality. *Trends in Ecology and Evolution, 11*(2), 98–102.

Thornhill, R., & Gangestad, S. W. (2006). Facial sexual dimorphism, developmental stability, and susceptibility to disease in men and women. *Evolution and Human Behavior, 27*(2), 131–144.

Thornhill, R., Gangestad, S. W., Miller, R., Scheyd, G., McCollough, J. K., & Franklin, M. (2003). Major histocompatibility complex genes, symmetry, and body scent attractiveness in men and women. *Behavioral Ecology, 14*(5), 668–678.

Thornhill, R., & Møller, A. P. (1997). Developmental stability, disease and medicine. *Biological Reviews, 72,* 497–548.

Tiggemann, M., & McGill, B. (2004). The role of social comparison in the effect of magazine advertisements on women's mood and body dissatisfaction. *Journal of Social and Clinical Psychology, 23*(1), 23–44.

Trivers, R. L. (1972). Parental investment and sexual selection. In B. Campbell (Ed.), *Sexual selection and the descent of man: 1871–1971* (pp. 136–179). Chicago: Aldine.

Turner, L. (2012). News media reports of patient deaths following medical tourism for cosmetic surgery and bariatric surgery. *Developing World Bioethics, 12*(1), 21–34.

Vaillancourt, T. (2013). Do human females use indirect aggression as an intrasexual competition strategy? *Philosophical Transactions of the Royal Society B, 368*(1631), 20130080.

Vaillancourt, T., & Sharma, A. (2011). Intolerance of sexy peers: Intrasexual competition among women, *Aggressive Behavior, 37*(6), 569–577.

Wheatley, J. R., Apicella, C. A., Burriss, R. P., Cárdenas, R. A., Bailey, D. H., Welling, L. L. M., & Puts, D. A. (2014). Women's faces and voices are cues to reproductive potential in industrial and forager societies. *Evolution and Human Behavior, 35*(4), 264–271.

Wiseman, C. V., Gray, J. J., Mosimann, J. E., & Ahrens, A. H. (1992). Cultural expectations of thinness in women: An update. *International Journal of Eating Disorders, 11*(1), 85–89.

Woodstock, L. (2001). Skin deep, soul deep: Mass mediating cosmetic surgery in popular magazines, 1968–1998. *Communication Review, 4,* 421–442.

Zebrowitz, L. A., Hall, J. A., Murphy, N. A., & Rhodes, G. (2002). Looking smart and looking good: Facial cues to intelligence and their origins. *Personality and Social Psychology Bulletin, 28*(2), 238–249.

Zhang, H., You, J., Teng, F., & Chan, D. K. S. (2014). Differential roles of physical attractiveness and earning capability in explaining sense of power among dating individuals in China: A gender comparison. *Sex Roles, 70*(7–8), 343–355.

Intrasexual Competition Among Beauty Pageant Contestants

Rebecca L. Shaiber, Laura L. Johnsen, *and* Glenn Geher

Abstract

We analyze beauty pageants from an evolutionary perspective, with the goal of providing a unique insight into a novel cultural practice. Through a detailed review of adult and children beauty pageants, we propose that pageants elicit intrasexually competitive behaviors that would typically be seen within a mating context. In real-world settings, women's intrasexual competition is often focused on gaining and possessing resources, typically through mate attraction and retention. While there is no mate to "win" in pageants, there is a substantial amount of status and resources to be gained by the winner. Further, the context also highlights individual differences in such mating-relevant attributes as physical attractiveness, talent, and compassion. We propose that beauty competitions feature traits that heterosexual men find attractive in a mate (e.g., indicators of youth, fertility, long-term commitment, virginity, intelligence, and creativity). Finally, we discuss future avenues of evolutionary research in the context of beauty pageants.

Key Words: pageants, beauty competitions, intrasexual competition, evolutionary theory, competitive strategies, self-promotion, competitor derogation, competitor manipulation, fashion

Human nature evolved over a long time, and our nature is reflected in many current contexts. While beauty pageants are novel and relatively modern, the traits that allow one to compete against rivals have a long, evolved history that match those that allow one to be successful in competing for mates. Over the past several decades, evolutionary psychologists have shed light on how such strategies affect so many modern cultural practices. Based on our analysis throughout this chapter, we believe that beauty pageants as a cultural practice are the sine qua non when it comes to explicating the mating psychology of women. We take a primarily evolution-based approach in our analysis for several reasons. Firstly, we use an evolutionary framework to facilitate a relatively deep analysis that cuts across all aspects of the human experience. Equally important, research on beauty pageants that has come from sociocultural, anthropological, and feminist approaches has focused largely on proximate causes for competition among women (e.g., how media have influenced

women's perceptions of themselves) (see Banet-Weiser, 1999; Reischer & Koo, 2004; Yamamiya, Cash, Melnyk, Posavac, & Posavac, 2005). We propose that through the lens of evolutionary theory, we are able to dig deeper in our examination of the ultimate causes of behavior that are relevant in beauty competitions.

Across historical and geographical space, implicit and explicit competitions between women that focus on physical attractiveness and other mating-relevant attributes have been observed (see Geher & Kaufman, 2013). Such explicit competitions can be seen in the somewhat recent phenomenon of beauty pageants—documented as taking place now for hundreds of years (Wolf, 1991). Simply put, a beauty competition involves women competing against each other in various events for the title of "Beauty Queen." Unlike the pageants and contests of our past (Library of Congress, n.d.), present-day beauty pageants no longer focus strictly on physical attractiveness. As we review, contestants in modern-day pageants invest a significant amount of time, energy, and money into their physical appearance, but they must also show high intelligence, excellent interpersonal skills, and confidence (Miss America, n.d.). While each pageant has its own format, rules, and judging system, the three pageants that will be the focus in this chapter—Miss America, Miss USA, and Miss Universe—contain four categories for judgment in: (1) an interview session with judges, (2) a swimsuit event (sometimes known as "lifestyle and fitness"), (3) a formal-wear event, and 4) a final onstage question-and-answer segment. Miss America also includes a "talent" event, where contestants perform a short routine of their choosing while displaying a specific talent (e.g., dancing).

Though the evolutionary themes found within beauty pageants may not be readily apparent, we argue that beauty competitions elicit similar intrasexually competitive behaviors observed in a mating context, such as self-promotion, competitor manipulation, and competitor derogation. That is, we argue that the structure of the pageant, the rules of the competition and the values they evoke, and the interaction between contestants during and after the pageant are all similar to behaviors and actions that would be observed when attracting and retaining a mate. The primping and priming for the competition largely mirror the preparations a woman might take before leaving the house for a night on the town. From an evolutionary perspective, a beauty contest is a novel platform for competition to be exhibited, given that it is unlikely that our early hominid ancestors engaged in such organized activity. The first documented beauty pageants were held in the early twentieth century (Miss America Organization, 2014). By applying evolutionary concepts to this new cultural practice, we are able to observe how women's mating-relevant competitive instincts can be seen in modern behavior.

For example, we propose that the structure of pageants showcases traits that heterosexual men find attractive in long-term mates. Each category highlights physical attractiveness, intelligence, and conservative sexual values. Additionally, we argue that beauty pageants offer women better access to high-ranking potential mates. Due to the national publicity campaigns that bring pageant winners into contact with high-ranking individuals, as well as potential advancement into fame-making careers in politics, literature, modeling, music, and acting, winners are likely to have a greater chance of partnering with a high-status mate than if they did not win or participate in pageants at all.

In the search for a long-term partner, women tend to emphasize a mate's status, resources, and long-term income potential, in addition to traits that signal long-term commitment ability such as kindness and honesty (Buss & Schmitt, 1993). Resources may be more important to women than men in most mammalian species because women tend to invest more in their children between gestation and postnatal care (Trivers, 1972). The disparity in prenatal investment begins even at the level of gametes, as an ovum plays a selective role in choosing which sperm that makes it up through the vaginal canal (Levitan & Ferrell, 2006; Palumbi, 1999) will fertilize it. Women's access to additional resources provided by a mate will aid in the survival of future children. If children have more access to resources such as food, shelter, and protection, they will be more likely to survive into reproductive age. Likewise, winners of beauty pageants gain access to numerous resources (e.g., scholarship money, endorsements, and gifts) and high-status positions. While their reign as a beauty queen lasts for only one year, winners are able to make connections for future high-status and lucrative careers in entertainment, politics, literature, and finance. In other words, winning a beauty pageant solidifies a beauty queen's social standing for years to come.

The rules of beauty pageants can also be seen as a direct reflection of men's evolved preferences for virginity in a mate (see Buss, 2003). For example, both Miss America and Miss USA have stipulations that prohibit married or divorced women from participating in the pageants. Rules such as this allude to the contestants' virginity status, which contribute to the wholesome image that the pageants strive to promote. When looking for a long-term partner, men find virginity desirable in a potential mate, especially in areas that have more conservative religious values concerning female sexuality, such as Iran (Buss & Schmitt, 1993). Virginity is significant from an evolutionary perspective because it is thought to be indicative of paternity certainty. If a woman is undoubtedly a virgin, then a man who mates with her can be considerably confident that he is the biological father of her children. Men who prefer women who are chaste, particularly in long-term mating contexts, may be more reproductively successful than men who are impartial to a woman's reproductive behavior (Buss & Schmitt, 1993).

Based on these evolutionary themes (i.e., the showcasing of attractive traits for a heterosexual man's gaze, and increased access to quality mates) found within pageants and the inherent structure of beauty competitions, we postulate that women participating in pageants engage in the three intrasexual competitive strategies that are used to attract mates: (1) self-promotion (Buss, 1988), (2) competitor derogation (Buss & Dedden, 1990), and (3) competitor manipulation (Fisher & Cox, 2011). *Self-promotion* is the display of one's physical attractiveness (e.g., wearing makeup) to increase one's mate value (Buss, 1988). This tactic is utilized when trying to appear appealing to a potential mate. *Competitor derogation* exists when a woman attempts to make a rival woman less appealing in the eyes of the potential mate (Buss & Dedden, 1990). For example, a woman may use her rival's sexual history as an insult. *Competitor manipulation* includes the manipulation of one's opponents, which usually entails distorting the qualities of the prize to be had (Fisher & Cox, 2011). In this scenario, a woman may describe a potential mate as lacking in relevant qualities (e.g., unambitious) to her competition, whereby she convinces her rival that the said mate is not worth pursuing. Additionally, although a physical mate is not a part of the contestant's winnings, the "prize" of resources and status grant women more access to high-status men, who have the potential of turning into long-term mates. We propose that beauty pageants tap into various processes and qualities that are vital to long-term mate acquisition.

This chapter begins with a detailed review of the adult beauty pageant world, wherein we provide a breakdown of pageant history, structure, rules, and real-life examples. We then delve into evolutionary themes found in the pageant world that are relevant to intrasexual competition in a mating context. We also provide a similarly detailed account of child beauty pageants, along with relevant evolutionary themes found in these pageants. Lastly, we focus on future directions in the application of evolutionary theory and intrasexual competition research in the realm of beauty competitions.

A History and the Structure of Adult Beauty Pageants

The two national adult pageants that will primarily be focused on in this chapter are Miss America and Miss USA, although we will also discuss local town and city pageants. We will also discuss Miss Universe, which is the international division for Miss USA. Miss America and Miss USA are two of the most widely recognized and long-established

beauty pageants, and have been the focus of much of the research in this area. The Miss America Pageant began in 1921 in Atlantic City, New Jersey, as a "popularity contest" in which contestants submitted their photographs to the competition (Miss America Organization, 2014). Five finalists were selected to attend the Second Annual Atlantic City Pageant, and upon their arrival the contestants were entered into the Inner-City Beauty Pageant. Contestants wore casual attire and were scored by both the judges and the public. Margaret Gorman, from Washington, D.C., was selected as the winner of "Inner-City Beauty, amateur" (Riverol, 1992). At the end of her reign as "Inner-City Beauty," she was expected to defend the title at the next pageant. However, another woman had been selected for the title of "Miss Washington D.C." The pageant officials decided that Gorman's official title would then be "Miss America," and thus an American tradition for nearly one hundred years was born (Miss America Organization, 2014).

Much has changed since the initial pageant. There are now formal rules for competing, formal categories for each event (such as the formal-wear component, lifestyle and fitness category, or talent category), no public voting, requirements of official duties that the winner must attend to, and a large grand prize that includes scholarship money (Miss America Organization, 2014). In 2014, Miss America reported providing $306,000 worth of scholarships to the women participating in the actual pageant (Miss America, 2014). The winner receives $50,000 of scholarship money plus endorsement deals, travel funds, and other gifts. To be eligible for the Miss America competition, participants must be 17 to 24 years old, must be US citizens, and must "meet residency requirements for competing in a certain town or state, meet character criteria as set forth by the Miss America Organization, be in reasonably good health to meet the job requirements, and be able to meet the time commitment and job responsibilities as set forth by the local program in which [they] compete" (Miss America Organization, 2014).

Currently, the Miss America pageant is conducted in two parts: the preliminary competition and the finals competition. During the preliminary competition, all contestants participate in each event. Out of the 52 (or 53) competitors (one participant from each state; one from Washington, D.C.; one from Puerto Rico; and, in 2015, one competitor from the Virgin Islands), 16 are selected to move on to the finals competition.

The following weightings of the various criteria for the preliminary competition versus the finals competition are taken directly from the Miss America website. The preliminary competition includes lifestyle and fitness in swimsuit evaluation (15%), evening wear (20%), talent (35%), private interview (25%), and onstage question-answering (5%). The finals competition includes, for the top 16 contestants, a composite score (25%) and lifestyle and fitness in swimsuit evaluation (10%); for the top 10 constants, a score for evening wear (15%); and for the top 8 contestants, a score for talent (30%), and onstage question-answering (20%) (Miss America Organization, 2016). There is also a final ballot, where each judge ranks the top 5 contestants in the order he/she believes they should each finish. The outcome of the pageant is based solely on the point totals resulting from the final ballot (Miss America Organization, 2014).

To be qualified for participation in the national and international pageants, participants must first participate in local- and state-level pageants (e.g., the winner of Miss Texas [and Miss New York, Miss California, etc.] automatically qualifies to compete for Miss America). There is no international-level competition associated with Miss America, unlike Miss USA who goes on to compete in Miss Universe.

Miss USA was founded and sponsored by Catalina Swimsuits as an advertising campaign (Miss America Organization, 2016) in 1952 (Miss Universe, n.d.) after a long history of working with Miss America (Catalina, 2015). Since then, it has grown into a larger competition that is on par with the scale of Miss America. It is also part of a larger pageant system, Miss Universe, in which over 85 countries participate (Miss Universe, 2016). Contestants are required to be between the ages of 18 to 27, have won their respective state titles, and have no record of marriage or pregnancy before or during their reign. Fifty-one women (one for each state and Puerto Rico) compete in three categories: swimsuit, evening wear, and a live interview. Miss USA has similar monetary prizes to Miss America, but winners of this competition also receive a year's worth of salary and living expenses in a luxury New York City apartment, thousands of dollars' worth of clothing and makeup, a wardrobe stylist, a scholarship to the New York Film Academy, skincare and hair treatments, a modeling portfolio, and the opportunity to be a representative for philanthropic work (Rosenfeld, 2014).

Although all participants participate in the opening ceremony, only 15 competitors are selected to move on to the swimsuit portion, 10 for evening wear, and five for the live interview. The Miss USA pageant recently added public voting to the scoring, labeled as "You be the Judge" (Miss USA, 2016). Audience participants rate the contestant on a scale of one through ten in each of the three categories (swimsuit, evening, and final question-and-answer segment). These scores account for a portion of their overall score. The winner of Miss USA moves on to compete in the Miss Universe Pageant.

Evolutionary Themes in Pageant Segments

As previously discussed, there are four categories that are found in most pageants: an interview with the judges, a swimsuit event, a formal-wear event, and a final onstage question-and-answer segment. Miss America also has a talent category. The categories are intended to display the well-roundedness of the winner; she is personable, intelligent, talented, and beautiful. The private interview with the judges is designed to allow them to learn more intimate details about each contestant. Contestants can be asked about past behaviors; their experiences, credentials, and opinions; and other personal details (Miss America Organization, 2011). The judges are looking to see a woman who "is a leader to all she serves, she is beautiful, well-spoken, talented, able to relate to young people, charismatic, reflective of women her age, and mature enough to handle the job and all of its responsibilities" (Miss America Organization, 2011, p. 28).

Markers of intelligence are implicitly included in beauty pageant criteria and may be understood from an evolutionary perspective. For instance, intelligence is a key quality that is sought in mates and in social partners more generally (see Geher & Kaufman, 2013; Geher, Garcia, Kaufman, Kaufman, & Dawson, 2016). The personal interview and onstage question segments are both used to assess qualities associated with intelligence such as communication, confidence, education, and how to handle pressure (Miss America Organization, 2007). Additionally, poise and attractiveness are relevant for these portions of the competition (Miss America Organization, 2007). On this point, note that intelligence has been found to be positively linked with physical attractiveness—thus suggesting that both intelligence and attractiveness may provide markers of a more general fitness factor (corresponding to the idea of "genetic fitness," or having positive heritable features). Evidence of a relationship between intelligence and attractiveness comes from Fink, Neave, Manning, and Grammer (2006), who found that people with highly symmetrical faces (i.e., faces that are typically rated as more attractive when they are symmetrical, meaning the left side aligns perfectly with the right side) were perceived by others to be sociable and intelligent compared to people with relatively asymmetrical faces (i.e., relatively less attractive).

The onstage question-and-answer session, which is the last category, truly tests the contestants' ability to formulate intelligent and logical answers to questions concerning current events. Many questions have a political focus, which means that the contestant must have knowledge of current events, at both global and national levels. While the questions in these pageants are designed to test the contestants' general intelligence and world knowledge, they also seem to capture the participants' political stances. However, they do not ask about contestants' personal politics (e.g., whom they voted for, what party they belong to). The answers to these questions often determine views on the contestants' success and intelligence. If the contestant does not give a logical and coherent answer, she will likely not win the overall competition. For example, Caitlin Upton, Miss South Carolina, from the 2007 Miss Teen USA pageant, gave a famously disastrous answer to a question asking why one-fifth of Americans cannot locate the United States on a map. Her answer was unintelligible, and while she placed in the top four, she did not go on to win the competition.

The questions may also serve as an indirect way to learn a contestant's sexual values, with the expectation that contestants are conservative and oriented toward long-term marriage. Contestants such as Vanessa Williams (discussed later) have had to return the crown after nude or suggestive photographs were uncovered, as this type of behavior goes against the conservative image of the pageant. If the answer hints at conservative political values, judges and viewers may think that the contestant is less likely to engage in promiscuous sexual behavior and may subsequently view her more favorably.

Beauty pageant criteria include behavioral markers beyond those that track intelligence. Such pageants also highlight the contestants' social grace and agreeableness. Interestingly, just as past research has shown that relatively attractive women are seen as relatively intelligent, physical attractiveness also has been linked with perceptions of positive personality attributes. Individuals with symmetrical faces are also rated as being more agreeable when compared to people with more asymmetrical faces (Noor & Evans, 2003). According to Miller (2000), agreeableness "always tops the charts" (p. 330) when people are asked to rate features of the personality of a potential mate. It can therefore be surmised that contestants in beauty pageants who appear to be agreeable, sociable, and intelligent will score higher than their counterparts.

When examining the costs associated with beauty pageants, we can easily see where competition among contestants comes into play. Pageant gowns, pageant trainers (i.e., someone who prepares the contestant for each segment of the pageant), physical trainers, competition fees, and other expenses can be quite overwhelming. To alleviate the cost to compete, contestants are encouraged to seek out sponsors. Their ability to charm and persuade vendors to donate to their cause likely contributes to their success during the overall competition. Contestants who have favorable personality traits would likely elicit more sponsorship than less favorable contestants, and therefore they can invest more money in their pageant training. Similarly, communication and charm are important in a mating context. Women's verbal proficiency (lexicon, fluency, and grammar) (Lange, Zaretsky, Schwarz, & Euler, 2014) and higher vocal pitch (Collins & Missing, 2003; Karthikeyan & Locke, 2015) are related to perceived attractiveness. We argue that contestants possessing higher vocal pitch in combination with eloquent speech may solicit more sponsors when compared to their lower-pitched, less vocally proficient peers.

In addition to conveying interpersonal skills both in the pageant (with judges and other contestants) and outside the pageant (with potential sponsors and the public at large), potential pageant winners must also display their creativity. Their creativity is showcased during a performance for the talent event. Creativity is considered to be a rather good indicator for intelligence, as the two factors have been found to be positively intercorrelated (Miller, 2000). Pageant contestants must display some kind of performable talent such as singing, dancing, or playing an instrument. The performance itself is left open to the contestants, though it is implied that it must be tasteful and "family-friendly." The talent portion is really where mastery of a skill (i.e., one's creativity) can shine through during the competition. The talent portion has such varied acts, and it is important that the contestants display their creative skills as being unique from the other contestants. For the 2014 Miss America pageant, the winner, Nina Davuluri, Miss New York, performed an electrifying Bollywood routine that was not only technically challenging but visually interesting as well. Another highly rated performance in that competition was by Myrrhanda Jones, Miss Florida, who performed a baton-twirling routine after injuring her knee—which demonstrated creativity, body coordination, and technical skill. Further, Jones received praise for performing well despite the injury she sustained during a preliminary rehearsal.

The swimsuit category is the only category where the focus is primarily on physical appearance. While physical appearance may be a secondary contributing factor to how a dress looks during the evening-wear portion of the competition, personality, poise, and confidence are important traits that are also incorporated into the judging for that portion. During the swimwear portion, contestants walk the runway in either a bikini or a one-piece bathing suit, pose in front of the judges for a few seconds, and then walk to the side of the stage. According to Buss (2003), physical attractiveness is one of the most relevant traits heterosexual men take into consideration when searching for a mate. As such, competition between women across various contexts has often focused on physical attributes. In fact, the term *beauty* itself, which is embedded in the phrase *beauty pageant*, typically corresponds to physical features such as a beautiful face or a beautiful figure (see Perilloux, Cloud, & Buss, 2013). Evolution-based research into attractiveness has shed much light on the features that are considered relatively beautiful, often demonstrating that markers of beauty (such as an hourglass-like waist-to-hip ratio) are often also markers of fertility (see Singh, 1993). As youth tends to track fertility in women (i.e., older women experience menopause), it makes sense, then, as to why beauty pageants have such strict age-related requirements.

Evolutionarily Relevant and Culturally Normative Physical Attractiveness

Body Mass Index (BMI) is an important indicator of body attractiveness. According to Tovée and colleagues (1999), a woman's BMI is the "primary determinant of the attractiveness of female bodies" (Tovée, Maisey, Emery, & Cornelissen, 1999, p. 216). It is no secret that all beauty pageant contestants spend a large portion of their pageant preparation exercising and dieting. In 2011, Bree Boyce

lost over one hundred pounds over three years and won Miss South Carolina. She then went on to compete in Miss America. During pageant season, Boyce reported exercising between two and three hours each day to become competition-ready (Leifer, 2011). Boyce's conscientious fitness regimen is an example of the intrasexual competitive tactic of self-promotion. She was exercising and dieting more to become more attractive relative to other women. When a woman uses self-promotion as an intrasexually competitive tactic, she is focusing on self-improvement *and* being superior relative to her peers. Attractive female bodies and faces tend to prime female competitive drives (see Fisher & Cox, 2009). In light of this feature of female mating psychology, the beauty pageant environment (wherein all contestants are surrounded by many physically attractive women) likely serves as an intensive platform for fostering competition among women.

Ideally attractive features of women's bodies have changed over time (see Singh, 1993). For instance, according to Singh (1993) and Mazur (1986), the ideal weight has decreased for Miss America contestants since the 1920s. Also, since the late 1960s, the ratio of bust-to-hip measurements has remained the same, but because the average height of contestants has increased and their weight has decreased, the women of the Miss America pageants still have an hourglass figure. However, according to more recent findings by Fisher and Voracek (2006), mainstream media examples of ideal female attractiveness, such as Miss America, *Vogue* models, and *Playboy* centerfolds, have shown a decrease in BMI measurements and have less of an hourglass figure over time.

Broadly speaking, the ideal body type for winning Miss America can be seen as a strong marker of physical standards for all American women. Miss America is supposed to be the representative of the perfect "All-American girl," and hence, she is a role model for physical beauty. Although the contestants are competing against each other for possessing the best body, women across America may potentially compare themselves to the contestants as well. There is evidence that suggests that women use Miss America, and other beauty pageant–style reality shows, to inform their own beauty habits (see Mazur, 1986). In the 1960s, when a slimmer shape became vogue, Miss America contestants also adopted the look. There was an increase in research concerning anorexia, as women began attempting to morph their shape into something unhealthy (Mazur, 1986). In *Miss America*, the PBS documentary, Margaret Cho, feminist commentator and comedian, explains what it is like to view the bodies of the contestants:

"When you see their bodies, it's so interesting because they seem so not real.

You don't see anything off. . ... There's no creases or lines, there's no stretch marks or nipples or hair. It's kind of jarring. You think god whose body is like that? And then you think, oh, maybe I'm not the woman. Maybe they're the women, and I'm not the woman. And then you kind of feel like an imposter too."
(Ferrari, 2002)

Here, it is exemplified that the intrasexual competition that exists between contestants (e.g., the competition for the best body) extends itself to the female viewers. Via these highly publicized pageants, women may see the idolized "American Beauty" and think that they have to look like the contestants to be beautiful and thus desirable by potential mates. Women watching Miss America in the context of broader media (which reflects the same trends Miss America contributes to) may be influenced to conform to these mainstream trends. Fashion advertisements and television have been shown to negatively influence women's perception of their bodies (Mask & Blanchard, 2011; Want, 2009; Yamamiya et al., 2005), suggesting that the constant inundation of a nearly unattainable body type in various media formats can contribute to bodily dissatisfaction among women.

We argue that Miss America reflects mainstream beauty trends such as thinness and symmetry. Cosmetic use, hairstyle, and dress style tend to reflect mainstream fashion trends (although the gowns veer toward gaudy and outlandish compared to designer gowns in other high-fashion media platforms). There has never been a winner of Miss America, Miss USA, or Miss Universe that could be categorized as "plus size" (i.e., typically a dress size 10 and up), nor has there been a beauty queen from these competitions that has an obvious asymmetrical facial disfigurement (such as from disease or injury). As time goes on and mainstream media (e.g., fashion, television, music, and film) become more diverse, these trends may change.

Currently, Miss America and Miss USA do not physically represent the average American woman. The organizations have often been criticized for their lack of diverse body representation, which more accurately reflects the average body type in the United States (Vagianos, 2015). The average dress size of an American woman is between 16 and 18 (Christel & Dunn, 2016), while the average size of Miss America is approximately 2 to 4 (PBS Online, 1999–2002; Women's Size Guide, 2016). The Miss America winner is supposed to be "the type which the American Girl might well emulate" (Hickman, as quoted by Miss America Pageant, n. d.). According to the Miss America Organization, "the American public has an expectation that she will be beautiful and physically fit. This is the same expectation they have for all of their celebrities, from music and film to sports, and Miss America is no exception. You must look at her physical beauty as well as her physical fitness" (Miss America Organization, 2012).

Beauty Pageants and the Evolution of Competition among Women

As explicated throughout this chapter, the facets of competition found in beauty pageants mirror the evolved nature of competition among women in general—particularly in long-term mating contexts. In a straightforward sense, these competitions lead to direct and tangible resources. As mentioned previously, the crowned Miss America and Miss USA receive fame and high status that could potentially lead to other career opportunities after their reigns are complete. For example, the 2014 Miss America winner, Nina Davuluri, has become a public speaker and advocate for diversity, civil rights, and the STEM fields (Davuluri, n.d.). Gretchen Carlson, the 1989 Miss America, is a FOX News Channel anchor on the show *Fox and Friends*. Rachel Smith, Miss USA 2007, is *Good Morning America*'s entertainment news correspondent and also hosts the entertainment fashion show *On the Red Carpet*. Such outcomes clearly lead to fiscal and social benefits.

Based on an evolutionary analysis of female mating psychology, competition among women is largely driven by two goals: to attain a mate and to attain status (Buunk & Fisher, 2009). The actual act of competition occurs when the necessary resources to reach these goals, such as a good mate or opportunity to gain status, are in limited supply (Cox & Fisher, 2008). Women strongly desire high-quality mates who have the capacity to offer resources for them and their offspring. Women also desire features in males that are indicative of robust genetic features that can be passed down to offspring (see Geher, 2014; Trivers, 1972). With respect to mates, women engage in intrasexually competitive behavior for various reasons: to attract a mate, to attain a mate, and to retain a mate (Campbell, 1999; Darwin, 1871).

Women are more likely to express their aggression indirectly (e.g., the silent treatment: not speaking to someone as a way to punish that person for perceived poor behavior) rather than directly (e.g., physically) (Cashdan, 1998; Griskevicius et al., 2009). *Indirect aggression* (Crick & Grotpeter, 1995), *relational aggression* (Archer & Coyne, 2005), and *social aggression* (Cairns, Cairns, Neckerman, Ferguson, & Gariépy 1989), are the preferred methods of aggression for women (Björkqvist, 1994). *Indirect aggression* refers to using "social manipulation, attacking the target in circuitous ways" (Österman et al., 1998, p. 1) and can include self-promotion. An example of indirect aggression would be spreading negative rumors about an individual. The attacker is not directly confronting her target, but using social communication to continue harassment. Relatedly, *relational aggression* and *social aggression* refer to styles of aggression that target the victim's relationships and friendships (Archer & Coyne, 2005). *Relational aggression* is usually stealthy but does have some more prominent behaviors. *Social aggression* also attempts to disrupt the victim's relationships; however, the ultimate end goal of the attacker is to harm the victim's social standing and social acceptance by a group (Archer & Coyne, 2005). *Social aggression* has both outward and concealed behaviors, but also includes behaviors such as dirty looks (short-lived facial expressions of anger or disgust that are intended to make the victim uncomfortable or upset while also emphasizing social undesirability), which can occur in both overt and covert contexts (Archer & Coyne, 2005).

Research has suggested that the display of indirect aggression (e.g., rumor spreading) is less *costly* to a woman than the display of direct aggression (e.g., punching) (Björkqvist, 1994). Indirect aggression allows the aggressor to both remain anonymous *and* hide her deleterious intentions while causing harm to her intended target. Indirect aggression also reduces the likelihood of the aggressor suffering from physical retaliation. If the victim of the aggression cannot identify her attacker, it is unlikely that the victim would be able to physically challenge that person. Physical aggression may also be avoided even if the attacker is known, as women physically or overtly fighting with each other may be viewed as less attractive to a potential mate (Campbell, 1999). We argue that *indirect, relational,* and *social aggressions* are the backbone for how women exhibit intrasexual competition in beauty pageants, and that the

behaviors that we document in the following discussion are direct reflections of these less overt displays of aggression.

Self-Promotion, Competitor Derogation, and Competitor Manipulation

Pageant contestants are forced to spend time with one another before, during, and after the competitive event segments. For example, during the Miss USA and Miss Universe pageants, the women share a hotel room with at least one other contestant. They attend meals, pageant rehearsals, and recreational activities together (Parker, 2000). Contestants have reported that they have formed lifelong friendships with other contestants (Zhang, 2013). While many contestants do form friendships with one another, there are also instances where relationships with other contestants can be used to a contestant's advantage. Information about one's opponents in a competitive situation may prove to be useful in the fight to win (Cox & Fisher, 2008). The phrase "keep your friends close, but your enemies *closer*" captures this sentiment. These women likely bond with each other because they are in close quarters and participating in group activities for several hours every day for the course of a week. However, as part of this bonding, they may exchange details about past indiscretions, current or past relationships, or other issues that may appear benign in a real-life context, but may subtly indicate that the contestant does not fit with the ideal "all-American" pageant responsibilities. This information may be then used for the purposes of intrasexual competition.

Self-Promotion

In mating-relevant contexts, people engage in various competitive strategies. One of these strategies is *self-promotion* (Buss, 1988), which can be defined as flaunting one's best assets (e.g., physical appearance, personality) when compared to members of the same sex. This strategy is one of the most commonly researched in the mating literature (Fisher & Cox, 2011), and is at the heart of beauty pageant competitions. One who engages in self-promotion does so to improve one's capability of competing, relative to potential rivals. This strategy is an obvious approach to take advantage of when competing in a beauty pageant. It could even be suggested that the strategy of self-promotion is the basic tenet of beauty competitions. While contestants are not judged in direct comparison to each other (pre–live competition scores are compared to the live competition scores, wherein "pre-live" refers to the portion of the competition that occurs prior to being televised, or the live competition), it is likely that they influence each other's scores to some degree. If contestant A scores highly in a specific segment and wows the judges, contestant B may feel like she has to overshadow contestant A's success in order to have a chance to win.

Self-promotion subthemes (i.e., *appearance, body and athleticism, personality advertisement, autonomy*, and *direct contact*) (Fisher & Cox, 2011) are highly relevant in the beauty pageant world. Beauty pageant competition is indicative of dressing in an attractive and sexy way (*appearance*); showing off one's body (*body and athleticism*); displaying a pleasant, funny, smart, and outgoing personality, while being social and acting innocent (*personality advertisement*); being surrounded with other women to cause jealousy in a potential mate (*autonomy*); flirting and smiling excessively (*direct contact*); and of course showing one's best qualities and talents, being the best, and displaying virginal qualities (*other self-promotion categories*) (see Fisher & Cox, 2011). Pageant contestants spend a substantial amount of time (and money) training and prepping in all of the aforementioned categories with the sole purpose of outperforming their competitors. Fisher and Cox (2011) suggest that self-promotion may be one of the most widely used intrasexually competitive tactics due to social desirability. Even though beauty pageant contestants are there to compete, it reflects more positively on a contestant to claim she is working on improving herself rather than outright competing with others when she's striving to outshine her peers. Beauty pageants are the epitome of self-promotion tactics at work.

Competitor Derogation and Pageant Scandals

A second mating-relevant competitive strategy is known as *competitor derogation* (Buss & Dedden, 1990). This approach is characterized by any behavior that will decrease an opponent's worth when compared to oneself. Women are most likely to target rivals' sexual behavior, fidelity, and physical attractiveness when engaging in competitor derogation. In the pageant world, it would not make as much sense to target a contestant's physical attractiveness, as it is clear that all of the competitors would rate highly in terms of attractiveness. However, rumors concerning sexual behavior and fidelity are harder to defend against because that behavior is not physically apparent (i.e., one cannot

guess someone's sexual history just by looking at her). If a rival was intending to do more damage to a contestant's reputation, she may communicate to other contestants or the press that the contestant engages in sexual behavior that deviates from the virginal image that the pageants present. A successful derogation strategy may include attacking behaviors that cannot be easily proven false, such as promiscuity.

Most, if not all, scandals that have led to pageant queens' downfalls and tarnished reputations are sexual in nature. It seems that each year, after each pageant, one of the finalists suffers publicly from leaked photographs, videos, and stories. Several prominent examples include Miss USA 2006, Tara Conner; Miss America 1983, Vanessa Williams; Miss Teen USA 2006, Katie Blair; Miss Nevada USA 2007, Katie Rees; and Miss USA 2010, Rima Fakih. It would be extremely interesting to discover how the person leaking the information is related to the winner, but sadly, this information is rarely disclosed. We predict that the information is leaked by other contestants (or their publicists, handlers, or supporters), or other rivals in the contestant's life (e.g., former friends), who would benefit from the fall of the title winner.

Deviations from the conservative image of the pageant expose the contestant to potential derogation from other competitors and their peers. "When you win a pageant, you automatically become a role model for many women and children. This is perhaps the most important aspect of your reign. . . . Remember, someone is always watching your actions, no matter where you are or what you are doing" (Parker, 2000, p. 69). Parker warns against being photographed smoking, drinking, or using drugs, as well as being caught gossiping or cursing. She specifically discusses not having a photograph with any drink, even nonalcoholic ones, because "even if it's water . . . someone will always assume it's liquor" (Parker, 2000, p. 69). Parker's advice is well-rooted; many pageant contestants in competitions, large and small, become caught up in scandals. These women have violated their contract of being a wholesome (almost virginal) representative of the pageant, and hence, their punishment can be drastic, including loss of the title and crown. Table 32.1 lists pageant scandals that made headlines over the past decade. In 10 years, we were able to find 16 noteworthy scandals based on contestant behavior. Nine out of 16 infractions resulted in the loss of the title, and all contestants involved suffered a negative backlash

Table 32.1. Beauty Pageant Scandals from 2006–2015*.

Year	Pageant	Participant	Infraction	Title	Title Retention (yes or no)
2006	Miss USA	Tara Conner, SC	Documented pictures and reports of partying	Miss USA	Yes
	Miss Teen USA	Kate Blair, MT	Documented pictures and reports of partying	Miss Teen USA	Yes
	Miss Great Britain	Danielle Lloyd	Posing for *Playboy* and dating a judge	Miss Great Britain	No
2007	Miss USA	Ashley Harder, NJ	Pregnancy	Miss NJ USA	No
	Miss America	Elyse Umemoto, WA	Documented pictures and reports of partying	Miss WA America	Yes
	Miss America	Amy Polumbo, NJ	Compromising photographs	Miss NJ America	Yes
2008	Miss USA	Kate Rees, NV	Compromising photographs	Miss NV USA	No
	Miss Teen USA	Lindsey Evans, LA	Leaving restaurant without paying, marijuana use	Miss Teen LA	No
	Miss Universe	Dayana Mendoza, Venezuela	Compromising photographs	Miss Universe	Yes
	Miss Universe	Valerie Begue, France	Compromising photographs	Miss France	No
2009	Miss USA	Carrie Prejean, CA	Derogatory comments about gay marriage	Miss CA USA	No
2010	Miss USA	Rima Fakih, MI	Compromising photographs	Miss MI USA	Yes
2011	Miss San Antonio	Dominique Ramirez	Gaining weight, missing events, attending events with boyfriend	Miss San Antonio	No
2013	Miss Teen USA	Melissa King, DE	Starring in adult film	Miss DE USA	No
2015	Miss Puerto Rico	Destiny Velez, PR	Derogatory comments against Muslims	Miss PR	Suspended indefinitely
	Miss Universe	Emily Kahote, Zimbabwe	Compromising photographs	Miss Zimbabwe	No

* The data collected for this chapter sourced several "listicle" articles that reported the top 10–23 scandals that have occurred throughout pageant history. Only events that were attributed to the misbehavior of the contestant were included in the table. The years 2012 and 2014 did not have scandals relevant to the analysis.

in the media. Even if the title is not lost, contestants must still suffer the consequences of public opinion.

One highly publicized example of these types of scandals is the story of Tara Conner, the 2006 Miss USA title winner. Conner almost had her title taken away when she tested positive for cocaine and was seen drinking in incriminating photographs with fellow contestants and past winners. Many criticized Donald Trump's (the owner of the Miss USA franchise) decision to give Conner a second chance instead of stripping her of the title (Time, 2009).

In 1983, Vanessa Williams was crowned the 1984 Miss America. Her win was groundbreaking, as she was the first African American woman to win the pageant. Unfortunately, her win was short-lived, as nude photographs taken before she had even entered pageants were sent to *Penthouse* magazine (Hampson, 1984). Williams ultimately had to give up her title to Suzette Charles, the runner-up. Though there is no evidence to suggest that Charles was involved in outing Williams, she greatly benefited from the negative reaction to Willam's nude photographs. All of the commercial opportunities that Williams received went to Charles, and despite Williams's successful acting career after winning the crown, the loss of her Miss America title is still remembered as one of the most infamous situations to befall the pageant. Runners-up gain a great deal from winners' downfalls, as they are the ones to then benefit financially and in terms of increased status.

Competitor Derogation at the Local Level

Contestants are under a microscope when they are competing, and consequently, we predict that they are less likely to openly or publicly derogate other contestants during the competition. However, the anonymity of online posting or leaks to media outlets creates an opportunity for contestants to derogate other contestants (including the winner) without serious consequences such as retaliation from those derogated against, or their families, friends, or pageant officials. If the contestant were to reveal herself as a bully, it would directly conflict with the pageants' emphasis on the importance of positive role models. Subsequently, any attacks on fellow contestants' characters need to be indirect and untraceable. Regional pageants often hold considerable prestige for the regions (Greenwood, 2010). Although the contestants do not receive many financial benefits from winning the pageant, they gain social status within their community (Greenwood, 2010). Contestants participating in

these pageants are familiar with the VoyForums, a website with various forums, some of which are dedicated to discussing events at various local pageants. Those who win the pageants experience an intense amount of cyberbullying at the hands of other contestants, other contestants' family and friends, and other pageant attendees. These online forums are also easy ways for rumors to start and spread about contestants (Greenwood, 2010).

While the scope of the local town pageants may be smaller than the national ones, the contestants feel similar pressure to maintain a positive image once they have won. For instance, the 2008 winner of the Frog Queen beauty pageant in Rayne, Louisiana, Chelsea Richard, was arrested for driving under the influence of alcohol during her reign (Greenwood, 2010). Her arrest was problematic for several reasons. One of the main issues was that she was underage for legal alcohol consumption, as she was 20 years old when arrested. Also, the pageant board had no real authority to strip her crown as her contract did not specifically indicate an arrest as a suitable reason for the loss of the title. Despite the loophole in the contract, the VoyForums were ablaze with slanderous attacks about Richard's moral character and indicated that the runner-up should take the title of Frog Queen. In the end, Richard held on to her crown, but her actions influenced her ability to win a larger title crown where all of the local pageant winners compete. Her arrest also forced the Frog Queen pageant and other local pageants to change their contracts. Moreover, Richard had to handle attacks on her character online and in person (Greenwood, 2010).

Competitor Manipulation

Beauty pageant contestants likely also employ the strategy of *competitor manipulation*, which is the manipulation of one's rivals (Fisher & Cox, 2011). This third competitive strategy often involves using persuasion to change the value of the prize or goal in the eyes of the opponent. Contestants are judged through a subjective lens (the scores of judges), rather than the usual objective approach used in many competitions (e.g., points earned in a tennis match). Therefore, it may be useful for a contestant to become friendly with the other contestants to observe and examine their qualities in a closer context, and then use this information to form manipulations that may, ultimately, cause the contestant to decrease her performance. From the perspective of a beauty pageant contestant who is employing competitor manipulation, there is presumably no better way to get to know her competition than befriending the other contestants. We predict that the results of employing competitor manipulation as a strategy would likely mimic the results of using competitor derogation. Like the derogator, the manipulator can push the target out of the competition and win the prize for herself. In-depth, qualitative research on the beauty pageant world, which takes the evolution-based approach suggested here, could systematically address the extent to which such strategies do indeed come into play in the beauty pageant environment.

Moreover, there is a fourth strategy, *mate manipulation*, that has been discussed within the intrasexual competition research on mating. Mate manipulation involves taking action to remove or diminish the presence of one's competition, or the removal of oneself from the competition (e.g., displacing a rival, or withdrawing from a beauty competition) (Fisher & Cox, 2011). Within the context of the present chapter, we propose that mate manipulation may take the form of leaking scandalous information on a fellow contestant if one believes this contestant is an imminent threat to one's success in the competition. Another potential avenue could involve manipulating judges' attention away from other competitors to increase one's own likelihood of winning. We do not address mate manipulation in more detail because pageant culture likely dictates that contestants should not make negative statements about interactions with the judges. While we suspect that a form of mate manipulation could take place at pageants, more investigation, such as candid interviews with past pageant contestants, would be needed.

Paternity Certainty and Pageant Rules

One of the most pervasive elements of some of the more famous beauty pageants is that the contestants must fit certain criteria with respect to their reproductive and matrimonial history. For example, the following rule was taken directly from the Miss Universe organization website (www.missuniverse.com/info/faq), which houses Miss Universe, Miss USA, and Miss Teen USA:

> *"Can contestants be married? No, contestants may not be married or pregnant. They must not have ever been married, not had a marriage annulled nor given birth to, or parented, a child. The titleholders are also required to remain single throughout their reign"* (Miss Universe Organization, n.d.).

It is unlikely that Miss USA and its sister competitions can ask about virginity for legal reasons;

however, the ban on married women and mothers circumvents that issue. If a woman is married, it is highly likely that she is no longer a virgin. Additionally, if she has biological children, it would be obvious that she is not a virgin. The importance that is placed on women's virginity, or more specifically, the appearance of virginity, has a strong evolutionary basis.

In a cross-cultural study that included 37 different cultures, Buss (2007) found that a mate's chastity holds more importance for men than for women in the majority of cultures examined. Specifically, in the United States, men were found to value virginity in a potential partner more than women. Buss argued that the reason for this sex difference in virginity preference is because men have evolved to seek indicators of paternal certainty and long-term commitment in potential mates. Many men may prefer virginal partners because there is no potential risk of raising a child that is not biologically their own, and hence, no risk of allocating resources and parental effort to an unrelated child.

To have children and not be married was not, and is still not, something that is accepted in many cultures around the world (as Buss [2007] points out). It is not surprising that pageants maintain this view, as beauty queens, after all, "must be of good health and moral character" (Miss New York US, 2014). There are several powerful examples of winners who have lost their crowns for violating these rules. In 2007, Miss New Jersey, Ashley Harder, had to resign because she became pregnant during her reign. Miss USA 1957, Leona Gage, also had her crown taken from her, just one day after winning. Her mother-in-law informed the public that Leona was in fact married with two children. In 2012, Carlina Duran, the former Miss Dominican Republic, lost her crown because she was in the process of annulling her marriage (Macatee, 2012).

The Importance of the Virginal Quality of the Evening Gown

In certain aspects of the competition, contestants who exude a virginal quality may be more likely to win, and therefore compete with one another, to appear "more virginal." One of the ways virginity could be conveyed is through dress choice (e.g., wearing white or showing less skin). One of the most well-known segments of beauty competitions is the evening gown portion. This element of pageants is framed as a forum for displaying contestants' personality, class, elegance, and poise.

According to Miss USA 1994, the judges are more concerned with how the contestant presents herself in the gown as opposed to the actual gown itself (Parker, 2000). Like the swimsuit event, contestants walk down the runway in an evening gown of their choosing, pose, and then walk offstage. They do not speak directly to the judges during this segment, but sometimes there are prerecorded short statements about what it means to be beautiful and sexy, their fashion role models, and how fashion plays a part in their life. Some statements also include information about their ties to family and religion. In these statements, they may be conveying a more virginal attitude by alluding to the choice of dress as being similar to their future wedding gown preference or alluding to their father's approval of the gown. They could also express conservative values by choosing a classic fashion icon, such as Audrey Hepburn or Jackie Kennedy, over sexy fashion icons like Britney Spears or the cartoon character Jessica Rabbit. Other conservative values, such as having close ties to family and religion, being a homebody, and having a strong desire to be married, are also discussed in these statements. Emphasis on staying at home or a desire to be married may be perceived as virginal as it would suggest that the contestant would not partake in events that may lead to casual sex (e.g., going out to bars and parties). Further, expressing a desire to be married would likely be perceived as a desire to engage in a long-term relationship and may also be related to the idea that she may be "saving herself" for that long-term partner. Future research could analyze the content of these statements to see if women who express more conservative values place higher than those who discuss the sexiness of the gown or sexy role models.

As the pageants want to emphasize a wholesome, virginal image as well as remarkable physical beauty, it is important that the gown design reflect a careful balance between being classy and sexy. If the gown is ill-fitting, it would likely distract from how the contestant presents herself (e.g., her poise), or indicate that she does not fully care about her appearance. If the gown is overly revealing, it would also distract the judges from considering how the contestant carries herself, and instead leave a negative perception; clothing that is too revealing is not virginal. Though the gown itself is not judged, there are some interesting trends between gown color and the winners. After conducting a brief review of the evening gown portion of Miss America competitions between 2006 and 2015, we found that the gown shape most popular with contestants was a trumpet or mermaid style, where the garment is form-fitting all the way down to the knee and then dramatically flares out. This dress style showcases or fakes an hourglass figure, emphasizing the contestant's waist-to-hip ratio. Further, most dresses had some form of beading, rhinestones, or sequins, and all contestants wore high heels. High heels have been shown to create a more flattering silhouette and gait for the woman wearing them as they help to emphasize the chest and buttocks (Cox, 2004; Semmelhack, 2006), and create a shorter stride (Morris, White, Morrison, & Fisher, 2013). High heels also create the illusion of a more slender ankle and smaller foot (Smith, 1999), which is thought to be an indicator of youth and fertility (Fessler et al., 2005).

Color also appears to be important, and reflects the theme of virginity or innocence. Table 32.2 shows the most popular color among Miss America contestants and the color worn by the winner. Between 2006 and 2015, the most popular color for the evening gowns was white, with 50% of the winners wearing this color. These data were gathered from videos posted to YouTube of each competition, and gown colors of winners were checked with photographs from the competition. The fact that white is the most popular choice for contestants overall may be due to the perception that contestants who wear white are those who will win. Cultural associations

Table 32.2. Popular and Winning Dress Colors in Miss America, 2006–2015.

Year	Popular Color*	Winner's Color
2006	White (4/10)	White
2007	Black (2/10)	Black
2008	White (4/10)	Silver
2009	Silver (3/12) Black (3/12)	White
2010	White (4/12)	Yellow
2011	White (5/12)	White
2012	White (5/13)	Black
2013	White (4/12)	White
2014	White (5/12)	Yellow
2015	White (9/12)	White

* Numbers in parentheses indicate how many participants wore that color during the evening gown segment, with the first number indicating number of wearers, and the second number indicating the total number of contestants.

of white are linked to purity (Aslam, 2006), which is the running theme in Western beauty pageants. In the same videos mentioned previously, several contestants discussed how putting on a white gown felt like they were going to their wedding, which implicitly signals the wearer has a "virginal quality." It would be interesting for future researchers to examine this effect cross-culturally. We predict that the color(s) that represent "pureness" or virginity are popular for contestants' clothing choices cross-culturally. In marked contrast, red gowns, though stunning and attention-grabbing, were not popular among the contestants, and no winning contestant wore a red gown in the ten reviewed competitions. The lack of red gowns is to be expected, given connections that people often make between the color red and sexuality and attention-seeking (see Aslam, 2006; Elliot & Pazda, 2012).

Interestingly, the color of the dress may be more important than the amount of skin the dress reveals. For example, in 2006, Jennifer Berry of Oklahoma wore a white halter-neck gown with a deep-plunging neckline, embellishments, and a high slit. Compared to some of the other contestants, her dress would likely be considered very sexy. A fellow contestant, Erica Powell of South Carolina, wore a much more conservative red dress with no exposed cleavage, leg slit, or embellishments. Berry went on to win the competition. We predict that formal analysis would establish that color is used more as an indicator of perceived promiscuity than dress style or cut. One potential avenue for future research would be to examine if variability in explicit sexiness of dress style (e.g., high slits) independently affects attractiveness judgments in light of color of dress (e.g., red vs. white).

In beauty pageants, fashion choices are meant to attract the judges' attention, flatter the contestants' bodies, and allow the wearer to feel confident as she models the gown. Even though the judges are not scoring the actual gown, there is still competition to find the perfect gown that exudes the personality of the wearer (Parker, 2000). Some pageant contestants bring multiple gowns to wear something that is completely unique, once they see the other contestant's gowns. For example, a contestant who was interviewed at a local state pageant stated that she brought dozens of dresses to make sure she would not wear the same color or style as any of the other contestants (Greenwood, 2010). Uniqueness is a signal of creativity, which has been hypothesized to serve as a fitness indicator in both men and women (see Miller, 2000).

In many ways, then, success in a beauty pageant mirrors success in the domain of long-term mating—coming across as attractive but not promiscuous. Research has shown that the implication of a woman's promiscuity either through nonverbal forms such as dress (Abbey, Cozzarelli, McLaughlin, & Hamish, 1987; Williamson & Hewitt, 1986), or through verbal communication such as rumor (Campbell, 1999; Clayton & Trafimow, 2007) often leads to that woman being negatively perceived by others. In a mating context, it could lead to the potential loss of a long-term mate, while in the pageant context, it may conflict with the wholesome family-friendly values the pageant promotes. The latter scenario would lead to the loss of the competition and therefore the potential loss of high-status mates and prized resources.

A History and the Structure of Child Beauty Pageants

Child beauty pageants, like adult beauty pageants, have had a long and controversial history. Over one hundred years after P.T. Barnum's adult pageants in the 1850s, the Palisades Park in New Jersey hosted one of the first modern beauty pageants for little girls in 1961. Six thousand girls came each week to compete for the title of "Little Miss America." Competitors between the ages of 5 and 10 were judged "on the basis of their beauty, charm, poise, and personality" (Gargiulo, 2006, p. 91). This pageant was then followed by the "Our Little Miss" pageant that was started in 1962 by Marge Hannaman, a former model and basketball player (Our Little Miss, n.d.).

Since the 1960s, the pageant business has grown exponentially. Such junior pageants now exist all across America as local, state, and national pageants, and they also exist internationally. The rules and winnings from each pageant may vary, but there are two basic kinds of pageants: those that focus on glitz and those that focus on natural features. *Glitz* and *natural*, as they are commonly known, refer to the amount of emphasis placed on enhanced beauty for judging. Natural pageants require that minimal or no cosmetics be worn for girls under 13 years of age, that dresses and swimsuits (some natural pageants do not have a swimsuit event) are age-appropriate, and there is an interview event to emphasize personality (Pageant Center, n.d.).

The Glass Slipper Beauty Pageant System, a natural pageant, is for girls aged newborn to 16 and is held in South Carolina. Competitors partake in two events, beauty and theme wear (Stripe Delight

Pageant, 2014). While *beauty* refers to the natural physical beauty of the contestant, *theme wear* refers to clothing that is worn based on a specific theme. For the Stripe Delight Pageant, which is a part of Glass Slipper Pageants, the theme is "stripes," and girls must wear an outfit that has stripes as a part of the costume. In this pageant, girls aged 4 years and older can wear light cosmetics. There are no swimsuit costumes allowed, no bare stomachs, no removal of clothing on stage, and no glitz modeling or talent routines. There are three division categories with three to four titles awarded per category (shown in Table 32.3).

Glitz pageants allow and encourage girls to wear full cosmetics, wear rhinestone-encrusted dresses, and have a pageant coach to create glitz routines (Pageant Center, n.d.). Glitz routines refer to the style of dancing, acting, or other performance during the talent event. The girls, even children as young as 2 years old, wear hairpieces, fake eyelashes, fake or manicured nails, false teeth, and spray tans during the competition. The pageant dresses are covered with light-catching rhinestones and cost hundreds to thousands of dollars.

The Universal Royalty Pageant, owned by Annette Hill, is a high-glitz pageant. *Toddlers and Tiaras*, a reality television program on the TLC Network that focuses on various national and state pageants across the United States, featured the Universal Royalty Pageant during its first season (Reddy, 2009). The Universal Royalty Pageant is a two-day competition. The pageant is divided into babies, toddlers, teens, and miss/misses (the mothers of the contestants) and consists of three parts: talent, beauty, and swimsuit. Any participant from these categories can take home the Ultimate Grand Supreme title (Reddy, 2009).

Both types of pageants have similar awards (see Tables 32.3 and 32.4), with slight variations based on the specific pageant. While both types of pageants are also open to adolescent boys entering the competition, contestants are mostly adolescent girls.

In many children's pageants, there is no "double crowning"; if one contestant wins the "Grand Supreme Queen" title, she cannot also win a "Division Princess" title or the "Age Beauty Princess" title. There are, however, secondary awards that can be double-crowned. These include "Best Eyes," "Best Personality," "Most Beautiful," and "Photogenic." Interestingly, in natural pageants, the photograph submitted to the "Photogenic" award must not be retouched. However, in glitz pageants, the photographs that are entered into the competition are heavily retouched to erase blemishes, add teeth, add a tan, and add full cosmetics. To be considered for these secondary titles, contestants must pay an additional fee for each title for which she wants to be nominated. Many pageants, in both the glitz and natural categories, adopt this type of pageant structure.

Glitz pageants have been especially criticized for oversexualizing young girls because of the heavy cosmetics use, revealing costumes, and flirty dancing and modeling (such as wiggling the hips and batting eyelashes). For these reasons, France has banned child beauty pageants for girls younger than 16 years of age (Rubin & de la Baume, 2013).

Evolutionary Themes in Children's Beauty Pageants

We propose that the pageant structure of many children's pageants is similar to adult pageants, with a strong emphasis on physical beauty in children's pageants (especially in glitz pageants). As a result, intrasexually competitive behavior may develop early or more aggressively in pageant participants. As previously discussed, girls are thought to engage in indirect aggression, as opposed to direct aggression (such as physical fighting), because there is less risk to the instigator (Campbell, 1999). Research from Björkqvist and colleagues (1992) has shown that girls are more furtive when directing aggression toward another peer. Even in early childhood, such

Table 32.3. Example of Division Titles and Ages from Stripe Delight Pageant*.

Division	Title	Age
Division I	Baby Miss	0–12 months
	Tiny Miss	13–23 months
	Wee Miss	2 years
	Toddler Miss	3 years
Division II	Precious Miss	4–5 years
	Petite Miss	6–7 years
	Little Miss	8–9 years
Division III	Young Miss	10–11 years
	Junior Miss	12–13 years
	Teen Miss	14–16 years

* Title names and age ranges may vary slightly between competitions.

Table 32.4. Example of Winning Titles and Descriptions from Stripe Delight Pageant*.

Title	Description
Grand Supreme Queen/Ultimate Grand Supreme	Highest-scoring contestant across 3 divisions
Mini Supreme Queen	Second-highest-scoring contestant across 3 divisions
Division Princess	Highest-scoring contestant in each division
Age Beauty Princess	Highest-scoring contestant in each age group

* Title names and descriptions may vary slightly between competitions.

as by 8 years of age, girls are more likely than boys to engage in gossip, shunning, and becoming friendly with someone else out of a motive of revenge. By age 11, these strategies are more significantly developed (Björkqvist, Lagerspetz, & Kaukiainen, 1992). In children's beauty pageants, younger girls may have to be better at employing these indirect strategies as they are competing for titles not only within their age group but also with other girls who are significantly older than themselves.

Children's pageants could be prime environments to foster the development of successful intrasexually competitive strategies. Not only are girls competing for status and resources, their mothers are constantly informing their daughters' competitive behavior. During the competitions, mothers and other helpers like makeup artists, pageant trainers, and other family members gather to support the contestant throughout the competition (Mirabello, 2009–2013). The contestants are constantly surrounded by maternal assistance; even during the onstage activities, mothers will quietly direct their daughters, literally behind the judges' backs, during the routine (Mirabello, 2009–2013). Any developing competitive behavioral strategies (e.g., the use of indirect aggression, expressing a desire to win the top prize, or extreme disappointment when losing) within the contestant could be reinforced by their mothers. The mothers, in turn, attempt to ensure the success of their daughters in the competition. Since facilitating the success of one's children is a basic evolutionary goal entrenched in parenting, it is not surprising that pageant mothers heavily assist in the development of their daughter's success. The competitive attitude fostered by the mother will

likely be carried into the child's life outside the pageant, which has the potential to be beneficial in education (e.g., getting the highest grade), sports (e.g., becoming the best player), business (e.g., taking more risks, going after promotions), and eventually in adult romantic relationships (e.g., winning access to the best mates).

Aside from the problematic hypersexualization of young girls, children's beauty pageants have been shown to have a negative impact on the contestants' adult lives. Wonderlich, Ackhard, and Henderson (2005) found that participation in child beauty pageants may be linked to higher levels of body dissatisfaction, high levels of distrust of peers, and lower levels of impulse control. These adverse psychological outcomes may well be thought of as the downside of female mating in general—with a large focus on physicality and negative social and psychological repercussions associated with failure on this front. The constant judgment solely on external appearance, pressure from competitive mothers, and indirect and direct aggression from peers could potentially be a major influence on why Wonderlich and colleagues (2005) found these results.

The practice of indirect aggression also carries over into adulthood (Björkqvist, Österman, & Lagerspetz, 1994). If the participants are constantly combative or engaging in indirect aggression, where friends turn out to be enemies and adults are reinforcing and nurturing devious behavior, it follows that past contestants would have higher rates of depression and interpersonal distrust of peers. At the same time, due to their enhanced competitive skills, we propose that winners of children's pageants may ultimately emerge as more apt at using indirect aggression and be more reproductively successful (i.e., have children that are healthier, who are able to accrue status and mates readily) than other peers who competed and consistently lost top titles. The continuous reinforcement and reward for winning the titles would boost confidence and potentially refine their ability to knock rivals out of the competition. With fewer rivals and greater access to top mates, one could infer that greater reproductive success would be inevitable. Those who repeatedly lose these competitions may negatively value their self-worth, lose confidence, and may not consider themselves to be worthy of high-status mates, thus removing themselves from the competition before working against a rival. This would lead to fewer mating opportunities and thus lower reproductive success. Future research into the social strategies of past childhood beauty pageant contestants (and winners in particular) would yield much insight into these possibilities.

Future Directions

In spite of their longstanding existence and popularity in a variety of modern cultures, there is a substantial lack of experimental psychological research on beauty pageants. Although a promising first step, Singh's (1993) research that tracked the waist-to-hip ratio measurements of Miss America winners is one of the only studies that applied evolutionary thinking to beauty competitions. Given that evolutionary theory speaks to human nature, as evidenced across all cultures, we hypothesize that empirical research on beauty pageant contestants would uncover a great deal in terms of universals in the social and mating-relevant strategies of women. Specifically, we propose that future researchers may want to examine the following topics among beauty pageant contestants individually and interactively: (a) past and current romantic relationship status, (b) ovulatory status and competition behavior, and (c) use of intrasexual competitive strategies. We now expand on each of these three topics.

The study of romantic relationships is a thriving area of research in psychological and evolutionary studies. While beauty pageant contestants are expected to be single, we believe romantic relationship status would be a fascinating area of study for two reasons. First, many contestants may have undisclosed sexual relationships. Such a pattern would speak to the fact that pageants are perceived as favoring long-term mating and relatively conservative approaches to relationships. Similarly, past romantic relationship data (i.e., relationship status, length of relationship, ratings of contestant's partners) on pageant contestants may be extremely interesting in shedding light on the actual mating and social strategies of beauty pageant contestants. Do pageant winners climb up the mating ladder, as compared to nonwinners? Are their post-winning partners more attractive and higher-status mates when compared to their pre-winning partners? Concerning current relationship status and competitive strategy use, partnered people have reported that they engage in more frequent competitive strategy use, especially competitor derogation, than those who are not involved in romantic relationships (Fisher & Cox, 2011). Future researchers should aim to empirically examine these trends among beauty pageant contestants and how they relate to actual pageant winnings. Given the nature of beauty competitions, we hypothesize that those contestants who are more skilled in competitive strategies (i.e., engage in competitive strategies more often and with more success than others) would be more likely to have had more romantic relationships and to win the title of "Beauty Queen." In fact, women who are particularly skilled at displaying prototypical long-term mating strategies may well be best positioned to win the crown.

There is also a large body of research and burgeoning interest in ovulatory status and various behavioral, dispositional, and physical traits. Normally (or naturally) cycling women (i.e., those not taking a hormonal contraceptive) are perceived to be more attractive, have more pleasant body odors, and have more attractive voices when in their fertile than infertile phase (Doty, Ford, Preti, & Huggins, 1975; Kirchengast & Gartner, 2002; Miller & Maner, 2010; Pipitone & Gallup, 2008; Thornhill et al., 2003). Interestingly, naturally cycling women in their fertile phase wear more revealing clothing than women in other phases of the menstrual cycle and are perceived as trying to look sexier (Durante, Li, & Haselton, 2008). These systematic cyclical changes have not been found among women who use hormonal contraceptives, which mimic physiological changes associated with pregnancy (Miller, Tybur, & Jordan, 2007; Seppo et al., 2004; Welling, Puts, Roberts, Little, & Burriss, 2012). Future researchers should test these findings directly among beauty pageant contestants. We hypothesize that contestants who are in their fertile phase would be rated as more attractive across the board (e.g., physical appearance, voice) than contestants who are not in their fertile phase at the time of scoring or those on hormonal contraception.

Although we review intrasexual competition within beauty pageants, there remain numerous directions for further investigation. We propose that many of the mating-relevant behaviors that are exhibited in beauty pageants are inherently competitive. As we discussed, contestants are judged on many qualities that are directly relevant to mating success (e.g., beauty, intelligence, creativity). It is therefore appropriate to examine the competitive tactics used by women in beauty pageants as being similar to competitive strategies used in the pursuit and retention of a mate. We propose that pageant winners increase their status as potential mates by directly competing with other women in categories that are directly representative of what is desired in a mate. We therefore hypothesize that pageant winners gain greater access and exposure to higher-status mates compared to their losing counterparts. Future research can easily test this hypothesis by examining and comparing the romantic partners of pageant contestants versus pageant title-holders.

Conclusion

Throughout this chapter, we have provided an overview of the histories and structures of adult and child beauty pageants in order to present the evolutionary themes found within these contests. We focused on how the structure of a pageant may foster an environment that provokes similar intrasexually competitive behavior from contestants that would be seen in a mating context from an evolutionary lens. We argued that the strategies underlying behaviors that are used in mating competition, such as self-promotion, competitor derogation, and competitor manipulation, are strategies that would also benefit potential competitors in a beauty pageant context. The microenvironment of the pageant is representative of a competition to attract a mate in order to obtain and retain status and resources. The winnings of the competition become the "resources," while the events (pre-interview, swimsuit, fashion, onstage questions, and [sometimes] talent) showcase the traits that men desire in a partner for a long-term relationship. We proposed that children's pageant environments may evoke and exacerbate indirect aggression seen in young girls because the pageant events mimic those of adult pageants (minus the pre-interview and onstage questions), place a great amount of emphasis on physical beauty, and have indirect competitive behaviors reinforced by contestants' mothers' encouragement. While there is some evidence to support these proposed ideas, more research into the evolutionary themes in pageants is necessary before we can draw any concrete conclusions.

References

Abbey, A., Cozzarelli, C., McLaughlin, K., & Hamish, R. (1987). The effects of clothing and dyad sex composition on perceptions of sexual intent: Do women and men evaluate these cues differently? *Journal of Applied Social Psychology, 17*(2), 108–126.

Archer, J., & Coyne, S. M. (2005). An integrated review of indirect, relational, and social aggression. *Personality and Social Psychology Review, 9*(3), 212–230.

Aslam, M. M. (2006). Are you selling the right colour? A cross-cultural review of colour as a marketing cue. *Journal of Marketing Communications, 12*, 15–30.

Banet-Weiser, S. (1999). *The most beautiful girl in the world: Beauty pageants and national identity*. Berkeley: University of California Press.

Björkqvist, K. (1994). Sex differences in physical, verbal, and indirect aggression: A review of recent research. *Sex Roles, 30*(3–4), 177–188.

Björkqvist, K., Lagerspetz, K. M., & Kaukiainen, A. (1992). Do girls manipulate and boys fight? Developmental trends in regard to direct and indirect aggression. *Aggressive Behavior, 18*(2), 117–127.

Björkqvist, K., Österman, K., & Lagerspetz, K. M. (1994). Sex differences in covert aggression among adults. *Aggressive Behavior, 20*(1), 27–33.

Buss, D. (1988). The evolution of human intrasexual competition: Tactics of mate attraction. *Journal of Personality and Social Psychology, 54*, 616–628.

Buss, D. (2003). *The evolution of desire: Strategies of human mating*. 4th ed. New York: Basic Books.

Buss, D. M. (2007). The evolution of human mating. *Acta Psychologica Sinica, 39*, 502–512.

Buss, D., & Dedden, L. (1990). Derogation of competitors. *Journal of Social and Personal Relationships, 7*, 395–422.

Buss, D. M., & Schmitt, D. P. (1993). Sexual strategies theory: An evolutionary perspective on human mating. *Psychological Review, 100*(2), 204–232.

Buunk, A. P., & Fisher, M. (2009). Individual differences in intrasexual competition. *Journal of Evolutionary Psychology, 7*(1), 37–48.

Cairns, R. B., Cairns, B. D., Neckerman, H. J., Ferguson, L. L., & Gariépy, J. (1989). Growth and aggression: I. Childhood to early adolescence. *Developmental Psychology, 25*(2), 320–330.

Campbell, A. (1999). Staying alive: Evolution, culture, and women's intrasexual aggression. *Behavioral and Brain Sciences, 22*(2), 203–252.

Cashdan, E. (1998). Are men more competitive than women? *British Journal of Social Psychology, 37*, 213–229.

Catalina. (2015). Celebrating 100 years of style at Catalina. Retrieved from http://www.catalinaswim.com/our-history/

Christel, D. A, & Dunn, S. C. (2016). Average American women's clothing size: comparing national health and nutritional examination surveys (1988–2010) to ASTM International misses & women's plus size clothing. *International Journal of Fashion Design, Technology, and Education*, 1–8.

Clayton, K. D., & Trafimow, D. (2007). A test of three hypotheses concerning attributions toward female promiscuity. *Social Science Journal, 44*(4), 677–686.

Collins, S. A., & Missing, C. (2003). Vocal and visual attractiveness are related in women. *Animal Behaviour, 65*(5), 997–1004.

Cox, C. (2004). *Stiletto*. New York: Harper Collins.

Cox, A., & Fisher, M. (2008). A framework for exploring intrasexual competition. Special Issue: Proceedings of the 2nd Annual Meeting of the NorthEastern Evolutionary Psychology Society. *Journal of Social, Evolutionary, and Cultural Psychology, 2*(4), 144–155.

Crick, N. R., & Grotpeter, J. K. (1995). Relational aggression, gender, and social-psychological adjustment. *Child Development, 66*, 710–722.

Darwin, C. (1871). *The descent of man and selection in relation to sex*. London: John Murray.

Doty, R. L., Ford, M., Preti, G., & Huggins, G. R. (1975). Changes in the intensity and pleasantness of human vaginal odors during the menstrual cycle. *Science, 190*(4221), 1316–1318.

Durante, K. M., Li, N. P., & Haselton, M. G. (2008). Changes in women's choice of dress across the ovulatory cycle: Naturalistic and laboratory task-based evidence. *Personality and Social Psychology Bulletin, 34*(11), 1451–1460.

Elliot, A. J., & Pazda, A. D. (2012). Dressed for sex: Red as a female sexual signal in humans. *PLoS ONE, 7*(4).

Ferrari, M. (writer) & Ades, L. (director). (2002). Miss America. [television program]. *The American Experience*, PBS.

Fessler, D. M., Nettle, D., Afshar, Y., de Andrade Pinheiro, I., Bolyanatz, A., Mulder, M. B., . . . Khaltourina, D. (2005). A cross-cultural investigation of the role of foot size in physical attractiveness. *Archives of Sexual Behavior, 34*(3), 267–276.

Fink, B., Neave, N., Manning, J. T., & Grammer, K. (2006). Facial symmetry and judgements of attractiveness, health and personality. *Personality and Individual Differences, 41*, 491–499.

Fisher, M. & Cox, A. (2009). The influence of female attractiveness on competitor derogation. *Journal of Evolutionary Psychology, 7*, 141–155.

Fisher, M. & Cox, A. (2011). Four strategies used during intrasexual competition for mates. *Personal Relationships, 18*, 20–38.

Fisher, M. L., & Voracek, M. (2006). The shape of beauty: determinants of female physical attractiveness. *Journal of Cosmetic Dermatology, 5*(2), 190–194.

Gargiulo, V. (2006). *Palisades amusement park: A century of fond memories*. New Brunswick: Rutgers University Press.

Geher, G. (2014). *Evolutionary Psychology 101*. New York: Springer.

Geher, G., Garcia, J. R., Kaufman, S. B., Kaufman, J., & Dawson, B. B. (2016). The validity and structure of mating intelligence. *Evolution, Mind, and Behaviour, 14*(1).

Geher, G., & Kaufman, S. B. (2013). *Mating intelligence unleashed*. New York: Oxford University Press.

Greenwood, D. (2010). *The rhinestone sisterhood: A journey through small-town American one tiara at a time*. New York: Crown Publishers.

Griskevicius, V., Tybur, J. M., Gangestad, S. W., Perea, E. F., Shapiro, J. R., & Kenrick, D. T. (2009). Aggress to impress: Hostility as an evolved context-dependent strategy. *Journal of Personality and Social Psychology, 96*(5), 980–994.

Hampson, R. (1984). Vanessa Williams gives up her Miss America Crown. *Gettysburg Times*, July 24, p. 4.

Karthikeyan, S., & Locke, J. L. (2015). Men's evaluation of women's speech in a simulated dating context: Effects of female fertility on vocal pitch and attractiveness. *Evolutionary Behavioral Sciences, 9*(1), 55–67.

Kirchengast, S., & Gartner, M. (2002). Changes in fat distribution (WHR) and body weight across the menstrual cycle. *Collegium Antropologicum, 26*, S47–S57.

Lange, B. P., Zaretsky, E., Schwarz, S., & Euler, H. A. (2014). Words won't fail: Experimental evidence on the role of verbal proficiency in mate choice. *Journal of Language and Social Psychology, 33*(5), 482–499.

Leifer, M. (2011). She lost 110 lbs.—and won beauty queen crown. *NBC News*, May 7 Retrieved from http://www.today.com/id/43676767/ns/today-today_style/t/she-lost-lbs-won-beauty-queen-crown/#slice-3.

Levitan, D. R., & Ferrell, D. L. (2006). Selection on gamete recognition proteins depends on sex, density, and genotype frequency. *Science, 312*(5771), 267–269.

Library of Congress. (n.d.). It's not a beauty pageant, it's a scholarship program. Retrieved from https://www.loc.gov/wiseguide/aug08/beauty.html.

Macatee, R. (2012). Another Miss Universe scandal: Miss Dominican Republic Carlina Duran dethroned for being a missus! April 26. Retrieved from http://www.eonline.com/news/311756/another-miss-universe-scandal-miss-dominican-republic-carlina-duran-dethroned-for-being-a-missus.

Mask, L., & Blanchard, C. M. (2011). The effects of "thin ideal" media on women's body image concerns and eating-related intentions: The beneficial role of an autonomous regulation of eating behaviors. *Body Image, 8*(4), 357–365.

Mazur, A. (1986). U.S. trends in feminine beauty and overadaptation. *Journal of Sex Research, 22*(3), 281–303.

Miller, G. F. (2000). *The mating mind: How sexual choice shaped the evolution of human nature*. New York: Doubleday.

Miller, S. L., & Maner, J. K. (2010). Evolution and relationship maintenance: Fertility cues lead committed men to devalue relationship alternatives. *Journal of Experimental Social Psychology, 46*(6), 1081–1084.

Miller, G., Tybur, J. M., & Jordan, B. D. (2007). Ovulatory cycle effects on tip earnings by lap dancers: Economic evidence for human estrus? *Evolution and Human Behavior, 28*(6), 375–381.

Mirabello, D. (2009–2013). *Toddlers and tiaras* [television series]. S. Raucher [producer].

Miss America Organization (2011). *2011 Miss America Judges Manual*. Retrieved from http://www.miss-sc.org/led-portal-forms/2011%20Miss%20America%20Judging%20Manual.pdf.

Miss America Organization. (2016). FAQ. Retrieved from http://missamerica.org/faq/.

Miss America Pageant. (n.d.). Retrieved from http://www.missamerica.org/default.aspx.

Miss New York USA. (2014). Events information. Retrieved from http://missnewyorkusa.com/faq/.

Miss Universe (n.d). Historical Highlights. Retrieved from press.missuniverse.com/listanevent.php?events=1462&section=presskit.

Miss Universe. (2016). About the competition. Retrieved from http://www.missuniverse.com/competition.

Miss USA. (2016). Miss U App. Retrieved from https://www.missuniverse.com/missusa/news/view/199.

Morris, P. H., White, J., Morrison, E. R., & Fisher, K. (2013). High heels as supernormal stimuli: How wearing high heels affects judgments of female attractiveness. *Evolution and Human Behavior, 34*(3), 176–181.

Noor, F., & Evans, D. C. (2003). The effect of facial symmetry on perceptions of personality and attractiveness. *Journal of Research in Personality, 37*, 339–347.

Österman, K., Björkqvist, K., Lagerspetz, K. M. J., Kaukiainen, A., Landau, S. F., Fraczek, A., & Caprara, G. V. (1998). Cross-cultural evidence of female indirect aggression. *Aggressive behavior, 24*(1), 1–8.

Our Little Miss. (n.d). Marge Hannaman (1924-2006)-Founder. Retrieved from http://www.ourlittlemiss.com/story-of-olm.html.

Pageant Center. (n.d.). What is the difference between glitz pageants and natural pageants. Retrieved from http://pageantcenter.com/pageants1/pageant-news/what-is-the-difference-between-glitz-pageants-and-natural-pageants/#.VW802M9VhHw.

Palumbi, S. R. (1999). All males are not created equal: fertility differences depend on gamete recognition polymorphisms in sea urchins. *Proceedings of the National Academy of Sciences*, *96*(22), 12632–12637.

Parker, L. (2000). *Catching the crown: The source for pageant competitions*. San Antonio, TX: Burke Publishing Company.

PBS Online. (1999–2002). "... The winners are." Retrieved from http://www.pbs.org/wgbh/amex/missamerica/sfeature/sf_list.html.

Perilloux, C., Cloud, J. C., & Buss, D. M. (2013). Women's physical attractiveness and short-term mating strategies. *Personality and Individual Differences*, *54*, 490–495.

Pipitone, R. N., & Gallup, G. G., Jr. (2008). Women's voice attractiveness varies across the menstrual cycle. *Evolution and Human Behavior*, *29*(4), 268–274.

Reddy, S. (writer). (2009). Universal Royalty Pageant. In L. Lexington (executive producer), T. Rogan (executive producer), S. Rauscher (co-executive producer), *Toddlers and Tiaas*. Silver Spring, MD: The Learning Channel.

Reischer, E., & Koo, K. S. (2004). The body beautiful: Symbolism and agency in the social world. *Annual Review of Anthropology*, *33*, 297–317.

Riverol, A. R. (1992). *Live from Atlantic City: The history of the Miss America Pageant before, after and in spite of television*. Bowling Green, OH: Bowling Green State University Popular Press.

Rosenfeld, L. (2014). What Does Miss USA Win? Commence Major Jealousy Sequence ... To A Degree. June 8. Retrieved from 1/3/16 http://www.bustle.com/articles/27091-what-does-miss-usa-win-commence-major-jealousy-sequence-to-a-degree.

Rubin, A. J., & de la Baume, M. (2013, September 18). French senate approves ban on pageants for young girls. *The New York Times*. Retrieved from http://www.nytimes.com/2013/09/19/world/europe/french-senate-passes-ban-on-beauty-pageants-for-girls.html.

Semmelhack, E. (2006). A delicate balance: Women, power, and high heels. In G. Reilo & P. McNeil (Eds.), *Shoes: A history from sandals to sneakers* (pp. 224–249). New York: Berg.

Seppo, K., Eriksson, C. J. P., Koskela, E., Mappes, T., Nissinen, K., & Rantala, M. J. (2004). Attractiveness of women's body odors over the menstrual cycle: The role of oral contraceptives and receiver sex. *Behavioral Ecology*, *15*(4), 579–584.

Singh, D. (1993). Adaptive significance of female physical attractiveness: Role of waist-to-hip ratio. *Journal of Personality and Social Psychology*, *65*, 293–307.

Smith, E. O. (1999). High heels and evolution: natural selection, sexual selection and high heels. *Psychology of Evolution and Gender*, *1*, 245–278.

Stripe Delight Pageant (2014). Application form. Retrieved from http://form.jotformpro.com/form/32325206991958.

Thornhill, R., Gangestad, S. W., Miller, R., Scheyd, G., McCullough, J., & Franklin, M. (2003). Major histocompatibility complex genes, symmetry and body scent attractiveness in men and women. *Behavioral Ecology*, *14*(5), 668–678.

Time (2009). Sex, Drugs, and The Donald. Retrieved from http://content.time.com/time/specials/packages/article/0,28804,1873790_1873792_1873896,00.html.

Tovée, M. J., Maisey, D. S., Emery, J. L., & Cornelissen, P. L. (1999). Visual cues to female physical attractiveness. *Proceedings of the Royal Society B*, *266*, 211–218.

Trivers, R. L. (1972). Parental investment and sexual selection. In B. Campbell (Ed.), *Sexual selection and the descent of man: 1871–1971*. Chicago: Aldine.

Vagianos, A. (2015). The eye-opening evolution of Miss America's body over 95 years. Retrieved from http://www.huffingtonpost.com/entry/the-eye-opening-evolution-of-miss-americas-body-over-95-years_us_55f078d9e4b002d5c077a6fb.

Want, S. C. (2009). Meta-analytic moderators of experimental exposure to media portrayals of women on female appearance satisfaction: Social comparisons as automatic processes. *Body Image*, *6*(4), 257–269.

Welling, L. L. M., Puts, D. A., Roberts, S. C., Little, A. C., & Burriss, R. P. (2012). Hormonal contraceptive use and mate retention behavior in women and their male partners. *Hormones and Behavior*, *61*(1), 114–120.

Williamson, S., & Hewitt, J. (1986). Attire, sexual allure, and attractiveness. *Perceptual Motor Skills*, *63*, 981–982.

Women's Size Guide. (2016). Women's size guide: US sizes. Retrieved from http://www.sizeguide.net/size-guide-women-size-chart.html.

Wolf, N. (1991). *The beauty myth: How images of beauty are used against women*. HarperCollins: New York.

Wonderlich, A. L., Ackard., D. M., Henderson, J. B. (2005). Childhood beauty pageant contestants: Associations with adult disordered eating and mental health. *Eating Dsiorders: Journal of Treatment and Prevention*, *13*(3), 219–301.

Yamamiya, Y., Cash, T. F., Melnyk, S. E., Posavac, H. D., & Posavac, S. S. (2005). Women's exposure to thin-and-beautiful media images: Body image effects of media-ideal internalization and impact-reduction interventions. *Body Image*, *2*(1), 74–80.

Zhang, C. (2013). What is it like to compete in a beauty pageant? September 6. Message posted to https://www.quora.com/What-is-it-like-to-compete-in-a-beauty-pageant.

Fashion as a Set of Signals in Female Intrasexual Competition

Laura L. Johnsen *and* Glenn Geher

Abstract

Fashion is one tool that women employ to enhance their overall attractiveness to increase mating opportunities and repel competition from other females. This essay first discusses how evolution has shaped the female form and how clothing is used to enhance desirable traits. Additionally, this essay addresses how fashion trends have endured throughout history because they have been continually successful in maintaining women's attractiveness. Further, the reasons why women... clothing when engaging in competitive strategies such as self-promotion and competitor manipulation is also explored. The second section covers how women's physiological occurrences influence the way they dress and how males perceive them. Third, this essay delves into the social perceptions and consequences of wearing certain kinds of clothing. It explores how fashion is used to attract and retain mates by enabling a woman to stand out among her potential rivals and/or forcing rivals to back down from pursuing a potential partner.

Key Words: clothing, intrasexual competition, mating, fashion trends, physiological occurrences, social perceptions

Introduction

Clothing may be one of the first features we notice about a person. People identify in-group and out-group affiliations through the use of designs that are specific to a certain group. Some evidence suggests that we can assign a person's personality, wealth, and interests just by looking at and evaluating his or her clothing choice (Howlett, Pine, Cahill, Orakçıoğlu, & Fletcher, 2015; Howlett, Pine, Orakçıoğlu, & Fletcher, 2013).

The original purpose of clothing is open to debate. It has been argued that clothing was used to mainly protect our bodies from the elements, specifically to provide warmth in cooler climates (Gilligan, 2010). In addition to providing protection from the environment, there is a secondary argument that clothing and adornment were also used by our ancestors for mate attraction (Roach & Eicher, 1965). When the first humans made a decision to decorate their animal-skin tunics,

mating-relevant signaling became part of clothing (provided we conceptualize art and design in sexual-selection terms). For example, certain iconography may indicate high status or religious affiliation. Decorating one's tunic with rare beads and paint and creating a design to reflect one's social affiliations was a way to communicate that one had access to valuable resources and possessed creativity. These qualities are desirable in potential mates (Buss & Schmitt, 1993). Additionally, complex clothing required making and using more sophisticated tools (Gilligan, 2007). Clothing manufacture likely showcased a diverse skill set, which could have been important when choosing a mate because it may have shown that the individual was better able to survive. On this point, skills required for clothing manufacture would have included hunting, sewing, manipulation and construction of tools (like needles and stone knives), as well as creative and abstract problem-solving. These skills could have applied to a diverse array of situations that could make the individual better adapted to his or her environment.

Clothing is made up of two different aspects: *adornment*, which refers to a modification of the body, and *dress*, which refers to the act of putting clothing on the body and the physical item of clothing (Roach & Eicher, 1965). Adornment was likely the first way in which humans began to cover their bodies and is a characteristic found in all cultures (Roach & Eicher, 1979).

Certain forms of adornment are likely conduits of risky signaling, commonly used to attract potential mates (Carmen, Guitar, & Dilion, 2012). In fact, body paint, permanent ink, piercing, and purposeful body scarring have little to no protective benefit, and, moreover, may present a risk of potential toxins entering the bloodstream (Koziel, Kretschmer, & Pawlowski, 2010). Thus, we must conclude that these actions were taken for alternative reasons; if they were not used to protect the body, they may have been used to enhance physical appearance and display status, such as tribal affiliation and societal rank, to potential mates (Carmen et al., 2012).

Adornment is not the only factor that serves as a medium for intrasexual competition. Clothing, as previously mentioned, has been used for more than protecting the body from the environment. If clothing were used only for protection and no other signaling, designs with beading, embroidery, and dying would not be found with the remains of garments, and current fashion would be more practical and geared toward improving our survival. Yet when one observes downtown streets on a cold Friday night and sees groups of women without coats, wearing short skirts and open-toed high heels making their way to the bar, it is obvious that clothing has strayed far from just protection from the elements and has become a way for humans to nonverbally express their personality (Feinberg, Mataro, & Burroughs, 1992; Johnson, Schofield, & Yurchisin, 2002), wealth and status (conveyed by wearing designer clothing), and even their sexual availability (Grammer, Renninger, & Fischer, 2005). While both men and women use fashion as a display of these traits, the focus of this essay is on how women use clothing and adornment as mediums of intrasexual competition.

Intrasexually competitive tactics have proven to increase reproductive success (i.e., the number of children one has; see Buss, 1988; Geher & Kaufman, 2013). According to much research (e.g., Campbell, 1999), the style of women's competitive behavior is less physical and instead more indirect (e.g., rumors, put-downs) compared to men's competitive behavior, which is more physically based. Intrasexual competition in the mating domain for women is often focused on defending and collecting resources, such as access to physical resources like food that has been picked and gathered or social resources, such as strong social in-groups. Such intrasexual competition facilitates the attraction of high-status mates (Campbell, 1999). Additionally, because men place an emphasis on the youth and physical attractiveness of potential mates, women's competitive tactics often center on emphasizing reproductive value (e.g., lustrous hair), which is often marked by youthful physical features (Buss, 1988). Youth and physical attractiveness are thought to be indicators of good general health and fecundity (discussed in depth later). Further, given that men's reproductive success was tied to women bearing genetically fit offspring, they would be attracted to women who possessed traits (e.g., youth, low waist-to-hip ratio [WHR]) that would indicate a higher likelihood of possessing the ability to have healthy children.

The indirect competitive female tactics described earlier are elaborated in some detail here. Such tactics include verbal competitor derogation, rumor spreading, and clothing/cosmetics choice (Campbell, 1999). These competitive behaviors have been categorized into two related strategies (Cox & Fisher, 2008): *self-promotion* (Buss, 1988) and *competitor derogation* (Buss & Dedden, 1990). Self-promotion refers to an individual making himself or herself appear more attractive relative to other peers of the same sex. Women engage in self-promotion to highlight their youthfulness and reproductive capability; they do this by wearing stylish clothing, jewelry, and cosmetics and portraying an overall groomed appearance—stimuli such as stylish female clothing often highlight youthful qualities (Buss, 1988). Competitor derogation refers to negatively portraying a rival to a potential mate. Buss and Dedden (1990) argue that members of both sexes engage in competitor derogation; however, women are more likely to derogate a competitor's appearance and sexual behavior, as those are two particularly important factors regarding mate value in women. Appearance and attractiveness, as previously mentioned, are indicators of genetic quality. Women's sexual history or proclivity toward promiscuity is linked to paternal certainty, so it makes sense from an evolutionary perspective that the sexual history of a woman is a target of intrasexual derogation.

As discussed later, women's promiscuity is viewed by men as an indicator that they may cheat in the future, thereby decreasing the certainty among men that any offspring born by these woman are actually theirs. As discussed later, a rival's clothing is a prime target for derogation. A short skirt and high heels or a loosely laced corset might be criticized by other women for looking too "slutty," which would decrease the target's mate value in the context of a long-term relationship but not necessarily for short-term relationships (Buss & Schmitt, 1993).

This essay explores the use of clothing in women's intrasexual competition for mates. In the first section of the essay, we discuss how evolution has shaped the female form and how clothing is used to enhance desirable traits. The second section covers how women's physiological occurrences, such as the menstrual and ovulatory cycles, influence the way women dress and how men perceive women as a result. Third, we delve into the social perceptions and consequences of wearing certain kinds of clothing. Each of these topics further explores how fashion is used to attract mates by enabling one to stand out among one's potential rivals and/or forcing rivals to back down from pursuing a potential partner.

The Evolutionary Basis of Emphasizing Fitness

Over the course of our evolutionary history, naturally and sexually selected traits have created our present-day form. Past studies have found that women tend to use more self-promotion as opposed to competitor derogation in order to attract a potential partner (Fisher, Cox, & Gordon, 2009). This pattern means that women are more likely to emphasize their own appearance instead of criticizing their competitor's appearance. Clothing and cosmetics have been used throughout history to aid in such self-promotion (Buss, 1988).

Due to the process of evolution, individuals with more desirable traits were more reproductively successful than were individuals who did not possess favorable traits. Though body shape varies across humankind, preferences for specific traits, such as facial symmetry and body proportionality, exist cross-culturally (Fink, Neave, Manning, & Grammer, 2006; Singh & Singh, 2006). This fact implies that the desire for specific body types has an evolutionary basis. Certain parts of the female body are thought to be evolved indicators of health and reproductive capability. These include clear and rosy skin, facial symmetry, WHR and fat deposition, and leg length (see Buss, 2003). In this section we discuss the evolutionary importance of each of these traits and how women have used fashion styles throughout history to enhance these traits in order to outcompete other women and attract a mate.

Skin Health and Facial Beauty

Attractiveness in general has been ranked as the first trait that men value in a potential partner (Buss & Schmitt, 1993). Women who are considered more attractive will have better access to quality mates—and this point connects with the fact that attractiveness is correlated with youth in populations of female adults (see Buss, 2003). As previously mentioned, youth is an indicator for fecundity given that, in our species, the reproductive window for females is a subset of the lifespan that corresponds largely to young adulthood. From an evolutionary perspective, skin can indicate age (Fink, Grammer, & Matts, 2006; Matts, Fink, Grammer, & Burquest, 2007), general health (Fink et al., 2006; Matts et al., 2007), and even ovulatory status (Keltner & Buswell, 1997). When the color of skin is more homogeneous, men tend to rate it as more youthful and attractive than skin that is less homogenous (Matts et al., 2007). During peak ovulation, women's skin tends to appear redder when flushed or while flirting due to the lightening of skin (Van den Berghe & Frost, 1986).

Symmetry has also been associated with attractiveness in both human and nonhuman animals; symmetry is often found as a marker of resistance to parasite load, so it has clear fitness-relevant implications (Møller & Swaddle, 1997). For example, in the species *Scatophaga stercoaria* (the common dung beetle), more symmetrical males are more reproductively successful than are less symmetrical males (Liggett, Harvey, & Manning, 1993). Many nonhuman animal studies focus on male symmetry, as females are more selective when choosing their mating partners. In humans, however, symmetry is preferred by both sexes. Fink, Neave, Manning, and Grammer (2006) found that both men and women rate symmetrical female faces as more attractive, intelligent, and healthy than nonsymmetrical faces. Less symmetrical faces were rated as more anxious than more symmetrical faces, suggesting something of a halo effect for facial symmetry (Fink et al., 2006). It would be important, then, for women to use a number of beauty products to improve their attractiveness and increase their facial symmetry and youthfulness, especially within a mating context.

Cosmetics have been a part of human life since ancient times. For example, ancient Egyptians, ~2000 BC, were known to use various kinds of eye cosmetics (makeup) and cosmetic powder (Walter et al., 1999). The ancient use of cosmetics has not been lost through the ages. Technology and scientific advances have revolutionized the beauty industry so that every aspect of the face can be embellished with cosmetics of all colors and textures. Relatedly, cosmetic surgery can smooth, tighten, clear, and add color to the skin or change the shape of a face. The use of cosmetics and surgery can be interpreted as "faking fitness" or faking genetic quality by obscuring traits that would make the wearer appear less attractive to potential mates. Cosmetics and enhancement surgery, thus, may be conceptualized as forms of self-promotion designed to attract mates.

Cosmetics are a relatively noninvasive and inexpensive way to correct any imperfections on an individual's face. Foundation, for example, is a liquid or powder substance that is sold in a variety of skin tones and is intended to make the skin look homogenous by hiding blemishes and blotchiness. Foundation covers up the skin's natural coloring, so blush is used to re-add color to the cheeks (Draelos, 2000).

The technique of contouring combines different shades of foundation to add highlights and shadows to emphasize the bone structure of the face, neck, clavicle, and chest. It can also be used to make the face appear more symmetrical, as the highlights and shadows can create the illusion of symmetry. Not only does it make skin appear younger and tauter, but it can completely transform the face so that the wearer is nearly unrecognizable after the cosmetics are removed. For interesting examples of contouring at work, see the work of makeup artist Melissa Murphy (Greening, 2014), who has documented the transformative power of heavy cosmetic usage.

Instead of simply using cosmetics, one may opt for plastic surgery, which is relatively costly and poses higher risks to the health of the individual undergoing the treatment. Botox, skin lifts, rhytidectomy (facial surgery), rhinoplasty (nose surgery), mentoplasty (chin surgery), and otoplasty (ear surgery) are just a few options that an individual can use to change his or her appearance. Surgery cannot, of course, change an individual's genetic composition; thus, regardless of one's modified morphology, one's original genes (unaffected by plastic surgery) will be passed on to one's children. However, if the goal is to attract a potential mate and outcompete a rival, then the use of cosmetics and surgery may be effective tools to help one be successful.

As many women invest in cosmetics and surgery with the intention to appear more attractive, one might wonder if men actually view women with cosmetic enhancement as more attractive. The answer is *yes*. Based on extant research, cosmetics do seem to make the wearer appear more attractive to men (and also to women). Mulhern, Feldman, Hussey, Lévêque, and Pineau (2003) analyzed the perception of different "levels" of cosmetics by both men and women. In Mulhern et al.'s study, ten Caucasian female volunteers between the ages of 31 and 38 had their cosmetics professionally applied under five different conditions: (a) no cosmetics, (b) foundation only, (c) eye cosmetics only, (d) lipstick only, and (d) full-face cosmetics. The color of cosmetics varied at the discretion of the makeup artist so that the cosmetics used enhanced each volunteer's individual attractiveness. Two hundred participants (100 men and 100 women) looked at ten sets of five color photographs showing each volunteer under the five cosmetics conditions. The ratings could only be used once within each set of photographs. Both men and women chose the full-face cosmetics as the most attractive for each set of photographs (54.8% for men, 51.4% for women). However, the next preferred choice for men was the foundation-only condition (22.1%), while women chose the eye-cosmetics condition as the next most attractive condition (29.5%). These results seem to suggest that males perceived the foundation and women the eye cosmetics as contributing more to the attractiveness of the full-face cosmetics (Mulhern et al., 2003). These findings indicate that although men consider women who use full-face cosmetics as attractive, they may prefer the use of cosmetics to replicate more of a natural face, as seen in the foundation-only condition.

A field study by Guéguen (2008) demonstrated that cosmetics are very important to men in a mating context. This study took place over the course of three hours at two different bars. In one condition, confederates wore no cosmetics, and in the second condition, a female makeup artist gave each confederate a specifically tailored makeover. The findings revealed that, based on unobtrusive behavioral measures, men were more likely to interact with the women in the cosmetics condition.

In support of the idea that women use cosmetics as a form of self-promotion to attract a mate, Guéguen (2012) found women's cosmetics preferences change over the course of their menstrual cycle. Women closer to ovulation, or in the "highly fertile" phase of their cycle, spent more time applying cosmetics, used a heavier amount of cosmetics, and had more attractive makeup than women in the nonfertile phase. The ratings for the amount of cosmetics and the attractiveness of application of the cosmetics came from professional makeup artists whose sex was not disclosed. Women are thought to increase their intrasexually competitive behavior closer to ovulation because they are trying to attract a high-quality mate and thereby improve the likelihood that they will conceive a child (Gangestad, Thornhill, & Garver, 2002). Women do not necessarily realize they are engaging in this behavior, but it is clear that ovulatory and menstrual cycle patterns impact on daily behavior (Gangestad et al., 2002), including clothing choice, as discussed later in this essay.

The use of cosmetics is only one small part of how women employ synthetic materials to increase their attractiveness. The next sections pertain to specific postcranial attributes, meaning parts of the body below the skull. In addition to cosmetics, women use clothing such as corsets, high heels, and peplums (i.e., attached strips of flared fabrics connected to skirts and blouses) to change their body shape for mate competition.

Waist-to-Hip Ratio and Fat Deposition

Body shape is often used in assessments of female attractiveness (Singh & Singh, 2006). Certain postcranial traits are thought to be indicators of female fecundity (Singh, 1993). Low waist-to-hip ratio (WHR) and increased fat deposition in the breasts and buttocks are the three traits we focus on in this section. Women use and have used clothing throughout history to emphasize or enhance these desired traits.

WHR, as the name implies, is the ratio of a person's waist measurement compared to his or her hip measurement. In women, high WHR (i.e., above .7) has been linked to problems with fertility (Kaye, Folsom, Prineas, Potter, & Gapstur, 1990; Zaadstra et al., 1993) and higher levels of testosterone (Rebuffe-Scrive, Cullberg, Lundberg, Lindstedt, & Björntorp, 1989). Lower WHR has been linked to higher fertility and femininity, and thus it is thought that a lower WHR is linked to women's attractiveness. Indeed, Singh (1993) found that men tend to prefer women with a WHR close to .7—and such an "optimally preferenced" WHR has been shown to be closely linked with effective

reproductive capabilities (see Lassek & Gaulin, 2008, for a detailed treatment of how WHR can be also understood as proxy for neurodevelopmental outcomes).

In support of Singh (1993), Platek and Singh (2010) showed several men photographs of women's bodies in pre- and postcondition after the target women had elective surgical procedures that altered their WHR. The men viewed the pictures in a functional magnetic resonance imaging machine and rated the women's attractiveness. These researchers found that the .7 WHR hourglass shape created from the surgery activates the right orbital frontal cortex, or the reward center of the brain. Additionally, body mass index (weight scaled for height) seemed to not play a large role in the activation of the reward center, providing more support for the unique importance of WHR.

Historically, fashion trends seem to have consistently returned to favoring an hourglass shape (Steele, 2001). Clothing has been used to emphasize the hourglass or create the illusion of an hourglass by color blocking or finding the balance of clothing to offset a body shape that is not naturally shaped like an hourglass. For example, a woman who has a narrow upper body and wide hips (commonly referred to as "pear shaped") can create the illusion of an hourglass figure by adding more volume to the shoulders. This styling would make the top portion of her body seem more proportional to her bottom half.

Specific pieces of clothing have been used to physically modify the body to create an hourglass figure. For example, the corset was a major staple in women's wardrobes for nearly 400 years (Steele, 2001) and played a large role in a woman's physical beauty and social status. In the next section, we argue that the corset may have been used for self-promotion and competitor derogation and thus for intrasexual competition.

The first corsets appeared during the late Renaissance and fell out of favor during the 1920s. Though there are a few precursors to the corset, the origins of the actual corset, designed to narrow the waist, dates to about the mid-16th century (Steele, 2001). The design of the corset flattens the stomach and cinches in the waist, thereby straightening the spine and pushing up the breasts. In conjunction with panniers (i.e., box-like contraptions made of fabric and wire that attached to the hips in order to fill out skirts), hoop skirts, and bustles (i.e., similar to panniers except there is added fabric to the rear instead of the hips, making it look larger and more full), the corset creates a hyper-hourglass figure with exaggerated breasts and hips.

The process of corseting (i.e., wearing a corset) began during infancy in order to prevent skeletal defects and to "procure an agreeable waist and a well-positioned bust" (Mme de Sévigné, cited in Steele, 2001, p. 12). The majority of small-scale corset manufacturers were female staymakers and corsetieres; they marketed their corsets as "natural" and an aid to "help Nature 'correct' defects" (Steele, 2001, p. 42). Like the use of cosmetics, the corset could redefine a woman's natural shape into a more attractive figure. By mimicking the hourglass figure, universally preferred by men (Singh, Dixion, Jessop, Morgan, & Dixson 2010), women likely increased their desirability to the opposite sex.

In conjunction with clever marketing, older female matriarchs, such as mothers and grandmothers, enforced the wearing of the corset in order to "maximize both their [daughters'] physical 'beauty' and their reputation for propriety" so that their daughters and granddaughters could attract a potential suitor for marriage (Steele, 2001, p. 51). In this case, the intrasexual competitive tactic of self-promotion was extended to a woman's daughter or granddaughter by her mother or grandmother. In a sense, the grandmothers or mothers were attempting to facilitate their own reproductive success (via indirect fitness) by helping their offspring and grand-offspring become more attractive to the opposite sex. That is, by helping their daughter or granddaughter be more desirable as a mate, they were increasing the likelihood that their own genes would be furthered (as advancing reproductive success of kin has the evolutionarily beneficial effect of advancing the reproductive success of the individual).

Corseting also supported the courtly practices of self-discipline and grace by controlling the body and correcting poor posture. Moreover, the corset was linked to women's sexuality. During the 18th century, English women were observed to wear little cosmetics but were "always laced" (Madame du Bocage, cited in Steele, 2001, p. 26), and popular literature described prostitutes as women who were unlaced (Steele, 2001). Slender waists also denoted status, as images of working-class women were often depicted with fuller waists than women of the bourgeoisie, even though the less expensive corsets that the working class could afford provided them with the same silhouette as the bourgeois women in real life (Steele, 2001).

Historically, a woman's reputation was incredibly important for her future marriage prospects (e.g., read any novel authored by Jane Austen to understand the intricacies of scandal and rumor-spreading among Regency women). Insinuating that a woman was "unlaced" (and therefore promiscuous or, perhaps, from a lower social class) could have potentially been a way for women to derogate their competitors and remove them from the mating game because virginity and family pedigree were so prized. Additionally, if a woman was rumored to not be a virgin, before marriage her reputation in mating contexts would be tainted. This outcome could have potentially removed several women from attracting mates, as any sisters of that woman labeled as promiscuous might suffer reputational effects by proxy, such as being labeled as *promiscuous by proxy* (Cominos & Vicinus, 1972).

A common misconception about corsetry is that many women practiced "tight-lacing" or the act of reducing the waist size far below its natural state. Stories supposedly written by women and published in *The English Woman's Domestic Magazine* reported women wearing corsets around 16 or 16.5 inches in diameter. However, Steele (2001) argues that these letters to the magazine read more like *Penthouse's* erotic letters to the editor and that the act of tight-lacing was relatively rare in the real world. Hyper-tight-lacing, which is essentially overtightening the corset to create a more wasp-like waist, had its own adverse consequences, as women who engaged in such behavior may have been perceived as focusing too much on fashion and their appearance. Male cartoonists satirized the process of tight-lacing by showing a vain and unattractive woman being laced by overwhelmed and flustered servants (Steele, 2001). Though tight-lacing may not have been common, the perception that tight-lacing was acceptable, and even attractive, was spread by other women (or men posing as female authors who fetishized the practice; Steele, 2001). Purporting the myth of tight-lacing could have been a form of competitor manipulation (a kind of mating tactic designed to reduce the mating-related outcomes for a competitor in some way) because it may have convinced potential rivals to look less attractive than their peers.

In modern life, research indicates that women consistently overestimate men's desire for underweight women (Rozin & Fallon, 1988). Rozin and Fallon found that mothers and daughters thought that men of their generation preferred thinner women than the men actually did prefer. Therefore, extending this finding to tight-lacing, if women could convince other women to engage in tight-lacing and to believe that it was considered attractive by men, competition would be reduced—such a strategy could be part of a subtle competitor manipulation approach. Tight-lacing was a practice frowned upon by potential mates, and hence it would possibly decrease the tight-lacer's mating opportunities while increasing the normal-lacer's mating prospects.

Though the use of corsets has been phased out of most current fashion, its descendants, the girdle (from the early 20th century) and SPANX™ as well as waist cinchers (from the late 20th century), are used to smooth out the body's imperfections. While girdles and SPANX™ products are not as ridged as corsets, they attempt to mold the body to a shape that is closer to an hourglass figure than it would be without these figure-enhancing garments. Thus, they allow women to essentially fake their reproductive value by molding their bodies into a shape that approximates a .7 WHR. Girdles, along with high heels (discussed later) and strategic cosmetics, may allow a woman to increase her sexual appeal and overall attractiveness.

Leg Length and Gait

Leg length also seems to be an indicator of general health, environmental background, and potential reproductive value (Lawlor, Smith, & Ebrahim, 2003). Extremely long legs or extremely short legs might be indicative of poor genetic quality or a history of disease, as conspicuous deviations from a physical norm often are unconsciously processed as such (see review in Sorokowskia & Palwloski, 2008).

This preference for leg length has been demonstrated in Sorokowskia and Palwloski's (2008) leg-length study. They had men and women rate the attractiveness of male and female silhouettes that varied in leg length and found that slightly longer than average legs were preferred for both sexes by all participants. Sorokowskia and Pawloski suggest that the reason for this preference may be because slightly longer legs might have had an adaptive advantage in running and good nutrition, and, for women specifically, leg length is indicative of a healthy offspring birth weight. Similar results for the preference for slightly longer legs have been found cross-culturally, which further indicates that leg-to-body ratio plays a significant role in perceived attractiveness for both men and women (Sorokowskia et al., 2011).

Based on these results, men should find women in high heels more attractive than women in flat shoes, as long as the perceived leg length is not extremely longer than the average leg length. In high heels, the posture of one's body is shifted forward, placing the pressure on the toes, shortening the hamstrings, and arching the lower back upwards and outwards (Eisenhardt, Cook, Preglerc, & Foehla, 1996; Speksnijdera, Munckhofa, Moonenb, & Walenkampa, 2005). This posture is attractive as it places an emphasis on the chest and buttocks (Cox, 2004; Semmelhack, 2006). It also gives the illusion of lengthening the leg, decreasing the size of the foot, and slimming the ankle, and creates a feminine gait that is characterized by small steps (Smith, 1999).

In support of a high-heeled gait being more attractive, Morris, White, Morrison, and Fisher (2013) found the gait of women in high heels (compared to those in flat shoes) was considered relatively attractive as rated by both men and women. The gait of women in high heels showed shorter strides, more pelvic rotation, and more knee flexion than those wearing flats. In addition, in a series of studies, Guéguen (2015) found that men's helping behavior toward women increased as the height of the woman's heels increased.

Though high heels increase attractiveness by lengthening the leg and feminizing one's gait, they also pose many health risks. These include balance (Gerber et al., 2012; Kim, Yi, Yoo, & Choi, 2011), hallux valgus (i.e., a foot deformity affecting the big toe; Menz & Morris, 2005), and pain in the legs and back (Lee, Jeong, & Freivalds, 2001). However, the price of the pain may be evolutionarily offset by increases in mating opportunities. That is, the minor cost of some pain that results from these shoes may be less than the benefits associated with being perceived as more attractive in mating contexts.

Evolution's Influence on the Maintenance of Fashion Trends

Evolutionary themes play a large role in the maintenance, persistence, and disappearance of fashion trends. Judging from the continuous popularity of these fashions in their various forms, fashions that go against evolutionary indicators of fitness, such as women's shoulder pads of the 1980s and 1990s, occur only sporadically and disappear quickly from women's fashion (Morris et al., 2013). The devolving popularity of shoulder pads in women's wear may stem from the fact that they gave women a more masculine physique by creating the illusion of a wider shoulder and a narrower hip (Morris, 1999). This body shape has been associated with dominance and masculinity, which would likely not attract a potential mate for women (Morris, 1999).

Of course, there are a multitude of factors that can explain why certain trends that emphasize beauty evolutionarily, like panniers or bustle skirts, disappeared. For one, such items may have grown to the point where they were completely impractical to wear because the environment changed and could not accommodate the size of the skirt (imagine trying to catch a subway train wearing a hoop skirt spanning six feet wide). Also, values concerning women's rights and sexuality drastically changed. For example, women's sexual liberation of the 1960s and the women's equality movement of the early 20th century caused a reaction against rigidity and the conservative nature of the partly Victorian-inspired fashion of the 1950s (Steele, 2001). However, fashions that emphasize the breasts, buttocks, waist, legs, and other parts of the female body that represent fertility still exist in a less extreme form.

Take, for example, the peplum, a short, flared layer of fabric at the top of a slim-fitted skirt or the bottom of a shirt, which has gained popularity in fashion on and off since the 1930s. Peplums add extra emphasis to the hips, and while the exaggeration is not as extreme as what a pannier would cause, there is still an illusion that the hips are wider than reality. In general, therefore, we argue that the popularity of emphasizing the hips, fitted bodices, and high heels would likely not have lasted as long if there was not an evolutionary undercurrent to fashion preferences. Based on the ability of clothing to enhance desirable traits, as described earlier, it seems that there is an evolutionary undercurrent that helps specific fashion trends endure or recur throughout history.

Fashion across the Ovulatory Cycle
Changes in Clothing Preferences

Women's fashion choices vary according to individual preference. Despite these differences, there are several trends in the types of clothing women prefer or wear depending on their ovulatory cycle status. Over the course of human evolution, human females lost the ability to conspicuously display estrus (i.e., genital swelling that occurs in the females of some species that signals sexual receptivity and fertility; Park, 2011), as compared to the flamboyant displays of other primates. For example, the genital region of female bonobos swells and emits pheromones to attract male bonobos for mating purposes (Paoli,

Palagi, Tacconi, & Tarli, 2006). However, that does not mean women lack visual cues to display where they are in their ovulatory cycle. During their most fertile phase, women go through a number of physical changes such as an increase in facial attractiveness (Roberts et al., 2004), emitting a more attractive scent (Singh & Bronstad, 2001), improved breast symmetry and symmetry of other soft tissue parts (Scutt & Manning, 1996), and an increase in vocal attractiveness (Pipitone & Gallup, 2008). Also, when flirting during this time, blushing is more easily seen (Keltner & Buswell, 1997) due to lightening of the skin (Van den Berghe & Frost, 1986). Furthermore, women exhibit behavioral changes across the ovulatory cycle. During the most fertile phase, women are able to better detect men's facial symmetry (Oinonen & Mazmanian, 2007), have a higher preference for more masculine and symmetrical faces (Little et al., 2007), have a stronger preference for cad-type characteristics in potential mates (Aitken, Lyons, & Jonason, 2013), and are even more likely to think about cheating on their current partner (Pillsworth, Haselton, & Buss, 2004).

These physical and behavioral changes imply that a woman at peak fertility is signaling to potential mates that she is healthy and ready to copulate. In general, women (compared to men) seem to prefer long-term relationships and place more emphasis on their potential partner's resources instead of his attractiveness (Buss & Schmitt, 1993). Parental investment theory suggests that women look for these long-term traits in men because they spend more energy caring for their offspring than men do. Women invest more energy in their children and are far more limited in the number of children they may have, and, consequently, they tend to be more selective when choosing a mate (Trivers, 1972). However, women's desired traits in a mate depend on type of relationship they are seeking. For instance, Kenrick, Sadalla, Groth, and Trost (1990) found that women rated good looks as being more important for a sexual relationship than for dating, steady dating, and marriage. They argue that this preference is due to women seeking men with high genetic quality, which physical attractiveness is thought to serve as an indicator of under ancestral conditions. Further, during peak fertility, women's sexual preferences tend to change, and they become more interested in a short-term sexual relationship (Aitken, Lyons, & Jonason, 2013). In a short-term mating context as well, women still place an emphasis on physical attractiveness over access to resources in terms of which trait is more important (Gangestad, Garver-Apgar, Simpson, & Cousins, 2007).

A woman's physical changes due to menstrual phase may not be obvious to men largely because the fluctuations are covered by clothing. Thus, we argue that clothing must play an important role in signaling female fertility, because it covers up many of the physical changes that occur at peak fertility. On this point, Haselton, Mortezaie, Pillsworth, Bleske-Rechek, and Frederick (2007) showed that photographs of women in their fertile phase were rated as trying to look more attractive by both men and women than when they were in the infertile phase of their cycle. These photographs were also rated by three female graduate assistants for how fashionable, nice, and sexy the clothing was; level of exposed skin; and whether the woman wore a skirt, accessories, or lacy top. The photographs of women in the high-fertility phase scored higher in all categories except sexiness, which may be due to the women wearing daytime attire appropriate for their environment when photographed (i.e., a classroom). The higher frequency of lacy tops during the fertile phase replicates Grammer, Renninger, and Fischer's (2005) finding that women with a higher motivation for sex wear more see-through or skin-revealing clothing.

In a related study by Durante, Li, and Haselton (2008), women were asked to come twice to the laboratory (i.e., when most and least fertile) to complete a series of scales. They were also asked to draw outfits on a female silhouette showing what they might wear at each time. The findings revealed that during the high-conception phase, women scored as being more promiscuous on several psychological measures. Further, their drawings revealed that the outfits they would wear were much more revealing in a literal sense, as they included less in the way of material.

In general, what these studies about women's dressing habits imply is that women use clothing as part of a mating strategy. Women seem to select revealing clothing in order to attract mates for sexual activity (Grammer et al., 2005). Moreover, according to the findings of Durante et al. (2008), during a highly fertile menstrual phase, women, specifically those not in romantic relationships, actively seek short-term relationships, perhaps to extract high-quality genes from a mate, given that there will be no other contribution (i.e., no parental investment from the male).

Lady in Red: Evolutionary Explanations of Color Preferences in Women's Fashion

One aspect not covered by the previously mentioned studies is the importance of color. Color, within a mating context, may signal information that could be highly important to intrasexual competition and for gaining access to mates. For example, in nature, red is linked to several different phenomena. Some animals, like the *Melanophryniscus montevidensis* (a toad from Uruguay), are red and poisonous (Mebs, Pogoda, Maneyro, & Kwet, 2005). Their brightly colored bellies are used to warn predators that they are poisonous (Lord, 2012). Aside from signaling danger, however, red is also an indicator of fertility in many species. When many nonhuman primates enter estrus, genital swelling occurs, and the genitals redden. Thus, it is hypothesized that humans have evolved to recognize red as an indicator of fertility. The color red, as the following studies demonstrate, has a unique effect on the way men perceive women. This use of red is highly consistent across primates, and it relates to the fact that red is a color that follows from genital and facial pigmentation morphology across various primate species—with much interindividual variability (Higham, MacLarnon, Ross, Heistermann, & Semple, 2008).

Research results indicate that women's color preferences for clothing change over the course of the menstrual cycle, similar to the discussed changes in the level of grooming, accessorizing, and amount of skin revealed. In one online study, women were asked what color shirt they were wearing and how many days since their last menses (Beall & Tracey, 2013). Their responses helped to classify them into either a high- or low-fertility menstrual phase. It was found that women in the high-fertility phase were more likely to be wearing red or pink than other colors. The authors conclude that wearing red or pink clothing is a potential indicator of ovulation (i.e., maximal fertility and the highest probability of conception), which supports the theory that although women have relatively concealed estrus, they have found other ways to signal their fertility to potential partners.

Similarly, women also wear red to express sexual desirability. Elliot and Pazda (2012) examined the relationship between clothing color choice and interest in casual sexual relationships. They found, across a series of three studies, women who expressed interest in casual sex were more likely to wear red than those who expressed interest in long-term relationships (Elliot & Pazda, 2012). Clearly, the color red, as opposed to other colors, signifies to potential partners a willingness to engage in casual sex.

The color red has cross-culturally been associated with love, desire, lust, and jealousy (Aslam, 2006). It may have these associations because of red's indication of fertility in other species. For example, the genital region of female chimpanzees swells and reddens when they are in estrus (Goodall, 1986). This external indication of fertility means males can easily track a female's cycle and mate with her at the appropriate time to maximize their reproductive potential (Goodall, 1986). In humans, there appears to be a carryover effect, whereby simply seeing red, even just in the background, seems to enhance female attractiveness (Elliot & Niesta, 2008). Elliot and Niesta found that men, but not women, rated women's photographs as more attractive if they were presented on a red as opposed to a white background. They also explored whether red was more associated with attraction versus personality traits like kindness or intelligence. They found women surrounded by a red background, as opposed to a gray or green background, were rated as more attractive and sexually desirable and were perceived as being more likely to engage in sexual behavior. In addition, they found that men rated a woman wearing a red shirt as more attractive than a woman wearing a blue shirt, and they were more likely to ask her on a date and spend money on that date.

This last point about spending more money when on a date with women in red clothing has also been evidenced by Guéguen and Jacob (2014), who measured the number and worth of financial tips received by female waitresses wearing different-colored clothing. They found that women who wore red received more tips from men, and received more money overall, compared to waitresses wearing other colors. There was no significant change in the amount left to the waitresses by women. Similarly, lap dancers who were in a highly fertile phase (e.g., ovulating) received more tips of a higher amount than those who were in their nonfertile phase and substantially more than those who were menstruating (Miller, Tybur, & Jordan, 2007). Interestingly, this phase effect was not documented for those using hormonal contraceptives (which is relevant as such technologies force a woman's body to mimic a pregnant state).

Although the results of these studies indicate that men exhibit behavioral changes when looking at women in red clothing, they have been obtained only in Western cultures. Color meanings vary cross-culturally, which suggests that if the effect of red is culturally based, the effects would be contrary or less noticeable in other cultures that do not associate red with love or sexuality. However, a study by Elliot, Tracy, Pazda, and Beall (2013) obtained clear cross-cultural evidence for the effects of red. Men from Burkina Faso, which is culturally conservative in terms of sexuality, and which happens to hold red in a negative light culturally, black-and-white photographs of women framed by a red or blue border. Men who viewed the red-bordered photographs rated the women as more attractive and were more likely to want to meet and date them compared with those in the blue-border condition. However, color did not alter ratings of men's desire to have sex with the woman or men's perceptions of her sexual interest. The authors explain that though the red effect is present, it is only relevant for "culturally appropriate expressions of attraction" (Elliot et al., 2013, p. 167). This finding supports the previous studies that the color red, whether in clothing or in some other kind of display, is interpreted by men as a signal of sexuality or fertility.

Based on the aforementioned studies, it is clear that women signal their fertility through clothing style and color choices and that men are the receivers of this information. The perfect item of clothing to attract a short-term mate is a short, tight, and revealing red dress (or shirt and shorts), as it would provide a woman with the opportunity to display many indicators of fertility, including changes in body shape and changes in skin color (which would make signals of flirtation more apparent); it would also help her express potential openness to sexual experience and possibly enhance her overall physical attractiveness. Wearing such an outfit could theoretically increase one's chances of accessing a high-quality mate in comparison to other women who are not dressed to signal ovulation or sexual interest. However, we do not always see women wearing such an outfit at peak fertility, as there are many other factors that influence the way women dress.

The Importance of Being Fashionable

As discussed by others in this volume (see, e.g., Nikiforidis, Arsena, & Durante, this volume), fashion has a clear and significant role in female relationship psychology. On the surface, keeping up with the latest fashion trends can seem like an impossible or even an unimportant way to expend energy, especially when fashion styles change constantly and people have their own unique tastes. However, participating in the latest trends, or at least wearing classic styles, may be somewhat necessary in order to avoid competitor derogation or female–female bullying. As Salmon (this volume) discusses in her essay, young women associate being fashionable with high status, dominance, and attractiveness.

In Veblen's (2003) *Theory of the Leisure Class*, fashion is viewed as an example of conspicuous consumption, where one flaunts one's wealth through buying certain products and thus acquiring status (Bagwell & Bernheim, 1996). However, status is only achieved through the judgments of others (Chai, Earl, & Potts, 2007). Veblen also discusses the constant drive to buy newer products to replace the old outdated ones:

> We readily, and for the most part with utter sincerity, find those things pleasing that are in vogue. Shaggy dress stuffs and pronounced color effects, for instance, offend us at times when the vogue is goods of a high, glossy finish and neutral colors. A fancy bonnet of this year's model unquestionably appeals to our sensibilities today much more forcibly than an equally fancy bonnet of the model of last year. (p. 88)

Fashions that are targeted to the upper class usually set the tone for clothing of the lower class. For example, noted luxury fashion designer Diane von Furstenberg sued Forever 21, a popular and inexpensive clothing store in North America, for plagiarizing the dress pattern and fabric print for her $325 "Cerisier" dress (Lo, 2007). Forever 21 sold its version of the dress for $32, which made the luxury style (but not quality) more affordable to a wider group of people. Once some kind of fashion stops being a signal of upper-tier wealth, it becomes psychologically devalued, as it no longer carries the same signaling capacity.

Fashions can be promoted by various types of individuals such as fashion designers, celebrities, and socialites. Some of these styles, such as those derived from celebrities including Audrey Hepburn, Michelle Obama, and Coco Chanel, are likely considered to be classic and long-lasting. Others, like John Travolta's white leisure suit in *Saturday Night Fever* or Nicole "Snooki" Polizzi's (of the reality show, *The Jersey Shore*) hair pouf, could be considered passing fads.

Distinguishing classic fashion from "trendy" fashion is highly subjective. However, it seems that classic fashion consists of neutral colors and simple silhouettes and possesses versatility (meaning that fashionable clothes can be worn with many other types of clothing and accessories). Fads may have louder colors, patterns, and fabrics that become indicative of the year/decade in which they were popular.

Specific fads or fashion trends, such as the paper dresses of the 1960s or white leisure suits of the 1970s, can be arbitrary and do not necessarily have an evolutionary basis, especially since they are culturally based. However, the act of following trends may grant an individual more reproductive access because of the signals they send to other individuals and groups. Trends can be followed or started by an individual at any point across the lifespan, but it seems that the intrinsic need to follow certain fashions begins during childhood and adolescence for both men and women.

Fashion can be used to gain acceptance into a social group and help one remain accepted within that group. This idea was represented in the 2004 hit movie, *Mean Girls*, where new girl. Cady Heron becomes a part of a popular group that sets the latest trends for the rest of the girls in high school. "I saw Cady Heron wearing army pants and flip flops, so I bought army pants and flip-flops," explains a girl, outside of Cady's group, who wishes to increase her popularity (Waters, 2004).

Though the film exaggerates the experiences of girls and women recorded in the parenting book *Queen Bees and Wannabes* (Wiseman, 2009), it accurately reflects the use of fashion as a way to fit into a peer group. The pressure to follow trends in order to fit into a group with higher status continues into young adulthood. In the movie, when Cady is first invited to sit at lunch with the popular girls, they create a detailed list of what clothing is acceptable to wear on specific days; she must follow these guidelines if she wants to sit with them. Thus, when one does not adhere to the standards set by a localized peer group, one may be subjected to exclusion.

In a similar vein, the book *Odd Girl Out* (Simmons, 2002) contains various anecdotal bullying experiences of women in childhood, adolescence, and young adulthood. Fashion is used by the "popular girls" to exclude girls from acceptance within the group. It also makes girls targets for abuse. Simmons relays a warning from a fifth-grade girl explaining how important it is to avoid committing a fashion faux pas. "Everyone's gonna remember that . . . because that's like baby and everything. Everyone will know that came from Kids 'R' Us. Everyone popular will be embarrassed to be her friend because they wear the updated clothes" (Simmons, 2002, p. 212).

Here, the fifth-grader is expressing wearing the wrong clothing as akin to social suicide.

By making unfashionable girls the targets for bullying, the female bullies are able to effectively decrease the self-esteem of rivals who might compete with them for access to mates. Though bullying can occur before girls are of reproductive age, the psychological effects of bullying are long-lasting and can carry into adulthood (Gladstone, Parker, & Malhi, 2006). If girls are able to lower the self-confidence and self-esteem of other girls early on, then they potentially may have fewer future rivals in the competition for mates as they age. Fashion is an easy characteristic to target; it is readily observable and may reflect many aspects of an individual, from his or her personality to the current environment. Thus, fashion provides a direct and simple way for female aggressors to alienate other women.

Being part of a group with high status provides several advantages. In nonhuman animals, such as chimpanzees, friends of the dominant male reap benefits such as access to mates and food (for a full review, see Muller & Mitani, 2005). Similarly, female baboons (*Papio cynocephalus*) have greater infant survival when they are part of a dominant female's social group. In humans, popularity and dominance are also linked to access to resources. By dressing fashionably, a woman can potentially fit into the popular crowd and look more attractive than her competitors, which could also put her a step above potential rivals. In effect, popularity may well increase one's pool of potential mates, as popularity is defined as being liked by a large number of others in a social community.

Janney (1941) found that different groups of women at an all-woman college were responsible for various fads (defined as a style lasting less than six months) and fashions (defined as a style that lasts six months or more), which slightly deviated from the general fashions of the time. Women in these groups appeared to have achieved admiration from their peers by excelling at different activities, including design, comedy, and choreography (Janney, 1941). Trends that are set at the local level by high-status individuals within a community might be more important than keeping up with global trends, since the consequences from violating community decorum are more immediate.

Fashion may also play a significant role in mate guarding. In a recent article by Wang and Griskevicius (2014), data suggested that women's attraction to designer clothing may be related to mate-retention tactics. After conducting a series of studies that had

women read several types of mate-guarding and non-mate-guarding scenarios, the researchers found that (a) women perceived women in designer clothing as having a more committed partner, especially if it was indicated that the man paid for the luxury items; (b) women were more likely to prefer large brand logos when having to engage in hypothetical mate guarding; (c) women were more likely to spend more money on conspicuous luxury products than nonconspicuous luxury products when having to engage in hypothetical mate guarding; (d) women were more likely to invest in designer clothing when their audience would be other women competitors; and (e) women were less likely to pursue men who had paid for luxury items in a hypothetical scenario. The authors concluded that the use of luxury items by women in a relationship can be used as a signal to other rivals to back down when attempting to poach a potential mate.

Virtuous to Vixen: Perceptions of Sexy Clothing

Following trends and being fashionable are not the only important factors when choosing clothing, as clothes also have to be perceived as appropriate for the situation. Wearing a crop top and miniskirt to a business meeting would likely be considered wildly inappropriate because it exposes too much skin for such a formal setting. This feeling of inappropriateness is related to women's perceptions of other women's sexiness and style, as well as the signals sexy clothing may send to males. Sexiness, in previous studies (Durante et al., 2008; Grammer et al., 2005; White, 1995), seems to be defined in terms of how much skin is exposed and the tightness of clothing fit.

Abbey, Cozzarelli, McLaughlin, and Hamish (1987) asked men and women to rate various traits such as sexiness, flirtatiousness, kindness, and sincerity of male and female experimenters in both revealing and nonrevealing clothing. Men, more than women, found more sexual cues in a female experimenter's clothing than a male experimenter's clothing. Also, the female experimenter in revealing clothing was thought to be less kind, intelligent, polite, and sincere by female participants. In this case, females might view the experimenter as a potential competitor for a partner. Males seemed to perceive the revealing nature of clothing as a nonverbal cue of sexual interest even when the female wearer was not consciously trying to send sexual cues (Abbey et al., 1987). This same phenomenon has also been documented by Williamson and

Hewitt (1986, p. 981), who studied perceptions of women wearing sexually provocative casual clothes (e.g., miniskirts, short shorts, shirts revealing the stomach) versus more conservative clothing (e.g., "regular-length" shorts, skirts, and shirts). Women rated the models wearing the more overtly sexual clothing as less attractive than the models wearing the more conservative clothing. Men found the models in sexier clothing to be more attractive (Williamson & Hewitt, 1986).

Many cultures have taboos concerning skin exposure and sexual display, although the degree to which exposed skin equals a sexual display varies across cultures and time. In an ethnographic study by Broude and Greene (1976), the majority of the examined cultures had a custom of wearing clothes that exposed little skin before puberty. This practice instills the belief during childhood that there are parts of the body that should be kept private, potentially because they are seen as sexualized after the body goes through development.

The burqa, a garment that covers the entire body except the eyes, is an example of an article of clothing from a non-Western culture that is designed specifically to prevent the female body from being sexualized. In instances where clothing, like the burqa, is the norm, most of the bodily cues of fertility cannot be seen. However, intrasexual competition through the use of fashion can still exist. The burqa promotes and protects modesty and thus may be a form of self-promotion (or self-promotion by way of pressure from relatives). Women who wear the burqa will be granted access to quality mates or other kinds of privileges because they comply with the social-modesty norms, while those who do not are unable to do so. For example, in Afghanistan women face social ostracization and may even be imprisoned for not wearing a burqa (Wing & Nadimi, 2011).

The association of sexy clothing and lack of modesty with promiscuous sexual behavior is also seen in more Westernized societies. Perception of the sexiness of women's clothing has been linked to negative feelings toward victims of rape, such that women in more revealing clothing were thought to be more responsible for their rape (Lewis & Johnson, 1989). Although the effect is more pronounced in men than women, the latter are more likely to attribute some blame to the victim in revealing clothing than nonrevealing clothing (Lewis & Johnson, 1989). However, sometimes women can also be criticized for dressing too conservatively and, in situations where clothing options are unlimited (such as in an office where a standard uniform is not worn), they have to find the socially and culturally acceptable balance between sexy and conservative. As seen in Hill, Nocks, and Gardner (1987), clothing traits, such as tightness and amount of skin revealed, can be used to judge the attractiveness of women for a sexual relationship or marriage. Future research could expand on previous studies to examine how women in different styles of clothing (ranging from most sexy to least sexy) are perceived by both men and women in various romantic contexts (e.g., long-term dating, short-term dating, sexual hookups). It would make sense that women who display a culturally appropriate balance between sexy and conservative attire will be perceived more favorably in terms of their promiscuity, personality, and intelligence than their relatively sexy rivals while also being rated as more physically attractive than their relatively conservative rivals.

This balance between sexy and conservative is a challenging one to attain, particularly for women in the workplace. Though dressing "professionally" can vary between individuals, one can expect that wearing an outfit intended for a night of dancing to a meeting with the CEO of a corporation will be met with a negative reaction. Women have more variety in their clothing options than men (White, 1995); in Western cultures, it is acceptable for women to wear skirts, pants, suits, and shirts, all of varying lengths, colors, and styles. By comparison, men's suit fashion since about the 19th century has experienced limited variability, typically consisting of some type of pant, shirt, jacket, and maybe a vest. Convention in Western society dictates that it is unacceptable for a man to go to work in a dress or skirt, while women, at least since the mid- to late 20th century onward, have been able to wear both pants and skirts acceptably in the workforce. As Glick, Larsen, Johnson, and Branstiter (2005, p. 389) state, "there is no male equivalent of the low-cut blouse or slit skirt." Based on these findings, it seems that fashion is used more by women than by men as a set of tools in the mating domain (Glick et al., 2005).

Glick et al. (2005) examined how a woman's clothing affected the perception of her various attributes. Her hypothetical career was the manipulated variable; she was either in a low-status position (receptionist) or a high-status position (manager). Among other variables, participants rated how positive (e.g., relaxed, fond, supportive) and negative (e.g., shame, disgust, frustration) they felt toward her. They also rated her competency (e.g., ineptitude and efficiency), and they rated her intelligence via estimated GPA scores. The sexy outfit was rated to be less appropriate for both the receptionist (low-status) and manager (high-status) position. Further, the woman in the sexy clothing evoked less positive and more negative assessments and was rated to be less competent and less intelligent than the woman in conservative clothing by both the men and the women participating in the study. These findings suggest that sexy clothing that mismatches the situational context, such as at a business meeting, influences how the wearer is perceived by others. In terms of intrasexual competition, these findings indicate that, perhaps, women who wear inappropriately sexy clothing may experience more competitor derogation that focuses on their past or current sexual behavior.

Conclusion

Clothing has played a major role in our evolutionary history. While clothing may have been originally used for practical purposes, humans have expanded on its original purpose so that it can now communicate personality, status, and group affiliation. Women's fashion has surpassed men's fashion in terms of variety, and there are limitless possibilities for outfit choice. However, evolution has guided what trends remain popular over time, what patterns we see in women's dressing style, and how clothing is perceived by both men and women. Women's clothing design, across history, has been used to exaggerate the female shape to show hyper-fecundity as evidenced by the corset, high heels, and bustle skirts. These items modify the natural female form to have an exaggerated WHR and longer legs, which are thought to be signs of fertility (Singh, 1993, 1995; Sorokowskia & Pawlowski, 2008).

Women use clothing for the purposes of intrasexual competition via self-promotion and competitor manipulation. Women recognize these cues in other women and can consciously or unconsciously use fashion as a way to compete with each other for access to mates. Additionally, men are apt to respond to how women use clothing to communicate their fecundity, personality, and sexual preferences (Guéguen, 2008, 2012, 2015).

While the studies discussed here provide an interesting look into how fashion is used for intrasexual competition, there are several limitations. First, all of these studies used cis-gendered women who identified as heterosexual. Such methodology excludes a large portion of women or non-gender-conforming individuals who wear women's fashion. We need to

study these populations as they could also provide further insight into the interaction between fashion and gender, broadly conceptualized. Second, many of the studies focused on Western/European populations. More cross-cultural studies in areas where people wear more traditional clothing are needed to see if the same effects are found in a more global context. Expanding the studied populations could benefit our understanding of the fashion/evolution interface.

There is also a need for more studies that observe fashion in real-life contexts. Guéguen's field studies are an excellent start, but we could also examine how clothing preferences change over the course of a relationship and how that relates to intrasexual competition. For example, women may wear more revealing clothing on a first date or when courting because they are trying to showcase their physical attractiveness and potential sexuality. More research into how dress relates to evolved mechanisms of mate retention and intrasexual competition need to be done in order to understand how humans use elements of fashion to manipulate their social environments for fitness-related benefits. At the end of the day, humans use many technologies in the extended-phenotype sense—utilizing products from their environments in evolutionarily relevant ways. In our species, given the universal attention that it attracts, the use of fashion to accentuate social and mating-relevant outcomes may well be conceptualized as *extended phenotype sine qua non*.

References

Abbey, A., Cozzarelli, C., McLaughlin, K., & Hamish, R. (1987). The effects of clothing and dyad sex composition on perceptions of sexual intent: Do women and men evaluate these cues differently? *Journal of Applied Social Psychology*, *17*(2), 108–126.

Aitken, S. J., Lyons, M., & Jonason, P. K. (2013). Dads or cads? Women's strategic decisions in the mating game. *Personality and Individual Differences*, *55*(2), 118–122.

Aslam, M. M. (2006). Are you selling the right colour? A cross-cultural review of colour as a marketing cue. *Journal of Marketing Communications*, *12*, 15–30.

Bagwell, L. S., & Bernheim, B. D. (1996). Veblen effects in a theory of conspicuous consumption. *American Economic Review*, *86*(3), 349–373.

Beall, A. T., & Tracy, J. L. (2013). Women are more likely to wear red or pink at peak fertility. *Psychological Science*, *24*, 1837–1841.

Broude, G. J., & Greene, S. J. (1976). Cross-cultural codes on twenty sexual attitudes and practices. *Ethnology*, *15*(4), 409–429.

Buss, D. M. (1988). The evolution of human intrasexual competition: Tactics of mate attraction. *Journal of Personality and Social Psychology*, *54*(4), 616–628.

Buss, D. M. (2003). *The evolution of desire: Strategies of human mating.* New York: Basic Books.

Buss, D. M., & Dedden, L. A. (1990). Derogation of competitors. *Journal of Social and Personal Relationships, 7,* 395–422.

Buss, D. M., & Schmitt, D. P. (1993). Sexual strategies theory: An evolutionary perspective on human mating. *Psychological Review, 100*(2), 204–232.

Campbell, A. (1999). Staying alive: Evolution, culture, and women's intrasexual aggression. *Behavioral and Brain Sciences, 22*(2), 203-214.

Carmen, R. A., Guitar, A. E., & Dillon, H. M. (2012). Ultimate answers to proximate questions: The evolutionary motivations behind tattoos and body piercings in popular culture. *Review of General Psychology, 16*(2), 134–143.

Chai, A., Earl, P. E., & Potts, J. (2007). Fashion, growth and welfare: An evolutionary approach. In M. Bianchi (Ed.), *The evolution of consumption: Theories and practices advances in Austrian economics* (Vol. 10, pp. 187–207). Bingley, England: Emerald Group.

Cominos, P. T., & Vicinus, M. (1972). *Suffer and be still: Women in the Victorian age.* Bloomington: Indiana University Press

Cox, A., & Fisher, M. (2008). A framework for exploring intrasexual competition. *Journal of Social, Evolutionary, and Cultural Psychology, 2*(4), 144–155.

Cox, C. (2004). *Stiletto.* New York: Harper Collins.

Draelos, Z. D. (2000). Colored facial cosmetics. *Dermatologic Clinics, 18*(4), 621–631.

Durante, K. M., Li, N. P., & Haselton, M. G. (2008). Changes in women's choice of dress across the ovulatory cycle: Naturalistic and laboratory task-based evidence. *Personality and Social Psychology Bulletin, 34,* 1451–1456.

Eisenhardt, J. R., Cook, D., Preglerc, I., & Foehla, H. C. (1996). Changes in temporal gait characteristics and pressure distribution for bare feet versus various heel heights. *Gait & Posture, 4*(4), 280–286.

Elliot, A. J., & Niesta, D. (2008). Romantic red: Red enhances men's attraction to women. *Journal of Personality and Social Psychology, 95*(5), 1150–1164.

Elliot, A. J., & Pazda, A. D. (2012). Dressed for sex: Red as a female sexual signal in humans. *PLoS ONE, 7*(4), e34607. doi:10.1371/journal.pone.0034607

Elliot, A. J., Tracy, J. L., Pazda, A. D., & Beall, A. T. (2013). Red enhances women's attractiveness to men: First evidence suggesting universality. *Journal of Experimental Social Psychology, 49*(1), 165–168.

Feinberg, R. A., Mataro, L., & Burroughs W. J. (1992). Clothing and social identity. *Clothing and Textiles Research Journal, 11*(1), 18–23.

Fink, B., Grammer, K., & Matts, P. J. (2006). Visible skin color distribution plays a role in the perception of age, attractiveness, and health in female faces. *Evolution and Human Behavior, 27*(6), 433–442.

Fink, B., Neave, N., Manning, J. T., & Grammer, K. (2006). Facial symmetry and judgements of attractiveness, health and personality. *Personality and Individual Differences, 41*(3), 491–499.

Fisher, M., Cox, A., & Gordon, F. (2009). Self-promotion versus competitor derogation: The influence of sex and romantic relationship status on intrasexual competition strategy selection. *Journal of Evolutionary Psychology, 7*(4), 287–308.

Gangestad, S. W., Garver-Apgar, C. E., Simpson, J. C., & Cousins, A. J. (2007). Changes in women's mate preferences across the ovulatory cycle. *Journal of Personality and Social Psychology, 92*(1), 151–163.

Gangestad, S. W., Thornhill, R., & Garver, C. E. (2002). Changes in women's sexual interests and their partners' mate-retention tactics across the menstrual cycle: Evidence for shifting conflicts of interest. *Proceedings of the Royal Society B, 269,* 975–982.

Geher, G., & Kaufman, S. B. (2013). *Mating intelligence unleashed: The role of the mind in sex, dating, and love.* New York: Oxford University Press.

Gerber, S. B., Costa, R. V., Grecco, L. A. C., Pasini, H., Correal, J. F. C., Lucareli, P. R. G., ... Oliveria, C. S. (2012), Interference of high-heel shoes in static balance among young women. *Gait & Posture, 36,* 1247–1252.

Gilligan, I. (2007). Neanderthal extinction and modern human behavior: The roles of climate change and clothing. *World Archaeology, 39,* 499–514.

Gilligan, I. (2010). The prehistoric development of clothing: Archaeological implications of a thermal model. *Journal of Archaeological Method and Theory, 17,* 15–80.

Gladstone, G. L., Parker, G. B., & Malhi, G. S. (2006). Do bullied children become anxious and depressed adults? A cross-sectional investigation of the correlates of bullying and anxious depression. *Journal of Nervous and Mental Disease, 194*(3), 201–208.

Glick, P., Larsen, S., Johnson, C., & Branstiter, H. (2005). Evaluations of sexy women in low- and high-status jobs. *Psychology of Women Quarterly, 29,* 389–395.

Goodall, J. (1986). *The chimpanzees of Gombe.* Cambridge, MA: Belknap Press.

Greening, T. (2014, July 30). 28 Before and afters that show the transformative power of makeup. Retrieved from https://www.buzzfeed.com/awesomer/makeup-before-and-afters?utm_term=.obE7YmYLQy#.au6qYZYV2o

Grammer, K., Renninger, L., & Fischer, B. (2005). Disco clothing, female sexual motivation, and relationship status: Is she dressed to impress? *Journal of Sex Research, 41,* 64–71.

Guéguen, N. (2008). Brief report: The effects of women's cosmetics on men's approach: An evaluation in a bar. *North American Journal of Psychology, 10*(1), 221–228.

Guéguen, N. (2012). Cosmetics and menstrual cycle: Near ovulation, women use more cosmetics. *Psychological Record, 62*(3), 541–548.

Guéguen, N. (2015). High heels increase women's attractiveness. *Archives of Sexual Behavior, 44,* 2227–2235.

Guéguen N., & Jacob, C. (2014). Clothing color and tipping: Gentlemen patrons give more tips to waitresses with red clothes. *Journal of Hospitality & Tourism Research, 38*(2), 275–280.

Haselton, M. G., Mortezaie, M., Pillsworth, E. G., Bleske-Rechek, A., & Frederick, D. A. (2007). Ovulatory shifts in human female ornamentation: Near ovulation, women dress to impress. *Hormones and Behavior, 51,* 40–45.

Higham, J. P., MacLarnon, A. M., Ross, C., Heistermann, M., & Semple, S. (2008). Baboon sexual swellings: Information content of size and color. *Hormones and Behavior, 53,* 452–462.

Hill, E. M., Nocks, E. S., & Gardner, C. (1987). Physical attractiveness: Manipulation by physique and status displays. *Ethology and Sociobiology, 8,* 143–154.

Howlett, N., Pine, K. J., Cahill, N., Orakçıoğlu, İ., & Fletcher, B. C. (2015). Unbuttoned: The interaction between provocativeness of female work attire and occupational status. *Sex Roles, 72*(3–4), 105–116.

Howlett, N., Pine, K., Orakçioğlu, I., & Fletcher, B. (2013). The influence of clothing on first impressions: Rapid and positive responses to minor changes in male attire. *Journal of Fashion Marketing and Management, 17*(1), 38–48.

Janney, J. E. (1941). Fad and fashion leadership among undergraduate women. *Journal of Abnormal and Social Psychology, 36*(2), 275–278.

Lassek, W. D., & Gaulin, S. J. (2008). Waist-hip ratio and cognitive ability: Is gluteofemoral fat a privileged store of neurodevelopmental resources? *Evolution and Human Behavior, 29*(1), 26-34.

Johnson, K. K. P., Schofield, N. A., & Yurchisin, J. (2002). Appearance and dress as a source of information: A qualitative approach to data collection. *Clothing and Textiles Research Journal, 20*(3), 125–137.

Kaye, S. A., Folsom, A. R., Prineas, R. J., Potter, J. D., & Gapstur, S. M. (1990). The association of body fat distribution with lifestyle and reproductive factors in a population study of postmenopausal women. *International Journal of Obesity, 14*(7), 583-591.

Keltner, D., & Buswell, B. (1997). Embarrassment: Its distinct form and appeasement functions. *Psychological Bulletin, 122,* 250–270.

Kenrick, D. T., Sadalla, E. K., Groth, G., & Trost, M. R. (1990). Evolution, traits, and the stages of human courtship: Qualifying the parental investment model. *Journal of Personality, 58,* 97–116.

Kim, M. H., Chung, H. Y., Yoo, W. G., & Choi, B. R. (2011). EMG and kinematics analysis of the trunk and lower extremity during the sit-to-stand task while wearing shoes with different heel heights in healthy young women. *Human Movement Science, 30*(3), 596–605.

Koziel, S., Kretschmer, W., & Pawlowski, B. (2010). Tattoo and piercings as signals of biological quality. *Evolution and Human Behavior, 31,* 187–192.

Lawlor, D. A., Smith, G. D., & Ebrahim, S. (2003). Association between leg length and offspring birth weight: Partial explanation for the trans-generational association between birth weight and cardiovascular disease: Findings from the British women's heart and health study. *Pediatric and Perinatal Epidemiology, 17,* 148–155.

Lee, C., Jeong, E., & Freivalds, A. (2001). Biomechanical effects of wearing high-heeled shoes. *International Journal of Industrial Ergonomics, 28*(6), 321–326.

Lewis, L., & Johnson, K. (1989). Effect of dress, cosmetics, sex of subject, and causal inference on attribution of victim responsibility. *Clothing and Textiles Research Journal, 8*(1), 22–27.

Liggett, A. C., Harvey, I. F., & Manning, J. T. (1993). Fluctuating asymmetry in *Scatophaga stercoraria* L.: successful males are more symmetrical. *Animal Behaviour, 45*(5), 1041–1043.

Little, A. C., Jones, B. C., Burt, M. B., & Perrett, D. I., (2007). Preferences or symmetry in faces change across the menstrual cycle. *Biological Psychology, 76,* 209–216.

Lo, D. (2007, March 29). Designer sues. *The New York Post.*

Lord, R. (2012). Reptiles and amphibians. *The Science Teacher, 79*(5), 81.

Matts, P. J., Fink, B., Grammer, K., & Burquest, M. (2007). Color homogeneity and visual perception of age, health, and attractiveness of female facial skin. *Journal of the American Academy of Dermatology, 57*(6), 977–984.

Mebs, D., Pogoda, W., Maneyro, R., & Kwet, A. (2005). Studies on the poisonous skin secretion of individual red bellied toads, *Melanophryniscus montevidensis (Anura, Bufonidae),* from Uruguay. *Toxicon, 46*(6), 641–650.

Menz, H. B., & Morris, M. E. (2005). Footwear characteristics and foot problems in older people. *Gerontology, 51*(5), 346–351.

Miller, G., Tybur, J. M., & Jordan, B. D. (2007). Ovulatory cycle effects on tip earnings by lap dancers economic evidence for human estrus? *Evolution and Human Behavior, 28,* 375–381.

Møller, A. P., & Swaddle, J. P. (1997). *Asymmetry, developmental stability, and evolution.* New York: Oxford University Press.

Morris, D. (1999). *The naked ape: A zoologist's study of the human animal.* New York: Random House.

Morris, P. H., White, J., Morrison, E. R., & Fisher, K. (2013). High heels as supernormal stimuli: How wearing high heels affects judgments of female attractiveness. *Evolution and Human Behavior, 34*(3), 176–181.

Mulhern, R., Fieldman, G., Hussey, T., Lévêque, J. L., & Pineau, P. (2003). Do cosmetics enhance female Caucasian facial attractiveness?. *International Journal of Cosmetic Science, 25*(4), 199-205.

Muller, M. N., & Mitani, J. C. (2005). Conflict and cooperation in wild chimpanzees. *Advances in the Study of Behavior, 35,* 275–331.

Oinonen, K. A., & Mazmanian, D. (2007). Facial symmetry detection ability changes across the menstrual cycle. *Biological Psychology, 75*(2), 136–145.

Park, M. A. (2011). *Introducing anthropology: An integrated approach.* New York: McGraw-Hill.

Paoli, T., Palagi, E., Tacconi, G., & Tarli, S. B. (2006). Perineal swelling, intermenstrual cycle, and female sexual behavior in bonobos (*Pan paniscus*). *American Journal of Primatology, 68*(4), 333–347.

Pipitone, N. R., & Gallup, G. G. Jr., (2008). Women's voice attractiveness varies across the menstrual cycle. *Evolution and Human Behavior, 29*(4), 268–274.

Pillsworth, E. G., Haselton, M. G., & Buss, D. M., (2004). Ovulatory shifts in female sexual desire. *Journal of Sex Research, 41*(1), 55–65.

Platek, S. M., & Singh D. (2010). Optimal waist-to-hip ratios in women activate neural reward centers in men. *PLoS ONE, 5*(2), e9042. doi:10.1371/journal.pone.0009042

Rebuffé-Scrive, M., Cullberg, G., Lundberg, P. A., Lindstedt, G., & Björntorp, P. (1989). Anthropometric variables and metabolism in polycystic ovarian disease. *Hormone and Metabolic Research, 21*(7), 391-397.

Roach, M. E., & Eicher, J. (1965). *Dress, adornment, and the social order.* New York: John Wiley.

Roach, M. E., & Eicher, J. B. (1979). The language of personal adornment. In J. M. Cordwell & R. A. Schwartz (Eds.) *The fabrics of culture: The anthropology of clothing and adornment* (pp. 7–22). Boston: Walter de Gruyter.

Roberts, S. C., Havlicek, J., Flegr, J., Hruskova, M., Little, A. C., Jones, B. C., . . . Petrie, M. (2004). Female facial attractiveness increases during the fertile phase of the menstrual cycle. *Proceedings of the Royal Society B, 271*(Suppl. 5), S270–S272.

Rozin, P., & Fallen, A. (1988). Body image, attitudes to weight, and misperceptions of figure preferences of the opposite sex: A comparison of men and women in two generations. *Journal of Abnormal Phenology 97*(3), 342–345.

Scutt, D., & Manning, J. T. (1996). Ovary and ovulation: Symmetry and ovulation in women. *Human Reproduction, 11*(11), 2477-2480.

Semmelhack, E. (2006). A delicate balance: Women, power, and high heels. In G. Reilo & P. McNeil (Eds.), *Shoes: A history from sandals to sneakers* (pp. 224-249). New York: Berg.

Simmons, R. (2002). *Odd girl out: The hidden culture of aggression in girls*. New York: Mariner Books.

Singh, D. (1993). Adaptive significance of waist-to-hip ratio and female physical attractiveness. *Journal of Personality and Social Psychology, 65*, 293–307.

Singh, D., & Bronstad, P. M. (2001). Female body odor is a potential cue to ovulation. *Proceedings of the Royal Society B, 268*, 797–801.

Singh, D., Dixson, B. J., Jessop, T. S., Morgan, B., & Dixson, A. F. (2010). Cross-cultural consensus for waist–hip ratio and women's attractiveness. *Evolution and Human Behavior, 31*(3), 176-181.

Singh, D., & Singh, D. (2006). Role of body fat and body shape on judgment of female health and attractiveness: An evolutionary perspective. *Psychological Topics, 15*(2), 331–350.

Singh, D., & Young, R. K. (1995). Body weight, waist-to-hip ratio, breasts, hips: Role in judgment in female attractiveness and desirability for relationships. *Ethology and Sociobiology, 1*(6), 483–507.

Smith, E. O. (1999). High heels and evolution: natural selection, sexual selection and high heels. *Psychology of Evolution and Gender, 1*, 245-278.

Sorokowskia, P. &, Pawlowski, B. (2008). Adaptive preferences for leg length in a potential partner *Evolution and Human Behavior, 29*, 86–91.

Sorokowskia, P., Szmajke, A., Sorokowska, A., Cunen, M. B., Fabrykant, M., Zarafshani, K., . . . Fang, T. (2011). Attractiveness of leg length: Report from 27 nations. *Journal of Cross-Cultural Psychology, 42*(1), 131–139.

Speksnijdera, C. M., Munckhofa, R. J. H., Moonenb, S. A., & Walenkampa, G. H. (2005). The higher the heel the higher the forefoot-pressure in ten healthy women. *The Foot, 15*(1), 17–21.

Steele, V. (2001). *The corset: A cultural history*. New Haven, CT: Yale University Press.

Trivers, R. (1972). Parental investment and sexual selection. In B. Campbell (Ed.), *Sexual selection and the descent of man, 1871–1971* (pp. 136–179). Chicago: Aldine.

Walter, P., Martinetto, P., Tsoucaris, G., Bréniaux, R., Lefebvre, M. A., Richard, G., . . . Dooryhee, E. (1999). Making make-up in Ancient Egypt. *Nature, 397, 483–494.*

Wang, Y., & Griskevicius, V. (2014). Conspicuous consumption, relationships, and rivals: Women's luxury products as signals to other women. *Journal of Consumer Research, 40*(5), 834–854.

Waters, M. (Dir.). (2004). *Mean girls* [Motion Picture]. Los Angeles: Paramount Pictures.

Wiseman, R. (2009). *Queen bees and wannabes: Helping your daughter survive cliques, gossip, boyfriends, and the new realities of girl world*. New York: Crown.

White, S. (1995). A content analytic technique for measuring the sexiness of women's business attire in media presentations. *Communication Research Reports, 12*(2), 178–185.

Williamson, S., & Hewitt, J. (1986). Attire, sexual allure, and attractiveness. *Perceptual Motor Skills, 63*, 981–982.

Wing, A. K., & Nadimi, P. P. (2011). Women's rights in the muslim world and the age of Obama. *Transnational Law & Contemporary Problems, 20*, 431.

Van den Berghe, P. L., & Frost, P. (1986). Skin color preference, sexual dimorphism, and sexual selection: A case of gene culture co-evolution. *Ethnic and Racial Studies, 9*, 87–113.

Veblen, T. (2003). The theory of the leisure class. (Original work published 1899). Retrieved from http://www.wilsonsd.org/cms/lib01/PA01000270/Centricity/Domain/185/Theory-Leisure-Class.pdf

Zaadstra, B. M., Seidell, J. C., Van Noord, P. A., te Velde, E. R., Habbema, J. D., Vrieswijk, B., & Karbaat, J. (1993). Fat and female fecundity: prospective study of effect of body fat distribution on conception rates. *BMJ, 306*(6876), 484–487.

Competition in Virtual Contexts

Female Virtual Intrasexual Competition and Its Consequences: An Evolutionary Mismatch Perspective

Jose C. Yong, Norman P. Li, Katherine A. Valentine, *and* April R. Smith

Abstract

Intrasexual competition is a key component of sexual selection. Evolutionarily, women compete for access to and retention of mates on key dimensions that men have evolved to value and prioritize in their long- and short-term mates, in particular physical attractiveness. Such competition evolved to be adaptive in ancestral environments as the perceived competition consisted of real individuals. However, underlying psychological mechanisms for competition are excessively triggered and more continuously engaged in modern environments, because these psychological mechanisms for social comparison and competition, at a deep level, do not differentiate between real people and imagined intrasexual competition in the form of mass media images. Utilizing an evolutionary mismatch framework, this chapter explores ways that women are psychologically influenced by the pervasive presence of virtual same-sex competitors for mates. Various negative psychological states in modern societies (e.g., depression, eating disorders) may be linked to virtual intrasexual competition.

Key Words: evolutionary psychology, mismatch, mating, intrasexual competition, mass media, self-esteem, eating disorders, depression

Mass Media and Women's Mental Health Problems

Many scholars have viewed the spread of mass media as an important global phenomenon, particularly researchers wishing to determine the source of women's mental health issues. *Mass media* here refers to media technologies that are intended to reach a large audience, and these include broadcast media (e.g., radio, recorded music, film, and television); print media (e.g., newspapers, books, pamphlets, and comics); digital media (e.g., websites, social networking sites, and smartphones); and outdoor media (e.g., billboards, signs, and placards placed inside or outside buildings, stations, and vehicles). Although the increasing utilization of mass media has its benefits, such as providing an efficient platform for communicating information about news and products, many researchers have focused on mass media for its negative effects on the psychological well-being of consumers (e.g., Durkin & Paxton, 2002; Harrison & Cantor, 1997; Stice, Schupak-Neuberg, Shaw, & Stein, 1994).

Mass media has been implicated in the apparent rise of women's mood and eating disorders in cultures where mass media containing idealized images of women is especially pervasive (Ahern, Bennett, & Hetherington, 2008; Culbertson, 1997; Makino, Tsuboi, & Dennerstein, 2004). The "thin ideal" has been conceptualized as a Western-led notion, in which the standard for female beauty is having a slender physique with a small waist and little body fat. Fashion or image-related mass media in the United States typically extols this image of thin women through the repeated presentation of such images. Women presumably internalize this ideal standard of beauty and then try to emulate the standard (Striegel-Moore, Silberstein, & Rodin, 1986).

Researchers have argued that cultures endorsing the thin ideal result in women from such cultures experiencing body dissatisfaction and, accordingly, attempting to reduce their weight and appear slim by engaging in maladaptive eating behaviors, like dietary restriction (Thompson & Stice, 2001). Indeed, body dissatisfaction has been identified as a key precursor to both depression and disordered eating (American Psychological Association, 2007; Stice & Shaw, 2002). Rather tellingly, when images of idealized thin women spread to previously unexposed cultures via the globalization of (typically American or Westernized) mass media, the same effects that the thin ideal images have on existing industrialized and Westernized populations (e.g., body image concerns and restricted eating) appear to be exhibited by women of those cultures too (e.g., Becker, Burwell, Herzog, Hamburg, & Gilman, 2002).

The theory of media exposure as a cause of female body dissatisfaction and mental health problems is appealing because it seems coherent and thus "provides an answer that is more understandable than esoteric claims about genetics, heritability, and diatheses," thereby creating an easy "villain" (Ferguson, Winegard, & Winegard, 2011, p. 15). However, blaming the media for body dissatisfaction without a thorough consideration of the underlying psychological mechanisms may be misleading. It is not clear why a thin ideal should be adopted as the gold standard for beauty in the cultures that endorse it in the first place, and importantly why rural, less developed, or non-Westernized cultures that have never endorsed such a thin ideal initially should be so easily receptive. Also, these explanations may simply elucidate proximate processes, or causes that are closest to or immediately responsible for female body dissatisfaction. Absent is an understanding of a higher-level ultimate or underlying root cause responsible for the disparate immediate causes observed across different lines of research.

Without a fundamental explanation to theoretically unify these disparate lines of arguments, our understanding of female body dissatisfaction and women's mental health problems remains incomplete. For instance, depression and eating disorders in women display an unusually high degree of comorbidity (Blinder, Cumella, & Sanathara, 2006), so another factor plausibly underlies these consistent trends alongside the spread of mass media and the proliferation of idealized female images. In this chapter, we investigate how images of attractive females in the media represent virtual mating competitors to women, contributing to the perception of many formidable mating rivals in the environment and triggering fundamental mechanisms for intrasexual competition. The prolonged engagement of intrasexual competition mechanisms, as well as accompanying perceptions that the competition is difficult to beat, could be a cause of body dissatisfaction and other subsequent psychopathological outcomes.

A Possible Underlying Role for Female Intrasexual Competition

A key process through which the media may influence women's body image, mood, and eating behaviors is intrasexual competition. Intrasexual competition is a form of sexual selection in which some individuals out-reproduce other same-sex conspecifics because they are better at attracting and securing mates (Darwin, 1871). Competition is thus tightly coupled with mate preference, as the traits providing the best chance of competitive success are also the most preferred by the opposite sex. Only when individuals have sufficient "mate value" as constituted by these traits will they be selected by interested members of the opposite sex for mating and reproduction.

Darwin (1871) proposed that sexual selection acts more strongly on males than on females, due to females generally being more of a limiting factor for the reproductive success of males. Stated another way, in many species (including humans) individual male reproductive success increases with the number of mating events, and a male can thus achieve greater reproductive success by competing with other males to access as many females as possible. As a consequence, the frequency and intensity of exaggerated traits and behaviors for competition tend to be greater in males than in females across various species. Physically aggressive and confrontational competition for mates among males is ubiquitous and readily observable in nature, as can be seen from the ominous antlers of stags and tusks of elephants. Male mate value is derived from both the actual ability to win at mating contests, such as when a stronger stag successfully subdues a weaker stag, and the *perceived* ability to win, such as when one stag has larger antlers than another stag, from which the likelihood of victory in mating contests can be inferred. Therefore, weapon size can be an honest indicator of male quality and mate value. The elaborate feathers of peacocks are also highly attractive to peahens because they serve as an honest indicator of mate value, as the quality of feathers may indicate the extent of a peacock's nourishment, disease, and parasite load, which are directly related to health status and genetic quality (Loyau, Saint Jalme, Cagniant, & Sorci, 2005).

Although intrasexual competition is most often associated with males, it is also a process occurring among females (e.g., Buss, 1988; Clutton-Brock et al., 2006; Palombit, Cheney, & Seyfarth, 2001). Even as Darwin considered females to be the sex that "remains passive," he also pointed out that females may have to struggle to excite or charm conspecific males (1871, p. 398), which means that competition exists among females to be the most charming and alluring of the lot. For instance, in animal populations where access to males is limited, such as when the ratio of males to females is low, or when high-quality males are selective, females in these populations have to compete for mates. Pairs of captive female house mice are more aggressive toward each other when presented with one male than when presented with three males (Rusu & Krackow, 2004). Among tidewater gobies, males create burrows through an effortful process of digging and cementing sand together with mucus. These burrows are a valuable resource that drives females to become competitive with other females, in terms of both physically attacking mating rivals and enticing males to open their burrows (Swenson, 1997). Female–female competitive interactions are also common in many insect species where there is variance in the quality of spermatophores provided by males to their mates (e.g., Gwynne & Bailey, 1999; Lewis, Cratsley, & Rooney, 2004). Females may also compete intrasexually not only to attract a mate but also to retain one. In the facultative polygynous starling, when mated males were given the opportunity to attract additional mates, the mates of these males reacted aggressively to potential female mating competitors in a bid to maintain their monogamous status (Sandell, 1998).

Human females are not spared from the need to compete for mates, and women therefore also compete on key dimensions that men have evolved to value and prioritize in their mates. Although female competitiveness evolved to be adaptive under certain circumstances in ancestral environments (such as when the sex ratio was skewed toward having more women than men or when men vary in their ability to provide a limited and therefore valuable resource), modern environments may induce women's perceived need to compete for mates to an inordinate degree. Psychological mechanisms that exist for the purpose of facilitating intrasexual competition may be triggered excessively for modern women, leading to maladaptive outcomes.

Evolved Psychological Mechanisms

From an evolutionary perspective, human psychology and behavior are products of evolved psychological mechanisms. Psychological mechanisms are adaptations that arise over time as a result of overcoming recurrent obstacles to survival and reproduction, and these often operate automatically at a subconscious level. In their simplest form, psychological mechanisms exist as if–then computational modules that take in input in the form of specific stimulus information that may be internal (e.g., one's hunger level) or external (e.g., how crowded the environment is) and transform the input through decision rules into output (which can be physiological activity, information to other psychological mechanisms, or manifest behaviors); this output is directed toward the solution to a specific adaptive problem (Tooby & Cosmides, 1992). For instance, consider the possible adaptive mechanism for obtaining nutrition. The experience of hunger serves as stimulus input into the evolved mechanism, which leads to the adaptive output response of seeking food according to the following computational logic: If hungry, then seek appropriate food sources. Such a mechanism solves the adaptive problem of malnutrition by getting the host organism to behave in evolutionarily appropriate ways.

The need to reproduce is a fundamental adaptive problem for humans, and a range of evolved psychological mechanisms exists to help optimize a behavioral solution to the problem. For example, consider mate selection as one part of the reproductive problem. To reproduce, one has to select a mate. Finding some individuals more attractive than others based on their appearance, background, or personality traits motivates the narrowing of attention toward a few individuals over others and creates the impetus to either approach these individuals or be receptive when these individuals approach. Much of this process happens without conscious deliberation. Likewise, the need to be able to signal high mate value is important as it attracts the attention of potential mates, creates mating opportunities, and allows one to be able to choose higher-quality mates among alternatives and retain mates in the event of competition. Psychological mechanisms that underlie intrasexual competition are likely to be triggered when the social environment is perceived to be threatening to one's mating success. When a man finds himself at a high-society party, intrasexual competition mechanisms are stimulated by perceiving the presence of many ambitious and competent men, which motivates him to signal high mate value, such as adopting a dominant posture, wearing a fashionable suit, or talking about his latest successful project in a bid to appear at least on par with, if not a cut above, the competition. Thus, psychological mechanisms underlying intrasexual competition facilitate the enactment of adaptive behaviors that serve to increase the chances of reproductive success.

Given the nature of the stimulus input that psychological mechanisms are attentive toward, these mechanisms can sometimes be triggered "incorrectly" by similar stimuli. For instance, early studies on herring gulls showed that when features of the parent gull's beak responsible for eliciting the begging response of gull chicks were isolated and artificial gull dummies exaggerating these features were created, the artificial gull dummies could elicit the same or stronger begging responses than the naturally occurring stimuli (Tinbergen & Perdeck, 1950). Stickleback fish, which instinctually attack conspecific males with bright red underbellies, could also be induced to attack models shaped unlike fish, as long as their undersides were painted red (Barrett, 2007). A psychological mechanism can therefore be "hijacked" by irrelevant stimuli resembling those for which the mechanism was designed to respond.

Virtual Competitors Contributed by the Media

In the modern world, women's psychological mechanisms for intrasexual competition may also respond not only to actual competitors but also to the plethora of two-dimensional images encountered through various forms of print and electronic media. Although we can consciously and rationally distinguish real people from virtual images of people seen on mass media, our evolved mechanisms that operate at a subconscious level may be less able to differentiate. Thus, the overrepresentation of attractive females by the mass media may, in women, contribute to frequent and lasting perceptions of stiff competition for mates. As such, we propose that mechanisms that were initially designed to facilitate competition are triggered, in a maladaptive manner, by the barrage of an unnaturally high number of perceived competitors, many of whom are virtual. As we explain in this chapter, a potential consequence of this process is the array of negative

psychological states associated with modern societies, including depression and eating disorders.

The following sections outline why attractive females are often depicted instead of attractive males in mass media, how these images engage psychological mechanisms underlying intrasexual competition for mates in women, and how the overengagement of these mechanisms interacts with other aspects of our evolved psychology, thus contributing to the various mental problems faced by women today.

Evolved Mate Preferences and Intrasexual Competition

Buss's (1989) large study on mate preferences across 37 cultures uncovered a range of important similarities and differences between the sexes. There was a considerable overlap between the sexes on preference for traits such as kindness, love, intelligence, and emotional stability in a marriage partner, which are essentially traits that people generally tend to value in people and, in particular, their mates. On the other hand, the sexes diverged on their mate preferences in ways that are predicted by evolutionary theories of mate selection. For example, women, more than men, value the ability of a partner to provide resources (Buss & Schmitt, 1993). In humans as well as other mammals, status is an effective proxy for abilities to acquire and retain resources (e.g., Cummins, 2005), and women thus place a premium on men's dominance and social status. For men more than for women, reproduction is constrained by access to reproductively valuable or fertile mates (Symons, 1979; Trivers, 1972). Because women's fertility declines sharply as a function of age, men tend to have a preference for younger women whose fertility peaks around the early and mid-20s (Dunson, Colombo, & Baird, 2002). The physical features that men find attractive in women (e.g., firm skin, long and luscious hair, and low waist-to-hip ratio [WHR]) are predictive of their health and fertility (e.g., Buss & Schmitt, 1993; Li, Bailey, Kenrick, & Linsenmeier, 2002; Singh, 1993). Likewise, these characteristics are age dependent; hence, because it is possible to infer a person's age from physical features, men find youthful physical features on women attractive. Thus, men's mate preferences generally revolve around the related aspects of youth and physical attractiveness.

As a direct consequence of these evolved mate preferences, it has been hypothesized that men and women will compete intrasexually on the traits that the opposite sex values (Buss, 1988; Walters &

Crawford, 1994). Indeed, people's version of their ideal selves mirrors what the opposite sex desires in their mates. Thus, men prioritize social status in themselves while women prioritize physical attractiveness in themselves (Li, 2007). Men are therefore expected to compete within the domain of status and dominance more than women, while women are expected to compete on physical attractiveness and youthfulness more than men.

A robust set of findings provides evidence for these predictions. In the realm of male intrasexual competition, men are more likely than women to utilize resource and status displays as a tactic of both mate attraction and mate retention (Buss, 1988; Buss & Shackelford, 1997; Schmitt & Buss, 1996). Men are also more likely than women to exaggerate their actual income (Hall, Park, Song, & Cody, 2010; Tooke & Camire, 1991) and, in line with the subjective importance of men's standing in relation to other men on status, more likely to derogate mating rivals on their resources and future job prospects (Buss & Dedden, 1990; Schmitt & Buss, 1996). This difference is reflected in subjective distress about mating rivals, as men are more distressed than women if a potential rival has impressive job prospects (Buss, Shackelford, Choe, Buunk, & Dijkstra, 2000).

Conversely, in female intrasexual competition, women are more likely than men to use beauty and appearance enhancements as mate attraction and retention tactics (Buss, 1988; Buss & Shackelford, 1997; Schmitt & Buss, 1996). Women are also more likely than men to misrepresent their age and weight in online dating sites (Hall et al., 2010). Moreover, women allocate a larger portion of their financial budgets than men to purchasing goods and services that enhance appearance (Hayhoe, Leach, Turner, Bruin, & Lawrence, 2000; Miller, 2009; Saad, 2007). Indeed, in times of economic crisis, while most industries suffer losses from the effects of the recession, beauty and cosmetic industries (where females are the primary consumers) either are unscathed or may even experience a boom, as the number of financially stable men drops and competition for them becomes more fierce (Elliott, 2008; Hill, Rodeheffer, Griskevicius, Durante, & White, 2012; Nelson, 2001). Similarly, women are more likely than men to derogate their rival's physical appearance (Buss & Dedden, 1990; Schmitt & Buss, 1996) and are more subjectively distressed than men if a potential mating rival is more physically attractive (Buss et al., 2000). Divorce across cultures reflects the consequences of defeats at intrasexual competition, as women are more likely to divorce a man due to his failure to provide economic resources, while men are more likely to divorce a woman due to her old age (Betzig, 1989). Youth and physical attractiveness are thus related and central components of female mate value for which women compete intensely with one another for access to, and retention of, mates.

Presentation of Female Mate Value Traits in the Media

Desirable female traits appear to drive how women are portrayed in mass media. Media images, such as those seen in advertisements, movies, television shows, and magazines, overwhelmingly present women as young and physically attractive (although the specific features underlying physical attractiveness may differ to some extent cross-culturally; e.g., Fisher & Voracek, 2005; Frith, Shaw, & Cheng, 2005). Women are also more often than men depicted in roles that are "decorative" (i.e., sexually objectified or of being concerned with physical attractiveness; Plakoyiannaki, Mathioudaki, Dimitratos, & Zotos, 2008; Saad, 2004).

Accordingly, in magazine advertisements and television commercials, women are more often depicted as attractive sex objects, whereas men are commonly portrayed as heavier and not quite as attractive and in a less sexually explicit manner (e.g., Lin, 1998; Saad, 2004). In video games, for instance, female characters are more likely than male characters to be scantily clad, expose more skin, and be sexually attractive. Research also shows that when female characters appear in video games, they are more likely than male characters to serve as victims or prizes, making them objects that are passive or that elicit desire (Provenzo, 1991). These differences stretch across various forms of mass media and have also been found in longitudinal studies to span generations and time periods ranging from the mid-1970s to at least the mid-1990s, suggesting a consistent trend (Ferguson, Kreshel, & Tinkham, 1990; Reichert, Lambiase, Morgan, Carstarphen, & Zavoina, 1999). Furthermore, the accentuation of female versus male youth, physical attractiveness, and sexuality can also be found in advertisements across cultures as diverse as those in Malaysia, Singapore, Japan, the United States, and Hispanic American countries (Ford, Voli, Honeycutt, & Casey, 1998; Fullerton & Kendrick, 2000; Maynard & Taylor, 1999; Wee, Choong, & Tambyah, 1995).

Female mate value traits are also highlighted in television programs and videos: Whereas male characters tend to be portrayed in roles that emphasize skill, profession, or seniority, female characters are more likely to be defined through physical appearance (i.e., being attractive, dressing provocatively, and being the object of another person's gaze) or having stereotyped roles such as homemaking or nursing (e.g., Davis, 1990; Signorielli & Bacue, 1999). Such tendencies in sex-differentiated portrayals are similarly found in movies (e.g., Haskell, 1987; Marjorie, 1973). Women are also less likely to be shown with gray hair compared to men, suggesting that it is more acceptable, or even attractive, for men—but not women—to display older age (Davis, 1990). In the United States, where there is a thin ideal for women, a content analysis of 33 television programs by Silverstein, Perdue, Peterson, and Kelly (1986) found that 69% of female characters were coded as "thin" compared to only 18% of male characters, while only 5% of female characters were coded as "heavy" vis-à-vis 26% of males, reflecting a relative emphasis on female bodily ideals of physical attractiveness. The authors also found that popular celebrities who serve as models for attractiveness are thinner than the average woman, and the normative standards of thinness have increased since the early 20th century.

Not only is this pattern limited to depictions of male and female appearance, but also behavioral expectancies congruent with mate value are espoused. As people are attuned toward resourceful information that may increase their odds at winning at intrasexual competition, mass media outlets such as magazines also feed consumers information relevant for intrasexual competition in a sex-differentiated manner. While men's magazines tend to focus on providing information about hobbies and activities, which may enable men to improve their mate value through skill and resource acquisition, a larger proportion of women's magazines focus on how women can increase their mate value by improving their physical appearance through fashion and cosmetics (Malkin, Wornian, & Chrisler, 1999). Taken as a whole, universal as well as culturally relevant determinants of a desirable woman (i.e., specifically youth, physical attractiveness, and sexuality) appear to be emphasized; women with these traits are shown as confident and happy and are extolled and upheld as winners by the mass media. The implication then is that women who fail to meet these standards become losers in the timeless game of intrasexual competition.

Use of Female Mate Value Traits to Increase Viewership or Consumption

Why would the mass media gravitate toward choosing to excessively display desirable female mate value traits in the women they present? The selection of content by mass media producers certainly is not an arbitrary process. Producers using media outlets in capitalistic societies for whatever communicative purpose—to advertise products, broadcast television shows, publish magazine articles—do so with the intention of generating returns on the product(s), typically monetary profits, by reaching as wide an audience as possible (Saad, 2004). An important point addressed in greater detail further in this chapter is also that people appear to respond to images of people in mass media (essentially artificial or unreal persons) as if they are real people (Kanazawa, 2002). Mass media producers have continued to utilize images of people precisely because artificial images of people are effective in engaging audience members' psychological mechanisms that are dedicated to perceiving and processing other people.

A significant part of the decision-making processes underlying the choosing and designing of content involves heightening audience members' awareness and attention—two major components of consciousness (Al-Hejin, 2004; Schmidt, 1994). In this regard, producers are motivated to select content that captures as much "attention, comprehension, retention, and/or behavioral impact" from the masses as possible (Pollay, 1986, p. 21). As consumers tend to stop and read or view materials they are already interested in (Bovee & Arens, 1986), the attention-grabbing and influential nature of mate value traits promise strong "returns on investment." Therefore, men and women are often portrayed according to their relevant mate value traits, with exemplary men typically shown as having high social status and exemplary women shown as young and physically attractive. Physically attractive women are also employed because attractive product endorsers have been found to produce better brand reputation and instill in viewers a stronger desire to consume the product (Till & Busler, 2000). Relatedly, sex appeal can stimulate the curiosity of consumers and increase the attention paid to associated product imagery, and this process crucially provokes a second look, enhances recall, forms focal discussion points, and leads to interest in any new trends or fashions (Reichert, Heckler, & Jackson, 2001). However, a more refined analysis also suggests important differences in the way mass media producers exploit how men and women perceive and react to female mate value stimuli.

The Exploitation of Male Mating Psychology

Humans spend more time in a juvenile state than other mammals, requiring more years of brain and social development before they are capable of functioning independently. Children thus greatly benefit from more than just the mother's investment (Bjorklund & Shackelford, 1999; Morris, 1967). Indeed, compared to other mammalian males, human fathers demonstrate higher levels of invested effort toward nurturing their offspring (Geary, 2005).

However, despite relatively high human male investment in offspring, humans still share a fundamental sex difference with other mammals: Obligatory physiological investment in offspring is much higher in females, who bear the costs of internal gestation (pregnancy) and nursing. Such costs place constraints on the number of offspring females can produce, resulting in the evolution of mammalian females as the typically more selective (and risk-averse) sex. Conversely, given the lower minimum reproductive investment and higher ceiling on males' potential production of offspring, males evolved to be generally less selective in mating and stand to benefit from a strategy that maximizes the quantity of offspring (Buss & Schmitt, 1993; Trivers, 1972). Therefore, males of various species are typically adapted to exhibit high eagerness toward sexual opportunities (Bateman, 1948; Dobzhansky & Pavlovsky, 1967), followed by minimal commitment to the mate and subsequent offspring after insemination.

For human males, a mating strategy that minimizes commitment yet maximizes the number of successful matings is largely constrained by the availability of fertile women. As such, men may have evolved to respond positively to cues of both availability and fertility (Buss & Schmitt, 1993; Symons, 1979). Indeed, men generally respond more strongly than women to visual sexual stimuli, such as pornography, by demonstrating greater interest and prolonged visual attention to sexual features of female targets, such as breasts and genitalia (Rupp & Wallen, 2008). While experiments with functional magnetic resonance imaging (fMRI) scans have found that there are many similar brain regions activated for both men and women when viewing visual sexual stimuli, it was also found that men had greater hypothalamic activation as well as

greater activation in the amygdala than women in response to sexually explicit images of heterosexual activities. This difference may reflect the cognitive processing of sexual stimuli like motivation and desire for sexual activity that are specific to men (Hamann, Herman, Nolan, & Wallen, 2004). Men also demonstrate a higher inclination than women to accept sexual offers from attractive opposite-sex strangers (Clark & Hatfield, 1989). When exposed to cues that signal desirable mating opportunities, such as being in the presence of attractive members of the opposite sex, men demonstrate greater disinhibition than women and take more risks (Pawlowski, Rajinder, & Dunbar, 2008; Ronay & von Hippel, 2010). Media producers, whose livelihoods depend on their ability to attract attention, viewership, or consumption, have realized the profitability of exploiting this male "eagerness" toward mating opportunities (Trivers, 2011, p. 19).

The deliberate display of female mate value traits takes advantage of men's visual sensitivity to cues of youth and fertility. Attractive women, particularly virtual images that have been artificially enhanced to emphasize youth and fertility, strongly capture the attention of men. Maner, Gailliot, and DeWall (2007) conducted a study utilizing a visual cueing task in which participants first focused on a particular stimulus and were next instructed to shift their attention to a different point on the computer screen. They found men had greater difficulty disengaging their attention to the new point on the screen when the initial stimulus was an attractive woman.

Presenting images of attractive females is also aimed at increasing men's arousal and their subsequent cognitive disinhibitions (i.e., reductions in the ability to engage psychological restraint), which creates impulsive receptivity to, and consumption of, purchases, subscriptions, and persuasive messages, just to name a few. Early research showed that when female targets instill a "drive" in male participants, perceptual distortion occurs so that female targets are seen as having high potential for "drive satisfaction," resulting in what is described as an "autistic" and automatic process aimed in the direction of gratification of the drive (Stephan, Berscheid, & Walster, 1971). In practical terms, this finding suggests that a man whose sexual interest is piqued by an attractive woman will be aroused with a desire that is ultimately aimed toward fulfilling his goal to mate, and his behavior thereafter will be more likely motivated narrowly in service of achieving that mating goal. He may now be less conscious of social conventions that normally block him from pursuing his goal or may be less visually attentive to things in his environment that are unrelated to mating. Indeed, a study exploring the effects of being "in the heat of the moment" revealed that college males who were induced by self-stimulation into a state of sexual arousal were less restricted toward a wide range of questionable behaviors and more willing to engage in unsafe sexual practices (Ariely & Loewenstein, 2006).

Such disinhibition is typically associated with an increased appetite for risk (Eysenck & Eysenck, 1978). When exposed to images of attractive women, men become more likely to take risks (Baker & Maner, 2008), and field experiments with male skateboarders have also found that the mere presence of an attractive woman elevates testosterone levels and produces an increase in risky stunts attempted (Ronay & von Hippel, 2010). "Discounting the future," or valuing of imminent goods over future goods, also occurs more in men viewing images of attractive women compared to women viewing images of attractive men (Wilson & Daly, 2004). Temporal discounting has consequences for reduced self-control, deficiency of deliberative decision-making, and desire for immediate gratification (Loewenstein, 1996), and indeed it has been shown to increase the likelihood of spending or acquiescing to persuasion messages (e.g., Loewenstein, 2000; Rook, 1987). Attractive women are often employed as models by organizers of car showroom events to attract the attention of men and induce disinhibited purchasing behavior. Similarly, media producers exploit men's mating psychology—specifically men's fixation on physically attractive women denoting mating opportunity and their subsequent narrow and specific behaviors in service of mating fulfillment—to attract more male viewers, make men pay more attention to the media content presented, and make men react in ways favorable to these media producers, such as accepting a message conveyed or buying a product marketed. As elaborated further in this chapter, mass media images of people can be as effective as real-life models in engaging our person perception mechanisms, such that we respond to them as if they are real.

The Exploitation of Female Intrasexual Competition Psychology

The same attention-grabbing power that attractive female images have on men also exerts itself on women. Although physically attractive others are generally preferred in mating and nonmating relationships, experimental studies have found that both men and women selectively attend to, and have the best recall for, physically attractive female faces, as opposed to physically attractive male faces or unattractive male and female faces (Becker, Kenrick, Guerin, & Maner, 2005; Maner et al., 2003). In fact, there is some evidence from these studies that people have a tougher time remembering handsome men than average-looking men. It thus appears that women, as much as men, preferentially fixate their attention on attractive women, both in real life as well as those presented in the media, albeit for different reasons.

Due to intrasexual competition for mates, women may be particularly perceptive of other women's appearance. This attention is logical given that players in a competitive game should pay attention to how formidable their opponents are to gauge their own chances of success. Attention is paid to specific critical features, and adjustments can then be made either to themselves or their behaviors to raise their odds of winning. A team of soccer players may observe, for instance, if their opponents are taller to see if a high-ball strategy will pay off; if their opponents are indeed generally taller, then the team will likely select another strategy that maximizes their own strengths, such as short-ball passing. Attention to key traits valued by the game is thus first necessary for self-assessment and strategic maneuvering.

Li (2007) has shown that people are aware of the traits that the opposite sex values, which results in greater sensitivity toward those traits. More specifically, because of intrasexual competition, men are attuned to traits related to dominance and social status in other men, while women are sensitive to indicators of youth and physical attractiveness in other women. Moreover, the excessive presentation of physically attractive people in mass media affects female viewers more negatively than male viewers. Researchers have found that exposure to physically attractive men does not affect women's appraisals of their mates or men's self-appraisals, whereas exposure to images of physically attractive women can undermine women's self-appraisals, as well as men's appraisals of their current mates (Gutierres, Kenrick, & Partch, 1999; Kenrick, Neuberg, Zierk, & Krones, 1994). Young and physically attractive intrasexual competitors thus pose more of a threat to women than to men (Dijkstra & Buunk, 1998; Kenrick et al., 1994), contributing to women's hypersensitivity toward young and physically attractive women. Indeed, in the aforementioned study by Maner et al. (2007) utilizing the visual cueing task, women were also more attentionally fixated on physically attractive females, and their fixation was stronger if they felt insecure about their current relationship. As imagery of physically attractive women is sufficient to induce these effects in women, women are therefore responding to these images as if they are real-life mating competitors.

The focus of playing on females' emotions in advertising has a longstanding history (cf. Lopate, 1977). Various scholars and practitioners have emphasized the effectiveness of appealing to women by highlighting flaws that may be resolved only by buying the advertised products and services. For example, Pease (1958) asserted that appealing to the family ideal and the importance of romantic love through marketing can create the impression that shopping provides solutions to these unfulfilled needs. As early as the 1920s, advertisements for products such as mouthwash and soap have insinuated that women need to care about their bodies and possess good looks (e.g., maintain good skin) to attract and retain a mate (Ewen, 1976). The use of attractive female models in advertisements fortifies this aspirational function as well, as the attractive models serve as high-level benchmarks of key female mate value traits. Indeed, numerous studies of female social comparison caused by exposure to idealized female images in advertising have demonstrated that such advertising raises women's comparison standards for attractiveness and induces women to experience negative affect and lowered satisfaction of the self in relevant comparison dimensions (Bower, 2001; Martin & Gentry, 1997; Richins, 1991). Being a desirable mate is a central theme of these advertising messages, and such aspirations are set by marketers through the use of attractive images and models.

The insecurities that are aroused by key marketing tactics tap into female intrasexual competition for mates, which draws attention to deficiencies in traits that are linked to mate value and that are compensable by the acquisition of advertised products. Women are willing, in the service of competing with same-sex rivals, to invest in these products to enhance their mate value traits (e.g., Hill et al., 2012). Taken together, the exploitation of the psychologies of male mating and female intrasexual competition account for the pervasiveness of attractive female images in today's mass media.

Interaction of Attractive Female Virtual Images and Intrasexual Competition and Its Consequences

The intensive presentation of attractive females in mass media has palpable consequences for women. Many of these effects are detrimental to women's psychological well-being, creating downstream effects on physical health, which is explicated further in the chapter. First, we address an important issue: Why are women affected by these images when the images are not real peers with whom they are competing? Evolutionary mismatch theory provides an answer.

EVOLUTIONARY MISMATCH THEORY AND THE PERCEPTION OF VIRTUAL OTHERS

Natural selection eliminates traits in organisms if these traits are nonadaptive or deleterious to the organism in a given environment, leading to the passing on of neutral and adaptive traits encoded in genes to later generations of the organism. A key issue, though, is that the current environment may be unlike the environments in which we evolved, thereby leading to a "mismatch" between psychological mechanisms—which developed over the course of human evolutionary history—and the modern environment in which they now function (Tooby & Cosmides, 1990). As such, humans have traits that are better suited to ancient ecologies but are maladaptive in some modern settings. One often-cited example is our preference for foods that are high in fat and sugar. In the ancient environments of the Pleistocene era where humans evolved (Barkow, Cosmides, & Tooby, 1992), having a preference for sugars and fats motivated ancestral humans to seek food sources that provided the best natural sources of nutrition and calories (e.g., ripe fruits, nuts, occasional meat). However, much like media producers capitalizing on the evolved mating psychologies of men and women, food producers often manufacture foods laden with sugars and fats that exploit our evolved taste preferences and increase our consumption rate. This manufacturing poses problems because a profusion of such foods combined with the human adaptation to prefer them can (and often does) contribute to undesirable outcomes, including tooth decay and, more important, obesity (Buss, 1995).

Another manifestation of this mismatch between our evolved psychology and the modern environment is the inability to discern between virtual and real persons. In ancestral times, all visual representations of people that actually resembled real people (i.e., excluding cave drawings and other abstract visual representations) *were* real people; thus, there was no need for mechanisms to distinguish otherwise. Indeed, various lines of research have demonstrated that people (or, more precisely, their evolved psychological mechanisms) cannot distinguish between real individuals encountered in the flesh and those seen on television, magazines, the Internet, and other forms of media (e.g., Kanazawa, 2002). A particularly striking example reflecting this mismatch is the multibillion-dollar pornography industry, which attests to the ability of psychological mechanisms designed for mating to be triggered by two-dimensional images (Kenrick, Gutierres, & Goldberg, 1989).

As outlined by Kanazawa (2002), the biological function of a penile erection is to enable men to have sexual intercourse with women in the service of reproduction. As erections are not metabolically costly, it paid off in reproductive terms for males to have erections whenever young and physically attractive females behaving in sexually responsive ways were encountered in the ancestral past. In error management terms, having erections even when sex did not eventually occur would constitute a Type I error, which is a less costly error than the Type II form of this error where one fails to have erections when sex is possible. By always having erections whenever physically attractive women were perceived to be sexually responsive, ancestral men were therefore more likely to have successful copulations and, thus, offspring. As a result, men today have erections when viewing naked or sexually suggestive attractive women in photographs and videos even though any occurrence of sexual intercourse with these women is impossible. Men's sexual adaptations have not updated themselves fast enough to keep up with the distinction between real and virtual females (consisting of images and videos that did not exist during evolutionarily critical periods in the past). Therefore, men unconsciously behave as if they could have sex with the virtual females they see in pornography.

Currently, people consume electronic media copiously given how tightly interwoven it is with modern living. Avid consumers of mass media can therefore expose themselves to more individuals in one day than our ancestors encountered in a lifetime, and such overexposure to these virtual others has real consequences. As demonstrated by Kenrick and colleagues (1994), men express reduced commitment to their long-term romantic partners after viewing pictures of physically attractive women. Relatedly, a recent study reported that many healthy men in their 20s who regularly consume Internet pornography cannot maintain erections with their actual partners ("Italian Men Suffer," 2011). As most women are less physically attractive relative to professional pornographic actresses, men who have habituated to the standards of physical attractiveness set by pornographic actresses find their actual partners unattractive in comparison, leading to erectile dysfunctions.

Exposure to media representations of other people does not always produce negative effects. A correlational study suggested that many people evaluate their social lives more positively after having watched television, as if the characters they saw on television were their actual friends (Kanazawa, 2002). Thus, the perception of virtual persons can engage the same social psychological mechanisms that were designed to respond to real people.

Female Virtual Intrasexual Competition

We have discussed why, in modern environments, a person's perceived intrasexual competitors are not limited to actual competitors. The influence of the mass media on women's perception of same-sex rivals in the environment is likely greater than the influence on men due to the overrepresentation of physically attractive women in media images (as compared to physically attractive men and less physically attractive women), as well as the greater role that physical attractiveness plays in female mate value (e.g., Buss, 1989). There is growing concern that mass media exposure is slowly affecting men as well, and some experimental evidence exists for men being negatively affected by viewing images of physically attractive men (such as tall, handsome, or muscular male models; e.g., Agliata & Tantleff-Dunn, 2004). A recent meta-analysis by Ferguson (2013) sheds important light on current trends in mass media effects on body dissatisfaction. Overall, experimental studies report stronger effect sizes than correlational studies, suggesting that priming effects found through experimental manipulations affect viewers temporarily, after which only viewers with preexisting insecurity traits remain strongly affected, while the effects attenuate for other more resilient viewers.

Negative effects of physically attractive imagery on women are by and large still greater than on men. First, where young and physically attractive people are used in mass media content, women are predictably more likely than men to be negatively affected viewing physically attractive same-sex individuals given the underlying processes of intrasexual competition concerned. Second, as demonstrated through reviews of mass media content previously in this chapter, more women in mass media, as opposed to men, are portrayed as young and physically attractive, which also drives these negative effects more strongly for women than for men. If we are indeed unable to differentiate between real and virtual individuals, then women in today's media-bombarded modern world will feel like they are facing an inordinate number of greatly formidable female competitors.

From an evolutionary perspective, direct competition involves one or more individuals enacting behaviors directed at achieving a goal by confronting another individual (or group) of the same species motivated by the same goal, such as social status, food, territory, or mating. When one individual is victorious in a competitive encounter, the chances of others' success diminishes; victory leads to a dominant status, while defeat leads to a subordinate status (Salvador, 2005). These dynamics of competition typically lead to the subjective experience of stress, and studies have found that stress from competition is a recurring theme in the lives of higher animal species (Blanchard, McKittrick, & Blanchard, 2001).

Competition affects people in various ways, and not all outcomes of competition are necessarily detrimental to psychological and physical well-being. Some healthy degree of competition can lead to increased performance (Stanne, Johnson, & Johnson, 1999; Tauer & Harackiewicz, 2004) and innovation (Aghion, Bloom, Blundell, Griffith, & Howitt, 2005), as well as the subjective experience of positive affect in the process of competing (Tauer & Harackiewicz, 2004; Tjosvold, Johnson, Johnson, & Sun, 2003) for both men and women. On the other hand, excessive competition has clearly been established across various streams of research to have negative consequences.

Studies of nonhuman populations provide some insight into the basic behavioral, physiological, and endocrinological outcomes associated with competition. When competition was experimentally imposed on house finches by making feeding sites scarce, those house finches exhibited higher aggression rates, lower antibody responses, and loss of body mass (Hawley, Lindström, & Wikelski, 2006). Steroid hormones, namely testosterone and cortisol, which aid functional responses to competition, have also been demonstrated to increase in bonobos and

chimpanzees when they were placed in situations where competition for food appeared imminent (Wobber et al., 2010). Indeed, these physiological changes present themselves in humans as well.

The link between stress and levels of cortisol secretion is well established (Djuric et al., 2008; Mason, 1968), and prolonged higher levels of cortisol in the bloodstream have various harmful effects on the body (e.g., Ebrecht et al., 2004). Testosterone, a key hormone associated with competition and aggression, has also been shown to impede immune functioning (e.g., Bobjer, Katrinaki, Tsatsanis, Giwercman, & Giwercman, 2013; Phillips, Pinkernell, & Jing, 1994). Taken together, these findings suggest that prolonged stress from competition can be physically harmful to the body.

At a social behavioral level, competition has a variety of consequences. For instance, competition can lessen group productivity due to group members being less willing to coordinate actions with each other (Stanne et al., 1999). Competition can also reduce the intrinsic motivation one has for a task because one's focus is on winning rather than the activity itself (Deci, Betley, Kahle, Abrams, & Porac, 1981). Further, competition undermines social relationships through the adoption of antisocial behaviors, ranging from guardedness and viewing others as threats (Kohn, 1992) to cheating and social manipulation (Stallman, 2012). It also erodes trust, as people cannot afford the vulnerability associated with trust in competitive situations (Deutsch, 1962). All in all, being in extended periods of competitiveness can lead to numerous negative reactions in humans. Further, while the majority of research has explored these effects on men, an emerging literature has also uncovered such effects on women (see in chapters this volume by Costa et al. and Cobey and Hahn).

Individuals living in high-density populations tend to subjectively experience more competition and stress (Jain, 1978; Milgram, 1970). Perceived higher density might result from believing there are more competitors in the local environment than truly exist. That is, highly attractive virtual females may, in lower-density areas, create similar conditions to high-density areas. Selected by media producers for their idealized youth and beauty, their presence translates into an overwhelming number of rivals whose quality in female mate value traits is often unsurpassably high. Thus, a woman may perceive that she is pitted against formidable opponents on a regular basis and that her mate value might be chronically low in relation to the perceived competition. Coupled with the general negative influence of competition, as well as women's perceived inability to control their physical attractiveness (Ben Hamida, Mineka, & Bailey, 1998), this perceived prevalence of attractive female rivals in the environment leading to virtual intrasexual competition provides a strong account for the psychological distress that is faced by many modern women. Here, we examine three problems reported more by women than men: low self-esteem, depression, and disordered eating (American Psychological Association, 2007), which we propose is caused by virtual intrasexual competition.

SELF-ESTEEM

Given that physical attractiveness is a central component of women's mate value, the proliferation of attractive virtual women may then lead women to have not only increased attractiveness concerns but also lower overall appraisals of self-worth, or self-esteem. Indeed, research findings (e.g., Davison & McCabe, 2006; Hagger & Stevenson, 2010; Levine & Smolak, 2002; Sabiston, Sedgwick, Crocker, Kowalski, & Mack, 2007) have indicated that young women, particularly those living in Westernized cultures with plentiful images of attractive females depicted by the mass media, express deep concerns about their physical appearance and their body's attractiveness. Importantly, such concerns have been linked to lowered self-esteem in females (Davison & McCabe, 2006; Hagger & Stevenson, 2010).

Self-esteem reflects a person's overall emotional evaluation of personal worth. The sociometer hypothesis of self-esteem established the functional nature of self-esteem as a "gauge" reflecting how an individual is valued by personally meaningful social groups (Leary, Tambor, Terdal, & Downs, 1995). The gauge is useful in that it allows individuals to fit into social hierarchies and adjust their expectations accordingly. More specifically, self-esteem may have domain-specific constituents, such as mating (Kirkpatrick & Ellis, 2001), that are evolutionarily important. Indeed, Kavanagh, Robins, and Ellis (2010) found mating aspirations were altered by the rejection or acceptance by romantic targets, and this link was mediated by self-esteem. In addition, humans may have evolved the competency to socially compare with others. As proposed by Gilbert, Price, and Allan (1995), if an individual's social comparisons indicate her or his relative value to be lower, then the individual's self-esteem, as an indicator and regulator of confidence in exerting influence, may fall. In the mating domain, the

capacity to exert greater mating choices may be a function of one's own mating desirability. Thus, constant reminders that one's mate value is low possibly exerts negative effects on self-esteem.

The perception of formidable intrasexual competitors contributed by the mass media may, from the vantage point of evolved social comparison competencies, lead to lowered self-perceived rank in the mating hierarchy, which predicts lower levels of self-esteem (Fournier, 2009). Experimental research has demonstrated that exposure to attractive, idealized female images has adverse effects (at least temporarily) on women's self-esteem. In the same experimental study by Kenrick and colleagues (1994) described previously, exposure to pictures of physically attractive women also led women to evaluate themselves more negatively as potential mates. Further, Little and Mannion (2006) used a within-subject design to demonstrate that when women view attractive female faces, they perceive themselves as less attractive, and they shift their mate preferences toward men of lower mate value. In another laboratory study, women who were exposed to photographs from popular magazines experienced increased body dissatisfaction, negative mood states, and decreased self-esteem (Hawkins, Richards, Granley, & Stein, 2004). Indeed, motivations related to social comparison drive the manner in which women experience dissatisfaction with themselves and lowered self-esteem when viewing idealized female images used in advertising (Martin & Gentry, 1997; Martin & Kennedy, 1994; Richins, 1991).

DEPRESSION

The dynamics of female virtual intrasexual competition are especially pertinent for understanding how media images of highly desirable females contribute to depressive symptoms in women. In particular, the social competition hypothesis of human depression draws attention to how competitive stress plays a key role in the etiology of depression (Fournier, Moskowitz, & Zuroff, 2002; Sloman & Gilbert, 2000). Social competition theorists assume that reproductively relevant resources, such as food, territory, and mating opportunities, were often in scarce supply over the course of human evolutionary history. Insights from studies of the spontaneous formation of social hierarchies suggest that hierarchies function to organize priority of access to scarce resources (e.g., Savin-Williams, 1977; Strayer & Strayer, 1976), and that humans are endowed with a stock of behavioral strategies to assess and pursue standing in social hierarchies. In the course of displaying talents and competencies to compete for dominance (e.g., Fournier, 2009), a proportion of competitors will lose because victory for some necessarily means defeat for others (Salvador, 2005). To assist them in the face of potential defeat, humans are equipped with a range of defensive strategies (Gilbert, 1992, 2001), which include responses such as fight (reinvesting efforts to win the contest), flight (redirecting efforts to escape the contest), and help-seeking (enlisting the aid of allies).

When a competitor is unable to enlist any defensive strategies, he or she may be left in a state of "entrapped defeat," with associated feelings of "personal failure, inferiority, inability, powerlessness, and hopelessness" (Sloman, Price, Gilbert, & Gardner, 1994, p. 405). Such a state, termed an *involuntary defeat strategy* (IDS), may function to discourage persistence in the face of inevitable defeat, and thus to limit the risk of injury or death and further losses of time and energy, and to facilitate the acceptance of the loss of a rank contest (Sloman & Gilbert, 2000). Usually, the IDS is activated for a short time as the individual accepts defeat, reconciles with her or his competitors, and then moves on. Brief activation of the IDS would likely manifest as a mild, temporary depression or dysphoria. However, if the state of entrapped defeat persists and the individual is unable to disengage from the competition, then the IDS may intensify into severe clinical depression (Sloman & Gilbert, 2000).

The hypothesized components of the IDS have been found to be closely related to the experience of depression. Depression is associated with feelings of inferiority (Cheung, Gilbert, & Irons, 2004; Gilbert & Allan, 1998; Zuroff, Fournier, & Moskowitz, 2007); submissive behavior (Gilbert & Allan, 1998; Irons & Gilbert, 2005; Zuroff et al., 2007); lack of dominance (Zuroff et al., 2007); inability to exert influence (Nezlek, Hampton, & Shean, 2000); and suppression of overt hostility (Allan & Gilbert, 2002; Gilbert, Gilbert, & Irons, 2004). Further, in accordance with the theory, depressive episodes are largely time limited, tending to naturally resolve within a period of 3 months to a year (American Psychiatric Association, 2013). Researchers have also uncovered links between entrapped defeat and depression.

Depression is correlated with the subjective experience of humiliation and defeat (Gilbert & Allan, 1998; Kendler, Hettema, Butera, Gardner, & Prescott, 2003); the desire to escape while feeling trapped (Gilbert & Allan, 1998; Gilbert et al., 2004); and the feeling that help from others is not available (Billings, Cronkite, & Moos, 1983). These components are also consistent with the learned helplessness model of depression (Seligman, 1975), where the experience of lack of control and the expectation of future uncontrollability (which comes with reduced agency by virtue of being subordinate in rank) is sufficient for the onset of depression.

This evolutionary framework of social rank underlies the dynamics of intrasexual competition, and status-negotiating behaviors benefit from knowledge of one's relative value in the mating market. In this regard, the formation of mental composites of the population is useful because it creates an awareness of one's standing in relation to others (Symons, 1979). Further, women may form composites of same-sex mating competitors to better understand their relative mate value and enact mating strategies more effectively. Such a calibration of one's composite for intrasexual competition is adaptive in a village setting comprising only 100–230 individuals (Dunbar, 1992), as it likely led to an accurate view of the competitive landscape. However, as the lives of modern humans become more intertwined with technology and mass media, the overgenerous portrayal and presentation of attractive females by media producers causes the perception of an overload of formidable same-sex competitors. When women compare themselves to the artificially skewed mental composites they derive from the physically attractive competitors contributed by the mass media in their environment, they may feel that their value in the mating hierarchy is habitually low despite any efforts they make.

The chronic perception that intrasexual competitors are too formidable increases the likelihood of feeling that defeat in mating is inevitable. The IDS, as a psychological mechanism to counteract prolonged participation in losing contests, may thus be activated to facilitate disengagement from mating competitions. As proposed by the social competition hypothesis of human depression, activation of the IDS for brief periods expresses itself as mild depressive symptoms (Fournier, 2009), which is adaptive as it compels the mildly depressed individual to reallocate time, energy, and resources away from competing. However, an extended mental state of inferiority and entrapped defeat where there is no way to escape can lead to a maladaptive state of severe depression (Cheung et al., 2004; Gilbert & Allan, 1998; Gilbert et al., 2004; Zuroff et al., 2007).

Depression patterns around the world converge with this view. Women are about twice as likely as men to develop depression and depressive symptoms across various demographics (Jenkins, Kleinman, & Good, 1991; Nolen-Hoeksema, 1990; Weissman et al., 1996). A closer look at cross-cultural variability in the size of the sex difference of depressive symptoms indicates support for the view that the increasing flux of media-presented attractive women exacerbates female intrasexual competition, which increases the incidence of depression in women.

First, cultural variables that positively correlate with the prevalence of pervasive modern electronic mass media (such as the Internet or television), including being more Westernized (Culbertson, 1997; Nolen-Hoeksema, 1987), having greater gender equality (Hopcroft & Bradley, 2007), and being more developed (Colla, Buka, Harrington, & Murphy, 2006; Culbertson, 1997; Nolen-Hoeksema, 1987), have been found to be associated with a greater sex difference in depression. In other words, the more women reside in environments that are likely to have more modern and pervasive forms of ideologies and electronic mass media, the more likely they are to be depressed in comparison to men.

Second, increasingly more traditional cultures and developing nations are gaining access to modern forms of mass media and media content due to increasing globalization and modernization pressures (Bhugra & Mastrogianni, 2004; Patil & Gayatri, 2012), and this growth in mass media consumption is occurring alongside growing rates of depression in these places (Hidaka, 2012; Stack, 1993). This correlation is consistent with the finding that women in modern societies are more depressed than women in traditional societies, with depression assessed using an algorithm based on widely acknowledged criteria to reduce cultural bias (Colla et al., 2006). Therefore, this cultural difference is not just an artifact of people in modern Westernized societies having more access to medical knowledge that results in more awareness of mental health issues or greater access to mental health practitioners they can go to for diagnoses. Thus, the widespread availability of media images laden with attractive females may contribute to the acceleration of depression among females in traditionally unexposed cultures. Consistent with this view of media exposure on depression, an experimental study on girls in the 7th and 10th grades found that viewing female advertising images led to overall significant increases in state depression over the course of a week, providing evidence for the short-term effects of idealized female images (Durkin & Paxton, 2002).

EATING DISORDERS

Over 24 million people in the United States and as many as 70 million people worldwide are afflicted with an eating disorder, and many more are undiagnosed (Renfrew Center Foundation for Eating Disorders, 2003). Disordered eating may involve avoiding foods, purging ingested food, or engaging in any other extreme weight control practices (Neumark-Sztainer, 2005). According to the American Psychiatric Association (2013), the three major categories of eating disorders are anorexia nervosa, bulimia nervosa, and binge eating disorder. Individuals with a clinically significant disorder of eating that does not meet the criteria for one of these three are diagnosed as having an "eating disorder not otherwise specified."

The perspective of virtual intrasexual competition makes an important contribution with respect to its integration with, and extension of, the intrasexual competition hypothesis of eating restriction. Two important primary variants of this hypothesis exist. One variant, as argued and elaborated by Salmon (this volume), asserts that dominant females succeed at intrasexual competition by inducing restricted eating in subordinates, which then lowers their body fat until they are unable to ovulate. In this case, women compete intrasexually by getting other females to stop eating. The other variant of this hypothesis, which is more relevant to women's self-imposed eating disorders, proposes that thinness was an indicator of youth and nubility in the ancestral past, and women therefore restrict their diets to signal fertility to mates (Abed, 1998; Li, Smith, Griskevicius, Cason, & Bryan, 2010; Li, Smith, Yong, & Brown, 2014).

The hourglass shape (i.e., WHR; Singh, 1993) and body mass (indexed by the body mass index [BMI]; measured by weight in kilograms divided by the square of the height in meters) have been argued to hold reliable information about a woman's reproductive condition. There is some debate with regard to the relative importance of BMI and WHR for women's attractiveness. Research that has sought to synthesize WHR and BMI include Lassek and Gaulin's (2008) work on fat distribution. The authors demonstrated that BMI was strongly related to body fat, and the relationship between WHR and BMI mediated the relationship between WHR and fat. Because women with low WHRs and BMIs generally have less body fat, they have less energy reserve to support the energy demands of pregnancy and to increase survival in times of famine.

Men evolved to prefer females with typically low WHRs and BMIs within a specific range as mates because such females had higher reproductive capacity, were not currently pregnant or lactating, and were also less likely to have had a history of pregnancies. Studies have determined these WHR and BMI figures as 0.68 ± 0.04 and 18.09 ± 1.21, respectively, in 300 *Playboy* models (Tovée, Mason, Emery, McClusky, & Cohen-Tovée, 1997) and 0.68 ± 0.04 and 18.4 ± 1.3, respectively, in 129 female adult film stars (Voracek & Fisher, 2006).

As women age, they not only lose the hourglass shape but also tend to gain body mass. These changes are especially apparent when women's bodies are subjected to cycles of pregnancy, childbirth, and nursing, as they would have been from a relatively earlier age in the ancestral past (e.g., Bourgeois-Pichat, 1967; Wood, 1990). Thus, the hourglass shape and bodily thinness may also have been reliably associated with being nubile—that is, in a state of fecundity with no reproductive history.

Importantly, these judgments do not occur in a vacuum and are instead made based on comparisons between people in the social environment, so whether a woman is judged as slim or not (and therefore whether she was likely nubile or not) depends on the other women around her. For instance, a study of men in an isolated Matsigenka village in Peru showed that "overweight" figures with a WHR of 0.9 (highly unattractive by modern Western standards) were rated as most attractive, but this WHR was characteristic of young women in the village before their first pregnancy (Yu & Shepard, 1998).

Women exposed to mass media thus perceive themselves to be surrounded by especially slim competitors, which leads them to experience pressure to be as thin as, if not thinner than, the slim women portrayed in mass media. This competitive pressure arises from the threat of losing out in the mating game. Whereas WHRs are largely influenced by estrogen levels (Cashdan, 2008; Singh, 1993), thinness not only may be influenced by hormones but also may be controllable to some extent through dieting. As such, women may have evolved to be sensitive to perceptions of premature obesity and to strive for being as thin as or thinner than the young female competitors in their environment (Abed, 1998).

The phenomenon of the thin ideal (e.g., Thompson & Stice, 2001) serves as an important illustration of this mechanism. Some scholars have argued that the thin ideal is most influentially spread via mass media, where slim female models are ubiquitous (e.g., Harrison & Cantor, 1997). Until recently, the thin ideal has been regarded as unique to the West. A review of attitudes toward female body fat (Anderson, Crawford, Nadeau, & Lindberg, 1992) found considerable cross-cultural variability in such attitudes. Thinness, body dissatisfaction, and eating disorders are reliable manifestations of the internalization of such thin ideal attitudes (Ahern et al., 2008; Stice & Shaw, 2002; Thompson & Stice, 2001), and these symptoms have generally been found to be more prevalent in Western versus non-Western (e.g., Makino et al., 2004) and in industrialized versus nonindustrialized countries (e.g., Choudry & Mumford, 1992).

However, there is also important growing evidence that such a thin ideal is spreading across the globe. Women in Japan, Iran, and Hong Kong are exhibiting increasing symptoms of adoption of the thin ideal, including decreased BMIs, increased rates of eating disorders, and greater bodily dissatisfaction, and this has typically been attributed to cultural outflows from the West, including urbanization and globalization (Makino et al., 2004). An examination of adolescent Fijian girls' eating behaviors before and after the arrival of Western television programs found that, after 3 years of Western television exposure, self-induced vomiting in the population went from being nonexistent to being endorsed by 11.3% of the population (Becker et al., 2002). The researchers further found a reported 16.5% increase in clinical levels of disordered eating attitudes. Relatedly, a negative perception about weight, which leads to a "fat stigma," is also gradually becoming a worldwide cultural norm. This stigma is increasingly found in places that have traditionally considered larger bodies to be more attractive, such as Puerto Rico, Paraguay, and American Samoa (Brewis, Wutich, Falletta-Cowden, & Rodriguez-Soto, 2011). While the size of the ideal female body is becoming thinner, the rate of female obesity in countries such as the United States is simultaneously increasing, indicating that this bodily ideal is only becoming more difficult for women to achieve or maintain (Pinhas, Toner, Ali, Garfinkel, & Stuckless, 1999).

A consideration of the evolutionary role of intrasexual competition in this globalizing phenomenon may be instructive. The prevalent thin ideal that is thought to be a product of Western culture may be rooted in the workings of women's innate mental composites (Symons, 1979) of their competitors for potential mates. While such composites might have been functional for setting comparison standards within the ancestral setting of a small village, in the modern world they include an unnaturally high number of thin, nubile-looking competitors, both real and virtual, thereby leading to perpetual shortcomings between one's self-evaluation and one's ideal, desired state (Li et al., 2014). Observing many thin women in the global and virtual environment today thus may lead to overbearing pressure to be equally, if not more, thin.

As described previously, in modern environments, advertisers strategically exploit the intrasexual competition psychology of women to encourage them to consume a host of services and goods, including beauty products. When engaged in these contexts, intrasexual competition compels women to take interest in attractive, thin models to socially compare themselves to same-sex individuals of higher mate value. The comparison process seems to be linked to disordered eating. For instance, in one study, eye movements of women presented with various target faces revealed women with relatively high bulimitypic symptomatology, which includes the desire to socially compare, tended to fixate on physically attractive female faces versus average female faces, average male faces, and attractive male faces (Maner et al., 2006). These comparison processes may also be responsible for various cognitive distortions and biases relating to one's own size and shape (e.g., Cooper, 1997), which, along with body dissatisfaction, serve to motivate eating restriction and weight loss. Hence, another result of all this virtual intrasexual competition is that, for some women, mechanisms to compete with same-sex rivals via dietary control may be excessively triggered, thereby leading to unhealthy dieting practices and, in the extreme, disordered eating practices such as anorexia nervosa and bulimia nervosa (Li et al., 2014).

Summary and Strengths of the Virtual Intrasexual Competition Framework

Virtual intrasexual competition provides an important and useful framework linking research on mental health issues to the proliferation of media images of attractive females. We have argued that attractive virtual females presented by various media outlets are perceived as formidable mating rivals,

triggering competitive mechanisms that lead to lowered self-esteem, a higher prevalence of depression and depressive symptoms, as well as increased rates of eating disorders.

A critical review (Ferguson, Winegard, et al., 2011) indicated that the effect size of the direct relationship between media exposure and body dissatisfaction typically does not reach the level of *practical* significance (e.g., Ferguson, 2009). Thus, according to some researchers, the media's *direct* impact on body dissatisfaction may be small and overstated (Ferguson, Winegard, et al., 2011; Holmstrom, 2004). On the other hand, multiple studies across cultures, as presented in this chapter, showed that symptoms of depression, eating disorders, and lower self-esteem do correlate with the prevalence of mass media. This pattern suggests the presence of a previously unidentified variable mediating the link between media exposure and body dissatisfaction, followed by subsequent depressive or disordered eating symptoms. Virtual intrasexual competition serves as a plausible mediating factor and provides a parsimonious explanation for how the idealized female images presented in the mass media may lead to lower self-esteem, depressive symptoms, and disordered eating—which exhibit high comorbidity—among women.

Experimental studies exploring the nuances of the effects of attractive female images suggested that media exposure might have an influence on women's body dissatisfaction insofar as it triggers mating competition mechanisms. For instance, when peer competition and television influences were compared, it was found that television influences were negligible, but women reported greater body dissatisfaction in the presence of attractive peers, especially when a desirable man was present (Ferguson, Winegard, et al., 2011). Female participants with high status aspirations (and who were therefore more competitive) experienced body dissatisfaction after viewing pictures and reading descriptions of women who were thin and successful, but not female participants with low status aspirations (Smith, Li, & Joiner, 2011). The female mate value traits emphasized by the media via attractive images of females must therefore first engage the intrasexual competition psychology of women before the symptoms of body dissatisfaction, depression, and restricted eating manifest. This account thus provides stronger explanatory power above and beyond traditional theories directly linking media exposure with self-esteem, depression, and disordered eating.

Virtual intrasexual competition, with its evolutionary focus, serves as a fundamental explanation and therefore also provides an important clarification for how and why body dissatisfaction even occurs. As suggested by Ferguson, Winegard, et al.'s (2011) review, because media exposure may not directly cause women to have depression or eating disorders, scholars have tried to identify body dissatisfaction as a mediator, but this construct still does not explain why some women will be more or less likely to have body dissatisfaction (Ferguson, Muñoz, Contreras, & Velasquez, 2011; Muñoz & Ferguson, 2012).

Media theorists and other researchers emphasizing social learning explanations have tried to pin the cause on Western thin ideals and gender role expectations that lead to women experiencing greater dissatisfaction with their bodies. However, this conjecture fails to explain the strange pattern wherein bodily dissatisfaction and eating disorders appear to affect heterosexual women and homosexual men at higher rates (Beren, Hayden, Wilfley, & Grilo, 1996; Striegel-Moore, Tucker, & Hsu, 1990). If there is no cultural model for homosexual men to learn from, given that the media primarily presents attractive females, then why should homosexual men exhibit such high rates of eating disorders when the aforementioned cultural causes—Western thin ideals and gender role expectations—are less salient for them? The intrasexual competition explanation for this phenomenon provides an ultimate cause and provides better clarity on these observed trends.

Utilizing the intrasexual competition perspective, Li and colleagues (2010) hypothesized that because heterosexual women and homosexual men both desire male partners, the male mate preference for youth and physical attractiveness instigates both homosexual men and heterosexual women to compete on looks, leading to insecurities with physical appearance for these two groups. Indeed, after being exposed to mating competition cues, homosexual men and heterosexual women, much more than heterosexual men or homosexual women, exhibited worse body image and eating attitudes.

Another study showed that body dissatisfaction for both homosexual and heterosexual men was correlated with muscle and fitness magazine consumption, indicating that when physical attractiveness as a mate value trait becomes salient, men may also experience greater body dissatisfaction from viewing idealized and attractive targets (Duggan &

McCreary, 2004). Therefore, body dissatisfaction occurs when cues trigger intrasexual competition mechanisms for individuals whose mate value is tied more closely to youth and physical attractiveness. Virtual intrasexual competition thus offers a more fundamental explanation for the psychological trends associated with mass media consumption than the variety of social learning explanations that currently dominate the literature.

Indeed, this account is also strengthened by research identifying media effects emphasizing females' mate preference for men's status. Gulas and McKeage (2000) argued that men make social comparisons to advertising imagery and that these comparisons have an impact on male self-perceptions when idealized images reflect "relevant features" other than physical attractiveness. Correspondingly, the authors experimentally demonstrated that showing idealized images of financial success to male participants significantly reduced their self-esteem, whereas idealized images of physical attractiveness had no effect. Tellingly, financial success in a mate is a trait that females value and prioritize more than males (e.g., Li & Kenrick, 2006; Li et al., 2013). Consistent with the virtual intrasexual competition framework, men who are subjected to images that induce comparisons on relevant female mate preference dimensions should experience feelings of heightened intrasexual competition.

Future Directions

Researchers and practitioners concerned with addressing how people might overcome detriments to psychological well-being may benefit from an understanding of evolutionary mismatch and a consideration of the virtual intrasexual competition perspective. Many aspects of our modern environment and lifestyle, including exercise, diet, exposure to chemicals, and hygiene practices, are mismatched to our bodies' physiological evolutionary state. If, owing to our prehistoric ancestors' hunter-gatherer lifestyles, our physiology is evolutionarily hardwired for low caloric intake and intense physical activity, our rich modern diets and sedentary lifestyles mismatch our innate metabolism (Neel, 1962; Wang & Mariman, 2008). A growing body of evolutionary medicine research demonstrates that many of today's so-called diseases of civilization that are highly prevalent and growing rapidly in incidence, such as diabetes, obesity, and cardiovascular disease, may be driven by a mismatch in the metabolic rate our bodies are currently subjected to in our modern environment versus the metabolic rate that our bodies evolved for (Leonard, 2007). Contemporary populations that have undergone a "nutrition transition" in which rapid socioeconomic, demographic, and technological changes have brought profound changes in diet and activity patterns often experience sudden and widespread increases in metabolic disorders. Therefore, an understanding of evolutionary mismatch can be useful for practitioners who seek to eliminate or reduce various forms of modern human suffering.

The virtual intrasexual competition perspective also predicts that both women and men should be susceptible to mass media exposure, except that men and women likely respond differently to various types of mass media stimuli. To date, there is scant research on the kinds of male archetypes presented in the media that may negatively affect men's self-perceptions and subsequent well-being. As predicted by evolutionary theories of mate preferences, women are more likely than men to value social status and dominance in a mate (Buss, 1989; Li et al., 2002). Therefore, if the mass media wishes to utilize idealized male exemplars, these exemplars are likely to be dominant men of high social status. The virtual intrasexual competition perspective predicts that men are more likely than women to be negatively affected when excessively exposed to media images of socially confident, ambitious, successful, and dominant individuals. Indeed, men are more likely than women to derogate competitors on dominance and status because insults on these traits are more likely to hurt male competitors than female competitors (Buss & Dedden, 1990), and women are more likely than men to rate their relationships less favorably when exposed to socially dominant opposite-sex targets (Kenrick et al., 1994). Future studies can determine the extent to which idealized male exemplars espoused by the media might contribute to decrements in men's self-worth.

Further research can also identify the effectiveness of buffers to reduce the influence of media imagery on women, such as encouraging media producers to explore a wider range of types of female images, encouraging females to partake in more non-media-related activities and reduce their consumption of media, and perhaps even simply educating females to be aware of the negative effects of intrasexual competition. Indeed, it has been argued that the effectiveness of evolved mechanisms might be compromised once we become conscious of

them (Nesse & Lloyd, 1992), so shining a spotlight on one's mental processes in this manner can lead to deliberate attempts to short-circuit the automaticity (and reduce the unavoidability) of the psychological process.

Conclusion

We have presented theory and findings outlining a virtual intrasexual competition perspective, with a focus on women. Increasingly, people are negatively affected by mass media images of perceived competitors, albeit in different ways. Women are inundated with images and portrayals of physically attractive virtual females that they interpret as competitors and respond by having lowered self-esteem, becoming depressed, or eating in a disordered fashion. Men, on the other hand, are more likely than women to experience depletions in self-worth from viewing financially successful men. Fundamentally, intrasexual competition underlies these reactions to disparate types of stimuli. As described in this chapter, these dysfunctional responses are the result of evolutionary mismatch—adaptations to ancestral environments that have become maladaptive in the technology-laden modern world.

Based on the evidence accumulated thus far, we believe that future studies building on the ideas presented here will likely contribute to our understanding of not only the issues identified currently but also many of the ills of modern society. Just as important, such research can facilitate the identification of means to counter the negative effects of psychological mechanisms mismatched to the environment and thus increase the well-being of many individuals worldwide.

References

Abed, R. T. (1998). The sexual competition hypothesis for eating disorders. *British Journal of Medical Psychology, 71*(4), 525–547.

Aghion, P., Bloom, N., Blundell, R., Griffith, R., & Howitt, P. (2005). Competition and innovation: An inverted-U relationship. *Quarterly Journal of Economics, 120*(2), 701–728.

Agliata, D., & Tantleff-Dunn, S. (2004). The impact of media exposure on males' body image. *Journal of Social and Clinical Psychology, 23*(1), 7–22.

Ahern, A. L., Bennett, K. M., & Hetherington, M. M. (2008). Internalization of the ultra-thin ideal: Positive implicit associations with underweight fashion models are associated with drive for thinness in young women. *Eating Disorders, 16*(4), 294–307.

Al-Hejin, B. (2004). Attention and awareness: Evidence from cognitive and second language acquisition research. *Columbia University Working Papers in TESOL and Applied Linguistics, 4*(1), 1–22.

Allan, S., & Gilbert, P. (2002). Anger and anger expression in relation to perceptions of social rank, entrapment and depressive symptoms. *Personality and Individual Differences, 32,* 551–565.

American Psychiatric Association. (2013). *Diagnostic and statistical manual of mental disorders* (5th ed). Arlington, VA: American Psychiatric Association.

American Psychological Association. (2007). *Report of the APA Task Force on the Sexualization of Girls.* Washington, DC: American Psychological Association.

Anderson, J. L., Crawford, C. B., Nadeau, J., & Lindberg, T. (1992). Was the Duchess of Windsor right? A cross-cultural review of the socioecology of ideals of female body shape. *Ethology and Sociobiology, 13,* 197–227.

Ariely, D., & Loewenstein, G. (2006). The heat of the moment: The effect of sexual arousal on sexual decision making. *Journal of Behavioral Decision Making, 19,* 87–98.

Baker, M. D., & Maner, J. K. (2008). Risk-taking as a situationally sensitive male mating strategy. *Evolution and Human Behavior, 29,* 391–395.

Barkow, J. H., Cosmides, L., & Tooby, J. (1992). *The adapted mind: Evolutionary psychology and the generation of culture.* Oxford: Oxford University Press.

Barrett, D. (2007). *Waistland: The (r)evolutionary science behind our weight and fitness crisis.* New York: Norton.

Bateman, A. J. (1948). Intra-sexual selection in *Drosophila. Heredity, 2*(3), 349–368,

Becker, A. E., Burwell, R. A., Herzog, D. B., Hamburg, P., & Gilman, S. E. (2002). Eating behaviours and attitudes following prolonged exposure to television among ethnic Fijian adolescent girls. *British Journal of Psychiatry, 180*(6), 509–514.

Becker, D. V., Kenrick, D. T., Guerin, S., & Maner, J. K. (2005). Concentrating on beauty: Sexual selection and sociospatial memory. *Personality and Social Psychology Bulletin, 31*(12), 1643–1652.

Ben Hamida, S., Mineka, S., & Bailey, J. M. (1998). Sex differences in perceived controllability of mate value: An evolutionary perspective. *Journal of Personality and Social Psychology, 75,* 953–966.

Beren, S. E., Hayden, H. A., Wilfley, D. E., & Grilo, C. M. (1996). The influence of sexual orientation on body dissatisfaction in adult men and women. *International Journal of Eating Disorders, 20*(2), 135–141.

Betzig, L. (1989). Causes of conjugal dissolution: A cross-cultural study. *Current Anthropology, 30*(5), 654–676.

Bhugra, D., & Mastrogianni, A. (2004). Globalisation and mental disorders. *British Journal of Psychiatry, 184,* 10–20.

Billings, A. G., Cronkite, R. C., & Moos, R. H. (1983). Social-environmental factors in unipolar depression: Comparisons of depressed patients and nondepressed controls. *Journal of Abnormal Psychology, 92,* 119–133.

Bjorklund, D. F., & Shackelford, T. K. (1999). Differences in parental investment contribute to important differences between men and women. *Current Directions in Psychological Science, 8*(3), 86–89.

Blanchard, R. J., McKittrick, C. R., & Blanchard, D. C. (2001). Animal models of social stress: Effects on behavior and brain neurochemical systems. *Physiology and Behavior, 73,* 261–271.

Blinder, B. J., Cumella, E. J., & Sanathara, V. A. (2006). Psychiatric comorbidities of female inpatients with eating disorders. *Psychosomatic Medicine, 68*(3), 454–462.

Bobjer, J., Katrinaki, M., Tsatsanis, C., Giwercman, Y. L., & Giwercman, A. (2013). Negative association between testosterone concentration and inflammatory markers in young men: A nested cross-sectional study. *PLoS ONE, 8*(4), e61466.

Bourgeois-Pichat, J. (1967). Social and biological determinants of human fertility in nonindustrial societies. *Proceedings of the American Philosophical Society, 111*(3), 160–163.

Bovee, C., & Arens, W. (1986). *Contemporary advertising.* Chicago: Irwin.

Bower, A. B. (2001). Highly attractive models in advertising and the women who loathe them: The implications of negative affect for spokesperson effectiveness. *Journal of Advertising, 30*(3), 51–63.

Brewis, A. A., Wutich, A., Falletta-Cowden, A., & Rodriguez-Soto, I. (2011). Body norms and fat stigma in global perspective. *Current Anthropology, 52*(2), 269–276.

Buss, D. M. (1988). The evolution of human intrasexual competition: Tactics of mate attraction. *Journal of Personality and Social Psychology, 54*(4), 616–628.

Buss, D. M. (1989). Sex differences in human mate preferences: Evolutionary hypotheses tested in 37 cultures. *Behavioral and Brain Sciences, 12,* 1–49.

Buss, D. M. (1995). Evolutionary psychology: A new paradigm for psychological science. *Psychological Inquiry, 6,* 1–30.

Buss, D. M., & Dedden, L. A. (1990). Derogation of competitors. *Journal of Social and Personal Relationships, 7,* 395–422.

Buss, D. M., & Shackelford, T. K. (1997). Susceptibility to infidelity in the first year of marriage. *Journal of Research in Personality, 31,* 193–221.

Buss, D. M., & Schmitt, D. P. (1993). Sexual strategies theory: An evolutionary perspective on human mating. *Psychological Review, 100*(2), 204–232.

Buss, D. M., Shackelford, T. K., Choe, J., Buunk, B. P., & Dijkstra, P. (2000). Distress about mating rivals. *Personal Relationships, 7,* 235–243.

Cashdan, E. (2008). Waist-to-hip ratio across cultures: Trade-offs between androgen- and estrogen-dependent traits. *Current Anthropology, 49,* 1099–1107.

Cheung, M. S.-P., Gilbert, P., & Irons, C. (2004). An exploration of shame, social rank and rumination in relation to depression. *Personality and Individual Differences, 36,* 1143–1153.

Choudry, I., & Mumford, D. B. (1992). A pilot study of eating disorders in Mirpur (Pakistan) using an Urdu version of the Eating Attitudes Test. *International Journal of Eating Disorders, 11,* 243–251.

Clark, R. D., & Hatfield, E. (1989). Gender differences in receptivity to sexual offers. *Journal of Psychology and Human Sexuality, 2,* 39–55.

Clutton-Brock, T. H., Hodge, S. J., Spong, G., Russell, A. F., Jordan, N. R., Bennett, N. C., … Manser, M. B. (2006). Intrasexual competition and sexual selection in cooperative mammals. *Nature, 444*(7122), 1065–1068.

Colla, J., Buka, S., Harrington, D., & Murphy, J. M (2006). Depression and modernization: A cross-cultural study of women. *Social Psychiatry and Psychiatric Epidemiology, 41*(4), 271–279.

Cooper, M. J. (1997). Cognitive theory of anorexia nervosa and bulimia nervosa: A review. *Behavioural and Cognitive Psychotherapy, 25,* 113–145.

Culbertson, F. (1997). Depression and gender: An international review. *American Psychologist, 52*(1), 25–31.

Cummins, D. D. (2005). Dominance, status, and social hierarchies. In D. M. Buss (Ed.), *The evolutionary psychology handbook* (pp. 676–697). New York: Wiley.

Darwin, C. (1871). *The descent of man and selection in relation to sex*. London: Murray.

Davis, D. M. (1990). Portrayals of women in prime-time network television: Some demographic characteristics. *Sex Roles, 23*, 325–332.

Davison, T. E., & McCabe, M. P. (2006). Adolescent body image and psychosocial functioning. *Journal of Social Psychology, 146*, 15–30.

Deci, E., Betley, G., Kahle, J., Abrams, L., & Porac, J. (1981). When trying to win: Competition and intrinsic motivation. *Personality and Social Psychology Bulletin, 7*, 79–83.

Deutsch, M. (1962). Cooperation and trust: Some theoretical notes. In M. Jones (Ed.), *Nebraska Symposium on Motivation* (pp. 275–320). Lincoln: University of Nebraska Press.

Dijkstra, P., & Buunk, B. P. (1998). Jealousy as a function of rival characteristics: An evolutionary perspective. *Personality and Social Psychology Bulletin, 24*, 1158–1166.

Djuric, Z., Bird, C. E., Furumoto-Dawson, A., Rauscher, G. H., Ruffin, M. T., IV, . . . Masi, C. M. (2008). Biomarkers of psychological stress in health disparities research. *The Open Biomarkers Journal, 1*(1), 7–19.

Dobzhansky, T., & Pavlovsky, O. (1967). Repeated mating and sperm mixing in *Drosophila pseudoobscura*. *American Naturalist, 101*(922), 527–533.

Duggan, S. J., & McCreary, D. R. (2004). Body image, eating disorders, and the drive for muscularity in gay and heterosexual men: The influence of media images. *Journal of Homosexuality, 47*(3–4), 45–58.

Dunbar, R. I. M. (1992). Neocortex size as a constraint on group size in primates. *Journal of Human Evolution, 22*(6), 469–493.

Dunson, D. B., Colombo, B., & Baird, D. D. (2002). Changes with age in the level and duration of fertility in the menstrual cycle. *Human Reproduction, 17*(5), 1399–1403.

Durkin, S. J., & Paxton, S. J. (2002). Predictors of vulnerability to reduced body image satisfaction and psychological wellbeing in response to exposure to idealized female media images in adolescent girls. *Journal of Psychosomatic Research, 53*(5), 995–1005.

Ebrecht, M., Hextall, J., Kirtley, L. G., Taylor, A., Dyson, M., & Weinman, J. (2004). Perceived stress and cortisol levels predict speed of wound healing in healthy male adults. *Psychoneuroendocrinology, 29*(6), 798–809.

Elliott, L. (2008, December 22). Into the red: "Lipstick effect" reveals the true face of the recession. *The Guardian*. Retrieved from http://www.guardian.co.uk

Ewen, S. (1976). *Captains of consciousness: Advertising and the social roots of the consumer culture*. New York: McGraw-Hill.

Eysenck, S. B. G., & Eysenck, H. J. (1978). Impulsiveness and venturesomeness: Their position in a dimensional system of personality description. *Psychological Reports, 43*, 1247–1255.

Ferguson, C. J. (2009). An effect size primer: A guide for clinicians and researchers. *Professional Psychology: Research and Practice, 40*, 532–538.

Ferguson, C. J. (2013). In the eye of the beholder: Thin-ideal media affects some, but not most, viewers in a meta-analytic review of body dissatisfaction in women and men. *Psychology of Popular Media Culture, 2*(1), 20–37.

Ferguson, C. J., Muñoz, E. M., Contreras, S., & Velasquez, K. (2011). Mirror, mirror on the wall: Peer competition, television influences, and body image dissatisfaction. *Journal of Social and Clinical Psychology, 30*(5), 458–483.

Ferguson, C. J., Winegard, B., & Winegard, B. M. (2011). Who is the fairest one of all? How evolution guides peer and media influences on female body dissatisfaction. *Review of General Psychology, 15*(1), 11–28.

Ferguson, J. H., Kreshel, P. J., & Tinkham, S. F. (1990). In the pages of *Ms.*: Sex role portrayals of women in advertising. *Journal of Advertising, 19*, 40–51

Fisher, M. L., & Voracek, M. (2005). The shape of beauty: Determinants of female physical attractiveness. *Journal of Cosmetic Dermatology, 5*, 190–194.

Ford, J. B., Voli, P. K., Honeycutt, E. D., Jr., & Casey, S. L. (1998). Gender role portrayals in Japanese advertising: A magazine content analysis. *Journal of Advertising, 27*, 113–124.

Fournier, M. A. (2009). Adolescent hierarchy formation and the social competition theory of depression. *Journal of Social and Clinical Psychology, 28*(9), 1144–1172.

Fournier, M. A., Moskowitz, D. S., & Zuroff, D. C. (2002). Social rank strategies in hierarchical relationships. *Journal of Personality and Social Psychology, 83*, 425–433.

Frith, K., Shaw, P., & Cheng, H. (2005). The construction of beauty: A cross-cultural analysis of women's magazine advertising. *Journal of Communication, 55*(1), 56–70.

Fullerton, J. A., & Kendrick, A. (2000). Portrayal of men and women in U.S. Spanish-language television commercials. *Journalism and Mass Communication Quarterly, 77*, 128–142.

Geary, D. C. (2005). Evolution of paternal investment. In D. M. Buss (Ed.), *The evolutionary psychology handbook* (pp. 483–505). Hoboken, NJ: Wiley.

Gilbert, P. (1992). *Depression: The evolution of powerlessness*. Hillsdale, NJ: Erlbaum.

Gilbert, P. (2001). Evolutionary approaches to psychopathology: The role of natural defences. *Australian and New Zealand Journal of Psychiatry, 35*, 17–27.

Gilbert, P., & Allan, S. (1998). The role of defeat and entrapment (arrested flight) in depression: An exploration of an evolutionary view. *Psychological Medicine, 28*, 585–598.

Gilbert, P., Gilbert, J., & Irons, C. (2004). Life events, entrapments and arrested anger in depression. *Journal of Affective Disorders, 79*, 149–160.

Gilbert, P., Price, J. S., & Allan, S. (1995). Social comparison, social attractiveness and evolution: How might they be related? *New Ideas in Psychology, 13*, 149–165.

Gulas, C. S., & McKeage, K. (2000). Extending social comparison: An examination of the unintended consequences of idealized advertising imagery. *Journal of Advertising, 29*(2), 17–28.

Gutierres, S. E., Kenrick, D. T., & Partch, J. (1999). Beauty, dominance, and the mating game: Contrast effects in self-assessment reflect gender differences in mate selection criteria. *Personality and Social Psychology Bulletin, 25*, 1126–1134.

Gwynne, D. T., & Bailey, W. J. (1999). Female-female competition in katydids: Sexual selection for increased sensitivity to a male signal? *Evolution, 53*, 546–551.

Hagger, M. S., & Stevenson, A. (2010). Social physique anxiety and physical self-esteem: Gender and age effects. *Psychology and Health, 25*(1), 89–110.

Hall, J. A., Park, N., Song, H., & Cody, M. J. (2010). Strategic misrepresentation in online dating: The effects of gender, self-monitoring, and personality traits. *Journal of Social and Personal Relationships, 27*(1), 117–135.

Hamann, S., Herman, R. A., Nolan, C. L., & Wallen, K. (2004). Men and women differ in amygdala response to visual sexual stimuli. *Nature Neuroscience, 7,* 411–416.

Harrison, K., & Cantor, J. (1997). The relationship between media consumption and eating disorders. *Journal of Communication, 47,* 40–67.

Haskell, M. (1987). *From reverence to rape: The treatment of women in the movies.* Chicago: University of Chicago Press.

Hawkins, N., Richards, P. S., Granley, H. M., & Stein, D. M. (2004). The impact of exposure to the thin-ideal media image on women. *Eating Disorders, 12,* 35–50.

Hawley, D., Lindström, K. M., & Wikelski, M. (2006). Experimentally increased social competition compromises humoral immune response in house finches. *Hormones and Behavior, 49,* 417–424.

Hayhoe, C. R., Leach, L. J., Turner, P. R., Bruin, M., & Lawrence, F. C. (2000). Differences in spending habits and credit use of college students. *Journal of Consumer Affairs, 34,* 113–133.

Hidaka, B. H. (2012). Depression as a disease of modernity: Explanations for increasing prevalence. *Journal of Affective Disorders, 140*(3), 205–214.

Hill, S. E., Rodeheffer, C. D., Griskevicius, V., Durante, K., & White, A. E. (2012). Boosting beauty in an economic decline: Mating, spending, and the lipstick effect. *Journal of Personality and Social Psychology, 103*(2), 275–291.

Holmstrom, A. (2004). The effects of the media on body image: A meta-analysis. *Journal of Broadcasting and Electronic Media, 48,* 196–217.

Hopcroft, R. L., & Bradley, D. B. (2007). The sex difference in depression across 29 countries. *Social Forces, 85*(4), 1483–1507.

Irons, C., & Gilbert, P. (2005). Evolved mechanisms in adolescent anxiety and depression symptoms: The role of the attachment and social rank systems. *Journal of Adolescence, 28,* 325–341.

Italian men suffer "sexual anorexia" after Internet porn use. (2011). Retrieved December 29, 2012, from http://www.ansa.it/web/notizie/rubriche/english/2011/02/24/visual-izza_new.html_1583160579.html

Jain, U. (1978). Competition tolerance in high- and low-density urban and rural areas. *Journal of Social Psychology, 105,* 297–298.

Jenkins, J. H., Kleinman, A., & Good, B. J. (1991). Cross-cultural studies of depression. In J. Becker & A. Kleinman (Eds.), *Psychosocial aspects of depression* (pp. 67–99). Mahwah, NJ: Erlbaum.

Kanazawa, S. (2002). Bowling with our imaginary friends. *Evolution and Human Behavior, 23,* 167–171.

Kavanagh, P. S., Robins, S. C., & Ellis, B. J. (2010). The mating sociometer: A regulatory mechanism for mating aspirations. *Journal of Personality and Social Psychology, 99*(1), 120–132.

Kendler, K. S., Hettema, J. M., Butera, F., Gardner, C. O., & Prescott, C. A. (2003). Life event dimensions of loss, humiliation, entrapment, and danger in the prediction of onsets of major depression and generalized anxiety. *Archives of General Psychiatry, 60,* 789–796.

Kenrick, D. T., Gutierres, S. E., & Goldberg, L. (1989). Influence of erotica on ratings of strangers and mates. *Journal of Experimental Social Psychology, 25,* 159–167.

Kenrick, D. T., Neuberg, S. L., Zierk, K. L., & Krones, J. M. (1994). Evolution and social cognition: Contrast effects as a function of sex, dominance, and physical attractiveness. *Personality and Social Psychology Bulletin, 20,* 210–217.

Kirkpatrick, L. A., & Ellis, B. J. (2001). An evolutionary-psychological approach to self-esteem: Multiple domains and multiple functions. In G. J. O. Fletcher & M. S. Clark (Eds.), *Blackwell handbook of social psychology: Interpersonal processes* (pp. 411–436). Oxford: Blackwell.

Kohn, A. (1992). *No contest: The case against competition.* New York: Houghton Mifflin.

Lassek, W. D., & Gaulin, S. J. C. (2008). Waist-hip ratio and cognitive ability: Is gluteofemoral fat a privileged store of neurodevelopmental resources? *Evolution and Human Behavior, 29,* 26–34.

Leary, M. R., Tambor, E. S., Terdal, S. K., & Downs, D. L. (1995). Self-esteem as an interpersonal monitor: The sociometer hypothesis. *Journal of Personality and Social Psychology, 68*(3), 518–530.

Leonard, W. R. (2007). Lifestyle, diet and disease: Comparative perspectives on the determinants of chronic health risks. In S. C. Stearns & J. C. Koella (Eds.), *Evolution in health and disease* (2nd ed., pp. 265–276). Oxford: Oxford University Press.

Levine, M. P., & Smolak, L. (2002). Body image development in adolescence. In T. F. Cash & T. Pruzinsky (Eds.), *Body image: A handbook of theory, research, and clinical practice* (pp. 74–82). New York: Guilford.

Lewis, S. M., Cratsley, C. K., & Rooney, J. A. (2004). Nuptial gifts and sexual selection in *Photinus* fireflies. *Integrative and Comparative Biology, 44,* 234–237.

Li, N. P. (2007). Mate preference necessities in long- and short-term mating: People prioritize in themselves what their mates prioritize in them. *Acta Psychologica Sinica, 39,* 528–535.

Li, N. P., Bailey, J. M., Kenrick, D. T., & Linsenmeier, J. A. W. (2002). The necessities and luxuries of mate preferences: Testing the tradeoffs. *Journal of Personality and Social Psychology, 82*(6), 947–955.

Li, N. P., & Kenrick, D. T. (2006). Sex similarities and differences in preferences for short-term mates: What, whether, and why. *Journal of Personality and Social Psychology, 90,* 468–489.

Li, N. P., Smith, A., Griskevicius, V., Cason, M. J., & Bryan, A. (2010). Intrasexual competition and eating restriction in heterosexual and homosexual individuals. *Evolution and Human Behavior, 31,* 365–372.

Li, N. P., Smith, A., Yong, J. C., & Brown, T. A. (2014). Intrasexual competition and other theories of eating restriction. In T. K. Shackelford & V. A. Weekes-Shackelford (Eds.), *Evolutionary perspectives on human sexual psychology and behavior* (pp. 323–346). New York: Springer.

Li, N. P., Yong, J. C., Tov, W., Sng, O., Fletcher, G. J. O., Valentine, K. A., … Balliet, D. (2013). Mate preferences do predict attraction and choices in the early stages of mate selection. *Journal of Personality and Social Psychology, 105,* 757–776.

Lin, C. A. (1998). Uses of sex appeals in prime-time television commercials. *Sex Roles, 38,* 461–475.

Little, A. C., & Mannion, H. (2006). Viewing attractive or unattractive same-sex individuals changes self-rated attractiveness and face preferences in women. *Animal Behaviour, 72,* 981–987.

Loewenstein, G. (1996). Out of control: Visceral influences on behavior. *Organizational Behavior and Human Decision Processes, 65*(5003), 272–292.

Loewenstein, G. (2000). Emotions in economic theory and economic behavior. *American Economic Review (Papers and Proceedings)*, *90*(2), 426–432.

Lopate, C. (1977). Selling to Ms. Consumer. *College English: Mass Culture, Political Consciousness and English*, *38*(8), 824–834.

Loyau, A., Saint Jalme, M., Cagniant, C., & Sorci, G. (2005). Multiple sexual advertisements honestly reflect health status in peacocks (*Pavo cristatus*). *Behavioral Ecology and Sociobiology*, *58*, 552–557.

Makino, M., Tsuboi, K., & Dennerstein, L. (2004). Prevalence of eating disorders: A comparison of Western and non-Western countries. *Medscape General Medicine*, *6*(3), 49.

Malkin, A. R., Wornian, K., & Chrisler, J. C. (1999). Women and weight: Gendered messages on magazine covers. *Sex Roles*, *40*, 647–655.

Maner, J. K., Gailliot, M. T., & DeWall, N. (2007). Adaptive attentional attunement: Evidence for mating-related perceptual bias. *Evolution and Human Behavior*, *28*, 28–36.

Maner, J. K., Holm-Denoma, J. M., Van Orden, K. A., Gailliot, M. T., Gordon, K. H., & Joiner, T. E., Jr. (2006). Evidence for attentional bias in women exhibiting bulimotypic symptoms. *International Journal of Eating Disorders*, *39*(1), 55–61.

Maner, J. K., Kenrick, D. T., Becker, D. V., Delton, A., Hofer, B., Wilbur, C., Neuberg, S. L. (2003). Sexually selective cognition: Beauty captures the mind of the beholder. *Journal of Personality and Social Psychology*, *85*, 1107–1120.

Marjorie, R. (1973). *Popcorn Venus: Women, movies, and the American dream*. New York: Coward, McCann & Geoghegan.

Martin, M. C., & Gentry, J. W. (1997). Stuck in the model trap: The effects of beautiful models in ads on female pre-adolescents and adolescents. *Journal of Advertising*, *26*, 19–33.

Martin, M. C., & Kennedy, P. F. (1994). Social comparison and the beauty of advertising models: The role of motives for comparison. *Advances in Consumer Research*, *21*, 365–371.

Mason, J. W. (1968). A review of psychoendocrine research on the sympathetic-adrenal medullary system. *Psychosomatic Medicine*, *30*(Suppl. 5), 631–653.

Maynard, M. L., & Taylor, C. R. (1999). Girlish images across cultures: Analyzing Japanese versus U.S. *Seventeen* magazine ads. *Journal of Advertising*, *28*, 39–48.

Milgram, S. (1970). The experience of living in cities. *Science*, *167*, 1461–1468.

Miller, G. F. (2009). *Spent: Sex, evolution, and consumer behavior*. New York: Viking.

Morris, D. (1967). *The naked ape: A zoologist's study of the human animal*. New York: McGraw-Hill.

Muñoz, M. E., & Ferguson, C. J. (2012). Body dissatisfaction correlates with inter-peer competitiveness, not media exposure: A brief report. *Journal of Social and Clinical Psychology*, *31*(4), 383–392.

Neel, J. V. (1962). Diabetes mellitus: A "thrifty" genotype rendered detrimental by "progress." *American Journal of Human Genetics*, *14*, 353–362.

Nelson, E. (2001, November 26). Rising lipstick sales may mean pouting economy. *The Wall Street Journal*, p. B1.

Nesse, R. M., & Lloyd, A. T. (1992). The evolution of psychodynamic mechanisms. In J. Barkow, L. Cosmides, & J. Tooby (Eds.), *The adapted mind* (pp. 602–624). New York: Oxford University Press.

Neumark-Sztainer, D. (2005). *I'm, like, SO fat!* New York: Guilford Press.

Nezlek, J. B., Hampton, C. P., & Shean, G. D. (2000). Clinical depression and day-to-day social interaction in a community sample. *Journal of Abnormal Psychology*, *109*, 11–19.

Nolen-Hoeksema, S. (1987). Sex differences in unipolar depression: Evidence and theory. *Psychological Bulletin*, *101*, 259–282.

Nolen-Hoeksema, S. (1990). *Sex differences in depression*. Stanford, CA: Stanford University Press.

Palombit, R. A., Cheney, D. L., & Seyfarth, R. M. (2001). Female-female competition for male "friends" in wild chacma baboons, *Papio cynocephalus ursinus*. *Animal Behavior*, *61*, 1159–1171.

Patil, N. H., & Gayatri, Y. (2012). Impact of television on rural women. *Golden Research Thoughts*, *1*(10), 1–4.

Pawlowski, B., Rajinder, A., & Dunbar, R. I. M. (2008). Sex differences in everyday risk-taking behavior in humans. *Evolutionary Psychologyzierk*, *6*(1), 29–42.

Pease, O. (1958). *The responsibilities of American advertising*. New Haven, CT: Yale University Press.

Phillips, G. B., Pinkernell, B. H., & Jing, T. Y. (1994). The association of hypotestosteronemia with coronary artery disease in men. *Arteriosclerosis and Thrombosis: A Journal of Vascular Biology*, *14*, 701–706.

Pinhas, L., Toner, B. B., Ali, A., Garfinkel, P. E., & Stuckless, N. (1999). The effects of the ideal of female beauty on mood and body satisfaction. *International Journal of Eating Disorders*, *25*(2), 223–226.

Plakoyiannaki, E., Mathioudaki, K., Dimitratos, P., & Zotos, Y. (2008). Images of women in online advertisements of global products: Does sexism exist? *Journal of Business Ethics*, *83*, 101–112.

Pollay, R. W. (1986). The distorted mirror: Reflections on the unintended consequences of advertising. *Journal of Marketing*, *50*(2), 18–36.

Provenzo, E. F. (1991). *Video kids: Making sense of Nintendo*. Cambridge, MA: Harvard University Press.

Reichert, T., Heckler, S. E., & Jackson, S. (2001). The effects of sexual social marketing appeals on cognitive processing and persuasion. *Journal of Advertising*, *30*(1), 13–27.

Reichert, T., Lambiase, J., Morgan, S., Carstarphen, M., & Zavoina, S. (1999). Cheesecake and beefcake: No matter how you slice it, sexual explicitness in advertising continues to increase. *Journalism and Mass Communication Quarterly*, *76*, 7–20.

Renfrew Center Foundation for Eating Disorders. (2003). *Eating disorders 101 guide: A summary of issues, statistics and resources*. Retrieved from Renfrew Center Foundation website: http://www.renfrew.org

Richins, M. (1991). Social comparison and the idealized images of advertising. *Journal of Consumer Research*, *18*, 71–83.

Ronay, R., & von Hippel, W. (2010). The presence of an attractive woman elevates testosterone and physical risk-taking in young men. *Social Psychological and Personality Science*, *1*, 57–64.

Rook, D. W. (1987). The buying impulse. *Journal of Consumer Research*, *14*, 189–199.

Rupp, H. A., & Wallen, K. (2008). Sex differences in response to visual sexual stimuli: A review. *Archives of Sexual Behavior*, *37*, 206–218.

Rusu, A. S., & Krackow, S. (2004). Kin-preferential cooperation, dominance-dependent reproductive skew, and competition for mates in communally nesting female house mice. *Behavioral Ecology and Sociobiology*, *56*, 298–305.

Saad, G. (2004). Applying evolutionary psychology in understanding the representation of women in advertisements. *Psychology and Marketing, 21*(8), 593–612.

Saad, G. (2007). *The evolutionary bases of consumption.* Mahwah, NJ: Erlbaum.

Sabiston, C. M., Sedgwick, W. A., Crocker, P. R. E., Kowalski, K. C., & Mack, D. E. (2007). Social physique anxiety in adolescence: An exploration of influences, coping strategies, and health behaviors. *Journal of Adolescent Research, 22*, 78–101.

Salvador, A. (2005). Coping with competitive situations in humans. *Neuroscience and Biobehavioral Reviews, 29*, 195–205.

Sandell, M. I. (1998). Female aggression and the maintenance of monogamy: Female behaviour predicts male mating status in European starlings. *Proceedings of the Royal Society B, 265*(1403), 1307–1311.

Savin-Williams, R. C. (1977). Dominance in a human adolescent group. *Animal Behavior, 25*, 400–406.

Schmidt, R. W. (1994). Deconstructing consciousness in search of useful definitions for applied linguistics. *AILA Review, 11*, 11–26.

Schmitt, D. P., & Buss, D. M. (1996). Strategic self-promotion and competitor derogation: Sex and context effects on the perceived effectiveness of mate attraction tactics. *Journal of Personality and Social Psychology, 70*(6), 1185–1204.

Seligman, M. E. P. (1975). *Helplessness: On depression, development and death.* San Francisco: Freeman.

Signorielli, N., & Bacue, A. (1999). Recognition and respect: A content analysis of prime-time television characters across three decades. *Sex Roles, 40*, 527–544.

Silverstein, B., Perdue, L., Peterson, B., & Kelly, E. (1986). The role of the mass media in promoting a thin standard of bodily attractiveness for women. *Sex Roles, 14*, 519–532.

Singh, D. (1993). Adaptive significance of female physical attractiveness: Role of waist-to-hip ratio. *Journal of Personality and Social Psychology, 65*(2), 293–307.

Sloman, L., & Gilbert, P. (2000). *Subordination and defeat: An evolutionary approach to mood disorders and their therapy.* Mahwah, NJ: Erlbaum.

Sloman, L., Price, J., Gilbert, P., & Gardner, R. (1994). Adaptive function of depression: Psychotherapeutic implications. *American Journal of Psychotherapy, 48*, 401–416.

Smith, A. R., Li, N. P., & Joiner, T. (2011). The pursuit of success: Can status aspirations negatively affect body satisfaction? *Journal of Social and Clinical Psychology, 30*, 531–547.

Stack, S. (1993). The effect of modernization on suicide in finland: 1800–1984. *Sociological Perspectives, 36*(2), 137–148.

Stallman, H. (2012). A qualitative evaluation of perceptions of the role of competition in the success and distress of law students. *Higher Education Research and Development, 31*(6), 891–904.

Stanne, M., Johnson, D., & Johnson, R. (1999). Does competition enhance or inhibit motor performance: A meta-analysis. *Psychological Bulletin, 125*, 133–154.

Stephan, W., Berscheid, E., & Walster, E. (1971). Sexual arousal and heterosexual perception. *Journal of Personality and Social Psychology, 20*, 93–101.

Stice, E., Schupak-Neuberg, E., Shaw, H. E., & Stein, R. I. (1994). Relation of media exposure to eating disorder symptomatology: An examination of mediating mechanisms. *Journal of Abnormal Psychology, 103*(4), 836–840.

Stice, E., & Shaw, H. E. (2002). Role of body dissatisfaction in the onset and maintenance of eating pathology. *Journal of Psychosomatic Research, 53*, 985–993.

Strayer, F. F., & Strayer, J. (1976). An ethological analysis of social agonism and dominance relations among preschool children. *Child Development, 47*, 980–989.

Striegel-Moore, R. H., Silberstein, L. R., & Rodin, R. (1986). Towards an understanding of risk factors for bulimia. *American Psychologist, 41*, 246–263.

Striegel-Moore, R. H., Tucker, N., & Hsu, J. (1990). Body image dissatisfaction and disordered eating in lesbian college students. *International Journal of Eating Disorders, 9*, 493–500.

Swenson, R. O. (1997). Sex-role reversal in the tidewater goby, *Eucyclogobius newberryi. Environmental Biology of Fishes, 50*, 27–40.

Symons, D. (1979). *The evolution of human sexuality.* New York: Oxford University Press.

Tauer, J. M., & Harackiewicz, J. M. (2004). The effects of cooperation and competition on intrinsic motivation and performance. *Journal of Personality and Social Psychology, 86*, 849–861.

Thompson, J. K., & Stice, E. (2001). Thin-ideal internalization: Mounting evidence for a new risk factor for body-image disturbance and eating pathology. *Current Directions in Psychological Science, 10*(5), 181–183.

Till, B., & Busler, M. (2000). The match-up hypothesis: Physical attractiveness, expertise, and the role of fit on brand attitude, purchase intent and brand beliefs. *Journal of Advertising, 29*(3), 1–13.

Tinbergen, N., & Perdeck, A. C. (1950). On the stimulus situation releasing the begging response in the newly hatched herring gull chick (*Larus argentatus* Pont.). *Behaviour, 3*, 1–39.

Tjosvold, D., Johnson, D. W., Johnson, R. T., & Sun, H. (2003). Can interpersonal competition be constructive within organizations? *Journal of Psychology: Interdisciplinary and Applied, 137*(1), 63–84.

Tooby, J., & Cosmides, L. (1990). The past explains the present: Emotional adaptations and the structure of ancestral environments. *Ethology and Sociobiology, 11*, 375–424.

Tooby, J., & Cosmides, L. (1992). The psychological foundations of culture. In J. Barkow, L. Cosmides, & J. Tooby (Eds.), *The adapted mind* (pp. 19–136). New York: Oxford University Press.

Tooke, W., & Camire, L. (1991). Patterns of deception in intersexual and intrasexual mating strategies. *Ethology and Sociobiology, 12*, 345–364.

Tovée, M. J., Mason, S., Emery, J. L., McClusky, S. E., & Cohen-Tovée, E. M. (1997). Supermodels: Stick insects or hourglasses? *Lancet, 350*, 1474–1475.

Trivers, R. L. (1972). Parental investment and sexual selection. In B. Campbell (Ed.), *Sexual selection and the descent of man, 1871–1971* (pp. 136–179). Chicago: Aldine.

Trivers, R. L. (2011). *The folly of fools: The logic of deceit and self-deception in human life.* New York: Basic Books.

Voracek, M., & Fisher, M. L. (2006). Success is all in the measures: Androgenousness, curvaceousness, and starring frequencies in adult media actresses. *Archives of Sexual Behavior, 35*, 297–304.

Walters, S., & Crawford, C. B. (1994). The importance of mate attraction for intrasexual competition in men and women. *Ethology and Sociobiology, 15*, 5–30.

Wang, P., & Mariman, E. D. M. (2008). Insulin resistance in an energy-centered perspective. *Physiology and Behavior, 94*(2), 198–205.

Wee, C. H., Choong, M. L., & Tambyah, S. K. (1995). Sex role portrayal in television advertising. *International Marketing Review, 12,* 49–64.

Weissman, M. M., Bland, R. C., Canino, G. J., Faravelli, C., Greenwald, S., Hwu, H.-G., . . . Yeh, E. K. (1996). Cross-national epidemiology of major depression and bipolar disorder. *Journal of the American Medical Association, 276,* 293–299.

Wilson, M., & Daly, M. (2004). Do pretty women inspire men to discount the future? *Proceedings of the Royal Society B, 271,* S177–S179.

Wobber, V., Hare, B., Maboto, J., Lipson, S., Wrangham, R., & Ellison, P. T. (2010). Differential changes in steroid hormones before competition in bonobos and chimpanzees. *Proceedings of the National Academy of Sciences, 107,* 12457–12462.

Wood, J. W. (1990). Fertility in anthropological populations. *Annual Review of Anthropology, 19,* 211–242.

Yu, D. W., & Shepard, G. H. (1998). Is beauty in the eye of the beholder? *Nature, 396,* 321–322.

Zuroff, D. C., Fournier, M. A., & Moskowitz, D. S. (2007). Depression, perceived inferiority, and interpersonal behavior: Evidence for the involuntary defeat strategy. *Journal of Social and Clinical Psychology, 26,* 751–778.

Facebook Frenemies and Selfie-Promotion: Women and Competition in the Digital Age

Amanda E. Guitar *and* Rachael A. Carmen

Abstract

Human communication has been largely influenced by the global popularization of social network sites such as Facebook over the past decade. From PCs to mobile phones, humans can now communicate in ways never before experienced during our history on Earth; moreover, sites like Facebook are providing a novel platform for engaging in female intrasexual competition. Through cyberbullying, selfies, and Facebook "stalking," females are engaging in traditional strategies of intrasexual competition (i.e., self-promotion, rival derogation, mate manipulation, and competitor manipulation) in an evolutionarily novel social environment. This chapter examines what is new about social interactions that take place online and what is an artifact of our evolutionary heritage. Additionally, it argues that the self-promoting material that Facebook users post to the site is indicative of underlying fitness; therefore Facebook postings are an example of a modern-day extended phenotype.

Key Words: intrasexual competition, extended phenotype, Facebook, evolutionary heritage, selfie

In the twenty-first century, much of our lives are consumed with evolutionarily novel stimuli. Cars, trains, and airplanes allow us to travel distances that would have been physically impossible just 100 years ago; similarly, the Internet allows us to share ideas on a mass scale and interact with individuals in ways never before imagined. This relatively recent change has facilitated the rapid sharing of many forms of knowledge, be it scholarly, cultural, or social. Additionally, it is now possible to communicate with others scattered throughout the world on a scale that humans have never before encountered during our history on Earth. Since the Internet was released to the public in the early 1990s, our lives increasingly take place online. From shopping to sharing personal news, websites now facilitate many components of our everyday experience.

In particular, social network sites have become an increasingly prominent part of the online experience,

with 72% of online adults reporting using a social network site in 2013, a drastic increase from the 8% who reported social network use in 2005 (Pew Internet & American Life Project, 2013b). Social network sites refer to "web-based services that allow individuals to construct a public or semi-public profile within a bounded system, articulate a list of other users with whom they share a connection, and view and traverse their list of connections and those made by others within the system" (boyd & Ellison, 2007, p. 211). Social network sites are popular among both adolescents and adults, with the largest age group in the United States being 18- to 29-year-olds (89%; Pew Internet & American Life Project, 2013a). Of the multitude of social media platforms currently available (e.g., Twitter, Instagram, Google+, LinkedIn, Tumblr, Myspace), Facebook (www.facebook.com) is the most popular, with over 1.44 billion users worldwide actively using the site each month (Facebook, 2014b). According to Facebook's information page, "People use Facebook to stay connected with friends and family, to discover what's going on in the world, and to share and express what matters to them" (Facebook, 2014a). In this chapter we argue that one of the reasons that females choose to "stay connected" and "share and express what matters to them" is because Facebook provides users with a novel platform for engaging in competition with other females (i.e., intrasexual competition).

Charles Darwin (1859) made many groundbreaking observations, including the ideas of *natural* and *sexual* selection. Essentially, the logic is as follows: natural selection is a mechanism (or "driving force") of evolution, and it acts on an individual's phenotype (i.e., observable physical traits). Observable traits are the product of generations and generations' worth of sexual selection, which is further broken down in terms of intra- and intersexual selection. *Intrasexual selection* refers to competition within the sexes, as opposed to *intersexual selection*, which is competition between the sexes (Darwin, 1859). Darwin emphasized male–male competition as the typical form of intrasexual selection and female choice as the typical form of intersexual selection (Buss, 1988; Darwin, 1871; Gray & Garcia, 2013). Fundamentally, this means that mate choice drives competition between same-sex conspecifics, and thus traits that are seen as more "attractive" are selected for through preferences of the opposite sex (Buss, 1988; Darwin, 1859; Fisher & Cox, 2010; Gray & Garcia, 2013).

An example of a potentially attractive phenotypic trait in females is waist-to-hip ratio (WHR) where the lower the number, the more drastic the difference between a female's waist and her hips (Gray & Garcia, 2013; Singh, 1993). When discussing this topic, it is important to keep in mind that WHR does *not* refer to a specific weight; instead it is in reference to how a female's body *distributes* fat. This example is particularly interesting because it refers to a secondary sexual characteristic (i.e., a characteristic that comes about after a surge of hormones experienced during puberty; Gray & Garcia, 2013). Early research into WHRs hypothesized that a female WHR of around .7 is universally preferred by males and is predictive of reproductive viability because a female's body taps into these fat reserves when she gets pregnant. Singh (1993) suggested that an "hourglass" figure distribution of fat makes it more likely for females to get pregnant and stay pregnant since the body pulls specifically on

gluteofemoral fat during the entirety of the gestation term. However, it is important to keep in mind that there is variability for this preference within and between various historical time periods and cultures (see Swami, Jones, Einon, & Furnham, 2009), suggesting that this variability can be seen as a product of various types of environments. Research has found that low WHRs tend to be preferred by those living in high-resource environments, while high WHRs are perceived more favorably in low-resource environments (Swami & Tovée, 2007). For example, in some subsistence societies, like the Hadza of Tanzania, men tend to prefer women who have high WHRs because this is linked with increased reproductive potential (Gray & Garcia, 2013). In contrast, research has found that men in the United States tend to prefer lower WHRs, possibly due to the prevalence of obesity in this society and the negative health outcomes associated with it (Marlowe & Wetsman, 2001). The fact that various types of WHR are seen as desirable depending on environmental factors speaks to the competition faced by same-sexed individuals to find an "appropriate" mate (Gray & Garcia, 2013; Singh, 1993). This is the essence of intrasexual competition.

Classically, intrasexual competition was conceptualized in terms of two strategies: self-promotion and rival derogation (e.g., Buss, 1988, Schmitt & Buss, 1996). However, Fisher and Cox (2010) found that individuals actually tend to utilize two additional strategies as well: mate manipulation and rival manipulation. The addition of the manipulation facet to the strategies that make up intrasexual competition is crucial because self-promotion and rival derogation do not speak to the strategy deployed by individuals vying for attention by potential mates. Mate manipulation is played out in terms of removing the potential mate from the competition by creating an illusion that makes the presence/actions of the rivals unbeknownst to the potential mate (Fisher & Cox, 2010). This occurs by actions that prevent potential competitors from gaining access to the current or potential mate. For example, mate manipulation may involve a couple going to a dance and, after seeing one's date dancing with someone else, telling him or her one does not feel well and asking to go home.

On the other hand, rival manipulation can take multiple forms, like reducing the worth of the "prize" (Fisher & Cox, 2010). In order to reduce competition from rivals, it would be beneficial to an individual to convince others that the "prize" is not worth the costs (e.g., convincing competitors that a potential mate is not worth their time because he is getting over an ex-partner). In an evolutionary sense, there is always a cost-benefit trade off; therefore, there is a good chance that if an individual "plays down" the potential mate's worth to other competitors, the costs of competing will outweigh the benefits and ultimately not be worth it (Fisher & Cox, 2010).

Of the four strategies of intrasexual competition, self-promotion has been found to be the most commonly used, with mate manipulation second and competitor derogation and manipulation strategies not significantly differing from one another in regard to usage (there were also no sex differences found; Fisher & Cox, 2010). Additionally, Fisher and Cox explain that strategies could possibly be used depending on the stage of competition for the mate. For example, self-promotion can be performed in the earliest stages of meeting an individual, with minimal knowledge about potential competitors. Once a potential mate has been "targeted," mate manipulation can begin to occur. If an individual is with a partner of high mate value, he or she might rethink his or her choice of target; however, if the person is single, or with an individual of estimated equal or lesser value, he or she might then engage in competitor manipulation or derogation (Fisher & Cox, 2010).

Ultimately, individuals compete in an arena of gray, not black and white. There are multiple ways in which one can compete, and these strategies are dependent on a tremendous amount of input from environmental stimuli. In this chapter we explore the ways in which women engage in various subfacets of intrasexual competition through the evolutionarily novel social platform of Facebook. After briefly covering the history and current design of Facebook, we examine what is evolutionarily novel about social interactions that take place online and what is an artifact of our evolutionary heritage. Specifically, we examine some of the ways in which many of the online behaviors that we see today on Facebook reflect the strategies of intrasexual competition that have been present in female relationships throughout history. We conclude by suggesting some of the areas that future research can explore in order to further study the competitive strategies that are utilized when competition takes place online.

The Age of Facebook

Founded in 2004, Facebook initially began as a platform for college students to connect online and required users to have a valid university e-mail address to create a profile. The site quickly expanded to include high school students in 2005 and eventually opened to the general public in 2006 (Facebook, 2014c). Currently Facebook is the second most visited website in the world (Alexa, 2014), and, in the United States, 71% of online adults report using Facebook, with more women (76%) than men (66%) using the site (Duggan & Smith, 2013). Regarded as a *friend-networking site* (Muscanell & Guadagno, 2011), Facebook, users accrue friends by "friend requesting" other users who vary from individuals whom they know outside of the Internet to creating new relationships with individuals whom they meet online. Some of the many features of the site include allowing users to upload photos and videos, post status updates, "like" content that others post, tag "friends" in content, create event invitations, and write to other users directly through private messaging or public comments. Moreover, there are two ways that users can access information on the site: a user's profile page and the News Feed.

A user's profile is formatted so that the top of the page contains a space where a photo can be uploaded as a profile image, as well as a rectangular space where a cover photo may be added. Research has found that women and men tend to differ in the types of profile images they select. Tifferet and Vilnai-Yavetz (2014) found that females' photos tended to emphasize familial relations and emotional expressions while males' photos were more likely to emphasize status and risk-taking. Additionally, profile photos were more likely to be of oneself, while cover photos were more likely to contain a different expression of identity (e.g., hobbies, values, lifestyle). While sex differences existed in self-presentation in profile pictures, females and males did not vary much in the content they displayed in their cover photos, with the only exception being that females were more likely to accentuate familial relations than males were. The authors of this study suggest that these sex differences may be a reflection of the evolutionary pressures that females and males have faced throughout human history. For example, females may have had more selective pressure to develop skills for attachment, sensitivity, and communication, which are all necessary for successful caregiving, while males may have had more selective pressure to maintain status through displays of power and dominance (Tifferet & Vilnai-Yavetz, 2014). Users may also choose to upload personal information about themselves to their "About" section, which includes information such as relationship status, sexual orientation, work history, education, places lived, birth date, and contact information. The profile page also links to photos that the individual has uploaded or was tagged in and includes a list of the user's "friends" on the site. Additionally, the profile page contains a user's wall (now referred to as the timeline), which is a space where Facebook friends can post comments or photos directly to another user.

However, many people spend less time on individual profiles and more time scanning the News Feed, a continuously updating stream of one's Facebook friends' activity. Introduced in September 2006, the News Feed feature in many ways revolutionized Facebook and the way in which users engage with the site. Prior to the News Feed, Facebook users would have to visit a friend's profile page in order to know of any activity that was going on; however, the News Feed suddenly changed that by putting on display in a compact format all of the actions of a user's Facebook friends. The feature was met with outrage by many Facebook users; groups such as "Students Against Facebook News Feeds" gained over 700,000 members and Facebook founder Mark Zuckerberg was compelled to create the "Free Flow of Information on the Internet" group where he hosted a live forum to address the backlash that the change was receiving (boyd, 2008). The main issue Facebook users had with the News Feed was that they felt it was an encroachment on their privacy, despite the fact that all of this information was previously available to Facebook users if they visited a friend's profile page. Eventually, Facebook users adjusted to the new design, and the News Feed has remained a salient part of the Facebook format ever since.

The News Feed was an important change because it not only increased the visibility of Facebook users' activity but also made viewing Facebook friend's postings normative since one no longer had to make the conscious effort to visit a particular person's profile page. This was quite a dramatic change, since looking at a friend's Facebook activity through their profile page was often considered "stalking" on the pre-News Feed format of Facebook (boyd, 2008). Now, however, with Facebook friends' activity openly displayed, it was informally accepted and no longer invasive to see the pictures that someone had posted or read a conversation occurring on the wall of two friends. This change in the social dynamic of Facebook broadened the audience of Facebook activity and, we argue, has allowed for the increased capabilities for competitive strategies such as self-promotion and surveillance of potential rivals and mates that are the focus of this chapter.

The introduction of the "Like" button in 2009 also had a dramatic impact on how Facebook users utilize the site. Prior to the Like button, the only way to engage with other user's activity was to write a comment underneath the posting, which required a more direct and personalized action. Additionally, the Like option introduced a new dimension of quantitative displays of social status. Now one could compare oneself with a competitor to see how many "likes" each of their postings received. Moreover, both the News Feed and Like button created a more passive manner for users to engage with others in their network, which added a new dimension to being on Facebook. Users could still have more personalized interactions with close friends; however, the introduction of these two changes to the Facebook's site interface created the option to casually interact with their network and Facebook friends that they might not have done otherwise.

While Facebook has been around for only a decade, several fundamental aspects of what makes it so appealing to many users have been present throughout human history. Recall Facebook's claim that "People use Facebook to stay connected with friends and family, to discover what's going on in the world, and to share and express what matters to them" (Facebook, 2014a). When broken down, these three motivations for Facebook use are similar to human behavior dating back to the Paleolithic era (2.6 mya–10 kya). For example, evidence for early human large-scale social organization and communication (i.e., "stay connected with family and friends") is derived from materials found at archaeological sites that were traced from a source hundreds of kilometers away (Boyd & Silk, 2006). This evidence suggests that some form of communication between groups was already commonplace during this time, be it through individuals traveling great distances to procure regional specialties or simply establishing some type of trading agreement. The interest in global expansion of early humans (i.e., "discover what's going on in the world") is also evident through archaeological remains across ecological regions (Boyd & Silk, 2006). Finally, symbolic expression (i.e., "share and express what matters") in the form of artistic displays and jewelry crafting was common among early hunter-gatherer societies (Boyd & Silk, 2006).

Boiled down, communication consists of basic *signals*, which have the potential to be reliable and honest or unreliable and deceptive (Searcy &

Nowicki, 2005). Signals in this case refer to "behavioral, physiological, or morphological characteristics fashioned or maintained by natural selection because they convey information to other organisms" (Otte, 1974, p. 385). A signal is reliable and honest if a characteristic of the signal is *regularly* correlated with actual attributes of the signaler and/or its environment (i.e., the signal matches the signaler) and receivers of the signal *benefit* from this information (Searcy & Nowicki, 2005). Unreliable and deceptive signals are when a signal (*x*) does not equal the signaler (*y*). Sometimes a deceptive signal can be *beneficial.* How, then, is one to tell if a signal is a reliable indicator of the individual signaling? Zahavi (1975) explained that in order to counter this problem, individuals with truly honest signals must confer a "handicap" on the survival of the individual. "Surviving" the test is an honest signal of quality.

In many ways, Facebook is a novel platform for communication, or signaling information. Electricity, satellites, and all of the other components that go into making Facebook function have only been around for a very brief part of *Homo sapiens'* history on Earth; yet we argue that Facebook is the outcome of an evolutionarily rooted need for communication with individuals from near and far. Granted, humans were not accustomed to communicating with individuals farther than their geography would permit, but this was an artifact of premature technology. Once nomadic tribes began settling into agricultural cities, individuals had a need to communicate with one another across vast distances for various reasons (e.g., family, trade of goods). Originally, signals of communication relied on physical, tangible input that was starkly evident to the receiver of the signal (i.e., communicating with the individual in person). This form of communication rested primarily on an individuals' input from five senses: visual, auditory, tactile, olfactory, and sometimes even gustatory. When the human population began expanding, individuals found themselves miles and miles away from loved ones, friends, and others whom they may have needed to communicate with for one reason or another. The "adaptive" result to these changes was to develop new forms of communication to cover immense distances. This new form of communication began with messengers and eventually evolved into a mail system in which individuals could send letters to one another's physical address.

It was not until 1858 and the advent of the telegraph that humans were able to electronically communicate at vast distances and speeds never before accomplished (Falconer, 2011). Although the operators of the first transatlantic telegraph cable communicated through Morse code, they were breaking down the barriers of distance and time in ways never before available to humans. The ability to communicate in real time with individuals miles away started at Morse code and took another big step with the invention of the telephone in the early twentieth century (Falconer, 2011). Of course the next big step was the invention of the Internet.

The Internet was originally conceptualized as a platform to connect a growing number of military computers worldwide, but it became increasingly evident that it had the potential to do much more than that (Glowniak, 1998). Between August 1981 and October 1990, the number of computers connected to the Internet went from 213 to 313,000, and by January 1998 nearly 30 million computers were connected. Though early testing for an Internet-like system began more than 50 years ago, the slow-to-start yet rapid expansion of ways to communicate with individuals over vast distances, in real time, became readily available to the general (Western) population in less than 20 years (Glowniak, 1998). Today individuals communicate with one another in multiple ways, in delayed time (letters), slightly delayed time (e-mails), real time (text messages/instant messages), and a combination of all three: Facebook.

Females as Competitors and Cooperators

Sociality is the result of a balance between the advantages and disadvantages of living in close proximity to conspecifics. Some of the main advantages to social living include the ease of acquiring and/or controlling resources and avoiding predators, both of which are imperative for survival. However, group living also has its costs, such as competition among conspecifics for access to resources (e.g., food, mates), vulnerability to disease, and cuckoldry, to name a few. Throughout the animal kingdom (including our closest primate ancestors), the competition for resources *within* groups encourages dominance hierarchies. When within-group competition is the primary form of competition, females' capacity to control access to resources is a direct function of their dominance rank (Boyd & Silk, 2006). This structure results in females higher up in the dominance hierarchy having the ability to exclude lower-ranking females from much-needed resources (e.g., food, mates). We see these same trends within humans as well, just played out in increasingly complex ways.

Intrasexual competition in women is more likely to take the form of *indirect* aggression (Campbell, 1999). According to Campbell, male aggression is motivated by social status and self-esteem (*status-oriented aggression*), while female aggression is less physically dangerous and covert to reduce the likelihood of physical threat (*indirect aggression*). Interestingly, the idea that women are indifferent to status acquisition is debatable. Benenson (1999) explains that the disparity between men and women's drive to acquire higher status is likely derived from a *male definition* of status. Status is often conceived as a type of "physical toughness," and, consequentially, since females do not seem to exhibit this behavior, they do not fit this definition of status (Benenson, 1999). However, research on the correlates of status has consistently found that both males and females are concerned with their status, although status was linked with different attributes depending on sex. In males, status is associated with strength, coordination, and being part of some type of athletic team; in females, status is associated with attractiveness and being close friends with individuals who are considered "popular" (i.e., higher status by association; Benenson, 1999).

Females tend to choose tactics that involve indirect aggression because of the low physical risk it promotes, as well as allowing a target to be attacked while the aggressor remains unidentified (Campbell, 1999). Examples of indirect aggression include criticizing a competitor's appearance, gossiping, and social exclusion (Vaillancourt, 2013). Engaging in indirect tactics of aggression has many positive outcomes, particularly the fact that a perpetrator's reputation is usually left unscathed and the threat of retaliation is also minimal due to the relative anonymity of the aggressor.

While the focus of this chapter is on competition, it is important to note the unique role that *cooperation* plays in female competition. Even a female at the top of her social hierarchy still relies heavily on her relationships with other females to maintain her dominance. One of the main reasons that females continuously rely on social bonds for survival is due to the challenges related to human offspring survival. The common adage "it takes a whole village to raise one child" is telling of the investment required to raise human young. There are many factors that play into why children are particularly difficult to raise without a network of support. Notably, human fetuses are born relatively underdeveloped compared

to other mammalian species and take a substantial amount of time to fully mature. Additionally, evidence suggests that around the time of *Homo erectus*, supplementary foods were being sought out to help support an increasing brain and body size (for a review see Hrdy, 2009). This new food source came in the form of tubers, which were difficult to extract from the ground and impossible for young offspring to process on their own. This reliance on others for both acquiring and processing the tubers may also have resulted in the need for alloparenting (i.e., care for a child provided by individuals who are not the biological parents). Due to these difficulties involved in raising children, assistance is an adaptive trait to have; thus, establishing a support network where one can collaboratively rear children (i.e., alloparenting) may have been a primary interest for women caring for young dating back as far as 1.8 mya (Hrdy, 2009).

Evidence for the female instinct to cooperate stems from the idea that females and males differ in their biobehavioral response to stressors. The idea of a "fight or flight" (Cannon, 1932) response to stressful events was widely accepted throughout the scientific community for decades as a sound theoretical framework for understanding how all humans respond to stress. However, this does not take into account the unique challenges females have experienced in our ancestral past. There are limitations to mobility when one is caring for young offspring, so it may not be adaptive for caretakers to "fight" when the action could potentially leave their young at risk of danger. Moreover, opting to "fight" is an arduous and dangerous option for a woman who is pregnant and in a vulnerable state. Additionally, the option of "flight" poses a risk when young are present and cannot escape at the same pace, which can potentially result in losing offspring. Therefore, the fight-or-flight model does not account for the unique challenges of caring for offspring.

Alternatively, Taylor et al. (2000) proposed a different adaptive response to threat referred to as "tend and befriend," or the affiliative response to stress. This theory suggests that another adaptive response in a threatening situation would be for individuals, primarily females who typically invest more in offspring, to begin by ensuring that young are out of the way of immediate danger (i.e., tend). It would also be adaptive to place an emphasis on establishing social bonds with other group members in order to have a network that one could rely on when faced with a dangerous situation (i.e., befriend; Taylor, 2006; Taylor et al., 2000). Beyond this theoretical rationale, the tend-and-befriend response has been supported on a neurobiological level with the hormone oxytocin implicated in the affiliative response (Taylor, 2006).

Although physiological stress responses evolved in a different environment than what we encounter today, novel modern-day occurrences can still trigger these evolved reactions. Nesse and Williams (1994) illustrate this point through the example of feeling anxiety over flying in an airplane. This activity involves great heights, enclosed spaces, and loud noises, which would all be indicators of a potentially dangerous situation outside of the modern context. Therefore, despite the fact that feeling anxiety over flying is a maladaptive trait in a world where air travel is a ubiquitous practice, this same stress response would have been quite adaptive in an ancestral environment. Similarly, although electricity, a computer or smartphone, and other components involved in accessing Facebook are recent developments, the physiological responses the website can elicit harken back to ancestral social situations. Thompson and Lougheed (2012) found that, in a sample of undergraduates, 80.24% reported using Facebook as part of their everyday activities. Interestingly, females were more likely than males to feel stress and anxiety caused by logging in to Facebook; specifically, females tended to *agree* or *strongly agree* with the idea that Facebook gave them a negative self-image due to the pictures that others post (Thompson & Lougheed, 2012). The anxiety and negative responses that many females report experiencing when logging in to Facebook (Thompson & Lougheed, 2012) may be a reflection of the interpretation of a social threat, an obstacle that has been faced throughout human history (Nesse & Ellsworth, 2009). Moreover, research has demonstrated that simulated socially threatening situations online elicit the same emotional responses that are predicted offline (Guitar, Glass, Saba, & Geher, 2012).

The underlying cause of intrasexual competition (i.e., *ultimate* motivation) can be thought of as displaying genetic fitness through *proximate* mechanisms (e.g., phenotypic fitness indicators); however, the way in which we display our genetic quality is not always limited to our own bodies (i.e., *extended phenotype*; Dawkins, 1982). Examples of extended phenotypes in nonhuman animals include beaver dams, bird nests, beehives, and spider webs, because these are genetically mediated behaviors that are recognized by conspecifics as honest signals of gene quality. In humans, extended phenotypes

are typically expressed as products of our culture. For instance, it has been argued that artwork can be seen as an indicator of fitness because it can signal high-fitness qualities such as hand–eye coordination, intelligence, creativity, and the ability to learn difficult skills (Miller, 2001). Additionally, body ornamentation (e.g., piercings, tattoos) has also been proposed to be an example of an extended phenotype in humans due to the potential signaling of adaptive traits in a variety of areas: psychological (e.g., the creativity involved in selecting a tattoo, the time commitment needed for larger pieces), physiological (e.g., pain tolerance, pathogen resistance), and social (e.g., individuality, group membership; Carmen, Guitar, & Dillon, 2012).

Another notable evolutionary strategy that we discuss in terms of Facebook behavior is that of costly signaling. Costly signaling is the idea that some genotypic traits are manifested phenotypically in ways that seem deleterious to the individual organism's survival but actually exhibit some form of fitness (Zahavi, 2003). The classic example of costly signaling in the animal kingdom comes from the peacock, where males of this species exhibit large, ornate trains that are indicative of genetic quality. Those peacocks with the biggest and most colorful trains are more likely to garner the attention of females and subsequently experience increased reproductive success (Zahavi, 2003). However, costly signaling is not limited to physiological displays. When gazelles are faced with a predator that they can outrun, they will engage in a behavior called stotting, which consists of continuously leaping into the air with all four legs held straight. At first glance, this energy-expending behavior seems like a deadly choice when faced with a predator; however, research has found that predators are less likely to pursue stotting gazelles and stotting gazelles are more likely to outrun predators if chased, suggesting that this behavior is an honest signal of fitness (FitzGibbon & Fanshawe, 1988).

Within human populations a multitude of behaviors can be considered costly signaling, such as wearing high heels, driving a motorcycle, or getting tattoos and piercings (Carmen et al., 2012). If an individual can successfully pull off a costly signal, it is thought to be indicative of underlying genetic quality. For instance, if an individual has tattoos and/or piercings, this means that he or she has successfully introduced a foreign body into his or her immune system and that immune system was healthy enough to fight off any bacteria or pathogens it might have been exposed to in the process

(Carmen et al., 2012). Interestingly, there are also *dishonest* signals, which refer to an individual using some type of deceitful physical signal to indicate "fitness." For example, humans may use beauty-enhancing tools such as cosmetics and corsets, or even cosmetic surgery (see Johnsen & Geher; Shaiber, Johnsen, & Geher this volume). These are considered dishonest signals because they do not truly convey an individual's genetic signal (i.e., getting liposuction and a breast enhancement mimic an "ideal" body shape). As we discuss in the proceeding sections, Facebook is a platform for displaying both honest and dishonest signals to both potential rivals and potential mates. In the remainder of this chapter, we explore how women are utilizing Facebook to engage in four different strategies of intrasexual competition: self-promotion, rival derogation, mate manipulation, and rival manipulation.

Selfie Promotion

Of all the strategies of intrasexual competition, females have been found to engage in self-promotion most frequently (Fisher & Cox, 2010). This preference has been suggested to occur because self-promotion can be concealed as the socially desirable trait of self-improvement (Fisher, 2013). For example, a female can argue that she is working out for health purposes rather than reveal that perhaps she is actually more motivated to enhance her physical appearance to gain an advantage against potential competitors. Self-promotion can come in a variety of forms, such as increasing one's physical appearance, advertising positive personality traits, and attempting to outshine others (Fisher & Candea, 2012). One clear way that females self-promote on Facebook is by posting selfies. The term *selfie* was introduced into the *Oxford Dictionary* in 2013 and is defined as "A photograph that one has taken of oneself, typically one taken with a smartphone or webcam and uploaded to a social media website" (http://www.oxforddictionaries.com/us/definition/american_english/selfie). Interestingly, the example sentence that is provided in this dictionary definition is telling of the attitudes that many have toward selfies: "Occasional selfies are acceptable, but posting a new picture of yourself everyday isn't necessary" (example sentence, para. 1).

A large-scale study titled *Selfiecity* was recently conducted across five major cities around the world and examined selfies posted to Instagram (i.e., a site for photo sharing that is owned by Facebook and that many users link their accounts to so that a post on Instagram is also immediately uploaded to Facebook). Researchers found that in all five cities studied, females posted significantly more selfies than males; additionally, females tend to take selfies from a higher angle than males do (Selfiecity, 2014). This finding has interesting implications in light of previous research that has found that males prefer feminine facial characteristics that reflect high estrogen levels (i.e., a hormone associated with reproductive benefits) such as large eyes, a small chin, and a larger top third than bottom third of the face (for a review see Grammer, Fink, Møller, & Thornhill, 2003). Preliminary research has demonstrated that the downward angle that selfies are often taken from actually accentuates these feminine traits, suggesting that females may be unconsciously selecting their selfie angle because the resulting photo emphasizes feminine features and signals reproductive viability through high estrogen levels (Guitar & Carmen, 2014). This downward angle can also emphasize the female's breasts, especially if a low-cut top is selected for the selfie. Moreover, males have also been found to prefer females with full lips (Jones, 1996), which we find an extreme example of in a selfie pose that is referred to in popular culture as "duck lips" due to the extreme protrusion of the lips that are exhibited with this pose. Given the preference males have for many of the features that we see accentuated in selfies, it is possible that females are selecting these photos as a form of self-promotion toward mates; however, it is also just as likely that the motivations behind these displays of fitness may actually be directed at other females as a way of engaging in intrasexual competition.

However, some selfies are more subtle in the way that they signal fitness and might even be considered a form of costly signaling. For example, a female who posts a selfie with a caption that specifies that no makeup or photo filter was involved may be attempting to demonstrate that she is attractive enough (i.e., fit) to post a photo without the aid of modern beauty enhancement tools (e.g., makeup, photo filters). Just as the stotting gazelle is engaging in a seemingly deleterious action when faced with a predator, a "natural" selfie may similarly seem counterintuitive when the selfie may be seen by potential mates and rivals unless the action is considered in terms of costly signaling. Moreover, some females may post a selfie where they are intentionally making an unattractive face. This too may be seen as costly signaling, where the message signaled is that this female is so fit that she can afford to make an unappealing expression and still be considered attractive.

While a selfie is a direct, and obvious, method for self-promotion, there are other indirect ways to self-promote on Facebook. For instance, advertising positive personality features and trying to outshine others can both be accomplished in more subtle ways (Fisher & Candea, 2012). When it comes to advertising positive personality features, one option is to post links to articles or videos that demonstrate some form of political or social awareness, often referred to as *slactivism*. The *Oxford Dictionary* defines *slactivism* as "Actions performed via the Internet in support of a political or social cause but regarded as requiring little time or involvement, e.g., signing an online petition or joining a campaign group on a social media website" (http://www.oxforddictionaries.com/us/definition/american_english/slacktivism). An example of how superficial slactivism can oftentimes be was revealed by a social experiment conducted in 2009 by the Danish psychologist Anders Colding-Jorgensen. In the experiment, Colding-Jorgensen created a Facebook group to oppose the destruction of the Stork Fountain, a famous landmark in Copenhagen; however, the cause was completely fictitious as there were not actually any plans for the destruction of the fountain (Morozov, 2011). The Facebook group went viral; with 27,500 members joining before Colding-Jorgensen shut the experiment down (Morozov, 2011). This is an example of how little research individuals often conduct into the background of many of the political issues that they support on Facebook (i.e., slactivism), suggesting that the motivations behind the support may be more influenced by the positive reputational benefits of *appearing* politically or socially conscious rather than actually being so.

Facebook also provides a useful platform for engaging in indirect self-promotion tactics such as trying to outshine others. The main way that this can be accomplished is by selectively posting content that shines a positive light on oneself and paints the picture that one's life is to be envied. For instance, limiting status updates to reveal only achievements or successes is one way of attempting to increase one's perceived worth. Additionally, posting photos of a night out that makes it appear that everyone is having a better time than they actually did is another example of how Facebook allows users to create the illusion that their life is more exciting than it might actually be. Moreover, it is important to consider that Facebook profiles are often the result of *favorable filtration* due to the ability to "untag" photos that other individuals have added. Essentially, by hiding undesirable photos that will not be linked to the user's profile, an individual has the ability to build an ideal identity in ways that are not possible offline. However, it is not just what an individual posts on Facebook that influences how others perceive him or her; Facebook friends also influence the judgments of others. For example, profile owners were rated significantly more attractive when they had content posted on their Facebook wall by physically attractive individuals (Walther, Van Der Heide, Kim, Westerman, & Tong, 2008). This suggests that who one associates with on Facebook is factored into judgments of attractiveness, and forming alliances with attractive females may also be used as a tactic for attempting to outshine rivals on Facebook.

It is clear that online settings create a novel opportunity for users to engage in a controlled environment where an ideal identity can be expressed outside of the projected traits that come forth in face-to-face communications. This is due to the fact that the user has the ability to control virtually all aspects of self-presentation in the digital realm (Mehdizadeh, 2010). Much like the Wizard of Oz created a powerful image of himself through the use of a machine and a large screen, Facebook also allows individuals to present an ideal and often more socially robust version of themselves that may not be as accurate when one looks behind the curtain.

Facebook Frenemies

As previously mentioned, throughout our ancestral past females have benefited from both competing and cooperating with one another; for this reason, the relationships between females are complex and can often fluctuate between competition and cooperation (Bleske-Rechek, 2010). In popular culture, these relationships can be referred to as *frenemies*, which the *Oxford Dictionary* defines as "A person with whom one is friendly despite a fundamental dislike or rivalry" (http://www.oxforddictionaries.com/us/definition/american_english/frenemy?q=frenemies). This relationship dynamic can often come about because most females rely on other females to help in their mate-seeking efforts; however, they also find themselves competing with one another for mates (Bleske & Buss, 2000). This seemingly contradictory relationship that comprises female friendships is expressed in interesting ways on Facebook, particularly in regards to rival derogation. In many ways, the term *frenemies* accurately captures not only the vacillating nature of female social relationships offline but also the relationship dynamic between many Facebook "friends."

Females can use a variety of tactics to engage in rival derogation on Facebook; however, we focus on two forms: direct written attacks (e.g., cyberbullying) and indirect social aggression (e.g., gossiping, shunning). Cyberbullying refers to using technology to engage in conscious, recurring, and antagonistic behavior that is intended to harm others (Li, 2007). Abeele and de Cock (2013) examined cyberbullying through mobile phone use and found that four social groups emerged from their sample of Belgian adolescents: popular controversial, popular liked, average, and rejected adolescents. Of these groups, it was found that popular controversial girls engaged in the most mobile phone gossiping, an act that is thought to be indicative of the tendency girls have to inflict reputational damage on their victims as a coercive strategy to increase/solidify their dominant social role. However, of the many technologies available to engage in cyberbullying (e.g., e-mail, text messaging, Twitter), research has found that Facebook is utilized most often (Walker, Sockman, & Koehn, 2011). Examples of cyberbullying a rival on Facebook might include posting derogatory comments under a photo or status update of a rival, or posting an insulting message to a rival's Facebook wall. One of the defining features of this form of rival derogation is that the aggressor is identified, making this a form of direct attack; however, this can be a risky strategy since females who engage in identifiable acts of competitor derogation have been found to be less desirable as a mate by males (Fisher, Shaw, Worth, Smith, & Reeve, 2010). For this reason, females may choose to compete indirectly where the goal is to conceal that any competition is occurring.

A primary way of engaging in indirect aggression toward a competitor is through behaviors such as gossiping and social exclusion (Vaillancourt, 2013). Gossiping on Facebook can take place through the private messaging or chat function; however, this can also be risky due to the written record of rival derogation that exists unless one can trust both parties to immediately delete all messages. Therefore, it can sometimes be the *absence* of an action (i.e., social exclusion) that denotes competition on Facebook. Social exclusion can take either a passive form (e.g., not liking the content that a rival has posted) or an active form (e.g., creating a Facebook event for a social engagement and purposely not inviting a rival). Posting photos of a social function that a rival was not invited to may be another way in which females can subtly devalue a rival (i.e., rival manipulation).

Interestingly, there is often a fine line between direct written attacks and indirect social aggression on Facebook. Recall the direct attack previously mentioned where a competitor writes a derogatory comment on the photo that a rival has posted. If this derogatory comment is followed by an acronym such as "LOL" (i.e., "laugh out loud") or "JK" (i.e., "just kidding"), the attack can suddenly fall more into the indirect category since the perpetrator could claim that she was simply "joking around" if confronted about the attack. Overall, Facebook provides the opportunity to select from a variety of rival derogation tactics, whether they are direct or subtle in nature.

Utilizing Facebook for Mate and Competitor Manipulation

As previously mentioned, mate and rival manipulation are also important strategies of intrasexual competition (Fisher & Cox, 2010), and Facebook provides many possibilities for females to engage in both. One method of mate manipulation is to sequester the target from rivals so that no competition is necessary (Fisher, 2013). On Facebook, females can sequester current mates by forming a shared Facebook profile. In this situation, not only do both parties have access to the account so that constant surveillance of a mate's Facebook interactions can take place, but it also sends a strong message to potential competitors that this mate is not available. While this is a more extreme example of mate manipulation on Facebook, other, more subtle tactics to decrease the likelihood that a mate will interact with a potential competitor exist as well. For instance, making it clear that a mate is taken by ensuring that a mate marks their relationship status as "in a relationship," encouraging one's mate to make his or her profile picture one that shows them as a happy couple, or simply posting frequently on a mate's profile page can all be interpreted as mate-guarding practices meant to deter potential competitors.

However, mate-manipulation tactics are not limited to those already in a relationship. Females pursing a potential target have the option to adopt a radical tactic for sequestering mates through *catfishing* (i.e., creating a fake online profile with the goal of seducing a target who believes the profile is of a real person). The term *catfish* was coined by a 2010 documentary (now also a popular television show of that name) that followed Nev Schulman on his quest to meet a woman with whom he had been having an online relationship. However, rather than meeting what he thought to be a young, single woman, Nev found out that he had actually been involved in an online relationship with a middle-aged married woman with children who had created a fake Facebook profile (Hevern, 2011). The title of the documentary, and now the term used in popular culture to describe this practice, came about from a story that the woman's husband tells Nev in the documentary:

> They used to tank cod from Alaska all the way to China. They'd keep them in vats in the ship. By the time the codfish reached China, the flesh was mush and tasteless. So this guy came up with the idea that if you put these cods in these big vats, put some catfish in with them and the catfish will keep the cod agile. And there are those people who are catfish in life. And they keep you on your toes. They keep you guessing, they keep you thinking, they keep you fresh. And I thank god for the catfish because we would be droll, boring and dull if we didn't have somebody nipping at our fin.
>
> *(Harris, 2013)*

Catfishing is truly the epitome of *dishonest* signalers, as the practice relies on displaying fictitious information to potential mates. Moreover, catfishing can also provide an opportunity to distract a potential target from other mate-seeking opportunities (i.e., mate manipulation) in ways that would not have been possible without the specific possibilities that online profiles provide.

Facebook can also provide many useful tools for engaging in competitor manipulation by keeping tabs on rivals. Recall that competitor manipulation refers to convincing a competitor that the target is not worth the effort of competition (Fisher, 2013); however, people cannot begin to engage in this manipulation unless they are aware that interest in a target exists. Therefore, a female can gain valuable insight into the intentions of a competitor by monitoring her Facebook interactions with a target. Facebook provides many tools to engage in such monitoring; the first step, however, is to ensure that one is Facebook "friends" with the competitor in order to ensure that privacy settings will not hinder the monitoring (i.e., Facebook frenemies). Once the competitor is in one's Facebook network, the female can acquire substantial information from monitoring the News Feed for updates on interactions between the competitor and target. Still, this leaves open the possibility of missing interactions, and so further steps can be taken such as selecting to receive notifications on the Facebook activity of a competitor or target. Moreover, Facebook provides an additional method for monitoring the interactions of the two parties through the "See Friendship" option. Introduced in 2010, Facebook allows users to select two of their Facebook friends and a "friendship page" will be produced. In the same format of an individual profile page, a friendship page provides an overview of all Facebook interactions that have taken place between the two individuals; a compilation of photos that both parties are tagged in; and a list of mutual friends, likes, and Facebook event invitations that both have accepted. This option provides a streamlined method for keeping tabs on all public Facebook activity between a target and competitor and can be a useful tool when attempting to monitor potential rivals.

Beyond these options simply being available, research supports the idea that females are, in fact, utilizing Facebook for rival surveillance. For instance, females have been found to be more likely than males to use Facebook to compare themselves with others (Haferkamp, Eimler, Papadakis, & Kruck, 2012) and report increased feelings of jealousy correlating with increased time that was spent on Facebook (Muise, Christofides, & Desmarais, 2009). Additionally, the way in which Facebook profiles are visually processed is dependent on factors such as the profile owner's sex and physical attractiveness. Specifically, both female and male participants spent more time looking at the main profile picture of females and more time focused on the personal information for profiles of males (Seidman & Miller, 2013). Moreover, more time was spent viewing information that was not relevant to the profile owner (e.g., advertisements) when the profile owner was rated as unattractive, as opposed to those categorized as attractive (Seidman & Miller, 2013). These results suggest that females may focus more on the profiles of individuals who are considered formidable rivals.

Given the evidence that Facebook is being used for rival surveillance, we suggest that women's Facebook "friends" fall into two general categories: "check-in" (i.e., cooperator) and "check-up" (i.e., competitor). A "check-in" Facebook friend is someone whom the individual does not assess as a threat and instead uses Facebook to connect with that individual (an example of the affiliative nature of female status acquisition). A "check-up" Facebook friend, however, is someone whom the individual may wish to keep tabs on; thus, the primary motivation behind adding her as a friend on Facebook is to increase access to monitoring her activities on the site (i.e., Facebook frenemies). To date, research has not looked directly at the motivations behind why females add other females as friends on Facebook and the possible links to intrasexual competition strategies that might exist, making this a ripe area for future study.

Discussion

Digital technologies have become an increasingly prevalent aspect of everyday life over the past decade. From PCs to mobile phones, devices are now available to connect people in ways never before imagined. We have argued in this chapter that the social network site Facebook is a particularly prominent aspect of modern-day social relations. Moreover, we have suggested that Facebook provides a rich environment for females to engage in four strategies of intrasexual competition: self-promotion, rival derogation, mate manipulation, and rival manipulation. First, Facebook provides females with the ability to self-promote by posting flattering content to Facebook that we argue reflects fitness indicators. Second, through cyberbullying and shunning, females can utilize Facebook to derogate rivals in both direct and subtle ways. Third, Facebook can be utilized for mate manipulation by engaging in a variety of public mate-guarding practices, as well as distracting targets from other mate-seeking opportunities through the act of catfishing. Fourth, the design of the Facebook platform allows for anonymous rival and mate surveillance that can be used to gain valuable information that can help with future mate-manipulation endeavors.

As we have argued, the way in which females use their Facebook profiles can be interpreted as possible displays of fitness indicators. Digital anthropologist Daniel Miller (2012) almost seems to be referencing an extended phenotype when he refers to online profiles as *interior decoration* or "the private space of the individual externalized onto this digital domain" (p. 156). Although the platform utilized (i.e., the Internet) may be novel, the information being transmitted has been communicated between females since the dawn of modern humans. As previously discussed, females rely heavily on a strong social network in order to raise their young. This can be described in evolutionary terms by looking at the proximate factor (e.g., making friends) as well as the ultimate motivation (e.g., passing genes to subsequent generations through successful rearing of offspring). Thus, the desire for

women to display a large number of friends is in no way a new consequence of the Internet; however, what *is* new is the ability to quantitatively display this information through online platforms such as Facebook.

In many ways Facebook allows users to gauge social prominence through factors such as the number of likes or positive comments that posted content receives, or simply the number of friends in their social network. Indeed, research has found that judgments are formed about users based on the size of their Facebook friend list. Interestingly, there appears to be a curvilinear effect, where Facebook users with around 300 friends were considered the most socially attractive, while those at the low end (e.g., 102 friends) or high end (e.g., 902 friends) of the spectrum were rated as less socially attractive (Tong, Van Der Heide, Langwell, & Walther, 2008). These results suggest that having what are considered to be too few friends, as well as having too many friends, are both socially unattractive on Facebook. At first glance, these results may seem counterintuitive since having more friends is generally perceived as a socially attractive trait. However, the authors suggest that a possible explanation for this finding might be that individuals with the highest number of friends may be judged as possessing unfavorable characteristics such as focusing too much on Facebook and computer-mediated interactions and/or adding friends out of desperation rather than popularity (Tong et al., 2008).

It is worth noting that often Facebook interactions are quite ambiguous in nature. For instance, people often "like" content that their friends have posted related to a personal tragedy or negative experience. Is this a reflection of cruel individuals who are happy that something bad happened, or, more likely, is this a form of showing solidarity? The important point here is that the platform itself does not allow us to clarify. Additionally, without any further cues (e.g., facial expressions, tone of voice), actions such as "liking" content leave the interpretation up to the individual, meaning that two people may perceive a "like" in different ways. Another ambiguous action on Facebook is the "poke" function, where one user selects the "poke" option and the other user receives a simple notification with the poker's name. According to Facebook, "People poke their friends or friends of friends on Facebook for a lot of reasons (ex: just saying hello, getting their attention)" (Facebook, 2014d). Unlike face-to-face interactions, however, there are no further clues to indicate what the motivation behind a "poke" might be. Like many actions on Facebook, whether a "poke" is a flirtatious, malicious, or benign act remains a mystery.

Relationship researchers tend to identify a main risk associated with rival derogation as the possibility that others will negatively perceive the aggressor as being mean-spirited (Fisher & Cox, 2010); however, online interactions can include a component of anonymity that eliminates the negative reputational effects that have been previously associated with rival derogation tactics. Outside of creating a fake profile (i.e., catfishing), Facebook limits the ability one has to engage in anonymous attacks. Therefore, anonymous websites such as Ask.fm have become increasingly popular in recent years. Founded in 2010, Ask.fm currently has around 120 million users globally, most of which are under the age of 17 (42%; Dickey, 2014). Ask.fm users create a public profile with basic information (e.g., name, profile photo) and then other users can anonymously ask them questions, with the basic idea being that anonymity will result in more truthful responses. However, this anonymity has resulted in the site gaining notoriety as a platform for cyberbullying and has been implicated in the suicides of at least 16 adolescents since 2012 (Dickey, 2014). Ask.fm serves as one example of how the Internet can provide a platform for anonymous rival derogation, often with devastating consequences for those being targeted.

Future Directions

While this chapter has mainly focused on cisgender (i.e., a person whose gender identity corresponds to the sex he or she was assigned at birth), heterosexual, adolescent, and/or young adult females in the United States, future research would benefit greatly from examining how other populations engage in competition online. For instance, social network sites are not a phenomenon of Western cultures. In fact, the first large-scale usage of a social network site was Cyworld in Korea in 2005 (Miller, 2012). Additionally, the Philippines boast the largest broadband network (Hjorth, 2008), and African countries such as Ghana have seen an upsurge in Internet presence (Burrell, 2012). Further, accounts of Facebook behaviors affecting relationships can be found globally. One example comes from Trinidad, where a marriage ended because the wife was constantly checking on women her husband had any contact with on Facebook, which was interpreted as reflecting the unfavorable cultural trait of being

nosy or *macotious* (Miller, 2011). While the Internet is spreading globally, it is important to note that not all individuals within a country have equal access to technologies. An example of this can be seen in the urban poor of São Paulo, where access to digital technologies is largely based on socioeconomic status (Heckenberger, 2012). This raises the question of how socioeconomic status and the *absence* of access to a social network site affect social relations in the Digital Age.

Future research should also look into what role age plays in intrasexual competition that takes place online. Multiple instances of mothers cyberbullying their daughters' rivals have been reported in the popular press. In the nation's first cyberbullying trial in 2006, a mother was found guilty of creating a fake Myspace profile of an older teenage boy (i.e., catfishing) and sending flirtatious messages to one of her daughter's rivals (Stelter, 2008). The woman then began to send harassing messages from the fake account that resulted in the 13-year-old committing suicide (Stelter, 2008). In a more recent case, a mother was arrested after sending over 65 harassing messages on Ask.fm to a teenage girl who had begun dating her daughter's ex-boyfriend (Walsh, 2014). Moreover, widespread cyberbullying between adult females on mommy blogs has been reported. These attacks generally center on disagreements pertaining to parenting practices (e.g., breastfeeding vs. formula feeding, co-sleeping) and can quickly escalate to name calling (e.g., a mom asking questions about baby bottles was called "a cop out" and "uneducated" because she was not breastfeeding; Wild, 2010). In sum, these cases suggest that it is not only adolescents who are engaging in cyberbullying; thus, future research should look into how older females, especially those with children, are engaging in intrasexual competition online.

Another area that has yet to be explored is if females' Facebook behavior changes near ovulation. To date, a substantial literature has established that women undergo a number of detectable changes over the ovulatory cycle (for a review see Haselton & Gildersleeve, 2011). Of particular interest for the current discussion, research has found that females near ovulation (i.e., the phase of the cycle reflecting the highest likelihood of conception) were more likely to derogate a rival's physical appearance (Fisher, 2004), as well as select more provocative clothing (Durante, Li, & Haselton, 2008; Grammer, Renninger, & Fischer, 2004). Given this evidence suggesting that women increase their competitive strategy use (e.g., rival derogation, self-promotion) offline, future research should look into whether these changes are also reflected in Facebook activity. For instance, research could explore whether females are more likely to engage in direct (e.g., writing a negative comment on a picture a rival posts) and/or indirect (e.g., *not* liking a photo that a frenemy posts) rival derogation on Facebook closer to ovulation. Moreover, researchers could examine the type of content that females are posting across the cycle to examine if, for example, more provocative photos are being posted closer to ovulation.

Additionally, research has found that males were more likely to engage in mate-guarding practices when their partners were near ovulation (Haselton & Gangestad, 2006). Interestingly, this trend seemed to be mediated by the female partner's attractiveness: females rated higher on attractiveness reported high levels of mate guarding throughout their ovulatory cycle, while females rated as less attractive reported higher instances of mate guarding around ovulation. Future research can also examine if males are more likely to engage in Facebook surveillance of their mates (a form of "cyber mate guarding") when they are near ovulation. Finally, research has yet to examine if these mate-guarding behaviors of fertile females are also present among nonheterosexual couples.

The changes discussed here are limited to those females who are not currently taking some form of hormonal contraceptives. This is important to control for because hormonal contraceptives often produce effects that mimic pregnancy by elevating pregnancy hormones in a female's body like estrogen and progesterone. When a female is naturally cycling, hormone levels vary depending on where she is in her ovulatory cycle, resulting in hormonal peaks and nadirs. Conversely, when a female is being regulated by hormonal contraceptives, hormones remain stable for the majority of the month. Hormones can play a large role when it comes to various human behaviors, particularly those that aid in finding a mate. Therefore, future research should also explore the possibility of differences in Facebook behavior of those women who are naturally cycling as compared to those taking hormonal contraceptives.

Limitations

A limitation of the current chapter that is worth considering comes from Morozov's (2011) thought-provoking book, *The Net Delusion*: "The biggest problem with most predictions about technology is that they are invariably based on how the world works today rather than how it will work tomorrow" (p. 284). It is important to keep this cautious message in mind, especially in light of some of the conclusions that were drawn in this chapter. While the trends discussed may be relevant today, this does not mean that other rapid changes cannot or will not occur. This brings us to the other point from Morozov that is pertinent to the current analysis; one must avoid *technological determinism*, or "the belief that certain technologies are bound to produce certain social, cultural, and political effects" (p. 289). While this chapter has suggested that Facebook is currently having an impact on female intrasexual competition, it does not go so far as to say that it *must* or that Facebook will replace other traditional venues of competition.

That being said, we see various types of social media, especially Facebook, as a novel platform for ancient social behaviors. Classically, social scientists acquire data through methods such as self-report measures from a single moment in time or, ideally, as a result of one or two trials from an experiment done within a lab. However, humans are constantly changing emotional entities, the result of genetic, environmental, and cultural influences, so although capturing data from a single point in time may be valuable, it only hints at the whole story. Facebook is interesting because it is both limiting and facilitating of research—limiting because we as researchers must abide by strict confidentiality rules (e.g., we cannot ask for expanded context displayed on an individual's public profile) yet facilitating because we have multiple converging lines of evidence that branch out from a single individual (e.g., family, partners, friends, colleagues). This provides the unique opportunity for future research to inquire about a participant's Facebook behavior through self-report measures and then compare those results to actual Facebook behavior. We argue that this will ultimately lead to a better understanding of individuals as changing, as opposed to static, entities.

Conclusion

Scholars have debated how to classify social interactions in the digital world. For instance, many digital researchers refer to interactions that occur offline as "real" or as occurring in the "real world." By classifying the physical as "real," it is then implied that the online is "unreal," which subsequently creates a false dichotomy (Boellstorff, 2012). It has been the goal of this chapter to demonstrate that interactions that occur online are, in fact, very "real" and have an impact on relationships offline.

Many fitness-related benefits come about from engaging in online communication (for a review see Crosier, Webster, & Dillon, 2012). Given the affiliative nature of females, maintaining social relationships online can have many positive outcomes, including bolstering one's status, or place in a social hierarchy. Further, Facebook provides individuals with opportunities to display a wide variety of fitness indicators. Through selfies and status updates, females now have the chance to extend their identity into the digital realm in what we have suggested to be an example of a modern-day extended phenotype. Female competition with rivals has changed in the Digital Age through the increased opportunities to engage in direct (e.g., cyberbullying) and indirect (e.g., social exclusion) competitor derogation, as well as rival surveillance (e.g., "check-up" Facebook friends). Although the platform for intrasexual competition in the twenty-first century has changed, the ultimate drive is still manifested in proximate contexts: women have survived throughout human history by finding a balance between cooperating and competing. Although the cyber-sphere is unique in many ways from the sub-Saharan environment of our ancestors, in the twenty-first century, women are still driven to find this balance.

References

Abeele, M. V., & De Cock, R. (2013). Cyberbullying by mobile phone among adolescents: The role of gender and peer group status. *Communications*, 38(1), 107–118.

Alexa. (2014). *The top 500 sites on the web*. Retrieved from http://www.alexa.com/topsites

Benenson, J. F. (1999). Females' desire for status cannot be measured using male definitions. *Behavioral and Brain Sciences*, 22(2), 216–217.

Bleske-Rechek, A. (2010). Attractiveness and rivalry in women's friendships with women. *Human Nature*, 21(1), 82–97.

Bleske, A. L., & Buss, D. B. (2000). Can men and women just be friends? *Personal Relationships*, 21, 131–151.

Boellstorff, T. (2012). Rethinking digital anthropology. In H. A. Horst & D. Miller (Eds.), *Digital anthropology* (pp. 39–60). New York: Bloomsbury Academic.

boyd, d. m. (2008). Facebook's privacy trainwreck: Exposure, invasion, and social convergence. *Convergence: The International Journal of Research into New Media Technologies*, 14(1), 13–20.

boyd, d. m., & Ellison, N. B. (2007). Social network sites: Definition, history, and scholarship. *Journal of Computer-Mediated Communication*, 13(1), 210–230.

Boyd, R., & Silk, J. B. (2006). *How humans evolved* (4th ed.). New York: W. W. Norton.

Burrell, J. (2012). *Invisible users: Youth in the Internet cafes of urban Ghana*. Cambridge, MA: MIT Press.

Buss, D. M. (1988). The evolution of human intrasexual competition: Tactics of mate attraction. *Journal of Personality and Social Psychology*, 54, 616–628.

Campbell, A. (1999). Staying alive: Evolution, culture, and women's intrasexual aggression. *Behavioral and Brain Sciences*, 22(2), 203–214.

Cannon, W. B. (1932). *The wisdom of the body*. New York: Norton.

Carmen, R. A., Guitar, A. E., & Dillon, H. M. (2012). Ultimate answers to proximate questions: The evolutionary motivations behind tattoos and body piercings in popular culture. *Review of General Psychology*, 16(2), 134–143.

Crosier, B. S., Webster, G. D., & Dillon, H. M. (2012). Wired to connect: Evolutionary psychology and social networks. *Review of General Psychology*, 16(2), 230–239.

Darwin, C. (1859). *Origin of species*. Princeton, NJ: Princeton University Press.

Darwin, C. (1871). *Sexual selection and the descent of man*. London: John Murray.

Dawkins, R. (1982). *The extended phenotype: The gene as the unit of selection*. New York: Oxford University Press.

Dickey, J. (2014, June). Meet the brothers behind the web's most controversial social network. *Time Magazine*. Retrieved from http://time.com/2923146/ask-fm-interview/

Duggan, M., & Smith, A. (2013). *Social media update*. Retrieved from Pew Research Internet Project website: http://www.pewinternet.org/2013/12/30/social-media-update-2013/

Durante, K. M., Li, N. P., & Haselton, M. G. (2008). Changes in women's choice of dress across the ovulatory cycle: Naturalistic and laboratory task-based evidence. *Personality and Social Psychology Bulletin*, 34(11), 1451–1460.

Facebook. (2014a) *Information*. Retrieved from https://www.facebook.com/facebook/info

Facebook. (2014b). *Key Facts*. Retrieved from https://newsroom.fb.com/Key-Facts

Facebook. (2014c). *Timeline*. Retrieved from https://newsroom.fb.com/Timeline

Facebook. (2014d). *What is a poke? How do I poke someone?* Retrieved from https://www.facebook.com/help/219967728031249

Falconer, D. (2011). History of equalization 1860–1980. *IEEE Communications Magazine*, 11, 42–50.

Fisher, M. L. (2004). Female intrasexual competition decreases female facial attractiveness. *Proceedings of the Royal Society*, 271(5), S283–S285.

Fisher, M. L. (2013). Women's intrasexual competition for mates. In M. L. Fisher, J. R. Garcia, & R. Sokol Chang (Eds.). *Evolution's empress: Darwinian perspectives on the nature of women* (pp. 19–41). Oxford: Oxford University Press.

Fisher, M. L., & Candea, C. (2012). You ain't woman enough to take my man: Female intrasexual competition as portrayed in songs. *Journal of Social, Evolutionary, and Cultural Psychology*, 6(4), 480.

Fisher, M., & Cox, A. (2010). Four strategies used during intrasexual competition for mates. *Personal Relationships*, 18(1), 20–38.

Fisher, M., Shaw, S., Worth, K., Smith, L., & Reeve, C. (2010). How we view those who derogate: Perceptions of female competitor derogators. *Journal of Social, Evolutionary, and Cultural Psychology*, 4(4), 265.

FitzGibbon, C. D., & Fanshawe, J. H. (1988). Stotting in Thomson's gazelles: an honest signal of condition. *Behavioral Ecology and Sociobiology, 23*(2), 69–74.

Glowniak, J. (1998). History, Structure, and function of the Internet. *Seminars in Nuclear Medicine, 28*(2), 135–144.

Grammer, K., Fink, B., Møller, A. P., & Thornhill, R. (2003). Darwinian aesthetics: Sexual selection and the biology of beauty. *Biological Reviews, 78*(3), 385–407.

Grammer, K., Renninger, L., & Fischer, B. (2004). Disco clothing, female sexual motivation, and relationship status: Is she dressed to impress? *Journal of Sex Research, 41*(1), 66–74.

Gray, P. B., & Garcia, J. R. (2013). *Evolution & human sexual behavior*. Cambridge, MA: Harvard University Press.

Guitar, A. E., & Carmen, R. A. (2014, April). *Facebook "frenemies" and social media as an extended phenotype: How do women engage in intrasexual competition in the digital age?* Paper presented at the Feminist Evolutionary Psychology Society Symposium, New Paltz, NY.

Guitar, A. E., Glass, D. J., Saba, A., & Geher, G. (2012, April). *Situation-specific emotional states: A test of evolutionary functionality*. Paper presented at the Northeastern Evolutionary Psychology Society, Plymouth, NH.

Haferkamp, N., Eimler, S. C., Papadakis, A., & Kruck, J. (2012). Men are from Mars, women are from Venus? Examining gender differences in self-presentation on social networking sites. *Cyberpsychology, Behavior and Social Networking, 15*(2), 91–98.

Harris, A. (2013, January). Who coined the term "catfish"? *Slate*. Retrieved from http://www.slate.com/blogs/browbeat/2013/01/18/catfish_meaning_and_definition_term_for_online_hoaxes_has_a_surprisingly.html

Haselton, M. G., & Gangestad, S. W. (2006). Conditional expression of women's desires and men's mate guarding across the ovulatory cycle. *Hormones and Behavior, 49*(4), 509–518.

Haselton, M. G., & Gildersleeve, K. (2011). Can men detect ovulation? *Current Directions in Psychological Science, 20*(2), 87–92.

Heckenberger, M. (2012). Marginal bodies, altered states, and subhumans. In. N. L. Whitehead & M. Wesch (Eds.), *Human no more* (pp. 199–216). Boulder, CO: University Press of Colorado.

Hevern, V. W. (2011). The self on Facebook and deceptive identity. *PsycCRITIQUES, 56*(45).

Hjorth, L. (2008). *Mobile media in the Asia-Pacific: Gender and the art of being mobile*. New York: Routledge.

Hrdy, S. B. (2009). *Mothers and others: The evolutionary origins of mutual understanding*. Cambridge, MA: Harvard University Press.

Jones, D. (1996). *Physical attractiveness and the theory of sexual selection*. Ann Arbor: Museum of Anthropology, University of Michigan.

Li, Q. (2007). New bottle but old wine: A research of cyberbullying in schools. *Computers in Human Behavior, 23*, 1777–1791.

Marlowe, F., & Wetsman, A. (2001). Preferred waist-to-hip ratio and ecology. *Personality and Individual Differences, 30*(3), 481–489.

Mehdizadeh, S. (2010). Self-presentation 2.0: Narcissism and self-esteem on Facebook. *Cyberpsychology, Behavior, and Social Networking, 13*(4), 357–364.

Miller, D. (2011). *Tales from Facebook*. Cambridge, MA: Polity Press.

Miller, D. (2012). Social networking sites. In H. A Horst & D. Miller (Eds.), *Digital anthropology* (pp. 146–161). London: Bloomsbury Academic.

Miller, G. F. (2001). *The mating mind: How sexual choice shaped the evolution of human nature*. New York: Anchor Books.

Morozov, E. (2011). *The net delusion: The dark side of Internet freedom*. New York: PublicAffairs Store.

Muise, A., Christofides, E., & Desmarais, S. (2009). More information than you ever wanted: Does Facebook bring out the green-eyed monster of jealousy? *Cyberpsychology and Behavior, 12*, 441–444.

Muscanell, N. L., & Guadagno, R. E. (2011). Make new friends or keep the old: Gender and personality differences in social networking use. *Computers in Human Behavior, 28*, 107–112.

Nesse, R. M., & Ellsworth, P. C. (2009). Evolution, emotions, and emotional disorders. *American Psychologist, 64*(2), 129.

Nesse, R. M., & Williams, G. C. (1994). *Why we get sick: The new science of Darwinian medicine*. New York: First Vantage Books.

Otte, D. (1974). Effects and function in the evolution of signaling systems. *Annual Review of Ecology and Systematics, 5*, 385–417.

Pew Internet & American Life Project. (2013a). *Social networking fact sheet*. Retrieved from http://www.pewinternet.org/fact-sheets/social-networking-fact-sheet/

Pew Internet & American Life Project. (2013b). *Social networking sites 2013*. Retrieved from http://pewInternet.org/Reports/2013/social-networking-sites/Findings.aspx

Schmitt, D. P., & Buss, D. M. (1996). Strategic self-promotion and competition derogation: Sex and conflict effects on perceived effectiveness of mate attraction tactics. *Journal of Personality and Social Psychology, 70*(6), 1185–1204.

Searcy, W. A., & Nowicki, S. (2005). *The evolution of animal communication: Reliability and deception in signaling systems*. Princeton, NJ: Princeton University Press.

Seidman, G., & Miller, O. S. (2013). Effects of gender and physical attractiveness on visual attention to Facebook profiles. *Cyberpsychology, Behavior, and Social Networking, 16*(1), 20–24.

Selfiecity. (2014). *Our main findings*. Retrieved from http://selfiecity.net/#findings

Singh, D. (1993). Adaptive significance of female physical attractiveness: Role of waist-to-hip ratio. *Journal of Personality and Social Psychology, 65*(2), 293–307.

Stelter, B. (2008, November 27). Guilty verdict in cyberbullying case provokes many questions over online identity. *The New York Times*. Retrieved from http://www.nytimes.com/2008/11/28/us/28internet.html?_r=0

Swami, V., Jones, J., Einon, D., & Furnham, A. (2009). Men's preferences for women's profile waist-to-hip ratio, breast size, and ethnic group in Britain and South Africa. *British Journal of Psychology, 100*, 313–325.

Swami, V., & Tovée, M. J. (2007). Differences in attractiveness preferences between observers in low-and high-resource environments in Thailand. *Journal of Evolutionary Psychology, 5*(1), 149–160.

Taylor, S. E. (2006). Tend and befriend: Biobehavioral bases of affiliation under stress. *Current Directions in Psychological Science, 15*(6), 273–277.

Taylor, S. E., Klein, L. C., Lewis, B. P., Gruenewald, T. L., Gurung, R. A. R., & Updegraff, J. A. (2000). Biobehavioral responses to stress in females: Tend-and-befriend, not fight-or-flight. *Psychological Review, 107*(3), 411–429.

Thompson, S. H., & Lougheed, E. (2012). Frazzled by Facebook? An exploratory study of gender differences in social network communication among undergraduate men and women. *College Student Journal, 46*(1), 88–98.

Tifferet, S., & Vilnai-Yavetz, I. (2014). Gender differences in Facebook self-presentation: An international randomized study. *Computers in Human Behavior, 35*, 388–399.

Tong, S. T., Van Der Heide, B., Langwell, L., & Walther, J. B. (2008), Too much of a good thing? The relationship between number of friends and interpersonal impressions on Facebook. *Journal of Computer-Mediated Communication, 13*, 531–549.

Vaillancourt, T. (2013). Do human females use indirect aggression as an intrasexual competition strategy? *Philosophical Transactions of the Royal Society B, 368*(1631), 20130080.

Walker, C. M., Sockman, B. R., & Koehn, S. (2011). An exploratory study of cyberbullying with undergraduate university students. *TechTrends, 55*(2), 31–38.

Walsh, M. (2014, May 22). Connecticut mom, teacher cyberbullied teen daughter's rival: cops. *New York Daily News.* Retrieved from http://www.nydailynews.com/news/crime/conn-mom-cyberbullied-daughter-rival-cops-article-1.1801992

Walther, J. B., Van Der Heide, B., Kim, S. Y., Westerman, D., & Tong, S. T. (2008). The role of friends' appearance and behavior on evaluations of individuals on Facebook: Are we known by the company we keep? *Human Communication Research, 34*(1), 28–49.

Wild, A. (2010, April 28). Grown up mean girls: Mom on mom cyberbullying. *ABC News.* Retrieved from http://abcnews.go.com/GMA/Parenting/grown-girls-mom-mom-cyberbullying/story?id=10180974

Zahavi, A. (1975). Mate selection—A selection for a handicap. *Journal of Theoretical Biology, 53*, 205–214.

Zahavi, A. (2003). Indirect selection and individual selection in sociobiology: My personal views on theories of social behaviour. *Animal Behaviour, 65*, 859–863.

Women's Use of Computer Games to Practice Intrasexual Competition

Tami M. Meredith

Abstract

Digital gaming, whether performed using a game console, cellular telephone, or desktop computer, is now a popular entertainment activity. While men still dominate among game developers and players, this disparity has been reduced as game designers shift their views and develop games that support women's style of play. In particular, women desire to practice and perform the competitive styles they use when performing real-world intrasexual competition: self-promotion, competitor derogation and manipulation, target manipulation, and the building of social hierarchies to obtain allies or spread information needed to support these strategies. Women play games and compete, both among each other and against game challenges, if given the opportunity to do so in a meaningful and realistic manner where they can practice their preferred competitive skills. This chapter examines digital gaming with respect to women's competitive strategies to identify how games can support these strategies and appeal to women.

Key Words: computer games, digital games, gaming, competitive skills, video games, intrasexual competition

Computer gaming, also referred to as digital gaming, which for this chapter includes console or video gaming on dedicated hardware such as the Microsoft XBox, Nintendo Wii, or Sony PlayStation, is now a popular entertainment activity. It was reported that in 2012, 58% of Americans played computer games as part of a $14.8 billion industry (Entertainment Software Association, 2013). As shown by historical data, there is evidence that there was an extreme male dominance within gaming. For example, a reported 75–85% of 1998 game sales were to male consumers (Cassell & Jenkins, 1998, p. 11). Steve Meretzky, the creator of the Infocom text games, stated that when he introduced these games in the early 1980s, the general audience of the time was less than 5% female, although, interestingly, Infocom's text-based games had an unusually high 25–30% female participation rate (Graner Ray, 2004, p. 22). This male domination persists: almost universally, research shows that more boys and men play computer games than do girls and women (e.g.,

Dawson, Cragg, Taylor, & Toombs, 2007; Hamlen, 2010, Hartmann & Klimmt, 2006; Ogletree & Drake, 2007; Willoughby, 2008).

However, as current data and trends indicate, male dominance of the gaming community has significantly declined. Recent data indicate that, in the United States, 45% of game players are female (Entertainment Software Association, 2013). Olson et al. (2007) surveyed 1,254 participants (53% female, 98% aged 12–14) and found only 17 (1.4%) had never played a computer game and only 63 (5.0%) had not played in the past 6 months. As reported by Kafai, Heeter, Denner, and Sun in the preface to their text, *Beyond Barbie and Mortal Kombat: New Perspectives on Gender and Gaming* (2008), the sex gap in game playing has significantly decreased over the past decade, although females still spend less time playing than do males. Thus, although a disparity exists, it is decreasing as more women investigate and play computer games.

When examining this disparity regarding a player's sex, researchers have often suggested that female aversion to competition is responsible. For example, Denner, Bean, and Werner (2005) suggest that if a game is to appeal to girls, it should minimize the focus on competition and conflict. In their summary of previous research, they state that girls prefer games that are not competitive and feature little meaningless violence. Similarly, Hartmann and Klimmt (2006), report that female respondents (online survey, N = 795) were less attracted to competitive elements in video games. Thus, there is a prevailing belief that women avoid video games as a consequence of their being less competitive than men or wanting to avoid competition.

However, there exist contradictory data that show women do not necessarily avoid competition within computer gaming. For example, Olson (2010) found that 61% of girls in a survey of 1,254 students (aged 12–14) enjoyed competition, including 28% who strongly agreed with this factor as a reason to play. Carr (2005) studied girls in a computer games club at an all-girls state school in the United Kingdom. She found "no evidence that competition was inherently unappealing for these girls, that it complicated friendship, or that overt competition at the console in any way conflicted with the performance of gendered identity" (p. 472). She also found that girls were happy to coach each other but showed no reluctance to compete.

According to international sales data, *Tetris* is the most paid-downloaded software of all time, with sales of exceeding 170 million copies (70 million copies in multiple formats and 100 million additional downloaded mobile/cellular telephone copies; Tetris, 2014). As of August 2014, the leaderboard for the website *Tetris Friends* (N-blox Leaderboard, 2014) identifies the highest score of any player as that of the German female player Integration (her online alias). E-Sports Earnings rated the top 100 female game players by earnings in computer gaming tournaments and reported that the top three players were Katherine Gunn, who has earned $122,000 playing *Halo: Reach*; Sasha Hostyn, who has earned $102,154 playing *Starcraft II*; and Marjory Bartell, who has earned $55,000 playing *Dead or Alive 4* (Top 100 Female Players, 2014). With respect to all game players worldwide, including men, Katherine Gunn ranks as number 132, Sasha Hostyn as number 170, and Marjory Bartell as number 363. As these examples demonstrate, women competitively play video games and can perform at world-class levels. Thus, it is not that

women are avoiding competition, but more likely that many are unmotivated by the style of competition required in many games.

In this chapter, competition is used as a mechanism to explore sex differences in computer gaming and to potentially explain the differences in game-play styles, preferences, and desires of men and women. It will be shown that women are competitive with respect to gaming but that their style of competition differs from men and requires a change in perspective by game designers to create more inclusive games and increase female participation. Specifically, women's use of indirect competitive skills will be explored as female players use games to practice realistic and meaningful competitive behaviors that they apply in the real world, such as self-promotion or advancement in social hierarchies. Glaubke, Miller, Parker, and Espejo (2001) note that a game is "girl-friendly" when it contains player-controlled female characters (i.e., their avatar—an icon or figure used to represent oneself within a computer game) and permits cooperative and creative play in a reality-based environment. Their observations can be interpreted as supporting the idea that women's gaming activities are mediated by the desire to develop useful and applicable real-world skills because one can consider that using an avatar of the same sex in a realistic environment is a prerequisite for women's practicing of naturalistic competitive skills.

The computer game market has likely been dominated by male consumers as a consequence of game developers and designers being predominantly male. That is, it is reasonable to assume that games created by men are best suited to male styles of competition and play and will thus be readily purchased and played by other men. When definitions of gaming are examined, one can see that men's competitive styles are supported, encouraged, and encompassed by most computer games, whereas women's styles are ignored or even discouraged. Thus, there is evidence that the sex disparity in players results from rigid views of competition within gaming that male designers have applied when creating the majority of the games available.

To begin, consider the definition of Adams (2010, p. 3) who describes a game as a "play activity, conducted in the context of a pretended reality, in which the participant(s) try to achieve at least one arbitrary, non-trivial goal by acting in accordance with the rules." In general, published definitions tend to have four elements: fun or play, abstraction of reality, goals/challenges, and some form of structure such as rules (Moore & Sward, 2007, p. 6). Due to this chapter's focus on competition, it is the third element—goals and challenges—upon which our attention will be placed. Goals are often guarded by challenges and obstacles that one must overcome during game play, and these challenges require competition, either against oneself or against the obstacle, to successfully complete.

Some game designers use a limited view of gaming as they attempt to differentiate games from toys and stories. Crawford (1984) goes so far as to state that conflict is fundamental to games and that purposeful obstacles require an intelligent agent who actively attempts to block players from reaching their goals to create this conflict. Although a human opponent is one such form of active intelligent agent, he also includes the many potentially adaptive, artificially intelligent, programmed agents (e.g., monsters, villains, foes) found in computer games. Salen and Zimmerman (2003, p. 80) describe a game as an "artificial conflict, defined by rules, that results in a quantifiable outcome" and exclude anything without a directly competitive element that is created by conflict. Such definitions are a trap that limits the perspectives and options of game developers to the extent that they consider a game to be a zero-sum system in which, for every winner, there must be an equivalent loser, as produced by the required conflict (Graner Ray, 2004, p. 41). This view manifested itself in early games as direct competition with a confrontational approach, in which there was a clear need for overt, often physical aggression to dominate and outwit an opponent (Lewis, 1998).

The games industry has gone so far as to create the term "software toy" to describe computer software such as *The Sims* that is not game-like in that it cannot be won or lost in a traditional sense (Rouse, 2005, p. 384). Thus, software that does not provide a distinctive goal that must be aggressively achieved (e.g., *Bratz Rock Angelz, Barbie Fashion Designer, SimCity*), even though created by game designers and sold as games, are often not considered to be games by traditional game developers (Queiroz, 2005). As suggested by Fron et al. (Fron, Fullerton, Ford Morie, & Pearce, 2007, p. 309) "the game industry is a predominately ... male-dominated corporate and creative elite" that has "systematically developed a rhetoric of play that is exclusionary, if not entirely alienating to 'minority' users (who, in numerical terms, actually constitute a majority) such as most women and girls." Despite that fact

that sexually inclusive games such as *The Sims* are among the best-selling games of their generation (Business Wire, 2002), many designers trivialize any software that does not match their belief that gaming is an arena for conflict and direct aggression.

These rigid views of game designers result in beliefs and statements that border on the ridiculous. For example, Crawford (1984) wrote, "games [that] emphasize cooperative efforts rather than conflict... have not been successful commercially; this suggests that few people enjoy them." If this was the case, then why, 30 years later, when network technology had advanced sufficiently to support cooperative play styles, are highly successful massively multiplayer online role-playing games (e.g., *World of Warcraft*) purposely built to encourage social interaction and reward socialization and the development of an in-game reputation (Ducheneaut & Moore, 2004)? Game designer William Wright, when developing the highly successful *The Sims,* presented his ideas to his corporate board of directors and was told "an interactive doll house? ... Doll houses were for girls and girls didn't play video games" (Seabrook, 2006). However, as the immense success of *The Sims* indicates—it went on to become the best-selling personal computer game of its time—girls (and boys) do enjoy playing computer games in a virtual doll house.

It is not that women will not play a game that is directly confrontational—there are plenty who will (e.g., the top 100 female players by earnings; www.esportsearnings.com)—but that, in general, women prefer to use a less direct and less confrontational style than men and prefer games such as *The Sims* that support this style of play. Defining gaming with respect to male preferences and tendencies, as decided by male game developers and designers, and focusing on confrontation that women often wish to avoid is a biased, sexist, and ineffective strategy to attract female players. The bias of some game designers goes so far as to exclude puzzles for which a goal without confrontation exists and thus prevents games like *Solitaire* and *Tetris* from being classified as games (e.g., Crawford, 1984).

Sheri Graner Ray, a successful female game designer, suggests that women prefer games that are activity-based, as opposed to goal-based, and states that the gaming industry needs to better understand and support this difference if it wishes to increase its sales to female game consumers (Graner Ray, 2004, p. 9). These activities are not necessarily without a goal because, if one is motivated to play, one usually does so for some reason and hence is using a self-selected goal as opposed to a predefined goal provided by the game designer. However, the game industry excludes, by categorizing them as software toys, any activity-based software such as puzzles and simulations. These so-called toys are not viewed as games because the players set their own goals, which are perhaps cooperative, social, and nonconfrontational. Thus, male game developers have historically rejected anything without direct competition and have produced only games of interest to male players (Graner Ray, 2004, p. 41).

The increase in female game playing is, in part, a result of more progressive views of gaming, such as that of Adams (2010, p. 9), who suggests that designers "think of a game as an activity rather than as a system of rules." Although new to the computer gaming community, this view was advocated by Suits (1967), who defines a game as "an activity directed towards bringing about a specific state of affairs, using only means permitted by specific rules ... and where the sole reason for accepting such limitation is to make possible such activity" (p. 148). As with Adams, Suits considers a game as an activity and suggests that rules exist only to provide an enabling framework that causes the activity have some meaning. In this chapter, a digital or computer game will be considered as *any activity, done for play, and for which a digital device, such as a computer, enables the activity.* Thus, the computer provides rules and limits the scope of any activities by way of the software used to perform the activity. That is, game players can only perform activities that the software is programmed to let them perform and in a manner that is subject to the software's limitations and constraints.

This wider perspective, of a game as a computer-enabled play activity, has likely helped to reduce the sex disparity in player demographics. Successful, activity-based software designed for female players, such as *Cosmo Virtual Makeover, Let's Talk About ME,* or *Barbie Fashion Designer,* all fit within this broader definition of a game and avoid the limiting trap of providing a rigid goal for which direct competition is likely needed. Thus, when the goals and challenges can be set by the players, the games become of more interest to women, consequently making it possible to explore how women actually compete within and using computer games.

How Women Compete

Before one can analyze women's competitive behaviors and preferences with respect to computer gaming, it is necessary to review women's competitive behaviors and strategies. Owing to the fact that a considerable portion of the research on female competition explores intrasexual competition and its use by women to obtain high-quality mates, it is used here as a focus for examining computer gaming.

In female intrasexual competition, women compete against each other for the attention and eventually the long-term commitment of healthy, attractive, and successful male partners (see Fisher, 2013, for a detailed review). As summarized by Campbell (1995), women compete using strategies in which they exercise choice by giving sexual access to the most desirable mates, and they seek to attract these mates by exhibiting the qualities men find most appealing. Furthermore, women show restraint in their use of direct intrasexual aggression and instead use indirect means to denigrate rivals so as to avoid the use of direct physical competition until such time as desirable mates are in short supply and more extreme competitive strategies are required (Campbell, 2004).

Within gaming, support for this view is provided by Lewis (1998), who reports that girls value games with covert competition whereas boys prefer overt competition. Similarly, Graner Ray (2004, p. 45) states that female preferences in gaming center on indirect, as opposed to direct, competition. Games with indirect competition, such as *Tetris* or *Farmville,* do not require players to act directly on an opponent to influence the outcome. Since indirect competition tends to hide and obscure the competitor, which women prefer due to higher parental investment than men and correspondingly greater reproductive costs associated with injury (Campbell, 2004), it is no surprise that women are often mistakenly viewed as being uncompetitive because their competitive activities are intentionally indirect and concealed.

Figure 36.1 illustrates a basic competitive scenario in which a woman is intrasexually competing against her rivals and for whom all competitors are potentially supported by allies to obtain the attention of a target male. In this form of competition, the target is active and makes a choice that the woman, her rivals, and everyone's allies can attempt to influence. It should be noted that men and women value different attributes in their partners (Buss, 1988), and the way that these qualities are viewed is subject to individual differences in preference as well as to contextual factors that may influence their evaluation. For example, whereas most men prefer attractive women, what they find

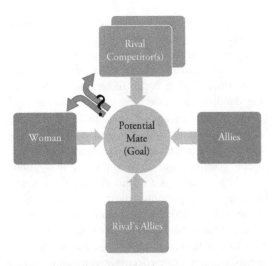

Figure 36.1 Typical competitive scenario (sexual selection). The potential male mate may select the woman or one of her competing rivals as a mating partner but is being influenced in his choice by the woman, her rivals, and any allies.

attractive will show individual variation and can be influenced by context, their mood, or other factors. Thus, the participants in the scenario can potentially influence or alter the male's choice and are not completely passive and inactive, although, as will be shown, their strategies do not rely on direct aggression. It should be noted that for the purposes of this chapter, an activity is considered competitive if it is performed to improve one's chance of success in a competitive situation such as mate acquisition. The activity does not need to be confrontational, aggressive, or performed against a specific rival; instead, it can be indirect, concealed, or self-directed.

Initially, researchers identified two strategies that women use in this scenario: self-promotion and competitor derogation (Buss, 1988; Buss & Dedden, 1990; Walters & Crawford, 1994). In self-promotion, a woman attempts to increase her ability to draw the target male to her by making herself appear more desirable and attractive, such as by using cosmetics or wearing appearance-enhancing clothing. One advantage of this strategy is that it does not need allies, although they may help influence the target by drawing attention to the woman's attractiveness and desirability. Furthermore, any act of self-promotion is effective against all rivals, whether known or not, and will be noticed by all target males if more than one is present. It can be seen that self-promotion is a very nonaggressive and indirect strategy in which the woman's efforts do not create direct confrontations with her rivals. In self-promotion, the woman attempts to manipulate

the perspectives of the target male and does not directly involve her rivals. Fisher and Cox (2010) have found that self-promotion is the most used strategy for female intrasexual competition.

With competitor derogation, the woman and her allies seek to convince the target of the rivals' undesirability by pointing out flaws, limitations, and other negative qualities. Competitor derogation can also be performed in a nonconfrontational style if the derogation is not observed by or reported to the rivals being derogated. As a strategy, competitor derogation is more limited than self-promotion in that it must be directed against specific rivals. However, similar to self-promotion, the goal is to manipulate the target's perceptions, not those of the rivals.

Fisher and Cox (2010) identified two additional strategies that women can use: competitor manipulation and mate manipulation. In competitor manipulation, a woman and her allies attempt to convince her rivals that they do not have the ability to win the competition because they lack the resources to compete successfully or because the target is either out of reach or not worth their efforts. The strategy revolves around attempts to change the rivals' perceptions, either with respect to the target male or with respect to the woman herself (i.e., the rivals' competitor).

Mate manipulation occurs when the goal or target is manipulated to reduce or remove the influence of the rivals. A typical example of target manipulation is mate guarding (Buss, 2002), where a potential target mate is shielded or hidden (e.g., "let's have dinner at my place tonight") from potential rivals. As with self-promotion and competitor derogation, competitor manipulation and mate manipulation tend to use indirect, nonaggressive means to influence and win a competition. Mate manipulation is not always seen as a competitive strategy because, when done successfully, competition can be avoided by removing the presence of the rivals. However, because the activities of mate manipulation allow a woman to win a competition against her rivals, it must be seen as a form of competition, particularly if the same activities are not performed when rivals are absent.

The use of allies to influence competitors and target mates means that a woman's position within social dominance hierarchies and her ability to direct her allies' actions will affect her competitive advantage. A woman high in her social hierarchy, with a large number of subordinates she can use to support her competitive strategies, will have an advantage over a rival with few allies or little ability to direct her allies. As suggested by Liesen (2013), social status has reproductive benefits with regards to access to resources for survival and reproduction that include food, shelter, and mates. Thus, social status and position within a female dominance hierarchy are also factors in women's intrasexual competition. To support one's position within a hierarchy, disseminate information about competitors (e.g., in support of competitor manipulation), and manipulate relationships, coalitions and gossip are an important component of competition (Hess & Hagen, 2002).

Although this chapter closely examines women's intrasexual competition with respect to mate acquisition, women compete for a variety of other reasons, primarily against other women (Burbank, 1987), using a wide range of behaviors such as teasing, verbal insults, social exclusion (i.e., snubbing), or destruction of property (Liesen, 2013). Although obtaining a high-quality mate is a prerequisite for reproduction, having a safe environment and plentiful resources to raise offspring is also needed. Thus, women compete for resources such as food and shelter, for themselves and for their children, as well as for status because it enables a greater access to resources (Anderson, John, Keltner, & Krieg, 2001). Women also compete to retain their mates in societies where resources are male-dominated (Cashdan, 1998). As detailed by Liesen, women's intrasexual competition in these areas, although sometimes requiring direct aggression, primarily relies more on indirect means that can be described as status seeking, prosocial, or coercive (Liesen, 2013).

Men, when competing for women's attention, do so directly and will sometimes resort to physical confrontations to inflict costs on competitors (Buss & Shackelford, 1997). Furthermore, the "fight-or-flight" response to stress (Cannon, 1932), which can be potentially induced by competition, adds to men's likelihood for resorting to aggressive activities. As suggested by Buss (2012, p. 302), male intrasexual competition provides the foundation for men's higher levels of violent and aggressive behaviors than females. Thus, it is easy to see how computer games, designed to produce an artificial conflict against a reactive competitor and requiring the use of aggression, are supportive of male competitive styles. In contrast, it has been suggested that, in response to stress, women are more likely to resort to a "tend-and-befriend" response (Taylor et al., 2000), in which women befriend within

affiliated social groups to reduce risk. With respect to competition, these social groups can form the allies that one relies on to improve competitive advantage. Hess and Hagen (2006) show that girls, more than boys, resort to indirect aggression during conflict, such as during competition for boys' attention, and that these activities involved gossip and reputational attacks. For these techniques to be effective, one must have social groups with whom to spread gossip in support of competitor derogation.

Although there is a wealth of research on female intrasexual competition against other females, there is surprisingly little on female intersexual competition against males. In part, this lack is due to the sexual dimorphism between men and women that limits women from effectively competing against comparatively larger and stronger men, particularly when men resort to direct physical confrontation. Bertozzi (2008) believes that the ability of games to facilitate intersexual competition can cause violations of sociocultural norms and dissuades females from playing games, thus providing some evidence that women do not play games to compete against men. However, women do compete against men for resource acquisition, and, as will be detailed in the next section, women do use games to practice their resource acquisition skills. Thus, regardless of the type of competition being performed (i.e., intersexual or intrasexual), games facilitate women's practicing of real-world competitive skills.

It has been well-established that men are more risk tolerant and take more risks than women (see Daly & Wilson, 2001, for a comprehensive review). As much as possible, women take fewer risks and accept risk only as a last resort or when the benefits are maximized and the costs minimized. In general, women tend to choose high-probability, low-payoff strategies, whereas, in similar situations, men tend to choose low-probability but high-payoff strategies (Daly & Wilson, 2001). Due to the fact that competitions can be lost and consequently require taking risks, women's risk-taking behavior will have an impact on their competitive strategies as they presumably attempt to minimize risk when competing. Within gaming, women's risk preferences will likely lead to styles of play that differ from men's as they seek to avoid unnecessary risks or risks for which the chance of success is too low.

There is evidence that women are more practical and less abstract than men, potentially as a risk-reduction technique. For example, in computer programming (McKenna, 2001; Turkle & Papert, 1992), women use a bottom-up strategy that is more likely to produce a working program but at the cost of an elegant design. Men prefer top-down strategies that focus on design, and, if they are successful (which is less likely), will create a more elegant program. A Lyra Research study (Digital Photography Review, 2005) found that women prefer simpler technologies with respect to digital cameras. Although one interpretation is that women are avoiding technology, it may also be that women are less interested in the abstract features of a camera and are more focused on the concrete goal of taking photographs. Women may simply be avoiding any complex or difficult-to-use features that reduce the probability of success (although improving the opportunity to produce higher-quality photographs).

When it comes to spatial navigation, women more than men tend to use less abstract, more concrete representations of the environment such as landmarks, whereas men tend to use more abstract representations such as cardinal directions (e.g., north, south; Lawton, 2001). Furthermore, more than women, men will use abstract mental maps as opposed to more concrete route-based strategies (Saucier, Bowman, & Elias, 2003). Postma et al. (Postma, Jager, Kessels, Koppeschaar, & van Honk, 2003) suggest that route-based navigation can be performed at both an abstract and a concrete level, but that the use of survey maps is predominately performed at an abstract level. If women tend toward the less abstract, then they should tend to use a route-based navigation strategy. Lawton (1994) confirmed this suggestion and found that women were more likely than men to use route-based strategies, whereas men were more likely than women to use survey navigation strategies. These examples, as a whole, show women's tendency to prefer practical and concrete approaches over abstract ones.

A meta-analysis of learning styles (Severiens & Ten Dam, 1994) found that men were likely to prefer an abstract conceptualization mode when learning and were more motivated by extrinsic rewards (e.g., qualifications), whereas women were more motivated by mastery of the material and skills. Within gaming, Morlock, Yando, and Nigolean (1985) similarly report that women have less interest in mastering the game itself and are motivated by intrinsic standards of performance, whereas men are motivated by extrinsic standards of performance. Further support was found by Philbin, Meier, Huffman, and Boverie (1995) who state that women learn better using hands-on approaches in practical settings whereas men prefer approaches

that are abstract and reflective. If games are used as environments for practicing and learning competitive skills, it can be seen that women will tend toward games that are realistic and less abstract, thus better permitting them to express their indirect competitive tactics. Glaubke, Miller, Parker, and Espejo (2001) provide evidence that supports this perspective and report that when developing a scale to rate a game's girl-friendliness, they gave a higher score to games with "a reality-based environment." Denner, Bean, and Werner (2005) examined 35 games created by 90 girls ranging from ages 10 to 13 and found that 74% used a realistic world. *The Sims*, a realistic game based on living a simulated life, was on its release the best-selling personal computer game of all time and had the highest percentage of female players (Fron, Fullerton, Ford Morie, & Pearce, 2007). These findings support the belief that women will prefer less abstract games and that female game players will correspondingly prefer, as realistically as possible, to practice activities they use during intrasexual competition as opposed to more abstract skills.

Koster (2004), in his disparagement of the distinction between toys, puzzles, and games, suggests that games are "edutainment" for teaching the skills needed in real life in a safe, low-stakes environment. Similarly, Reiber (1996) advocates that research on play involving children or adults is an important mediator for learning and socialization throughout life. Based on these observations, we have strong evidence that women play games to practice and learn real-world skills.

In games, goals are often unresponsive and abstract, such as trying to achieve the highest score or the fastest time. Players can only improve their performance directly, via changes in their play, because the games provide no method for them to influence how their performance is scored and viewed. For example, practicing self-promotion and having a more attractive avatar within the game environment does not influence the avatar's ability to slay opponents and gain points. Thus, it is often difficult to see how many existing games permit female players to use and practice the indirect competitive skills that they use for mate acquisition. However, in the next section, women's gaming behaviors will be explored and ties to their four competitive strategies will be considered. It will be shown that women do use video games to practice their competitive skills but that they do so less obviously than men, thus leading to the mistaken claim that women do not practice or enjoy competition.

Women's Gaming Behaviors

Jenson (2005) notes that there is a tendency in the literature pertaining to girls/women and computer game playing to construct their gaming choices and play styles as distinctly and essentially "female," characterizing those who choose to play as "liking collaboration," "nonviolent," and "easy" (i.e., noncompetitive) computer games. An example of this viewpoint is provided by Phan et al. (Phan, Jardina, Hoyle, & Chaparro, 2012), who suggest that male gamers are more likely than female gamers to be drawn to games from the strategy, role-playing, action, and fighting genres whereas female gamers are more likely than male gamers to play games from the social, puzzle, music/dance, educational, and simulation genres. Similarly, Bertozzi (2008) states that females, although now much more involved in computer games than before, generally play games that stress traditionally feminine values such as socializing with others, shopping, and nurturing. Shopping could be considered as supportive of self-promotion activities, whereas socializing permits one to practice competitor evaluation and the construction of supportive social hierarchies. Durchin (2000) states that girls value fashion and glamour play among other activities in gaming—play that is very supportive of the competitive strategy of self-promotion. Although one could view socialization and shopping as being noncompetitive, it would be potentially more accurate to view them as practice for women's real-world competitive activities and as elements of self-promotion and competitor derogation.

In support of this perspective, Greenberg et al. (Greenberg, Sherry, Lachlan, Lucas, & Holmstrom, 2010) found that younger players opted for the fantasy motive in their playing and older players more so for competition. One way to explain this difference is to consider that intrasexual competition is less important until the onset of puberty, when mating concerns arise. Similarly, Björkqvist et al. (Björkqvist, Lagerspetz, & Kaukiainen, 1992) found dramatic increases in indirect aggression among girls who were approximately 11 years of age, followed by still higher rates at age 15. Thus, as children mature and begin to need skills for mate acquisition and retention, they are more motivated by competition and see the need to practice and develop competitive strategies.

Although it has been subject to criticism, the hunter-gatherer hypothesis (Eagly & Wood, 1999) suggests that men will prefer the aggressive (i.e., hunting) aspects of gaming, whereas women will prefer to explore "gathering" behavior. Jesyca Durchin, a former executive at Mattel, observes that girls prefer collecting "stuff" as part of gaming, and that collection play is highly appealing for female players (Durchin, 2000). This view provides additional evidence of a game's need to satisfy players' real-world activities, in that scouring a game for new or rare items is much the same as foraging/gathering and will exercise the same skills, such as object location memory. Additionally, players' large collections of in-game resources are equivalent to high scores but can be more concrete because players have something to show for their efforts, perhaps showing women's preference for minimizing abstraction by using a more concrete method for evaluating success.

Durchin (2000) also suggests that, in addition to fashion and glamour play, which are supportive of self-promotion, girls prefer games with communication and social play, which can be seen as supportive of competitor manipulation and derogation. Communication is also useful for building a network of supportive allies to support competitive strategies. She further states that girls like to reproduce daily life within their play, providing evidence that play is realistic and consequently may be used to practice real-world competitive skills for mate acquisition and retention.

Kaye Elling, a creative manager for Blitz games, has proposed several characteristics for games that increase their inclusivity and accessibility to girls. In summary, women are more aware of a game's aesthetic context, prefer games that give players more control, enjoy customizing the game more, and desire more opportunity to express creativity (Elling, 2006). Each of these characteristics can be viewed as supporting women's styles of competing and women's need to pay attention to attractiveness (even though in a very indirect manner). Self-promotion is about using cosmetics and fashion, for example, to maximize attractiveness, often in creative ways. Practicing these behaviors on their avatars and game interfaces to create attractive environments supports self-promotion.

A key preference, stated by Elling (2006), is that girls like to feel that they are in control of the game, particularly over decisions involving risks. Risk-and-reward styles of game play appeal less to girls than to boys because girls do not enjoy risk-taking as much and limit it to situations where it is necessary and the rewards are justified. Elling suggests that women dislike game play that harshly punishes failure because it discourages experimentation. One could also consider that this dislike is a component of risk-avoidance because the punishment for failure and the risk that it creates is not sufficiently motivating. In an experiment in which same-sex groups of 9- to 10-year-olds were asked to design a game to teach fractions, boys and girls produced very different solutions in accord with their preferences toward punishment (Kafai, 1993). Boys created games that were goal-based and required objects to be recovered and won, whereas girls created games that were activity-based, with tasks such as landing a plane or exploring a spider web. The boys punished failure in violent manners, often resulting in the player's "death" and with the death ending the game. The girls used passive feedback by withholding items or blocking progress, thus providing an element of forgiveness and permitting players to resume play and try again. In the girl's games, risk was minimized, punishment less severe, and play focused on activities instead of goals.

Turkle (1988) suggests that women, when working with formal systems such as computing, prefer paradigms that support multiple approaches for problem solving. Since women tend to be more intrinsically motivated, this preference may stem from their desire to fully explore the problem space as they learn its properties; by contrast, men are motivated by the more extrinsic and abstract measure of their score. When games are rigidly scripted such that only one possible set of actions leads to its successful completion and exploration of the problem space is unnecessary except to identify the sole solution path, as do many contemporary computer games, girls will be less motivated to play and will likely experience less enjoyment.

Aggression and Violence

Adams (2010, p. 627) suggests that it is a fallacy that, within computer games, girls want "everything to be happy and sweet." He expands his view to explain that girls are comfortable with realism, suspense, mystery, danger, and even violence, provided it is meaningful and not random or pointless. Female game players know that phenomena such as violence occur, but that it is occasional, and they want their games to reflect this fact. As suggested by Denner, Bean, and Werner (2005), violence is acceptable as long as it is meaningful. Additional support is provided by Meredith (2013), who provides examples in which women engage in combat and directly aggressive activities when they are motivated to do so, such as fighting to defend their homes and families. By extension, it is suggested that if there is a lack of other options, women will engage in violent and directly aggressive activities in games if these activities have a meaningful purpose and goal.

Ultima 7, created with the input of female designer Lisa Smith, had strong sales in 1993 and was nominated by *Strategy Plus Magazine* as the role-playing game of the year (Graner Ray, 2004, p. 46). This game appealed to female game players because it permitted combat to be avoided since each conflict point was designed to permit an indirect or nonconfrontational solution, such as distracting hostile monsters using food. It is likely frustrating for female players when game designers such as Oxland (2004, p. 218) consider it cheating when a player finds a way to avoid the challenges that the designer emplaced. Such an attitude can be seen as detrimental to the use of indirect strategies for competition and the avoidance of direct physical aggression that was found to be appealing to women in *Ultima 7*.

Elling (2006) also states that women generally avoid hostile environments because hostility often leads to direct aggression—a strategy that women tend to avoid because of the risk of physical harm. As explained by Campbell (2002), women have a more involved role in childrearing than do men and thus need to avoid harm because it will have more impact on their offspring than will injuries to their male partners. Furthermore, women's smaller size and strength with respect to men means that women are less likely to win a direct physical confrontation against men. For these reasons, when possible, women avoid direct hostility, aggression, and confrontation. However, Elling does extend her stance on violence and suggests that it is more acceptable to women when it is defensive or provoked. This view is in keeping with the perspective that women will engage in combat and other direct aggression when other options have been exhausted and confrontation is inevitable and unavoidable, such as to defend oneself or respond to provocation (Meredith, 2013).

Women's attitudes toward fighting within games mean that if combat is excessive, they usually become bored (Graner Ray, 2004, p. 49). That is, women generally do not mind purposeful conflict, but once an opponent has been defeated, further violence or having to repeatedly slay that opponent is considered boring. Women will engage in direct physical aggression and confrontation to overcome an obstacle, but they become disinterested when it is unnecessary because they likely see no need to repetitively practice a skill they use only as a last resort. As a consequence of intrasexual competition among women being indirect, rarely physical, and sometimes focussing on the self (e.g., self-promotion), women will compete in and play games that permit this style of competition to be practiced, explored, and developed and, conversely, will avoid games that focus on combat, aggression, and direct competition.

Avatar Attachment and In-Game Socialization

As described by O'Riordan (2001), game players strongly associate with their avatars through "the incorporation of self into avatar while playing" (p. 235). This phenomena is referred to as "avatar attachment" (Wolfendale, 2009), and it has been suggested that one's "avatar is a truer reflection of their identity than their real life persona" (p. 10). Similarly, Taylor (2002, p. 55) states "people often say that it was through their avatar that they found a 'better' version of themselves, one that felt even more right than their offline body." Conrad, Neale, and Charles (2010, p. 242) found that as technology improves, "the distinction between the avatar and the self seems to be blurring." Such statements support the view that gaming environments provide effective and seemingly realistic locales for exploring and practicing competitive behaviors via a surrogate presence—one's representative avatar.

Elling (2006) suggests that women identify more with their avatar than do male players and are more likely to view it as a representation of themselves rather than as an object to control. This perspective supports the view that women see a game as an environment in which to practice and explore real-world behaviors and that, when gaming, their avatar is their representation within the game for performing behaviors. The lack of association with the avatar is one of the reasons that male players have no issues with controlling a female avatar such as Lara Croft in the *Tomb Raider* series, although part of males' tolerance for Lara is her performance of masculine activities (Adams, 2010, p. 133). Men see this hypersexualized avatar as eye candy to enjoy (Adams, 2010, p. 138), whereas women struggle to associate with her unrealistic proportions and attire (Graner Ray, 2004, p. 33). However, although Barbie-like in her femininity, women find it easier to associate with Lara than with, for example, the muscular super-soldier Master Chief of the *Halo* game series (Xenakis, 2001).

Social interaction, for practicing indirect aggression or building alliances and maintaining social relationships, requires emotional involvement that games often lack. Designers frequently focus on making games visually and not emotionally stimulating. As discussed by Adams (2010, p. 155), game designers debate the issue of whether storylines are actually needed in games. There are some male designers who feel that stories, and the intellectual and emotional involvement they provide, are distracting from the mechanics of game play. That is, they feel that defeating one's opponents is reason enough to play and that motivating stories and plots do little more than add to production and development costs. Oxland (2004, p. 161) provides an explanation of why games do not need stories by discussing the noninteractive nature of stories and the lack of challenge they provide, disregarding the ability of stories to provide context, meaning, and purpose to the game. Stories, such as those in the game *Myst* where players solve challenges to help the former inhabitants of an island, provide social and emotional contexts that women enjoy and desire (Graner Ray, 2004, p. 56). Indirect competition, such as competitor manipulation, requires social interaction that stories facilitate and support by making games less abstract and more realistic.

Although some game players may be explorative and perform unrealistic behaviors—particularly adolescents (Beavis & Charles, 2005)—most players tend to adhere to conventional storylines influenced by their culture, education, and the environment itself (Nutt & Railton, 2003). Yee, Bailensen, and Urbanek (2007) examined how social norms and behaviors in online gaming communities compared to those of real life. They report that social norms for sex, eye gaze transfer, and interpersonal distance in the game *Second Life* (see Rymaszewski et al., 2007, for a detailed overview of *Second Life*; http://www.secondlife.com) mimic real-life interactions. In fact, the quality of the online interactions is sufficient to permit users to develop real emotions, such as trust for each other (Donath, 2007). Such interactions permit individuals to practice and express competitive skills by using their avatars as their in-world surrogate. It is likely that women have a stronger attachment to their avatars than do men, so that they feel a stronger presence within the game world and a greater sense of realism.

Cole and Griffiths (2007) note that women are drawn to socially oriented video games (e.g., *The Sims, Second Life, World of Warcraft*), resulting in less domination by male users than more traditional games. Virtual environments such as *Second Life* are social in nature and tend to be activity-based and not goal-based. This difference enables and encourages users to develop their own agendas and styles of play and avoid sex-biased elements, which is in line with the activity-based style suggested by Graner Ray (2004).

Williams et al. (2006) explored socialization in *World of Warcraft*. They report that players in this game believe that the social aspect is the most important part of the game and that they have formed real friendships with those with whom they interact online. These friendships go beyond mere discussions of situations in the virtual environment (e.g., game goals such as defeating an opponent) and include discussions of the player's life outside the game (e.g., their current boyfriend/girlfriend; Steinkeuhler & Williams, 2006). The willingness to share personal information in an online environment is correlated with the strength of one's relationship to another player (Chiu, Hsu, & Wang, 2006). Users are thus demonstrating social interactions with other users, which presumably include competitive interactions (e.g., competitor derogation) and that tend to match those they would develop outside the game environment.

Some online environments attempt to mimic reality in as much detail as possible. The online world of *Second Life* permits players the expression of sexual appearance and gendered behavior with regard to fashion, body shape, genitals, hairstyle, and cosmetic use, among other attributes. The environment is sufficiently realistic that players can intrasexually compete to form partnerships (i.e., the equivalent of getting married) using avatars that can now be made almost identical in appearance to one's real-world self or, alternatively, to one's idealized self. To facilitate partnering, women regularly practice self-promotion to create a more attractive avatar for dating (Vasalou & Joinson, 2009) and improve their looks while designing an avatar (Messinger et al., 2008). Although some suggest that these virtual environments would permit women to violate gender and social norms, for the most part, women "construct identities in *Second Life* only to serve themselves up as objects of sexual desire, [and] reassert an existing belief system" (Brookey & Cannon, 2009, p. 162). This evidence can be used to support the view that, when given the opportunity to intrasexually compete in a virtual environment such as a game, women do so without hesitation using techniques with which they are comfortable and familiar (e.g., self-promotion) while using an avatar

that represents an idealized and attractive version of themselves.

Gaming in Context

Women are very much aware of games' abstract nature. Although competitive skills can be learned and practiced within a gaming environment, it is of little value to do so if such practice harms one's ability to compete outside the gaming environment. Support for this perspective comes from Kowert, Griffiths, and Oldmeadow (2012), who have shown that "gamers" are considered low in social status and thus penalized for their practicing and development of social skills in a virtual environment. Console games in particular are considered "boy's toys" (Cooper & Weaver, 2003, p. 14, but also computers in general, Turkle, 1988) because boys tend to play three times as long as girls (Kaiser Family Foundation, 1999), thus requiring girls to violate gender roles if they wish to use them. Self-identified "grrl gamers," such as Nikki Douglas, dispute the need for female game players to satisfy traditional feminine gender roles and advocate the use of aggressive, masculine perspectives (Yates & Littleton, 1999). As seen in the many online discussions concerning "grrl gamers," where the deliberate misspelling is used to convey a sense of rebellion against gender norms, the term has come to represent hard-core female game players who interact within the gaming community using aggressive and directly competitive behaviors.

As the tension between girl game players and the stereotypical "grrl gamer" suggests, girls who associate with game culture are often viewed as less feminine or perhaps even "butch" (Jenkins & Cassell, 2008). Although for some girls being viewed this way is empowering (Yates & Littleton, 1999), for many it is not and thus discourages their use and enjoyment of electronic games. However, when viewed as a casual social activity, women do not feel the same aversion to gaming. As indicated by Meretzky, 70% of online casual gamers are female (Graner Ray, 2004, p. xvi).

Adams (2010, p. 627) believes that games perpetuate an unfortunate stereotype of masculinity that rewards men and players who are violent, greedy, wanton, and self-obsessed. When building social hierarchies and practicing social communication, actions that can be considered as greedy, violent, wanton, and selfish are not very likely to succeed. Thus, to succeed in games designed to satisfy this type of male player, women would require a skill set that is in opposition to the skills they need for life success. Therefore, from a perspective of practicing competitive skills, there is good cause for women avoiding unrealistic, violence-oriented, antisocial games.

Although there have been suggestions that women's technological skills are a factor in the male domination of computer gaming, Hamlen (2010) examined girls' comfort with technology use and found that girls feel just as competent as boys at video games but that boys experience an increased sense of reward from achievement. Robinson-Stavely and Cooper (1990) explored sex differences in play of the game *Zork*. They found that social context affected girls' performance in that girls outperformed boys in private, but, when observed by others, girls' scores dropped to below that of boys, who correspondingly improved. This finding shows that sex differences in game play are not likely a result of technological skills but rather are influenced by other factors. In a follow-up study (Robinson-Stavely & Cooper, 1990), it was found that women perform equivalently to men when they have an expectation of success and that decreases in performance are associated with expectations of failure. As a result, it can be suggested that women do not expect to do well at computer gaming, experience decreased performance as a result, and choose not to play games in response to their perceived inability rather than for any actual technological impediments.

Competition by boys differs from that of girls in regards to what they compete against. When playing a game, girls and women tend to see the computer as a tool or platform to facilitate play, and, by extension, they see the game as an environment in which to complete the game's challenges. Boys, however, tend to see the computer as a device to dominate, and, for them, competition has a "them versus the machine" element. Whereas girls are frustrated by games containing hidden components (e.g., special combat moves not described in the documentation), boys consider discovering these components as an enjoyable challenge when learning to master the software (Graner Ray, 2004, p. 12). Girls want to play the game and compete against the challenges within the game, not against the challenges in learning to use the game. Women view computers and related software, such as games, as tools to achieve a goal and focus on the goal, not the tool (Cooper & Weaver, 2003, p. 16). As with the aforementioned study regarding digital cameras (Digital Photography Review, 2005), women are more concerned with the achievement of a successful result and not with the means and tools needed to achieve that result.

Games containing direct aggression, combat, and violence are common within the gaming industry and seemingly fill the shelves of game stores. In these games, success is measured in terms of opponents slain or defeated. What seems to be missing are games in which success is achieved using the skills needed for female intrasexual competition because self-promotion and competitor derogation are virtually ignored as possible game-play actions. Facebook games, such as *Sorority Life* and *Fashion Wars*, partially permit the use of women's competitive strategies but are highly abstract and focus on supporting collection behaviors (e.g., accumulating outfits and fashion accessories) and not on social interactions. There is clearly an opportunity for game designers to better exploit women's desires to practice their real-world competitive skills by providing games that support social interactions needed for successful mate acquisition. Computer networking is now sufficiently established that online gaming against other human opponents makes it possible for women to intrasexually compete, albeit in "non-games" such as *Second Life*. There is ample opportunity for future games to explicitly support strategies such as competitor manipulation, thus exercising players' social and interpersonal skills as an alternative to combat.

The Influence of Ubiquitous Computing

As the data for 2012 indicate, 45% of game players are now female (Entertainment Software Association, 2013). This marked increase can be attributed to several factors that include changes in the pervasiveness of computers in society, improvements in computer and communication technology, changes in social attitudes toward computing, and an increased awareness by game designers and developers of women's gaming preferences. Computers are increasingly a part of our daily lives as we surround ourselves with them, albeit sometimes unintentionally. Devices such as MP3 players and e-readers are nothing more than specialized computers for specific applications, with complete operating systems and network interfaces, although most users are unaware of this fact. However, it is the evolution of the mobile telephone from what was originally a hand-held radio transceiver into a "smartphone" (e.g., Apple iPhone) that has potentially had the biggest impact on our views about computing and our usage of computers. Current mobile phones match the computing power of a desktop computer from a decade ago, run an industrial-strength Unix operating system (e.g., a derivative of BSD Unix in Apple's iOS), provide multiple communications interfaces (e.g., Bluetooth, WiFi, and cellular telephony), and are nothing more than physically small computers with integrated support for telephone communication. However, because they are viewed as telephones, using a smartphone lacks the social stigmas that are associated with computer use, thus causing women to own and use them in equal numbers to men (Lenhart, Purcell, Smith, & Zickuhr, 2010). As well, the workplace is increasingly becoming computerized. Recordkeeping, document preparation, and communication (e.g., electronic mail) are predominantly done on computers as paper files, typewriters, and postal mail become less frequently used and needed or—as in the case of the typewriter—obsolete. Women now comprise about half of the workforce (e.g., 46.2% in the United States; World Bank, 2014) and are in contact with computers daily. Point-of-sale systems in retail environments are typically computer-based, causing even lower socioeconomic employment to require some computer skills. Although female pursuit of technical computing degrees has significantly decreased from 40% of US bachelor's degrees in the 1980s to 17.7% in 2008, matched by a similar decrease in women's participation in computing professions, the pervasiveness of computers in society and their integration within people's lives has helped decrease negative stereotypes (Butterfield & Crews, 2012) and consequently increased women's use of computers for all purposes, including gaming. However, women are not rushing to use their smartphones to play combat games, race automobiles, or play simulated sports such as football and hockey. Games, within frameworks such as Facebook or mobile telephone "apps," are social in nature, requiring large networks of friends to be successful, and are thus played on devices that require strong communications technology, such as smartphones. As seen with the currently popular app *The Ville*, a clear copy of the successful *The Sims* with an added social element, game designers are finally learning what is appealing to women.

In support of women's participation, game developers have leveraged the flexibility provided by software product lines and sometimes release a suite of games with virtually identical game play but different context. For example, with a minimum of effort, Zynga has created games that appeal to men (*Mafia Wars*), women (*Fashion Wars*), and both sexes (*Vampire Wars*) simply by using different themes that only required minor changes to the user interface. As well, when presented in Facebook, these games are viewed in the familiar interface of a web browser, such as Firefox, Chrome, or Internet Explorer, and do not require any special skills to use. To play a game on a web browser for which one has previously developed competence, a player needs only to learn the rules of the game, not the complexities of the user interface. Bunz (2009) has found that men and women exhibit equal levels of WWW fluency (i.e., browser use), although younger women still express more computer anxiety than do younger men. Interestingly, Bunz found that there was no sex difference in computer anxiety among older users. Women's WWW fluency thus permits them to play browser-based games using skills that are equal to those of men.

Server-based games, such as *World of Warcraft* and *Second Life*, allow developers to continuously change and extend the virtual environment in which the game is played. This dynamism prevents the repetition that bores female players. Furthermore, these games now support women's desire to customize the environment and their avatar through the ability to upload textures, photographs, 3D mesh models, and animation sequences and to combine them with in-world building and scripting tools. For example, *Second Life* has developed a virtual economy selling user-created content, such as fashion and avatar enhancements, at a level that has prompted some economists to suggest that it is suitable for taxation (Lederman, 2007).

Conclusion

In this chapter, it has been shown that women use games to practice the skills needed for intrasexual competition. In order to expand their target audience, game designers could leverage this tendency and develop games for which intrasexual competition is necessary for success. For example, one such approach could involve limiting an avatar's lifespan such that continued play would require a player to use an avatar's offspring, thus introducing a need for reproduction and the opportunity to apply intrasexual competition in the pursuit of reproductive partners. Reproduction could also be introduced by making an avatar's offspring more effective at overcoming a game's obstacles, thus necessitating the need to produce offspring to overcome advanced challenges. Alternatively, one could give different attributes, such as flying and teleportation, to differently sexed avatars and then provide obstacles for which the combination of attributes—and hence cooperation—is needed to overcome obstacles. Players could then practice intrasexual competition in the formation of effective cooperative teams. It falls on game designers to creatively apply sex differences in competitive behavior in the development of more inclusive games.

However, before game developers can fully exploit sex differences, these differences need to be better explored. In large, multiplayer, online games, such as *World of Warcraft*, do women prefer to compete intrasexually as opposed to intersexually? When pursing abstract goals such as an increase in a player's skill level, do women have different strategies or preferences when competing against other women as opposed to against men? Is sex even necessary to facilitate women's application of their preferred competitive styles? Could a science fiction game using different alien species provide opportunities for inter- and intraspecies competition that mimics inter- and intrasexual competition among humans? Although competitive strategy is generally influenced by the sex of the player, and most players tend to use avatars of the same sex, how does the use of an opposite-sex avatar influence game play? To support the development of more sexually inclusive games, there remains much for researchers to explore with regard to in-game competition.

Improvements in technology and communication, shifts in the attitudes of game developers, and increases in the prevalence of computers that have turned them from toys for geek boys into essential, portable, and ubiquitous devices have radically impacted the participation of women in computer games. These changes have influenced social attitudes toward using computers and decreased technological barriers that have almost certainly affected women's attitudes toward game play. However, it is unlikely that the influence of these factors would have been as significant if game designers had not shifted their views and started to develop games that supported women's style of play. In particular, women's style of play can be seen as revolving around their desire to practice the indirect competitive styles they use when performing intrasexual competition: self-promotion, competitor derogation and manipulation, target manipulation, and the building of social hierarchies to obtain allies and spread information needed to support these strategies. Whereas men generally enjoy traditional games in which they can practice direct aggression to achieve a clearly identifiable victory, women tend to prefer activity-based games for which they can set their own goals and in which they can practice their preferred strategies for intrasexual competition.

References

Adams, E. (2010). *Fundamentals of game design* (2nd ed.) Berkeley, CA: New Riders Press.

Anderson, C., John, O., Keltner, D., & Krieg, A. (2001). Who attains social status? Effects of personality on physical attractiveness in social groups. *Journal of Personality and Social Psychology, 81*(1), 116–132.

Beavis, C., & Charles, C. (2005). Challenging notions of gendered game play: Teenagers playing *The Sims. Discourse: Studies in the Cultural Politics of Education, 26*(3), 355–367.

Bertozzi, E. (2008). You play like a girl! Cross-gender competition and the uneven playing field. *Convergence, 14*(4), 473–487.

Björkqvist, K., Lagerspetz, K., & Kaukiainen, A. (1992). Do girls and boys fight? Developmental trends in regard to direct and indirect aggression. *Aggressive Behavior, 18*, 117–127.

Brookey, A., & Cannon, L. (2009). Sex lives in *Second Life. Critical Studies in Media Communication, 26*(2), 145–164.

Bunz, U. (2009). A generational comparison of gender, computer anxiety, and computer-email-web fluency. *Studies in Media & Information Literacy Education, 9*(2), 54–69.

Burbank, V. (1987). Female aggression in cross-cultural perspective. *Behavioral Science Research, 21*, 71–100.

Business Wire. (2002, March 21). The Sims becomes the best selling game of all time. *Business Wire*. Retrieved from http://www.thefreelibrary.com/The+Sims+Becomes+The+Best+Selling+PC+Game+of+All+Time.-a084043760.

Buss, D. (1988). The evolution of human intrasexual competition: Tactics of mate attraction. *Journal of Personality and Social Psychology, 54*, 616–628.

Buss, D. (2002). Human mate guarding. *Endocrinology Letters, 23*(Supp. 4), 23–29.

Buss, D. (2012). *Evolutionary psychology: The new science of the mind*. Boston: Allyn & Bacon.

Buss, D., & Dedden, L. (1990). Derogation of competitors. *Journal of Social and Personal Relationships, 7*, 395–422.

Buss, D., & Shackelford, T. (1997). Human aggression in evolutionary psychological perspective. *Clinical Psychology Review, 17*(6), 605–619.

Butterfield, J., & Crews, T. (2012). Casting a wider net: A longitudinal study of exploring gender differences, influences, and attitudes impacting academic major selection in computing. *Computer and Information Science, 5*, 2–10.

Campbell, A. (1995). A few good men: Evolutionary psychology and female adolescent aggression. *Ethnology and Sociobiology, 16*, 99–123.

Campbell, A. (2002). *A mind of her own: The evolutionary psychology of women*. New York: Oxford University Press.

Campbell, A. (2004). Female competition: Causes, constraints, content, and contexts. *Journal of Sex Research, 41*, 16–26.

Cannon, W. (1932). *The wisdom of the body*. New York: Norton.

Carr, D. (2005). Contexts, gaming pleasures, and gendered preferences. *Simulation and Gaming, 36*(4), 464–482.

Cashdan, E. (1998). Women's mating strategies. *Evolutionary Anthropology, 5,* 134–143.

Cassell, J., & Jenkins, H. (1998). Chess for girls? Feminism and computer games. In J. Cassell & H. Jenkins (Eds.), *From Barbie to Mortal Kombat: Gender and computer games* (pp. 2–45). Boston: MIT Press.

Chiu, C., Hsu, M., & Wang, E. (2006). Understanding knowledge sharing in virtual communities: An integration of social capital and social cognitive theories. *Decision Support Systems, 42*(3), 1872–1888.

Cole, H., & Griffiths, M. (2007). Social interactions in massively multiplayer online role-playing gamers. *CyberPsychology and Behavior, 10*(4), 573–583.

Conrad, M., Neale, J., & Charles, A. (2010). Of mice or men?— The avatar in the virtualscape. Published in Proceedings, *IEEE International Conference on Information Society,* 242–247.

Cooper, J., & Weaver, K. (2003). *Gender and computers: Understanding the digital divide.* Mahwah, NJ: Lawrence Erlbaum Associates.

Crawford, C. (1984). *The art of computer game design.* Berkeley, CA: Osborne Media.

Daly, M., & Wilson, M. (2001). Risk-taking, intrasexual competition, and homicide. *Proceedings of the Nebraska Symposium on Motivation, 47,* 1–36.

Dawson, C., Cragg, A., Taylor, C., & Toombs, B. (2007). Video games: Research to improve understanding of what players enjoy about video games, and to explain their preferences for particular games. *British Board of Film Classification.* Retrieved from http://www.bbfc.co.uk/sites/default/files/attachments/BBFC Video Games Report.pdf.

Denner, J., Bean, S., & Werner, L. (2005). Girls creating games: Challenging existing assumptions about game content. *Paper presented at the DiGRA 2005 Conference: Changing Views—Worlds in Play.* Vancouver, BC, Canada.

Digital Photography Review. (2005). *Women prefer Kodak digital cameras.* Retrieved from http://www.dpreview.com/news/2005/4/21/women_kodak.

Donath, J. (2007). Virtually trustworthy. *Science, 317*(5834), 53–54.

Ducheneaut, N., & Moore, R. (2004). The social side of gaming: A study of interaction patterns in a massively multiplayer online game. In *Proceedings of the ACM Conference on Computer Supported Cooperative Work* (pp. 360–369). Chicago: Association of Computing Machinery.

Durchin, J. (2000, March). *Developing software for girls.* Lecture delivered at Game Developers' Conference, San Jose, CA.

Eagly, A., & Wood, W. (1999). The origins of sex differences in human behavior: Evolved dispositions versus social roles. *American Psychologist, 54*(6), 408–423.

Elling, K. (2006). *Inclusive games design [Presentation].* Lecture delivered at Animex International Festival of Animation and Computer Games. University of Teesside, Middlesbrough, UK. Retrieved from http://www.designersnotebook.com/Media/Inclusive_Games_Design.ppt.

Entertainment Software Association. (2013). *2013 sales, demographic, and usage data: Essential facts about the computer and video game industry.* Minneapolis, MN: Ipsos MediaCT. Retrieved from http://www.isfe.eu/sites/isfe.eu/files/attachments/esa_ef_2013.pdf.

Fisher, M. (2013). Women's intrasexual competition for mates. In M. Fisher, J. Garcia, & R. Sokol Chang (Eds.), *Evolution's empress: Darwinian perspectives on the nature of women* (pp. 19–42). New York: Oxford University Press.

Fisher, M., & Cox, A. (2010). Four strategies used during intrasexual competition for mates. *Personal Relationships, 18*(1), 20–38.

Fron, J., Fullerton, T., Ford Morie, J., & Pearce, C. (2007). The hegemony of play. In A Baba (Ed.), *Proceedings, Digital Games Research Association: Situated Play* (pp. 309–318). Tokyo: DiGRA Japan.

Glaubke, C., Miller, P., Parker, M., & Espejo, E. (2001). *Fair play: Violence, gender and race in computer games.* Oakland, CA: Children NOW.

Graner Ray, S. (2004). *Gender inclusive game design: Expanding the market.* Hingham, MA: Charles River Media.

Greenberg, B., Sherry, J., Lachlan, K., Lucas, K., & Holmstrom, A. (2010). Orientations to video games among gender and age groups. *Simulations & Gaming, 41*(2), 238–259.

Hamlen, K. (2010). Re-examining gender preferences in video game play: Time spent and feelings of success. *Journal of Educational Computing Research, 43*(3), 293–306.

Hartmann, T., & Klimmt, C. (2006). Gender and computer games: Exploring females' dislikes. *Journal of Computer Mediated Communication, 11*(4), 910–931.

Hess, N., & Hagen, E. (2002). Informational warfare. Retrieved from http://cogprints.org/2112/3/gossip.pdf.

Hess, N., & Hagen, E. (2006). Sex differences in indirect aggression: Psychological evidence from young adults. *Evolution and Human Behavior, 27,* 231–245.

Jenkins, H., & Cassell, J. (2008). From Quake Grrls to desperate housewives. In Y. Kafai, C. Heeter, J. Denner, & J. Sun (Eds.), *Beyond Barbie and Mortal Kombat: New perspectives on gender and gaming* (pp. 5–20). Boston: MIT Press.

Jenson, J. (2005). Her own boss: Gender in the pursuit of incompetent play. *Paper presented at the DiGRA 2005 Conference: Changing Views—Worlds in Play.* Vancouver, BC, Canada.

Kafai, Y. B. (1993). *Minds in play: Computer game design as a context for children's learning* (Unpublished doctoral dissertation). Harvard, Cambridge.

Kafai, Y. B., Heeter, C., Denner, J., & Sun, J. Y. (Eds.). (2008). *Beyond Barbie and Mortal Kombat: New perspectives on gender and gaming.* Cambridge, MA: MIT Press.

Kaiser Family Foundation. (1999). *Kids & media @ The new millennium.* Retrieved from http://kff.org/hivaids/report/kids-media-the-new-millennium/.

Koster, R. (2004). *A theory of fun for game design.* Scottsdale, AZ: Paraglyph Press.

Kowert, R., Griffiths, M., & Oldmeadow, J. (2012). Geek or chic? Emerging stereotypes of online gamers. *Bulletin of Science, Technology & Society, 32*(6), 471–479.

Lawton, C. (1994). Gender differences in way-finding strategies: Relationship to spatial ability and spatial anxiety. *Sex Roles, 30*(11/12), 765–779.

Lawton, C. (2001). Gender and regional differences in spatial references used in direction giving. *Sex Roles, 44*(5/6), 321–337.

Lederman, L. (2007). Stranger than fiction: Taxing virtual worlds. *New York University Law Review, 82,* 1620–1672.

Lenhart, A., Purcell, K., Smith, A., & Zichuhr, K. (2010). *Social media & mobile internet use among teens and young adults.* Washington, DC: Pew Research Center.

Lewis, M. (1998). *Sugar, spice, and everything nice: Computer games girls play*. Retrieved from http://www.slate.com/articles/arts/millionerds/1998/02/sugar_spice_and_everything_nice.html.

Liesen, L. (2013). The tangled web she weaves: The evolution of female-female aggression and status-seeking. In M. Fisher, J. Garcia, & R. Sokol Chang (Eds.), *Evolution's empress: Darwinian perspectives on the nature of women* (pp. 43–62). New York: Oxford University Press.

Meredith, T. (2013). A new view of evolutionary psychology using women's priorities and motivations. In M. Fisher, J. Garcia, & R. Sokol Chang (Eds.), *Evolution's empress: Darwinian perspectives on the nature of women* (pp. 371–389). New York: Oxford University Press.

Messinger, P., Ge, X., Stroulia, E., Lyons, K., Smirnov, K., & Bone, M. (2008). On the relationship between my avatar and myself. *Journal of Virtual Worlds*, 1(2).

McKenna, P. (2001). Programmers: Concrete women and abstract men? *Journal of Computer Assisted Learning*, 17(4), 386–395.

Moore, M., & Sward, J. (2007). *Introduction to the game industry*. Upper Saddle River, NJ: Pearson Prentice Hall.

Morlock, H., Yando, T., & Nigolean, K. (1985). Motivation of video game players. *Psychological Reports*, 57, 247–250.

N-blox Leaderboard. (2014). *Tetris friends*. Retrieved from http://www.tetrisfriends.com/leaderboard/index.php.

Nutt, D., & Railton, D. (2003). *The Sims*: Real life as genre. *Information, Communication and Society*, 6(4), 577–592.

Ogletree, S., & Drake, R. (2007). College student's video game participation and perceptions: Gender differences and implications. *Sex Roles*, 56(7–8), 537–542.

Olson, C. (2010). Children's motivations for video game play in the context of normal development. *Review of General Psychology*, 14(2), 180–187.

Olson, C., Kutner, L., Warner, D., Almerigi, J., Baer, L., Nicholi, A., & Beresin, E. (2007). Factors correlated with violent video game use by adolescent boys and girls. *Journal of Adolescent Health*, 41, 77–83.

O'Riordan, K. (2001). Playing with Lara in virtual space. In S. Munt (Ed.), *Technospaces: Inside the new media* (pp. 124–138). London: Continuum.

Oxland, K. (2004). *Gameplay and design*. London: Addison-Wesley.

Phan, M. H., Jardina, J. R., Hoyle, S., & Chaparro, B. S. (2012, September). Examining the role of gender in video game usage, preference, and behavior. *In Proceedings of the Human Factors and Ergonomics Society Annual Meeting* (Vol. 56, No. 1, pp. 1496–1500). Thousand Oaks, CA: Sage.

Philbin, M., Meier, E., Huffman, S., & Boverie, P. (1995). A survey of gender and learning styles. *Sex Roles*, 32(7/8), 485–494.

Postma, A., Jager, G., Kessels, R., Koppeschaar, H., & van Honk, J. (2003). Sex differences for selective forms of spatial memory. *Brain and Cognition*, 54, 24–34.

Queiroz, C. (2005). *Insular: Critical appraisal* (Unpublished master's thesis). Surrey Institute of Art and Design, Farnham, UK.

Reiber, L. (1996). Seriously considering play: Designing interactive learning environments based on the blending of microworlds, simulation, and games. *Educational Technology Research and Development*, 44, 43–58.

Robinson-Stavely, K., & Cooper, J. (1990). Mere presence, gender, and reactions to computers: Studying human-computer interaction in the social context. *Journal of Experimental Social Psychology*, 26, 168–183.

Rouse, R. (2005). *Game design: Theory and practice*. Plano, TX: Wordware Publishing.

Rymaszewski, M., Au, W., Wallace, M., Winters, C., Ondrejka, C., & Batstone-Cunningham, B. (2007). *Second Life: The official guide*. Indianapolis, IN: Wiley.

Salen, K., & Zimmerman, E. (2003). *Rules of play: Game design fundamentals*. Boston: MIT Press.

Saucier, D., Bowman, M., & Elias, L. (2003). Sex differences in the effect of articulatory or spatial dual-task interference during navigation. *Brain and Cognition*, 53, 346–350.

Seabrook, J. (2006, November 6). Game master. *The New Yorker*, 405–414.

Severiens, S., & Ten Dam, G. (1994). Gender differences in learning styles: A narrative review and quantitative meta-analysis. *Higher Education*, 27, 487–501.

Steinkeuhler, C., & Williams, D. (2006). Where everybody knows your (screen) name: Online games as "third places." *Journal of Computer-Mediated Communication*, 11, 885–909.

Suits, B. (1967). What is a game? *Philosophy of Science*, 34, 148–156.

Taylor, S., Cousino Klein, L., Lewis, B., Gruenewald, T., Gurung, R., & Updegraff, A. (2000). Biobehavioral responses to stress in females: Tend-and-befriend, not fight-or-flight. *Psychological Review*, 107(3), 411–429.

Taylor, T. (2002). Living digitally: Embodiment in virtual worlds. In R. Schroeder (Ed.), *The social life of avatars: Presence and interaction in shared virtual environments* (pp. 40–62). London: Springer-Verlag.

Tetris. (2014). *Wikipedia, the free encyclopedia*. Retrieved from http://en.wikipedia.org/wiki/Tetris.

Top 100 Female Players. (2014). *E-sports earnings*. Retrieved from http://www.esportsearnings.com/players/female_players.

Turkle, S. (1988). Computational reticence: Why women fear the intimate machine. In C. Kramare (Ed.), *Technology and women's voices: Keeping in touch* (pp. 41–61). New York: Routledge & Kegan Paul.

Turkle, S., & Papert, S. (1992). Epistemological pluralism and revaluation of the concrete. *Journal of Mathematical Behavior*, 11(1), 3–33.

Vasalou, A., & Joinson, A. (2009). Me, myself and I: The role of interactional context on self-presentation through avatars. *Computers in Human Behavior*, 25(2), 510–520.

Walters, S., & Crawford, C. (1994). The importance of mate attraction for intrasexual competition in men and women. *Ethology and Sociobiology*, 15, 5–30.

Williams, D., Duchenaut, N., Xiong, L., Zhang, Y., Yee, N., & Nickell, E. (2006). From tree house to barracks: The social life of guilds in *World of Warcraft*. *Games and Culture*, 1(4), 338–361.

Willoughby, T. (2008). A short-term longitudinal study of internet and computer game use by adolescent boys and girls: Prevalence, frequency of use, and psychosocial predictors. *Developmental Psychology*, 44(1), 195–204.

Wolfendale, J. (2009). Virtual harm and attachment. Australian Institute of Family Studies. *ACSSA Newsletter*, 21, 9–11.

World Bank. (2014). Labor force, female (% of total labor force). Retrieved from http://data.worldbank.org/indicator/SL.TLF.TOTL.FE.ZS

Xenakis, J. (2001). *Online games for girls: E-commerce's next frontier?* Retrieved from http://www.cfo.com/printable/article.cfm/2991753?f=options.

Yates, S., & Littleton, K. (1999). Understand computer game cultures. *Information, Communication and Society, 2*(4), 566–583.

Yee, N., Bailenson, J., & Urbanek, M. (2007). The unbearable likeness of being digital: The persistence of nonverbal social norms in online virtual environments. *Cyberpsychology and Behavior, 10*(1), 115–121.

Competition in Applied Settings

The Buzz on the Queen Bee and Other Characterizations of Women's Intrasexual Competition at Work

Lucie Kocum, Delphine S. Courvoisier, *and* Saundra Vernon

Abstract

Competition is a normal part of working life. It is expected of both women and men as they enter the workforce, and as they ascend the corporate ladder. Interestingly, women are often vilified for engaging in competition, particularly with members of their own sex. The focus of this essay is intrasexual competition among women in the workplace. It provides a description of workplace competition and its positive and negative consequences for workers and organizations, followed by similarities and differences in women's and men's competitive experiences and styles. The ways zero-sum contexts such as tokenism affect social identity and give rise to the intrasexual prejudice and discrimination—most notably, the queen bee—are discussed. The essay ends with a discussion based on the authors' experimental evidence of intragroup favoritism among women, and a growing body of work underscoring the importance of not expecting women to be allies without accompanying organizational change.

Key Words: intrasexual competition, women, gender, queen bee, social identity

Competition is a normal part of working life. We compete with other candidates for jobs and with our colleagues for career advancement. In fact, the free-market economy is predicated on the tenet of free and fair competition. Although competition is expected and is something in which both women and men engage, competition among women is sometimes vilified, particularly in popular culture. One example is the film *Mean Girls* (Waters, 2004), based on the book *Queen Bees and Wannabes: Helping Your Daughter Survive Cliques, Gossip, Boyfriends, and Other Realities of Adolescence* (Wiseman, 2002; updated 2009). In *Mean Girls*, two adolescent girls vie for top spot in a clique of popular girls because, presumably, there can be only one *most* popular girl. Although this example presents intrasexual competition among women at its most sensational, even workplace competition among women is characterized differently, and

sometimes more negatively, than it is among men. This is partly because women approach competition differently than men (Niederle & Vesterlund, 2007), and partly because people stereotypically expect women to cooperate rather than compete (Eagly & Karau, 2002), especially with each other (Sheppard & Aquino, 2013).

The focus of this essay is intrasexual competition among women in the workplace. We start with a general description of workplace competition and its positive and negative consequences for workers and organizations. We follow with a more specific explanation of intrasexual competition among women and men, and the organizational and psychological contexts that result in negative sex-based perceptions and consequences for women. We discuss how tokenism (Kanter, 1977) and the glass ceiling (Hymowitz & Schellhardt, 1986) affect social identity (Tajfel, 1978, 1982; Tajfel & Turner,

1986) to give rise to the "queen bee." This term was introduced to the literature by Staines, Travis, and Jayaratne (1974), and was used to denote a woman who has achieved success in a "man's world" but is unwilling to extend a hand to more junior women.

We also discuss social role theory (Eagly, 1987) and how sex-based stereotypes are applied, by both women and men, to female professionals (Cuddy, Fiske, & Glick, 2004), including managers (Powell, Butterfield, & Parent, 2002; Rudman & Glick, 2001). We also explain how women, unlike men, use these stereotypes as an identity-saving strategy in competition with other women (Heilman, Wallen, Fuchs, & Tamkins, 2004). Not all women denigrate their same-sex colleagues, and we thus end with a discussion based on our experimental evidence of intragroup favoritism (Kocum, Tougas, Courvoisier, & Brazeau, 2014), as well as a growing body of work underscoring the importance of not expecting women to be allies (Mavin, 2008; Sheppard & Aquino, 2013, 2014) without accompanying organizational changes that facilitate cooperation. The extent to which negative intrasexual discrimination stifles professional women is put into larger perspective of the consequences of males' intersexual dismissal of women as viable competiton (Saad & Gill, 2001).

Workplace Competition: The Good, the Bad, and the Ugly

Most organizations are set up in a way that rewards success in competition, employing competitive hiring and promotion practices, among other praxes. Though stress is heightened when people compete (Wilder & Shapiro, 1989), organizations favor competition. This is because it can have positive outcomes such as increased individual effort (Stanne, Johnson, & Johnson, 1999) and corporate productivity (Nickell, 1996). However, competition can have negative outcomes for individuals and organizations as well. Especially in zero-sum competition contexts, in which outcomes are interdependent (i.e., my gain equals your loss), "the contrastive feelings of pride, scorn, and *schadenfreude* or depression, resentment, and envy, depending who has gained or lost the advantage" are evoked (Smith, 2000, p. 193). Envy, in particular, is associated with lower work self-esteem, reduced performance, and a higher rate of turnover intentions, among other negative effects (for a review, see Duffy, Shaw, & Schaubroeck, 2008). This kind of competitive environment also engages "positional bias" (Hill & Buss, 2006), wherein a person would rather choose

to have fewer total resources if it meant having more resources as compared to others (e.g., they would choose an income of $40,000 if others made $35,000 rather than choosing a higher income of $45,000 if others made $50,000). In fact, in the presence of such a ranking reward system, employees are more likely to engage in counterproductive work behavior (a term coined by Sackett & DeVore, 2002), sabotaging competitors and even incurring a cost so that their overall ranking outperforms that of others (Charness, Masclet, & Villeval, 2014). In sum, there are clear disadvantages of a competitive work environment to both the worker and the organization, particularly if the focus of the competition for the worker is individual gain/loss.

Because most companies favor competition, most workers are expected to engage in competition. For both females and males, winning at competition is an inherent part of corporate success. The research on competition summarized in the previous paragraph applies to both sexes equally. That is to say, both females and males feel heightened stress in competitive environments, and both react negatively to competitive-rank compensation schemes.

There are several other similarities between the sexes. Females and males are equally driven to influence others and feel equivalently rewarded after a victory and discouraged after a defeat (Schultheiss et al., 2005). Also, females and males prefer to compete intrasexually (for a review, see Buunk, Pollet, Dijkstra, & Massar, 2011), which means that the targets of their social comparisons—and ensuing envy, scorn, resentment, and sabotage, should the outcome of the comparison disfavor them—are most often members of their own sex. That said, the higher the woman's income, the more likely she is to make job-related comparisons with men (Steil & Hay, 1997).

It may be surprising to learn that females and males have so much in common when it comes to competition. In their recent book, Bronson and Merryman (2013) contend that males are eager and overconfident competitors, whereas females are more hesitant and calculated in their approach. It has been long thought that males' higher testosterone levels are responsible for their proclivity for competition. Biologically, males have significantly more testosterone—a hormone that has been more clearly associated with status-seeking behavior in men than in women (Mazur & Booth, 1998). Recently, though, researchers have discovered that the relationship between testosterone and competition is not as straightforward as once thought. In both males and females, testosterone increases prior to competition and after a victory. However, after a defeat, women's testosterone levels increase, while men's levels drop (Schultheiss et al., 2005). Vongas and Hajj (2014) posit that females' rise in testosterone after a defeat may explain why women (but not men) are more tenacious and more willing to continue the competitive pursuit after a defeat, while males tend to drop it.

Do women tend to shy away from competition? The essays in this volume provide ample evidence that women actively engage in competition, particularly within the context of mating. In the context of work, however, mating competition and matters of financial success are uncorrelated among women (unlike men; Cashdan, 1998). Experimental research examining men and women's approach to competition has found that women tend to avoid competitive situations whereas men gravitate toward them, particularly if these competitions are "tournament" style in which the winner takes all. In contrast to this tendency toward avoidance, research shows that in these contexts, women perform as well as, and sometimes outperform, men. Niederle and Vesterlund (2007) conducted a series of experiments in which women and men were given a choice of being compensated for a task in a piecemeal fashion (i.e., a fixed rate per correct answer) or a tournament fashion (i.e., the winner who solves the most problems correctly takes all). In this study, twice as many men as women selected the competitive "tournament" as their preferred compensation scheme. Niederle and Vesterlund's conclusion was that men "embrace" competition whereas women "shy away from it."

A replication a half-decade later (Price, 2012) corroborated this tendency for women to choose the less competitive work option for compensation. However, Price extended his experiment to also compare performance on a simple set of math tasks for women and men who were told their compensation scheme would be tournament style (i.e., no choice in the matter), compared to their performance when the compensation scheme was assigned to them by a "manager" working with them in a dyad. Women and men performed similarly well when simply instructed to solve problems under the condition of tournament-style payment. However, when the manager in their dyad assigned the tournament style to them, women significantly outperformed the men also selected for this payment scheme. Thus, women performed equally well under two different competitive payment schemes,

whereas the performance of men significantly declined when the scheme was chosen for them. Therefore, although women may not prefer competitive contexts when given a choice, they perform well under them and outperform men when given a vote of confidence by someone acting as their manager.

If women do compete in many arenas, are as driven to succeed, and, in fact, are more tenacious in the face of defeat than are men, why would they avoid competitive task contexts? Moreover, if they are just as successful at competitive tasks as are men—and sometimes even more successful—why do they still form a minority in the upper echelons of the corporate world? In the next section, we argue that prescriptive gender stereotypes (endorsed and applied by both women and men; Cuddy, Fiske, & Glick, 2004; Heilman, Wallen, Fuchs, & Tamkins, 2004), social roles (Eagly & Karau, 2002), and the social dynamics of tokenism (Kanter, 1977) act together to heighten competition among women, particularly in male-dominated professions. This unhealthy competitive environment induces envy, sabotage, and other counterproductive work behaviors leveled at same-sex targets, thereby buttressing the glass ceiling.

To be clear, we do not engage in victim blaming here. On the contrary, acknowledging that women and men share attitudes that may lead to women's subjugation necessarily situates stereotyping as a social process available to all people, regardless of sex. Recognizing that the nature of intrasexual competition is different among women and men due to their different (often opposing) social role expectations, and also status in the workplace, is an important step in understanding why women sometimes scrutinize their same-sex competitors more heavily than they would men. We thus place women's social psychology on an equal footing to that of men, and permit ourselves to entertain the notion that women may be key contributors to maintaining their disadvantaged status quo. We also explore possible ways in which females propagate this status quo by discussing what they think of women and how they compete with them, given the constraints of stereotypes, social role norms, and their minority status in traditionally male spheres of employment.

Making It in a Man's World: A Prescription for Unsuccess

There's an overlap in people's minds between the qualities that we associate with leadership and the qualities we associate with masculinity—decisiveness, aggressiveness, competence. There is much less overlap between leadership qualities and those we associate with being feminine—an inclination toward consensus building, to being communal, expressive, nurturing. That's why for many people it was rather disturbing that I was Prime Minister. A woman wasn't supposed to be Prime Minister.

—*The Right Honourable Kim Campbell, in Campbell & Morse, 2002, p. 20*

Adopted by Parliament in 1977, the Canadian Human Rights Act (1976–1977) rendered sex discrimination illegal in the Canadian workplace. The achievement of this legislation was a major milestone in the Canadian labor movement and served as a catalyst for women's career progress. Recent figures indicate that women constitute 47% of North American workers (Bureau of Labor Statistics, 2016; Statistics Canada, 2016), with a labor force participation rate of between 58% in the United States and 61% in Canada. The strongest female representation is in the health-care, trade, and education sectors (Statistics Canada, 2001). Perhaps one of the best exemplars of women's professional progress has been the trajectory of women in management. Historically dominated by men, the proportion of women in management has increased by more than 40% in recent years (Statistics Canada, 2003).

It might be tempting to conclude that, in time, women managers will gain an equal footing to men and that continued investigations of inequity are outdated and unnecessary, but such conclusions would be precipitous. At present, female managers are still segregated in terms of earnings, power, and prestige (Gibelman, 2003; Statistics Canada, 2003). The top of the corporate ladder remains prohibitive, as women continue to occupy a minority of senior management positions. Currently, women hold just 4.4% of S&P 500 chief executive officer positions, and, at that, only 9.5% of top earner positions (Catalyst, 2016). The resistance to female leadership is also evidenced in the public sector, where women currently constitute only 25% of ministers of Parliament. These statistics are disconcerting, given that equity programs have been legislated for nearly three decades with the specific mandate of eliminating workplace inequality (Employment Equity Act, 1986).

Why does sex segregation persist in field of management? Two root causes have been explored in the literature. Some researchers have argued that women avoid entering traditionally male fields of employment as a matter of personal choice, because such workplaces are competitive and hierarchical, and women are thought to prefer work settings offering collaborative relationships with coworkers and power structures that are more egalitarian. A more pervasive and contemporary view attributes the proportional asymmetry to contextual rather than person-centered factors. The most prevalent and damaging of these factors is stereotyping, or the view that women simply do not possess the ideal combination of traits and dispositions to succeed as managers. Therefore, those espousing gender-prescriptive views would argue that there is a lack of female managers because females are not *supposed* to be managers.

Males have been targeted as the main instigators of such perceptions because, by virtually all accounts and measures, they have displayed significantly higher levels of stereotyping than females. It is argued that their obstinate view of women as not measuring up to an ideal (i.e., stereotypically male) standard of management is particularly harmful because they are situated in positions of authority and hold the power to maintain the status quo. By attributing stereotyping to males, however, researchers have reverted to a person-centered approach to understanding the sexual asymmetry in the distribution of top jobs, this time blaming men's perceptions as opposed to women's choices. Researchers have often ignored the participation of women in this social process as little more than helpless victims. However, some research has shown that, under certain circumstances, women also hold prejudicial views against members of their own sex. Acknowledging women, not only as targets but also as agents of stereotyping, is the necessary ingredient for jarring the stalemate generated and maintained by the assumptions that women are all egalitarian and that their negative views of women have benign consequences. For these reasons, we challenge the assumption of biological sex as a precursor to stereotyping and present attitudes toward the distribution of sex roles as the more important factor prompting people—both women and men—to hold stereotyped perceptions of women.

Illustrative of the tendency to see women as victims of male oppression and ignoring the role women play as active agents in their own subjugation is Wood and Eagly's (2010) review of existing gender literature in the *Handbook of Social Psychology* (Fiske, Gilbert, & Lindzey, 2010). Their review demonstrates that the extant literature does not address directly the specific question of women's intragroup prejudice and discrimination. Instead, women are normally viewed as the targets—the passive victims and not the instigators—of stereotyping and sexism. When their perceptions and attitudes *are* measured, the detection of sexism and stereotyping is attributed to the social learning of male-defined prejudice rather than motivational factors (Glick & Fiske, 1996), and these interpretations tend to occur post hoc, after results have gone "unexpectedly" counter to the proposed hypotheses (e.g., Biernat & Fugen, 2001). Most often, though, women's egalitarianism toward their own sex has been assumed without question (e.g., Swim, Aikin, Hall, & Hunter, 1995), or their prejudice has gone unnoticed (for a discussion on this tendency in research, see Baron, Burgess, & Kao, 1991). Others have concluded that, whereas women once viewed the world in a sex-typed fashion, they have now become egalitarian (Schein, 2001).

As targets of workplace discrimination, there are significant costs to women identifying too closely with a marginalized group, particularly as they strive to climb the corporate ladder. Women compete with each other in the workplace, and, sometimes, this competition involves sex-based discrimination, particularly in cases in which women violate gender norms and in token environments, in which women are a minority. Using Deaux and Lafrance's (1998) gender belief system as a framework, we explain how gender role stereotypes, negative attitudes toward women, gender identity, and, importantly, women's token status work together to foster an environment in which successful women serve as gatekeepers of the glass ceiling, keeping other women down who would otherwise threaten their privileged position.

Gender Belief System: Stereotyping and Sexism

According to Deaux and Lafrance (1998), three components are integral to the gender belief system: stereotypes, attitudes, and identity. To define the terms further, gender stereotypes are a set of beliefs about the characteristics that women and men possess (descriptive stereotypes) and ought to possess (injunctive or prescriptive stereotypes; Cialdini & Trost, 1998; Fiske & Stevens, 1993). Sexism, in its contemporary form known as neosexism (Tougas, Brown, Beaton, & Joly, 1995), is the "resistance to role modifications and support of a differential view of men and women" (Tougas, Beaton, Brown, & St.-Pierre, 1999, p. 1496). Gender identity, from the social identity perspective (Tajfel, 1978, 1982;

Tajfel & Turner, 1986), has three aspects: awareness of belonging to a gender group (cognitive aspect), recognition of the gender group as important (evaluative aspect), and positive or negative feelings about one's gender group (affective aspect). In addition, a relational aspect has been added to gender identity to account for the "common fate" aspect often experienced by low-status groups (Luhtanen & Crocker, 1992). It is argued that these three components of the gender belief system correlate and interact in specific ways to give rise to intragroup disfavoring biases.

Role congruity theory asserts that women are perceived as less suitable for positions of power and leadership (Eagly & Karau, 2002). For nearly three decades, Schein and her colleagues (see Schein, 2001, for a review) have examined the discord between traits ascribed to typical managers and those to female managers in the United States and, more recently, in the UK, Germany, China, and Japan. The point of departure for Schein's research is the *think manager, think male* hypothesis. This hypothesis purports that people view the role of manager androcentrically. In other words, when people think of a typical manager, the image of a male—possessing stereotypically male characteristics—comes to mind: the image of a female is simply not evoked.

To operationalize this sex-typing phenomenon, Schein developed the Schein Descriptive Index (SDI; Schein, 1973). A list of ninety-two traits typically associated with either females or males (but not both), the SDI asks participants to rate the extent to which each trait applies to one of three categories of people: *women in general, men in general,* or *successful middle managers*. Of note is that the last of these conditions makes no reference to the sex of the managers. Participants in the *successful middle managers* condition are thereby prompted to characterize what they view to be prototypical managers. Stereotyping is signaled by a lack of correspondence between ratings of the prototype and ratings of female targets (or between the prototype and male targets).

Schein's initial (1973, 1975) findings among middle managers in the United States showed that both female and male raters sex-typed the managerial role. A reliable correspondence was found between the traits ascribed to males and those ascribed to the protoypical manager (e.g., logical, competent). There was a mismatch, however, between the traits ascribed to the prototypical manager and those ascribed to females. Females were perceived to lack traits requisite to managing. In addition, traits typically associated with females (e.g., helpful, aware of other's feelings) did not correspond to the managerial profile. More recent SDI replications in the United States (Brenner, Tomkiewicz, & Schein, 1989; Deal & Stevenson, 1998; see Schein, 2001, for a review) indicate that women have come to perceive women and men to be equally capable as leaders. Although males continue to perceive a woman–manager discord, there is no longer a gap between how women perceive females and how they characterize managers. Schein (2001), as well as researchers corroborating the attenuation of stereotyping among women (Deal & Stevenson, 1998), have identified perceiver sex as the key predictor of sex stereotyping. In fact, Schein suggests that women may serve as a "barometer of change" (p. 681).

Schein's own cross-cultural replications, however, clearly indicate that perceiver sex is not a panacea. These studies have revealed that women in the UK and Germany (Schein & Mueller, 1992) and in the People's Republic of China and Japan (Schein, Mueller, Lituchy, & Liu, 1996) sextype the managerial position as much as do men (though to a greater extent in Japan than in China, the UK, and Germany). Both female and male managers and business management students were found to share the view that women lack leadership and analytical abilities, business skills, and a desire for responsibility. Males (but not females) additionally were found to view women as lacking a desire for competition (a point we return to later), whereas females were found to view women as lacking self-confidence.

Furthermore, critics of sample segregation, or the drawing of conclusions based on subject and not causal variables (i.e., Condor, 1988, 1989; Henwood, 1994), have argued that studies drawing conclusions based on variables such as race or sex, without exploring the underlying reasons for those differences, assume that "differences between groups are simply natural, intractable and non-negotiable" (Henwood, 1994, p. 44). Although Schein (2001) conjectures that the shift in females' perceptions may be due to changing attitudes among women, the link between attitudes and sex-typing under the SDI paradigm has not been assessed. A handful of studies have emerged recently that have gone beyond demographics and have examined attitudes toward women as a qualifier for sex as a predictor (Konrad & Hartmann, 2001; Konrad & Spitz, 2003; O'Connor, Gutek, Stockdale, Geer, & Melançon, 2004). In all cases,

it was demonstrated that attitudes fully or partially supplant sex differences.

For instance, in their examination of sexual harassment judgments, O'Connor and colleagues (2004) found that although women were more likely than men to define a case as sexual harrassment and identify with the victim, sexism partially accounted for these effects. Both women and men with lower as opposed to higher sexism were more likely to define a case as sexually harassing and were more likely to identify with the victim.

Konrad and Hartmann (2001) and Konrad and Spitz (2003) sought to explain sex (as well as other demographic) differences regularly found in studies examining attitudes toward affirmative action programs. They hypothesized that traditional attitudes toward women would qualify (i.e., render nonsignificant) sex as a predictor of affirmative action attitudes, as people who hold such attitudes believe that women and men are suited to differential roles and would consequently oppose measures to correct this difference. Indeed, sex was fully qualified by attitudes toward women. In other words, regardless of sex, people (i.e., women as well as men) with more negative attitudes toward women were less likely to endorse affirmative action programs. These findings help researchers move beyond demographics in understanding attitudes toward equalizing programs and identify attitudes toward women, in particular, as a worthwhile qualifier of sex to consider in other contexts where sex roles are evaluated. A more direct challenge to Schein's (2001) contention of female egalitarianism is a model of neosexism tested by Tougas et al. (1999). To clarify what the construct means, someone low in neosexism, for example, would acknowledge inequity in the present employment system, whereas someone high in neosexism would report finding it difficult to work for a female boss. Tougas and her colleagues (1999) found that women who endorse neosexist attitudes view male managers to be more competent and qualified than female managers.

In sum, the ostensible disappearance of intrasexual stereotyping among women has been disconfirmed. In other words, women do endorse negative attitudes toward women, and these negative attitudes are associated with an increased propensity to apply gender stereotypes to women. In the following section, we not only provide evidence of intrasexual sex-typing among women but also reveal a "shifting standard" (Biernat & Vescio, 2002), whereby women scrutinized against a higher standard are penalized for being successful in a man's world.

Women in Competition: Damned If They Do

Women are not supposed to compete. This view is dictated by the stereotypic norm that women are meant to be cooperative. In fact, some argue that it is precisely this gender normative lens that has been applied in perceiving competition among women as more problematic than it is among men (Mavin, 2008; Sheppard & Aquino, 2013, 2014). It is possible that some women avoid competition so that they may retain their feminine identity. It also possible that they avoid competition to avoid the social sanctions that ensue when women break traditional gender roles. These sanctions are used by both women and men and, in some cases, are applied more harshly by women.

Women can be warm or competent but not both. Robust findings under the stereotype content model (Fiske, Cuddy, Glick, & Xu, 2002) tell us that there are two distilled stereotype dimensions, warmth and competence, by which people are characterized. A housewife, for example, is stereotypically perceived as very high on warmth but very low on competence. A businesswoman, conversely, is perceived as highly competent but very low on warmth. Cuddy, Fiske, and Glick (2004) conducted a series of experiments to assess whether parenthood added to professionals' warmth ratings. They found that professional males who were identified as fathers maintained competence and gained in warmth ratings, whereas professional females lost in competence what they gained in warmth. Indeed, similar dimensions play out comparably across other experiments. When presented as successful, particularly in a male domain of employment, women professionals are adjudged as less likeable and, as a result, are allocated fewer organizational rewards and more disfavorable evaluations (Heilman, Wallen, Fuchs, & Tamkins, 2004). In sum, in terms of these perceived stereotypic dimensions of warmth/likeableness and competence, it seems that men can have it all, but women cannot.

Though the previous results apply to both women and men equally, women have been found to be particularly threatened when presented with a professional female target who is both warm and competent. In a series of experiments, Parks-Stamm, Heilman, and Hearns (2008) replicated the findings of Heilman et al. (2004). Moreover, they found that when presented with female targets who were described as both successful and highly likeable, females' (but not males') self-ratings of competence were significantly lower. The researchers suggest women's lower self-evaluations were the result of social comparisons with professional female targets whom female participants could not "penalize" through lower likeability ratings. It seems that female participants were envious of the targets and took a loss to their self-esteem in the absence of an opportunity to apply their stereotypical judgment against the target.

Another interesting finding regarding competence is that women have been shown to judge each other more harshly in hiring situations. Biernat and Fuegan (2001) found that when asked to provide thresholds for competence in hiring male versus female candidates, women (but not men) raised their standards of competence for hiring females. One can imagine how this counterproductive double standard would play out in the workforce.

Why might professional women feel especially threatened by their female counterparts? What follows is a closer examination of the social psychological processes, namely social identity in the context of a token environment, underlying why and how sexist attitudes and gender-based prejudice are used in ultimately counterproductive intrasexual competition among women.

Tokenism Begets a Tournament: Women's Intrasexual Competition as a Status Minority

We have already described how tournament-style competitions beget counterproductive work behaviors and envy, among other negative consequences, in both women and men. In the case of women in traditionally male spheres of employment such as management, it has been argued (Duguid, 2011; Sheppard & Aquino, 2013, 2014) that their token status (Kanter, 1977) creates a perception that there is a limited amount of room for women (Ely, 1994), which gives rise to a heightened sense of competition over a perceived smaller territory. Whereas males face competition at work, they do not face this added competitive subcontext of being a minority.

We posit women and men are not competing on a level playing field, particularly in organizational contexts in which females form a minority. In such token (Kanter, 1977) environments, women may perceive the number of positions for women to be limited (Ely, 1994) and therefore feel relegated to competing over a "smaller piece of the pie" (Sheppard & Aquino, 2014, p. 10). As already discussed at the outset of this essay, these kinds of zero-sum competitive environments elicit feelings of envy and threat in everyone—females and males alike; in majority-male occupations, however, males would not feel the pressure of such a threat. Women, however, feel two kinds of threat from other women: competitive, or a personal threat that another woman may threaten some of her limited resources, and collective, or a threat that the presence of another woman—especially if she performs poorly—will lead others to generalize the performance to all women (Duguid, 2011).

> *When we were growing up, many of us could not see ourselves beyond the age of twenty-one. We had no image of our own future, of ourselves as women.*
> —*Friedan, 1963, p. 69*

Over forty years ago, Betty Friedan's (1963) book *The Feminine Mystique* signaled a crisis in the identity of women. Friedan argued that "the feminine mystique [i.e., the predominant view of postindustrial North American women as wives and mothers and nothing else] permits, even encourages, women to ignore the question of their identity" (Friedan, 1963, p. 71). By "identity" Friedan was referring to the "private image" (p. 72) or imagined sense of self beyond the socially prescribed role of housewife and mother. According to Friedan, breaking out of this normative role in the 1950s and 1960s was stressful for women for two reasons. First, there was a lack of variety in the roles occupied, and the spheres populated, by women. Although there was increasing encouragement of women to feel as free as and equal to men, there were few exemplars to prepare them for the challenge of assuming their role as women in male domains. Second, Friedan suggested, women were experiencing stress arising from "growing pains" associated with attaining levels of personal growth hitherto *verboten* or unnecessary within the scope of the housewife/mother role.

In some respects, times have changed since Friedan wrote her social *exposé*. Certainly in contemporary North America, both the public (i.e., social) and private images of women include a career component. These figures demonstrate that there is still a significant need to bolster female numbers in higher-level management positions, as this paucity of women in the upper echelons continues to be cited as stifling female career progress (Catalyst, 2005). Furthermore, as targets of prejudicial scrutiny by superiors, colleagues, and subordinates (Chung, Marshall, & Gordon, 2001; Schein, 2001; Sinclair & Kunda, 2000), it is doubtful that women in the contemporary workplace have the support they need to work through the growing pains to which Friedan alludes. Finally—and perhaps most important—women continue to have difficulty imagining themselves in influential professional roles (Killeen, López-Zafra, & Eagly, 2006).

How do women react to their workplace marginalization and heavy scrutiny—that which is self-directed and that which is dispatched by others? Social identity theory is often applied in understanding intergroup conflicts. The fundamental premise of the social identity approach is that the perceptions held, attitudes endorsed, and behaviors carried out by individuals are largely piloted by the groups to which they belong. In others words, how one perceives, feels, and acts toward members of a given social group is determined, in large part, by one's own social groups and the relation among one's in-groups and relevant out-groups. In technical terms, social identity is defined as "that part of an individual's self-concept which derives from his knowledge of his membership in a social group (or groups) together with the value and emotional significance attached to that membership" (Tajfel, 1981, p. 255)". Thus, the extent to which social behavior is influenced by one's group membership depends on how strongly aware one is of one's group membership (cognitive aspect), one's recognition of one's group as important (evaluative aspect), and one's feelings about the group (affective aspect).

According to social identity theory's self-esteem hypothesis (best articulated by Abrams & Hogg, 1988), invidious social comparisons—and the threat to self-esteem they invoke—are the trigger for in-group enhancing strategies (i.e., either in-group favoritism or out-group derogation). Individuals are motivated to maintain a positive self-esteem, and when the status of their in-group is threatened, they elevate their group status by forcing down that of another. There is an important qualification to this hypothesis, however. Members of low-status groups (such as designated minority groups in a mostly white male context) who perceive their self-concept to be in jeopardy may choose to derogate *in-group* rather than *out-group* members. For women in organizations in which few females assume top positions, their sex may be viewed as a marker of lower status. In order to bolster their personal identity, members of low-status groups may adopt an individual mobility strategy (Taylor & McKirnan, 1984) by seeking membership in the higher-status group, thereby distancing themselves from the negative identifiers associated with the low-status group. This strategy has been called the "queen bee" strategy (Ellemers, Rink, Derks, & Ryan, 2012; Ellemers, van den Heuvel, de Gilder, Maass, & Bonvini, 2004) and plays out as a lack of support of women superiors for their subordinates.

In particular, when there are differences in status among members of the same in-group, and that in-group is a low-status group, members can then find it difficult to maintain a positive group identity. Consequently, their in-group interactions can become strained as powerful members attempt to distance themselves from their group (Sheppard & Aquino, 2013). There may be significant costs to women who identify too closely with their sex, particularly as they strive to climb the corporate ladder within a male-dominated corporation. Threatened personal self-esteem resulting from the knowledge that one is a member of a low-status group may cause women to lash out at the other members of their low-status group. Additionally, when a woman comes to understand that membership in her low-status group does not pay and is in fact a hindrance to her success, she will hold less positive group identification. As noted by Ely (1994), identification with one group is only strong when the member feels his or her success is tied to the success of other members of the group.

There is some evidence supporting the social identity explanation of intragroup derogation. Dennis and Kunkel (2004) assessed the influence of gender identity on perceptions of female CEOs using the Bem Sex-Role Inventory (BSRI; Bem, 1974) to measure gender identity and the Schein Descriptive Index (Schein, 1973, 1975) to assess stereotyped perceptions of female, male, and non-gender-specified CEOs. Dennis and Kunkel found that both female and male undergraduates who identified themselves in masculine terms perceived women as not measuring up to the CEO role. Those who characterized themselves in feminine terms did not display these sex-typed judgments. Thus, these findings support the hypothesis that those who distance themselves from the low-status group by adopting self-categorizations stereotypical of the higher-status group (i.e., males), and very few stereotypical of the low-status group (i.e., females), tend to underestimate the capabilities of the low-status group.

In a professional context, Ellemers et al. (2004) found that female professors' masculine identity exacerbated their negative evaluations of female graduate students. Also using the BSRI (Bem, 1974) as a measure of gender group identity, these researchers found that female (as opposed to male) professors who identified more strongly on masculine (as opposed to feminine) traits viewed female graduate students as lacking commitment to the academe. Moreover, older (as opposed to younger) female professors engaged in this derogation of their female subordinates through their ratings of them. Ellemers and colleagues consequently attributed their findings to the *queen bee* phenomenon (changed here from the original term "queen bee syndrome" to avoid the proliferation of a pathologization of women; Staines, Travis, & Jayaratne, 1974). "Queen bee," as described earlier, is a woman who disparages other women in order to keep her distinct (usually high-status) position in a (usually male-dominated) hierarchy. Further evidence of the queen bee may be found in the results of Lortie-Lussier and Rinfret (2002). In their examination of the impact of proportional representation on attitudes toward women, their perceived status, and their contribution to the corporate culture, they found that the oldest female managers in their sample (51 years and over) had the least favorable attitudes toward women as managers—as Ellemers and colleagues found, more negative still than the males in the sample.

Ellemers et al. (2004) and Lortie-Lussier and Rinfret (2002) attribute their findings to the professional context of older women. They assert that in order to have achieved success in a male-dominated profession, women had to adopt a strategy of personal mobility by identifying more strongly with men in their profession at a time when women were a rarity—if not completely absent. The consequence has been a distancing from other women and the derogation of same-sex colleagues as a means of shaking the stigma associated with women, demonstrating that they are not "like" other women and possess the same (desirable) traits as do men for the job. What is not entirely clear in Ellemers et al.'s and Lortie-Lussier and Rinfret's findings is the content of the derogation. Ellemers and colleagues use only one item, namely the perceived lack of commitment to the academe, as a stereotype indicator. Though they were careful to choose measures that were highly relevant to the context (i.e., commitment to career is an important component on which graduate students are judged and influences the quality of mentoring offered by a supervisor), it would be prudent to triangulate the measure by including additional items for evaluation.

Lortie-Lussier and Rinfret (2002) used the Women as Managers Scale (Peters, Terborg, & Taynor, 1974) as a measure of attitudes. However, this scale is largely composed of both stereotype ratings and items measuring attitudes and beliefs. Many questions are double-barreled (e.g., "On the average, a woman who stays at home all the time with her children is a better mother than a woman who works outside the home at least half of the time"), or necessarily compare women to men (e.g., "Women would not more allow their emotions to influence their managerial behavior than would men"). Examining the influence of age on ratings of female professionals using a variety of relevant trait dimensions would provide a clearer picture of where exactly older women perceive trait deficiencies—or the threats—to exist. Women are competing for what is thought to be fewer jobs at the top for women. Tokenism creates the illusion of a zero-sum competitive environment wherein there are limited spots for women, and, thus, every gain for one woman represents a direct loss for another (Duguid, 2011; Ely, 1994; Sheppard & Aquino, 2013, 2014).

Intrasexual Cooperation: Women Helping Women

Although the aforementioned investigations have highlighted the importance of identity to negative judgments of one's in-group, they are limited both methodologically and theoretically. The first critique questions the use of the BSRI (Bem, 1974) as a measure of social identification to one's gender group. Bem herself notes that the "masculinity" and "femininity" scale dimensions of the BSRI can foster a polarized view of women as intrinsically feminine and men as intrinsically masculine, with deviants possessing some combination of both or neither sets of traits. Although she presents a more sophisticated view of gender identity in schematic terms in her subsequent work (Bem, 1993), with gender-congruent trait adoption represented as a sex-typed tendency rather than a reflection of one's gender identity, researchers have ignored this theoretical development and continue to use the BSRI as gender-group social identity measure. Of 180 peer-reviewed studies appearing in PsycInfo since 2010, 22 used the BSRI as measure of gender identity.

Research also shows that people are flexible with the traits that they adopt, depending on the social context. In traditional BSRI terms, both women and men are more masculine at work and more feminine at home (Echabe & Castro, 1999), and the

traits people adopt fluctuate for both sexes across a variety of contexts (Smith, Noll, & Bryant, 1999). Since the BSRI is a set of characteristics deemed desirable for one sex or the other (but not both), which are a product of the social roles that women and men have traditionally occupied (Eagly, 1987), it is an inadequate measure of identity in a context in which women are directly challenging those gender roles. By occupying the role of a manager, for instance, women would be expected to be "competitive" and to "act as leaders"; both traits are items on the masculinity scale of the BSRI. Certainly, the adoption of these traits cannot be interpreted as rendering female managers as less identified with women. When used as a measure of gender identity, the BSRI confounds sex and occupational roles and is not an accurate measure of in-group ties, especially among women with career aspirations in traditionally male contexts.

A final shortcoming with using the BSRI is that traits, per se, may be construed as personal rather than social identity (Tougas, Lagacé, de la Sablonnière, & Kocum, 2004). Gurin and Markus (1988) argue that gender identity is not simply a matter of possessing a list of traits commonly ascribed to one sex or the other but rather the "internal representation of belonging to the social category, women" (p. 157). In fact, using the BSRI as an indicator of identity ignores the active role the individual plays in the identification process. To recapitulate, identifying with a group means that an individual is aware that he or she belongs to the group, feels that the group membership is important to his or her sense of self, and perceives of the group as worthwhile. As the BSRI does not apply to any of these aspects of social identity, predictions using the BSRI under the social identity paradigm are arguably misguided.

In addition to the shortcomings of using the BSRI as a measure of social identity, a second critique of the queen bee findings is leveled at the assumption that low-status group members necessarily have a negative social identity necessitating "corrective" measures. In fact, it has been found that members of low-status groups often take pride in their in-group membership because they share a common struggle with their group members (Crocker & Major, 1989; Smith & Tyler, 1997). As opposed to reacting to one's low status with a strategy of personal mobility, stronger in-group ties have been linked to collective strategies of coping with status differentials and enhanced in-group favoritism, particularly if they are viewed to be illegitimate (Tougas & Veilleux, 1988). Researchers have thus expanded social identity theory to include this shared aspect of "common fate" (Gurin & Markus, 1988) in women's identity as a low-status group and have included a relational aspect to their respective operationalizations (Luhtanen & Crocker, 1992; Phinney, 1992).

One such measure is the Collective Self-Esteem (CSE) scale developed by Luhtanen and Crocker (1992). The CSE scale was created as a measure of social identity and was intended to provide researchers with a tool for assessing under what circumstances (i.e., high vs. low identity) in-group favoritism would emerge. The CSE scale was designed to tap all of the aspects of social identity theorized to give rise to collective, group-enhancing strategies, namely how one feels about one's group (i.e., private collective self-esteem), how others view one's group (i.e., public collective self-esteem [PCSE]), and how important the group is to the individual (i.e., identity). Luhtanen and Crocker originally conceived this scale to assess global esteem for all of one's ascribed social groups (i.e., sex, race, religion, nationality, ethnicity, and socioeconomic class), but they suggested that collective self-esteem with respect to specific target groups—both acquired (e.g., managers) and ascribed (e.g., women)—could be assessed with this scale.

Of all the aspects of social identity captured by the CSE, it is the PCSE subscale that has been found to be strongly related to in-group favoring bias and out-group derogation. (Hunter et al., 2005; Hunter et al., 2004; Long & Spears, 1998). PCSE comprises four items tapping judgments of how others view one's social group (e.g., "In general, others respect female managers"). An individual with low PCSE holds the view that others do not value his or her in-group, and, conversely, an individual with high PCSE perceives that others hold his or her in-group in high regard. Though support for the self-esteem hypothesis (according to which individuals should be motivated to maintain a positive self-esteem) has been mixed (see Rubin & Hewstone, 1998) since it was introduced theoretically by Tajfel and colleagues (Tajfel, 1978, 1982; Tajfel & Turner, 1979), findings using the PCSE subscale have been consistent with theory. Specifically, low PCSE has been found to be associated with elevated in-group favoritism in both lab-generated and natural groups (Hunter et al., 2004, 2005) and to increased out-group derogation (Long & Spears, 1998). For example, Hunter et al. (2005) demonstrated that, both in the lab and with real groups (New Zealanders [in-group] vs. Australians [out-group]), those with lower PCSE

allocated more points to their in-group and allocated a significantly shorter period of white noise (noxious sound) to their in-group members. Lower PCSE has also been found to be related to higher perceived discrimination based on sex (Luhtanen & Crocker, 1992, in their validation of the scale). Conversely, higher PCSE scores have been found among self-identified antifeminists (Smith, 1999), suggesting a possible corollary of these findings could be that group members with *higher* PCSE would have higher levels of intragroup discrimination. In other words, those who perceive that others value their group, particularly if that group has been traditionally a target group for discrimination, might be denying that discrimination exists and therefore perceiving their in-group with greater scrutiny.

A re-examination of the link between age, identity, and in-group bias (both disfavoring and favoring), using PCSE as a measure of identity and the SDI paradigm as a gauge of intragroup stereotyping, reveals evidence of intrasexual discrimination. Kocum, Tougs, Courvoisier, and Brazeau (2014) conducted an online experiment among female managers of the Federal Public Service of Canada in which female managers served as both raters and targets. The Schein paradigm was modified, and a within-subjects strategy was employed to measure and analyze the responses of the 308 female manager participants (i.e., all managers rated two targets: *successful female managers* and *managers in general*). As such, a Correlated Trait Correlated Method-1 (Courvoisier, Nussbeck, Eid, Geiser, & Cole, 2008; Eid, Lischetzke, Nussbeck, & Trierweiler, 2003) model was employed to test the discrepancy between ratings of successful female managers and the successful managerial prototype. For the present purposes, we report only the latent factor discrepancy scores (for more detailed results, see Kocum et al., 2014).

As can be seen in Figure 37.1, the expected association between lower PCSE and in-group favoritism is evidenced among older managers (i.e., over 40 years old). Female managers who perceived their in-group (i.e., female managers) to be threatened (i.e., not viewed well by others) displayed in-group favoritism by rating female managers' competence as higher than the managerial standard for success. However, they did not significantly derogate female managers with lower competence scores when their PCSE level was higher. Younger female managers (i.e., 40 years and younger) who perceived an in-group threat derogated their in-group

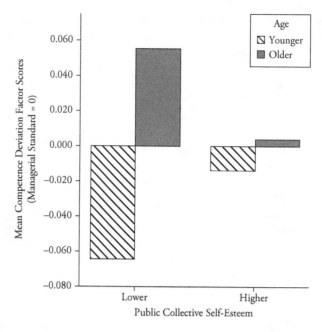

Figure 37.1 Competence deviation factor scores as a function of PCSE and age.

with significantly lower ratings of female managerial competence as compared to the perceived managerial standard. In sum, older female managers who perceived that others devalue female managers adjudged female managers as above standard on competence; younger female managers who perceived that others devalue female managers adjudged female managers as below standard on competence.

A similar pattern of in-group derogation/favoritism can be seen with the evaluative measure democratic approach (which is composed of traits such as democratic, strategic, diplomatic, empowers and motivates others, good communicator, democratic, fair, and able to resolve conflicts; Figure 37.2). Again, when PCSE is low, older managers favor their in-group, whereas younger managers disfavor it.

Regarding Activity/Potency (which is composed of traits such as dominant, confident, firm, high need for power, forceful, aggressive, and ambitious; Figure 37.3), older managers with lower PCSE perceived female managers to be somewhat (but not significantly) less active/potent than the managerial standard, whereas younger women with low PCSE viewed female managers to be significantly *more* active/potent. High PCSE showed the opposite pattern. Among older women, high PCSE yielded a slight increase in in-group derogation; among

younger women, however, it yielded activity/potency scores significantly lower than the standard, suggesting that younger women are stereotyping no matter what they perceive others think of female managers. If their in-group identity is threatened, they view female managers as too hostile; if they view female managers to be valued by others, they perceive females to be too docile for managerial success.

Overall, these results suggest that, when their identity is threatened, younger and older female professionals react in opposite ways—by either disfavoring or favoring their in-group. Most notably, two findings refute both previous research and theory. First, the highest levels of sex-typing were found among younger—not older—female professionals. Therefore, when social identity is considered in context, there is little support for the queen bee phenomenon. In fact, older women are more likely to *favor* other women when their group identity is threatened, providing evidence of a collective mobility strategy among older women. Second, whereas higher levels of PCSE increase in-group derogation significantly with regard to younger managers' perception of female managers' lack of potency, they significantly diminish both in-group favoring and disfavoring biases on dimensions of competence and democratic approach.

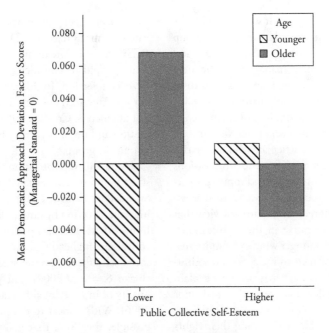

Figure 37.2 Democratic approach deviation factor scores as a function of PCSE and age.

Why do these results differ from those found by Ellemers et al. (2004) and Lortie-Lussier and Rinfret (2002)? In Ellemers et al.'s study, female professors evaluated graduate students; thus, there was a status difference between perceivers and targets. It is possible that this bias would be attenuated if participants were to rate female colleagues who had obviously crossed a status threshold into the same status category. With regard to Lortie-Lussier and Rinfret, age was found to predict a composite of stereotypes and attitudes. In fact, Kocum et al. (2014) found no simple mean differences in stereotyping when

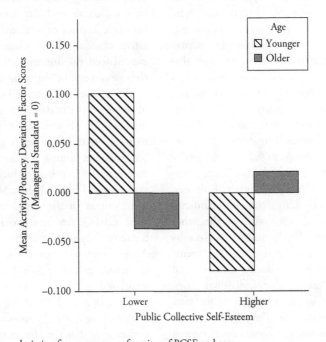

Figure 37.3 Activity/potency deviation factor scores as a function of PCSE and age.

age was considered on its own. It was only with the inclusion of identity moderated by age that in-group bias was revealed. Furthermore, Lortie-Lussier and Rinfret found that female managers in the next age bracket down (i.e., female managers ages 46 to 50 years) had the most favorable attitudes.

Further interpreting the findings of Kocum et al. (2014), it is younger women who perceive that society devalues women, in particular, who are at risk for perpetuating stereotypes of women in positions of power as being less competent and more competitive (that would be expected of a standard successful manager). Even more, they endorse the view that women are less collaborative in their professional dealings. Why would younger women be more susceptible than older women to intrasexual discrimination? Generational context may serve to explain some differences. Older managers witnessed and/or were raised during the first wave of feminism, when women were visible, articulating their rights and changing laws to reflect their political demands. Younger managers lived at a time when women were already seeing the benefits of feminism, and political action began to be deemed unnecessary. In fact, the current social climate of up-and-coming professionals would suggest a rather hostile attitude toward the foremothers who paved their way (e.g., a popular site: http://womenagainstfeminism.tumblr.com/).

Why would PCSE have the opposite influence among older versus younger workers, and why would younger workers' perceptions run counter to those predicted under social identity theory? Perhaps older workers, having lived through discriminatory experiences and having attained a certain stature and stability in their position, feel secure enough to protest the scrutiny of the corporate culture. Younger women may feel more threatened and, as a result, more competitive. Why are younger women's perceptions so volatile? An analysis of the influence of PCSE on the quality of interpersonal interactions (Downie, Mageau, Koestner, & Liodden, 2006) was framed under sociometer theory (Leary, 1999), a theory with an altogether different presentation of self-esteem motives as compared to social identity theory. The basic premise of sociometer theory is similar to that of social identity theory and asserts that individuals constantly monitor their social environment for cues regarding their acceptance or rejection by others. In contrast to social identity theory's self-esteem hypothesis, however, which contends that individuals are motivated to maintain a positive self-esteem,

sociometer theory purports that people are motivated to curtail rejection. Downie et al. submit that PCSE, as a measure of how valued one's group is by others, could be considered a gauge, or *sociometer*, of social rejection. In this manner, social identity as per the American definition (Cheek, 1989, as cited in Luhtanen & Crocker, 1992), reflecting one's reputation and popularity, may be guiding evaluations of one's in-group.

Using this interpretation, it is possible that the stress found to be associated with low PCSE (Katz, Swindell, & Farrow, 2004) is actually the stress arising from rejection by (and lack of support in general from) others. It is also perhaps for this reason that, conversely, higher PCSE is associated with general social self-efficacy among students with disabilities (Blake & Rust, 2002) and greater intimacy and quality of interpersonal interactions (Downie et al., 2006). With respect to the present discussion, it is possible, therefore, that younger female managers who perceive that female managers are not valued are avoiding rejection by disfavoring other female managers. In fact, this conjecture is in line with the personal mobility response proposed by social identity theory for group members with threatened identities. In other words, younger female managers may be distancing themselves from those that are devalued. All the while, ironically (given the literature on the queen bee attributing this behavior to older women), older female managers are engaged in a collective mobility strategy, providing more favorable ratings of women. The argument seems rather circular, but it seems that, if these women experienced no discrimination to which to react, they would not be engaging in either type of bias.

Of course, age cannot be construed as a *cause* of intragroup disfavoritism or favoritism. Further investigation should explore the factors associated with age that would elicit unstable, impressionable reactions among younger managers. Status, as measured by earnings (which increase with position in the Federal Public Service hierarchy), was ruled out as an alternative explanation by Kocum et al. (2014). Another correlate for consideration, however, might be number of mobility attempts. Applications for promotion are conceivably more numerous as one ages and have been found to be associated with lower neosexism among women (Tougas et al., 1999). A high and stable personal identity might also be associated with age, as it is conceivable that the longer one is in a profession, the less negatively one may react to negative evaluations of others. Meta-analytic results suggest that age is negatively correlated with counterproductive work behaviors (Ng & Feldman, 2008).

Conclusion

This essay has described workplace competition, similarities and differences between men's and women's approaches and reactions to competition, and how women's token status in majority male work contexts gives rise to stereotyping and negative attitudes toward women. We have explained how a threatened gender identity may lead to counterproductive workplace behavior, such as discrimination, when women perceive their token status to be indicative of a zero-sum competitive environment in which only a limited number of positions are reserved for women. We have provided evidence that contradicts findings of Ellemers and colleagues (2004), which suggested that queen bee behavior is reserved for older female professionals. Our experimental work suggests that, in fact, younger female managers are those more susceptible to the perceived view of others—and when that view is negative, they react by derogating other women.

It must be stated explicitly that this essay does not intend to vilify women or blame them for their marginalization, nor does it posit that women and men share the same drive to keep the women's movement at bay. The effects of male prejudice are well documented and are widely acknowledged as devastating, as their higher social and employment status affords them the power and authority to limit women's access to resources, and research shows that they tend to exercise that advantage. However, the "sting" of female prejudice is also painful—so much so that Mizrahi (2004) argues for the introduction of legal guidelines aimed at detecting female-versus-female hostility in the workplace.

Recent research programs investigating stereotypes, prejudice, and discrimination have shifted their focus from the instigators of these debilitating social perceptions and behaviors to their victims (e.g., Marx & Stapel, 2006; Matheson & Cole, 2004). Though researchers are making an effort to understand the role women are playing in their own subordination, such as the investigation of the correlates of the tendency for women fail to recognize sexism, thus leaving it unchallenged (e.g., Barreto & Ellemers, 2005a, 2005b), research continues to position women as passive players. The research presented here has recognized women as active agents in their subjugation and has examined the impact of women's negative attitudes toward women, as well as their social context, on their intragroup judgments.

Women, particularly those in leadership positions, are in positions of decision and evaluation over the careers of other women. Therefore, it is important to understand if, when, and how they may be applying commonly held gender stereotypes, as well as negative judgments, to members of their own sex.

Critics (Skevington & Baker, 1989) argue that social identity theory is a "male theory" focused on individual gain rather than collective investment. It predicts that those in lower-status groups will strive to become members of the higher-status group and, once they are successful, will adopt the views of that group. As it stands, social identity theory provides an insufficient account of the occupational mobility of women. If one follows the logic of social identity theory, then sex bias would be predicted among all women who "make it in a man's world" by virtue of their having chosen to participate in a system that disfavors them. However, there is a qualitative difference between climbing the organizational hierarchy as an individual and climbing it as a group member (Schmitt, Ellemers, & Branscombe, 2003). In fact, women's occupational mobility, with respect to social (i.e., not personal) identity, could theoretically be the result of at least one of two motivations. On one hand, women may be dissociating from other women by entering what they believe to be a rightfully male (i.e., high-status) vocation, thus attaining an individually gratifying social and occupational status. On the other hand, women entering management may have a collective mobility strategy in mind, characterized by the desire to bolster the proportion of women in male-dominated occupations and the encouragement of women to participate in (re)defining that system.

Women do compete, and those in token contexts in which women form a minority compete on two fronts: against all colleagues, according to the rules prescribed by the overt organizational system, and against female colleagues under the pressure of the zero-sum competitive "subenvironment" they perceive as tokens. It is in the latter environment where women run the risk of engaging in counterproductive work behaviors, engaging in sex typing and discrimination in similar ways to men, and engaging in their own brand of professional sabotage that is entirely sex-based. Besides leading to a host of negative outcomes for the worker (target and perpetrator) and organization, sex-based harassment from men and women should be a great concern for occupational health psychologists.

In sum, competition is not the problem. Unfair competition resulting from perceived threat due to a discriminatory context is the problem. All workers are expected to engage in competition in the workplace, and women should not be scrutinized for engaging in this expected behavior or judged as "hostile" when they are engaged in competition, especially with members of their own sex. There is a growing body of literature suggesting that our focus on women in competition is likely due to cognitive dissonance experienced because our gender norm expectations of women as cooperative are violated when we witness women competing (Sheppard & Aquino, 2013, 2014). In this essay, we have carefully ensured that we are not viewing women through a gendered lens, expecting them to cooperate and collaborate just because they are women. However, we have also not avoided a direct examination of women's gender belief system and how it is in part responsible for their own marginalized position.

In part, women share the same gender-typed prescriptions as do men and apply them in adjudging women's capacities for jobs that are traditionally in the male domain. However, the psychological impact of being members of a numerical minority must not be disregarded. Must women remain a persistent minority in fields traditionally occupied by men? In more sex-integrated, egalitarian contexts, women's attitudes are significantly more positive toward their female colleagues (Ely, 1994). It makes sense that, without the pressure of the token environment, women would have little use for endorsing negative, sex-typed attitudes, perceptions, and behaviors. Recommendation 1, then, is that firms take seriously the importance of bolstering the numbers of women at all strata of their organizations, not only for the sake of their female workers but also for the sake of business.

Recommendation 2 is for organizations to avoid tournament-style competition as much as possible. At the outset of this essay, we described the negative consequences for this type of competition for all workers, not just women. We would go further in our recommendation and suggest that organizations work toward eliminating even the perception of zero-sum competitive contexts. If sex parity is not possible at the current moment in an organization, then divert the focus from interindividual competition to intergroup competition by creating teams. Research has shown that men perform equivalently, but women fare significantly better in performance and affective ratings when competing as part of a team, where the focus is not on individual but on team accomplishment (Wittchen,

Krimmel, Kohler, & Hertel, 2013). Fewer individual social comparisons associated with intergroup competition would reduce instances of envy and the host of other negative worker and organizational outcomes associated with zero-sum competition.

Finally, it is important not to discount the role of males in the continued subordination of women in traditionally male spheres of employment. Statistics show that 24% of women report having experienced workplace sexual harassment (Ilies, Hauserman, Schwochau, & Stibal, 2003), with the negative psychological and job impact lasting for years after the incident (Munson, Hulin, & Drasgow, 2000). In addition to sex-typing women and holding negative attitudes toward them, one particular finding about men and competition was striking: they do not seem to see women as competitive rivals, even when engaged in a competitive task (Saad & Gill, 2001). Perhaps men simply dismiss women as adversaries in the workplace, and that is why the boys' club persists and they are such persistent gatekeepers of the glass ceiling. It may very well be that, in most cases, women in the role of workplace competitors are simply not on their radar. In this case, Recommendation 2 would still hold, as intergroup competition would not require interindividual competition. It would be highly frustrating for a woman of a higher income, who is more likely to compare socially to males, to be disregarded as a competitor. Women's elevated testosterone levels in the face of defeat seem quite adaptive, given all the adverse experiences women face when simply striving to succeed in the workplace.

References

Abrams, D., & Hogg, M. A. (1988). *Social identifications: A social psychology of intergroup relations and group processes.* London: Routledge.

Baron, R. S., Burgess, M. L., & Kao, C. F. (1991). Detecting and labeling prejudice: Do female perpetrators go undetected? *Personality and Social Psychology Bulletin, 17*(2), 115–123.

Barreto, M., & Ellemers, N. (2005a). The burden of benevolent sexism: How it contributes to the maintenance of gender inequalities. *European Journal of Social Psychology, 35*(5), 633–642.

Barreto, M., & Ellemers, N. (2005b). The perils of political correctness: Men's and women's responses to old-fashioned and modern sexist views. *Social Psychology Quarterly, 68*(1), 75–88.

Bem, S. L. (1974). The measurement of psychological androgeny. *Journal of Consulting and Clinical Psychology, 42*, 155–162.

Bem, S. L. (1993). *The lenses of gender: Transforming the debate on sexual inequality.* New Haven, CT: Yale University Press.

Biernat, M., & Fuegen, K. (2001). Shifting standards and the evaluation of competence: Complexity in gender-based judgement and decision-making. *Journal of Social Issues, 57*(4), 707–724.

Biernat, M., & Vescio, T. K. (2002). She swings, she hits, she's great, she's benched: Implications of gender-based shifting standards for judgment and behavior. *Personality and Social Psychology Bulletin, 28*(1), 66–77.

Blake, T. R., & Rust, J. O. (2002). Self-esteem and self-efficacy of college students with disabilities. *College Student Journal, 36*(2), 214–221.

Brenner, O. C., Tomkiewicz, J., & Schein, V. E. (1989). The relationship between sex role stereotypes and requisite management characteristics revisited. *Academy of Management Journal, 32*(3), 662–669.

Bronson, P., & Merryman, A. (2013). *Top dog: The science of winning and losing*. New York: Hachette Book Group.

Bureau of Labor Statistics. (2016). Current population survey, "Table 3: Employment status of the civilian noninstitutional population by age, sex, and race." *Household Data Annual Averages 2015*. Retrieved from Labor Force Statistics: http://www.bls.gov/cps/cpsaat03.htm

Buunk, A. P., Pollet, T. V., Dijkstra, P., & Massar, K. (2011). Intrasexual competition within organizations. In G. Saad (Ed.), *Evolutionary psychology in the business sciences* (pp. 41–70). Berlin: Springer-Verlag.

Campbell, K., & Morse, G. (2002, September). The emancipated organization: a conversation with Kim Campbell. *Harvard Business Review, 80*, 20–21.

Cashdan, E. (1998). Are men more competitive than women? *British Journal of Social Psychology, 37*, 213–229.

Catalyst. (2005). Women "take care," men "take charge:" Stereotyping of U.S. business leaders exposed. Retrieved from http://www.catalyst.org/knowledge/women-take-care-men-take-charge-stereotyping-us-business-leaders-exposed

Catalyst. (2016). Women CEOs of the S&P 500. Retrieved from Knowledge Center: http://www.catalyst.org/knowledge/women-ceos-sp-500

Charness, G., Masclet, D., & Villeval, M. C. (2014). The dark side of competition for status. *Management Science, 60*, 38–55.

Cheek, J. M. (1989). Identity orientations and self-interpretation. In D. M. Buss & N. Cantor (Eds.), *Personality psychology: Recent trends and emerging directions* (pp. 275–285). New York: Springer-Verlag.

Chung, Y. B., Marshall, J. A., & Gordon, L. L. (2001). Racial and gender biases in supervisory evaluation and feedback. *Clinical Supervisor, 20*(1), 99–111.

Cialdini, R. B., & Trost, M. R. (1998). Social influence: Social norms, conformity and compliance. In D. T. Gilbert, S. T. Fiske, & G. Lindzey (Eds.), *The handbook of social psychology* (4th ed., Vol. 2, pp. 151–192). New York: McGraw-Hill.

Condor, S. (1988). Race stereotypes and racist discourse. *Text, 8*, 69–90.

Condor, S. (1989). "Biting into the future": Social change and the social identity of women. In S. Skevington & D. Baker (Eds.), *The social identity of women* (pp. 15–39). London: Sage.

Courvoisier, D. S., Nussbeck, F. W., Eid, M., Geiser, C., & Cole, D. A. (2008). Analyzing the convergent and discriminant validity of states and traits: Development and applications of multimethod latent state-trait models. *Psychological Assessment, 20*(3), 270–280.

Crocker, J., & Major, B. (1989). Social stigma and self-esteem: The self-protective properties of stigma. *Psychological Review, 96*(4), 608–630.

Cuddy, A. C., Fiske, S. T., & Glick, P. (2004). When professionals become mothers, warmth doesn't cut the ice. *Journal of Social Issues, 60*(4), 701–718.

Deal, J. J., & Stevenson, M. A. (1998). Perceptions of female and male managers in the 1990s: Plus ça change . . . *Sex Roles, 38*(3–4), 287–300.

Deaux, K., & Lafrance, M. (1998). Gender. In D. T. Gilbert, S. T. Fiske, & G. Lindzey (Eds.), *The handbook of social psychology* (4th ed., Vol. 2, pp. 788–827). New York: McGraw-Hill.

Dennis, M. R., & Kunkel, A. D. (2004). Perceptions of men, women, and CEOs: The effects of gender identity. *Social Behavior and Personality, 32*(2), 155–172.

Downie, M., Mageau, G. A., Koestner, R., & Liodden, T. (2006). On the risk of being a cultural chameleon: Variations in collective self-esteem across social interactions. *Cultural Diversity and Ethnic Minority Psychology, 12*(3), 527–540.

Duffy, M. K., Shaw, J. D., & Schaubroeck, J. M. (2008). Envy in organizational life. In R. H. Smith (Ed.), *Envy: Theory and research* (pp. 167–189). New York: Oxford University Press.

Duguid, M. (2011). Female tokens in high-prestige work groups: Catalysts or inhibitors of group diversification. *Organizational Behaviour and Human Decision Processes, 116*(1), 104–115. doi: 10.1016/j.obhdp.2011.05.009

Eagly, A. H. (1987). *Sex differences in social behavior: A social-role interpretation*. Hillsdale, NJ: Lawrence Erlbaum.

Eagly, A. H., & Karau, S. (2002). Role congruity theory of prejudice toward female leaders. *Psychological Review, 109*, 573–598.

Echabe, A. E., & Castro, J. L. G. (1999). The impact of context on gender social identities. *European Journal of Social Psychology, 29*(2–3), 287–304.

Eid, M., Lischetzke, T., Nussbeck, F. W., & Trierweiler, L. (2003). Separating trait effects from trait-specific method effects in multitrait-multimethod analysis: A multiple indicator CTC(M-1) model. *Psychological Methods, 8*, 38–60.

Ellemers, N., Rink, F., Derks, B., & Ryan, M. K. (2012). Women in high places: When and why promoting women into top positions can harm them individually or as a group (and how to prevent this). *Research in Organizational Behavior, 32*, 163–187. doi: 10.1016/j.riob.2012.10.003

Ellemers, N., van den Heuvel, H., de Gilder, D., Maass, A., & Bonvini, A. (2004). The underrepresentation of women in science: Differential commitment or the queen bee syndrome? *British Journal of Social Psychology, 43*(3), 315–338.

Ely, R. J. (1994). The effects of organizational demographics and social identity on relationships among professional women. *Administrative Science Quarterly, 39*, 203–238.

Employment Equity Act. (1986, c. C 44-5). Retrieved from the Department of Justice of Canada website: http://laws.justice.gc.ca/eng/acts/e-5.401/page-2.html#h-6

Fiske, S. T., Cuddy, A. J., Glick, P., & Xu, J. (2002). A model of (often mixed) stereotype content: Competence and warmth respectively follow from perceived status and competition. *Journal of Personality and Social Psychology, 82*(6), 878–902.

Fiske, S. T., Gilbert, D. T., & Lindzey, G. (2010). *Handbook of social psychology* (Vol. 1). Hoboken, NJ: John Wiley & Sons.

Fiske, S. T., & Stevens, L. E. (1993). What's so special about sex? Gender stereotyping and discrimination. In S. Oskamp & M. Costanzo (Eds.), *Gender issues in contemporary society* (pp. 173–196). Thousand Oaks, CA: Sage.

Friedan, B. (1963). *The feminine mystique*. Oxford: Norton.

Gibelman, M. (2003). The non-profit sector and gender discrimination. *Nonprofit Management and Leadership, 10*(3), 251–269. doi: 10.1002/nml.10303

Glick, P., & Fiske, S. T. (1996). The Ambivalent Sexism Inventory: Differentiating hostile and benevolent sexism. *Journal of Personality and Social Psychology, 70*(3), 491–512.

Gurin, P., & Markus, H. (1988). Group identity: The psychological mechanisms of durable salience. *Revue Internationale de Psychologie Sociale, 1*(2), 257–274.

Heilman, M. E., Wallen, A. S., Fuchs, D., & Tamkins, M. M. (2004). Penalties for success: Reactions to women who succeed at male gender-typed tasks. *Journal of Applied Psychology, 89*(3), 416–427.

Henwood, K. L. (1994). Resisting racism and sexism in academic psychology: A personal/political view. *Feminism & Psychology, 4*(1), 41–62.

Hill, S. E., & Buss, D. M. (2006). Envy and positional bias in the evolutionary psychology of management. *Managerial and Decision Economics, 27*, 131–143.

Hunter, J. A., Cox, S. L., O'Brien, K., Stringer, M., Boyes, M., Banks, M., . . . Crawford, M. (2005). Threats to group value, domain-specific self-esteem and intergroup discrimination amongst minimal and national groups. *British Journal of Social Psychology, 44*(3), 329–353.

Hunter, J. A., Kypri, K., Stokell, N. M., Boyes, M., O'Brien, K. S., & McMenamin, K. E. (2004). Social identity, self-evaluation and intragroup bias: The relative importance of particular domains of self-esteem to the intragroup. *British Journal of Social Psychology, 43*(1), 59–81.

Hymowitz, C., & Schellhardt, T. D. (1986, March 24). The glass ceiling: Why women can't seem to break the invisible barrier that blocks them from the top jobs. *Wall Street Journal*, D1, D4–D5.

Ilies, R., Hauserman, N., Schwochau, S., & Stibal, J. (2003). Reported incidence rates of work-related sexual harassment in the United States: Using meta-analysis to explain reported rate disparities. *Personnel Psychology, 56*, 607–631.

Kanter, R. M. (1977). *Men and women of the corporation*. New York: Basic Books.

Katz, J., Swindell, S., & Farrow, S. (2004). Effects of participation in a first women's studies course on collective self-esteem, gender-related attitudes, and emotional well-being. *Journal of Applied Social Psychology, 34*(10), 2179–2199.

Killeen, L. A., López-Zafra, E., & Eagly, A. H. (2006). Envisioning oneself as a leader: Comparisons of women and men in Spain and the United States. *Psychology of Women Quarterly, 30*(3), 312–322.

Kocum, L., Tougas, F., Courvoisier, D. S., & Brazeau, T. (2014). *The buzz on the queen bee phenomenon, or women at the crossroads of occupational and gender identities*. Manuscript in preparation.

Konrad, A. M., & Hartmann, L. (2001). Gender differences in attitudes toward affirmative action programs in Australia: Effects of beliefs, interests, and attitudes toward women. *Sex Roles 45*(5–6), 415–432.

Konrad, A. M., & Spitz, J. (2003). Explaining demographic group differences in affirmative action attitudes. *Journal of Applied Social Psychology, 33*(8), 1618–1642.

Leary, M. R. (1999). Making sense of self-esteem. *Current Directions in Psychological Science, 8*(1), 32–35.

Long, K. M., & Spears, R. (1998). Opposing effects of personal and collective self-esteem on interpersonal and intergroup comparisons. *European Journal of Social Psychology, 28*(6), 913–930.

Lortie-Lussier, M., & Rinfret, N. (2002). The proportion of women managers: Where is the critical mass? *Journal of Applied Social Psychology, 32*(9), 1974–1991.

Luhtanen, R., & Crocker, J. (1992). A collective self-esteem scale: Self-evaluation of one's social identity. *Personality and Social Psychology Bulletin, 18*(3), 302–318.

Marx, D. M., & Stapel, D. A. (2006). Distinguishing stereotype threat from priming effects: On the role of the social self and threat-based concerns. *Journal of Personality and Social Psychology, 91*(2), 243–254.

Matheson, K., & Cole, B. M. (2004). Coping with a threatened group identity: Psychosocial and neuroendocrine responses. *Journal of Experimental Social Psychology, 40*(6), 777–786.

Mavin, S. (2008). Queen bees, wannabees, and afraid to bees: No more "best enemies" for women in management? *British Journal of Management, 19*(Suppl. 1), 75–84.

Mazur, A., & Booth, A. (1998). Testosterone and dominance in men. *Behavioral and Brain Sciences, 21*, 353–397.

Mizrahi, R. (2004). "Hostility to the presence of women": Why women undermine each other in the workplace and the consequences for Title VII. *Yale Law Journal, 113*, 1579–1621.

Munson, L. J., Hulin, C., & Drasgow, F. (2000). Longitudinal analysis of dispositional influences and sexual harassment: Effects on job and psychological outcomes. *Personnel Psychology, 53*, 21–46.

Ng, T. H., & Feldman, D. C. (2008). The relationship of age to ten dimensions of job performance. *Journal of Applied Psychology, 93*(2), 392–423.

Nickell, S. J. (1996). Competition and corporate performance. *Journal of Political Economy, 104*, 724–746.

Niederle, M., & Vesterlund, L. (2007). Do women shy away from competition? Do men compete too much? *Quarterly Journal of Economics, 122*(3), 1067–1101. doi: 10.1162/qjec.122.3.1067

O'Connor, M., Gutek, B. A., Stockdale, M., Geer, T. M., & Melançon, R. (2004). Explaining sexual harassment judgements: Looking beyond gender of the rater. *Law & Human Behavior, 28*(1), 69–95.

Parks-Stamm, E. J., Heilman, M. E., & Hearns, K. A. (2008). Motivated to penalize: Women's strategic rejection of successful women. *Personality and Social Psychology Bulletin, 34*, 237–247.

Peters, L. H., Terborg, J. R., & Taynor, J. (1974). Women as Managers Scale (WAMS): A measure of attitudes toward women in management positions. *JSAS Catalogue of Selected Documents in Psychology, 4*, 1–43.

Phinney, J. S. (1992). The multigroup ethnic identity measure: A new scale for use with diverse groups. *Journal of Adolescent Research, 7*(2), 156–176.

Powell, G. N., Butterfield, D. A., & Parent, J. D. (2002). Gender and managerial stereotypes: Have the times changed? *Journal of Management, 28*(2), 177–193.

Price, C. R. (2012). Does the gender preference for competition affect job performance? Evidence from a real effort experiment. *Managerial and Decision Economics, 33*, 531–536.

Rubin, M., & Hewstone, M. (1998). Social identity theory's self-esteem hypothesis: A review and some suggestions for clarification. *Personality and Social Psychology Review, 2*(1), 40–62.

Rudman, L. A., & Glick, P. (2001). Perscriptive gender stereotypes and backlash toward agentic women. *Journal of Social Issues, 57*(4), 743–762. doi: 10.1111/0022-4537.00239

Saad, G., & Gill, T., (2001). Sex differences in the ultimatum game: An evolutionary psychology perspective. *Journal of Bioeconomics, 3*, 171–193.

Sackett, P. R., & DeVore, C. J. (2002). Counterproductive behaviors at work. In N. Anderson, D. S. Ones, H. K. Sinangil, & C. Viswesvaran (Eds.), *Handbook of industrial, work and organizational psychology*, Vol. 1: *Personnel psychology* (pp. 145–164). Thousand Oaks, CA: Sage.

Schein, V. (1973). The relationship between sex role stereotypes and requisite management characteristics. *Journal of Applied Psychology, 57*(2), 95–100.

Schein, V. E. (1975). The relationship between sex role stereotypes and requisite management characteristics among female managers. *Journal of Applied Psychology, 60*, 340–344.

Schein, V. (2001). A global look at psychological barriers to women's progress in management. *Journal of Social Issues, 57*(4), 675–688.

Schein, V. E., & Mueller, R. (1992). Sex role stereotyping and requisite management characteristics: A cross cultural look. *Journal of Organizational Behavior, 13*(5), 439–447.

Schein, V. E., Mueller, R., Lituchy, T., & Liu, J. (1996). Think manager—think male: A global phenomenon? *Journal of Organizational Behavior, 17*(1), 33–41.

Schmitt, M. T., Ellemers, N., & Branscombe, N. R. (2003). Perceiving and responding to sex discrimination at work. In S. A. Haslam, D. van Knippenberg, M. J. Platow, & N. Ellemers (Eds.), *Social identity at work: Developing theory for organizational practice* (pp. 277–292). New York: Psychology Press.

Schultheiss, O. C., Wirth, M. M., Torges, C. M., Pang, J. S., Villacorta, M. A., & Welsh, K. M. (2005). Effects of implicit power motivation on men's and women's implicit learning and testosterone changes after social victory or defeat. *Journal of Personality and Social Psychology, 88*, 174–188.

Sheppard, L. D., & Aquino, K. (2013). Much ado about nothing? Observers' problematization of women's same-sex conflict at work. *Academy of Management Perspectives, 27*, 52–62.

Sheppard, L. D., & Aquino, K. (2014). Sisters at arms: A theory of female same-sex conflict and its problematization in organizations. *Journal of Management.* Advanced online publication. doi:10.1177/0149206314539348

Sinclair, L., & Kunda, Z. (2000). Motivated stereotyping of women: She's fine if she praised me but incompetent if she criticized me. *Personality and Social Psychology Bulletin, 26*(11), 1329–1342.

Skevington, S., & Baker, D. (1989). 'Biting into the future': Social change and the social identity of women. In S. Skevington & D. Baker (Eds.), *The social identity of women* (pp. 15–39). London: Sage.

Smith, C. A. (1999). I enjoy being a girl: Collective self-esteem, feminism, and attitudes toward women. *Sex Roles, 40*(3–4), 281–293.

Smith, C. J., Noll, J. A., & Bryant, J. B. (1999). The effect of social context on gender self-concept. *Sex Roles, 40*(5–6), 499–512.

Smith, H. J., & Tyler, T. R. (1997). Choosing the right pond: The impact of group membership on self-esteem and group-oriented behavior. *Journal of Experimental Social Psychology, 33*(2), 146–170.

Smith, R. H. (2000). Assimilative and contrastive emotional reactions to upward and downward social comparisons. In J. Suls & L. Wheeler (Eds.), *Handbook of social comparison: Theory and research* (pp. 173–200). Dordrecht, Netherlands: Kluwer Academic.

Staines, G., Travis, C., & Jayaratne, T. (1974). The queen bee syndrome. *Psychology Today, 9*, 55–60.

Stanne, M. B., Johnson, D. W., & Johnson, R. T. (1999). Does competition enhance or inhibit motor performance? A meta-analysis. *Psychological Bulletin, 125*, 133–154.

Statistics Canada. (2001). National occupational classification for statistics (Table No. 97F0012XCB2001017). Retrieved from http://www5.statcan.gc.ca/olc-cel/olc.action?objId=97F0012X2001017&objType=46&lang=en&limit=0

Statistics Canada. (2003, February). The changing profile of Canada's labour force (Catalogue no. 96F0030XIE2001009). Retrieved from Statistics Canada Analysis Series: http://www12.statcan.ca/access_acces/archive.action-eng.cfm?/english/census01/Products/Analytic/companion/paid/pdf/96F0030XIE2001009.pdf

Statistics Canada. (2016). *Labour Force Characteristics by Sex and Age Group.* Retrieved from Employment and Unemployment tables: http://www.statcan.gc.ca/tables-tableaux/sum-som/l01/cst01/labor05-eng.htm

Steil, J. M., & Hay, J. L. (1997). Social comparison in the workplace: A study of 60 dual-career couples. *Personality and Social Psychology Bulletin, 23*, 427–438.

Swim, J. K., Aikin, K. J., Hall, W. S., & Hunter, B. A. (1995). Sexism and racism: Old-fashioned and modern prejudices. *Journal of Personality and Social Psychology, 68*(2), 199–214.

Tajfel, H. (1978). *Differentiation between social groups: Studies in the social psychology of intergroup relations.* London: Academic.

Tajfel, H. (1981). *Human groups and social categories.* Cambridge: Cambridge University Press.

Tajfel, H. (Ed.). (1982). *Social identity and intergroup relations.* Cambridge: Cambridge University Press.

Tajfel, H., & Turner, J. C. (1979). An integrative theory of intergroup conflict. In W. G. Austin & S. Worschel (Eds.), *The social psychology of intergroup relations* (pp. 33–47). Monterey, CA: Brooks and Cole.

Tajfel, H., & Turner, J. C. (1986). The social identity theory of intergroup behaviour. In S. Worschel & W. G. Austin (Eds.), *Psychology of intergroup relations* (2nd ed., pp. 7–24). Chicago: Nelson-Hall.

Taylor, D. M., & McKirnan, D. J. (1984). A five-stage model of intergroup relations. *British Journal of Social Psychology, 23*, 291–300.

Tougas, F., Brown, R., Beaton, A. M., & Joly, S. (1995). Neosexism: Plus ça change, plus c'est pareil. *Personality and Social Psychology Bulletin, 21*(8), 842–849.

Tougas, F., Brown, R., Beaton, A. M., & St-Pierre, L. (1999). Neosexism among women: The role of personally experienced social mobility attempts. *Personality and Social Psychology Bulletin, 25*(12), 1487–1497.

Tougas, F., Lagace, M., de la Sablonniere, R., & Kocum, L. (2004). A new approach to the link between identity and relative deprivation in the perspective of ageism and retirement. *International Journal of Aging & Human Development, 59*(1), 1–23.

Tougas, F., & Veilleux, F. (1988). The influence of identification, collective relative deprivation, and procedure of implementation on women's response to affirmative action: A causal modelling approach. *Canadian Journal of Behavioural Science, 20*(1), 15–28.

Vongas, J. G., & Hajj, R. A. (2014). Competing sexes, power, and testosterone: How winning and losing affect people's empathic responses and what this means for organisations. *Applied Psychology, 64*(2), 308–337. doi: 10.1111/apps.12030

Waters, M. (Dir.). (2004). *Mean girls* [Motion Picture]. Los Angeles: Paramount Pictures.

Wilder, D. A., & Shapiro, P. N. (1989). Role of competition-induced anxiety in limiting the beneficial impact of positive behavior by an out-group member. *Journal of Personality and Social Psychology, 56*, 60–69.

Wittchen, M., Krimmel, A., Kohler, M., & Hertel, G. (2013). The two sides of competition: Competition-induce effort and affect during intergroup versus interindividual competition. *British Journal of Psychology, 104*(3), 320–338. doi: 10.1111/j.2044-8295.2012.0213.x

Wiseman, R. (2002). *Queen bees and wannabes: Helping your daughter survive cliques, gossip, boyfriends, and other realities of adolescence.* New York: Three Rivers.

Wiseman, R. (2009). *Queen bees and wannabes: Helping your daughter survive cliques, gossip, boyfriends, and other realities of adolescence* (2nd ed.). New York: Three Rivers.

Wood, W., & Eagly, A. H. (2010). Gender. In S. T. Fiske, D. T. Gilbert, & G. Lindzey (Eds.), *Handbook of social psychology* (Vol. 1, 5th ed., pp. 629–667). Hoboken, NJ: Wiley.

Food as a Means for Female Power Struggles

Charlotte J. S. De Backer, Liselot Hudders, *and* Maryanne L. Fisher

Abstract

Food often brings to mind diet and health, but it also has important social functions. Food is about so much more than just caloric intake and providing nourishment to oneself and others under one's care. It signals, for example, care about oneself and others by means of careful planning, preparation, and consumption. After reviewing several perspectives on the social dynamics of food, this chapter connects food to women's intrasexual competition. Specifically, it addresses how cooking and food intake are self-promotion strategies, not only due to one's demonstration of an excellent domestic ability to a potential audience but also by boosting one's physical attractiveness via controlling food intake. While there exists little direct, empirical evidence on the relationship between interpersonal competition and food preparation and consumption, research from a wide array of topics offers support. The chapter closes with numerous directions for future research in the area of food studies.

Key Words: food studies, self-promotion, intrasexual competition, social dynamics, food intake

Introduction

"There is no spectacle on earth more appealing than that of a beautiful woman in the act of cooking dinner for someone she loves."
—*Thomas Wolfe*

In this chapter, we demonstrate the tight link between food and women's intrasexual competition for mates. Food often brings to mind diet and health, but it also has an important social function (Fischler, 2011). Food is about so much more than just caloric intake and concerns of caring for oneself and others by means of food preparation and consumption. In particular, cooking can be considered as an act of intrasexual competition, as women may outdo other women by cooking lavish meals. The importance of cooking as an act of intrasexual competition has been explored by Walters and Crawford (1994), who examined various tactics used by men and women to outcompete same-sex rivals. Not only did they notice that cooking was listed by

both sexes, but they also found that "demonstrating domestic ability" (including cooking) and "attracting attention to appearances" are the most frequently used female tactics, while these were much less important for males. Moreover, these tactics are also perceived as being more effective for competition when performed by women compared to men. In this chapter, we review how cooking and food intake are self-promotion strategies undertaken not only to demonstrate one's excellent domestic ability but also to boost one's physical attractiveness via controlling food intake.

We start by explaining why cooking and making certain food choices labels women as "caring." Combining this material with the fact that caring and commited are highly valued features in the context of long-term commitment, we present how and why cooking may become an arena for female intrasexual competition. Second, while preparing food is a way to care for others, consuming food is a means to care for oneself. Carefully selecting what one eats, how much is eaten, and when one eats influences one's physical and even psychological well-being. Food is a means to achieve a desirable physical appearance, as well as a threat of losing attractiveness (e.g., due to obesity problems). Since female physical appearance is crucial in the context of intersexual attraction and intrasexual selection, it is no surprise that food consumption may become a battlefield for some women. We support this theory using findings from food studies and evolutionary psychology.

Cooking Is Caring: Food Preparation and Female Competition over Motherhood

Intrasexual competition occurs when individuals compete to gain access to limited resources that they do not want to share (Cox & Fisher, 2008). This involves same-sex competition for access to potential and desirable mates (Rosvall, 2011) and competition to retain a mate (Schmitt & Buss, 1996). For parsimony, the focus in this chapter is on sex-specific preferences and behaviors involved in mate acquisition. Women often want longer sexual relationships, and often more strongly desire long-term relationships, than men, whereas men have a stronger desire for short-term mating (Buss & Schmitt, 1993). Since this chapter focuses on features that are desired by the opposite sex and consequently used to outcompete same-sex competitors, we believe that focusing on what women believe men desire for long-term commitment is valuable. Moreover, we support the contention that both men and women are very well aware of which personal assets are most valued by potential mates (Geher & Miller, 2008). Focusing on which traits are valued in the context of courtship, it is clear that both men and women desire multiple traits in potential partners and that these qualities are multifaceted and complex. Although these overlap between the sexes, especially with regard to what traits are desired for long-term mates, they are also sexually differentiated (Buss, 2003). In this chapter, we focus on just some of the traits that are highly desired by men—the ones that matter most and that can best be linked to food and cooking.

In the context of long-term commitment, men, on average, lower their premium on physical attractiveness and put greater emphasis on other desirable traits, such as loyalty and caring (Buss & Schmitt, 1993). From an evolutionary perspective, it makes sense that valuing traits such as these will secure good motherhood qualities, which men typically pursue when opting for long-term commitment.

Thus, because women generally strongly desire long-term commitment and men in this context value women who are loyal, loving, and caring, we start by focusing on these traits. Framing these traits in the context of food, we ask how food can help women appear loving and caring toward others or, in other words, how they can become "domestic goddesses."

A "domestic goddess" refers to a woman who excels at housework of all sorts but cooking and baking in particular (*Oxford Dictionaries*, 2013). She knows how to select the best ingredients and turn them into true feasts for her family and friends. Although a woman may be labeled a "goddess," many hate this female stereotype. For example, those using feminist approaches (e.g., Charles & Kerr, 1988; DeVault, 1991; Murcott 1982) would rather call these women "domestic slaves" who comply to the wishes of others, in particular their children and partner. Women's primary responsibility for food planning and preparation has many times been regarded as a site of gender oppression within the household and society (Charles & Kerr, 1988; DeVault, 1991; Murcott 1982). However, the metaphor exists, and to understand the origin we use an evolutionary perspective with a reanalysis of the literature on this topic. After reviewing how one learns to cook, we first explain why (some) cooking and baking captures the heart to such an extent that it elevates women to the level of goddess. Second, we illustrate how selecting and processing foods, as well as the sharing of food knowledge, can become genuine arenas of female competition.

Learning How to Cook: The Transfer of Food Skills and Intergenerational Intrasexual Competition

While Walters and Crawford (1994) reported "cooking lavish dishes" as one of the twenty-six strategies men and women use to outcompete same-sex competitors, cooking a lavish dish or even a simple everyday meal is a challenge for the inexperienced cook. This is difficult because cooking depends on learning a skill. Humans have innate taste preferences, and these tastes might come alive in elaborate dishes, yet the art of creating a meal that highlights these preferences is a matter of cultural transfer of knowledge. If women want to impress potential mates with their cooking skills and outcompete same-sex competitors, they need to acquire a range of skills and knowledge about food selection and processing. Not surprisingly, the most effective strategy for a woman to outcompete same-sex competitors, according to Walters and Crawford, is not so much about demonstrating and attracting attention to domestic skills but about acquiring domestic skills.

Where to start when one wants to learn how to cook? In Western societies, perhaps a cookbook would be considered a great starting point for learning how to cook. Yet, as Leonardi (1989) has carefully explained, recipes are not just about lists of ingredients and directions of use; they are about the act of giving and represent a social exchange of knowledge. "I think I can safely claim that a cookbook that consisted of nothing but rules for various dishes would be an unpopular cookbook indeed. Even the root of recipe—the Latin *recipere*—implies an exchange, a giver and a receiver. Like a story, a recipe needs a recommendation, a context, a point, a reason to be" (Leonardi, 1989, p. 340). Recipes are about the accumulated knowledge of previous trial and errors of others. Children mainly learn to cook by observing their (grand)parents cook (Bowen & Devine, 2010; Norazmir et al. 2012; Stringer, 2009). This happens both on a conscious and subconscious level, as Kaufman (2010) explains. As children, we might not be actively engaged in the cooking process, but we observe countless details, albeit unintentionally. This information is stored in our passive memory and is activated when necessary, later on in life. From an evolutionary perspective, the passing over of cooking skills within the family appears obvious in light of the aforementioned evidence of cooking and eating occurring in intimate family settings. Moreover, passing on valuable information on how to acquire and process foods in optimal ways is also a way for women to pass on fitness-relevant information and skills that may have reproductive consequences to ensure future reproductive success (in as far as finding a mate and feeding one's child).

Investigating the acquisition of cooking skills, several social scientists have documented how especially women transfer cooking skills (Meyers, 2001) and perceive this as a joyful activity (Hocking, Wright-St Clair, & Bunrayong, 2002). In general, these women are expressing intergenerational caregiving in a variety of ways. For example, they construct and maintain a family identity that resists the commodification of food (Moisio, Arnould, & Price, 2004). They reassure the existence of family traditions and pass on valuable knowledge to the next generation. Mothers are the first and most important sources of food knowledge, and their role in passing on knowledge and skills related to food is greater than fathers' role (Caraher, Dixon,

Lang, & Carr-Hill 1999; Lang & Caraher, 2001; Ternier, 2010). Likewise, these findings are apparent for grandmothers compared to grandfathers. However, another interesting finding is apparent when focusing on the grandparents; a matrilineal pattern appears in the use of family recipes (De Backer, 2013), as well as in the influence on food choice (Johnson, Sharkey, McIntosh, & Dean, 2010). Similarly, it has been documented that maternal grandmothers positively influence the nutritional status of children in rural Gambia, while paternal grandmothers had a negligible influence (Sear, Mace, & McGregor, 2000). In their cross-cultural review of studies on child investment, Sear and Mace (2008) documented that maternal grandmothers in general appear to be more reliable helpers compared to paternal grandmothers. These findings collectively support the "grandmother hypothesis" explanation for the evolution of the menopause (Hamilton, 1966; Williams, 1957). The grandmother hypothesis suggests that, in terms of inclusive fitness, women in menopause fare better by investing in their children and grandchildren than by continuing to reproduce themselves. Paternal uncertainty explains why grandmothers will invest more in the children of their daughters compared to the children of their sons. That is, there is a higher probability that one's daughter's children are biological kin in comparison to one's son's children, due to the possibility of cuckoldry.

This grandmother hypothesis has been contested, and it has recently been suggested that a model incorporating reproductive competition may improve our understanding of the evolution of menopause (Cant & Johnstone, 2008). These authors suggest that the "the human fertility trajectory has been shaped, in substantial part, by selection to minimize reproductive competition between generations within the same social unit" (p. 5332). They provide that menopause usually starts at the time when women (or at least ancestral women) would have entered into competition with women from the next generation. In ancestral times, this new generation most often consisted of immigrant females entering the social group. Moreover, these newcomers had an advantage in reproductive conflict with older women in that they were often much younger. In the end, this intergenerational intrasexual form of competition may explain why the best strategy for older women would be to invest in their maternal offspring, including grandchildren. One way to fulfill this strategy is to monitor the nutritional status of grandchildren; ensuring food provisioning and teaching cooking skills would have given the youngest generation a substantial advantage to ensure their own survival and potentially increase their reproductive success by acquiring future mates. Regardless of whether the grandmother hypothesis or an alternative variation involving immigrant females is correct, it is clear that, even today, cooking skills are transferred within the female family, which we contend is a strategy to outcompete other women across generations.

Food Preparation Signals Caring and Commitment

We have all heard the old saying, "the way to capture a man's heart is through his stomach." Cooking a meal for someone is an intimate act of commitment. An invitation for dinner not only invites guests into the private sphere of one's home, but the act of sharing food and eating together signals intimacy. When we see people dine together, we automatically assume they are closely connected in some way. For example, a couple is perceived as having an intimate relationship when they are observed to be sharing a meal, especially if they use the same utensils or both eat from the same, single dish of food (Alley, 2012). As Kniffin and Wansink (2012) have recently shown, it is not "just lunch"; eating together is perceived as an intimate act to such a degree that we get jealous when our partner is having dinner or lunch with a former romantic partner. When cooking is added into this situation, it becomes even more intimate, since cooking, caring, and commitment are perceived to be closely intertwined. To understand why cooking, in our mind, equals caring, we start with a study of the opposite: those who do not cook, and how people who skip meal preparations are perceived by society.

Pancakes on Sunday and Lazy Suzies. We can distinguish between several groups of people who often skip meal preparations, based on several human traits. For example, based on sex, we can set men apart from women. Women generally outscore men in terms of frequency of food shopping, displayed food skills and knowledge, and performing the majority of food preparation (Beardsworth & Keil, 1993; Larson, Nelson, Neumark-Sztainer, Story, & Hannan, 2009; Mancino & Newman, 2007; Smith et al., 2010; Tashiro & Lo, 2012). However, men have a long history of cooking. Compared to women, men do not engage as much in daily cooking but more often prepare meals for

special occasions, which includes, for example, a family meal or the typical pancakes on Sunday (Adler, 1981; Lange & Caraher, 2001). Sex differences are also observed in one's approach to cooking. On average, women are pragmatic cooks, while their male counterparts see cooking as an excellent opportunity to demonstrate competence and skills (Meah & Jackson, 2012). This fits the evolutionary framework on heterosexual courtship strategies and mating intelligence (Geher & Miller, 2008). On average, women desire ambitious and skillful men, and men's demonstration of these desired traits is part of their tactic to capture the heart of a woman. In the past decades cooking increasingly has become a recreational pastime to demonstrate skills, rather than a daily burden (Lange & Caraher, 2001). Therefore, one may have expected an increase in males' contributions to cooking. Yet, at the turn of the twenty-first century the balance was still the same: women still outscore men in terms of cooking skills, knowledge, and practice (Lange & Caraher, 2001; Larson et al., 2009; Mancino & Newman, 2007; Smith et al., 2010). This said, the magnitude of the sex differences might be decreasing, as some studies indicate that men's contributions to everyday cooking are increasing (Moser, 2010). Perhaps these subtle changes are more often due to the fact than men "have to" rather than "want to" cook, for instance because their partner is still at work when cooking needs to be done (Bell & Valentine, 1997; Devine, Connors, Sobal, & Bisogni, 2003). Kaufman (2010) talks about the *male assistant cook*, ready to stand in when necessary and to assist the female daily cook. But what happens when there is no other daily cook? Consider, for example, men who are single, living by themselves. Do they cook, or do they turn to alternatives from the preprocessed food shelves? Research suggests that they do both. A study of Sellaeg and Chapman (2008) among young Canadian men living alone showed they regularly make an effort to prepare food. Moreover, their study shows that single men cook not only for themselves but for others (e.g., friends, guests) as well. Another reason it can be assumed that the gap in the sexes' cooking behavior is closing is the influence of fathers' home cooking on their sons. From a study with university students, we learned that male students more often engage in daily cooking when they recall their father doing so during childhood (De Backer, 2013).

In sum, it can be concluded that mothers are still the first and most important sources of food knowledge, and their role in passing on knowledge and skills related to food is greater than fathers' role (Caraher et al. 1999; Lang & Caraher, 2001; Ternier, 2010). This said, the fathers' role is not to be neglected; when they cook, the odds are more likely that their sons will also cook later on in life. It should be noted that these results are based on a study that was done in Belgium, where daily cooking is well embedded in family life (Daniels, Glorieux, Minnen, & van Tienoven, 2012). More studies are needed to see if similar results can be found elsewhere, and longitudinal research is necessary to investigate the continuous effect of this observation. For now, we can conclude that men cook and that men have always cooked, but often only if there is no one to fall back on, or if they want an opportunity to show off their skills.

Turning to women who skip meal preparations, a different situation emerges. When a woman does not feel like cooking (or have the time to do so), she needs to turn to others to take over this task. Where this option has long been a privilege for the wealthy, the industrialization of food in the twentieth century offered a solution for all socio-economic classes: convenience food. In 1950, Mason Haire investigated social perceptions of consumers of preprocessed and fresh foods. Haire gave respondents a shopping list and asked them to characterize the woman shopping for these groceries. Two versions of the shopping list were used, and only one item was different on these lists. On one list, the woman bought fresh coffee (traditional drip ground). According to the alternative list, the woman bought instant coffee. In this study, the respondents regarded the woman who bought instant coffee as lazy. She was seen as an insufficient household planner, showing little care for her family. The woman who bought fresh coffee was seen as compassionate, showing concern for her family. Replicating this study with a premade blueberry pie filling as the distinguishing product, similar results emerged. Customers who bought convenience foods were stigmatized. Rather than being a domestic goddess, a consumer of convenience food was regarded as a "lazy Suzy" who cares little about what is brought to the table. In the following years, however, replications of the Haire studies reached somewhat different results. Starting in the 1970s, American researchers could not replicate these findings (Arndt, 1973; Webster & Pechmann, 1970) and explained their null results by the fact that convenience food was already much more accepted in society and no longer elicited negative thoughts.

Consequent replications yielded similar null findings in the United States and abroad (Lane, 1975). Recently, a study using the shopping-list technique for ready-to-eat salad versus ingredients to make a salad also indicated, again, that people no longer see the woman buying the ready meal as "lazy" but merely as "short in time" (Vidal, Ares, & Gimenez, 2013). Does this finding imply that the cooking/caring stereotype was a cultural fad that is now outdated? We propose that this conclusion cannot be supported without further research. From an evolutionary perspective, the most interesting finding in the original Haire study is not that the woman who bought ready-meals was seen as lazy but that the woman who bought fresh products was labeled as more caring. In other words, it does not matter if women are seen as lazy; on the contrary, we argue that time-saving strategies in food acquisition should be praised. What does matter, though, is the question of whether these women are perceived as less loving toward their family members. Future replications of the Haire study should therefore focus on grocery lists that focus on *family meals* rather than on meals for personal consumption, such as a single serving of salad.

Moreover, it would be interesting not only to focus on how women who buy preprocessed foods are perceived but to examine perceptions of men too. Women also desire caring traits in potential mates, and, as mentioned, men's cooking is a way of showing of their skills and competency, which may be valued. Then again, women put a higher premium on access to resources than domestic skills when evaluating potential mates (Li, Bailey, Kenrick, & Linsenmeier, 2002). It can therefore be assumed that men who buy expensive, ready-made meals will receive more positive ratings compared to men who spend money on cheaper, yet home-cooked, food. That is, buying preprocessed foods might not harm the reputation of men so much, as long as they pay a high enough price for it. In contrast, we predict that a woman who opts for the lavish, ready-made meal will not outscore the woman who spends less but invests more time and labor. This difference is because, in the end, we propose men will place a higher premium on the woman's hard work, which signals her loving and caring capacities rather than her access to resources.

Standard social scientists might not agree on these assumptions, especially if these scholars adhere to the works of Pierre Bourdieu. On a proximate level, Bourdieu (1984) has explained how food and cooking are means to climb the social ladder. In his work on culinary capital, he explains how, just like any other form of consumption, food consumption is a class struggle where the middle classes have better opportunities to capitalize on their assets. Framed in this theory, references have been made to, for example, the 1980s nouvelle cuisine where visual and oral aesthetics were clearly privileged over the idea that food needs to satisfy basic needs of hunger (Ashley, Hollows, Jones, & Taylor, 2004). Applying Bourdieu's work on women's cooking, DeVault (1991) arrived at some interesting conclusions. Based on her field work, she concluded that especially middle-class American women had a desire to gain cultural capital, and they used exclusive media resources, such as fancy food magazines and cookbooks, to achieve this goal (DeVault, 1991). What we do not know from DeVault's work, and what would be interesting to further investigate, is what mattered most in these exclusive recipes. That is, was it the use of expensive ingredients, the use of elaborate techniques that signal high cooking skills, and/or the fact that the recipe/dish is exclusive for certain groups? DeVault's and Bourdieu's view is that foods are exclusive as long as they can set groups apart; they are available to some (i.e., the upper class) and not to others (i.e., those in lower socioeconomic classes). From an evolutionary point of view, we predict that the techniques will overrule the price of the ingredients and the availability of the product. In other words, from Bourdieu's and DeVault's point of view, serving macaroons (i.e., a French type of cookie that is challenging to make) will no longer increase the status of the cook if macaroons become widely available in the food chain (e.g., when certain fast-food chains start offering them) and everyone is making them at home. In contrast, an evolutionary scientist would predict that it will not matter how exclusive the product is (or has become), nor does it matter if a fortune has been spent on the ingredients; what is important is the hard work and labor that one invests in creating these little wonders. A woman serving homemade macaroons to her guests perhaps has endured a series of trials and errors, engaging in a labor of love to create the perfect little cookie to impress her guests. This effort will be moot if her guests do not like macaroons, which would mean she has chosen the wrong food to please the crowd. Thus, we propose that showing that one cares is also reflected in making correct food choices.

When is dinner ready and what are we having?
Also using Haire's (1950) projective methodology, Jones, McVie, and Noble (2008) investigated parents' perceptions of the food choices that women make for their children. They concluded that women who select healthy foods for their children are rated more favorably compared to women who make less healthy food choices. Moreover, the respondents of this study, who were all parents themselves, also believed that the women who made healthy food choices spent more quality time with their children (Jones et al., 2008). Thus, in our perception of women, we attribute caring characteristics to women who select healthy nutrition for their offspring. Therefore cooking is not just about time management; it is also, and perhaps above all, about selecting the right food. It is a matter of making choices on what to eat and what not to eat to stay healthy and survive. Cooking and caring for others is really a way of making choices to maintain and increase the health of those whom one feeds. Women generally have well-developed skills to locate healthy foods, according to an intriguing study in which men and women were led by a circuitous route to several food stalls at a California farmer's market. At each food stall, they were given a food item to eat and asked some questions. What the participants did not know was that the researchers were testing their spatial skills; after the tour of the market, all participants were shown the foods they had sampled and asked to give directions (standing from a central place) to the food stall that had offered them each of these items. The results showed that, in contrast to the dominant belief that men outscore women in terms of spatial skills, the female respondents in this study outscored their male counterparts (New, Krasnow, Truxaw, & Gaulin, 2007). Therefore, while other findings suggest men generally have superior spatial abilities (e.g., Moffat, Hampson, & Hatzipantelis, 1998), meta-analyses on sex differences in spatial skills have revealed that much depends on the context of the task and the interest of the participants (Voyer, Voyer, & Bryden, 1995). When it comes to finding the right foods, women know their way around.

Of course, women also may prepare less healthy foods for their loved ones, based on the latter's desires. That is, women often make food choices that will please the ones they feed. In her classic book *Feeding the Family*, DeVault (1991) elaborated the "caring for others" idea, outlining women's "caring work" in the family. In her analyses, she stressed the fact that women, wives, and mothers do not just cook any old thing but rather carefully select their ingredients and recipes. By engaging in this task, they consider not their own food preferences as mattering most but rather those of their partner and children. "The food provided for a family cannot just be any food, but must be food that will satisfy them," as DeVault writes (p. 40). Framing this in an evolutionary perspective, it makes sense that the caring signal attributed to food preparation perhaps mainly stems from the actual selection of food and not so much from the time investment. Although humans are omnivores, capable of digesting a wide range of foods (Teaford, Ungar, & Grine, 2002), a human diet is typically quite narrow, consisting of chosen elements. It has even been suggested that human-specific characteristics—a long lifespan, extended juvenile period, male support and grandparental investment in offspring, extreme intelligence—have evolved because of a dietary shift toward high-quality, nutrient-dense, and difficult-to-acquire food resources among our ancestors (Kaplan, Hill, Lancaster, & Hurtado, 2000). Being able to select nutrient-dense foods with the least time investment was the most adaptive strategy in an environment of food scarcity. In an ancestral environment, lazy Suzy would have outcompeted the domestic goddess who spent all her time on selecting only the best "fresh" (i.e., raw) foods. Cooking, defined as applying heat to improve the nutritional quality of food, played a crucial role in this dietary shift (Wrangham & Conklin-Brittain, 2003). The modern and seemingly trendy raw-food diet may work in the context of a relatively sedentary and well-supported urbanized lifestyle, but switching from a raw-food diet to cooked food was a major turning point in human evolution. Cooked food increases the amount of energy our bodies can obtain from food. In cost-benefit terms, cooked foods are more effective at providing nourishment, as compared to raw foods that deliver less energy and take longer to chew and digest (Carmody & Wrangham, 2009). By switching to a cooked-food diet, our ancestors gained extra energy and time. Of course time had to be reallocated and devoted to the cooking process, and most likely this also generated new forms of relational cooperation and conflict. Cooking necessitates the collection of food into piles, and decisions must be made about who contributes to which piles and how the cooked food is to be redistributed (Wrangham & Conklin-Brittain, 2003).

The shift toward cooking foods also carried with it perceptions of relationships between people, as mentioned earlier. In anthropological records, there is some evidence that sharing cooking facilities and eating from "the same pot" signals intimacy. For instance, while in some cultures multiple families share housing, they often do not share cooking facilities. The sharing of cooking facilities and meals, not cohabitation, seems to be an indicator of what constitutes a household. The right to use and eat from one pot is restricted to people belonging to the same group. This has been documented among several hunter-gatherer societies, such as the Wolof in Senegal (Venema, 1978), the Mewun of Malekula (Larcom, 1980), the Vedda villages in Sri Lanka (Brow, 1978), the Saramaka in Suriname (Price, 1975), and the Navajo in New Mexico (Lamphere, 1977). To illustrate this, Lamphere reports that "Navajos recognize a cluster of people 'who cook and eat together,' expressed in the phrase 'ałahji' ch'iiyáán dił' dóó 'ałahjí da'ííy' (together food is prepared, and together they eat)" (p. 75). In many cases, the sharing of food signals relatedness, often but not always in terms of biological kinship. By inviting newcomers to a meal, a signal of close connectedness is given, as Larcom accounts: "Mewun who lived in the same ples [pidging for 'citizen'], even if they were not blood relations, could become strongly tied to one another by the labor involved in regular gesture of commensality" (p. 101).

In sum, the preparation and offering of food signals commitment to the receiver as well as to outside viewers. Selecting ingredients and cooking them into a meal is an act that appears to be deeply rooted in our ancestry, dating back a long time in human history and leaving its traces in perceptions of people today. Cooking and the selection of ingredients symbolizes caring and commitment on a level that is seeded in our automatic perceptions of the social world. Further, because caring and commitment are such important criteria for women within the context of a long-term romantic commitment, a woman who cannot cook may feel embarrassed because she lacks a critical skill that would display these attributes. To our knowledge, it has not yet been investigated if women who cannot cook (or at least cannot cook well) feel worried or concerned about their ability to display their care for others. It is known that men and women who cannot cook worry about their health, because the alternatives to not cooking (e.g., ready-made meals) are less healthy, and cooking skills are therefore regarded as an important threshold to physical health (Stead et al., 2004). Therefore, food and cooking are about far more than just the caloric intake; they are highly symbolic and have important social functions (Fischler, 2011) that need to be studied.

To Eat or Not to Eat: Food Consumption and Female Competition Over Beauty

So far we have focused on food as a means to signal care toward others, a highly valued trait for long-term relationships. However, food is, of course, also a means to care for oneself. Food fuels the body; we need food to survive, but overconsumption of food also puts our health at risk. In addition, others may influence our decisions about what to eat, or how much to eat, and both of these actions will in turn influence what others think about us. In this section, we discuss the relationship between food consumption and female intrasexual competition, via beauty, for the purposes of mate acquisition. We begin, though, with an examination of how food consumption shapes the female body.

Eating Our Way to Beauty

What one eats, and especially how much one eats, will influence body weight. Given the recent obesity epidemic, this simple relationship of food type(s) and quantity with healthy body size is challenging to master. From an evolutionary point of view, it is not surprising that people overeat. In ancestral times, food was scarce, and those who seized opportunities to consume available food resources likely had an advantage over contemporaries who were perhaps picky and subsequently starved to death. Further, our minds are designed to indulge in calorically dense foods whenever available; these would be highly rare in the ancestral environment and represent a nutrient "jackpot" that would allow some buffering against the demand of locating and preparing food.

However, in an environment of supermarkets, fast-food chains, and restaurants at every corner of the street (and in between), our cravings for fatty and sugar-rich foods have become maladaptive (Lowe, 2003). Obesity is one of the key health issues of the twenty-first century. For example, the global epidemic increase in overweight individuals and obesity is listed by the World Health Organization as a leading challenge for the twenty-first century (Lobstein, Baur, & Uauy, 2004). It is generally accepted that this adverse trend in eating behavior and subsequent changes in nutritional status will affect other chronic diseases like diabetes, cardiovascular disease, and cancer in the long run (Esposito, Fisher, Mennella, Hoelscher, & Huang, 2009).

Apart from worrying about their health, most women have other issues on their mind when gaining some (or many) extra pounds. As we review, many women become concerned with increases in weight gain because it may cause decreases in perceived physical attractiveness. The reason for this concern is because men put a high premium on the physical attractiveness of women (Buss & Schmitt, 1993; Li et al., 2002), and as a result of their mating intelligence, women know that their looks matter (Geher & Miller, 2008). Consequently, physical attractiveness is one of the most critical characteristics women can display in any competition over a short-term or a long-term mate.

Food consumption and body weight among women. Body weight is a key component of a woman's physical attractiveness. Men have a fairly robust preference for a particular body mass index (weight divided by height squared) range representing a woman who is neither overweight nor too thin (Cornelissen, Tovée, & Bateson, 2009; Tovée & Cornelissen, 2001; Tovée, Reinhardt, Emery, & Cornelissen, 1998). Thus, women who want to appear healthy and attractive should eat enough but not too much, resulting in an ideal body mass index. However, it is not just a matter of quantity or food portion size but also the quality of the food one eats. For instance, it is known that higher salt consumption is linked to a higher risk of obesity. The intake of salt, most commonly consumed via the consumption of preprocessed foods, correlates positively with body weight (Libuda, Kersting, & Alexy, 2012). Therefore, reduced salt intake is recommended for weight maintenance.

Second, it is also known that a vegetarian diet (cutting back on or eliminating meat) helps to maintain body weight. The average body weight of male and female vegetarians is lower compared to nonvegetarians, and obesity is less prevalent among vegetarians (Berkow & Barnard, 2006). It is therefore not surprising that omitting meat from one's diet is a popular practice among women who want to lose weight (Gilbody, Kirk, & Hill, 1999; Smith, Burke, & Wing, 2000). In extreme cases, some women seem to use their vegetarian diet as a socially accepted reason to majorly reduce their caloric intake, disguising an eating disorder (Bardone-Cone et al., 2012; Hansson, Bjorck, Birgegard, & Clinton, 2011; Klopp, Heiss, & Smith, 2003). This "false" drive for vegetarianism, as it is sometimes labeled, is most popular among semi-vegetarians, who occasionally reduce their meat intake (Timko, Hormes, & Chubski, 2012). Perhaps this approach is the healthiest option, as meat consumption should not be avoided at all times. Meat has been shown to be a crucial element of a balanced diet, although moderate consumption of it is advised (Pereira & Vicente, 2013). Semi-vegetarians are thus making a smart decision, in terms of both their health and weight maintenance.

Losing weight or maintaining weight may also be obtained by the *increased* intake of certain foods. Green tea, for example, has been considered to have a positive effect on weight maintenance and has been promoted as one of the Asian wonders. However, results from scientific studies testing the effect of green tea consumption on body weight are inconclusive. For example, one meta-analysis of studies on the effect of green tea concluded that there might be a positive effect, but it is moderated by the intake of caffeine and the ethnicity of the individual. Consuming green tea to maintain weight works best for those who consume considerable levels of caffeine and for Asians compared to Caucasians (Hursel, Viechtbauer, & Westerterp-Plantenga, 2009). The safest strategy when it comes to food intake and body weight appears to be cutting back on what damages the most, rather than increasing the intake of some "miracle foods." In other words, in order to lose weight, one needs to eat less food overall.

Food consumption and female facial attractiveness. A woman's beauty depends not only on her body weight or shape; facial appearance matters too and might even be more important than body weight and body shape (Currie & Little, 2009). In terms of female facial attractiveness, facial symmetry and averageness are important criteria (Perrett et al., 1998, 1999). Facial symmetry is a signal of good health; for example, a lack of nutritional deficits during development affects facial symmetry (Jones et al., 2001). The beauty industry is well aware of this finding and makes a fortune on products that can help us achieve facial symmetry, for instance by offering foundation creams that smooth out imperfections that cause an asymmetric look (Etcoff, Stock, Haley, Vickery, & House, 2011; Nash, Fieldman, Hussey, Leveque, & Pineau, 2006).

Can food do this too? Are there foods that can improve skin tone—for example, allowing one to achieve smooth, evenly colored skin, given that this is a feature of facial attractiveness (e.g., Matts, Fink, Grammer, & Burquest, 2007)?

Women's magazines and popular books want us to believe that food and facial traits are very much related, prescribing special diets to make wrinkles disappear and skin to become tight and glowing. As for scientific support for these claims, the results are rather negligible. Starting with green tea, a meta-study investigating the effect of green tea polyphenols on photoaging skin revealed no improvement. Compared to the placebo group, those who consumed green tea polyphenols for two years did not achieve better skin condition (Janjua et al., 2009). Another often-promoted Asian wonder is soy isoflavone, found in soy products (e.g., beans, milk, tofu). With regard to physical attractiveness, the daily oral intake of soy (isoflavones) appears to significantly improve the extent of fine wrinkles after twelve weeks (Izumi et al., 2007). This study was performed by means of pills containing the soy isoflavones, and we have not yet heard of scientific outcomes to truly know the effect of drinking soymilk and eating edamame beans on a regular basis. Other studies have investigated the effect of actual food intake, and fruits and vegetables appear to do more than just benefit our health: they are effective beauty boosters. The intake of fruit and vegetables, and subsequently the intake of β-carotene, correlates positively with higher skin carotenoid levels and yellower skin, which in general is rated as healthier and prettier than skin with fewer carotenoid pigments (Stephen, Coetzee, & Perrett, 2011). Moreover, modest dietary changes with regard to the intake of fruit and vegetables appear to be sufficient to cause significant changes in the skin-color appearance of an individual after merely six weeks. Increasing one's daily intake of fruit and vegetables with 2.91 portions per day results in a healthier appearance, and boosting one's daily intake to 3.30 portions results in better attractiveness scores in perception research (Whitehead, Re, Xiao, Ozakinci, & Perrett, 2012). Thus, women who want to appear healthy *and* pretty fare best by consuming their daily vegetables and fruits. Likewise, they should fear or envy other women who do this rigorously, as these women become healthy and attractive competitors.

Contextual Influences on Women's Food Choice and Food Intake

Deciding what and how much to eat is not just a matter of personal desires and choices. These decisions also depend on contextual factors, ranging from how the food is being presented, to the atmosphere surrounding the meal, to the presence of others. Brian Wansinck (2004) provides a strong overview of these environmental factors. For our purposes, we highlight here the presence of others, women in particular, in our discussion. However, we first briefly review the influence of another contextual factor influencing most women: their menstrual cycle.

Hormonal influence on women's food choice and food intake. In reality, most women rarely crave vegetables and fruit but often have a strong desire to eat calorically dense snacks, such as chocolate. Moreover, women's desires and will to resist sugar cravings appear to fluctuate. The explanation for this fluctuation simply comes from hormonal influences; the menstrual cycle influences women's appetite. Both what women eat and how much they eat of it are influenced by their hormonal balance. In general, women tend to eat less during the fertile phase and increase their food intake, and especially the intake of high-calorie foods (such as chocolate), during the late luteal phase (see, e.g., Fessler, 2003, Saad & Stenstrom, 2012). A possible evolutionary explanation for these changes is that ancestral women had to trade off between investing time and energy in food acquisition versus mating strategies. It makes sense to invest most in mating strategies during fertile periods, while switching the balance again during the luteal phase (Fessler, 2003). Saad and Stenstrom provide convincing evidence showing that women, on average, spend more money on food during the luteal phase compared to the fertile phase, while more money is spent on clothing during the fertile phase compared to the luteal phase. Moreover, the women in this (diary) study reported feeling less hungry in the fertile compared to the luteal phase (Saad & Stenstrom, 2012).

I'll have what she's having: Eating in the presence of a woman. In general, when eating in the presence of others, women change their intake behavior. The results are, however, not entirely straightforward, as it is not the case that the presence of other people always influences the food intake of individuals in the same way, and, overall, the results appear somewhat inconclusive.

Young, Mizzau, Mai, Sirisegaram, and Wilson (2009) conducted a study in which they observed people eating in their natural habitat. Their results show that the presence of other women increases the food intake of an observed woman, whereas her caloric intake appears to be negatively correlated with the number of men present at the table.

That is, the more men present, the less calories a woman consumes. This indicates that while the priming of intersexual attraction may lower women's food intake, the presence of other women has an opposite effect. To explain this pattern, laboratory experiments in which certain conditions can be manipulated are useful; the downside is that most of these studies pertain to snack behavior rather than the actual consumption of meals (Hermans, Herman, Larsen, & Engels, 2010). One of the factors that has been manipulated a few times is the level of acquaintance between the women eating together. For instance, women tend to eat more with same-sex friends, whereas eating with same-sex strangers does not influence food intake (Hetherington, Anderson, Norton, & Newson, 2006). Thus, it is logical that, in the natural observations study, women eating in the presence of other women ate more, since natural occasions of shared meals are most often meals eaten with friends. Interestingly, however, this experimental study did not find an effect in the condition where unknown women ate in each other's presence, while other experimental studies arrive at different conclusions. Some researchers have found that women ate *less* when eating with female strangers (Bellisle, Dalix, Airinei, Hercberg, & Peneau, 2009), or that the effect is mediated by the food intake of other women, such that women eat as much or as little as the other women do (Herman, Koenig-Nobert, Peterson, & Polivy, 2005; Salvy, Jarrin, Paluch, Irfan, & Pliner, 2007). It has even been shown that women (including those who are strangers) mimic each other while eating; they take a bite when the other takes a bite and wait/rest when the other woman delays before her next bite (Hermans et al., 2012).

In their search for the variables that may influence the relationship between social presence and food intake, researchers have looked at distraction effects and cognitive restraint (Bellisle & Dalix, 2001), body weight (Conger, Conger, Costanzo, Wright, & Matter, 1980), and personality matches between the eaters (Herman et al., 2005). None of these variables appeared to have an effect. In contrast, social presence and imitation of eating behavior were considered to have a robust effect, such that women ate less when other women ate less and ate more when other women ate more. Yet there are some exceptions to this robust finding. First, when running a study with an actual meal (i.e., a breakfast), results indicate that women do not eat less when the other woman (a confederate) is eating little compared to a substantial quantity of food. The only condition in which women ate less in this study was in the condition where the confederate ate nothing at all. The authors concluded that, except for a situation where another woman does not eat, most women fall back on their personal habits during mealtimes, even in the presence of another, unknown woman (Hermans et al., 2010).

However, not all meals allow one to fall back on habits or personal routines. For instance, when eating an unfamiliar type of meal with unknown women, the mimicry affect reappears; women do what other women do (Hermans, Larsen, Herman, & Engels, 2012). To make matters even more complex, another study (Hermans, Larsen, Herman, & Engels, 2008) showed that the body weight of the confederate moderates the effect. Women eat more/less, when other women ate more/less, yet only when the other woman has a normal body weight. When the woman appeared slim (same confederate not wearing her silicon belt), participants ate significantly less, regardless of how much the confederate was eating. The authors primarily explain this effect by referring to the fact that overeating has negative connotations and that slim women may trigger competition over weight maintenance and weight loss. Interestingly, another study found that competition in general may trigger lower food intake among women. The mere presence of another women in a competitive situation causes women to opt for lower-calorie foods (Pliner, Rizvi, & Remick, 2009). Together, these results indicate that women do opt for a low-calorie diet when other women are present, as long as these other women are seen as competitors.

An examination of the range of findings from an evolutionary perspective, especially the last results, appears promising, in that they enable us to start to unravel the complex relationship between eating and social presence. That is, considering that food intake affects weight maintenance and therefore physical attractiveness, it can be expected that women will carefully monitor and restrict their food intake when they feel threatened by other women who represent potential rivals. Since men, on average, are attracted to physically attractive, slim, and younger women (Buss & Schmitt, 1993), it can be predicted that any confederate with these traits will lower the food intake of other women

eating in her presence. That is what some of the previously mentioned studies also find. For example, women indeed eat less when faced with a slim, unknown companion (Hermans et al., 2008). Moreover, some evolutionary psychologists have even tested this prediction in a slightly different though very clever setting, measuring women's attitudes toward eating before and after they were shown photographs of attractive other women while also being primed into intrasexual competition. After seeing the photographs, the women reported more restrictive eating (i.e., preventing the consumption of certain foods) attitudes and body-image concerns (Li, Smith, Griskevicius, Cason, & Bryan, 2010). Building on this work, and tying it to mass media, it would be interesting to investigate if the mere consumption of women's magazines may lead not only to body dissatisfaction (see meta-analyses by Grabe, Ward, & Hyde, 2008; Groesz, Levine, & Murnen, 2002) but to restrictive eating patterns as well. That is, by presenting media images of attractive women, and especially showing what these women eat, female consumers might be triggered to engage in intrasexual competition over weight maintenance and restrict their food intake as a result. Casual observation suggests that followers of mass media are interested in what female celebrities eat, as people regularly post photographs online that show celebrities' plates of food.

There is one obvious application of this theory, and that is toward the study of eating disorders. The unhealthy pursuit of thinness has been called a manifestation of female intrasexual competition (Abed, 1998; Abed et al., 2012; Mealey, 2000). Faer, Hendriks, Abed, and Figueredo (2005) investigated if it was competition for mates or competition for status that explains female eating disorders. Their model illustrated that intrasexual competition for mates was the driving force behind intrasexual competition for status and drive for thinness (among other factors they investigated; Faer et al., 2005). The chapter by Salmon (this volume) elaborates on this topic in more detail. It would be interesting to replicate the social presence effect on eating behavior in the future, controlling for these variables, to see if the results could provide benefit in the treatment of those with unhealthy eating habits that promote thinness. As mentioned earlier, we advise any researcher investigating the eating behavior of women to control for their menstrual cycle, since this influences not only eating habits (see previous discussion) but also their level of intrasexual competition (Fisher, 2004).

Food for Talk: The Influence of Food Intake on Women's Reputation

So far we have focused on how eating is related to physical attractiveness and therefore triggers direct competition among women, resulting in restricted eating as a way to self-promote or enhance one's appearance. Although intrasexual competition often involves strategies of self-promotion, it also involves the derogation of competitors (e.g., Walters & Crawford, 1994). While self-promotion strategies appear to be most often used (Fisher & Cox 2010) and are the most obvious in this chapter as well, we should not overlook the fact that eating habits may also appear in the derogation of competitors. Women often use indirect aggression techniques such as manipulating the reputation of competitors (Hess & Hagen, 2006a, 2006b). A woman's eating behavior also feeds into this type of backstabbing, because what one eats influences her reputation. In other words, to use a colloquialism, "a giant steak puts a woman's reputation at stake." Popular perceptions suggest that steaks and burgers are "men's food," whereas salad and sweets are "women's food." Similar to the earlier mentioned shopping-list studies, projective methods have also been used to evaluate how people judge women (as well as men, which we do not discuss here for brevity) based on what they eat. Using a range of different projective methods, Rozin, Hormes, Faith, and Wansink (2012) thoroughly investigated the metaphoric relation between meat and maleness and concluded that both are connected and that women avoid meat to maintain their gender identity. It is not just the steak that puts women's reputation at stake; in general, women's unhealthy and/or excessive eating appear to elicit negative stereotypes (Vartanian, Herman, & Polivy, 2007). For example, when people are shown food diaries merely consisting of what a person ate for breakfast, lunch, and dinner, they attribute smaller food portions to attractive women (Rock & Kanarek, 1995). Likewise, when male and female students watch images of similar-looking women eating different meals, a woman's social appeal increases when she is eating a smaller-sized, light meal (Basow & Kobrynowicz, 1993). Although most of these studies focus on Western populations, similar research has been conducted in, for example, Japan. In this Asian context similar results appear;

low-fat foods are perceived as feminine, high-fat foods as masculine (Kimura et al., 2009).

Therefore, excessive eating and opting for nutrition-dense foods appears to put a woman at risk of derogation strategies by same-sex competitors who might attack her reputation. This definitely calls for further investigation in the domain of gossip; do women try to attack other women's reputation via gossip about her eating habits? Are women afraid of reputation attacks with regard to their cooking skills, and might this explain why Walters and Crawford (1994) found that women regard the acquisition of domestic skills as more important compared to the display of these skills? So far, analyses of gossip have not yet focused on such questions. This is an especially intriguing area for future work, since stereotyping and gossiping about the fact that a woman consumes or buys preprocessed foods not only is a means to downgrade her reputation about her own grooming (i.e., her ability to keep her own body fit and attractive) but also attacks her reputation as a caretaker (see first part of this chapter).

Conclusion: Food for Future Thought

Although Walters and Crawford (1994) listed cooking as a female strategy to outcompete same-sex competitors, to date, there has been little attention to this topic. Nutritionists have intensively studied the eating habits of women, and social psychologists have looked at contextual factors influencing eating behavior (e.g., Wansink, 2004). The cooking behavior of women has also been the topic of many studies, mainly from the field of food anthropology and nutrition (e.g., Lange & Caraher, 2001) or feminist studies (e.g., Charles & Kerr, 1988; DeVault, 1991; Murcott, 1982). However, so far there has been little attention paid toward the evolved strategies and connotations related to cooking and eating. In this chapter we provided an overview of interesting fields of research that have examined women and food, adding evolutionary explanations and results whenever possible, and gave suggestions for future research.

This chapter was divided in two main parts. The first part focused on cooking and caring, and the second part dealt with eating and physical attractiveness. Of course in reality both topics show considerable overlap; for example, women cook and dine in each other's company. Therefore future studies must also aim to investigate how both processes influence each other and determine which aspect is more important. Ideally, studies from one domain will spark new ideas to investigate the other. For instance, merging all the knowledge from social presence and eating behavior studies with what we know about women's cooking behavior and the transfer of recipes, the following research questions arise. First, will women share successful recipes with other women, controlling for the level of acquaintance, physical appearance, and age? Do women cook different meals for potential lovers, compared to same-sex friends and same-sex rivals? More specifically, would women cook more calorie-rich meals for same-sex competitors in an attempt to sabotage these women's physical appeal? What about a woman who cooks lavish, impressive meals for potential lovers, or even her husband, but barely eats anything herself; does this behavior provide a boost to her attractiveness, as compared to engaging in only one of these acts? Or does the discrepancy between her cooking and eating result in credibility issues, since a thin cook may not be considered a reliable cook? In October 2013, a famous French chef, Raymond Blanc, tweeted the following comment on the final show of the Great British Bake-Off contest, starring three attractive young women: "the great British bake off. Not much skills, female tears. And a winner so thin who makes me doubt of her love for great cooking, baking." Do people in general put stock into such stereotypes—and, if so, then what matters most: being a great cook and thus carrying some extra weight or being pretty and thin but not knowing how to boil an egg? From an evolutionary point of view, we predict the chubby domestic goddess will win against the pretty yet cooking-inept woman when it comes to long-term engagement, but a reverse result is predicted within the context of casual flings. Therefore, depending on what a woman prefers for her romantic relationships may influence what she focuses on most: cooking proper meals and acquiring further domestic skills or dieting at all times and looking maximally physically attractive.

Furthermore, it would be interesting to compare how women using opposing strategies to lose weight are perceived. That is, consider one woman who is not entirely concerned with what she eats but puts effort into downsizing her portions a little. She still mainly eats preprocessed foods and engages in a high level of exercise to lose weight. Consider in contrast a second woman who is not exercising excessively but carefully monitors what she eats. She selects healthy foods to nourish her body while avoiding excessive weight gain. It would be

interesting to ask women (and men) which strategy they believe is more successful, and what characteristics (e.g., how caring she is, her physical appearance) they associate with each strategy.

Finally, it is important to note that we are by no means promoting the idea that women *should* be domestic goddesses and cook lavish meals in accordance to the desires of their partner and offspring. On the contrary, we embrace the fact that the gap in women's and men's level of everyday cooking might be growing toward a closure and hope many young men will follow the example of their cooking fathers (see De Backer, 2013). With this chapter, we sought to explain why so many women across the globe still engage in everyday cooking, despite the abundant availability of alternatives in many Westernized cultures. Similarly, we sought to explain why women might feel guilty if they do not cook and instead turn to ready-made meals and preprocessed foods. The literature on how women, and mothers in particular, feel about feeding their children foods that have been prepared by others is very scant. Some researchers have found mothers feel guilty about not feeding children "proper," as in "healthy," foods (Devine et al., 2003). Perhaps, though, the guilt and shame also stems from a deeper-rooted awareness that cooking and caring are strongly connected, so that not cooking equals less caring. It is timely and necessary to investigate this possible connection further.

Moreover, the knowledge we can gain from this line of inquiry might be useful for health practitioners who often have a hard time endorsing healthy diets to particular groups. It is not easy to change eating habits, especially if some of these habits have evolutionary roots (Lowe, 2003). Promoting fruits and vegetables while our bodies desperately crave sugar and fats is rowing against the stream of our evolved psychological mechanisms. To put it simply, we are hardwired to prefer calorically dense foods, and for some individuals, it might be too difficult to change these preferences or eat them only in moderation. However, what if we fight these unhealthy food cravings with other hardwired mechanisms? That is, could we cause women to change toward a healthier diet not because it is good for their overall health but because their beauty will benefit from this shift? A study among African American women, who generally consume little fresh fruits and vegetables, has shown that promoting a healthier diet via a beauty salon can significantly increase the intake of fruit and vegetables (Johnson, Ralston, & Jones, 2010).

During a six-week period, a cosmetologist from the beauty salon discussed the importance of a healthy lifestyle and motivated her clients to consume more water, fruits, and vegetables and engage in more physical activities. Participants were given an information package and a starter kit with samples of fruits, vegetables, and water, and they received three motivational sessions from the cosmetologist during the program. Results showed that daily servings of fruit and vegetables increased and were significantly higher at posttest (Johnson et al., 2010). Fighting our maladaptive sweet tooth with an adaptive desire to be physically attractive seems to work, and we hope more researchers will explore this approach.

The same logic can be applied toward the promotion of cooking foods, rather than relying on preprocessed or ready-made meals. Cooking can be a burden, and it may be difficult to schedule time to cook into hectic schedules. It is easy to turn to fast alternatives, for which we have an evolved taste preference, since most of these foods contain high levels of salt and fat. Moreover, foraging for nutrient-dense foods is also an evolutionary adaptive strategy. On top of these issues, health practitioners who want to motivate people to cook are faced with another problem: the lack of skills and confidence (Stead et al., 2004). To combat these obstacles, we believe that playing on evolved psychological mechanisms related to cooking might be a worthy strategy. Convincing women, and men, that cooking is not only good for their health and that of their offspring but is a deeply rooted signal of care and social bonding may convince people to cook more often. We note that there is some disagreement with this conclusion; one study concluded that family meals are not directly benefiting the physical and psychological well-being of family members (Musick & Meier, 2012) but rather income and family coherence are tied to well-being. It is possible, though, that these authors are perhaps overlooking other factors than the "eating together," which appears to be equalized to "spending time together." Of course the authors are correct in that people can also connect by talking, playing, commuting together, and so on, yet if food and care have been so closely connected throughout our evolutionary history, we wonder if it is not still one of the most *genuine* signals of love and care. Moreover, a recent study has shown that sharing food, such as dividing dishes for multiple members, and not merely eating together, as in sitting in each other's company while consuming food, corresponds to the socialization of a caring

personality (De Backer, Fisher, Poels, & Ponnet, 2015). More precisely, these authors found that the more often children consumed home-cooked meals that had to be shared by multiple (family) members, the higher they scored on a self-report measure for altruism as young adults. In contrast, how often they ate in the presence of their parents and siblings (i.e., "eating together") did not influence their scores on the self-report altruism scale. Sharing food thus not only signals caring but endorses caring characteristics in offspring as well. Sharing food is not about restaurant visits and ordering every family member's favorite dish from a delivery company that caters to individual demands. Sharing food is about cooking as a process of selecting ingredients with care, processing them with love, and consuming them together, as a feast. In this view, a meal is the celebration of successful cooperation in food selection and preparation, or, at least, that is how it has been for most of our evolutionary history (Jones, 2007). Every meal should be a celebration of the hard work that has been put in it, and only under these circumstances, we believe, does the "family meal" perform an important social function distinct from other activities that allow for quality time together.

We are hopeful that the merging of knowledge from social food studies, food anthropologists, nutritionists, health practitioners, and evolutionary psychologists will bring about new recipes to convince people about what matters most: selecting and processing what we put inside our bodies and that of others. Food is not just fuel for the body. Food fuels our reputation, our identity, and our social relations in a multitude of ways—many of which still need to be discovered.

References

Abed, R. T. (1998). The sexual competition hypothesis for eating disorders. *British Journal of Medical Psychology, 71,* 525–547.

Abed, R., Mehta, S., Figueredo, A. J., Aldridge, S., Balson, H., Meyer, C., & Palmer, R. (2012). Eating disorders and intrasexual competition: Testing an evolutionary hypothesis among young women. *Scientific World Journal,* Article 290813. doi:10.1100/2012/290813

Adler, T. A. (1981). Making pancakes on Sunday: The male cook in family tradition. *Western Folklore, 40,* 45–54.

Alley, T. R. (2012). Contaminated and uncontaminated feeding influence perceived intimacy in mixed-sex dyads. *Appetite, 58,* 1041–1045.

Arndt, J. (1973). Haires' shopping list revisited. *Journal of Advertising Research, 13,* 57–61.

Ashley, B., Hollows, J., Jones, S., & Taylor, B. (2004). *Food and cultural studies.* Oxford: Routledge.

Bardone-Cone, A. M., Fitzsimmons-Craft, E. E., Harney, M. B., Maldonado, C. R., Lawson, M. A., Smith, R., & Robinson, D. P. (2012). The inter-relationships between vegetarianism and eating disorders among females. *Journal of the Academy of Nutrition and Dietetics, 112,* 1247–1252.

Basow, S. A., & Kobrynowicz, D. (1993). What is she eating? The effects of meal size on impressions of a female eater. *Sex Roles, 28,* 335–344.

Beardsworth, A. D., & Keil, E. T. (1993). Contemporary vegetarianism in the UK: Challenge and incorporation. *Appetite, 20,* 229–234.

Bell, D., & Valentine, G. (1997). *Consuming geographies: We are where we eat.* London: Routledge.

Bellisle, F., & Dalix, A. M. (2001). Cognitive restraint can be offset by distraction, leading to increased meal intake in women. *American Journal of Clinical Nutrition, 74,* 197–200.

Bellisle, F., Dalix, A. M., Airinei, G., Hercberg, S., & Peneau, S. (2009). Influence of dietary restraint and environmental factors on meal size in normal-weight women. A laboratory study. *Appetite, 53,* 309–313.

Berkow, S. E., & Barnard, N. (2006). Vegetarian diets and weight status. *Nutrition Reviews, 64,* 175–188.

Bourdieu, P. (1984). *Distinction: A social critique on the judgment of taste.* Cambridge, MA: Harvard University Press.

Bowen, R. L., & Devine, C. M. (2010). "Watching a person who knows how to cook, you'll learn a lot". Linked lives, cultural transmission, and the food choices of Puerto Rican girls. *Appetite, 56*(2), 290–298.

Brow, J. (1978). *Vedda villages of Anuradhapura: The historical anthropology of a community in Sri Lanka* (No. 33). Seattle: University of Washington Press.

Buss, D. M. (2003). Sexual strategies: A journey into controversy. *Psychological Inquiry, 14,* 219–226.

Buss, D. M., & Schmitt, D. P. (1993). Sexual strategies theory: An evolutionary perspective on human mating. *Psychological Review, 100,* 204–232.

Cant, M. A., & Johnstone, R. A. (2008). Reproductive conflict and the separation of reproductive generations in humans. *Proceedings of the National Academy of Sciences of the United States of America, 105,* 5332–5336.

Caraher, M., Dixon, P., Lang, T., & Carr-Hill, R. (1999). The state of cooking in England. The relationship of cooking skills to food choice. *British Food Journal, 101*(8), 590–609.

Carmody, R. N., & Wrangham, R. W. (2009). The energetic significance of cooking. *Journal of Human Evolution, 57,* 379–391.

Charles, N., & Kerr, M. (1988). *Women, food and families.* Manchester: Manchester University Press.

Conger, J. C., Conger, A. J., Costanzo, P. R., Wright K. L., & Matter, J. A. (1980). The effect of social cues on the eating behavior of obese and normal subjects. *Journal of Personality, 48,* 258–271.

Cornelissen, P. L., Tovée, M. J., & Bateson, M. (2009). Patterns of subcutaneous fat deposition and the relationship between body mass index and waist-to-hip ratio: Implications for models of physical attractiveness. *Journal of Theoretical Biology, 256,* 343–350.

Cox, A., & Fisher, M. (2008). A framework for exploring intrasexual competition. *Journal of Social, Evolutionary, and Cultural Psychology, 2,* 144–155.

Currie, T. E., & Little, A. C. (2009). The relative importance of the face and body in judgments of human physical attractiveness. *Evolution and Human Behavior, 30,* 409–416.

Daniels, S., Glorieux, I., Minnen, J., & van Tienoven, T. P. (2012). More than preparing a meal? Concerning the meanings of home cooking. *Appetite, 58,* 1050–1056.

De Backer, C. J. S. (2013). Family meal traditions. Comparing reported childhood food habits to current food habits among university students. *Appetite, 69,* 64–70.

De Backer, C. J., Fisher, M. L., Poels, K., & Ponnet, K. (2015). "Our" food versus "my" food. Investigating the relation between childhood shared food practices and adult prosocial behavior in Belgium. *Appetite, 84,* 54–60.

DeVault, M. L. (1991). *Feeding the family: The social organisation of caring as gendered work.* Chicago: Chicago University Press.

Devine, C. M., Connors, M. M., Sobal, J., & Bisogni, C. A. (2003). Sandwiching it in: Spillover of work onto food choices and family roles in low- and moderate-income urban households. *Social Science & Medicine, 56,* 617–630.

Devine, C. M., Jastran, M., Jabs, J., Wethington, E., Farell, T. J., & Bisogni, C. A. (2006). "A lot of sacrifices": Work-family spillover and the food choice coping strategies of low-wage employed parents. *Social Science & Medicine, 63,* 2591–2603.

Esposito, L., Fisher, J. O., Mennella, J. A., Hoelscher, D. M., & Huang, T. T. (2009). Developmental perspectives on nutrition and obesity: From gestation to adolescence. *Preventing Chronic Disease, 6*(3), 1–11.

Etcoff, N. L., Stock, S., Haley, L. E., Vickery, S. A., & House, D. M. (2011). Cosmetics as a feature of the extended human phenotype: Modulation of the perception of biologically important facial signals. *PLoS One, 6*(10), e25656.

Faer, L. M., Hendriks, A., Abed, R. T., & Figueredo, A. J. (2005). The evolutionary psychology of eating disorders: Female competition for mates or for status? *Psychology and Psychotherapy: Theory Research and Practice, 78,* 397–417.

Fessler, D. M. T. (2003). No time to eat: An adaptationist account of periovulatory behavioral changes. *Quarterly Review of Biology, 78,* 3–21.

Fischler, C. (2011). Commensality, society and culture. *Social Science Information Sur les Sciences Sociales, 50,* 528–548.

Fisher, M. L. (2004). Female intrasexual competition decreases female facial attractiveness. *Proceedings of the Royal Society B, 271,* S283–S285.

Geher, G., & Miller, G. (2008). *Mating intelligence: Sex, relationships, and the mind's reproductive system.* New York: Lawrence Erlbaum Associates.

Gilbody, S. M., Kirk, S. F. L., & Hill, A. J. (1999). Vegetarianism in young women: Another means of weight control? *International Journal of Eating Disorders, 26,* 87–90.

Grabe, S., Ward, L. M., & Hyde, J. S. (2008). Role of the media in body image concerns among women: A meta-analysis of experimental and correlational studies. *Psychological Bulletin, 134,* 460–476.

Groesz, L. M., Levine, M. P., & Murnen, S. K. (2002). The effect of experimental presentation of thin media images on body satisfaction: A meta-analytic review. *International Journal of Eating Disorders, 31,* 1–16.

Haire, M. (1950). Projective techniques in marketing research. *Journal of Marketing, 14,* 649–656.

Hamilton, W. D. (1966). Moulding of senescence by natural selection. *Journal of Theoretical Biology, 12*(1), 12–45.

Hansson, L. M., Bjorck, C., Birgegard, A., & Clinton, D. (2011). How do eating disorder patients eat after treatment? Dietary habits and eating behaviour three years after entering treatment. *Eating and Weight Disorders: Studies on Anorexia, Bulimia, and Obesity, 16*, E1–E8.

Herman, C. P., Koenig-Nobert, S., Peterson, J. B., & Polivy, J. (2005). Matching effects on eating: Do individual differences make a difference? *Appetite, 45*, 108–109.

Hermans, R. C. J., Herman, C. P., Larsen, J. K., & Engels, R. C. M. E. (2010). Social modeling effects on young women's breakfast intake. *Journal of the American Dietetic Association, 110*, 1901–1905.

Hermans, R. C. J., Larsen, J. K., Herman, C. P., & Engels, R. C. M. E. (2008). Modeling of palatable food intake in female young adults. Effects of perceived body size. *Appetite, 51*, 512–518.

Hermans, R. C. J., Larsen, J. K., Herman, C. P., & Engels, R. C. M. E. (2012). How much should I eat? Situational norms affect young women's food intake during meal time. *British Journal of Nutrition, 107*, 588–594.

Hermans, R. C. J., Lichtwarck-Aschoff, A., Bevelander, K. E., Herman, C. P., Larsen, J. K., & Engels, R. C. M. E. (2012). Mimicry of food intake: The dynamic interplay between eating companions. *PLoS One, 7*, e31027.

Hess, N. H., & Hagen, E. H. (2006a). Psychological adaptations for assessing gossip veracity. *Human Nature: An Interdisciplinary Biosocial Perspective, 17*, 337–354.

Hess, N. H., & Hagen, E. H. (2006b). Sex differences in indirect aggression—Psychological evidence from young adults. *Evolution and Human Behavior, 27*, 231–245.

Hetherington, M. M., Anderson, A. S., Norton, G. N. M., & Newson, L. (2006). Situational effects on meal intake: A comparison of eating alone and eating with others. *Physiology & Behavior, 88*, 498–505.

Hocking, C., Wright-St Clair, V., & Bunrayong, W. (2002). The meaning of cooking and recipe work for older Thai and New Zealand women. *Journal of Occupational Science, 9*, 117–127.

Hursel, R., Viechtbauer, W., & Westerterp-Plantenga, M. S. (2009). The effects of green tea on weight loss and weight maintenance: A meta-analysis. *International Journal of Obesity, 33*, 956–961.

Izumi, T., Saito, M., Obata, A., Arii, M., Yamaguchi, H., & Matsuyama, A. (2007). Oral intake of soy isoflavone aglycone improves the aged skin of adult women. *Journal of Nutritional Science and Vitaminology, 53*, 57–62.

Janjua, R., Munoz, C., Gorell, E., Rehmus, W., Egbert, B., Kern, D., & Chang, A. L. (2009). A two-year, double-blind, randomized placebo-controlled trial of oral green tea polyphenols on the long-term clinical and histologic appearance of photoaging skin. *Dermatologic Surgery, 35*, 1057–1065.

Johnson, C. M., Sharkey, J. R., McIntosh, A. W., & Dean, W. R. (2010). "I'm the Momma": Using photo-elicitation to understand matrilineal influence on family food choice. *BioMed Central Womens Health, 10*, 21–35.

Johnson, L. T., Ralston, P. A., & Jones, E. (2010). Beauty salon health intervention increases fruit and vegetable consumption in African-American women. *Journal of the American Dietetic Association, 110*, 941–945.

Jones, B. C., Little, A. C., Penton-Voak, I. S., Tiddeman, B. P., Burt, D. M., & Perrett, D. I. (2001). Facial symmetry and judgements of apparent health: Support for a "good genes" explanation of the attractiveness-symmetry relationship. *Evolution and Human Behavior, 22*, 417–429.

Jones, M. (2007). *Feast: Why humans share food.* Oxford: Oxford University Press.

Jones, S. C., McVie, D., & Noble, G. (2008). You are what your children eat: Using projective techniques to investigate parents' perceptions of the food choices parents make for their children. *Open Communication Journal, 2*, 23–28.

Kaplan, H., Hill, K., Lancaster, J., & Hurtado, A. M. (2000). A theory of human life history evolution: Diet, intelligence, and longevity. *Evolutionary Anthropology, 9*, 156–185.

Kaufman, J. C. (2010). *The meaning of cooking.* Malden, MA: Polity.

Kimura, A., Wada, Y., Asakawa, A., Masuda, T., Goto, S., Dan, I., & Oka, T. (2012). Dish influences implicit gender-based food stereotypes among young Japanese adults. *Appetite, 58*, 940–945.

Kimura, A., Wada, Y., Goto, S., Tsuzuki, D., Cai, D., Oka, T., & Dan, I. (2009). Implicit gender-based food stereotypes. Semantic priming experiments on young Japanese. *Appetite, 52*, 521–524.

Klopp, S. A., Heiss, C. J., & Smith, H. S. (2003). Self-reported vegetarianism may be a marker for college women at risk for disordered eating. *Journal of the American Dietetic Association, 103*, 745–747.

Kniffin, K. M., & Wansink, B. (2012). It's not just lunch: Extra-pair commensality can trigger sexual jealousy. *PLoS One, 7*, e40445.

Lamphere, L. (1977). *To run after them: Cultural and social bases of cooperation in a Navajo community.* Tucson: University of Arizona Press.

Lane, G. S. (1975). A Canadian replication of Mason Haire's "shopping list" study. *Journal of the Academy of Marketing Science, 3*, 48–59.

Lange, T., & Caraher, M. (2001). Is there a culinary skills transition? Data and debate from the UK about changes in cooking culture. *Journal of the HEIA, 8*, 2–14.

Larcom, J. C. (1980). *Place and the politics of marriage: The Mewun of Malekula, New Hebrides/Vanuaaku.* Stanford, CA: Stanford University.

Larson, N. I., Nelson, M. C., Neumark-Sztainer, D., Story, M., & Hannan, P. J. (2009). Making time for meals: Meal structure and associations with dietary intake in young adults. *Journal of the American Dietetic Association, 109*, 72–79.

Leonardi, S. J. (1989). Recipes for reading: Summer pasta, Lobster à la Riseholme, and key lime pie. *PMLA, 104*, 340–347.

Li, N. P., Bailey, J. M., Kenrick, D. T., & Linsenmeier, J. A. W. (2002). The necessities and luxuries of mate preferences: Testing the tradeoffs. *Journal of Personality and Social Psychology, 82*, 947–955.

Li, N. P., Smith, A. R., Griskevicius, V., Cason, M. J., & Bryan, A. (2010). Intrasexual competition and eating restriction in heterosexual and homosexual individuals. *Evolution and Human Behavior, 31*, 365–372.

Libuda, L., Kersting, M., & Alexy, U. (2012). Consumption of dietary salt measured by urinary sodium excretion and its association with body weight status in healthy children and adolescents. *Public Health Nutrition, 15*, 433–441.

Lobstein, T., Baur, L., & Uauy, R. (2004). Obesity in children and young people: A crisis in public health. *Obesity Reviews, 5*, 4–104.

Lowe, M. R. (2003). Self-regulation of energy intake in the prevention and treatment of obesity: Is it feasible? *Obesity Research, 11*(S10), 44S–59S.

Mancino, L., & Newman, C. (2007). *Who has time to cook? How family resources influence food preparation.* USDA

Economic Research Report, No. 40. Washington, DC: US Department of Agriculture.

Matts, P. J., Fink, B., Grammer, K., & Burquest, M. (2007). Color homogeneity and visual perception of age, health, and attractiveness of female facial skin. *Journal of the American Academy of Dermatology*, 57(6), 977–984.

Meah, A., & Jackson, P. (2012). Crowded kitchens: The "democratisation" of domesticity? *Gender, Place and Culture: A Journal of Feminist Geography*, 19, 1–19.

Mealey, L. (2000). Anorexia: A "losing" strategy? *Human Nature: An Interdisciplinary Biosocial Perspective*, 11, 105–116.

Meyers, M. (2001). *A bite off Mama's plate: Mothers' and daughters' connections through food*. London: Bergin & Harvey.

Moffat, S. D., Hampson, E., & Hatzipantelis, M. (1998). Navigation in a "virtual" maze: Sex differences and correlation with psychometric measures of spatial ability in humans. *Evolution and Human Behavior*, 19(2), 73–87.

Moisio, R., Arnould, E., & Price, L. L. (2004). Between mothers and markets: Constructing family identity through homemade food. *Journal of Consumer Culture*, 4, 361–384.

Moser, A. (2010). Food preparation patterns in German family households. An econometric approach with time budget data. *Appetite*, 55, 99–107.

Murcott, A. (1982). On the social significance of the cooked dinner in South-Wales. *Social Science Information Sur les Sciences Sociales*, 21, 677–696.

Musick, K., & Meier, A. (2012). Assessing causality and persistence in associations between family dinners and adolescent well-being. *Journal of Marriage and Family*, 74, 476–493.

Nash, R., Fieldman, G., Hussey, T., Leveque, J. L., & Pineau, P. (2006). Cosmetics: They influence more than Caucasian female facial attractiveness. *Journal of Applied Social Psychology*, 36, 493–504.

New, J., Krasnow, M. M., Truxaw, D., & Gaulin, S. J. C. (2007). Spatial adaptations for plant foraging: Women excel and calories, count. *Proceedings of the Royal Society B*, 274, 2679–2684.

Norazmir, N. M., Sharif, M. S. M., Zahari, M. S. M., Salleh, H. M., Isha, N., & Muhammad, R. (2012). The transmission modes of Malay traditional food knowledge within generations. *Procedia-Social and Behavioral Sciences*, 50, 79–88.

Oxford Dictionaries. (2013). Domestic goddess [in English]. www.oxforddictionaries.com

Pereira, P. M. D. C., & Vicente, A. F. D. B. (2013). Meat nutritional composition and nutritive role in the human diet. *Meat Science*, 93, 586–592.

Perrett, D. I., Burt, D. M., Penton-Voak, I. S., Lee, K. J., Rowland, D. A., & Edwards, R. (1999). Symmetry and human facial attractiveness. *Evolution and Human Behavior*, 20, 295–307.

Perrett, D. I., Lee, K. J., Penton-Voak, I., Rowland, D., Yoshikawa, S., Burt, D. M., & Akamatsu, S. (1998). Effects of sexual dimorphism on facial attractiveness. *Nature*, 394, 884–887.

Pliner, P., Rizvi, S., & Remick, A. K. (2009). Competition affects food choice in women. *International Journal of Eating Disorders*, 42, 557–564.

Price, R. (1975). *Saramaka social structure: Analysis of a Maroon society in Surinam*. Institute of Caribbean Studies, University of Puerto Rico.

Rock, B. C., & Kanarek, R. B. (1995). Women and men are what they eat: The effects of gender and reported meal size on perceived characteristics. *Sex Roles*, 33, 109–119.

Rosvall, K. A. (2011). Intrasexual competition in females: Evidence for sexual selection? *Behavioral Ecology*, 22, 1131–1140.

Rozin, P., Hormes, J. M., Faith, M. S., & Wansink, B. (2012). Is meat male? A quantitative multimethod framework to establish metaphoric relationships. *Journal of Consumer Research*, 39, 629–643.

Saad, G., & Stenstrom, E. (2012). Calories, beauty, and ovulation: The effects of the menstrual cycle on food and appearance-related consumption. *Journal of Consumer Psychology*, 22, 102–113.

Salvy, S. J., Jarrin, D., Paluch, R., Irfan, N., & Pliner, P. (2007). Effects of social influence on eating in couples, friends and strangers. *Appetite*, 49, 92–99.

Schmitt, D. P., & Buss, D. M. (1996). Strategic self-promotion and competitor derogation: Sex and context effects on the perceived effectiveness of mate attraction tactics. *Journal of Personality and Social Psychology*, 70, 1185–1204.

Sear, R., & Mace, R. (2008). Who keeps children alive? A review of the effects of kin on child survival. *Evolution and Human Behavior*, 29, 1–18.

Sear, R., Mace, R., & McGregor, I. A. (2000). Maternal grandmothers improve nutritional status and survival of children in rural Gambia. *Proceedings of the Royal Society B*, 267, 1641–1647.

Sellaeg, K., & Chapman, G. E. (2008). Masculinity and food ideals of men who live alone. *Appetite*, 51, 120–128.

Smith, C. F., Burke, L. E., & Wing, R. R. (2000). Vegetarian and weight-loss diets among young adults. *Obesity Research*, 8, 123–129.

Smith, K. J., McNaughton, S. A., Gall, S. L., Blizzard, L., Dwyer, T., & Venn, A. J. (2010). Involvement of young Australian adults in meal preparation: Cross-sectional associations with sociodemographic factors and diet quality. *Journal of the American Dietetic Association*, 110, 1363–1367.

Stead, M., Caraher, M., Wrieden, W., Longbottom, P., Valentine, K., & Anderson, A. (2004). Confident, fearful and hopeless cooks. Findings from the development of a food-skills initiative. *British Food Journal*, 160, 274–287.

Stephen, I. D., Coetzee, V., & Perrett, D. I. (2011). Carotenoid and melanin pigment coloration affect perceived human health. *Evolution and Human Behavior*, 32, 216–227.

Stringer, R. E. (2009). The domestic foodscape of young low-income women in Montreal. Cooking practices in the context of an increasingly processed food supply. *Health Education and Behaviour*, 37(2), 211–226.

Tashiro, S., & Lo, C. P. (2012). Gender difference in the allocation of time: Preparing food cooked at home versus purchasing prepared food. *Food Culture and Society*, 15, 455–471.

Teaford, M. F., Ungar, P. S., & Grine, F. E. (2002). Paleontological evidence for the diets of African Plio-Pleistocene hominins with special reference to early Homo. In P. S. Ungar & M. F. Teaford (Eds.), *Human diet: Its origin and evolution* (pp. 143–166). Westport, CT: Bergin & Garvey.

Ternier, S. (2010). Understanding and measuring cooking skills and knowledge as factors influencing convenience food purchases and consumption. *Studies by Undergraduate Researchers at Guelph*, 3(2), 69–76.

Timko, C. A., Hormes, J. M., & Chubski, J. (2012). Will the real vegetarian please stand up? An investigation of dietary restraint and eating disorder symptoms in vegetarians versus non-vegetarians. *Appetite, 58,* 982–990.

Tovée, M. J., & Cornelissen, P. L. (2001). Female and male perceptions of female physical attractiveness in front-view and profile. *British Journal of Psychology, 92,* 391–402.

Tovée, M. J., Reinhardt, S., Emery, J. L., & Cornelissen, P. L. (1998). Optimum body-mass index and maximum sexual attractiveness. *Lancet, 352,* 548.

Vartanian, L. R., Herman, C. P., & Polivy, J. (2007). Consumption stereotypes and impression management: How you are what you eat. *Appetite, 48,* 265–277.

Venema, L. B. (1978). *The Wolof of Saloum: Social structure and rural development in Senegal.* Wageningen University, Wageningen.

Vidal, L., Ares, G., & Gimenez, A. (2013). Projective techniques to uncover consumer perception: Application of three methodologies to ready-to-eat salads. *Food Quality and Preference, 28,* 1–7.

Voyer, D., Voyer, S., & Bryden, M. P. (1995). Magnitude of sex differences in spatial abilities: A meta-analysis and consideration of critical variables. *Psychological Bulletin, 117*(2), 250–270.

Walters, S., & Crawford, C. B. (1994). The importance of mate attraction for intrasexual competition in men and women. *Ethology and Sociobiology, 15*(1), 5–30.

Wansink, B. (2004). Environmental factors that increase the food intake and consumption volume of unknowing consumers. *Annual Review of Nutrition, 24,* 455–479.

Webster, F. E., & Pechmann, F. V. (1970). Replication of shopping list study. *Journal of Marketing, 34,* 61–63.

Whitehead, R. D., Re, D., Xiao, D. K., Ozakinci, G., & Perrett, D. I. (2012). You are what you eat: Within-subject increases in fruit and vegetable consumption confer beneficial skincolor changes. *PLoS One, 7,* e32988.

Williams, G. C. (1957). Pleiotropy, natural-selection, and the evolution of senescence. *Evolution, 11,* 398–411.

Wrangham, R., & Conklin-Brittain, N. (2003). Cooking as a biological trait. *Comparative Biochemistry and Physiology A: Molecular & Integrative Physiology, 136,* 35–46.

Young, M. E., Mizzau, M., Mai, N. T., Sirisegaram, A., & Wilson, M. (2009). Food for thought: What you eat depends on your sex and eating companions. *Appetite, 53,* 268–271.

Evolution of Artistic and Aesthetic Propensities through Female Competitive Ornamentation

Marco Antonio Corrêa Varella, Jaroslava Varella Valentova, *and* Ana María Fernández

Abstract

This chapter highlights and discusses the role of women's competitive ornamentation as one of the relevant, and so far overlooked, ancestral selective pressures in the evolution of artistic propensities. The authors critically discuss how and why sex differences and sexual selection processes acting on women have been disregarded for more than a decade. The authors review available convergent evidence about sex differences in aesthetics and artistic propensities showing that, overall, women outnumber men. Then the authors propose and show evidence that higher women's inclination toward artistic domains, including ornamentation of body, behavior, and objects/places, can serve as a social arena for attracting/maintaining mates and dealing with rivals, primarily through self-promotion via competitive ornamentation. The chapter concludes by developing connections with related theories that broaden the scope of the field and highlight predictions for future research.

Key Words: arts, music, sex differences, sexual selection, female competition, ornaments

Introduction

The National Museum of Women in the Arts in Washington D.C. is the only major museum in the world exclusively dedicated to recognizing women's artistic contributions. It was founded in 1987, and, by focusing on women artists, the museum aims to directly overcome an imbalance in the presentation of art in the world, thus assuring great women artists a place of honor now and into the future.

The importance of women to the artistic domain is being reconsidered in art, as well as most recently in the science of the evolution of artistic propensities. This shift is accompanied by many important questions that are relevant for the purposes of this chapter. For example, are there sex differences that affect the psychological basis of artistic propensities? And, if so, what do they indicate in terms of their evolution? How can women compete through various artistic venues without being violent? How does the shift from men to women in the evolutionary thinking of artistic inclination contribute to the integration and expansion of existing theories?

The evolutionary roots of human cross-cultural capacities, motivations, and preferences to create, enjoy, and engage in a whole array of artistic expression have been a fascinating and controversial topic since before Darwin (1871) (cf. Kleinman, 2015). Although painting, music, and theater, for example, are intuitively easy to grasp to some extent (e.g., one can spontaneously like them or not), their phylogenetic origins and adaptive functions are neither straightforward nor obvious. Darwin (1871) wrote that "as neither the enjoyment nor the capacity of producing musical notes are faculties of the least use to man in reference to his daily habits of life, they must be ranked amongst the most mysterious with which he is endowed" (pp. 569–570). The paradox mystery of the evolutionary status of arts has motivated the creation of varied theories concerning the possible proximal functions, ontogenetic development, phylogeny, and evolutionary functions of artistic behavior and led to specific hypotheses (cf. Dissanayake, 2008).

Framing "Arts" for Performing Evolutionary Analysis

An evolutionary approach does not focus on explanations of particular individual behavioral outcomes, such as why Beethoven composed his *5th Symphony*. It neither aims to focus on specific cultural particularities, such as why certain cultures lack separate concepts of dance and music, nor explains why Western individuals consider some works masterpieces and others crafts.

Arts are not simply and only fine arts. When considering the possible evolutionary aspects of artistic works, one should assume the point of view of an "alien" researcher to avoid Western-centrism (Boyd, 2009; Dissanayake, 2008; Dutton 2009) and human exceptionalism (Endler, 2012; Taylor, 2013). Thus, one must contemplate the phenomena broadly, in such a way that allows both cross-cultural and cross-species comparison. Therefore, art is not merely what people think it is within each culture, nor is it only art works, artistic performance, or appreciative evaluations. Instead, the artistic domain encompasses all that and more, and thus, art is a vaguely defined concept. Art may be determined by the products, as well as by the behaviors that led to the creation of a product, and furthermore, as the underlying mental capacities that result in the performance of any type of artistic behavior or product. From an evolutionary view, we argue that neither behaviors nor products of behaviors are candidate adaptations per se; instead, they are the consequences of fully developed psychological adaptations interacting with particular cultural, historical, and ecological backgrounds (Andrews, Gangestad, & Mattews, 2002; Cosmides & Tooby, 1992; Pinker, 1999).

With that in mind, evolutionarily oriented researchers have tried to define art broadly, grasping its essential features and aspects. For instance, Coe (2003) conceives of visual art as the modification of an object or body through color, line, pattern, and form, done solely to attract attention to that object or body. In contrast, according to Boyd (2005), art is an attempt to engage an audience's attention by transforming objects and/or actions in order to appeal to species-wide cognitive preferences exclusively for the sake of the response they evoke. Yet another alternative view is from Ramachandran and Hirstein (1999), who state that the purpose of all forms of art is to enhance, transcend, or even distort reality. This view is supported by theorists such as Dissanayake (2008), who contends that the single goal of all art is making ordinary elements of everyday objects and social interactions extraordinary, special. Likewise, while focusing on ornaments, Glăveanu (2014) defines these as patterned "markings" in the world, resulting from acts of decoration or embellishment that, when "added" to objects or processes, contribute to their aesthetic quality, as well as to individual and social value.

Building on these and other authors (e.g., Varella, Ferreira, & Souza, 2011; Varella, Souza, & Ferreira, 2011), the core of all artistic manifestation may be seen as a multimodal communication through enhancement activities that require physical, material, creative, and appreciative effort to produce extraordinary behaviors and/or products that attract attention, inspire aesthetic evaluations, and induce emotional reaction in others. Such evaluations and reactions, in turn, induce affiliative or nonaffiliative/neutral interpersonal reactions, influencing the reputation of the individual and of the social group to which they belong. In other words, as in all communication, those who create such products or behaviors are assessed by an audience, and this assessment has important bearing for the audience and the creators' social standing and reputation. This is in line with a recent challenge in the field, which redefines and situates artistic manifestations within the scope of nonhuman species' communication dynamics, thereby importing methods and concepts used to recognize specific benefits to producers and to receivers and to analyze the design of artistic signals, among other attributes (c.f. Endler, 2012; Huron, 2015; Snowdon, Zimmerman, & Altenmüller, 2015; Varella, Souza, & Ferreira, 2011).

Artisticality

In this chapter, we focus broadly on artistic propensities as a whole, seen as artistic instincts. "Artisticality" is the term we use to generically encompass the instinctive propensities to develop psychological faculties that underlie a whole array of multimodal and extraordinary aesthetically enhancing activities, including behaviors, its products, and appreciations across cultures, historical periods, and species. In this sense, what artisticality is to all arts, musicality is to all music. Artisticality broadly encompasses instinctive propensities in five interrelated subdomains. Visual/plastic arts are mostly focused on images and aesthetically enhancing objects, such as painting, drawing, engraving, sculpting, carving, weaving, handiwork, photography, maquillage, body and environmental decoration, designing costumes and masks, or creative cooking (food presentation). Literary/scenic arts are mostly concerned with stories and aesthetically enhancing narratives, such as acting, telling or writing stories, poetry, or jokes. Musical arts are mostly focused on aesthetically enhancing sounds, such as singing, playing, whistling, drumming, clapping, and dancing. Circus arts are mostly focused on aesthetically enhancing body movements, such as acrobatics, juggling, balancing act, contortionism, illusionism, and artistic sports. Finally, olfactory arts are primarily concerned with scent and aesthetically enhancing odors, such as the development of fragrances, perfumes, incense sticks, smoking and other flavor enhancing techniques, and other uses of scents.

In general, artisticality includes at least three main psychological components: artistic motivations, capacities for creative production, and aesthetic appreciation (for a similar distinction on musicality see Bispham, 2009). All humans are capable of engaging in artistic expression and can perform, independently or simultaneously, the role of a producer, in which role they are evaluated by others, as well as the role of appreciator/spectator, in which they evaluate the artistic works of others. The importance of describing the array of psychological processes underlying artisticality is crucial because it is easy to conflate motivations, with capacities and those with overt behavior, but they do not always need to be aligned. Furthermore, the evolution of art production and aesthetic appreciation may be relatively independent from each other (see, Varella, Souza, & Ferreira, 2011).

In the following section, we outline the most relevant theories that explain the existence and ancestral functions of artistic propensities from an evolutionary perspective. We discuss how and why sex differences and sexual selection as acting on women have been disregarded in this literature for more than a decade. After demonstrating how embracing and prevalent artistic tendencies are in women, we will show that artisticality taps into women's main social arena for attracting and maintaining mates and for dealing with rivals through self-promotion. We argue that the evolutionary role of female behavior, including the extended competitive ornamentation of the body and objects/places, opens the opportunity for a new line of research regarding artisticality. In the conclusion

section, we point to connections to related theories that broaden the scope of the field and highlight predictions for future research.

Evolutionary Theories of the Arts

Most authors agree that a trait is adaptive when it increases the relative reproductive success of individuals in a given population, and it becomes an adaptation when it has been modified by selection and has a near-optimal and special design showing efficiency, precision, and reliability (e.g., Andrews et al., 2002, Cosmides & Tooby, 1992, p. 165). One line of reasoning suggests that, given the nonobvious survival value of artistic tendencies, these were not adaptive either in humans' ancestral time nor in the current environment (e.g., Patel, 2010, Pinker, 1999; Souza, 2004). However, given enough time and recurrent selective pressures, pre-existing neuropsychologically adapted mechanisms (such as creativity to solve practical problems or aesthetic tendencies to appreciate people, animals, food, and landscape) could have became interconnected and phylogenetically exapted. That is, perhaps they were reused for a different domain, which could have been the origin of our artistic mental adaptations, and later have suffered further modifications from different selective pressures (Varella, Souza, & Ferreira, 2011).

Nowadays, most researchers agree that artisticality is an adapted feature of human nature, or at least that there is an heuristic value in viewing artisticality using adaptationism. However, as we review later, each scholar defends a slightly different theory. To organize the diversity of adaptive functions, Dissanayake (2008) described four general categories of proposed functions of artistic propensities. We build on her classification, expanding and updating her summary and also highlighting the plausible selective mechanisms for each category. First, artisticality could have improved cognition in general, through play or simulating possible situations, and thus have an indirect effect on fitness (e.g., Boyd, 2009; Cross, 2007, 2009; Honing, 2011; Tooby & Cosmides, 2001). That is, individuals with slightly superior artistic propensities, as a consequence, could have had improved overall mental development and better motor, perceptual, emotional, and social capacities that, in turn, improved their chances of survival and reproduction. Furthermore, the arts could have been adaptive in promoting social propaganda and manipulation via redirecting attention and emotion to indoctrinating messages, and thus have a direct effect on fitness through reciprocal altruism and multilevel or kin selection mechanisms (e.g., Brown, 2000; Scalise-Sugiyama, 1996). For example, ancestral people could have used artistic manifestations, such as songs or dances, costumes, and story-telling, in group rituals or parades to promote specific religious or political views against other views and/or groups. The artistic manifestation might enhance the aesthetic and emotional appeal of the ritual or manifestation, which helps justify in-group survival and reproductive privileges against others. Third, through enhancing cooperation and contributing to social cohesion, the arts could have reinforced sociality, thus enabling higher in-group familiarity and mutual help even in times of crises, with the same effects as listed in the second point (e.g., Coe, 2003; Dissanayake, 1988, 2008; Dunbar, 2012). Finally, the arts could have increased mating opportunities and the desirability of individuals or groups by manipulating the sensory bias of the perceivers and/or by showing off fitness indicators that help in attracting, maintaining, and competing for mates and thus have a direct effect on fitness (e.g., Dutton, 2009; Miller, 1999, 2000, 2001; Power, 1999; Varella, Souza, & Ferreira, 2011). For example, individuals with slightly superior artistic propensities (dancer, jewelry maker, or poet) relative to others could have gained more attention and made a better first impression, thus increasing their mate value and, through the increased likelihood of matings, gaining a higher number of children. Any of the four categories of proposed adaptive value to artisticality could have plausibly happened sequentially or in combination throughout human evolution. These adaptive propositions do not suggest that expressions of artisticality are *the only way* to improve the development of cognition or to improve cohesion, cooperation, or mate value and overall fitness. Rather, artisticality would be another available viable strategy to enhance survival and reproduction, working side by side with the most ancient strategies, such as play behavior, grooming, and flirting.

Another important point is realizing that some traits can be adaptive without being an adaptation, such as the ability to read and write, which are crucial for surviving and reproducing in the modern environments but did not exist in ancestral times (Parkinson & Wheatley, 2015). On the other hand, not all adaptations need to be adaptive in today's context. The overconsumption of high-calorie food, which was adaptive in times of ancestral scarcity, leads today, in a time of food abundance, to obesity and heart disease (for the distinction between adaptation and adaptiveness, see Laland & Brown, 2002). Therefore, it is important to remember that not all ancestral adaptations need to function properly in today's current environment. Keeping in mind this distinction between adaptation and current adaptiveness can clarify some contraintuitive conclusions. That is, even in case of a total absence of any current fitness enhancement, a trait does not need to be only a by-product of another adaptation: it can still be considered a past adaptation if it can be shown that it has been favored by natural selection for its design and effectiveness in a particular ancestral function (Andrews et al., 2002). Furthermore, due to their apparent simplicity and historical misuses, evolutionary accounts of the human mind and behavior can elicit many erroneous interpretations. Consequently, one must be aware of the variety of existing misunderstandings, especially regarding adaptationism (for a systematic review, see Varella et al., 2013).

The basic evolutionary view of the arts implies two relatively independent dimensions of the potentially adaptive role of artisticality: survival and reproduction. In this chapter, we focus mostly on the role of sexual selection (thus reproduction) as one of the possible adaptive roles of artisticality. In comparison with theories focused on survival advantages, theories focusing on reproductive advantages can predict a higher degree of sex differences in artisticality, but not always. In the next section, we explore how and why sex differences, together with sexual selection and the role of women in the evolution of artisticality, have been dismissed.

Overlooking Sex Differences, Sexual Selection, and the Female Role in the Evolutionary Accounts of Artistic Propensities

Before we present the existing evidence of sex differences in artisticality, we briefly summarize the previous literature claiming a lack of sex differences in this area. Far from being an extensive review, this section pinpoints flaws in specific arguments about the influences of sexual selection in human artisticality by authors who otherwise offered their own well-founded theories. In order to provide direct evidence, we cite actual, exact phrases and statements from each author's work. Moreover, we want to demonstrate that there are changes to the story; for example, Miller and Brown alter their view as time progresses, but others working from Miller's original model do not. In any case, by stressing these flaws, we do not aim to simply criticize the authors, but rather to show that these flaws can create a widespread bias in the empirical literature.

The denial of sex differences in artisticality without empirical support started when modern evolutionary thinking was applied to musicality. It seems to have been used as a rhetorical device to weaken or dismiss possible influences of any sexual selection processes on artisticality. In 1999, Miller proposed that age and sex would influence the amount of publicity that individuals aim to get using "behaviours such as telling stories, wearing clothes, dancing, making music, decorating artifacts, expressing belief in certain ideas, and so forth" (p. 77). He wrote that "cultural production should increase rapidly after puberty, peak at young adulthood when sexual competition is greatest, and gradually decline over adult life as parenting eclipses courtship. Males should also show much higher rates of cultural production than females, because they are competing more intensely for mates" (p. 81). Miller (1999) then analyzed rates of released jazz and rock albums, gallery paintings, and published books and found "persistent sexual dimorphism in cultural production rates, with males producing about 10 times more cultural output, across all media, than females" (p. 86). Recently Miller (2013) admits he exaggerated by stating that "for a while in the early 1990s, I was indeed 'an ape that thought it was a peacock'" (p. 207) and changed his perspective to include more mutual mate choice and competition in both men and women. Despite this revised focus, his original exaggerated view of sex differences of the arts has heavily influenced later theoretical discussion.

As a reaction to Miller's early approach (1999), sexual selection as applied to artisticality has been frequently simplified to the form of ornamented males attracting nonornamented females. This oversimplification of strong male superiority led scholars to challenge the application of sexual selection theory to artisticality. For example, Brown (2000) stated, "Importantly, musical capacity is not a sexually dimorphic trait and this weakens claims that music evolved by sexual selection as a device for men to court women" (p. 247). Similarly, Fitch (2006) concluded "as for language . . ., musical abilities show a remarkably egalitarian sexual distribution pattern. This is a serious problem for the hypothesis that sexual selection was the major driving force in music evolution" (p. 201). Following the same line of reasoning, Ball (2010) argued that "if music is an adaptation via sexual selection, we might expect it to be developed to different degrees in men and women. There's no evidence that it is (even though there may be slight differences in how music is processed in the brain). . . . This doesn't mean that music can't be unique . . ., but it does warrant some skepticism about the idea" (p. 21).

Moreover, when comparing humans with other species, sex differences have been considered mainly categorical, meaning that researchers expect either large sex differences or none at all, rather than viewing them as being on a continuum, such that there would be various degrees of sex differences. In this sense, Fitch (2006) wrote, "In birds, where sexual selection for song is most clear, it is mostly males that sing, . . . [as in] whales and seals. This is definitely not the case in humans, where women sing in most cultures, and male and female musical abilities do not clearly differ" (p. 201). Similarly, Huron (2001) pointed out that "there is nothing to indicate that one sex is more musical than the other, and so there is no evidence of the dimorphism commonly symptomatic of sexual selection. Women may be impressed by men who serenade them outside their balcony windows, but unlike female songbirds, female humans are perfectly capable of serenading men" (pp. 47–48). Likewise, Patel (2008) wrote, "sexual selection for male song production typically results in salient male-female differences in anatomy and/or behavior (e.g., among birds, whales, frogs, crickets), yet there is no evidence that human males and females differ in any substantial way in their music production or perception abilities" (p. 368). Approaching all artistic manifestations, Dissanayake (2009) stated that "Although some animals and a number of birds perform art-like behaviors, . . . humans as a species are unique in that, without being constrained by season or gender or genetic program, they deliberately . . . make their bodies, vocalizations, movements, and surroundings extraordinary or special" (p. 165). Finally, Chang, Fisher, and Meredith (2012) stated that "contra to the stunning sex differences in pea fowl appearance, women display artistic ability and creativity as well as men when given the chance to do so. In the case of the arts, many of the sex differences can be interpreted as a lack of exposure rather than a lack of aptitude" (p. 444).

The described approach oscillates between human exceptionalism, which considers humans as special, distinct, and thus noncomparable to other species (for more details, see Taylor, 2013), to contrasting humans with other species that are known to be highly sexually dimorphic. Under such circumstances, humans certainly appear more monomorphic. The problem is that this approach shows a specific way of conducting interspecies comparisons by illustrating differences between humans and highly sex-differentiated species rather than focusing on where humans fit into the continuum of all species, ranging from those that are extremely monomorphic to extremely sexually dimorphic.

The comparative approach just described gives the impression that sexual selection happens only in extreme cases of sexual dimorphism. As Ball (2010) noticed, "We know of no . . . example of sexual selection that is manifested the same way in both sexes" (p. 21). However, sexual selection theory can be applied not only to highly sex-dimorphic species, but also to relatively monomorphic species, such as humans. Also, in socially monogamous species, which tend to be more monomorphic, sexual selection can still drive the evolution of costly signaling ornamentation, as long as the trait is sufficiently heritable and allows positive assortative mating (Hooper & Miller, 2008). In a review of the animal behavior literature about mutual ornaments, Kraaijeveld, Kraaijeveld-Smit, and Komdeur (2007) concluded that there is strong evidence that mutual ornaments can have a signaling function in both sexes, especially in terms of mate choice, so that even without sex differences there is still sexual selection acting on ornaments.

Furthermore, sexual selection is often misunderstood as being directly related to courtship for the sole purpose of gaining mating access, rather than as being composed of many processes ranging from competing for resources and access to partners, attracting partners, to maintaining the partnership and parental investments (Andersson, 1994; Hoquet, 2015). In other words, sexually selected traits are expected to be directly connected only to intercourse, desire to copulate, and/or seduction and romance. This oversimplified assumption is frequently contradicted in order to dismiss sexual selection entirely. For instance, Brown (2000) proposed that "Music's role in courtship is at best indirect. Courtship and marriage are certainly matters of collective importance, and so we shouldn't be surprised that music plays a role in these functions. However, ethnographic evidence argues strongly against the idea that music evolved to serve a direct and primary role in human courtship" (p. 250). Similarly, Cross (2007) pointed out that "Although music is certainly used for courtship in most, if not all, societies, as the ethnomusicological evidence indicates its roles are always more multifarious" (p. 658). In the same line, Patel (2008) also assumed that if sexual selection had influenced

musicality, then all flirting should be fully musical. He used the lack of evidence to support his point and stated that "Courtship is only one of music's many functions, and there is no evidence that music is either necessary or sufficient for successful courtship across human cultures" (p. 368). However, sexual selection mechanisms have consequences reaching far beyond courtship, such as maintaining a stable relationship, parenting, and territorial behavior, which can be extrapolated to an array of other social behaviors, such as alliance formation or indirect competition (Andersson, 1994; Hoquet, 2015). At the same time, sexual selection applied to musicality, or artisticality in general, does not mean only individuals possessing such abilities reproduce. Instead, such traits might be one of many available strategies helping to increase one's mating success, at least under certain circumstances.

Another reaction to Miller's original contribution (1999) consists of the argument that any ancestral evolutionary function should be the only, or the prevailing, social function of art in today's society. For example, Boyd (2005) stated, "If art were sexually selected, this would predict that it is overwhelmingly male and directed to females, it begins only with puberty, it peaks just before mate selection, and it diminishes drastically afterward, . . . but mothers of all cultures sing to infants; . . . infants of both sexes engage in cooing and singing, clapping, and dancing as soon as they can; adolescent girls go wild over all-female bands . . .; Hokusai . . . was still producing masterpieces in his ninetieth year" (p. 161). However, the fact that art is not only directed toward fertile members of the opposite sex, but is also present in children or elders, during major life events such as funerals, as part of ritualized sacrifice and cannibalism, in same-sex groups, and so on, does not rule out sexual selection's influence on human artisticality in the ancestral environments (Varella, Souza, & Ferreira, 2011, 2012). By analogy, this logic is akin to saying that heterosexual sex did not evolve to foster direct reproduction because people cross-culturally engage in sex during nonfertile phases of the female menstrual cycle, during pregnancy or after menopause, perform oral or anal sex, conduct same-sex sexual activities, and use various methods of contraception.

In another publication, Miller (2000) emphasized the "nature" side of artisticality by stating that "it seems likely that most music at all levels, from local pub bands to internationally televised concerts, is produced by young men. And that is exactly the pattern sexual selection would produce . . . The behavioral demographics of music production are just what we would expect for a sexually selected trait, with young males greatly overrepresented in music making" (pp. 355–356). This simplistic approach concerning artistic display as disconnected from sociocultural influences revealed reactions that emphasized the "nurture" side of the phenomenon. For example, Patel (2008) wrote that males producing musical displays "can be explained by cultural factors, such as the importance of music in identity formation in adolescence and male dominance in the control of the recording industry" (p. 369). Similarly, Aiken (2001) pointed out that artistic manifestation is "a behavior or trait that has evolved via sexual selection calls for males to be the artists. Although it can be said that most recognized artists historically have been men, that fact is confounded by the lack of opportunity for women" (p. 6). Barash (2012) considered both the ultimate influence of sexual selection and the proximate explanation of sociocultural norms and concluded a moderate view was needed: "On the one hand, the fact that there are so many more 'great masters' than 'great mistresses' in every major artistic discipline is consistent with the sexual selection hypothesis, since males . . . would be more strongly selected to be sexual/artistic/creative show-offs than would females" (p. 189). "But on the other hand, it is clear that cultural biases and social norms have long restricted the creative outlets for women. . . [A]s the cultural prohibitions against women's artistic creativity have fallen, the ranks of women artists have swollen. This suggests that women's artistic capacity may well be at least as great as their manly counterparts, and not limited to being an appreciative—albeit discerning—audience" (p. 190). Finally, Fitch (2006) noticed that orchestras are male-biased, but states that "such numerical differences appear to stem more from cultural power relations rather than innate dimorphism" (p. 201). Recently, Brown as a part of the author team (Savage, Brown, Sakai, & Currie, 2015) changed his initial view that musical capacity is not a sexually dimorphic trait. They analyzed world-wide data on musical performances and found that "music tends to be performed predominantly in groups and by males. The bias toward male performance is true of singing, but even more so of instrumental performance" (p. 3). However, although the authors acknowledge that group cohesion and sexual selection explanations are not mutually exclusive, and that the reasons why music evolved in the past might not necessarily correspond with its current functions, they also chose to attribute patriarchy for causing the sex difference. They stated that "the predominance of male performers in our sample may perhaps be more reasonably explained by widespread patriarchal restrictions on female performance" (p. 5). Sociocultural influences, without doubt, highly impact on the dimension of artistic display; since the feminist movement(s), Western-style society is systematically moving away from the heavily male patriarchal way of thinking and influencing sex and gender roles in cultural behavior (Cook, 1994). On the other hand, lack of opportunities because of cultural influences does not explain, for instance, cross-cultural sex differences in occupational preferences, where females systematically and freely choose different types of jobs than do men (see later discussion). Thus, culture can certainly bias sex differences, but, at the same time, it is not a sufficient explanation for all of them (Geary, 2010).

Several authors have used a different approach and instead tried to weaken the simplistically expected male supremacy in artisticality by showing the undoubted role of women. For example, Boyd (2005) stated, "Differential parental investment—higher male competitiveness, higher female choosiness—can then hint at part of the reason for the preponderance of males over females in art for public display, although women seem always to have participated in song, dance, weaving, and storytelling, especially near the home, as much as or more than men" (pp. 160–161). Similarly, Aiken (2001) stressed that women have always woven beautiful cloth and baskets with elaborate designs, sewn decorated clothing, set beautiful tables, and made themselves beautiful with cosmetics, hair dye, and carefully chosen clothes. Nevertheless, she concluded that "The question of gender specificity still nags, however." Finally, Cross (2007) reminded us that "the manifestation of musicality that is perhaps most culturally widespread, in the form of the use of proto-musical and musical forms of interaction between caregiver and infant, is primarily evidenced by females" (p. 658).

Interestingly, in the same chapter in which Miller (1999) overemphasized artistic display in men, he also pointed to the female side of arts:

> A different version of the cultural courtship model could emphasize sex differences not in display rates, but in display channels that show off particular components of phenotypic quality desired by the opposite sex. For example, one could take the standard evolutionary psychology view that males

pay relatively more attention to youth and physical attractiveness in mate choice than females do (Buss, 1989), to predict that body ornamentation (e.g., cosmetics, jewelry, costly clothes) will show a display profile with a similar age peak, but with more ornamentation worn by females than by males. (p. 86)

In this line, Miller (1999) continued, "there are also strong incentives for females to display cultural creativity during courtship to attract high-quality male mates. But the costs of male sexual harassment probably favoured a female display strategy of targeting desired prospects rather than broadcasting one's fertility and attractiveness to all males indiscriminately" (p. 86). He argued that "we would expect much of female 'courtship' to occur after a sexual relationship forms and even after children are produced, with the cultural displays directed specifically at one's partner, and designed to solicit his continued attention and investment" (p. 86). Furthermore, he specified in which area he would expect sex differences: "These arguments suggest a sexually dimorphic motivational system, with equal capacities for cultural production in both sexes, but with males much more prone to publicly broadcast their cultural production and thereby to leave their mark on historical records of culture" (pp. 86–87).

Later, Miller (2001) revisited his previous statements by emphasizing that in socially monogamous species such as humans, both sexes tend to be choosy, and both sexes evolve sexual ornamentation. He wrote,

> a sexual selection theory of art evolution need not imply higher male art-production ability and higher female aesthetic-judgment ability. . . . Although males have produced vastly more public art in agricultural and industrial societies (Miller, 1999), the sexual dimorphism in art output among prehistoric hunter-gatherers may have been smaller. In any case, sexual selection is likely to have produced more dimorphism at the level of artistic motivation than at the level of artistic capacity, given the overlapping perceptual and cognitive abilities required to produce and to appreciate art . . . (p. 23)

More recently, he evaluated the role of artistic displays in the male-compete/female-choose debate and stressed the necessity of more sophisticated and demanding evolutionary models to study mutual-mate-choice systems (Miller, 2013). Indeed, this wave of counterreactions against the exaggeration of intersexual female choice and intrasexual male competition has been elaborated by Stewart-Williams and Thomas (2013), who generated awareness about the improvement of methodological and theoretical complexity of sexual selection models applied to humans.

The recently growing empirical literature has been nevertheless influenced by the early simplified views about sexual selection. For example, Miller's idea was tested by examining only the influence of a male artist on females, thus omitting women from the productive part and men from the appreciative part and reinforcing a one-sided view of how sexual selection operates (e.g., Guéguen, Meineri, & Fischer-Lokou, 2013). Other empirical examinations included both male and female artists, but they investigated whether artisticality leads to an increased quantity of sexual partners (e.g., Beaussart, Kaufman, & Kaufman, 2012; Clegg, Nettle, & Miell, 2011). Numbers of sexual partners were thus simplistically equaled to reproductive success; although being a questionable measure in men due to biased self-reporting and a very low likelihood of conception through one copulation (Wilcox, Dunson, Weinberg, Trussell, & Baird, 2001), this is a highly inappropriate measure of female success because of limits introduced by gestation and lactation. A high number of sexual partners does not signal increased female reproductive success because women typically aim more for high-quality partners, rather than for high number of partners, as Clegg et al. (2011) admit. It is thus not surprising that the results were significant only in case of males, giving somewhat biased support for Miller's theory.

Long before this debate, Darwin (1871) first connected aesthetics and music with sexual selection in humans. Although aware of sex differences in animals, he did not imply that we should find more musical and artistic capacity in men than in women. By his own words "it appears probable that the progenitors of man, either the males or females or both sexes, before acquiring the power of expressing their mutual love in articulate language, endeavoured to charm each other with musical notes and rhythm" (p. 246). In fact, he further stressed the female display by stating that "we have no means of judging whether the habit of singing was first acquired by our male or female ancestors. Women are generally thought to possess sweeter voices than men, and as far as this serves as any guide, we may infer that they first acquired musical powers in order to attract the other sex" (p. 337).

It is thus worth mentioning that the role of women in artisticality has not been completely overlooked. One of the few exceptions is Duarte (2014), who proposed that artistic manifestations had a survival advantage. He suggested that the fitness advantages to ancient humans of using shells and red ochre, in terms of providing supplies of docosahexaenoic acid (DHA), possibly iron, and other essential nutrients for brain development and reproductive health coming from seafood, might have selected for artistic and symbolic expression and thereby led to social cohesion. When Duarte (2014) recognized that the elaborated deposits of shells with processed red ochre indicated that "the individuals involved spent substantial time working in their caves to process these materials and decorate their walls and their own bodies" (p. 563), he wrote, "A further speculation, for which no evidence is available as yet, is that some of these early artists might have been women in advanced pregnancy stages, with reduced mobility and agility to gather food outside the cave. Indeed, it is women and their babies who benefit the most from dietary supplements in DHA, omega 3, iodine, and iron" (p. 563). In support of this, Snow (2013) has shown evidence that the majority of prehistoric cave hand stencils were in fact made by women.

We know of only three fully developed evolutionary accounts for artistic propensities that focus mostly on females. These theories were not mere reactions to Miller's early contribution and were mostly articulated by women (for the role of women researchers in evolutionary theories concerning female adaptive issues, see Fernandez, 2013). The first one, developed by Dissanayake (1988, 1992, 2008), is based on developmental and cross-cultural evidence and suggests that artification, which underlies all artistic manifestations, is the behavioral tendency for "making especial," for transforming ordinary experience, objects, movements, sounds, surroundings into extraordinary ones. Her adaptationist theory is divided into artistic origins, motivations, and manifestations. She proposed that proto-aesthetic tendencies originated from the ritualization of mother–infant interactions, such as exaggeration, repetition, and delayed expectancy during the parent–infant communication. The motivations of ancestral humans to engage in artistic manifestations primarily stemmed from motivations to reduce basic tensions, in particular those stemming from uncertainty of socioecological circumstances. In keeping with this line of thinking, she interprets artistic manifestations as an essential part of ceremonies and rituals, which "create and reinforce emotionally satisfying and reassuring feelings of belonging to a group" (Dissanayake, 2008, p. 22). Although Dissanayake stressed the role of females in the origins of the artification processes by maternal interactive care and group ritual participation, she did not emphasize or predict any sex differences in artisticality.

Another way to conceptualize the evolution of artisticality was offered by Power (1999), who proposed that art, especially visual art and dance, started off as body ornamentation. In particular, menstruating females were controlled, ornamented, and displayed by their female coalitions to attract and manipulate attention, resources, and care from males. The males, who presumably assumed that the displaying females would be soon receptive to courtship, would give them valuable gifts and other honest signals of commitment and compete for access to them. She predicts that in the ancestral times "Whenever a coalition member menstruated, the whole coalition joined in advertising this valuable signal as widely as possible to recruit available male energy to the coalition" (p. 98). "Between female coalitions, a competitive dynamic is expected as they strive to attract available male muscle power. This should drive an evolutionary 'arms race' of increasingly elaborate 'sham' menstrual advertising [mimicking of true menstruation signal], resulting in ritualistic amplification of displays. This could involve use of red pigment to amplify and broadcast the menstrual signal, with multimedia effects of movement, song and dance" (p. 99). In contrast to Miller (1999), Power (1999) would predict public artistic displays being made mostly by coalitions of women, and she presents supporting ethnographic studies of rituals in sub-Saharan Africa. Despite stressing female coalitional competition, she did not predict further sex differences in artisticality.

Finally, Coe (2003) also suggested that, cross-culturally, visual art has been more of a female than a male tradition. In her view, art started as family marks (e.g., patterns of body paintings, tattoos) through which ancient ancestresses influenced their descendants to be more cooperative with each other. This cooperation was influenced by the use of visual tagging, which may have been a specific tattoo, body painting, or hairstyle to identify maternal relatives, ancestors, and co-descendants. She presented ethnographic material and fieldwork from many cultures to show how the visual arts transmit traditions within kin groups, especially from mothers to children, and encourage cooperation among those identified as co-descendants of a common ancestress. In contrast to uncertainty of paternity (i.e., fathers not having absolute knowledge of their biological relatedness to their children), certainty of maternity allowed the framework of kin selection (i.e., investing in own relatives) to explain the observed female prevalence in visual art.

As outlined earlier, in addition to these three theories, most of the male authors seem to have found an absence of scientific evidence about sex differences in artisticality or based their conclusions on anecdotal data. Nevertheless, since even the presumed absence of evidence is not an evidence of absence, we turn to the existing empirical findings on sex differences in artisticality stemming from diverse sources.

Empirical Evidence for Sex Differences in Artisticality

From the previous section, it seems that a considerable number of evolutionary accounts of artisticality expect either no sex differences or a male bias in artistic tendencies. In contrast, we present a brief overview of empirical evidence pertaining to the potential sex differences in artistic propensities. In order to find a general pattern based on the results of various studies, we rely on meta-analyses and comprehensive overviews across human populations, ages, and historical periods that are aimed at artisticality in general, ranging from its prerequisites (e.g., perceptual sensitivity, fine motor skills, and creativity) to the social recognition of production, including aesthetics and topics indirectly associated with artistic propensities.

Ellis et al. (2008) conducted an extensive meta-analysis summarizing the published literature on sex differences and similarities about every aspect of humans and other species. They covered more than 18,000 studies and more than a century of research. A considerable part of the investigations they examined focus not only on young adult populations, but also on children, adolescents, and elderly adults. Importantly, many studies were conducted in different locations within North America, and there is also cross-cultural and cross-ethnic evidence from Europe, Asia, Oceania, and Latin America, which gives their conclusions a broader representative spectrum. In Tables 39.1 and 39.2, we present an overview of all art-related traits, divided into those that showed male predominance, female predominance, or no sex difference.

As shown in Tables 39.1 and 39.2, both sexes are artistic; however, women are generally more prone

to artisticality. This claim is supported by other studies on various ages that are not included in Ellis et al. (2008). One such study was aimed at education (Lightbody, Siann, Stocks, & Walsh, 1996) and surveyed 1,068 secondary school pupils about their enjoyment of school subjects. Compared to boys, girls reported that they liked drama and music, whereas boys reported that they liked crafts and design technology.

Concerning young adults, Varella et al. (Varella, Ferreira, Cosentino, Ottoni, & Bussab, 2010) surveyed 202 women and 179 men across different undergraduate studies from two universities in São Paulo, Brazil. Women reported that they liked singing, appreciated music, and considered music more important in their lives than did men, whereas men liked playing musical instruments more than did women. They were then asked to listen to one of three unfamiliar instrumental tunes and rate how much they liked the tunes. Women rated all the tunes as more "inspiring" and that they liked the tunes more in general than did men. Varella et al. (Varella, Ferreira, & Bussab, 2011) further analyzed sex differences based on real-life outcomes of young adult applicants for admission exams to university art education programs at four Brazilian universities between 1980 and 2010. They compiled information from more than 71,000 applicants. Irrespective of the historical period, they found an overwhelming female prevalence in the majority of arts courses: dance, theater arts, plastic arts, visual arts, and art and technology. Men, on the other hand, applied more often for most music courses, such as playing instruments, composing, conducting, and teaching, although the singing specialization was dominated by women. Thus, women show higher appreciation and motivation for professional artistic production than do men in most artistic modalities, without any significant change over the course of 30 years.

In a similar line, Holahan, Sears, and Cronbach (1995) analyzed the famous Terman longitudinal study of intellectually gifted individuals, which started in 1922 when the participants were 11 years old and finished in 1986 when they were 75 years old. In 1977, when the group was 67 years old, women reported higher participation than men in all activities relating to artisticality, such as listening to recorded music; going to concerts, plays, lectures, museums; playing a musical instrument; playing or singing within a musical group; and participating in creative writing, painting, sculpture, and dramatics.

Table 39.1. Selection of meta-analytical conclusions related to the prerequisites for artistic appreciation and production divided according to their sex-specificity.

	Precursors for artistic appreciation	Precursors for artistic production
Art-related traits more salient in men/boys	1. Faster and more accurate identification of various features of the Rorschach (or inkblot) (p. 227) 2. Stronger preference for complex visual stimuli (p. 413) 3. Boys spend more time looking at inanimate objects than at human faces (p. 414)	1. Higher performance on the ability to rhythmically tap one's fingers in a particular sequence and speed (p. 238) 2. School-aged boys more creative than girls (p. 302) 3. Dream in the third person, as though a story is being told (p. 343) 4. Preference for tasks and games that involve greater amounts of skill relative to mere chance in affecting outcome (p. 417)
Art-related traits more salient in women/girls	1. Greater auditory acuity (p. 219) 2. Higher pitch discrimination and pure tone detection (p. 220) 3. Higher tactile sensitivity (p. 222) 4. Higher sensitivity to tastes (p. 223) 5. Higher sensitivity to most odors (p. 223) 6. Better odor discrimination, identification (p. 224) 7. Faster, more accurate, and better at discriminating subtle differences in colors (p. 225) 8. Higher susceptibility to emotional contagion in gatherings (p. 249) 9. Higher inclination to exhibit facial expressions in response to emotion-provoking stimuli (p. 275) and to surprise-provoking stimuli (p. 276) 10. Postpubertal females recall more dreams (p. 341) 11. Dreaming more about clothing (p. 342) 12. Higher frequency of fantasizing (p. 343) 13. Usage of aesthetic rather than functional terms as criteria to assess the adequacy of their bodies (p. 353) 14. Higher ratings to their reading abilities (p. 358) 15. More likely to assert that they have a favorite color (p. 410) 16. Spending more time looking at faces of adult humans than at objects (p. 414) 17. Greater interest in dreams (p. 416)	1. Faster and more accurate on tests of fine motor skills (p. 238)
Art-related traits without sex difference	1. Habituation to visual stimuli in general (p. 413) 2. Music-related knowledge (p. 328)	1. Preferences for skilled manual labor occupations in adolescents (p. 474)

The division by sex is based on vote-counting of studies compiled by Ellis et al. (2008). For example, if more particular studies showed a sex difference in favor of women than in favor of men, it is reported as a characteristic/ability more typical of women.

Using a structural model, McManus and Furnham (2006) investigated the influences of education, personality, and demographic factors, including age and sex. They found sex had no relationship to aesthetic activity and neither did attitude. Nevertheless, women reported higher rates of attending classical music concerts/opera, reading novels, reading poetry, going to classical or modern ballet/dance, and going dancing, and they had an overall higher aesthetic activity score. There was

Table 39.2. Selection of meta-analytical conclusions related to artistic appreciation and production divided according to their sex-specificity.

	Art appreciation	Art production
Art-linked traits more salient in men/boys	1. Stronger preference for adventure (and away-from-home) stories (p. 456)	1. Self-assessed musical ability (p. 358) 2. Preferring musical instruments that are larger, louder, and with lower-pitched tones from childhood on (p. 446) 3. Telling more dirty jokes (p. 674) 4. Engagement in occupations of artisan or skilled craftsperson (p. 791) 5. Writing and producing of plays, television programs, and the like (p. 795) 6. Considered among the "great musicians" (p. 816) 7. Most or all shamans in 40 cultures were males, whereas most or all shamans in only seven cultures were females (p. 803)
Art-linked traits more salient in women/girls	1. Higher interest in art and the humanities as subjects of study (p. 419) 2. Preference of "highbrow" tastes in aesthetics and culture (p. 429) 3. Greater interest in aesthetic aspects of sports such as social dancing, gymnastics, and ice skating (p. 433) 4. More interest in personal appearance and one's own attractiveness (p. 432) 5. Stronger preferences for clothing fashions (p. 446) 6. Stronger preference for watching movies and television programs overall (p. 446) 7. Stronger preference for music, art, and literature (p. 455) 8. Stronger preference/interest in fictional stories when reading (p. 456) 9. Stronger preference for stories about home life, school, or children (p. 456) 10. Preference for reading mystery and romance material (p. 457) 11. Keener aesthetic sense, the assessment of the beauty and artistic merit of an object or an experience (p. 605)	1. Drawing ability (p. 302) 2. Either more musical ability or there are no sex differences (p. 302) 3. Stronger preference for making crafts (small objects without moving parts that reflect a substantial aesthetic element) and interest in artistic activities (p. 452) 4. Higher preference for dancing, at least during childhood (p. 452) 5. Playing dress-up more (p. 452) 6. More interested in being an actor/actress or entertainer (p. 464), an artist (p. 465), a hairdresser (p. 467), an interior or landscape designer (p. 467), a musician (p. 469), and careers related to creative, aesthetic, and artistic matters (p. 473) 7. Engage more in artistic activities in general (p. 630) 8. Write more toilet stall graffiti specifically on romantic topics (p. 679) 9. Communication through writing more (p. 687) 10. More likely to major or take advanced courses in the fine arts (p. 772) 11. Operate textile sewing machines more (p. 805) 12. Stereotyped as being more artistic (p. 819), more attractive or beautiful (p. 819), more dreamy (p. 825), more imaginative (p. 832), more interested in art (p. 833), and more tactful (p. 876)
Art-linked traits without sex-difference	1. Knowledge surrounding the arts and humanities (p. 328)	1. Preference for humor/cartoons/comedic mass entertainment (p. 447) 2. Writing toilet stall graffiti in general (p. 679) 3. Evaluation of the quality of writing according to the presumed sex of the writer (p. 854)

The division by sex is based on vote-counting of studies compiled by Ellis et al. (2008). For example, if more particular studies showed sex difference in favor of women than in favor of men, it is reported as a characteristic/ability more typical of women.

no sex difference in rates of listening to pop and classical music; attending pop concerts; playing musical instruments; going to museums or art galleries; reading about art in newspapers, magazines, or books; drawing and painting; going to the cinema or theater; and taking part in the theater. Men reported higher rates of anti-art attitudes (e.g., that all kinds of art should be censored), and attitudes about artistic inclusivity (e.g., that sport is an art) were higher than women.

Creativity, a prerequisite for artisticality, was reviewed by Baer and Kaufman (2008), who analyzed sex differences in 75 studies. These studies included various measurement tools and were based in various cultures. They concluded that "if there were to be an overall 'winner' in the number of studies in which one gender outperformed the other, it would be women and girls over men and boys" (p. 28). Likewise, Cheung and Lau (2010) studied 2,476 4th- to 9th-graders. They found that girls excelled over boys in verbal flexibility and drawing creativity. Furthermore, Kaufman, Niu, Sexton, and Cole (2010) examined stories and poems written by 205 students that were then rated by 108 different students. Their results indicate that females wrote poems that were judged to be more creative.

Occupational choice reflects these sex differences. A recent meta-analysis (Su, Rounds, & Armstrong, 2009) including more than 500,000 individuals reported that women showed higher preferences for artistic occupations than did men. Similarly, Ellis, Ratnasingam, and Wheeler (2012) examined occupation preferences according to sex and sexual orientation in approximately 3,000 male and 6,000 female students from colleges and universities in the United States and Canada. They found that women prefer to be actresses, artists, beauticians, dress designers, and novelists more so than did men, whereas men prefer to be comedians, musicians, and wildlife photographers more so than did women. In general, homosexual men and women showed gender-atypical patterns of occupation preferences. That is, gay men were more interested in occupations preferred by straight women and gay women in those preferred by straight men. Contrary to the field of evolution of artisticality, in the field of hobbies and occupation preferences, sex differences toward arts are well-known and systematically replicated (Su et al., 2009). Interestingly, even when jobs, occupations, and the evolution of the arts appear in the same book, the evidence for sex differences found within hobbies and occupations is

not taken into account with regards to the evolution of artistic propensities (Varella, 2014).

Although the reviewed studies are diverse in the age ranges and geographic areas they include and their reliance on large samples, they are mostly focused on modern Western, educated, industrialized, rich, and democratic (WEIRD) societies, which, from a cross-cultural perspective, can be seen as outliers (Henrich, Heine, & Norenzayan, 2010). Despite the rarity of cross-cultural reviews of artistic manifestations, some ethnographers agree that there is a female prominence in the arts (Coe, 2003). In a similar vein, Snow (2013) showed sex differences related to art production in prehistoric humans. In particular, he studied sexual dimorphism of hand stencils found in the Upper Paleolithic (between 35,000 and 15,000 years ago) cave sites of France and Spain. He discovered that the prints are clear enough to allow empirical determination of the sexes of the individuals who made some of them. The results showed that out of 32 hand stencils in eight Upper Paleolithic caves 75% were made by females and only a quarter of all cases were made by men, and, where it could be determined, 10% of them by adults and 15% by subadults. Taken together, these results show that women's prevalence in artisticality might not be only present in modern and Western types of societies. Rather, it seems to be widespread in space and deep in time.

It is important to stress that the sex differences mentioned here are continuous rather than categorical (e.g., Reis & Carothers, 2014). Thus, although in most aspects of aesthetics and artisticality females, on average, outnumber males, there is a considerable overlap between female and male distributions. In addition to a possible publishing bias against null results, statistically speaking, there has been a tendency to underestimate the magnitude of psychological sex differences given the lack of use of multivariate effect sizes (Del Giudice, 2009). On the theoretical level, sex differences in mating psychology have been generally overestimated because of the emphasis placed on distinct parental investments of females and males, overlooking humans' mutual mate-selection criteria (Stewart-Williams & Thomas, 2013). Therefore, it is important to be aware of possible misleading theoretical framing and statistical procedures that hinder an accurate view of the degree of human sexual dimorphism. Among other misunderstandings, finding or stressing any sex difference, although more or less universal, does not justify any inequality of treatment or rights between the sexes (Varella et al., 2013).

To sum up, the empirical evidence we have outlined indicates that, overall, despite similarities and overlapping between the sexes, women prevail in their artisticality and aesthetic propensities including predispositions, sensitivity, talent, interest, behavior, and motivation. Even though this conclusion contradicts some of the reviewed theories, it does not automatically reject them, given that there is great overlap between the theories and the fact that artisticality might have multiple adaptive values. Rather, the reported pattern in artisticality may provide partial support for theories focusing on females and those predicting some degree of sex differences. Thus, any existing or future theory must take into consideration this pattern of higher female artisticality, at least as reviewed here.

Artisticality as a Social Arena for Female Competitive Ornamentation

From the evolutionary point of view, any selective pressure acting differently on females and males may have led to sex differences. It is argued that the majority of secondary sexual traits and mating intelligence originated from sexual selection, although this selective pressure does not explain all sex differences (Cronin, 1991; Geher & Miller, 2008). In a similar vein, sexual selection might be a plausible candidate for the origins of sex differences in artisticality despite that, at face value, it contradicts the males-compete/females-choose paradigm and that it is mainly females who display artisticality.

The traditional and still prevailing view of sexual selection is that males use ornamentation and competition to increase their reproductive success, more than females. Current reasoning points to the evolutionary processes that originated female ornaments and competitive tactics in nonhuman species (Clutton-Brock, 2009; Rubenstein, 2012; Stockley & Bro-Jørgensen, 2011) and also in humans (e.g., Campbell, 2002; Faer, Hendriks, Abed, & Figueredo, 2005; Fisher, 2004, 2015; Fisher, Shaw, Worth, Smith, & Reeve, 2010; Fisher & Fernandez, this volume; Puts, Barndt, Welling, Dawood, & Burriss, 2011; Thornhill & Gangestad, 2008).

Recent evolutionary reviews emphasize the fact that in humans and also in some other mammalian, bird, and fish species, both parents heavily invest in reproduction (Clutton-Brock, 2009; Gangestad & Simpson, 2000; Stockley & Bro-Jørgensen, 2011), although, according to parental investment theory, when restricted to mammalian species, females

always invest more than males (Trivers, 1972). Thus, sexual selection is not solely based on female choice and male competition because the requirements of high biparental care in our species create opportunities for mutual mate choice and contest, which leads females to display and compete and males to choose (for more details on the mutual mate choice model, see Stewart-Williams & Thomas, 2013, and related comments).

Indeed, although not the most important trait in human mating, artisticality seems to be an influential part of mate selection. For example, out of 13 traits for choosing a potential partner, females and males from various cultures ranked "creative and artistic" in sixth and seventh place, respectively (Buss, 1989). Li, Bailey, Kenrick, and Linsenmeier (2002) found that for long-term mate choice, after ensuring the necessities (i.e., intelligence and income favored by women, and physical attractiveness and intelligence favored by men), both sexes prefer creativity in their potential partners. Kaufman, Kozbelt, Silvia, Kaufman, Ramesh, and Feist (2014) showed that both men and women prefer ornamental/aesthetic forms of creativity (e.g., writing music, poetry, or plays; performing in a band, comedy troupe, or play) in a prospective sexual partner than everyday/domestic (e.g., interior and exterior decorating, inventing new recipes, or making useful or decorative objects) and applied/technological forms of creativity (e.g., writing magazine or journal articles or making websites). Men preferred more than women everyday/domestic forms of creativity in their potential partners, whereas women preferred more ornamental/aesthetic forms of creativity in their prospective male partners. The study also showed assortative mating (e.g., likes prefer likes) in both sexes.

Both sexes not only actively choose appropriate mates: they also actively compete among themselves for sexual partners, resources, and territories, although their competition domains might substantially differ (Cashdan, 1998). Sometimes they even use the same traits—meaning that ornaments are armaments (Berglund, Bisazza, & Pilastro, 1996). As reviewed in many chapters in this volume, women often compete because men vary in their ability to protect and provide resources for their partners and offspring. According to Puts (2010), one of the reasons why the sexes compete differently is because ancestral females could not monopolize high-quality men through physical force but could compete to be the most attractive and desirable. In general, men compete for mates more through displays of masculinity, physical contest, and indicators of social status (Buss, 1988; Cashdan, 1998; Puts, 2010), which tend to be part of the mating necessities for women (Buss, 1989; Cronin, 1991; Li et al., 2002). On the other hand, women typically compete for mates mainly through indicators of youth, femininity, and beauty (Cashdan, 1998; Fisher, 2004), which are traits most valued by men (Li et al., 2002; Puts, 2010).

We argue that women's intrasexual competition, especially through self-promotion strategies (Buss, 1988; Fisher, Cox, & Gordon, 2009), is a crucial factor leading to a greater female inclination to artisticality and other aesthetic domains. We suggest that women's self-promotion, in comparison to men's, is more prone to be manifested via aesthetics and artisticality (i.e., ornaments that can be displayed in both phenotypic traits and in behavior and its products), which are both attractants for potential mates and effective social weapons against potential same-sex rivals. Moreover, the ornament should attract opposite-sex individuals and also same-sex allies who might help in competition against other same-sex group members. In other words, artisticality, in a broad sense, might be seen as a part of the female competitive arena for displaying and appreciating extended beauty and attractiveness. Thus, the artistic domain is a field dominated by females at least partly because of their underlying tendency to compete for a better aesthetic appearance (i.e., bodily attractiveness including self-grooming or self-ornamentation), behavioral performance (i.e., dancing, singing, acting), and the final product (i.e., handcrafts, visual and plastic arts).

Self-promotion is one of the strategies of intrasexual competition, along with mate manipulation, competitor derogation, and competitor manipulation, and it goes far beyond direct rivalry with potential rivals; it also can be a part of dominance hierarchies, territorial behavior, and mate-guarding, for example (Buss, 1988; Fisher et al., 2010). Thus, competitive strategies can also assume indirect and subtle forms through ornaments, such as gossiping about the unfashionable way the rival dresses, the horrible combination of colors she wears, the awkwardness of her dancing movements, and her singing out of tune. Moreover, through self-promotion strategies, people try to make the best impression possible on their potential rivals, as well as on actual and potential mates. Thus, attracting mates and repelling rivals are intertwined behaviors in females, and it might be difficult to distinguish between them (Berglund et al., 1996). If we assume that

the social organization of early *Homo* was rather polygynous, we might infer from modern polygynous societies that female–female conflict among female partners of one male is (and was) rather high (Jankowiak, Sudakov, & Wilreker, 2005). We might speculate that in such a social system, self-decorations, such as body paintings or jewelry, and other aesthetic displays, such as house decoration or singing, might have served as weapons against other co-wives and as attractants for the male partner in order to monopolize his sexual attention and material support.

This thinking is in line with social competition theory and, in particular, the ability to elicit positive attention and social rewards, which Gilbert (1997) called Social Attention Holding Power (SAHP). This ability is actually referred to as *social attractiveness*, which is suggested to create affiliative states in the minds of others and elicit their approval, appraisal, support, admiration, acceptance, respect, or desire, which increases one's chances to be chosen as a lover, friend, leader, or ally, for example. Social attractiveness is a specific way for individuals to compete in a nonagonistic way, other than in a direct physical contest. Price (1995) describes it as *prestige competition*, which promotes affiliative behavior from the group, in opposition to *agonist competition*, in which one aims to intimidate. One can gain social attention and prestige through displaying various outstanding high-cost characteristics or talents, such as intelligence, altruism, or artistic competency, that tend to elicit positive reactions. We suggest that this strategy is a basic, indirectly competitive tactic in ancestral and modern women.

It is important to keep in mind that intrasexual and intersexual evolutionary processes do not always lead heterosexual females and males to be rivals of same-sex individuals, and to be impressed only by opposite-sex individuals. Cooperation among individuals of the same sex leads frequently to the development of same-sex coalitions, which can more successfully attract opposite-sex coalitions and/or threaten rival coalitions. On the individual level, we should mention the *idol effect*, which suggests that people usually imitate the appearance and behavior of same-sex persons possessing traits desired by others. Studies have shown that, in addition to family members, boys admire mostly athletes and actors in action movies as role models, whereas girls admire mostly their teachers and female artists, such as popular singers and movie actresses, as role models (e.g., Read, 2011). These models are the targets of imitation because they have proved to possess some extraordinary and desirable characteristics, such as talent, prestige, dominance, and/or physical attractiveness. By copying these models, one may receive similar prestige among same-sex peers and attention from opposite-sex peers. Learning from and mimicking successful individuals can be highly adaptive because it brings advantages for both copiers (in the sense of enhancing their social acceptance and prestige) and models (by having more fans who, through imitation, create free advertisement of the idol, thus increasing his or her fame and prestige; see, e.g., Henrich & Gil-White, 2001).

Next, we highlight the small but growing body of literature related to the production and appreciation of bodily ornamentation, behavioral performance, and artistic production in women, and we make predictions according to our model of competitive ornamentation.

Bodily Ornamentation

Female facial and physical bodily attractiveness is a crucial aspect of human mating (for a review, see Buggio et al., 2012; Weeden & Sabini, 2005). In Western societies, women's physical attractiveness is positively related to their health (Weeden & Sabini, 2005) and predicts their actual reproductive success (Jokela, 2009). A potential partner's physical attractiveness is generally preferred by males more so than by females, and physical attractiveness is also more preferred in potential partners of sons than of daughters (Apostolou, 2008; Buss, 1989). Thus, for these evolutionary reasons, women are prone to spend more time and effort enhancing the aesthetics of their physical appearance than are men (Singh & Randall, 2007).

In the meta-analysis of sex differences previously mentioned, Ellis et al. (2008) presented studies showing that, compared to men, women provide higher ratings of self-assessed physical attractiveness (p. 353), are more likely to use aesthetic rather than functional terms as criteria to assess the adequacy of their bodies (p. 353), want to lose weight (p. 354) and diet more (p. 639), use more cosmetics (p. 732), are believed to be more graceful (p. 830), wear clothes that most people consider more in sexual terms than men's clothing (p. 851), and are more likely to be portrayed in the mass media as physically attractive or sexy than are men (p. 904). Furthermore, women are not only focused on their own physical appearance, they also pay more attention to the appearance of other individuals, particularly other women. For instance, compared to men, women

report being more aware of obesity in others with whom they interact (Ellis et al., 2008, p. 345); women gossip more (p. 686); and they talk more about body figure, clothing style, and hairstyles than do men (p. 690).

Likewise, interactions with other attractive women can directly impact on women's feelings, mood, and behaviors (Fernandez, Muñoz-Reyes, & Dufey, 2014). A brief, nonpersonal contact with an unknown attractive female can have an immediate effect on a woman's mood. After exposure to an attractive potential rival, women report more negative feelings, including higher depressiveness and anger (e.g., Groesz, Levine, & Murnen, 2002). The facts that women undergo nine times more plastic/aesthetic surgical and nonsurgical aesthetic treatments than men (American Society for Aesthetic Plastic Surgery, 2012) and that women suffer more from eating disorders and self-image disorders (Faer et al., 2005) illustrate their preoccupation with their own and others' appearance. Accordingly, Faer et al. (2005) concluded that female intrasexual competition for mates was the driving factor that contributed to female competition for status, general competitiveness, perfectionism, body dissatisfaction, drive for thinness, and both bulimia and anorexia.

By extension, consumption of luxury beauty products, such as expensive clothes or accessories, can serve as a female mate-retention strategy (Wang & Griskevicius, 2014), intrasexual competition strategy (Hudders, DeBacker, Fisher, & Vyncke, 2014), and intersexual attractant, particularly in periods of economic recession (Hill, Rodeheffer, Griskevicius, Durante, & White, 2012). These results apply only to the consumption of attractiveness-enhancing products, not to products not related to attractiveness per se, such as electronics. Furthermore, it seems that women choose more provocative attire when they are motivated by the possibility of sexual involvement (Grammer, Renninger, & Fischer, 2004).

Use of cosmetics and makeup can be considered as another example of self-decorating artisticality, in Western societies particularly in women. It was suggested that the use of makeup is not random; women systematically exaggerate sex dimorphic traits, such as eye proportion and prominence of cheekbones, and they also use makeup to enhance neotenic features, such as lip fullness or skin smoothness (Jones, Russell, & Ward, 2015). Women wearing makeup are consistently rated as more attractive, more healthy, confident, and with greater financial potential than women without makeup (e.g., Nash, Fieldman, Hussey, Lévêque, & Pineau, 2006). By this self-enhancement strategy, women can manipulate the perception of others, which may have advantages in the social lives. Importantly, women can use makeup not only to attract the attention of attractive men, they can also avoid using this tactic when expecting an interaction with an unattractive man (Regan, 2011). Besides the effect of makeup on individuals of the opposite sex, women also use more makeup when expecting an interaction with an attractive woman (Regan, 2011), which suggests that women use self-decorations as a mean of communication with other women, in particularly a potential rival.

Thus, from an evolutionary point of view, female physical attractiveness and the concern with one's own and other's physical appearance seems to be an important factor in attracting potential mates of high quality and beating potential rivals (Fisher, 2004; Puts et al., 2011). Furthermore, women can also use their own body as a canvas and/or a medium for creating an aesthetic and artistic impression, which can communicate to both desired males and rival females.

Ornamented Performance

Interestingly, even beauty contests, such as the Miss America pageant, are concerned not only with the contestant's physical attractiveness per se because the talent competition contributes almost half of the total score. Indeed, it is often considered to be the most important part of the whole competition (Banet-Weiser, 1999). The most popular choices of talent display are vocal and instrumental numbers, whereas the choices that often lead to relative failure are stand-up comedy, ventriloquism, and contemporary dance (Banet-Weiser, 1999). Although directly connected to physical appearance, behavioral display, such as dancing, broadens the ways to attract potential mates and/or discourage potential rivals. Behavior, as the extended phenotype, has a longer outreach into the world than the phenotype alone (Dawkins, 1982). That is, the phenotype is mostly restricted to the body, such as physical attractiveness, symmetry, or color, whereas the extended phenotype refers to the behavior and its product, such as energetic dances or singing. Typical examples of extended phenotypes from nonhuman species are beaver dams and bower birds' ornamented bowers (for an updated review see Dawkins, 2004). In this sense, we stress the continuity of bodily into behavioral artistic ornaments. In other words, the

attractiveness of the body, behavior, and its products are linked with each other through the same social dynamics and underlying evolutionary processes.

It has been suggested that women's search for potential high-quality mates appears in a more pronounced way during the fertile phase of their menstrual cycles (Gildersleeve, Haselton, & Fales, 2014). Also, it has been reported that women during this same fertile phase show more intrasexual competition, particularly subtle forms of competitor derogation (Fisher, 2004). If artisticality is an important component of human mating intelligence (Geher & Kaufman, 2013; Geher & Miller, 2008), especially when used by women during mating display and competition, then we might expect it to be most apparent during the fertile phases of women's menstrual cycle.

The majority of previous studies focusing on possible changes in mating psychology during women's menstrual cycles were targeting changes in women's appreciation of other individuals, in particular of potential partners (Gildersleeve et al., 2014). As far as we know, only one study showed that, during the fertile phase, women prefer creative men over wealthy ones, although this seems to be restricted to a short-term mating context (Haselton & Miller, 2006). Similarly, ovulating (i.e., in the maximally fertile phase) women showed elevated preferences for short-term relationships with men displaying more complex music, although there was no effect of menstrual cycle on preferences for males displaying visual arts (Charlton, 2014, but see Charleton, Filippi, & Fitch, 2012).

However, the influence of fertility on women's artisticality goes far beyond simple appreciation of such traits in other individuals, and thus, we suggest that women also show variation in their artistic production during their cycle. In line with this reasoning, women should also display higher creativity during their fertile phase, which is supported by Krug, Stamm, Pietrowsky, Fehm, and Born, (1994). In this study, ovulating females showed higher scores in several measures of divergent thinking and lower stereotypical hand movements, which are related to less predictive and more innovative moves. Moreover, these changes appeared in normally cycling women but not in the group using hormonal contraceptives. From this perspective, the appreciation and manifestation of creativity seem to be linked to fertility.

Furthermore, we predict that women show a stronger tendency for self-ornamentation and self-grooming during their fertile phase. This proposal is supported by research that demonstrates women dress in a more attractive way when in this maximally fertile phase (Durante, Li, & Haselton, 2008), and they even increase their purchasing of products that are used to enhance their physical appearance (Durante et al., 2010).

Finally, we predict that, during ovulation, women also show more of their own artistic behavior and production, such as singing, dancing, painting, creative writing, and poetry. However, there is not much research directly testing women's artistic displays across their menstrual cycle. It has been shown, for instance, that women's spontaneous dance is evaluated by men as more attractive during the fertile phase than non-fertile phase (Fink, Hugill, & Lange, 2012); and that female lap dancers earn more money from tips during the fertile phase of their menstrual cycle in comparison to other phases (Miller, Tybur, & Jordan, 2007), which is evidence that females' dance displays are perceived as more appealing and more likely to attract mates and extract their resources. Furthermore, Guéguen (2009) found that ovulating women in nightclubs have a higher tendency to accept men's invitations to dance, which indicates a higher interest in interacting with men through dance movements.

Theoretically, we speculate that there is shift in singing due to the menstrual cycle phase, based on previous research on vocal attractiveness. Both productive and appreciative facets of women's vocalization are influenced by the fertile phase of the cycle. Near ovulation, women's voices appear to increase in femininity (Bryant & Haselton, 2009) and attractiveness (Pipitone & Gallup, 2008), and they prefer more masculine male voices (Feinberg et al., 2006). Also, the same parameters that men find attractive in women's voice are used by other women to track the threat of potential competitors (Puts et al., 2011). Collectively, this research exemplifies the double function of vocal display, which is to compete with rivals and attract mates, and is in line with the ornament/armament theory of Berglund, Bisazza, and Pilastro (1996).

Menstrual cycle phase is an important hormonal monthly shift occurring in women, and it certainly influences women's artistic performance. In addition, other hormones closely related to competitive behavior, such as androgens (produced in the adrenal glands of men and women), may affect ornamented performance in a way that motivates women toward prestige competition, as described by Gilbert (1997). For instance, Hassler (1991b) found that creative musical behavior is associated with relatively low testosterone

values in males but high testosterone levels in females, indicating that the main hormone related to aggressiveness and competitiveness boosts female musical performance in particular. Along related lines, Fukui (2001) found that listening to familiar and especially to favorite songs decreased testosterone levels in men, whereas it increased testosterone levels in women. This finding indicates that not only producing but also appreciating musical performance is associated with increased testosterone in women. In a competitive context, it makes sense that both the displayer and appreciator would have a similar physiological basis preparing for competition. Hassler (1992) further showed that an optimal testosterone level for the expression of creative musical behavior is at the bottom of the normal male range and at the top of the normal female range. Hassler (1991a) also reported that male composers attained significantly lower testosterone values than male instrumentalists and male nonmusicians, whereas female composers had significantly higher testosterone values than female instrumentalists and female nonmusicians. In this study, painters of both sexes did not differ from controls in terms of their testosterone levels. It seems that productive and appreciative components of musicality have co-evolved in females and males, in the direction of increasing competitiveness of females and decreasing competitiveness in males.

The increased testosterone influence on artistic performance, found especially in women who are music composers, would influence the content of songs such that they show increased competitiveness. In fact, Fisher and Candea (2012) found a wide array of competitive topics in selected female popular songs, such as reactions to mate poaching, feelings of ownership for mates, attempts to persuade a mate that the rival is not a suitable alternative, and notions of differences in mate value between oneself and a perceived potential rival.

In this line, a study on singing offered an additional convergent evidence on competition among women through self-promotion of musical talents by focusing on face-saving, or non-promotion of one's weakness (Garland & Brown, 1972). Individuals engage in face-saving when they sacrifice even tangible (monetary) rewards to keep a deficiency from public visibility. The question was whether sex and level of expertise of the audience modulate face-saving. Twenty men and 20 women were asked to sing a ballad before an audience of male or female evaluators. Face-saving was measured by an abbreviated singing time in front of the audience; the shorter the time the more the individuals wanted to hide their bad singing from others. They found that face-saving was greater among women than men, and also that it was more pronounced among women facing a female audience. In another experiment of the same study, the authors found that face-saving was greater before an audience believed to be composed of excellent singers (Garland & Brown, 1972). So it seems that women know the competitive consequences of exposing their weak vocal aesthetic performance, in particular to other women. Thus, the need to prevent deficiencies from becoming visible to others is an integral part of female competitive ornamentation of performance.

Artistic Products

After exploring women's competitive ornamentation of their own bodies and of their own behavior as artistic performances, we focus on the artistic product. This includes visual/plastic or the non-performatic modalities of literary arts, which are at the furthest end of the extended phenotype of artisticality because they are spatially separated from the body and from performance.

One of the oldest paleoanthropological findings indicates that the most original *Homo sapiens sapiens* artifacts were handmade for body decoration (e.g., perforated and pigment-stained marine shells with use-wear marks) dating to 70,000–120,000 years ago (d'Errico et al., 2009); in *Homo neanderthalensis*, body ornaments date back at least to 50,000 years ago (Zilhão et al., 2010). Thus, self-decoration and ornamented artifacts have probably been linked for a substantial proportion of time in both *Homo* species. Along with self-decoration, mostly women also ornamented caves with hand stencils, as shown by Snow (2013).

Considering modern human populations, several researchers have reported results that might be best explained by intrasexual competition. For instance, when women were asked to judge paintings by other females, they evaluated them to be significantly worse than when they thought that the same paintings were created by men (Clifford & Hatfield, 1972; Pheterson, Kiesler, & Goldberg, 1971). Interestingly, this sex difference in judgments did not apply for works that were supposedly winning pieces, showing that recognized competence might decrease derogation by other females. This conclusion is supported by Johnson and Gurung's study (2011), in which women assigned rather negative characteristics (e.g., promiscuity) to attractive females who did not show any kind of professional competence (in this case, either academic or athletic). Thus, competition through artistic display might become pronounced under conditions where all females are on a similar proficiency level and where desirable mates are rare. Partial support for this possibility comes from one study where girls in single-sex high schools scored higher on creative writing than did girls in co-ed schools (Mcvay, 2003).

Regarding the effects of ovulation on artistic products, Haselton et al. (Haselton, Mortezaie, Pillsworth, Bleske-Recheck, & Frederick, 2007) found that women in the fertile phase, especially single ones, drew sexier and more revealing clothing on an outline of a feminine figure, as assessed by male and female raters. This finding indicates that the fertile phase might influence not only female appearance as an artistic performance, but also the actual product of artistic behavior. This interpretation is novel because the purpose of the study was to address female intrasexual competition according to menstrual phase. That is, the context of female competition is evident because the drawings were supposed to reflect their choice of dress for a social evening.

In a similar vein, Griskevicius, Cialdini, and Kenrick (2006) explored whether stimuli designed to activate mating motives, such as reading a romantic story, trigger displays of creativity in story writing. They found that men and women seem to have different mate-quality thresholds for displaying creativity. For men, the requirements are relatively low because any cue designed to activate a short- or a long-term mating goal boosted creative story writing. In contrast, for women, the requirements were high because only a cue designed to activate the desire for a high-quality long-term mate, perceived to be trustworthy and committed to the relationship, boosted their creativity in story writing.

Throughout historical periods and cultures, the content of artistic products made by women may suggest under which evolved motivation the production occurred. Chang, Fisher, and Meredith (2012) analyzed Western paintings between 1700 and 1940 in order to explore whether these works reflected issues specific to women's evolutionary history. They found that women tended to paint topics related to their evolved motivations, such as creating and maintaining alliances and family relations using depictions of motherhood, family life, and portraits. More generally, they displayed private life over public life and landscape. The predominance of themes about family and private life is in accordance with the earlier-mentioned findings of long-term romantic motivation boosting female creative display.

The ornamentation of places and interiors also belongs to the realm of female extended artisticality, as pointed out by historical accounts of the handcraft and interior design produced by women (Edwards, 2006). It seems that women from the 18th and 19th centuries at various levels of society took up crafts for the house and customizing house interiors. For Edwards (2006), the improvement and decoration of the home by the occupier seemed to have many similarities with handcrafted artifacts made by women in and for the home throughout the period he reviewed (1750–1900). Both home decorations and handcraft artifacts appeared to reflect aspects of artistic self-expression together with the turning of ordinary products into artifacts with personal associations, aspects of leisure pursuits and the desire to be creative, and the need for economy. There was also often a recognized sense of satisfaction in being able to personalize and customize the home. According to the proposed model of female extended competitive ornamentation, we predict that women would be more willing to aesthetically enhance their private spaces, particularly during the fertile phase and when engaged in long-term relationships. However, at the same time, we predict that they would become more acidic and critical toward other females' interior decorations near ovulation and, similarly, also during long-term relationships in comparison to being single.

Bridges among Different Evolutionary Theories for Artisticality

We argue that because of the higher importance of physical attractiveness and self-grooming for female mate value, women would prevail not only in the aesthetics domain, but in the artistic domain in general. Thus, general aesthetics and physical attractiveness are mainly the female arenas for competition, and sexual selection might be one of the possible ways to explain the female role in the evolution of artisticality. We are aware that our account of the evolution of artisticality does not—and is not aimed to—explain all aspects of its origins and maintenance during human evolution, but we are proposing a heuristic framework to integrate various existing theories based on available empirical evidence.

In general, evolutionary theories about artistic propensities are fairly recent and more speculative and untestable in nature, rather than based on evidence (Loersch & Arbuckle, 2013; Miller,

2000; Nadal, Capó, Munar, Marty, & Cela Conde, 2009). Although empirical studies are beginning to appear, the debate is still theoretical, which often leads to the impression that different evolutionary accounts are incompatible and competing alternatives. In fact, most of the evolutionary approaches to artisticality are not mutually exclusive, and more effort is needed to show how different theories interact with each other, their distinct predictions, and which of their empirical findings are supportive (Fitch, 2006).

Our evolutionary view is aligned with Miller's (1999) argument that females and males use different display channels to emphasize those particular components of their phenotypic quality that are desired by the opposite sex. It is still open to empirical confirmation whether body ornamentation used by females would increase rapidly after puberty and peak at young adulthood, as Miller suggested. We predict that during the peak reproductive age women would most frequently display not only body ornamentation, but also those behaviors emphasizing their body ornamentation, such as dancing or acting, and they would display products developed by females for body and house decoration. Griskevicious et al. (2006) have already shown the importance of long-term mating motivations for boosting female creativity, and more empirical support is needed for Miller's expectation that much of female display of ornamentation would appear after forming a sexual relationship and even after having offspring, with the cultural display directed specifically at the partner and family. However, because females can also get important evolutionary benefits out of short-term sexual strategies (Gangestad & Simpson, 2000), we predict that women would be willing to show a public artistic display, although under more specific internal and external contexts, such as within female coalitions.

This point leads to Power's theory (1999), who suggested that female coalitions would exhibit their artisticality in public, at least for friends and relatives (i.e., familiar people), particularly during menstruation. Contrary to her theory, we expect the increase of artistic production and publicity during the fertile phase rather than during nonfertile phases of the menstrual cycle.

The coalitional context in which female competition and display occur is further related to the theory proposed by Coe (2003), who stressed that artistic behavior displayed among groups of female relatives has played an important cooperative role against other rival groups. Following this line, we predict that mothers and grandmothers would use art as a family marker (such as specific body painting or clothing style) and that their attempts to enhance the mate value of kin (i.e., influencing appearance and aesthetic quality of behavior and the product of behaviors of their children and grandchildren) would be more numerous than that of fathers or grandfathers. Also, we predict that women would be more willing to encourage their children and grandchildren, but also other—particularly female—relatives to develop their artisticality via teaching them or signing them up for art classes. Furthermore, we predict that mothers would be the ones most defending and being fans of their children's aesthetic and artistic expressions. There is also a growing interest in parental influence on mate choice, and the beauty of a male offspring's mate seems to be at the center of parent–offspring conflict (Apostolou, 2008).

Parent–offspring interactions are a central part of Dissanayake's (2008) adaptive model of multimodal ritualized activities strengthening the attachment between mother and infant. Artistic displays dominated by women, such as higher preference for singing (Varella et al., 2010), can be related to lullabies and the "motherese" supporting the mother–infant interaction model, which was also stressed by Cross (2007). Moreover, as Dissanayake (2008) wrote, once mother–infant attachment evolved, it could have exapted to romantic attachment and group affiliation. This would explain the "loverese" way of talking and the infantile behaviors observed between romantic partners (Chang & Garcia, 2010); this could indicate commitment and a parental care disposition, which in turn fosters cohesion of the couple.

Furthermore, our perspective is connected to Dunbar's grooming and gossip theory about music, dance, and language (2012). According to this theory, mutual tactile grooming between a dyad has changed with the growing size and complexity of human society and turned into vocal grooming—such as laughter, singing, or gossip—that expands beyond the touching dyad. As such, vocal grooming is more efficient in regulating complex social relationships, particularly because it can be aimed at a greater number of individuals at the same time. In this sense, the female average supremacy in the aesthetic and artistic domain is closely related to female predominance in the areas of sociability and grooming. Ellis et al. (2008) reported on studies showing that, in comparison to males, females during childhood and adolescence express a greater desire

for popularity and acceptance from others (p. 421); throughout a wide age spectrum, females prefer to maintain interpersonal harmony and cooperation in their social interactions (p. 422) and to form strong interpersonal relationships with others (p. 423). As well, female ungulates, rodents, nonhuman primates, and humans are more likely than males to engage in grooming behavior (p. 647), and women gossip more than men (p. 686). Thus, similar patterns of interaction through social grooming that led to actual levels of sociality and complex communication in females also gave rise to alliances, courtship, and subtle forms of competition through artisticality.

The seeming contradiction between theories focusing on group cohesion on one hand and hypotheses driven by the sexual selection theory on the other can be smoothly surpassed by a new trend in evolutionary theorizing aimed at social selection (Rubenstein, 2012). Lyon and Montgomerie (2012) stated that social selection includes interaction processes that are not related directly to mating, such as both social hierarchy and parent–offspring interactions. Interestingly, in humans, even interactions aimed primarily at mating, such as courtship, are not overtly manifested but rather are covert and ritualized, as in the form of indirect flirting (Gersick & Kurzban, 2014). We propose that artisticality might have evolved, among other possibilities, as an indirect form of female social and sexual competition over mates, status, and/or family success. The overlap between social and sexual competition has direct support in Gilbert's (1997) overlooked concept of SAHP, in which social attraction is connected not only to mating but also to social prestige and status.

Importantly, because it is highly possible that artisticality has had multiple evolutionary functions, both successively and concomitantly, different evolutionary explanations do not need to be mutually exclusive. Thus, results supporting ancestral influences of sexual selection do not need to directly weaken other theories and vice versa. Here, we tried to highlight the possible interconnections between our approach and the closest related theories, stressing similar and dissimilar predictions. Before we are able to discard theories, more empirical evidence is needed to falsify or support the outlined predictions.

Conclusion

At the heart of this chapter, we argue that, from the evolutionary perspective, women's intrasexual competition, especially through self-promotion strategies, is one of the crucial factors leading to a greater female inclination to artistic and other aesthetic domains. In light of the current evidence indicating the scope and importance of female ornamentation and competition through producing and appreciating artistic behaviors and products, we proposed that artisticality can be considered as a female strategy for competing through self-/group promotion on the level of body decorations, behavioral displays, and production of nonbodily artifacts. To support this position, we highlighted the evidence pointing to variations in female artisticality along the menstrual cycle, particularly its boost during the fertile phase, and we also showed evidence for the role of hormonal levels, such as testosterone, in artistic production and appreciation. Furthermore, we accentuated the importance of female artists as role models for other females and the importance of romantic motivations and other aspects influencing both the productive and appreciative subdomains of female artisticality.

This reasoning was partly based on a careful consideration of the existing evidence suggesting a rather higher prevalence of women in the artistic domain in general. We presented available cross-cultural convergent evidence indicating that, overall, although there are some sex similarities and overlaps between females and males, women seem to prevail in artisticality and aesthetic propensities, including sensitivity, talent, interest, behavior, and motivation. This view was supported by evidence from several Paleolithic caves containing art, where most artists were probably women (Snow, 2013). This conclusion is apparently in contradiction to several existing evolutionary theories concerning artisticality, in which the prominent role of females has mostly been overlooked and sexual selection easily dismissed. We discussed this prevailing theoretical presumption, which was based on personal experience and anecdotal evidence arguing for the lack of sex difference in musicality and/or other artistic propensities.

By considering both the existing evolutionary theories of artisticality and available empirical evidence, we stressed our approach for understanding female artisticality as an indirect way to attract and compete for mates and to maintain and promote long-term relationships and families. In our view, all theories have something to gain from an empirically oriented and conciliatory approach, particularly when taking into account aspects of females' extended competitive ornamentation, production,

and appreciation. Our approach is not designed to be the only way to consider sexual selection, nor the only possible evolutionary approach. Instead, we are showing only one possible path of integrating the fragmented theoretical landscape of evolutionary artisticality.

Throughout the chapter, we touched on some of the most prominent misunderstandings about the evolutionary approach to human mind and behavior, and we aimed to ground evolutionary explanations within available evidence from a variety of sources. In the same line, we stressed the importance of clearly setting the realms of artisticality and the implications of considering art as an instinctive tendency, as psychological faculty, and as behavior, and in comparison to artistic objects. We propose that these distinctions are as crucial as distinguishing its individual, social, and evolutionary functions, as well as the importance of realizing the differences between artisticality as an evolved adaptation and as being currently adaptive behavior.

Future Directions

The implications of our approach are highly relevant for future research on the evolution of artistic propensities. More effort should be put into reviewing, organizing, and extracting testable empirical predictions from the evolutionary accounts for artisticality, as well as stressing their similarities and dissimilarities. Furthermore, future studies might consider and explicitly correct misunderstandings about sexual selection and evolutionary psychology in order to promote a more informative and effective debate.

Future studies should test and expand the specific predictions of the proposed model of female extended competitive ornamentation for evolution of artisticality, particularly regarding the nature, quality, and number of women's artistic manifestations throughout the lifespan, from childhood, through puberty and young adulthood, until late adulthood and the postmenopausal period. For instance, given that there might be two reproductive peaks in females, one when they have their own offspring and the other later in life when they have grandchildren (e.g., Hrdy, 2009), we might predict also two peaks in artisticality in women that would follow these reproductive peaks. Moreover, further aspects of romantic and reproductive life, such as being in love, getting married, or getting divorced; one's current level of mate value and attractiveness; feelings of body satisfaction; or the occurrence of extramarital affairs, should be integrated into the model and tested correspondingly.

Concerning sex differences in artisticality, we might predict average higher artistic propensities and manifestations not only in women but, similarly, also in gender-nonconforming men (i.e., feminine men). McManus and Furnham (2006) found that femininity increases some artistic activities and attitudes. Thus, we suggest that there should be a connection between gender nonconformity and sex-specific dimensions of artisticality that might be reflected, for instance, in research on sexual orientation because homosexuals, on average, show higher gender nonconformity than do heterosexuals (Bailey & Zucker, 1995). This has been partly supported by Ellis, Ratnasingam, and Wheeler (2012), who found that male and female homosexuals prefer gender-atypical occupations. Moreover, Bailey and Oberschneider (1997) found that homosexual men tend to engage in some artistic occupations, such as professional dance, at a higher frequency than do heterosexual males.

In this chapter, we touched on sex differences in several layers of the artisticality domain. We encourage future researchers to investigate in detail the proximate factors, such as neurocognitive and developmental aspects related to the artistic domain, that might be studied by the whole array of scientific branches, such as molecular and behavioral genetics; physiology; neuropsychology; cognitive, behavioral, and social sciences; history; ethnography; paleoanthropology; and comparative animal behavior. In agreement with Boyd (2005), to be fully comprehensive on evolutionary grounds, adaptive explanations of artistic propensities need to consider all four types of questions that ethologist Tinbergen proposed: proximate functional mechanisms, developmental processes, adaptive values, and phylogenetic origins (see Hogan, 2014, for a recent expansion). Importantly, more effort needs to be put into comparisons between proximate markers of particular artistic modalities to test whether they are separate adaptations or integrated components of a general artistic mental adaptation. Furthermore, nonadaptationist accounts might go beyond simple identification of preartistic neuropsychological processes co-opted for artisticality by also testing exaptationist hypotheses (see Andrews et al., 2002).

Finally, the male role in artisticality should not be forgotten in future studies. Human males have their artistic specificities and are particularly prone to public display. Through assortative mating men and women of high artistic talent can pass their artisticality to offspring of both sexes, strengthening co-evolution. Male mate preferences and ornamented competition patterns should be integrated with female ones, stressing co-evolutionary processes and connecting parental investments and mutual mate choice models of sexual selection with kin selection and group cohesion models to draw a broader picture of the relevant aspects involved in the evolution of artistic propensities.

To conclude, women's prevalence in artistic production and appreciation has been overlooked so far. This chapter reviews both how it has been neglected and the empirical evidence showing support for its occurrence. One evolutionary explanation is that the female prevalence in art represents women's competitive tendencies toward beauty, aesthetics, and self-promotion. Here, we proposed that artisticality—human cross-cultural artistic propensities—entered female competitive dynamics in human ancestral environments. We put together evidence supporting competitive ornamentation within bodily ornaments, behavioral performance, and artistic products. Moreover, within this framework, we specified predictions for future research and we stressed the overlaps and confluences between the proposed theories of evolution of artistic propensities that emphasize women as crucial agents. This chapter also addresses the co-evolutionary dynamics between females and males as crucial to the evolution of artistic propensities. By doing so, we hope to improve the debate about the role of women and sexual selection on the evolution of artistic propensities by clearing misunderstanding and argumentation biases from the path where the fields should develop.

References

Aiken, N. E. (2001). An evolutionary perspective on the nature of art. *Bulletin of Psychology and the Arts, 2*, 3–7.

American Society for Aesthetic Plastic Surgery. (2012). *Cosmetic surgery national data bank statistics.* Retrieved from http://www.surgery.org/sites/default/files/ASAPS-2012-Stats.pdf

Andersson, M. B. (1994). *Sexual selection.* Princeton, NJ: Princeton University Press.

Andrews, P. W., Gangestad, S. W., & Mattews, D. (2002). Adaptationism: How to carry out an exaptationist program. *Behavioral and Brain Sciences, 25*, 489–553.

Apostolou, M. (2008). Parent-offspring conflict over mating: The case of beauty. *Evolutionary Psychology, 6*, 303–315.

Baer, J., & Kaufman, J. C. (2008). Gender differences in creativity. *Journal of Creative Behavior, 42*, 75–106.

Bailey, J. M., & Oberschneider, M. (1997). Sexual orientation and professional dance. *Archives of Sexual Behavior, 26*(4), 433–444.

Bailey, J. M., & Zucker, K. J. (1995). Childhood sex-typed behavior and sexual orientation: A conceptual analysis and quantitative review. *Developmental Psychology, 31*(1), 43.

Ball, P. (2010). *The music instinct: How music works and why we can't do without it.* New York: Oxford University Press.

Banet-Weiser, S. (1999). *The most beautiful girl in the world: Beauty pageants and national identity.* Berkeley: University of California Press.

Barash, D. P. (2012). *Homo mysterious: Evolutionary puzzles of human nature.* New York: Oxford University Press.

Beaussart, M. L., Kaufman, S. B., & Kaufman, J. C. (2012). Creative activity, personality, mental illness, and short-term mating success. *Journal of Creative Behavior, 46*(3), 151–167.

Berglund, A., Bisazza, A., & Pilastro, A. (1996). Armaments and ornaments: An evolutionary explanation of traits of dual utility. *Biological Journal of the Linnean Society, 58*, 385–399.

Bispham, J. C. (2009). Music's "design features": Musical motivation, musical pulse, and musical pitch. *Musicae Scientiae, 13*(2), 41–61.

Boyd, B. (2005). Evolutionary theories of art. In J. Gottschall & D. S. Wilson (Eds.), *Literature and the human animal: Evolution and the nature of narrative* (pp. 147–176). Evanston, IL: Northwestern University Press.

Boyd, B. (2009). *On the origin of stories: Evolution, cognition, and fiction.* Cambridge, MA: Harvard University Press.

Brown, S. (2000). Evolutionary models of music: From sexual selection to group selection. In T. Tonneau & N. S. Thompson (Eds.), *Perspectives in ethology 13: Behavior, evolution and culture* (pp. 231–281). New York: Plenum.

Bryant, G. A., & Haselton, M. G. (2009). Vocal cues of ovulation in human females. *Biology Letters, 5*, 12–15.

Buggio, L., Vercellini, P., Somigliana, E., Viganò, P., Frattaruolo, M. P., & Fedele, L. (2012). "You are so beautiful": Behind women's attractiveness towards the biology of reproduction: a narrative review. *Gynecological Endocrinology, 28*, 753–757.

Buss, D. M. (1988). The evolution of human intrasexual competition: Tactics of mate attraction. *Journal of Personality and Social Psychology, 54*, 616–628.

Buss, D. M. (1989). Sex differences in human mate selection: Evolutionary hypotheses tested in 37 cultures. *Behavioral and Brain Sciences, 12*, 1–49.

Campbell, A. (2002). *A mind of her own: The evolutionary psychology of women.* New York: Oxford University Press.

Cashdan, E. (1998). Are men more competitive than women? *British Journal of Social Psychology, 37*(Pt 2), 213-229.

Chang, R. S., Fisher, M. L., & Meredith, T. M. (2012). Evolutionary perspectives on what women paint. *Journal of Social, Evolutionary, and Cultural Psychology, 6*, 442–452.

Chang, R. S., & Garcia, J. R. (2010). *Loverese: Bonding through intimate baby talk.* Paper presented at the 4th Annual North Eastern Evolutionary Psychology Society conference, State University of New York, New Paltz.

Charlton, B. D. (2014). Menstrual cycle phase alters women's sexual preferences for composers of more complex music. *Proceedings of the Royal Society B, 281*(1784), 20140403.

Charlton, B. D., Filippi, P., & Fitch, W. T. (2012). Do women prefer more complex music around ovulation? *PloS One, 7*(4), e35626.

Cheung, P. C., & Lau, S. (2010). Gender differences in the creativity of Hong Kong school children: Comparison by using the new electronic Wallach–Kogan Creativity Tests. *Creativity Research Journal, 22*, 194–199.

Clegg, H., Nettle, D., & Miell, D. (2011). Status and mating success amongst visual artists. *Frontiers in Psychology, 2*, 1–4.

Clifford, M. M., & Hatfield, E. (1972). The effect of sex on college admission, work evaluation, and job interviews. *Journal of Experimental Education, 41*, 1–5.

Clutton-Brock, T. (2009). Sexual selection in females. *Animal Behaviour, 77*, 3–11.

Coe, K. (2003). *The ancestress hypothesis: visual art as adaptation.* New Brunswick, NJ: Rutgers University Press.

Cook, R. J. (Ed.). (1994). *Human rights of women: National and international perspectives.* Philadelphia: University of Pennsylvania Press.

Cosmides, L., & Tooby, J. (1992). Cognitive adaptations for social exchange. In J. H. Barkow, L. Cosmides, & J. Tooby (Eds.), *The adapted mind: Evolutionary psychology and the generation of culture* (pp. 163–228). New York and Oxford: Oxford University Press.

Cronin, H. (1991). *The ant and the peacock: Altruism and sexual selection from Darwin to today.* Cambridge, UK: Cambridge University Press.

Cross, I. (2007). Music and cognitive evolution. In R. I. M. Dunbar & L. Barrett (Eds.), *The Oxford handbook of evolutionary psychology* (pp. 649–667). New York: Oxford University Press.

Cross, I. (2009). The nature of music and its evolution. In S. Hallan, I. Cross, & M. Thaut (Eds.), *The Oxford handbook of music psychology* (pp. 3–13). New York: Oxford University Press.

Darwin, C. (1871). *The descent of man and selection in relation to sex.* London: John Murray.

Dawkins, R. (1982). *The extended phenotype.* Oxford: Oxford University Press.

Dawkins, R. (2004). Extended phenotype–but not too extended. A reply to Laland, Turner and Jablonka. *Biology and Philosophy, 19*(3), 377–396.

Del Giudice, M. (2009). On the real magnitude of psychological sex differences. *Evolutionary Psychology, 7*, 264–279.

d'Errico, F., Vanhaeren, M., Barton, N., Bouzouggar, A., Mienis, H., Richter, D., . . . Lozouet, P. (2009). Additional evidence on the use of personal ornaments in the Middle Paleolithic of North Africa. *Proceedings of the National Academy of Sciences USA, 106*, 16051–16056.

Dissanayake, E. (1988). *What is art for?* Seattle: University of Washington Press.

Dissanayake, E. (1992). *Homo aestheticus: Where art comes from and why.* Seattle: University of Washington Press.

Dissanayake, E. (2008). The arts after Darwin: Does art have an origin and adaptive function? In K. Zijilmans & W. van Damm (Eds.), *World art studies: Exploring concepts and approaches* (pp. 241–263). Amsterdam: Valiz.

Dissanayake, E. (2009). The artification hypothesis and its relevance to cognitive science, evolutionary aesthetics, and neuroaesthetics. *Cognitive Semiotics, 9*(5), 136–158.

Duarte, C. M. (2014). Red ochre and shells: clues to human evolution. *Trends in Ecology & Evolution, 29*(10), 560–565.

Dunbar, R. I. M. (2012). On the evolutionary function of song and dance. In N. Bannan (Ed.), *Music, language and human evolution* (pp. 201–214). Oxford: Oxford University Press.

Durante, K. M., Griskevicius, V., Hill, S. E., Perilloux, C., Li, N. P., & Nordqvist, C. (2010). Ovulation, female competition, and product choice: Hormonal influences on consumer behavior. *Journal of Consumer Research, 37*, 921–934.

Durante, K. M., Li, N. P., & Haselton, M. G. (2008). Changes in women's choice of dress across the ovulatory cycle: Naturalistic and laboratory task-based evidence. *Personality and Social Psychology Bulletin, 34*, 1451–1460.

Dutton, D. (2009). *The art instinct*. Oxford: Oxford University Press.

Edwards, C. (2006). "Home is where the art is": Women, handicrafts and home improvements 1750–1900. *Journal of Design History, 19*, 11–21.

Ellis, L., Hershberger, S., Field, E., Wersinger, S., Pellis, S., Geary, D., … Karadi, K. (2008). *Sex differences: Summarizing more than a century of scientific research*. New York: Taylor & Francis.

Ellis, L., Ratnasingam, M., & Wheeler, M. (2012). Gender, sexual orientation, and occupational interests: Evidence of their interrelatedness. *Personality and Individual Differences, 53*, 64–69.

Endler, J. A. (2012). Bowerbirds, art and aesthetics: Are bowerbirds artists and do they have an aesthetic sense?. *Communicative & Integrative Biology, 5*(3), 281–283.

Faer, L. M., Hendriks, A., Abed, R. T., & Figueredo, A. J. (2005). The evolutionary psychology of eating disorders: Female competition for mates or for status? *Psychology and Psychotherapy: Theory, Research and Practice, 78*, 397–417.

Feinberg, D. R., Jones, B. C., Law Smith, M. J., Moore, F. R., DeBruine, L. M., Cornwell, R. E., … Perrett, D. I. (2006). Menstrual cycle, trait estrogen level, and masculinity preferences in the human voice. *Hormones and Behavior, 49*, 215–222.

Fernandez, A. M. (2013). The feminine touch in the shaping of modern evolutionary theory. *Journal of Social, Evolutionary, and Cultural Psychology, 7*(4), 311–331.

Fernandez, A. M., Muñoz-Reyes, J. A., & Dufey, M. (2014). BMI, age, mate value, and intrasexual competition in Chilean women. *Current Psychology, 33*, 435–450.

Fink, B., Hugill, N., & Lange, B. P. (2012). Women's body movements are a potential cue to ovulation. *Personality and Individual Differences, 53*, 759–763.

Fisher, M. L. (2004). Female intrasexual competition decreases female facial attractiveness. *Proceedings of the Royal Society B, 271*, 283–285.

Fisher, M. L. (2015). Women's competition for mates: Experimental findings leading to ethological studies. *Human Ethology Bulletin, 30*(1), 53–70.

Fisher, M. L., & Candea, C. (2012). You ain't woman enough to take my man: Female intrasexual competition as portrayed in songs. *Journal of Social, Evolutionary, and Cultural Psychology, 6*, 480–493.

Fisher, M., Cox, A., & Gordon, F. (2009). Self-promotion versus competitor derogation: The influence of sex and romantic relationship status on intrasexual competition strategy selection. *Journal of Evolutionary Psychology, 7*(4), 287–308.

Fisher, M., Shaw, S., Worth, K., Smith, L., & Reeve, C. (2010). How we view those who derogate: Perceptions of female competitor derogators. *Journal of Social, Evolutionary, and Cultural Psychology, 4*(4), 265–276.

Fitch, W. T. (2006). The biology and evolution of music: A comparative perspective. *Cognition, 100*, 173–215.

Fukui, H. (2001). Music and testosterone. A new hypothesis for the origin and function of music. *Annals of the New York Academy of Sciences, 930*, 448–451.

Gangestad, S. W., & Simpson, J. A. (2000). The evolution of human mating: Trade-offs and strategic pluralism. *Behavioral and Brain Sciences, 23*, 573–578.

Garland, H., & Brown, B. R. (1972). Face-saving as affected by subjects' sex, audiences' sex and audience expertise. *Sociometry*, 280-289.

Geary, D. C. (2010). *Male, female: The evolution of human sex differences*. Washington, American Psychological Association.

Geher, G., & Kaufman, S. B. (2013). *Mating intelligence unleashed*. New York: Oxford University Press.

Geher, G., & Miller, G. (2008). *Mating intelligence: sex, relationships, and the mind's reproductive system*. New York: Lawrence Erlbaum.

Gersick, A., & Kurzban, R. (2014). Covert sexual signaling: Human flirtation and implications for other social species. *Evolutionary Psychology, 12*(3), 549–569.

Gilbert, P. (1997). The evolution of social attractiveness and its role in shame, humiliation, guilt and therapy. *British Journal of Medical Psychology, 70*(2), 113–147.

Gildersleeve, K., Haselton, M. G., & Fales, M. M. (2014). Do women's mate preferences change across the ovulatory cycle? A meta-analytic review. *Psychological Bulletin, 140*(5), 1205–1259.

Glăveanu, V. (2014). The function of ornaments: A cultural psychological exploration. *Culture & Psychology, 20*(1), 82–101.

Grammer, K., Renninger, L., & Fischer, B. (2004). Disco clothing, female sexual motivation, and relationship status: is she dressed to impress? *Journal of Sex Research, 41*, 66–74.

Griskevicius, V., Cialdini, R. B., & Kenrick, D. T. (2006). Peacocks, Picasso, and parental investment: The effects of romantic motives on creativity. *Journal of Personality and Social Psychology, 91*, 63–76.

Groesz, L. M., Levine, M. P., & Murnen, S. K. (2002). The effects of experimental presentation of thin media images on body satisfaction: A meta-analytic review. *International Journal of Eating Disorders, 31*, 1–16.

Guéguen, N. (2009). Menstrual cycle phase and female receptivity to a courtship solicitation: An evaluation in a nightclub. *Evolution and Human Behavior, 30*, 351–355.

Guéguen, N., Meineri, S., & Fischer-Lokou, J. (2013). Men's music ability and attractiveness to women in a real-life courtship context. *Psychology of Music, 42*(4), 545–549.

Haselton, M. G., & Miller, G. F. (2006). Women's fertility across the life cycle increases the short-term attractiveness of creative intelligence. *Human Nature, 17*, 50–73.

Haselton, M. G., Mortezaie, M., Pillsworth, E. G., Bleske-Recheck, A. M., & Frederick, D. A. (2007). Ovulation and human female ornamentation: near ovulation, women dress to impress. *Hormonal Behaviour, 51*, 40–45.

Hassler, M. (1991a). Testosterone and artistic talents. *International Journal of Neuroscience, 56*, 25–38.

Hassler, M. (1991b). Testosterone and musical talent. *Experimental and Clinical Endocrinology, 98*, 89–98.

Hassler, M. (1992). Creative musical behavior and sex hormones: musical talent and spatial ability in the two sexes. *Psychoneuroendocrinology, 17*, 55–70.

Henrich, J., & Gil-White, F. (2001). The evolution of prestige: Freely conferred deference as a mechanism for enhancing the benefits of cultural transmission. *Evolution and Human Behavior 22*, 165–196.

Henrich, J., Heine, S. J., & Norenzayan, A. (2010). The weird-est people in the world? *Behavioral and Brain Sciences*, *33*, 61–135.

Hill, S. E., Rodeheffer, C. D., Griskevicius, V., Durante, K., & White, A. E. (2012). Boosting beauty in an economic decline: mating, spending, and the lipstick effect. *Journal of Personality and Social Psychology*, *103*(2), 275–291.

Hogan, J. A. (2014). A framework for the study of behavior. *Behavioural Processes*, May 22. pii: S0376-6357(14)00123-5. doi: 10.1016/j.beproc.2014.05.003 [Epub ahead of print].

Holahan, C. K., Sears, R. R., & Cronbach, L. J. (1995). *The gifted group in later maturity*. Palo Alto, CA: Stanford University Press.

Honing, H. (2011). *Musical cognition. A science of listening*. New Brunswick, NJ: Transaction Publishers.

Hooper, P. L., & Miller, G. F. (2008). Mutual mate choice can drive costly signaling even under perfect monogamy. *Adaptive Behavior*, *16*, 53–70.

Hoquet, T. (Ed.) (2015). *Current perspectives on sexual selection: What's left after Darwin?* (Vol. 9). New York: Springer.

Hrdy, S. B. (2009). *Mothers and others: The evolutionary origins of mutual understanding*. Cambridge, MA: Harvard University Press.

Hudders, L., De Backer, C., Fisher, M., & Vyncke, P. (2014). The rival wears Prada: Luxury consumption as a female competition strategy. *Evolutionary Psychology*, *12*(3), 570–587.

Huron, D. (2001). Is music an evolutionary adaptation? *Annals of the New York Academy of Sciences*, *930*(1), 43–61.

Huron, D. (2015). Affect induction through musical sounds: An ethological perspective. *Philosophical Transactions of the Royal Society B*, *370*(1664), 122–128.

Jankowiak, W., Sudakov, M., & Wilreker, B. C. (2005). Co-wife conflict and co-operation. *Ethnology*, *44*, 81–98.

Johnson, V., & Gurung, R. A. R. (2011). Defusing the objectification of women by other women: The role of competence. *Sex Roles*, *65*, 177–188.

Jokela, M. (2009). Physical attractiveness and reproductive success in humans: Evidence from the late 20th century United States. *Evolution and Human Behavior*, *30*, 342–350.

Jones, A. L., Russell, R., & Ward, R. (2015). Cosmetics alter biologically-based factors of beauty: Evidence from facial contrast. *Evolutionary Psychology: An International Journal of Evolutionary Approaches to Psychology and Behavior*, *13*(1), 210–229.

Kaufman, J. C., Niu, W., Sexton, J. D., & Cole, J. C. (2010). In the eye of the beholder: differences across ethnicity and gender in evaluating creative work. *Journal of Applied Social Psychology*, *40*, 496–511.

Kaufman, S. B., Kozbelt, A., Silvia, P., Kaufman, J. C., Ramesh, S., & Feist, G. J. (2014). Who finds Bill Gates sexy? Creative mate preferences as a function of cognitive ability, personality, and creative achievement. *Journal of Creative Behavior*, *0*(0), 1–19.

Kleinman, K. (2015). Darwin and Spencer on the origin of music: Is music the food of love? *Progress in Brain Research*, *217*, 3–15.

Kraaijeveld, K., Kraaijeveld-Smit, F. J., & Komdeur, J. (2007). The evolution of mutual ornamentation. *Animal Behaviour*, *74*(4), 657–677.

Krug, R., Stamm, U., Pietrowsky, R., Fehm, H. L., & Born, J. (1994). Effects of menstrual cycle on creativity. *Psychoneuroendocrinology*, *19*, 21–31.

Laland, K. N., & Brown, G. R. (2002). *Sense and nonsense: Evolutionary perspectives on human behaviour*. New York: Oxford University Press.

Li, N. P., Bailey, J. M., Kenrick, D. T., & Linsenmeier, J. A. W. (2002). The necessities and luxuries of mate preferences: Testing the tradeoffs. *Journal of Personality and Social Psychology*, *82*, 947–955.

Lightbody, P., Siann, G., Stocks, R., & Walsh, D. (1996). Motivation and attribution at secondary school: The role of gender. *Educational Studies*, *22*, 13–25.

Loersch, C., & Arbuckle, N. L. (2013). Unraveling the mystery of music: Music as an evolved group process. *Journal of Personality and Social Psychology*, *105*(5), 777–798.

Lyon, B. E., & Montgomerie, R. (2012). Sexual selection is a form of social selection. *Philosophical Transactions of the Royal Society B*, *367*(1600), 2266–2273.

McManus, I. C., & Furnham, A. (2006). Aesthetic activities and aesthetic attitudes: Influences of education, background and personality on interest and involvement in the arts. *British Journal of Psychology*, *97*(4), 555–587.

Mcvay, L. A. (2003). *Single-sex schooling and girls' gender-role identity and creativity* (Unpublished doctoral dissertation). Fordham University, New York.

Miller, G. F. (1999). Sexual selection for cultural displays. In R. Dunbar, C. Knight, & C. Power (Eds.), *The evolution of culture* (pp. 71–91). New Brunswick, NJ: Rutgers University Press.

Miller, G. F. (2000). Evolution of human music through sexual selection. In N. L. Wallin, B. Merker, & S. Brown (Eds.), *The origins of music* (pp. 329–360). Cambridge, MA: MIT Press.

Miller, G. F. (2001). Aesthetic fitness: How sexual selection shaped artistic virtuosity as a fitness indicator and aesthetic preferences as mate choice criteria. *Bulletin of Psychology and the Arts*, *2*, 20–25.

Miller, G. F. (2013). Mutual mate choice models as the red pill in evolutionary psychology: Long delayed, much needed, ideologically challenging, and hard to swallow. *Psychological Inquiry: An International Journal for the Advancement of Psychological Theory*, *24*(3), 207–210.

Miller, G., Tybur, J. M., & Jordan, B. D. (2007). Ovulatory cycle effects on tip earnings by lap dancers: economic evidence for human estrus? *Evolution and Human Behavior*, *28*, 375–381.

Nadal, M., Capó, M. A., Munar, E., Marty, G., & Cela Conde, C. J. (2009). Constraining hypotheses on the evolution of art and aesthetic appreciation. In M. Skov & O. Vartanian (Eds.), *Neuroaesthetics* (pp. 103–129). Amityville, NY: Baywood.

Nash, R., Fieldman, G., Hussey, T., Lévêque, J. L., & Pineau, P. (2006). Cosmetics: They influence more than Caucasian female facial attractiveness. *Journal of Applied Social Psychology*, *36*(2), 493–504.

Parkinson, C., & Wheatley, T. (2015). The repurposed social brain. *Trends in Cognitive Sciences*, *19*(3), 133–141.

Patel, A. D. (2008). *Music, language, and the brain*. New York: Oxford University Press.

Patel, A. D. (2010). Music, biological evolution, and the brain. In M. Bailar (Ed.), *Emerging disciplines* (pp. 91–144). Houston, TX: Rice University Press.

Pheterson, G. I., Kiesler, S. B., & Goldberg, P. A. (1971). Evaluation of the performance of women as a function of their sex, achievement, and personal history. *Journal of Personality and Social Psychology*, *19*, 114–118.

Pinker, S. (1999). *How the mind works*. New York: Penguin Books.

Pipitone, N. R., & Gallup, G. G. Jr. (2008). Women's voice attractiveness varies across the menstrual cycle. *Evolution and Human Behavior*, *29*, 268–274.

Power, C. (1999). "Beauty magic": The origins of art. In R. Dunbar, C. Knight, & C. Power (Eds.), *The evolution of culture* (pp. 92–112). New Brunswick, NJ: Rutgers University Press.

Price, J. (1995). Agonistic versus prestige competition: A possible basis for a distinction between the agonic and hedonic modes. *Across-Species Comparisons and Psychiatry Newsletter, 8*(9), 6–12.

Puts, D. A. (2010). Beauty and the beast: Mechanisms of sexual selection in humans. *Evolution and Human Behavior, 31*(3), 157–175.

Puts, D. A., Barndt, J. L., Welling, L. L. M., Dawood, K., & Burriss, R. P. (2011). Intrasexual competition among women: Vocal femininity affects perceptions of attractiveness and flirtatiousness. *Personality and Individual Differences, 50,* 111–115.

Ramachandran, V. S., & Hirstein, W. (1999). The science of art: A neurological theory of aesthetic experience. *Journal of Consciousness Studies, 6,* 15–51.

Read, B. (2011). Britney, Beyoncé, and me: Primary school girls' role models and constructions of the "popular" girl. *Journal of Gender and Education, 23,* 1–13.

Regan, P. C. (2011). Cinderella revisited: Women's appearance modification as a function of target audience sex and attractiveness. *Social Behavior and Personality: An International Journal, 39*(4), 563–576.

Reis, H. T., & Carothers, B. J. (2014). Black and white or shades of gray: Are gender differences categorical or dimensional? *Current Directions in Psychological Science, 23*(1), 19–26.

Rubenstein, D. R. (2012). Sexual and social competition: Broadening perspectives by defining female roles. *Philosophical Transactions of the Royal Society B, 367,* 2248–2252.

Savage, P. E., Brown, S., Sakai, E., & Currie, T. E. (2015). Statistical universals reveal the structures and functions of human music. *Proceedings of the National Academy of Sciences USA,* June 29. doi: 10.1073/pnas.1414495112 [Epub ahead of print].

Scalise-Sugiyama, M. (1996). On the origins of narrative: Storyteller bias as a fitness-enhancing strategy. *Human Nature, 7,* 403–425.

Singh, D., & Randall, P. K. (2007). Beauty is in the eye of the plastic surgeon: Waist-hip ratio (WHR) and women's attractiveness. *Personality and Individual Differences, 43,* 329–340.

Snow, D. R. (2013). Sexual dimorphism in European upper Paleolithic cave art. *American Antiquity, 78*(4), 746–761.

Snowdon, C. T., Zimmermann, E., & Altenmüller, E. (2015). Music evolution and neuroscience. *Progress in Brain Research, 217,* 17–34.

Souza, R. (2004). Is art an adaptation? Prospects for an evolutionary perspective on aesthetic emotions. *Journal of Aesthetics and Art Criticism, 62,* 109–118.

Stewart-Williams, S., & Thomas, A. G. (2013). The ape that thought it was a peacock: Does evolutionary psychology exaggerate human sex differences? *Psychological Inquiry, 24,* 137–168.

Stockley, P., & Bro-Jørgensen, J. (2011). Female competition and its evolutionary consequences in mammals. *Biological Reviews, 86,* 341–366.

Su, R., Rounds, J., & Armstrong, P. I. (2009). Men and things, women and people: A meta-analysis of sex differences in interests. *Psychological Bulletin, 135*(6), 859.

Taylor, H. (2013). Connecting interdisciplinary dots: Songbirds, "white rats" and human exceptionalism. *Social Science Information, 52,* 287–306.

Thornhill, R., & Gangestad, S. W. (2008). *The evolutionary biology of human female sexuality.* New York: Oxford University Press.

Tooby, J., & Cosmides, L. (2001). Does beauty build adapted minds? Toward an evolutionary theory of aesthetics, fiction and the arts. *SubStance, 30,* 6–27.

Trivers, R. L. (1972). Parental investment and sexual selection. In B. Campbell (Ed.), *Sexual selection and the descent of man* (pp. 136–179). Chicago: Aldine Atherton.

Varella, M. A. C. (2014). The human evolution and the nature of societies. Book review. *Human Ethology Bulletin, 29*(4), 38–43.

Varella, M. A. C., Ferreira, J. H. B. P., & Bussab, V. S. R. (2011). *Sex differences in motivation for music and arts careers in Brazil: evolutionary implications.* Paper presented at the 3rd Summer Institute of the International Society for Human Ethology, Prague, Czech Republic. Abstract retrieved from http://media.anthro.univie.ac.at/ishe_conferences/index.php/isi/isi_2011/paper/viewPaper/77

Varella, M. A. C., Ferreira, J. H. B. P., Cosentino, L. A. M., Ottoni, E., & Bussab, V. S. R. (2010). Sex differences in aspects of musicality in a Brazilian sample: Adaptive hypotheses. *Cognition & Musical Arts, 4,* 10–16.

Varella, M. A. C., Ferreira, J. H. B. P., & Souza, A. A. L. (2011). Reply: Approaches, concepts, universalities and sexual selection on the evolution of paleoart appreciation. *Rock Art Research, 28,* 179–186.

Varella, M. A. C., Santos, I. B. C., Ferreira, J. H. B. P., & Bussab, V. S. R. (2013). Misunderstandings in applying evolution to human mind and behavior and its causes: a systematic review. *Journal of the Evolutionary Studies Consortium, 5,* 81–107.

Varella, M. A. C., Souza, A. A. L., & Ferreira, J. H. B. P. (2011). Evolutionary aesthetics and sexual selection in the evolution of rock art aesthetics. *Rock Art Research, 28,* 153–163.

Varella, M. A. C., Souza, A. A. L., & Ferreira, J. H. B. P. (2012). Considering both proximal and distal explanations for (rock) art production and appreciation as fruitful. *Rock Art Research, 29,* 227–229.

Wang, Y., & Griskevicius, V. (2014). Conspicuous consumption, relationships, and rivals: women's luxury products as signals to other women. *Journal of Consumer Research, 40*(5), 834–854.

Weeden, J., & Sabini, J. (2005). Physical attractiveness and health in Western societies: A review. *Psychological Bulletin, 131,* 635–653.

Wilcox, A. J., Dunson, D. B., Weinberg, C. R., Trussell, J., & Baird, D. D. (2001). Likelihood of conception with a single act of intercourse: Providing benchmark rates for assessment of post-coital contraceptives. *Contraception, 63*(4), 211–215.

Zilhão, J., Angelucci, D. E., Badal-García, E., d'Errico, F., Daniel, F., Dayet, L., . . . Zapata, J. (2010). Symbolic use of marine shells and mineral pigments by Iberian Neanderthals. *Proceedings of the National Academy of Sciences USA, 107,* 1023–1028.

"Playing Like a Girl": Women in Competition in Sport and Physical Activity

Hayley C. Russell, Julia Dutove, *and* Lori Dithurbide

Abstract

This chapter reviews the theoretical and research evidence on women in competition in the context of sport. First, it explores the history of women in competitive sport and physical activity, and then reviews the relevant theories of competition in sport and sex- and gender-based differences in sport. Next, the chapter examines women's experiences in sport from a developmental perspective and reviews women's competition in youth sport, high-performance sport, and nontraditional physical activities. This chapter also examines how women learn about competition, what gender/sex differences do or do not exist in dispositional competitiveness, the behavioral outcomes of competitiveness, and the overall consequences—both positive and negative—of competition in sport on women and girls. The chapter concludes by discussing the current research gaps and future directions in the study of women in competition in the context of sport.

Key Words: competition, women, sport, physical activity, gender, sex, social, biological, theory

"I don't see any point in playing the game if you don't win."

—*Mildred "Babe" Didrikson Zaharias*

It has been suggested that women are underrepresented in business, the arts, and natural sciences because women dislike competition (Comeig, Grau-Gray, Jaramillo-Gutierrez, & Ramirez, 2016; Deaner, 2013). Research contends, however that women with a background in competitive sport are more likely to enter other competitive domains such as corporate business and sciences (Comeig et al., 2016). In fact, a recent research report by the Ernst and Young Women Athletes Business Network and espnW indicates that the majority of female executives have experience in competitive sport (EY & espnW, 2014). Nevertheless, the question of whether women are more or less competitive

than men in sport remains a point of debate in the academic literature.

The term "sport" is almost synonymous with competition (Grindstaff & West, 2006). Yet from a historical perspective, the goals of sport participation for males and females have been very different. Typically, boys were encouraged to participate in sport to reinforce dominant masculine norms, including assertiveness, achievement orientation, and competition. Girls, on the other hand, were often discouraged from participating in sport because it challenged dominant feminine norms (Coakley, 1994). The very values that were being encouraged in boys were being discouraged in girls.

Over time, the meaning of competitiveness in sport changed for women to the point that today men and women look more similar than different on the field of play (Frick, 2011). Nonetheless, our conversations and even the academic literature continue to focus on sex-based (e.g., biological differences between males and females) or gender-based (e.g., socially constructed differences between males and females; Unger 1979) influences that mark differences in competition. For example, in her book *Sisterhood in Sports: How Female Athletes Collaborate and Compete*, psychologist Joan Steidinger (2014) argues that there are sex-based differences in sport whereby women prefer cooperation over competition, because cooperation serves the larger purpose of maintaining long-term relationships. Critics of this book, however, suggest that the relationship between sex and competition, and gender and competition, is not so simple. Wade and Stabb (2015) argue Steidinger's perspective on women in competitive sport is reductionist and largely ignores the influence of socialization, power structures, and gender roles in women's lives. Such a reductionist perspective serves to reinforce gender stereotypes in sport, while failing to acknowledge the preponderance of evidence that men and women are more alike than different when it comes to competitiveness in sport (Kilpatrick, Hebert, & Bartholomew, 2005; Warner & Dixon, 2013).

Despite this recognition of similarity between men and women in sport, gender/sex inequities continue to persist. For example, sport remains a largely male-dominated domain with men occupying a disproportionate number of positions of power in sport, such as athletic directors, head coaches, and owners (Acosta & Carpenter, 2014; Lapchick, 2013; LaVoi, 2015). Sport is a domain in which the masculine worldview is normative and often preferable; masculine characteristics are highly valued and rewarded. In these and even more subtle ways, women are reminded that they are considered to be less well suited for sport (Messner, 1998).

Interestingly, attempts to address the gender/sex inequities in sport have focused largely on efforts to "fix the women" (Shaw & Frisby, 2006, p. 487). According to Shaw and Frisby (2006), much less effort has been directed at addressing structural problems in sport. The "fix the women" approach reinforces the notion that the problem resides in women; if women could just be more like men, they could be more successful in sport. This notion, of course, ignores individual differences (i.e., makes assumptions about *all* men and *all* women) as well as the full range of motives for, and benefits of,

sport participation. For example, people participate in sport for reasons beyond competition, such as enjoyment, socializing, and self-improvement (Warner & Dixon, 2013).

The purpose of this chapter is to review the theoretical and research evidence on women in competition in the context of sport. We begin by exploring the history of women in competitive sport and physical activity, and then review the relevant theories of competition in sport and sex- and gender-based differences in sport. Next we explore women's experiences in sport from a developmental perspective and review competition in youth sport, high-performance sport, and women in nontraditional physical activity contexts (e.g., CrossFit, marathon/ultra running). Within these sport contexts, we examine how women learn about competition, what gender/sex differences do or do not exist in dispositional competitiveness and the behavioral outcomes of competitiveness, women's preferences for competition and competitive behavior, and the overall consequences—both positive and negative—of competition in sport on women and girls.

Historical Context of Women in Sport

In order to understand the current state of women's sport participation, it is important to acknowledge the historical factors that have influenced women's sport participation in the last two centuries. Barriers to women's sport participation throughout history have included social, psychological, and biological factors, which are often not based on evidence. For example, Little League Baseball's director of research Dr. Creighton Hale cited "incontrovertible facts substantiating the physiological and anatomical differences between girls and boys which made it unsafe for girls to play baseball with boys" (Hudson, 1978, p. 19). In part, Hale was referring to an increased risk of bone fractures for girls. The research used to support his claim, however, was based on studies of Japanese cadavers. Ironically, the only recognized difference in skeletal development of boys and girls ages 8 to 12 (the ages of interest to Hale) is that girls' bones are more mature than boys' bones (Hudson, 1978). Myths such as these have been perpetuated in order to limit girls' opportunities to participate in sport. From a social-psychological standpoint, concerns of sport making a women undesirable for marriage, or causing "hysteria," have been perpetuated as a way of discouraging female sport participation (Sage & Eitzen, 2016). Moreover, there was a great deal of fear surrounding women's participation in sport. Having women and girls participating in sport risked disrupting the social order of men in powerful positions in society (Mrozek, 1987).

Throughout history sport has been used as a way to encourage masculinity and define gender roles. As Coakley (2009) notes, the goal of putting boys in sports was historically to "turn these 'overfeminized' boys into assertive, competitive, achievement-oriented men who would be leaders in business, politics, and the military" (Coakley, 2009, p. 73). Women's initial participation in sport had opposing goals because "competition was eliminated or controlled so that physical activity emphasized personal health, the dignity of beauty, and good form" (Coakley, 2009, p. 75).

In order to promote these gender roles within sports, the historical context of men's and women's participation in sport and physical activity differed greatly (Gill & Kamphoff, 2010; Park, 1987). Physical activity of men and boys was considered the norm and was public. Men and boys boasted about sport participation as evidence of their masculinity (Mrozek, 1987). For women, however, prior to the 1970s sport participation was somewhat hidden. Although in the nineteenth century colleges such as Vassar and Wellesley required physical activity in their academic programs, the philosophy of early physical educators followed the classic phrase "a game for every girl and every girl in a game" (National Amateur Athletic Federation, 1930, p. 41). This philosophy advocated "putting athletes first, preventing exploitation, downplaying competition, emphasizing enjoyment and sportsmanship, and promoting activity for all rather than just an elite few" (Gill & Kamphoff, 2010, p. 565). In describing the purpose of competition for women, the National Amateur Athletic Federation noted they aimed to "promote competition that stresses enjoyment of sport and development of good sportsmanship and character rather than those types that emphasize the making and breaking of records and the winning of championships" (Sefton, 1941, p. 13). Furthermore, the National Amateur Athletic Federation reported that "play and joy make good companions, because when a game is pursued for its own sake, with no end in view but the game itself, the element of joy is usually present" (Sefton, 1941, p. 13). These objectives of the governing organization for women's collegiate sport in the United States highlight a clear distinction in competitive objectives for male and female athletes. Male athletes were expected to focus on winning, whereas female athletes were expected to focus on the joy of play instead of competitive outcomes.

The historical structure of family played an important role in sportswomen's experiences during the formative years of women's sports (i.e., mid-nineteenth century to early twentieth century; Hargreaves, 1987). The relationship between men and women during this period was reciprocal, with women taking the role of bearing and raising children and maintaining a household, while men were responsible for the financial well-being of the family. Women were also considered role models for children in terms of morality, obedience, division of labor, and loyalty. Women at this time were viewed as the weaker sex and, as such, participated in leisure activities that required little physical strain or competitiveness, such as croquet. Hargreaves (1987) described women's recreational play at the time by saying it "embodied the characteristics of passivity rather than activity, subordination rather than ascendancy" (p. 133). Women's demeanor during physical activity was also important, as "in all form of exercise for women, a 'proper' demeanor, decency, and modesty were required: the avoidance of over-exertion, bodily display and sensual pleasure was essential" (Hargreaves, 1987, p. 136).

In the early twentieth century, women became increasingly involved in sports such as badminton, skating, and tennis, and they began to exhibit increasing levels of aggression and competitiveness. Men's and women's sport participation became insular, and since men and women never competed against one another their competitiveness was seen as qualitatively different (Hargreaves, 1987). Generally, women's participation in sport during the Victorian era was seen as a threat to the "cult of athleticism," which was "in essence a cult of manliness" (Hargreaves, 1987, p. 62). Participating in sport was seen as competing with men and often resulted in harsh ridicule; therefore it was important for women to maintain "ladylike" behavior both on and off the field (Hargreaves, 1987).

This philosophy of differentiating women's sport participation from men's existed in professional sport as well. For example, The All-American Girls' Professional Baseball League was established in 1943 as an alternative to Major League Baseball, many players from which were fighting in World War II. The league was controlled by a central organization that promoted high moral and social standards. League officials had the authority to sign and trade players among teams as necessary to maintain competitiveness throughout the league. The structure of each team promoted a patriarchal system where men occupied positions of power (i.e., coaches and managers), and women were employed by each team as chaperones to enforce feminine values of the organization including dress, behavior, and social interactions. Philip Wrigley, the founder of the league, insisted on traditional values for the league's players in order the market the league and players as feminine, attractive, and consistent with social norms of women in the 1940s (Fidler, 2006). Similarly, the marketing of early professional women's hockey teams also focused on femininity and differences from male sports as a marketing strategy. Women's hockey in the 1910s and 1920s was promoted as a suitable alternative to many of the unsavory aspects of men's hockey, such as fighting; however, men's hockey continued to be viewed as the "real game" (Holman, 2005).

Despite many advances in women's sports since in the 1970s, including the passing of Title IX in the United States, sport continues to be a gendered institution. Even the study of sport focuses on sex- rather than gender-based differences (Gill & Kamphoff, 2010), highlighting biological differences rather than socially constructed differences between men and women. The remainder of this chapter will focus on contemporary research in women and girls in sport.

Theory and Definitions

In this section we will review the relevant theories and definitions related to competitiveness in sport, as well as sex/gender differences in competition in sport.

Sex and Gender Definitions

For the purposes of this chapter we will use the terms "sex" and "gender" to describe the differences between males and females in competition in sport. Specifically, "sex" refers to biological traits that males and females possess, whereas "gender" refers to socially constructed characteristics and expectations of males and females (Unger, 1979). At points in this chapter we will use the term "sex" intentionally when citing research related to biological differences; however, more often the focus of this chapter will be gender-based similarities or differences in sport.

Competition and Sport Theories and Definitions

Although there are many theories in sport psychology that could be relevant to the understanding of gender differences in competition in sport, in the following section we highlight theories that are the most widely used and supported in sport psychology literature.

Competition. Unlike other chapters in this volume, we approach the study of competition in sport from a more social than biological approach. This is consistent with the seminal and contemporary research in sport psychology, where competition is defined as a social process by which rewards are given based on other-referenced performance (Coakley, 1994; Martens, 1975). Specially, Kohn (1986) notes that competition is a learned social phenomenon, and sport is one social context in which competition is most visible and pervasive (Warner & Dixon, 2013). Competition is discussed in the sport psychology literature in two key ways. First, it is often suggested that competition is a source of intrinsic and extrinsic motivation to participate (or not) in sport (Warner & Dixon, 2013). Second, competition is studied as a predictor of performance relative to others or other behavioral outcomes, such as training volume or commitment (i.e., achievement motivation; Deaner, Masters, Ogles, & LaCaille, 2011; Kohn, 1986).

Franken and Brown (1994) note that there are three key reasons why people like competition: (1) it provides individuals an opportunity to win, (2) it allows people to improve their performance, and (3) it provides a source of motivation. However, these authors also argue that not all people like competition. Gill (1986) suggests that some athletes thrive in competitive settings, are eager to seek out competitions, and give their best performances in competitive settings. Others, however, find competition unpleasant, avoid competition, or "choke" in competitive situations. The reasons for this are unknown; however, put in simple terms, some physical activity participants/athletes are competitive and others are not. The term "competitiveness" is described by Martens (1976) as "a disposition to strive for satisfaction when making comparisons with some standard of excellence in the presence of evaluative others in sport" (p. 326). Generally, competitiveness has its roots in achievement motivation or the propensity to strive for success and take pride in accomplishments.

Competition in sport theory. Martens (1975) described competition in sport as a four-step process—objective competitive situation, subjective competitive situation, response, and consequences.

This competitive process is an essential element of sport. The first stage of this model—objective competitive situation—involves an athlete being placed in a situation where his or her performance will be compared to others or a standard of excellence, with at least one other person present. The second stage of this process is the subjective competitive situation where the athlete appraises the objective competitive situation, which will be influenced by personality factors, including competitiveness. The third phase of this model is the response. Based on the subjective assessment of the competitive situation, the athlete will decide whether to approach or avoid the situation. Finally, the athlete will experience the consequences of the situation, which will involve the evaluation of his or her performance in the given situation.

Achievement motivation theories. Gender differences are often suggested in the subjective competitive situation phase of Marten's (1975) model. In sport psychology, competitiveness, or more specifically how athletes measure their own success, has been assessed in a number of different ways (Hanrahan & Biddle, 2002). Achievement orientation, or how a person defines success, has two major domains—task and ego orientation. An athlete with a high task orientation defines success by self-referenced criteria such as improvement of skills, whereas an athlete with high ego orientation defines success by other-referenced criteria such as outperforming someone else or winning (Nicholls, 1984).

Achievement goals are based on displaying competency. Nicholls (1984) described two distinct goals—task and ego—also known as mastery or performance goals. Task (mastery) goals involve displaying competency through mastering the task, whereas ego (performance) goals focus on displaying competency through comparison to others. These two achievement orientations can determine the outcome or consequences of an achievement task such as sport. Researchers have demonstrated task goal orientation to be more adaptive as compared to ego orientation. This difference is because, regardless of perceived competence, athletes with a task orientation would be expected to have adaptive motivational patterns (i.e., positive emotions, selection of challenging tasks), while those with ego orientation will only be expected to have an adaptive motivational pattern if they have high-perceived competence. Those athletes who are ego-oriented and have low perceived competence would be expected to have a maladaptive motivational pattern (i.e., selection of easier tasks, escape or withdrawal behavior; Gill & Williams, 2008).

In their measurement of achievement orientations, Gill and Deeter (1988) developed the Sport Orientation Questionnaire, which divides achievement domains into three subscales—"desire to reach personal goals (task), win (ego), and general competitiveness or the desire to strive for success in sport achievement situations" (Hanrahan & Biddle, 2002, p. 2). In other scales, however, competitiveness has been considered a part of ego orientation (e.g., Perception of Success Questionnaire; Roberts & Balague, 1989). For the purpose of this chapter we will consider the term "competitiveness" to include an athlete's perception of success in sport as other-referenced and the propensity to strive for success in sport situations.

Gender Differences in Competition in Sport Theories

Theories regarding gender/sex differences in competition in sport suggest men and women view competition differently and as such respond differently. Men are thought to seek out and thrive in competitive situations, whereas women do not like competition and do not perform well in competitive situations (Warner & Dixon, 2013). Researchers, however, suggest this perspective is an oversimplification of the relationship between gender and competition (Tjosvold, Johnson, Johnson, & Sun, 2006; Warner & Dixon, 2013). In sport a variety of theories have been used to explain the relationship between gender and competition.

There are four major theories regarding the gender differences in competition (Frick, 2011). The first theory suggests that gender differences are genetic and have evolved based on the fitness of those individuals who possess competitiveness and associated traits (Deaner, 2006). For example, Deaner (2013) argues that male distance runners outperform female distance runners because of greater motivation for training. Specifically, men have benefited evolutionarily from displaying physical competence, and therefore men have evolved to be more competitive than women. Notably, Deaner describes this difference as a "sex" difference, not a "gender" difference. In the second theory, hormones, strength, risk of injuries, body fat, and response to training are responsible for differences in competitiveness (Cheuvront, Carter, DeRuisseau, & Moffatt, 2005). For example, Hamilton, van

Anders, Cox, and Watson (2009) found that men's levels of testosterone increased significantly during competition and that these testosterone levels were related to outcomes of the competition. Although women's testosterone levels also increased, they did not increase as much as men's and were not related to the outcome. This research suggests a physiological difference in response to competition between men and women, again a sex rather than a gender difference.

The third major theory is a social science approach, which suggests it is the socialization of boys and girls into sport that explains gender differences in competitiveness (Henslin, 1999). Specifically, parents tend to place more value on competition for boys than for girls and therefore provide more experiences at earlier ages for competitive sport (Warner & Dixon, 2013). The final theory is an economic approach, suggesting that differences in competitiveness are a result of opportunities and incentives that differ by gender (Becker, 1993). The overall evidence on the gender gap in competitiveness in sport suggests that the gender gap is narrowing. This narrowing refutes early ideas that gender difference in competitiveness is a biological or psychological predisposition and supports the hypothesis that gender differences in competitiveness are much more a result of sociocultural or economic conditions (Frick, 2011). As Frick (2011) suggested, "the social change and economic incentives are far more important in explaining gender differences in competitiveness than biological characteristics and/or evolved psychological predispositions" (p. 394).

Gender and Sport Appropriateness Theory

Another gender-focused, rather than sex-focused, competition theory centers around appropriate sports for men and women. Metheny (1965) proposed her theory of socially accepted sports for women, which has since been adapted and challenged by Kane (1995). In Metheny's work, she described certain sports as more or less socially acceptable for female athletes. "Masculine sports" were those that included aspects such as body contact (e.g., hockey), face-to-face competition (e.g., American football), and projecting the body through space (e.g., track and field jumping events). Conversely, acceptable sports for women included those that focused on feminine characteristics such as beauty and poise (e.g., dance, figure skating). Based on Metheny's theory, it was not that men and women were more or less competitive than one another but rather that

it was more socially acceptable for men to compete through direct body contact, while women competed through demonstrations of beauty, graceful movement, and the use of light equipment such as a tennis racket (Mathes, 1978).

Kane (1995) has challenged this idea by arguing that sport exists on a continuum where some women outperform men in a variety of sports. Kane's theory opposed the binary of men's and women's sports and the biological reductionism that is inherent in Metheny's (1965) theory, instead contending that when we make comparisons in this way we are comparing the average man against the average woman rather than considering the spectrum of individual abilities of both men and women. Sport naturally lends itself to a separation based on sex, as virtually all athletic competition consists of separate events for men and women. In terms of competition in sport, this theory would posit that competition of men and women is not limited by sport but rather that "best performance" is defined by the best *male* performance, and therefore most women are not considered to be as good in sport and by extension are seen as less competitive.

Gender Differences in Competition in Sport

As outlined in the previous sections, there are four major theories as to why and how gender differences exist in competitive sport. From a sport psychology perspective, competitiveness appears to show both similarities and differences between males and females. We begin by exploring the experience of young athletes in youth sport and then move on to adult athletes in high-performance sport as well as athletes in other sport contexts.

Youth Sport

Despite a dramatic increase in girls' participation in sport since Title IX in 1972, there remain differences in the way sport is framed for girls and boys. Title IX is a constitutional amendment passed in the United States in 1972. It mandates that any educational settings receiving federal funding must provide equal opportunities for both male and female students. One of the ways this legislation played out was to greatly increase funding and opportunities for girls to participate in school sports. At the high school level, for example, girls accounted for just 7% of participants in 1971–72 compared to 42% in 2015–16 (NFHS 2015). In this section, we examine how boys and girls are socialized into sport, reasons for participation in competitive sport, intrateam competition, and trends in youth sport.

Historically, boys and girls were socialized differently into sport participation. In the late 1980s and early 1990s girls were not as explicitly praised for physical activity/motor skills as boys, which acted as a subtle discouragement for girls' sport participation (Greendorfer, Lewko, & Rosengren, 1996). What appeared to be a natural preference of boys toward sport and more competitive activity is more likely a socialization process, as girls were not encouraged in the same way as boys to participate in sport. Little to no difference has been found in the development of motor skills between boys and girls, and in fact girls often display fine and gross motor skills earlier than boys (Greendorfer et al., 1996). The lack of biological difference between boys and girls again points to differences in socialization around participation in sport. This socialization process may have shifted somewhat today, as evidenced by increased participation by girls in a wider variety of sports. For example, in 1971 there were 14 sports available for girls at the high school level in the United States, compared to 48 sports in 2001 and 61 in 2015 (NFHS, 2014, 2015), including 1,806 schools offering wrestling for boys and girls and 510 schools offering American football for girls in the 2014–15 school year (NFHS, 2015), both traditionally male-only sports.

Similar trends in socialization are found in physical education classes. In such classes, teachers reported similar expectations of participation for girls and boys (Constantinou, Manson, & Silverman, 2009). Girls reported they liked having boys in class as they felt it increased competitiveness in the class, even though they thought boys were sometimes too competitive. Although some sports were still viewed as "girlish" or "boyish" (Constantinou et al., 2009, p. 91) by students, girls viewed themselves as competitive and were willing to play "boy" sports (e.g., football) as long as they learned how to play the sport.

Parents have strongly held stereotypes about girls' participation in sport. In a study of parental influence on sport participation, Fredricks and Eccles (2005) found both mothers and fathers reported gender-stereotyped beliefs and behaviors about their children's sport participation, and were strong socializing agents for their children in sport. Specifically, parents believed their sons had higher sport abilities and thought sport was more important for their sons than daughters. Additionally, parents provided their sons with more opportunities and more encouragement in sport than they provided their daughters. Similarly, some girls thought that their parents would be concerned about their participation in some sports (e.g., American football) because of a perceived risk of injury (Constantinou et al., 2009).

With respect to motives for participation, many children report participation motives such as wanting to have fun, learning new skills, status and rewards for participation, inherent excitement related to competition, and being part of a team (e.g., Hedstrom & Gould, 2004; Seefeldt, Ewing, & Walk, 1992; Walters, Payne, Schluter, & Thomson, 2015; Weinberg et al., 2000). In a study of Swedish boys and girls competing in running, skipping rope, and dancing, the authors found no significant differences in competitiveness of boys and girls on these tasks (Dreber, von Essen, & Ranehill, 2011). However, a study of youth aged 13 to 18 years old in the United States, New Zealand, and Australia "found that competitive motives and social/energy motives were more important for males than females, whereas motives relating to fun/fitness and teamwork were more important for females than males" (Weinberg et al., 2000, p. 342). It appears that younger children (both boys and girls) may be less motivated by competition, and competition becomes more important, especially for boys, as children move into adolescence, although the research on this is limited.

Partridge and Knapp (2015) found that peer conflict seemed to influence the experience of competition for adolescent girls. Specifically, adolescent female athletes reported conflict often resulted from jealousy based on the sport performance or experience of other athletes (e.g., playing time or status such as a starting position on a team). Competitive anxiety was an outcome of this peer conflict. When peer conflict was present, adolescent female athletes indicated they had more competitive anxiety (i.e., they were concerned teammates would be mad at them if they did not perform well) than when there was an absence of peer conflict on their team. However, this study only examined the experience of adolescent girls, so it is unclear if this is similar to or different than adolescent boys.

Overall, the trends in youth sports indicate that much of the difference between boys' and girls' competitiveness is rooted in gender differences in socialization into sport. In the past five decades we have seen an increase in overall participation of girls in sport, as well as an increase in the number of sports offered for girls in school and community settings, including sports traditionally considered "boy" sports like American football. In the next section, women's participation in high-performance sport will be discussed at length, but it is important to note that there are increasing opportunities for elite and professional sport for women (e.g., the National Women's Hockey League, the first professional ice hockey league to pay female players, started in 2015). Increasing opportunities for high-performance sport fosters role models for young girls, which can serve to further increase interest and competition in sport at the youth level. As more girls participate in sports and, especially, are given opportunities to participate at higher levels, it is possible that the gap in competitiveness between boys and girls will continue to shrink.

Women in Sport

The previous section focused on youth experience in sport. The next sections will focus on the gender differences in adult sport participation, including both high-performance sport and nontraditional sport contexts such as CrossFit.

High-performance sport. High-performance sport broadly describes elite competitive sport, including college, national, international, and professional sport participation. Much of the research on the gender gap in competitiveness has been conducted with high-performance athletes. In this section we review the literature on male and female high-performance athletes' preferences for competition and cooperation, as well as the motivational orientations of these athletes.

There has been some disagreement on the gender-based differences of competitiveness or competition orientation between high-performance male and female athletes. Gill (1988) found that female athletes were more goal-oriented than win-oriented, whereas male athletes displayed the opposite pattern. Reeve, Kobayashi, and Eklund (1994) examined the competitive orientations of male and female athletes' gender (i.e., level of masculinity or femininity, as measured by the Bem Sex-Roles Inventory) and did not find significant differences in competitive orientation due to gender. Duda, Olson, and Templin (1991), however, found that male athletes were significantly more likely to endorse unsportsmanlike play (e.g., cheating, intentionally injurious acts) in order to win, perhaps a demonstration of being more competitive.

Warner and Dixon (2015) examined the gender differences in perceptions of competition and the relationship to experience in sport. Through a quantitative analysis, the authors found that there were both similarities and differences between male and female college athletes in terms of perceptions of competition. When asked whether competition added to or detracted from the sport experience, men overwhelmingly thought it added to the sport experience, whereas most women indicated it detracted from the sport experience. The biggest differences appeared to be in perceptions of internal competition (intragroup), as compared to external competition (intergroup) competition. For women, internal competition seemed to be the most negative aspect of competition, with participants indicating it fostered personal vendettas, especially in zero-sum situations against teammates. Men also responded more positively to external competition than to internal competition; however, they also expressed being less likely to take the internal competition to a "personal level" and saw internal competition as a means of improvement. For both genders, external competition was viewed as more positive and facilitative than internal competition.

When asked where gender differences in competitive preferences originated, male athletes focused on a biological perspective, proposing that differences in testosterone are responsible and that competition comes naturally to men. Conversely, women endorsed both biological and social perspectives; they thought competition came more naturally to men but also acknowledged social influences on women in competition, specifically an expectation for men to be competitive and for women to tend to moderate competitiveness (Warner & Dixon, 2015).

Results of this research by Warner and Dixon (2015) highlight the multidimensional and complex nature of the relationship between competition and gender. Both men and women acknowledged positive and negative elements of the competitive process and differences between perceptions of internal and external competition. Based on these findings, external competition and internal cooperation are preferable dynamics, particularly for female athletes.

When it comes to the behavioral or performance outcomes of competitiveness, Deaner et al. (2011) found that the outcomes of competitiveness appear similar between male and female marathon runners. Specifically, they documented that for both male and female runners, marathon performance (e.g., lifetime best marathon time) was predicted by training volume and competitiveness. Male marathon runners, however, reported significantly higher competitiveness as a motivation for marathon running.

In their examination of gender differences in competitive tennis, Anbarci, Lee, and Ulker (2016) proposed that the most successful male and female tennis players would be those who are highly skilled in competitiveness and in risk management. They explored gender differences in a risk-taking behavior in tennis—line-calling challenges. Line-calling challenges are when a player challenges the call of an umpire. It is considered a risk-taking behavior because if the player is successful the decision can be reversed; however, an unsuccessful player will lose one of his or her limited number of line-call challenges. Andarci and colleagues found no gender differences in the number of line-call challenges by male and female tennis players; however, there were gender differences related to certain situational factors. First, male players' likelihood of challenging a line-call was based on their own ranking, while female players' likelihood of challenging a line-call was based on their opponent's ranking. There was also a significant gender difference in the success of line-call challenges during a tiebreak, with female players being significantly more likely to make a correct challenge and males significantly more likely to make an incorrect challenge. Finally, the likelihood of making an "embarrassing" line-call increased significantly for male players as their opponent's ranking increased; however, this pattern was not observed for female players. The authors suggest that these findings indicate males are more likely to demonstrate competitive behavior or a win-at-all-costs attitude in situations such as tie-breakers where the outcome is important, whereas women are more likely to "accept losing more gracefully" (p. 327), which could also be viewed as women making more correct line-calls in high-pressure situations (i.e., ties) and being less likely to make "embarrassing" line-calls. The authors attribute these differences to gender differences in psychological constructs, with men being higher in confidence and pride and women being higher in risk aversion and shame.

Some gender differences have also been found with respect to competitive anxiety. Competitive anxiety or precompetitive anxiety is anxiety experienced prior to a competition. Both the interpretation (i.e., positive or negative) and intensity (i.e., high or low) of competitive anxiety have been associated with performance in sport (Neil, Wilson, Mellalieu, Hanton, & Taylor, 2012), but with mixed results. For example, in an examination

of tennis players, few gender differences were observed. Specifically, male and female tennis players did not differ on measures of self-confidence or level of competitive anxiety; where they did differ, however, was in the interpretation of competitive anxiety. Male athletes interpreted the anxiety as more facilitative than female athletes (Perry & Williams, 1998). Gender differences in intensity of anxiety symptoms have been found in other studies (e.g., Martens et al., 1990; Thuot, Kavouras, & Kenefick, 1998), with males reporting less intensity of anxiety symptoms than females. Similarly, Wolf, Eys, and Kleinert (2015) examined predictors of anxiety responses prior to a competition. In a sample of 252 collegiate athletes, they found that athletes who were male, had more experience, and were starters had less anxiety intensity and a higher facilitative interpretation of the anxiety, with trait anxiety being the strongest predictor of precompetition anxiety.

Team sport. Not all sports are individual competitions. Many involve teams, and consequently team dynamics in sport has been a popular area of research in the context of sport and physical activity psychology. One of the most-studied group phenomena in sport is cohesion, which has been defined in the sport context as "a dynamic process which is reflected in the tendency for a group to stick together and remain united in the pursuit of its instrumental objectives and/or for the satisfaction of member affective needs" (Carron, Brawley, & Widmeyer, 1998, p. 213). Due to the considerable amount of research examining the relationship between cohesion and sport performance, Carron, Colman, Wheeler and Stevens (2002) conducted a meta-analysis and found an overall moderate to large effect. While individual studies have failed to find any gender differences in team cohesion (Spink, 1990) or moderating effects of gender (e.g., Halbrook, Blom, Hurley, Bell, & Holden, 2012), Carron and colleagues' (2002) meta-analysis found that the association between cohesion and performance is significantly greater in female teams than in male teams.

Spink (1995) also examined whether cohesion could predict intentions to return to sport in elite female ringette athletes. He found that athletes' perceptions of social cohesion were reliable predictors of intention to participate in the same sport the following season. That is, elite female ringette athletes who indicated that they would return for another season were most likely to perceive the social cohesiveness with their team as high; however, it is unclear if this relationship also exists for male athletes.

Other physical activity contexts. Adults, whether former participants in high-performance sport or not, participate in other physical activity that may or may not have competitive motives or competitive achievement motives. Ogles and Masters (2003) have done extensive work examining the motives of marathon runners. In their 2003 study, they found motives that fell into the "competitive achievers" category were by far the least common motives for marathon participation. Motives included social motives, enjoyment motives, and personal goal achievement. This pattern held true for both male and female runners. Men, however, were more likely to endorse competitive motives than were female runners (Ogles & Masters, 2003).

Ziegler (1991), however, in her examination of perceived benefits of marathon running in both competitive and recreational runners, found no significant gender differences in the benefits they saw running having on their lives. Specifically, Ziegler found that males endorsed physical (e.g., increased energy, improved muscle tone) and affective benefits (e.g., decreased anxiety) more often than females, yet variables associated with competition were no more likely endorsed by one gender over the other. Women also reported that running had a more positive impact on their lives, specifically in terms of social perceptions of running as "normal" or "healthy."

CrossFit presents an interesting context for examining gender differences in competition. CrossFit is a fast-growing workout program that involves all participants in completing the same workout of the day (WOD), which focuses on a range of physical fitness outcomes such as strength, endurance, and agility. Partridge, Knapp, and Massengale (2014) examined gender differences in motivational variables in male and female CrossFit participants using Achievement Goal Theory. Specifically, the authors examined how CrossFit participants defined competence (i.e., mastery or performance) and how it is valenced (i.e., approach success or avoid failure). They found the women scored higher on mastery avoidance goal orientation. Women measured competence by an absolute standard or their own ability on the task and are negatively valenced, meaning they are motivated to avoid failure—for example, being motivated to not look incompetent or to avoid the embarrassment of not being able to complete the WOD. Male CrossFit participants, however, scored significantly higher on performance approach goals. These goals are preferable because they have been found to be associated with better performance, self-confidence, and self-concept.

Conclusions

Theoretical and research evidence now suggests that there are more similarities than differences between men and women, and much of the difference that may exist seems to be socially constructed rather than rooted in evolution or biology. Although there are four broad theories explaining the sex/gender differences in competition in sport, based on evolutionary, biological, psychological, and social factors, the research supports a strong social influence on gender-based differences in competition in sport. For example, socialization into sport (Greendorfer et al., 1996), the reward structure of sport (Sage & Eitzen, 2016), and expectations of competitiveness between men and women (Warner & Dixon, 2015) all contribute to observed differences in competition and competitiveness between men and women. In addition, the differences noted through a biological perspective can be reductionist and make assumptions about all men and all women that are not necessarily true in every context.

Looking in different contexts and levels of sport, the socialization into sport in different ways for boys and girls may have influenced the perception of competition by these athletes in the past; however, more recent research may suggest that differences in competitiveness are placed on young athletes by others (e.g., parents, teachers, coaches) rather than the actual perception of the athletes (Fredricks & Eccles, 2005; Greendorfer et al., 1996). There is also evidence to suggest that this may be changing with increased opportunities for girls in sports and in female role models for young female athletes (NFHS, 2015).

For adult athletes, the gender differences in competition seem to be in athletes' perceptions of competition rather than levels of competitiveness or competitive behavior (Warner & Dixon, 2015). Notably, women were more likely than men to find that competition detracted from sport, while both men and women preferred external competition (intergroup) over internal competition (intragroup; Warner & Dixon, 2015). Further, in the team sport context, cohesion has been found to be more associated with performance for women than for men (Carron et al., 2002), highlighting an aversion for intragroup competition. Finally, in nontraditional sports such as CrossFit and marathon/ultra marathon running, few gender differences appeared to exist and competition in general seemed less important than in more traditional sport forms for both men and women (Ogles & Masters, 2003; Ziegler, 1991).

Research Gaps and Future Directions

Overall, we see that the relationship between sex/gender and competition in sport is complicated, and despite the extent of research we can only conclude there are both similarities and differences between competition in sport for men and women, although competition for men and women seems to be more similar than it is different. There are several areas that could be fruitful for future research, including more recent studies on children's perceptions of competition, a comparison between preferences for competition between children and adults, and consequences of competitive versus noncompetitive environments.

It is important that we have current research on the experience of males and females in competition in sport. Much of the research we cited in this chapter was dated, and although it certainly extends our understanding of sex/gender differences in competitive sport it may not reflect the ever-changing landscape of sport. Since the passing of Title IX, there have been monumental changes for women in sport; however, even in the past ten years there have been significant changes to the sport landscape for women. In particular, an increase in playing opportunities for girls and women in traditionally "male sports" (e.g., American football, wrestling) and the increase in professional playing opportunities for women (e.g., National Women's Soccer League) have provided girls with the opportunity to play different sports and have visible role models of female athletes. It is possible that these changes could lead to changes in perceptions of competition for young female athletes, their coaches, and their families and as such should be examined. Replications of studies such as Greendorfer et al. (1996) regarding gender differences in socialization and motor skill development could yield an interesting comparison of young female athletes twenty years ago to today. Moreover, as women's professional sports increase and there are opportunities for female athletes to play professionally in several sports today, it would be interesting to examine whether young female athletes view competition differently in light of these new professional opportunities.

A second area of investigation that may be of interest lies in the experiences of competition for girls and women. To date there has not been a longitudinal study examining the experiences of sex/gender in competition in sport over time. It would be interesting to examine how the experiences of females in sport change across the lifetime, specifically during transitional periods where girls/women develop more agency over their sport experience. For example, young girls may have less say about their sport experiences (e.g., parents may require participation in certain sports over others, families may not be able to afford certain sports, or some sports may not exist in geographic areas). Over the lifespan women will develop increased autonomy over sport participation and as such may view competition differently.

Finally, there is little research examining the consequences of competitive environments. Are girls participating in less competitive sport environments than boys, and if so, does this impact their ability to be competitive in sports as adolescents? Do competitive environments experienced by children impact the physical activity and sport pursued later in life, or in future career decisions? There is evidence suggesting that competitive athletes are more likely to enter more competitive work domains (Comeig et al., 2016). Further exploration of this could involve longitudinal studies to address questions such as the following: Are athletes predisposed to enjoy competition (i.e., nature) or do they become accustomed to competition through exposure to more competitive environments (i.e., nurture)? And if exposure to competition at young ages can improve work opportunities in the future, there may be merit to increasing competition in sport for youth athletes.

Summary

In summary, although there are both similarities and differences between competition (and perception of competition) for men and women in sport men and women appear so be more similar than they are different in competition in sport. Despite theoretical evidence from a wide variety of perspectives (e.g., evolutionary, biological, social, and psychological), the relationship between sex/gender and competitiveness is not completely clear. From a historical context we saw significant differences between the experience of males and females in sport. Sport was seen as a way to promote masculinity, which was highly valued for men whereas women's participation in sport challenged the status quo (Gill & Kamphoff, 2010). Historically the philosophy behind sport was very different for men and women, primarily focused on teaching masculinity to young men as compared to the less competitive, "sport for all" ideals found in women's sport. While sport today physically does not look all that different for men and women, these stereotypes persist in the way sport and competition are framed even when these stereotypes are not evidence-based.

References

Acosta, R. V., & Carpenter, L. J. (2014). *Women in intercollegiate sport: A longitudinal, national study thirty-seven year update.* Retrieved from http://acostacarpenter.org/2014%20Status%20of%20Women%20in%20Intercollegiate%20Sport%20-37%20Year%20Update%20-%201977-2014%20.pdf.

Anbarci, N., Lee, J., & Ulker, A. (2016). Win at all costs or lose gracefully in high-stakes competition? Gender difference in professional tennis. *Journal of Sport Economics, 17*, 323–353.

Becker, G. S. (1993). Nobel lecture: The economic way of looking at behavior. *Journal of Political Economy, 101*, 385–409.

Carron, A. V., Brawley, L. R., & Widmeyer, W. N. (1998). The measurement of cohesiveness in sport groups. In J. L. Duda (Ed.), *Advances in sport and exercise psychology measurement* (pp. 213–226). Morgantown, WV: Fitness Information Technology.

Carron, A., Colman, M., Wheeler, J., & Stevens, D. (2002). Cohesion and performance in sport: A meta analysis. *Journal of Sport & Exercise Psychology, 24*, 168–188.

Cheuvront, S. N., Carter III, R., DeRuisseau, K. C., & Moffatt, R. J. (2005). Running performance differences between men and women. *Sports Medicine, 35*(12), 1017–1024.

Coakley, J. (1994). *Sport in society: Issues and controversies.* New York: McGraw-Hill.

Coakley, J. (2009). *Sport in society: Issues and controversies.* New York: McGraw-Hill.

Comeig, I., Grau-Gray, A., Jaramillo-Gutiérrez, A., & Ramírez, F. (2016). Gender, self-confidence, sports, and preferences for competition. *Journal of Business Research, 69*, 1–5.

Constantinou, P., Manson, M., & Silverman, S. (2009). Female students' perceptions about gender-role stereotypes and their influence on attitude toward physical education. *Physical Educator, 66*(2), 85.

Deaner, R. O. (2006). More males run fast: A stable sex difference in competitiveness in U.S. distance runners. *Evolution and Human Behavior, 27*, 63–84.

Deaner, R. O. (2013). Distance running as an ideal domain for showing a sex difference in competitiveness. *Archives of Sexual Behavior, 42*, 413–428.

Deaner, R. O., Masters, K. S., Ogles, B. M., & LaCaille, R. A. (2011). Marathon performance as a predictor of competitiveness and training in men and women. *Journal of Sport Behavior, 34*, 325–342.

Dreber, A., von Essen, E., & Ranehill, E. (2011). Outrunning the gender gap—boys and girls compete equally. *Experimental Economics, 14*, 567–582.

Duda, J. L., Olson, L. K., & Templin, T. J. (1991). The relationship of task and ego orientation to sportsmanship attitudes and the perceived legitimacy of injurious acts. *Research Quarterly for Exercise and Sport, 62*(1), 79–87.

EY & espnW. (2014). *Where will you find your next leader?* Retrieved from: http://www.ey.com/Publication/vwLUAssets/EY-where-will-you-find-your-next-leader/$FILE/where-will-you-find-your-next-leader-report-from-EY-and-espnw.pdf.

Fidler, M. A. (2006). *The origins and history of the All-American Girls Professional Baseball League.* Jefferson, NC: McFarland.

Franken, R. E., & Brown, D. J. (1994). Why do people like competition? The motivation for running, putting forth effort, improving one's performance, performing well, being instrumental, and expressing forceful/aggressive behavior. *Personal and Individual Differences, 19*, 175–184.

Fredricks, J. A., & Eccles, J. S. (2005). Family socialization, gender, and sport motivation and involvement. *Journal of Sport and Exercise Psychology, 27*, 3–31.

Frick, B. (2011). Gender differences in competitiveness: Empirical evidence from professional distance running. *Labour Economics, 13*, 389–398.

Gill, D. L. (1986). Competitiveness among females and males in physical activity classes. *Sex Roles, 15*, 233–257.

Gill, D. L. (1988). Measurement of achievement orientations: Psychometric measures, gender, and sport differences. *European Journal of Sport Science, 2*, 1–12.

Gill, D. L., & Deeter, T. E. (1988). Development of the sport orientation questionnaire. *Research Quarterly for Exercise and Sport, 59*, 191–202.

Gill, D. L., & Kamphoff, C. S. (2010). Gender in sport and exercise psychology. In J. C. Chrisler & D. R. McCreary (Eds.), *Handbook of gender research in psychology* (pp. 563–585). New York: Springer.

Gill, D. L. & Williams, L. (2008). *Psychological dynamics of sport and exercise.* Champaign, IL: Human Kinetics.

Greendorfer, S. L., Lewko, J. H., & Rosengren, K. S. (1996). Family and gender-based influences in sport socialization of children and adolescents. In F. Smoll & R. Smith (Eds.), *Children and Youth in Sport.* (pp. 89–111). Madison, WI: Brown & Benchmark Publishers.

Grindstaff, L., & West, E. (2006). Cheerleading and the gendered politics of sport. *Social Problems, 53*(4), 500–518.

Halbrook, M., Blom, L. C., Hurley, K., Bell, R. J., & Holden, J. E. (2012). Relationships among motivation, gender, and cohesion in a sample of collegiate athletes. *Journal of Sport Behavior, 35*(1), 61–77. Retrieved from http://ezproxy.library.dal.ca/login?url=http://search.proquest.com/docview/922364018?a countid=10406.

Hamilton, L. D., van Anders, S. M., Cox, D. N., & Watson, N. V. (2009). The effect of competition on salivary testosterone in elite female athletes. *Age, 20*, 1–8.

Hanrahan, S. J., & Biddle, S. J. H. (2002). Measurement of achievement orientations: Psychometric measures, gender, and sport differences. *European Journal of Sport Science, 2*, 1–12.

Hargreaves, J. A. (1987). Victorian familism and the formative years of female sports. In J. A. Mangan & R. J. Parks (Eds.), *From "fair sex" to feminism: Sport and the socialization of women in the industrial and post-industrial eras* (pp. 130–143). Totowa, NJ: Frank Cass.

Hedstrom, R., & Gould, D. (2004). *Research in youth sports: Critical issues status.* Retrieved from http://www.pysc.org/projects/documents/ResearchinYouthSports-CriticalIssuesStatus.pdf.

Henslin, J. M. (1999). On becoming male: Reflections of a sociologist on childhood and early socialization. In J. M. Henslin (Ed.), *Down to earth sociology: Introductory readings* (10th ed., pp. 142–152). New York: Simon & Schuster.

Holman, A. C. (2005). Stops and starts: Ideology, commercialism and the fall of American Women's Hockey in the 1920s. *Journal of Sport History, 32*, 328–350.

Hudson, J. (1978). Physical parameters used for female exclusion from law enforcement and athletic. In C. A. Oglesby (Ed.), *Women and sport from myth to reality* (pp. 19–57). Philadelphia: Lea & Febiger.

Kane, M. J. (1995). Resistance/transformation of the oppositional binary: Exposing sport as a continuum. *Journal of Sport and Social Issues, 19*, 191–218.

Kilpatrick, M., Hebert, E., & Bartholomew, J. (2005). College students' motivation for physical activity: differentiating men's and women's motives for sport participation and exercise. *Journal of American College Health, 54*, 87–94.

Kohn, A. (1986). *No contest: The case against competition.* New York: Mariner Books.

Lapchick, R. E. (2013). *Beyond the competition: 2013 racial and gender report card.* Retrieved from http://nebula.wsimg.com/728474de65f7d28b196a0fbb47c05a91?AccessKeyId=DAC3A56D8FB782449D2A&disposition=0&alloworigin=1.

LaVoi, N. M. (2015). *Head coaches of women's collegiate teams: A report of select NCAA Division-I mid-major institutions.* Retrieved from http://www.cehd.umn.edu/tuckercenter/library/docs/research/2014-15_WCR-Head-Coaches-Report_Mid-Majors_Oct-29.pdf.

Martens, R. (1975). *Social psychology and physical activity.* New York: Harper & Row.

Martens, R. (1976). Competition: In need of a theory. In D. M. Landers (Ed.), *Social problems in athletics* (pp. 9–17). Urbana: University of Illinois Press.

Martens, R. Burton, D., Vealey, R. S., Bump, L. A, & Smith, D. E. (1990). Development and validation of the competitive state anxiety inventory-2 (CSAI-2). In R. Martens, R. S. Vealey, & D. Burton (Eds.), *Competitive anxiety in sport* (pp. 117–213). Champaign, IL: Human Kinetics.

Mathes, S. (1978). Body image and sex stereotyping. In C. A. Oglesby (Eds.), *Women and sport from myth to reality* (pp. 59–72). Philadelphia: Lea & Febiger.

Messner, M. A. (1998). Sport and male domination: The female athlete as contested ideological terrain. *Sociology of Sport Journal, 5*, 197–211.

Metheny, E. (1965). *Connotations of movement in sport and dance.* Dubuque, IA: WC Brown.

Mrozek, D. J. (1987). "Amazon" and the American "lady": Sexual fears of women as athletes. In J. A. Mangan & R. J. Parks (Eds.), *From "fair sex" to feminism: Sport and the socialization of women in the industrial and post-industrial eras* (pp. 282–296). Totowa, NJ: Frank Cass.

National Amateur Athletic Foundation, Women's Division. (1930). *Women and athletics.* New York: Barnes.

Neil, R., Wilson, K., Mellalieu, S. D., Hanton, S., & Taylor, J. (2012). Competitive anxiety intensity and interpretation: A two-study investigation into their relationship with performance. *International Journal of Sport and Exercise Psychology, 10*, 96–111.

NFHS. (2014). Sports participation survey. Retrieved from http://www.nfhs.org/ParticipationStatics/PDF/Participation%20Survey%20History%20Book.pdf.

NFHS. (2015). *2014–15 high school athletics participation survey.* Retrieved from http://www.nfhs.org/ParticipationStatistics/PDF/2014-15_Participation_Survey_Results.pdf.

Nicholls, J. G. (1984). Achievement motivation: Conception of ability, subjective experience, mastery choice, and performance, *Psychological Review, 91*, 328–346.

Ogles, B. M., & Masters, K. S. (2003). A typology of marathon runners based on cluster analysis of motivations. *Journal of Sport Behavior, 26*, 69–85.

Park, R. J. (1987). Sport, gender and society in a transatlantic Victorian perspective. In J. A. Mangan & R. J. Park (Eds.), *From "fair sex" to feminism: Sport and socialization of women in the industrial and postindustrial areas* (pp. 58–93). London: Cass.

Partridge, J. A., & Knapp, B. A. (2015). Mean girls: Adolescent female athletes and peer conflict in sport. *Journal of Applied Sport Psychology, 28*, 113–127.

Partridge, J. A., Knapp, B. A., & Massengale, B. D. (2014). An investigation of motivational variables in CrossFit facilities. *Journal of Strength and Conditioning Research, 28*, 1714–1721.

Perry, J. D., & Williams, J. M. (1998). Relationship of intensity and direction of competitive trait anxiety to skill level and gender in tennis. *Sport Psychologist, 12*, 169–179.

Reeve, T. G., Kobayashi, M., & Eklund, R. C. (1994). Gender-role and competitiveness of female athletes. *Journal of Sport Sciences, 12*, 207.

Roberts, G. C., & Balagué, G. (1989). *The development of a social-cognitive scale in motivation.* Seventh World Congress of Sport Psychology, Singapore, August.

Sage, G. H., & Eitzen, D. S. (2016). *Sociology of North American sport.* New York: Oxford University Press.

Seefeldt, V., Ewing, M., & Walk, S. E. (1992). *An overview of youth sports.* Carnegie Council of Adolescent Development for Its Task Force on Youth Development and Community Programs.

Sefton, A. A. (1941). *The Women's Division, National Amateur Athletic Federation: Sixteen years of progress in athletics for girls and women, 1923-1939.* New York: Stanford University Press.

Shaw, S., & Frisby, W. (2006). Can gender equity be more equitable?: Promoting an alternative frame for sport management research, education, and practice. *Journal of Sport Management, 20*, 483–509.

Spink, K. (1990). Group cohesion and collective efficacy of volleyball teams. *Journal of Sport & Exercise Psychology, 12*, 301–311.

Spink, K. (1995). Cohesion and intention to participate of female sport team athletes. *Journal of Sport & Exercise Psychology, 17*, 416–427.

Steidinger, J. (2014). *Sisterhood in sports: How female athletes collaborate and compete.* Lanham, MD: Rowman & Littlefield.

Thuot, S., Kavouras, S., & Kenefick, R. (1998). Effect of perceived ability, game location, and state anxiety on basketball performance. *Journal of Sport Behavior, 21*, 311.

Tjosvold, D., Johnson, D. W., Johnson, R. T., & Sun, H. (2006). Competitive motives and strategies: Understanding constructive competition. *Group Dynamics: Theory, Research, and Practice, 10*, 87.

Unger, R. K. (1979). Toward a redefinition of sex and gender. *American Psychologist, 34*, 1085–1094.

Wade, A., & Stabb, S. D. (2015). Sisterhood in sports: How female athletes collaborate and compete: A book review. *Psychology of Women Quarterly, 39*, 557–558.

Walters, S. R., Payne, D., Schluter, P. J., & Thomson, R. W. (2015). "It just makes you feel invincible": A Foucauldian analysis of children's experiences of organized team sports. *Sport, Education and Society, 20*, 241–257.

Warner, S., & Dixon, M. A. (2013). Sports and community on campus: Constructing a sports experience that matters. *Journal of College Student Development, 54*(3), 283–298.

Warner, S., & Dixon, M. A. (2015). Competition, gender and the sport experience: An exploration among college athletes. *Sport, Education and Society, 20*, 1–19.

Weinberg, R., Tenenbaum, G., McKenzie, A., Jackson, S., Anshell, M., Grove, R., & Fogarty, G. (2000). Motivation for youth participation in sport and physical activity: Relationships to culture, self-reported activity levels, and gender. *International Journal of Sport Psychology, 31*, 321–346.

Wolf, S. A., Eys, M. A., & Kleinert, J. (2015). Predictors of the precompetitive anxiety response: Relative impact and prospects of anxiety regulations. *International Journal of Sport and Exercise Psychology, 4*, 344–358.

Ziegler, S. G. (1991). Perceived benefits of marathon running in males and females. *Sex Roles, 25*, 119–127.

Conclusion

Conclusion

Gregory L. Carter *and* Maryanne L. Fisher

Abstract

This handbook has presented a wide range of theoretical perspectives on the motivations, attitudes, and behaviors involved in female competition. Using a metatheoretical framework, the contributors have examined how, when, and why women compete. This conclusion articulates the book's main themes, beginning with evidence regarding women as active, competitive individuals and the value of mating information, addressing topics such as women's competitive choices regarding mate copying, mate poaching, and mate retention. It then considers the role of intrasexual aggression in adolescence in relation to dating and reproduction, the importance of Operational Sex Ratio (OSR) to female competition, the concept of cooperative mothering or allomothering, and infanticide. It also discusses women as competitors in both traditional and novel social arenas as well as the role of women's physiology in their competitive behaviors. Finally, it suggests directions for future research on topics that warrant further scrutiny.

Key Words: female competition, women, mating, mate poaching, intrasexual aggression, dating, reproduction, Operational Sex Ratio, allomothering, infanticide

The study of human and nonhuman behavior, to a greater or lesser extent, has been beset by androcentrism since Darwin, Freud, and their many, usually male, antecedents. These two men in particular, however, greatly influenced scholarly thought about cognition and motivation in the twentieth century, and will no doubt continue to do so in the twenty-first century. This history is relevant, as many of the articles and books cited by the contributors to this volume are grounded in research from this time frame, meaning that the work in this book has been, to varying extents, influenced by these two men.

As Degler (1991) says, Darwin "rephrased, as no one before him, what it meant to be human" (p. 6). Darwin's statement from his book introducing the theory of sexual selection (*The Descent of Man and Selection in Relation to Sex*; 1871/1998) makes his views transparent: "man has ultimately become superior to woman" (Darwin, 1871/1998, p. 585). Perhaps his belief about women stemmed from the ethos of the Victorian society in which he was living. That milieu, though, did not prevent others from noticing Darwin's conclusion was problematic and lacked empirical comparison of the sexes (e.g., Blackwell, 1875). Others have written impressive accounts of Darwin's lack of accuracy, and scholarly omission in portraying females of many species, including our own (e.g., Gowaty, 1992; Hrdy, 1997; Liesen, 1995; Vandermassen, 2005). Indeed, Gowaty foresaw the importance of female intrasexual competition when she wrote, "I consider the long-standing theoretical primacy of male-male competition to be one of the most potentially misleading notions in evolutionary biology" (1992, p. 229).

Likewise, Freud had a substantial impact on our views of human nature, despite his highly limited insights into women. In his infamous essay, *Some Psychical Consequences of the Anatomical Distinction Between the Sexes* (1925), he considers women's psychological development to be simply analogous to that of men. His writings about women (and girls) are relatively sparse, as compared with his far more extensive considerations about men (and boys). However, even today, scholars argue that Freud's influence has largely shaped our thinking about human nature: Mitchell and Black (2016) write, "Today, Freud's contributions are so broadly accepted, so tightly woven into the fabric of our culture and our experience of ourselves, that, in the broadest sense, we are all 'Freudians'" (p. iv). In Freud's theorizing about sexuality, he proposed that women were identical to men, simply lacking penises (Cohler & Galatzer-Levy, 2008), which caused women to become stuck at the phallic stage of psychosexual development and experience a so-called phallic crisis (Bernstein, 1983, p. 187). Others have commented at length about Freud's views of women (e.g., Schafer, 1974), suggesting that Freud was, to put it simply, not complimentary, or accurate, and at times his thoughts were very underdeveloped, particularly in terms of female sexuality.

Doubtlessly, androcentrism in scientific thought preceded these two figures, as immediately evidenced by a cursory scan of historical psychological, biological, anatomical, and medical texts. Moreover, Darwin and Freud had many contemporaries who followed similar lines of thinking; for example, in his analysis of what he called "secondary sexual characteristics," Havelock Ellis (1894) writes that

> women are more docile and amenable to discipline; that they can do light work equally well [to men]; that they are steadier in some respects; but that, on the other hand, they are oftener absent on account of slight indisposition, they break down sooner under strain (although consideration is shown them in the matter of hours, etc.), and exhibit less intelligence outside the ordinary routine, not showing the same ability of willingness (possibly because they look forward to marriage) to acquire technical knowledge. (p. 183)

Although coming from very different viewpoints about the origins of human behavior, what sets Darwin and Freud apart from their contemporaries is that they significantly influenced the course of scholarly research in the decades that followed. Many researchers currently working in fields that address human (and nonhuman animal) behavior have been exposed to their androcentric thinking, perhaps receiving university courses on Freudian thought, or Darwinian theory, for example. At the

same time, though, they have hopefully also been exposed to opposing views; ones where women (as well as nonhuman female animals) may be seen as actively engaging in contests and competition, rather than sitting on the sidelines. The growth of the literature devoted toward women and competition was slow, initially, but has since gained significant momentum, as outlined in the Introduction to this volume.

We must conclude, then, that contemporary researchers, and some pioneering forebears, have, since the time of Darwin and Freud and their immediate academic descendants, encouraged the field to adopt a broader mindset. This handbook represents a milestone in how current, active researchers seek to understand and further our knowledge of women's competition. Multiple issues are reviewed; multiple roles that women play are reconceptualized. In this volume, we consider women as lovers, women as mothers, and women as fighters. Their many and various critical stakes and positions within the human condition, and human evolution, cannot be ignored. We broaden these considerations to include nonhuman female primates and animals, and provide deeper insight into the multitude of issues faced by females of multiple species and the challenges that human women have faced over the course of evolutionary time.

The chapters that make up this book are diverse in tone and content, yet they are united by a common theme: women are competitive. Women compete as, and for, potential mates. Women compete for resources for both themselves and their children. And women compete in sports and physical activity, for status, and for friendships. In general, women adopt inter- and intrasexual competitive tactics.

The myth of the "coy female," by which we mean "the presupposed existence of a highly discriminating ... female who is courted by sexually undiscriminating males," is dead (Hrdy, 1986, p. 119; see, for a review, Chapter 3 in Workman & Reader, 2008). Others have remarked on the inaccuracy of this myth (e.g., Hrdy, 1986; Vandermassen, 2005), so we leave that theoretical discussion at this point. However, it is important to note that while theorists have shown that women are far from coy and passive, this idea continues to pervade contemporary thought, including the ways in which women are shown in mass media. For example, an analysis of video game covers shows that sales are negatively related to the presence of women as central characters (Near, 2013). Likewise, an examination of children's picture books reveals that adult women are often displayed in passive, nurturing roles, while adult men are typically depicted to be active, aggressive, and assertive (Koss, 2015). The portrayal of women as passive, influencing primarily or exclusively domestic spheres, is demonstrably not new. In their writings about feminist media theory, Parry and Karam (2001) document that media often negatively portray "women as women"; they elucidate that popular forums rarely show women as active, competing effectively for limited resources, or displaying a highly competent level of planning a course of action. Findings such as these clearly highlight how the utter lack of acceptance of women as "active" pervades modern thinking.

We have ample evidence that women are frequently ferocious in competition. Women's goals and tactics may vary from those of men, however. Though this last point is hardly novel, it bears revisiting in drawing this volume to a conclusion. Researchers, lecturers, and students alike would do well to attune themselves to the presence of any last, archaic bastions of misogyny that have yet to recognize that women compete, yet frequently do so in different ways, and avoid inadvertently subscribing to these views themselves.

Moreover, there remain other topics pertaining to women that warrant far closer scrutiny than they have yet received. For example, the perpetuated assumption that mothers commit to nurturing and will forevermore care for their young is simply false. As Hrdy (1986) outlines, mothers "cut-bait far more often than is generally recognized, and ... skipped ovulations, spontaneous abortions, and abandonment of young by mothers are fairly routine events in nature" (p. 136). The ramifications of assuming not only that mothers are good at nurturing but also that all women have a natural propensity to be nurturers is harmful and needlessly limiting. For example, it may limit men from occupying professions that involve interacting with children, or assuming that women would be better at interacting with children (Bhana, 2016), regardless of an examination of the individual characteristics that people possess. Moreover, given that mothers are thought to be natural nurturers, it is hardly surprising that maternal competition has remained understudied until recently (e.g., Fisher & Moule, 2013; Linney, Korologou-Linden, & Campbell, 2016; Sokol-Chang, Burch, & Fisher, this volume), despite the fact that it clearly influences the well-being and survival of infants and children.

Readers can debate whether chapters in this book adopt a feminist or postfeminist perspective.

What they unequivocally represent is a sustained reflection on the motivations, attitudes, and behaviors involved in female competition. At no point do the chapters within this volume propose the unsubstantiated argument that men and women are directly comparable with respect to their competitive natures. Instead, they take a nuanced look at the wide-ranging domains in which evidence indicates that women are competitive. These arguments are then incorporated into a wider metatheoretical framework. Asking if women compete is redundant; these chapters break new ground in advancing ideas with respect to how, when, and why women compete.

The theoretical perspectives the authors of these chapters adopt varies. Some (e.g., Russell, Dutove, & Dithurbide) adopt a social-constructionist angle. Many others (e.g., Sutton & Oaten) utilize the metatheoretical toolkit provided by evolutionary psychology to explain females' many motivations and arenas of competition.

In respect to the latter, an outdated perspective sees female sexual competition as an evolutionary spandrel. Within the chapters that take an evolutionary perspective, arguments are presented that show it is germanely purposeful; it is adaptive. It is a response to the specific issues women face with respect to successful mating, primarily biparental care, and the high variance in men's value as candidate mates (Arnocky & Vaillancourt). Importantly, the chapters in this handbook recognize individual differences within women, relative not only to their mate value but also to their relationship status. They then go further, addressing how competition serves multiple purposes in terms of social standing and resource acquisition at home, in the schoolyard, at the workplace, and online, transcending the lifespan.

Chapters contained within this book necessarily articulate multiple theoretical approaches and cover diverse subject areas. This conclusion will articulate the main themes, referring back to specific chapters, and propose new directions in which we should now head in our continued studies of women's competition.

Women as Lovers, Mates, and Long-Term Partners

Evidence is articulated across a number of chapters (Adair et al.; Anderson) regarding women as active, competitive maters. Women compete as mates directly and vicariously. They use information on and from fellow competitors within the local ecology to establish their own and potential rivals' mate value, alongside the value of candidate mates. Fisher and Fernández discuss the importance of accurate self-assessments of mate value, in order to establish one's comparative worth. This information supports a strategic approach according to the local ecology, and competing intrasexually to alter one's own or rivals' mate values. Additionally, it allows for an appraisal of the likelihood of retaliatory aggression.

Also regarding the value of mating information, Morris, Beaussart, Reiber, and Krajewski consider mate loss via poaching. They argue this experience can represent a valuable learning process via self-reflection. Morris et al. assert that relationship breakdown of this nature, while potentially distressing, can be instructive regarding relative mate value and the potential need for competitive retention tactics. In this way, women may enhance their competitive abilities, and develop new strategies to retain future, high-quality partners. Moreover, it may enhance female–female social relationships via social support provision.

Considering single and partnered women, Brewer outlines the differential underlying motivations for female competition across groups. Single women, broadly speaking, compete for mates of demonstrably high quality—a fact echoed in multiple chapters. Information on candidate mate quality is valuable to acquire and costly to get wrong. Women benefit from acquiring this information vicariously, minimizing risk and potentially maximizing benefit. Adair reflects on how this information shapes women's competitive choices regarding mate copying, mate poaching, and mate retention.

Gallup focuses on the role of intrasexual aggression in adolescence in relation to dating and reproduction, showcasing evidence that intrasexual competition in adolescent girls represents an adaptive approach to dating and sex. Moreover, such aggression can disrupt rivals' attempts to access desirable mates, limiting their value and, potentially, future reproductive potential (related outcomes for rivals are also discussed by Salmon). Gallup makes a case for the continued study of adolescent populations to improve our understanding of female sexual competition, as part of the lifetime trajectory and relevance of such behaviors (similar points are also made by Costa et al. and Cobey and Hahn).

The importance of Operational Sex Ratio (OSR) to female competition is addressed by Dillon, Adair, and Brase. A scarcity of (quality) men breeds intensity in female competition for mates, and is critical

to understanding competitive female behaviors and broader social interactivity in relevant environments. Stone makes a similar point in assessing a comparable evolutionary psychological hypothesis, as well as a biological model. The latter pertains to whether a surfeit of mates might increase competition, with the potential of increased returns on investment. Initial results are mixed, warranting ongoing investigation. In respect of this, Dillon et al. and Stone both highlight the relevance of cross-cultural research, including in traditional societies, to understanding and providing evidence on this issue.

For partnered women, competition takes on a more defensive role, protecting investment and guarding against mate poaching (Brewer). Female family members act as allies in this endeavor (i.e., fellow, but not rival, competitors), aiding mate retention and offsetting future costs on their own part. Such costs include investment in their own genetic successors in the event of paternal abandonment.

Women as Mothers, Allomothers, and Offspring-Related Conflict

Maternal (sororital; materteral; grandmaternal) investment is another area of focus. Sokol-Chang, Burch, and Fisher discuss the challenges that motherhood poses, not just to the mother herself, but in the context of the related and unrelated women who surround her. cooperation in the form of bidirectional opportunities for vicarious learning and the provisioning of direct care are discussed alongside maternal competition for mates and resources. Ultimately, Sokol-Chang et al. stress the need to explore cooperation and competition in tandem, as inseparable parts of the whole that is motherhood: cooperative mothering, or allomothering, is just one side of a coin. Competitive mothering warrants continued study from evolutionary psychologists, across social, personality, and developmental fields. Indeed, this argument is also advanced by MacEacheron and Campbell.

Valentine, Li, and Yong similarly reflect on competitive motherhood, comparing humans with nonhuman mammals and emphasizing comparable pressures on mothers regarding status, resources, and mates (for themselves and their offspring). Like Low, Valentine et al. also highlight the existence of competition beginning with conception.

Several others chapters address "light" and "dark" sides of maternal and familial competition. De Backer, Hudders, and Fisher provide an example of the former with the presentation of an argument for "positive" competition via food preparation. A self-enhancement strategy and potential illustration of genuine love and care, family meal preparation benefits health and unity. This unity may also help guard against mate poaching, strengthening the cohesion of the familial unit.

The darker side of female parenthood is addressed elsewhere. Kennair and Biegler discuss mother–daughter and intersibling conflict. An absence of harmony in mother–daughter priorities for mate qualities in the latter's partner(s) may cause internal familial disunity. Where one party values direct and the other indirect signs of fitness (which may be either mother or daughter), relationships can sour. Moreover, where maternal influence restricts mate choice, female siblings are more likely to compete between themselves for a limited pool of acceptable mates.

Infanticide, where genetic quality or survival likelihood will adversely affect women's intrasexual "ranking," is discussed in a powerful chapter by Cousins and Porter. Noted as a "morally dark" form of competition, this has previously been associated with stepmothers but is not exclusively enacted by women at a genetic distance. An unwanted child can limit a woman's mate value, which may be particularly potent in an environment with a female-heavy OSR. It is important, in looking to advance our understanding of female competition, not to avoid discussion of reality. More research into what Cousins and Porter term a "homicide adaptation" would be prudent.

Women as Competitors in Novel Social Arenas

Several chapters address evolutionarily novel, or dissonant, forms and forums of female competition. Guitar and Carmen articulate the need to consider the online world no less "real" than the offline version. Facebook "frenemies," stalking, self(ie) promotion, and cyberbullying are pervasive contemporary forms of female competition. Ostracizing one's competitors online can be devastatingly effective, reminding us to reflect on the ways in which the twenty-first century has enhanced the suite of available competitive tactics.

In another chapter, Meredith expands on the ways in which video gaming provides an opportunity for women to practice and perform both problem-solving and intrasexual competition. Typically, their behavior is of a covert rather than overt nature (contrasting with men), including self-promotion, competitor derogation, and competitor manipulation.

These tactics also form part of women's—and girls'—involvement in contemporary beauty pageants (Shaiber, Johnsen, & Geher). Shaiber et al. explain that, while beauty pageants do not feature competition for mates per se, they provide an opportunity to assess (and advertise) comparative mate value (per, e.g., Fisher & Fernández) and, potentially, to acquire status and resources. The attributes that typically determine a victorious outcome (e.g., indicators of youth, fertility, and potentially virginity and intelligence) are highly germane to mate value. This societally sanctioned form of competition is in a sense no less gladiatorial than men's physical sparring, and provides valuable information regarding women's relative status as a mate.

Comparably, as discussed by Russell, Dutove, and Dithurbide, sport provides another fertile ground for female–female competition. In a consideration of historical sex and gender roles, Russell et al. consider how these may have affected women's participation in sporting endeavors, and how such participation may affect women's views on competition more broadly. Sporting competition may provide women with information on comparative health in terms of athleticism, and victories can dramatically enhance social standing (e.g., Olympic success). Russell et al. note that the sporting domain has been dominated by consideration of male competition, and propose that future work is needed on female sports.

Other contemporary advances have provided for increasing accessibility and variety in cosmetic enhancement. This development has intensified what DelPriore, Prokosch, and Hill term "competitive beautification." This process, too, may involve online tactics, including trolling (e.g., regarding women's Instagram uploads), posting targeted "fitspiration" memes, and engaging in fat-shaming.

Yong, Li, Valentine, and Smith discuss other multiplatform media portrayals of desirable female mate values. Exploitative virtual intersexual competition can adversely affect women's impression formation. This arises from an evolutionary mismatch in failing to distinguish between real and virtual "competitors." While DelPriore et al. suggested that such advertising may ultimately "backfire" against companies, Yong et al. propose that severe body dissatisfaction and mental health outcomes will, in the current climate, result.

Forms of competition, and rival and media exploitation thereof, can thus be deleterious to women's psychical and psychological health. In addition to Yong et al.'s chapter, Dubbs, Kelly and Barlow refer to women's potential "appearance fixation." The discrepancy between female perception of male preferences and actual male preferences is a strong indicator that female competition is a potent, if not the primary, driving force behind this effect. Such fixation, potentially resulting in undertaking cosmetic techniques, can even lead to a lower mate value, and being branded as a "cheater" or "faker."

Women as Competitors in Traditional Social Arenas

Less extreme forms of self-enhancing competitive tactics, in the form of fashion choices, are advanced as potent competitive signals by Johnsen and Geher. These can be extremely effective online (e.g., via Tinder) or offline. The persistence of certain fashion trends over time, such as corsets, contemporary "body con" dresses, and high heels, enhances specific fitness indicators. Women may also select clothes of specific colors (i.e., red, pink) to imply fertility at peak times. Johnsen and Geher additionally make the point that, in several cultures, the burqa may benefit a woman's social standing, and a willingness to wear it increases her appeal to high-quality partners. Thus, fashion represents self-promotion, competitor manipulation, and mate-manipulation tactics.

Nagamuthu and Page-Gould address competition between female friends, manifest through comparison-drawing and status-seeking, and align certain behaviors with nonhuman primates (similar to Salmon and Scott). They present friendships as featuring both competition and competition-nullification, set against the comparative power of friendship dyads. Ultimately, they look to disabuse a sense that friendships are always egalitarian, and frame unequal friendships as potentially providing a source of healthy female–female competition, calling on the field to expand theories of friendship accordingly.

Rucas, in a chapter supplying evidence from women of the Tsimane tribe in the Bolivian Amazon, discusses similar themes, focusing on female social capital. Investment in female–female relationships may yield improved inclusive fitness (e.g., allomothering) with respect to offspring. Rucas describes the appeal of cooperative others but also acknowledges the potential for "cheats" to take advantage of species—and group-typical cooperation—for personal gain (see also Honey).

Miller and Rucas, presenting data from Sidama women in rural southwestern Ethiopia, reflect on the effects of female networks on women's health, particularly with respect to sleep. Female competition may be detrimental to women's health via intrasexual conflict that adversely affects sleep, such that it causes the assorted negative outcomes that insufficient sleep entails (e.g., low energy, poor rejuvenation of internal systems). Competitive co-wife scenarios, or other socially stressful relationships, can ultimately hamper fitness. In addition to adverse health outcomes, poor sleep can increase aggression levels, incurring further costs. Thus, disrupting the sleep of a rival who is competing for status or mates, via (anti)social interaction, can be beneficial.

In further consideration of female–female relationships, Hess discusses coalitional gossiping. Coalitions (of friends and allies) serve to improve information collection, analysis, dissemination, believability, and defense. Primarily, Hess argues, coalitional gossiping can draw on these functions to enhance reputational management, for the self, friends, and rivals, as a form of "informational warfare." McAndrew extends this reflection on gossip and its potential role in establishing a valuable social network. Forming such a network has the potential to improve, for example, access to cooperative mothering or allomothering, as well as excluding rivals for status and mates. In this way, gossip can be extremely limiting to rivals' success (see also Salmon). Importantly, McAndrew notes that despite the ubiquity of gossip—or perhaps because of it—it is an understudied area; this could also be said of the focus of the volume as a whole.

Informational warfare of this nature is thus proposed to be particularly useful for women, as a form of indirect aggression (see also Gallup), the benefits of which in comparison to direct aggression are discussed at length throughout this volume. However, Sutton and Oaten discuss the role of general and targeted gossip (i.e., regarding others' sexual activity) as a comparatively low-risk tool in competition for men and women. Notably, they conclude that gossip appears to be a non–sex-specific strategy, suggesting that there is some overlap in the deployment of specific intrasexually competitive tactics.

Salmon considers the role of well-established intrasexual competitive tactics alongside ecological factors (and comparatively novel media influence) on reproductive suppression. The approach dominant women may adopt in competition can absolutely limit the reproductive mate value of a rival, although Salmon also contemplates the role of women themselves in reproductive suppression. Ultimately, further, longitudinal work would enhance our understanding of this extremely potent and restrictive outcome of female competition.

Broadening Theoretical and Societal Perspectives

A persistent theme across several chapters is the cognitive dissonance that some—men and women—have in viewing women as competitive. In particular, Kocum, Courvoisier, and Vernon discuss adverse perceptions of female competitiveness in the workplace. The discriminatory vocational backdrop that many women face presents double-standard expectations for male and female competition and is deleterious.

Similarly, the Dark Triad in women receives much-needed attention from Honey. Narcissism, Machiavellianism, and psychopathy have been well-documented in men, with respect to enhancing mate competition, predicting an array of sexual tactics, and engaging in duplicitous, criminal behaviors. Female exemplars of these traits have largely been overlooked. In the context of other chapters, it seems eminently possible that the "darker" side of maternal and familial conflict (per, e.g., Cousins & Porter; Sokol-Chang et al.) is a predictable outcome for women high in these traits. That society might not expect this behavior is another in the list of reasons the chapters in this volume are of vital importance.

Additionally, the Dark Triad, and especially behaviorally flexible Machiavellianism, may enhance women's abilities to navigate social groups and social competition. After providing a valuable overview of previously invisible female competition, brought forward by feminist evolutionary psychology, Liesen reflects on the challenges faced by women in social networks. In particular, Liesen stresses the importance of both competition and cooperation as factors within women's social networks that may positively or adversely affect individual women's reproductive strength.

Varella, Varella Valentová, and Fernández discuss a different domain that has been shaped by female competition: artistic production and appreciation. Varella et al. propose a view of art as a reflection of women's competitive approach to aesthetics, and self-promotion, as discussed in multiple other chapters. They adopt a broad definition of art, encompassing bodily ornamentation and performative art, as well as artistic products, and their commentary

proposes that future work consider male roles in the same domain.

Scott engages in a commentary on nonhuman primates (as also discussed by Valentine et al.) and the ways in which humans, and women, would compete if living in comparable ecologies. Similar themes are discussed in those chapters, which have focused on human women: competition for resources and social status, friendships, the drive for reproductive success, and infanticide. Tactics adopted by the featured species are varied but include, for example, reproductive suppression (also addressed by Salmon), which has undoubted parallels with respect to human competitor derogation and manipulation. Scott aptly concludes that human exceptionalism may be overstated in respect of competition.

Women's Physiology; the Relevance of Cycle, Hormones, and Age

Several chapters have boldly tackled comparatively novel areas, and the hope is that these represent the start, rather than end, of a discussion. A multifaceted, multimethod, multicultural approach will be needed to advance this field further. Costa et al. propose a psychobiological model, reflecting on the relationship between competition and hormonal responses to competition, and the ways in which these may differ between men and women. Moreover, they draws attention to the importance of age, a point echoed in other chapters. Cobey and Hahn, likewise, draw attention to both these matters: the complex interrelated role of multiple hormones, including cortisol, estrogen, progesterone, and testosterone, and the variation of these across the female lifespan.

MacEacheron and Campbell argue the need to extend consideration of female competition beyond the 18- to 25-year-old women who make up approximately 75% of samples. They propose that the entirety of a woman's reproductive career features intrasexual competition, and that sexual strategies and mate preferences shift over time. Women who have a proven maternal history and have potentially accrued sizable resources over their lifespan may have a competitive edge in attracting high-value mates. Low, equally, calls for attention to female competition across the lifespan, from being in the womb to being a grandmother. Low considers multiple aspects of lifelong competition, across survival and reproductive domains.

Nikiforidis, Arsena, and Durante champion an ovulatory competition hypothesis, documenting the well-established effects on female mating-related competition at times of peak fertility. They note, however, that time-related female appearance enhancement is not undertaken to impress men, but to outcompete rival women. This extends beyond dress, too, and includes luxury-item consumption and financial decision-making. In concluding, Nikiforidis et al. also make the case for the study of female behavior during the luteal phase, and the role of progesterone, adding to the aforementioned call by Cobey and Hahn.

Future Directions

As Fisher notes in her introduction, this volume is timely. There is much more to be done, however. The broader spectrum of female competition encompasses nonmonogamous mating systems, nonheterosexual relationships, and non–gender-conforming women (see mention in the chapters by Brewer; Johnsen & Geher). Further, while cross-cultural work has been cited within the preceding chapters, studying more diverse ethnicities and cultures will deepen and broaden our knowledge, and may reveal similarities or differences in the female experience (see DelPriore et al.).

This future research should include studying ecologies of differing operational sex ratios (see Dillon et al.; Stone). Such work may consider not only mating behaviors but also the effect this may have on female–female friendship (per Nagamuthu and Page-Gould).

Much work has yet to be done on the interrelated nature of many of the issues discussed in this volume, both within and across specific areas. The study of hormonal influence on female competition is a prime example of the former (per Cobey & Hahn). The role of hormones in reproductive suppression, and how this varies across environments, is an example of the latter (see Salmon).

A rich, varied suite of methodological approaches will be key to further advancing this field. Observational analyses will provide richer, more ecologically valid data (per Liesen). So, too, will cross-temporal, longitudinal work, charting variations in female competition across the entire lifespan (per Cobey & Hahn; Costa et al.; Low; Salmon; and others).

Hrdy (1986) documents the influential shift caused by female academics entering research fields formerly occupied by men. However, decades later, there is evidence that women are still not being heard to the same degree as men. For example, Isbell, Young, and Harcourt (2012) analyzed 21 annual meetings of the American Association of Physical Anthropologists. In the subfield of primatology, a discipline that is typically biased with more female than male academics, women presented more academic posters than conference talks, with the reverse true for men. They also document the incredible importance of the sex of organizers for symposia, which are typically by invitation to participate. Symposia organized by men had the lowest rate of female first-authored presentations (29%), as compared with symposia organized by women (64%), or those chaired by both men and women (58%). There remains much work to be done to arrive at a science of human behavior that has representation of ideas from men and women equally. With those changes, perhaps women's intrasexual competition will be viewed as an everyday occurrence, and media representations of women as active will catch up to the theoretical advances from the past few decades.

Women's (and, more broadly, female nonhuman animals') competition is not a deviation from a norm; it is a norm. We argue that competition is not inherently negative or that it somehow detracts from the benefits of friendships and familial ties. Instead, we describe how women's competition exists; we accept, acknowledge, and outline how it enables women to attain and retain mates. We discuss and describe how it functions for women in acquiring the resources that are necessary to raise their children and care for their families, and to sustain friendships and bond with others, among other tasks. It is not a "problem" that requires a solution, as suggested by recent mass-media books (as reviewed in the Introduction). Science, and the general public, must accept that women compete in many different ways, just as they have seemingly accepted that men compete in the areas that matter most to them. This applies as much to our species as to nonhuman species. This book provides insight into how and why women compete, and it is our sincere hope that future work will continue in the same vein.

References

Bernstein, D. (1983). The female superego: A different perspective. *International Journal of Psycho-Analysis, 64,* 187–201.

Bhana, D. (2016). Teachers are mothers: Can men teach young children? In D. Bhana (Ed.), *Gender and childhood sexuality in primary school: Series perspectives on children and young people* (pp. 45–64). Singapore: Springer.

Blackwell, A. (1875/1976). *The sexes through nature.* Westport, CT: Hyperion Press.

Cohler, B. J., & Galatzer-Levy, R. M. (2008). Freud, Anna, and the problem of female sexuality. *Psychoanalytic Inquiry, 28,* 3–26.

Darwin, C. R. (1998). *The descent of man, and selection in relation to sex.* London: John Murray. (Original work published 1871.)

Degler, C. N. (1991). *In search of human nature: The decline and revival of Darwinism in American social thought.* New York: Oxford University Press.

Ellis, H. (1894). *Man and woman: A study of human secondary sexual characters.* London: Walter Scott.

Fisher, M., & Moule, K. (2013). A new direction for intrasexual competition research: Cooperative versus competitive motherhood. *Journal of Social, Evolutionary and Cultural Psychology, 7,* 318–325.

Freud, S. (1925). Some psychical consequences of the anatomical distinction between the sexes. *Standard Edition, 19,* 243–258.

Gowaty, P. (1992). Evolutionary biology and feminism. *Human Nature, 3*(3), 217–249.

Hrdy, S. B. (1986). Empathy, polyandry, and the myth of the coy female. In R. Bleier (Ed.), *Feminist approaches to science* (pp. 119–146). New York: Pergamon.

Hrdy, S. (1997). Raising Darwin's consciousness: Female sexuality and the prehominid origins of patriarchy. *Human Nature, 8*(11), 1–49.

Isbell, L. A., Young, T. P., & Harcourt, A. H. (2012). Stag parties linger: Continued gender bias in a female-rich scientific discipline. *PLoS One, 7*(11), 49–53.

Koss, M. D. (2015). Diversity in contemporary picture-books: A content analysis. *Journal of Children's Literature, 41*(1), 32–42.

Liesen, L. (1995). Feminism and the politics of reproductive strategies. *Politics and the Life Sciences, 14*(2), 145–162.

Linney, C., Korologou-Linden, L., & Campbell, A. (2016). Maternal competition in women. *Human Nature, 28*(1), 92–116.

Mitchell, S. A., & Black, M. J. (1995/2016). *Freud and beyond: A history of modern psychoanalytic thought.* New York: Basic Books.

Near, C. E. (2013). Selling gender: Associations of box art representation of female characters with sales for teen- and mature-rated video games. *Sex Roles, 68*(3), 252–269.

Parry, L., & Karam, B. (2001). Feminist media theory. In P. J. Fourie (Ed.), *Media studies. Institutions, theories, and issues* (Vol. 1, pp. 383–446). Landsdowne, South Africa: Juta Company.

Schafer, R. (1974). Problems in Freud's psychology of women. *Journal of the American Psychoanalytic Association, 22*(3), 459–485.

Vandermassen, G. (2005). *Who's afraid of Charles Darwin: Debating feminism and evolutionary theory.* New York: Rowman & Littlefield.

INDEX

Note: Page references followed by a "*t*" indicate table; "*f*" indicate figure.

A

abdominoplasty (tummy tuck), 598
abstract conceptualization model, 704–5
academic domains
  competition within, 7, 808
  physical attractiveness and, 578–79
achievement motivation theories, 789
acquaintanceships, 133, 134
active distress, in grief, 340
active mate choice, 322
adaptations
  of adolescent peer aggression, 89–92
  or mismatch, for adolescent
    girls, 443–44
  of primates, 43
  for progenicide, 569
  of women jealousy, 345–46
adaptive behavioral strategy
  of appearance enhancement, 31, 250
  female competition as, 25
  of women, 35
adaptive competition tactic, of appearance
    enhancement, 31, 250
adaptive dating outcomes, peer aggression
    and, 96–98, 99
adaptive purpose, of grief, 342
adaptive self-deception, 180
adaptive sexual behaviors, peer aggression
    and, 98
adolescence and young adulthood, 3
  See also preadolescence
  ancestral selective process for, 91
  in cultural context, 19
  dating behavior in, 91
  direct mate competition sex
    differences, 19
  educational settings competition, 19
  family conflict during, 426
  female-female competition in, 19
  fitness advantages over peers, 94
  popularity aim, 19
  socialization during, 19
  sports during, 19
  winning sex differences, 19
adolescent girls
  competition in patriarchal culture, 4, 19
  dating overinvolvement outcomes, 97
  dominance structures of, 72
  fashion importance of, 440
  indirect and relational aggression
    impact on, 81

relational aggression of, 75
social manipulation by, 385
status and, 439–40
subfertility of, 81
teasing and exclusion use, 75
violent actions age of, 8, 93
adolescent peer aggression
  as adaptation, 89–92
  bullying, 89–90
  cost-benefit ratio of, 101
  female reproductive competition and,
    95–99, 439
  females and earlier dating onset, 97, 99
  forms and trends of, 92–93
  indirect, 92, 95
  intrasexual competition strategies, 93–95
  mate competition link with, 96, 100
  opposite-sex friendship and, 96, 99
  physical, 92–93, 100
  relational, 92
  sex differences in, 92–93
  social, 92, 100
adolescents
  aggressive expression, 94–95
  dominance of, 440–41
  life history theory on, 81–82
  peer relationships and sleep of, 419
  reproductive capacity in lifespan, 91
  social network sites popularity with, 681
  social status and, 440
adornment, in clothing, 638
adultery. *See* infidelity
adults, aggressive expression of, 93–94
adult sex ratio, OSR compared to, 251–52
advertisement
  female emotions and, 665
  of genetic quality, 435
affiliation, 8
  benefits of, 51
  friendships through behaviors of, 52
  immigrant females use of, 51
  in primate female competition, 43
age, 301. *See also* aging
  of adolescent girls violent action, 93
  competition responses and, 366
  facial symmetry and, 458
  female-female competition and, 453–73
  fertility and, 304
  importance of, 303–5
  marital status of American women by,
    303, 303*f*

of menarche and menopause, 453
pregnancy likelihood by, 461
public collective self-esteem and,
    729–30, 730*f*, 731*f*, 732
reduced physical attractiveness and,
    457, 471
single and married women percentages
    by, 303–5, 304*f*
social boundaries, of single and married
    women, 307
agents, women as, 4, 149
age-related changes, female-female
    competition and, 456, 807
  desire for children, 459
  extended family role, 461
  life history theory and, 457–59
  older, mated women competition with
    mate poachers, 459–60
  ornament concealment, 457–59, 471
  reduced attractiveness, 457, 471
  resource accumulation, 460–61
  sexual strategy change, 457–59
aggression, 6. *See also specific types*
  attractive signaling link to, 183–84
  biological expressions of, 169
  children development of, 170–71
  cognitive association models, 174
  communication and, 50, 170–71
  in computer gaming, 707–8
  empathy lack and, 154
  environmental triggers and, 8
  evolutionary account on, 172, 174–75
  frustration-aggression hypothesis, 171
  general aggression model, 171
  jealousy as motivator for, 94, 184–85
  to maintain status hierarchies, 172
  male-male competition and, 59, 97,
    256, 435
  media witnessing of, 169
  physical attractiveness link to,
    172, 179–81
  during preadolescence, 19
  primatologists definition of, 72
  proximate explanation of, 174–75
  during puberty, 382
  sex differences, 151, 174
  situational triggers for, 170, 171
  social context of, 90
  social learning models, 174
  within social networks, 9
  sociocultural explanations of, 171

gossip, 72, 169, 174, 446, 690. *See also*
    evolutionary psychology, of gossip;
    reputation-based gossip
  aggressive use of, 8, 198–200
  aging reduction of, 179
  bad, selfish within own group,
    195–96
  bullying and, 416
  about celebrities, 196, 201–2
  coalitional relationships effective, 77
  control through, 77
  cosmetic surgery and, 609
  defined, 208, 228
  from derogated individual
    perspective, 216–17
  Ducking Stool for, 193–94, 193*f*
  to enforce group norms, 197
  evaluative, 212
  Facebook spreading and tracking, 200
  female competition role,
    200–202, 435
  female representation of, 192–93,
    198–200
  function of, 208
  good, serving group interests, 196–98
  good provider indicators in, 213
  group norms enforced by, 197
  individual differences in, 198
  as informational aggression, 8, 227–32
  information management of, 229, 232
  as intrasexual competition form, 207–9
  low and high frequency, 198
  male intrasexual competition and, 308
  for mate poaching, 8, 207–19
  mate value and, 292–93
  motivations for, 191–92
  natural selection and, 194–95
  to promote solidarity, 232–33
  relationships and, 209, 215–16, 218
  religious sanctions against, 192–93
  as reputational information
    manipulation, 8, 227–32
  research on sex differences in, 212–15
  risk-acceptance mechanisms, 211
  Scold's Bridle for, 193, 193*f*
  sex, mate competition, and mate
    poaching relationships, 207–19
  show-off hypothesis for men, 212
  sneering physical appearance
    comments, 95
  as social control mechanism, 197, 208
  social networks functions of, 77, 416
  social status and, 196
  strategy learning, 208
  time engaged in, 212–13
  among Tsimane women, 110, 111, 121
  in workplace, 198, 199
grandchildren, grandmothers survivors
    influence, 22
grandiosity, in narcissism, 154
grandmother hypothesis, 21–22,
    387, 741–42
grandmothers, 8, 21–22

grandchildren survivorship
    influenced by, 22
  human lifetime fertility
    influenced by, 22
  Tsimane women as, 109
grief
  active distress in, 340
  adaptive purpose of, 342
  inactive, depressed state, 340
  maladaptive behavior from, 340, 342
  mate loss and, 340
grooming and gossip theory, 777
group decision-making, Lost on the Moon
    task measure, 141–42, 142*f*
group formations, female
  bad gossip, selfish within, 195–96
  food competition and, 50
  good gossip, serving interests
    within, 196–98
  for predation risk, 50
group norms, gossip to enforce, 197
grrl gamers, 709
guilt, sex differences in, 149
guppies, mate copying behavior of,
    325–26, 333

H

hamadryas baboons
  caretaking behaviors, 57
  dispersal and reproduction, 57
  dispersing-egalitarian, 49
  dominance and friendships, 58–59
  fission-fusion society, 57
  harems of, 57
  herding of, 57
  social structure, 57
hammer-headed bats, 327
happiness
  after divorce, 347
  materialism dimension of, 404
harassment
  infertility and spontaneous abortions
    from, 74, 79
  by primates subordinate females, 28
  to reduce fertility, 460
  sexual, 587, 724
harems, of hamadryas baboons, 57
health, 302. *See also* mental health
  consequences, 7, 9
  in fashion, 639–41
  female competition costs for, 417
  friendships psychological and
    physiological, 52, 115
  lack of studies on women, 355
  positive social support and, 415
  of Sidama women, 420–26,
    424*f*, 806
  sleep and, 7, 9, 417, 420–23,
    427, 806
  social networks benefits of, 74–75,
    415, 427
  WHR correlation with, 32
  women fertility predictor, 401

health-insurance theories, 227
herding, by hamadryas baboons, 57
heterogamy, 283
hierarchies, 5, 6
  aggression to maintain status, 172
  benefits of, 137
  dominance, in contest competition, 225
  human dominance, informational
    warfare and, 234–35
high frequency gossip, 198
high-performance sports, 792–93
high status
  mate guarding and, 345
  reproductive rewards from, 17
  women mating opportunities
    for, 172–73
homogamy, in romantic
    relationships, 283–84
hormonal contraceptive use
  competition and, 383–87
  mate guarding behavior and, 386
  mate preferences and choice influenced
    by, 398–99
  ovulatory phase and, 398
  psychosocial behavior negatively
    impacted by, 386
hormonal mechanisms
  competition associated with, 356
  influencing intrasexual competition,
    311–12, 333
hormonal regulation, of behavior, 9, 371,
    372, 375
hormonal trade-offs, 9, 365, 371, 372,
    375, 377
hormonal variations, 378–79
  across female lifespan, 371, 380–89
hormones, 397
  reproductive suppression and, 438
  trade-offs regulation, 9, 365, 371, 372,
    375, 377
  women food choice and intake
    influenced by, 748
HPA. *See* hypothalamus-pituitary-adrenal
HPG. *See* hypothalamic-pituitary-gonadal
HRAF. *See* Human Relations Area Files
human competition, sexual selection
    applied to, 28–29
human evidence, of OSR
  cross-cultural research, 274
  demographic research, 273–74
  laboratory research, 274–75
human evolution, 505
  on aggression, 172, 174–75
  of children and aggression, 175
  of communication, 175
  of indirect aggression, 169–70
  women active influence on, 4
  of women aggression, 173–74
human lifetime fertility, grandmothers
    influence on, 22
Human Relations Area Files (HRAF)
  on organized sports, 19
  on polygynous societies, 255

Facebook and, 201, 219
low physical attractiveness and, 34, 94
mate retention and guarding, 328
over female friends, 231
over previous partners, 304
of partnered women, 305
in relationships, 345
rivalry and, 302
women adaptations of, 345–46
juvenility, 81

K

kin-preference marriages, 111–12
kin selection, 51
kin support, 52–53
knowledge, 17

L

legal outcomes, physical attractiveness
and, 579
leg length, fashion and, 643
lethal risks, for reproductive rewards, 16
LH. *See* luteinizing hormone
life history theory, 8, 15, 17, 22, 414
on adolescents, 81–82
age-related changes and, 457–59
group living roles and women, 509–10
mate poaching and, 332
partner investment and offspring in, 442
progenicide and, 555–58
on reproductive strategies, 78, 81–82
trade-offs in, 371, 457
women pursuit slow life-history, 458
lifespan, 9, 15
adolescent reproductive capacity, 91
nutrition in, 17
limited resources, 356, 361
Darwin on competition for, 15
female competition for, 436–37
mate quality, 7, 208, 414
primates coalitional behavior for, 224
lipstick effect, 583
local resource competition, 273, 482–84
long-term mates, 288
Dark Triad personality traits and, 154
female standards for, 338–39
men choosiness in selection of, 35
motivation for, 303
sexual strategies theory and, 338
women preference for, 173
long-term relationships, short-term
relationships compared to, 458–59
Lost in the Moon task, 141–42, 142*f*
lovers, women as, 804–5
low frequency gossip, 198
luteinizing hormone (LH), 380, 381,
383, 398
lying, 151

M

Machiavellianism, 8, 116, 807
cold and manipulative individuals, 154
examples, 158–60

males higher scores for, 155, 161
maladaptive behavior, from grief, 340, 342
male competition. *See also* contest
competition
through dominance, resources and
social status, 28
over resources within groups, 225–26
physical aggression and, 28–29, 112, 235,
400, 401, 414
T and, 357, 361, 375, 400
male disadvantaged mating markets, 272
male friends, 136–37
anti-infanticide hypothesis, 138
male intrasexual competition, 514, 605–6.
See also contest competition
gossip and, 308
intensity of, 16
mating and aggression, 235, 704
in mating markets, 321
OSR and, 272
parental investment and, 267, 302, 321
resource and status display in, 661
women observation of, 324
male-male competition, 273, 321, 436, 605,
801. *See also* contest competition
aggression and, 59, 97, 256, 435
Darwin on, 682
in organized sports, 19
pair-bonding reduction of, 112
physical harm in, 237
risk taking behaviors in, 597
sexual dimorphism and, 112
male preference
in gaming, 701
for low WHR, 582
for nulliparous women, 471, 472
for physical attractiveness, 31, 111
for sexual variety, 30
for status, 686
for virginity, 618
males, 29, 311. *See also* men
body scent, ovulatory cycle and
preference for, 399–400
evolutionary process for reproductive
success, 107–8
exclusive sports, 19
higher Machiavellianism and
psychopathy scores, 155, 161
infertility of, 238–39
intrasexual competition, 605–6
low WHR preference, 582
mothering tasks value, 465–66
multiple mating opportunities, 27, 97
penile erection, 666
philopatric primate species, 485–86
physical attractiveness preferences,
31, 111
reproductive fitness and, 96
with resources, women competition for,
492, 618, 704, 802
self-promotion by, 199
sexually dimorphic features, 27
sexual variety preference, 30

surviving and reproducing
importance of, 16
tolerance and dominance, 55
visual stimuli arousal, 602
wealth and status mate preference, 282,
319, 435
women less agency than, 149
workplace and, 722–23
younger women partnering, 465, 580,
604–5, 638, 673
mammals
female competition in, 436–37
reproductive suppression in, 437–39
managers, sex segregation for, 722,
723–24, 729
manipulation, 72, 437
adolescent girls social, 385
coalitional, of reputation, 230–31
gossip as reputational information,
8, 227–32
in Machiavellian individuals, 154
of mate value, 291–93
reproductive self-suppression and
RSH, 445
rival, 682–83
marital conflicts, women psychological
detriments from, 415
marital status, of American women by age,
303, 303*f*
marketing strategies, physical
attractiveness and, 589
marriages. *See also* mating systems
arranged, 20, 296, 309, 330, 424*f*, 425*f*
consanguineous, 111–12
cooperative, 112
faithful as your options hypothesis, 253
kin-preference, 111–12
mating supply and demand
hypothesis, 253
reproduction and, 253
reproductive success influenced by, 255
systems as indicators, 255–56
teen, 303
T levels and, 376
mass media, 674
cultures access to, 670
eating disorders and, 657–58
women mental health and, 657–58
mate acquisition
female resource production priority, 108
peer aggression and, 98–99, 100, 101
physical attractiveness, of Tsimane
women and, 111
Tsimane conflicts over, 109, 111, 116, 457
Tsimane long-term mate bonds, 111
mate choice, 249, 256, 296, 319, 529, 606
Bayesian modeling approach to,
324–25, 333
behavior for, 283–84
bidirectional, 321–22
evolutionary ecological theory on, 112
female consequences for, 321
by females, 93